T0235923

Lecture Notes in Computer Science   11898

More information about this series at http://www.springer.com/series/7410

Feng Hao · Sushmita Ruj ·
Sourav Sen Gupta (Eds.)

Progress in Cryptology – INDOCRYPT 2019

20th International Conference on Cryptology in India
Hyderabad, India, December 15–18, 2019
Proceedings

 Springer

Editors
Feng Hao
University of Warwick
Warwick, UK

Sushmita Ruj
CSIRO Data61
Marsfield, NSW, Australia

Sourav Sen Gupta
Nanyang Technological University
Singapore, Singapore

Indian Statistical Institute
Kolkata, India

ISSN 0302-9743   ISSN 1611-3349   (electronic)
Lecture Notes in Computer Science
ISBN 978-3-030-35422-0   ISBN 978-3-030-35423-7   (eBook)
https://doi.org/10.1007/978-3-030-35423-7

LNCS Sublibrary: SL4 – Security and Cryptology

This Springer imprint is published by the registered company Springer Nature Switzerland AG
The registered company address is: Gewerbestrasse 11, 6330 Cham, Switzerland

Preface

It is our great pleasure to present the proceedings of INDOCRYPT 2019, the 20th International Conference on Cryptology in India, held at the Novotel Hyderabad Convention Centre, Hyderabad, India, during December 15–18, 2019.

This year marked two eventful decades of the INDOCRYPT conference series organized under the aegis of the Cryptology Research Society of India (CRSI). The conference began in 2000 under the leadership of Prof. Bimal Roy of Indian Statistical Institute, Kolkata, and since then, this annual event has gained its place among prestigious cryptology conferences in the world. It is considered as the leading Indian venue on the subject. Over the last two decades, the conference took place in various cities of India—Kolkata (2000, 2006, 2012, 2016), Chennai (2001, 2004, 2007, 2011, 2017), Hyderabad (2002, 2010), New Delhi (2003, 2009, 2014, 2018), Bangalore (2005, 2015), Kharagpur (2008), and Mumbai (2013). This was the third time the conference was hosted in Hyderabad.

INDOCRYPT 2019 attracted 110 submissions from 20 different countries. Out of these, papers that were withdrawn before the deadline and the ones that violated the submission policy, were not reviewed. Finally, 90 papers were reviewed normally by 4 reviewers, with at least 3 reviewers per paper (2 in only 2 cases). The double-blind review phase was followed by a week-long discussion that generated additional comments from the Program Committee members and the external reviewers. After the discussions, and after shepherding in a few cases, 28 papers were accepted for inclusion in the program, with authors from 14 different countries. These 28 papers were presented during the conference, and revised versions of these papers are included in these proceedings. In addition to the traditional presentations, the conference hosted a number of interesting short-talks and announcements during the Rump Session.

The conference would not have been possible without the hard work of the 60 Program Committee members and the 69 external reviewers, who took part in the process of reviewing and subsequent discussions. We take this opportunity to thank the Program Committee members and the external reviewers for their tremendous job in selecting the current program. It was an honor to work with them. The submissions, reviews, discussions, and proceedings were effectively managed using the EasyChair conference management system. We would also like to express our appreciation to Springer for their active cooperation and timely production of these conference proceedings.

In addition to the contributed talks and the Rump Session, the program included three invited talks and two tutorials. Elaine Shi from Cornell University, USA, introduced "Streamlined Blockchains: A Simple and Elegant Approach," Bart Preneel from KU Leuven, Belgium, discussed "Blockchain and Distributed Consensus: Hype or Science," and Manoj Prabhakaran from IIT Bombay, India, spoke on "Extending the Foundations of Differential Privacy." Tutorials by Satya Lokam, Microsoft Research, India, and Feng Hao, University of Warwick, UK, introduced the attendees to "Zero

Knowledge Proofs for Fun and Profit" and "More Practical Multi-Party Computation," respectively. The abstracts of the invited talks and tutorials are also included in these proceedings.

INDOCRYPT 2019 was conducted by C. R. Rao Advanced Institute of Mathematics, Statistics, and Computer Science (AIMSCS), jointly with University of Hyderabad (UoH), National Technical Research Organisation (NTRO), and Defence Research and Development Organization (DRDO). We are indebted to the general chairs, Anand Achuthan (ARCC), Siddani Bhaskara Rao (C. R. Rao AIMSCS), and Daggula Narasimha Reddy (C. R. Rao AIMSCS), for smoothly coordinating all matters related to local organization of the event. We would also like to thank the chief patrons, the organizing chairs, the organizing secretary, the treasurer, the convenors and co-convenors, and all members of the Organizing Committee, for their support in successfully hosting the conference in Hyderabad. We would also like to thank the team at Indian Statistical Institute, Kolkata, for maintaining the conference website, and the local organizing team at Hyderabad for their hard work to make the conference a success.

We are especially grateful to our sponsors Department of Science and Technology (DST), Google, Microsoft Research India, Ministry of Electronics and Information Technology (MEITY), National Board of Higher Mathematics (NBHM), Reserve Bank of India (RBI), and Robert Bosch Engineering and Business Solutions Pvt. Ltd, for their generous support towards the conference.

Finally, we would like to thank each one of the 240 authors who submitted their work to INDOCRYPT 2019, and all the cryptology practitioners and enthusiasts who attended the event. Without their spirited participation, the conference would not have been a success. We hope you enjoy these proceedings of INDOCRYPT 2019.

December 2019   Feng Hao
                                                    Sushmita Ruj
                                                 Sourav Sen Gupta

Organization

General Chairs

Anand Achuthan   Applied Research Centre for Cryptology, India
Siddani Bhaskara Rao   C. R. Rao AIMSCS, India
Daggula Narasimha Reddy   C. R. Rao AIMSCS, India

Program Committee Chairs

Feng Hao   University of Warwick, UK
Sushmita Ruj   CSIRO Data61, Marsfield, NSW, Australia,
     and Indian Statistical Institute, Kolkata, India
Sourav Sen Gupta   Nanyang Technological University, Singapore

Chief Patrons

C. R. Rao (Founder)   C. R. Rao AIMSCS, India
C. Rangarajan   RBI, India
  (Former Governor)
V. K. Saraswat (Member)   NITI Aayog, India
Appa Rao P. (Vice-chancellor)   University of Hyderabad, India

Organizing Chairs

C. E. Veni Madhavan   C. R. Rao AIMSCS, India
K. Narayana Murthy   University of Hyderabad, India

Web Chairs

Prabal Banerjee   Indian Statistical Institute, Kolkata, India
Laltu Sardar   Indian Statistical Institute, Kolkata, India

Program Committee

Anand Achuthan   Applied Research Centre for Cryptology, India
Divesh Aggarwal   National University of Singapore, Singapore
Diego F. Aranha   Aarhus University, Denmark,
     and University of Campinas, Brazil
Frederik Armknecht   Universität Mannheim, Germany
Man Ho Au   The Hong Kong Polytechnic University,
     Hong Kong, China
Daniel Augot   Inria and École polytechnique, France

Samiran Bag	The University of Warwick, UK
Subhadeep Banik	École Polytechnique Fédérale de Lausanne, Switzerland
Rishiraj Bhattacharyya	NISER Bhubaneswar, India
Avik Chakraborti	NTT, Japan
Debrup Chakraborty	Indian Statistical Institute, Kolkata, India
Anupam Chattopadhyay	Nanyang Technological University, Singapore
Liqun Chen	University of Surrey, UK
Sherman S. M. Chow	The Chinese University of Hong Kong, Hong Kong, China
Michele Ciampi	The University of Edinburgh, UK
Mauro Conti	University of Padua, Italy
Nilanjan Datta	Indian Statistical Institute, Kolkata, India
Keita Emura	National Institute of Information and Communications Technology, Japan
Chaya Ganesh	Aarhus University, Denmark
Esha Ghosh	Microsoft Research, Redmond, USA
Feng Hao	The University of Warwick, UK
Martin Hell	Lund University, Sweden
Xinyi Huang	Fujian Normal University, China
Takanori Isobe	University of Hyogo, Japan
Bhavana Kanukurthi	Indian Institute of Science, Bengaluru, India
Aniket Kate	Purdue University, USA
Ayesha Khalid	Queen's University Belfast, UK
Kaoru Kurosawa	Ibaraki University, Japan
Alptekin Küpçü	Koç University, Turkey
Kwok Yan Lam	Nanyang Technological University, Singapore
Kaitai Liang	University of Surrey, UK
Joseph Liu	Monash University, Australia
Zhe Liu	Nanjing University of Aeronautics and Astronautics, China
Subhamoy Maitra	Indian Statistical Institute, Kolkata, India
Mary Maller	University College London, UK
Giorgia Azzurra Marson	NEC Laboratories Europe, Germany
Tarik Moataz	Brown University, USA
Pratyay Mukherjee	Visa Research, Palo Alto, USA
Shishir Nagaraja	University of Strathclyde, UK
Seetharam Narasimhan	Intel Corporation, USA
Rajesh Pillai	DRDO, India
Shashwat Raizada	Robert Bosch Engineering and Business Solutions Private Limited, India
Somindu Chaya Ramanna	Indian Institute of Technology, Kharagpur, India
Chester Rebeiro	Indian Institute of Technology, Madras, India
Mike Rosulek	Oregon State University, USA
Sushmita Ruj	CSIRO Data61, Marsfield, NSW, Australia, and Indian Statistical Institute, Kolkata, India

Reihaneh Safavi-Naini	University of Calgary, Canada
Kouichi Sakurai	Kyushu University, Japan
Santanu Sarkar	Indian Institute of Technology, Madras, India
Sumanta Sarkar	TCS Innovation Labs, India
Peter Schwabe	Radboud University, The Netherlands
Sourav Sen Gupta	Nanyang Technological University, Singapore
Binanda Sengupta	Singapore Management University, Singapore
Siamak Shahandashti	University of York, UK
Maliheh Shirvanian	Visa Research, Palo Alto, USA
Sujoy Sinha Roy	University of Birmingham, UK
Willy Susilo	University of Wollongong, Australia
Alwen Tiu	The Australian National University, Australia
Qingju Wang	University of Luxembourg, Luxembourg
Kan Yasuda	NTT, Japan
Jiangshan Yu	Monash University, Australia
Bin Zhang	Chinese Academy of Sciences, China
Bingsheng Zhang	Lancaster University, UK

Additional Reviewers

Aghili, Seyed Farhad
Agrawal, Shashank
Anada, Hiroaki
Anshu, Anurag
Baksi, Anubhab
Balli, Fatih
Bao, Zhenzhen
Barooti, Khashayar
Biçer, Osman
Chakraborty, Kaushik
Charpin, Pascale
Chatterjee, Sanjit
Cheng, Chen-Mou
Choi, Gwangbae
Costa Massolino, Pedro Maat
Daemen, Joan
Dalai, Deepak
Dey, Chandan
Dobraunig, Christoph
Dutta, Avijit
Dutta, Sabyasachi
Fauzi, Prastudy
Ferradi, Houda
Ge, Chunpeng
Ghosh, Satrajit

Gupta, Indivar
Han, Runchao
Hubáček, Pavel
Huguenin-Dumittan, Loïs
Inoue, Akiko
İşler, Devriş
Jana, Amit
Karati, Sabyasachi
Khairallah, Mustafa
Kumar Singh, Nikhilesh
Kumar, Nishant
Kumar, Satyam
Kumar, Yogesh
Kundu, Samir
Larangeira, Mario
Li, Wei
Lin, Chao
Lin, Fuchun
Liu, Fukang
Livsey, Lee
Ma, Jack P. K.
Ma, Jinhua
Mancillas-López, Cuauhtemoc
Matsuda, Takahiro
Meier, Willi

Mikhalev, Vasily
Mishra, Prasanna
Mishra, Surya Prakash
Nuida, Koji
Ogata, Wakaha
Ohigashi, Toshihiro
Papachristodoulou, Louiza
Patanjali, Slpsk
Pooranian, Zahra
Poostindouz, Ali
Rathee, Mayank
Ravi, Prasanna
Rohit, Raghvendra
Rozic, Vladimir
Sakumoto, Koichi
Salehi Shahraki, Ahmad
Saraswat, Vishal
Sasaki, Yu
Sharifian, Setareh
Shojafar, Mohammad
Siniscalchi, Luisa

Song, Ling
Stankovski Wagner, Paul
Stephens-Davidowitz, Noah
Su, Jiawei
Sun, Siwei
Taheri Boshrooyeh, Sanaz
Tiwari, Sharwan Kumar
Todo, Yosuke
Treiber, Amos
Udovenko, Aleksei
Velichkov, Vesselin
Wagner, Kim
Wan, Zhiguo
Wang, Gaoli
Yang, Rupeng
Yang, Shaojun
Yang, Wenjie
Yang, Xu
Zamani, Mahdi
Zhao, Hong
Zhao, Liangrong

Organizing Committee

Organizing Secretary

Appala Naidu Tentu   C. R. Rao AIMSCS, India

Treasurer

Neelima Jampala   C. R. Rao AIMSCS, India

Convenors

Y. V. Subbarao   University of Hyderabad, India
Ashtalakshmi J.   Applied Research Centre for Cryptology, India

Co-convenors

N. Rukhma Rekha   University of Hyderabad, India
G. Padmavathi   C. R. Rao AIMSCS, India

Members

Anand Achuthan   Applied Research Centre for Cryptology, India
Suman Balwan   Applied Research Centre for Cryptology, India
Chakravarthy Bhagavati   University of Hyderabad, India
Supriya Goel   C. R. Rao AIMSCS, India
M. Arun Kumar   ITI Limited, Bengaluru, India

D. Ravi Kumar	Applied Research Centre for Cryptology, India
Arpita Maitra	C. R. Rao AIMSCS, India
Ashish Mishra	Applied Research Centre for Cryptology, India
Priyanka Mekala	C. R. Rao AIMSCS, India
Chaitanya Palli	C. R. Rao AIMSCS, India
Digambar Pawar	University of Hyderabad, India
K. V. Pradeepti	C. R. Rao AIMSCS, India
D. N. Reddy	C. R. Rao AIMSCS, India
Sumanta Sarkar	TCS Innovation Labs, India
Ashutosh Saxena	C. R. Rao AIMSCS, India
Sirisha Velampalli	C. R. Rao AIMSCS, India
V. Ch. Venkaiah	University of Hyderabad, India
U. Yugandhar	C. R. Rao AIMSCS, India

Abstracts of Invited Talks
and Tutorials

Streamlined Blockchains: A Simple and Elegant Approach

Elaine Shi

Cornell University, USA

Abstract. A blockchain protocol (also called state machine replication) allows a set of nodes to agree on an ever-growing, linearly ordered log of transactions. In this talk, we present a new paradigm called "streamlined blockchains." This paradigm enables a new family of protocols that are extremely simple and natural: every epoch, a proposer proposes a block extending from a notarized parent chain, and nodes vote if the proposal's parent chain is not too old. Whenever a block gains enough votes, it becomes notarized. Whenever a node observes a notarized chain with several blocks of consecutive epochs at the end, then the entire chain chopping off a few blocks at the end is final. By varying some parameters, we illustrate two variants for the partially synchronous and synchronous settings respectively. We present very simple proofs of consistency and liveness. We hope that this talk provides a compelling argument why this new family of protocols should be used in lieu of classical candidates (e.g., PBFT, Paxos, and their variants), both in practical implementation and for pedagogical purposes.

Blockchain and Distributed Consensus: Hype or Science

Bart Preneel

Katholieke Universiteit Leuven, Belgium

Abstract. This talk will offer a perspective on blockchain and distributed consensus. It will try to explain why technologies from the 1980s and early 1990s are suddenly perceived as highly innovative. Part of the story is related to the hype related to Bitcoin, a distributed cryptocurrency that managed to solve the Byzantine generals problem with a clever proof of work. Bitcoin generated a flurry of research on other cryptocurrencies and distributed consensus mechanisms. Several governments are now planning to issue centrally banked digital currency and large organizations are considering stablecoins. In this talk, we explain how several blockchain variants attempt to improve the complex tradeoffs between public verifiability, robustness, privacy, and performance. We discuss how Markov Decision processes can be used to compare in an objective way the proposed improvements in terms of chain quality, censorship resistance, and robustness against selfish mining and double spending attacks. We conclude with a discussion of open problems.

Extending the Foundations of Differential Privacy

Manoj Prabhakaran

Indian Institute of Technology Bombay, India

Abstract. Differential Privacy (DP) has been a highly influential framework to analyze and obtain privacy guarantees for "big data". A rich body of literature has used DP and its extensions to enable a fruitful balance of privacy and utility, in a variety of contexts. We identify and address two limitations of the current DP framework that seem to have evaded attention. At a high-level, these limitations follow from a seemingly natural choice: accuracy guarantees of a mechanism are in terms of distances in the output space, and privacy demands are in terms of distances in the input space (neighboring inputs). Somewhat surprisingly, these choices turn out to be not always adequate. We introduce two new notions – flexible accuracy and robustness – that address these limitations. The machinery we develop also naturally lets us extend the notion of DP to randomized functions over a metric space, for which distances are measured using a (generalization of) Wasserstein distance.

Zero Knowledge Proofs for Fun and Profit

Satyanarayana V. Lokam

Microsoft Research, India

Abstract. Zero knowledge proofs were introduced by Goldwasser, Micali, and Rackoff more than three decades ago. Since then, this notion found numerous applications within the field of cryptography. In recent years, the gap between theoretical foundations and practical implementations of zero knowledge proof systems has been rapidly shrinking. Much of the recent work has been motivated by applications such as privacy in blockchains and credential systems. This synergy between theory and practice also gives rise to several research challenges. In this tutorial, we will survey some of the recent developments in the design and implementation of zero knowledge proof systems.

More Practical Multi-Party Computation

Feng Hao

University of Warwick, UK

Abstract. A general multi-party computation (MPC) protocol allows a group of participants to jointly compute an arbitrary function over their inputs while keeping each input private. While versatile in theory, it has several practical limitations. First of all, a lack of efficiency is commonly acknowledged. Second, it typically requires pairwise secret channels among the participants in addition to a public authenticated channels, but pairwise secret channels are difficult to realize in practice. Third, due to the existence of pairwise secret channels, certain operations in the protocol are impossible to be verified publicly, say by third-party observers. Finally, its security model normally relies on the assumption that a majority of the players are honest. However, this assumption is questionable in practice. In this tutorial, I will present examples to show how to construct more practical MPC protocols that overcome these limitations. I will cover a diversified range of application areas including key exchange, e-voting, and e-auction. The protocols that we present enjoy exceptional efficiency, are publicly verifiable without involving secret channels, and remain secure even when the vast majority of the players are corrupted. The public verifiability makes it suitable to implement these protocols as smart contracts on a blockchain where the public verification process is guaranteed by the consensus mechanism that underpins the blockchain.

Contents

Theory: Oblivious Transfer, Obfuscation and Privacy Amplification

Mathematics: Boolean Functions, Elliptic Curves and Lattices

Quantum: Algorithms, Attacks and Key Distribution

Hardware: Efficiency, Side-Channel Resistance and PUFs

Constructions: Signatures and Filter Permutators

PKP-Based Signature Scheme

Ward Beullens[1]([✉]), Jean-Charles Faugère[2], Eliane Koussa[3],
Gilles Macario-Rat[4], Jacques Patarin[5], and Ludovic Perret[2]

[1] imec-COSIC, KU Leuven, Leuven, Belgium
`ward.beullens@esat.kuleuven.be`
[2] Inria and Sorbonne Universities/UPMC Uni Paris 6, Paris, France
`jean-charles.faugere@inria.fr`, `ludovic.perret@lip6.fr`
[3] Versailles Laboratory of Mathematics, UVSQ, Versailles, France
`EJKoussa@outlook.com`
[4] Orange, Meylan, France
`gilles.macariorat@orange.com`
[5] Versailles Laboratory of Mathematics, UVSQ, CNRS, University of Paris-Saclay,
Versailles, France
`jpatarin@club-internet.fr`

Abstract. In this document, we introduce PKP-DSS: a Digital Signature Scheme based on the Permuted Kernel Problem (PKP) [23]. PKP is a simple NP-hard [10] combinatorial problem that consists of finding a kernel for a publicly known matrix, such that the kernel vector is a permutation of a publicly known vector. This problem was used to develop an Identification Scheme (IDS) which has a very efficient implementation on low-cost smart cards. From this zero-knowledge identification scheme, we derive PKP-DSS with the traditional Fiat-Shamir transform [9]. Thus, PKP-DSS has a security that can be provably reduced, in the *(classical) random oracle model*, to the hardness of random instances of PKP (or, if wanted, to any specific family of PKP instances). We propose parameter sets following the thorough analysis of the State-of-the-art attacks on PKP presented in [17]. We show that PKP-DSS is competitive with other signatures derived from Zero-Knowledge identification schemes. In particular, PKP-DSS-128 gives a signature size of approximately 20 KBytes for 128 bits of classical security, which is approximately 30% smaller than MQDSS. Moreover, our proof-of-concept implementation shows that PKP-DSS-128 is an order of magnitude faster than MQDSS which in its turn is faster than Picnic2, SPHINCS, ...

Since the PKP is NP-hard and since there are no known quantum attacks for solving PKP significantly better than classical attacks, we believe that our scheme is post-quantum secure.

Keywords: Public-key cryptography · Fiat-Shamir · Post-quantum cryptography · 5-pass identification scheme · Public-key Signature · Permuted Kernel Problem

© Springer Nature Switzerland AG 2019
F. Hao et al. (Eds.): INDOCRYPT 2019, LNCS 11898, pp. 3–22, 2019.
https://doi.org/10.1007/978-3-030-35423-7_1

1   Introduction

The construction of large quantum computers would break most public-key cryptographic schemes in use today because they rely on the discrete logarithm problem or the integer factorization problem. Even though it isn't clear when large scale quantum computation would be feasible, it is important to anticipate quantum computing and design new public key cryptosystems that are resistant to quantum attacks. Therefore, there currently is a large research effort to develop new post-quantum secure schemes, and a Post-Quantum Cryptography standardization process has been initiated by the American National Institute of Standards and Technology (https://www.nist.gov/). Because of this, there has been renewed interest in constructing signature schemes by applying the Fiat-Shamir transform [9] to Zero-Knowledge Identification Schemes. In particular, we are interested in post-quantum cryptographic schemes whose security relies on the quantum hardness of some NP-Hard problem [2]. One of those problems is the Permuted Kernel Problem: the problem of finding a permutation of a known vector such that the resulting vector is in the kernel of a given matrix. This is a classical NP-Hard combinatorial problem which requires only simple operations such as basic linear algebra and permuting the entries of a vector. For quite some time, no new attacks on PKP have been discovered, which makes it possible to confidently estimate the concrete hardness of the problem.

In 1989, Shamir [23] introduced a five-pass ZK-Identification scheme, based on the PKP. This work uses the Fiat-Shamir transform [9] on this identification scheme to develop a signature scheme that is provably secure in the Random Oracle Model (ROM). However, since our goal is to have a post-quantum scheme, we should also consider attackers in the Quantum Random Oracle Model (QROM). The security of the Fiat-Shamir transform in the QROM has been studied in [25–27], where the authors of [25,27] explain that the Fiat-Shamir transform might not be secure against quantum computers. Thus, new techniques with extra properties (such as "lossy IDS") were developed to obtain a quantum-secure transform. However, more recently, a number of works have proven the Fiat-Shamir construction secure in the QROM [13,26] under very mild conditions. So far, none of these works apply to five-round protocols (which is the kind of protocol we are considering in this work), but it is conceivable that the results can be generalized to five-pass protocols, including ours. We consider this an important open problem in post-quantum cryptography.

Previous Work and State-of-the-Art. Since quantum computers are expected not to be capable of solving *NP*-Hard problems in sub-exponential time (in worst case), Zero-knowledge Identification schemes based on such problems are interesting candidates for Post-Quantum Cryptography. The Fiat-Shamir transform [9] is a technique that can convert such a zero-knowledge authentication scheme into a signature scheme. This approach was taken by Chen et al. [7], who applied the Fiat-Shamir transform to a 5-pass identification scheme of Sakumoto et al. [22]. This identification scheme relies on the hardness of the (*NP*-Hard) problem of finding a solution to a set of multivariate quadratic equations. Chen et al. proved that, in the random oracle model, applying the Fiat-Shamir transform to this 5-pass identification scheme results in a secure signature scheme. A concrete parameter choice and an efficient implementation of this signature scheme (which is called MQDSS) were developed, and this was one of the submissions to the NIST PQC standardization project. At a security level of 128 bits, the MQDSS scheme comes with a public key of 46 Bytes, a secret key of 16 Bytes and a signature size of approximately 28 Kilobytes.

A different line of work resulted in the Picnic signature scheme. Chase et al. [6] constructed this digital signature scheme by applying the Fiat-Shamir transform to an identification scheme whose security relies purely on symmetric primitives. At the 128-bit security level Picnic has a public key of 32 Bytes, a secret key of 16 Bytes and signatures of approximately 33 Kilobytes. There is a second version of this signature scheme, where the signatures are only 13.5 Kilobytes, but Picnic2 is 45 times slower than the original Picnic for signing and 25 times slower for verification.

Main Results. The main contribution of this paper is to present PKP-DSS, a new post-quantum secure signature scheme. Similar to the approaches cited above, we use the Fiat-Shamir transform to construct a signature scheme from the 5-pass PKP identification scheme by Shamir [23]. Following the complexity analysis of the PKP [17], we choose secure parameter sets of the signature scheme for 128/192/256 of classical security level. To date, there are no known quantum algorithms for solving PKP (other than combining Grover search with the classical algorithms), so we claim that our signatures achieve the NIST security levels I/III and V respectively. However, we recognize that the (quantum) hardness of PKP deserves more research, and we hope that this work will inspire researchers to investigate this topic further.

We have developed a constant-time C implementation of the new signature scheme. By constant-time we mean that the running time and the memory access pattern of the implementation are independent of secret material, therefore blocking attacks from timing side channels. The resulting signature scheme compares well with MQDSS and Picnic/Picnic2. Our scheme is much faster than MQDSS and Picnic/Picnic2 in terms of signing and verification, we have small public and private keys, and the signature sizes of our scheme are comparable to those of MQDSS and Picnic2. This makes our signature scheme based on PKP competitive with state of the art post-quantum signature schemes.

2   Preliminaries

2.1   The Permuted Kernel Problem (PKP)

The Permuted Kernel Problem (PKP) [10,23] is the problem on which the security of PKP-DSS is based. PKP is a linear algebra problem which asks to find a kernel vector of a given matrix under a vector-entries constraint. It's a generalization of the Partition problem [10, pg. 224]. More precisely, it is defined as follows:

Definition 1 (Permuted Kernel Problem). *Given a finite field* $\mathbb{F}_p$, *a matrix* $\mathbf{A} \in \mathbb{F}_p^{m \times n}$ *and a n-vector* $\mathbf{v} \in \mathbb{F}_p^n$, *find a permutation* $\pi \in S_n$ *such that* $\mathbf{A}\mathbf{v}_\pi = 0$, *where* $\mathbf{v}_\pi = (v_{\pi(1)}, \cdots, v_{\pi(n)})$

A reduction of the 3-Partition problem proves PKP to be NP-Hard [10]. Moreover, solving random instances of PKP seems hard in practice. In fact, this is the fundamental design assumption of PKP-DSS. The hardness of PKP comes from, on the one hand, the big number of permutations, on the other hand, from the small number of possible permutations that satisfy the kernel equations. Note that, to make the problem more difficult, the n-vector $\mathbf{v}$ should have distinct coordinates. Otherwise if there are repeated entries, the space of permutations of $\mathbf{v}$ gets smaller. In the next section, we give the best known algorithm to solve the PKP problem.

Best Known Algorithms for Solving PKP. The implementation's efficiency of the first IDS, proposed by Shamir [23], based on PKP problem has led to several solving tools. There are various attacks for PKP, which are all exponential. We will not describe them here. Instead, we refer to [17] for further details. To estimate the concrete security of PKP, the authors of [17] review and compare the efficiency of the best known attacks in terms of the number of operations performed, for different finite fields. They bring together the Patarin-Chauvaud attack [21] and Poupard's algorithm [18] to provide an accurate program. The paper gives security estimates that we used to pick secure parameters sets for the Permuted Kernel Problem.

2.2 Commitment Schemes

In our protocol, we use a commitment scheme $\mathsf{Com} : \{0,1\}^\lambda \times \{0,1\}^\star \to \{0,1\}^{2\lambda}$, that takes as input λ uniformly random bits bits, where λ is the security parameter, and a message $m \in \{0,1\}^\star$ and outputs a 2λ bit long commitment $\mathsf{Com}(\mathsf{bits}, m)$. In the description of our protocols, we often do not explicitly mention the commitment randomness. We write $\mathsf{S} \leftarrow \mathsf{Com}(m)$, to denote the process of picking a uniformly random bit string r, and setting $\mathsf{C} \leftarrow \mathsf{Com}(\mathsf{r}, m)$. Similarly, when we write check $\mathsf{C} = \mathsf{Com}(m)$, we actually mean that the prover communicates r to the verifier, and that the verifier checks if $\mathsf{C} = \mathsf{Com}(\mathsf{r}, m)$.

We assume that Com is computationally binding, which means that no computationally bounded adversary can produce a $\mathsf{r}, \mathsf{r}', m, m'$ with $m \neq m'$ such that $\mathsf{Com}(\mathsf{r}, m) = \mathsf{Com}(\mathsf{r}', m')$. We also assume that Com is computationally hiding, which means that for every pair of messages m, m', no computationally bounded adversary can distinguish the distributions of $\mathsf{Com}(m)$ and $\mathsf{Com}(m')$.

2.3 2q-Identification Schemes and 2q-Extractors

In this paper, we will describe a so-called 2q-Identification Scheme [24]. This is a 5-round identification scheme, where the first challenge is drawn uniformly at random from a challenge space of size q, and the second challenge is a random bit. Therefore, a transcript of an execution of a $2q$-protocol looks like $(\mathsf{com}, c, \mathsf{rsp}_1, b, \mathsf{rsp}_2)$. We now state the properties of a $2q$-protocol more formally:

Definition 2 ($2q$-Identification scheme, [24]). *A $2q$-Identification scheme is a canonical five-pass identification scheme $(\mathsf{KeyGen}, \mathcal{P}, \mathcal{V})$ with challenge spaces $\mathcal{Ch}_1$ and $\mathcal{Ch}_2$ for which it holds that $|\mathcal{Ch}_1| = q$ and $|\mathcal{Ch}_2| = 2$. Moreover, we require that the probability that the commitment com take a certain value is a negligible function of the security parameter.*

Definition 3 (Completeness). *An Identification scheme $(\mathsf{KeyGen}, \mathcal{P}, \mathcal{V})$ is called complete if when both parties follow the protocol honestly, the verifier accepts with probability 1. That is, we have*

$$\Pr \left[\begin{array}{c} (\mathsf{pk}, \mathsf{sk}) \leftarrow \mathsf{KeyGen}(1^\lambda) \\ \langle \mathcal{P}(\mathsf{sk}), \mathcal{V}(\mathsf{pk}) \rangle = 1 \end{array} \right] = 1 \, ,$$

where $\langle \mathcal{P}(\mathsf{sk}), \mathcal{V}(\mathsf{pk}) \rangle$ stands for the common execution of the protocol between $\mathcal{P}$ with input sk and $\mathcal{V}$ with input pk.

Definition 4 (Soundness with soundness error κ). *An identification scheme $(\mathsf{KeyGen}, \mathcal{P}, \mathcal{V})$ is called Sound with soundness error κ, if for any probabilistic polynomial time adversary $\mathcal{A}$, we have*

$$\Pr \left[\begin{array}{c} (\mathsf{pk}, \mathsf{sk}) \leftarrow \mathsf{KeyGen}(1^\lambda) \\ \langle \mathcal{A}(1^\lambda, \mathsf{pk}), \mathcal{V}(\mathsf{pk}) \rangle = 1 \end{array} \right] \le \kappa + \epsilon(\lambda) \, ,$$

for some negligible function $\epsilon(\lambda)$.

Definition 5 ((computational) Honest-Verifier Zero-Knowledge). *We say an identification scheme $(\mathsf{KeyGen}, \mathcal{P}, \mathcal{V})$ is HVZK if there exists a probabilistic polynomial time Simulator $\mathcal{S}$ that outputs transcripts that are computationally indistinguishable from transcripts of honest executions of the protocol.*

Finally, we define the notion of a $2q$-extractor, which is an algorithm that can extract the secret key from 4 transcripts that satisfy some properties. This is useful because when there exists a $2q$-extractor for a $2q$-Identification scheme, this implies that the identification scheme has soundness with knowledge error at most $\frac{q+1}{2q}$. Moreover, this implies that applying the Fiat-Shamir transform to the identification scheme results in a secure signature scheme.

Definition 6 ($2q$-extractability). *We say a $2q$-identification scheme $(\mathsf{KeyGen}, \mathcal{P}, \mathcal{V})$ has $2q$-extractability, if there exists a polynomial-time algorithm that given four transcripts $(\mathsf{com}, c^{(i)}, \mathsf{rsp}_1^{(i)}, b^{(i)}, \mathsf{rsp}_2^{(i)})$ for i from 1 to 4, such that*

$$c^{(1)} = c^{(2)} \neq c^{(3)} = c^{(4)}$$
$$\mathsf{rsp}_1^{(1)} = \mathsf{rsp}_1^{(2)} \quad \mathsf{rsp}_1^{(3)} = \mathsf{rsp}_1^{(4)}$$
$$b^{(1)} = b^{(3)} \neq b^{(2)} = b^{(4)}$$

can efficiently extract a secret key.

Theorem 1 ([24], Theorem 3.1 and Theorem 4.3). *A $2q$-extractable $2q$-identification scheme is sound with knowledge error at most $\frac{q+1}{2q}$. Moreover, applying the Fiat-Shamir transform to such an identification scheme results in a EUF-CMA secure signature scheme in the Random Oracle Model.*

3   Identification Scheme (IDS) Based on PKP

In this section, we first present the 5-pass Zero-Knowledge Identification Scheme (ZK-IDS) based on the computational hardness of PKP [19,23], noted here PKP-IDS. Then, we introduce our optimized version of PKP-IDS and we prove that the optimized identification scheme is secure.

3.1   The Original 5-Pass PKP IDS

In this section, we present the original PKP-IDS [19,23], and we propose its slightly modified version. It consists of three probabilistic polynomial time algorithms $IDS = (\text{KeyGen}, \mathcal{P}, \mathcal{V})$ which we will describe now.

Generation of the Public Key and Secret Key in PKP-IDS. The users first agree on a prime number p, and on n, m, the dimensions of the matrix $\mathbf{A}$. The public-key in PKP-IDS is an instance of PKP, a solution to this instance is the secret-key. Thus, the prover picks a (right) kernel-vector $\mathbf{w} \in \text{Ker}(A)$, then randomly generates a secret permutation of n elements $\mathsf{sk} = \pi$ and finishes by computing $\mathbf{v} = \mathbf{w}_{\pi^{-1}}$. We summarize the key generation algorithm in Algorithm 1.

5-Pass Identification Protocol: Prover $\mathcal{P}$ and Verifier $\mathcal{V}$.
The prover and verifier are interactive algorithms that realize the identification protocol in 5 passes. The 5 passes consist of one commitment and two responses transmitted from the prover to the verifier and two challenges transmitted from the verifier to the prover. The identification protocol is summarized in Algorithm 1.

Algorithm 1. KeyGen(n,m,p)

$\mathbf{A} \xleftarrow{\$} \mathbb{F}_p^{m \times n}$
$\mathbf{w} \xleftarrow{\$} \text{Ker}(\mathbf{A})$
$\pi \xleftarrow{\$} S_n$
$\mathbf{v} \leftarrow \mathbf{w}_{\pi^{-1}}$
Return $(\mathsf{pk} = (\mathbf{A}, \mathbf{v}), \mathsf{sk} = \pi)$

Theorem 2. *PKP-IDS is complete, moreover, if the used commitment scheme is computationally hiding then PKP-IDS is computationally honest-verifier zero-knowledge and if the commitment scheme is computationally binding, then PKP-IDS is sound with soundness error $\kappa = \frac{p+1}{2p}$.*

Algorithm 2. The original 5-pass PKP identification protocol

$\mathcal{P}(\mathsf{sk}, \mathsf{pk})$		$\mathcal{V}(\mathsf{pk})$

$\sigma \xleftarrow{\$} S_n$

$\mathbf{r} \xleftarrow{\$} \mathbb{F}_p^n$

$\mathsf{C}_0 \leftarrow \mathrm{Com}(\sigma, \mathbf{Ar})$

$\mathsf{C}_1 \leftarrow \mathrm{Com}(\pi\sigma, \mathbf{r}_\sigma)$

$\xrightarrow{\quad \mathsf{C}_0, \mathsf{C}_1 \quad}$

$c \xleftarrow{\$} \mathbb{F}_p$

$\xleftarrow{\quad c \quad}$

$\mathbf{z} \leftarrow \mathbf{r}_\sigma + c\mathbf{v}_{\pi\sigma}$

$\xrightarrow{\quad \mathbf{z} \quad}$

$b \xleftarrow{\$} \{0, 1\}$

$\xleftarrow{\quad b \quad}$

if $b = 0$ **then**
   $\mathsf{rsp} \leftarrow \sigma$
else
   $\mathsf{rsp} \leftarrow \pi\sigma$
end if

$\xrightarrow{\quad \mathsf{rsp} \quad}$

if $b = 0$ **then**
   accept if $\mathsf{C}_0 = \mathrm{Com}(\sigma, A\mathbf{z}_{\sigma^{-1}})$
else
   accept if $\mathsf{C}_1 = \mathrm{Com}(\pi\sigma, \mathbf{z} - c\mathbf{v}_{\pi\sigma})$
end if

Proof. We refer to [23] for the complete proof.

In such ZK-IDS, it is usually possible to cheat if a cheater can correctly guess some challenges, so there is a nonzero probability (called the soundness error) that the verifier accepts the proof, even though the prover does not know the witness. In the case of PKP-IDS, this soundness error is $\frac{p+1}{2p}$. Thus, it is necessary to repeat the protocol several times to reduce the probability of fraud. Sequentially repeating the zero-knowledge proof N times results in an Identification scheme with knowledge error $\kappa_{\mathrm{repeated}} = \kappa^N$, hence it suffices to repeat the protocol $\lceil \lambda / \log_2(\frac{2p}{p+1}) \rceil$ times to get a soundness error $\kappa \leq 2^{-\lambda}$. The systems are constructed such that executing the protocol does not reveal any secrets (Zero-knowledge).

3.2   The Modified Version of PKP-IDS

We now describe several optimizations to reduce the communication cost of the identification scheme, as well as the computational cost of the algorithms. We will start by explaining a few standard optimizations that are common for identification protocols based on zero-knowledge proofs. Then, we will explain some novel optimizations that apply to the specific context of PKP-IDS.

Hashing the Commitments. In the commitment phase of the protocol, instead of transmitting all the $2N$ commitments $C_0^{(1)}, C_1^{(1)}, \cdots, C_0^{(N)}, C_1^{(N)}$ the prover can just hash all these commitments together with a collision resistant hash function $\mathcal{H}$ and only transmit the hash $h = \mathcal{H}(C_0^{(1)}, \cdots, C_1^{(N)})$. Then, the prover includes the N commitments $C_{1-b_i}^{(i)}$ in the second response. Since the verifier can reconstruct the $C_{b_i}^i$ himself, he now has all the $2N$ commitments, so he can hash them together and check if their hash matched h. With this optimization, we reduce the number of communicated commitments from $2N$ to N, at the cost of transmitting a single hash value.

Use Seeds and PRG. Instead of directly choosing the permutation σ at random, we can instead choose a random seed of λ bits and use a PRG to expand this seed into a permutation σ. This way, instead of transmitting σ, we can just transmit the λ-bit seed. This reduces the communication cost per permutation from $\log_2(n!)$ bits to just λ bits. For example for 128-bits of security, we have $n = 69$, so the communication cost per permutation drops from $\log_2(69!) \approx 327$ bits to just 128 bits.

Matrix A in Systematic Form. Now we get to the PKP-IDS-specific optimizations. With high probability, we can perform elementary row operations on $\mathbf{A}$ to put it in the form $(I_m \ \mathbf{A}')$, for some $(n-m)$-by-m matrix $\mathbf{A}'$. Since row operations do not affect the right kernel of A, we can just choose the matrix $\mathbf{A}$ of this form during key generation, without affecting the security of the scheme. This makes the protocol more efficient because multiplying by a matrix of this form requires only $(n-m) * m$ multiplications instead of $n * m$ multiplications for a general matrix multiplication.

Optimizing Key Generation. It is of course not very efficient to include in the public key the matrix $\mathbf{A} = [\mathbf{c}_i^{\mathbf{A}}, \mathbf{i} \in \{1, \cdots, \mathbf{n}\}]$, where c_i^A is the i-th column of A. The first idea is to just pick a random seed, and use a PRG to expand this seed to obtain the matrix $\mathbf{A}$. The public key then consists of a random seed, and the vector $\mathbf{v}$ of length n. However, we can do slightly better than this. We can use a seed to generate $\mathbf{A^*}$ which is formed by the first $n-1$ columns $c_1^A, \cdots, c_{n-1}^A$

of $\mathbf{A}$ and the vector v. Then we pick a random permutation π, and we solve for the last column c_n^A of $\mathbf{A}$ such that $\mathbf{v}_\pi$ is in the right kernel of $\mathbf{A}$. Now the public key only consists of a seed and a vector of length m (instead of a vector of length n). Another important advantage of this approach is that we do not need to do Gaussian elimination this way (and if fact this was the motivation behind this optimization). The optimized key generation procedure is given in Algorithm 3.

Algorithm 3. KeyGen(n,m,p)

$sk.seed \leftarrow$ Randomly sample λ *bits*
$(seed_\pi, pk.seed) \leftarrow \mathsf{PRG}_0(sk.seed)$
$\pi \leftarrow \mathsf{PRG}_1(seed_\pi)$
$(\mathbf{A}^*, \mathbf{v}) \leftarrow \mathsf{PRG}_2(pk.seed)$
Compute $\mathbf{c}_n^A$ from A^* and $\mathbf{v}_\pi$
sk $\leftarrow$ **sk.seed**
pk $\leftarrow$ (**pk.seed**, $\mathbf{c}_n^A$)
Return (pk, sk)

Sending Seeds Instead of Permutations. Because of the second optimization, we can send a λ-bit seed instead of σ, if the challenge bit $b = 0$. However, in the case $b = 1$, we still need to send the permutation $\pi\sigma$, because we cannot generate both σ and $\pi\sigma$ with a PRG. However, this problem can be solved. We can generate $\mathbf{r}_\sigma$ with a PRG, and then we can send this seed instead of $\pi\sigma$. This seed can be used to compute $\pi\sigma$, because if the verifier knows $\mathbf{z}$ and $\mathbf{r}_\sigma$, then he can compute $\mathbf{z} - \mathbf{r}_\sigma = c\mathbf{v}_{\pi\sigma}$. And since $\mathbf{v}$ and c are known, it is easy to recover $\pi\sigma$ from $c\mathbf{v}_{\pi\sigma}$ (we choose the parameters such that the entries of v are all distinct, so there is a unique permutation that maps $\mathbf{v}$ to $\mathbf{v}_{\pi\sigma}$). Moreover, sending the seed for $\mathbf{r}_\sigma$ does not reveal more information than sending $\pi\sigma$, because given $\mathbf{z}$ and $\pi\sigma$ it is trivial to compute $\mathbf{r}_\sigma$, so this optimization does not affect the security of the scheme. However, there is a problem: If $c = 0$, then the $c\mathbf{v}_{\pi\sigma} = 0$, and so the verifier cannot recover $\pi\sigma$. To solve this problem we just restrict the challenge space to $\mathbb{F}_p \setminus \{0\}$. This increases the soundness error to $\frac{p}{2p-2}$ (instead of $\frac{p+1}{2p}$), but this is not a big problem. An important advantage of this optimization is that the signature size is now constant. Without this optimization, a response to the challenge $b = 0$ would be smaller than a response to $b = 1$. But with the optimization, the second response is always a random seed, regardless of the value of b. We summarize the one round of the optimized IDS modified version in Algorithm 4.

Algorithm 4. The modified 5-pass of PKP-IDS

$$\mathcal{P}(\mathsf{sk}, \mathsf{pk}) \qquad\qquad\qquad \mathcal{V}(\mathsf{pk})$$

$\mathsf{seed}_0, \mathsf{seed}_1 \xleftarrow{\$} \{0,1\}^\lambda$
$\sigma \leftarrow \mathrm{PRG}_1(seed_\sigma)$
$\mathbf{r}_\sigma \leftarrow \mathrm{PRG}_2(\mathbf{r}_\sigma.seed)$
$\mathsf{C}_0 \leftarrow \mathrm{Com}(\sigma, \mathbf{A}\mathbf{r})$
$\mathsf{C}_1 \leftarrow \mathrm{Com}(\pi\sigma, \mathbf{r}_\sigma)$

$$\xrightarrow{\quad \mathsf{C}_0, \mathsf{C}_1 \quad}$$

$$c \xleftarrow{\$} \mathbb{F}_p \setminus \{0\}$$

$$\xleftarrow{\qquad c \qquad}$$

$\mathbf{z} \leftarrow \mathbf{r}_\sigma + c\mathbf{v}_{\pi\sigma}$

$$\xrightarrow{\qquad \mathbf{z} \qquad}$$

$$b \xleftarrow{\$} \{0,1\}$$

$$\xleftarrow{\qquad b \qquad}$$

$\mathsf{rsp} \leftarrow \mathsf{seed}_b$

$$\xrightarrow{\qquad \mathsf{rsp} \qquad}$$

> **if** $b = 0$ **then**
> $\sigma \leftarrow \mathrm{PRG}_1(\mathsf{rsp})$
>   accept if $\mathsf{C}_0 = \mathrm{Com}(\sigma, A\mathbf{z}_{\sigma^{-1}})$
> **else**
> $\mathbf{r}_\sigma \leftarrow \mathrm{PRG}_2(\mathsf{rsp})$
>   **if** $\mathbf{z} - \mathbf{r}_\sigma$ is not a permutation of $c\mathbf{v}$
>   **then**
>   **Return** reject
>   **else**
>   Let $\rho \in S_n$ such that $c\mathbf{v}_\rho = \mathbf{z} - \mathbf{r}_\sigma$.
>   **end if**
>   accept if $\mathsf{C}_1 = \mathrm{Com}(\rho, \mathbf{r}_\sigma)$
> **end if**

3.3   Security Proof of the Optimized Scheme

Theorem 3. – *The modified version of PKP-IDS is complete.*
  – *If the commitment scheme is computationally binding, then the scheme is sound with soundness error* $\kappa = \frac{p}{2p-2}$.
  – *If the used commitment scheme is computationally hiding and the output of* PRG$_1$ *and* PRG$_2$ *is indistinguishable from uniform randomness, then the scheme is computationally honest-verifier zero-knowledge.*

Proof. **Completeness.** In the case $b = 0$, if the prover acts honestly, then the commitment check will succeed if $\mathbf{Ar} = A\mathbf{z}_\sigma^{-1} = \mathbf{A}(\mathbf{r} + \mathbf{v}_{\pi\sigma\sigma^{-1}})$, which holds if and only if $\mathbf{Av}_\pi = 0$. Therefore, if π is a solution to the PKP problem, then the verifier will accept the transcript. In an honest execution with $b = 1$ the verifier will always accept, regardless of whether π was a solution to the PKP problem or not.

Soundness. First, we prove that the scheme has a $q2$-extractor [24]. That is, we show that, given four accepted transcripts $(C_0, C_1, c^{(i)}, \mathbf{z}^{(i)}, b^{(i)}, \mathsf{rsp}^{(i)})$ for i from 1 to 4, such that

$$c^{(1)} = c^{(2)} \neq c^{(3)} = c^{(4)}$$
$$\mathbf{z}^{(1)} = \mathbf{z}^{(2)} \quad \mathbf{z}^{(3)} = \mathbf{z}^{(4)}$$
$$b^{(1)} = b^{(3)} \neq b^{(2)} = b^{(4)}$$

one can efficiently extract a solution for the PKP problem.

By relabeling the transcripts if necessary, we can assume that $b^{(1)} = b^{(3)} = 0$ and $b^{(2)} = b^{(4)} = 1$. Let us first look at transcripts 1 and 3. Let $\sigma = \mathsf{PRG}_1(\mathsf{rsp}^{(1)})$ and $\sigma' = \mathsf{PRG}_1(\mathsf{rsp}^{(3)})$, and let $\mathbf{x} = \mathbf{A}\mathbf{z}^{(1)}_{\sigma^{-1}}$ and $\mathbf{x}' = \mathbf{A}\mathbf{z}^{(3)}_{\sigma'^{-1}}$. Then, because both transcripts are accepted, we have

$$C_0 = \mathsf{Com}(\sigma, \mathbf{x}) = \mathsf{Com}(\sigma', \mathbf{x}').$$

Therefore, the computationally binding property of Com implies that with overwhelming probability we have $\sigma = \sigma'$ and $\mathbf{x} = \mathbf{x}'$.

Now, lets look at transcripts 2 and 4. Let $\mathbf{y} = \mathsf{PRG}_2(\mathsf{rsp}^{(2)})$ and $\mathbf{y}' = \mathsf{PRG}_2(\mathsf{rsp}^{(4)})$. Since both transcripts are accepted, we know that $\mathbf{z}^{(2)} - \mathbf{y}$ and $\mathbf{z}^{(4)} - \mathbf{y}'$ are permutations of $c^{(2)}\mathbf{v}$ and $c^{(4)}\mathbf{v}$ respectively. Let ρ and ρ' be the permutations such that $c^{(2)}\mathbf{v}_\rho = \mathbf{z}^{(2)} - \mathbf{y}$ and $c^{(4)}\mathbf{v}'_\rho = \mathbf{z}^{(4)} - \mathbf{y}'$. Since both transcripts are accepted, we have

$$C_1 = \mathsf{Com}(\rho, y) = \mathsf{Com}(\rho', y'),$$

so the computationally binding property of Com implies that with overwhelming probability we have $\rho = \rho'$ and $\mathbf{y} = \mathbf{y}'$. Now, we put everything together to get

$$\begin{aligned}
0 &= \mathbf{A}(\mathbf{z}^{(1)}_{\sigma^{-1}} - \mathbf{z}^{(3)}_{\sigma^{-1}}) \\
&= \mathbf{A}(\mathbf{z}^{(2)}_{\sigma^{-1}} - \mathbf{z}^{(4)}_{\sigma^{-1}}) \\
&= \mathbf{A}(c^{(2)}\mathbf{v}_{\rho\sigma^{-1}} - \mathbf{y}_{\sigma^{-1}} - c^{(4)}\mathbf{v}_{\rho\sigma^{-1}} + \mathbf{y}_{\sigma^{-1}}) \\
&= (c^{(2)} - c^{(4)})\mathbf{A}\mathbf{v}_{\rho\sigma^{-1}}.
\end{aligned}$$

Since $c^{(2)} - c^{(4)}$ is nonzero, this means that $\rho\sigma^{-1}$ is a solution to the permuted kernel problem. Moreover the extractor can efficiently extract this solution, because he can extract ρ from either transcript 2 or 4, and he can extract σ from either transcript 1 or 3.

It is known that $2q$-extractability implies soundness with error $\frac{q+1}{2q}$, where q is the size of the first challenge space [22, 24]. In our case, the first challenge space has $p - 1$ elements, so the optimized IDS has soundness error $\frac{p}{2p-2}$.

Honest-Verifier Zero-Knowledge. To prove Honest-Verifier Zero-Knowledge we construct a simulator that outputs transcripts that are computationally indistinguishable from transcripts of honest executions of the identification scheme. First, the simulator picks a uniformly random value $c \in \mathbb{F}_p \setminus \{0\}$ and a uniformly random bit b. We treat the cases $b = 0$ and $b = 1$ separately.

Case $b = 0$: The simulator picks a random seed seed_0, a uniformly random vector $\mathbf{z}$, and computes $\sigma = \mathsf{PRG}_1(\mathsf{seed}_0)$ and $\mathsf{C}_0 = \mathsf{Com}(\sigma, \mathbf{Az})$. The simulator also commits to a dummy value to get C_1. Now the simulator outputs $(\mathsf{C}_0, \mathsf{C}_1, c, \mathbf{z}, b, \mathsf{seed}_\sigma)$.

This distribution is indistinguishable from honestly generated transcripts with $b = 0$. Indeed, the values $c, \mathbf{z}, \mathsf{seed}_0$ are indistinguishable from uniformly random in both the simulated transcripts and the honest transcripts (here we use the assumption that the output of PRG_2 is indistinguishable from the uniform distribution). The first commitment $\mathsf{C}_0 = \mathsf{Com}(\sigma, \mathbf{Az}_{\sigma^{-1}})$ is a function of seed_0 and $\mathbf{z}$, so it also has the same distribution in the simulated and the honest transcripts. Finally, the commitment C_1 is never opened, so the computationally hiding property of Com guarantees that C_1 in the simulated transcript is computationally indistinguishable from the C_1 in an honest transcript.

Case $b = 1$: The simulator picks a uniformly random seed seed_1 and a uniformly random permutation ρ and computes $\mathbf{r}_\sigma = \mathsf{PRG}_2(\mathsf{seed}_1)$, $z = c\mathbf{v}_\rho + \mathbf{r}_\sigma$ and $\mathsf{C}_1 = \mathsf{Com}()$. The simulator also commits to a dummy value to produce a commitment C_0, then the simulator outputs the transcript $(\mathsf{C}_0, \mathsf{C}_1, c, \mathbf{z}, b, \mathsf{seed}_1)$.

We now show that the simulated transcripts are indistinguishable from honestly generated transcripts with $b = 1$. It is clear that c and seed_1 are uniformly random in both the simulated transcripts and the honestly generated transcripts. Moreover, in both the simulated and the real transcripts, $\mathbf{z}$ is equal to $\mathsf{PRG}_2(\mathsf{seed}_1) + c\mathbf{v}_\rho$, and $\mathsf{C}_1 = \mathsf{Com}(\rho, \mathsf{PRG}_2(\mathsf{seed}_1))$ where ρ is indistinguishable from a uniformly random permutation (here we need the assumption that the output of PRG_1 is indistinguishable from a uniformly random permutation). Therefore $\mathbf{z}$ and C_1 have the same distribution in the simulated and the honest transcripts. Finally, the computationally hiding properties of Com guarantee that the value of C_0 in the simulated transcripts is indistinguishable from that of C_0 in honestly generated transcripts.

3.4   Communication Cost

We can now provide the communication complexity of N rounds of the modified IDS, of which the soundness error is $\left(\frac{p}{2p-2}\right)^N$. The commitment consists of a single hash value, which is only 2λ bits. The first response consists of N vectors of length n over $\mathbb{F}_p$, so this costs $Nn\lceil \log_2 p \rceil$ bits of communication. Lastly, the second responses consist of N random λ-bit seeds, N commitments (which consist of 2λ bits each) and N commitment random strings (which consist of λ bits each), so this costs $4N\lambda$ bits of communication. In total, the communication cost (ignoring the challenges) is

$$2\lambda + N\left(n\lceil \log_2 p\rceil + 4\lambda\right).$$

4   Digital Signature Scheme (DSS) Based on PKP

We present here the main contribution of this work which is to construct a digital signature scheme, based on the PKP problem, from the optimized IDS defined in Sect. 3. This is simply a direct application of the well-known Fiat Shamir transformation [9].

The key generation algorithm is identical to the key generation algorithm for the identification scheme. To sign a message m, the signer executes the first phase of the commitment scheme to get a commitment com. Then he derives the first challenge $\mathbf{c} = (c_1, \cdots, c_N)$ from m and com by evaluating a hash function $\mathcal{H}_1(m\|\text{com})$. Then he does the next phase of the identification protocol to get the N response vectors $\text{rsp}_1 = (\mathbf{z}^{(1)}, \cdots, \mathbf{z}^{(N)})$. Then he uses a second hash function to derive $\mathbf{b} = (b_1, \ldots, b_N)$ from m, com and rsp_1 as $\mathcal{H}_2(m\|\text{com}, \text{rsp}_1)$. Then he finishes the identification protocol to obtain the vector of second responses $\text{rsp}_2 = (\text{rsp}^{(1)}, \cdots, \text{rsp}^{(N)})$. Then, the signature is simply $(\text{com}, \text{rsp}_1, \text{rsp}_2)$.

To verify a signature $(\text{com}, \text{rsp}_1, \text{rsp}_2)$ for a message m, the verifier simply uses the hash function $\mathcal{H}_1$ and $\mathcal{H}_2$ to obtain $\mathbf{c}$ and $\mathbf{b}$ respectively. Then, he verifies that $(\text{com}, \mathbf{c}, \text{rsp}_1, \mathbf{b}, \text{rsp}_2)$ is a valid transcript of the identification protocol.

The signing and verification algorithms are displayed in Algorithms 5 and 6 in more detail.

We then get the same security result as Th. 5.1 in [7].

Theorem 4. *PKP-DSS is Existential-Unforgeable under Chosen Adaptive Message Attacks (EU-CMA) in the random oracle model, if*

- *the search version of the Permuted Kernel problem is intractable,*
- *the hash functions and pseudo-random generators are modeled as random oracles,*
- *the commitment functions are computationally binding, computationally hiding, and the probability that their output takes a given value is negligible in the security parameter.*

The proof is the same as in [7].

Algorithm 5. Sign(sk, m)

1: derive $\mathbf{A}, \mathbf{v}$ and π from sk.
2: **for** i from 1 to N **do**
3:    pick λ-bit seeds $\text{seed}_0^{(i)}$ and $\text{seed}_1^{(i)}$ uniformly at random
4:    $\sigma^{(i)} \leftarrow \text{PRG}_1(\text{seed}_0^{(i)})$
5:    $\mathbf{r}_\sigma^{(i)} \leftarrow \text{PRG}_2(\text{seed}_1^{(i)})$
6:    $\mathsf{C}_0^{(i)} = \text{Com}(\sigma^{(i)}, \mathbf{Ar}^{(i)})$,
7:    $\mathsf{C}_1^{(i)} = \text{Com}(\pi\sigma^{(i)}, \mathbf{r}_\sigma^{(i)})$.
8: **end for**
9: $\text{com} := \mathcal{H}_{\text{com}}(\mathsf{C}_0^{(1)}, \; \mathsf{C}_1^{(1)}, \cdots, \mathsf{C}_0^{(N)}, \; \mathsf{C}_1^{(N)})$
10: $c^{(1)}, \cdots, c^{(N)} \leftarrow \mathcal{H}_1(m \| \text{com})$. $c^i \in \mathbb{F}_p \setminus \{0\}$
11: **for** i from 1 to N **do**
12:    $\mathbf{z}^{(i)} \leftarrow \mathbf{r}_\sigma^{(i)} + c^{(i)} \mathbf{v}_{\pi\sigma^{(i)}}$
13: **end for**
14: $\text{rsp}_1 \leftarrow (\mathbf{z}^{(1)}, \cdots, \mathbf{z}^{(N)})$
15: $b^{(1)}, \cdots, b^{(N)} \leftarrow \mathcal{H}_2(m \| \text{com} \| \text{rsp}_1)$
16: **for** i from 1 to N **do**
17:    $\text{rsp}_2^{(i)} \leftarrow (\text{seed}_{b^{(i)}}^{(i)} \| \mathsf{C}_{1-b^{(i)}}^{(i)})$
18: **end for**
19: $\text{rsp}_2 \leftarrow (\text{rsp}_2^{(1)}, \cdots, \text{rsp}_2^{(N)})$
20: **Return** $(\text{com}, \text{rsp}_1, \text{rsp}_2)$

Algorithm 6. Verify(m, pk, $\sigma = (\text{com}, \text{rsp}_1, \text{rsp}_2)$)

1: $c^{(1)}, \cdots, c^{(N)} \leftarrow \mathcal{H}_1(m \| \text{com})$.
2: $b^{(1)}, \cdots, b^{(N)} \leftarrow \mathcal{H}_2(m \| \text{com} \| \text{rsp}_1)$
3: Parse rsp_1 as $\mathbf{z}^{(1)}, \cdots, \mathbf{z}^{(N)}$
4: Parse rsp_2 as $\text{seed}^{(1)}, \cdots, \text{seed}^{(N)}, \mathsf{C}_{1-b^{(1)}}^{(1)}, \cdots, \mathsf{C}_{1-b^{(N)}}^{(N)}$
5: **for** i from 1 to N **do**
6:    **if** $b^{(i)} = 0$ **then**
7:        $\sigma^{(i)} \leftarrow \text{PRG}_1(\text{seed}^{(i)})$
8:        $\mathsf{C}_0^{(i)} \leftarrow \text{Com}(\sigma^{(i)}, \mathbf{Az}_{\sigma^{(i)}-1})$
9:    **else**
10:       $\mathbf{r}_\sigma^{(i)} \leftarrow \text{PRG}_2(\text{seed}^{(i)})$
11:       **if** $\mathbf{z}^{(i)} - \mathbf{r}_\sigma$ is not a permutation of $c\mathbf{v}$ **then**
12:           **Return** reject
13:       **else**
14:           $\pi\sigma^{(i)} \leftarrow$ the permutation that maps $c\mathbf{v}$ to $\mathbf{z}^{(i)} - \mathbf{r}_\sigma$.
15:       **end if**
16:       $\mathsf{C}_1^{(i)} \leftarrow \text{Com}(\pi\sigma^{(i)}, \mathbf{r}_\sigma^{(i)})$
17:    **end if**
18: **end for**
19: $\text{com}' := \mathcal{H}_{\text{com}}(\mathsf{C}_0^{(1)}, \; \mathsf{C}_1^{(1)}, \cdots, \mathsf{C}_0^{(N)}, \; \mathsf{C}_1^{(N)})$
20: **Return** accept if and only if $\text{com} = \text{com}'$

4.1   Generic Attack

If the number of iterations N is chosen such that $(\frac{p}{2p-2})^N \leq 2^{-\lambda}$, then the cheating probability of the identification protocol is bounded by $2^{-\lambda}$. However, a recent attack by Kales and Zaverucha on MQDSS reveals that this does not meant that the Fiat-Shamir signature scheme has λ bits of security [16]. They give a generic attack that also applies to PKP-DSS. The attack exploits the fact that if an attacker can guess the first challenge **or** the second challenge, he can produce responses that the verifier will accept. The idea is to split up the attack in two phases. In the first phase, the attacker guesses the values of the N first challenges, and uses this guess to produce commitments. Then, he derives the challenges from the commitment and he hopes that at least k of his N guesses are correct. This requires on average

$$\mathsf{Cost}_1(N, k) = \sum_{i=k}^{N} \left(\frac{1}{p-1}\right)^k \left(\frac{p-2}{p-1}\right)^{N-k} \binom{N}{k}$$

trials. In the second phase, the attacker guesses the values of second challenges, and uses these guesses to generate a response. Then he derives the second challenges with a hash function and he hopes that his guess was correct for the $N-k$ rounds of the identification protocol where he did not guess the first challenge correctly. This requires on average 2^{N-k} tries. Therefore, the total cost of the attack is

$$\min_{0 \leq k \leq N} \mathsf{Cost}_1(N, k) + 2^{N-k}.$$

5   Parameter Choice and Implementation

5.1   Parameter Choice

The PKP-DSS is mainly affected by the following set of parameters: (p, n, m). We now explicitly detail the choice of these parameters. Recall that firstly the IDS [23] was designed to suit small devices. Thus, Shamir proposed $p = 251$. To have an efficient implementation we choose p to be a prime number close to a power of 2, such as 251, 509 and 4093. A solution of a random instance of PKP is to find a kernel n-vector $(\mathbf{v}_\pi)$ with distinct coordinates in $\mathbb{F}_p$. Hence, the probability to find such a vector shouldn't be too small. The probability of an arbitrary vector to be in the kernel of the matrix $A \in \mathcal{M}_{m \times n}$ whose rank is equal to m, is p^{-m}. Moreover, if the n-vector v has no repeated entries, its orbit under the possible permutations π contains $n!$ vectors. Thus, to get on average one solution, we have the following constraint: $n! \approx p^m$. And finally, using the complexity of Poupard's algorithm [18] combined with Patarin-Chauvaud's method (See Sect. 2.1), triplets of (p, n, m) were selected matching the security requirements and optimizing the size of the signature. With these parameter choices, the scheme is secure against all the attacks described in [17]. We pick the value of N just large enough such that

$$\min_{0 \leq k \leq N} \mathsf{Cost}_1(N, k) + 2^{N-k} \geq 2^\lambda,$$

such that the scheme is secure against the generic attack of Kales and Zaverucha [16]. The chosen parameter sets for three different security levels are shown in Table 1.

Table 1. PKP-DSS parameters sets

Parameter set	Security level	p	n	m	Iterations N	Attack cost
PKP-DSS-128	128	251	69	41	157	2^{130}
PKP-DSS-192	192	509	94	54	229	2^{193}
PKP-DSS-256	256	4093	106	47	289	2^{257}

5.2 Key and Signature Sizes

Public Key. A public key consists of the last column $\mathbf{c}_n^A$ of $\mathbf{A}$ and a random seed **pk.seed**, which is used to generate $\mathbf{A}^*$ which is formed by all but the last column of $\mathbf{A}$ and the vector $\mathbf{v}$. Therefore, the public key consist of $\lambda + m\lfloor\log_2(p)\rfloor$ bits.

Secret Key. A secret key is just a random seed **pk.seed** that was used to seed the key generation algorithm, therefore it consists of only λ bits.

Signature. Finally, a signature consists of a transcript of the identification protocol (excluding the challenges, because they are computed with a hash function). In Sect. 3.4 we calculated that a transcript can be represented with $2\lambda + N\left(n\lceil\log_2 p\rceil + 4\lambda\right)$ bits, so this is also the signature size.

In Table 2 we summarize the key and signature sizes for the parameter sets proposed in the previous section.

Table 2. Key and signature sizes for PKP-DSS with the three proposed parameter sets.

Security level	Parameters (p, n, m, N)	|sk| Bytes	|pk| Bytes	|sig| Kilobytes
128	$(251, 69, 41, 157)$	16	57	20.4
192	$(509, 94, 54, 229)$	24	85	43.4
256	$(4093, 106, 47, 289)$	32	103	76.5

5.3 Implementation

To showcase the efficiency of PKP-DSS and to compare the performance to existing Fiat-Shamir signatures we made a proof-of-concept implementation in plain C. The code of our implementation is available on GitHub at [4]. We have used SHA-3 as hash function and commitment scheme, and we have used

SHAKE128 as extendable output function. The running time of the signing and verification algorithms is dominated by expanding seeds into random vectors and random permutations. This can be sped up by using a vectorized implementation of SHAKE128, and using vector instructions to convert the random bitstring into a vector over $\mathbb{F}_p$ or a permutation in S_n. We leave this task for future work.

Making the Implementation Constant Time. Most of the key generation and signing algorithms is inherently constant time (signing branches on the value of the challenge bits b, but this does not leak information because b is public). The only problem was that applying a secret permutation to the entries of a vector, when implemented naively, involves accessing data at secret indices. To prevent this potential timing leak we used the "djbsort" constant time sorting code [3]. More specifically, (see Algorithm 7) we combine the permutation and the vector into a single list of n integers, where the permutation is stored in the most significant bits, and the entries of the vector are stored in the least significant bits. Then we sort this list of integers in constant time and we extract the permuted vector from the low order bits. Relative to the naive implementation this slows down signing by only 11%. There is no significant slowdown for key generation.

Algorithm 7. Constant time computation of $v' = v_\sigma$

1: Initialize a list of integers $L \leftarrow \emptyset$
2: $L := [\sigma[1] * B + v[1], \cdots, \sigma[n] * B + v[n]]$, where $B > n$ is a constant
3: sort L in constant time
4: $v' := [L[1] \bmod B, \cdots, L[n] \bmod B]$
5: Return v'

5.4   Performance Results

To measure the performance of our implementation we ran experiments on a laptop with a i5-8250U CPU running at 1.8 GHz. The C code was compiled with gcc version 7.4.0 with the compile option -O3 . The cycle counts in Table 3 are averages of 10000 key generations, signings, and verifications.

5.5   Comparison with Existing FS Signatures

In Table 4, we compare PKP-DSS to MQDSS, Picnic, and Picnic2. We can see that for all the schemes the public and secret keys are all very small. The main differences are signature size and speed. When compared to MQDSS, the signature sizes of PKP-DSS are roughly 30% smaller, while being a factor 14 and 30 faster for signing and verification respectively. Compared to Picnic, the PKP-DSS signatures are roughly 40% smaller, and signing and verification are 4 and 9 times faster respectively. Compared to Picinc2 our scheme is 153 and 170 times faster for signing and verification, but this comes at the cost of 50% larger signatures.

Finally, compared to SUSHSYFISH [12], a different scheme based on the Permuted Kernel Problem, our scheme is 3.4 and 6.6 times faster, but at the cost of 45% larger signatures.

Table 3. Average cycle counts for key generation, signing and verification, for our implementation of PKP-DSS with the three proposed parameter sets.

Security level	Parameters (p, n, m, N)	KeyGen 10^3 cycles	Sign 10^3 cycles	Verify 10^3 cycles
128	$(251, 69, 41, 157)$	72	2518	896
192	$(509, 94, 54, 229)$	121	5486	2088
256	$(4093, 106, 47, 289)$	151	7411	3491

Table 4. Comparison of different post-quantum Fiat-Shamir schemes

Security level	Scheme	Secret key (Bytes)	Public key (Bytes)	Signature (KBytes)	Sign 10^6 cycles	Verify 10^6 cycles
128	PKP-DSS-128	16	57	20.4	2.5	0.9
	MQDSS-31-48	16	46	28.0	36	27
	Picnic-L1-FS	16	32	33.2	10	8.4
	Picnic2-L1-FS	16	32	13.5	384	153
	SUSHSYFISH-1	16	72	14.0	8.6	6
192	PKP-DSS-192	24	85	43.4	5.5	2.1
	MQDSS-31-64	24	64	58.6	116	85
	Picnic-L3-FS	24	48	74.9	24	20
	Picnic2-L3-FS	24	48	29.1	1183	357
	SUSHSYFISH-3	24	108	30.8	22.7	16.5
256	PKP-DSS-256	32	103	76.5	7.4	3.5
	Picnic-L5-FS	32	64	129.7	44	38
	Picnic2-L5-FS	32	64	53.5	2551	643
	SUSHSYFISH-5	32	142	54.9	25.7	18

6 Conclusion

We introduce a new post-quantum secure signature scheme PKP-DSS, which is based on a PKP Zero-knowledge identification scheme [23]. We optimized this identification scheme, and to make it non-interactive, we used the well-known Fiat-Shamir transform.

We developed a constant-time implementation of PKP-DSS and we conclude that our scheme is competitive with other Post-Quantum Fiat-Shamir signature schemes such as MQDSS, Picnic/Picnic2, and SUSHSYFISH. The main advantages of our scheme are that signing and verification are much faster than existing Fiat-Shamir signatures and that the scheme is very simple to implement. Our implementation takes only 440 lines of C code.

Acknowledgments. This work was supported by the European Commission through the Horizon 2020 research and innovation program under grant agreement H2020-DS-LEIT-2017-780108 FENTEC, by the Flemish Government through FWO SBO project SNIPPET S007619N and by the IF/C1 on Cryptanalysis of post-quantum cryptography and by the French Programme d'Investissement d'Avenir under national project RISQ P141580. Ward Beullens is funded by an FWO fellowship.

References

1. Baritaud, T., Campana, M., Chauvaud, P., Gilbert, H.: On the security of the permuted kernel identification scheme. In: Brickell, E.F. (ed.) CRYPTO 1992. LNCS, vol. 740, pp. 305–311. Springer, Heidelberg (1993). https://doi.org/10.1007/3-540-48071-4_21
2. Bennett, C.H., Bernstein, E., Brassard, G., Vazirani, U.: Strengths and weaknesses of quantum computing. SIAM J. Comput. **26**(5), 1510–1523 (1997)
3. The djbsort software library for sorting arrays of integers or floating-point numbers in constant time. https://sorting.cr.yp.to/
4. Beullens, Ward. PKPDSS (2019). Public GitHub repository. https://github.com/WardBeullens/PKPDSS
5. Beullens, W.: On sigma protocols with helper for MQ and PKP, fishy signature schemes and more. Cryptology ePrint Archive, Report 2019/490 (2019). https://eprint.iacr.org/2019/490
6. Chase, M., et al.: Post-quantum zero-knowledge and signatures from symmetric-key primitives. In: Proceedings of the 2017 ACM SIGSAC Conference on Computer and Communications Security, pp. 1825–1842. ACM, October 2017
7. Chen, M.S., Hülsing, A., Rijneveld, J., Samardjiska, S., Schwabe, P.: MQDSS specifications (2018)
8. Damgård, I.: Commitment schemes and zero-knowledge protocols. In: Damgård, I.B. (ed.) EEF School 1998. LNCS, vol. 1561, pp. 63–86. Springer, Heidelberg (1999). https://doi.org/10.1007/3-540-48969-X_3
9. Fiat, A., Shamir, A.: How to prove yourself: practical solutions to identification and signature problems. In: Odlyzko, A.M. (ed.) CRYPTO 1986. LNCS, vol. 263, pp. 186–194. Springer, Heidelberg (1987). https://doi.org/10.1007/3-540-47721-7_12
10. Gary, M., Johnson, D.: Computers and Intractability: A Guide to NP-Completeness. W H., New York (1979)
11. Georgiades, J.: Some remarks on the security of the identification scheme based on permuted kernels. J. Cryptol. **5**(2), 133–137 (1992)
12. Beullens, W.: On sigma protocols with helper for MQ and PKP, fishy signature schemes and more IACR Cryptology ePrint Archive 2019 (2019). https://eprint.iacr.org/2019/490
13. Don, J., Fehr, S., Majenz, C., Schaffner, C.: Security of the fiat-shamir transformation in the quantum random-oracle model. Cryptology ePrint Archive, Report 2019/190 (2019). https://eprint.iacr.org/2019/190

14. Haitner, I., Nguyen, M.H., Ong, S.J., Reingold, O., Vadhan, S.: Statistically hiding commitments and statistical zero-knowledge arguments from any one-way function. SIAM J. Comput. **39**(3), 1153–1218

15. Jaulmes, É., Joux, A.: Cryptanalysis of PKP: a new approach. In: Kim, K. (ed.) PKC 2001. LNCS, vol. 1992, pp. 165–172. Springer, Heidelberg (2001). https://doi.org/10.1007/3-540-44586-2_12

16. Kales, D., Zaverucha, G.: Forgery attacks against MQDSSv2.0 Note postes on the NIST PQC forum. https://groups.google.com/a/list.nist.gov/forum/?utm_medium=email&utm_source=footer#!msg/pqc-forum/LlHhfwg73eQ/omM6TWwlEwAJ

17. Koussa, E., Macario-Rat, G., Patarin, J.: On the complexity of the Permuted Kernel Problem. IACR Cryptology ePrint Archive 2019:412 (2019)

18. Poupard, G.: A realistic security analysis of identification schemes based on combinatorial problems. Eur. Trans. Telecommun. **8**(5), 471–480 (1997)

19. Lampe, R., Patarin, J.: Analysis of Some Natural Variants of the PKP Algorithm. IACR Cryptology ePrint Archive, 2011:686

20. NIST categories: Security strength categories. https://csrc.nist.gov/CSRC/media/Projects/Post-Quantum-Cryptography/documents/call-for-proposals-final-dec-2016.pdf

21. Patarin, J., Chauvaud, P.: Improved algorithms for the permuted kernel problem. In: Stinson, D.R. (ed.) CRYPTO 1993. LNCS, vol. 773, pp. 391–402. Springer, Heidelberg (1994). https://doi.org/10.1007/3-540-48329-2_33

22. Sakumoto, K., Shirai, T., Hiwatari, H.: Public-key identification schemes based on multivariate quadratic polynomials. In: Rogaway, P. (ed.) CRYPTO 2011. LNCS, vol. 6841, pp. 706–723. Springer, Heidelberg (2011). https://doi.org/10.1007/978-3-642-22792-9_40

23. Shamir, A.: An efficient identification scheme based on permuted kernels (extended abstract). In: Brassard, G. (ed.) CRYPTO 1989. LNCS, vol. 435, pp. 606–609. Springer, New York (1990). https://doi.org/10.1007/0-387-34805-0_54

24. Chen, M.-S., Hülsing, A., Rijneveld, J., Samardjiska, S., Schwabe, P.: From 5-pass $\mathcal{MQ}$-based identification to $\mathcal{MQ}$-based signatures. In: Cheon, J.H., Takagi, T. (eds.) ASIACRYPT 2016. LNCS, vol. 10032, pp. 135–165. Springer, Heidelberg (2016). https://doi.org/10.1007/978-3-662-53890-6_5

25. Kiltz, E., Lyubashevsky, V., Schaffner, C.: A new identification scheme based on syndrome decoding. In Annual International Conference on the Theory and Applications of Cryptographic Techniques, pp. 552–586. Springer, Cham (2018)

26. Unruh, D.: Post-quantum security of fiat-shamir. In: Takagi, T., Peyrin, T. (eds.) ASIACRYPT 2017. LNCS, vol. 10624, pp. 65–95. Springer, Cham (2017). https://doi.org/10.1007/978-3-319-70694-8_3

27. Unruh, D.: Non-interactive zero-knowledge proofs in the quantum random oracle model. In: Oswald, E., Fischlin, M. (eds.) EUROCRYPT 2015. LNCS, vol. 9057, pp. 755–784. Springer, Heidelberg (2015). https://doi.org/10.1007/978-3-662-46803-6_25

28. Leurent, G., Nguyen, P.Q.: How risky is the random-oracle model? In: Halevi, S. (ed.) CRYPTO 2009. LNCS, vol. 5677, pp. 445–464. Springer, Heidelberg (2009). https://doi.org/10.1007/978-3-642-03356-8_26

29. Halevi, S., Krawczyk, H.: Strengthening digital signatures via randomized hashing. In: Dwork, C. (ed.) CRYPTO 2006. LNCS, vol. 4117, pp. 41–59. Springer, Heidelberg (2006). https://doi.org/10.1007/11818175_3

Modification Tolerant Signature Schemes: Location and Correction

Thaís Bardini Idalino[✉], Lucia Moura, and Carlisle Adams

University of Ottawa, Ottawa, Canada
{tbardini,lmoura,cadams}@uottawa.ca

Abstract. This paper considers malleable digital signatures, for situations where data is modified after it is signed. They can be used in applications where either the data can be modified (collaborative work), or the data must be modified (redactable and content extraction signatures) or we need to know which parts of the data have been modified (data forensics). A classical digital signature is valid for a message only if the signature is authentic and not even one bit of the message has been modified. We propose a general framework of modification tolerant signature schemes (MTSS), which can provide either location only or both location and correction, for modifications in a signed message divided into n blocks. This general scheme uses a set of allowed modifications that must be specified. We present an instantiation of MTSS with a tolerance level of d, indicating modifications can appear in any set of up to d message blocks. This tolerance level d is needed in practice for parametrizing and controlling the growth of the signature size with respect to the number n of blocks; using combinatorial group testing (CGT) the signature has size $O(d^2 \log n)$ which is close to the best known lower bound of $\Omega(\frac{d^2}{\log d}(\log n))$. There has been work in this very same direction using CGT by Goodrich et al. (ACNS 2005) and Idalino et al. (IPL 2015). Our work differs from theirs in that in one scheme we extend these ideas to include corrections of modification with provable security, and in another variation of the scheme we go in the opposite direction and guarantee privacy for redactable signatures, in this case preventing any leakage of redacted information.

Keywords: Modification tolerant signature · Redactable signature · Content extraction signature · Malleable signature · Modification localization · Modification correction · Digital signature · Combinatorial group testing · Cover-free family

1 Introduction

Classical digital signature schemes (CDSS) are used to guarantee that a document was created by the sender (authenticity) and has not been modified along

T. B. Idalino—Funding granted from CNPq-Brazil [233697/2014-4] and OGS.

F. Hao et al. (Eds.): INDOCRYPT 2019, LNCS 11898, pp. 23–44, 2019.
https://doi.org/10.1007/978-3-030-35423-7_2

the way (integrity); they also help to prevent the signer from claiming s/he did not sign a message (non-repudiation). The verification algorithm has a boolean output: a successful outcome is achieved if and only if both the signature is valid and the document has not been modified. In this paper, we consider more general digital signature schemes which we call *modification-tolerant signature schemes* (MTSS), which go beyond the ability of **detecting** modifications provided by CDSS, and have the ability of **locating** modifications or **locating and correcting** modifications. We discuss two types of modification-tolerant signature schemes: a general MTSS that allows the location of modified blocks of the data, and an MTSS with *correction capability*, that allows the correction of the modified blocks, recovering the original message. We give three instantiations of the scheme for the purpose of location, correction, and redaction.

In which situations can modifications be allowed or even desired in the context of digital signatures? One situation where modifications are desirable is the so-called redactable signatures [13], also called content extraction signatures [21]. In redactable signature schemes [13,18,21], some blocks of a document are redacted (blacked out) for privacy purposes, without interacting with the original signer and without compromising the validity of the signature. Related to these are the "sanitizable" signatures introduced by Ateniese et al. [1] which are also used for the purpose of privacy of (parts of) the original message, but the modifications are done by a semi-trusted third party (the sanitizer) who can modify blocks of the document and sign the modified version, without the need of intervention by the original signer. Thus, in both redactable and sanitizable signature schemes, the privacy of the (redacted or modified parts of the) original message must be preserved. For MTSS, privacy of the original data that has been modified is not required. An MTSS with only location capability that guarantees privacy can be used for implementing redactable signatures, but that is not an intrinsic requirement for MTSS. Indeed, as pointed out in [18] the scheme provided in [12] does not meet standard privacy requirements. In the case of MTSS with correction capability, privacy cannot be guaranteed by definition, since the method permits the recovery of the original document.

A different scenario where a moderate amount of modification is desirable involves collaborative work. The authors of a document can use MTSS to allow further modifications as long as the original parts can be identified as their own. Other collaborators may apply modifications to the original document and append the original document's signature, which provides information about which blocks were modified, as well as a guarantee of integrity of the original blocks. MTSS can separate the original blocks from the modified ones, while correction capability further provides retrieval of the original version of the document.

Locating modifications has also been considered in situations where modifications are not desired, but their localization is used as a mechanism to mitigate damage. Indeed, in the context of message authentication codes for data structures, Goodrich et al. [11] propose a message authentication code (MAC) with modification locating capabilities. They propose their use in data forensics applications since the identification of which information was modified can be used to identify the perpetrator of the crime (for example: the salary of a person or the grade of a student was modified on a database). In [12], in the context of MTSS with only location capability, the authors mention the advantage of being able to guarantee the integrity of part of the data instead of the all-or-nothing situation given by a CDSS boolean outcome. For example, the integrity of 95% of a document or database may contain enough information needed for a specific application, whereas it would have been considered completely corrupted and unusable in the case of CDSS. In the case of MTSS with correction capability, we can go beyond mitigating the damage, and actually recover the originally signed document.

The mechanism behind the MTSS schemes instantiated here, like in [11,12], is the use of cover-free families (CFF) in the same way as it is traditionally employed in combinatorial group testing. Combinatorial group testing has been used in cryptography in the context of digital signatures [23], broadcast communication [8,20], and many others. The main idea is to test t groups, which are subsets of the n blocks, together (with enough redundancy and intersections between groups), and each group is used to produce a distinct hash. The tuple of t hashes is then signed and provided that no more than d blocks were modified, it is possible to identify precisely which blocks have been modified. The main efficiency concern is the compression ratio: the order of growth of n/t as n grows, for a fixed modification tolerance d. Using cover-free families, it is possible to achieve a compression ratio of $O(n/(d^2 \log n))$, which is not much worse than the $O(n)$ compression ratio given by modification intolerant schemes such as CDSS.

Our Contributions: In the present paper, we propose a general framework for MTSS, and a specific MTSS scheme for modification correction and another for redacted signatures. Both schemes are based on a modification tolerance d, indicating the maximum number of modifications or redactions. The security of the schemes rely only on an underlying classical digital signature scheme and on collision resistant hash functions; therefore the schemes can be used in the context of postquantum cryptography as long as these underlying building blocks are postquantum secure.

First, we extend methods that use cover-free families for modification location [11,12] to further provide modification correction (Scheme 2 in Sect. 4.2), provided that the size of the blocks are small enough, say bounded by a constant s where an algorithm with 2^s steps can run in an acceptable amount of time. In short, the localization of the modified blocks is done using CFF similarly to [11,12] with an extra constraint on blocks of size at most s, and an exhaustive search is used to correct the block to a value that makes the concatenation of a specific group of blocks match its original hash. The assumption that a collision resistant hash function does not cause collisions for messages of small size up to s is not only reasonable, but can be tested before employing it in the method.

Second, we propose a variation of the scheme for modification location to ensure total privacy of the modified blocks in order to extend it for the purpose of redactable signatures (Scheme 3 in Sect. 6). In this case, a block modification can be a redaction to hide private information. Unlike the modification correction scheme, this scheme does not need a restriction on block size.

Paper Organization: In Sect. 2, we discuss related work. In Sect. 3, we give a general framework for modification tolerant signature schemes with and without modification correction. In Sect. 4, we instantiate the schemes for location and/or correction that allows any modifications in up to d blocks using cover-free families. In Sect. 5, we prove the unforgeability of the schemes under the adaptive chosen message attack. In Sect. 6, we extend and instantiate the modification location scheme for redactable signatures, and prove it guarantees total privacy. In Sect. 7, we discuss implementation issues of the schemes proposed in this paper. In Sect. 8, we consider the relationship of parameters and the impact on the size of the signature and the ability to locate and correct modifications. A conclusion is given in Sect. 9.

2   Related Work

The idea of error detection and correction of corrupted data is well established in coding theory. Combinatorial group testing can help locating where errors (modification of data) occurred, which can be considered an intermediate goal, which is stronger than error detection and more efficient than error correction. In the context of cryptography, localization of modified portions of data has been studied in the context of hash functions [4,5], digital signatures [3,12], and message authentication codes [7,11]. Correction of modifications is proposed by some schemes, but they have severe limitations on the correction capability [3,7]. Schemes such as the ones in [4,5,11,12] use techniques related to cover-free families to generate redundant information, which is used later to locate the modified portions of the data. The benefit of cover-free families is that they require a small amount of redundant data for a fixed threshold d in location capability.

The methods that provide location at the hash level [4,5] are based on superimposed codes, which are binary codes equivalent to d-cover-free families (d-CFF). These codes are used in two steps of the process: to generate a small set of hash tags from an input message, and to verify the integrity of the message using these tags. Because of the d-CFF property, the scheme allows the identification of up to d corrupted data segments [4,5]. A digital signature scheme with location of modifications is presented in [12]. Their scheme uses d-CFF matrices to generate a digital signature scheme that carries extra information for location of modifications. In this case, data is divided into n blocks which are concatenated and hashed according to the rows of the d-CFF. This set of hash values is signed using any classical digital signature algorithm, and both the signature and the set of hashes form the new signature of the message. The verification algorithm uses this information to precisely locate up to d blocks that contain modified content [12]. This is presented in detail in Sect. 4.2 as Scheme 1. In [11], the authors propose a solution for locating the items that were modified inside a data structure. They compute a small set of message authentication tags based on the rows of a d-disjunct matrix, which is equivalent to d-CFFs. These tags are stored within the topology of the data structure, and an auditor can later use these tags to determine exactly which pieces of data were modified and perform forensics investigation.

The methods described above have a common approach: they all compute extra integrity information based on combinatorial group testing techniques and use this information to locate up to d modified pieces of data. In our work, we show that if these pieces are small enough, it is possible to actually correct them to the originally-signed values. In the literature, we find signature and message authentication schemes that provide the correction of modifications, such as in [3, 7]. These schemes use different approaches than the ones previously discussed, and the capacity of location and correction is very limited. In [3] only a single error can be corrected, while in [7] the data is divided into blocks, and only one bit per block can be corrected.

Error correcting codes (d-ECC) are related to this work, as we could use them to provide authentication and correction of d modifications as we explain next. For a message m formed by blocks of up to $\log_2 q$ bits each, sign it using a CDSS and compute the corresponding codeword c_m using a d-ECC over alphabet q. Send the codeword c_m and the signature σ. The receiver obtains c', which may differ from c_m in at most d blocks, and by decoding c', obtains c_m and thus the original message m. Then, the verifier can check its authenticity and integrity by verifying (m, σ). We call this scheme *Scheme E*. In Sect. 4.3, we compare Scheme E and Scheme 2 using d-CFF, and find that they have very similar compression ratios. Scheme 2 has the advantage of giving more information in the failing case, of being more efficient when we do not need correction, and of being a simple variation of Schemes 1 and 3, facilitating comparison among the different approaches.

There is also a solution proposed in [2] for location of modifications in images with digital signatures, using a different approach than d-CFFs. Their scheme consists of partitioning the image into n blocks, and generating one digital signature per block (with dependency on neighbours to avoid attacks). Although we can use signature schemes with very small signature sizes, the total number of signatures in this scheme is linear with the number of blocks n, while in [12], for example, the amount of extra information produced is logarithmic in n because of the d-CFF.

Redactable or content extraction digital signatures [6, 13, 21] are used when the owner of a document signed by another party, needs to show parts of that document to a third party, but wants to keep parts of the document private. In Sect. 6, we give a variation of an MTSS scheme that implements redactable signatures. More on related work involving redactable signatures is discussed in that section.

3   Framework for Modification-Tolerant Digital Signatures

3.1   Classical Digital Signature Schemes (CDSS)

Classical digital signature schemes are based on public-key cryptography and consist of three algorithms: KEYGENERATION, SIGN, and VERIFY. We consider that any document or piece of data to be signed is a sequence of bits called a *message*.

Definition 1. *A classical digital signature scheme (CDSS) is a tuple Σ of three algorithms:*

- KEYGENERATION(ℓ) *generates a pair of keys (secret and public) (SK, PK) for a given security parameter ℓ.*
- SIGN(m, SK) *receives the message m to be signed, the secret key SK, and outputs the signature σ.*
- VERIFY(m, σ, PK) *takes as input a message m, signature σ, and public key PK. Using PK, outputs 1 if the pair (m, σ) is valid (as in Definition 2), and outputs 0 otherwise.*

Definition 2. *Let Σ be a CDSS as defined above, and let (SK, PK) be a pair of secret and public keys. A pair of message and signature (m, σ) is valid if σ is a valid output[1] of Σ.SIGN(m, SK).*

Generally speaking, we say CDSS is *unforgeable* if a signature that verifies using PK can only be generated by the signer who has SK. In more detail, we consider the model of *adaptive chosen message attack*, where the attacker $\mathcal{A}$ adaptivelly chooses a list of messages $m_1, \ldots, m_q$, and requests the respective signatures $\sigma_1, \ldots, \sigma_q$ from an oracle $\mathcal{O}$. Given this information, we say the attacker performs an *existential forgery* if he is able to produce a valid signature σ on a new message m chosen by him, $m \neq m_i, 1 \leq i \leq q$ [15,22]. Because with unlimited time an adversary can perform all possible computations, we limit the computational power of the attacker by requiring an efficient algorithm to be one that runs in probabilistic polynomial time (PPT). Moreover, we say a function f is *negligible* if for every polynomial p there exists an N such that for all $n > N$ we have that $f(n) < 1/p(n)$ [14].

Definition 3 (Unforgeability). *A digital signature scheme is existentially unforgeable under an adaptive chosen message attack if there is no PPT adversary $\mathcal{A}$ that can create an existential forgery with non-negligible probability.*

---

[1] We use "valid output" instead of Σ.SIGN(m, SK) $= \sigma$ because the signing algorithm does not need to be deterministic.

3.2 Description of MTSS

Now we define the algorithms of the modification tolerant signature scheme (MTSS). We assume that the message m to be signed has size $|m|$ in bits, and is split into n blocks, not necessarily of the same size. A message split into blocks is represented as a sequence $m = (m[1], \ldots, m[n])$, where $m[i]$ represents the ith block of message m. For two messages m and m', each split into n blocks, we denote $\mathrm{diff}(m, m') = \{i \in \{1, \ldots, n\} : m[i] \neq m'[i]\}$. An *authorized modification structure* is a collection $S \subseteq P(\{1, \ldots, n\})$, where P is the power set of $\{1, \ldots, n\}$, that contains each set of blocks that the signer allows to be modified. The idea is that if σ is a valid signature for m, then σ is a valid signature for m' if and only if $\mathrm{diff}(m, m') \in S$. Of course, to prevent inconsistencies we must have $\emptyset \in S$. Indeed, an MTSS is equivalent to a CDSS if $S = \{\emptyset\}$. A more general example is $S = \{\emptyset, \{2\}, \{3\}, \{5\}, \{2, 3\}, \{2, 5\}, \{3, 5\}\}$ for $n = 5$ blocks, which specifies blocks 1 and 4 cannot be changed and any change of at most two other blocks is allowed. The authorized modification structure is used to provide flexibility of modifications while providing control for the signer. In practice, we do not expect S to be stored explicitly, but instead to be implicitly enforced by the scheme.

Definition 4. *A modification tolerant signature scheme (MTSS) for authorized modification structure $S \subseteq P(\{1, \ldots, n\})$ on messages with n blocks is a tuple Σ of three algorithms:*

- MTSS-KEYGENERATION(ℓ) *generates a pair of secret and public keys (SK, PK) for a given security parameter ℓ.*
- MTSS-SIGN(m, SK) *receives the message m to be signed, the secret key SK, and outputs the signature σ.*
- MTSS-VERIFY(m, σ, PK) *takes as input a message m, signature σ, and public key PK. Outputs $(1, I)$ if (m, σ) is valid for modification set I (as in Definition 5), and outputs 0 otherwise.*

Definition 5. *Let Σ be an MTSS for authorized modification structure $S \subseteq P(\{1, \ldots, n\})$, and let (SK, PK) be a pair of secret and public keys. A pair (m, σ) of message and signature is valid if there exists m' such that σ is a valid output[2] of Σ.MTSS-SIGN(m', SK) and diff$(m, m') \in S$. In this case, we say (m, σ) is valid for modification set I (where $I = $ diff(m, m')).*

The definition of unforgeability of an MTSS scheme is exactly like Definition 3, but the existential forgery now needs to produce a valid signature as given in Definition 5. This is in alignment with the notions introduced in [6].

Definition 6. *An MTSS Σ for authorized modification structure $S \subseteq P(\{1, \ldots, n\})$ has correction capability if it is a tuple Σ of four algorithms, which, in addition to the algorithms in Definition 4, has the following algorithm:*

---

[2] We use "valid output" instead of Σ.MTSS-SIGN(m', SK) $= \sigma$ because the signing algorithm does not need to be deterministic.

- MTSS-VERIFY&CORRECT(m, σ, PK): takes as input a message m, signature σ, and public key PK. Outputs a pair (ver, m') where:
    1. $ver = \Sigma.\text{MTSS-VERIFY}(m, \sigma, PK)$.
    2. m' is a message with $m' \neq \lambda$ (the corrected message) if $ver = (1, I)$, $I = \text{diff}(m, m')$, and (m', σ) is a valid pair for modification set $I' = \emptyset$; in all other cases $m' = \lambda$, which indicates failure to correct.

Location of modifications with MTSS would be trivial for any $\mathcal{S} \subseteq P(\{1, \ldots, n\})$ if the signer simply produced σ as a tuple of n signatures, one for each block. However, this would be extremely inefficient for a large number of blocks n. We must reconcile the objectives of having a large $\mathcal{S}$ and having a compact signature. Of course, the signature size depends on the security parameter, but once this is fixed, we would like the signature to grow moderately as a function of n. This motivates the following definition of compression ratio.

Definition 7. *An MTSS Σ^n for messages with n blocks and signature σ with $|\sigma| \leq s(n)$ has compression ratio $\rho(n)$ if $\frac{n}{s(n)}$ is $O(\rho(n))$.*

The compression ratio measures how efficient our signature is with respect to the trivial scheme of keeping one signature per block, with $\rho(n) = O(1)$, supporting $\mathcal{S} = P(\{1, \ldots, n\})$. Classical signatures have $\rho(n) = n$ (best possible), but $\mathcal{S} = \{\emptyset\}$. In the next section we present a tradeoff, where $\rho(n) = \frac{n}{\log n}$ and $\mathcal{S}$ is the set of all sets of up to d modifications, for fixed d. Indeed, when using cover-free families it is possible to have a compression ratio of $O(\frac{n}{d^2 \log n})$ using known CFF constructions [19], while a lower bound on $s(n)$ [10] tells us we cannot have $\rho(n)$ larger than $\Theta(\frac{n}{(d^2/\log d)\log n})$.

4 d-Modification Tolerant MTSS Based on Combinatorial Group Testing

Here we propose an MTSS that allows the modification of any set of up to d blocks in the message, for a constant d which we call a tolerance level. In other words, the authorized modification structure is $\mathcal{S} = \{T \subseteq \{1, \ldots, n\} : |T| \leq d\}$. To obtain a compact signature size, we rely on combinatorial group testing, which we summarize in Sect. 4.1 before we describe the scheme in Sect. 4.2. Similar modification location methods based on combinatorial group testing have been proposed in [11,12], and the instantiation we propose for the first three algorithms of MTSS (Sect. 4.2) are based on [12]. Our new contributions in this section include proof of security for the MTSS scheme based on cover-free families and the addition of error correction capability by proposing algorithm MTSS-VERIFY&CORRECT that corrects modifications in this context.

4.1   Cover-Free Families and Group Testing

Combinatorial group testing deals with discovering d defective items in a set of n items, via testing various groups of items for the presence of defects in each group. In nonadaptive combinatorial group testing, the groups are determined before the testing process starts. For the problems considered in this paper, a modified block is a defective item, and the groups are sets of blocks combined and hashed together. In our case, we must use nonadaptive combinatorial group testing, as the tests are generated at time of signing, while verification is done later. Cover-free families allow for a small number of groups that help to identify the modified blocks.

Recall that a permutation matrix of dimension l is an $l \times l$ matrix that is obtained from permuting rows of the identity matrix.

Definition 8. *A d-cover-free family (d-CFF) is a $t \times n$ binary matrix $\mathcal{M}$ such that any set of $d + 1$ columns contains a permutation submatrix of dimension $d + 1$.*

Each column of $\mathcal{M}$ corresponds to a block of the message, and each row corresponds to a group of blocks that will be tested together. A test fails if a group contains a modified block and passes if every block in a group is unchanged. The definition of d-CFF guarantees that for any column index j and any other set of d column indices $j_1, \ldots, j_d$, there will be a row i s.t. $\mathcal{M}_{i,j} = 1$, and $\mathcal{M}_{i,j_1} = \ldots = \mathcal{M}_{i,j_d} = 0$. In other words, for any unchanged block, there exists a test that contains that block but none of the up to d modified blocks.

Figure 1 shows an example of how to use a 2-CFF$(9, 12)$ to test a message with 12 blocks (represented by the columns) by testing 9 groups of blocks (the rows). Every unchanged block is in at least one group that passes the test (with result 0), and every group that failed the test (result **1**) contains at least one modified block, which in this example are blocks 3 and 12. We note that column "result" is the bitwise-or of the columns corresponding to modified blocks 3 and 12.

blocks	1	2	3	4	5	6	7	8	9	10	11	12	
	✓	✓	X	✓	✓	✓	✓	✓	✓	✓	✓	X	result:
t_1	1	0	0	1	0	0	1	0	0	1	0	0	0
t_2	1	0	0	0	1	0	0	1	0	0	1	0	0
t_3	1	0	0	0	0	1	0	0	1	0	0	1	1
t_4	0	1	0	1	0	0	0	0	1	0	1	0	0
t_5	0	1	0	0	1	0	1	0	0	0	0	1	1
t_6	0	1	0	0	0	1	0	1	0	1	0	0	0
t_7	0	0	1	1	0	0	0	1	0	0	0	1	1
t_8	0	0	1	0	1	0	0	0	1	1	0	0	1
t_9	0	0	1	0	0	1	1	0	0	0	1	0	1

Fig. 1. Example of a 2-CFF$(9, 12)$.

The next theorem is important for the efficiency of MTSS-VERIFY& CORRECT. Indeed, it ensures that for each modified block, we can find a test that contains it together with only other unchanged blocks. Therefore, an exhaustive trial-and-error can be used to guess this block until the hash of this group of blocks matches the original hash.

Theorem 1. *Let $j_1, \ldots, j_d$ be the column indices that represent invalid elements. There is a row i such that $\mathcal{M}_{i,j_1} = 1, \mathcal{M}_{i,j_2} = \ldots = \mathcal{M}_{i,j_d} = 0$.*

Proof. Since $\mathcal{M}$ is a d-CFF, it is also a $(d-1)$-CFF, therefore one of the rows in the permutation submatrix indexed by $j_1, \ldots, j_d$ is as stated.

4.2   Description of d-Modification Tolerant Signature Scheme

The main idea of a d-modification tolerant signature scheme is to sign a message split into blocks by concatenating the hashes of these blocks according to a d-CFF matrix. This allows us to locate up to d modified blocks in the signed message, and correct these modifications. In this context, we represent a concatenation of two strings a and b as $a||b$, and λ represents an empty string.

Definition 9. *A d-modification tolerant signature scheme (d-MTSS) is an MTSS with authorized modification structure $\mathcal{S} = \{T \subseteq \{1, \ldots, n\} : |T| \leq d\}$.*

We now give an instantiation of d-MTSS using d-cover-free families based on [12].

Scheme 1: A d-Modification Tolerant Signature Scheme

The scheme requires an underlying CDSS Σ, a public hash function h, and a d-CFF(t, n) matrix $\mathcal{M}$. The algorithms are given next:

- MTSS-KEYGENERATION(ℓ): generates a key pair (SK, PK) using algorithm Σ.KEYGENERATION(ℓ).
- MTSS-SIGN(m, SK): Takes as input a secret key SK and a message $m = (m[1], \ldots, m[n])$, and proceeds as follows.
  1. Calculate $h_j = h(m[j]), 1 \leq j \leq n$.
  2. For each $1 \leq i \leq t$, compute c_i as the concatenation of all h_j such that $\mathcal{M}_{i,j} = 1, 1 \leq j \leq n$. Set $T[i] = h(c_i)$.
  3. Compute $h^* = h(m)$ and set $T = (T[1], T[2], \ldots, T[t], h^*)$.
  4. Calculate $\sigma' = \Sigma$.SIGN(T, SK). Output signature $\sigma = (\sigma', T)$.
- MTSS-VERIFY(m, σ, PK): takes as input a message $m = (m[1], \ldots, m[n])$, signature $\sigma = (\sigma', T)$ for $T = (T[1], T[2], \ldots, T[t], h^*)$, and public key PK, and proceeds as follows.
  1. Ensure that Σ.VERIFY(T, σ', PK) $= 1$, otherwise stop and output $(0, -)$.
  2. Check if $h^* = h(m)$. Stop and output $(1, \emptyset)$ if that is the case, continue otherwise.
  3. Use $\mathcal{M}$ and m and do the same process as in steps 1 and 2 of MTSS-SIGN to produce hashes $T'[1], \ldots, T'[t]$.

4. Start with an empty set V, and for each $1 \leq i \leq t$ such that $T[i] = T'[i]$, compute the set of indices of unmodified blocks $V_i = \{j : \mathcal{M}_{i,j} = 1\}$, and accumulate these values in the set of all indices of unmodified blocks $V = V \cup V_i$. Compute $I = \{1, \ldots, n\} \setminus V$. If $|I| \leq d$ output $(1, I)$, else output $(0, I)$.

The correctness of the scheme is shown next.

Theorem 2. *Consider a valid signature σ generated by MTSS-SIGN for a message m and key pair (SK, PK), and let m' be a possibly modified message with $|diff(m, m')| \leq d$. Then, MTSS-VERIFY$(m', \sigma, PK) = (1, diff(m, m'))$.*

Proof. Since σ is valid, MTSS-VERIFY(m', σ, PK) does not stop at step 1. If $m = m'$, then $h(m) = h(m')$ and the algorithm will stop in step 2, with $(1, \mathrm{diff}(m, m') = \emptyset)$. It remains to check the case it stops in step 4. The d-CFF property guarantees that if a block has not been modified, it is contained in at least one valid concatenation with $T[i] = T'[i]$, since there is a row i that avoids all modified blocks. Therefore, this block is contained in V_i. For each row i that contains a modified block, we have $T[i] \neq T'[i]$, so modified blocks are not contained in any V_i. Therefore I consists of precisely the modified blocks. Thus, $|I| \leq d$, and the algorithm outputs $(1, I = \mathrm{diff}(m, m'))$. □

The next theorem shows that when step 4 outputs $(0, I)$, Scheme 1 may give more information than required in Definition 4, as it may identify some unmodified blocks, even if not all.

Theorem 3. *Consider a valid signature σ generated by MTSS-SIGN for a message m and key pair (SK, PK), and let m' be a modified message with $|diff(m, m')| > d$. Then, MTSS-VERIFY$(m', \sigma, PK) = (0, I)$, and for any $i \in \{1, \ldots, n\} \setminus I$, block $m[i]$ is guaranteed to be unmodified.*

Proof. This case will lead MTSS-VERIFY to step 4, and since $|\mathrm{diff}(m, m')| > d$, the output will be $(0, I)$. Any block in $\{1, \ldots, n\} \setminus I$ is guaranteed to be part of matching row i, and must be unmodified, even though not every unmodified block will necessarily be placed in $\{1, \ldots, n\} \setminus I$. □

Scheme 1 has been proposed in [12]. One of our main contributions here is to add correcting capability to d-MTSS. We require the size of each block to be upper bounded by a value s that is small enough that guessing each of the (up to) d modified blocks is "computationally feasible". Basically, by brute force we compute up to $O(d2^s + n)$ hashes to accomplish the modification correction (see the algorithm under Scheme 2). We use the indices of the modified blocks in I and do an exhaustive search to recover their original values.

Scheme 2: A d-MTSS with Correction Capability

The scheme requires an underlying CDSS Σ, a public hash function h, and a d-CFF(t, n) matrix $\mathcal{M}$. It further requires that the message is divided into n blocks of size at most s. The scheme has the three algorithms from Scheme 1, and additionally the algorithm below:

– MTSS-VERIFY&CORRECT(m, σ, PK): receives as input a message $m = (m[1], \ldots, m[n])$, a signature $\sigma = (\sigma', T)$ where $T = (T[1], T[2], \ldots, T[t], h^*)$, and a public key PK, and proceeds as follows.

1. Compute $result = $ MTSS-VERIFY(m, σ, PK). If $result = (0, X)$, then stop and output $(0, X)$, otherwise $result = (1, I)$. If $|I| = 0$ go to step 6, otherwise run steps $2 - 5$ for each $k \in I$.
2. Identify a row i in $\mathcal{M}$ such that $\mathcal{M}_{i,k} = 1$ and $\mathcal{M}_{i,j} = 0$, for all $j \in I \backslash \{k\}$.
3. Compute $h_j = h(m[j])$ for all j such that $\mathcal{M}_{i,j} = 1, j \neq k$, i from step 2. Set $corrected[k] = false$.
4. For every possible binary string b of size $\leq s$, proceed as follows:
   - Compute $h_k = h(b)$.
   - For i obtained in step 2 and $1 \leq j \leq n$, compute c_i as the concatenation of every h_j such that $\mathcal{M}_{i,j} = 1$ and set $T'[i] = h(c_i)$.
   - If $T'[i] = T[i]$ and $corrected[k] = false$, set $corrected[k] = true$ and correct the block $m[k] = b$.
   - Else, if $T'[i] = T[i]$ and $corrected[k] = true$, stop and output $(1, I, \lambda)$.
5. Return to step 2 with the next $k \in I$.
6. Output $(1, I, m)$.

We note that the flag $corrected[k]$ is used to identify a possible collision of two different bit strings b giving the same hash value $h(m[k])$. Since the correct block cannot be determined, we exit with λ indicating failure. The next proposition has details on the correctness of this algorithm.

Proposition 1. *Let (m, σ) be a valid pair of message and signature produced by* MTSS-SIGN*(m, SK), using a hash function h and with $m = (m[1], \ldots, m[n])$. Let m' be a message and let $I = diff(m, m')$ with $|I| \leq d$. If for every $k \in I$, $h(m[k])$ has no other preimage of size up to s, then* MTSS-VERIFY&CORRECT*$(m', \sigma, PK) = (1, I, m)$.*

Proof. As seen in Theorem 2, the set I contains precisely the indices of the modified blocks, and Theorem 1 guarantees that such a row i in step 2 of the algorithm exists. Finally, if for every $k \in I$ the hash $h(m[k])$ has no second preimage, then step 4 of the algorithm computes a unique replacement for each modified block, and the algorithm outputs the corrected message in step 6. □

Now we prove that when selecting a good hash function, we can always guarantee the correction of any up to d modified blocks.

Theorem 4. *Consider Scheme 2 restricted to messages with blocks of size at most s, and such that h is a hash function where no two inputs of size up to s have the same hash value. Then,* MTSS-VERIFY&CORRECT*(m', σ, SK) can always correct a message with up to d modified blocks.*

Proof. Easily obtained by Proposition 1 since no matter what is the value of the block, no other block of size up to s can have the same image under h. □

Next, we show that the assumption of existence of such hash function is realistic, and in fact very easy to find.

Proposition 2. *Consider a family of hash functions $h : X \to Y$ where $|Y| = 2^l$ and a subset of the inputs $S \subseteq X$ where $|S| \leq 2^{s+1}$. The probability that there is collision in S, i.e. the probability that there exists x, z in S with $h(x) = h(z)$, is approximately $\epsilon = 1 - e^{-2^{2s-l+1}}$.*

Proof. This comes from the fact that the probability of finding at least one collision after Q hash calculations is approximately $1 - e^{-\frac{Q^2}{2^{l+1}}}$, and in our application $Q = |S| = 2^{s+1}$.

In practice, we will set $2s \ll l$. This ensures via Proposition 2 that h is very likely to have the desired property of being injective on S, the set of binary strings with size at most s. In the unlikely event that h fails this property, we try another hash function until we succeed. The expected number of attempts will be very close to 1. For example, if we consider SHA-256 as the hash function, $|Y| = 2^{256}$, and for $s = 20$, the probability of a collision within the set of size at most 20 is $\epsilon = 1 - e^{-2^{40-256+1}} \approx 3.70 \times 10^{-68}$. Indeed, we experimentally verified that SHA-256 has no collisions for $s = 20$.

Theorem 5. *Consider Scheme 2 with tolerance level d, and let m be a message split into n blocks, each block of size at most s. Let $\sigma = $ MTSS-SIGN(m, SK) and m' be a message with $I = \text{diff}(m, m')$ with $|I| \leq d$. Then, MTSS-VERIFY&COR-rect(m', σ, PK) returns $(1, I, m)$ and uses $O(n + d^2 \log n + d2^s)$ hash computations.*

Proof. By choosing a suitable hash function, Theorem 4 guarantees that MTSS-VERIFY&CORRECT returns $(1, I, m)$. The algorithm starts with the location of the modified blocks. This step uses a d-CFF for which we can use a construction with $t = O(d^2 \log n)$ rows [19], and therefore a total of $n + t$ hash calculations are required to locate these modifications. After locating up to d modified blocks, we need to perform the following computations for each one of them. We compute every possible block of size up to s and their corresponding hash values (total of $2^{s+1} - 1$), and according to the row of the CFF matrix, we compute a few extra hashes (in total not more than n, if storing h_i instead of recomputing among different runs of of line 3). This gives a total of $O(d2^s + n)$ hash computations for the correction step.

4.3 Comparing Scheme 2 with Scheme E

Let an $(l, n, D)_q$-ECC $\mathcal{C}$ be an error correcting code with minimum distance D, codewords of length l that encode messages of size n over an alphabet of size q. The alphabet must be so that it can distinguish each possible block considered in Scheme 2, so $q \geq 2^s$. For simplification, assume $c_m = (m, b_m)$ where b_m is a tuple of $l - n$ letters ("check bits"). This code can correct $d = \lfloor \frac{D-1}{2} \rfloor$ errors (modifications in the message). Next, we describe signature and verification using Scheme E. Using the same inputs as MTSS-SIGN, algorithm ECC-SIGN(m, SK) do the following steps: (1) Compute $\sigma' = \Sigma.\text{SIGN}(m, SK)$;

(2) Compute $c_m = (m, b_m)$ according to ECC $\mathcal{C}$ and return $\sigma = (b_m, \sigma')$. Then, algorithm ECC-VERIFY&CORRECT$(m, \sigma = (b, \sigma'), PK)$ do the following steps: (1) Decode $c = (m, b)$ to m' using $\mathcal{C}$; (2) If $\Sigma.$VERIFY$(m', \sigma, PK) = 1$ then return $(1, \mathrm{diff}(m, m'), m')$, else return 0.

Since $\mathcal{C}$ can correct up to d errors, if the signature σ is valid (σ' is authentic for m' and $|\mathrm{diff}(m, m')| \leq d$), then ECC-VERIFY&CORRECT will behave in the same way as MTSS-VERIFY&CORRECT and will return $(1, \mathrm{diff}(m, m'), m')$. However, when ECC-VERIFY&CORRECT returns 0, it does not distinguish between the two failing cases obtained by MTSS-VERIFY&CORRECT, namely: **Case 1)** output $(0, -)$, which means the CDSS signature σ' is not authentic; **Case 2)** output $(0, I)$, which means σ' is authentic and message m differs from the signed m' in more than d blocks, and also if $|I| < n$, then $|\{1, \ldots, n\} \setminus I| > 0$ and we are sure of at least one unmodified block. Therefore, while the Scheme E is an MTSS scheme according to Definition 4, it provides less information than Scheme 2.

A comparison of Scheme 2 with Scheme E shows they have similar compression ratios. Indeed, we first note that given an $(l, n, D)_q$-ECC, it is possible to construct a d-CFF$(l \cdot q, q^n)$, with $d = \lfloor (l-1)/(l-D) \rfloor$ [16]. Then, we consider some families of error correcting codes, and for each family we restrict Scheme 2 to only use CFFs constructed using codes from this family. In the next table, we summarize the compression ratios obtained for 3 families of codes, but we omit the details of our calculations due to lack of space.

code:	Hamming, $n = 2^{2^r-1}$	Reed-Solomon, $n = q^{\frac{(q-1)}{d}+1}$	PR-code [19]
Scheme 2	$\approx 2^{2^r-2r-2}$	$q^{\frac{(q-1)}{d}-1}$	$\Theta(\frac{n}{d^2 \log n})$
Scheme E	$\approx 2^{2^r-2r-1}$	$\frac{q^{\frac{(q-1)}{d}+1}}{2d+1}$	$O(\frac{(\log d)n}{d^2 \log n})$

In conclusion, both schemes serve the same purpose with similar compression ratios, but Scheme 2 has several advantages. First, Scheme 2 gives more information in the failing case where ECC returns 0, as discussed above. Second, Scheme 2 provides a non-correcting version of the verification algorithm (MTSS-VERIFY) which in the case of unmodified messages is basically as time efficient as $\Sigma.$VERIFY (see step 1 of MTSS-VERIFY); in this case, Scheme E still needs to run a decoding algorithm, with complexity influenced by $q \geq 2^s$, where s is the largest size of a block. Finally, Scheme 2 is part of a family of similar schemes presented here (Schemes 1–3), which can be more easily compared.

5 Security

In this section, we present the security proof of d-MTSS for Schemes 1 and 2. In order to do this, we need to check that the security of the hash function h and the unforgeability of the underlying CDSS can together ensure unforgeability of

d-MTSS. Note that although Scheme 1 appeared in [12], no security proof has been given in that paper. For the next proof we assume a *collision-resistant* hash function, i.e. a hash function in which a collision cannot be efficiently found [22].

When we consider d-MTSS using d-CFFs, a valid (m, σ) as in Definition 5 implies that there exists m' such that σ is an output of MTSS-SIGN(m', SK) and $|\text{diff}(m, m')| \leq d$. In the next theorem we suppose there is a valid (m, σ) as a forgery to our scheme. We consider two types of forgery: a *strong forgery* consists of (m, σ) such that MTSS-VERIFY$(m, \sigma, PK) = (1, I), |I| \leq d$; a *weak forgery* consists of (m, σ) such that MTSS-VERIFY$(m, \sigma, PK) = (1, \emptyset)$.

Theorem 6. *Let X be a d-MTSS as described in Scheme 1 based on an existentially unforgeable CDSS Σ and on a collision resistant hash function h. Then, X is existentially unforgeable.*

Proof. (By contradiction) Suppose X is not existentially unforgeable. Then, there is an adversary $\mathcal{A}$ that, after q adaptive queries to a signing oracle $\mathcal{O}$, obtains pairs $(m_1, \sigma_1), \ldots, (m_q, \sigma_q)$, with $\sigma_i = (\sigma'_i, T_i), 1 \leq i \leq q$, and with non-negligible probability, outputs a valid pair (m, σ), with $\sigma = (\sigma', T)$, $T = (T[1], T[2], \ldots, T[t], h^*)$, and $|\text{diff}(m, m_i)| > d$, for all $1 \leq i \leq q$.

We show that if such $\mathcal{A}$ exists, then we can build a probabilistic polynomial time algorithm $\mathcal{A}'$ which has the following input and output:

Input: an existentially unforgeable CDSS Σ and a collision-resistant hash function h, both with security parameter ℓ.

Output: either a existential forgery (T, σ') of Σ or a collision pair for h.
  Next we describe the steps of such $\mathcal{A}'$.

1. Simulate the probabilistic polynomial time adversary $\mathcal{A}$ forging an MTSS based on Σ and h using queries mentioned above. With non-negligible probability, this will produce a forgery $(m, \sigma = (\sigma', T))$ in X, as described above. Otherwise, return "FAIL".
2. If $T \neq T_i$, for all $1 \leq i \leq q$, $\mathcal{A}'$ presents (T, σ') as a forgery in Σ, for σ' the corresponding signature of T.
3. If $T = T_i$, for some $1 \leq i \leq q$, first calculate I by computing MTSS-VERIFY(m, σ, PK). Then, we have:
   - In the case of weak forgery, we must have $I = \emptyset$, and so the final element of T is $h(m)$ and the final element of T_i is $h(m_i)$, and since $m \neq m_i$, $\mathcal{A}'$ presents (m, m_i) as a collision pair for h.
   - Otherwise, we must have a strong forgery with $1 \leq |I| \leq d$. So, there exists m' such that MTSS-VERIFY$(m', \sigma, PK) = (1, \emptyset)$ and $|\text{diff}(m, m')| \leq d$. Since $|\text{diff}(m, m_i)| > d$, there must be a block $m[k], k \in \{1, \ldots, n\} \setminus I$, that is considered valid in m but $m[k] \neq m_i[k]$. Let p be any row of the CFF matrix $\mathcal{M}$ with $\mathcal{M}_{p,k} = 1$. Because $T = T_i$, this implies $T[p] = h(c) = h(c') = T_i[p]$, for $c = h(m[j_1])||h(m[j_2])||\ldots||h(m[j_s])$ and $c' = h(m_i[j_1])||h(m_i[j_2])||\ldots||h(m_i[j_s])$, where $k \in \{j_1, j_2, \ldots, j_s\}$. If $h(m[k]) = h(m_i[k])$, then $\mathcal{A}'$ presents $(m[k], m_i[k])$ as a collision pair for h. Otherwise, $\mathcal{A}'$ presents (c, c') as a collision pair for h.

The probability $p(\ell)$ that $\mathcal{A}'$ succeeds is the same as the probability that $\mathcal{A}$ succeeds, where ℓ is the security parameter. Whenever $\mathcal{A}'$ succeeds, we have either an existential forgery of Σ or a collision for h, corresponding to steps 2 and 3, respectively. For each ℓ, one of these steps is at least as likely to occur as the other, so it has probability at least $1/2$. So, for any security parameter ℓ, use one of two algorithms (an existential forger for Σ, or a collision finder for h) that runs in probabilistic polynomial time and succeeds with probability at least $p(\ell)/2$. In other words, we can technically design two adversaries $\mathcal{A}'_1$ and $\mathcal{A}'_2$ based on $\mathcal{A}'$. $\mathcal{A}'_1$ forges Σ by proceeding as $\mathcal{A}'$ but returning "FAIL" if it falls in the case of step 3. Similarly, $\mathcal{A}'_2$ finds a collision for h or returns "FAIL" if it falls in the case of step 2. Then, either $\mathcal{A}'_1$ or $\mathcal{A}'_2$ will succeed with probability at least $p(\ell)/2$ for infinitely many ℓ. This contradicts either the unforgeability of Σ or the collision resistance of h. □

6   Using MTSS for Redactable Signatures

Now we turn our attention to using MTSS in general and using similar algorithms to our proposed d-MTSS for redactable signature schemes. Redactable and sanitizable signature schemes allow for parts of a message to be removed or modified while still having a valid signature without the intervention of the signer. Sanitizable signatures usually requires the existence of a semi-trusted party called the *sanitizer* who is entrusted to do the modifications and recomputation of the signature, in some schemes done in a transparent way (see [18]). Our proposed scheme does not deal with sanitizable, but rather with redactable signatures.

Redactable signatures have been proposed in several variants also under the names of content extraction signatures [21] and homomorphic signatures [13]. Redactable signature schemes (RSS) "allow removing parts of a signed message by any party without invalidating the respective signature" [6] and without interaction with the signer. In [21], the authors mention content extraction for privacy protection or bandwidth savings. Suppose Bob is the owner of a document signed by Alice and does not want to send the whole document to a third verifying party Cathy but only some extracted parts of the document; however, Cathy still needs to verify that Alice is the signer of the original document. Alice is agreeable with future redactions when she signed the document. An example given in [21] is that Bob has his university transcripts signed by the issuing university (Alice) and wants to submit the transcripts to a prospect employer (Cathy) without revealing some of his private information such as his date of birth. Cathy must be able to verify that the signature came from the university in spite of the redaction. In addition to the privacy application, content extraction can be used in a similar way when only part of a large document needs to be passed by Bob to Cathy for the purpose of reducing the communication bandwidth [21].

The notion of redactable signatures we consider next is in line with our general definition of MTSS, but differs in that we add another algorithm called

MTSS-REDACT and we require total privacy of the redacted parts. We give next a d-MTSS version that is redactable based on ideas similar to Scheme 1 but modifying it to guarantee total privacy of redacted blocks. As mentioned in [18], the scheme proposed in [12] which was presented as Scheme 1 does not meet standard privacy requirements and in particular leaks the original message's hash value. The scheme we propose below addresses this issue by individually signing each of the hashes of the groups of blocks, and at the time of redaction of blocks, also redacting from the signature tuple any hashes involving concatenations of the modified blocks. To avoid more complex forms of forgery, that could take advantage of combining individual signatures of concatenations coming from different signed messages, we add the same random string to the various hashes of concatenations to link the individual parts that are signed at the same time; in addition, to avoid reordering of blocks within the same message via reordering the groups, we add a group counter to these hashes before signing.

In the description below, a redaction is represented by the symbol ■.

Scheme 3: A Redactable d-MTSS with Privacy Protection

The scheme requires an underlying CDSS Σ, a public hash function h, a d-CFF(t, n) matrix $\mathcal{M}$ and a random number generator RAND. The algorithms are given next:

- MTSS-KEYGENERATION(ℓ): generates a key pair (SK, PK) using algorithm Σ.KEYGENERATION(ℓ).
- MTSS-SIGN(m, SK): Takes as input SK and a message $m = (m[1], \ldots, m[n])$, and proceeds as follows.
  1. Calculate $h_j = h(m[j]), 1 \leq j \leq n$. Compute a random string $r =$RAND().
  2. For each $1 \leq i \leq t$, compute c_i as the concatenation of all h_j such that $\mathcal{M}_{i,j} = 1, 1 \leq j \leq n$, and set $T[i] = h(c_i)||r||id(i, t+1)$, where $id(i, t+1)$ encodes the numbers i and $t+1$.
  3. Compute $h^* = h(m)$, set $T[t+1] = h^*||r||id(t+1, t+1)$ and set $T = (T[1], \ldots, T[t+1])$.
  4. Calculate $\sigma'[i] = \Sigma$.SIGN($T[i], SK$), for each $1 \leq i \leq t+1$ and set $\sigma' = (\sigma'[1], \sigma'[2], \ldots, \sigma'[t+1])$. Output signature $\sigma = (\sigma', r)$.
- MTSS-VERIFY(m, σ, PK): takes as input a message $m = (m[1], \ldots, m[n])$, a signature $\sigma = (\sigma', r)$, and a public key PK, and proceed as follows.
  1. Check if Σ.VERIFY($h(m)||r||id(t+1, t+1), \sigma'[t+1], PK$) = 1. Stop and output $(1, \emptyset)$ if that is the case; continue otherwise.
  2. Use $\mathcal{M}$, m, r and do the same process as in steps 1–3 of MTSS-SIGN to produce tuple $T' = (T'[1], \ldots, T'[t])$.
  3. For each $1 \leq i \leq t$ such that Σ.VERIFY($T'[i], \sigma'[i], PK$) = 1, compute the set of indices of intact blocks $V_i = \{j : \mathcal{M}_{i,j} = 1\}$ and do $V = V \cup V_i$. Compute $I = \{1, \ldots, n\} \setminus V$. Output $(1, I)$ if $|I| \leq d$; output 0 otherwise.
- MTSS-REDACT(m, σ, R): takes as input a message $m = (m[1], \ldots, m[n])$, a signature $\sigma = (\sigma', r)$, and a set $R \subseteq \{1, \ldots, n\}$ of blocks to be redacted, with $|R| \leq d$, and proceeds as follows.
  1. If $R = \emptyset$, then stop and output (m, σ).

2. Create copies of the message and signature: $\overline{m} = m$, $\overline{\sigma} = \sigma$, so that $\overline{\sigma} = (\overline{\sigma}', r)$.
3. Set $\overline{\sigma}'[t+1] = \blacksquare$.
4. For each $j \in R$: set $\overline{m}[j] = \blacksquare$ and for each index i such that $\mathcal{M}_{i,j} = 1$ set $\overline{\sigma}'[i] = \blacksquare$
5. Output $(\overline{m}, \overline{\sigma} = (\overline{\sigma}', r))$.

The correctness of the first three algorithms follows similar reasoning using the CFF properties as argued in Theorem 2, taking into account the different approach used here where t CDSS signatures and t CDSS verifications are required. The redaction offers total privacy in the sense of information theory, as no information related to the redacted blocks is kept in the signature, which are erased in steps 3 and 4 of MTSS-REDACT. The redacted blocks and redacted parts of the signature will only affect the verification of the parts of the signatures involving redacted blocks; all other block indices will be indicated as unmodified in the output of line 3 of MTSS-VERIFY, as long as no more than d blocks have been redacted.

In the next theorem, we establish the unforgeability of this scheme.

Theorem 7. *Let X be a redactable d-MTSS given in Scheme 3 based on an existentially unforgeable CDSS Σ, on a collision-resistant hash function h, and on a random Oracle. Then, X is existentially unforgeable.*

Sketch of the Proof. Similar reasoning as in Theorem 6 can be used to argue that the unforgeability of Σ and the collision resistance of the hash function are sufficient to protect against forgery at the level of individual parts of the tuple signature. However, we need to rule out more complex forgery attempts that could try to combine individual signatures in the signature tuple in different ways as well as different blocks from different messages. The use of a common random string in the creation of each $T[i]$ in lines 2 and 3 of algorithm MLSS-SIGN prevents an adversary from trying to combine message blocks and signature parts of $(m_1, \sigma_1), \ldots, (m_q, \sigma_q)$ coming from different calls to the random Oracle to create a new valid signature since, by definition, two different calls to the oracle will, with high probability, not produce the same random string. Furthermore, the concatenation of the encoding of the test index and the number of tuple elements, $id(i, t+1)$, within each tuple position $T[i]$ in line 2 and 3, makes it highly unlikely that blocks are added, removed or reordered, since this would amount to finding a collision in the hash function. □

7   Implementation Issues

When implementing Schemes 1–3, there are a few details that need to be considered regarding efficiency, security, and even flexibility on the inputs or outputs of the algorithms. For example, we consider a message divided into blocks that we represented as a sequence, but blocks may be represented using different data structures depending on the application and the type of data. Pohls [18] discusses sequence, set and tree data structures for blocks, which could be employed.

When signing a message using MTSS-SIGN as described in Schemes 1–3, we could consider not hashing every block before concatenation, especially if the sizes of the blocks are small enough that a hash function will end up increasing the size of the data being concatenated. This approach needs to be carefully considered, since a simple concatenation does not insert a delimitation on where the individual blocks start or end, and therefore blocks with a shared suffix or prefix may lead to wrong identifications of valid/invalid. To be safe, we can hash each block before concatenating them as presented in our schemes, or ensure the concatenations use delimiters to separate blocks, or require blocks of fixed size.

The correction algorithm MTSS-VERIFY&CORRECT computes the set of indices of modified blocks I and tries to correct these blocks to their original value. If there is at least one position where two different blocks match the hash of the original one (a second preimage on the hash function), the algorithm aborts the correction process and outputs an empty string λ to represent correction error. As seen in Proposition 2 and the discussion that follows, it is very unlikely for such event to occur, and we could always choose another hash function with no collisions for certain block sizes. However, if some specific application is not flexible in the choice of hash functions and such an event happens, an interesting approach can be to correct as many modified blocks as possible, and return some information regarding the ones with collisions (such as a fail message or even a list of possible values for those specific blocks). This approach allows for partial correction of modified data, that may be interesting for some applications. Moreover, if we already know that the chosen hash function has no collisions for blocks of size up to s, we do not need to run step 4 for every possible block of size $\leq s$, and we could stop this loop as soon as we find the first match, improving the efficiency of the method.

Regarding the multiple hash computations that happen in the correction algorithm, one could consider some improvements. Note that we already compute the hashes of all unmodified blocks when we do the call of MTSS-VERIFY to obtain the set I, so these hashes of unmodified blocks could be reused in step 2. Moreover, we repeat for every modified block in I the same process of computing all blocks of size $\leq s$ and their corresponding hash values. For the cases where we have a big set of modified blocks (big d), one may consider to pre-compute all these values, in case the application can handle the storage that this will require.

8 Parameter Relations

For MTSS with modification location only (Scheme 1), a message m is split into n blocks of no specific size, and a location capability parameter d needs to be decided. These parameters are used to construct a d-CFF(t, n) with number of rows $t = \Theta(d^2 \log n)$ if using [19], $t = d\sqrt{n}$ if using [17], and $t = q^2$ when using [9], for any prime power q and positive integer k that satisfy $q \geq dk + 1$. The signature size is impacted by d and n, since there are $t + 1$ hashes as part of the signature. Therefore, while smaller sizes of blocks and larger d give a more precise location of modifications, they also increase the size of the signature.

Now consider the exact same message m, but for the case of an MTSS with correction capabilities (Scheme 2). This scheme requires that the blocks have a small size of up to s bits, which implies that the very same message m now has many more blocks $n' \gg n$. A larger number of blocks directly increases the size of the signature. But now, the d that was enough to locate the modifications before may not be enough anymore, since modifications that were in one big block before now may be spread over several small blocks. When locating the modifications, the algorithm aborts the process if the number of modified blocks is larger than the expected location capability d, which may cause the scheme to fail to correct more often if this value is not increased as n' increases.

The size of the signature σ in Schemes 1 and 2 is $|\sigma| = |h(.)| \times (t+1) + |\sigma'|$, and in Scheme 3 is $|\sigma| = |\sigma'| \times (t+1) + |r|$, for σ' a classical digital signature, r a random bit string, $h(.)$ a traditional hash function, and t the number of rows of a d-CFF(t,n). The input consists of a message of size $|m| = N$ in bits, divided into n blocks, each of size at most s, so $N \approx n \times s$. In Scheme 2, given N, we need to wisely choose s so it is small enough to allow corrections of blocks, while guaranteeing n is small enough to have a reasonable $|\sigma|$. We cannot expect our signature to be as small as the ones from classical digital signature schemes, since we require extra information in order to be able to locate and correct portions of the data. In summary what we want is $n \times s \gg |\sigma|$.

The next examples show that even for small $s = 8$, we still have a reasonably small signature.

Example 1: $N = 1$ GB $= 2^{30}$ bytes $= 2^{30}2^3 = 2^{33}$ bits, $h =$ SHA-256, $s = \log|h| = \log 2^8 = 8$ bits, $d = 4$, and we use RSA with a 2048-bit modulus. Then we have $n = N/s = 2^{33}/2^3 = 2^{30}$ blocks, with 8 bits each. Consider the d-CFF(q^2, q^{k+1}) from [9], with $k = 6, q = 25, t = 25^2, n = 25^7$. Now, since $|\sigma| = |h(.)| \times (t+1) + |\sigma'|$ in Schemes 1 and 2, we have $|\sigma| = 2^8 \times (25^2 + 1) + 2048 = 162304$ bits, which is 20288 bytes, or ~ 20 KB.

Example 2: For the same message and parameters as in Example 1, now we use a random bit string r of size 128 bits and create a signature as in Scheme 3. Since $|\sigma| = |\sigma'| \times (t+1) + |r|$, we have $|\sigma| = 2048 \times (25^2 + 1) + 128 = 1282176$ bits, which is 160272 bytes, or ~ 160 KB.

For Scheme 3, small blocks like in Example 2 are not required, so we can get a much smaller signature. The choice of s and n in this case depends on the application, and on whether we wish to correct non-redactable blocks.

9 Conclusion

We introduce modification tolerant signature schemes (MTSS) as a general framework to allow localization and correction of modifications in digitally signed data. We propose a scheme based on d-CFFs that allows correction of modifications, and a variation without correction that gives redactable signatures. The presented schemes are provably secure and present a digital signature of size close to the best known lower bound for d-CFFs.

Interesting future research includes an implementation of the schemes proposed here, with practical analysis of parameter selection for specific applications. In addition, new solutions for MTSS beyond d-CFFs can also be of interest. The d-CFF treats every block the same and allows for any combination of up to d blocks to be modified. Specific applications can have different requirements about what combinations of blocks can be modified by specifying a different authorized modification structure. Moreover, other hypotheses about more likely distribution of modifications throughout the document can be used for efficiency; for example, modified blocks may be concentrated close to each other. One idea in this direction is to use blocks with sub-blocks for increasing granularity of modification location and to aid correction. This would involve matrices with a smaller d for the bigger blocks and a larger d for sub-blocks of a block, picking these parameters with the aim of decreasing t and consequently signature size. It is out of the scope of this paper to go into detailed studies of other types of modification location matrices, which we leave for future work.

References

1. Ateniese, G., Chou, D.H., de Medeiros, B., Tsudik, G.: Sanitizable signatures. In: di Vimercati, S.C., Syverson, P., Gollmann, D. (eds.) ESORICS 2005. LNCS, vol. 3679, pp. 159–177. Springer, Heidelberg (2005). https://doi.org/10.1007/11555827_10
2. Barreto, P.S.L.M., Kim, H.Y., Rijmen, V.: Toward secure public-key blockwise fragile authentication watermarking. IEE Proc. Vis. Image Sig. Process. **149**(2), 57–62 (2002)
3. Biyashev, R.G., Nyssanbayeva, S.E.: Algorithm for creating a digital signature with error detection and correction. Cybernet. Syst. Anal. **48**(4), 489–497 (2012)
4. De Bonis, A., Di Crescenzo, G.: Combinatorial group testing for corruption localizing hashing. In: Fu, B., Du, D.-Z. (eds.) COCOON 2011. LNCS, vol. 6842, pp. 579–591. Springer, Heidelberg (2011). https://doi.org/10.1007/978-3-642-22685-4_50
5. De Bonis, A., Di Crescenzo, G.: A group testing approach to improved corruption localizing hashing. Cryptology ePrint Archive, Report 2011/562 (2011). https://eprint.iacr.org/2011/562
6. Derler, D., Pöhls, H.C., Samelin, K., Slamanig, D.: A general framework for redactable signatures and new constructions. In: Kwon, S., Yun, A. (eds.) ICISC 2015. LNCS, vol. 9558, pp. 3–19. Springer, Cham (2016). https://doi.org/10.1007/978-3-319-30840-1_1
7. Di Crescenzo, G., Ge, R., Arce, G.R.: Design and analysis of dbmac, an error localizing message authentication code. In: IEEE Global Telecommunications Conference, GLOBECOM 2004, vol. 4, pp. 2224–2228 (2004)
8. D'Arco, P., Stinson, D.R.: Fault tolerant and distributed broadcast encryption. In: Joye, M. (ed.) CT-RSA 2003. LNCS, vol. 2612, pp. 263–280. Springer, Heidelberg (2003). https://doi.org/10.1007/3-540-36563-X_18

9. Erdös, P., Frankl, P., Füredi, Z.: Families of finite sets in which no set is covered by the union of R others. Israel J. Math. **51**, 79–89 (1985)
10. Füredi, Z.: On r-cover-free families. J. Comb. Theory **73**, 172–173 (1996)
11. Goodrich, M.T., Atallah, M.J., Tamassia, R.: Indexing information for data forensics. In: Ioannidis, J., Keromytis, A., Yung, M. (eds.) ACNS 2005. LNCS, vol. 3531, pp. 206–221. Springer, Heidelberg (2005). https://doi.org/10.1007/11496137_15
12. Idalino, T.B., Moura, L., Custódio, R.F., Panario, D.: Locating modifications in signed data for partial data integrity. Inf. Process. Lett. **115**(10), 731–737 (2015)
13. Johnson, R., Molnar, D., Song, D., Wagner, D.: Homomorphic signature schemes. In: Preneel, B. (ed.) CT-RSA 2002. LNCS, vol. 2271, pp. 244–262. Springer, Heidelberg (2002). https://doi.org/10.1007/3-540-45760-7_17
14. Katz, J., Lindell, Y.: Introduction to Modern Cryptography. Chapman & Hall/CRC, Washington (2007)
15. Menezes, A.J., Vanstone, S.A., Van Oorschot, P.C.: Handbook of Applied Cryptography, 1st edn. CRC Press Inc., Boca Raton (1996)
16. Niederreiter, H., Wang, H., Xing, C.: Function fields over finite fields and their applications to cryptography. In: Garcia, A., Stichtenoth, H. (eds.) Topics in Geometry, Coding Theory and Cryptography. Algebra and Applications, pp. 59–104 (2006)
17. Pastuszak, J., Pieprzyk, J., Seberry, J.: Codes identifying bad signatures in batches. In: Roy, B., Okamoto, E. (eds.) INDOCRYPT 2000. LNCS, vol. 1977, pp. 143–154. Springer, Heidelberg (2000). https://doi.org/10.1007/3-540-44495-5_13
18. Pöhls, H.C.: Increasing the Legal Probative Value of Cryptographically Private Malleable Signatures. Ph.D. Thesis, University of Passau (2018)
19. Porat, E., Rothschild, A.: Explicit nonadaptive combinatorial group testing schemes. IEEE Trans. Inf. Theory **57**, 7982–7989 (2011)
20. Safavi-Naini, R., Wang, H.: New results on multi-receiver authentication codes. In: Nyberg, K. (ed.) EUROCRYPT 1998. LNCS, vol. 1403, pp. 527–541. Springer, Heidelberg (1998). https://doi.org/10.1007/BFb0054151
21. Steinfeld, R., Bull, L., Zheng, Y.: Content extraction signatures. In: Kim, K. (ed.) ICISC 2001. LNCS, vol. 2288, pp. 285–304. Springer, Heidelberg (2002). https://doi.org/10.1007/3-540-45861-1_22
22. Stinson, D., Paterson, M.: Cryptography: Theory and Practice, 4th edn. CRC Press, Boca Raton (2018)
23. Zaverucha, G.M., Stinson, D.R.: Group testing and batch verification. In: Kurosawa, K. (ed.) ICITS 2009. LNCS, vol. 5973, pp. 140–157. Springer, Heidelberg (2010). https://doi.org/10.1007/978-3-642-14496-7_12

Rerandomizable Signatures Under Standard Assumption

Sanjit Chatterjee and R. Kabaleeshwaran[(⊠)]

Department of Computer Science and Automation, Indian Institute of Science,
Bangalore, India
{sanjit,kabaleeshwar}@iisc.ac.in

Abstract. The Camenisch-Lysyanskaya rerandomizable signature (CL-RRS) scheme is an important tool in the construction of privacy preserving protocols. One of the limitations of CL-RRS is that the signature size is linear in the number of messages to be signed. In 2016, Pointcheval-Sanders introduced a variant of rerandomizable signature (PS-RRS) scheme which removes the above limitation. However, the security of PS-RRS scheme was proved under an interactive assumption. In 2018, Pointcheval-Sanders improved this to give a reduction under a parameterized assumption.

In 2012, Gerbush et al. introduced the dual-form signature technique to remove the dependency on interactive/parameterized assumption. They applied this technique on the CL-RRS scheme (for single message) and proved its unforgeability under static assumptions instead of the interactive assumption used in the original work but in the symmetric composite-order pairing setting.

In this work, we realize a fully rerandomizable signature scheme in the prime order setting without random oracle based on the SXDH assumption. The signature structure is derived from Ghadafi's structure-preserving signature. We first apply the dual-form signature technique to obtain a composite-order variant, called RRSc. A signature in RRSc consists of only two group elements and is thus independent of the message block length. The security of the proposed scheme is based on subgroup hiding assumptions. Then we use the dual pairing vector space framework to obtain a prime-order variant called RRS and prove its security under the SXDH assumption.

Keywords: Rerandomizable signatures · Dual-form signatures · Dual pairing vector spaces · Standard assumption

1 Introduction

In their seminal work, Camenisch and Lysyanskaya [10] introduced a rerandomizable signature (henceforth denoted as CL-RRS) scheme. The rerandomizability property says that, given a signature σ on some message m under the public key PK, anybody can compute another valid signature on the same message which

© Springer Nature Switzerland AG 2019
F. Hao et al. (Eds.): INDOCRYPT 2019, LNCS 11898, pp. 45–67, 2019.
https://doi.org/10.1007/978-3-030-35423-7_3

is indistinguishable from the original signature. The rerandomizability property aids in replacing costly zero knowledge proof system in many privacy-preserving protocols. The CL-RRS scheme has an additional desirable property that a signature can be generated on multiple message blocks in a single invocation of the signing algorithm. Due to these attractive properties, CL-RRS scheme has been used as a building block in many applications such as group signature [3], anonymous attestation [4], aggregate signature [23] and E-cash [14].

The main drawbacks of the CL-RRS scheme are (i) the signature size depends on the length of the message block signed and (ii) unforgeability is proved under the interactive LRSW assumption. In 2016, Pointcheval-Sanders [29] introduced a new rerandomizable signature (henceforth called PS-RRS) scheme in the Type-3 pairing setting: $e : \mathbb{G} \times \mathbb{H} \to \mathbb{G}_T$ [19]. They considered the signature space to be $\mathbb{G}$ while the public key comes from $\mathbb{H}$. Separating the signature space from the public key space allows them to optimize the signature size. Using an ℓ-wise independent function in the signature structure, the PS-RRS construction can make the signature length constant. However, the unforgeability of PS-RRS is proved under a new interactive assumption (called as the PS assumption).

In 2018, their follow-up work [30] presented a weak unforgeability proof for the PS-RRS scheme under a parameterized (called as q-MSDH-1) assumption. They also modified the original PS-RRS (henceforth called mPS-RRS) scheme a bit and proved its unforgeability under the q-MSDH-1 assumption. However, they could achieve only weak rerandomizability for the mPS-RRS scheme, as one of the random exponents has to be provided explicitly as part of the signature. They also showed that mPS-RRS scheme can be modified to realize full rerandomizability, but its unforgeability is proved only in the random oracle model. [30] further described a modified CL-RRS (henceforth called mCL-RRS) scheme under a new parameterized assumption (called as q-MSDH-2), instead of an interactive assumption. However, mCL-RRS achieves only weak rerandomizability and to achieve fully rerandomizability random oracle based argument is required for the unforgeability.

Usually, the hardness of parameterized assumption is ensured in the generic group model, which provides only the lower bound. Also the parameters in the parameterized assumptions are related to the number of oracle queries in the security reduction of the protocol and become stronger as the parameter grows. For example, Cheon [7] showed that the q-SDH problem can be solved using $O(\sqrt{p/q})$ group operations, where p is the underlying group order. Hence, in the literature there are several efforts [12,13,18] to remove the dependence on parameterized assumption for the security reduction.

In 2012, Gerbush et al. [18] introduced an interesting technique called dual-form signature. They applied this technique in the composite order pairing setting to argue security of several signature schemes based on static assumptions. This way they were able to remove the dependency on interactive or parameterized (q-type) assumptions in some existing signature schemes [2,5,10]. In particular, they constructed a dual-form variant of Camenisch-Lysyanskaya signature (for the case of single message) in the symmetric composite-order setting. Since then the dual form proof technique has been used to argue security of structure preserving signature, group signature etc. [22,24,25] based on some static assumption.

While [18] did achieve a dual-form variant of CL-RRS scheme for single message block, the scheme is instantiated in the composite-order pairing setting. Due to the relative inefficiency [16,20] of the composite-order pairing, a construction in the prime-order setting is usually preferable. Since the PS-RRS scheme is instantiated in the prime-order and has constant size signature, the authors [29] demonstrated that it is a better alternative of the dual-form CL-RRS scheme in several privacy-preserving applications, such as group signatures [3], anonymous credentials [1,10]. However, the unforgeability of PS-RRS (or, mPS-RRS) can be proved only under some interactive/parameterized assumption. So in this work we explore the applicability of the dual-form signature technique to realize an RRS scheme with constant size signature as in [29,30] based on some standard (static) assumptions.

The dual-form signature [18] consists of two signing algorithms, namely Sign_A and Sign_B that will respectively return two forms of signature both of which verify under the same public key. To argue security, the forgery space is partitioned into two types, namely Type-I and Type-II that respectively correspond to the signatures returned by Sign_A and Sign_B.

The approach that [18] had taken to argue security of the signature variants under static assumption, consists of two steps. The first step is to construct a dual-form of the signature variants and argue its security under some static assumptions. Next, they obtained the actual signature scheme by removing any one of the Sign_A or Sign_B algorithm. Finally, they argued that the security of the signature scheme is reducible from the security of the dual-form signature variants.

1.1   Our Contribution

We realize a fully rerandomizable signature scheme based on the SXDH assumption without random oracle in the prime order setting. Towards this goal, we first construct a rerandomizable signature scheme (denoted as RRSc), whose construction is inspired from [17]'s structure-preserving signature scheme, in the composite-order setting with $N = p_1 p_2$. We argue the unforgeability of RRSc under subgroup hiding assumptions. Then we convert the above RRSc scheme to the prime-order setting (denoted as RRS) which is instantiated using the dual pairing vector space (DPVS) framework [21]. We argue the security of RRS under the SXDH assumption. We also describe a variant of RRS (denoted as PS-RRS) constructed from PS-RRS scheme [29]. Table 1 compares the proposed rerandomizable signature schemes with the existing ones.

Our approach is similar to the previous works that used the dual form signature technique [22,24,25,31]. Rather than first defining a dual-form variant of (rerandomizable) signature as in some of the previous works [8,18,32], we directly apply the dual-form signature techniques in the unforgeability proof. In other words, we use Sign_A in the actual scheme construction while Sign_B is used

Table 1. Comparing rerandomizable signatures in the standard model.

Scheme	Pairing Setting	Group Order	#σ	Rand.	EUF-CMA
CL-RRS [10]	Symmetric	prime	$2\ell+1$	Full	LRSW (interactive)
mCL-RRS [30]			$2\ell+3$	Weak	q-MSDH-1
PS-RRS [29]	Asymmetric	prime	2	Full	PS (interactive)
mPS-RRS [30]			2	Weak	q-MSDH-2
DF-CL-RRS ‡ [18]	Symmetric	composite	3	Full	SGH, Static
RRSc Sect. 3	Asymmetric	composite	2	Full	SGH
RRS Sect. 4	Asymmetric	prime	1 †	Full	SXDH

† RRS scheme consists of a single signature component, but in the DPVS setting it requires four atomic group elements. ‡ Dual-form of CL-RRS scheme that signs a single message, whereas the other schemes sign a message block of length ℓ.

only in the unforgeability proof. Similar to previous results, security is argued using a hybrid argument.

Organization of the Paper. In Sect. 2, we recall a few definitions that will be used in this paper. In Sects. 3 and 4, we present the rerandomizable signature scheme in the composite and prime order settings respectively. In Sect. 4.4, we present a variant of rerandomizable signature scheme and provide a comparative analysis in Sect. 4.5.

2 Preliminaries

2.1 Notation

For a prime p, $\mathbb{Z}_p^*$ denotes the set of all non-zero elements from $\mathbb{Z}_p$. We denote $a \xleftarrow{\$} A$ to be an element chosen uniformly at random from the non-empty set A. For $n > 1$, $\boldsymbol{b} \in \mathbb{Z}_p^n$ denotes the vector $(b_1, \ldots, b_n)$, where $b_j \in \mathbb{Z}_p$, for all $j \in [1, n]$. For any two vectors $\boldsymbol{b} = (b_1, \ldots, b_n), \boldsymbol{b}^* = (b_1^*, \ldots, b_n^*)$ from $\mathbb{Z}_p^n$, the 'dot' product is denoted as $\boldsymbol{b} \cdot \boldsymbol{b}^*$ which is same as $\boldsymbol{b}(\boldsymbol{b}^*)^\top$, since both are equal to $\sum_{i=1}^n b_i b_i^*$. We denote $GL(n, \mathbb{Z}_p)$ to be the set of all non-singular matrix of order n over $\mathbb{Z}_p$ and A^{-1} to be the inverse of the matrix $A \in GL(n, \mathbb{Z}_p)$. For any matrix M from $\mathbb{Z}_p^{m \times n}$, $M^\top$ denotes the transposition of the matrix M.

2.2 Bilinear Pairing Setting

We recall the definition of bilinear group generator from [16].

Definition 1. *A bilinear group generator $\mathcal{G}$ is a probabilistic polynomial time (PPT) algorithm which takes the security parameter λ as input and outputs (N, G, H, G_T, e, μ), where N is either prime or composite, G, H and G_T are the groups such that $|G| = |H| = k_1 N$ and $|G_T| = k_2 N$ for $k_1, k_2 \in \mathbb{N}$, all the elements of G, H, G_T are of order at most N and $e : G \times H \longrightarrow G_T$ is a bilinear map which satisfies,*

(i) *Bilinearity: For all $g, g' \in G$ and $h, h' \in H$, one has $e(g \cdot g', h \cdot h') = e(g, h) \cdot e(g, h') \cdot e(g', h) \cdot e(g', h'),*$

(ii) *Non degeneracy: If a fixed $g \in G$ satisfies $e(g, h) = 1$ for all $h \in H$, then $g = 1$ and similarly for a fixed element $h \in H$ and*

(iii) *Computability: The map e is efficiently computable.*

The additional parameter μ is optional and defined as follows. Whenever G and H are prime-order cyclic groups, μ contains their respective generators g and h. Whenever the groups G and H are decomposed into their cyclic subgroups $G_1, \ldots, G_n$ and $H_1, \ldots, H_n$ respectively, μ contains the description of these subgroups and/or their generators.

The bilinear group generator $\mathcal{G}$ is said to be of composite-order (resp. prime-order), if N is composite (resp. prime). In this paper we use both prime-order and composite-order bilinear group settings. Hence, for ease of readability, we use the following notation to differentiate between these two settings. In the prime-order setting, we denote $\mathcal{P} = \mathcal{G}$, $\mathbb{G} = G$, $\mathbb{H} = H$, $\mathbb{G}_T = G_T$ and we could obtain only trivial subgroups, hence the generators g and h of the respective groups $\mathbb{G}$ and $\mathbb{H}$. In the composite-order setting, we denote $\mathcal{G}_N = \mathcal{G}$ and we decompose the groups $G \cong G_1 \oplus \ldots \oplus G_n$ and $H \cong H_1 \oplus \ldots \oplus H_n$ for $N = p_1 \ldots p_n$ with μ containing required subgroup(s) information i.e., $\{g_i, h_i\}_{i=1}^n$, where g_i (resp. h_i) is the generator of the subgroup G_i (resp. H_i).

The Dual Pairing Vector Space (DPVS) was introduced by [27,28], though the following definition is taken from [11]. Here we consider the concrete case of $n = 4$, however, one can define the DPVS for any $n > 1$.

Definition 2. *Given the parameters $p, n = 4$, the dual orthogonal basis generator is denoted as $\mathsf{Dual}(\mathbb{Z}_p^4)$ and it returns two random bases $\mathbb{B} = (b_1, \ldots, b_4)$ and $\mathbb{B}^* = (b_1^*, \ldots, b_4^*)$ which are defined from $\mathbb{Z}_p^4$ such that $b_i \cdot b_j^* = 0 \bmod p$, for $i \neq j$ and $b_i \cdot b_i^* = \psi \bmod p$, for all $i, j \in [1, 4]$ with $\psi \in \mathbb{Z}_p^*$.*

From the above definition, we denote $\mathcal{P}_{(\perp,4)}$ to be the bilinear group generator which takes the security parameter λ and an integer $n = 4$ as input and outputs $(p, G, H, G_T, e, \{G_i, H_i\}_{i=1}^4, g, h)$. Here $G = G_1 \oplus \ldots \oplus G_4 \approx \mathbb{G}^4$ and $H = H_1 \oplus \ldots \oplus H_4 \approx \mathbb{H}^4$. Also, g (resp. h) is the generator of the group $\mathbb{G}$ (resp. $\mathbb{H}$). Let g^{b_i} (resp. $h^{b_j^*}$) be the generator of the subgroup G_i (resp. H_j), for $i, j \in [1, 4]$ such that $e(g^{b_i}, h^{b_j^*}) = 1$, for $i \neq j$ and $e(g^{b_i}, h^{b_i^*}) = e(g, h)^\psi$, for $i, j \in [1, 4]$. Any element $\tilde{g} \in G$ can be written as $\tilde{g} = g^{\sum_{i=1}^4 \gamma_i b_i}$, for some $\gamma_i \in \mathbb{Z}_p$. We say that γ_i is the coefficient of the term $\tilde{g}$ with respect to the basis b_i, for any $i \in [1, 4]$.

2.3 Complexity Assumptions

Composite-Order Setting. Recall that the subgroup hiding (SGH) assumptions in [15,26] are defined in the symmetric composite-order setting. Whereas, [6] defined the SGH assumption in the asymmetric composite-order setting with $N = p_1 p_2 p_3$. In this section we recast the SGH assumption of [6] in the asymmetric bilinear group of composite-order $N = p_1 p_2$. Let us denote $\Theta_N = (N = p_1 p_2, G, H, G_T, e, g, h)$, where g (resp. h) is the generator of G

(resp. H) and the pairing is defined as $e : G \times H \to G_T$. Now we define the SGH assumptions as follows.

Assumption 1. SGH$_{p_1 \to p_1 p_2}^H$ *Given* $(\Theta_N, \mu = \{g_1, h_1, h_2\}, \hat{T})$, *it is hard to decide whether* $\hat{T} \in H_1$ *or* $\hat{T} \in H$.

Assumption 2. SGH$_{p_1 \to p_1 p_2}^G$ *Given* $(\Theta_N, \mu = \{g_1, g_2, h_1\}, T)$, *it is hard to decide whether* $T \in G_1$ *or* $T \in G$.

Assumption 3. SGH$_{p_2 \to p_1 p_2}^H$ *Given* $(\Theta_N, \mu = \{g_2, g_1^{\tau_1} g_2^{\tau_2}, h_1, h_2\}, \hat{T})$, *it is hard to decide whether* $\hat{T} \in H_2$ *or* $\hat{T} \in H$, *for* $\tau_1, \tau_2 \xleftarrow{\$} \mathbb{Z}_N$.

Prime-Order Setting. Now we define some variant of subspace assumptions similar to [11]. Here we consider the bilinear group generator $\mathcal{P}_{(\perp, 4)}$ which outputs $(p, G, H, G_T, e, \{G_i, H_i\}_{i=1}^4)$. Let g (resp. h) be the generator of the group $\mathbb{G}$ (resp. $\mathbb{H}$), where $G \approx \mathbb{G}^4$ and $H \approx \mathbb{H}^4$. Let us denote $\Theta = (p, G, H, G_T, e, g, h)$ in the following definitions.

Assumption 4. *Given* Θ *and* $g^{b_1}, g^{b_2}, h^{b_1^*}, h^{b_2^*}, h^{b_3^*}, h^{b_4^*}, U_1 = g^{\mu_1 b_1 + \mu_2 b_3}, U_2 = g^{\mu_1 b_2 + \mu_2 b_4}, T_1 = h^{\tau_1 b_1^* + \tau_2 b_3^*}, T_2 = h^{\tau_1 b_2^* + \tau_2 b_4^*}$, *it is hard to decide whether* $\tau_2 = 0$ *mod p or not.*

Assumption 5. *Given* Θ *and* $g^{b_1}, g^{b_2}, g^{b_3}, g^{b_4}, h^{b_1^*}, h^{b_2^*}, U_1 = h^{\mu_1 b_1^* + \mu_2 b_3^*}, U_2 = h^{\mu_1 b_2^* + \mu_2 b_4^*}, T_1 = g^{\tau_1 b_1 + \tau_2 b_3}, T_2 = g^{\tau_1 b_2 + \tau_2 b_4}$, *it is hard to decide whether* $\tau_2 = 0$ *mod p or not.*

We observe that Assumption 5 can be directly obtained from the subspace assumption in $\mathbb{G}$ [11, Definition 12] by removing the coefficient μ_2 from the latter instance and taking $N = 4$ and $k = 2$. Hence Assumption 5 is reducible to the subspace assumption in $\mathbb{G}$ [11, Definition 12]. Now from Lemma 2 of [11], DDH$_\mathbb{G}$ is reducible to the subspace assumption in $\mathbb{G}$, and hence to Assumption 5. Similarly, Assumption 4 is obtained from the subspace assumption in $\mathbb{H}$. Also, from Lemma 2 of [11], we infer that DDH$_\mathbb{H}$ is reducible to the subspace assumption in $\mathbb{H}$ and hence to Assumption 4. Now we recall the decisional Diffie-Hellman assumption (DDH) in $\mathbb{G}$ (denoted as DDH$_\mathbb{G}$) as follows.

Assumption 6. *Given* $(p, \mathbb{G}, \mathbb{H}, \mathbb{G}_T, e, g, h, g^a, g^b)$ *and* $T = g^{ab+\theta}$, *it is hard to decide whether* $\theta = 0$ *or not, for* $a, b \xleftarrow{\$} \mathbb{Z}_p$.

In the same way, we can define the DDH assumption in $\mathbb{H}$ (denoted as DDH$_\mathbb{H}$). When $\mathcal{P}$ satisfies the DDH assumption in both $\mathbb{G}$ and $\mathbb{H}$, then we say that $\mathcal{P}$ satisfies the symmetric external Diffie-Hellman (SXDH) assumption.

3 RRS in the Composite-Order Setting

In this section, we present the rerandomizable signature scheme (denoted as RRSc) in the asymmetric composite-order setting. The structure of the signature is inspired from Ghadafi's [17] structure-preserving signature (SPS) scheme.

We prove unforgeability of the RRSc scheme under subgroup hiding assumptions. We follow the standard definition of signature scheme and its security as recalled in the full version [9]. Our main goal is to realize a rerandomizable signature scheme in the prime-order setting, which is described in Sect. 4. However we present the RRSc scheme in the composite-order setting as a stepping stone towards that goal.

3.1 Construction

First we describe our RRSc construction idea in brief. The construction is instantiated in the bilinear group of composite-order $N = p_1 p_2$. Here the source groups are decomposed into two orthogonal subgroups i.e., $G \approx G_1 \oplus G_2$ and $H \approx H_1 \oplus H_2$ such that $e(g_i, h_j) = 1$, for $i \neq j$, where g_i (resp. h_j) is the generator of the subgroup G_i (resp. H_j). In the RRSc construction, we mimic the [17] SPS structure to obtain a signature on ℓ block of messages, for some $\ell \in \mathbb{N}$. In particular, we use the exponent of the form $(x + m_1 + \sum_{j=2}^{\ell} m_j y_j)/y_1$ suitably randomized in the subgroup G_1 to obtain a rerandomizable signature component B. For verification, the variables x and y_j's are provided in the exponent of H_1 component of the public key. To verify a signature, the randomness used in signing needs to be given in the subgroup G_1's exponent separately. The subgroup G_2 is used to define another signing algorithm, which is used only in the security proof. The subgroup H_2 is used in the proof to determine the forgery type returned by the forger.

Run the bilinear group generator $\mathcal{G}_N$ on λ which outputs $(\Theta_N, \mu = \{g_i, h_i\}_{i=1}^{2})$, where $\Theta_N = (N = p_1 p_2, G, H, G_T, e)$ and g_i (resp. h_i) is a random element from the p_i-order subgroup G_i (resp. H_i) of G (resp. H), for $i \in [1, 2]$. The pairing is defined as $e : G \times H \to G_T$.

Table 2. RRSc scheme in the composite-order setting.

KeyGen(λ)	Sign($SK, \boldsymbol{m} = (m_1, \ldots, m_\ell)$)
Run $\mathcal{G}_N(\lambda) \to (\Theta_N, \mu = \{g_1, h_1\})$, where $\Theta_N = (N = p_1 p_2, G, H, G_T, e)$. Choose $x, \{y_j\}_{j=1}^{\ell} \xleftarrow{\$} \mathbb{Z}_N$ and set $PK := \{\Theta_N, h_1, \{Y_j := h_1^{y_j}\}_{j=1}^{\ell},$ $X := h_1^x\}$ and $SK := \{x, \{y_j\}_{j=1}^{\ell}, g_1\}$. Return (SK, PK).	Choose $r \xleftarrow{\$} \mathbb{Z}_N$ and set $A := g_1^r$, $B := g_1^{\frac{r}{y_1}(x + m_1 + \sum_{j=2}^{\ell} m_j y_j)}$. Return $(\boldsymbol{m}, \sigma := (A, B))$.
	Ver($PK, \boldsymbol{m}, \sigma$)
	Accept if $e(A, h_1) \neq 1$ and $e(B, Y_1) = e(A, X h_1^{m_1} \prod_{j=2}^{\ell} Y_j^{m_j})$.

The RRSc scheme consists of three PPT algorithms, which are defined in Table 2. Notice that, we avoid the trivial forgery by checking $e(A, h_1) \neq 1$. Suppose we do not check the above condition, then anyone can output $\sigma = (1, 1)$ as a (trivial) forgery on any message $\boldsymbol{m} \in \mathbb{Z}_N^\ell$. The correctness of the scheme can be verified using the following equalities,

$$e(B, Y_1) = e(g_1^{\frac{r}{y_1}(x+m_1+\sum_{j=2}^{\ell} m_j y_j)}, h_1^{y_1})$$

$$= e(g_1^r, h_1^{x+m_1+\sum_{j=2}^{\ell} m_j y_j}) = e(A, X h_1^{m_1} \prod_{j=2}^{\ell} Y_j^{m_j}).$$

The second equality follows from the linearity of the pairing and the last equality follows from the definition of X and Y_j's.

3.2 Randomizability

An additional feature of a rerandomizable signature scheme is the so-called *rerandomizable property*. This feature has been utilized effectively in the construction of several other protocols, such as group signature [3] and anonymous credential scheme [10].

It is easy to see that the RRSc scheme satisfies rerandomizability property. Consider the signature $\sigma = (A, B)$ on the message m as defined in Table 2, which can be randomized by choosing a random $t \xleftarrow{\$} \mathbb{Z}_N$ and computing $\sigma' = (A^t, B^t)$. One can verify that σ' is a valid signature on m under the PK.

3.3 Unforgeability

As mentioned before, we use the dual-form signature technique [18,22,31] to prove unforgeability of the RRSc scheme under subgroup hiding assumptions. First we define the forgery classes as follows. Let $\mathcal{V}$ be the set of all message and signature pairs (m^*, σ^*) such that they verify under the public key PK, where $m^* = (m_1^*, \ldots, m_\ell^*) \in \mathbb{Z}_N^\ell$ and $\sigma^* = (A^*, B^*) \in G^2$. Now we partition the forgery class $\mathcal{V}$ into two disjoint sets $\mathcal{V}_I$ and $\mathcal{V}_{II}$ which are defined as follows.

Type I: $\mathcal{V}_I = \{(m^*, \sigma^*) \in \mathcal{V} : (A^*)^{p_2} = 1, (B^*)^{p_2} = 1\}$,
Type II: $\mathcal{V}_{II} = \{(m^*, \sigma^*) \in \mathcal{V} : (A^*)^{p_2} \neq 1 \text{ or } (B^*)^{p_2} \neq 1\}$.

From the above definition, for any message and signature pair (m^*, σ^*) satisfying verification equation, the signature $\sigma^* = (A^*, B^*)$ can be written as $A^* = g_1^r g_2^{\delta_1}$ and $B^* = g_1^{\frac{r}{y_1}(x+m_1^*+\sum_{j=2}^{\ell} m_j^* y_j)} g_2^{\delta_2}$, for some r, δ_1, δ_2 from $\mathbb{Z}_N$. In order to prove unforgeability, we use the subgroup hiding assumptions defined in Sect. 2.3.

Theorem 1. *If the assumptions,* $SGH_{p_1 \to p_1 p_2}^H$, $SGH_{p_1 \to p_1 p_2}^G$ *and* $SGH_{p_2 \to p_1 p_2}^H$ *hold in* $\mathcal{G}_N$, *then the RRSc scheme is EUF-CMA secure.*

Proof. Let Sign_A be same as the Sign algorithm defined in Table 2. Next we define the following Sign_B algorithm, which is used by the simulator in the security argument. The Sign_B algorithm takes the secret key SK along with an element $g_2 \in G_2$ and the message $m \in \mathbb{Z}_N^\ell$ and outputs a message-signature pair.

Sign$_B(SK \cup \{g_2\}, \boldsymbol{m} = (m_1, \ldots, m_\ell))$:

   Choose $r \xleftarrow{\$} \mathbb{Z}_N, \delta_1, \delta_2 \xleftarrow{\$} \mathbb{Z}_N$ and
   set $A := g_1^r g_2^{\delta_1}, B := g_1^{\frac{r}{y_1}(x + m_1 + \sum_{j=2}^\ell m_j y_j)} g_2^{\delta_2}$.
   Return $(\boldsymbol{m}, \sigma := (A, B))$.

Note that $e(g_2, h_1) = 1$ and hence the signature returned by Sign_B can be verified under PK. Now we use a hybrid argument to prove this theorem in terms of the following games.

Game$_R$. This is the original EUF-CMA game. Recall that, after receiving the PK from the challenger, the forger $\mathcal{A}$ makes q many signing oracle queries adaptively and then returns a forgery from $\mathcal{V}$.

Game$_0$. Same as Game$_R$ except that $\mathcal{A}$ returns a forgery from $\mathcal{V}_I$. Let E be the event that $\mathcal{A}$ returns a forgery from $\mathcal{V}_{II}$ in Game$_0$. In Lemma 2, we prove that the event E happens with negligible probability under SGH$^H_{p_1 \to p_1 p_2}$ assumption. Thus we deduce that Game$_R$ and Game$_0$ are computationally indistinguishable under SGH$^H_{p_1 \to p_1 p_2}$ assumption. In particular we have,

$$|Adv_{\mathcal{A}}^{\mathsf{Game_R}} - Adv_{\mathcal{A}}^{\mathsf{Game_0}}| \leq Pr[E] \leq Adv_{\mathcal{B}}^{SGH^H_{p_1 \to p_1 p_2}}.$$

Game$_k$. Same as Game$_0$ except that the first k signing queries are answered using Sign$_B$, for $k \in [1, q]$, whereas the last $q - k$ queries are answered using Sign$_A$. For $k \in [1, q]$, in Lemma 3, we prove that Game$_{k-1}$ and Game$_k$ are computationally indistinguishable under SGH$^G_{p_1 \to p_1 p_2}$ assumption. In particular we have,

$$|Adv_{\mathcal{A}}^{\mathsf{Game_{k-1}}} - Adv_{\mathcal{A}}^{\mathsf{Game_k}}| \leq Adv_{\mathcal{B}}^{SGH^G_{p_1 \to p_1 p_2}}.$$

Finally in Lemma 4, we prove that $Adv_{\mathcal{A}}^{\mathsf{Game_q}}$ is negligible under SGH$^H_{p_2 \to p_1 p_2}$ assumption. In particular we have,

$$Adv_{\mathcal{A}}^{\mathsf{Game_q}} \leq Adv_{\mathcal{B}}^{SGH^H_{p_2 \to p_1 p_2}}.$$

Hence by the hybrid argument and from Eqs. 1, 2 and 3, described below, we have,

$$Adv_{\mathcal{A}}^{UF} = Adv_{\mathcal{A}}^{\mathsf{Game_R}} = |Adv_{\mathcal{A}}^{\mathsf{Game_R}} - Adv_{\mathcal{A}}^{\mathsf{Game_0}} + Adv_{\mathcal{A}}^{\mathsf{Game_0}} - Adv_{\mathcal{A}}^{\mathsf{Game_1}} +$$
$$\ldots + Adv_{\mathcal{A}}^{\mathsf{Game_{k-1}}} - Adv_{\mathcal{A}}^{\mathsf{Game_k}} + \ldots + Adv_{\mathcal{A}}^{\mathsf{Game_q}}|$$
$$\leq Pr[E] + q\, Adv_{\mathcal{B}}^{SGH^G_{p_1 \to p_1 p_2}} + Adv_{\mathcal{B}}^{SGH^H_{p_2 \to p_1 p_2}}$$
$$\leq Adv_{\mathcal{B}}^{SGH^H_{p_1 \to p_1 p_2}} + q\, Adv_{\mathcal{B}}^{SGH^G_{p_1 \to p_1 p_2}} + Adv_{\mathcal{B}}^{SGH^H_{p_2 \to p_1 p_2}}.$$

$\square$

Lemma 2. *If* $SGH^H_{p_1 \to p_1 p_2}$ *assumption holds in* $\mathcal{G}_N$, *then* $Pr[E]$ *is negligible.*

Proof. Assume that the event E happens with some non-negligible probability. Then we construct a simulator $\mathcal{B}$ to break the $SGH^H_{p_1 \to p_1 p_2}$ problem as follows. $\mathcal{B}$ is given $\Theta_N, g_1, h_1, h_2, \hat{T}$ and his goal is to decide whether $\hat{T}$ is from H_1 or H. Now $\mathcal{B}$ chooses x, y_j from $\mathbb{Z}_N$, for $j \in [1, \ell]$ and defines the PK and SK as described in Table 2. Given the PK, $\mathcal{A}$ makes the signing oracle queries to $\mathcal{B}$. Since $\mathcal{B}$ knows the secret key SK, he computes σ_i using Sign_A algorithm and sends to $\mathcal{A}$. After q many queries, $\mathcal{A}$ returns a forgery $(\boldsymbol{m}^*, \sigma^*)$, where $\boldsymbol{m}^* = (m_1^*, \ldots, m_\ell^*)$ and $\sigma^* = (A^*, B^*)$. Then $\mathcal{B}$ checks (i) the forgery $(\boldsymbol{m}^*, \sigma^*)$ is valid and (ii) the message $\boldsymbol{m}^*$ is not queried earlier. If any of these checks fail to hold, $\mathcal{B}$ returns a random bit to his challenger. Otherwise, $\mathcal{B}$ checks whether $\mathcal{A}$ is returning a Type-II forgery. From the definition of forgery types, it is sufficient for $\mathcal{B}$ to check whether $e(A^*, h_2) \neq 1$ or $e(B^*, h_2) \neq 1$ holds.

As mentioned before, since the forgery returned by $\mathcal{A}$ is valid, $\mathcal{B}$ writes $A^* = g_1^r g_2^{\delta_1}$ and $B^* = g_1^{\frac{r}{y_1}(x + m_1^* + \sum_{j=2}^\ell m_j^* y_j)} g_2^{\delta_2}$, for some r, δ_1, δ_2 from $\mathbb{Z}_N$ unknown to $\mathcal{B}$. Now $\mathcal{B}$ defines the following backdoor verification test (BVT),

$$S := B^*(A^*)^{-\frac{1}{y_1}(x + m_1^* + \sum_{j=2}^\ell m_j^* y_j)} \overset{?}{=} 1.$$

Note that the correctness of the forgery ensures that $e(S, h_1) = 1$. Hence the above BVT can be simplified as $S = g_2^{\delta_2 - \frac{\delta_1}{y_1}(x + m_1^* + \sum_{j=2}^\ell m_j^* y_j)} \overset{?}{=} 1$. We argue that for a Type-II forgery, the event $S = 1$ happens with negligible probability. From the exponent of S, it is sufficient to prove that for a Type-II forgery, the event $\delta_2 - \frac{\delta_1}{y_1}(x + m_1^* + \sum_{j=2}^\ell m_j^* y_j) = 0$ modulo p_2 happens with negligible probability.

Suppose $\delta_1 = 0$ modulo p_2, then the condition $\delta_2 - \frac{\delta_1}{y_1}(x + m_1^* + \sum_{j=2}^\ell m_j^* y_j) = 0$ modulo p_2 ensures that δ_2 must be zero modulo p_2. This means the forgery cannot be Type-II, by definition. Hence assume that $\delta_1 \neq 0$ modulo p_2. We re-write the above condition as $(x + m_1^* + \sum_{j=2}^\ell m_j^* y_j)/y_1 = \delta_2/\delta_1$ modulo p_2. Since x and y_js are chosen uniformly at random from $\mathbb{Z}_N$, by Chinese Remainder Theorem (CRT), x (resp. y_j) modulo p_2 and x (resp. y_j) modulo p_1 are independent. Hence x and y_j modulo p_2 are information theoretically hidden to $\mathcal{A}$. Thus $\mathcal{A}$ have to guess the value of δ_2/δ_1. Hence the probability that $(x + m_1^* + \sum_{j=2}^\ell m_j^* y_j)/y_1 = \delta_2/\delta_1$ modulo p_2 is at most $1/N$, which is negligible.

Now $\mathcal{B}$ checks whether $S \overset{?}{=} 1$ or not. Suppose $S \neq 1$, then $\mathcal{B}$ checks whether $e(S, \hat{T}) \overset{?}{=} 1$ or not. If $e(S, \hat{T}) = 1$, then $\mathcal{B}$ returns 1 indicating $\hat{T} \in H_1$, else 0 indicating $\hat{T} \in H$. For the case of $S = 1$, $\mathcal{B}$ simply returns a random guess to his challenger. For a Type II forgery, the latter can happen only with a negligible probability. So we conclude,

$$Pr[E] \leq Adv_{\mathcal{B}}^{SGH^H_{p_1 \to p_1 p_2}}. \tag{1}$$

$\square$

Lemma 3. *If* $\text{SGH}^G_{p_1 \to p_1 p_2}$ *assumption holds in* $\mathcal{G}_N$, *then* $\text{Game}_{k-1} \approx_c \text{Game}_k$, *for* $k \in [1, q]$.

Proof. Suppose that, there exists a PPT adversary $\mathcal{A}$ who distinguishes between Game_{k-1} and Game_k with some non-negligible probability. Then we construct a simulator $\mathcal{B}$ to break the $\text{SGH}^G_{p_1 \to p_1 p_2}$ problem as follows. $\mathcal{B}$ is given Θ_N and g_1, g_2, h_1, T and his goal is to decide whether $T \in G_1$ or $T \in G$. Now $\mathcal{B}$ chooses x, y_j and constructs the PK and SK as described in Table 2. After receiving PK, $\mathcal{A}$ makes signing queries on some message $\boldsymbol{m}_i = (m_{i1}, \dots, m_{i\ell})$. For the first $k-1$ (resp. last $q-k$) queries, $\mathcal{B}$ uses Sign_B (resp. Sign_A) algorithm to answer for signing queries, as he knows g_2 and all the secret key components. For the k-th query, $\mathcal{B}$ embeds the challenge term T to construct the signature $\sigma_k = (A_k, B_k)$, where $A_k = T, B_k = T^{(x+m_{k1}+\sum_{j=2}^{\ell} m_{kj} y_j)/y_1}$. Suppose $T \in G_1$, then the signature σ_k is distributed as an output of Sign_A. Thus $\mathcal{B}$ is simulating Game_{k-1}. Suppose $T \in G$, then from CRT, x (resp. y_j) modulo p_2 and x (resp. y_j) modulo p_1 are independent. Also from the definition of Sign_A and Sign_B, the values $x, y_j \bmod p_2$ are information theoretically hidden to $\mathcal{A}$. Hence the G_{p_2} part of σ_k is randomly distributed from the view of $\mathcal{A}$. Thus σ_k is distributed as an output of Sign_B and hence $\mathcal{B}$ is simulating Game_k.

Finally, $\mathcal{A}$ returns a forgery $(\boldsymbol{m}^*, \sigma^*)$, where $\boldsymbol{m}^* = (m_1^*, \dots, m_\ell^*)$ and $\sigma^* = (A^*, B^*)$. Notice that σ_k is generated using the challenge term of the SGH assumption. Since $\mathcal{B}$ knows all the SK components in addition to the random element g_2 from G_2, he can generate the k-th signature of any type properly. However, $\mathcal{B}$ cannot on its own decide the type of the signatures generated using the problem instance as $\mathcal{B}$ is not given any element of H_2. In other words, $\mathcal{B}$ needs to rely on the advantage of $\mathcal{A}$.

As long as $\mathcal{A}$ distinguishes between Game_{k-1} and Game_k, $\mathcal{B}$ leverages $\mathcal{A}$ to solve the $\text{SGH}^G_{p_1 \to p_1 p_2}$ assumption. Thus we have

$$|Adv_{\mathcal{A}}^{\text{Game}_{k-1}} - Adv_{\mathcal{A}}^{\text{Game}_k}| \leq Adv_{\mathcal{B}}^{\text{SGH}^G_{p_1 \to p_1 p_2}}. \tag{2}$$

$\square$

Lemma 4. *If* $\text{SGH}^H_{p_2 \to p_1 p_2}$ *assumption holds in* $\mathcal{G}_N$, *then* $Adv_{\mathcal{A}}^{\text{Game}_q}$ *is negligible.*

Proof. Suppose that, there exists a PPT adversary $\mathcal{A}$ playing Game_q and winning with some non-negligible probability. Then we construct a simulator $\mathcal{B}$ to break the $\text{SGH}^H_{p_2 \to p_1 p_2}$ problem as follows. $\mathcal{B}$ is given $\Theta_N, g_2, g_1^{\tau_1} g_2^{\tau_2}, h_1, h_2, \hat{T}$ and his goal is to decide whether $\hat{T} \in H_2$ or $\hat{T} \in H$. Next $\mathcal{B}$ chooses x, y_j uniformly at random from $\mathbb{Z}_N$ and defines the PK as described in Table 2. $\mathcal{B}$ also defines the SK containing only $\{y_j\}_{j=1}^{\ell}$ and x. Since no random element of G_1 is given, $\mathcal{B}$ cannot define the SK component g_1 which is from G_1. Once PK is given to $\mathcal{A}$, he makes the signing queries on some message $\boldsymbol{m}_i = (m_{i1}, \dots, m_{i\ell})$. Even without knowing the random element g_1 from G_1 as part of SK, $\mathcal{B}$ can simulate the Sign_B algorithm. In particular, $\mathcal{B}$ computes the signature as $\sigma_i = (A_i, B_i)$, where

$$A_i = (g_1^{\tau_1} g_2^{\tau_2})^{r'} g_2^{\delta_1'}, \quad B_i = (g_1^{\tau_1} g_2^{\tau_2})^{\frac{r'}{y_1}(x+m_{i1}+\sum_{j=2}^{\ell} m_{ij} y_j)} g_2^{\delta_2'},$$

for $r', \delta_1', \delta_2' \xleftarrow{\$} \mathbb{Z}_N$. It is easy to check that the above signature is properly distributed by substituting the randomness r, δ_1 and δ_2 by $\tau_1 r'$, $\delta_1' + \tau_2 r'$ and $\delta_2' + \tau_2 \frac{r'}{y_1}(x + m_{i1} + \sum_{j=2}^{\ell} m_{ij} y_j)$ respectively. After q many signing queries, $\mathcal{A}$ returns a forgery $(\boldsymbol{m}^*, \sigma^*)$, where $\boldsymbol{m}^* = (m_1^*, \ldots, m_\ell^*)$ and $\sigma^* = (A^*, B^*)$. As before, $\mathcal{B}$ checks (i) the forgery $(\boldsymbol{m}^*, \sigma^*)$ is valid and (ii) the message $\boldsymbol{m}^*$ is not queried earlier. If any of these checks fail to hold, then $\mathcal{B}$ aborts. Otherwise, $\mathcal{B}$ proceeds as follows. As mentioned before, from the valid forgery, σ^* can be written as,

$$A^* = g_1^s, \quad B^* = g_1^{\frac{s}{y_1}(x + m_1^* + \sum_{j=2}^{\ell} m_j^* y_j)},$$

for some $s \in \mathbb{Z}_N$. By our initial assumption, $\mathcal{A}$ returns a Type-I forgery with some non-negligible probability. Now $\mathcal{B}$ checks whether $e(A^*, \hat{T}) \overset{?}{=} 1$. Notice that, $e(A^*, \hat{T}) = 1$ holds if and only if $\hat{T} \in H_2$, as A^* and $\hat{T}$ are non-trivial elements from G and H respectively. Thus we have,

$$Adv_{\mathcal{A}}^{\mathsf{Game}_q} \leq Adv_{\mathcal{B}}^{SGH_{p_2 \to p_1 p_2}^H}. \tag{3}$$

$\square$

Remark 1. *In the above Lemma 4, we can use the following computational assumption. Given $\Theta_N, g_2, g_1^{\tau_1} g_2^{\tau_2}, h_1, h_2$, for $\tau_1, \tau_2 \in \mathbb{Z}_N$, it is hard to compute g_1^s, for some $s \in \mathbb{Z}_N$. Also, it is easy to see that the $SGH_{p_2 \to p_1 p_2}^H$ assumption (Assumption 3) implies this computational assumption.*

4   RRS in the Prime-Order Setting

Recall that Yuen et al. [32] presented the dual-form Boneh-Boyen signature scheme in the prime-order setting through the dual pairing vector space (DPVS) [27,28] framework. Following a similar approach, we use the DPVS framework to convert the RRSc scheme in the prime-order setting, which we call RRS scheme. We prove unforgeability of the scheme under the SXDH assumption.

4.1   Construction

In the DPVS setting, the underlying source groups are decomposed into four orthogonal subgroups i.e., $G \approx \oplus_{i=1}^4 G_i$ and $H \approx \oplus_{i=1}^4 H_i$ such that $e(g_i, h_j) = 1$, for $i \neq j$, where g_i (resp. h_i) is the generator of the subgroup G_i (resp. H_i). In the RRS construction, the subgroup $G_1 \oplus G_2$, which is of rank 2, is utilized to generate the signature. In particular, we use exponent of the form $\frac{1}{y_1}(x + m_1 + \sum_{j=2}^{\ell} m_j y_j)$ in the subgroup G_2 component while the corresponding randomness r is provided in the exponent of G_1 component. The rank 2 subgroup enables us to construct a signature having only one group element instead of two components in the RRSc construction. The associated public key structure is provided in the subgroup $H_1 \oplus H_2$. In particular, we retain the variables x, $\{y_j\}_{j \neq 1}$ in the subgroup H_1 while the variable y_1 is encoded in the subgroup H_2.

Table 3. RRS in the prime order setting.

KeyGen(λ)	
Run $\mathcal{P}_{(\perp,4)} \rightarrow (\Theta, \{G_i, H_i\}_{i=1}^4)$, where $\Theta = (p, G, H, G_T, e, g, h)$. Choose $x, \{y_j\}_{j=1}^\ell \xleftarrow{\$} \mathbb{Z}_p$, $g^{d_i} \xleftarrow{\$} G_i$ and $h^{d_i^*} \xleftarrow{\$} H_i$, for $i \in [1,2]$. Set $PK := \{\Theta, h^{d_1^*}, X := h^{xd_1^*},$ $Y_1 := h^{y_1 d_2^*}, \{Y_j := h^{y_j d_1^*}\}_{j=2}^\ell\}$, $SK := \{x, \{y_j\}_{j=1}^\ell, g^{d_1}, g^{d_2}\}$. Return (SK, PK).	**Sign**($SK, \boldsymbol{m} = (m_1, \dots, m_\ell)$) Choose $r \xleftarrow{\$} \mathbb{Z}_p$ and set, $\sigma := g^{r d_1 - \frac{r}{v_1}(x + m_1 + \sum_{j=2}^\ell m_j y_j) d_2}$. Return $(\boldsymbol{m}, \sigma)$. **Ver**($PK, \boldsymbol{m} = (m_1, \dots, m_\ell), \sigma$) Accept if $e(\sigma, h^{d_1^*}) \neq 1$ and $e(\sigma, Y_1 X(h^{d_1^*})^{m_1} \prod_{j=2}^\ell Y_j^{m_j}) = 1$.

The RRS scheme consists of three PPT algorithms, which are defined in Table 3. Notice that we avoid the trivial forgery by checking $e(\sigma, h^{d_1^*}) \neq 1$. As mentioned before, if this checking is removed, any one can produce $\sigma = 1$ as a (trivial) forgery on any message $\boldsymbol{m} \in \mathbb{Z}_p^\ell$. The correctness of the scheme can be verified using the following equation,

$$e(\sigma, Y_1 X(h^{d_1^*})^{m_1} \prod_{j=2}^\ell Y_j^{m_j})$$

$$= e(g^{r d_1 - \frac{r}{v_1}(x + m_1 + \sum_{j=2}^\ell m_j y_j) d_2}, h^{(x + m_1 + \sum_{j=2}^\ell m_j y_j) d_1^* + y_1 d_2^*})$$

$$= e(g, h)^{r(x + m_1 + \sum_{j=2}^\ell m_j y_j)\psi - r(x + m_1 + \sum_{j=2}^\ell m_j y_j)\psi} = 1.$$

The first equality follows from the definition of X and Y_j's. In the second equality, we use the fact that, $\boldsymbol{d}_i \cdot \boldsymbol{d}_i^* = \psi$ and $\boldsymbol{d}_i \cdot \boldsymbol{d}_j^* = 0$, for $i, j \in [1,4]$ and $i \neq j$.

4.2 Randomizability

It is easy to see that RRS scheme satisfies rerandomizability property. Consider the signature σ on the message $\boldsymbol{m} \in \mathbb{Z}_p^\ell$, which can be randomized by choosing a random $t \xleftarrow{\$} \mathbb{Z}_p$ and computing $\sigma' = \sigma^t$. One can verify that σ' is a valid signature on $\boldsymbol{m}$ under the PK.

4.3 Unforgeability

Recall that, in Sect. 3.3 we established the unforgeability proof for RRSc scheme using the orthogonality property and the CRT in the composite-order setting. However, in the prime-order setting, we will be using the parameter-hiding property [21] instead of CRT. This necessitates instantiating the prime-order variant using DPVS framework, as it captures both orthogonality and parameter-hiding property.

Now we define the forgery classes. Let $\mathcal{V}$ be the set of all message and signature pairs such that they verify under the public key PK.

Type I: $\mathcal{V}_I = \{(\boldsymbol{m}^*, \sigma^*) \in \mathcal{V} : e(\sigma^*, h^{\boldsymbol{d}_3^*}) = 1, e(\sigma^*, h^{\boldsymbol{d}_4^*}) = 1\}$,
Type II: $\mathcal{V}_{II} = \{(\boldsymbol{m}^*, \sigma^*) \in \mathcal{V} : e(\sigma^*, h^{\boldsymbol{d}_3^*}) \neq 1 \text{ or } e(\sigma^*, h^{\boldsymbol{d}_4^*}) \neq 1\}$.

Consider the message and signature pair $(\boldsymbol{m}^*, \sigma^*)$ satisfying the verification equation, where $\boldsymbol{m}^* = (m_1^*, \ldots, m_\ell^*)$. Suppose the forgery is Type-I, then the signature σ^* can be written as

$$\sigma^* = g^{r\boldsymbol{d}_1 - \frac{r}{y_1}(x + m_1^* + \sum_{j=2}^{\ell} m_j^* y_j)\boldsymbol{d}_2}, \tag{4}$$

for some $r \in \mathbb{Z}_p^*$. This is because, by definition, a Type-I forgery does not have any non-zero component of $\boldsymbol{d}_3$ and $\boldsymbol{d}_4$. Suppose the forgery is Type-II, then the signature σ^* can be written as

$$\sigma^* = g^{r\boldsymbol{d}_1 - \frac{r}{y_1}(x + m_1^* + \sum_{j=2}^{\ell} m_j^* y_j)\boldsymbol{d}_2 + \delta_3 \boldsymbol{d}_3 + \delta_4 \boldsymbol{d}_4}, \tag{5}$$

for some $r, \delta_3, \delta_4 \in \mathbb{Z}_p$ where $r \neq 0$. This is because, a Type-II forgery contains some non-zero component of either $\boldsymbol{d}_3$ or $\boldsymbol{d}_4$. We will use the subspace assumptions (Assumptions 4 and 5) and DDH$_\mathbb{H}$ assumption defined in Sect. 2.3 to prove unforgeability.

Theorem 5. *The* RRS *scheme is EUF-CMA secure under the SXDH assumption.*

Proof. Recall that DDH$_\mathbb{H}$ (resp. DDH$_\mathbb{G}$) is reducible to Assumption 4 (resp. Assumption 5). Let Sign$_A$ be same as the Sign algorithm defined in Table 3. Next we define the following Sign$_B$ algorithm, which is used by the simulator in the security argument.

Sign$_B(SK \cup \{g^{\boldsymbol{d}_3}, g^{\boldsymbol{d}_4}\}, \boldsymbol{m} = (m_1, \ldots, m_\ell))$:

Choose $r, \delta_3, \delta_4 \overset{\$}{\leftarrow} \mathbb{Z}_p$ and set
$$\sigma := g^{r\boldsymbol{d}_1 - \frac{r}{y_1}(x + m_1^* + \sum_{j=2}^{\ell} m_j^* y_j)\boldsymbol{d}_2 + \delta_3 \boldsymbol{d}_3 + \delta_4 \boldsymbol{d}_4},$$
Return $(\boldsymbol{m}, \sigma)$.

Note that the elements $g^{\boldsymbol{d}_3}$, $g^{\boldsymbol{d}_4}$ are orthogonal to the subgroup $H_1 \oplus H_2$, in which PK is defined. Hence the signature returned by Sign$_B$ can be verified under PK. Now we use a hybrid argument to prove this theorem. First, we define the following games.

Game$_R$. This is the original EUF-CMA game. Recall that, after receiving the PK from the challenger, the forger $\mathcal{A}$ makes q many signing oracle queries adaptively and then returns a forgery from $\mathcal{V}$.

Game$_0$. Same as Game$_R$ except that $\mathcal{A}$ returns a forgery from $\mathcal{V}_I$. Let E be the event that $\mathcal{A}$ returns a forgery from $\mathcal{V}_{II}$ in Game$_0$. In Lemma 6, we prove that the event E happens with negligible probability under Assumption 4. Thus we deduce that Game$_R$ and Game$_0$ are computationally indistinguishable under Assumption 4. In particular we have,

$$|Adv_{\mathcal{A}}^{\mathsf{Game_R}} - Adv_{\mathcal{A}}^{\mathsf{Game_0}}| \leq Pr[E] \leq Adv_{\mathcal{B}}^{Ass\ 4}.$$

Game$_k$. Same as Game$_0$ except that the first k signing queries are answered using Sign$_B$, for $k \in [1, q]$, whereas the last $q - k$ queries are answered using Sign$_A$. For $k \in [1, q]$, in Lemma 7, we prove that Game$_{k-1}$ and Game$_k$ are computationally indistinguishable under Assumption 5. In particular we have,

$$|Adv_{\mathcal{A}}^{\mathsf{Game}_{k-1}} - Adv_{\mathcal{A}}^{\mathsf{Game}_k}| \leq Adv_{\mathcal{B}}^{Ass\ 5}.$$

Finally in Lemma 8, we prove that $Adv_{\mathcal{A}}^{\mathsf{Game}_q}$ is negligible under DDH$_{\mathbb{H}}$ assumption. In particular we have,

$$Adv_{\mathcal{A}}^{\mathsf{Game}_q} \leq Adv_{\mathcal{B}}^{DDH_{\mathbb{H}}}.$$

Hence by the hybrid argument and from Eqs. 11, 12 and 13, described below, we have,

$$\begin{aligned}
Adv_{\mathcal{A}}^{UF} = Adv_{\mathcal{A}}^{\mathsf{Game}_R} &= |Adv_{\mathcal{A}}^{\mathsf{Game}_R} - Adv_{\mathcal{A}}^{\mathsf{Game}_0} + Adv_{\mathcal{A}}^{\mathsf{Game}_0} - Adv_{\mathcal{A}}^{\mathsf{Game}_1} + \\
&\quad \dots + Adv_{\mathcal{A}}^{\mathsf{Game}_{k-1}} - Adv_{\mathcal{A}}^{\mathsf{Game}_k} + \dots + Adv_{\mathcal{A}}^{\mathsf{Game}_q}| \\
&\leq Adv_{\mathcal{B}}^{Ass\ 4} + q\, Adv_{\mathcal{B}}^{Ass\ 5} + Adv_{\mathcal{B}}^{DDH_{\mathbb{H}}} \\
&\leq (q + 2)\, Adv_{\mathcal{B}}^{SXDH}.
\end{aligned}$$

$\square$

Lemma 6. *If Assumption 4 holds in $\mathcal{P}_{(\perp,4)}$, then $Pr[E]$ is negligible.*

Proof. Assume that the event E happens with some non-negligible probability. Then we construct a simulator $\mathcal{B}$ to break the Assumption 4 as follows. $\mathcal{B}$ is given $\Theta, \{g^{b_i}\}_{i=1}^{2}, \{h^{b_j^*}\}_{j=1}^{4}, U_1 = g^{\mu_1 b_1 + \mu_2 b_3}, U_2 = g^{\mu_1 b_2 + \mu_2 b_4}, T_1 = h^{\tau_1 b_1^* + \tau_2 b_3^*}, T_2 = h^{\tau_1 b_2^* + \tau_2 b_4^*}$ and his goal is to decide whether $\tau_2 = 0 \mod p$ or not. First $\mathcal{B}$ chooses a matrix A uniformly at random from $GL(2, \mathbb{Z}_p)$ and defines the orthogonal basis as, $\boldsymbol{d}_i = \boldsymbol{b}_i$, $\boldsymbol{d}_i^* = \boldsymbol{b}_i^*$, for $i \in [1, 2]$ and

$$(\boldsymbol{d}_3, \boldsymbol{d}_4)^{\top} = A^{-\top}(\boldsymbol{b}_3, \boldsymbol{b}_4)^{\top}, \quad (\boldsymbol{d}_3^*, \boldsymbol{d}_4^*)^{\top} = A(\boldsymbol{b}_3^*, \boldsymbol{b}_4^*)^{\top}.$$

Now $\mathcal{B}$ chooses x, y_j uniformly at random from $\mathbb{Z}_p$, for $j \in [1, \ell]$ and defines the PK and SK as described in Table 3. Recall that PK includes Θ which contains the description of G and H such that $G = \oplus_{i=1}^{4} G_i$, $H = \oplus_{i=1}^{4} H_i$. Notice that the information about the matrix A is given indirectly to the adversary $\mathcal{A}$ only through the description of the source groups G and H. However, from the parameter-hiding property [21, Lemma 3], we can ensure that the matrix A is information theoretically hidden to the adversary $\mathcal{A}$.

Once PK is given to $\mathcal{A}$, he makes q many signing oracle queries to $\mathcal{B}$. Since he knows all the SK components, $\mathcal{B}$ can answer for the signing queries using Sign$_A$ algorithm. Finally $\mathcal{A}$ returns a forgery $(\boldsymbol{m}^*, \sigma^*)$. Then $\mathcal{B}$ checks (i) the forgery $(\boldsymbol{m}^*, \sigma^*)$ is valid and (ii) the message $\boldsymbol{m}^*$ is not queried earlier. If any of these checks fail to hold, $\mathcal{B}$ returns a random bit to his challenger. Otherwise, $\mathcal{B}$ checks whether $\mathcal{A}$ returns a Type-II forgery. From the definition of forgery types, it is sufficient for $\mathcal{B}$ to check whether $e(\sigma^*, h^{\boldsymbol{d}_3^*}) \neq 1$ or $e(\sigma^*, h^{\boldsymbol{d}_4^*}) \neq 1$ holds.

As $\mathcal{A}$ outputs a valid forgery $(\boldsymbol{m}^*, \sigma^*)$, from Eq. 5, $\mathcal{B}$ can write the signature $\sigma^* := g^{rd_1 - \frac{r}{y_1}(x + m_1^* + \sum_{j=2}^{\ell} m_j^* y_j)d_2 + \delta_3 d_3 + \delta_4 d_4}$, for some r from $\mathbb{Z}_p^*$ and δ_3, δ_4 from $\mathbb{Z}_p$ unknown to $\mathcal{B}$. Now $\mathcal{B}$ defines the following backdoor verification test (BVT),

$$e(\sigma^*, \Delta) \overset{?}{=} 1, \tag{6}$$

where $\Delta := (h^{b_1^*} h^{b_3^*})^{(x + m_1^* + \sum_{j=2}^{\ell} m_j^* y_j)} (h^{b_2^*} h^{b_4^*})^{y_1}$. Note that,

$$e(\sigma^*, \Delta) = e(g^{rd_1 - \frac{r}{y_1}(x + m_1^* + \sum_{j=2}^{\ell} m_j^* y_j)d_2}, (h^{d_1^*})^{(x + m_1^* + \sum_{j=2}^{\ell} m_j^* y_j)} (h^{d_2^*})^{y_1})$$

$$e(g^{\delta_3 d_3 + \delta_4 d_4}, (h^{b_3^*})^{(x + m_1^* + \sum_{j=2}^{\ell} m_j^* y_j)} (h^{b_4^*})^{y_1})$$

$$= e(g^{\delta_3 d_3 + \delta_4 d_4}, (h^{b_3^*})^{(x + m_1^* + \sum_{j=2}^{\ell} m_j^* y_j)} (h^{b_4^*})^{y_1}). \tag{7}$$

The first equality follows from the orthogonality of the basis and the last equality follows from the correctness of the forgery.

Next we consider the coefficient of Δ with respect to the basis $(\boldsymbol{b}_3^*, \boldsymbol{b}_4^*)$, which is $((x + m_1^* + \sum_{j=2}^{\ell} m_j^* y_j), y_1)^\top$. However, from the change of basis techniques, we obtain the coefficient of Δ with respect to the basis $(\boldsymbol{d}_3^*, \boldsymbol{d}_4^*)$ as $A^{-1}((x + m_1^* + \sum_{j=2}^{\ell} m_j^* y_j), y_1)^\top$. Then we simplify the BVT Eq. 6 as,

$$(\delta_3, \delta_4) \cdot A^{-1}((x + m_1^* + \sum_{j=2}^{\ell} m_j^* y_j), y_1)^\top \overset{?}{=} 0 \bmod p. \tag{8}$$

Now we argue that for a Type-II forgery, Eq. 8 holds with only a negligible probability. Recall that, Lewko [21, Lemma 3] ensures that the matrix A is information theoretically hidden to $\mathcal{A}$. Also, $\mathcal{A}$ is given Sign_A oracle access and PK contains the variables x, y_j in the exponent of $H_1 \oplus H_2$. Hence the value $A^{-1}((x + m_1^* + \sum_{j=2}^{\ell} m_j^* y_j), y_1)^\top$ is randomly distributed to $\mathcal{A}$. However, $\mathcal{A}$ has to produce a Type-II forgery which is having a non-zero coefficient of the basis $(\boldsymbol{d}_3, \boldsymbol{d}_4)$. The only possibility for $\mathcal{A}$ is to guess the values of δ_3 and δ_4 from $\mathbb{Z}_p$ such that Eq. 8 holds. Thus $\mathcal{A}$ can create a Type-II forgery that satisfies BVT Eq. 6 with probability atmost $1/p^2$, which is negligible.

Now $\mathcal{B}$ checks whether the BVT Eq. 6 holds or not. Suppose BVT does not hold, then $\mathcal{B}$ checks whether

$$e(\sigma^*, T_1^{(x + m_1^* + \sum_{j=2}^{\ell} m_j^* y_j)} T_2^{y_1}) \overset{?}{=} 1 \tag{9}$$

holds or not. Similar to Eq. 7, we can simplify Eq. 9 as,

$$e(\sigma^*, T_1^{(x + m_1^* + \sum_{j=2}^{\ell} m_j^* y_j)} T_2^{y_1}) = e(g^{rd_1 - \frac{r}{y_1}(x + m_1^* + \sum_{j=2}^{\ell} m_j^* y_j)d_2},$$

$$h^{\tau_1(x + m_1^* + \sum_{j=2}^{\ell} m_j^* y_j)d_1^* + \tau_1 y_1 d_2^*})$$

$$e(g^{\delta_3 d_3 + \delta_4 d_4}, h^{\tau_2(x + m_1^* + \sum_{j=2}^{\ell} m_j^* y_j)b_3^* + \tau_2 y_1 b_4^*})$$

$$= e(g^{\delta_3 d_3 + \delta_4 d_4}, h^{(x + m_1^* + \sum_{j=2}^{\ell} m_j^* y_j)b_3^* + y_1 b_4^*})^{\tau_2}. \tag{10}$$

The first equality follows from the orthogonality of the basis and the last equality follows from the correctness of the forgery. We already argued that Eq. 8 holds only with a negligible probability. From the Eq. 10, we have (i) if $\tau_2 \neq 0$, then Eq. 9 does not hold except with a negligible probability and (ii) if $\tau_2 = 0$, then Eq. 9 must hold. Hence, $\mathcal{B}$ returns 1 if Eq. 9 holds, indicating $\tau_2 = 0$, else $\mathcal{B}$ returns 0 to its challenger. So we conclude,

$$Pr[E] \leq Adv_{\mathcal{B}}^{Ass\ 4}. \tag{11}$$

$\square$

Lemma 7. *If Assumption 5 holds in $\mathcal{P}_{(\perp,4)}$, then $\mathsf{Game}_{k-1} \approx_c \mathsf{Game}_k$, for $k \in [1, q]$.*

Proof. Suppose that, there exists a PPT adversary $\mathcal{A}$ who distinguishes between Game_{k-1} and Game_k with some non-negligible probability. Then we construct a simulator $\mathcal{B}$ to break the Assumption 5 as follows. $\mathcal{B}$ is given $\Theta, \{g^{b_i}\}_{i=1}^4, \{h^{b_j^*}\}_{j=1}^2, U_1 = h^{\mu_1 b_1^* + \mu_2 b_3^*}, U_2 = h^{\mu_1 b_2^* + \mu_2 b_4^*}, T_1 = g^{\tau_1 b_1 + \tau_2 b_3}, T_2 = g^{\tau_1 b_2 + \tau_2 b_4}$ and his goal is to decide whether $\tau_2 = 0 \bmod p$ or not. Now $\mathcal{B}$ chooses a matrix A uniformly at random from $GL(2, \mathbb{Z}_p)$ and defines the orthogonal basis as,

$$\boldsymbol{d}_i = \boldsymbol{b}_i,\ \ \boldsymbol{d}_i^* = \boldsymbol{b}_i^*,\ \ (\boldsymbol{d}_3, \boldsymbol{d}_4)^\top = A(\boldsymbol{b}_3, \boldsymbol{b}_4)^\top,\ \ (\boldsymbol{d}_3^*, \boldsymbol{d}_4^*)^\top = A^{-\top}(\boldsymbol{b}_3^*, \boldsymbol{b}_4^*)^\top,$$

for $i \in [1, 2]$. Next $\mathcal{B}$ chooses x, y_j uniformly at random from $\mathbb{Z}_p$, for $j \in [1, \ell]$ and defines the PK and SK as described in Table 3. Once $\mathcal{B}$ sends the PK, $\mathcal{A}$ makes q many signing queries on some message $\boldsymbol{m}_i = (m_{i1}, \ldots, m_{i\ell})$. $\mathcal{B}$ uses Sign_A algorithm to answer for the last $q - k$ signing queries, as he knows all the SK components. $\mathcal{B}$ uses Sign_B algorithm to answer for the first $k - 1$ signing queries, as he knows the elements g^{d_3} and g^{d_4} in addition to all the SK components. For the k-th signing query, $\mathcal{B}$ embeds the challenge terms T_1 and T_2 to compute $\sigma_k = T_1 T_2^{\frac{-1}{y_1}(x + m_{k1} + \sum_{j=2}^\ell m_{kj} y_j)}$. Then $\mathcal{B}$ sends σ_k to $\mathcal{A}$. Here $\mathcal{B}$ implicitly sets τ_1 as r modulo p. If $T_1 = g^{\tau_1 b_1}$ and $T_2 = g^{\tau_1 b_2}$, then the k-th signature σ_k is distributed as an output of Sign_A. Thus $\mathcal{B}$ is simulating Game_{k-1}. Suppose $T_1 = g^{\tau_1 b_1 + \tau_2 b_3}$ and $T_2 = g^{\tau_1 b_2 + \tau_2 b_4}$, with $\tau_2 \neq 0$. Then the coefficient of σ_k with respect to the basis $(\boldsymbol{d}_3, \boldsymbol{d}_4)$ is $\tau_2 A^{-1}(1, \frac{-1}{y_1}(x + m_{k1} + \sum_{j=2}^\ell m_{kj} y_j))^\top$. Since the matrix A is chosen uniformly at random, the coefficient of the σ_k with respect to the basis $\boldsymbol{d}_3$ and $\boldsymbol{d}_4$ are also random. By taking $r = \tau_1$ and $(\delta_3, \delta_4) = \tau_2 A^{-1}(1, \frac{-1}{y_1}(x + m_{k1} + \sum_{j=2}^\ell m_{kj} y_j))$, it is easy to see that the signature σ_k is properly distributed as an output of Sign_B. Thus $\mathcal{B}$ is simulating Game_k.

Finally $\mathcal{A}$ returns a forgery $(\boldsymbol{m}^*, \sigma^*)$. As before, $\mathcal{B}$ checks (i) the forgery is valid and (ii) the message $\boldsymbol{m}^*$ is not queried earlier. Notice that $\mathcal{B}$ is not given with the elements $h^{b_3^*}$ and $h^{b_4^*}$ to check the forgery types. Hence, as similar to Lemma 3, $\mathcal{B}$ cannot compare the signature σ_k constructed above with the signature obtained by using SK components, to break the underlying assumption. In other words, $\mathcal{B}$ has to rely on the advantage of $\mathcal{A}$.

As long as $\mathcal{A}$ distinguishes between Game_{k-1} and Game_k with some non-negligible probability, $\mathcal{B}$ leverages $\mathcal{A}$ to break the Assumption 5. Thus we have

$$|Adv_{\mathcal{A}}^{\mathsf{Game}_{k-1}} - Adv_{\mathcal{A}}^{\mathsf{Game}_k}| \leq Adv_{\mathcal{B}}^{Ass\ 5}. \tag{12}$$

□

Lemma 8. *If DDH$_{\mathbb{H}}$ assumption holds in $\mathcal{P}$, then Adv^{Game_q} is negligible.*

Proof. Suppose that, there exists a PPT adversary $\mathcal{A}$ playing Game_q and winning with some non-negligible probability. Then we construct a simulator $\mathcal{B}$ to break the DDH$_{\mathbb{H}}$ assumption as follows. $\mathcal{B}$ is given $(p, \mathbb{G}, \mathbb{H}, \mathbb{G}_T, e, g, h, h^a, h^b, h^{ab+\theta})$ and his goal is to decide whether $\theta = 0$ or not. Now $\mathcal{B}$ chooses $(\mathbb{F}, \mathbb{F}^*)$ uniformly at random from $\mathsf{Dual}(\mathbb{Z}_p^4)$, where $\mathbb{F} = \{\boldsymbol{f}_i\}_{i=1}^4$ and $\mathbb{F}^* = \{\boldsymbol{f}_i^*\}_{i=1}^4$. Next $\mathcal{B}$ defines the orthogonal basis $(\mathbb{D}, \mathbb{D}^*)$ as,

$$\boldsymbol{d}_1 = \boldsymbol{f}_1 - a\boldsymbol{f}_3, \quad \boldsymbol{d}_2 = \boldsymbol{f}_2, \quad \boldsymbol{d}_3 = \boldsymbol{f}_3, \quad \boldsymbol{d}_4 = \boldsymbol{f}_4,$$
$$\boldsymbol{d}_1^* = \boldsymbol{f}_1^*, \quad \boldsymbol{d}_2^* = \boldsymbol{f}_2^*, \quad \boldsymbol{d}_3^* = \boldsymbol{f}_3^* + a\boldsymbol{f}_1^*, \quad \boldsymbol{d}_4^* = \boldsymbol{f}_4^*.$$

$\mathcal{B}$ computes $\{g^{\boldsymbol{d}_i}\}_{i=2}^4$ and $\{h^{\boldsymbol{d}_i^*}\}_{i=1}^4$, whereas he cannot compute $g^{\boldsymbol{d}_1}$, as he does not know g^a. $\mathcal{B}$ chooses μ_1', μ_2' uniformly at random from $\mathbb{Z}_p$ and computes,

$$U := g^{\mu_1' \boldsymbol{f}_1 + \mu_2' \boldsymbol{f}_3} = g^{\mu_1' \boldsymbol{d}_1 + (\mu_2' + a\mu_1')\boldsymbol{d}_3} = g^{\mu_1 \boldsymbol{d}_1 + \mu_2 \boldsymbol{d}_3},$$

where $\mathcal{B}$ implicitly sets $\mu_1 = \mu_1'$ and $\mu_2 = \mu_2' + a\mu_1'$ modulo p. Next $\mathcal{B}$ chooses x, y_j uniformly at random from $\mathbb{Z}_p$, for $j \in [1, \ell]$ and defines the PK as described in Table 3. $\mathcal{B}$ also defines the SK containing only $\{y_j\}_{j=1}^\ell$ and x. Since g^a is not given, $\mathcal{B}$ cannot simulate the SK component $g^{\boldsymbol{d}_1}$. After receiving PK, $\mathcal{A}$ makes signing queries for some message $\boldsymbol{m}_i = (m_{i1}, \dots, m_{i\ell})$. Since $\mathcal{B}$ knows $U = g^{\mu_1 \boldsymbol{d}_1 + \mu_2 \boldsymbol{d}_3}$ and $\{g^{\boldsymbol{d}_i}\}_{i=2}^4$, he can answer for the $\mathsf{Sign}_{\mathcal{B}}$ queries by computing,

$$\sigma_i := U^{r'} (g^{\boldsymbol{d}_2})^{-\mu_1 \frac{r'}{y_1}(x + m_{i1} + \sum_{j=2}^\ell m_{ij} y_j)} (g^{\boldsymbol{d}_3})^{\delta_3'} (g^{\boldsymbol{d}_4})^{\delta_4'},$$

for r', δ_3', δ_4' uniformly chosen from $\mathbb{Z}_p$ with $r' \neq 0$. Now, it is easy to check that the above signature is properly distributed by implicitly setting the randomness r as $\mu_1' r'$ and δ_3 as $\delta_3' + (\mu_2' + a\mu_1')r'$. After q many signing queries, $\mathcal{A}$ returns a forgery $(\boldsymbol{m}^*, \sigma^*)$, where $\boldsymbol{m}^* = (m_1^*, \dots, m_\ell^*)$.

As before, $\mathcal{B}$ checks (i) the forgery is valid and (ii) $\boldsymbol{m}^*$ is not queried earlier. If any of these checks fail to hold, $\mathcal{B}$ aborts. Otherwise, first $\mathcal{B}$ checks whether $\mathcal{A}$ returns Type-I forgery by checking $e(\sigma^*, h^{\boldsymbol{d}_3^*}) = 1$ and $e(\sigma^*, h^{\boldsymbol{d}_4^*}) = 1$.

As mentioned in Eq. 4, for the valid forgery, $\mathcal{B}$ writes the signature as, $\sigma^* = g^{sd_1 - \frac{s}{y_1}(x + m_1^* + \sum_{j=2}^\ell m_j^* y_j)\boldsymbol{d}_2}$, for some $s \in \mathbb{Z}_p^*$. Since $\mathcal{B}$ knows $\{\boldsymbol{f}_i, \boldsymbol{f}_i^*\}_{i=1}^4$, he computes g^s and g^{sa} as follows. Writing σ^* in-terms of the orthogonal basis $(\mathbb{F}, \mathbb{F}^*)$, we have

$$\sigma^* = g^{sd_1 - \frac{s}{y_1}(x + m_1^* + \sum_{j=2}^\ell m_j^* y_j)\boldsymbol{d}_2} = g^{s(\boldsymbol{f}_1 - a\boldsymbol{f}_3) - \frac{s}{y_1}(x + m_1^* + \sum_{j=2}^\ell m_j^* y_j)\boldsymbol{f}_2}.$$

Then using the orthonormal basis $\{\boldsymbol{f}_i, \boldsymbol{f}_i^*\}$, $\mathcal{B}$ computes the projection of σ^* with respect to the subspace generated by $\boldsymbol{f}_1^*$ and $\boldsymbol{f}_3^*$ to obtain g^s and g^{sa} respectively. In other words, $\mathcal{B}$ computes, $g^s = (\sigma^*)^{(\boldsymbol{f}_1^*)^\top}$ and $g^{sa} = (\sigma^*)^{-(\boldsymbol{f}_3^*)^\top}$. The condition $e(\sigma^*, h^{\boldsymbol{d}_1^*}) \neq 1$ ensures that $s \neq 0$ modulo p.

Now $\mathcal{B}$ checks whether $e(g^s, h^{ab+\theta}) \stackrel{?}{=} e(g^{sa}, h^b)$. Notice that the equality holds only when $\theta = 0$. Hence we obtain,

$$Adv_{\mathcal{A}}^{\mathsf{Game_q}} \leq Adv_{\mathcal{B}}^{DDH_{\mathbb{H}}}. \tag{13}$$

$\square$

Remark 2. *In the above Lemma 8, we can use the following computational assumption. Given $p, \mathbb{G}, \mathbb{H}, \mathbb{G}_T, e, g, h, h^a$ it is hard to compute (g^s, g^{sa}), for some $s \in \mathbb{Z}_p^*$. It is easy to see that the $DDH_{\mathbb{H}}$ assumption implies this computational assumption.*

4.4   Another Variant

Here we present a variant of the above signature scheme, denoted as PS-RRS scheme. This construction is derived from [29] rerandomizable signature scheme. In particular, we use the $(\ell + 1)$-wise pairwise independent function of the form $(x + \sum_{i=1}^{\ell} m_i y_i)$ in our construction. Along with the above structure, the random term r is given in the exponent of the subgroup G_1's generator $g^{\boldsymbol{d}_1}$. The public key components will be defined appropriately to validate the signature. We describe the PS-RRS scheme in Table 4.

Table 4. PS-RRS scheme in the prime-order setting.

KeyGen(λ)	**Sign($SK, \boldsymbol{m} = (m_1, \ldots, m_\ell)$)**
Run $\mathcal{P}_{(\perp,4)} \to (\Theta, \{G_i, H_i\}_{i=1}^4)$, where $\Theta = (p, G, H, G_T, e, g, h)$. Choose $x, \{y_j\}_{j=1}^\ell \stackrel{\$}{\leftarrow} \mathbb{Z}_p$, $g^{\boldsymbol{d}_i} \stackrel{\$}{\leftarrow} G_i$ and $h^{\boldsymbol{d}_i^*} \stackrel{\$}{\leftarrow} H_i$, for $i \in [1,2]$. Set $PK := \{\Theta, h^{\boldsymbol{d}_1^*}, h^{\boldsymbol{d}_2^*}, X := h^{x\boldsymbol{d}_1^*}, \{Y_j := h^{y_j \boldsymbol{d}_1^*}\}_{j=1}^\ell\}$ and $SK := \{x, \{y_j\}_{j=1}^\ell, g^{\boldsymbol{d}_1}, g^{\boldsymbol{d}_2}\}$. Return (SK, PK).	Choose $r \stackrel{\$}{\leftarrow} \mathbb{Z}_p$ and set, $\sigma := g^{r\boldsymbol{d}_1 - r(x + \sum_{j=1}^\ell m_j y_j)\boldsymbol{d}_2}$. Return $(\boldsymbol{m}, \sigma)$. **Ver($PK, \boldsymbol{m} = (m_1, \ldots, m_\ell), \sigma$)** Accept if $e(\sigma, h^{\boldsymbol{d}_1^*}) \neq 1$ and $e(\sigma, X \prod_{j=1}^\ell Y_j^{m_j} h^{\boldsymbol{d}_2^*}) = 1$.

One can easily check the correctness of the scheme and that the signature components are rerandomizable. We only give a high level idea for the unforgeability proof of PS-RRS scheme, as it essentially mimics that of Theorem 5. Recall that in the proof of Lemmas 6, 7 and 8, the variables x, y_j's are chosen by the simulator. Hence it does not matter whether we are arguing the unforgeability of the signature whose exponent structure is of the form $r(x + m_1 + \sum_{i=2}^\ell m_i y_i)/y_1$ (for RRS scheme) or $r(x + \sum_{i=1}^\ell m_i y_i)$ (for PS-RRS scheme). Thus one can use the same set of assumptions to argue the unforgeability proof of PS-RRS scheme.

4.5   Comparison

We compare our rerandomizable signature schemes instantiated in the prime-order setting with the existing schemes in Table 5.

Table 5. Comparing rerandomizable signatures for multiple block messages.

	$|PK|$	$|\sigma|$	Signing Cost	Verification Cost	Rand.	Assum.
CL-RRS	$(\ell+2)|\mathbb{G}|$	$(2\ell+1)|\mathbb{G}|$	$(2\ell+1)E_{\mathbb{G}}$	$4\ell\mathbb{P}+\ell E_{\mathbb{G}}+\ell M_{\mathbb{G}}$	Full	LRSW
mCL-RRS	$(\ell+3)|\mathbb{G}|$	$(2\ell+3)|\mathbb{G}|$ $+1|\mathbb{Z}_p|$	$(2\ell+3)E_{\mathbb{G}}$	$4(\ell+1)\mathbb{P}+(\ell+1)E_{\mathbb{G}}$ $+(\ell+1)M_{\mathbb{G}}$	Weak	q-MSDH-1
PS-RRS	$(\ell+2)|\mathbb{H}|$	$2|\mathbb{G}|$	$2E_{\mathbb{G}}$	$2\mathbb{P}+\ell E_{\mathbb{H}}+\ell M_{\mathbb{H}}$	Full	PS
mPS-RRS	$(\ell+3)|\mathbb{H}|$	$2|\mathbb{G}|+1|\mathbb{Z}_p|$	$2E_{\mathbb{G}}$	$2\mathbb{P}+(\ell+1)E_{\mathbb{H}}$ $+(\ell+1)M_{\mathbb{H}}$	Weak	q-MSDH-2
PS-RRS	$(4\ell+13)|\mathbb{H}|+1|\mathbb{G}|$	$4|\mathbb{G}|$	$8E_{\mathbb{G}}+4M_{\mathbb{G}}$	$8\mathbb{P}+6M_{\mathbb{G}_T}+4\ell E_{\mathbb{H}}$ $+4(\ell+1)M_{\mathbb{H}}$	Full	SXDH
RRS	$(4\ell+9)|\mathbb{H}|+1|\mathbb{G}|$					

For any group $X \in \{\mathbb{G}, \mathbb{H}, \mathbb{G}_T\}$, E_X, M_X respectively denote the cost of the exponentiation, multiplication in X and $|X|$ is the bit size of X whereas $\mathbb{P}$ denotes pairing computation cost.

Notice that both CL-RRS [10] and modified CL-RRS (denoted as mCL-RRS) [30, Section 6.2] are defined in the symmetric prime-order setting. However, the signature size in both CL-RRS and mCL-RRS schemes depends on the message block length ℓ. The remaining schemes such as PS-RRS [29] and modified PS-RRS (denoted as mPS-RRS) [30, Section 4.2] are defined in the asymmetric prime-order setting, whose signature size is independent of the message block length ℓ. However, the unforgeability of CL-RRS and PS-RRS (resp. mCL-RRS and mPS-RRS) schemes is proved under interactive (resp. parameterized) assumption. Notice that both mCL-RRS and mPS-RRS schemes achieve only weakly rerandomizable property.

In contrast, both RRS (Sect. 4.1) and PS-RRS (Sect. 4.4) schemes are instantiated in the asymmetric prime-order setting. Both schemes ensure full rerandomizable property and unforgeability under the SXDH assumption. Also, the signature size of RRS and PS-RRS schemes is constant and thus independent of the message block length. PS-RRS scheme is having one more public key component (i.e., four atomic group elements) as compared to the RRS scheme. Hence RRS scheme is slightly better than PS-RRS scheme.

5   Concluding Remark

We proposed the first construction of fully rerandomizable signature scheme in the standard model based on the SXDH assumption in the prime order bilinear pairing setting. This is achieved by applying the dual form signature technique in the DPVS setting on an RRS inspired by Ghadafi's SPS. Our proposal retains the desirable properties of RRS, namely full randomizability and constant size signature on a block of messages.

References

1. Au, M.H., Susilo, W., Mu, Y.: Constant-size dynamic k-TAA. In: De Prisco, R., Yung, M. (eds.) SCN 2006. LNCS, vol. 4116, pp. 111–125. Springer, Heidelberg (2006). https://doi.org/10.1007/11832072_8
2. Boneh, D., Boyen, X.: Efficient selective-id secure identity-based encryption without random oracles. In: Cachin, C., Camenisch, J.L. (eds.) EUROCRYPT 2004. LNCS, vol. 3027, pp. 223–238. Springer, Heidelberg (2004). https://doi.org/10.1007/978-3-540-24676-3_14
3. Bichsel, P., Camenisch, J., Neven, G., Smart, N.P., Warinschi, B.: Get shorty via group signatures without encryption. In: Garay, J.A., De Prisco, R. (eds.) SCN 2010. LNCS, vol. 6280, pp. 381–398. Springer, Heidelberg (2010). https://doi.org/10.1007/978-3-642-15317-4_24
4. Bernhard, D., Fuchsbauer, G., Ghadafi, E., Smart, N.P., Warinschi, B.: Anonymous attestation with user-controlled linkability. Int. J. Inf. Secur. **12**(3), 219–249 (2013)
5. Boldyreva, A., Gentry, C., O'Neill, A., Yum, D.H.: Ordered multisignatures and identity-based sequential aggregate signatures, with applications to secure routing. In: Ning, P., De Capitani di Vimercati, S., Syverson, P.F. (eds.) ACM CCS, pp. 276–285 (2007)
6. Chen, J., Gong, J., Kowalczyk, L., Wee, H.: Unbounded ABE via bilinear entropy expansion, revisited. In: Nielsen, J.B., Rijmen, V. (eds.) EUROCRYPT 2018. LNCS, vol. 10820, pp. 503–534. Springer, Cham (2018). https://doi.org/10.1007/978-3-319-78381-9_19
7. Cheon, J.H.: Security analysis of the strong Diffie-Hellman problem. In: Vaudenay, S. (ed.) EUROCRYPT 2006. LNCS, vol. 4004, pp. 1–11. Springer, Heidelberg (2006). https://doi.org/10.1007/11761679_1
8. Chatterjee, S., Kabaleeshwaran, R.: Towards static assumption based cryptosystem in pairing setting: further applications of DéjàQ and Dual-Form signature (Extended Abstract). In: Baek, J., Susilo, W., Kim, J. (eds.) ProvSec 2018. LNCS, vol. 11192, pp. 220–238. Springer, Cham (2018). https://doi.org/10.1007/978-3-030-01446-9_13
9. Chatterjee, S., Kabaleeshwaran, R.: Rerandomizable Signatures under Standard Assumption. IACR Cryptology ePrint Archive, 2019:1144 (2019)
10. Camenisch, J., Lysyanskaya, A.: Signature schemes and anonymous credentials from bilinear maps. In: Franklin, M. (ed.) CRYPTO 2004. LNCS, vol. 3152, pp. 56–72. Springer, Heidelberg (2004). https://doi.org/10.1007/978-3-540-28628-8_4
11. Chen, J., Lim, H.W., Ling, S., Wang, H., Wee, H.: Shorter IBE and signatures via asymmetric pairings. In: Abdalla, M., Lange, T. (eds.) Pairing 2012. LNCS, vol. 7708, pp. 122–140. Springer, Heidelberg (2013). https://doi.org/10.1007/978-3-642-36334-4_8
12. Chase, M., Meiklejohn, S.: Déjà Q: using dual systems to revisit q-type assumptions. In: Nguyen, P.Q., Oswald, E. (eds.) EUROCRYPT 2014. LNCS, vol. 8441, pp. 622–639. Springer, Heidelberg (2014). https://doi.org/10.1007/978-3-642-55220-5_34
13. Chase, M., Maller, M., Meiklejohn, S.: Déjà Q all over again: tighter and broader reductions of q-type assumptions. In: Cheon, J.H., Takagi, T. (eds.) ASIACRYPT 2016. LNCS, vol. 10032, pp. 655–681. Springer, Heidelberg (2016). https://doi.org/10.1007/978-3-662-53890-6_22
14. Canard, S., Pointcheval, D., Sanders, O., Traoré, J.: Divisible e-cash made practical. In: Katz, J. (ed.) PKC 2015. LNCS, vol. 9020, pp. 77–100. Springer, Heidelberg (2015). https://doi.org/10.1007/978-3-662-46447-2_4

15. Chen, J., Wee, H.: Semi-adaptive attribute-based encryption and improved delegation for boolean formula. In: Abdalla, M., De Prisco, R. (eds.) SCN 2014. LNCS, vol. 8642, pp. 277–297. Springer, Cham (2014). https://doi.org/10.1007/978-3-319-10879-7_16

16. Freeman, D.M.: Converting pairing-based cryptosystems from composite-order groups to prime-order groups. In: Gilbert, H. (ed.) EUROCRYPT 2010. LNCS, vol. 6110, pp. 44–61. Springer, Heidelberg (2010). https://doi.org/10.1007/978-3-642-13190-5_3

17. Ghadafi, E.: More efficient structure-preserving signatures - or: bypassing the type-III lower bounds. In: Foley, S.N., Gollmann, D., Snekkenes, E. (eds.) ESORICS 2017. LNCS, vol. 10493, pp. 43–61. Springer, Cham (2017). https://doi.org/10.1007/978-3-319-66399-9_3

18. Gerbush, M., Lewko, A., O'Neill, A., Waters, B.: Dual form signatures: an approach for proving security from static assumptions. In: Wang, X., Sako, K. (eds.) ASIACRYPT 2012. LNCS, vol. 7658, pp. 25–42. Springer, Heidelberg (2012). https://doi.org/10.1007/978-3-642-34961-4_4

19. Galbraith, S.D., Paterson, K.G., Smart, N.P.: Pairings for cryptographers. Discrete Appl. Math. **156**(16), 3113–3121 (2008)

20. Guillevic, A.: Arithmetic of Pairings on Algebraic Curves for Cryptography. École Normale Supérieure, Paris (2013). PhD thesis

21. Lewko, A.: Tools for simulating features of composite order bilinear groups in the prime order setting. In: Pointcheval, D., Johansson, T. (eds.) EUROCRYPT 2012. LNCS, vol. 7237, pp. 318–335. Springer, Heidelberg (2012). https://doi.org/10.1007/978-3-642-29011-4_20

22. Libert, B., Joye, M., Yung, M., Peters, T.: Concise multi-challenge CCA-secure encryption and signatures with almost tight security. In: Sarkar, P., Iwata, T. (eds.) ASIACRYPT 2014. LNCS, vol. 8874, pp. 1–21. Springer, Heidelberg (2014). https://doi.org/10.1007/978-3-662-45608-8_1

23. Lee, K., Lee, D.H., Yung, M.: Aggregating CL-signatures revisited: extended functionality and better efficiency. In: Sadeghi, A.-R. (ed.) FC 2013. LNCS, vol. 7859, pp. 171–188. Springer, Heidelberg (2013). https://doi.org/10.1007/978-3-642-39884-1_14

24. Libert, B., Mouhartem, F., Peters, T., Yung, M.: Practical "Signatures with efficient protocols" from simple assumptions. In: Chen, X., Wang, X., Huang, X. (eds.) AsiaCCS, pp. 511–522. ACM (2016)

25. Libert, B., Peters, T., Yung, M.: Short group signatures via structure-preserving signatures: standard model security from simple assumptions. In: Gennaro, R., Robshaw, M. (eds.) CRYPTO 2015. LNCS, vol. 9216, pp. 296–316. Springer, Heidelberg (2015). https://doi.org/10.1007/978-3-662-48000-7_15

26. Lewko, A., Waters, B.: New techniques for dual system encryption and fully secure hibe with short ciphertexts. In: Micciancio, D. (ed.) TCC 2010. LNCS, vol. 5978, pp. 455–479. Springer, Heidelberg (2010). https://doi.org/10.1007/978-3-642-11799-2_27

27. Okamoto, T., Takashima, K.: Homomorphic encryption and signatures from vector decomposition. In: Galbraith, S.D., Paterson, K.G. (eds.) Pairing 2008. LNCS, vol. 5209, pp. 57–74. Springer, Heidelberg (2008). https://doi.org/10.1007/978-3-540-85538-5_4

28. Okamoto, T., Takashima, K.: Fully secure functional encryption with general relations from the decisional linear assumption. In: Rabin, T. (ed.) CRYPTO 2010. LNCS, vol. 6223, pp. 191–208. Springer, Heidelberg (2010). https://doi.org/10.1007/978-3-642-14623-7_11

29. Pointcheval, D., Sanders, O.: Short randomizable signatures. In: Sako, K. (ed.) CT-RSA 2016. LNCS, vol. 9610, pp. 111–126. Springer, Cham (2016). https://doi.org/10.1007/978-3-319-29485-8_7

30. Pointcheval, D., Sanders, O.: Reassessing security of randomizable signatures. In: Smart, N.P. (ed.) CT-RSA 2018. LNCS, vol. 10808, pp. 319–338. Springer, Cham (2018). https://doi.org/10.1007/978-3-319-76953-0_17

31. Waters, B.: Dual system encryption: Realizing fully secure IBE and HIBE under simple assumptions. IACR Cryptology ePrint Archive, 2009:385 (2009)

32. Yuen, T.H., Chow, S.S.M., Zhang, C., Yiu, S.-M.: Exponent-inversion Signatures and IBE under Static Assumptions. IACR Cryptology ePrint Archive, 2014:311 (2014)

Improved Filter Permutators for Efficient FHE: Better Instances and Implementations

Pierrick Méaux[1]($\boxtimes$), Claude Carlet[2,3], Anthony Journault[1], and François-Xavier Standaert[1]

[1] ICTEAM/ELEN/Crypto Group, Université catholique de Louvain, Louvain-la-Neuve, Belgium
pierrick.meaux@uclouvain.be
[2] LAGA, University of Paris 8, Saint-Denis, France
[3] Department of Informatics, University of Bergen, Bergen, Norway

Abstract. We revisit the design of filter permutators as a general approach to build stream ciphers that can be efficiently evaluated in a fully homomorphic manner. We first introduce improved filter permutators that allow better security analyses, instances and implementations than the previously proposed FLIP family of ciphers. We also put forward the similarities between these improved constructions and a popular PRG design by Goldreich. We then propose a methodology to evaluate the performance of such symmetric cipher designs in a FHE setting, which primarily focuses on the noise level of the symmetric ciphertexts (hence on the amount of operations on these ciphertexts that can be homomorphically evaluated). Evaluations through HElib show that instances of improved filter permutators using direct sums of monomials as filter outperform all existing ciphers in the literature based on this criteria. We also discuss the (limited) overheads of these instances in terms of latency and throughput.

Keywords: Filter permutator · Homomorphic encryption · Boolean functions

1 Introduction.

State-of-the-Art. Block cipher designs with reduced multiplicative complexity (*e.g.* number of AND gates per ciphertext bit or AND depth) have recently attracted significant attention in symmetric cryptography research. Such ciphers are motivated by new constraints raised by emerging security applications. For example, limited multiplicative complexity allows preventing side-channel attacks via masking more efficiently [24,27,40], can improve the throughput and latency of Multi-Party Computation (MPC) protocols [2,26], and mitigates the noise increase and the ciphertext expansion in Fully Homomorphic Encryption (FHE) schemes [2,3,10,19,36]. Concretely, thanks to innovative (and sometimes aggressive) design choices, recent ciphers (*e.g.* LowMC [2,3]) can encrypt with as little of four ANDs per bit, or with a multiplicative depth of four (*e.g.* FLIP [36]). In a recent work by Dobraunig et al., the authors even go as far as minimizing both metrics jointly for a single cipher (called Rasta [19]). In this

© Springer Nature Switzerland AG 2019
F. Hao et al. (Eds.): INDOCRYPT 2019, LNCS 11898, pp. 68–91, 2019.
https://doi.org/10.1007/978-3-030-35423-7_4

paper, we are concerned with the question whether the reduction of the multiplicative depth can be pushed even further (yet, with "reasonable" key sizes).

More specifically, we are interested in the exploitation of Symmetric Encryption for FHE applications (SE-FHE), which we will sometimes call "hybrid FHE framework", and in stream ciphers based on Filter Permutators (FPs) introduced at Eurocrypt 2016 by Méaux et al. [36]. While the simple structure of FPs is particularly appealing for FHE, early instances of the FLIP cipher[1] have been cryptanalyzed by Duval et al. thanks to guess-and-determine attacks [20]. These attacks led the authors of FLIP to tweak the designs published at Eurocrypt with conservative choices (hence reducing their performances). They also highlighted a lack of theoretical understanding of the exact properties needed for the Boolean functions used in FPs, due to the fact that these designs exploit Boolean functions with non-uniformly distributed inputs. As later observed by Carlet et al. such a structure leads to new research problems related to the analysis of Boolean functions [12, 34, 37, 38]. Besides, recent results confirmed that the design principles of FPs are at least theoretically sound (thanks to an analysis in the random oracle model) [13], hence leaving ample room for improved constructions and analyzes of stream ciphers taking advantage of the FP principles in order to enable efficient SE-FHE.[2]

Contributions. Building on this state-of-the-art, our first contribution is to propose a new family of stream ciphers, namely Improved Filter Permutators (IFPs) that takes advantage of recent advances on FPs and the cipher FLIP. It mostly tweaks FPs in two directions. First, IFPs exploit an extended key register, so that the key size N is larger than the input of the Boolean function used as a filter. This allows the input of the filter to be increasingly close to uniformly distributed as N increases (which is not the case for FPs). Second, IFPs use a whitening stage. That is, before being sent to the filter the permuted key bits are XORed with a random public value. This allows simplifying the analysis of guess-and-determine attacks (and to mitigate them), while having no impact on the noise increase and a very mild impact on the latency and throughput of a SE-FHE implementation. The register extension also makes the IFP designs more similar to a PRG construction proposed by Goldreich [25]. So despite most known results on Goldreich's PRG are asymptotic [5, 6, 18, 39], they also give confidence that the general principles of IFPs are sound and motivate the quest for efficient instances.

We provide a detailed security analysis of IFPs (considering all published attacks we are aware of) and use it to propose new cipher instances exploiting Boolean filters made of Direct Sums of Monomials (DSMs). We denote these new instances as FiLIP$_{DSM}$ and observe that they allow reduced multiplication complexity compared to existing instances of FLIP. The security analysis largely depends on cryptographic criteria of Boolean functions, and more particularly on the properties of sub-functions derived from the filtering function. Therefore we develop the tools required for this analysis, and we exhibit the parameters of any DSM function relatively to these relevant criteria.

---

[1] More precisely, instances presented at the "Journées C2", a French workshop for PhD students held in La Londe Les Maures, in October 2015.

[2] To some extent, the Rasta cipher actually exploits one of the FPs' ideas, which is to make a part of the cipher computations independent of the key.

We then use these new instances as a basis to compare IFPs with other published ciphers aimed at efficient FHE evaluation. In this respect, we first observe that the usual approach for assessing such performances is to compare latency and throughput [2, 10, 19, 36]. The best performances are then typically achieved for FHE parameters such that the ciphertexts will "just enable decryption", or a few levels of multiplications more. Directly optimizing the latency and throughput of the obtained homomorphic ciphertexts forces to fix the ciphertext size and error. On the one hand, this methodology gives accurate timings relatively to the targeted function, or close ones. On the other hand, it makes the evaluations quite application-specific since the estimation of these metrics is quite dependent of the targeted function. More precisely, this optimization leads to tailor the homomorphic ciphertext parameters for the SE evaluation. Thus, the ciphertexts have different sizes, so involving different times to evaluate the same function, and different quantities of noise which lead to different security levels. We therefore argue that in order to evaluate various symmetric schemes for application in a hybrid-FHE framework in an application-dependent manner, a more relevant comparison metric is based on the noise level of the ciphertexts. This leads to a more stable metric than latency and throughput (since it avoids the aforementioned specialization to a given target function). It is also connected to a generally desirable goal (since one may expect that the ability to perform as much homomorphic operations as possible is a useful feature for practical applications).

We formalize our comparison methodology, by (i) setting the FHE security parameters at a level that is comparable to the SE ones (i.e. 80-bit or 128-bit), (ii) using ciphertexts of comparable size for all the cipher designs to compare (so basing the comparison on the most expensive cipher in terms of noise), and (iii) monitoring the noise (e.g. provided by HElib) not only for the ciphertexts but also after one and two levels of additional multiplications on the ciphertexts. Concrete estimations carried out using HElib put forward that the noise of Rasta and FiLIP is orders of magnitudes smaller than the one of LowMC, and that new instances of FiLIP with reduced multiplicative depth allow performing two more levels of multiplications on its ciphertexts than the recommended Rasta designs. We further observe that even non-recommended versions of Rasta (with comparable multiplicative depth) would not compare favorably to FiLIP due to a (much) larger key size. We complement our analyzes with an evaluation of best-case latency and throughput (i.e. when ciphertexts can just be decrypted), as performed previously. We believe that it remains an informative alternative metric and clarify that it has to be understood as the best possible performances of a cipher since any concrete application (where symmetric ciphertexts are manipulated homomorphically) will require ciphertext expansion.

2   Preliminaries

In addition to classic notation we use the log to denote the logarithm in basis 2, and $[n]$ to denote the subset of all integers between 1 and n: $\{1, \ldots, n\}$. For readability we use the notation $+$ instead of $\oplus$ to denote the addition in $\mathbb{F}_2$.

2.1 Boolean Functions and Criteria

We introduce here some core notions of Boolean functions in cryptography, restricting our study to the following definition of Boolean function, more restrictive than a vectorial Boolean function. We recall the main cryptographic properties of Boolean functions, mostly taken from [11]: balancedness, resiliency, nonlinearity and (fast) algebraic immunity. We give notions relatively to bit-fixing (as defined in [6]) due to there important when guess-and-determine attacks are investigated (see Sect. 4.3). Finally we define the direct sums of monomials and recall some of their properties.

A Boolean function f with n variables is a function from $\mathbb{F}_2^n$ to $\mathbb{F}_2$. The set of all Boolean functions in n variables is denoted by $\mathcal{B}_n$. We call Algebraic Normal Form (ANF) of a Boolean function f its n-variable polynomial representation over $\mathbb{F}_2$ (*i.e.* belonging to $\mathbb{F}_2[x_1, \ldots, x_n]/(x_1^2 + x_1, \ldots, x_n^2 + x_n)$):

$$f(x) = \sum_{I \subseteq [n]} a_I \left(\prod_{i \in I} x_i \right) = \sum_{I \subseteq [n]} a_I x^I,$$

where $a_I \in \mathbb{F}_2$. The algebraic degree of f equals the global degree $\max_{\{I \mid a_I = 1\}} |I|$ of its ANF. Any term $\prod_{i \in I} x_i$ is called a monomial and its degree equals $|I|$. A function with only one non-zero coefficient a_I, $|I| > 0$, is called a monomial function.

A Boolean function $f \in \mathcal{B}_n$ is said to be balanced if its output is uniformly distributed over $\{0, 1\}$. f is called m-resilient if any of its restrictions obtained by fixing at most m of its coordinates is balanced. We denote by $\mathrm{res}(f)$ the maximum resiliency m of f and set $\mathrm{res}(f) = -1$ if f is unbalanced. The nonlinearity NL of a Boolean function f is the minimum Hamming distance between f and all the affine functions in $\mathcal{B}_n$: $\mathrm{NL}(f) = \min_{g, \deg(g) \leq 1} \{d_H(f, g)\}$, with $d_H(f, g) = \#\{x \in \mathbb{F}_2^n \mid f(x) \neq g(x)\}$ the Hamming distance between f and g; and $g(x) = a \cdot x + \varepsilon$, $a \in \mathbb{F}_2^n$, $\varepsilon \in \mathbb{F}_2$ (where $\cdot$ is some inner product in $\mathbb{F}_2^n$; any choice of an inner product will give the same definition). The algebraic immunity of a Boolean function, denoted as $\mathrm{AI}(f)$, is defined as:

$$\mathrm{AI}(f) = \min_{g \neq 0} \{\deg(g) \mid fg = 0 \text{ or } (f + 1)g = 0\},$$

where $\deg(g)$ is the algebraic degree of g. The function g is called an annihilator of f (or $f + 1$). We additively use the notation $\mathrm{AN}(f)$ for the minimum algebraic degree of non null annihilator of f, and $\mathcal{DAN}(f)$ for the dimension of the vector space made of the annihilators of f of degree $\mathrm{AI}(f)$ and the zero function. The fast algebraic immunity, denoted as $\mathrm{FAI}(f)$, is defined (*e.g.* [7]) as:

$$\mathrm{FAI}(f) = \min\{2\mathrm{AI}(f), \min_{1 \leq \deg(g) < \mathrm{AI}(f)} (\max[\deg(g) + \deg(fg), 3\deg(g)])\}.$$

Definition 1 (Bit-fixing Descendants and Bit-fixing Families). *Let f be a Boolean function in n variables (x_i, for $i \in [n]$), let ℓ be an integer such that $0 \leq \ell < n$, let $I \subset [n]$ be of size ℓ (i.e. $I = \{I_1, \ldots, I_\ell\}$ with $I_i < I_{i+1}$ for all $i \in [\ell - 1]$), and let $b \in \mathbb{F}_2^\ell$, we denote as $f_{I,b}$ the ℓ-bit fixing descendant of f on subset I with binary vector b the Boolean function in $n - \ell$ variables:*

$$f_{I,b}(x') = f(x) \mid \forall i \in [\ell], \ x_{I_i} = b_i, \quad \text{where } x' = (x_i, \text{ for } i \in [n] \backslash I).$$

For $\mathcal{F}$ a family of Boolean functions, $\mathcal{F}$ is called bit-fixing stable, or stable relatively to guess and determine, if for all $f \in \mathcal{F}$ all its descendants belong to $\mathcal{F}$.

Definition 2 (Direct Sum of Monomials and Direct Sum Vector). Let $f \in \mathcal{B}_n$, we call f a Direct Sum of Monomials (or DSM) if the following holds for its ANF:

$$\forall (I, J) \text{ such that } a_I = a_J = 1, \ I \cap J \in \{\emptyset, I \cup J\}.$$

We define its Direct Sum Vector (or DSV) $\mathbf{m}_f$ of length $k = \deg(f)$ where $m_i, i \in [k]$, is the number of monomials of degree i:

$$\mathbf{m}_f = [m_1, m_2, \ldots, m_k], \quad m_i = |\{a_I = 1, \text{ such that } |I| = i\}|.$$

By default when we refer to the vector $\mathbf{m}_F = [m_1, m_2, \ldots, m_k]$, it corresponds to the function in $N = \sum_{i=1}^{k} i m_i$ variables with constant term being null.

Remark 1. Some properties of two particular families of DSM have been studied in [36], the family of triangular functions, *i.e.* $\mathbf{m}_F$ is the all-1 vector of length k, and FLIP functions, *i.e.* $\forall i \in [3, k] \ m_i = m_k, m_1 > m_k$, and $m_2 > m_k$.

Note also that DSM functions form a bit-fixing stable family: fixing $\ell < n$ variables (influencing $f(x)$ of not) does not change the property on the ANF defining a DSM.

2.2 Fully Homomorphic Encryption

We recall here the definition of (fully) homomorphic encryption, a kind of encryption enabling to perform computations on plaintexts only manipulating the ciphertexts, without requiring the ability of decrypting. We introduce the vocabulary relative to homomorphic encryption we will use in this paper. For more details we refer to [22] for FHE, and to [31,36] for hybrid homomorphic encryption.

Definition 3 (Homomorphic Encryption Scheme). *Let $\mathcal{M}$ be the plaintext space, $\mathcal{C}$ the ciphertext space and λ the security parameter. A homomorphic encryption scheme consists of four probabilistic polynomial-time algorithms:*

- *$H.\mathsf{KeyGen}(1^\lambda)$. Generates a pair $(\mathsf{pk}^H, \mathsf{sk}^H)$, public and secret keys of the scheme.*
- *$H.\mathsf{Enc}(m, \mathsf{pk}^H)$. From the plaintext $m \in \mathcal{M}$ and pk^H, outputs a ciphertext $c \in \mathcal{C}$.*
- *$H.\mathsf{Dec}(c, \mathsf{sk}^H)$. From the ciphertext $c \in \mathcal{C}$ and the secret key, outputs $m' \in \mathcal{M}$.*
- *$H.\mathsf{Eval}(f, c_1, \cdots, c_k, \mathsf{pk}^H)$. With $c_i = H.\mathsf{Enc}(m_i, \mathsf{pk}^H)$ for $1 \le i \le k$, outputs a ciphertext $c_f \in \mathcal{C}$.*

Homomorphic Encryption: Simple, Leveled, Somewhat, Fully. Different notions of homomorphic encryption exist, depending on the set over which the function f can be taken, that is, on the operations which are possible. For all these kinds we assume a compactness property: $|\mathcal{C}|$ is finite, and the size of a ciphertext does not depend on the number of operations performed to obtain it. When only one kind of operation is permitted the scheme is simply homomorphic, it is called somewhat homomorphic when more than one operation can be performed, at least partially. Leveled homomorphic schemes correspond to f being any polynomial of bounded degree (defining the level) and bounded coefficients. Fully Homomorphic Encryption (FHE) corresponds to f being any function defined over $\mathcal{M}$. Gentry [22] proved that FHE can be constructed by combining a leveled homomorphic scheme with a bootstrapping technique. As this technique is still a bottleneck for homomorphic evaluation, we consider a framework where no bootstrapping (or at least less bootstrappings) are performed, and then when we refer to FHE or HE it refers more precisely to this context.

Noise or Error-Growth. Any known FHE scheme is based on noise-based cryptography, so that an homomorphic ciphertext is associated to a part of error (or noise). The more homomorphic operations are performed, the higher is the noise (if no bootstrapping is used), this quantity of noise can be measured in terms of standard deviation of the distribution followed by the error part. The error-growth involved in an homomorphic evaluation is then the evolution of this parameter.

FHE Generations. Since Gentry's breakthrough [22], various FHE schemes following this blueprint appeared. We call second generation the schemes where the error of the product is symmetric in the factors, as BGV [9] which is often considered for efficiency comparisons as implemented in the HElib library [28]. We call third generation the schemes where the error of the product is asymmetric in the factors, the most recent generation of FHE, initiated with GSW [23].

2.3   Filter Permutators and FLIP Instances

The Filter Permutator or FP is the general design of stream ciphers introduced in [36], and FLIP is an instance of this design where the filtering function is taken from a subfamily of DSM functions. The main design principle of FPs is to filter a constant key register with a variable (public) bit permutation. More precisely, at each cycle, the key register is (bitwise) permuted with a pseudo-randomly generated permutation, and then a non-linear filtering function is applied to the output of this permuted key register. The general structure of FPs is depicted in the left part of Fig. 1. It is composed of three parts: A register where the key is stored, a (bit) permutation generator parametrized by a Pseudo Random Number Generator (PRNG) which is initialized with a public IV, and a filtering function which generates a key-stream.

3   Improved Filter Permutators: A New Design for Better Security and Better Performances

Two main tweaks are performed on the Filter Permutators blueprint to increase its security and its performances as a SE scheme in the SE-FHE framework. The first goal of these modifications is to generalize the original design, in a way which provides more flexibility to choose the functions used, and the number of variables involved in the computations. The second goal consists in simplifying the security analysis, erasing some particularities of the FP which make the security difficult to evaluate.

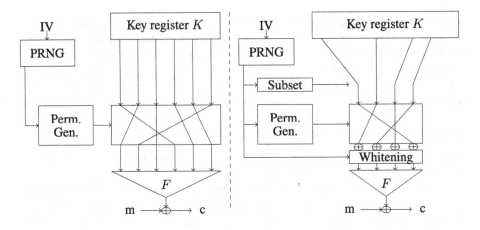

Fig. 1. Filter permutator and improved filter permutator constructions.

3.1 Description

The design of Improved Filter Permutators (IFPs) deviates from filter permutators blueprint in two ways. First, the size of the key register and the number of variables of the filtering function is not forced to be equal. The IFP key can be longer than the number of inputs of the filtering function (in practice we consider a small factor between both, between 2 and 32). Second, at each clock cycle a whitening of the size of F input's is derived from the PRNG and bitwise XORed with the permuted sub-part of the key.

It gives a new design depicted in the right part of Fig. 1, with the following particularities: N is the size of the key register, $n \leq N$ is the number of selected bits from the key register at each clock cycle, and $F \in \mathcal{B}_n$ is the filtering function.

For a security parameter λ, to encrypt $m \leq 2^\lambda$ bits under a secret key $K \in \mathbb{F}_2^N$ (such that $w_H(K) = N/2$), the public parameters of the PRNG are chosen and then the following process is executed for each key-stream bit s_i (for $i \in [m]$):

- The PRNG is updated, its output determines the subset, the permutation, and the whitening at time i,
- the subset S_i is chosen, as a subset of n elements over N,
- the permutation P_i from n to n elements is chosen,
- the whitening w_i from $\mathbb{F}_2^n$ is chosen,
- the key-stream bit s_i is computed as $s_i = F(P_i(S_i(K)) + w_i)$, where $+$ denotes the bitwise XOR.

Note that for each clock cycle i we consider that the PRNG gives enough pseudorandom bits to independently determine the subset ($\log \binom{N}{n}$ bits), the permutation ($\log(n!)$ bits), and the whitening (n bits). Its effect on the performances of IFPs in a hybrid FHE framework is negligible anyway. Note that if the number of pseudorandom bits given by the instance of the PRNG used is limited to b, it enables to compute $\lfloor b/(\log \binom{N}{n} + \log(n!) + n) \rfloor$ bits of ciphertexts only. If this quantity is smaller than m, then another instance of PRNG is used, and so forth until the m bits of ciphertexts are produced (an instantiation of the whole scheme is given in Sect. 5). Any pseudorandom sequence not adversarially chosen could be used instead of the PRNG's output, the use of the PRNG is only motivated by the storage limitation [36] of one of the participants in the hybrid FHE framework.

3.2 Impact on Security

The two modifications from FPs to IFPs, *i.e.* the register extension and the whitening, are generalizing the design and strictly improving the security. The register extension has two main advantages. First, it enables to increase the security without using more complex functions (allowing then more flexibility in the design). Indeed, keeping invariant the filtering function, increasing N decreases the probability of each key-bit to appear in a key-stream equation, directly increasing the complexity of all attacks known to apply on the Filtering Permutator. Second, the Hamming weight of F's input is not constant anymore. Since $N \geq 2n$, F can be evaluated on any element of $\mathbb{F}_2^n$ (being the weight of $S_i(K)$ at time i), it makes the attacks based on restricted input considerations [12] even less efficient.

The main advantage of the whitening is to facilitate the analysis of security against guess-and-determine attacks [20]. When a guess-and-determine strategy is used by the attacker, some key bits (ℓ) are fixed and then the key-stream bits do not correspond to evaluations of F anymore, but to evaluations of descendants of F, which are functions acting on a number of variables between n and $n - \ell$. The complexity of these attacks depends on the properties of the descendants rather than the ones of F. In the security analysis of [36], the descendant with the worst parameter was considered for each Boolean criterion, giving a lower bound on the complexity of the corresponding attack. By randomizing the choice of the descendant, the whitening enables the security of IFPs to be based on average properties rather than worst-case ones (as the probability of getting a function with the worst parameters is not equal to 1).

Finally, note that increasing the register size makes the construction very similar to Goldreich's PRG [25]. For more details on this PRG, we refer to the initial article of Goldreich and to the survey of Applebaum [5]. In the following we give the necessary explanations to understand the connection between this PRG and IFPs. Goldreich's PRG is an asymptotic construction with interesting conjectured security [4–6], and many implications such as secure computation with constant computational overhead [29], or indistinguishability obfuscation [32,33]. We can define this PRG in the following way: let n and m be two integers, let $(S_1, \ldots, S_m)$ be a list of m subsets of $[n]$ of size d, and let $P \in \mathcal{B}_d$ (often called predicate), we call Goldreich's PRG the functions $G : \mathbb{F}_2^n \mapsto \mathbb{F}_2^m$ such that for $x \in \mathbb{F}_2^n$, $G(x) = P(S_1(x)), P(S_2(x)), \ldots, P(S_m(x))$. The integer d is called the locality of the PRG and many works have focused on polynomial-stretch local PRG. Local means that d is a constant, and polynomial-stretch means that $m = n^s$ where s is the called the stretch: these PRG extend a short random seed into a polynomially longer pseudorandom string. These local PRG are conjectured secure based on some properties of the subsets and on the function P. Considering the (n, m, d)-hypergraph given by the subsets $(S_1, \ldots, S_m)$, the PRG cannot be secure if the hypergraph is not sufficiently expending (we refer to [5] for the notions and references). In practice, an overwhelming portion of (n, m, d)-hypergraphs are sufficiently expanding, making the choice of a random (n, m, d)-hypergraph an usual and adequate strategy. For the function P, the PRG cannot be secure if P is not resilient enough [39] or if its algebraic degree, or more generally its algebraic immunity, is insufficient [6], both quantity being related to s. For these constructions, the security is considered asymptotically, relatively to classes of polynomial adversaries as linear distinguishers [39] or the Lasserre/Parrilo semidefinite programming hierarchy. Regarding concrete parameters, very few is known up to now, we are only aware of the recent work [17], which concretely studies the security of an instance of a super-linear (but less than quadratic) stretch.

3.3 Impact on Homomorphic Evaluation

The modifications from FPs to IFPs are almost free. The size of the key register does not modify the function F so the homomorphic error-growth given by the evaluation of F is independent of N. The whitening is given by the output of the PRNG, so considered as public, therefore each bit of the whitening is encrypted as a zero-noise homomorphic ciphertext. Adding homomorphically these zero-noise ciphertexts to the input of F does not increase the error-growth, giving a final noise identical to the one obtained with a FP instantiated with the same function. Only the time of the evaluation is modified, but the search in a longer list and the addition of zero-noise ciphertexts has a minor impact compared to the evaluation of the filtering function.

3.4 Key-Size Consideration

A general idea behind FPs and Improved FPs is to have the main part of the encryption process which would have no cost when homomorphically evaluated. This specificity leads to consider longer keys than the traditional λ-bits key for a bit-security of λ. We argue that in the SE-FHE context this specificity has a very low impact. Indeed, even bounding the total key-size to 2^{14} it is still way smaller that the size of only one homomorphic ciphertext. Then, the encryption of each bit depending only on a subpart of fixed length of the key, the total length of the key has no impact for the majority of the hybrid FHE framework. Since the user can store a key of this size, and the server can store this amount of homomorphic ciphertexts, the key size is not a bottleneck in the considered framework. Note that for the schemes with key size of λ bits, more computations are needed for the encryption or decryption, having an important impact on the size of the homomorphic ciphertexts required, impacting the majority of the hybrid FHE framework, and mostly the application part.

4 Security Analysis of the Improved Filter Permutators

Due to the similarity of (improved) filter permutators to the filter register model, we investigate the attacks known to apply on this model. We consider that no additional weakness arises from the PRNG which is chosen to be forward secure to avoid malleability. The subsets and the whitenings are chosen without any bias, and Knuth-shuffle is used to choose the permutations. As a consequence, on this pseudorandom system non adversarially chosen, the attacks applying target the filtering function and they are adaptations from the one applying on filtered registers. The first part of the security analysis is similar to the one in [36], the same kind of attacks are explored but the complexity is computed differently, using new algorithms enabling to consider any functions. We consider the attacks in the single-key setting, in the known ciphertext model, focusing particularly on key-recovery attacks.

4.1   Algebraic-Like Attacks

We qualify as algebraic-like attacks the kind of attacks consisting in manipulating the system of equations given by the key-stream to build a system of smaller degree, easier to solve. Algebraic attacks [16], fast algebraic attacks [14], or approaches using Grobner bases (such as [21]) are examples of this type. To determine the security of IFP relatively to this class of attacks we study more particularly the complexity of algebraic and fast algebraic attacks, as their complexity can be estimated from Boolean criteria.

The main idea of algebraic attacks as defined in [16] (in a context of filtered LFSR) is to build an over-defined system of equations with the initial state of the LFSR as unknown, and to solve this system with Gaussian elimination. The principle is to find a nonzero function g such that both g and $h = gF$ have low algebraic degree, allowing the attacker to get various equations of small degree d. Then, the degree-d algebraic system is solved, by linearization if it is possible, using Grobner basis method or SAT solvers otherwise; linearization is the only method for which evaluating the complexity is easy. The degree of g is at least $\mathsf{AI}(F)$, and g is chosen to be a non null annihilator of F or $F + 1$ of minimal degree. Then the adversary is able to obtain $\mathcal{DAN}(F)$ (respectively $\mathcal{DAN}(F + 1)$) equations with monomials of degree $\mathsf{AI}(F)$ in the key bits variables, for each equation. After linearization, the adversary obtains a system of equations in $D = \sum_{i=0}^{\mathsf{AI}(F)} \binom{N}{i}$ variables, where N is the number of original indeterminates. Therefore, the time complexity of the algebraic attack is $\mathcal{O}(D^{\omega}) \approx \mathcal{O}(N^{\omega \mathsf{AI}(F)})$, where ω is the exponent in the complexity of Gaussian elimination (we assume $\omega = \log(7)$ for all our security estimations[3]). The data complexity is $\mathcal{O}(D/\mathcal{DAN}(F))$.

Fast algebraic attacks [14] are a variation of the previous attacks. Still considering the relation $gF = h$, their goal is to find and use functions g of low algebraic degree e, possibly smaller than $\mathsf{AI}(f)$, and h of low but possibly larger degree d. Then, the attacker lowers the degree of the resulting equations by an off-line elimination of the monomials of degrees larger than e (several equations being needed to obtain each one with degree at most e). Following [7], this attack can be decomposed into four steps. The search for the polynomials g and h generating a system of $D + E$ equations in $D + E$ unknowns, where $D = \sum_{i=0}^{d}\{N \text{ choose } i\}$, and $E = \sum_{i=0}^{e}\{N \text{ choose } i\}$. The search for linear relations which allow the suppression of the monomials of degree more than e, with a time complexity in $\mathcal{O}(D \log^2(D))$. The elimination of monomials

---

[3] For a sparse system of equations we could use $\omega = 2$, but, note that even if the filtering function has a sparse ANF, it does not imply that this property holds on its annihilators. Then, the systems targeted by the (fast) algebraic attacks have a lower degree but are denser, justifying this more common choice for ω.

of degree larger than e using the Berlekamp-Massey algorithm, corresponding to a time complexity in $\mathcal{O}(ED\log(D))$. Finally, the resolution of the system, in $\mathcal{O}(E^\omega)$. This attack is very efficient on filtered LFSR ciphers as the search of linear relations between equations is simple. For IFPs, the first step could be trivial for our choice of F. Then, as the subset of variables and the permutation chosen at each clock cycle are given by the PRNG, there is no trivial linear relation between one equation and the next ones. It is always possible to simplify some equations using the system, for example forcing collisions on the monomials of higher degree, so other techniques of eliminations could apply. We stress that the time complexity of these techniques would be higher than the one of Berlekamp-Massey. Thus we consider the (time) complexity of the fast algebraic attack, $O(D\log^2(D) + ED\log(D) + E^\omega) \approx \mathcal{O}(N^{\mathsf{FAI}})$, as an upper bound on the time complexity of any attack of the algebraic kind on IFPs, and a data complexity of D.

4.2   Correlation-Like Attacks

We qualify as correlation-like attacks the kind of attacks that use the bias of the filtering function relatively to uniform, or to a low degree function. Correlation attacks, Learning Parity with Noise (LPN) solvers, correlations based on the XL algorithm [15] are examples of this kind. To determine the security of IFP relatively to this class of attacks, we study more particularly the complexity of correlation attacks, and show how it complexity can be estimated using Boolean criteria.

The principle of correlation attacks is to distinguish the output of IFPs from random. For example if the filtering function is unbalanced an attack can consist in averaging the key-stream and observing a bias towards $1/2$. If the function is balanced, this strategy does not apply, but instead of averaging on all the key-stream, the attack can target one sub-part only, depending on a small portion of the variables. As the goal of these attacks is to distinguish the key-stream from random, then we assume that key-recovery attacks have at least the same complexity. Two points influence the effectiveness of this attack: the possibility to get equations relatively to an unbalanced function, and the bias.

Two criteria enable us to study the functions relatively to these points: the resiliency and the nonlinearity. The resiliency of a function gives the number of variables that have to be fixed to make it unbalanced, and can be used for the first point. Then, the nonlinearity gives the distance with the closest affine function, determining the bias to $1/2$. Note that to detect the bias to $1/2$ the data complexity would be $\mathcal{O}(\delta^{-2})$, with $\delta = 1/2 - \mathsf{NL}(F)/2^n$. For LPN solvers, correlation based on XL, or other attacks of this kind, a similar bias has to be observed. The smaller is δ, the more distant is the algebraic system from a linear one, which decreases the efficiency of these attacks. When combinations of vectors are required to observe a bias, the higher is the resiliency, the higher is the attack complexity. We adopt a conservative approach to thwart this variety of attacks: we assume that guaranteeing both $\delta^{-2} \geq 2^\lambda$ and a resiliency of $\lambda - 1$ avoids any attack of this kind with time or data complexity of less that 2^λ operations.

Note that in the context of Goldreich's PRG only the resiliency is studied. The underlying principle is, as the output is bounded (polynomial) and as the subsets are well distributed, the probability of repetitively finding subsets of the key-stream bits whose sum gives an unbalanced function is low, with enough resilience. In this context the nonlinearity is not studied, as any bias is considered as giving a polynomial attack.

4.3 Guess-and-Determine Strategies

As shown in [20] guess-and-determine attacks apply on FPs. Thus, we consider this class of attacks relatively to IFPs. The principle of the guess-and-determine attack consists in guessing ℓ key bits in order to target simpler functions, obtaining a system of equations easier to solve or with a distribution easier to distinguish. In our context it can be less costly for an attacker to consider the 2^ℓ possible systems given by fixing the value of ℓ variables than attacking the initial system of equation given by the keystream. Hence, both kinds of attacks presented before can be generalized with guess-and-determine. We explain the principle relatively to the algebraic attack: the attacker selects ℓ variables and gives a value of its guess, it simplifies the algebraic system. Then, the attacker considers all equations such that the descendant function has algebraic immunity at most k, and generates the corresponding degree k algebraic system. Once linearized, the attacker solves the system, if it is not consistent, then another guess is tried. As one of the 2^ℓ values of the guess is the correct one, the attack will succeed. Similarly for the other attacks, once the value of the guess is fixed, the attack is mounted on the new system relatively to a specific value of a parameter (the value of e and d for the fast algebraic attack, the value of δ, or the value of the resiliency).

A bound on the complexity of these attacks can be derived from the complexity of the attack without guess-and-determine. For the time complexity, it corresponds to multiplying by 2^ℓ the complexity of the attack using the parameter of value k on a system with $N - \ell$ variables. For the data complexity, the probability of getting a function with parameter k is important, the whole complexity can then be bounded by the inverse of this probability multiplied by the complexity of the attack using the parameter of value k on a system with $N - \ell$ variables. To determine this probability, it requires to determine the parameters relatively to the Boolean criteria of all descendant functions of F up to $\ell \leq \lambda$ variables. Some descendants may have extreme parameters (called recurrent criteria in [36]), but very low probability of appearing. Then for attacks with guess-and-determine, it is important to investigate both time and data complexities.

Note that the particular guess-and-determine attacks investigated in [20] on FLIP uses two properties. First, the fact that the filtering functions has a very sparse ANF so the descendant obtained by fixing zeros is the one with worse parameters, and then, the crucial fact that for filter permutators the guesses made on the key bits are directly in input of F. The whitening changes the latter property, then targeting a weak function requires to have both the guesses and the whitenings coinciding. It leads to an higher data complexity, as shown by the algorithms estimating the complexity at the end of this section.

4.4 Other Attacks

Besides the previous attacks that will be taken into account quantitatively when selecting concrete instances, we also investigated other cryptanalyses, so we develop some explanations on those which are known to apply on filter permutators [36].

First, weak key attacks can be considered: if the Hamming weight of the key is extreme the input of F is far away from the uniform distribution. The probability of this weight to be extreme is very low due to the register extension, and as explained before the whitening avoids simple attacks using the unusual distribution of F's inputs. Restricting our instances to keys of Hamming weight $N/2$ handles these attacks. Second, higher-order correlation attacks [15] consist in approximating the filtering function by a function of degree $d > 1$ and to solve the approximated algebraic system of degree d with a Grobner basis algorithm such as F4 [21]. The attack could be efficient if the function was very close to a degree d function (which corresponds to a small nonlinearity of order d), and if d was low enough as one part of the attack consists in solving a degree d system. This attack can easily be combined with guess-and-determine techniques, but up to now for the filtering functions we tried, the complexity of this attack is always superior to the one considered for fast algebraic attacks or for correlation-like attacks. Eventually, restricted input attacks [12] using the behavior of F on a restricted part of its input are handled by the register size and the whitening. Since the input of F is not restricted to a subset of $\mathbb{F}_2^n$, but to the whole set, it seems unrealistic to adapt this attacks in this context. It would require to combine equations to obtain a set of equations corresponding with high probability to a known small subset of $\mathbb{F}_2^n$. Moreover the function should also have some flaws relatively to this particular subset, which we leave as a scope for further investigations.

4.5 Estimating the Attacks Complexity

Based on the previous parts of this section, relatively to a Boolean function F and the register size N, we can estimate the security of IFPs by computing the parameters of each descendant up to λ variables. We describe the principle of the algorithm used to determine the complexity of an attack relatively to a parameter. To illustrate it, we consider (a simplified version for) the attack based on the algebraic immunity.

Algorithm's Principle. Determining the security from any filtering function F:

1. From F and λ, the profile of the function relatively to algebraic immunity is computed. The profile corresponds to the probability of getting a descendant of F with algebraic immunity less than or equal to k ($0 \le k \le \mathsf{AI}(F)$) by fixing ℓ bits of F inputs. The probability is taken over all choices of ℓ over n variables ($0 \le \ell \le \lambda$) and over the 2^ℓ possible values taken by these variables. To compute the profile, the probability of getting each descendant is computed iteratively, from step 0 to λ. Step 0 corresponds to the function F with probability 1, the profile for 0 guess gives a probability of 0 for $k < \mathsf{AI}(F)$ and 1 for $k \ge \mathsf{AI}(F)$. Then, from step ℓ to step $\ell+1$, for each descendant of step ℓ and its probability, all descendants obtained by fixing one of its variables (to 0 and to 1) are computed, together with their probability. It gives then all descendants of step $\ell + 1$, the algebraic immunity of each one is computed, and the profile for ℓ guesses at value k is the sum of the probabilities of all these descendants with algebraic immunity less than or equal to k.
2. From the profile and N, for each L with $0 \le L \le \lambda$, and for each possible value k of the algebraic immunity ($0 \le k \le \mathsf{AI}(F)$), we compute the time and data complexity of the attack targeting functions with AI less than or equal to k. The time complexity is then 2^L multiplied by the time complexity of an algebraic attack with AI equal to

k on a system in $N - L$ variables. The data complexity depends on the probability of obtaining an equation with such a parameter of AI. This probability depends on the profile and on N. It corresponds to $P = \sum_{\ell=0}^{L} P_{L=\ell} \cdot P_{(\text{AI} \leq k) \mid \ell}$, where $P_{L=\ell} = \binom{L}{\ell}\binom{N-L}{n-\ell}\binom{N}{n}^{-1}$ is the probability that ℓ over the L guesses of the adversary are in the n input's variables of F. The quantity $P_{(\text{AI} \leq k) \mid \ell}$ is the probability that the function has algebraic immunity less than or equal to k conditioned on the number of variables fixed in F to get this function. This probability is what the profile gives. The data complexity is finally P^{-1} multiplied by the data complexity of an algebraic attack with algebraic immunity equal to k on a system in $N - L$ variables.

3. For each pair (L, k), we determine the maximum between the time and data complexity, the minimum over all pairs gives the final complexity of the attack.

Potential Modifications. The advantage of this methodology is to apply on any filtering function F, and any register size N, giving a general framework to determine the security of IFPs instances. This general algorithm being exhaustive, it has a high time and storage complexity. Indeed, note that the number of descendants of a function is exponential. The algorithm can be modified in order to be more efficiently evaluated, but sometimes at the cost of underestimating the cost of the attacks.

A first modification, which does not underestimates the cost of the attacks, consists in finding the descendants which are equivalent. That is, the ones which have exactly the same parameters for each criterion and that give the same descendants with identical probabilities. When such equivalent descendants are found, which can be handled through the representation of the function, the number of descendant at step ℓ can be less than the initial bound of $2^{\ell}\binom{n}{\ell}$. A second modification, underestimating the cost of the attacks, consists in replacing each value of the parameter (which can take in some cases numerous values) by the nearest one among those which are more favorable to the attacker in a shorter list, and summing the probabilities corresponding to each such approximation. A third modification, also underestimating the cost of the attacks, can be achieved by not considering all descendants but only descendants which have worse parameters. It is possible when, for each number of guesses considered, for each criterion, the profile of a function is worse than the profile of another one. Then the probability of the function with better profiles can be added to the probability of the function with worse profiles. In other words, a (stronger) function can be neglected and its probability added to another one, if the probability of its descendants to reach a particular weak value of parameter is always inferior than the corresponding probability for the descendants of the other (weaker) function.

5   Instantiating the Improved Filter Permutators with DSM Functions: FiLIP$_{\text{DSM}}$ Instances

We now instantiate the IFP paradigm with filtering functions being direct sums of monomials, and denote these instances as FiLIP$_{\text{DSM}}$. This choice is motivated by the functions considered in [36] under the name of FLIP functions, which are a sub-family of DSM functions. DSM functions are very structured functions, are easy to represent through their direct sum vector, and we can determine all their parameters relatively to Boolean criteria. Recall that to estimate the most correctly the security given by a filtering function, it is necessary to determine the parameters of all its descendants (up to λ variables). As DSM are bit-fixing stable (see Remark 1), knowing the standard properties of all the family enables to determine the bit-fixing properties of any DSM filtering function, giving a very accurate estimation of the security against guess-and-determine attacks. Finally, it is a good choice in terms of homomorphic error-growth due to their low multiplicative depth, which is considered as the main parameter influencing second generation FHE schemes such as BGV [9]. Evaluating DSM functions consists in summing products of binary ciphertexts only, which corresponds to a very low error-growth, both in second, and in third generations. More precisely, the evaluation of a DSM function with a 3G scheme produces only a quasi-linear (in n) error-growth ([35], Lemma 22).

We instantiate the forward secure PRNG following Bellare and Yee [8] construction, using the AES as underlying block cipher. The PRNG is set with two constants C_0 and C_1, For each K_i the first block $AES(K_i, C_0)$ gives the key K_{i+1} of the next iteration and the second block $AES(K_i, C_1)$ gives 128 bits being the i-th part of the PRG's output. For each key-stream bit the PRNG outputs $\lceil \log \binom{N}{n} \rceil$ bits used to select the subset considering the variables in lexicographic order. Then, the permutation over n bits is instantiated with the Knuth shuffle [30] with the following bits output by the PRNG. Finally, n last bits are used to generate the whitening. If the number of ciphertext bits $m \leq 2^\lambda$ requires more pseudorandom bits that the secure limitation of the PRNG, another instance is used with other constants. The number of possible instances for the PRNG makes that for the parameters we consider the limitation comes from m.

5.1 Simplifying the Attack Complexities Algorithms for DSM Functions

In Sect. 4 we give the general framework to compute the complexity of the attacks. Even if DSM functions form a bit-fixing stable family, computing exactly the parameters of all descendants of a non trivial DSM in more than 300 variables is out of reach. Then, we use general properties proven on these functions in [35] to modify the algorithms as explained in Sect. 4.5. We describe in the following these modifications which greatly improve the complexity and finally enable to find concrete instances.

First note that the criteria of resiliency, nonlinearity, algebraic immunity and fast algebraic immunity can exactly be determined using the DSV notation (for the $\mathcal{D}$AN the constant term of the function matters). Therefore, two functions with the same DSV are considered as equivalent, and the number of descendants to consider decreases using this property, it corresponds to the first modification mentioned in Sect. 4.5. Then, the number of descendants with different DSV is still very important, and the number of different parameters also. consequently, we use the second modification relatively to the nonlinearity, the $\mathcal{D}$AN and the fast algebraic immunity. For DSM functions, the exact value of the bias δ varies a lot, hence we consider only the values of $-\lfloor (\log(\delta)) \rfloor$. For the $\mathcal{D}$AN we use an upper bound (compatible with the DSV notation), considering the maximum over all DSM of degree at most k. For fast algebraic attack we consider only 1 and 2 as possible values for e and the reached algebraic immunity as possible value for d. Finally, we decide to not consider all descendants, and attribute the probability of the ones with good parameters to others (third modification). It is the modification affecting most the complexity of the algorithm. It is realized through proving relations between the parameters of DSM functions and an order on their DSV. In the case of DSM, the descendants obtained by fixing zeros are always with worse parameter.

First Modification, Parameters Given by the Direct Sum Vector. As far as we know DSM functions constitute the first bit-fixing stable family for which all the parameters (mentioned in Sect. 4) are determined. Note that for a DSM function f with $\mathbf{m}_f = [m_1, m_2, \ldots, m_k]$ there are at most $M = \prod_{i=1}^{k}(m_i + 1)$ different DSV in the descendants obtained by fixing zeros (as fixing a variable to 0 decreases one of the m_i by 1). To compute the profiles of a DSM, we use the following representation, as only the descendants obtained by fixing zeros are considered, we store a vector of length M and each index represent one descendant. The number of descendants at each step being the most expensive part of the algorithm in term of storage and time, the algorithm is better suited for function with relatively small M. It justifies why we will focus on instances with sparse DSV.

Lemma 1 (Direct Sum of Monomials and Boolean Criteria, [35] Lemmata 2, 3 and Theorem 1). *Let $f \in \mathbb{F}_2^n$ be a Boolean function obtained by direct sums of monomials with associated direct sum vector $= [m_1, \ldots, m_k]$, its parameters are:*

- *Resiliency:* $\mathsf{res}(f) = m_1 - 1$.
- *Nonlinearity:* $\mathsf{NL}(f) = 2^{n-1} - \dfrac{1}{2}\left(2^{(n-\sum_{i=2}^{k} im_i)} \prod_{i=2}^{k} (2^i - 2)^{m_i} \right)$.
- *Algebraic immunity:* $\mathsf{AI}(f) = \min_{0 \leq d \leq k}\left(d + \sum_{i=d+1}^{k} m_i \right)$.

Second Modification, Bounding FAI and $\mathcal{D}$AN. We recall the lower bound on the FAI and the upper bound of the $\mathcal{D}$AN of a DSM in the following proposition. The bound on the FAI is tight for most functions, whereas the situation is opposite for the bound on the $\mathcal{D}$AN. It is very common that all descendant of a DSM with a different DSV have a different value of $\mathcal{D}$AN. Hence, the bound allows us to reduce from $\prod_{i=1}^{k}(m_i + 1)$ possible values to $2k$ only. This modification simplifies greatly the estimation of the algebraic attack complexity, as it requires to jointly use AI and $\mathcal{D}$AN profiles.

Proposition 1 (Bounds on FAI and $\mathcal{D}$AN, [35] Propositions 4 and 5). *For any DSM function f of degree $k > 0$:*

$$\mathsf{FAI}(f) \geq \mathsf{bFAI}(f) = \begin{cases} \mathsf{AI}(f) + 2 & \text{if } \mathsf{AI}(f) = \deg(f), \mathsf{AI}(f) > 1, \text{and } m_k > 1, \\ \mathsf{AI}(f) + 1 & \text{otherwise.} \end{cases}$$

$$\mathcal{D}\mathsf{AN}(f) \leq \mathsf{b}\mathcal{D}\mathsf{AN}(f) = k^k + 1 \text{ if } m_1 = 0, \text{ and } k^{k-1} + 1 \text{ if } m_1 > 0.$$

Third Modification, Determining DSM Descendant with Worse Properties. In the previous paragraphs we consider the number of descendants obtained by fixing zeros and not the total number of descendants, the reason is that a relation between the descendant greatly decreases the algorithms complexity. We use this relation between the 2^ℓ descendants to bound the parameters relatively to the standard criteria of all descendant functions on a same subset by the parameters of only one of these descendant. The purpose of these results is to be able to upper bound the number of descendants of a function which parameter is equal to a targeted value. More specifically, for all $b \in \mathbb{F}_2^\ell$, the parameters of all descendant functions relatively to the same subset can be bound using the direct sum vectors of the all-0 or all-1 descendant:

Proposition 2 (DSM Descendants Properties, [35] Proposition 6). *Let $\ell \in \mathbb{N}^*$, 0^ℓ and 1^ℓ denote the all-0 and all-1 vectors of $\mathbb{F}_2^\ell$. Let f be a DSM function in n variables, for any $\ell \mid 1 \leq \ell < n$, and any subset $I \subseteq [n]$ such that $|I| = \ell$, and for any $b \in \mathbb{F}_2^\ell$:*

$$\mathsf{res}(f_{I,b}) \geq \mathsf{res}(f_{I,0^\ell}), \quad \mathsf{NL}(f_{I,b}) \geq \mathsf{NL}(f_{I,0^\ell}), \quad \mathsf{AI}(f_{I,b}) \geq \mathsf{AI}(f_{I,0^\ell}),$$
$$\mathsf{bFAI}(f_{I,b}) \geq \mathsf{bFAI}(f_{I,0^\ell}), \quad \mathsf{b\mathcal{D}AN}(f_{I,b}) \leq \mathsf{b\mathcal{D}AN}(f_{I,1^\ell}).$$

5.2 Concrete Instances with DSM Functions

Based on the security estimations we propose the following instances of $\mathsf{FiLIP}_{\mathsf{DSM}}$ in Table 1, $\mathbf{m}_F$ is the DSV notation of F, n is the number of variables of F, N is the size of the key register, d is the multiplicative depth of the function, and λ is the conjectured security parameter.

Table 1. $\mathsf{FiLIP}_{\mathsf{DSM}}$ Instances.

$\mathbf{m}_F$	n	N	d	λ	Name
$[89, 67, 47, 37]$	512	16384	2	80	FiLIP-512
$[80, 40, 15, 15, 15, 15]$	430	1792	3	80	FiLIP-430
$[80, 40, 0, 20, 0, 0, 0, 10]$	320	1800	3	80	FiLIP-320
$[128, 64, 0, 80, 0, 0, 0, 80]$	1216	16384	3	128	FiLIP-1216
$[128, 64, 0, 0, 0, 0, 0, 0, 0, 0, 0, 0, 0, 0, 0, 64]$	1280	4096	4	128	FiLIP-1280

6 Performance Evaluation

Ultimately, the goal of SE-FHE applications is to obtain the result of the homomorphic computations with the best latency and throughput. However, such performance metrics can only be evaluated if the functions to be evaluated by the Cloud are known in advance. In previous evaluations of symmetric ciphers for FHE evaluation, this issue was (partially) circumvented by studying the latency and throughput of homomorphic ciphertexts that will just enable decryption or a fixed number of levels of multiplications. This allows getting lower bounds on the timings necessary to evaluate any function, and the performances are reasonably accurate for simple functions with the given multiplicative depth. Yet, one important drawback of this approach remains that optimizing latency and throughput requires to fix parameters such as the size of the ciphertexts and the quantity of noise (which set the security of the FHE scheme). More precisely, in HE, it is the quantity of noise that determines the size of the ciphertexts required to correctly handle the operations. This size is in turn the main factor determining the latency and throughput of the homomorphic operations. Therefore, optimizing throughput and latency is ideal for one specific function, but it looses its accuracy when the application deviates from this particular function. We next propose an alternative comparison methodology, based on the homomorphic noise, that aims to be more independent of the applications.

6.1 Methodology

Considering the performances of SE-FHE relatively to the homomorphic noise is based on two simple principles. The smaller is the noise, the wider is the class of functions still evaluable on these ciphertexts. The smaller is the noise, the smaller are the homomorphic ciphertexts, the faster are the evaluations. It means that the homomorphic noise dictates the ciphertext parameters, and eventually the latency and throughput of the final application. Consequently, an appealing performance evaluation could consist in determining exactly the error-growth (in average or with overwhelming probability) given by an SE scheme for a specific FHE scheme. As there is no simple parameter (such as the multiplicative depth) which encompasses totally the error-growth, we use a simpler methodology consisting in measuring the noise just after evaluating the symmetric decryption or after some additive levels of multiplications.

In contrast with the aforementioned latency/throughput oriented methodology, which leads to fix the homomorphic parameters to optimize the timings for a given target function, a noise-oriented methodology can ensure that the ciphertext parameters are the same for all SE schemes to be compared. This has two advantages. First, all homomorphic ciphertexts obtained have the same security, that we fix to λ, the security level of the SE scheme. Second, once the symmetric decryption is performed, the evaluation time of any function will be independent of the SE scheme used for the transciphering. Such a scheme is then only limited by the ciphertext noise, which determines the quantity of operations that can be performed until decryption becomes impossible. Consequently, with this methodology, the smaller is the measured noise, the better suited is the SE scheme. We believe this approach provides interesting insights for the comparison of SE schemes in an application-dependent manner.

Additionally, and for completeness, we give some indications on the time performances, using the strategy of previous works. To do so, for each SE scheme we select homomorphic parameters that are sufficient to evaluate the decryption circuit, but no more. It gives an idea on the minimal size of homomorphic ciphertext and minimal evaluation time required for each SE scheme relatively to the library used. The result corresponds to a minimum as for any application, bigger ciphertexts are necessary to make the evaluations of the computation part.

6.2   Performances and Comparisons

We chose to compare the following symmetric schemes: LowMC [2], FLIP [36], Rasta and Agrasta [19] and FiLIP$_{DSM}$, all designed for the SE-FHE framework. We did not consider Kreyvium [10] as its implementation is very different (based on previous studies the related numbers would be slightly better than the one of LowMC due to a multiplicative depth of 12 and 13). All implementations were made with the HElib library [28]. The LowMC implementations were taken from the publicly available code (https://bitbucket.org/malb/lowmc-helib). The one of Rasta were built from this implementation and the publicly available one (https://github.com/iaikkrypto/rasta). We use the same code for computing the "Four Russians" method, used for multiplying binary matrices. The FLIP and FiLIP$_{DSM}$ implementations were made ad hoc. These implementations were evaluated on laptop computer with processor Intel(R) Core(TM) i5-4210M CPU at 2.60 GHz.

Accordingly to the previously described methodology, we chose parameters in HElib enabling to evaluate the decryption of all these schemes. These parameters are dictated by LowMC (due to its higher multiplicative depth), so we choose the minimal parameters such that LowMC ciphertexts can be decrypted while keeping an FHE security of at least the security of the symmetric ciphers. The noise level after evaluation is estimated thanks to HElib function log_of_ratio() which returns the difference $\log(\sigma) - \log(q)$ where σ^2 is the noise variance (derived from bounds on the error-growth of addition, product, automorphism, and switchings) of the error part of the ciphertext, and q is the modulus. In order to have a glimpse of what this noise level represents, we also computed 1 (respectively 2) level(s) of multiplications between ciphertexts (after the homomorphic evaluation of the symmetric schemes). The results for 80-bit security and 128-bit security are given in Tables 2 and 3[4]. Symbol d denotes the multiplicative depth of the decryption circuit of the SE scheme, N is the key size, symbol b denotes the number of produced bits. The latency refers to the time required to have the first ciphertext after evaluation, the noise columns refer to the output of the log_of_ratio() function, with respectively 0, 1 and 2 levels of multiplications (after evaluation of the SE decryption function).

From these results we can conclude that LowMC ciphertexts have the biggest error-growth. For the 80-bit security instances the noise after evaluating FLIP, Rasta or Agrasta is similar whereas the instances of FiLIP$_{DSM}$ enable 1 or 2 additional levels of multiplications. For 128 bits of security, FiLIP-1280 ciphertexts are slightly less noisy than Agrasta and FLIP ciphertexts, whereas FiLIP-1216 offers an additional level of multiplications. In terms of evaluation time, the parameters are more suited for LowMC, but relatively to this size of ciphertexts we can conclude that Agrasta evaluations produce more ciphertexts per second. The instances of FiLIP$_{DSM}$ produce the ciphertexts one by one, and have then a throughput around 50 times slower for 80-bit instances and 200 for 128-bit instances. These results confirm the excellent behavior of FiLIP$_{DSM}$ in terms of noise, enabling 1 or 2 supplementary levels of multiplication (at the cost of a moderate decrease of the time performances detailed next).

---

[4] These security levels are the one given by HElib, more accurate estimations are given in [1].

Table 2. Noise comparison for 80-bit security. HElib parameters: LWE dimension 15709, HElib Depth L 14, B = 28 (Bit per level parameter that influence BGV security), BGV security 84.3, Nslots 682, log_of_ratio() of fresh ciphertext -237.259.

Cipher	d	N	b	Latency (s)	noise	noise $\times$	noise $\times^2$
LowMCv2 (12, 31, 128)	12	80	128	329.38	-2.966	n/a	n/a
LowMCv2 (12, 49, 256)	12	80	256	699.10	-2.495	n/a	n/a
Agrasta (81, 4)	4	81	81	67.48	-155.722	-139.423	-119.459
Rasta (327, 4)	4	327	327	290.99	-154.502	-139.423	-119.459
Rasta (327, 5)	5	327	327	366.30	-135.727	-119.459	-100.641
FLIP-530	4	530	1	42.06	-157.201	-139.423	-119.459
FiLIP-512	2	16384	1	33.74	-194.342	-177.739	-158.241
FiLIP-430	3	1792	1	31.25	-176.039	-158.241	-139.423
FiLIP-320	3	1800	1	21.41	-176.588	-158.241	-139.423

Table 3. Noise comparison for 128-bit security. HElib parameters: LWE dimension of the underlying lattice = 24929, HElib Depth L = 16, B = 30, BGV security = 132.1, Nslots = 512, log_of_ratio() of fresh ciphertext = -293.929.

Cipher	d	N	b	Latency (s)	noise	noise $\times$	noise $\times^2$
LowMCv2 (14, 63, 256)	14	128	256	1629.03	-3.418	n/a	n/a
Agrasta (129, 4)	4	128	129	207.68	-207.478	-190.086	-169.011
Rasta (525, 5)	5	525	525	1264.30	-185.885	-169.011	-148.313
Rasta (351, 6)	6	351	351	967.62	-164.945	-148.313	-129.716
FLIP-1394	4	1394	1	272.31	-207.831	-190.086	-169.011
FiLIP-1216	3	16384	1	251.28	-227.93	-210.437	-190.086
FiLIP-1280	4	4096	1	325.04	-208.112	-190.086	-169.011

Note that the gain in depth of FiLIP$_{DSM}$ relatively to Agrasta or Rasta is obtained at the price of larger key sizes. When choosing which scheme to use in the hybrid homomorphic framework, a trade-off can be considered between these schemes, depending on the number of levels of multiplications required (computation phase) and constraints on the key-size (initialization phase). The more computations over the data will be considered, the more important will be the influence of the error-growth, making negligible the impact of the key-size.

Table 4. Performances for minimal FHE parameters.

Cipher	B	m	L	λ'	ns	Latency (s)	noise
LowMCv2(12, 31, 128)	28	15709	14	84.3	682	329.38	-2.966
LowMCv2(12, 49, 256)	28	15709	14	84.3	682	699.10	-2.495
Agrasta (81, 4)	26	5461	5	82.9	378	12.97	-2.03
Rasta (327, 4)	26	8435	5	84.6	240	76.33	-1.903
Rasta (327, 5)	25	7781	7	85.1	150	90.78	-14.42
FLIP-530	21	4859	5	85.3	168	6.48	-1.23
FiLIP-512	21	4859	5	85.3	168	7.05	-29.09
FiLIP-430	21	4859	5	85.3	168	6.01	-15.457
FiLIP-320	21	4859	5	85.3	168	5.04	-16.02
LowMCv2(14, 63, 256)	30	24929	16	132.1	512	1629.3	-3.418
Agrasta (129, 4)	27	7781	5	134.7	150	20.26	-3.03
Rasta (525, 5)	27	10261	7	128.9	330	277.24	-20.441
Rasta (351, 6)	27	10261	8	128.9	330	195.40	-1.92
FLIP-1394	28	8191	6	146.8	630	26.53	-5.11
FiLIP-1216	22	7781	5	186.3	150	24.37	-15.94
FiLIP-1280	28	8191	6	146.8	630	26.59	-5.11

We also note that in [19], instances with a smaller multiplicative depth are considered, but the authors recommend a depth at least 4 for security reason. These instances always involve way bigger keys than FiLIP$_{DSM}$ instances with the same multiplicative depth, and due to the high number of XORs in these instances, the error-growth is higher. Rasta ciphers were not optimized for the metric we consider, instances designed for the error-growth could lead to better performances. We argue that minor modifications would benefit to evaluation over HElib, but by design the noise remain larger than the one from IFPs. For example, the high number of additions occurring at different levels between multiplications prohibits Rasta design to be used in a SE-FHE framework using 3G FHE, whereas IFPs are performing well for all known FHE.

We also study the performance results in time for the different SE ciphers considered. For this purpose, we chose the HElib parameters such that the ciphers can just be decrypted (by setting the appropriate L value), while keeping a similar security level for the HE scheme (by modifying with trial and errors the other parameters). These numbers have to be taken as a global behavior of the achievable performances of the ciphers. Optimizations can still be made in the code itself but also in the choice of the FHE parameters. We report the results in Table 4, B is the bit per level parameter, m is the LWE dimension, L is the HElib depth, λ' is the BGV security estimated by HElib, ns the number of slots. The latency refers to the time required to have the first ciphertext after evaluation, the noise columns refers to the output of the log_of_ratio() function after evaluation of the decryption. These results show that, adapting the FHE parameters to the decryption of the SE scheme only, the throughput can be sensibly increased.

Note that, for some lines the ciphertexts are still usable for more evaluations, it comes from the fact that HElib rejects smaller values of L, whereas the multiplicative depth of the scheme is inferior.

Acknowledgments. Pierrick Méaux is funded by a FSE Incoming Post-Doc Fellowship of the Université catholique de Louvain. François-Xavier Standaert is a Senior Associate Researcher of the Belgian Fund for Scientific Research (FNRS-F.R.S.). Work funded in parts by the CHIST-ERA project SECODE and the ERC Project SWORD.

References

1. Albrecht, M.R.: On dual lattice attacks against small-secret LWE and parameter choices in HElib and SEAL. In: Coron, J.-S., Nielsen, J.B. (eds.) EUROCRYPT 2017, Part II. LNCS, vol. 10211, pp. 103–129. Springer, Cham (2017). https://doi.org/10.1007/978-3-319-56614-6_4
2. Albrecht, M.R., Rechberger, C., Schneider, T., Tiessen, T., Zohner, M.: Ciphers for MPC and FHE. In: Oswald, E., Fischlin, M. (eds.) EUROCRYPT 2015, Part I. LNCS, vol. 9056, pp. 430–454. Springer, Heidelberg (2015). https://doi.org/10.1007/978-3-662-46800-5_17
3. Albrecht, M.R., Rechberger, C., Schneider, T., Tiessen, T., Zohner, M.: Ciphers for MPC and FHE. IACR Cryptology ePrint Archive, p. 687 (2016)
4. Applebaum, B.: Pseudorandom generators with long stretch and low locality from random local one-way functions. In: Karloff, H.J., Pitassi, T. (eds.) 44th ACM STOC, pp. 805–816. ACM Press, May 2012
5. Applebaum, B.: Cryptographic hardness of random local functions–survey. In: Sahai, A. (ed.) TCC 2013. LNCS, vol. 7785, p. 599. Springer, Heidelberg (2013). https://doi.org/10.1007/978-3-642-36594-2_33
6. Applebaum, B., Lovett, S.: Algebraic attacks against random local functions and their countermeasures. In: Wichs, D., Mansour, Y. (eds.) 48th ACM STOC, ACM Press, June 2016
7. Armknecht, F., Carlet, C., Gaborit, P., Künzli, S., Meier, W., Ruatta, O.: Efficient computation of algebraic immunity for algebraic and fast algebraic attacks. In: Vaudenay, S. (ed.) EUROCRYPT 2006. LNCS, vol. 4004, pp. 147–164. Springer, Heidelberg (2006). https://doi.org/10.1007/11761679_10
8. Bellare, M., Yee, B.: Forward-security in private-key cryptography. In: Joye, M. (ed.) CT-RSA 2003. LNCS, vol. 2612, pp. 1–18. Springer, Heidelberg (2003). https://doi.org/10.1007/3-540-36563-X_1
9. Brakerski, Z., Gentry, C., Vaikuntanathan, V.: (Leveled) fully homomorphic encryption without bootstrapping. In: Goldwasser, S. (ed.) ITCS 2012, pp. 309–325. ACM, January 2012
10. Canteaut, A., et al.: Stream ciphers: a practical solution for efficient homomorphic-ciphertext compression. In: Peyrin, T. (ed.) FSE 2016. LNCS, vol. 9783, pp. 313–333. Springer, Heidelberg (2016). https://doi.org/10.1007/978-3-662-52993-5_16
11. Carlet, C.: Boolean functions for cryptography and error-correcting codes. In: Encyclopedia of Mathematics and its Applications, pp. 257–397. Cambridge University Press (2010)
12. Carlet, C., Méaux, P., Rotella, Y.: Boolean functions with restricted input and their robustness; application to the FLIP cipher. IACR Trans. Symmetric Cryptol. **2017**(3), 192–227 (2017)
13. Cogliati, B., Tanguy, T.: Multi-user security bound for filter permutators in the random oracle model. Des. Codes Crypt. **87**(7), 1621–1638 (2018)
14. Courtois, N.T.: Fast algebraic attacks on stream ciphers with linear feedback. In: Boneh, D. (ed.) CRYPTO 2003. LNCS, vol. 2729, pp. 176–194. Springer, Heidelberg (2003). https://doi.org/10.1007/978-3-540-45146-4_11

15. Courtois, N.T.: Higher order correlation attacks, XL algorithm and cryptanalysis of toy-ocrypt. In: Lee, P.J., Lim, C.H. (eds.) ICISC 2002. LNCS, vol. 2587, pp. 182–199. Springer, Heidelberg (2003). https://doi.org/10.1007/3-540-36552-4_13

16. Courtois, N.T., Meier, W.: Algebraic attacks on stream ciphers with linear feedback. In: Biham, E. (ed.) EUROCRYPT 2003. LNCS, vol. 2656, pp. 345–359. Springer, Heidelberg (2003). https://doi.org/10.1007/3-540-39200-9_21

17. Couteau, G., Dupin, A., Méaux, P., Rossi, M., Rotella, Y.: On the concrete security of Goldreich's pseudorandom generator. In: Peyrin, T., Galbraith, S. (eds.) ASIACRYPT 2018, Part I. LNCS, vol. 11273, pp. 96–124. Springer, Cham (2018). https://doi.org/10.1007/978-3-030-03329-3_4

18. Cryan, M., Miltersen, P.B.: On pseudorandom generators in NC^0. In: Sgall, J., Pultr, A., Kolman, P. (eds.) MFCS 2001. LNCS, vol. 2136, pp. 272–284. Springer, Heidelberg (2001). https://doi.org/10.1007/3-540-44683-4_24

19. Dobraunig, C., et al.: Rasta: a cipher with low ANDdepth and few ANDs per bit. In: Shacham, H., Boldyreva, A. (eds.) CRYPTO 2018. LNCS, vol. 10991, pp. 662–692. Springer, Cham (2018). https://doi.org/10.1007/978-3-319-96884-1_22

20. Duval, S., Lallemand, V., Rotella, Y.: Cryptanalysis of the FLIP family of stream ciphers. In: Robshaw, M., Katz, J. (eds.) CRYPTO 2016, Part I. LNCS, vol. 9814, pp. 457–475. Springer, Heidelberg (2016). https://doi.org/10.1007/978-3-662-53018-4_17

21. Faugère, J.C.: A new efficient algorithm for computing Groebner bases. J. Pure Appl. Algebra 139(1–3), 61–88 (1999)

22. Gentry, C.: Fully homomorphic encryption using ideal lattices. In: Mitzenmacher, M. (ed.) 41st ACM STOC, pp. 169–178. ACM Press, May/June 2009

23. Gentry, C., Sahai, A., Waters, B.: Homomorphic encryption from learning with errors: conceptually-simpler, asymptotically-faster, attribute-based. In: Canetti, R., Garay, J.A. (eds.) CRYPTO 2013, Part I. LNCS, vol. 8042, pp. 75–92. Springer, Heidelberg (2013). https://doi.org/10.1007/978-3-642-40041-4_5

24. Gérard, B., Grosso, V., Naya-Plasencia, M., Standaert, F.-X.: Block ciphers that are easier to mask: how far can we go? In: Bertoni, G., Coron, J.-S. (eds.) CHES 2013. LNCS, vol. 8086, pp. 383–399. Springer, Heidelberg (2013). https://doi.org/10.1007/978-3-642-40349-1_22

25. Goldreich, O.: Candidate one-way functions based on expander graphs. Electron. Colloq. Comput. Complex. (ECCC) 7(90) (2000)

26. Grassi, L., Rechberger, C., Rotaru, D., Scholl, P., Smart, N.P.: MPC-friendly symmetric key primitives. In: Weippl, E.R., Katzenbeisser, S., Kruegel, C., Myers, A.C., Halevi, S. (eds.) ACM SIGSAC Conference on Computer and Communications Security (2016)

27. Grosso, V., Leurent, G., Standaert, F.-X., Varıcı, K.: LS-designs: bitslice encryption for efficient masked software implementations. In: Cid, C., Rechberger, C. (eds.) FSE 2014. LNCS, vol. 8540, pp. 18–37. Springer, Heidelberg (2015). https://doi.org/10.1007/978-3-662-46706-0_2

28. Halevi, S., Shoup, V.: Algorithms in HElib. In: Garay, J.A., Gennaro, R. (eds.) CRYPTO 2014, Part I. LNCS, vol. 8616, pp. 554–571. Springer, Heidelberg (2014). https://doi.org/10.1007/978-3-662-44371-2_31

29. Ishai, Y., Kushilevitz, E., Ostrovsky, R., Sahai, A.: Cryptography with constant computational overhead. In: 40th ACM STOC, pp. 433–442. ACM Press, May 2008

30. Knuth, D.E.: The Art of Computer Programming: Seminumerical Algorithms. vol. 2, 3rd edn. Addison-Wesley Professional, November 1997

31. Lauter, K., Naehrig, M., Vaikuntanathan, V.: Can homomorphic encryption be practical? Cryptology ePrint Archive, Report 2011/405 (2011)

32. Lin, H., Tessaro, S.: Indistinguishability obfuscation from trilinear maps and block-wise local PRGs. Cryptology ePrint Archive, Report 2017/250 (2017)

33. Lin, H., Vaikuntanathan, V.: Indistinguishability obfuscation from DDH-like assumptions on constant-degree graded encodings. In: 57th FOCS, pp. 11–20 (2016)
34. Maitra, S., Mandal, B., Martinsen, T., Roy, D., Stănică, P.: Tools in analyzing linear approximation for boolean functions related to FLIP. In: Chakraborty, D., Iwata, T. (eds.) INDOCRYPT 2018. LNCS, vol. 11356, pp. 282–303. Springer, Cham (2018). https://doi.org/10.1007/978-3-030-05378-9_16
35. Méaux, P., Carlet, C., Journault, A., Standaert, F.: Improved filter permutators: combining symmetric encryption design, boolean functions, low complexity cryptography, and homomorphic encryption, for private delegation of computations. Cryptology ePrint Archive, Report 2019/483 (2019)
36. Méaux, P., Journault, A., Standaert, F.-X., Carlet, C.: Towards stream ciphers for efficient FHE with low-noise ciphertexts. In: Fischlin, M., Coron, J.-S. (eds.) EUROCRYPT 2016, Part I. LNCS, vol. 9665, pp. 311–343. Springer, Heidelberg (2016). https://doi.org/10.1007/978-3-662-49890-3_13
37. Mesnager, S.: On the nonlinearity of Boolean functions with restricted input. In: Talk at The 13th International Conference on Finite Fields and their Applications (2017)
38. Mesnager, S., Zhou, Z., Ding, C.: On the nonlinearity of Boolean functions with restricted input. Crypt. Commun. 11(1), 63–76 (2018)
39. Mossel, E., Shpilka, A., Trevisan, L.: On e-biased generators in NC0. In: 44th FOCS, pp. 136–145. IEEE Computer Society Press, October 2003
40. Piret, G., Roche, T., Carlet, C.: PICARO – a block cipher allowing efficient higher-order side-channel resistance. In: Bao, F., Samarati, P., Zhou, J. (eds.) ACNS 2012. LNCS, vol. 7341, pp. 311–328. Springer, Heidelberg (2012). https://doi.org/10.1007/978-3-642-31284-7_19

Cryptanalysis: Symmetric Key Ciphers and Hash Functions

RC4: Non-randomness in the Index j and Some Results on Its Cycles

Chandratop Chakraborty[1], Pranab Chakraborty[2], and Subhamoy Maitra[3]([✉])

[1] Department of Computer Science and Engineering, PES University,
100 Feet Ring Road, BSK III Stage, Bangalore 560085, India
chandratop@protonmail.ch
[2] Learning and Development, Human Resources, Wipro Limited, Doddakannelli,
Sarjapur Road, Bangalore 560035, India
kojagori@gmail.com
[3] Applied Statistics Unit, Indian Statistical Institute,
203 B T Road, Kolkata 700108, India
subho@isical.ac.in

Abstract. In this paper we provide several theoretical evidences that the pseudo-random index j of RC4 is indeed not pseudo-random. First we show that in long term $\Pr(j = i+1) = \frac{1}{N} - \frac{1}{N^2}$, instead of the random association $\frac{1}{N}$ and this happens for the non-existence of the condition $S[i] = 1$ and $j = i + 1$ that is mandatory for the non-existence of the Finney cycle. Further we also identify several results on non-existence of certain sequences of j. We further discuss the cycle structure in RC4 and provide several theoretical results. The results are supported by experimental observations with reduced versions of RC4. In this direction we point out that certain non-randomness in j is closely related to the short cycles in RC4.

Keywords: Cycles · RC4 · Non-randomness · Pseudo-random index · Sequence · Stream cipher

1 Introduction

As we all know, there are many results related to non-randomness of RC4 that received the attention in flagship level cryptology conferences and journals (see for example [7–9] and the references therein). Even after intense research for more than three decades on a few lines of RC4 algorithm, we are still amazed with new discoveries in this area of research. While there are many evidences that RC4 is going out of business in the domain of secure communication, the algorithms and protocols based on this cipher are still in use at large. Thus, both from the theoretical interest of analysing this elegant cipher and from practical implications of studying a symmetric key system which is still present in commercial domain, it is quite tempting to put yet another effort on analysing RC4 in cryptologic context. In this backdrop, let us now present the algorithm briefly.

© Springer Nature Switzerland AG 2019
F. Hao et al. (Eds.): INDOCRYPT 2019, LNCS 11898, pp. 95–114, 2019.
https://doi.org/10.1007/978-3-030-35423-7_5

In RC4, there is a $N = 256$ length array of 8-bit integers 0 to $N - 1$, that works as a permutation. There is also an l length array of bytes K (the secret key), where l may vary from 5 to 32, depending on the key length. There are also two bytes i, j, where i is the deterministic index that increases by 1 in each step and j is updated in a manner so that it behaves pseudo-randomly. The Key Scheduling Algorithm (KSA) of RC4 is as follows:

- $j = 0$; for $i = 0$ to $N - 1$: $S[i] = i$;
- for $i = 0$ to $N - 1$:

$$j = j + S[i] + K[i \bmod l]; \text{ swap}(S[i], S[j]);$$

Next the pseudo-random bytes z are generated during the Pseudo Random Generator Algorithm (PRGA) as follows:

- $i = j = 0$;
- for $i = 0$ to $N - 1$:

$$i = i + 1; j = j + S[i]; \text{ swap}(S[i], S[j]); z = S[S[i] + S[j]];$$

Note that all the additions here are modulo N and we will use the same notation while discussing about operations that are related to RC4.

ORGANIZATION AND CONTRIBUTION. The organization and contribution of the paper can be summarized as follows. We mainly divide the paper in two parts.

- The first section is related to non-randomness in the pseudo-random index j. In Sect. 2, we show that the condition for removal of Finney cycle directly injects non-randomness in j. In Sect. 2.1, we provide several other non-randomness results related to non-existence of certain sequences in j. Further, we continue with some more non-randomness results of j in Sect. 2.2. To the best of our knowledge, this is the first disciplined study related to the pseudo-random index j. There were some sporadic results earlier (one may see [8] and the references therein) on j, but we could find long term biases for this pseudo-random index for the first time. In fact, most of our results are glimpses of j given the key stream byte z at different rounds. We show that the knowledge of z reveals information regarding the value of the pseudorandom index j, which is an weakness of the cipher from a cryptanalytic point of view.
- In Sect. 3, we try to revisit the cycles of RC4 following the initial idea of [6]. We start with some theoretical results related to the cycle structures in RC4. We theoretically show how the permutation is shifted with certain specific values of i, j and thus generates a cycle. In this direction, we present some ideas related to short cycles in Sect. 3.1. We note that in [6], some experimental results have been presented for $N = 8$. Surprisingly, there were no other published results after that. In this initiative, we run experiments for $N = 16$ and find certain interesting patterns for short cycles in the reduced version ($N = 16$) of RC4. We note that such short cycles (this occurs when we start the PRGA with $i = j = 0$, i.e., not Finney cycles) are related with non-randomness of j. Unfortunately, we could not theoretically characterize the

non-Finney short cycles and thus could not obtain any such cycle for $N = 256$. However, our experimental observations may be used to explore a theoretical technique in this direction.

The cryptanalytic motivation behind this analysis is quite evident in terms of predicting the key-stream. If a cycle is small, then same key-stream will appear quickly, providing an immediate route to cryptanalysis. Further, if from an initial portion of the key-stream, future key-stream can be predicted, that is also a serious weakness in a stream cipher. Our results related to cycles have clear cryptanalytic implications in this regard.

2   Non-randomness in j

While the researchers had suspicion that there could be problems with the pseudo-randomness of j, it has not been explored in a disciplined manner. In fact, in [8, Section 3.4], non-randomness of j has been studied for initial rounds and it has been commented that the distribution of j is almost uniform for higher rounds. Thus, no long term pseudo-randomness of the index j has been reported prior to this work.

It has been observed by Finney [2] that if $S[i] = 1$ and $j = i + 1$, then RC4 lands into a short cycle of length $N(N - 1)$. Note that the condition is $S[i] = 1$ in the pre-swap stage, that is before swapping $S[i]$ and $S[j]$ in the PRGA. Fortunately (or knowing this very well), the design of RC4 by Rivest considers the initialization of RC4 PRGA as $i = j = 0$. Thus, during RC4 PRGA, the Finney cycle cannot occur, i.e., if $\Pr(S[i] = 1)$, then $\Pr(j = i + 1) = 0$. This provides non-randomness in j.

Theorem 1. *During RC4 PRGA, $\Pr(j = i+1) = \frac{1}{N} - \frac{1}{N^2}$, under certain usual assumptions.*

Proof. We have

$$\begin{aligned}
\Pr(j = i + 1) &= \Pr(j = i + 1, S[i] = 1) + \Pr(j = i + 1, S[i] \neq 1) \\
&= 0 + \Pr(j = i + 1 | S[i] \neq 1) \cdot \Pr(S[i] \neq 1) \\
&= \frac{1}{N} \cdot (1 - \frac{1}{N}) = \frac{1}{N} - \frac{1}{N^2}.
\end{aligned}$$

Here we consider $\Pr(j = i+1 | S[i] \neq 1) = \frac{1}{N}$ under usual randomness assumption (it has been checked by experiments too). Further, considering S as a random permutation, we get $\Pr(S[i] \neq 1) = 1 - \frac{1}{N}$. $\qquad\square$

In fact, one can sharpen this result slightly by using Glimpse Theorem [3] as follows. Though it happens generally once out of N rounds during the PRGA.

Corollary 1. *During RC4 PRGA, $\Pr(j = i + 1 | i = z + 1) = \frac{1}{N} - \frac{2}{N^2} + \frac{1}{N^3}$.*

Proof. We refer to Glimpse theorem [3] that says, $\Pr(S[j] = i - z) = \frac{2}{N} - \frac{1}{N^2}$ after the swap of $S[i]$ and $S[j]$. Consider the situation when $S[i] = 1$ before the swap.

That means $S[j] = 1$ after the swap. Thus, $\Pr(S[i] = 1 | i = z + 1) = \frac{2}{N} - \frac{1}{N^2}$. Hence, we have the following:

$$\begin{aligned}
\Pr(j = i + 1 | i = z + 1) &= \Pr(j = i + 1, S[i] = 1 | i = z + 1) \\
&\quad + \Pr(j = i + 1, S[i] \neq 1 | i = z + 1) \\
&= 0 + \Pr(j = i + 1 | S[i] \neq 1, i = z + 1) \cdot \\
&\quad \Pr(S[i] \neq 1 | i = z + 1) \\
&= \frac{1}{N} \cdot (1 - \frac{2}{N} + \frac{1}{N^2}) = \frac{1}{N} - \frac{2}{N^2} + \frac{1}{N^3}.
\end{aligned}$$

We consider the usual assumptions as in Theorem 1.   □

Since we make a few assumptions, it is important to validate the results and the experimental data indeed supports the theoretical claims mentioned above. Theorem 1 and Corollary 1 were first reported in [4] and in Sect. 2.2 we present further results in that direction.

2.1   Non-existence and Biases in Certain Sequences of j over Several Rounds

In this section, we point out that over several rounds certain sequences of j cannot exist at all. Since j is believed to be pseudo-random, the probability of any specific pattern of j over t rounds should be $\frac{1}{N^t}$, considering independence. Needless to mention that the value of j in one round is clearly dependent on earlier rounds as RC4 is a finite state machine after fixing the secret key. Thus it is natural that the disciplined analysis should reveal the true nature of j and explores its deviation from actual uniform randomness. This is what we present in this section showing the non-existence of several sequences of j and thus the probability of obtaining such sequences is zero during RC4 evolution. We also present some results where the events have certain biases away from the uniform random value.

For terminology, we consider $S_r[k]$ as the value of the array at k-th index after the swap is done in round r.

Theorem 2. *During RC4 PRGA, in 3 consecutive rounds (r, $r + 1$ and $r + 2$), j cannot take 3 consecutive integer values. In other words, there is no r such that $j_{r+2} = j_{r+1} + 1 = j_r + 2$.*

Proof. Let us first consider the situation where j has been increased by 1 from round r to round $r+1$. So $j_r + 1 = j_{r+1}$, which implies $S_r[i_r + 1] = S_{r+1}[j_{r+1}] = 1$. It should be noted that in RC4 PRGA, a Finney cycle cannot happen. Hence, i_{r+1} cannot take the value of $(j_{r+1} - 1)$. Hence $S_{r+1}[i_{r+1} + 1]$ cannot be 1. Thus it would not be possible to have $j_{r+2} = j_{r+1} + 1$.   □

We have the following corollary.

Corollary 2. *Under certain usual assumptions, during RC4 PRGA, $\Pr(j_{r+2} = j_r + 2) = \frac{1}{N} - \frac{1}{N^2}$.*

Proof. We have

$$\begin{aligned}
\Pr(j_{r+2} = j_r + 2) &= \Pr(j_{r+2} = j_r + 2, j_{r+1} = j_r + 1) \\
&\quad + \Pr(j_{r+2} = j_r + 2, j_{r+1} \neq j_r + 1) \\
&= 0 + \Pr(j_{r+2} = j_r + 2 | j_{r+1} \neq j_r + 1) \cdot \Pr(j_{r+1} \neq j_r + 1) \\
&= \frac{1}{N} \cdot (1 - \frac{1}{N}) = \frac{1}{N} - \frac{1}{N^2}.
\end{aligned}$$

Here we consider $\Pr(j_{r+2} = j_r + 2 | j_{r+1} \neq j_r + 1) = \frac{1}{N}$ under usual randomness assumption. Further, considering S as a random permutation, we get $\Pr(j_{r+1} \neq j_r + 1) = 1 - \frac{1}{N}$. $\square$

Then similar to Corollary 1, we can show that the Corollary 2 can be extended as follows. Here the Glimpse theorem [3] is used in the $(r+1)$-th round.

Corollary 3. *Under certain usual assumptions, During RC4 PRGA, $\Pr(j_{r+2} = j_r + 2 | i_{r+1} = z_{r+1} + 1) = \frac{1}{N} - \frac{2}{N^2} + \frac{1}{N^3}$.*

The next result is related to equality of j in consecutive rounds and we show that such events cannot occur.

Theorem 3. *The value of j can remain constant, i.e., $(j_r = j_{r+1} = j_{r+2})$ for at most three consecutive rounds $(r, r+1 \text{ and } r+2)$. In other words there cannot exist any r for which $(j_r = j_{r+1} = j_{r+2} = j_{r+3})$.*

Proof. Let us denote the difference between the j values of two consecutive rounds as $\delta_{r+1} = (j_{r+1} - j_r)$. Clearly, $S_r[i_r + 1] = S_{r+1}[j_{r+1}] = \delta_{r+1}$. We now prove the claim now by contradiction.

Let us assume that it is possible to find an r and a permutation S such that $j_r = j_{r+1} = j_{r+2} = j_{r+3}$. Thus, $\delta_{r+1} = \delta_{r+2} = \delta_{r+3} = 0$, which implies

1. $S_{r+1}[j_{r+1}] = S_{r+1}[i_{r+1} + 1] = 0$ and
2. $S_{r+2}[i_{r+2} + 1] = 0$.

From 1, one can derive that $j_{r+1} = i_{r+1} + 1 = i_{r+2}$. Since $S_{r+1}[i_{r+1} + 1] = 0$, the j value will not change from $(r+1)$ to $(r+2)$ round. Therefore, $j_{r+2} = j_{r+1} = i_{r+2}$ and $S_{r+2}[j_{r+2}] = S_{r+2}[i_{r+2}] = 0$.

Hence, $S_{r+2}[i_{r+2} + 1]$ cannot be 0 and that contradicts Eq. 2. Thus we prove this by contradiction. $\square$

This immediately provides the following corollaries. The first one directly follows from the proof of the previous theorem.

Corollary 4. *If $(j_r = j_{r+1} = j_{r+2})$ then $i_{r+2} = j_{r+2}$ and $S_{r+1}[j_{r+1}] = S_{r+2}[i_{r+2}] = S_{r+2}[j_{r+2}] = 0$.*

Corollary 5. *In two consecutive rounds $(r \text{ and } r+1)$, if the value of j remains constant (i.e., $j_r = j_{r+1}$) then $S_{r+1}[j_{r+1}]$ must be 0.*

Proof. Using the same notation as used in Corollary 3 we observe that $\delta_{r+1} = (j_{r+1} - j_r) = 0$. Therefore, $S_{r+1}[j_{r+1}] = S_r[i_r + 1] = \delta_{r+1} = 0$.   □

Corollary 6. *Once a value of j gets repeated in three consecutive rounds (r, $r + 1$ and $r + 2$), no value can immediately be repeated in the subsequent two rounds (for $N > 2$). In other words, if $j_r = j_{r+1} = j_{r+2}$ it is not possible to have $j_{r+3} = j_{r+4}$.*

Proof. From Corollary 3, we know that if $j_r = j_{r+1} = j_{r+2}$ then $S_{r+1}[j_{r+1}] = S_{r+2}[i_{r+2}] = S_{r+2}[j_{r+2}] = 0$. Thus, $S_{r+2}[i_{r+2} + 1]$ cannot be 0 and hence j_{r+3} must be different from j_{r+2}. Therefore, $S_{r+3}[i_{r+3}]$ as well as $S_{r+3}[j_{r+3}]$ would be non-zero (please note that it is possible for both i and j to be same in this round). Next, $(i_{r+3} + 1)$ cannot be same as i_{r+2} for $N > 2$. This implies, $S_{r+3}[i_{r+3} + 1]$ cannot be 0. Thus, j_{r+4} cannot be equal to j_{r+3}.   □

Now let us present certain results related to non-existence of decreasing or increasing sequence of j.

Theorem 4. *During RC4 PRGA, there cannot be a continuously decreasing sequence of j having length more than 3. In other words there cannot exist any r for which $(j_r - j_{r+1}) = (j_{r+1} - j_{r+2}) = (j_{r+2} - j_{r+3}) = k$ where $(k < N - 1)$.*

Proof. Let us consider an r such that $(j_r - j_{r+1}) = (j_{r+1} - j_{r+2}) = k$ where $(k < N - 1)$. Since, $(j_r - j_{r+1}) = k$, it can be said that $S_r[i_r + 1] = (N - k)$. Similarly, as $(j_{r+1} - j_{r+2}) = k$, $S_{r+1}[i_{r+1} + 1] = (N - k)$. Thus, it can be concluded that $i_{r+1} = j_{r+1} - 1$.

In RC4 PRGA, since a Finney cycle cannot happen, k cannot take the value of $(N - 1)$ and hence $(k < N - 1)$. After the swap operation is completed in round $(r + 2)$, $S_{r+2}[j_{r+2}] = (N - k)$. Moreover, we know that $(j_{r+1} - j_{r+2}) = k$ which implies $j_{r+2} = j_{r+1} + (N - k)$. As $(k < N - 1)$, it is not possible to have $j_{r+2} = j_{r+1} + 1$. Thus, i_{r+2} cannot be one less than j_{r+2} implying it would not be possible to have $(j_{r+2} - j_{r+3}) = k$.   □

Corollary 7. *During RC4 PRGA, there cannot be a continuously increasing sequence of j of length more than 3. In other words there cannot exist any r for which $(j_{r+1} - j_r) = (j_{r+2} - j_{r+1}) = (j_{r+3} - j_{r+2}) = k$ where $(k > 1)$.*

Proof. Any increase in the value of j between two successive rounds by k can be considered as a decrease of the j value between two successive rounds by $(N - k)$. Here, $(k > 1)$. Hence, we may apply the previous theorem and arrive at this result.   □

2.2   Further Results on Non-randomness in j

Let us also present a few other technical results in this direction that provides further evidences of non-randomness in j. The following result is a simple generalization of [5] that shows $\Pr(z_2 = 0) \approx \frac{2}{N}$. However, we explain it for continuity and better understanding.

Lemma 1. *During RC4 PRGA, in any arbitrary round r, if $j_r = 0$, $S_r[i_r+1] \neq (i_r+2)$ and $S_r[i_r+2] = 0$, then in round $(r+2)$, the value of z must be 0, i.e., $z_{r+2} = 0$.*

Proof. Let us consider that, in round r, $S_r[i_r+1] = x$ and $S_r[x] = y$. In that case, at the end of round $(r+1)$, the index values would be $i_{r+1} = (i_r+1)$ and $j_{r+1} = (j_r + S_r[i_r+1]) = (0+x) = x$. Since, it is given that $S_r[i_r+1] \neq (i_r+2)$, we have $y \neq 0$, which means 0 would not be swapped out at the end of round $(r+1)$. Also, the array values in the index positions (post-swap) would be as follows.

$$S_{r+1}[i_{r+1}] = y \text{ and}$$
$$S_{r+1}[j_{r+1}] = x.$$

In the same way, at the end of round $(r+2)$, the index values would be $i_{r+2} = (i_r+2)$ and $j_{r+2} = (j_{r+1} + S_r[i_r+2]) = (x+0) = x$. The array values in the index positions (post-swap) would be as follows.

$$S_{r+2}[i_{r+2}] = x \text{ and}$$
$$S_{r+2}[j_{r+2}] = 0.$$

Using the above values we can now find the value of z.

$$z_{r+2} = S_{r+2}[S_{r+2}[i_{r+2}] + S_{r+2}[j_{r+2}]] = S_{r+2}[x + 0] = S_{r+2}[x] = 0$$

$\square$

This provides the following corollary.

Corollary 8. *During RC4 PRGA, (i) $\Pr(z_{r+2} = 0 | j_r = 0) = \frac{2}{N} - \frac{1}{N^2}$, and (ii) $\Pr(j_r = 0 | z_{r+2} = 0) = \frac{2}{N} - \frac{1}{N^2}$, under certain usual assumptions.*

Proof. We calculate the probability as follows: $\Pr(z_{r+2} = 0 | j_r = 0) = \Pr(z_{r+2} = 0, S_r[i_r+2] = 0 | j_r = 0) + \Pr(z_{r+2} = 0, S_r[i_r+2] \neq 0 | j_r = 0)$. Based on Lemma 1, we know that $\Pr(z_{r+2} = 0, S_r[i_r+2] = 0 | j_r = 0) = \Pr(S_r[i_r+2] = 0 | j_r = 0) = \frac{1}{N}$, under the usual randomness assumptions (which has been verified experimentally as well). (Here, we ignore the condition $S_r[i_r+1] \neq (i_r+2)$, since it would not alter the calculations significantly.)

Similarly, using the randomness assumptions, we can say that $\Pr(z_{r+2} = 0, S_r[i_r+2] \neq 0 | j_r = 0) = (1 - \frac{1}{N}) \cdot \frac{1}{N}$.

Therefore, $\Pr(z_{r+2} = 0 | j_r = 0) = \frac{1}{N} + (1 - \frac{1}{N}) \cdot \frac{1}{N} = \frac{2}{N} - \frac{1}{N^2}$.

The other result can be shown using Bayes' theorem. $\square$

One may note that while initiating the RC4 PRGA, $j_0 = 0$ and thus it was noted in [5] that $\Pr(z_2 = 0) = \frac{2}{N} - \frac{1}{N^2}$. In this direction, we provide the following two technical results.

Lemma 2. *During RC4 PRGA, $\Pr(j_{r-1} = j_r | i_r = z_r) = \frac{2}{N} - \frac{1}{N^2}$, under certain usual assumptions.*

Proof. According to the Glimpse theorem, $\Pr(S_r[j_r] = i_r - z_r) = \frac{2}{N} - \frac{1}{N^2}$. In any arbitrary round r, when $(i_r = z_r)$, there can be two different possibilities.

- Case 1: $S_r[j_r] = (i_r - z_r) = 0$ implying $j_{r-1} = j_r$,
- Case 2: $S_r[j_r] \neq (i_r - z_r)$, i.e., $S_r[j_r] \neq 0$ implying $j_{r-1} \neq j_r$.

Therefore, $\Pr(j_{r-1} = j_r | i_r = z_r) = \Pr(S_r[j_r] = 0 | i_r = z_r) = \frac{2}{N} - \frac{1}{N^2}$. $\qquad\square$

Lemma 3. *During RC4 PRGA, if the value of index j remains constant for three consecutive rounds $(r, r+1$ and $r+2)$, i.e., $j_r = j_{r+1} = j_{r+2}$, then z_{r+1} can not be equal to z_{r+2}.*

Proof. We have proved in Corollary 3 that if $(j_r = j_{r+1} = j_{r+2})$ then $i_{r+2} = j_{r+2}$ and $S_{r+1}[j_{r+1}] = S_{r+2}[i_{r+2}] = S_{r+2}[j_{r+2}] = 0$. This implies $j_r = (i_r + 2)$.

Let us now consider, $S_r[i_r] = x$ and $S_r[j_r] = y$. As, $S_{r+1}[j_{r+1}] = 0$, it is easy to derive that $S_r[i_r+1] = 0$. Therefore, at the end of round $(r+1)$, $S_{r+1}[i_{r+1}] = y$ and $S_{r+1}[j_{r+1}] = 0$. Based on these, we can derive the z values in the $(r+1)$ and $(r+2)$ rounds as follows:

$$z_{r+1} = S_{r+1}[y + 0] = S_{r+1}[y] \text{ and}$$
$$z_{r+2} = S_{r+2}[0 + 0] = S_{r+2}[0].$$

Since the permutation array remained unchanged from $(r+1)$ round to $(r+2)$ round and $y \neq 0$, z_{r+1} must be different from z_{r+2}. $\qquad\square$

We also have the following result that shows the effect of $j = 0$ on the key stream byte z, given that $i \neq 0$.

Lemma 4. *During RC4 PRGA, in any arbitrary round r, if $j_r = 0$, $i_r \neq 0$ and $S_r[0] = 0$, then $z_r \neq 0$. Similarly, in round r, if $j_r = 0$, $i_r \neq (N-1)$ and $S_r[i_r + 1] = 0$, then $z_{r+1} \neq 0$.*

Proof. Let us consider that, in round r, $S_r[i_r] = x$. It is also given that, $j_r = 0$, $i_r \neq 0$ and $S_r[0] = 0$. Hence, $i_r \neq j_r$, which implies $x \neq 0$. Therefore, $z_r = S_r[S_r[i_r] + S_r[j_r]] = S_r[x + 0] = S_r[x] \neq 0$.

Similarly, in the other case, let us consider that $S_r[0] = x$. Now the given conditions are, $j_r = 0$, i_r has any value other than $(N-1)$ and $S_r[i_r + 1] = 0$. As $i_r \neq (N-1)$, x can't be 0.

In round $(r+1)$, $j_{r+1} = j_r + S_r[i_{r+1}] = j_r + 0 = j_r = 0$. Therefore, after the swap operation, $S_{r+1}[j_{r+1}] = 0$ and $S_{r+1}[i_{r+1}] = x$. Thus, we obtain $z_{r+1} = S_{r+1}[S_{r+1}[i_{r+1}] + S_{r+1}[j_{r+1}]] = S_{r+1}[x + 0] = S_{r+1}[x] \neq 0$. Hence the proof. $\qquad\square$

One can also note that, during the RC4 PRGA, in any arbitrary round r, if $i_r = 0$, $j_r \neq 0$ and $S_r[0] = 0$, then also $z_r \neq 0$. The proof would be identical to the proof given in the first part of Lemma 4. Following Lemma 4, we present certain biases in z given $j = 0$, as explained below.

Corollary 9. *During RC4 PRGA, $\Pr(z_r = 0 | j_r = 0, i_r \neq 0) = \frac{1}{N} - \frac{1}{N^2}$ and $\Pr(z_{r+1} = 0 | j_r = 0, i_r \neq (N-1)) = \frac{1}{N} - \frac{1}{N^2}$, under certain usual assumptions.*

Proof. We have, $\Pr(z_r = 0|j_r = 0, i_r \neq 0) = \Pr(z_r = 0, S_r[0] = 0|j_r = 0, i_r \neq 0) + \Pr(z_r = 0, S_r[0] \neq 0|j_r = 0, i_r \neq 0)$. Based on Lemma 4, we obtain $\Pr(z_r = 0, S_r[0] = 0|j_r = 0, i_r \neq 0) = 0$.

Also, using the randomness assumptions, one can consider $\Pr(z_r = 0, S_r[0] \neq 0|j_r = 0, i_r \neq 0) = (1 - \frac{1}{N}) \cdot \frac{1}{N}$ (verified experimentally as well). Therefore, $\Pr(z_r = 0|j_r = 0, i_r \neq 0) = \frac{1}{N} - \frac{1}{N^2}$.

Similarly, $\Pr(z_{r+1} = 0|j_r = 0, i_r \neq (N-1)) = \Pr(z_{r+1} = 0, S_r[i_r + 1] = 0|j_r = 0, i_r \neq (N-1)) + \Pr(z_{r+1} = 0, S_r[i_r + 1] \neq 0|j_r = 0, i_r \neq (N-1))$. Based on Lemma 4, we know that $\Pr(z_{r+1} = 0, S_r[i_r + 1] = 0|j_r = 0, i_r \neq (N-1)) = 0$. Using the randomness assumptions, we can write $\Pr(z_{r+1} = 0, S_r[i_r + 1] \neq 0|j_r = 0, i_r \neq (N-1)) = (1 - \frac{1}{N}) \cdot \frac{1}{N}$.

Therefore, $\Pr(z_{r+1} = 0|j_r = 0, i_r \neq (N-1)) = \frac{1}{N} - \frac{1}{N^2}$. Hence the proof. $\square$

From Corollary 9 and using Bayes' theorem, we have the following result.

Corollary 10. *During RC4 PRGA, $\Pr(j_r = 0|z_r = 0, i_r \neq 0) = \frac{1}{N} - \frac{1}{N^2}$ and $\Pr(j_r = 0|z_{r+1} = 0, i_r \neq (N-1)) = \frac{1}{N} - \frac{1}{N^2}$, under certain usual assumptions.*

Thus, in this section we provide a series of results related to non-randomness of the pseudo-random index j. We show in detail how the key stream output byte z is affected by the non-randomness in j and in turn we could also prove that z reveals information related to j as well. As we had to assume certain randomness during the proofs, all the results are checked with sufficient amount of experimental effort.

3   Properties of RC4 Cycles

In this section, we prove certain properties on RC4 cycles. For some of these properties, we refer to the concept of cycle partitioning explained in [6, Section 4.2], where the authors showed that RC4 cycles can be partitioned into "equivalent" subsets in which, for every RC4 state (i, j, S) in one subset, one can find $(N-1)$ other equivalent RC4 subsets of the form $(i+d, j+d, S^{\gg d})$ for an integer $0 < d < N$. Here, $S^{\gg d}$ signifies a right-rotated permutation of S by d places. It is easy to note that a rotation of a permutation by N places is identical to a shift of the array by 0 place (i.e., no-shift). In the following discussion, "right-shift" and "right-rotation" are used interchangeably to imply the "right-rotation" of the permutation array.

Theorem 5. *Let S_0 be the initial permutation of S-Box $(i = 0, j = 0)$ in an RC4 cycle with right-shifts that appear as per sequence of $(d_1, d_2, ..., d_{k-1})$ where $d_0(= d_k)$ represents the original permutation or in other words a complete rotation by $N(= 2^n)$ places. In that case,*

(i) $k = \frac{LCM(N, d_1)}{d_1}$, where LCM stands for Least Common Multiplier;
(ii) k must be of the form of 2^m where m is in $[1, 2, ..., n]$;
(iii) If T is the length of the cycle that starts with $(i = 0, j = 0, S_0)$, then there must be at least $\frac{N}{2^m} = 2^{(n-m)}$ disjoint cycles in the state space of RC4 having cycle length of T;

(iv) $(\frac{T}{k} - d_1)$ *must be divisible by* N *apart from the condition that* T *must be divisible by* N;

Proof. The claim for each part of the theorem is proved below.

(i) As d_1 is the first shifted occurrence in the cycle, it is clear that after repeating the same shift k number of times it must come back to the original permutation. Hence, k times d_1 must be a multiple of N.

Let us assume $l \cdot d_1 = LCM(N, d_1)$. Clearly $l \leq k$. If $l < k$, the permutation array would come back to the original state S_0, even before the completion of the cycle, which is not possible. Therefore, l must have the same value as k. Hence, $k = \frac{LCM(N,d_1)}{d_1}$.

(ii) Since $k \cdot d_1 = LCM(N, d_1)$ and $N = 2^n$, k does not need to have any factor other than a power of 2. This implies, k must be of the form 2^m. Since $d_1 < N$, k can't be 1. Hence, possible values for m are $(1, 2, \ldots, n)$.

(iii) Since k is of the form of 2^m where $(m > 0)$, there would be at least $2^{(n-m)}$ disjoint cycles in the state space of RC4 with the cycle length T and each containing k number of right-shifted permutations (including the original permutation that corresponds to N-place or 0-place right-shift). Note that it is possible that some of these cycles may never appear in real RC4, in case they do not contain any state with $(i = 0, j = 0)$. The reason of qualifying the result with 'at least' is to highlight that there may be other cycles in RC4 state space that have the same length (T) as the current cycle.

(iv) When the permutation reaches the first right-shifted pattern in the sequence (corresponding to d_1), the value of index i should also be d_1. At this point, the number of rounds that would have got completed would be $\frac{T}{k}$ and d_1 rounds earlier to this point the value of i must have been 0.

Hence, $(\frac{T}{k} - d_1)$ must be divisible by N apart from the condition that T must be divisible by N.   □

Examples with $N = 8$. Let us first illustrate the above theorem using some of the cycles corresponding to $N = 8$. Note that such cycles have also been noted in [6]. However, we try to explain the analysis in greater detail. We first examine a cycle of length 322120 that has an initial state $(i = 0, j = 0)$ corresponding to the permutation: $[6, 4, 3, 1, 7, 0, 5, 2]$. After 40265 rounds, it reaches the state: $(i = 1, j = 1, [2, 6, 4, 3, 1, 7, 0, 5])$.

Evidently, this pattern is a right-shifted version of the initial pattern (by one place) and i and j both got incremented by 1. As we know, the sequence of j values of a right-shifted pattern (by one place) can be derived from the sequence of j values of the initial pattern, except for each position the j value would get incremented by 1. After 8 right-shifts, the permutation array comes back to the original state. The right-shifted patterns would be as follows:

$$(i = 0, j = 0, [6, 4, 3, 1, 7, 0, 5, 2]) \text{ for round} = 0$$
$$(i = 1, j = 1, [2, 6, 4, 3, 1, 7, 0, 5]) \text{ for round} = 40265$$
$$(i = 2, j = 2, [5, 2, 6, 4, 3, 1, 7, 0]) \text{ for round} = 80530$$

$$(i = 3, j = 3, [0, 5, 2, 6, 4, 3, 1, 7]) \text{ for round} = 120795$$
$$(i = 4, j = 4, [7, 0, 5, 2, 6, 4, 3, 1]) \text{ for round} = 161060$$
$$(i = 5, j = 5, [1, 7, 0, 5, 2, 6, 4, 3]) \text{ for round} = 201325$$
$$(i = 6, j = 6, [3, 1, 7, 0, 5, 2, 6, 4]) \text{ for round} = 241590$$
$$(i = 7, j = 7, [4, 3, 1, 7, 0, 5, 2, 6]) \text{ for round} = 281855$$
$$(i = 0, j = 0, [6, 4, 3, 1, 7, 0, 5, 2]) \text{ for round} = 322120$$

In case of the above mentioned cycle $d_1 = 1$, $k = 8$ and $LCM(N, d_1) = LCM(8, 1) = 8$. Hence, $k \cdot d_1 = LCM(N, d_1)$. Here, k is of the form of 2^m where $m = 3$. Since $\frac{N}{2^m}$ is 1, all possible right-shifted patterns of any permutation in the cycle are contained in this cycle. In fact, there is no other cycle in the RC4 state space corresponding to $N = 8$ with the length of 322120. We also notice that $(\frac{322120}{8} - 1) = 40264$, which is divisible by $N(= 8)$. Therefore, all the statements of the previous theorem hold in this example.

Let us consider another example of a cycle (in RC4 for $N = 8$) that has a length of 955496 starting from any initial state, the first right-shifted pattern that is reached is shifted by 2 places from the original permutation, which means $d_1 = 2$. Clearly, after 4 such right-shifts, the pattern and state must come back to the initial configuration (since $4 \cdot 2 = 8$), thus, $k = 4$. Hence, $k \cdot d_1 = LCM(N, d_1)$ holds. We also observe that k is a power of 2. If we divide N by k, we obtain 2. Hence, it is expected that at least two disjoint cycles would be present in RC4 with the same length (955496), which is found to be true. Also, $(\frac{T}{k} - 2) = 238872$ is divisible by $N(= 8)$.

Examples with $N = 16$. We also present here an example with $N = 16$. The experiments in these cases are more time consuming and that we will discuss later. We chose the permutation, where all the locations (0 to 15) are sorted in increasing order as $(0, 1, 2, 3, 4, 5, 6, 7, 8, 9, 10, 11, 12, 13, 14, 15)$ and started the iteration of PRGA from the initial state $(i = 0, j = 0)$ to check after how many rounds it may come back to the original permutation or any of its right-shifted permutation and correspondingly shifted indices (of i and j).

After 112,807,642,475,803 rounds, the PRGA reached the state $[i = 11, j = 11, (5, 6, 7, 8, 9, 10, 11, 12, 13, 14, 15, 0, 1, 2, 3, 4)]$. This example corresponds to a right-shifted version of the original permutation by 11 places with correspondingly incremented values of i and j. Applying Theorem 5, we can derive that the total number of shifts in the cycle k to be equal to $\frac{LCM(16,11)}{11} = 16$ and the cycle length $T = 16 \cdot 112807642475803 = 1804922279612848$, which is in the range of 1.8 quadrillion. We also verify that $(\frac{T}{k} - d_1) = (112807642475803 - 11) = 112807642475792$ is divisible by $N(= 16)$ as predicted in Theorem 5(iv).

We also counted the number of rounds where i and j values matched within the first 112807642475803 rounds and it is 7078127287425. This value would be the same as the number of rounds in the entire cycle where $(i = j = 0)$ occurred. That means that in the state space of RC4 PRGA for $N = 16$, in around 33.83% of instances, the initial state would belong to this particular long cycle.

Corollary 11. *If an RC4 contains right-shifted pattern(s), then its length must be of $N(2p+1)$ form, where p is an integer.*

Proof. From the previous theorem, we know that $(\frac{T}{k} - d_1) = t \cdot N$ for some integer t. Hence, $T = t \cdot k \cdot N + k \cdot d_1 = t \cdot k \cdot N + LCM(N, d_1)$. Now, $LCM(N, d_1)$ must be of the form $N \cdot r$, for some odd integer r. Therefore, $T = N(t \cdot 2^m + r)$. Since, $t \cdot 2^m$ is an even integer and r is an odd integer, we prove that T must have a length of the form $N \cdot (2p+1)$, where p is an integer. □

Corollary 12. *In RC4, if a cycle length T is such that $\frac{T}{N}$ is an even number, the cycle cannot contain any shifted pattern. In such a case, there must be N analogous copies of the given cycle, each being a shifted version of the original cycle by 1 or 2 or ... $(N-1)$ places.*

Proof. The first part of the result directly follows from the previous corollary. The second part follows from the fact that if we create a shifted pattern of one of the initial states from the first cycle, it would also form a cycle of the same length (as the original one) by going through analogous state transitions. Since there are $(N-1)$ shifts possible for any permutation, the number of disjoint cycles having the same length would be at least N in number.

However, one must be cautious about the fact that if the cycle length T is such that $\frac{T}{N}$ is an odd number, we can't necessarily conclude that the cycle would contain right-shifted patterns.

In RC4 with $N = 8$, there is a cycle of length 3008. We observe that $\frac{3008}{8} = 376$, which is an even number. Hence it should not have any right-shifted pattern as part of the cycle. Experimental result matches with the prediction and it is also found out that there are 8 disjoint cycles in RC4 state space (for $N = 8$) having the same cycle length.

From the length of a cycle and the number of cycles present in RC4 with that length, one may (in some cases) derive the sequence of shifts that cycle would contain. Let us once again take the example of the RC4 cycle of length 322120 for $N = 8$.

Once it is given that in RC4 with $N = 8$, there is only one cycle of length 322120, it would be clear that all 8 shifts would be present in that cycle. That means, we can rule out the possibility of an even numbered right-shift as the first occurrence of a shift in the cycle. Initially, it may appear that the sequence of the shifts can be any one of the following:

$$(0, 1, 2, 3, 4, 5, 6, 7),$$
$$(3, 6, 1, 4, 7, 2, 5, 0),$$
$$(5, 2, 7, 4, 1, 6, 3, 0),$$
$$(7, 6, 5, 4, 3, 2, 1, 0).$$

Now, the first right-shifted pattern cannot be shifted by 3, 5 or 7 places because in that case $(\frac{T}{8} - d_1)$ would yield fractional number. Hence, the only possibility for the sequence of right shifts would be $(0, 1, 2, 3, 4, 5, 6, 7)$, which indeed matches with the actual result.

Theorem 6. *In RC4, all the non-Finney states together can not form a single cycle.*

Proof. We prove the above claim by contradiction. Let us assume that for some value of N (of the form 2^n), all the non-Finney states form a complete cycle. Total number of permutations (of S-Box of length N together with i and j) is $(N!) \cdot (N^2)$.

Hence, by eliminating the permutations pertaining to Finney cycle, we get that the cycle length or (number of permutations as part of one single non-Finney cycle) would be $T = (N!) \cdot (N^2) - (N!)$. We now use the results derived by Mister and Tavares [6].

Let us denote by S_0, any permutation of S-Box where $i = 0$ and $j = 0$. Since we consider that there is only one non-Finney cycle, all possible $(N - 1)$ right shifts of S_0 must be part of the same cycle. Let the right-shifts appear in the cycle as per the sequence $d_1, d_2, ..., d_{N-1}$, where $d_0 (= d_N)$ is understood to be same 0 (no-shift) or N-shift (complete rotation). As per the Cycle Partitioning Theorem [6, Theorem 2, Section 4.2]) one can say that if L is the distance (number of rounds required to reach d_{i+1} from d_i), then $L = \frac{T}{N} = (N-1)! \cdot (N^2) - (N-1)!$.

Let S_1 be the permutation of S-box corresponding to the d_1-shift. S_0 starts with $i = 0$, hence after d_1 shifts $i = d_1$. So $(L - d_1)$ must be divisible by N, as d_1 steps before S_1, i must be equal to 0.

Now $(L - d_1)$ is same as $\frac{T}{N} - d_1$ which equals $(N - 1)! \cdot (N^2) - (N - 1)! - d_1$. Since N is of the form 2^n, the first two terms of the above expression would be divisible by N, provided $N \geq 8$. However, the third term would not be divisible by N.

Hence we reach a contradiction. This implies our initial assumption is incorrect. Therefore, in RC4, there must be more than one non-Finney cycles.   □

Theorem 7. *If an RC4 cycle contains all the N shifts, then one can find a fixed interval of rounds (say r_f) such that the z values taken after every r_f round from any arbitrary permutation S_r in that cycle, reveal the permutation in reverse sequence.*

Proof. Let us consider the RC4 state after an arbitrary round r is given by (i, j, S_r). Since the cycle contains all possible shifts, there would exist certain number of rounds (say r_f) after which the RC4 state would become $(i + 1, j + 1, S_{r+r_f}^{\gg 1})$. Clearly, array values of S at i and j positions would remain unchanged.

Hence, the value of z would necessarily differ and the value after $r + r_f$ rounds would be one place left to the array value that contained the z value in round r. In this way, after repeating this process for $(N - 1)$ times the array values would be revealed in reverse sequence. The permutation array S_r can be derived by trying out N possible rotations of the permutation so as to match the z value.   □

The above result can be further sharpened based on the observation that if in a permutation array $(N - 1)$ values and their corresponding positions are known, then remaining value and position would also be known.

3.1   On Short Cycles in Reduced Version of RC4

We have already discussed that it has been pointed out by Finney [2] that if $S[i] = 1$ and $j = i + 1$, then RC4 lands into a short cycle of length $N(N-1)$. However, the RC4 PRGA considers the initialization as $i = j = 0$ and thus Finney cycle cannot occur. On the other hand, it is still an open problem to obtain a short cycle in RC4 for $N = 256$ with the given initial condition $i = j = 0$. It is surprising, that there has been no published effort to study this even by experiment for small N. One may note that running a program for $N = 8$ provides immediate answer in present days and this has been completed in [6] two decades back. In case we consider N as power of 2, then the next choice is $N = 16$. For this, we need to run the programs for around two weeks in a system with 160 shared cores (see complete description in Sect. 3.2). We obtain very interesting observations that shows that there are indeed short cycles for $i = j = 0$ and such cycles are related to non-randomness of j. Indeed we could not theoretically characterize the combinatorial structures for the short cycles. However, we present the experimental results and highlight certain observations that should be of interest to the community.

While we are discussing short cycles, one immediate definition could be a cycle which is less than Finney cycle or of the same order. The size of the Finney cycle is $N(N-1)$, and we will try to discover cycles in our experiment having length not more than $4N(N-1)$. Before proceeding further, let us revisit some of the interesting properties of a Finney cycle. In such cycles, the value of j in each round is always 1 more than the value of i in that round. This implies that the sequences of j do not display sufficient pseudo-randomness in Finney cycles. A more interesting aspect of the sequence is that the consecutive values of j differ from each other by 1 and $S[i] = 1$ in each round immediately prior to the swap of $S[i]$ and $S[j]$. The difference between the values of j in two consecutive rounds (say, r and $r + 1$) reveal the array value ($S[i]$) of the permutation immediately prior to the swap operation of round $r + 1$. We have already denoted the difference of j values between r and $r + 1$ rounds as δ_r (in the sequel, we may skip the r). Since, in Finney cycles, only the value of 1 gets revealed from the array, the cycle is effectively independent of rest of the $(N-1)$ values. So each of the $(N-1)!$ possible permutations corresponding to the same pair of values of (i, j) would form a Finney cycle. It is easy to note that out of these $(N-1)!$ possible permutations, $(N-1)$ permutations are part of one cycle, leading to $(N-2)!$ separate Finney cycles. The fact that there are many missing values in the sequence of δ, can be considered a strong indicator to the shorter length for a Finney cycle.

This property of missing δ value(s) can be observed in case of a short cycle of RC4 PRGA for $N = 8$. For example, a cycle that starts with an initial state of ($i = 0, j = 0, [5, 4, 1, 7, 6, 2, 0, 3]$) has a cycle length of 24 and the value 2 is missing in the sequence of $delta$. For this cycle, all the z values are present, but the frequencies of different values of z are significantly skewed. We expect that such short cycles could exist having similar properties in case of RC4 PRGA for $N = 16$ as well. With experiments, we obtained three different sets of short cycles for $N = 16$ with cycle-lengths 80, 96 and 336 respectively. We first illustrate some of the interesting properties of the set of short cycles of length 96. The following 6 initial states are part of a single cycle of length 96. Let us designate this cycle as 96-Cycle$_1$. The following 6 initial states are part of a single cycle of length 96.

1. $(i = 0, j = 0, [13, 15, 10, 11, 0, 6, 8, 12, 2, 5, 3, 1, 7, 9, 14, 4])$
2. $(i = 0, j = 0, [13, 4, 5, 11, 15, 6, 8, 12, 2, 10, 3, 7, 14, 9, 1, 0])$
3. $(i = 0, j = 0, [13, 15, 10, 11, 0, 6, 8, 12, 2, 5, 3, 14, 1, 9, 7, 4])$
4. $(i = 0, j = 0, [13, 4, 5, 11, 15, 6, 8, 12, 2, 10, 3, 1, 7, 9, 14, 0])$
5. $(i = 0, j = 0, [13, 15, 10, 11, 0, 6, 8, 12, 2, 5, 3, 7, 14, 9, 1, 4])$
6. $(i = 0, j = 0, [13, 4, 5, 11, 15, 6, 8, 12, 2, 10, 3, 14, 1, 9, 7, 0])$

The above 6 permutations belong to two different forms.

- Permutation number 1, 3 and 5 belong to the form of
  $[13, 15, 10, 11, *, 6, 8, 12, 2, 5, 3, *, *, *, *, 4]$
- Permutation number 2, 4 and 6 belong to the form of
  $[13, 4, 5, 11, 15, 6, 8, 12, 2, 10, 3, *, *, *, *, *]$

Generic short-cycle features of 96-Cycle$_1$

1. Certain values (0, 1, 7, 9 or 14) are missing in δ
2. Due to the reason mentioned above, each possible in-place permutation of the set $\{0,1,7,9,14\}$ in the S-box corresponding to the initial state $(i = 0, j = 0)$, would result in a short cycle of length 96. This also allows prediction of additional short cycles by observing one cycle (which is 96-Cycle$_1$). By inspecting the current cycle it is possible to ascertain the exact nature of the predicted cycles.
3. The z values are not uniformly distributed across all possible values.

Since $5! = 120$, and each cycle contains 3 members from each form, there can be 40 such cycles (96-Cycle$_1$ to 96-Cycle$_{40}$). We have verified that these short cycles do exist as per the above analysis and prediction.

Special features of 96-Cycle$_1$

1. Since the cycle length $T = 96$ and $\frac{T}{N} = 6$ is an even number, as per Corollary 8, these cycles can not contain any shifted permutation. This has been verified by inspecting the cycle.
2. Certain values are missing in the sequence of z. For example, (2, 6 or 8) do not appear as z values.
3. It is interesting to note that, whenever $i = 0$ in any round, j is also 0. Similarly, whenever $i = 5$ or $i = 10$, $i = j$ as well. Except for $i = 1$ condition, whenever for any two rounds there is a match for the i value, the value of j matches too. Further, for all the rounds, the S-box array positions at 0, 5 and 10 do not change at all.

Table 1. Short cycle of length 96 for $N = 16$

#	i	j	permutation	δ	z
0.	0	0	[dfab068c253179e4]	f	b
1.	1	f	[d4ab068c253179ef]	a	f
2.	2	9	[d45b068c2a3179ef]	b	1
3.	3	4	[d450b068c2a3179ef]	b	3
4.	4	f	[d450f68c2a3179eb]	6	7
5.	5	5	[d450f68c2a3179eb]	8	4
6.	6	d	[d450f69c2a3178eb]	c	9
7.	7	9	[d450f69a2c3178eb]	2	0
8.	8	b	[d450f69a1c3278eb]	c	9
9.	9	7	[d450f69c1a3278eb]	3	9
10.	a	a	[d450f69c1a3278eb]	2	a
11.	b	c	[d450f69c1a3728eb]	2	d
12.	c	e	[d450f69c1a37c82b]	8	4
13.	d	6	[d450f68c1a37e92b]	2	0
14.	e	8	[d450f68c2a37e91b]	b	7
15.	f	3	[d45bf68c2a37e910]	d	3
16.	0	0	[d45bf68c2a37e910]	4	b
17.	1	4	[df5b468c2a37e910]	5	0
18.	2	9	[dfab068c2537e910]	b	0
19.	3	4	[dfa4b68c2537e910]	b	3
20.	4	f	[dfa4068c2537e91b]	6	e
21.	5	5	[dfa4068c2537e91b]	8	f
22.	6	d	[dfa4069c2537e81b]	c	f
23.	7	9	[dfa406952c37e81b]	2	c
24.	8	b	[dfa406957c32e81b]	c	f
25.	9	7	[dfa4069c7532e81b]	3	9
26.	a	a	[dfa4069c7532e81b]	2	d
27.	b	c	[dfa4069c753e281b]	2	4
28.	c	e	[dfa4069c753e182b]	8	f
29.	d	6	[dfa4068c753e192b]	2	5
30.	e	8	[dfa4068c253e197b]	b	4
31.	f	3	[dfab068c253e1974]	d	3
32.	0	0	[dfab068c253e1974]	f	b
33.	1	f	[d4ab068c253e197f]	a	f
34.	2	9	[d45b068c2a3e197f]	b	e
35.	3	4	[d450b068c2a3e197f]	b	3
36.	4	f	[d450f68c2a3e197b]	6	1
37.	5	5	[d450f68c2a3e197b]	8	4
38.	6	d	[d450f69c2a3e187b]	c	9
39.	7	9	[d450f69a2c3e187b]	2	d
40.	8	b	[d450f69aec32187b]	c	9
41.	9	7	[d450f69cea32187b]	3	9
42.	a	a	[d450f69cea32187b]	2	0
43.	b	c	[d450f69cea31287b]	2	a
44.	c	e	[d450f69cea3187b]	8	4
45.	d	6	[d450f68cea31792b]	2	d
46.	e	8	[d450f68c2a3179eb]	b	1
47.	f	3	[d45bf68c2a3179e0]	d	3
48.	0	0	[d45bf68c2a3179e0]	4	b
49.	1	4	[df5b468c2a3179e0]	5	0
50.	2	9	[dfab068c253179e0]	b	0
51.	3	4	[dfa4b68c253179e0]	b	1
52.	4	f	[dfa4068c253179eb]	6	7
53.	5	5	[dfa4068c253179eb]	8	f
54.	6	d	[dfa4069c253178eb]	c	f
55.	7	9	[dfa406952c3178eb]	2	4
56.	8	b	[dfa406951c3278eb]	c	f
57.	9	7	[dfa4069c153278eb]	3	9
58.	a	a	[dfa4069c153278eb]	2	5
59.	b	c	[dfa4069c153728eb]	2	d
60.	c	e	[dfa4069c1537e82b]	8	f
61.	d	6	[dfa4068c1537e92b]	2	4
62.	e	8	[dfa4068c2537e91b]	b	4
63.	f	3	[dfab068c2537e914]	d	3
64.	0	0	[dfab068c2537e914]	f	b
65.	1	f	[d4ab068c2537e91f]	a	f
66.	2	9	[d45b068c2a37e91f]	b	7
67.	3	4	[d450b068c2a37e91f]	b	3
68.	4	f	[d450f68c2a37e91b]	6	e
69.	5	5	[d450f68c2a37e91b]	8	e
70.	6	d	[d450f69c2a37e81b]	c	9
71.	7	9	[d450f69a2c37e81b]	2	c
72.	8	b	[d450f69a7c32e81b]	c	9
73.	9	7	[d450f69c7a32e81b]	3	9
74.	a	a	[d450f69c7a32e81b]	2	a
75.	b	c	[d450f69c7a3e281b]	2	0
76.	c	e	[d450f69c7a3e182b]	8	e
77.	d	6	[d450f68c7a3e192b]	2	a
78.	e	8	[d450f68c2a3e197b]	b	4
79.	f	3	[d45bf68c2a3e1970]	d	3
80.	0	0	[d45bf68c2a3e1970]	4	b
81.	1	4	[df5b468c2a3e1970]	5	0
82.	2	9	[dfab468c253e1970]	b	0
83.	3	4	[dfa4b68c253e1970]	b	e
84.	4	f	[dfa4068c253e1970]	6	1
85.	5	5	[dfa4068c253e197b]	8	f
86.	6	d	[dfa4069c253e187b]	c	f
87.	7	9	[dfa406952c3e187b]	2	d
88.	8	b	[dfa40695ec32187b]	c	f
89.	9	7	[dfa4069ce532187b]	3	9
90.	a	a	[dfa4069ce532187b]	2	4
91.	b	c	[dfa4069ce531287b]	2	5
92.	c	e	[dfa4069ce531782b]	8	f
93.	d	6	[dfa4068ce531792b]	2	d
94.	e	8	[dfa4068c253179eb]	b	4
95.	f	3	[dfab068c253179e4]	d	3
96.	0	0	[dfab068c253179e4]	f	b

4. This cycle does not include any right-shifted permutation. Thus, as per Theorem 5(iii), there must be 16 analogous disjoint cycles for each of the cycles in (96-Cycle$_1$ to 96-Cycle$_{40}$). Therefore, in the state space of RC4 PRGA for $N = 16$, there must be 640 cycles of length 96. However, not all of these cycles would include initial states corresponding to $(i = 0, j = 0)$. Since each of the 40 cycles (96-Cycle$_1$ to 96-Cycle$_{40}$) has the property of $i = j$ whenever $i = 0$ or $i = 5$ or $i = 10$, there must be $3 \cdot 40 = 120$ cycles out of the 640 cycles that correspond to initial states of $(i = 0, j = 0)$.

The details of the cycle starting with [13,15,10,11,0,6,8,12,2,5,3,1,7,9,14,4] is presented in Table 1 in hexadecimal format. Next let us discuss regarding the length 80 cycle. This starts with [8, 14, 9, 15, 6, 2, 11, 0, 13, 4, 10, 1, 5, 7, 12, 3]. Since the cycle length is $T = 80$ and $\frac{T}{N} = 5$ is an odd number, there can be right-sifted permutations in the cycle. By inspecting the cycle we observe that it contains a right-shifted permutation by 8 bytes. One can immediately verify part (i), (ii) and (iv) of Theorem 5 based on this observation. As per part (iii) of Theorem 5, there can be 8 disjoint cycles for each of the 120 cycles (80-Cycle$_1$

Table 2. Short cycle of length 80 for $N = 16$

0.	$i = 0, j = 0$,	$[8e9f62b0d4a157c3]$,	$\delta = e, z = a$
1.	$i = 1, j = e$,	$[8c9f62b0d4a157e3]$,	$\delta = 9, z = 4$
2.	$i = 2, j = 7$,	$[8c0f62b9d4a157e3]$,	$\delta = f, z = a$
3.	$i = 3, j = 6$,	$[8c0b62f9d4a157e3]$,	$\delta = 6, z = 1$
4.	$i = 4, j = c$,	$[8c0b52f9d4a157e3]$,	$\delta = 2, z = 8$
5.	$i = 5, j = e$,	$[8c0b5ef9d4a16723]$,	$\delta = f, z = 7$
6.	$i = 6, j = d$,	$[8c0b5e79d4a16f23]$,	$\delta = 9, z = 8$
7.	$i = 7, j = 6$,	$[8c0b5e97d4a16f23]$,	$\delta = d, z = b$
8.	$i = 8, j = 3$,	$[8c0d5e97b4a16f23]$,	$\delta = 4, z = 1$
9.	$i = 9, j = 7$,	$[8c0d5e94b7a16f23]$,	$\delta = a, z = 9$
10.	$i = a, j = 1$,	$[8a0d5e94b7c16f23]$,	$\delta = 1, z = a$
11.	$i = b, j = 2$,	$[8a1d5e94b7c06f23]$,	$\delta = 6, z = a$
12.	$i = c, j = 8$,	$[8a1d5e9467c0bf23]$,	$\delta = f, z = 4$
13.	$i = d, j = 7$,	$[8a1d5e9f67c0b423]$,	$\delta = 2, z = 2$
14.	$i = e, j = 9$,	$[8a1d5e9f62c0b473]$,	$\delta = 3, z = 7$
15.	$i = f, j = c$,	$[8a1d5e9f62c0347b]$,	$\delta = 8, z = 4$
16.	$i = 0, j = 4$,	$[5a1d5e9f62c0347b]$,	$\delta = a, z = 7$
17.	$i = 1, j = e$,	$[571d8e9f62c034ab]$,	$\delta = 1, z = 3$
18.	$i = 2, j = f$,	$[57bd8e9f62c034a1]$,	$\delta = d, z = 5$
19.	$i = 3, j = c$,	$[57b38e9f62c0d4a1]$,	$\delta = 8, z = 5$
20.	$i = 4, j = 4$,	$[57b38e9f62c0d4a1]$,	$\delta = e, z = 2$
21.	$i = 5, j = 2$,	$[57e38b9f62c0d4a1]$,	$\delta = 9, z = 2$
22.	$i = 6, j = b$,	$[57e38b0f62c9d4a1]$,	$\delta = f, z = 9$
23.	$i = 7, j = a$,	$[57e38b0c62f9d4a1]$,	$\delta = 6, z = 9$
24.	$i = 8, j = 0$,	$[67e38b0c52f9d4a1]$,	$\delta = 2, z = 6$
25.	$i = 9, j = 2$,	$[67238b0c5ef9d4a1]$,	$\delta = f, z = 0$
26.	$i = a, j = 1$,	$[6f238b0c5e79d4a1]$,	$\delta = 9, z = 6$
27.	$i = b, j = a$,	$[6f238b0c5e97d4a1]$,	$\delta = d, z = e$
28.	$i = c, j = 7$,	$[6f238b0d5e97c4a1]$,	$\delta = 4, z = 4$
29.	$i = d, j = b$,	$[6f238b0d5e94c7a1]$,	$\delta = a, z = a$
30.	$i = e, j = 5$,	$[6f238a0d5e94c7b1]$,	$\delta = 1, z = f$
31.	$i = f, j = 6$,	$[6f238a1d5e94c7b0]$,	$\delta = 6, z = 2$
32.	$i = 0, j = c$,	$[cf238a1d5e9467b0]$,	$\delta = f, z = 3$
33.	$i = 1, j = b$,	$[c4238a1d5e9f67b0]$,	$\delta = 2, z = e$
34.	$i = 2, j = d$,	$[c4738a1d5e9f62b0]$,	$\delta = 3, z = 0$
35.	$i = 3, j = 0$,	$[347c8a1d5e9f62b0]$,	$\delta = 8, z = 2$
36.	$i = 4, j = 8$,	$[347c5a1d8e9f62b0]$,	$\delta = a, z = 4$
37.	$i = 5, j = 2$,	$[34ac571d8e9f62b0]$,	$\delta = 1, z = 2$
38.	$i = 6, j = 3$,	$[34a157cd8e9f62b0]$,	$\delta = d, z = d$
39.	$i = 7, j = 0$,	$[d4a157c38e9f62b0]$,	$\delta = 8, z = d$
40.	$i = 8, j = 8$,	$[d4a157c38e9f62b0]$,	$\delta = e, z = 9$
41.	$i = 9, j = 6$,	$[d4a157e38c9f62b0]$,	$\delta = 9, z = c$
42.	$i = a, j = f$,	$[d4a157e38c0f62b9]$,	$\delta = f, z = 0$
43.	$i = b, j = e$,	$[d4a157e38c0b62f9]$,	$\delta = 6, z = b$
44.	$i = c, j = 4$,	$[d4a167e38c0b52f9]$,	$\delta = 2, z = d$
45.	$i = d, j = 6$,	$[d4a167238c0b5ef9]$,	$\delta = f, z = 2$
46.	$i = e, j = 5$,	$[d4a16f238c0b5e79]$,	$\delta = 9, z = d$
47.	$i = f, j = e$,	$[d4a16f238c0b5e97]$,	$\delta = d, z = 8$
48.	$i = 0, j = b$,	$[b4a16f238c0d5e97]$,	$\delta = 4, z = d$
49.	$i = 1, j = f$,	$[b7a16f238c0d5e94]$,	$\delta = a, z = 2$
50.	$i = 2, j = 9$,	$[b7c16f238a0d5e94]$,	$\delta = 1, z = 7$
51.	$i = 3, j = a$,	$[b7c06f238a1d5e94]$,	$\delta = 6, z = 7$
52.	$i = 4, j = 0$,	$[67c0bf238a1d5e94]$,	$\delta = f, z = 0$
53.	$i = 5, j = f$,	$[67c0b4238a1d5e9f]$,	$\delta = 2, z = a$
54.	$i = 6, j = 1$,	$[62c0b4738a1d5e9f]$,	$\delta = 3, z = 9$
55.	$i = 7, j = 4$,	$[62c0347b8a1d5e9f]$,	$\delta = 8, z = e$
56.	$i = 8, j = 6$,	$[62c0347b5a1d8e9f]$,	$\delta = a, z = 2$
57.	$i = 9, j = 6$,	$[62c034ab571d8e9f]$,	$\delta = 1, z = 8$
58.	$i = a, j = 7$,	$[62c034a157bd8e9f]$,	$\delta = d, z = 6$
59.	$i = b, j = 4$,	$[62c0d4a157b38e9f]$,	$\delta = 8, z = 6$
60.	$i = c, j = c$,	$[62c0d4a157b38e9f]$,	$\delta = e, z = 7$
61.	$i = d, j = a$,	$[62c0d4a157e38b9f]$,	$\delta = 9, z = 7$
62.	$i = e, j = 3$,	$[62c9d4a157e38b0f]$,	$\delta = f, z = 3$
63.	$i = f, j = 2$,	$[62f9d4a157e38b0c]$,	$\delta = 6, z = 3$
64.	$i = 0, j = 8$,	$[52f9d4a167e38b0c]$,	$\delta = 2, z = 5$
65.	$i = 1, j = a$,	$[5ef9d4a167238b0c]$,	$\delta = f, z = a$
66.	$i = 2, j = 9$,	$[5e79d4a16f238b0c]$,	$\delta = 9, z = 5$
67.	$i = 3, j = 2$,	$[5e97d4a16f238b0c]$,	$\delta = d, z = f$
68.	$i = 4, j = f$,	$[5e97c4a16f238b0d]$,	$\delta = 4, z = 3$
69.	$i = 5, j = 3$,	$[5e94c7a16f238b0d]$,	$\delta = a, z = 7$
70.	$i = 6, j = d$,	$[5e94c7b16f238a0d]$,	$\delta = 1, z = e$
71.	$i = 7, j = e$,	$[5e94c7b06f238a1d]$,	$\delta = 6, z = 9$
72.	$i = 8, j = 4$,	$[5e9467b0cf238a1d]$,	$\delta = f, z = f$
73.	$i = 9, j = 3$,	$[5e97b0c4238a1d]$,	$\delta = 2, z = 4$
74.	$i = a, j = 5$,	$[5e9f62b0c4738a1d]$,	$\delta = 3, z = d$
75.	$i = b, j = 8$,	$[5e9f62b0347c8a1d]$,	$\delta = 8, z = e$
76.	$i = c, j = 0$,	$[8e9f62b0347c5a1d]$,	$\delta = a, z = e$
77.	$i = d, j = a$,	$[8e9f62b034ac571d]$,	$\delta = 1, z = 7$
78.	$i = e, j = b$,	$[8e9f62b034a157cd]$,	$\delta = 8, z = 8$
79.	$i = f, j = 8$,	$[8e9f62b0d4a157c3]$,	$\delta = 8, z = 8$
80.	$i = 0, j = 0$,	$[8e9f62b0d4a157c3]$,	$\delta = e, z = a$

to 80-Cycle$_{120}$) amounting to 960 total cycles out of which $3 \cdot 120 = 360$ cycles contain initial states. The factor of 3 comes here due to the fact that each of the 120 cycles contain the states $i = j$ for 3 cases $i = 0$, $i = 4$ and $i = 8$. The details of this cycle is presented in Table 2.

We also obtained a cycle of length 336 with the initial state [10, 9, 6, 11, 15, 7, 4, 14, 12, 5, 3, 2, 8, 13, 1, 0]. Since the cycle length $T = 336$ and $\frac{T}{N} = 21$ is an odd number, there can be right-sifted permutations in this cycle. By inspecting the cycle we observe that it contains right-shifted permutations by (10, 4, 14, 8, 2, 12, 6, 0) places in the same sequence. We can immediately verify part (i), (ii) and (iv) of Theorem 5 based on these observations. As per part (iii) of Theorem 5, there can be 2 disjoint cycles for each of the 120 cycles (336-Cycle$_1$ to 336-Cycle$_{120}$) amounting to 240 total cycles out of which 120 cycles contain initial states. We do not present the cycle in tabular form here as it is longer than the earlier ones.

3.2   Computational Effort

Experimentation of RC4 cycles, even in the reduced version of $N = 16$, is time consuming due to the daunting size of its state space in the range of 5.36 quadrillion. The exact size of the state space is $16! \cdot 16^2 = 5,356,234,211,328,000$. Even if we restrict the search to always start from the initial states (i.e., $i = 0, j = 0$), an attempt to find short cycles of a size comparable to the length of a Finney cycle (i.e., $16 \cdot 15 = 240$), results in generation of more than 5.02 quadrillion ($16! \cdot 240 = 5,021,469,573,120,000$) data. Clearly, a practical approach would be to divide the problem to independent parts and to run those in one or more machines, each equipped with multi-core processors. We came up with the following basic idea and used the same to accomplish the parallelism.

Any permutation of N distinct objects from a set X can be constructed by partitioning X to two arbitrary non-empty subsets Y and Z (where $X = Y \cup Z$ and $Y \cap Z = \emptyset$), selecting two specific permutations from Y and Z respectively and combining the two permutations according to a unique N-tuple of $\{0, 1\}$ in which number of 0's (or number of 1's) is same as the number of elements in the set Y.

The explanation for this goes as follows. Let us first choose a specific permutation of the elements in X and represent it as $(x_1, x_2, ..., x_N)$. Let us now construct an N-tuple of $\{0, 1\}$, a permutation of Y as $(y_1, y_2, ...)$ and a permutation of Z as $(z_1, z_2, ...)$ by using the following algorithmic step.

For every x_i, if $x_i \in Y$, we append x_i as the next element in the permutation of Y and place 0 (or 1) in i-th position of an N-tuple under construction. If $x_i \in Z$, we append x_i as the next element in the permutation of Z and place 1 (or 0) in i-th position of an N-tuple under construction.

Clearly, at the end of N-steps, we get an N-tuple of $\{0, 1\}$ in which number of 0's (or number of 1's) is the same as the number of elements in the set Y, a specific permutation of Y that corresponds to the order (from left to right) in which the elements of Y appear in the original permutation of X and a specific permutation of Z that corresponds to the order (from left to right) in which the elements of Z appear in the original permutation of X. Given any two partitions Y and Z of X, two distinct permutations of X would necessarily differ in at least one of the 3 permutations that we have constructed $(y_1, y_2, ...)$ of Y, $(z_1, z_2, ...)$ of Z and the N-tuple of $\{0, 1\}$.

If we now start with the permutation of Y and the permutation of Z as created in the N steps described above, we can reconstruct the original permutation $(x_1, x_2, ..., x_N)$, by referring to the N-tuple of $\{0, 1\}$. In case, the i-th element of the N-tuple happens to be 0 (or 1), we choose the next available element from the permutation of Y as x_i or otherwise we choose the next available element from the permutation of Z as x_i. It is also apparent from the construction and reconstruction, that number of 0's (or 1's) would match with the number of elements in Y.

One may note that the above mentioned process of construction and reconstruction preserves the uniqueness of the permutations. We have already proved the fact in case of construction. Similarly, for the re-construction step, in case we make any change in the permutation of Y or in the permutation of Z, the re-constructed permutation would be different from the original one as the order of the elements of Y or the order of elements of Z in the final permutation would differ. On the other hand, if we choose a different N-tuple of $\{0, 1\}$ (without altering the number of 0s in it), the values of x_is would differ in all the positions where the N-tuple has different values. The bijection of the mapping proves that such a construction and re-construction would always be possible.

Utilizing this idea, we first partition the set of array elements of S-box in two sets, namely $Y = \{0, 1, 2, 3, 4, 5, 6, 7\}$ and $Z = \{8, 9, 10, 11, 12, 13, 14, 15\}$. Next, we create two data files where the first data file contains all possible $8!(= 40320)$ permutations of Y, while the second data file contains all possible 40320 permutations of Z. We also create a third data file containing all possible permutations of $\{0, 1\}$ of 16-byte length where the number of 0's and the number of 1's in each permutation is 8 each. The number of such permutations is $\frac{16!}{8! \cdot 8!} = 12870$.

Based on the theorem, we can say that each permutation of S-box for $N = 16$ can be constructed from a specific permutation of the partition Y (contained in the first data file), a specific permutation of the partition Z (contained in the second data file) and a specific permutation of 0's and 1's (as contained in the third data file). Moreover, we can segregate any one (or more) of these data files in multiple parts so as to run each part in separate processor cores and achieve the desired parallelism.

Eventually, we decided to run the program in two machines with 39 processes in each of those. The third data file was logically divided to 78 partitions (each having 165 permutation elements) and the i-th process focused on constructing the S-box permutations from each of the permutations from the first and second data file and by choosing the i-th partition of the third data file (having 165 such permutations of 0's and 1's).

To find the short cycles, we allowed each of the 78 processes to start with a permutation of the S-box (by constructing it from the first two data files and the relevant partition of the third data file as described in the paragraph above) with initial indices of $(i = 0, j = 0)$ and check up to the iteration of 960 rounds at maximum (which is 4 times the length of a Finney cycle) for possible cycle completion and then go back to start with the next permutation. For finding a possible long cycle, we used a separate program that started with the permutation of $(0, 1, 2, 3, 4, 5, 6, 7, 8, 9, 10, 11, 12, 13, 14, 15)$ and stopped at the point where it reached the first right-shifted version of the initial state. We used two separate variables to hold the number of rounds: one for the number of billion rounds completed and the other for the number of million rounds completed. Clearly, the extent of parallelism can be increased with more number of machines and/or more number of cores per processor.

4   Conclusion

The pseudo-randomness of the index j in RC4 has been an open question for quite some time and there were only a few sporadic results in this direction. In this paper we show that j is indeed not pseudo-random in long term evolution of RC4 PRGA where we consider S as a pseudo-random permutation. The implication of these results could be interesting to obtain further non-randomness in the evolution of this cipher. Moreover, the results may be utilized to obtain additional biases at the initial stage of RC4 PRGA where the permutation S has certain non-randomness. Further, theoretical and experimental results on the distribution of the sequences of j might be an interesting exercise, and we are working in that direction. One important direction could be to exploit many such biases and attempt a state recovery attack in an effort similar to [1]. We note that several sequences of j cannot exist during the RC4 evolution. Many of the results obtained here are consequences of non-existence of Finney Cycle, that were not noted earlier during long span of RC4 related research.

We also study certain results related to the cycle length of RC4. In the process, we have obtained enough evidence that there might be short cycles in RC4, even with the initialization fixing $i = j = 0$, for which Finney cycle cannot appear. We provide certain interesting observations in this regard through experiment for reduced version of RC4 with $N = 16$. While we could not characterize the short cycles theoretically, our experimental observations may provide a direction towards obtaining them for $N = 256$. This is indeed an important question for future research.

References

1. AlFardan, N.J., Bernstein, D.J., Paterson, K.G., Poettering, B., Schuldt, J.C.N.: On the security of RC4 in TLS and WPA. In: 22nd USENIX Security Symposium (2013). http://www.isg.rhul.ac.uk/tls/RC4biases.pdf. Accessed 1 Oct 2019
2. Finney, H.: An RC4 cycle that can't happen. Sci. Crypt, September 1994
3. Jenkins, R.J.: ISAAC and RC4 (1996). http://burtleburtle.net/bob/rand/isaac.html. Accessed 1 Oct 2019
4. Maitra, S.: The index j in RC4 is not pseudo-random due to non-existence of Finney Cycle. https://eprint.iacr.org/2015/1043. Accessed 1 Oct 2019
5. Mantin, I., Shamir, A.: A practical attack on broadcast RC4. In: Matsui, M. (ed.) FSE 2001. LNCS, vol. 2355, pp. 152–164. Springer, Heidelberg (2002). https://doi.org/10.1007/3-540-45473-X_13
6. Mister, S., Tavares, S.E.: Cryptanalysis of RC4-like ciphers. In: Tavares, S., Meijer, H. (eds.) SAC 1998. LNCS, vol. 1556, pp. 131–143. Springer, Heidelberg (1999). https://doi.org/10.1007/3-540-48892-8_11
7. Paterson, K.G., Poettering, B., Schuldt, J.C.N.: Big bias hunting in amazonia: large-scale computation and exploitation of RC4 biases (Invited Paper). In: Sarkar, P., Iwata, T. (eds.) ASIACRYPT 2014. LNCS, vol. 8873, pp. 398–419. Springer, Heidelberg (2014). https://doi.org/10.1007/978-3-662-45611-8_21
8. SenGupta, S., Maitra, S., Paul, G., Sarkar, S.: (Non-)random sequences from (non-)random permutations - analysis of RC4 stream cipher. J. Cryptol. **27**(1), 67–108 (2014). https://doi.org/10.1007/s00145-012-9138-1
9. Sepehrdad, P., Vaudenay, S., Vuagnoux, M.: Statistical attack on RC4. In: Paterson, K.G. (ed.) EUROCRYPT 2011. LNCS, vol. 6632, pp. 343–363. Springer, Heidelberg (2011). https://doi.org/10.1007/978-3-642-20465-4_20

Automatic Tool for Searching for Differential Characteristics in ARX Ciphers and Applications

Mingjiang Huang[1,2] and Liming Wang[1(✉)]

[1] SKLOIS, Institute of Information Engineering, CAS, Beijing, China
{huangmingjiang,wangliming}@iie.ac.cn
[2] School of Cyber Security, University of Chinese Academy of Sciences,
Beijing, China

Abstract. Motivated by the algorithm of differential probability calculation of Lipmaa and Moriai, we revisit the differential properties of modular addition. We propose an efficient approach to generate the input-output difference tuples with non-zero probabilities. A novel concept of combinational DDT and the corresponding construction algorithm are introduced to make it possible to obtain all valid output differences for fixed input differences. According to the upper bound of differential probability of modular addition, combining the optimization strategies with branch and bound search algorithm, we can reduce the search space of the first round and prune the invalid difference branches of the middle rounds. Applying this tool, the provable optimal differential trails covering more rounds for SPECK32/48/64 with tight probabilities can be found, and the differentials with larger probabilities are also obtained. In addition, the optimal differential trails cover more rounds than exisiting results for SPARX variants are obtained. A 12-round differential with a probability of $2^{-54.83}$ for SPARX-64, and a 11-round differential trail with a probability of 2^{-53} for SPARX-128 are found. For CHAM-64/128 and CHAM-128/*, the 39/63-round differential characteristics we find cover 3/18 rounds more than the known results respectively.

Keywords: SPECK · SPARX · CHAM · ARX · Differential cryptanalysis · Automatic search · Block cipher

1 Introduction

ARX-based ciphers rely on modular addition to provide non-linearity while rotation and XOR provide diffusion, hence the name: Addition, Rotation, XOR [7]. Benefiting from the high efficiency of modular addition in software implementation, the ARX construction is favored by many cryptography designers. In recent years, a large number of primitives based on the ARX construction have emerged, such as HIGHT [15], LEA [14], SPECK [5], SPARX [11], CHAM [18] and the augmented ARX ciphers SIMON [5] and SIMECK [30]. On April 18,

© Springer Nature Switzerland AG 2019
F. Hao et al. (Eds.): INDOCRYPT 2019, LNCS 11898, pp. 115–138, 2019.
https://doi.org/10.1007/978-3-030-35423-7_6

2019, in the Round 1 Candidates of *Lightweight Cryptographic* (LWC) standards announced by NIST [1], the permutations of COMET, Limdolen, SNEIK and SPARKLE [2] etc. also adopt ARX construction (all available online at [1]).

Since the ARX-based primitives are not so well understood as the S-box based ciphers, the security analysis on them is more difficult. And the proof of the rigorous security of the ARX ciphers is still a challenging task. In the cryptographic community, investigations on ARX ciphers are still going on.

Differential cryptanalysis [6,25] is one of the most important means to evaluate the security of ARX ciphers. For differential attack, the first step is to find some differentials with high probabilities, as well as covering enough rounds. Differentials with high probabilities can be used to mount key recovery attack with less data and/or time complexity, and differentials with longer rounds can be utilized to attack more rounds in the iterative block ciphers. To obtain good differentials of ARX ciphers, an effective method is with the help of automated analysis tools at present. Therefore, constructing efficient automated analysis tools to get the differential characteristics on ARX ciphers worth the effort.

Related Works. There are mainly three types of automated analysis tools for ARX ciphers until now. The first one, by characterizing the properties of components in ARX ciphers as a set of satisfiability problems, then use the SAT/SMT solvers (MiniSAT, STP, Boolector, etc.) to search for the characteristics, such as in [3,4,17,22,26,28,29]. The second ones are based on the inequality solving tools, by converting the cryptographic properties into inequalities characterization problems, constructing (mixed) integer linear programming (MILP) models, and solving them by third-party softwares (such as Gurobi, SAGE, etc.). MILP method is also very efficient in searching differential characteristics for ARX ciphers [13,31–33]. The third ones, which are constructed directly by the branch and bound search algorithm (Matsui's approach) under the Markov assumption [19]. By investigating the differential propagation properties of the round function, the differential characteristics can be searched according to depth-first [8,10,16,23,24] or breadth-first strategies [9]. The execution efficiency in the search phase of the first two tools depend on the performance of the third-party softwares and the representation of the equalities/inequalities of differential properties, while the third tool mostly depends on the optimizing strategies to reduce the invalid difference branches for improving the search efficiency.

In 2014, Biryukov et al. applied Matsui's approach to the differential analysis on SPECK, and proposed a concept of partial difference distribution table (pDDT) [8,9]. Based on some heuristic strategies, the differential trails they obtained can not be guaranteed as optimal ones. Then, at FSE'16 [10], Biryukov et al. further improved the branch and bound algorithm for SPECK. In the first round, they traversed the input-output difference space by gradually increasing the number of active bits of the input-output difference tuple, according to the monotonicity of the differential probability of modular addition. In the middle rounds, they used the calculation algorithm of Lipmaa and Moriai to compute the differential probability directly. The optimal differential characteristic covering 9-round for SPECK32 with a probability of 2^{-30} was obtained in [10]. Fu et al. applied the MILP method in [13] and Song et al. adopted the SAT method in [28] to search for the optimal differential characteristics of SPECK, and the obtained optimal differential trails cover 9/11-round for SPECK32/48 with probabilities of $2^{-30}/2^{-45}$ respectively. In [13,28], for SPECK64/96/128, the good differential trails were obtained by connecting two or three short trails from the extention of one intermediate difference state with a differential probability weight of 0. For SPECK64/96/128, it is still difficult to directly search for the optimal differential trails that cover more rounds and tight probabilities. In [4], Ankele et al. analyzed the differential characteristics of SPARX-64 by suing the SAT method, and they got a 10-round optimal differential trail with a probability of 2^{-42}. Up to now, there are still no third-party differential cryptanalysis results for SPARX-128 and CHAM.

Our Contributions. Firstly, we propose a method to construct the space of the valid input-output difference tuples of certain differential probability weight. We adopt the way to increase the differential probability weight monotonously, which can exclude the search space of impossible large probability weight of the first round. Secondly, in order to quickly obtain the possible output differences with non-zero probabilities correspond to the fixed input differences, we propose a concept of combinational difference distribution table (cDDT) with feasible storage complexity. All valid output differences can be combined dynamically by looking up the pre-computed tables. Thirdly, in the middle rounds, we achieve more delicate pruning conditions based on the probability upper bound of modular addition. Finally, combining these optimization strategies, the automatic tool to search for the differential characteristics on ARX ciphers can be constructed.

Applying this tool to several ciphers, better differential characteristics are obtained comparing to the existing results. For SPECK64, a 15-round optimal differential trail with probability of 2^{-62} is found. Meanwhile, a new 12-round differential for SPECK48 with probability of $2^{-47.3}$ is found. For SPARX-64, a 11-round optimal differential trail with probability of 2^{-48}, a 12-round good differential trail with probability of 2^{-56} and the corresponding 12-round differential with probability of $2^{-54.83}$ are obtained. For SPARX-128, a 10-round differential with probability of $2^{-39.98}$ is obtained. For CHAM-64/128, we find a 39-round optimal differential trail with probability of 2^{-64}. For CHAM-128/*, the 63-round optimal differential trail we obtained with probability of 2^{-127} is a good improvement compared to the results already announced.

Outline. The remainder of this paper is organized as follows. In Sect. 2, we present some preliminaries encountered in this paper. In Sect. 3, we present the approach to construct the space of input-output difference tuples and the construction method of cDDT. We introduce an automatic search tool for ARX ciphers in Sect. 4. And we apply the new tool to SPECK, SPARX and CHAM in Sect. 5. Finally, we conclude our work in Sect. 6.

2   Preliminaries

2.1   Notation

In this paper, we mainly focus on the XOR-difference probability of modular addition, which is marked by xdp$^+$. If not specified, the differential probabilities in this paper all represent xdp$^+$. For modular addition $x \boxplus y = z$ with input difference (α, β) and output difference γ, the XOR-difference probability of modular addition is defined by

$$\text{xdp}^+((\alpha, \beta) \to \gamma) = \frac{\#\{(x,y)|((x \oplus \alpha) \boxplus (y \oplus \beta)) \oplus (x \boxplus y) = \gamma\}}{\#(x,y)}. \quad (1)$$

Modular addition is the only nonlinear component in ARX ciphers that produces differential probabilities. The differential probability of each round is decided by the number of active modular additions (i.e N_A) in it. Let $(\alpha^{i,j}, \beta^{i,j}, \gamma^{i,j})$ be the differences of the jth addition in the ith round, there have,

$$\Pr(\Delta x_{i-1} \to \Delta x_i) = \prod_{j=1}^{N_A} \text{xdp}^+((\alpha^{i,j}, \beta^{i,j}) \to \gamma^{i,j}). \quad (2)$$

Under the *Markov assumption*, when the round keys are choosen uniformly, the probability of a differential trail is the product of the probabilities of each round. For a r-round reduced iterative cipher, with input difference Δx_0 and output difference Δx_r, the probability of the differential trail is denoted by

$$\Pr(\Delta x_0 \xrightarrow{r} \Delta x_r) = \prod_{i=1}^{r} \prod_{j=1}^{N_A} \text{xdp}^+((\alpha^{i,j}, \beta^{i,j}) \to \gamma^{i,j}). \quad (3)$$

For the differential effect, the differential probability (DP) can be counted by the probabilities of the differential trails with the same input and output differences. Let N be the number of trails be counted, it will contribute to get a more compact DP when N is large enough.

$$\text{DP}(\Delta x_0 \xrightarrow{r} \Delta x_r) = \sum_{s=1}^{N} \Pr(\Delta x_0 \xrightarrow{r} \Delta x_r)_s. \quad (4)$$

In this paper, we let $\mathbb{F}_2^n$ be the n dimensional vector space over binary filed $\mathbb{F}_2^1 = \{0,1\}$. We use the symbols $\lll$, $\ggg$ to indicate rotation to the left and right, and $\ll$, $\gg$ to indicate the left and right shift operation, respectively. The binary operator symbols $\oplus, \wedge, ||, \neg$ represent XOR, AND, concatenation, and bitwise NOT respectively. For a vector x, its Hamming weight is denoted by $\text{wt}(x)$. x_i represents the ith bit in vector x, and $x_{[j,i]}$ represents the vector of bits i to j in x. $\Delta x = x \oplus x'$ represents the XOR difference of x and x'. $\mathbf{0}$ represents a zero vector. For a r-round optimal differential trail with probability of Pr, $Bw_r = -\log_2 \text{Pr}$ represents the obtained differential probability weight of it, and $\overline{Bw_{r+1}}$ is the expected differential probability weight of the $(r+1)$-round optimal differential trail.

2.2   Differential Probability Calculation for Modular Addition

In [20], Lipmaa and Moriai proposed an algorithm to compute the XOR-difference probability of modular addition, which can be rewritten by *Theorem 1*.

Theorem 1 *(Algorithm 2 in [20]). Let α, β be the two n-bit input differences and γ is the n-bit output difference of addition modulo 2^n, $x, x', y, y' \in \mathbb{F}_2^n$, $f(x, y) = x \boxplus y$, $x = x' \oplus \alpha$, $y = y' \oplus \beta$, and $\gamma = f(x, y) \oplus f(x', y')$. For arbitrary α, β and γ, let $\mathrm{eq}(\alpha, \beta, \gamma) := (\bar{\alpha} \oplus \beta) \wedge (\bar{\alpha} \oplus \gamma)$, $\mathrm{mask}(n) := 2^n - 1$, and $g(\alpha, \beta, \gamma) := \mathrm{eq}(\alpha \ll 1, \beta \ll 1, \gamma \ll 1) \wedge (\alpha \oplus \beta \oplus \gamma \oplus (\beta \ll 1))$. The differential probability of (α, β) propagate to γ is denoted by*

$$\Pr\{(\alpha, \beta) \to \gamma\} = \begin{cases} 2^{-\mathrm{wt}(\neg \mathrm{eq}(\alpha, \beta, \gamma) \wedge \mathrm{mask}(n-1))}, & \text{if } g(\alpha, \beta, \gamma) = 0; \\ 0, & \text{else.} \end{cases}$$

Theorem 2. *Let α, β be the two n-bit input differences and γ is the n-bit output difference of addition modulo 2^n, the number of input-output difference tuples with probability of 2^{-w} is $4 \cdot 6^w \cdot \binom{n-1}{w}$, for any $0 \le w < n$ (Theorem 6 in [21], which is derived from Theorem 2 in [20]).*

3 The Input-Output Differences and the Differential Probabilities of Modular Addition

3.1 The Input-Output Difference Tuples of Non-zero Probability

In branch and bound search strategy, a naive method is to traverse the full space of the input-output difference tuples of each modular addition in the first round. However, it will lead to very large time complexity, when the word size n of modular addition is too large. To address this, it's possible to reduce the search complexity by removing those impossible tuples of modular addition at the starting of the search. Here, we will introduce an efficient algorithm to achieve this goal.

Lemma 1. *Let α, β be the two n-bit input differences and γ is the n-bit output difference of modular addition with non-zero differential probability. Let δ be a n-bit auxiliary vector, for $0 \le i \le n - 1$, the ith bit of δ is denoted by*

$$\delta_i = \begin{cases} 0, \text{if } \alpha_i = \beta_i = \gamma_i; \\ 1, \text{else.} \end{cases}$$

Therefore, there have $\delta = \neg \mathrm{eq}(\alpha, \beta, \gamma)$, and

$$\Pr\{(\alpha, \beta) \to \gamma\} = 2^{-\mathrm{wt}(\delta \wedge \mathrm{mask}(n-1))}.$$

Let $w = \mathrm{wt}(\delta \wedge \mathrm{mask}(n - 1))$ be the differential probability weight, there should be $0 \le w \le n - 1$. The Hamming weight of the vector $\delta_{[n-2,0]}$ equals to the differential probability weight w.

Definition 1. *For $w \ge 1$, we define an array $\Lambda := \{\lambda_w, \cdots, \lambda_1\}$, which contains w elements. The elements in Λ record the subscripts of the non-zero bits of vector $\delta_{[n-2,0]}$, called as the probability weight active positions. For $1 \le j \le w$, each element is denoted by $\lambda_j = i$, when $\delta_i \ne 0$, for $i = 0$ to $n - 2$. For example, $\Lambda = \{3, 2, 0\}$, when $\delta_{[0,6]} = (0001101)_2$.*

Definition 2. *Let* (α, β, γ) *be the input-output difference tuples of addition modulo* 2^n *with non-zero probability. Let's define an array* $D := \{d_{n-1}, \cdots, d_0\}$, *which contains* n *elements. Where* $d_i = \alpha_i||\beta_i||\gamma_i = 4d_{i,2} + 2d_{i,1} + d_{i,0}$, $d_i \in \mathbb{F}_2^3$, *and* $d_{i,2}, d_{i,1}, d_{i,0} \in \mathbb{F}_2^1$, *for* $0 \leq i \leq n-1$.

Definition 3. *Let's define four sets to represent the possible values that* d_i *might belongs to, i.e.* $U_0 = \{0, 3, 5, 6\}$, $U_0^* = \{3, 5, 6\}$, $U_1 = \{1, 2, 4, 7\}$, $U_1^* = \{1, 2, 4\}$.

Corollary 1. *Let* (α, β, γ) *be the input-output difference tuples of addition modulo* 2^n *with probability weight of* w. *For* $1 \leq j \leq w$, $1 \leq w \leq n-1$ *and let* $\lambda_0 = 0$ *when* $\lambda_1 > 0$, *there should have,*

- *for every element* λ_j *in* Λ, *the* λ_j-*th octal word in* D *should s.t.* $d_{\lambda_j} \notin \{0, 7\}$;
- *the elements between* d_{λ_j} *and* $d_{\lambda_{j-1}}$ *should be all 0, if and only if* $d_{\lambda_j} \in U_0^*$;
- *the elements between* d_{λ_j} *and* $d_{\lambda_{j-1}}$ *should be all 7, if and only if* $d_{\lambda_j} \in U_1^*$;
- *and* $d_{\lambda_1} \in U_0^*$ *in any case.*

Corollary 1 can be derived directly from Theorem 1. Inspired by the idea of finite-state machine (FSM) in [27], we take the most significant octal word d_{n-1} as the initial state to construct the state transition process of the elements in array D. The state transition diagram of octal word sequence that satisfy Corollary 1 is shown in Fig. 1. According to the distribution patterns of *probability weight active positions*, we introduce Algorithm 1 (marked as $Gen(w)$) to construct the $4 \cdot 6^w \cdot \binom{n-1}{w}$ input-output difference tuples of a certain differential probability weight w. All combinations of $\binom{n-1}{w}$ are produced by only single bit exchanges [12]. The output tuples do not need to be stored. The element d_i in D correspond to the bit values $(\alpha_i, \beta_i, \gamma_i)$ of the input-output difference tuples. Algorithm 1 traverses the values of the n elements in D and assigns them to the bits $(\alpha_i, \beta_i, \gamma_i)$, the total complexity of it will not be greater than $4 \cdot 6^w \cdot \binom{n-1}{w} \cdot 3n$.

3.2 The Combinational DDT

Generating a DDT that can be looked up is an efficient method to obtain the valid output differences for fixed input difference. For addition modulo 2^n, when n is too large, the full DDT will be too large to store. Hence, an intuitive idea is to store only a part of it. In [9], pDDT is introduced to precompute and store the difference tuples with probabilities above a fixed threshold. However, for the tuples that cannot be looked up in pDDT, their probabilities need to be calculated by the algorithm of Lipmaa and Moriai. In order to index all tuples, we propose a concept of combinational DDT (cDDT). cDDT represents the difference distribution tables for m-bit chunks of the n-bit words. By cDDT, the full DDT can be dynamically reconstructed on-the-fly during search. And the probabilities of the tuples can also be calculated by Lemma 2.

Lemma 2. *Let* α, β, γ *be the input-output differences of addition modulo* 2^n, $\alpha' = \alpha \ll 1$, $\beta' = \beta \ll 1$, $\gamma' = \gamma \ll 1$, $\alpha, \alpha', \beta, \beta', \gamma, \gamma' \in \mathbb{F}_2^n$ *and* $n = mt$. *Splitting* $\alpha, \alpha', \beta, \beta', \gamma, \gamma'$ *into* t *m-bit sub-vectors. If the equations*

$$\text{eq}(\alpha'_{[(j+1)m-1,jm]}, \beta'_{[(j+1)m-1,jm]}, \gamma'_{[(j+1)m-1,jm]}) \wedge$$
$$(\alpha_{[(j+1)m-1,jm]} \oplus \beta_{[(j+1)m-1,jm]} \oplus \gamma_{[(j+1)m-1,jm]} \oplus \beta'_{[(j+1)m-1,jm]}) = \mathbf{0}$$

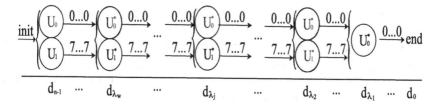

Fig. 1. The state transition diagram of the octal word sequence in D.

are satisfied for $0 \leq j \leq t - 1$, there should be

$$- \log_2 \Pr = \sum_{j=0}^{t-2} \mathrm{wt}(\neg \mathrm{eq}(\alpha_{[(j+1)m-1,jm]}, \beta_{[(j+1)m-1,jm]}, \gamma_{[(j+1)m-1,jm]}) \wedge \mathrm{mask}(m))$$

$$+ \mathrm{wt}(\neg \mathrm{eq}(\alpha_{[n-1,n-m]}, \beta_{[n-1,n-m]}, \gamma_{[n-1,n-1m]}) \wedge \mathrm{mask}(m-1)).$$

Algorithm 1: $Gen(w)$. Generating the input-output difference tuples of differential probability weight w for modular addition, $0 \leq w \leq n - 1$.

Input: The patterns of the *probability weight active positions* can be calculated from the combinations algorithm in [12], i.e. $\Lambda := \{$*the patterns of* $\binom{n-1}{w}\}$.

1 **Func_MSB:** // Constructing the most significant bits of α, β, γ.
2 **for** *each* $d_{n-1} = d_{n-1,2} || d_{n-1,1} || d_{n-1,0} \in \mathbb{F}_2^3$ **do**
3   **if** $d_{n-1} \in U_0$ **then**
4         $\alpha = d_{n-1,2} || \overbrace{0 \cdots 0}^{all\ 0s}, \beta = d_{n-1,1} || \overbrace{0 \cdots 0}^{all\ 0s}, \gamma = d_{n-1,0} || \overbrace{0 \cdots 0}^{all\ 0s}$;
5   If $w \geq 1$, call Func_Middle(w); else output each tuple (α, β, γ);
6   **else**
7         $\alpha = d_{n-1,2} || \overbrace{1 \cdots 1}^{all\ 1s}, \beta = d_{n-1,1} || \overbrace{1 \cdots 1}^{all\ 1s}, \gamma = d_{n-1,0} || \overbrace{1 \cdots 1}^{all\ 1s}$; //$d_{n-1} \in U_1$.
8   If $w \geq 1$, call Func_Middle(w); else output each tuple (α, β, γ);
9   **end**
10 **end**

11 **Func_Middle(j):** // Constructing the middle bits of α, β, γ.
12 **if** $j \leq 1$ **then**
13   call Fun_LSB;
14 **end**
15 **for** *each* $d_{\lambda_j} \in U_0^* \cup U_1^*$ **do**
16     $\alpha_{\lambda_j} = d_{\lambda_j,2}, \beta_{\lambda_j} = d_{\lambda_j,1}, \gamma_{\lambda_j} = d_{\lambda_j,0}$;
17   **if** $d_{\lambda_j} \in U_0^*$ **then**
18   Set the bit strings of α, β, γ with subscripts $\lambda_{j-1} \to \lambda_j - 1$ to all 0;
19   **else**
20   Set the bit strings of α, β, γ with subscripts $\lambda_{j-1} \to \lambda_j - 1$ to all 1; // $d_{\lambda_j} \in U_1^*$.
21   **end**
22   call Func_Middle($j - 1$);
23 **end**

24 **Func_LSB:** // Constructing the bits of α, β, γ with subscripts $0 \to \lambda_1$.
25 **if** $\lambda_1 > 0$ **then**
26   Set the bit strings of (α, β, γ) with subscripts $0 \to \lambda_1 - 1$ to all 0;
27 **end**
28 **for** *each* $d_{\lambda_1} \in U_0^*$ **do**
29     $\alpha_{\lambda_1} = d_{\lambda_1,2}, \beta_{\lambda_1} = d_{\lambda_1,1}, \gamma_{\lambda_1} = d_{\lambda_1,0}$;
30   Output each tuple (α, β, γ);
31 **end**

Proof. When $\Pr \neq 0$, $g(\alpha, \beta, \gamma) = \mathbf{0}$ should be satisfied, which is equivalent to each m-bit sub-vector of $g(\alpha, \beta, \gamma)$ should be zero vector. As $-\log_2 \Pr = \text{wt}(\delta_{[n-2,0]})$, the Hamming weight of vector $\delta_{[n-2,0]}$ can be split into $\text{wt}(\delta_{[n-2,0]}) = \sum_{j=0}^{t-2} \text{wt}(\delta_{[(j+1)m-1,jm]}) + \text{wt}(\delta_{[n-2,n-m]})$. Hence, the probability weight is the sum of the weights of each m-bit sub-vector of $\delta_{[n-2,0]}$, when all m-bit sub-vectors of $g(\alpha, \beta, \gamma)$ are zero vectors. $\qquad \square$

For each sub-vector tuple $(\alpha_{[(j+1)m-1,jm]}, \beta_{[(j+1)m-1,jm]}, \gamma_{[(j+1)m-1,jm]}$, or called as *sub-block*, its corresponding probability weight also depends on bits α_{jm-1}, β_{jm-1}, and γ_{jm-1}. Let $c[j] = \alpha_{jm-1}||\beta_{jm-1}||\gamma_{jm-1} \in \mathbb{F}_2^3$ (called as *carry bits*), and $\alpha_{[(j+1)m-1,jm]}, \beta_{[(j+1)m-1,jm]}, \gamma_{[(j+1)m-1,jm]} \in \mathbb{F}_2^m$, by traversing the 2^{3m+3} bits, a m-bit difference distribution table with non-zero probabilities can be pre-computed.

During the search process, the input differences (α, β) of modular addition are known, while the output difference γ and corresponding probability are unknown. For each m-bit sub-block $(\alpha_{[(j+1)m-1,jm]}, \beta_{[(j+1)m-1,jm]}, \gamma_{[(j+1)m-1,jm]})$, where $(\alpha_{[(j+1)m-1,jm]}, \beta_{[(j+1)m-1,jm]})$ are known. Considering the $\ll 1$ operator, the bits $\alpha_0', \beta_0', \gamma_0'$ should be all zeros. By traversing the m-bit sub-vector $\gamma_{[m-1,0]}$, the possible probability weights of the least significant sub-block can be generated. And for a definite $\gamma_{[m-1,0]}$, the bits $\alpha_{m-1}||\beta_{m-1}||\gamma_{m-1}$ can also be obtained.

Recursively, by traversing the other $t-1$ sub-vectors of γ, the corresponding probability weight of each sub-block can also be generated. Therefore, all valid n-bit output differences γ can be concatenated by the t sub-vectors of γ, and the probability weight of this modular addition is the sum of probability weight of each sub-block. The dynamic generation process of γ is shown in Fig. 2.

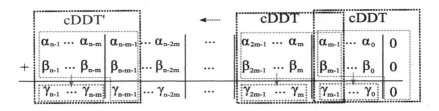

Fig. 2. The process of generating γ by looking up the difference distribution table.

For fixed input differences (α, β), the possible output difference γ with non-zero probability can be combined recursively by (5), where $c[0] = 0$ and $0 \leq j \leq t-1$. For each sub-block, the mapping can be pre-computed and stored by Algorithm 2, called as combinational DDT (cDDT) of modular addition. For each m-bit sub-vector of γ, it can be indexed by α, β, *carry bits* $c[j]$, corresponding probability weight w and the number of counts $N[w]$. It should be noted that, from the LSB to MSB direction, the *carry bits* $c[j]$ are obtained by the highest bits of the adjacent lower sub-block.

$$\begin{cases} c[j] = \alpha_{jm-1}||\beta_{jm-1}||\gamma_{jm-1}; \\ \gamma_{[(j+1)m-1,jm]} := \text{cDDT}(\alpha_{[(j+1)m-1,jm]}, \beta_{[(j+1)m-1,jm]}, c[j], w, N[w]). \end{cases} \quad (5)$$

Algorithm 2: Pre-computing the m-bit combinational DDTs.

```
 1  for each α, β ∈ F₂ᵐ do
 2  │   α' = α ≪ 1, β' = β ≪ 1, AB = α||β;
 3  │   for each c = c₂||c₁||c₀ ∈ F₂³ do
 4  │   │   Assign arrays N and N' with all zero;
 5  │   │   for each γ ∈ F₂ᵐ do
 6  │   │   │   γ' = γ ≪ 1, α'₀ = c₂, α* = ¬α', β'₀ = c₁, γ'₀ = c₀;
 7  │   │   │   eq = (α* ⊕ β') ∧ (α* ⊕ γ') ∧ (α ⊕ β ⊕ γ ⊕ β');
 8  │   │   │   if eq = 0 then
 9  │   │   │   │   w = wt(¬((¬α ⊕ β) ∧ (¬α ⊕ γ)));
10  │   │   │   │   cDDT[AB][c][w][N[w]] = γ;  // 0 ≤ w ≤ m.
11  │   │   │   │   N[w] + +;  // Number of γ with probability weight of w.
12  │   │   │   │   w' = wt(¬((¬α ⊕ β) ∧ (¬α ⊕ γ)) ∧ mask(m − 1));
13  │   │   │   │   cDDT'[AB][c][w'][N'[w']] = γ;  // 0 ≤ w' ≤ m − 1.
14  │   │   │   │   N'[w'] + +;  // Number of γ with probability weight of w'.
15  │   │   │   end
16  │   │   end
17  │   │   for 0 ≤ i ≤ m do
18  │   │   │   cDDT_num[AB][c][i] = N[i];  // The number of γ with probability weight of i.
19  │   │   end
20  │   │   cDDT_wt_min[AB][c] = min{i|N[i] ≠ 0};  // The minimum probability weight.
21  │   │   for 0 ≤ i ≤ m − 1 do
22  │   │   │   cDDT'_num[AB][c][i] = N'[i];
23  │   │   end
24  │   │   cDDT'_wt_min[AB][c] = min{i|N'[i] ≠ 0};
25  │   end
26  end
```

For fixed word size n, when m is large, the number of sub-blocks t should be small, and less times of queries in the combination phase. However, when m is too large, the complexity of the pre-computing time and storage space of Algorithm 2 will also be too large. After the trade-off in storage size and lookup times, we choose $m = 8$. Before the procedure to search for the differential characteristics, we first run Algorithm 2 to generate cDDT and cDDT', where cDDT' is used for the most significant sub-block. Algorithm 2 takes about several seconds[1] and about 16 GB of storage space when $m = 8$. Analogously, when only input difference α is fixed, the input difference β and output difference γ can also be indexed by a similar construction method, this variant of cDDT is omitted here.

3.3   Probability Upper Bound and Pruning Conditions

The exact probability upper bound can be used to prune the branches in the intermediate rounds and reduce the unnecessary search space.

Corollary 2. *Let α, β be the two input differences of addition modulo 2^n, for any n-bit output difference γ with differential probability $\Pr \neq 0$, the upper bound of the probability should s.t. $\mathrm{wt}((\alpha \oplus \beta) \wedge \mathrm{mask}(n-1)) \leq -\log_2 \Pr$.*

Proof. When $\Pr \neq 0$, it's easy to get that the elements in array D should s.t. $d_i \in U_0^* \cup U_1^*$. When $d_i \in \{2, 3, 4, 5\}$, there have $\delta_i = \alpha_i \oplus \beta_i$, and for $d_i \in \{1, 6\}$ there

---

[1] The time cost depends on the ability of the computation environment. On a 2.5 GHz CPU, it takes about 9 s.

should be $\delta_i > \alpha_i \oplus \beta_i$. Therefore, $\mathrm{wt}(\delta \wedge \mathrm{mask}(n-1)) \geq \mathrm{wt}((\alpha \oplus \beta) \wedge \mathrm{mask}(n-1))$ always hold when $\mathrm{Pr} \neq 0$. $\qquad\qquad\qquad\qquad\qquad\qquad\qquad\qquad\qquad\qquad\qquad\quad\square$

For fixed input difference (α, β), the probability weight correspond to all valid output difference γ can be obtained by summing the probability weights of all sub-blocks. The possible probability weight should subject to (6).

$$
\begin{aligned}
-\log_2 \mathrm{Pr} \geq\ & \mathrm{wt}((\alpha_{[n-1,n-m]} \oplus \beta_{[n-1,n-m]}) \wedge \mathrm{mask}(m-1)) \\
& + \sum_{j=0}^{t-2} \mathrm{wt}(\alpha_{[(j+1)m-1,jm]} \oplus \beta_{[(j+1)m-1,jm]}).
\end{aligned}
\tag{6}
$$

Let probability weights of each sub-block be $W_{XOR}[j] = \mathrm{wt}(\alpha_{[(j+1)m-1,jm]} \oplus \beta_{[(j+1)m-1,jm]})$ for $0 \leq j \leq t-2$, and $W_{XOR}[t-1] = \mathrm{wt}(\alpha_{[n-2,n-m]} \oplus \beta_{[n-2,n-m]})$. For fixed input differences (α, β), $0 \leq j \leq t-1$, the probability weight of each valid γ should also subject to (7).

$$
\begin{aligned}
-\log_2 \mathrm{Pr} \geq\ & \sum_{l=j+1}^{t-1} W_{XOR}[l] \\
& + \sum_{k=0}^{j} -\log_2 \mathrm{Pr}((\alpha_{[(k+1)m-1,km]}, \beta_{[(k+1)m-1,km]}) \rightarrow \gamma_{[(k+1)m-1,km]}).
\end{aligned}
\tag{7}
$$

Expressions (6) and (7) can be adopted as the pruning conditions to prune the branches delicately in the process of combine the n-bit γ, which can eliminate a large number of γ that will not be the intermediate difference states of the optimal differential trails.

4   Automatic Search Tool for ARX Ciphers

We combine Algorithms 1 and 2 and the pruning conditions with the branch-bound search approach to construct the efficient automatic search tool. The core idea is to prune the difference branches with impossible small probabilities by gradually increasing the probability weights of each modular addition.

Assuming w_1 is the probability weight of the first round in the r-round optimal differential trail, there should be $w_1 + Bw_{r-1} \leq \overline{Bw_r}$. Hence, the total search space of the first round is no more than $\sum_{w_1=0}^{\overline{Bw_r}-Bw_{r-1}} 4 \cdot 6^{w_1} \cdot \binom{n-1}{w_1}$. By gradually increasing the probability weight w_1 of the first round and traversing all input-output difference tuples correspond to it, the search space with probability weight be greater than w_1 can be excluded.

In the intermediate rounds, we firstly split the input differences (α, β) of each modular addition into t m-bit sub-vectors respectively. Then, according to (6), verifying whether the minimum probability weight correspond to (α, β) satisfies the condition or not. For valid possible (α, β), call $Cap(\alpha, \beta)$. By looking up cDDTs and pruning the branches by (7), the valid γ and possible probability

---

Algorithm 3: Searching for the optimal differential trails of ARX ciphers, and taking the application to SPECK as an example, where $n = mt, r > 1$.

Input: The cDDTs are pre-computed by Algorithm 2. $Bw_1, \cdots, Bw_{r-1}$ have been recorded;

1   **Program entry:** $//Bw_1$ can be derived manually for most ARX ciphers.
2   Let $\overline{Bw_r} = Bw_{r-1} - 1$, and $Bw_r =$ null;
3   **while** $\overline{Bw_r} \neq Bw_r$ **do**
4      $\overline{Bw_r} + +$; $//$The r-round expected weight increases monotonously from Bw_{r-1}.
5   Call Procedure Round-1;
6   **end**
7   Exit the program and record the differential trail be found.;

8   **Round-1:** $//w_1$ increases monotonously.
9   **for** $w_1 = 0$ to $n - 1$ **do**
10   **if** $w_1 + Bw_{r-1} > \overline{Bw_r}$ **then**
11   Return to the upper procedure with FALSE state;
12   **end**
13   Call Algorithm 1 $Gen(w_1)$ and traverse each tuple (α, β, γ);
14   **if** *call Round-I(2,γ, β) and the return value is TRUE* **then**
15   Break from $Gen(w_1)$ and return TRUE;
16   **end**
17   **end**
18   Return to the upper procedure with FALSE state;

19   **Round-I**(i, α, β): $//$Intermediate rounds, $2 \leq i \leq r$.
20   $\alpha' = \alpha \ggg r_a$, $\beta' = \alpha \oplus (\beta \lll r_b)$; $//$ (r_a, r_b): rotation parameters.
21   Let $W_{XOR}[t-1] = \text{wt}((\alpha'_{[n-1,n-m]} \oplus \beta'_{[n-1,n-m]}) \wedge \text{mask}(m-1))$;
22   Let $W_{XOR}[j] = \text{wt}(\alpha'_{[(j+1)m-1,jm]} \oplus \beta'_{[(j+1)m-1,jm]}$, for $0 \leq j \leq t - 2$;
23   **if** $w_1 + ... + w_{i-1} + \sum_{j=0}^{t-1} W_{XOR}[j] + Bw_{r-i} > \overline{Bw_r}$ **then**
24   Return to the upper procedure with FALSE state;
25   **end**
26   Let $AB[j] = \alpha'_{[(j+1)m-1,jm]}||\beta'_{[(j+1)m-1,jm]}$, for $0 \leq j \leq t - 1$;
27   Call $Cap(\alpha', \beta')$, and traverse each possible γ; $//$Where $w_i = -\log_2 xdp^+((\alpha', \beta') \rightarrow \gamma)$.
28   **if** $i = r$ and $w_1 + ... + w_{i-1} + w_i = \overline{Bw_r}$ **then**
29   Let $Bw_r = \overline{Bw_r}$, break from $Cap(\alpha', \beta')$ and return TRUE; $//$The last round.
30   **end**
31   **if** *call Round-I $(i + 1, \gamma, \beta')$ and the return value is TRUE,* **then**
32   Break from $Cap(\alpha', \beta')$ and return TRUE;
33   **end**
34   Return to the upper procedure with FALSE state;

35   $Cap(\alpha, \beta)$: $//$Combining all possible γ correspond to (α, β).
36   **for** $k = 0$ to $t - 2$, and let $k' = t - 1$, $c[0] = 0$ **do**
37   **for** $w_i^k = \text{cDDT}_{\text{wt}_{min}}[AB[k]][c[k]]$ to m **do**
38   **if** $\sum_{s=1}^{i-1} w_s + \sum_{l=k+1}^{t-1} W_{XOR}[l] + \sum_{j=0}^{k} w_i^j + Bw_{r-i} \leq \overline{Bw_r}$ **then**
39   **for** $x = 0$ to $\text{cDDT}_{num}[AB[k]][c[k]][w_i^k] - 1$ **do**
40            $\gamma_{[km+m-1,km]} = \text{cDDT}[AB[k]][c[k]][w_i^k][x]$;
41            $c[k+1] = \alpha_{km+m-1}||\beta_{km+m-1}||\gamma_{km+m-1}$; $//$The *carry* bits.
42   **if** $k = t - 2$ **then**
43   **for** $w_i^{k'} = \text{cDDT}'_{\text{wt}_{min}}[AB[k']][c[k']]$ to $m - 1$ **do**
44   **if** $\sum_{s=1}^{i-1} w_s + \sum_{j=0}^{t-1} w_i^j + Bw_{r-i} \leq \overline{Bw_r}$ **then**
45   **for** $y = 0$ to $\text{cDDT}'_{num}[AB[k']][c[k']][w_i^{k'}] - 1$ **do**
46                    $\gamma_{[n-1,n-m]} = \text{cDDT}'[AB[k']][c[k']][w_i^{k'}][y]$;
47   Output each $\gamma = \gamma_{[n-1,n-m]}|| \cdots ||\gamma_{[m-1,0]}$ and
                      $w_i = \sum_{j=0}^{t-1} w_i^j$;
48   **end**
49   **end**
50   **end**
51   **end**
52   **end**
53   **end**
54   **end**
55   **end**

weight will be generated dynamically. The pseudo code given by Algorithm 3 which is applied to SPECK as an example.

In the subroutine $Cap(\alpha, \beta)$, the least significant $t - 2$ sub-blocks will look up the cDDT. And the pruning condition $\sum_{s=1}^{i-1} w_s + \sum_{l=k+1}^{t-1} W_{XOR}[l] + \sum_{j=0}^{k} w_i^j + Bw_{r-i} \leq \overline{Bw_r}$ should be satisfied, in which w_i^j increases monotonously. For the most significant sub-block, to get all possible outputs of it by querying cDDT'. Then combining all sub-blocks' outputs to reconstruct the n-bit output difference with probability weight of $w_i = \sum_{j=0}^{t-1} w_i^j$, and $\sum_{s=1}^{i-1} w_s + w_i + Bw_{r-i} \leq \overline{Bw_r}$, where $\gamma = \gamma_{[n-1,n-m]} || \cdots || \gamma_{[m-1,0]}$. Nevertheless, the delicate pruning condition $\sum_{s=1}^{i-1} w_s + \sum_{l=k+1}^{t-1} W_{XOR}[l] + \sum_{j=0}^{k} w_i^k + Bw_{r-i} \leq \overline{Bw_r}$ will exclude most branches with small probabilities.

Formula (8) is adopted to count the probability of differential effect. In this tool, the pruning condition can be modified as $\sum_{s=1}^{i-1} w_s + w_i + Bw_{r-i} \leq w_{max}$ (*statistical condition*) to filter out the trails with probability weights be larger than w_{max}. w_{min} is the probability weight of the optimal differential trail be selected. The DP is counted by all trails with probability weights between w_{min} and w_{max}. When the probabilities of corresponding trails are too small, these trails cannot or need not to be searched, as their contribution to the DP can be ignored. $\#Trails[w]$ is the number of differential trails with probability of 2^{-w}.

$$\text{DP} = \sum_{w=w_{min}}^{w_{max}} 2^{-w} \times \#\text{Trails}[w] \tag{8}$$

5   Applications and Results

5.1   Differential Characteristics for SPECK32/48/64

The SPECK [5] family ciphers are typical ARX ciphers that proposed by NSA in 2013, which have five variants, i.e. SPECK32/48/64/96/128. The state of the ith round can be divided into two parts according to Feistel structure, i.e. X_r^i and X_l^i. Therefore, the round function transition process can be denoted by $X_l^{i+1} = ((X_r^i \ggg r_a) \boxplus X_l^i) \oplus rk^i$ and $X_r^{i+1} = X_l^{i+1} \oplus (X_r^i \lll r_b)$, in which the rk^i is the round subkey of the ith round, and (r_a, r_b) are the rotation parameters of left and right part respectively. $(r_a, r_b) = (7, 2)$ for SPECK32, and $(r_a, r_b) = (8, 3)$ for other variants.

Property 1. For SPECK variants, let $(\alpha^i, \beta^i, \gamma^i)$ be the input-output differences of modular addition in the ith round, $(\Delta X_l^i, \Delta X_r^i)$ and $(\Delta X_l^{i+1}, \Delta X_r^{i+1})$ are the input and output difference of ith round. There are $\alpha^i \lll r_a = \Delta X_l^i$, $\beta^i = \Delta X_r^i$, $\gamma^i = \Delta X_l^{i+1}$, and $\gamma^i \oplus (\beta^i \lll r_b) = \Delta X_r^{i+1}$.

By Algorithm 3, the optimal differential trails we obtained are shown in Tables 1 and 2. The runtime[2] and the differential probabilities are slightly improved comparing to the existing results, and the obtained optimal differential trails can cover more rounds. A new 12-round differential for SPECK48

---

[2] All experiments in this paper are carried out serially on a HPC with Intel(R) Xeon(R) CPU E5-2680 v3 @ 2.50 GHz. All differences are represented in hexadecimal.

Table 1. Runtime and the probabilities of the optimal differential trails for SPECK variants. In the following tables, $w = -\log_2 \Pr$, the 's', 'm', 'h', 'd' represent the time in seconds, minutes, hours, and days respectively. The columns of 'tw' indicate the time cost in this work, and the time for pre-calculating the cDDTs are not counted.

/	SPECK32			SPECK48			SPECK64			SPECK96			SPECK128		
r	w	time		w	time		w	time		w	time		w	time	
		[10]	tw		[10]	tw		[10]	tw		[10]	tw		[10]	tw
1	0	0 s	0 s	0	0 s	0 s	0	0 s	0 s	0	0 s	0 s	0	0 s	0 s
2	1	0 s	0 s	1	0 s	0 s	1	0 s	0 s	1	0 s	0 s	1	0 s	0 s
3	3	0 s	0 s	3	0 s	0 s	3	0 s	0 s	3	0 s	0 s	3	0 s	0 s
4	5	0 s	0 s	6	0 s	0 s	6	0 s	0 s	6	6 s	0 s	6	22 s	2 s
5	9	0 s	0 s	10	1 s	0 s	10	1 min	8 s	10	5 min	2 s	10	26 min	13 min
6	13	1 s	1 s	14	3 s	0 s	15	26 min	10 min	15	5 h	11 min	15	2 d	80 min
7	18	1 min	7 s	19	1 min	17 s	21	4 h	19 min	21	5 d	18 min	21	3 h	2 h
8	24	34 min	35 s	26	9 min	77 s	29	22 h	18 h	30	>3 d	162 h	≤30	>2 d	>32 d
9	30	12 min	3 min	33	7 d	6 h	34	>1 d	1 h	≤39		>32 d	≤39		>28 d
10	34	6 min	2 min	40	>3 h	16 h	38		40 min						
11				45		2 h	42		11 min						
12				49		40 min	46		5 min						
13							50		5 min						
14							56		20 min						
15							62		1 h						
16							70		91 h						

Table 2. The 9/11/15-round optimal differential trails for SPECK32/48/64.

r	SPECK32		SPECK48		SPECK64	
	ΔX_r	w	ΔX_r	w	ΔX_r	w
0	8054A900	3	080048080800	3	4000409210420040	5
1	0000A402	3	400000004000	1	8202000000120200	4
2	A4023408	8	000000020000	1	0090000000001000	2
3	50C080E0	4	020000120000	3	0000800000000000	1
4	01810203	5	120200820200	4	0000008000000080	1
5	000C0800	3	821002920006	9	8000008080000480	3
6	20000000	1	918236018202	12	0080048000802084	6
7	00400040	1	0C1080000090	4	80806080848164A0	13
8	80408140	2	800480800000	2	040F240020040104	8
9	00400542	-	008004008000	3	2000082020200001	4
10			048080008080	3	0000000901000000	2
11			808400848000	-	0800000000000000	1
12					0008000000080000	2
13					0008080000480800	4
14					0048000802084008	6
15					0A0808081A4A0848	-

is obtained, shown in Table 3. For SPECK96/128, due to the large word size, the time complexity is still too large to directly search for the optimal differential trails covering more rounds with probabilities close to the security bound ($Pr = 2^{-n}$).

Table 3. The differentials for SPECK32/48/64.

2n	r	Δin	Δout	w_{min}	w_{max}	DP	Reference
32	9	8054,A900	0040,0542	30	N/A	2^{-30}	[8]
	9	8054,A900	0040,0542	30	N/A	$2^{-29.47}$	[28]
	10	2040,0040	0800,A840	35	N/A	$2^{-31.99}$	[28]
	10	0040,0000	0814,0844	36	48	$2^{-31.55}$	This paper
48	11	202040,082921	808424,84A905	47	N/A	$2^{-46.48}$	[8]
	11	504200,004240	202001,202000	46	N/A	$2^{-44.31}$	[28]
	11	001202,020002	210020,200021	45	54	$2^{-43.44}$	This paper
	11	080048,080800	808400,848000	45	54	$2^{-42.86}$	This paper
	12	080048,080800	840084,A00080	49	52	$2^{-47.3}$	This paper
64	14	00000009,01000000	00040024,04200D01	60	N/A	$2^{-59.02}$	[8]
	15	04092400,20040104	808080A0,A08481A4	62	N/A	$2^{-60.56}$	[28]
	15	40004092,10420040	0A080808,1A4A0848	62	71	$2^{-60.39}$	This paper

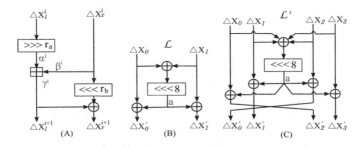

Fig. 3. The differential propagation of SPECK/SPECKEY is shown in (A), and the differential propagation of $\mathcal{L}/\mathcal{L}'$ are shown in (B) and (C).

5.2 Differential Characteristics for SPARX Variants

SPARX [11] was introduced by Dinu et al. at ASIACRYPT'16, which is designed according to the *long trail strategy* with provable bound. The SPECKEY component in SPARX, or called as ARX-Box, which is modified from the round function of SPECK32. The differential properties of SPECKEY are similar to that of the round function in SPECK32, see *Property* 1. For the 3 variants of SPARX, we mark them as SPARX-64 and SPARX-128 according to the block size. For the linear layer functions $\mathcal{L}/\mathcal{L}'$ (shown in Fig. 3), their differential properties are listed in *Property* 2, 3.

Property 2. For SPARX-64, $(X_0', X_1') = \mathcal{L}(X_0, X_1)$, let $a = (\Delta X_0 \oplus \Delta X_1) \lll 8$, there should be $\Delta X_0' = \Delta X_0 \oplus a$, and $\Delta X_1' = \Delta X_1 \oplus a$.

Property 3. For SPARX-128, $(X_0', X_1', X_2', X_3') = \mathcal{L}'(X_0, X_1, X_2, X_3)$, let $a = (\Delta X_0 \oplus \Delta X_1 \oplus \Delta X_2 \oplus \Delta X_3) \lll 8$, there should be $\Delta X_0' = \Delta X_2 \oplus a$, $\Delta X_1' = \Delta X_1 \oplus a$, $\Delta X_2' = \Delta X_0 \oplus a$, and $\Delta X_3' = \Delta X_3 \oplus a$.

To obtain the optimal differential trails of SPARX, there should make some modifications to Algorithm 3. In the first round, it is necessary to call Algorithm 1 for each addition modulo 2^{16} to generate its input-output difference tuples with probability weight increase monotonously. There should be nested call Algorithm 1 2/4 times for SPARX-64/SPARX-128 respectively. For every modular additions in each intermediate round, $Cap(\alpha, \beta)$ needs to be nested multiple times to produce its valid output differences. The *Property* 2/3 of linear layer functions $\mathcal{L}/\mathcal{L}'$ will be used to replace the linear properties of SPECK. The optimal differential trails and differentials for SPARX-64 are listed in Tables 4[3] and 5. The 12-round optimal differential trail for SPARX-64 cover 2 more rounds than the existing results in [3,4]. The 12-round good differential trail is obtained by taking the input difference of the 11-round optimal differential trail as a fixed value. Refer to expression (8), if the searched w_{max} is large enough, the time complexity and the differential probability also should be larger[4].

Table 4. Probabilities of the optimal differential trails for SPARX-64.

r	$-\log_2 \Pr$	Δin	Δout	Time
1	0	0040 0000 0000 0000	8000 8000 0000 0000	0 s
2	1	0040 0000 0000 0000	8100 8102 0000 0000	0 s
3	3	0040 0000 0000 0000	8A04 8E0E 8000 840A	0 s
4	5	0000 0000 2800 0010	8000 840A 0000 0000	0 s
5	9	0000 0000 2800 0010	850A 9520 0000 0000	1 s
6	13	0000 0000 0211 0A04	AF1A BF30 850A 9520	2 s
7	24	0000 0000 1488 1008	8000 8C0A 8000 840a	2 h38 min
8	29	0000 0000 0010 8402	0040 0542 0040 0542	4 h16 min
9	35	2800 0010 2800 0010	D761 9764 D221 9224	4 h54 min
10	42	2800 0010 2800 0010	0204 0A04 0204 0A04	80 h
11	48	2800 0010 2800 0010	0200 2A10 0200 2A10	194 h35 min
12	$\leq$56	2800 0010 2800 0010	0291 0291 2400 B502	-

The differential characteristics for SPARX-128 are shown in Table 6, and the 12/11-round good differential trail for SPARX-64/SPARX-128 are shown

---

[3] For the 7-round optimal differential trail with probability weight of 24, we limit the first round probability weight $w_1 \leq 5$ to speed up the search process.

[4] When the *statistical condition* is omitted in the last round, #Trails will perhaps be greater than the sum of the number of trail with probability weight $\leq w_{max}$.

Table 5. Comparison of the differentials for SPARX-64.

r	Δin	Δout	w_{min}	w_{max}	DP	#Trails	Time	Reference
7	000000007448B0F8	80048C0E8000840A	24	60	$2^{-23.95}$	56301	28 min	[3,4]
	0000000014881008	80008C0A8000840A	24	30	$2^{-23.82}$	4	12 s	This paper
8	0000000000508402	0040054200400542	29	60	$2^{-28.53}$	37124	17 min	[3,4]
	0000000000108402	0040054200400542	29	46	$2^{-28.54}$	194	48 min	This paper
9	2800001028000010	5761176452211224	35	58	$2^{-32.87}$	233155	7 h42 min	[3,4]
	2800001028000010	D7619764D2219224	35	47	$2^{-32.96}$	399	12 h19 min	This paper
10	2800001028000010	8081828380008002	42	73	$2^{-38.12}$	1294158	35 h18 min	[3,4]
	2800001028000010	02040A0402040A04	42	49	$2^{-38.05}$	362	17 h18 min	This paper
11	2800001028000010	02002A1002002A10	48	53	$2^{-43.91}$	922	98 h21 min	This paper
12	2800001028000010	029102912400B502	56	58	$2^{-54.83}$	9	17 h37 min	This paper

in Table 7. T_{opt}, T_{diff} are the time cost for searching the optimal differential trails and differentials respectively. The 9/10/11-round good differential trail with probability weight of 34/41/53 are obtained by limiting the probability weight $w_1 \leq 1$ of the first round, and T_{opt} is the corresponding time cost.

Table 6. The differential characteristics for SPARX-128.

r	w_{opt}	T_{opt}	Δin	Δout	w_{min}	w_{max}	DP	#Trails	T_{diff}
4			0000 0000 0000 0000	0000 0000 0000 040A					
	5	0 s	0000 0000 2800 0010	0000 0000 0000 0000	5	6	2^{-3}	63	16 s
5			0000 0000 0000 0000	0000 0000 850A 9520					
	9	3 min25 s	0000 0000 2800 0010	0000 0000 0000 0000	9	12	2^{-9}	1	15 s
6			0000 0000 0000 0000	0000 0000 850A 9520					
	13	7 min	0000 0000 0211 0A04	0000 0000 0000 0000	13	16	2^{-13}	1	14 s
7			0000 0000 0000 0000	0000 0000 850A 9520					
	18	17 h18 min	0000 0000 0a20 4205	0000 0000 0000 0000	18	22	2^{-18}	1	15 s
8			0000 0000 0000 0000	AF1A 2A10 2A10 BF30					
	24	24d17 h	0000 0000 1488 1008	0000 0000 850A 9520	24	28	$2^{-23.83}$	2	9 s
9	≥ 29		0000 0000 0000 0000	0010 0010 0800 2800					
	≤ 34	27 min	0000 0000 2040 0040	0000 0000 0810 2810	34	42	$2^{-31.17}$	238	2 h31 min
10	≥ 38		0000 0000 0000 0000	8040 8140 A040 2042					
	≤ 41	16 h31 min	0000 0000 0050 A000	0000 0000 2000 A102	41	48	$2^{-39.98}$	40	45 h22 min
11			0000 0000 0000 0000	0040 0542 A102 200A					
	≤ 53	17d19 h	0000 0000 0050 A000	0000 0000 6342 E748	53	53	2^{-53}	1	-

5.3 Differential Characteristics for CHAM Variants

CHAM [18] is a family of lightweight block ciphers that proposed by Koo et al. at ICISC'17, which combines the good design features of SIMON and SPECK. CHAM adopts a 4-branch generalized Feistel structure, and contains three variants which are denoted by CHAM-n/k with a block size of n-bit and a key size of k-bit. For CHAM-64/128, the word size w of each branch is 16 bits, and for CHAM-128/*, $w = 32$. The rotation parameters of every two consecutive rounds

Table 7. The 12/11-round good differential trail for SPARX-64 and SPARX-128.

12-round trail for SPARX-64					11-round trail for SPARX-128						
r	$\Delta X_r^0\|\|\cdots\|\|\Delta X_r^3$	w_r^0	w_r^1	w_r	r	$\Delta X_r^0\|\|\Delta X_r^1\|\|\cdots\|\|\Delta X_r^6\|\|\Delta X_r^7$	w_r^0	w_r^1	w_r^2	w_r^3	w_r
1	2800001028000010	2	2	4	1	000000000000000000000000000050A000	0	0	0	1	1
2	0040000000400000	0	0	0	2	00000000000000000000000000008002	0	0	0	2	2
3	8000800080008000	2	1	3	3	0000000000000000000000008006800C	0	0	0	6	6
$\mathcal{L}$	8300830281008102	-	-	-	4	00000000000000000000009D0C9D3E	0	0	0	7	7
4	0000000083008302	0	5	5	$\mathcal{L}'$	000000000000000000008478F082	-	-	-	-	-
5	000000008404880E	0	6	6	5	000000008478F0820000000000000000	0	6	0	0	6
6	00000000911AB120	0	8	8	6	00000000C08A0281000000000000000000	0	7	0	0	7
$\mathcal{L}$	00000000C4060084	-	-	-	7	000000000A00000400000000000000000	0	2	0	0	2
7	C406008400000000	8	0	8	8	0000000000100000000000000000000	0	1	0	0	1
8	0A14080400000000	4	0	4	$\mathcal{L}'$	00000000200020000000000000000000	-	-	-	-	-
9	2010000000000000	2	0	2	9	2000000000000200000000000020002000	1	1	0	2	4
$\mathcal{L}$	2040204000000000	-	-	-	10	004000402000A0000000000002040A040	1	2	0	2	5
10	2040204020402040	2	2	4	11	80408140A0402042000000002000A102	2	4	0	6	12
11	A0002100A0002100	3	3	6	12	00400542A102200A000000006342E748	-	-	-	-	-
12	2040A4402040A440	3	3	6							
$\mathcal{L}$	2400B5022400B502	-	-	-							
13	029102912400B502	-	-	-							

are $(1, 8)$ and $(8, 1)$ respectively, and it iterates over $R = 80/80/96$ rounds for the three variants.

Let $X_{r+1} = f_r(X_r, K)$ be the round function of the rth round of CHAM, $1 \le r \le R$. Let's divide the input state $X_r \in \mathbb{F}_2^n$ of the rth round into four w-bit words, i.e. $X_r = X_r[0]\|X_r[1]\|X_r[2]\|X_r[3]$. The state transformation of the round function can be represented by

$$X_{r+1}[3] = ((X_r[0] \oplus (r-1)) \boxplus ((X_r[1] \lll r_a) \oplus RK[(r-1) \bmod 2k/w])) \lll r_b,$$

$$X_{r+1}[j] = X_r[j+1], \; for \; 0 \le j \le 2.$$

When $r \bmod 2 = 1$, there have $(r_a, r_b) = (1, 8)$, otherwise $(r_a, r_b) = (8, 1)$.

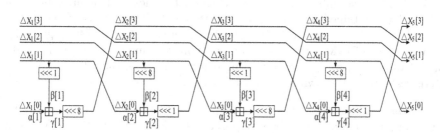

Fig. 4. The difference propagation for the first 4 rounds of CHAM.

For a master key $K \in \mathbb{F}_2^k$ of CHAM, the key schedule process will generate $2k/w$ w-bit round keys, i.e. $RK[0], RK[1], \cdots, RK[2k/w - 1]$. For $0 \le i < k/w$,

Let $K = K[0]||K[1]|| \cdots ||K[k/w - 1]$, the round keys can be generated by

$$RK[i] = K[i] \oplus (K[i] \lll 1) \oplus (K[i] \lll 8),$$

$$RK[(i + k/w) \oplus 1] = K[i] \oplus (K[i] \lll 1) \oplus (K[i] \lll 11).$$

The input difference $\Delta X_r = X_r \oplus X'_r$ of the rth round can be denoted by $\Delta X_r = \Delta X_r[0]||\Delta X_r[1]||\Delta X_r[2]||\Delta X_r[3]$, where $\Delta X_r[j] \in \mathbb{F}_2^w$, for $0 \le j \le 3$. Therefore, the differential propagation property of the round function of CHAM can be denoted by *Property* 4. The differential propagation process of the first 4 consecutive rounds of CHAM is shown in Fig. 4.

Property 4. Let $\Delta X_r, \Delta X_{r+1}$ be the input and output difference of the rth round of CHAM, there are $\Delta X_{r+1}[0] = \Delta X_r[1]$, $\Delta X_{r+1}[1] = \Delta X_r[2]$, $\Delta X_{r+1}[2] = \Delta X_r[3]$, and $\Delta X_{r+1}[3] := \delta_{\mathrm{Pr}}(\Delta X_r[0], \Delta X_r[1] \lll r_a) \lll r_b$. Where $\gamma := \delta_{\mathrm{Pr}}(\alpha, \beta)$ represents the output difference γ of modular addition that generated by input differences (α, β) with differential probability of Pr.

In the search process, the input-output difference tuples $(\alpha[1], \beta[1], \gamma[1])$ can be generated by Algorithm 1 directly. Then $(\beta[2], \gamma[2])$ can be obtained by querying a variant of cDDT based on $\alpha[2] = \beta[1] \ggg 1$. And, $(\beta[3], \gamma[3])$ can also be queried by $\alpha[3] = \beta[2] \ggg 8$. When $r \ge 4$, the input differences $\Delta X_r[0]||\Delta X_r[1]||\Delta X_r[2]||\Delta X_r[3]$ can be determined, so, $\Delta X_{r+1}[3]$ can be obtained by querying cDDT based on $(\Delta X_r[0], \Delta X_r[1] \lll r_a)$. The probability weights of each splitted sub-blocks of the input-output difference tuples increase monotonously, and the *Property* 4 should also be introduced, for $r \ge 2$.

It should be noted that, the rotation parameters in two consecutive rounds of CHAM are different. Let Bw_r^* be the probability weights of the truncated optimal differential trails that starting with rotation parameter $(r_a, r_b) = (8, 1)$. Hence, when searching for the optimal differential trail of CHAM, in the pruning condition $\sum_{s=1}^{i-1} w_s + w_i + Bw_{r-i} \le \overline{Bw_r}$, if current round i is odd, the pruning condition should be replaced with $\sum_{s=1}^{i-1} w_s + w_i + Bw_{r-i}^* \le \overline{Bw_r}$. Correspondingly, when searching for Bw_r^*, if current round i is even, the pruning condition should be $\sum_{s=1}^{i-1} w_s + w_i + Bw_{r-i}^* \le \overline{Bw_r^*}$, otherwise $\sum_{s=1}^{i-1} w_s + w_i + Bw_{r-i} \le \overline{Bw_r^*}$.

For CHAM variants, the differential characteristics with a probability of $P \ge 2^{-n}$ we obtained are listed in Tables 8 and 9. The details of the differential characteristics are shown in Table 11. Compared to the results given by the authors of CHAM, our results can cover more rounds, shown in Table 10. For CHAM-128/*, we get an interesting observation from the differential characteristics obtained, shown in *Observation* 1.

Observation 1. For CHAM-128/*, let $\Delta X_0^1|| \cdots ||\Delta X_3^1 \xrightarrow{16} \Delta X_0^{17}|| \cdots ||\Delta X_3^{17}$ be a 16-round differential trail Υ_1 with a probability of P_1, and $\Delta X_j^{17} = \Delta X_j^1 \lll 4$ for $0 \le j \le 3$. Hence, for consecutive $16t$-round reduced CHAM-128/*, there have such a differential trail, i.e. $\Delta X_0^1|| \cdots ||\Delta X_3^1 \xrightarrow{r=16t} \Delta X_0^{r+1}|| \cdots ||\Delta X_3^{r+1}$ with a probability of $P = P_1 \times \cdots \times P_t$, $t \ge 1$. Where $P_2, \cdots, P_t$ can be derived from the probability of Υ_1, the input differences of each round of the differential trail can be denoted by $\Delta X_j^i = \Delta X_j^{i \bmod 16} \lll (4\lfloor \frac{i}{16} \rfloor)$, for $0 \le j \le 3$ and $i > 16$.

Table 8. The probability weights of the best differential trails for CHAM-64.

Round	1	2	3	4	5	6	7	8	9	10	11	12	13	14	15	16	17	18	19	20
Bw_r	0	0	0	0	1	1	2	3	4	5	6	7	8	9	11	14	15	16	19	22
Bw_r^*	0	0	0	0	1	1	2	3	4	5	6	7	8	9	11	13	15	16	18	22
Round	21	22	23	24	25	26	27	28	29	30	31	32	33	34	35	36	37	38	39	
Bw_r	23	26	29	30	32	35	38	39	41	44	46	48	49	51	55	56	58	61	64	
Bw_r^*	23	25	29	31	34	36	38	40	42	45	47	48	50	52	54	57	58	60	64	

Table 9. The probability weights of the best differential trails for CHAM-128/*.

Round	1	2	3	4	5	6	7	8	9	10	11	12	13	14	15	16	17	18	19	20	21	22
Bw_r	0	0	0	1	1	2	2	3	5	6	7	8	9	11	13	16	17	18	21	24	26	28
Bw_r^*	0	0	0	1	1	2	2	3	5	6	7	8	9	11	13	16	17	18	21	24	26	28
Round	23	24	25	26	27	28	29	30	31	32	33	34	35	36	37	38	39	40	41	42	43	44
Bw_r	31	33	35	43	46	48	53	57	61	65	67	70	72	73	75	78	80	81	83	86	87	
Bw_r^*	31	34	36	39	43	46	49	51	55	62	64	67	69	72	74	76	78	81	82	83	85	88
Round	45	46	47	48	49	50	51	52	53	54	55	56	57	58	59	60	61	62	63	64		
Bw_r	88	90	93	96	97	99	102	104	105	107	110	113	114	116	119	121	122	124	127	130		
Bw_r^*	90	92	94	96	99	100	102	105	107	108	110	113	115	116	118	121	123	125	127	130		

Table 10. Comparison of the differential characteristics on CHAM.

Variants	r	Pr	Δin	Δout	Reference
CHAM-64/128	36	2^{-63}	0004 0408 0A00 0000	0005 8502 0004 0A00	[18]
	39	2^{-64}	0020 0010 1020 2800	1008 0010 2000 1000	This paper
CHAM-128/*	45	2^{-125}	01028008 08200080	00000000 00110004	[18]
			04000040 42040020	04089102 00080010	
	63	2^{-127}	80000000 40000000	00400010 00008000	This paper
			00408000 00200080	00004000 80000040	

Let $(\Delta X_0^1 || \cdots || \Delta X_3^1) = (8000000040000000004080000 0200080)$, the probabilities of the 16-round differential trails $\Upsilon_1/\Upsilon_2/\Upsilon_3/\Upsilon_4$ are $P_1 = 2^{-32}$, $P_2 = 2^{-33}$, $P_3 = 2^{-31}$, and $P_4 = 2^{-34}$. We can experimentally deduce the probabilities of the additional two 16-round differential trail Υ_5 and Υ_6, where $P_5 = 2^{-33}$, $P_6 = 2^{-32}$. Therefore, for the full round of CHAM-128/128 and CHAM-128/256, we can get the differential characteristics $\Upsilon_1 \to \cdots \to \Upsilon_5$ and $\Upsilon_1 \to \cdots \to \Upsilon_6$ of 80/96-round with probabilities of 2^{-163} and 2^{-195} respectively.

Υ_1 : 800000004000000000408000002000 80 $\to$ 00000000800000004040800000200 0800

Υ_2 : 0000000080000000404080000020008 00 $\to$ 0000080000004040800000200080 00

Υ_3 : 0000080000004040800000200080 00 $\to$ 0000080000004000800000400080002

Υ_4 : 0000080000004000800000400080002 $\to$ 000080000004000800000400080002 0

Υ_5 : 000080000004000800000400080002 0 $\to$ 0008000000400000000040808000020 0

Υ_6 : 0008000000400000000040808000020 0 $\to$ 00800000004000000000408080002000

Table 11. The best differential trails for CHAM-64/128 and CHAM-128/*.

	39-round trail for CHAM-64/128				64-round trail for CHAM-128/*		
r	$\Delta X_0^r \|\| \cdots \|\| \Delta X_3^r$	w_r	r	$\Delta X_0^r \|\| \cdots \|\| \Delta X_3^r$	w_r
1	0020 0010 1020 2800	1	1	80000000 40000000 00408000 00200080	0
2	0010 1020 2800 0000	2	2	40000000 00408000 00200080 00000000	2
3	1020 2800 0000 4000	3	3	00408000 00200080 00000000 01000000	3
4	2800 0000 4000 2040	2	4	00200080 00000000 01000000 00810000	2
5	0000 4000 2040 5000	0	5	00000000 01000000 00810000 00400100	1
6	4000 2040 5000 0080	2	6	01000000 00810000 00400100 00000002	1
7	2040 5000 0080 0040	2	7	00810000 00400100 00000002 00000001	3
8	5000 0080 0040 4080	2	8	00400100 00000002 00000001 01020000	3
9	0080 0040 4080 A000	1	9	00000002 00000001 01020000 00800200	1
10	0040 4080 A000 0000	1	10	00000001 01020000 00800200 00000000	2
11	4080 A000 0000 0001	3	11	01020000 00800200 00000000 04000000	3
12	A000 0000 0001 8100	1	12	00800200 00000000 04000000 02040000	2
13	0000 0001 8100 4001	1	13	00000000 04000000 02040000 01000400	1
14	0001 8100 4001 0200	2	14	04000000 02040000 01000400 00000008	2
15	8100 4001 0200 0100	2	15	02040000 01000400 00000008 00000004	3
16	4001 0200 0100 0201	3	16	01000400 00000008 00000004 04080000	3
17	0200 0100 0201 8003	1	17	00000008 00000004 04080000 02000800	1
18	0100 0201 8003 0000	2	18	00000004 04080000 02000800 00000000	2
19	0201 8003 0000 0004	4	19	04080000 02000800 00000000 10000000	3
20	8003 0000 0004 0402	2	20	02000800 00000000 10000000 08100000	2
21	0000 0004 0402 0007	1	21	00000000 10000000 08100000 04001000	1
22	0004 0402 0007 0800	2	22	10000000 08100000 04001000 00000020	2
23	0402 0007 0800 0400	4	23	08100000 04001000 00000020 00000010	3
24	0007 0800 0400 0004	4	24	04001000 00000020 00000010 10200000	3
25	0800 0400 0004 0002	1	25	00000020 00000010 10200000 08002000	1
26	0400 0004 0002 0000	1	26	00000010 10200000 08002000 00000000	2
27	0004 0002 0000 0000	1	27	10200000 08002000 00000000 40000000	3
28	0002 0000 0000 0000	1	28	08002000 00000000 40000000 20400000	2
29	0000 0000 0000 0004	0	29	00000000 40000000 20400000 10004000	0
30	0000 0000 0004 0000	0	30	40000000 20400000 10004000 00000080	2
31	0000 0004 0000 0000	1	31	20400000 10004000 00000080 00000040	3
32	0004 0000 0000 0800	1	32	10004000 00000080 00000040 40800000	3
33	0000 0000 0800 0008	0	33	00000080 00000040 40800000 20008000	1
34	0000 0800 0008 0000	1	34	00000040 40800000 20008000 00000000	1
35	0800 0008 0000 0010	2	35	40800000 20008000 00000000 00000001	3
36	0008 0000 0010 1008	1	36	20008000 00000000 00000001 81000000	2
37	0000 0010 1008 0010	1	37	00000000 00000001 81000000 40010000	2
38	0010 1008 0010 2000	2	38	00000001 81000000 40010000 00000200	2
39	1008 0010 2000 1000	3	39	81000000 40010000 00000200 00000100	2
40	0010 2000 1000 2810	–	40	40010000 00000200 00000100 02000001	3
			41	00000200 00000100 02000001 80020000	1
			42	00000100 02000001 80020000 00000000	2
			43	02000001 80020000 00000000 00000004	3
			44	80020000 00000000 00000004 04000002	1
			45	00000000 00000004 04000002 00040001	1
			46	00000004 04000002 00040001 00000800	2
			47	04000002 00040001 00000800 00000400	3
			48	00040001 00000800 00000400 08000004	3
			49	00000800 00000400 08000004 00080002	1
			50	00000400 08000004 00080002 00000000	2
			51	08000004 00080002 00000000 00000010	3
			52	00080002 00000000 00000010 10000008	2
			53	00000000 00000010 10000008 00100004	1
			54	00000010 10000008 00100004 00002000	2
			55	10000008 00100004 00002000 00001000	3
			56	00100004 00002000 00001000 20000010	3
			57	00002000 00001000 20000010 00200008	1
			58	00001000 20000010 00200008 00000000	2
			59	20000010 00200008 00000000 00000040	3
			60	00200008 00000000 00000040 40000020	2
			61	00000000 00000040 40000020 00400010	1
			62	00000040 40000020 00400010 00008000	2
			63	40000020 00400010 00008000 00004000	3
			64	00400010 00008000 00004000 80000040	3
			65	00008000 00004000 80000040 00800020	–

6   Conclusions

In this paper, we revisit the differential properties of modular addition. An algorithm to obtain all input-output difference tuples of specific probability weight, a novel concept of cDDT, and the delicate pruning conditions are proposed. Combining these optimization strategies, we can construct the automatic search algorithms to achieve efficient search for the differential characteristics on ARX ciphers. As appling, more tight differential probabilities for SPECK32/48/64 have been obtained. The differential characteristics obtained for SPARX variants are the best so far, although it does not threaten the claimed security. When considering key recovery attacks on CHAM-128/128 and CHAM-128/256 based on the differential characteristics of CHAM we obtained, and as its authors claimed that one can attack at most $4 + 2(k/w - 4) + 3$ rounds more than that of the differential characteristics obtained, therefore, the security margin of CHAM-128/* will be less than 20%. It can be believed that, our tool can also be utilized to differential cryptanalysis on other ARX-based primitives.

Acknowledgements. The authors will be very grateful to the anonymous reviewers for their insightful comments. And we are especially thankful to Qingju Wang and Vesselin Velichkov for their helpful suggestions. This work was supported by the National Key Research and Development Program of China (No. 2017YFB0801900).

A. How to Apply to Other ARX Ciphers

For an iterated ARX cipher, assuming that there are N_A additions modulo 2^n in each round, for example, $N_A = 1/2/4/1$ for SPECK/SPARX-64/SPARX-128/CHAM respectively. And the difference propagation properties of the linear layer between adjacent rounds can also be deduced, for example, as shown in *Property 1/2/3/4*. The following four steps demonstrate how to model the search strategy for the r-round optimal differential trail of an ARX cipher.

Step 1. Pre-compute and store cDDT. Call **Program entry** and gradually increase the expected probability weight $\overline{Bw}_r$.

Step 2. Gradually increasing the probability weights w_i $(1 \le i \le r_1)$ of each round for the front r_1 rounds. Simultaneously, generating the input-output difference tuples $(\alpha_{i,j}, \beta_{i,j}, \gamma_{i,j})$ for each addition by $Gen(w_{i,j})$. Where $w_{i,j} = 0$ to $n - 1$, and $w_i = \sum_{j=1}^{N_A} w_{i,j}$. Make sure all input differences $(\alpha_{r_1+1,j}, \beta_{r_1+1,j})$ of each modular addition in the $(r_1 + 1)$-round can be determined after the propagation. For example, $r_1 = 1/1/3$ for SPECK/SPARX/CHAM respectively.

Step 3. In the middle rounds $(r_1 < r_m \le r)$, for each addition, splitting its input differences $(\alpha_{r_m,j}, \beta_{r_m,j})$ into n/m m-bit sub-blocks and verifying the pruning condition (7). Call $Cap(\alpha_{r_m,j}, \beta_{r_m,j})$ for fine-grained pruning, and get the possible $\gamma_{r_m,j}$ and probability weight $w_{r_m,j}$, where $w_{r_m} = \sum_{j=1}^{N_A} w_{r_m,j}$.

Step 4. Iteratively call **Step 3** till the last round. Checking whether the expected probability weight $\overline{Bw}_r = \sum_{s=1}^{r} w_s$ or not. If it is, record the trail and stop, otherwise the execution should continue.

References

1. https://csrc.nist.gov/Projects/Lightweight-Cryptography
2. https://www.cryptolux.org/index.php/Sparkle
3. Ankele, R., Kölbl, S.: Mind the gap - a closer look at the security of block ciphers against differential cryptanalysis. In: Cid, C., Jacobson Jr., M.J. (eds.) Selected Areas in Cryptography - SAC 2018, pp. 163–190. Springer, Cham (2019). https://doi.org/10.1007/978-3-030-10970-7_8
4. Ankele, R., List, E.: Differential cryptanalysis of round-reduced Sparx-64/128. In: Preneel, B., Vercauteren, F. (eds.) ACNS 2018. LNCS, vol. 10892, pp. 459–475. Springer, Cham (2018). https://doi.org/10.1007/978-3-319-93387-0_24
5. Beaulieu, R., Shors, D., Smith, J., Treatman-Clark, S., Weeks, B., Wingers, L.: The SIMON and SPECK families of lightweight block ciphers. Cryptology ePrint Archive, Report 2013/404 (2013). https://eprint.iacr.org/2013/404
6. Biham, E., Shamir, A.: Differential cryptanalysis of DES-like cryptosystems. J. Cryptol. 4(1), 3–72 (1991)
7. Biryukov, A., Perrin, L.: State of the art in lightweight symmetric cryptography. IACR Cryptol. ePrint Arch. 2017, 511 (2017)
8. Biryukov, A., Roy, A., Velichkov, V.: Differential analysis of block ciphers SIMON and SPECK. In: Cid, C., Rechberger, C. (eds.) FSE 2014. LNCS, vol. 8540, pp. 546–570. Springer, Heidelberg (2015). https://doi.org/10.1007/978-3-662-46706-0_28
9. Biryukov, A., Velichkov, V.: Automatic search for differential trails in ARX ciphers. In: Benaloh, J. (ed.) CT-RSA 2014. LNCS, vol. 8366, pp. 227–250. Springer, Cham (2014). https://doi.org/10.1007/978-3-319-04852-9_12
10. Biryukov, A., Velichkov, V., Le Corre, Y.: Automatic search for the best trails in ARX: application to block cipher SPECK. In: Peyrin, T. (ed.) FSE 2016. LNCS, vol. 9783, pp. 289–310. Springer, Heidelberg (2016). https://doi.org/10.1007/978-3-662-52993-5_15
11. Dinu, D., Perrin, L., Udovenko, A., Velichkov, V., Großschädl, J., Biryukov, A.: Design strategies for ARX with provable bounds: SPARX and LAX. In: Cheon, J.H., Takagi, T. (eds.) ASIACRYPT 2016. LNCS, vol. 10031, pp. 484–513. Springer, Heidelberg (2016). https://doi.org/10.1007/978-3-662-53887-6_18
12. Ehrlich, G.: Loopless algorithms for generating permutations, combinations, and other combinatorial configurations. J. ACM 20(3), 500–513 (1973). https://doi.org/10.1145/321765.321781
13. Fu, K., Wang, M., Guo, Y., Sun, S., Hu, L.: MILP-based automatic search algorithms for differential and linear trails for speck. In: Peyrin, T. (ed.) FSE 2016. LNCS, vol. 9783, pp. 268–288. Springer, Heidelberg (2016). https://doi.org/10.1007/978-3-662-52993-5_14
14. Hong, D., Lee, J.-K., Kim, D.-C., Kwon, D., Ryu, K.H., Lee, D.-G.: LEA: a 128-bit block cipher for fast encryption on common processors. In: Kim, Y., Lee, H., Perrig, A. (eds.) WISA 2013. LNCS, vol. 8267, pp. 3–27. Springer, Cham (2014). https://doi.org/10.1007/978-3-319-05149-9_1
15. Hong, D., et al.: HIGHT: a new block cipher suitable for low-resource device. In: Goubin, L., Matsui, M. (eds.) CHES 2006. LNCS, vol. 4249, pp. 46–59. Springer, Heidelberg (2006). https://doi.org/10.1007/11894063_4
16. Huang, M., Wang, L., Zhang, Y.: Improved automatic search algorithm for differential and linear cryptanalysis on SIMECK and the applications. In: Naccache, D., et al. (eds.) ICICS 2018. LNCS, vol. 11149, pp. 664–681. Springer, Cham (2018). https://doi.org/10.1007/978-3-030-01950-1_39

17. Kölbl, S., Leander, G., Tiessen, T.: Observations on the SIMON block cipher family. In: Gennaro, R., Robshaw, M. (eds.) CRYPTO 2015. LNCS, vol. 9215, pp. 161–185. Springer, Heidelberg (2015). https://doi.org/10.1007/978-3-662-47989-6_8

18. Koo, B., Roh, D., Kim, H., Jung, Y., Lee, D.-G., Kwon, D.: CHAM: a family of lightweight block ciphers for resource-constrained devices. In: Kim, H., Kim, D.-C. (eds.) ICISC 2017. LNCS, vol. 10779, pp. 3–25. Springer, Cham (2018). https://doi.org/10.1007/978-3-319-78556-1_1

19. Lai, X., Massey, J.L., Murphy, S.: Markov ciphers and differential cryptanalysis. In: Davies, D.W. (ed.) EUROCRYPT 1991. LNCS, vol. 547, pp. 17–38. Springer, Heidelberg (1991). https://doi.org/10.1007/3-540-46416-6_2

20. Lipmaa, H., Moriai, S.: Efficient algorithms for computing differential properties of addition. In: Matsui, M. (ed.) FSE 2001. LNCS, vol. 2355, pp. 336–350. Springer, Heidelberg (2002). https://doi.org/10.1007/3-540-45473-X_28

21. Lipmaa, H., Wallén, J., Dumas, P.: On the additive differential probability of exclusive-or. In: Roy, B., Meier, W. (eds.) FSE 2004. LNCS, vol. 3017, pp. 317–331. Springer, Heidelberg (2004). https://doi.org/10.1007/978-3-540-25937-4_20

22. Liu, Y., Wang, Q., Rijmen, V.: Automatic search of linear trails in ARX with applications to SPECK and Chaskey. In: Manulis, M., Sadeghi, A.-R., Schneider, S. (eds.) ACNS 2016. LNCS, vol. 9696, pp. 485–499. Springer, Cham (2016). https://doi.org/10.1007/978-3-319-39555-5_26

23. Liu, Z., Li, Y., Wang, M.: Optimal differential trails in SIMON-like ciphers. IACR Trans. Symmetric Cryptol. 2017(1), 358–379 (2017)

24. Liu, Z., Li, Y., Wang, M.: The security of SIMON-like ciphers against linear cryptanalysis. IACR Cryptol. ePrint Arch. 2017, 576 (2017)

25. Matsui, M.: On correlation between the order of S-boxes and the strength of DES. In: De Santis, A. (ed.) EUROCRYPT 1994. LNCS, vol. 950, pp. 366–375. Springer, Heidelberg (1995). https://doi.org/10.1007/BFb0053451

26. Mouha, N., Preneel, B.: Towards finding optimal differential characteristics for ARX: application to Salsa20. Cryptology ePrint Archive, Report 2013/328 (2013)

27. Mouha, N., Velichkov, V., De Cannière, C., Preneel, B.: The differential analysis of S-functions. In: Biryukov, A., Gong, G., Stinson, D.R. (eds.) SAC 2010. LNCS, vol. 6544, pp. 36–56. Springer, Heidelberg (2011). https://doi.org/10.1007/978-3-642-19574-7_3

28. Song, L., Huang, Z., Yang, Q.: Automatic differential analysis of ARX block ciphers with application to SPECK and LEA. In: Liu, J.K., Steinfeld, R. (eds.) ACISP 2016. LNCS, vol. 9723, pp. 379–394. Springer, Cham (2016). https://doi.org/10.1007/978-3-319-40367-0_24

29. Sun, L., Wang, W., Wang, M.: Automatic Search of bit-based division property for ARX ciphers and word-based division property. In: Takagi, T., Peyrin, T. (eds.) ASIACRYPT 2017. LNCS, vol. 10624, pp. 128–157. Springer, Cham (2017). https://doi.org/10.1007/978-3-319-70694-8_5

30. Yang, G., Zhu, B., Suder, V., Aagaard, M.D., Gong, G.: The Simeck family of lightweight block ciphers. In: Güneysu, T., Handschuh, H. (eds.) CHES 2015. LNCS, vol. 9293, pp. 307–329. Springer, Heidelberg (2015). https://doi.org/10.1007/978-3-662-48324-4_16

31. Yin, J., et al.: Improved cryptanalysis of an ISO standard lightweight block cipher with refined MILP modelling. In: Chen, X., Lin, D., Yung, M. (eds.) Inscrypt 2017. LNCS, vol. 10726, pp. 404–426. Springer, Cham (2018). https://doi.org/10.1007/978-3-319-75160-3_24

32. Zhang, Y., Sun, S., Cai, J., Hu, L.: Speeding up MILP aided differential character-istic search with Matsui's strategy. In: Chen, L., Manulis, M., Schneider, S. (eds.) ISC 2018. LNCS, vol. 11060, pp. 101–115. Springer, Cham (2018). https://doi.org/10.1007/978-3-319-99136-8_6
33. Zhou, C., Zhang, W., Ding, T., Xiang, Z.: Improving the MILP-based security evaluation algorithms against differential cryptanalysis using divide-and-conquer approach. IACR Cryptol. ePrint Arch. **2019**, 19 (2019)

Improved Related-Tweakey Rectangle Attacks on Reduced-Round Deoxys-BC-384 and Deoxys-I-256-128

Boxin Zhao[1,2], Xiaoyang Dong[3], Keting Jia[4(✉)], and Willi Meier[5]

[1] Key Laboratory of Cryptologic Technology and Information Security (Shandong University), Ministry of Education, Jinan, People's Republic of China
[2] School of Cyber Science and Technology, Shandong University, Jinan, People's Republic of China
boxinzhao@mail.sdu.edu.cn
[3] Institute for Advanced Study, Tsinghua University, Beijing, People's Republic of China
xiaoyangdong@mail.tsinghua.edu.cn
[4] Department of Computer Science and Technology, Tsinghua University, Beijing, People's Republic of China
ktjia@mail.tsinghua.edu.cn
[5] FHNW, Institute ISE, Windisch, Aargau, Switzerland
willimeier48@gmail.com

Abstract. Deoxys-BC is the core internal tweakable block cipher of the authenticated encryption schemes Deoxys-I and Deoxys-II. Deoxys-II is one of the six schemes in the final portfolio of the CAESAR competition, while Deoxys-I is a 3rd round candidate. By well studying the new method proposed by Cid *et al.* at ToSC 2017 and BDT technique proposed by Wang and Peyrin at ToSC 2019, we find a new 11-round related-tweakey boomerang distinguisher of Deoxys-BC-384 with probability of $2^{-118.4}$, and give a related-tweakey rectangle attack on 13-round Deoxys-BC-384 with a data complexity of $2^{125.2}$ and time complexity of $2^{186.7}$, and then apply it to analyze 13-round Deoxys-I-256-128 in this paper. This is the first time that an attack on 13-round Deoxys-I-256-128 is given, while the previous attack on this version only reaches 12 rounds.

Keywords: CAESAR · Authenticated encryption · Deoxys-BC · Rectangle attack

1 Introduction

During recent years, Authenticated encryption (AE) schemes have attracted increasing attention of cryptanalysts all around the world. In addition to assuring the confidentiality and authenticity for messages simultaneously, authenticated encryption also provides security resisting the chosen ciphertext attack. In order to meet the increasing demand for AE schemes, and with the aim to receive

© Springer Nature Switzerland AG 2019
F. Hao et al. (Eds.): INDOCRYPT 2019, LNCS 11898, pp. 139–159, 2019.
https://doi.org/10.1007/978-3-030-35423-7_7

new AE algorithms that can offer advantages over the most widely used AE scheme AES-GCM [1], the CAESAR [2] competition organised by the international cryptologic research community was launched in 2014. In February 2019, the final portfolio for different use cases was announced, only six AE schemes out of the 57 candidates survived.

Deoxys-II [3], which was submitted to CAESAR by Jérémy Jean et al., is one of the six AE schemes listed in the final portfolio. The designers proposed two AE modes as a Deoxys family, i.e., Deoxys-I and Deoxys-II. Deoxys-I is one of the third round candidates and Deoxys-II is in the finalists. Both modes are based on two tweakable block ciphers (TBC) Deoxys-BC-256 or Deoxys-BC-384, which are AES-based designs.

The concept of tweakable block cipher was first invented by Liskov, Rivest and Wagner [4] at CRYPTO 2002. It not only adopts the two standard inputs, the secret key and the plaintext, but also takes a third public element called *tweak*. Most tweakable block ciphers take an existing block cipher as a black box and employ a tweak to change the input/output of the cipher. At ASIACRYPT 2014, Jean, Nikolic and Peyrin [5] introduced a new TWEAKEY framework to construct tweakable block ciphers. They use a unified view of the key and tweak, denoted as *tweakey*, and generate subtweakeys for each round by a key schedule. Deoxys-BC follows the TWEAKEY framework.

Related Work. Since the birth of the Deoxys AE family, there have been many public security evaluation results on both internal tweakable block ciphers Deoxys-BC and the Deoxys AE schemes. At ToSC 2017, Cid et al. [6] introduced a related-tweakey rectangle attack on Deoxys-BC, which was the first third-party analysis for it. They gave a new lower bound on the number of active Sboxes of the differential characteristic, and developed a new method to search related-tweakey boomerang differentials utilizing a Mixed Integer Linear Programming (MILP) model, and launched attacks on Deoxys-BC-256 up to 10 rounds and Deoxys-BC-384 for 13 rounds. In addition, key-recovery attacks on 9-round Deoxys-I-128-128 and 12-round Deoxys-I-256-128 were given. Then, Sasaki [7] improved the boomerang attack with lower complexity by a structural technique. Later, Mehrdad et al. [8] and Zong et al. [9] evaluated Deoxys-BC-256 against impossible differential attacks. Li and Jin [10] gave meet-in-the-middle attacks on Deoxys-BC. At EUROCRYPT 2018, a new technique called Boomerang Connectivity Table (BCT) proposed by Cid et al. [11] was used to increase the probability of the 10-round related-tweakey boomerang distinguisher on Deoxys-BC-384 by a factor of $2^{0.6}$. Later, at ToSC 2019, Wang and Peyrin [12] studied the boomerang switch in multiple rounds and introduced a new technique named Boomerang Difference Table (BDT), and finally they improved the 9-round distinguisher of Deoxys-BC-256 by a factor of $2^{1.6}$.

Our Contribution. In this paper, we focus on the versions of Deoxys-BC-384 and its AE mode Deoxys-I-256-128 against the related-tweakey rectangle attacks. Based on the method proposed in [6], we add some more constraints to the MILP model and obtain a new 11-round related-tweakey boomerang distinguisher of Deoxys-BC-384 with probability 2^{-120}, which has fewer active Sboxes when extending two forward rounds. With the help of the BDT technique, we increase the probability of the distinguisher by a factor of $2^{1.6}$, resulting in a probability of $2^{118.4}$. With the new and more efficient distinguisher, we can append two rounds to the end of the differential trail without activating all the output bytes. Besides, we can guess part of the key bytes involved in the extending two rounds step by step. Finally, we gain an improved related-tweakey rectangle attack on 13-round Deoxys-BC-384 with $2^{125.2}$ chosen plaintexts and $2^{186.7}$ encryptions. Note that the time complexity is reduced by a factor of $2^{83.3}$ when comparing with the best previous work by Cid et al. [6]. Therefore, we could break one more round on a Deoxys AE scheme, Deoxys-I-256-128, to 13 rounds, while the best previous attack could only reach to 12 rounds. We summarize the results of Deoxys-BC-384 and the AE scheme Deoxys-I-256-128 in Table 1.

Table 1. Summary of analysis results of Deoxys-BC-384.

Deoxys-BC-384, "KR" represents key recovery attack							
Rounds	Approach	Goal	Time	Data	Memory	Size set up	Ref.
12/16	Rectangle	KR	2^{127}	2^{127}	2^{125}	$t = 128, k = 256$	[6]
	Boomerang		2^{148}	2^{148}	2^{17}	$t = 128, k = 256$	[7]
	Boomerang		2^{148}	2^{100}	2^{100}	$t = 128, k = 256$	[7]
13/16	Rectangle	KR	2^{270}	2^{127}	2^{144}	$t < 114, k > 270$	[6]
	Boomerang		$2^{191.3}$	2^{125}	2^{136}	$t = 128, k = 256$	[13]
	Rectangle		$2^{186.7}$	$2^{125.2}$	2^{136}	$t = 128, k = 256$	Sect. 6.1
14/16	Rectangle	KR	$2^{286.2}$	2^{127}	2^{136}	$t < 98, k > 286$	[13]
	Rectangle		$2^{282.7}$	$2^{125.2}$	2^{136}	$t < 102, k > 282$	Sect. 6.2
Deoxys-I-256-128							
Rounds	Goal	Key size	Time	Data	Memory	Approach	Ref.
12/16	KR	256	2^{236}	2^{126}	2^{124}	Rectangle	[6]
12/16	KR	256	2^{208}	2^{115}	2^{113}	Rectangle	[13]
13/16	KR	256	$2^{186.7}$	$2^{125.2}$	2^{136}	Rectangle	Sect. 7

Notations. In follows, X_i, Y_i denote the internal states before and after the AddRoundTweakey operation in Round i ($0 \leq i \leq r-1$) of the r-round cipher; Z_i is the state after the ShiftRows ∘ SubBytes operation in Round i; ΔX means the difference of the state X; ∇X is the difference of the state X in the lower part of the boomerang distinguisher; $X_i[j \cdots k]$ is the jth byte, $\cdots$, k^{th} byte of X_i. $IK_i[j]$ is the equivalent key byte in Round i with the same index as $Y_i[j]$.

2 Specifications of Deoxys and Deoxys-BC

Deoxys-BC, including Deoxys-BC-256 and Deoxys-BC-384, is a tweakable block cipher [3]. Both versions of the authenticated encryption scheme Deoxys have

Deoxys-BC as its internal primitive. Deoxys-BC conforms the TWEAKEY framework [5], so besides a plaintext P (or a ciphertext C) and a secret key K, it will take another variable named tweak T as its standard inputs. According to the TWEAKEY framework, the concatenation of the tweak and key can be named a tweakey to provide a unified view. For Deoxys-BC-n ($n = 256, 384$), the length of tweakey is n which is the sum of the size of tweak and key. Both Deoxys-BC-256 and Deoxys-BC-384 have a 128-bit block size, and the size of tweak and key can vary according to users as long as the key size is greater or equal to the block size, i.e. 128 bits. In the following part of this section, we specify the details of the block cipher Deoxys-BC and the authenticated encryption operating modes Deoxys.

Deoxys-BC is an iterative substitution-permutation network (SPN) and adopts an AES-like design. It transforms the initial plaintext through a series of AES [14] round functions to a ciphertext. Different from AES, Deoxys-BC generates the round subkeys by linear operations and doesn't omit the MixColumns operation (defined below) in the last round. Besides, the state of Deoxys-BC is also seen as a 4×4 matrix of bytes, but the index of the 16 bytes is defined as

$$\begin{bmatrix} 0 & 4 & 8 & 12 \\ 1 & 5 & 9 & 13 \\ 2 & 6 & 10 & 14 \\ 3 & 7 & 11 & 15 \end{bmatrix}.$$

The round number r is 14 for Deoxys-BC-256 and 16 for Deoxys-BC-384, respectively. The same to AES, Deoxys-BC transforms the internal state in each round by the following four ordered transformations:

- AddRoundTweakey (AK) - Obtain a new internal state by XOR of the former internal state with the 128-bit round subtweakey, i.e. STK_i in round i ($0 \le i \le r - 1$) defined further below.
- SubBytes (SB) - Apply the 8-bit Sbox **S** of AES to the each byte of the internal state separately.
- ShiftRows (SR) - Rotate the 4 bytes of the j-th ($j \in \{1, 2, 3, 4\}$) row left by $j - 1$ positions.
- MixColumns (MC) - Multiply an invertible 4×4 MDS matrix left to the state.

At the end of the last round, there is an additional AddRoundTweakey operation to obtain the ciphertext.

Definition of the Subtweakeys. The round function is the same as in AES, but different from AES, the key production process of Deoxys-BC is simply composed of linear operations. With the same representation as [3], denote the concatenation of key K and tweak T as KT, *i.e.* the master tweakey $KT = K \parallel T$. For Deoxys-BC-256, the 256-bit tweakey KT is divided into two 128-bit words denoted by TK^1 (most significant) and TK^2. And for Deoxys-BC-384, the 384-bit tweakey is divided into three 128-bit words denoted by TK^1, TK^2 and TK^3. Then a series of 128-bit subtweakeys STK_i will be produced in Round i ($i \ge 0$) used in the AddRoundTweakey operation by $STK_i = TK_i^1 \oplus TK_i^2 \oplus$

RC_i for Deoxys-BC-256, whereas defined as $STK_i = TK_i^1 \oplus TK_i^2 \oplus TK_i^3 \oplus RC_i$ for Deoxys-BC-384. The 128-bit TK_i^1, TK_i^2, TK_i^3 are produced by several fixed linear algorithms or permutations in the tweakey schedule, initialized with $TK_0^1 = TK^1, TK_0^2 = TK^2$ for Deoxys-BC-256, while $TK_0^1 = TK^1, TK_0^2 = TK^2$ and $TK_0^3 = TK^3$ for Deoxys-BC-384. The tweakey schedule algorithm operates as: $TK_{i+1}^1 = h(TK_i^1), TK_{i+1}^2 = LFSR_2(h(TK_i^2)), TK_{i+1}^3 = LFSR_3(h(TK_i^1))$, where h is a linear byte permutation defined by:

$$h = \begin{pmatrix} 0 & 1 & 2 & 3 & 4 & 5 & 6 & 7 & 8 & 9 & 10 & 11 & 12 & 13 & 14 & 15 \\ 1 & 6 & 11 & 12 & 5 & 10 & 15 & 0 & 9 & 14 & 3 & 4 & 13 & 2 & 7 & 8 \end{pmatrix}.$$

The $LFSR_2$ and $LFSR_3$ are two linear feedback shift registers applied to each byte of the internal state. More precisely, the definitions of $LFSR_2$ and $LFSR_3$ are listed in Table 2:

Table 2. The two LFSRs used in Deoxys-BC tweakey schedule.

$LFSR_2$	$(x_7\|\|x_6\|\|x_5\|\|x_4\|\|x_3\|\|x_2\|\|x_1\|\|x_0) \rightarrow (x_6\|\|x_5\|\|x_4\|\|x_3\|\|x_2\|\|x_1\|\|x_0\|\|x_7 \oplus x_5)$
$LFSR_3$	$(x_7\|\|x_6\|\|x_5\|\|x_4\|\|x_3\|\|x_2\|\|x_1\|\|x_0) \rightarrow (x_0 \oplus x_6\|\|x_7\|\|x_6\|\|x_5\|\|x_4\|\|x_3\|\|x_2\|\|x_1)$

Finally, RC_i are the round constants used in the tweakey schedule. For more clarity, we give an instantiation of the framework of Deoxys-BC-384 in Fig. 1.

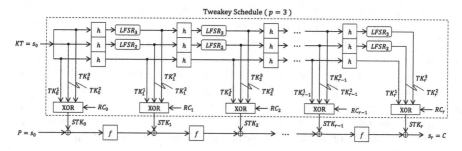

Fig. 1. Tweakey schedule and encryption process of Deoxys-BC-384 [6].

The Authenticated Encryption Deoxys. Utilizing the tweakable block cipher Deoxys-BC as its internal primitive, Deoxys provides two AE modes named Deoxys-I and Deoxys-II. The two modes are both nonce-based AEAD, but Deoxys-I is assumed to be nonce-respecting for the adversary, meaning that the same nonce N can not be used twice for the same key in encryption. This variant is similar to TAE [15]. While Deoxys-II adopts a nonce-misuse setting that allows users to reuse the same N under the same key.

When employing Deoxys-BC-256 as their internal primitive, the two AE modes, Deoxys-I-128-128 and Deoxys-II-128-128, lead to a 128-bit key version. While when based on Deoxys-BC-384, Deoxys-I-256-128 and Deoxys-II-256-128 are two 256-key variants. With the parameters given in [3], there is a 4-bit prefix for the tweak input to represent the different types of encryption/authentication blocks. Therefore, the adversary can not get more than 2^{124} plaintext-ciphertext pairs with the same key.

3   The Boomerang Attack and Rectangle Attack

The boomerang attack, proposed by Wagner [16] in 1999, is an adaptive chosen-plaintext or chosen-ciphertext differential attack that allows adversary to connect two short differential paths to get a longer distinguisher. After an adaptive chosen plaintext and ciphertext process, adversary can get a quartet structure by exploiting the two shorter differentials.

The attacker treats the whole encryption process $E(\cdot)$ as a decomposition of two sub-ciphers $E = E_1 \circ E_0$, where E_0 represents the upper part and E_1 denotes the lower half of the cipher. For the sub-cipher E_0, there exists a short differential characteristic $\alpha \to \beta$ with probability p, and there exists a differential characteristic $\gamma \to \delta$ over E_1 with probability q. With the assumption that the two differentials are independent, the adversary can get a boomerang distinguisher with property:

$$Pr[E^{-1}(E(m) \oplus \delta) \oplus E^{-1}(E(m \oplus \alpha) \oplus \delta) = \alpha] = p^2 q^2. \tag{1}$$

Thus, a correct plaintext quartet $(m, m', \bar{m}, \bar{m}')$ with the corresponding ciphertext $(c, c', \bar{c}, \bar{c}')$ can be generated with a probability of $p^2 q^2$ that meets the conditions $m \oplus m' = \alpha$, $c \oplus \bar{c} = \delta$, $c' \oplus \bar{c}' = \delta$, $\bar{m} \oplus \bar{m}' = \alpha$. If $p^2 q^2 > 2^{-n}$, we can distinguish E from an ideal cipher.

A variant of boomerang attack called amplified boomerang attack [17] or rectangle attack [18] only needs chosen plaintexts. In the amplified boomerang attack, one could find a right quartet with probability of $2^{-n} p^2 q^2$ while for an ideal cipher the probability is 2^{-2n}. At EUROCRYPT 2001, Biham et al. [18] proposed the rectangle attack, where only the differences α and δ are fixed, and any of the possible values of β and γ except $\beta \neq \gamma$ are considered. The probability of obtaining a correct quartet can be increased to $2^{-n} \hat{p}^2 \hat{q}^2$, where n is the size of state, and

$$\hat{p} = \sqrt{\sum_{\beta_i} Pr^2(\alpha \to \beta_i)} \quad and \quad \hat{q} = \sqrt{\sum_{\gamma_j} Pr^2(\gamma_j \to \delta)}.$$

At EUROCRYPT 2005, Biham *et al.* [19] proposed the related-key boomerang and rectangle attack. Different from the single-key attack, each plaintext in a quartet $(m, m', \bar{m}, \bar{m}')$ will be encrypted under different keys. Denote them by K_1, K_2, K_3 and K_4 respectively. Assume there exists a related-key differential $\alpha \to \beta$ over E_0 under a key difference ΔK with probability p and a related-key differential $\gamma \to \delta$ over E_1 under a key difference ∇K with probability q. With the related-key rectangle distinguisher, one finds a right quartet $(m, m', \bar{m}, \bar{m}')$ as follows shown in Fig. 2:

1. Randomly choose a plaintext m and compute another plaintext m' by $m' = m \oplus \alpha$, then make queries to the encryption oracle to get the corresponding ciphertexts c and c' under K_1 and K_2 respectively, i.e. $c = E_{K_1}(m), c' = E_{K_2}(m')$.
2. Randomly choose another plaintext $\bar{m}$ and get the plaintext $\bar{m}'$ by $\bar{m}' = \bar{m} \oplus \alpha$, then make queries to the encryption oracle to get the corresponding ciphertexts $\bar{c}$ and $\bar{c}'$ under K_3 and K_4 respectively, i.e. $\bar{c} = E_{K_3}(\bar{m}), \bar{c}' = E_{K_4}(\bar{m}')$.
3. Check whether both the constraints $c \oplus \bar{c} = \delta$ and $c' \oplus \bar{c}' = \delta$ are satisfied. If yes, a correct quartet $(m, m', \bar{m}, \bar{m}')$ is obtained, otherwise go to step 1 for other plaintexts.

Note that if any one of the K_i $(i = 1, 2, 3, 4)$ such as K_1 is known, all other keys can be computed by $K_2 = K_1 \oplus \Delta K$, $K_3 = K_1 \oplus \nabla K$, $K_4 = K_1 \oplus \Delta K \oplus \nabla K$.

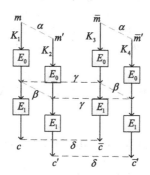

Fig. 2. Related-key rectangle attack framework.

4   The Boomerang Difference Table (BDT)

At EUROCRYPT 2018, a new technique called Boomerang Connectivity Table (BCT) proposed by Cid et al. [11] was used to increase the probability of the 10-round related-tweakey boomerang distinguisher on Deoxys-BC-384 by a factor of $2^{0.6}$. Later, at ToSC 2019, Wang and Peyrin [12] studied the boomerang switch in multiple rounds and introduced a new technique named Boomerang Difference Table (BDT), and finally they improved the 9-round distinguisher of Deoxys-BC-256 by a factor of $2^{1.6}$. Since our paper is highly related to the BDT technique, we briefly recall it in this section.

Definition 1. *Boomerang Difference Table (BDT) [12]. Let S be an invertible function which is from $\mathbb{F}_2^n$ to $\mathbb{F}_2^n$, and a 3-tuple $(\Delta_0, \Delta_1, \nabla_0) \in \mathbb{F}_2^n$. The boomerang difference table (BDT) of S is a three-dimensional table, in which each 3-tuple entry $(\Delta_0, \Delta_1, \nabla_0)$ can be computed by*

$$BDT(\Delta_0, \Delta_1, \nabla_0) = \#\{x \in \{(0,1)\}^n | S^{-1}(S(x) \oplus \nabla_0) \oplus S^{-1}(S(x \oplus \Delta_0) \oplus \nabla_0)$$
$$= \Delta_0, S(x) \oplus S(x \oplus \Delta_0) = \Delta_1\}.$$

(2)

To make the description more clear, the generation of boomerang difference table (BDT) can be visualized in Fig. 3.

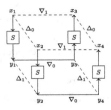

Fig. 3. Generation of a right quartet at the Sbox level [12].

Definition 2. *BDT' [12]. When the boomerang returns back, decryption operation will be considered first. The difference ∇_1 of the Sbox determines the differential characteristic in the backward rounds. Therefore, a variants of BDT called BDT' that takes into account a 3-tuple $(\nabla_0, \nabla_1, \Delta_0)$ can be obtained by*

$$BDT'(\nabla_0, \nabla_1, \Delta_0) = \#\{x \in \{(0,1)\}^n | S(S^{-1}(x) \oplus \Delta_0) \oplus S(S^{-1}(x \oplus \nabla_0) \oplus \Delta_0)$$
$$= \nabla_0, S^{-1}(x) \oplus S^{-1}(x \oplus \nabla_0) = \nabla_1\}.$$

$$(3)$$

Application in Two-round Boomerang Switch. In the two-round boomerang switch, we can only consider the two Sbox layers (SL) and the linear layer (R) in between, which is illustrated in Fig. 4.

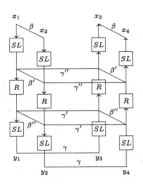

Fig. 4. A 2-round switch which only considers two Sbox layers and one linear layer [12].

When analyzing the two-round boomerang switch, the BDT will be applied to the first Sbox layer and the BDT' will be applied to the second one. Denote the probability of the two Sbox layers by p_1 and p_2, respectively. They can be computed by

$$p_1 = \prod_{(\Delta_0, \Delta_1, \nabla_0) \in L_1} BDT(\Delta_0, \Delta_1, \nabla_0)/2^n, \tag{4}$$

$$p_2 = \prod_{(\nabla_0, \nabla_1, \Delta_0) \in L_2} BDT'(\nabla_0, \nabla_1, \Delta_0)/2^n, \tag{5}$$

where L_1 and L_2 contain the 3-tuple difference of the Sbox in $(\beta, \beta', \gamma'')$ and $(\gamma, \gamma', \beta'')$, respectively.

Given the truncated differential pattern, there might exist three cases for the 2-round boomerang switch as follows:

- There is no active Sbox at the same position in both Sbox layers: the probability can be computed only by DDT.
- There are active Sboxes at the same position in only one of the two Sbox layers: we can use BDT to compute the probability for this Sbox layer.
- There are active Sboxes at the same position in both of the two Sbox layers. BDT will be applied to both of them but we must check the compatibility.

In [12], they specify the processes how to compute the probability for the 2-round boomerang switch. For more details, we refer to [12].

5   New Related Tweakey Distinguisher of Deoxys-BC-384

5.1   Searching Truncated Differentials by MILP Model

In this subsection, we simply describe the method proposed by Cid et al. [6] to search truncated differentials by MILP model. For simplicity, we omit the numerous inequality constraints. Let x_i, stk_i, y_i denote the activeness of a state byte before the AddRoundTweakey operation, the subtweakey byte, and the state byte after the AddRoundTweakey operation, respectively.

In the AddRoundTweakey operation, we only need to exclude all the solutions of $x_i + stk_i + y_i = 1$, and record the number of cancellations between x_i and stk_i in each column which can be denoted by c. For the MixColumns operation, we only need to guarantee that the branch number is at least 5. Cid et al. also introduced d to denote the degrees of freedom in the MILP model. If a, b are the number of active bytes before the MixColumns operation and inactive bytes after the MixColumns operation in each column, then this column will consume $-(a - b - c)$ degrees only when $(a - b - c) < 0$. If $stk_i = 0$ but $stk_{16+h(i)} > 0$ or $stk_{-16+h^{-1}(i)} > 0$, another degree consumption occurs. Suppose the number of active bytes in subtweakey of i-th round is $d_i(i = 1, 2, 3 \cdots)$, then the total degrees that could be consumed are $d = 3 \cdot \max\{d_1, d_2, d_3, ...\}$ in Deoxys-BC-384. Taking all the former constraints into account, when the sum of the degree consumption is smaller than the total degrees d, a truncated related-tweakey differential is obtained by the MILP model. By generating the MILP model for the upper part and lower part, respectively, and adding some connection constraints between them, a truncated related-tweakey boomerang differential can be obtained. For more details, we refer to [6].

Inspired by the MILP method proposed in [20], we add two more rounds of constraints to the MILP model. Here, we will specify the details of the extra constraints.

- **For the first extra round.** When processing a related-key boomerang or rectangle attack under a specific characteristic, the differences at the end of the characteristic are known. Therefore, the differences before the SubBytes operation can be deduced, and the cancellation may occur in the AddRoundKey operation. Thus when we treat them as truncated differences, the constraints on the AddRoundKey operation are the same as those in [6]. However, the differences after the SubBytes operation will be unknown, the branches of the MixColumns operation will be not 5, all the four output bytes of a column under the MixColumns operation will be active if any input byte of the column is active. Let Boolean variables $(y_i, y_{i+1}, y_{i+2}, y_{i+3})$ denote the activeness of the input 4-byte of MixColumns operation and $(x_i, x_{i+1}, x_{i+2}, x_{i+3})$ denote the activeness of the output 4-byte, then the constraints are as follows:

$$d_k - y_i \geq 0, \ d_k - y_{i+1} \geq 0, \ d_k - y_{i+2} \geq 0, \ d_k - y_{i+3} \geq 0,$$

$$y_i + y_{i+1} + y_{i+2} + y_{i+3} - d_k \geq 0,$$

$$x_i - d_k = 0, \ x_{i+1} - d_k = 0, \ x_{i+2} - d_k = 0, \ x_{i+3} - d_k = 0,$$

where d_k is a dummy variable so that $d_k = 0$ only when $y_i, y_{i+1}, y_{i+2}, y_{i+3}$ are all zero.

- **For the second extra round.** When processing the specific attack, the differences at the start of the second extended round are unknown, and cancellation can not occur in the AddRoundKey operation, *i.e.* for the Boolean variables (x_i, stk_i, y_i) that $x_i \oplus stk_i = y_i$, y_i must be active if x_i or stk_i are active. The constraints are different from those in [6] and expressed as

$$y_i - x_i \geq 0, \quad y_i - stk_i \geq 0, \quad x_i + stk_i - y_i \geq 0.$$

Since we omit the last MixColumns operation in the key recovery attacks, there are no constraints for it.

At the end of the MILP model, we add a group of extra constraints to constrain the number of active columns. Let Boolean variables $(x_i, x_{i+1}, \cdots, x_{i+15})$ denote the activeness of the 16 bytes after the SubBytes operation, we will constrain the number of the active columns being not bigger than 3 as:

$$d_k - y_{4k+i} \geq 0, \ d_k - y_{4k+i+1} \geq 0, \ d_k - y_{4k+i+2} \geq 0, \ d_k - y_{4k+i+3} \geq 0,$$

$$y_{4k+i} + y_{4k+i+1} + y_{4k+i+2} + y_{4k+i+3} - d_k \geq 0,$$

for $k \in \{0, 1, 2, 3\}$ and

$$d_0 + d_1 + d_2 + d_3 \leq 3.$$

5.2   The Method of Deriving Paths Given the Truncated Differential

Given the truncated differential of Deoxys-BC, we can search the detailed differential paths in two steps:

1. Deduce all the master tweakey differences that satisfy the truncated differential;
2. For each master tweakey difference, check the compatibility by the MixColumns operation and the difference distribution table (DDT) of Sbox.

We specify the process to get the path listed in Table 4.

Deduce the Tweakey Difference. We first deduce the master tweakey difference from the truncated differential shown in Table 4, where we just ignore the concrete values of the bytes and only care for the activeness or inactiveness of the bytes.

We first consider the upper part of Table 4, and note that we convert all the constraints in the differential into the constraints of the 3 tweakeys ΔTK_1^1, ΔTK_1^2 and ΔTK_1^3 in the 1st round. According to Table 4 and the definition of degree of freedom in Cid et $al.$ [6], we get the knowledge that there are totally 15 active bytes in the 3 tweakeys ΔTK_1^1, ΔTK_1^2 and ΔTK_1^3. We find that the indices of the five active bytes in ΔSTK_1 are $\{6, 9, 12, 13, 15\}$. According to the h permutation of the tweakey schedule, the active bytes will shift to $\Delta STK_2[1, 8, 3, 12, 6]$, respectively. However, all the active bytes are canceled in ΔSTK_2. Similarly, we could get the indices in Table 3, which the active bytes in ΔSTK_1 will shift to in the following 7 rounds. Note that, the indices in red mean inactive bytes, where the differences are canceled.

Table 3. The index of subtweakey difference.

Round	Index				
1	6	9	12	13	15
2	1	8	3	12	6
3	0	15	10	3	1
4	7	6	5	10	0
5	14	1	4	5	7
6	9	0	11	4	14
7	8	7	2	11	9

In Table 3, the active byte $\Delta STK_1[6]$ will be canceled in $\Delta STK_2[1]$ in the 2nd round and $\Delta STK_5[14]$ in the 5-th round. According to the tweakey schedule, we deduce the following equations for ΔTK_1^1, ΔTK_1^2 and ΔTK_1^3:

$$\Delta TK_1^1[6] \oplus LFSR_2^1(\Delta TK_1^2[6]) \oplus LFSR_3^1(\Delta TK_1^3[6]) = 0,$$
$$\Delta TK_1^1[6] \oplus LFSR_2^4(\Delta TK_1^2[6]) \oplus LFSR_3^4(\Delta TK_1^3[6]) = 0,$$

where $\Delta TK_j^i[k]$ means the k-th byte of ΔTK_j^i, $i \in \{0, 1, 2\}$ in j-th round, and $LFSR_i^j$, $i \in \{2, 3\}$ means executing the linear operation $LFSR_i$ for j times successively. Similarly, we can also write two equations for each of the other four indices as:

$$\Delta TK_1^1[9] \oplus LFSR_2^1(\Delta TK_1^2[9]) \oplus LFSR_3^1(\Delta TK_1^3[9]) = 0,$$
$$\Delta TK_1^1[9] \oplus LFSR_2^4(\Delta TK_1^2[9]) \oplus LFSR_3^4(\Delta TK_1^3[9]) = 0,$$

$$\Delta TK_1^1[12] \oplus LFSR_2^1(\Delta TK_1^2[12]) \oplus LFSR_3^1(\Delta TK_1^3[12]) = 0,$$
$$\Delta TK_1^1[12] \oplus LFSR_2^5(\Delta TK_1^2[12]) \oplus LFSR_3^5(\Delta TK_1^3[12]) = 0,$$

$$\Delta TK_1^1[13] \oplus LFSR_2^1(\Delta TK_1^2[13]) \oplus LFSR_3^1(\Delta TK_1^3[13]) = 0,$$
$$\Delta TK_1^1[13] \oplus LFSR_2^3(\Delta TK_1^2[13]) \oplus LFSR_3^3(\Delta TK_1^3[13]) = 0,$$

$$\Delta TK_1^1[15] \oplus LFSR_2^1(\Delta TK_1^2[15]) \oplus LFSR_3^1(\Delta TK_1^3[15]) = 0,$$
$$\Delta TK_1^1[15] \oplus LFSR_2^2(\Delta TK_1^2[15]) \oplus LFSR_3^2(\Delta TK_1^3[15]) = 0.$$

Totally, we can get ten equations for ΔTK_1^1, ΔTK_1^2 and ΔTK_1^3 by the cancellations of the differences in the subtweakeys.

Besides, we can also get some equations by the cancellations between the differences in the internal state and subtweakey. For example, as shown in Fig. 4, at the end of the 4-th round and the start of the 5-th round, the second column of the internal state is transformed in truncated form as:

$$(1,0,0,1) \xrightarrow{\text{MC}} (1,1,0,1) \xrightarrow[\oplus(1,1,0,1)]{\text{AK}} (0,0,0,0),$$

which means, the second column of ΔSTK_5 is equal to the second column of ΔX_5 in 5-th round. By looking up in Table 3, the three bytes of ΔSTK_5 are corresponding to byte $12, 13, 15$ of ΔSTK_1. By utilizing the MC^{-1} operation, we can get the following equations:

$$09 \cdot \Delta STK_5[4] \oplus 0e \cdot \Delta STK_5[5] \oplus 0d \cdot \Delta STK_5[7] = 0,$$
$$0d \cdot \Delta STK_5[4] \oplus 09 \cdot \Delta STK_5[5] \oplus 0b \cdot \Delta STK_5[7] = 0,$$

where

$$\Delta STK_5[4] = \Delta TK_1^1[12] \oplus LFSR_2^4(\Delta TK_1^2[12]) \oplus LFSR_3^4(\Delta TK_1^3[12]),$$
$$\Delta STK_5[5] = \Delta TK_1^1[13] \oplus LFSR_2^4(\Delta TK_1^2[13]) \oplus LFSR_3^4(\Delta TK_1^3[13]),$$
$$\Delta STK_5[7] = \Delta TK_1^1[15] \oplus LFSR_2^4(\Delta TK_1^2[15]) \oplus LFSR_3^4(\Delta TK_1^3[15]).$$

Similarly, we can obtain another two equations by the second column in 4-th round as:

$$03 \cdot \Delta STK_4[5] \oplus \Delta STK_4[6] = 0,$$
$$02 \cdot \Delta STK_4[6] = 0 \oplus \Delta STK_4[7] = 0,$$

where

$$\Delta STK_4[5] = \Delta TK_1^1[12] \oplus LFSR_2^3(\Delta TK_1^2[12]) \oplus LFSR_3^3(\Delta TK_1^3[12]),$$
$$\Delta STK_4[6] = \Delta TK_1^1[9] \oplus LFSR_2^3(\Delta TK_1^2[9]) \oplus LFSR_3^3(\Delta TK_1^3[9]),$$
$$\Delta STK_4[7] = \Delta TK_1^1[6] \oplus LFSR_2^3(\Delta TK_1^2[6]) \oplus LFSR_3^3(\Delta TK_1^3[6]).$$

With the above 14 equations for ΔTK_1^1, ΔTK_1^2 and ΔTK_1^3, since there are only 15 active bytes in ΔTK_1^1, ΔTK_1^2 and ΔTK_1^3, we can deduce 256 concrete values for ΔTK_1^1, ΔTK_1^2 and ΔTK_1^3.

Search for the Differential Path with the Highest Probability. For each value of ΔTK_1^1, ΔTK_1^2 and ΔTK_1^3, the subtweakey differences in any round can be computed since the key schedule is linear. Then the difference of every byte of the internal states is determined by combining the truncated differential: when the cancellation occurs between state bytes and subtweakey difference, the state difference is equal to the subtweakey difference; the other bytes can be computed by **MC** and **MC**$^{-1}$ operation.

Since the input and output differences of the SubBytes operation in each round are all known, it will be easy to verify the compatibility of the differential path by the difference distribution table (DDT) of Sbox. Note that there exist 6 active Sboxes in the upper part, and each input-output difference pair could pass the DDT of a Sbox with probability about 2^{-1} (the entry of the DDT is not zero). So only 4 values out of the 256 values for ΔTK_1^1, ΔTK_1^2 and ΔTK_1^3 are expected to survive from the verification. Finally, we find three 7-round differential paths having the probability 2^{-42}, and the other one is of probability 2^{-41}. The differential paths of the lower part can be deduced in similar process, and we omit it.

5.3 Computing the Accurate Probability of the Distinguisher by BDT

As shown in Table 4, $\Delta Y_6[0] = 0x9a$ in the upper part and $\nabla Z_7[0] = 0x1f$ in the lower part of the boomerang distinguisher are known. Therefore, $\Delta_0 = \Delta Y_6[0] = 0x9a$ used in BDT and $\nabla_0 = \nabla Z_7[0] = 0x1f$ used in BDT$'$ are know. So we can get the differential characteristic in the 2 switch rounds by the following step:

- Step 1. As shown in Fig. 3, in BDT, we fix $\Delta_0 = \Delta Y_6[0] = 0x9a$ in BDT, traverse all the values of $\nabla_0 = \nabla Z_6[0]$ and obtain all the 3-tuples $(0x9a, \Delta_1, \nabla_0)$ whose corresponding entry in BDT is greater than 0, where $\Delta_1 = \Delta Z_6[0]$.
- Step 2. For each tuple we obtained, $\Delta_1 = \Delta Z_6[0]$ and $\nabla_0 = \nabla Z_6[0]$ are known, therefore $\Delta Y_7[0]$ can be deduced. Hence, the value of $\Delta_0 = \Delta Y_7[0]$ used in BDT$'$ is known, so we can construct BDT$'$ with the fixed Δ_0.
- Step 3. In the BDT$'$, extract all the 3-tuples $(0x1f, \nabla_1, \Delta_0)$ whose entry in BDT$'$ obtained in step 2 is greater than 0, and $\nabla_1 = \nabla Y_7[0]$ in lower part will be determined.

In total, we get two differential characteristics in the 2-round switch, which are listed in Tables 4 and 5. In Table 4, the entry for $(0x9a, 0xdb, 0x23)$ in the BDT is 4 which gives probability 2^{-6}, and the entry for $(0x1f, 0xad, 0xad)$ in the BDT' is 2 which results in the probability 2^{-7}. Therefore, probability of the switch is 2^{-13}. For the other differential characteristic listed in Table 5, the entries for $(0x9a, 0xbf, 0xbf)$ in the BDT and the entries for $(0x1f, 0x65, 0x65)$ in the BDT' are all 2, which has probability 2^{-14}. So the switching probability in round 6 and 7 is $2^{-13} + 2^{-14} = 2^{-12.4}$, and the total probability of the boomerang distinguisher is $2^{118.4}$.

Experimental Verification. We used 2^{20} data and iterated it for 1000 times for randomly chosen plaintexts and keys for the 2-round switch. And the result shows that the average probability of obtaining a right quartet is $2^{12.4}$.

5.4   The Advantage of Our New Distinguisher

We have well studied the paper of Cid *et al.* [6], and since the difference δ in the 11-round distinguisher is $\delta = (00\ 00\ 00\ 00\ 00\ 00\ 00\ 00\ 00\ 00\ 00\ 00\ 08\ 00\ 7f\ 00)$, if we append two rounds at the end of the distinguisher, all of the 16 bytes shown in Fig. 5.

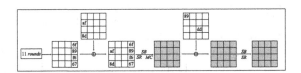

Fig. 5. Appending two rounds for Cid et al.'s 11-round distinguisher of Deoxys-BC-384.

Based on the method proposed in [6] and BDT technique in [12], we find a new 11-round boomerang distinguisher of Deoxys-BC-384 with the probability of $2^{-118.4}$, which holds with higher probability than that in [6]. More impressively, it is more effective to recover the key, since the only active column at the end of the path is $(9e, 1d, 00, 00)$, and it will become $(00, a4, 83, a4)$ after the MixColumns operation. If we append two rounds to the end of the trail, there are only 12 active bytes after the SubBytes operation in the last round as illustrated in Fig. 6. This helps us mount a 13-round related-tweakey rectangle attack on Deoxys-BC-384 with $\leq 2^{124}$ queries under the same key and time complexity $\leq 2^{256}$. Hence, it leads to the first 13-round attack on the corresponding AE scheme Deoxys-I-256-128, which are given in the following section.

Table 4. New 11-round distinguisher of `Deoxys-BC-384`. The probabilities marked with † are only spent once.

$$\Delta TK_0^1 : \texttt{00 00 00 00 00 00 8b 00 00 c4 00 00 a6 7a 00 c5}$$
$$\Delta TK_0^2 : \texttt{00 00 00 00 00 00 ad 00 00 c4 00 00 d8 73 00 21}$$
$$\Delta TK_0^3 : \texttt{00 00 00 00 00 00 a3 00 00 9a 00 00 2e 3b 00 0d}$$
$$\nabla TK_0^1 : \texttt{00 00 00 00 00 00 00 51 00 00 ea 00 00 00 00 00}$$
$$\nabla TK_0^2 : \texttt{00 00 00 00 00 00 00 f0 00 00 74 00 00 00 00 00}$$
$$\nabla TK_0^3 : \texttt{00 00 00 00 00 00 00 e6 00 00 7d 00 00 00 00 00}$$

R	ΔX	ΔK	ΔY	ΔZ	pr
1	00 00 00 50 00 00 9a 32 00 85 00 00 00 00 00 e9	00 00 00 50 00 00 9a 32 00 85 00 00 00 00 00 e9	00 00 00 00 00 00 00 00 00 00 00 00 00 00 00 00	00 00 00 00 00 00 00 00 00 00 00 00 00 00 00 00	1
2	00 00 00 00 00 00 00 00 00 00 00 00 00 00 00 00	00 00 00 00 00 00 00 00 00 00 00 00 00 00 00 00	00 00 00 00 00 00 00 00 00 00 00 00 00 00 00 00	00 00 00 00 00 00 00 00 00 00 00 00 00 00 00 00	1
3	00 00 00 00 00 00 00 00 00 00 00 00 00 00 00 00	57 00 00 00 00 00 00 00 00 00 4f 00 7a 00 00 f1	57 00 00 00 00 00 00 00 00 00 4f 00 7a 00 00 f1	6b 00 00 00 00 00 00 00 2a 00 00 00 15 a6 00 00	2^{-28}
4	e9 a6 00 00 00 a6 00 00 00 f1 00 00 bd 57 00 00	e9 00 00 00 00 a6 00 00 00 f1 00 00 00 57 00 00	00 a6 00 00 00 00 00 00 00 00 00 00 bd 00 00 00	00 2b 00 00 00 00 00 00 00 00 00 00 00 19 00 00	2^{-13}
5	00 4f 00 00 00 32 00 00 00 00 00 00 00 4f 00 00	00 4f 00 00 00 32 00 00 00 00 00 00 00 4f 00 00	00 00 00 00 00 00 00 00 00 00 00 00 00 00 00 00	00 00 00 00 00 00 00 00 00 00 00 00 00 00 00 00	1
6	00 00 00 00 00 00 00 00 00 00 00 00 00 00 00 00	9a 34 00 00 00 00 85 00 00 00 00 b9 00 00 00 00	9a 34 00 00 00 00 85 00 00 00 00 b9 00 00 00 00	db 00 00 00 00 00 00 00 00 00 00 00	2^{-6} †

7	ad 00 00
	db 00 00
	db 00 00
	76 00 00
		00 00 1b 00
		00 00 08 00
		50 00 00 00
		00 13 09 00
			ad 00
			    00
			00 00
			  00
				00
				  00
				00 00
				00
					1

6			00
			   00
			     00
			00
				23 00
				d2 00
				60 00
				e6 00
					1

7	ad 00 da 00 00 00 00 00	00 00 da 00 00 00 00 00	ad 00 00 00 00 00 00 00 00 00 00	1f 00 00 00 00 00 00 00 00 00 00	2^{-7} †
8	8a 00 00 00 00 00 00 00 00 00 00 00 21 00 00 00	8a 00 00 00 00 00 00 00 00 00 00 00 21 00 00 00	00 00 00 00 00 00 00 00 00 00 00 00 00 00 00 00	00 00 00 00 00 00 00 00 00 00 00 00 00 00 00 00	1
9	00 00 00 00 00 00 00 00 00 00 00 00 00 00 00 00	00 00 00 00 00 00 00 00 00 00 00 00 00 00 00 00	00 00 00 00 00 00 00 00 00 00 00 00 00 00 00 00	00 00 00 00 00 00 00 00 00 00 00 00 00 00 00 00	1
10	00 00 00 00 00 00 00 00 00 00 00 00 00 00 00 00	00 00 00 00 00 00 00 00 00 00 00 00 00 00 00 00	00 00 00 00 00 00 00 00 00 00 00 00 00 00 00 00	00 00 00 00 00 00 00 00 00 00 00·00 00 00 00 00	1
11	00 00 00 00 00 00 00 00 00 00 00 00 00 00 00 00	00 21 00 00 00 00 8a 00 00 00 00 00 00 00 00 00	00 21 00 00 00 00 8a 00 00 00 00 00 00 00 00 00	00 9e 00 00 00 1d 00 00 00 00 00 00 00 00 00 00	2^{-12}

Table 5. Another 2-round switch for round 6 to 7. The probabilities marked with †
are only spent once.

R	ΔX	ΔK	ΔY	ΔZ	pr
6	00 00 00 00 00 00 00 00 00 00 00 00 00 00 00 00	9a 34 00 00 00 00 85 00 00 00 00 b9 00 00 00 00	9a 34 00 00 00 00 85 00 00 00 00 b9 00 00 00 00	bf 00 00 00 00 00 00 00 00 00 00 00	2^{-7} †
7	65 00 00 bf 00 00 bf 00 00 da 00 00	00 00 1b 00 00 00 08 00 50 00 00 00 00 13 09 00	65 00 00 00 00 00	00 00 00 00 00 00 00 00	1
6			00 00 00 00	bf 00 00 00 bf 00 bf 00	1
7	65 00 da 00 00 00 00 00	00 00 da 00 00 00 00 00	65 00 00 00 00 00 00 00 00 00 00	1f 00 00 00 00 00 00 00 00 00 00	2^{-7} †

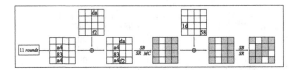

Fig. 6. Appending two rounds for our 11-round distinguisher of Deoxys-BC-384.

6   Rectangle Attack on Round-Reduced Deoxys-BC-384

6.1   Attack on 13-Round Deoxys-BC-384

Different from AES, Deoxys-BC does not omit the MixColumns operation in the
last round. However, as MixColumns is a linear operation, the attacker can get
the same differential cryptanalysis result by deleting it in the last round. For the
sake of simplicity, we omit the MixColumns operation in the last round.

Based on the new distinguisher listed in Tables 4 and 5, we construct a 13-
round related-tweakey rectangle attack on Deoxys-BC by extending two rounds
at the end of the 11-round trail, which is illustrated in Fig. 7. The upper
part of the trail through E_0 is under the related key $\Delta K = \{\Delta TK_0^1, \Delta TK_0^2,$
$\Delta TK_0^3\}$, and the lower part through E_1 is under the related key $\nabla K =$
$\{\nabla TK_0^1, \nabla TK_0^2, \nabla TK_0^3\}$.

As we can see from Tables 4 and 5 and Fig. 7, the initial difference of the
rectangle distinguisher is $\alpha = (00\ 00\ 00\ 00\ 00\ 00\ 85\ 00\ 00\ 9a\ 00\ 00\ 50\ 32\ 00\ e9)$,
and the final difference is $\delta = (00\ 00\ 00\ 00\ 9e\ 1d\ 00\ 00\ 00\ 00\ 00\ 00\ 00\ 00\ 00\ 00)$.
After two-round transition, difference δ will propagate to

$$\eta = (*\ 00\ *\ *\ 00\ *\ *\ *\ *\ *\ *\ 00\ *\ *\ 00\ *)$$

where '*' means active but unknown bytes, and note that there are four inactive
bytes in difference η. We follow the generalized related-key rectangle attacks on
block ciphers with linear key schedule that was proposed in [21], the detailed
attack process is as follows:

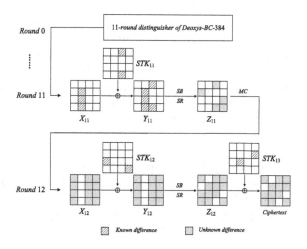

Fig. 7. Key-recovery attack against 13-round Deoxys-BC-384.

Data Collection. Randomly choose 2^t plaintext pairs (m, m') such that they all satisfy $m \oplus m' = \alpha$, where $\alpha = (00\ 00\ 00\ 00\ 00\ 00\ 85\ 00\ 00\ 9a\ 00\ 00\ 50\ 32\ 00\ e9)$. For all the 2^t plaintext pairs, we make queries to the encryption oracle under K_1 and K_2 respectively, so that we can receive the corresponding ciphertext pairs (c, c'), i.e. every plaintext-ciphertext pair (m, m', c, c') is computed by $c = E_{K_1}(m), c' = E_{K_2}(m')$.

Figure 7 shows that there are four zero-difference bytes in the ciphertext pair ($\Delta c[1, 4, 11, 14] = 0$), and since the goal of `Data Collection` is to collect quartets $(c, c', \bar{c}, \bar{c}')$ following the same form as η, i.e. the bytes $1, 4, 11, 14$ of $c \oplus \bar{c}$ and $c' \oplus \bar{c}'$ are all zeros. So we can insert all the elements formed by (m, m', c, c') into a hash table H indexed from 0 to $2^{64} - 1$ by 8 bytes $(c[1, 4, 11, 14], c'[1, 4, 11, 14])$.

Then for each of the 2^t plaintext pairs, denoted by $(\bar{m}, \bar{m}')$, we make queries to the encryption oracle under K_3 and K_4 respectively to get the corresponding ciphertext pair $(\bar{c}, \bar{c}')$. The required quartets are obtained, where the 8-byte difference of $\bar{c} \| \bar{c}'$ and $c \| c'$ have the same value, by looking up the hash table. As a result of 2^{64} indices, there will remain $2^t \cdot (2^t \cdot 2^{-64}) = 2^{2t-64}$ quartets.

Key Recovery. As we can see from the Fig. 7, in the partial computation from ciphertext to Y_{11}, there are totally 17 bytes of subkeys being involved including 12 bytes of STK_{13} and 5 bytes of equivalent keys of STK_{12}. Guessing all the possible values of the 17 bytes of subkeys simultaneously will cost much time complexity. Therefore, we guess partial involved keys step by step.

Firstly, we should initialize a list of 2^{136} counters, where each index means a corresponding guessed 136-bit value. Then for each of the 2^{2t-64} remaining quartets $(c, c', \bar{c}, \bar{c}')$, the detailed key recovery proceeds as follows.

1. Note that there are three zero-difference bytes in the first column of ΔZ_{11}, so guessing the involved keys from ciphertext to the first column of Y_{12} may be a wise choice.

   For each of the guessed 2^8 values of $STK_{13}[0]$, both the value and difference of $Y_{12}[10]$ can be deduced by $(c, \bar{c})$. Since there are three known zero-difference bytes in the first column of ΔZ_{11}, $\Delta Y_{12}[1, 2, 3]$ can be computed utilizing the property of the MixColumns operation[1]. Besides, the difference values of $\Delta Z_{12}[7, 10, 13]$ that are equal to the difference of ciphertext pair $(c, \bar{c})$ are known. With the input and output differences of the SBoxes being known, we can get the corresponding value of $STK_{13}[7, 10, 13]$. Then partially decrypt $(c', \bar{c}')$ to compute $\Delta Y_{12}[0, 1, 2, 3]$, and verify whether $\Delta Z_{11}[0, 2, 3] = 0$ or not. If so, we keep the 32-bit subkeys and the quartet. Otherwise, jump to Step 1 for a next quartet. Note that, about $2^{2t-64-16} = 2^{2t-80}$ quartets can enter Step 2.

2. Utilize the value of $\Delta Y_{12}[0, 1, 2, 3]$ computed in Step 1 to get the value of $\Delta Z_{11}[1]$ corresponding to $(c, \bar{c})$. With the known difference $\Delta Y_{11}[5]$, 8-bit equivalent subkeys can be deduced, and verify it using the corresponding pair $(c', \bar{c}')$. If the 8-bit equivalent subkeys pass the verification, we keep them and the quartet, otherwise go to Step 1. About 2^{2t-88} quartets remain with 40-bit subkeys.

3. Similarly, guess the value of $STK_{13}[5, 8]$, and we can compute both the value and difference of $Y_{12}[8, 9]$ with corresponding ciphertext pair $(c, \bar{c})$. Utilizing the two zero-difference bytes in the third column of ΔZ_{11}, $\Delta Y_{12}[0, 11]$ can be computed, and we can deduce the value of $STK_{13}[2, 15]$ by studying the input and output differences of the SBoxes in a similar way as in Step 1. Partially decrypt $(c', \bar{c}')$ and compute the third column of ΔZ_{11}. If $\Delta Z_{11}[9, 10] = 0$, keep the quartet and 72-bit subkeys. About 2^{2t-88} quartets remain.

4. With the deduced 32-bit subkeys of STK_{13} in Step 3, we can get the value of $\Delta Z_{11}[8, 11]$ corresponding to $(c, \bar{c})$. Figure 7 shows that $\Delta Y_{11}[7, 8]$ are known, and 16-bit equivalent subkeys of STK_{12} related to $Z_{11}[8, 11]$ will be deduced, and the subkey is verified using $(c', \bar{c}')$. It can pass the verification with a probability of 2^{-16}. Keep the quartet and the 88-bit subkeys if they can pass the check. Up to now, there are about 2^{2t-104} quartets that can enter next step.

5. Using a similar method as in Step 3 and 4, by guessing the 2^{16} values of $STK_{13}[9, 12]$, we can deduce the 16-bit subkeys $STK_{13}[3, 6]$ and verify them by partially decrypting $(c', \bar{c}')$. Then partially decrypt $(c, \bar{c})$ to deduce the 16-bit equivalent subkeys of STK_{12} and verify them by $(c', \bar{c}')$. Totally, about 2^{2t-120} quartets remain with the corresponding 136-bit subkeys.

6. We count the 136-bit subkeys and choose the higher count values as the candidate subkeys.

Complexity. Since each plaintext pair is queried under (K_1, K_2) and (K_3, K_4) successively, the data complexity is $2 \cdot 2 \cdot 2^t = 2^{t+2}$ queries. In the key recovery process, the attacker processes about $2^{2t-64} \cdot 2^8 = 2^{2t-56}$ one-round encryptions, which are equivalent to $2^{24-56}/13 \approx 2^{2t-59.7}$ encryptions.

Since the probability of the 11-round related-tweakey rectangle distinguisher is $\hat{p}^2 \cdot \hat{q}^2 \cdot 2^{-128} = 2^{-246.4}$, 2^t plaintext pairs can provide about $2^{2t-246.4}$ right quartets. The right subkey will be counted once a right quartet occurs. Finally,

---

[1] Note that if 4 out of 8 input-output bytes of MixColumns are known, all other bytes could be deduced.

there are 2^{2t-120} quartets to count the 136-bit subkeys, and the expected value of the right subkey counter is $2^{2t-246.4}$, and the expected counter of wrong guess is 2^{2t-256}.

In conclusion, we choose $t = 123.2$. Then the data complexity is $2^{125.2}$ queries and the time complexity is bounded by the key recovery process which is $2^{186.7}$. The memory complexity equals to the size of the subkey counter which is 2^{136}. Under the right key, the expected number of the counter is 1, while under the wrong key, the expected number of the counter is $2^{-9.6}$. The success probability is about 68% using Poisson distribution.

6.2   Attack on 14-Round Deoxys-BC-384

By prefixing one more round to the start of the related-tweakey boomerang distinguisher than the 13-round attack in sect. 6.1, a 14-round related-tweakey rectangle attack can be proceeded, which is illustrated in Fig. 8.

There are 96 bits of subtweakey involved in the first round and 136 bits of subtweakey involved in the last two rounds. According to the generalized attack model described in [13] and [21], the time complexity is $2^{282.7}$ encryptions, the data complexity is $2^{125.2}$ chosen plaintexts and the time complexity is 2^{136}.

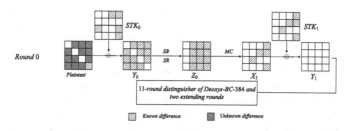

Fig. 8. Key-recovery attack against 14-round Deoxys-BC-384. The last 13 rounds are the same to the 13-round attack.

7   Impact on Deoxys Authenticated Encryption

As mentioned in [3], both versions of Deoxys adopts a 4-bit prefix for the tweak input to properly separate the different phases of authentication/encryptiong blocks. So differential paths that can be used to analyze Deoxys can not contain a difference in the 4 bits. Fortunately, the new related-tweakey rectangle distinguisher satisfies this constraint that no difference occurs in these 4 bits.

Besides, the designers of Deoxys recommend that the maximum length of a message can not exceed 2^{60} 128-bit blocks, and the maximum number of messages that can be encrypted under the same key is 2^{64}. So the adversary can not make more than 2^{124} queries under the same key.

For the version Deoxys-I, the concatenation of the nonce and the block counter is used as tweak input for Deoxys-BC. The adversary can make queries easily with the controllable tweak. So the related-tweakey rectangle attack with a data complexity of $\leq 2^{126}$ ($\leq 2^{124}$ per key) and a time complexity $\leq 2^{128}$ for Deoxys-BC-256 or $\leq 2^{256}$ for Deoxys-BC-384 can be applied to analyze the AE mode Deoxys-I.

Deoxys-BC-384 is the internal primitive of Deoxys-I-256-128. We present a related-tweakey rectangle attack on 13-round Deoxys-BC-384 in the previous section, and our attack has no difference in these 4 bits mentioned before. So the attack with a data complexity of $2^{125.2}$ ($\leq 2^{124}$ per key) and a time complexity of $2^{186.7}$ ($\leq 2^{256}$) can be applied to analyze to 13-round AE mode Deoxys-I-256-128.

However, Deoxys-II generates a *tag* utilizing the message, nonce and key. Then the *tag* is used as a part of tweak input to obtain the ciphertexts, which implies that the tweak input of Deoxys-BC can not be controlled. So the previous attack can not impact the security of Deoxys-II.

8   Conclusion

The 11-round related-tweakey distinguisher given in [6] has the lowest number of active Sboxes, but it can only extend one round forward when analyze Deoxys-BC-384. Motivated by the method of searching differential paths, we successfully find a 11-round distinguisher with comparable probability to that in [6], but with fewer active Sboxes when appending two rounds. Therefore, we can attack Deoxys-BC-384 with lower complexity and analyze Deoxys-I-256-128 for one more round. Our attack can not be applied to Deoxys-II.

Acknowledgments. We would like to thank the anonymous reviewers for their insightful comments. This work is supported by the National Key Research and Development Program of China (No. 2017YFA0303903), the National Natural Science Foundation of China (No. 61902207), the National Cryptography Development Fund (No. MMJJ20180101, MMJJ20170121), Zhejiang Province Key R&D Project (No. 2017C01062).

References

1. National Institute of Standards and Technology. Advanced Encryption Standard. In: FIPS PUB 197, Federal Information Processing Standards Publication (2001)
2. The CAESAR committee. CAESAR: Competition for authenticated encryption: Security, applicability, and robustness (2014). http://competitions.cr.yp.to/caesar.html
3. Jean, J., Nikolić, I., Peyrin, T., Seurin, Y.: Submission to caesar: Deoxys v1.41, October 2016. http://competitions.cr.yp.to/round3/deoxysv141.pdf
4. Liskov, M., Rivest, R.L., Wagner, D.: Tweakable block ciphers. In: Yung, M. (ed.) CRYPTO 2002. LNCS, vol. 2442, pp. 31–46. Springer, Heidelberg (2002). https://doi.org/10.1007/3-540-45708-9_3
5. Jean, J., Nikolić, I., Peyrin, T.: Tweaks and keys for block ciphers: the TWEAKEY framework. In: Sarkar, P., Iwata, T. (eds.) ASIACRYPT 2014, Part II. LNCS, vol. 8874, pp. 274–288. Springer, Heidelberg (2014). https://doi.org/10.1007/978-3-662-45608-8_15

6. Cid, C., Huang, T., Peyrin, T., Sasaki, Y., Song, L.: A security analysis of Deoxys and its internal tweakable blockciphers. IACR Trans. Symmetric Cryptol. **2017**(3), 73–107 (2017)

7. Sasaki, Y.: Improved related-tweakey boomerang attacks on Deoxys-BC. In: Joux, A., Nitaj, A., Rachidi, T. (eds.) AFRICACRYPT 2018. LNCS, vol. 10831, pp. 87–106. Springer, Cham (2018). https://doi.org/10.1007/978-3-319-89339-6_6

8. Mehrdad, A., Moazami, F., Soleimany, H.: Impossible differential cryptanalysis on Deoxys-BC-256. Cryptology ePrint Archive, Report 2018/048 (2018). https://eprint.iacr.org/2018/048

9. Zong, R., Dong, X., Wang, X.: Related-tweakey impossible differential attack on reduced-round Deoxys-BC-256. Cryptology ePrint Archive, Report 2018/680 (2018). https://eprint.iacr.org/2018/680

10. Li, R., Jin, C.: Meet-in-the-middle attacks on round-reduced tweakable block cipher Deoxys-BC. IET Inf. Secur. **13**(1), 70–75 (2019)

11. Cid, C., Huang, T., Peyrin, T., Sasaki, Y., Song, L.: Boomerang Connectivity table: a new cryptanalysis tool. In: Nielsen, J.B., Rijmen, V. (eds.) EUROCRYPT 2018, Part II. LNCS, vol. 10821, pp. 683–714. Springer, Cham (2018). https://doi.org/10.1007/978-3-319-78375-8_22

12. Wang, H., Peyrin, T.: Boomerang switch in multiple rounds. Application to AES variants and Deoxys. IACR Trans. Symmetric Cryptol. **2019**(1), 142–169 (2019)

13. Zhao, B., Dong, X., Jia, K.: New related-tweakey boomerang and rectangle attacks on Deoxys-BC including BDT effect. IACR Trans. Symmetric Cryptol. **2019**(3), 121–151 (2019)

14. Daemen, J., Rijmen, V.: The Design of Rijndael: AES - The Advanced Encryption Standard. Information Security and Cryptography. Springer, Heidelberg (2002). https://doi.org/10.1007/978-3-662-04722-4

15. Liskov, M., Rivest, R.L., Wagner, D.A.: Tweakable block ciphers. J. Cryptol. **24**(3), 588–613 (2011)

16. Wagner, D.: The boomerang attack. In: Knudsen, L. (ed.) FSE 1999. LNCS, vol. 1636, pp. 156–170. Springer, Heidelberg (1999). https://doi.org/10.1007/3-540-48519-8_12

17. Kelsey, J., Kohno, T., Schneier, B.: Amplified boomerang attacks against reduced-round MARS and serpent. In: Goos, G., Hartmanis, J., van Leeuwen, J., Schneier, B. (eds.) FSE 2000. LNCS, vol. 1978, pp. 75–93. Springer, Heidelberg (2001). https://doi.org/10.1007/3-540-44706-7_6

18. Biham, E., Dunkelman, O., Keller, N.: The rectangle attack — rectangling the serpent. In: Pfitzmann, B. (ed.) EUROCRYPT 2001. LNCS, vol. 2045, pp. 340–357. Springer, Heidelberg (2001). https://doi.org/10.1007/3-540-44987-6_21

19. Biham, E., Dunkelman, O., Keller, N.: Related-key boomerang and rectangle attacks. In: Cramer, R. (ed.) EUROCRYPT 2005. LNCS, vol. 3494, pp. 507–525. Springer, Heidelberg (2005). https://doi.org/10.1007/11426639_30

20. Sun, S., Hu, L., Wang, P., Qiao, K., Ma, X., Song, L.: Automatic security evaluation and (related-key) differential characteristic search: application to SIMON, PRESENT, LBlock, DES(L) and other bit-oriented block ciphers. In: Sarkar, P., Iwata, T. (eds.) ASIACRYPT 2014, Part I. LNCS, vol. 8873, pp. 158–178. Springer, Heidelberg (2014). https://doi.org/10.1007/978-3-662-45611-8_9

21. Zhao, B., Dong, X., Meier, W., Jia, K., Wang, G.: Generalized related-key rectangle attacks on block ciphers with linear key schedule: applications to SKINNY and GIFT. Cryptology ePrint Archive, Report 2019/714 (2019). https://eprint.iacr.org/2019/714

Some Cryptanalytic Results on TRIAD

Abhishek Kesarwani[1], Santanu Sarkar[1(✉)], and Ayineedi Venkateswarlu[2]

[1] Department of Mathematics, Indian Institute of Technology Madras,
Chennai 600036, India
1907abhi@gmail.com, sarkar.santanu.bir1@gmail.com
[2] Computer Science Unit, Indian Statistical Institute,
Chennai Centre, Chennai 600029, India
venku@isichennai.res.in

Abstract. In this paper, we study TRIAD-AE, which is submitted in the on-going NIST Lightweight competition. We first estimate an upper bound of the algebraic degree of internal state and *key-stream bit* seen as multivariate Boolean polynomials. Using this estimation, we find good cubes to analyze reduced round TRIAD-AE. We get a cube of size 32 which gives zero-sum up to 540 rounds, and a cube of size 34 which can distinguish TRIAD-AE up to 550 rounds with a confidence level around 95%. Further, we also obtained some small size good cubes which distinguishes TRIAD-AE from a random generator. We believe that our analysis can help to understand the security of the cipher better.

Keywords: Stream cipher · Non-linear feedback shift register (NFSR) · Cube attack · Cube tester · TRIAD

1 Introduction

Lightweight cryptography nowadays is a very popular research area due to its tremendous applications for devices with constrained resources. Recently NIST has organized a competition on lightweight cryptographic algorithms for standardization. There are 56 submissions in the first round of the competition. TRIAD, proposed by Banik et al. [2], is one of them. It consists of an authenticated encryption mode TRIAD-AE, and a hash function TRIAD-HASH. TRIAD-AE adopts the structure of Trivium-like stream ciphers. Its state size is 256 bits and key size is 128 bits, whereas the state size of Trivium is 288 and its key size is 80. Some parameters value of TRIAD-AE are given in Table 1. The hardware requirements of TRIAD-AE are low compared to Trivium and the designers claim 112-bit security. It has several phases: key nonce initialization phase with 1024 rounds, encryption phase and tag generation phase.

Cube attack, introduced by Dinur and Shamir [3] in 2009, has attracted a lot of attention from the cryptographic research communities, and has been extensively used to cryptanalyse many ciphers. Cube attacks are very efficient on stream ciphers based on low degree NFSRs. It can recover a secret key through

© Springer Nature Switzerland AG 2019
F. Hao et al. (Eds.): INDOCRYPT 2019, LNCS 11898, pp. 160–174, 2019.
https://doi.org/10.1007/978-3-030-35423-7_8

Table 1. Parameters of TRIAD-AE

Key Size	Nonce Size	State Size	Initialization Rounds
128	96	256	1024

queries to a black box polynomial using initial value (nonce) bits. One may also relate cube attacks with higher-order differential cryptanalysis [6] proposed long back. Trivium has been studied extensively and there are several results with reduced initialization rounds of Trivium. Dinur and Shamir [3] proposed key recovery attack on Trivium up to 774 rounds. In FSE 2013, Fouque and Vannet [4] proposed a cube attack for 799 rounds of Trivium using a cube of size 37.

Cube tester [1] is a similar concept related to cube attacks; it gives a distinguisher involving some of the nonce bits (or, sometimes non-randomness involving some of the key bits as well). Cube tester is an important tool to analyze Stream/Block ciphers. Using cube tester analysis, Aumasson et al. [1] build a distinguisher on Trivium for 790 round, and a non-randomness up to 885 rounds; which are later improved by others [5,7–9]. However, finding a good cube is a difficult task.

TRIAD-AE has a similar structure as Trivium, but no such result (except for the designers' claim in [2, Section 4.3]) has been reported till date. In this paper, we present some heuristics to find good cubes for cube tester for TRIAD-AE. Using our heuristics, we get some cubes to distinguish reduced round TRIAD-AE from a random generator. We obtain clear biases of TRIAD-AE upto 550 rounds with practical complexity.

Our Contribution and Roadmap

1. In Sect. 2, we discuss some preliminaries related to cube attack, cube tester and structure of TRIAD-AE.
2. Next, in Sect. 3, we present an algorithm to estimate the algebraic degree of keystream bits for TRIAD-AE. For this purpose, we consider the feedback functions of the NFSRs and provide an estimate for an upper bound on the algebraic degree of the internal state bits. From the experimental results, we observe that our estimated upper bound is close to the actual values.
3. Then in Sect. 4, we provide a method to search good cubes for distinguishing attacks for the reduced version of the cipher. In our method, we follow a greedy approach together with degree estimation to construct good cubes. From the experimental results, we get a cube of size 32, which gives zero-sum upto 540 rounds, and cube shows a bias upto 546 initialization rounds. We also obtain a cube of size 34 which provides zero-sum for 540 initialization rounds and it distinguishes TRIAD-AE upto 550 rounds with a confidence around 95%. We summarized our results in Table 2. In the table, a separate column is given with "# keys" which means the number of random keys taken

to do the experiments. We ran our experiments enough number of trails to get accuracy.

4. Section 5 concludes the paper.

2   Preliminaries

Let $\mathbb{F}_2^n$ be the n-dimensional vector space over the binary field $\mathbb{F}_2$ for some integer $n \geq 1$, and a Boolean function f in n variables is a map from $\mathbb{F}_2^n$ to $\mathbb{F}_2$. We denote the set of all Boolean functions in n variables by $\mathbb{B}_n$. It is easy to see that the cardinality of the set $\mathbb{B}_n$ is 2^{2^n}. A Boolean function $f \in \mathbb{B}_n$ can also be expressed as a multivariate polynomial in n variables over $\mathbb{F}_2$ as

$$f(x_1, x_2, \ldots, x_n) = \sum_{t \in \mathbb{F}_2^n} c_t x_1^{t_1} \ldots x_n^{t_n}, \tag{1}$$

where $c_t \in \mathbb{F}_2$ and $t = (t_1, t_2, \ldots, t_n)$. The above expression is known as the algebraic normal form (ANF for short) of f. The algebraic degree of f (denoted by $\deg(f)$) is the number of variables in the highest order monomial with non-zero coefficient in the ANF of f. Observe that for any f chosen uniformly at random from $\mathbb{B}_n$, each monomial (and in particular, the highest degree monomial $x_1 x_2 \cdots x_n$) appears in the ANF of f with probability $\frac{1}{2}$. Therefore we can see that a random element of $\mathbb{B}_n$ has maximal degree n with probability $\frac{1}{2}$. Similarly, we can also see that for any random element f of $\mathbb{B}_n$, it has degree $\deg(f) \leq (n-2)$ with probability $\frac{1}{2^{n+1}}$.

In 2017, Liu [7] provided a general framework for iterative estimation of algebraic degree for NFSR-based cryptosystems. For this purpose, a new technique called numeric mapping was introduced. Based on this general framework, an algorithm to find an upper bound on the algebraic degree for Trivium-like ciphers was presented in that paper. Now we recall the technique of Liu, which plays a central role in this work. Let $f \in \mathbb{B}_n$ be a Boolean function. The *numeric mapping* (denoted by DEG) is a map DEG : $\mathbb{B}_n \times \mathbb{Z}^n \to \mathbb{Z}$ given by

$$\text{DEG}(f, D) = \max_{c_t \neq 0} \{\sum_{i=1}^n t_i d_i\},$$

where $D = (d_1, d_2, \ldots, d_n)$ and c_t's are the coefficients in the ANF of f (see Eq. (1)). Let $G = (g_1, g_2, \ldots, g_n)$, where g_i's are Boolean functions in m variables. We define $\deg(G) = (\deg(g_1), \deg(g_2), \ldots, \deg(g_n))$. The numeric degree, denoted by DEG(h), of the composite function $h = f \circ G$ is defined as DEG($f, \deg(G)$). Then we have

$$\deg(h) = \deg(f(g_1, g_2, \ldots, g_n)) \leq \text{DEG}(h) = \max_{c_t \neq 0} \{\sum_{i=1}^n t_i \deg(g_i)\}.$$

From the above analysis we have the following proposition.

Proposition 1 ([7], Proposition 1). *The algebraic degree of a composite function is less than or equal to its numeric degree.*

2.1   Cube Attack

In 2009, Dinur and Shamir [3] introduced cube attack. Here we give a brief overview of this attack model. Stream cipher generally uses one secret key (K) and one nonce (N) to initialize its state. The secret key remains secret, and it is known only to the encryptor and the decryptor. But the nonce (or the initialization vector) is considered as a public variable. Generally, after many initialization/finalization rounds, the cipher outputs a key-stream bit. We can interpret the key-stream bit (z) as a Boolean polynomial over secret key and nonce, and so it can be expressed as $z = f(K, N)$. For general discussion, let a stream cipher takes secret-key variable $K = (k_0, \ldots, k_{l-1})$ and public variable $N = (n_0, \ldots, n_{m-1})$ as input. The main idea of cube attack is to simplify the polynomial $z = f(K, N)$ in order to solve for the secret variables involved. Let I be the set of indices $I = \{i_1, \ldots, i_c\} \subset \{0, 1, \ldots, m-1\}$, which we refer as *cube indices*. Consider a monomial of the form $t_I = n_{i_1} \cdots n_{i_c}$. We refer t_I as *term* and the variables $\{n_{i_1}, \ldots, n_{i_c}\}$ involved in t_I are referred as *cube variables*. Then we can express $f(K, N)$ as

$$f(K, N) = t_I p_{s(I)}(K, N) + q(K, N),$$

where the polynomial $p_{s(I)}$ corresponding to t_I is known as *superpoly*, and it is independent of the variables in t_I. Moreover, the polynomial $q(K, N)$ misses at least one variable from $\{n_{i_1}, \ldots, n_{i_c}\}$ or we can say t_I does not divide any monomial of the polynomial $q(K, N)$. It can also be observed that if we perform sum over all 0/1 possible values of the cube variables on z, then we will get the value of superpoly as the other terms will come even number of times and so they cancel out. To express this statement mathematically, we consider $C_I = \{(n_{i_1}, \ldots, n_{i_c}) : n_j \in \{0, 1\}$ for $j \in \{i_1, \ldots, i_c\}\}$. Note that $|C_I| = 2^c$. Now the above statement can be expressed as

$$\sum_{(n_{i_1}, \ldots, n_{i_c}) \in C_I} z = p_{s(I)}.$$

The set C_I represents the c-dimensional *cube* corresponding to the cube indices I, since it has 2^c vectors in C_I which is an analogue of a cube ($c = 3$) a closed, compact and convex figure. We present below a small example to explain the above statement.

Example 1. Consider the polynomial $z = f(k_0, k_1, k_2, n_0, n_1, n_2) = k_0 k_1 k_2 n_2 + k_0 k_1 n_1 + k_0 n_0 n_1 n_2 + k_1 n_0 n_1 n_2 + n_1 n_2$. This polynomial can also be expressed as $z = f(k_0, k_1, k_2, , n_0, n_1, n_2) = n_0 n_1 n_2 (k_0 + k_1) + k_0 k_1 k_2 n_2 + k_0 k_1 n_1 + n_1 n_2$. Let us take $t_I = n_0 n_1 n_2$. Observe that $p_{s(I)} = k_0 + k_1$ and t_I does not divide any monomial of $q = k_0 k_1 k_2 n_2 + k_0 k_1 n_1 + n_1 n_2$. Further, if we perform addition over all possible 0/1 values of $\{n_0, n_1, n_2\}$ then we will have $\sum z = p_{s(I)} = k_0 + k_1$.

Based on these observations, Dinur and Shamir proved the following theorem.

Theorem 1 *([3], Theorem 1). For any polynomial p and an index set I, $p_I \equiv p_{s(I)} \bmod 2$, where p_I is the addition of all the outputs of p corresponding to each 0/1 values of the cube variables.*

Now to use this observation in an attack model on stream cipher, the attacker first finds some cube variables and then computes the sum on the output bit for all $0/1$ possible values of the cube variables to get the value of the superpoly. The goal of the adversary is to choose the cube variables and fix the remaining public variables in such a way that the superpoly becomes a simple function (expected linear function) in secret variables. The main point of concern is that after a large number of initialization rounds, the expression of the output bit always becomes very complicated. In fact, it is not possible to compute the algebraic expression of the output bit after a few initialization rounds. To tackle this, the attacker uses the cipher as a black box. He randomly chooses the cube variables, and the black box provides the output bits corresponding to all possible $0/1$ values of the cube variables. By performing the sum on the obtained values, the attacker can recover the value of the superpoly. To check the linearity of the superpoly, the attacker performs the satisfiability of the following equation for many pairs of random values K_1, K_2:

$$p_{s(I)}(K_1) + p_{s(I)}(K_2) + p_{s(I)}(K_1 + K_2) + p_{s(I)}(0) = 0,$$

where K_1 and K_2 are the keys. If the above test passes for many random keys, then it is highly likely that the superpoly is linear. Further, with a few more queries, the attacker can recover the algebraic expression of the superpoly. In this way, the attacker chooses some more cubes to construct a system of equations using linear superpolys. Finally, the attacker solves the system of equations to get the unknown secret key. A detailed description of the cube attack is available in [3].

2.2   Cube Tester

Cube testers are basically some algorithms which can be used to check non-randomness of a given function. By using the cube attack technique, Aumasson et al. [1] proposed cube tester to check non-randomness of a Boolean function. Presence of a monomial, balancedness, constantness, presence of linear variables, and presence of neutral variables can be checked by using cube tester. A Boolean function is said to be vulnerable if it can be distinguished by some property like the ones mentioned above. Below we discuss one such cube tester which we use in this work to explain the above statement.

Upper Bound of Degree

Given a Boolean polynomial f in n variable, we want to find its algebraic degree after fixing some variables. Let $x_1, \ldots, x_n$ be the variables of the function f. Assume that $x_1, \ldots, x_k$ are initially fixed to 0. Now we are interested to check whether the reduced polynomial (after fixing $x_1, \ldots, x_k$ to 0) has degree $n - k$ or not. For this purpose, we do the following.

1. Consider $x_{k+1}, x_{k+2}, \ldots, x_n$ as cube variables.

2. Calculate the cube sum on the reduced polynomial over the prescribed cube variables.
3. If the cube sum is zero, then we conclude that the degree of the reduced polynomial is strictly less than $n - k$.

2.3   Structure of TRIAD

TRIAD is a family of stream ciphers submitted to the lightweight crypto standardization process to National Institute of Standards and Technology (NIST). It consists of an authenticated encryption mode cipher TRIAD-AE and a hash function TRIAD-HASH. TRIAD-AE provides authenticated encryption with associated data (AEAD) and generates a 64-bit tag for the confidentiality of the message. TRIAD-AE has encryption mode Triad-SC and message authentication code (MAC) mode Triad-MAC. Since we are interested in the key-stream generator part of the cipher, we exclude the details of the TRIAD-HASH and Triad-MAC (see [2] for more details).

The size of the internal state of TRIAD-AE is 256 bits[1], and it is divided into three NFSRs (Non-linear feedback shift register) denoted by $\mathbf{a} = (a_1||a_2||\ldots||a_{80})$, $\mathbf{b} = (b_1||b_2||\ldots||b_{88})$, and $\mathbf{c} = (c_1||c_2||\ldots||c_{88})$ of lengths $80, 88$ and 88 respectively. As in most stream ciphers, TRIAD-AE also has two phases: first the registers (internal state) are initialized with 128-bit key K, 96-bit nonce N and 32-bit constant C and the internal state is repeatedly updated for 1024 rounds using TriadUpd before generating key-stream bits. The initialization phase of the Triad-SC is described in Algorithm 2. For generating key-stream bits TriadUpd is used, and in each iteration of TriadUpd the internal state is updated and it outputs 1-bit key-stream (z).

We consider the reduced round version of the cipher and assume that it outputs the key-stream bit just after the initialization. We always fix the input variable msg with 0 in TriadUpd. In [2], the authors use byte array representation to describe the key, nonce, and messages. To express as byte arrays, the 128-bit key K and the 96-bit nonce N are denoted by

$$K = (K[0], K[1], \ldots, K[15]),$$

$$N = (N[0], N[1], \ldots, N[11]),$$

where $K[i]$ and $N[i]$ denote the ith memory of K and N respectively. Also the jth-bit of $K[i]$ is denoted by $K[i]_j$, i.e.,

$$K[i] = K[i]_1||K[i]_2||\ldots,||K[i]_8],$$

where $K[i]_1$ is the msb of $K[i]$. The constant C is a 32-bit hexadecimal number divided into 4 byte array which is given by:

$$(con[3]||con[2]||con[1]||con[0]) = \texttt{0xFFFFFFFE}.$$

---

[1] In order to make efficient in low-area implementation its state size is less than that of Trivium (Trivium has 288 bit state size).

We also use k_i for $0 \leq i \leq 127$ to denote the key bits and n_i for $0 \leq i \leq 95$ to denote the nonce bits. The authors [2] claim that the key recovery attack on TRIAD-AE requires at least 2^{112} computations on a classical computer. We now describe TriadUpd and Triad-SC in Algorithms 1 and 2 respectively.

Algorithm 1. TRIAD-AE Update Function

1: **procedure** TRIADUPD($\mathbf{a}, \mathbf{b}, \mathbf{c}, \mathbf{msg}$)
2:    $t_1 \leftarrow a_{68} \oplus a_{80} \oplus b_{85} \cdot c_{85}$
3:    $t_2 \leftarrow b_{64} \oplus b_{88}$
4:    $t_3 \leftarrow c_{68} \oplus c_{88}$
5:    $z \leftarrow t_1 \oplus t_2 \oplus t_3$
6:    $t_1 \leftarrow t_1 \oplus a_{73} \cdot a_{79} \oplus b_{66} \oplus \mathbf{msg}$
7:    $t_2 \leftarrow t_2 \oplus b_{65} \cdot b_{87} \oplus c_{84} \oplus \mathbf{msg}$
8:    $t_3 \leftarrow t_3 \oplus c_{77} \cdot c_{87} \oplus a_{74} \oplus \mathbf{msg}$
9:    $(a_1, a_2, \ldots, a_{80}) \leftarrow (t_3, a_1, \ldots, a_{79})$
10:    $(b_1, b_2, \ldots, b_{88}) \leftarrow (t_1, b_1, \ldots, b_{87})$
11:    $(c_1, c_2, \ldots, c_{88}) \leftarrow (t_2, c_1, \ldots, c_{87})$
12:    **return** $(\mathbf{a}, \mathbf{b}, \mathbf{c}, z)$
13: **end procedure**

Algorithm 2. Triad-SC

1: **procedure** TRIADSC(K, N, M)
2:    $(a_1|| \ldots ||a_{80}) \leftarrow (N[0]||K[4]||con[3]||K[3]||con[2]||K[2]||con[1]||K[1]||con[0]||K[0])$
3:    $(b_1|| \ldots ||b_{88}) \leftarrow (N[11]|| \ldots ||N[1])$
4:    $(c_1|| \ldots ||c_{88}) \leftarrow (K[15]|| \ldots ||K[5])$
5:    **for** $i = 1$ to 1024 **do**
6:        $(\mathbf{a}, \mathbf{b}, \mathbf{c}, z) \leftarrow$ TriadUpd($\mathbf{a}, \mathbf{b}, \mathbf{c}, 0$)
7:    **end for**
8:    **return** $(\mathbf{a}, \mathbf{b}, \mathbf{c})$
9: **end procedure**

---

3   Approximation of Algebraic Degree of TRIAD-AE

In this section, we present a method to estimate the degree of the output bit of TRIAD-AE in each round of the initialization phase. For this purpose, we first discuss an upper bound of the degree of feedback functions in terms of the initial variables. Let A, B and C be the three NFSRs of length n_A, n_B and n_C respectively. Let $s^{(t)} = (A_t, B_t, C_t)$ denote the internal state of the cipher at time t, where

$$A_t = (a_t, a_{t-1}, \ldots, a_{t-n_A+1}),$$
$$B_t = (b_t, b_{t-1}, \ldots, b_{t-n_B+1}),$$
$$C_t = (c_t, c_{t-1}, \ldots, c_{t-n_C+1}).$$

TRIAD-AE differs from Trivium by tapping positions, so the degree approximation of TRIAD-AE is different from that of Trivium. Also the feedback function
for b_t contains two AND gates as given in (3). The feedback functions for a_t and
c_t contain only one AND gate, but the tapping positions are not consecutive.
The feedback functions are as given below.

$$a_t = c_{t-i_1} \cdot c_{t-i_2} \oplus l_A(s^{(t-1)}), \tag{2}$$

$$b_t = a_{t-j_1} \cdot a_{t-j_2} \oplus b_{t-j_3} \cdot c_{t-j_3} \oplus l_B(s^{(t-1)}), \tag{3}$$

$$c_t = b_{t-k_1} \cdot b_{t-k_2} \oplus l_C(s^{(t-1)}), \tag{4}$$

Here l_A, l_B and l_B denote the linear functions corresponding to NFSRs A, B, and
C respectively. The variables with non-positive indices are the initial variables.

We discuss our method to estimate the degree for b_t, and the same method
can be applied for a_t and c_t as well. We have $1 \leq j_1 < j_2 < n_A$ and $j_2 < j_3 <$
$n_B = n_C$. Let $g_B^{(t)}$ denote the quadratic part of $b_{(t)}$ given by $g_B^{(t)} = a_{t-j_1} \cdot a_{t-j_2} \oplus$
$b_{t-j_3} \cdot c_{t-j_3}$. To estimate the algebraic degree of $g_B^{(t)}$, denoted by $\deg(g_B^{(t)})$, we
have four different cases for t.

Case (i): If $(t - j_1) \leq 0$ then the algebraic degree of $g_B^{(t)}$ satisfies

$$\deg(g_B^{(t)}) \leq \max\{\deg(a_{t-j_1}) + \deg(a_{t-j_2}), \deg(b_{t-j_3}) + \deg(c_{t-j_3})\}.$$

We have $0 \geq (t - j_1) > (t - j_2)$, and so $(t - j_2) \leq 0$ and $(t - j_3) \leq 0$. Therefore
we can see that all the variables are the initial variables.

Case (ii): If $1 + j_1 \leq t \leq j_2$ then we can write $a_{t-j_1} = c_{t-j_1-i_1} \cdot c_{t-j_1-i_2} \oplus$
$l_A(s^{(t-j_1-1)})$ using (2), and therefore

$$\deg(g_B^{(t)}) \leq \max\{\max\{\deg(c_{t-j_1-i_1}) + \deg(c_{t-j_1-i_2}), \mathrm{DEG}(l_A, D^{(t-j_1-1)})\} +$$
$$\deg(a_{t-j_2}), \deg(b_{t-j_3}) + \deg(c_{t-j_3})\}$$

Case (iii): If $1 + j_2 \leq t \leq j_3$ then from Eqs. (2) and (4) we have

$$a_{t-j_1} \cdot a_{t-j_2} = (c_{t-j_1-i_1} \cdot c_{t-j_1-i_2} + l_A(s^{(t-j_1-1)})) \cdot a_{t-j_2}$$
$$= c_{t-j_1-i_1} \cdot c_{t-j_1-i_2} \cdot a_{t-j_2} + l_A(s^{(t-j_1-1)}) \cdot a_{t-j_2}$$
$$= c_{t-j_1-i_1} \cdot c_{t-j_1-i_2} \cdot (c_{t-j_2-i_1} \cdot c_{t-j_2-i_2} + l_A(s^{(t-j_2-1)}))$$
$$+ l_A(s^{(t-j_1-1)}) \cdot a_{t-j_2}$$
$$= c_{t-j_1-i_1} \cdot c_{t-j_1-i_2} \cdot c_{t-j_2-i_1} \cdot c_{t-j_2-i_2} + c_{t-j_1-i_1} \cdot c_{t-j_1-i_2} \cdot$$
$$l_A(s^{(t-j_2-1)}) + l_A(s^{(t-j_1-1)}) \cdot a_{t-j_2}.$$

We denote the three summands in the last row of the above identity by Y_1, Y_2
and Y_3 respectively. We have $\deg(a_{t-j_1}) \geq \deg(c_{t-j_1-i_1} \cdot c_{t-j_1-i_2})$ from (2).

Therefore, we can write

$$\deg(Y_1) \leq \min\{\deg(a_{t-j_1}) + \deg(a_{t-j_2}), \deg(a_{t-j_1}) + \deg(c_{t-j_2-i_1}) +$$
$$\deg(c_{t-j_2-i_2}), \deg(c_{t-j_1-i_1}) + \deg(c_{t-j_1-i_2}) + \deg(a_{t-j_2}),$$
$$\deg(c_{t-j_1-i_1}) + \deg(c_{t-j_1-i_2}) + \deg(c_{t-j_2-i_1}) + \deg(c_{t-j_2-i_2})\} = d_1,$$
$$\deg(Y_2) \leq \deg(a_{t-j_1}) + \mathrm{DEG}(l_A, D^{(t-j_2-1)}) = d_2,$$
$$\deg(Y_3) \leq \deg(a_{t-j_2}) + \mathrm{DEG}(l_A, D^{(t-j_1-1)}) = d_3.$$

Let $h_1 = \max\{d_1, d_2, d_3\}$. Consequently, we get $\deg(g_B^{(t)}) \leq \max\{h_1, \deg(b_{t-j_3}) + \deg(c_{t-j_3})\}$.

Case (iv): If $(t - j_3) \geq 1$ then all the variables are new, and so we need to express $a_{t-j_1}, a_{t-j_2}, b_{t-j_3}$ and c_{t-j_3} in terms of the variables appearing in the previous round. Consider the product $b_{t-j_3} \cdot c_{t-j_3}$, and using Eqs. (3) and (4) we have

$$b_{t-j_3} \cdot c_{t-j_3} = (a_{t-j_3-j_1} \cdot a_{t-j_3-j_2} \oplus b_{t-2j_3} \cdot c_{t-2j_3} \oplus l_B(s^{(t-j_3-1)})) \cdot c_{t-j_3}$$
$$= a_{t-j_3-j_1} \cdot a_{t-j_3-j_2} \cdot c_{t-j_3} \oplus b_{t-2j_3} \cdot c_{t-2j_3} \cdot c_{t-j_3}$$
$$\oplus l_B(s^{(t-j_3-1)}) \cdot c_{t-j_3}$$
$$= a_{t-j_3-j_1} \cdot a_{t-j_3-j_2} \cdot (b_{t-j_3-k_1} \cdot b_{t-j_3-k_2} \oplus l_C(s^{(t-j_3-1)}))$$
$$\oplus b_{t-2j_3} \cdot c_{t-2j_3} \cdot (b_{t-j_3-k_1} \cdot b_{t-j_3-k_2} \oplus l_C(s^{(t-j_3-1)}))$$
$$\oplus l_B(s^{(t-j_3-1)}) \cdot c_{t-j_3}$$
$$= a_{t-j_3-j_1} \cdot a_{t-j_3-j_2} \cdot b_{t-j_3-k_1} \cdot b_{t-j_3-k_2} \oplus a_{t-j_3-j_1} \cdot a_{t-j_3-j_2} \cdot$$
$$l_C(s^{(t-j_3-1)}) \oplus b_{t-2j_3} \cdot c_{t-2j_3} \cdot b_{t-j_3-k_1} \cdot b_{t-j_3-k_2} \oplus b_{t-2j_3} \cdot$$
$$c_{t-2j_3} \cdot l_C(s^{(t-j_3-1)}) \oplus l_B(s^{(t-j_3-1)}) \cdot c_{t-j_3}.$$

We denote the five summands appearing in the last row of the above identity by Z_1, Z_2, Z_3, Z_4 and Z_5 respectively. From Eqs. (3) and (2), we can see that $\deg(b_{t-j_3}) \geq \deg(a_{t-j_3-j_1} \cdot a_{t-j_3-j_2})$ and $\deg(c_{t-j_3}) \geq \deg(b_{t-j_3-k_1} \cdot b_{t-j_3-k_2})$. Using these inequalities, we can write

$$\deg(Z_1) \leq \min\{\deg(b_{t-j_3}) + \deg(c_{t-j_3}), \deg(a_{t-j_3-j_1}) + \deg(a_{t-j_3-j_2}) +$$
$$\deg(c_{t-j_3}), \deg(b_{t-j_3}) + \deg(b_{t-j_3-k_1}) + \deg(b_{t-j_3-k_2}), \deg(a_{t-j_3-j_1}) +$$
$$\deg(a_{t-j_3-j_2}) + \deg(b_{t-j_3-k_1}) + \deg(b_{t-j_3-k_2})\} = e_1,$$
$$\deg(Z_2) \leq \deg(b_{t-j_3}) + \mathrm{DEG}(l_C, D^{(t-j_3-1)}) = e_2,$$
$$\deg(Z_3) \leq \min\{\deg(b_{t-j_3}) + \deg(c_{t-j_3}), \deg(b_{t-2j_3}) + \deg(c_{t-2j_3}) + \deg(c_{t-j_3}),$$
$$\deg(b_{t-j_3}) + \deg(b_{t-j_3-k_1}) + \deg(b_{t-j_3-k_2}), \deg(b_{t-2j_3}) + \deg(c_{t-2j_3})$$
$$+ \deg(b_{t-j_3-k_1}) + \deg(b_{t-j_3-k_2})\} = e_3,$$
$$\deg(Z_4) \leq \deg(b_{t-j_3}) + \mathrm{DEG}(l_C, D^{(t-j_3-1)}) = e_4.$$
$$\deg(Z_5) \leq \deg(c_{t-j_3}) + \mathrm{DEG}(l_B, D^{(t-j_3-1)}) = e_5.$$

Since e_2 and e_4 are the same, and so we ignore e_4 in estimating the upper bound. Let $h_2 = \max\{e_1, e_2, e_3, e_5\}$. Therefore, we have $\deg(g_B^{(t)}) \leq \max\{h_1, h_2\}$.

Similarly, we can get an upper bound for the algebraic degree of the quadratic parts of a_t and c_t and the estimates are denoted by $\deg(g_A^{(t)})$ and $\deg(g_C^{(t)})$ respectively. We use $\mathtt{DEG}(l_\lambda, D^{(t-1)})$ to approximate the degree of the linear part $l_\lambda(s^{(t-1)})$ for each $\lambda \in \{A, B, C\}$. It satisfies $\mathtt{DEG}(l_\lambda, D^{(t-1)}) \geq \deg(l_\lambda(s^{(t-1)}))$. We denote by $d_A^{(t)}$, $d_B^{(t)}$ and $d_C^{(t)}$ the estimated upper bounds of the algebraic degrees of a_t, b_t and c_t respectively. They are given by

$$d_\lambda^{(t)} = \max\{\deg(g_\lambda^{(t)}), \mathtt{DEG}(l_\lambda, D^{(t-1)})\},$$

where $\lambda \in \{A, B, C\}$. We now present our technique to get an upper bound on the algebraic degree of the output function $z = f(K, N)$ after R rounds in Algorithm 3. In the algorithm, $s^{(0)} = (s_1^{(0)}, \ldots, s_n^{(0)})$ denotes the initial state at time 0 with size n. For a given subset X of state variables, $\deg(s^{(0)}, X) = (\deg(s_1^{(0)}, X), \ldots, \deg(s_n^{(0)}, X))$, where $\deg(s_i^{(0)}, X)$ denotes the algebraic degree of $s_i^{(0)}$ with X as variables. Especially, $\deg(0, X) = -\infty$, $\deg(c, X) = 0$ for some nonzero c containing no variables from X. In the algorithm, $D^{(0)}$ is initialized with $\deg(s^{(0)}, X)$ for some subset X of state variables. Then the degrees of the state bits are estimated iteratively. It has been demonstrated in [7] that for all t with $1 \leq t \leq R$ the estimated degrees $d_A^{(t)}$, $d_B^{(t)}$, $d_C^{(t)}$ of a_t, b_t, c_t are greater than or equal to their corresponding algebraic degrees, and therefore the output $\mathtt{DEG}(f, D^{(R)})$ of Algorithm 3 gives an upper bound on the algebraic degree of the R-round output bit of TRIAD-AE.

Algorithm 3. Estimation of the algebraic degree of TRIAD-AE

Require: Given the initial internal state (A_0, B_0, C_0) and the set of variables X.
1: Initialize the degree of initial internal state, i.e., $D^{(0)} = \deg(s^{(0)}, X)$;
2: **for** t from 1 to R **do**
3:     **for** λ *in* $\{A, B, C\}$ **do**
4:         $d_\lambda^{(t)} \leftarrow \max\{\deg(g_\lambda^{(t)}), \mathtt{DEG}(l_\lambda, D^{(t-1)})\}$;
5:     **end for**
6:     Update the degree state $D^{(t)}$ from $D^{(t-1)}$;
7: **end for**
8: **return** $\mathtt{DEG}(f, D^{(R)})$

---

4   Analysis of Reduced Round TRIAD-AE

The major issue in a cube attack or a cube tester is to find a good cube in the sense that it provides a distinguisher for a large number of initialization rounds. First of all, from degree evaluation algorithm we have an upper bound of the degree of keystream bit over cube variables. Then we look at the maximum number of rounds up to which the calculated upper bound is strictly less than the size of the cube. This will give a zero-sum distinguisher of the cipher. Moreover, exploiting degree estimation method, we also describe a method to find new cubes in Algorithm 5.

In the algorithm, we first fix cube variables ($\mathbf{C}$) from a set of nonce bit variables. Suppose that the size of the cube $\mathbf{C}$ is c. We set all other nonce bit variables that are not in $\mathbf{C}$ to zero and the key as parameter (initialized with $\deg(k_i, \mathbf{C}) = 0$, same as in [7]). With this setup (i.e., input data for Algorithm 3), we run Algorithm 3 and check the round upto which, the degree of keystream bit is strictly less than c. Suppose Algorithm 3 returns r as output. Based on this observation, we perform cube sum on the first keystream bit by selecting the same cube variables for several random keys, and we will get the superpoly as zero at r-th round. One may note that Algorithm 3 gives an upper bound of the degree of the keystream bit in r-th round, and the computed degree is strictly less than the size of the cube. It is easy to see that at this round, the superpoly corresponding to this cube must be zero.

4.1   Our Approach to Find Cube Variables for TRIAD-AE

Very few cube finding algorithms are available in the literature, which are widely used to find good cubes. In [10], the authors proposed a GreedyBitSet algorithm to find cube variables, this algorithm heuristically generates a set of cube variables for which the cube sum on the output bit over these cube variables is zero for maximum rounds. We now describe a new cube finding method, our approach is similar to [5], but for completeness, we describe the details.

Our method relies on the degree estimation algorithm for TRIAD-AE, which is described in Sect. 3. Our aim is to find a cube which gives zero-sum on the keystream bit at r^{th} round, for large r. We use the ideas of GreedyBitSet algorithm with degree evaluation of TRIAD-AE. Similar to the greedy approach, in each iteration we add one nonce bit into cube set until we get a desired size of the cube.

In Algorithm 4, we calculate two attributes attached to the given cube variables $\mathbf{C}$ of size c at some fixed round p. For this purpose, we estimate the degree of the keystream bit, i.e., $\deg(z_p, \mathbf{C})$ at round p. We then calculate the last round L_R at which the superpoly of $\mathbf{C}$ is zero. Observe that L_R is the last round upto which $\deg(z_p, \mathbf{C})$ is strictly less than the size of the cube. The rationale behind this is that we look for a cube whose approximate degree of the keystream bit is strictly less than the size of a cube for a maximum round. Therefore, the superpoly corresponding to this cube will be zero.

We first start with an empty cube set and keep adding only one nonce bit at a time, using Algorithm 6. Algorithm 6 uses Algorithm 4, which returns two values ($\deg(z_p, \mathbf{C}), L_R$). Based on these values, we define our priorities to select which bit to include in the cube. We choose a cube variable bit according to the priority order given below:

- **Priority 1**: Select the bit among the bits as a cube variable whose first component $\deg(z_p, \mathbf{C})$ is minimum.

Algorithm 4. Estimation of the degree of the keystream bit at round p

---

Require: Cube variables $\mathbf{C} = \{n_{i_1}, n_{i_2}, \ldots, n_{i_c}\}$ of size c and fixed round p.
Ensure: Calculate two attributes related to cube $\mathbf{C}$ at round p
 1: Set all key bits as parameters, i.e., $\deg(k_i, \mathbf{C}) = 0$
 2: Set $\deg(n_i, \mathbf{C}) = 1$ for $n_i \in \mathbf{C}$, and set the remaining ($96 - c$ many) nonce bits to
    0, i.e., $\deg(n_i, \mathbf{C}) = -\infty$
 3: Initialize internal states A, B, and C using initialization Algorithm 2
 4: Run Algorithm 3, with input from Step 3, over the cube variable $\mathbf{C}$
 5: Return the following two attributes:
    – $\deg(z_p, \mathbf{C})$,
    – L_R.

– Priority 2: If there is a tie in the first priority then select the bit as a cube variable whose L_R is maximum.

If there is again a clash in L_R values, our priority is to choose the first variable among those according to the ordering of the variables considered. We now describe our main Greedy Algorithm for finding cubes of desired sizes, in Algorithm 5.

Algorithm 5. Finding a cube using Greedy approach

Require: Set of nonce bits N, cube size c, round p.
Ensure: A good cube $\mathbf{C} \subset N$ of size c.
 1: $\mathbf{C} = \emptyset$
 2: **for** $i = 1$ **to** $i = c$ **do**
 3:     $\mathbf{C} \leftarrow AddOneBit(N, \mathbf{C}, p)$
 4: **end for**
 5: **return** $\mathbf{C}$

How to Choose Return Round p?

We generate cube sets of size (say c), by looking at the degree of the keystream bit z at p-th round. We repeat this by varying p from 1 to R, where R is the number of initialization rounds, and generate many such cube sets. Among these cubes, we select the one which gives maximum zero-sum rounds.

Reverse the Nonce Bits Ordering During Cube Selection

We also consider some other heuristics for obtaining good cubes. We observe that if we reverse the ordering of the nonce bits N during the cube selection process in Algorithm 6 then we may have an advantage of getting good cubes. From the design of TRIAD-AE one can see that the update function involve initial nonce bits. Therefore, in order to get minimum degree we give priority to last nonce bits. In fact we used some permutation of the indices of nonce bits $\{0, 1, \ldots, 95\}$. Based on these two observations, we get some good cubes, and it is evident from the experiments.

Algorithm 6. *AddOneBit*$(N, \mathbf{C}, p)$

Require: Set of nonce bits N, cube $\mathbf{C}$ of size l, round p.
Ensure: Cube $\mathbf{C}$ of size $l + 1$.
1: good *bit* $\leftarrow$ *None*, $min_d \leftarrow \infty$, $max_R \leftarrow -1$
2: **for** all $x \in N \setminus \mathbf{C}$ **do**
3:     $\bar{\mathbf{C}} = \mathbf{C} \cup \{x\}$
4:     Call Algorithm 4 with input $(\bar{\mathbf{C}}, |\bar{\mathbf{C}}|, p)$
5:     **if** $\deg(z_p, \mathbf{C}) < min_d$ **then**
6:         $min_d \leftarrow \deg(z_p, \mathbf{C})$, $max_R \leftarrow L_R$, good *bit* $\leftarrow x$
7:     **end if**
8:     **if** $\deg(z_p, \mathbf{C}) == min_d$ **then**
9:         **if** $L_R > max_R$ **then**
10:             $max_R \leftarrow L_R$, good *bit* $\leftarrow x$
11:         **end if**
12:     **end if**
13: **end for**
14: **return** $\mathbf{C} = \mathbf{C} \cup \{$good *bit*$\}$

4.2   Experiment Results

In our experiments, we use C programming language and compile it with GCC in Unix environments. We first choose some good cube variables of length c ($10 \leq c \leq 96$) by using Algorithm 5. We compute the round up to which the degree of the first keystream bit is strictly less than c by using Algorithm 4 i.e., L_R rounds. For a fixed random key and a cube, we calculate the superpoly by summing over all possible cube variables and look for exact zero-sum and bias in the superpoly. We verify this by carrying out cube tester experiment for different random keys. Some best cubes and the corresponding output is provided in Table 2. We record that, whatever the experimental degree evaluation result is obtained for zero-sum distinguisher rounds, it matches all of time with exact cube tester. In [2], the authors also estimated the upper bound of the degrees of internal state bits, using mixed-integer linear programming (MILP) and mentioned that the maximum degree of keystream bit reaches 93 at 500 rounds by taking all the states bits as variables. In our search, we get a cube of size 10, which gives exact zero-sum for 501 rounds. We also obtain a cube of size 32, which gives exact zero-sum for 540 rounds. We obtain this cube by the reverse ordering of the cube indices. Then we perform cube tester experiments and find that its superpoly gives bias up to 546 rounds. We have tested it for 4800 random keys.

Remark 1. Let $\mathcal{A}$ and $\mathcal{B}$ be two sequence of bits where $\mathcal{A}$ is generated from random source and $\mathcal{B}$ is generated from stream cipher. Suppose an event E happens in $\mathcal{A}$ with probability p and the same event happens in $\mathcal{B}$ with probability $p(1 + q)$. Then one requires $\mathcal{O}(\frac{1}{pq^2})$ many samples to distinguish between $\mathcal{A}$ and $\mathcal{B}$. In fact for 90% confidence level, one requires $\frac{6.6}{pq^2}$ random samples.

We have obtained a cube of size 34 which distinguishes TRIAD-AE with 550 initialization rounds. One may note (from Table 2) the bias in the corresponding superpoly is very significant (approximately 0.423). To achieve a good confidence level, we have performed our experiment for 896 random keys. For our 34 size cube, we have $p = 0.5$ and $p(1 + q) = 0.423$, which gives $\frac{10.62}{pq^2} = 896$. Since we are doing for 896 trails, our confidence level is approximately 94.8%. In Table 2, we have mentioned that the number of random keys taken to perform the experiments. It can be observed that in all those cases, the probability of success (confidence) is always more than 90%. This is the first distinguishing attack on TRIAD-AE in terms of the initialization rounds.

Table 2. Some good cubes of different sizes for TRIAD-AE obtained from Algorithm 5

Cube Size	distinguisher round		# key	Confidence level	Cube Variable Indices
	exact zero-sum	(round, bias)			
10	501	(501, 0.00)	10000	≈ 100%	2, 3, 4, 5, 6, 7, 10, 88, 89, 93
20	519	(520, 0.464)	6400	≈ 97.9%	2, 3, 6, 7, 8, 9, 21, 22, 23, 24, 27, 28, 32, 47, 51, 75, 83, 89, 92, 94
30	533	(534, 0.213)	1856	≈ 99.7%	2, 6, 7, 8, 12, 13, 17, 18, 22, 23, 24, 25, 26, 31, 36, 37, 49, 54, 55, 60, 61, 72, 73, 74, 78, 79, 84, 90, 91, 92
32	540	(546, 0.473)	4800	≈ 90.1%	1, 5, 6, 9, 10, 11, 15, 19, 22, 23, 24, 28, 29, 30, 34, 35, 39, 43, 47, 48, 53, 54, 58, 66, 67, 71, 72, 77, 81, 90, 91, 95
34	540	(550, 0.423)	896	≈ 94.8%	1, 4, 5, 6, 9, 10, 11, 15, 19, 22, 23, 24, 28, 29, 30, 34, 39, 43, 47, 48, 53, 57, 58, 63, 66, 67, 71, 72, 76, 77, 81, 90, 91, 95
36	536	(542, 0.333)	1074	≈ 100%	0, 2, 3, 4, 7, 8, 9, 10, 17, 19, 20 21, 24, 25, 28, 29, 33, 44, 48, 52, 59, 61, 62, 63, 67, 71, 75, 76, 79, 86, 87, 90, 91, 93, 94, 95

5 Conclusion

In this paper, we have studied TRIAD-AE. We have shown how to estimate the algebraic degree of keystream bit considering as a polynomial over nonce for a fixed key. We have used this estimation together with some heuristics to find good cubes. We have got a cube of size 34 which can distinguish 550 initial rounds of TRIAD-AE. However, the number of initialization rounds proposed in TRIAD-AE is 1024. Hence the results presented in the paper does not invalidate any security claims of the designers.

References

1. Aumasson, J.-P., Dinur, I., Meier, W., Shamir, A.: Cube testers and key recovery attacks on reduced-round MD6 and Trivium. In: Dunkelman, O. (ed.) FSE 2009. LNCS, vol. 5665, pp. 1–22. Springer, Heidelberg (2009). https://doi.org/10.1007/978-3-642-03317-9_1

2. Banik, S., Isobe, T., Meier, W., Todo, Y., Zhang, B.: TRIAD v1- a lightweight AEAD and hash function based on stream cipher (2018)

3. Dinur, I., Shamir, A.: Cube attacks on tweakable black box polynomials. In: Joux, A. (ed.) EUROCRYPT 2009. LNCS, vol. 5479, pp. 278–299. Springer, Heidelberg (2009). https://doi.org/10.1007/978-3-642-01001-9_16

4. Fouque, P.-A., Vannet, T.: Improving key recovery to 784 and 799 rounds of Trivium using optimized cube attacks. In: Moriai, S. (ed.) FSE 2013. LNCS, vol. 8424, pp. 502–517. Springer, Heidelberg (2014). https://doi.org/10.1007/978-3-662-43933-3_26

5. Kesarwani, A., Roy, D., Sarkar, S., Meier, W.: New cube distinguishers onNFSR-based stream ciphers. Des. Codes Crypt. (2019). https://doi.org/10.1007/s10623-019-00674-1

6. Knellwolf, S., Meier, W.: High order differential attacks on stream ciphers. Cryptogr. Commun. 4(3–4), 203–215 (2012). https://doi.org/10.1007/s12095-012-0071-9

7. Liu, M.: Degree evaluation of NFSR-based cryptosystems. In: Katz, J., Shacham, H. (eds.) CRYPTO 2017. LNCS, vol. 10403, pp. 227–249. Springer, Cham (2017). https://doi.org/10.1007/978-3-319-63697-9_8

8. Liu, M., Lin, D., Wang, W.: Searching cubes for testing Boolean functions and its application to Trivium. In: IEEE International Symposium on Information Theory, ISIT, pp. 496–500. IEEE (2015). https://doi.org/10.1109/ISIT.2015.7282504

9. Sarkar, S., Maitra, S., Baksi, A.: Observing biases in the state: case studies with Trivium and Trivia-SC. Des. Codes Crypt. 82(1–2), 351–375 (2017). https://doi.org/10.1007/s10623-016-0211-x

10. Stankovski, P.: Greedy distinguishers and nonrandomness detectors. In: Gong, G., Gupta, K.C. (eds.) INDOCRYPT 2010. LNCS, vol. 6498, pp. 210–226. Springer, Heidelberg (2010). https://doi.org/10.1007/978-3-642-17401-8_16

Cryptanalysis of Round-Reduced KECCAK Using Non-linear Structures

Mahesh Sreekumar Rajasree[✉]

Center for Cybersecurity, Indian Institute of Technology Kanpur, Kanpur, India
mahesr@cse.iitk.ac.in

Abstract. In this paper, we present new preimage attacks on KECCAK-384 and KECCAK-512 for 2, 3 and 4 rounds. The attacks are based on non-linear structures (structures that contain quadratic terms). These structures were studied by Guo et al. [13] and Li et al. [18,19] to give preimage attacks on round reduced KECCAK. We carefully construct non-linear structures such that the quadratic terms are not spread across the whole state. This allows us to create more linear equations between the variables and hash values, leading to better preimage attacks. As a result, we present the best theoretical preimage attack on KECCAK-384 and KECCAK-512 for 2 and 3-rounds and also KECCAK-384 for 4-rounds.

Keywords: KECCAK · SHA-3 · Hash function · Cryptanalysis · Preimage attack

1 Introduction

Cryptographic hash functions are widely used in modern cryptography such as in digital signatures, message integrity and authentication. The U.S. National Institute of Standards and Technology (NIST) announced the "NIST hash function competition" for the Secure Hash Algorithm-3 (SHA-3) in 2006. They received 64 proposals from around the world. Among these, KECCAK designed by Bertoni, Daemen, Peeters, and Van Assche [4] became one of the candidates for SHA-3. It won the competition in October 2012 and was standardized as a "Secure Hash Algorithm 3" [12].

The KECCAK hash family is based on the sponge construction [5]. Its design was made public in 2008 and since then, it has received intense security analysis. In 2016, Guo et al. [13] formalised the idea of linear structures and gave practical preimage attacks for 2 rounds KECCAK-224/256. They also gave better preimage attacks for KECCAK-384/512, all variants of 3-rounds KECCAK as well as preimage attacks for 4-rounds KECCAK-224/256. Li et al. [19] improved the complexity of preimage attack for 3-rounds KECCAK-256 by using a new type of structure called cross-linear structure. The best-known attacks for 3 and 4 rounds KECCAK-224/256 are given by Li et al. [18] using a new technique called allocating approach, which consists of two phases - Precomputation phase

© Springer Nature Switzerland AG 2019
F. Hao et al. (Eds.): INDOCRYPT 2019, LNCS 11898, pp. 175–192, 2019.
https://doi.org/10.1007/978-3-030-35423-7_9

and Online phase. They gave the first practical preimage attack for 3-rounds KECCAK-224. Theoretical preimage attacks for higher rounds on KECCAK are considered in [2,7,20]. Apart from the attacks mentioned above, there are several other attacks against KECCAK such as preimage attacks in [16,17,21,22], collision attacks in [8–10,15,23] and distinguishers in [1,6,11,13,14].

Table 1. Summary of preimage attacks

Rounds	Instances	Complexity	References
1	224	Practical	[17]
	256		
	384		
	512		
2	224	Practical	[13]
	256	Practical	
	384	2^{129}	
	512	2^{384}	
2	384	Time 2^{89}	[16]
		Space 2^{87}	
2	384	$\mathbf{2^{113}}$	Subsection 3.2
	512	$\mathbf{2^{321}}$	Subsection 3.1
3	224	2^{38}	[18]
	256	2^{81}	
3	384	2^{322}	[13]
	512	2^{482}	
3	384	$\mathbf{2^{321}}$	Subsection 3.4
	512	$\mathbf{2^{475}}$	Subsection 3.5
4	224	2^{207}	[18]
	256	2^{239}	
4	384	2^{378}	[20]
	512	2^{506}	
4	384	$\mathbf{2^{371}}$	Subsection 3.6

Our Contributions: In this paper, we give the best theoretical preimage attacks for KECCAK-384 for $2, 3, 4$ rounds and KECCAK-512 for $2, 3$ rounds. This is achieved by carefully constructing non-linear structures such that the quadratic terms are not spread throughout the whole state and the number of free variables in the system of equations is more. Table 1 summaries the best theoretical preimage attacks up to four rounds and our contributions. The space complexity is most of the attacks is constant unless it is explicitly mentioned.

Organization: The rest of the paper contains the following sections. In Sect. 2, we will give a brief description about KECCAK, some preliminaries and notations that are used throughout the paper and useful observations about KEC-CAK. Section 3 contains detailed description of all our preimage attacks. Finally, we conclude in Sect. 4.

2   Structure of KECCAK

KECCAK hash function is based on sponge construction [5] which uses a padding function *pad*, a bitrate parameter r and a permutation function f as shown in Fig. 1.

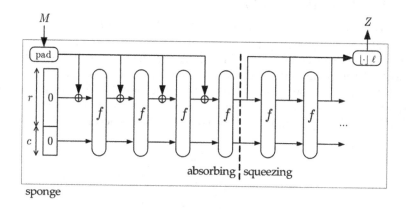

Fig. 1. Sponge function [5]

2.1   Sponge Construction

As shown in Fig. 1, the sponge construction consists of two phases - absorbing and squeezing. It first applies the padding function *pad* on the input string M which produces M' whose length is a multiple of r. In the absorbing phase, M' is split into blocks of r bits namely $m_1, m_2, ...m_k$. The initial state (IV) is a b bit string containing all 0. Here $b = r + c$ where c is called the capacity. The first r bits of IV is XORed with first block m_1 and is given as input to f. The output is XORed with the next message block m_2 and then is given as input to f again. This process is continued till all the message blocks have been absorbed.

The squeezing phase extracts the required output, which can be of any length. Let ℓ be the required output length. If $\ell \leq r$, then the first ℓ bits of the output of absorbing phase is the output of the sponge construction. Whereas, if $\ell > r$, then more blocks of r bits are extracted by repeatedly applying f on the output of the absorbing phase. This process is repeated enough number of times until we have extracted at least ℓ bits. The final output of the sponge construction is the first ℓ bits that have been extracted.

In the KECCAK hash family, the permutation function f is a KECCAK-$f[b]$ permutation, and the *pad* function appends 10*1 to input M. KECCAK-f is a specialization of KECCAK-p permutation.

$$\text{KECCAK-}f[b] = \text{KECCAK-p}[b, 12 + 2\gamma]$$

where $\gamma = log_2(b/25)$.

The official version of KECCAK have $r = 1600 - c$ and $c = 2\ell$ where $\ell \in \{224, 256, 384, 512\}$ called KECCAK-224, KECCAK-256, KECCAK-384 and KECCAK-512.

2.2 KECCAK-p Permutation

KECCAK-p permutation is denoted by KECCAK-p$[b, n_r]$, where $b \in \{25, 50, 100, 200, 400, 800, 1600\}$ is the length of the input string and n_r is the number of rounds of the internal transformation. The parameter b is also called the width of the permutation. The b bit input string can be represented as a $5 \times 5 \times w$ 3-dimensional array known as state as shown in Fig. 2. A lane in a state S is denoted by $S[x,y]$ which is the substring $S[x,y,0]|S[x,y,1]|\ldots|S[x,y,w-1]$ where w is equal to $b/25$ and "|" is the concatenation function.

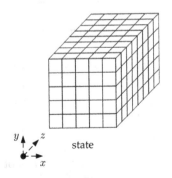

Fig. 2. KECCAK state [3]

In each round, the state S goes through 5 step mappings θ, ρ, π, χ and ι, i.e. $Round(S, i_r) = \iota(\chi(\pi(\rho(\theta(S)))), i_r)$ where i_r is the round index. Except for χ, rest of the step mappings are linear. In the following, S' is the state after applying the corresponding step mapping to S, "$\oplus$" denotes bitwise XOR and "." denotes bitwise AND.

1. θ: The θ step XOR's $S[x,y,z]$ with parities of its neighbouring columns in the following manner.

$$S'[x,y,z] = S[x,y,z] \oplus P[(x+1) \bmod 5][(z-1) \bmod 64]$$
$$\oplus P[(x-1) \bmod 5][z]$$

where $P[x][z]$ is the parity of a column, i.e.,

$$P[x][z] = \bigoplus_{i=0}^{4} S[x, i, z]$$

2. ρ: The ρ step simply rotates each lane by a predefined value given in the table below, i.e.

$$S'[x, y] = S[x, y] << r[x][y]$$

where $<<$ means bitwise rotation towards MSB of the 64-bit word.

4	18	2	61	56	14
3	41	45	15	21	8
2	3	10	43	25	39
1	36	44	6	55	20
0	0	1	62	28	27
$y\backslash x$	0	1	2	3	4

3. π: The π step interchanges the lanes of the state S.

$$S'[y, 2x + 3y] = S[x, y]$$

4. χ: The χ step is the only non-linear operation among the 5 step mappings due to the quadratic term.

$$S'[x, y, z] = S[x, y, z] \oplus ((S[(x + 1) \bmod 5, y, z] \oplus 1) \cdot$$
$$S[(x + 2) \bmod 5, y, z])$$

5. ι: The ι step is the only step that depends on the round number.

$$S'[0, 0] = S[0, 0] \oplus RC_i$$

where RC_i is a constant which depends on i where i is the round number.

2.3   Preliminaries and Notations

In this paper, we will be using the following observations made by Guo et al. [13]. The χ step mapping is a row dependent operation. Let a_0, a_1, a_2, a_3, a_4 be the 5 input bits to the χ operation and b_0, b_1, b_2, b_3, b_4 be the 5 output bits.

Observation 1. *Let d_0, d_1, d_2, d_3, d_4 be the elements of a column. Then, the parity of column can be fixed to a constant c by choosing for any $i \in \{0, 1, 2, 3, 4\}$*

$$d_i = c \oplus \left(\bigoplus_{j=1}^{j=4} d_{i+j} \right)$$

Observation 2. *If the output of χ for an entire row is known, i.e.* $\chi([a_0, a_1, a_2, a_3, a_4]) = [b_0, b_1, b_2, b_3, b_4]$, *then we have*

$$a_i = b_i \oplus (b_{i+1} \oplus 1) \cdot (b_{i+2} \oplus (b_{i+3} \oplus 1) \cdot b_{i+4}$$

Observation 3. *If we are given two consecutive bits b_i, b_{i+1} of the output of χ, we can set up the following linear equation on the input bits.*

$$b_i = a_i \oplus (b_{i+1} \oplus 1) \cdot a_{i+2}$$

In the rest of the paper, all the message variables and hash values are represented in the form of lanes (array) of length 64, and we will use $+$ symbol in place of $\oplus$. For a state A, $A[x, y]$ denotes a lane where $0 \leq x, y \leq 4$. In all the equations, the value inside the brackets '()' indicates the offset by which the lane is shifted. For example, $A[x, y](k)$ denotes lane $A[x, y]$ rotated by an offset of k. Every operation between two lanes is bitwise.

3   Our Preimage Attacks

In this section, we present the preimage attacks for round reduced KECCAK. In [13], the authors try to set up linear equations between message bits (variables) and hash bits by controlling the diffusion due to θ and χ from producing any non-linear terms. Observation 1 is used to manage the diffusion due to θ. Lanes are fixed to constant to prevent χ from creating any non-linear terms. Furthermore, for KECCAK-384/512, the first row of the hash digest can be inverted due to Observation 2.

In most cases, the number of linear equations between the variables and hash values is strictly less than the hash length. Therefore, they repeat the whole procedure enough number of times by appropriately changing the constants in the system of linear equations. This gives a successful preimage attack. In [18, 19], similar techniques are used to restrict χ from producing many non-linear terms. Here, we allow χ to produce non-linear terms, but at the same time, we control the number of non-linear terms in the state.

3.1   Preimage Attack on 2 Rounds KECCAK-512

In this subsection, we describe our preimage attack for 2-rounds KECCAK-512. The best-known attack for this variant of KECCAK is by Guo et al. [13] with a complexity of 2^{384}. Their preimage attack is based on a linear structure by keeping four lanes as variables. We give two preimage attacks using six lanes as variables. In the first preimage attack, we keep the lanes in column 1, 3, 4 as variables and get an attack of complexity 2^{337} which can be improved to 2^{321}. However, the second preimage attack chooses a different set of lanes as variables and also has complexity of 2^{321}.

Preimage Attack with Complexity 2^{337}: In Fig. 3, we set the lanes in column 1, 3 and 4 as variables, and the rest of the lanes are set to some constant. Therefore, we have $6 \times 64 = 384$ variables. To avoid the propagation by θ in the first round, we use Observation 1, i.e., $\bigoplus_{j=0}^{4} A[i,j] = \alpha_i, \forall i \in [0,2,3]$ where α_i is some constant and hence include $3 \times 64 = 192$ linear constraints to the system. Also, since the hash length is 512, we can invert the first row of the hash value due to Observation 2.

Observe that after the application of the χ operation in the first round, state (4) contains a lane with quadratic terms. Due to the θ of the second round, these will get propagated only to the neighbouring columns. Hence, majority of the lanes in the state (5) contains only linear terms. But, while equating state (6) and state (7), we are only able to obtain $2 \times 64 = 128$ linear equations between the hash values and the variables. Observe that we have set up only 320 linear equations but have 384 variables.

Applying the techniques used in [13], we can linearize the quadratic term and use them to create more linear equations between hash value and the variables. Notice that in state (5), there is atmost one quadratic term in each polynomial. This is because the state before the application of θ in the second round has only one lane containing polynomials with only one quadratic term. More precisely, $A[4,4]$ of state (4) contains a polynomial of the form $p_1 + \overline{p_2}.p_3$ where p_i's are linear polynomials. This non-linear polynomial can be linearlized by adding one more linear equation to the system, say $p_3 = \beta$ where β is a constant. Therefore, if we linearize one quadratic term in state (4), we will be able to linearize 11 quadratic terms in state (5). But, only 3 out of the 11 linearized terms can be equated to the values in state (7). Therefore, we can set up an additional 64 linear equations of which $3\lfloor 64/4 \rfloor = 48$ equations are between message bits and hash values. But, we need to include one more linear equation for the last message bit to be 1 to satisfy the padding condition of KECCAK. Therefore, we have a system of linear equation in 384 variables and 384 equations. Since, we have $128 + 48 - 1 = 175$ linear equations between hash values and variables, we get a valid preimage with probability $1/2^{337}$.

To get a successful preimage attack, we must repeat the above procedure for at least 2^{337} times where the system of linear equations are different each time. Observe that there is enough degrees of freedom to perform this, i.e. 192 bits from $A[1,0], A[1,1]$ and $A[4,0]$ and 192 bits from α_i for $i \in [0,2,3]$ which sums up to 384 bits. Therefore, we have a preimage attack for 2-rounds KECCAK-512 with complexity of 2^{337}.

Improved Analysis: In the previous analysis, by equating state (6) and (7), we were able to obtain 128 linear equations between the hash values and variables. Let us now focus on the second χ operation on the second row of state (6). Observe that the second and fourth lanes of second row in state (6) are linear whereas we know the values of the first three consecutive lanes of the output of the second χ operation. Using Observation 3, we can set up an additional 64 linear equations which sums up to $128 + 64 - 1$ linear equations between the

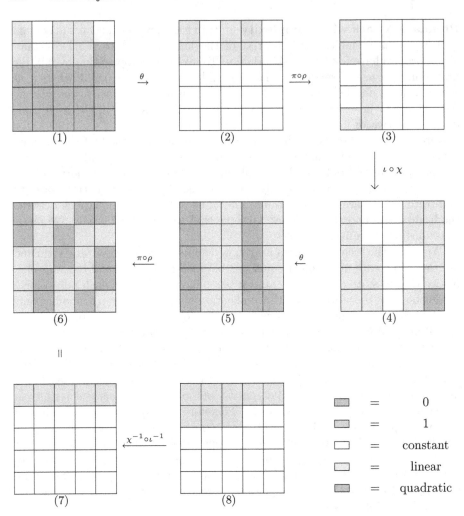

Fig. 3. Preimage attack on 2-round KECCAK-512

hash value and variables. Therefore, we have a preimage attack for 2-rounds KECCAK-512 with complexity of 2^{321}.

By choosing a different set of lanes as variables, we have another preimage attack with complexity 2^{321}. In Fig. 4, columns $1, 2$ and 4 are set as variables and the rest are set to constant. We also set $\bigoplus_{j=0}^{4} A[i, j] = \alpha_i, \forall i \in [0, 1, 3]$ where α_i is some constant, thus adding 192 linear equations to the system. Observe that in this case, we can set up $3 \times 64 - 1$ linear equations between the hash values and the variables. We must also include one more linear constraint for the last bit of message to be 1 to satisfy the padding condition for KECCAK. Therefore, we have a system of linear equation in 384 variables and 384 equations.

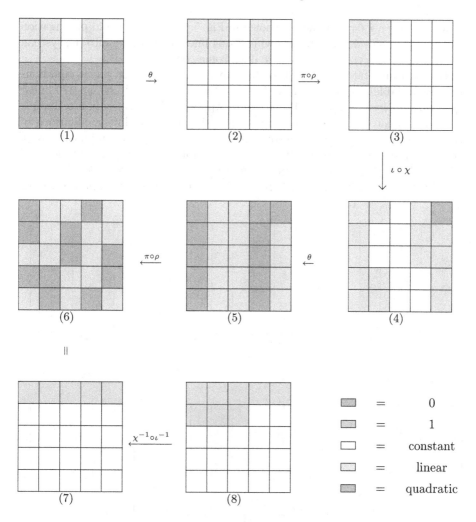

Fig. 4. Better preimage attack on 2-round KECCAK-512

Since we are able to set up only 191 linear equations between the hash values and the variables, we get a valid preimage with probability $1/2^{321}$. Observe that there is enough degrees of freedom to repeat this procedure for 2^{321} due 192 bits from $A[2,0], A[2,1]$ and $A[4,0]$ and 192 bits from α_i for $i \in [0,1,3]$ which sums up to 384 bits. Therefore, we have a preimage attack for 2-rounds KECCAK-512 with complexity of 2^{321}.

3.2 Preimage Attack on 2 Rounds KECCAK-384

The preimage attack given by Guo et al. [13] for 2 rounds KECCAK-384 has a complexity of 2^{129} by constructing a linear structure with 6×64 variables. In our attack, we use 8×64 variables as shown in Fig. 5. In-order to avoid propagation by θ in first round, we add the following 3×64 linear constraints into the system, $\bigoplus_{j=0}^{4} A[i,j] = \alpha_i, \forall i \in [0,2,3]$ where α_i is some constant.

By equating state (5) and state (6), we get $2 \times 64 = 128$ linear equations between variables and hash values. Observe that we have only set up 320 linear equations but have $8 \times 64 = 512$ variables. Applying the linearization technique used in Subsect. 3.1, we can set up an additional 3×64 linear equations of which $3\lfloor (3 \times 64)/4 \rfloor = 144$ equations are between message bits and hash values. After satisfying the padding rule, we have a complexity gain over brute force of $2^{128+144-1} = 2^{271}$ and hence a preimage attack of complexity $2^{384-271} = 2^{113}$. Observe that we have enough degrees of freedom to repeat this procedure for

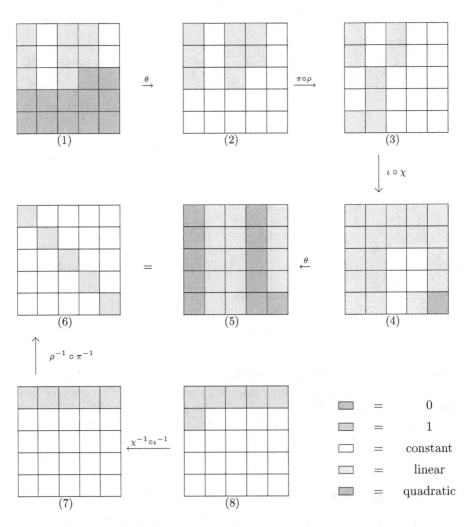

Fig. 5. Preimage attack on 2-round KECCAK-384

2^{113} times. Note that this result cannot be compared with the preimage attack given by Kumar et al. [16] because their attack has a space complexity of 2^{87}.

3.3 Preimage Attack for Higher Rounds

In the previous subsections, we were able to get better preimage attack due to the fact the states are not filled with quadratic terms. If we were to find a similar attack for 3-rounds, we need to keep the following guidelines in mind.

1. The state after the application of second θ must be sparse of lanes with linear terms and comprised mostly of lanes with constant terms. This is because it would lead to a state with lesser quadratic terms after the application of χ of the second round.
2. Even if the propagation due to the θ in the third round cannot be restricted, the state before the application of the third θ must contain all its quadratic terms either in a single column or in two columns adjacent to each other. This would lead to a state with at least one column containing linear terms only after the application of θ.

3.4 Preimage Attack on 3 Rounds KECCAK-384

The following is our attack on KECCAK-384 for 3-rounds which uses two message blocks as shown in Fig. 6. The first message block is chosen in such a way that after the application of 3 round KECCAK on this block, we get a state such that $A[1,3] = A[3,3] = 0$ and $A[1,4] = A[4,4] = 1$ where A is state (2) as shown in Fig. 6. The first message block can be found by randomly choosing $2^{4\times64}$ message block and expecting one of them to give the required output. This works because the output of a hash function is random and therefore the complexity for brute force preimage attack is $1/2^l$ where l is the number of bits in the hash digest. The same technique has been used in [18] subsection 4.3.

The second message block contains $6 \times 64 = 384$ variables. We want to keep the columns 2, 4 and 5 unchanged after the application of first θ. For this, we first set $\bigoplus_{j=0}^{4} A[i,j] = \alpha_i$, for $i \in [0,2]$ and then set up equation between column 1 and column 3 so that column 2 does not get affected after the application of first θ. This means that the α_i's are dependent. Similarly, c_2 and c_3 can be set according to α_i's such that column 4 and 5 do not get affected after the first θ. Therefore, we have 2×64 linear equations in our system. c_1 can be fixed to some randomly chosen value.

To avoid propagation after second θ, we set up 3×64 linear equations to make the column parties equal to some constant β_i. Observe that after the application of the second χ, there are two lanes with quadratic terms in state (8). But after the application of the third θ, the fourth column will contain only linear terms. By equating state (9) and state (10), we can set up 63 linear equations between message bits and hash values. Also, we have one more equation to keep the last message bit equal to 1. Therefore, we have a preimage attack with a time of complexity $2^{384-63} = 2^{321}$ because computing the first message block has a complexity of 2^{256}.

Note that there are enough degrees of freedom due to the 256 bits from α_i's and the β_i's, 64 bits from c_1 and enough bits from the first message block.

3.5 Preimage Attack on 3 Rounds KEECAK-512

We use two message blocks and $4 \times 64 = 256$ variables for this attack as shown in Fig. 7. The first message block is used so that we get enough degree of freedom to launch a preimage attack. Observe that after the application of θ in first round, we require certain lanes to be $1/0$ in state (4). To achieve this, we first set $A[1,0] \oplus A[1,1] = \alpha_1$ where α_1 is some constant. Then, we set up 64 linear equations of the form $\bigoplus_{i=0}^{4} (A[1,i] \oplus A[3,i](1) = e_2 + 1)$. Observe that due to this constraint, after the application of first θ, we will get $A[2,0] = A[2,4] = 1$ and $A[2,1] = 0$ where A is state (4). Similarly, by fixing x_6 and x_2 appropriately, we can get the required state (4).

To avoid propagation due to the θ in second round, we add only 64 linear equations to the system to make the parity of the first columns in state (6) as a constant. Observe that after the application of θ of the third round, the lanes in the first two columns will contain only one quadratic term. So, if we linearize one quadratic term in $A[2,4]$ of state (9), then we have linearized five polynomials in column 2 of state (10). Similarly, if we linearize one quadratic term in $A[4,2]$ of state (9), then we have linearized five polynomial in column 1 of state (10).

But, out of these 6 linearized polynomials, only one can be used to create a linear equation between message bits and hash value by equating state (10) and state (11). Therefore, we have $\lfloor 64/2 \rfloor = 32$ linear equations between message bits and hash value and hence obtained a preimage of complexity $2^{512-32+1} = 2^{481}$. Due to the first message block, we have enough degree of freedom.

Improved Analysis. Observe that if we carefully linearize one quadratic term from $A[2,4]$ and one from $A[4,2]$ of state (9), we also linearize one more polynomial in column 4 of state (10), i.e. we have also linearized a polynomial in the lane $A[3,3]$. Therefore, now we have $3\lfloor \frac{64}{5} \rfloor + 2 = 3 \times 12 + 2 = 38$. Therefore, we have an improved preimage attack of complexity $2^{512-38+1} = 2^{475}$.

3.6 Preimage Attack on 4 Rounds KEECAK-384

This attack requires two message blocks and $6 \times 64 = 384$ variables as shown in Fig. 8. As done in Subsect. 3.4, the first message block is found by trying randomly many message blocks so that after the application of 4-rounds and XORing the second message block, we get state (2). Observe that in state (2), there are two lanes with entries c and $\bar{c}$. We also require state (2) to satisfy one more equation.

$$d(-1) + \bar{b}(-2) + (g(-1) + (\bar{c} + a + b)(-2))(-2) + (a+b)(1) = \bar{k} \qquad (1)$$

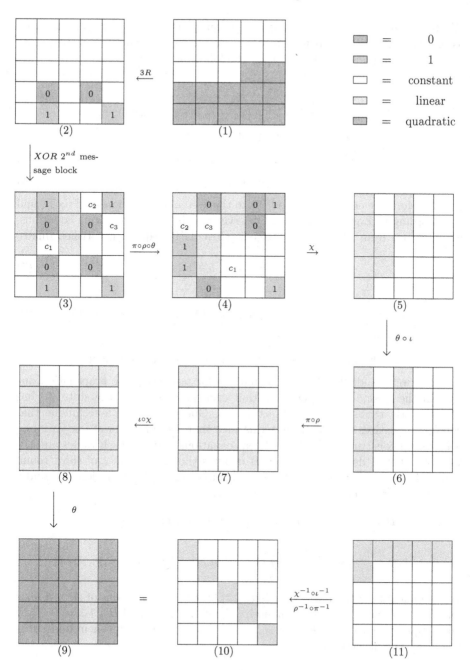

Fig. 6. Preimage attack on 3-round KECCAK-384

Therefore, we would require a complexity of 2^{128} to find the appropriate first message block. We will use the following strategy to obtain state (3). We include

$A[0,0] = A[0,2]$ to the system of linear equations, fix $x_1 = 0$ and randomly assign value to x_7 whereas we fix $x_2 = \bar{c}, x_3 = d, x_5 = g$. Since we require state (3) after the application of θ, we have the following equations.

$$(a + b) + (A[2,0] + A[2,2] + e)(1) = \bar{c} \tag{2}$$

$$(A[2,0] + A[2,2] + e) + (x_6 + x_7 + i + j + k)(1) = g \tag{3}$$

$$(x_6 + x_7 + i + j + k) + (A[1,0] + A[1,2] + c)(1) = \bar{b} \tag{4}$$

$$(A[1,0] + A[1,2] + c) + (x_4 + f + h)(1) = d \tag{5}$$

$$(x_4 + f + h) + (a + b)(1) = \bar{k} \tag{6}$$

Therefore, we add Eqs. (7) and (9) to the system of equations and fix x_6 and x_4 according to Eqs. (8) and (10). Observe that due to the following equations, all equations from (2)–(6) are satisfied, particularly, Eq. (6) is satisfied due to Eq. (1).

$$A[2,0] + A[2,2] = (\bar{c} + a + b)(-1) + e \tag{7}$$

$$x_6 = g(-1) + (\bar{c} + a + b)(-2) + x_7 + i + j + k \tag{8}$$

$$A[1,0] + A[1,2] = \bar{b}(-1) + (g(-1) + (\bar{c} + a + b)(-2))(-1) + c \tag{9}$$

$$x_4 = d(-1) + f + h + (\bar{b} + x_6 + x_7 + i + j + k)(-2)$$
$$= d(-1) + f + h + \bar{b}(-2) + (g(-1) + (\bar{c} + a + b)(-2))(-2) \tag{10}$$

Also, we include 2×64 linear equations for restricting the propagation due to θ in the second round. Observe that each polynomial in the state (9) has 11 quadratic terms. In [13] subsection 6.3, Guo et al. gave a technique that carefully linearizes the quadratic terms such that if the number of free variables is t, we can construct $2\lfloor (t-5)/8 \rfloor$ linear equations between hash values and the variables. Let A denotes state (8), B denotes the state after χ of third round and C denotes the state after θ of fourth round. From the definition of χ and θ and neglecting ι step for the sake of simplicity,

$$B[x,y,z] = A[x,y,z] \oplus (A[x+1,y,z] \oplus 1) \cdot A[x+2,y,z]$$

$$C[x,y,z] = B[x,y,z] \oplus \bigoplus_{y'=0}^{4} B[x-1,y',z] \oplus \bigoplus_{y'=0}^{4} B[x+1,y',z-1]$$

We can linearize $B[x-1,y,z]$ and $B[x,y,z]$ by guessing the value of $A[x+1,y,z]$ for $0 \leq y \leq 4$. Similarly, we can linearize $B[x+1,y,z-1]$ and $B[x+2,y,z-1]$ by guessing the value of $A[x+3,y,z-1]$ for $0 \leq y \leq 4$. This helps us in linearizing $C[x,y,z]$, but observe that

$$C[x+1,y+1,z] = B[x+1,y+1,z] \oplus \bigoplus_{y'=0}^{4} B[x,y',z] \oplus \bigoplus_{y'=0}^{4} B[x+2,y',z-1]$$

which contain a quadratic part in $B[x+1,y+1,z]$. By linearizing this term, we set up 13 linear equations of which two equations are between message bits and hash

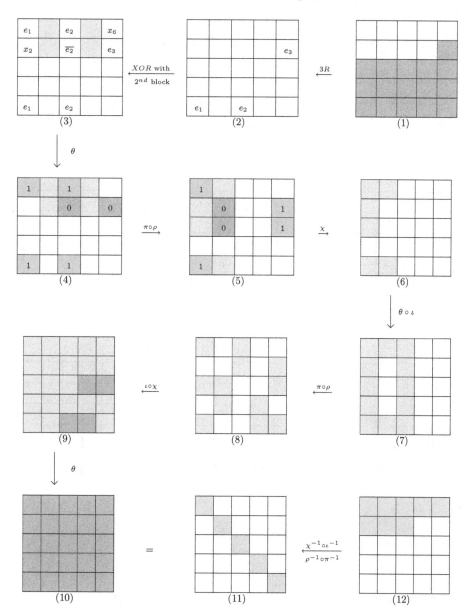

Fig. 7. Preimage attack on 3-round KECCAK-512

values. Similarly, by carefully observing $C[x+2, y+2, z-1]$ and $C[x+3, y+3, z-1]$ and linearizing them, we can set up another 8 linear equations of which two equations are between message bits and hash values. For more details, refer [13]. In our case, the number of free variable $t = 64$ and therefore, we can set up 14 linear equations between message bits and hash values. Observe that we have

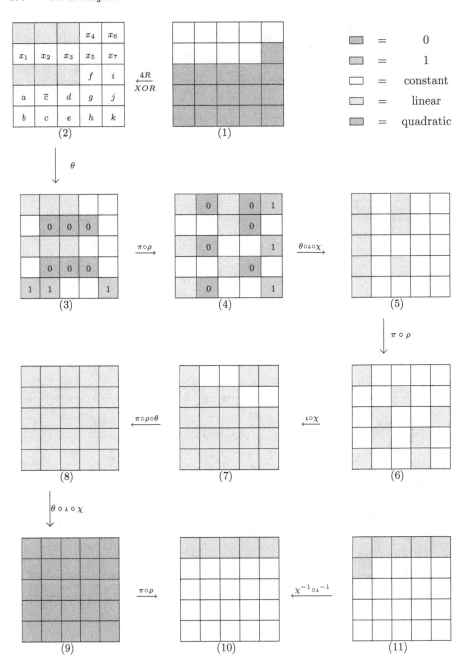

Fig. 8. Preimage attack on 4-round KECCAK-384

enough degree of freedom due to x_7, the parity of the two columns of the second θ and rest from the first message block. Therefore, the complexity of our attack is 2^{371}.

4 Conclusion

In this paper, we give the best theoretical preimage attacks on $2, 3$ rounds KECCAK-512 and $2, 3, 4$ rounds KECCAK 384 by studying non-linear structures carefully. It would be interesting to see whether non-linear structures along with other techniques can be used to find better preimage attacks for higher rounds.

Acknowledgement. We would like to thank Rajendra Kumar for valuable discussions and anonymous reviewers of INDOCRYPT 2019 for their helpful comments.

References

1. Aumasson, J.P., Meier, W.: Zero-sum distinguishers for reduced Keccak-f and for the core functions of Luffa and Hamsi. In: Rump Session of Cryptographic Hardware and Embedded Systems-CHES 2009, p. 67 (2009)
2. Bernstein, D.J.: Second preimages for 6 (7?(8??)) rounds of Keccak. NIST mailing list (2010)
3. Bertoni, G., Daemen, J., Peeters, M., Assche, G.: The Keccak reference (2011). http://keccak.noekeon.org/keccak-reference-3.0.pdf
4. Bertoni, G., Daemen, J., Peeters, M., Van Assche, G.: Keccak specifications. Submission to NIST (round 2), pp. 320–337 (2009)
5. Bertoni, G., Daemen, J., Peeters, M., Van Assche, G.: Cryptographic sponges (2011). http://sponge.noekeon.org
6. Boura, C., Canteaut, A., De Cannière, C.: Higher-order differential properties of KECCAK and *Luffa*. In: Joux, A. (ed.) FSE 2011. LNCS, vol. 6733, pp. 252–269. Springer, Heidelberg (2011). https://doi.org/10.1007/978-3-642-21702-9_15
7. Chang, D., Kumar, A., Morawiecki, P., Sanadhya, S.K.: 1st and 2nd preimage attacks on 7, 8 and 9 rounds of Keccak-224,256,384,512. In: SHA-3 workshop, August 2014
8. Dinur, I., Dunkelman, O., Shamir, A.: New attacks on Keccak-224 and Keccak-256. In: Canteaut, A. (ed.) FSE 2012. LNCS, vol. 7549, pp. 442–461. Springer, Heidelberg (2012). https://doi.org/10.1007/978-3-642-34047-5_25
9. Dinur, I., Dunkelman, O., Shamir, A.: Collision attacks on up to 5 rounds of SHA-3 using generalized internal differentials. In: Moriai, S. (ed.) FSE 2013. LNCS, vol. 8424, pp. 219–240. Springer, Heidelberg (2014). https://doi.org/10.1007/978-3-662-43933-3_12
10. Dinur, I., Dunkelman, O., Shamir, A.: Improved practical attacks on round-reduced Keccak. J. Cryptol. **27**(2), 183–209 (2014)
11. Duc, A., Guo, J., Peyrin, T., Wei, L.: Unaligned rebound attack: application to Keccak. In: Canteaut, A. (ed.) FSE 2012. LNCS, vol. 7549, pp. 402–421. Springer, Heidelberg (2012). https://doi.org/10.1007/978-3-642-34047-5_23
12. Dworkin, M.J.: SHA-3 standard: permutation-based hash and extendable-output functions. Technical report (2015)

13. Guo, J., Liu, M., Song, L.: Linear structures: applications to cryptanalysis of round-reduced KECCAK. In: Cheon, J.H., Takagi, T. (eds.) ASIACRYPT 2016. LNCS, vol. 10031, pp. 249–274. Springer, Heidelberg (2016). https://doi.org/10.1007/978-3-662-53887-6_9

14. Jean, J., Nikolić, I.: Internal differential boomerangs: practical analysis of the round-reduced Keccak-f permutation. In: Leander, G. (ed.) FSE 2015. LNCS, vol. 9054, pp. 537–556. Springer, Heidelberg (2015). https://doi.org/10.1007/978-3-662-48116-5_26

15. Kölbl, S., Mendel, F., Nad, T., Schläffer, M.: Differential cryptanalysis of Keccak variants. In: Stam, M. (ed.) IMACC 2013. LNCS, vol. 8308, pp. 141–157. Springer, Heidelberg (2013). https://doi.org/10.1007/978-3-642-45239-0_9

16. Kumar, R., Mittal, N., Singh, S.: Cryptanalysis of 2 round KECCAK-384. In: Chakraborty, D., Iwata, T. (eds.) INDOCRYPT 2018. LNCS, vol. 11356, pp. 120–133. Springer, Cham (2018). https://doi.org/10.1007/978-3-030-05378-9_7

17. Kumar, R., Rajasree, M.S., AlKhzaimi, H.: Cryptanalysis of 1-round KECCAK. In: Joux, A., Nitaj, A., Rachidi, T. (eds.) AFRICACRYPT 2018. LNCS, vol. 10831, pp. 124–137. Springer, Cham (2018). https://doi.org/10.1007/978-3-319-89339-6_8

18. Li, T., Sun, Y.: Preimage attacks on round-reduced KECCAK-224/256 via an allocating approach. In: Ishai, Y., Rijmen, V. (eds.) EUROCRYPT 2019. LNCS, vol. 11478, pp. 556–584. Springer, Cham (2019). https://doi.org/10.1007/978-3-030-17659-4_19

19. Li, T., Sun, Y., Liao, M., Wang, D.: Preimage attacks on the round-reduced Keccak with cross-linear structures. IACR Trans. Symmetric Cryptol. 39–57 (2017)

20. Morawiecki, P., Pieprzyk, J., Srebrny, M.: Rotational cryptanalysis of round-reduced KECCAK. In: Moriai, S. (ed.) FSE 2013. LNCS, vol. 8424, pp. 241–262. Springer, Heidelberg (2014). https://doi.org/10.1007/978-3-662-43933-3_13

21. Morawiecki, P., Srebrny, M.: A SAT-based preimage analysis of reduced Keccak hash functions. Inf. Process. Lett. **113**(10–11), 392–397 (2013)

22. Naya-Plasencia, M., Röck, A., Meier, W.: Practical analysis of reduced-round KECCAK. In: Bernstein, D.J., Chatterjee, S. (eds.) INDOCRYPT 2011. LNCS, vol. 7107, pp. 236–254. Springer, Heidelberg (2011). https://doi.org/10.1007/978-3-642-25578-6_18

23. Song, L., Liao, G., Guo, J.: Non-full sbox linearization: applications to collision attacks on round-reduced KECCAK. In: Katz, J., Shacham, H. (eds.) CRYPTO 2017. LNCS, vol. 10402, pp. 428–451. Springer, Cham (2017). https://doi.org/10.1007/978-3-319-63715-0_15

Protocols: Blockchain, Secure Computation and Blind Coupon Mechanism

Nummatus: A Privacy Preserving Proof of Reserves Protocol for Quisquis

Arijit Dutta[1], Arnab Jana[2], and Saravanan Vijayakumaran[1(✉)]

[1] Department of Electrical Engineering, Indian Institute of Technology Bombay, Mumbai, India
arijit.dutta@iitb.ac.in, sarva@ee.iitb.ac.in
[2] Department of Computer Science and Engineering, Indian Institute of Technology Bombay, Mumbai, India
arnabjanacse@cse.iitb.ac.in

Abstract. Quisquis is a recently proposed design for a privacy-focused cryptocurrency. We present *Nummatus*, a privacy preserving proof of reserves protocol for Quisquis. Nummatus enables exchanges to create a Pedersen commitment to the amount of Quisquis coins they own, without revealing the exact accounts they own. These commitments can be combined with a commitment to the total liabilities of an exchange to generate a proof of solvency. The Nummatus protocol also facilitates detection of account sharing collusion between exchanges. Our simulations show that the cost of using Nummatus instead of a non-private proof of reserves protocol is not prohibitive.

Keywords: Proof of reserves · Quisquis · Cryptocurrency · Privacy in blockchain

1 Introduction

Cryptocurrency exchanges arose to enable cryptocurrency acquisition without mining. They provide custodial wallets and trading services to their customers. Custodial wallets not only free customers from the burden of storing private keys but also allow for more efficient trading (as they do not need trades to be recorded on the blockchain). The downside of custodial wallets is that customer funds are lost when the exchange gets hacked or when the exchange operators execute an exit scam. In both these undesirable scenarios, corrective measures can be more effective if the attacks are detected early.

Proofs of solvency can enable early detection of loss of customer funds from cryptocurrency exchanges [11,12,21]. These proofs show that the cryptocurrency reserves of an exchange exceed its liabilities (the amount of coins the exchange has sold to customers). Exchanges are more likely to provide proofs of solvency if they are privacy preserving, i.e. the proofs do not reveal which outputs or accounts on the blockchain belong to the exchange and they also do not reveal the actual amounts corresponding to the total reserves and total liabilities.

© Springer Nature Switzerland AG 2019
F. Hao et al. (Eds.): INDOCRYPT 2019, LNCS 11898, pp. 195–215, 2019.
https://doi.org/10.1007/978-3-030-35423-7_10

A popular method of providing proofs of solvency is using Pedersen commitments [11,16]. First, a Pedersen commitment p_{liab} to the total amount of coins the exchange has sold to customers (the liabilities) is created. The protocol used to ensure that p_{liab} is in fact a commitment to the exchange's total liabilities is called a *proof of liabilities* protocol. Second, a Pedersen commitment p_{res} to the total amount of coins owned by the exchange (the reserves) is created. The protocol used to ensure that p_{res} is a commitment to the exchange's total reserves is called a *proof of reserves* protocol. Third, a range proof on the quantity $p_{\text{res}}p_{\text{liab}}^{-1}$ is provided to show that the difference between the reserves and liabilities is non-negative and in the correct range.[1] Proof of reserves protocols use the data available on the blockchain. Consequently, reasonable proof of reserves protocols have been proposed for Bitcoin [11], Monero [13], and Mimblewimble [14]. On the other hand, proof of liabilities protocols need to use an exchange's customer database to generate the proofs. As a malicious exchange can conceal some customer records to reduce its liabilities, the proofs of liabilities protocols proposed so far are not robust. In this paper, we limit our attention to a privacy preserving proof of reserves protocol for Quisquis [15].

Quisquis is a recently proposed design for privacy-focused cryptocurrency. It solves the problem of the always growing *unspent transaction output (UTXO)* set which plagues other privacy-focused cryptocurrencies like Monero [3] and Zcash [6]. While no reference implementation of Quisquis exists, the design is novel enough to warrant designing proof of reserves protocol for it. So when an implementation does emerge and the Quisquis cryptocurrency becomes available on exchanges, the Nummatus proof of reserves protocol can be employed in proofs of solvency.

Our Contribution. We propose Nummatus, a proof of reserves protocol for Quisquis exchanges[2]. It is, to the best of our knowledge, the first such protocol for Quisquis. Our protocol is privacy preserving in the sense that it only reveals that the exchange-owned accounts belong to a larger anonymity set of accounts, without identifying which ones are exchange-owned. The protocol gives a technique to detect collusion between exchanges who use the same account to generate their respective proofs of reserves. We also describe a non-private proof of reserves protocol for Quisquis exchanges called Simplus, with the intention of quantifying the cost of deploying a privacy preserving protocol. We give simulation results to compare the performance of the Nummatus and Simplus protocols. These simulations show that, while privacy has a cost, deploying Nummatus is a practical proposition.

---

[1] We present elliptic curve group operations in multiplicative notation to be consistent with the presentation in the Quisquis paper [15].

[2] *Quisquis* is Latin for "whoever, whatever" [19]. *Nummatus* is Latin for "moneyed, rich" [18]. We chose this name for our protocol as it enables an exchange to show that it is *rich enough* to meet its liabilities.

2   Overview of Quisquis

Privacy-focused cryptocurrencies like Monero and Zcash allow users to conceal the source of coins in a transaction using ring signatures [17] or zk-SNARKs [5]. As the true source of coins is not revealed, a one-time address in Monero and a commitment in Zcash cannot be considered spent.[3] Consequently, these cryptocurrencies have poor scalability in the long term without the opportunity to prune spent outputs from the blockchain.

Quisquis is a cryptocurrency proposal which offers both privacy and scalability [15]. It is an account-based design (as opposed to a UTXO-based design), where each account consists of a public key and a commitment to the balance in the account. The public key is generated from the secret key and a randomizing scalar. Hence there are many possible public keys corresponding to a secret key (unlike Bitcoin where the public key is a deterministic function of the secret key).

Each Quisquis transaction involves some *input accounts* and an *equal* number of *output accounts*. Each output account is an updated version of exactly one of the input accounts, where the update consists of an update of the input account's public key (the account secret key remains unchanged) *and/or* an update of the input account's balance. Unlike Bitcoin where the input UTXOs in a transaction represent the source of funds and output UTXOs represent destinations, the input accounts in a Quisquis transaction consist of both source accounts and destination accounts. Additionally, some *passive accounts* are added to the list of input accounts in the transaction to obfuscate the sources and destinations of funds. Only the public keys of the passive accounts are updated in a transaction and their balances are unchanged. On the other hand, the balances of source accounts are reduced and the balances of destination accounts are increased. For both source and destination accounts, the public keys are updated. The output accounts are presented in a lexicographical order to prevent linking of specific output accounts with input accounts. Once a Quisquis transaction appears on the blockchain, the input accounts can be pruned. Quisquis has special transactions for creation and deletion of accounts. Regular transactions do not create new accounts and this is the main reason for the scalability of the design. In the following subsections, we present a more precise description of those aspects of Quisquis that are necessary to present Nummatus.

2.1   Quisquis Accounts

Let $\mathbb{G}$ be a group with prime order p and generator g. The Decisional Diffie-Hellman (DDH) problem is assumed to be hard in $\mathbb{G}$. A Quisquis account based on $\mathbb{G}$ is specified by four group elements (a, b, c, d). The first two group elements specify a *public key* $\mathsf{pk} = (a, b) = (g^t, g^{k \cdot t})$ where $t \in \mathbb{F}_p$ is an arbitrary scalar

---

[3] Source addresses in Monero transactions where the sender deliberately chose a ring size of one can be considered spent. But this kind of behavior is seen only in old transactions as the default ring size was set to 11 in October 2018 [2].

and $k \in \mathbb{F}_p$ is the *secret key*. The last two group elements specify a *commitment* which depends on pk and is given by $\mathtt{com} = (c,d) = (a^r, g^v b^r)$ where $r \in \mathbb{F}_p$ is an arbitrary scalar. Here $v \in \mathbb{F}_p$ is the value being committed to by com. In summary, a Quisquis account is of the form

$$\mathtt{acct} = (a,b,c,d) = (a,b,a^r,g^v b^r) = \left(g^t, g^{k \cdot t}, g^{t \cdot r}, g^{v+k \cdot t \cdot r}\right) \tag{1}$$

where k is the secret key, v is the value in the account, and r, t are arbitrary scalars.

In the Quisquis design, knowledge of the secret key k is sufficient to prove ownership of an account and to create transactions which transfer value out of it, i.e. knowledge of the scalars r and t is not required. This feature allows an entity to perform a *secret key preserving update* of an account, even when the entity has no knowledge of the secret key, value, or scalars used to create the account elements. An update of an account $\mathtt{acct} = (a,b,c,d)$ to an account $\mathtt{acct}' = (a_1, b_1, c_1, d_1)$ preserves the secret key k and changes the amount from v to $v + \delta$ if the following equations hold.

$$b = a^k, \quad d = g^v c^k,$$
$$b_1 = a_1^k, \quad d_1 = g^{v+\delta} c_1^k. \tag{2}$$

A Quisquis transaction involves account updates of this kind in addition to range proofs on the values $v + \delta$ to ensure that the amount changes are valid.

The account update procedure is as follows:

1. Suppose acct in (1) is the account to be updated.
2. The updater chooses scalars $t_1, r_1, \delta \in \mathbb{F}_p$. While t_1, r_1 are chosen arbitrarily, δ represents the change in the value stored in the account.
3. The updater computes the updated public key as

$$\mathtt{pk}' = (a_1, b_1) = (a^{t_1}, b^{t_1}). \tag{3}$$

4. The updater computes the updated commitment as

$$\mathtt{com}' = (c_1, d_1) = (ca^{r_1}, dg^\delta b^{r_1}). \tag{4}$$

Note that this update can be interpreted as the coordinate-wise product of the commitment (c,d) with the commitment $(a^{r_1}, g^\delta b^{r_1})$.
5. The updated account is $\mathtt{acct}' = (\mathtt{pk}', \mathtt{com}') = (a_1, b_1, c_1, d_1)$.

It is easy to check that the equations in (2) hold. Since $b = a^k$, we have

$$b_1 = b^{t_1} = \left(a^k\right)^{t_1} = \left(a_1^t\right)^k = a_1^k. \tag{5}$$

Since $d = g^v c^k$ and $c_1 = ca^{r_1}$, we have

$$d_1 = dg^\delta b^{r_1} = g^v c^k g^\delta \left(a^k\right)^{r_1} = g^{v+\delta} \left(ca^{r_1}\right)^k = g^{v+\delta} c_1^k. \tag{6}$$

To see that the updated account has the structure specified in (1), consider the following version of acct'.

$$\texttt{acct}' = (a_1, b_1, c_1, d_1) = \left(a^{t_1}, b^{t_1}, ca^{r_1}, dg^{\delta}b^{r_1}\right) \tag{7}$$

$$= \left(g^{t \cdot t_1}, g^{k \cdot t \cdot t_1}, g^{t(r+r_1)}, g^{v+\delta+k \cdot t \cdot (r+r_1)}\right) \tag{8}$$

$$= \left(g^{t'}, g^{k \cdot t'}, g^{t' \cdot r'}, g^{v+\delta+k \cdot t' \cdot r'}\right), \tag{9}$$

where $t' = t \cdot t_1$ and $r' = t_1^{-1} \cdot (r + r_1)$.

In the subsequent discussion, we will find it convenient to denote the above account update procedure by the notation $\texttt{UpdateAcct}(\texttt{acct}, t_1, r_1, \delta)$.

2.2 Quisquis Transactions

Suppose Alice owns account $\texttt{acct}_1$ and wants to transfer δ amount to account $\texttt{acct}_2$. Alice will choose $n-2$ additional accounts from the blockchain which will play the role of passive accounts. Let these passive accounts be denoted by $\texttt{acct}_3, \texttt{acct}_4, \ldots, \texttt{acct}_n$. Alice will construct a transaction with input accounts given by $\texttt{inputs} = \{\texttt{acct}_1, \texttt{acct}_2, \ldots, \texttt{acct}_n\}$. The input accounts will be listed in a canonical order like lexicographical ordering to conceal the identity of the non-passive accounts. Alice will update each of the input accounts to generate output accounts given by $\texttt{outputs} = \{\texttt{acct}_1', \texttt{acct}_2', \ldots, \texttt{acct}_n'\}$ where

$$\texttt{acct}_1' = \texttt{UpdateAcct}(\texttt{acct}_1, t_1, r_1, -\delta),$$
$$\texttt{acct}_2' = \texttt{UpdateAcct}(\texttt{acct}_2, t_2, r_2, \delta),$$
$$\texttt{acct}_3' = \texttt{UpdateAcct}(\texttt{acct}_3, t_3, r_3, 0),$$

$$\vdots \quad = \quad \vdots$$

$$\texttt{acct}_n' = \texttt{UpdateAcct}(\texttt{acct}_n, t_n, r_n, 0),$$

where the t_is and r_is are arbitrarily chosen scalars. Note that the balance in the source account $\texttt{acct}_1$ is reduced by δ and the balance in the destination account $\texttt{acct}_2$ is increased by δ. The balances of the passive accounts remain the same. The output accounts will also be presented in a canonical ordering to conceal the mapping from the inputs to the outputs. Alice then constructs a zero knowledge proof π that convinces the verifier of the following statements.

1. Each account in outputs is an update of exactly one of the accounts in inputs.
2. The account updates cumulatively satisfy preservation of balances i.e. $\sum \delta_i = 0$, where δ_i is the update of balance of $\texttt{acct}_i$.
3. The balance of the source account does not become negative after the update.
4. The balance of the destination account after the update is in the correct range of values (range proof).
5. The balances of the passive accounts remain unchanged.

The transaction txn itself consists of the sets inputs, outputs, and the zero knowledge proof π, i.e. txn = (inputs, outputs, π). While our illustrative example had only one source account and one destination account, transactions with multiple sources and destinations are allowed in Quisquis.

The implication of this transaction model to our context is that exchange-owned accounts may be updated several times before they are used in the proof of reserves protocol. If the exchange is not involved in all the updates of an account, it will not know the discrete logarithm of the group elements forming the public key and commitment with respect to the generator g. This fact has to be taken into consideration in the proof of reserves protocol design.

3   Nummatus Proof of Reserves Protocol

The overall design of the Nummatus protocol is similar to the proof of reserves protocols which have appeared in the literature [11,13,14]. However, unlike these previously proposed protocols, the Nummatus protocol requires a sequence of elements $h_1, h_2, h_3, \ldots$ from $\mathbb{G}$ whose discrete logarithms with respect to g and each other are unknown. The sequence $\{h_j \in \mathbb{G} \mid j = 1, 2, \ldots\}$ can be generated by repeatedly hashing g while ensuring the result falls in the group $\mathbb{G}$. All the exchanges need to agree upon the specific sequence generation procedure. A Nummatus proof which is generated after the jth Quisquis block has appeared and before the $(j + 1)$th block has appeared on the blockchain will use the jth element h_j. We will see that this sequence will be used to serve three purposes, namely, (1) to compute the commitment to the total reserves amount of the exchange, (2) to reveal collusion between exchanges sharing account to generate proof of reserves, and (3) to conceal the identity of the exchange's accounts across multiple Nummatus proofs.

Suppose an exchange is generating the Nummatus proof of reserves after the jth Quisquis block. We give a high-level description the procedure followed by the exchange below (a more precise description is given in Sect. 3.1).

1. Let $\mathcal{A}_{\text{all}}$ be the set of all accounts and let $\mathcal{A}_{\text{own}} \subset \mathcal{A}_{\text{all}}$ be the accounts owned by the exchange.[4] The exchange chooses a set of accounts $\mathcal{A}_{\text{oth}}$ not owned by it, i.e. $\mathcal{A}_{\text{oth}} \subset \mathcal{A}_{\text{all}} \setminus \mathcal{A}_{\text{own}}$. These other accounts are added to the set of exchange-owned accounts to form the *anonymity set* $\mathcal{A}_{\text{anon}} = \mathcal{A}_{\text{own}} \cup \mathcal{A}_{\text{oth}}$.
2. Let $\mathcal{A}_{\text{anon}} = [\text{acct}_1, \text{acct}_2, \ldots, \text{acct}_n]$ where

$$\text{acct}_i = (a_i, b_i, c_i, d_i) = \left(a_i, a_i^{k_i}, a_i^{r_i}, g^{v_i} a_i^{k_i \cdot r_i} \right). \tag{10}$$

Here $k_i \in \mathbb{F}_p$ is the secret key, $v_i \in \mathbb{F}_p$ is the account balance, $r_i \in \mathbb{F}_p$ is an arbitrary scalar, and $a_i = g^{t_i}$ for an arbitrary $t_i \in \mathbb{F}_p$.

---

[4] Sets $\mathcal{A}_{\text{all}}$ and $\mathcal{A}_{\text{own}}$ may change everytime a new block is added to the Quisquis blockchain. Here we consider particular instances of these sets after the jth block is added to the blockchain.

For each $\mathtt{acct}_i$, the exchange creates a Pedersen commitment p_i and a non-interactive zero knowledge proof of knowledge (NIZKPoK) σ_i which proves the *disjunction* of the following statements:

(i) Account $\mathtt{acct}_i$ is owned by the exchange, i.e. the exchange knows the secret key k_i associated with $\mathtt{acct}_i$, and p_i is a Pedersen commitment to the balance v_i in $\mathtt{acct}_i$.

(ii) Pedersen commitment p_i is a commitment to the zero amount.

Note that the proof σ_i proves that *one of these two statements* is true without revealing which one.

3. The exchange publishes the anonymity set $\mathcal{A}_{\mathrm{anon}}$, Pedersen commitments $[p_1, p_2, \ldots, p_n]$, and NIZKPoKs $[\sigma_1, \sigma_2, \ldots, \sigma_n]$. It claims that $p_{\mathrm{res}} = \prod_{i=1}^{n} p_i$ is a Pedersen commitment to the total reserves of the exchange.

To understand the different parts of the protocol, we need to look at the structure of the individual Pedersen commitments p_i. As discussed above, the discrete logarithms g and h_j are unknown with respect to each other. A Pedersen commitment to an amount $v \in \mathbb{F}_p$ with respect to bases g and h_j is given by $g^v h_j^w$ where $w \in \mathbb{F}_p$ is the blinding factor.

When $\mathtt{acct}_i \in \mathcal{A}_{\mathrm{own}}$, the Nummatus protocol sets $p_i = g^{v_i} h_j^{k_i}$. So p_i is a commitment to the balance v_i of $\mathtt{acct}_i$ and the secret key k_i is the blinding factor in this case. When $\mathtt{acct}_i \notin \mathcal{A}_{\mathrm{own}}$, the Nummatus protocol sets $p_i = h_j^{w_i}$ for a randomly chosen $w_i \in \mathbb{F}_p$, making p_i a commitment to the zero amount. Let $\mathcal{I}_{\mathrm{own}}$ be the indices in $\{1, 2, \ldots, n\}$ corresponding to accounts in $\mathcal{A}_{\mathrm{own}}$, i.e. $\mathtt{acct}_i \in \mathcal{A}_{\mathrm{own}}$ for all $i \in \mathcal{I}_{\mathrm{own}}$. Let $\mathcal{I}_{\mathrm{own}}^c$ denote those indices in $\{1, 2, \ldots, n\}$ which are not in $\mathcal{I}_{\mathrm{own}}$. Then we have

$$p_{\mathrm{res}} = \prod_{i=1}^{n} p_i = \prod_{i \in \mathcal{I}_{\mathrm{own}}} g^{v_i} h_j^{k_i} \prod_{i \in \mathcal{I}_{\mathrm{own}}^c} h_j^{w_i} = g^{v_{\mathrm{res}}} h_j^{w_{\mathrm{res}}}, \qquad (11)$$

where

$$v_{\mathrm{res}} = \sum_{i \in \mathcal{I}_{\mathrm{own}}} v_i, \qquad (12)$$

$$w_{\mathrm{res}} = \sum_{i \in \mathcal{I}_{\mathrm{own}}} k_i + \sum_{i \in \mathcal{I}_{\mathrm{own}}^c} w_i. \qquad (13)$$

Thus p_{res} is a Pedersen commitment to the exchange's total reserves v_{res}. If $p_{\mathrm{liab}} = g^{v_{\mathrm{liab}}} h_j^{w_{\mathrm{liab}}}$ is a Pedersen commitment to the total liabilities of the exchange, then a proof of solvency reduces to showing that

$$p_{\mathrm{res}} p_{\mathrm{liab}}^{-1} = g^{v_{\mathrm{res}} - v_{\mathrm{liab}}} h_j^{w_{\mathrm{res}} - w_{\mathrm{liab}}} \qquad (14)$$

is a commitment to a non-negative amount in the correct range.

If two exchanges share an account $\mathtt{acct}_i$ while generating their respective proofs of reserves after the jth Quisquis block, then the account will appear in both the anonymity sets. But this is not enough to prove account sharing collusion between the exchanges. However, the commitment $p_i = g^{v_i} h_j^{k_i}$ corresponding to a shared account will appear in both lists of commitments, revealing the collusion.

The reason for choosing a different base h_j for generating the Pedersen commitments after each block is to prevent leaking the identity of exchange-owned accounts across multiple Nummatus proofs. Suppose the same base h is used to generate commitments in all Nummatus proofs given by an exchange. Then the commitments of exchange-owned accounts will remain same across proofs assuming the balances of the accounts (the v_is) remain same. However, the commitments of unknown accounts will be different in different proofs because of different w_is. Thus an observer will be able identify which accounts belong to the exchange.

A consequence of this design is that exchanges cannot use the same secret key for multiple accounts if they want to use the Nummatus proof of reserves protocol. This is not a serious restriction as the convenience afforded by having the same secret key for multiple accounts is negligible compared to the security provided by having different keys for different accounts. This issue is further discussed in Sect. 4.2.

Note that the proof σ_i proves that p_i is a Pedersen commitment of the form which is either $g^{v_i} h_j^{k_i}$ or $h_j^{w_i}$. If an exchange does not own the account acct_i, it will be forced to set p_i to the form $h_j^{w_i}$. When exchange does own the account, it can set p_i to be of the form $g^{v_i} h_j^{k_i}$. In the latter scenario, there is nothing stopping the exchange from setting p_i to be of the form $h_j^{w_i}$. But this will mean that the balance v_i of account acct_i is not counted in the total reserves amount v_{res}. In other words, the exchange is under-reporting the reserves it owns. This is not a problem as long as the reserves exceed the liabilities, since proving solvency is the final goal.

Due to the DDH assumption in the underlying group $\mathbb{G}$, the Nummatus proof of reserves protocol satisfies the following properties:

- *Inflation resistance*: No probabilistic polynomial time (PPT) exchange will be able to generate a commitment to an amount which exceeds the reserves it actually owns.
- *Proof of non-collusion between exchanges*: If two exchanges share an account while generating their respective proofs of reserves (from the same blockchain state), then such collusion can be detected.
- *Privacy of accounts*: No PPT adversary will be able to distinguish whether an account in the anonymity set belongs to the exchange or not.

3.1   Proof Generation

Suppose a Quisquis exchange wants to generate a Nummatus proof corresponding to its reserves after the jth Quisquis block. It performs the following procedure:

1. The exchange chooses the anonymity set of accounts $\mathcal{A}_{\text{anon}}$ from the set of all accounts $\mathcal{A}_{\text{all}}$ present on the blockchain after the jth Quisquis block has

appeared and before the $(j+1)$th block appeared. The exchange owns a subset $\mathcal{A}_{\text{own}}$ of $\mathcal{A}_{\text{anon}} = [\texttt{acct}_1, \texttt{acct}_2, \ldots, \texttt{acct}_n]$.

2. For each $\texttt{acct}_i \in \mathcal{A}_{\text{anon}}$ such that $\texttt{acct}_i = \left(a_i, a_i^{k_i}, c_i, g^{v_i} c_i^{k_i}\right)$, the exchange generates a Pedersen commitment p_i of the form

$$p_i = \begin{cases} g^{v_i} h_j^{k_i} & \text{if } \texttt{acct}_i \in \mathcal{A}_{\text{own}}, \\ h_j^{w_i} & \text{if } \texttt{acct}_i \notin \mathcal{A}_{\text{own}}, \end{cases} \tag{15}$$

where the w_is are chosen independently and uniformly from $\mathbb{F}_p$.

3. For each $\texttt{acct}_i \in \mathcal{A}_{\text{anon}}$ given by $\texttt{acct}_i = (a_i, b_i, c_i, d_i) = \left(a_i, a_i^{k_i}, c_i, g^{v_i} c_i^{k_i}\right)$, the exchange generates a NIZKPoK $\sigma_i = (e_{i,1}, e_{i,2}, s_{i,1}, s_{i,2}) \in \mathbb{F}_p^4$ of the form

$$\text{PoK}\left\{(\alpha, \beta) \,\Big|\, \left(b_i = a_i^{\alpha} \,\wedge\, p_i d_i^{-1} = \left(c_i^{-1} h_j\right)^{\alpha}\right) \vee \left(p_i = h_j^{\beta}\right)\right\}. \tag{16}$$

The NIZKPoK σ_i proves that the exchange knows scalars α, β such that *either* $p_i = h_j^{\beta}$ or $b_i = a_i^{\alpha}$ and $p_i d_i^{-1} = \left(c_i^{-1} h_j\right)^{\alpha}$. The algorithm for generating σ_i is given in Appendix A.

4. The exchange publishes the base h_j, the anonymity set $\mathcal{A}_{\text{anon}}$, Pedersen commitments $[p_1, p_2, \ldots, p_n]$, and NIZKPoKs $[\sigma_1, \sigma_2, \ldots, \sigma_n]$. It claims that $p_{\text{res}} = \prod_{i=1}^{n} p_i$ is a Pedersen commitment to the total reserves of the exchange.

Equation (15) reflects the requirement that p_i is a commitment to the account balance for exchange-owned accounts and a commitment to the zero amount for other accounts. The choice of blinding factor in each case makes p_i a deterministic function of the secret key and the balance for exchange-owned accounts and a random group element for other accounts. The NIZKPoK condition in (16) in fact ensures that an exchange does not deviate from the constructions of p_i given in (15). It states that either p_i is a commitment to the zero amount or the following conditions (in italics) hold:

(i) *The discrete logarithm of b_i with respect a_i is known to the party generating the proof σ_i.*
As $b_i = a_i^{k_i}$, this condition implies that the secret key k_i is known to the exchange.

(ii) *The party generating the proof σ_i knows the discrete logarithm of $p_i d_i^{-1}$ with respect to $c_i^{-1} h_j$. Furthermore, the discrete logarithm is equal to the discrete logarithm of b_i with respect to a_i.*
As $b_i = a_i^{k_i}$, from (16) we have

$$p_i d_i^{-1} = \left(c_i^{-1} h_j\right)^{k_i}. \tag{17}$$

Since $d_i = g^{v_i} c_i^{k_i}$, from the above equation we get

$$p_i g^{-v_i} c_i^{-k_i} = c_i^{-k_i} h_j^{k_i} \implies p_i = g^{v_i} h_j^{k_i}. \tag{18}$$

Thus p_i is a commitment to the balance v_i in the account $\texttt{acct}_i$ with blinding factor k_i as given in (15).

3.2 Proof Verification

Given a Nummatus proof of reserves from an exchange referring to the blockchain state after the jth Quisquis block, the verifier checks the following conditions:

1. All the accounts in the anonymity set $\mathcal{A}_{\text{anon}}$ must appear on the blockchain immediately after the jth block. If an account in $\mathcal{A}_{\text{anon}}$ does not appear on the blockchain, the proof is considered invalid.
2. For each i, the NIZKPoK σ_i must pass the verification procedure given in Appendix A.
3. The commitments $p_i, i = 1, 2, \ldots, n$, must not appear in another exchange's Nummatus proof. If the same commitments p_i appears in the Nummatus proofs of two different exchanges, then collusion is declared and the proof of reserves is considered invalid.

4 Nummatus Security Properties

In this section, we discuss the security properties of the Nummatus protocol. We are concerned with inflation resistance, collusion resistance, and account privacy (as defined in Sect. 3).

4.1 Inflation and Collusion Resistance

Inflation resistance refers to the requirement that a PPT exchange should not be able to use the Nummatus protocol to generate a Pedersen commitment p_{res} to an amount v_{res} which is greater than the total reserves it owns. Suppose p_{res} is a commitment to v_{res} which is greater than $\sum_{i \in \mathcal{I}_{\text{own}}} v_i$. Then since

$$p_{\text{res}} = \prod_{i=1}^{n} p_i = \prod_{i \in \mathcal{I}_{\text{own}}} p_i \prod_{i \in \mathcal{I}_{\text{own}}^c} p_i, \tag{19}$$

it must be that either p_i is not a commitment to zero for some $i \in \mathcal{I}_{\text{own}}^c$ or p_i is a commitment to an amount larger than the account balance v_i for some $i \in \mathcal{I}_{\text{own}}$. For $i \in \mathcal{I}_{\text{own}}^c$, the exchange does not know the secret key k_i and consequently it must generate the NIZKPoK σ_i by setting p_i to be commitment to the zero amount. For $i \in \mathcal{I}_{\text{own}}$, if a PPT exchange sets p_i to be a commitment to a nonzero amount then σ_i forces this amount to be the account balance v_i (see Eq. (18)). So the inflation resistance property of Nummatus follows from the unforgeability of the NIZKPoKs σ_i.

When p_i is not a commitment to zero, the account acct_i must be owned by the exchange as the private key k_i is needed to create p_i as $g^{v_i} h_j^{k_i}$. This form of p_i is a deterministic function of v_i and k_i. So two exchanges sharing acct_i after the jth Quisquis block will produce same p_i in their proofs. If this happens, then account sharing collusion is immediately detected.

4.2   Account Privacy

Account privacy refers to the requirement that a PPT distinguisher $\mathcal{D}$, which is given a polynomial number of Nummatus proofs as input, cannot identify exchange-owned accounts in the anonymity set $\mathcal{A}_{\text{anon}}$ except with a negligible probability. Our proof that the Nummatus protocol preserves account privacy relies on the DDH problem being hard in the group used to implement Quisquis.

Let $\lambda \in \mathbb{N}$ be a security parameter. Suppose $\texttt{Setup}(1^\lambda)$ is a group generation algorithm which gives $(\mathbb{G}, g, p)$ where $\mathbb{G}$ is a group with generator g and prime order p. We assume that there is no algorithm which can solve the DDH problem in $\mathbb{G}$ with a running time which is polynomial in λ.

To define account privacy security, we will use an experiment with name $\texttt{AccountPriv}$.

- Let us consider an exchange which has generated $f(\lambda)$ Nummatus proofs where f is a polynomial.
- Let $\mathcal{A}_{\text{anon}}^1, \mathcal{A}_{\text{anon}}^2, \ldots, \mathcal{A}_{\text{anon}}^{f(\lambda)}$, be the anonymity sets used in these $f(\lambda)$ proofs having sizes $N_1, N_2, \ldots, N_{f(\lambda)}$, respectively.
- For $l = 1, 2, \ldots, f(\lambda)$, assume that the lth Nummatus proof was created after the j_lth block appeared and before the $(j_l + 1)$th block appeared on the blockchain. So the lth Nummatus proof will use bases g and h_{j_l} to create Pedersen commitments.
- The lth Nummatus proof consists of the base h_{j_l}, the anonymity set $\mathcal{A}_{\text{anon}}^l$, Pedersen commitments $[p_{l,1}, p_{l,2}, \ldots, p_{l,N_l}]$, and NIZKPoKs $[\sigma_{l,1}, \sigma_{l,2}, \ldots, \sigma_{l,N_l}]$.

We make two assumptions:

(i) *The secret keys of all exchange-owned accounts in the lth anonymity set $\mathcal{A}_{\text{anon}}^l$ are all distinct.* This is necessary as the Nummatus protocol cannot provide account privacy without this constraint. To see why, suppose two accounts in $\mathcal{A}_{\text{anon}}^l$ share the same secret key k. Let their corresponding Pedersen commitments be $p_{l,i} = g^v h_{j_l}^k$ and $p_{l,i'} = g^{v'} h_{j_l}^k$ where i, i' are the account indices and v, v' are the account balances. An adversary can figure out that these two accounts are exchange-owned accounts by checking if the equality $p_{l,i} g^{-v_1} = p_{l,i'} g^{-v_2}$ holds for some $(v_1, v_2) \in V^2$ where V is the set of all possible amounts. As the size of V is small, this attack is practical. In fact, the receiver of a funds in a regular Quisquis transaction has to search through all possible values in V to figure out the amount received [15, Section 5.2.3].

(ii) *There is an exchange-owned account with secret key k which appears in the anonymity sets of all the $f(\lambda)$ Nummatus proofs.* This assumption serves to simplify the notation. In the $\texttt{AccountPriv}$ experiment, we want to consider an adversary which can identify an exchange-owned account based on multiple Nummatus proofs. The existence of such an adversary who can successfully identify an exchange-owned account with a non-negligible probability will lead to a contradiction of the DDH assumption. An adversary who succeeds only if the account appears in all the $f(\lambda)$ Nummatus proofs is weaker than an adversary who can succeed even if the account appears in a subset of the $f(\lambda)$ Nummatus proofs. Thus obtaining a contradiction from the non-negligible success probability of the weaker adversary is sufficient. Let i_l be the index of the account with secret key k in the lth anonymity set $\mathcal{A}^l_{\text{anon}} = [\text{acct}^l_1, \text{acct}^l_2, \ldots, \text{acct}^l_{N_l}]$. Let v_l be the non-zero balance of this account when the lth Nummatus proof is created. Thus we have

$$p_{l,i_l} = g^{v_l} h^k_{j_l} \text{ or } p_{l,i_l} = h^{w_{l,i_l}}_{j_l}, \tag{20}$$

where $w_{l,i_l} \in \mathbb{F}_p$.

The experiment `AccountPriv` proceeds as follows.

1. The group parameters are generated as $(\mathbb{G}, g, p) \leftarrow \texttt{Setup}(1^\lambda)$. A sequence of group elements $h_1, h_2, h_3, \ldots$ are chosen uniformly and independently from $\mathbb{G}$.
2. From the sequence generated in the previous step, the exchange chooses a subsequence $h_{j_1}, h_{j_2}, \ldots, h_{j_{f(\lambda)}}$ where f is a polynomial.
3. The exchange chooses a bit $\mathfrak{b}$ uniformly from $\{0, 1\}$.
4. If $\mathfrak{b} = 0$, the exchange sets $p_{l,i_l} = h^{w_{l,i_l}}_{j_l}$ for some uniformly chosen w_{l,i_l} from $\mathbb{F}_p$ for all $l = 1, 2, \ldots, f(\lambda)$, i.e. the i_lth account does not contribute to the reserves in all the $f(\lambda)$ Nummatus proofs. The exchange generates the NIZKPoKs σ_{l,i_l} accordingly.
   The other commitments $p_{l,i}$ for all $l = 1, 2, \ldots, f(\lambda)$ and $i = 1, 2, \ldots, N_l, i \neq i_l$ are generated arbitrarily. The corresponding NIZKPoKs $\sigma_{l,i}$ are generated accordingly.
5. If $\mathfrak{b} = 1$, the exchange sets $p_{l,i_l} = g^{v_l} h^k_{j_l}$ for all $l = 1, 2, \ldots, f(\lambda)$, i.e. the i_lth account contributes its balance to the reserves in all the $f(\lambda)$ Nummatus proofs. The exchange generates the NIZKPoKs σ_{l,i_l} accordingly.
   The other commitments $p_{l,i}$ for all $l = 1, 2, \ldots, f(\lambda)$ and $i = 1, 2, \ldots, N_l, i \neq i_l$ are generated arbitrarily. The corresponding NIZKPoKs $\sigma_{l,i}$ are generated accordingly.
6. Let $\mathfrak{N}_l = \left(h_{j_l}, \mathcal{A}^l_{\text{anon}}, [p_{l,1}, \ldots, p_{l,N_l}], [\sigma_{l,1}, \ldots, \sigma_{l,N_l}] \right)$ be the lth Nummatus proof. Let the account index vector be $\mathcal{I} = [i_1, i_2, \ldots, i_{f(\lambda)}]$ and the account balance vector be $\mathcal{V} = [v_1, v_2, \ldots, v_{f(\lambda)}]$. The $f(\lambda)$ Nummatus proofs $\{\mathfrak{N}_l\}^{f(\lambda)}_{l=1}$, $\mathcal{I}$, and $\mathcal{V}$ are given as input to a distinguisher $\mathcal{D}$ which then outputs a bit $\mathfrak{b}'$, i.e.

$$\mathfrak{b}' = \mathcal{D}\left(\mathfrak{N}_1, \mathfrak{N}_2, \ldots, \mathfrak{N}_{f(\lambda)}, \mathcal{I}, \mathcal{V}\right). \tag{21}$$

7. $\mathcal{D}$ succeeds if $\mathfrak{b}' = \mathfrak{b}$. Otherwise it fails.

Definition 1. *The Nummatus proof of reserves protocol provides account privacy if for every PPT distinguisher $\mathcal{D}$ in the* `AccountPriv` *experiment with a probability which is negligibly close to $\frac{1}{2}$.*

This definition captures the requirement that a distinguisher should not be able to tell if an account was used in a sequence of Nummatus proofs even if it knew the account index in the anonymity set and the account balance in all the proofs. Note that distinguisher who knows $\mathcal{I}$ and $\mathcal{V}$ is more likely to succeed than a distinguisher which does not know these vectors, i.e.

$$\Pr\left[\mathcal{D}\left(\mathfrak{N}_1, \mathfrak{N}_2, \ldots, \mathfrak{N}_{f(\lambda)}\right) = \mathfrak{b}\right] \leq \Pr\left[\mathcal{D}\left(\mathfrak{N}_1, \mathfrak{N}_2, \ldots, \mathfrak{N}_{f(\lambda)}, \mathcal{I}, \mathcal{V}\right) = \mathfrak{b}\right]. \quad (22)$$

So if we can show that for every distinguisher $\mathcal{D}$ with knowledge of $\mathcal{I}$ and $\mathcal{V}$, there is a negligible function `negl` such that

$$\Pr\left[\mathcal{D}\left(\mathfrak{N}_1, \mathfrak{N}_2, \ldots, \mathfrak{N}_{f(\lambda)}, \mathcal{I}, \mathcal{V}\right) = \mathfrak{b}\right] \leq \frac{1}{2} + \texttt{negl}(\lambda), \quad (23)$$

then the same upper bound applies holds on the success probability of distinguishers which do not know $\mathcal{I}$ and $\mathcal{V}$. We will use a distinguisher of the form $\mathcal{D}\left(\mathfrak{N}_1, \mathfrak{N}_2, \ldots, \mathfrak{N}_{f(\lambda)}, \mathcal{I}, \mathcal{V}\right)$ to construct an adversary who can solve the generalized DDH problem [7] resulting in the following theorem.

Theorem 1. *The Nummatus proof of reserves protocol provides account privacy in the random oracle model under the DDH assumption provided that the exchange uses distinct secret keys for its accounts in the anonymity set.*

Proof. Suppose $\mathcal{E}$ is an adversary which wants to solve the generalized DDH problem given a tuple $\left(g_1, \ldots, g_{f(\lambda)}, u_1, \ldots, u_{f(\lambda)}\right) \in \mathbb{G}^{2f(\lambda)}$ [7]. Specifically, it want to distinguish between the following two situations:

- In the tuple $\left(g_1, \ldots, g_{f(\lambda)}, u_1, \ldots, u_{f(\lambda)}\right)$, each of the g_is and u_is are uniformly and independently chosen from $\mathbb{G}$.
- In the tuple $\left(g_1, \ldots, g_{f(\lambda)}, u_1, \ldots, u_{f(\lambda)}\right)$, each of the g_is are uniformly and independently chosen from $\mathbb{G}$. Each $u_l = g_l^k$ for all $l = 1, 2, \ldots, f(\lambda)$ where k is chosen uniformly from $\mathbb{F}_p$.

Let $\mathfrak{d} = 0$ denote the former situation and $\mathfrak{d} = 1$ denote the latter situation. If $\mathfrak{d}'$ is the output of a PPT $\mathcal{E}$, then $\Pr\left[\mathfrak{d}' = \mathfrak{d}\right]$ must be negligibly close to $\frac{1}{2}$.

The adversary $\mathcal{E}$ will construct a valid input for the distinguisher $\mathcal{D}$ in the `AccountPriv` experiment in the following manner:

1. For $l = 1, 2, \ldots, f(\lambda)$, $\mathcal{E}$ chooses anonymity set sizes N_l and test account indices i_l where $1 \leq i_l \leq N_l$. It also chooses non-zero values v_l for the test account balances from the allowed set of amount values V.
2. For each l, the accounts in the anonymity set $\mathcal{A}_{\text{anon}}^l = [\texttt{acct}_1^l, \ldots, \texttt{acct}_{N_l}^l]$ are constructed as

$$\texttt{acct}_i^l = (a_{l,i}, b_{l,i}, c_{l,i}, d_{l,i}) = \begin{cases} \left(g^{t_{l,i}}, g^{k_{l,i} \cdot t_{l,i}}, g^{t_{l,i} \cdot r_{l,i}}, g^{v_{l,i} + k_{l,i} \cdot t_{l,i} \cdot r_{l,i}}\right) & \text{if } i \neq i_l \\ \left(g_l^{t_{l,i}}, u_l^{k' \cdot t_{l,i}}, g_l^{t_{l,i} \cdot r_{l,i}}, g^{v_l} u_l^{k' \cdot t_{l,i} \cdot r_{l,i}}\right) & \text{if } i = i_l \end{cases}$$

where $k', k_{l,i}, t_{l,i}, r_{l,i}$ are chosen uniformly and independently from $\mathbb{F}_p$ and $v_{l,i}$ are chosen uniformly and independently from V. From Eq. (1), it follows that $\texttt{acct}_i^l$ is a valid account for $i \neq i_l$. For $i = i_l$ and $u_l = g_l^k$, i.e. the case of $\mathfrak{d} = 1$, it again follows that $\texttt{acct}_l^l$ is a valid account with secret key $k \cdot k'$. For $\mathfrak{d} = 0$,

Table 1. Proof generation and verification performance of Nummatus and Simplus

$\mathcal{A}_{anon}$ size	$\mathcal{A}_{own}$ size	Nummatus proof size	Nummatus Generat. time	Nummatus verification time	Simplus proof size	Simplus Generat. time	Simplus verification time
100	25	0.02 MB	1.15 s	1.15 s	0.005 MB	0.29 s	0.28 s
100	50	0.02 MB	1.16 s	1.16 s	0.011 MB	0.58 s	0.57 s
100	75	0.02 MB	1.19 s	1.19 s	0.017 MB	0.91 s	0.91 s
1000	250	0.29 MB	11.94 s	11.76 s	0.057 MB	3.00 s	2.98 s
1000	500	0.29 MB	11.92 s	11.77 s	0.114 MB	5.97 s	5.95 s
1000	750	0.29 MB	11.83 s	11.74 s	0.171 MB	8.92 s	8.74 s
10000	2500	2.93 MB	112.65 s	113.36 s	0.572 MB	28.99 s	28.06 s
10000	5000	2.93 MB	112.08 s	113.23 s	1.145 MB	56.40 s	56.63 s
10000	7500	2.93 MB	111.71 s	112.87 s	1.717 MB	85.07 s	85.72 s

the u_ls are independent of the g_ls. But since the g_ls are generators of the prime order group $\mathbb{G}$, we have $u_l = g_l^{s_l}$ for some $s_l \in \mathbb{F}_p$. Even though the s_ls are not known to $\mathcal{E}$, acct_i^l can be expressed as $\left(g_l^{t_{l,i}}, g_l^{k' \cdot s_l \cdot t_{l,i}}, g_l^{t_{l,i} \cdot r_{l,i}}, g^{v_l} g_l^{k' \cdot s_l \cdot t_{l,i} \cdot r_{l,i}} \right)$ which is a valid account structure.

3. For each l, $\mathcal{E}$ sets $h_{j_l} = g_l$ and $p_{l,i_l} = g^{v_l} u_l^{k'}$. As $\mathcal{E}$ does not know the discrete logarithm of $u_l^{k'}$ with respect to $h_{j_l} = g_l$, it generates valid NIZKPoKs σ_{l,i_l} using the random oracle assumption on H (see [13] for a similar argument). It involves changing the outputs of H for some inputs such that Eq. (31) is satisfied. We omit the details due to space constraints.

   The other commitments $p_{l,i}$ for all $l = 1, 2, \ldots, f(\lambda)$ and $i = 1, 2, \ldots, N_l, i \neq i_l$ are generated arbitrarily. The corresponding NIZKPoKs $\sigma_{l,i}$ are generated accordingly using knowledge of $k_{l,i}$.

4. $\mathcal{E}$ gives the $f(\lambda)$ Nummatus proofs generated in the previous steps, the index vector $\mathcal{I}$, and the balance vector $\mathcal{V}$ to a distinguisher $\mathcal{D}$ in the `AccountPriv` experiment. Let $\mathfrak{b}' = \mathcal{D}\left(\mathfrak{N}_1, \mathfrak{N}_2, \ldots, \mathfrak{N}_{f(\lambda)}, \mathcal{I}, \mathcal{V} \right)$. $\mathcal{E}$ outputs $\mathfrak{d}' = \mathfrak{b}'$. If $\mathcal{D}$ is a PPT algorithm, then so is $\mathcal{E}$.

Suppose the $\mathfrak{d} = 0$ situation occurs, i.e. $u_l = g_l^{s_l}$ for uniform $s_l \in \mathbb{F}_p$. Then irrespective of the values of v_l, the terms $p_{l,i_l} = g^{v_l} u_l^{k'}$ are uniformly distributed over $\mathbb{G}$. This corresponds to the situation of $\mathfrak{b} = 0$ in the `AccountPriv` experiment. On the other hand if the $\mathfrak{d} = 1$ situation occurs, then $u_l = g_l^k$ for a fixed $k \in \mathbb{F}_p$ for all l. Then for $h_{j_l} = g_l$, we have $p_{l,i} = g^{v_l} u_l^{k'} = g^{v_l} g_l^{k \cdot k'} = g^{v_l} h_{j_l}^{k \cdot k'}$. This corresponds to the situation of $\mathfrak{b} = 1$ in the `AccountPriv` experiment. Thus we have $\Pr[\mathfrak{d}' = \mathfrak{d}] = \Pr[\mathfrak{b}' = \mathfrak{b}]$.

   If there exists a PPT distinguisher $\mathcal{D}$ whose success probability $\Pr[\mathfrak{b}' = \mathfrak{b}]$ is larger than $\frac{1}{2} + \frac{1}{q(\lambda)}$ for some polynomial q, then this will imply that the success probability $\Pr[\mathfrak{d}' = \mathfrak{d}]$ of $\mathcal{E}$ is also larger than $\frac{1}{2} + \frac{1}{q(\lambda)}$. As a PPT adversary who can solve the generalized DDH problem is equivalent to a PPT adversary who can solve classical DDH problem [7], we get a contradiction. Thus any PPT distinguisher $\mathcal{D}$ in the AccountPriv experiment can only succeed with a probability which is negligibly close to $\frac{1}{2}$. □

5 Performance

To the best of our knowledge, Nummatus is the first proof of reserves protocol for Quisquis exchanges which keeps the identities of the exchange accounts private. For benchmarking purposes, we compare Nummatus to a simple non-private protocol which we will call *Simplus*.[5] In the Simplus protocol, the exchange reveals the accounts it owns, i.e. the set $\mathcal{A}_{own}$ is revealed. Like Nummatus, this protocol outputs a Pedersen commitment to the total reserves of the exchange. While the Simplus protocol does not provide account privacy, it provides reserve amount privacy. The proof generation in Simplus proceeds as follows:

1. The exchange chooses a set $\mathcal{A}_{own} = \{acct_1, acct_2, \ldots, acct_m\}$ of its own accounts which are sufficient to meet its liabilities. These accounts need to be present on the blockchain after the jth Quisquis block has appeared and before the $(j+1)$th block appeared.

2. For each $acct_i \in \mathcal{A}_{own}$ given by $acct_i = (a_i, b_i, c_i, d_i) = \left(a_i, a_i^{k_i}, c_i, g^{v_i} c_i^{k_i}\right)$, the exchange generates a Pedersen commitment $p_i := g^{v_i} h^{k_i}$ and a NIZKPoK $\psi_i = (e_{i,1}, s_{i,1}) \in \mathbb{F}_p^2$ of the form

$$PoK\left\{\alpha \,\middle|\, \left(b_i = a_i^{\alpha} \,\wedge\, p_i d_i^{-1} = \left(c_i^{-1} h\right)^{\alpha}\right)\right\}. \tag{24}$$

   Note that in case of Nummatus, we need to use h_j as base of p_i to make exchange's accounts indistinguishable from accounts not owned by the exchange across multiple Nummatus proofs. But in case of Simplus, the exchange has already revealed the accounts owned by it. Therefore we can simply use h instead of h_j as a base of p_i. The algorithm for generating ψ_i is given in Appendix B.

3. The exchange publishes the set $\mathcal{A}_{own}$, Pedersen commitments $[p_1, p_2, \ldots, p_m]$, and NIZKPoKs $[\psi_1, \psi_2, \ldots, \psi_m]$. It claims that $p_{res} = \prod_{i=1}^{m} p_i$ is a Pedersen commitment to the total reserves of the exchange.

The NIZKPoK in (24) ensures that the exchange knows the private key k_i for each account $acct_i$. Furthermore, by the argument presented in the Nummatus protocol discussion, the NIZKPoK ensures that p_i is a commitment to the account balance v_i of $acct_i$. As the exchange's accounts are revealed in the Simplus protocol, collusion between exchanges can be detected if the same account appears in the own account lists of two different exchanges.

---

[5] Simplus is Latin for "simple" [20].

The Simplus proof verification proceeds as follows:

1. All the accounts in the set $\mathcal{A}_{\text{own}}$ must appear on the blockchain immediately after the jth block. If not, the proof is considered invalid.
2. For each i, the NIZKPoK ψ_i must pass the verification procedure given in Appendix B.

The simulation code was implemented in Rust using the rust-secp256k1-zkp library [1] which has also been used for Revelio [14]. The source code is available at [4]. Performance of the Nummatus proof generation and verification algorithms is given in Table 1 for anonymity list $\mathcal{A}_{\text{anon}}$ having sizes 100, 1000, and 10000. For each case, the percentage of accounts belonging to the exchange is either 25%, 50%, or 75%. Table 1 also shows the performance of the Simplus protocol as a function of $\mathcal{A}_{\text{own}}$ size (the $\mathcal{A}_{\text{anon}}$ parameter is irrelevant here). The execution times were measured on single core of an Intel i7-7700 3.6 GHz CPU. The Nummatus protocol is at most 3 to 4 times slower and its proof size is at most 4 to 5 times larger compared to the Simplus protocol. The proof size and execution time of Nummatus protocol are practical and can be reduced further by parallel signature generations and verifications for different accounts in $\mathcal{A}_{\text{anon}}$. The higher values of performance parameters for Nummatus than that of Simplus can be considered as the price we are paying for privacy.

6   Conclusion

We give Nummatus, the first privacy preserving proof of reserves protocol for Quisquis [15] exchanges. Using Nummatus, a Quisquis exchange can prove that it holds more reserves than what it owes to its customers without revealing the reserves amount or the identity of owned accounts. Nummatus also detects the account sharing collusion between exchanges provided all exchanges generate their proofs after a particular block is added to the Quisquis blockchain. We give the performance comparison of Nummatus and a non-private proof of reserves protocol which we call Simplus. Our simulation shows that deployment of Nummatus is practical and feasible.

A   Nummatus NIZKPoK Generation and Verification Algorithms

In this appendix, we present algorithms for generating and verifying the NIZKPoK σ_i that is used in Nummatus. In the notation proposed by Camenisch and Stadler [8,9], the NIZKPoK is of the form

$$\text{PoK}\left\{(\alpha, \beta) \,\middle|\, \left(b_i = a_i^{\alpha} \,\wedge\, p_i d_i^{-1} = \left(c_i^{-1} h_j\right)^{\alpha}\right) \vee \left(p_i = h_j^{\beta}\right)\right\}.$$

The above proof is for a disjunction of two statements. We motivate the structure of σ_i by first describing methods to prove these two statements individually. Then the method first proposed by Cramer et al. [10] is used to generate a proof for the disjunction of the two statements.

Let $H : \{0,1\}^* \mapsto \mathbb{F}_p$ be a cryptographic hash function which is modeled as a random oracle. Let $\|$ denote the bitstring concatenation operator. For notational convenience, we write $H(x, y, z)$ to denote $H(x\|y\|z)$ where x, y, z are group elements represented as bitstrings.

Definition 2. *An ordered pair $(e, s) \in \mathbb{F}_p^2$ is a NIZKPoK of the discrete logarithm of a group element p_i with respect to a base h_j if*

$$e = H(h_j, p_i, h_j^s p_i^e). \tag{25}$$

The pair (e, s) is said to be of the form $PoK\{\beta \mid p_i = h_j^\beta\}$.

The proof (e, s) is generated by first choosing a scalar r uniformly from $\mathbb{F}_p$ and calculating $e = H(h_j, p_i, h_j^r)$. The second element of the pair is calculated as $s = r - e\beta$ where β is the discrete logarithm of p_i with respect to h_j, which is known to the prover. It now follows that

$$e = H(h_j, p_i, h_j^r) = H(h_j, p_i, h_j^{s+e\beta}) = H(h_j, p_i, h_j^s p_i^e). \tag{26}$$

The verification of the proof (e, s) simply consists of checking the equality in Eq. (25).

Definition 3. *An ordered pair $(e, s) \in \mathbb{F}_p^2$ is a NIZKPoK of*

(i) *the knowledge of the discrete logarithms of the group elements b_i with respect to base a_i, **and***

(ii) *the knowledge of discrete logarithms of the group element $p_i d_i^{-1}$ with respect to base $c_i^{-1} h_j$, **and***

(iii) *the equality of the discrete logarithm of b_i with respect to a_i and of $p_i d_i^{-1}$ with respect to $c_i^{-1} h_j$,*

if it satisfies

$$e = H\left(\mathtt{stmt}_i, a_i^s b_i^e, \left(c_i^{-1} h_j\right)^s \left(p_i d_i^{-1}\right)^e\right). \tag{27}$$

where $\mathtt{stmt}_i = (h_j, a_i, b_i, c_i, d_i, p_i)$ is the tuple of group elements appearing in the statement being proved. The ordered pair (e, s) is said to be of the form

$$PoK\left\{\alpha \mid b_i = a_i^\alpha \wedge p_i d_i^{-1} = \left(c_i^{-1} h_j\right)^\alpha\right\}.$$

A prover who knows α can generate the proof (e, s) as follows:

- The prover chooses scalars r uniformly from $\mathbb{F}_p$ and calculates

$$e = H\left(\mathtt{stmt}_i, a_i^r, \left(c_i^{-1} h_j\right)^r\right). \tag{28}$$

- The second scalar in the proof is calculated as

$$s = r - e\alpha \tag{29}$$

It follows that

$$
\begin{aligned}
e &= H\left(\mathbf{stmt}_i, a_i^r, \left(c_i^{-1} h_j\right)^r\right)\\
&= H\left(\mathbf{stmt}_i, a_i^{s+ea}, \left(c_i^{-1} h_j\right)^{s+ea}\right)\\
&= H\left(\mathbf{stmt}_i, a_i^s b_i^e, \left(c_i^{-1} h_j\right)^s \left(p_i d_i^{-1}\right)^e\right).
\end{aligned}
\tag{30}
$$

The verification of the proof (e, s) simply consists of checking the equality in Eq. (27).

The NIZKPoK σ_i in Nummatus is a proof of the disjunction of the two statements proved above.

Definition 4. *The tuple* $\sigma_i = (e_1, e_2, s_1, s_2) \in \mathbb{F}_p^4$ *is a NIZKPoK of the knowledge of the discrete logarithm of a group element* p_i *with respect to base* h_j ***or***

- *the knowledge of the discrete logarithm of the group element* b_i *with respect to base* a_i, ***and***
- *the knowledge of discrete logarithm of the group element* $p_i d_i^{-1}$ *with respect to base* $c_i^{-1} h_j$, ***and***
- *the equality of the discrete logarithm of* b_i *with respect to* a_i *and of* $p_i d_i^{-1}$ *with respect to* $c_i^{-1} h_j$,

if it satisfies

$$
e_1 + e_2 = H\left(\boldsymbol{stmt}_i, a_i^{s_1} b_i^{e_1}, \left(c_i^{-1} h_j\right)^{s_1} \left(p_i d_i^{-1}\right)^{e_1}, h_j^{s_2} p_i^{e_2}\right).
\tag{31}
$$

where $\boldsymbol{stmt}_i = (h_j, a_i, b_i, c_i, d_i, p_i)$ *is the tuple of group elements appearing in the statement being proved. The tuple* (e_1, e_2, s_1, s_2) *is said to be of the form*

$$
PoK\left\{(\alpha, \beta) \,\middle|\, \left(b_i = a_i^\alpha \,\wedge\, p_i d_i^{-1} = \left(c_i^{-1} h_j\right)^\alpha\right) \vee \left(p_i = h_j^\beta\right)\right\}.
$$

Suppose the prover know the discrete logarithm β of p_i with respect to base h_j. Then she can create the proof σ_i as follows:

(i) She chooses scalars r_2, e_1, s_1 uniformly and independently from $\mathbb{F}_p$. She calculates e_2 as

$$
e_2 = H\left(\mathbf{stmt}_i, a_i^{s_1} b_i^{e_1}, \left(c_i^{-1} h_j\right)^{s_1} \left(p_i d_i^{-1}\right)^{e_1}, h_j^{r_2}\right) - e_1.
\tag{32}
$$

(ii) Using her knowledge of β, she calculates s_2 as

$$
s_2 = r_2 - e_2 \beta.
\tag{33}
$$

It follows that

$$
\begin{aligned}
e_1 + e_2 &= H\left(\mathbf{stmt}_i, a_i^{s_1} b_i^{e_1}, \left(c_i^{-1} h_j\right)^{s_1} \left(p_i d_i^{-1}\right)^{e_1}, h_j^{s_2 + e_2 \beta}\right)\\
&= H\left(\mathbf{stmt}_i, a_i^{s_1} b_i^{e_1}, \left(c_i^{-1} h_j\right)^{s_1} \left(p_i d_i^{-1}\right)^{e_1}, h_j^{s_2} p_i^{e_2}\right).
\end{aligned}
\tag{34}
$$

On the other hand, if the prover knows α such that $b_i = a_i^\alpha$, and $p_i d_i^{-1} = \left(c_i^{-1} h_j\right)^\alpha$, then she can create the proof σ_i as follows:

(i) She chooses scalars r_1, e_2, s_2 uniformly and independently from $\mathbb{F}_p$. She calculates e_1 as

$$e_1 = H\left(\mathtt{stmt}_i, a_i^{r_1}, \left(c_i^{-1}h_j\right)^{r_1}, h_j^{s_2}p_i^{e_2}\right) - e_2. \tag{35}$$

(ii) Using her knowledge of α, she calculates s_1 as

$$s_1 = r_1 - e_1\alpha. \tag{36}$$

It follows that

$$
\begin{aligned}
e_1 + e_2 &= H\left(\mathtt{stmt}_i, a_i^{r_1}, \left(c_i^{-1}h_j\right)^{r_1}, h_j^{s_2}p_i^{e_2}\right) \\
&= H\left(\mathtt{stmt}_i, a_i^{s_1+e_1\alpha}, \left(c_i^{-1}h_j\right)^{s_1+e_1\alpha}, h_j^{s_2}p_i^{e_2}\right) \\
&= H\left(\mathtt{stmt}_i, a_i^{s_1}b_i^{e_1}, \left(c_i^{-1}h_j\right)^{s_1}\left(p_id_i^{-1}\right)^{e_1}, h_j^{s_2}p_i^{e_2}\right).
\end{aligned} \tag{37}
$$

In both cases, the verification of the proof (e_1, e_2, s_1, s_2) consists of checking the equality in Eq. (31). In the proof of disjunction of statements, the prover has one degree of freedom as only the sum $e_1 + e_2$ has to be equal to the hash function output (whose argument contains the scalars). This freedom is exploited to choose which knowledge is used to prove the disjunction.

B   Simplus NIZKPoK Generation and Verification Algorithms

Compared to the NIZKPoK in the Nummatus protocol, the NIZKPoK ψ_i in the Simplus protocol is simpler to compute.

Definition 5. *An ordered pair $\psi_i = (e, s) \in \mathbb{F}_p^2$ is a NIZKPoK of*

(i) *the knowledge of the discrete logarithm of the group element b_i with respect to base a_i, and*
(ii) *the knowledge of discrete logarithm of the group element $p_id_i^{-1}$ with respect to base $c_i^{-1}h$, and*
(iii) *the equality of the discrete logarithm of b_i with respect to a_i and of $p_id_i^{-1}$ with respect to $c_i^{-1}h$,*

if it satisfies

$$e = H\left(\mathtt{stmt}_i, a_i^s b_i^e, \left(c_i^{-1}h\right)^s \left(p_id_i^{-1}\right)^e\right). \tag{38}$$

where $\mathtt{stmt}_i = (h, a_i, b_i, c_i, d_i, p_i)$ is the tuple of group elements appearing in the statement being proved. The ordered pair (e, s) is said to be of the form

$$PoK\left\{\alpha \mid b_i = a_i^\alpha \wedge p_id_i^{-1} = \left(c_i^{-1}h\right)^\alpha\right\}.$$

A prover who knows α can generate the proof (e, s) as follows:

- The prover chooses scalars r uniformly from $\mathbb{F}_p$ and calculates

$$e = H\left(\mathtt{stmt}_i, a_i^r, \left(c_i^{-1}h\right)^r\right). \tag{39}$$

- The second scalar in the proof is calculated as

$$s = r - e\alpha \tag{40}$$

It follows that

$$
\begin{aligned}
e &= H\left(\mathtt{stmt}_i, a_i^r, \left(c_i^{-1}h\right)^r\right) \\
&= H\left(\mathtt{stmt}_i, a_i^{s+e\alpha}, \left(c_i^{-1}h\right)^{s+e\alpha}\right) \\
&= H\left(\mathtt{stmt}_i, a_i^s b_i^e, \left(c_i^{-1}h\right)^s \left(p_i d_i^{-1}\right)^e\right).
\end{aligned}
\tag{41}
$$

The verification of the proof (e, s) simply consists of checking the equality in Eq. (38).

References

1. Grin rust-secp256k1-zkp github repository. https://github.com/mimblewimble/secp256k1-zkp/
2. Monero 0.13.0 Beryllium Bullet Release Notes. https://src.getmonero.org/2018/10/11/monero-0.13.0-released.html. Accessed 02 Aug 2019
3. Monero website. https://getmonero.org/
4. Nummatus simulation code. https://github.com/Arnabjana1999/Nummatus
5. What are zk-SNARKs? https://z.cash/technology/zksnarks/. Accessed 02 Aug 2019
6. Zcash website. https://z.cash/
7. Bao, F., Deng, R.H., Zhu, H.F.: Variations of Diffie-Hellman problem. In: Qing, S., Gollmann, D., Zhou, J. (eds.) ICICS 2003. LNCS, vol. 2836, pp. 301–312. Springer, Heidelberg (2003). https://doi.org/10.1007/978-3-540-39927-8_28
8. Camenisch, J.: Group signature schemes and payment systems based on the discrete logarithm problem. Ph.D. dissertation, ETH Zürich (1998)
9. Camenisch, J., Stadler, M.: Proof systems for general statements about discrete logarithms. Technical report (1997)
10. Cramer, R., Damgård, I., Schoenmakers, B.: Proofs of partial knowledge and simplified design of witness hiding protocols. In: Desmedt, Y.G. (ed.) CRYPTO 1994. LNCS, vol. 839, pp. 174–187. Springer, Heidelberg (1994). https://doi.org/10.1007/3-540-48658-5_19
11. Dagher, G.G., Bünz, B., Bonneau, J., Clark, J., Boneh, D.: Provisions: Privacy-preserving proofs of solvency for Bitcoin exchanges. In: Proceedings of the 22nd ACM SIGSAC Conference on Computer and Communications Security (ACM CCS), New York, NY, USA, pp. 720–731 (2015)

12. Decker, C., Guthrie, J., Seidel, J., Wattenhofer, R.: Making Bitcoin exchanges transparent. In: Pernul, G., Ryan, P.Y.A., Weippl, E. (eds.) ESORICS 2015. LNCS, vol. 9327, pp. 561–576. Springer, Cham (2015). https://doi.org/10.1007/978-3-319-24177-7_28
13. Dutta, A., Vijayakumaran, S.: MProve: A proof of reserves protocol for Monero exchanges. In: 2019 IEEE European Symposium on Security and Privacy Workshops (EuroS&PW), pp. 330–339, June 2019. https://doi.org/10.1109/EuroSPW.2019.00043
14. Dutta, A., Vijayakumaran, S.: Revelio: A MimbleWimble proof of reserves protocol. In: 2019 Crypto Valley Conference on Blockchain Technology (CVCBT), pp. 7–11, June 2019. https://doi.org/10.1109/CVCBT.2019.000-5
15. Fauzi, P., Meiklejohn, S., Mercer, R., Orlandi, C.: Quisquis: A new design for anonymous cryptocurrencies. Cryptology ePrint Archive, Report 2018/990 (2018). https://eprint.iacr.org/2018/990
16. Pedersen, T.P.: Non-interactive and information-theoretic secure verifiable secret sharing. In: Feigenbaum, J. (ed.) CRYPTO 1991. LNCS, vol. 576, pp. 129–140. Springer, Heidelberg (1992). https://doi.org/10.1007/3-540-46766-1_9
17. Saberhagen, N.v.: CryptoNote v 2.0. White paper (2013). https://cryptonote.org/whitepaper.pdf
18. Wiktionary contributors: nummatus – Wiktionary, the free dictionary. https://en.wiktionary.org/wiki/nummatus. Accessed 02 Aug 2019
19. Wiktionary contributors: quisquis – Wiktionary, the free dictionary. https://en.wiktionary.org/wiki/quisquis. Accessed 02 Aug 2019
20. Wiktionary contributors: simplus – Wiktionary, the free dictionary. https://en.wiktionary.org/wiki/simplus. Accessed 02 Aug 2019
21. Wilcox, Z.: Proving your Bitcoin reserves. Bitcoin Talk Forum Post, May 2014. https://bitcointalk.org/index.php?topic=595180.0

Optimality of a Protocol by Feige-Kilian-Naor for Three-Party Secure Computation

Sibi Raj B. Pillai[1], Manoj Prabhakaran[1(✉)], Vinod M. Prabhakaran[2]⊙, and Srivatsan Sridhar[1]⊙

[1] Indian Institute of Technology Bombay, Mumbai, India
bsraj@ee.iitb.ac.in, mp@cse.iitb.ac.in, ssrivatsan97@gmail.com
[2] Tata Institute of Fundamental Research, Mumbai, India
vinodmp@tifr.res.in

Abstract. In an influential work aimed at understanding the communication requirements of secure computation, Feige, Kilian and Naor introduced a minimal model of secure computation (STOC 1994). In that work, among other results, Feige et al. presented a simple protocol for the 2 input AND function. It has remained an intriguing question whether the communication and randomness used in this protocol are optimal. While previous work of Data et al. (CRYPTO 2014) showed that the communication from the two parties with inputs (Alice and Bob) to the third party who gets the output is optimal, the question of optimality for the third message in the protocol – a common reference string shared between Alice and Bob – remained open. In this note we show that in fact, this message (and hence all the randomness used in the protocol) is also optimal in the protocol of Feige et al. This improves on a previous result of Rajan et al. (ISIT 2016), which showed this optimality restricted to protocols where Alice and Bob are deterministic. Further, our result holds even if only a weak secrecy condition is required of the protocol.

Keywords: Secure multiparty computation · Private simultaneous messages · Randomness complexity · Lower bound

1 Introduction

Secure multi-party computation (MPC) is one of the cornerstones of modern cryptography. While a wealth of literature in this area has uncovered several fundamental aspects of MPC (see, e.g. [4,10,13]), many basic questions remain open. One such problem relates to the communication complexity of MPC. As an attempt towards understanding communication complexity of MPC and as a model of independent interest, Feige, Kilian and Naor introduced a simplified

---

The last author is the primary author. The author list is sorted alphabetically.

© Springer Nature Switzerland AG 2019
F. Hao et al. (Eds.): INDOCRYPT 2019, LNCS 11898, pp. 216–226, 2019.
https://doi.org/10.1007/978-3-030-35423-7_11

model of secure computation [8], which we shall refer to as the FKN model in this work.[1] In a protocol for computing a function f in the FKN model, two parties Alice and Bob are given inputs x and y respectively and a third party Carol should be able to compute $f(x, y)$, without learning anything else about (x, y). All parties are computationally unbounded. The simplicity of the model is that Alice and Bob are allowed to send a single message each to Carol, with no communication between them after they receive the inputs. Prior to receiving their inputs, they can communicate, or equivalently, are given a common random string from a fixed distribution. This is illustrated in Fig. 1.

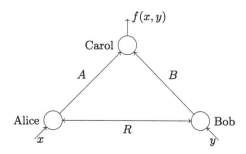

Fig. 1. The FKN model. Alice and Bob have a common reference string R. On being given inputs x and y, respectively, they send a single message each – A and B, respectively – to Carol, who computes $f(x, y)$ from it. Carol, who does not see R, should learn nothing about x, y other than $f(x, y)$.

Unfortunately, despite being a much simpler model, understanding the communication complexity in the FKN model too remains largely open. In this work, we present a new lower bound result that establishes the optimality of a protocol in [8] for the AND function, 25 years after it was devised by Feige, Kilian and Naor. The protocol itself is simple, but the question of its optimality remained largely unaddressed till recently. In [7] and subsequently in [14] significant advances were made towards showing the optimality of this protocol. Specifically, [7] established that the communication received by Carol from Alice and Bob is optimal in the protocol of [8], and [14] further showed that if Alice and Bob are deterministic, then the communication (common randomness) between Alice and Bob is also optimal in this protocol. Here we show that even if Alice and Bob are randomized, the amount of communication between every pair of parties is optimal in the protocol of [8].

---

[1] This model is also known as the *Private Simultaneous Messages* (PSM) model, after [11]. The PSM model was originally introduced for a variant of the FKN model with an asymptotically growing number of input parties. Since our focus, similar to [8], is on the setting of 2 input parties, we shall refer to the model as the FKN model.

Interestingly, while [7,14] relied on information-theoretic tools to establish their results, we use elementary (but elaborate) set-theoretic arguments to close the remaining gap. On the other hand, their results yield lower bounds on entropy of the messages, whereas our results are only about the size of the support of the messages. Further, the result of [7] applies not just to the FKN model, but to the full-fledged MPC model (with an arbitrary, multi-round communication pattern among the three parties), whereas our approach exploits the non-interactive nature of the FKN model.

1.1 Our Contribution

Consider the following protocol for the AND function from [8].[2]

Protocol 1. *FKN Protocol for AND(x, y)*

1. *Alice and Bob receive a randomly and uniformly picked permutation of $(0, 1, 2)$, $R = (\alpha, \beta, \gamma)$ as the common randomness.*
2. *Alice sends A to Carol, where $A = \gamma$ if $x = 1$ and $A = \alpha$ if $x = 0$.*
3. *Bob sends B to Carol, where $B = \gamma$ if $y = 1$ and $A = \beta$ if $y = 0$.*
4. *Carol declares her output to be 1 if $A = B$, and 0 otherwise.*

Note that in this protocol, the alphabet size for A and B is 3 each, whereas that for R is 6. Our main result is that each of these alphabet sizes is optimal in any protocol for AND in the FKN model, even when Alice and Bob are allowed to be probabilistic (while they are deterministic in the above protocol). Previously, it was known that the alphabet sizes for A, B are optimal [7]. The alphabet size for R is also optimal in the setting where Alice and Bob are deterministic [14]. However, when Alice and Bob can be randomized, the best known lower bound on the alphabet size of R was 4 (in fact, from [7], a lower bound of 1.826 bits on the *entropy* of R was known).

Our lower bounds on the alphabet sizes hold even if only a weak secrecy condition is required of the protocol. The weak secrecy condition only requires that Carol cannot fully rule out any of the three possible input combinations when the output is 0, but she is allowed to identify the correct input with probability arbitrarily close to 1. We point out that the previously established lower bounds on the alphabet sizes of A, B in [7] did not address the case of weak security. Along with the lower bound on the alphabet size of R, we reestablish the lower bounds for A, B as well, for the case of weak security. Thus, the AND protocol of [8] remains optimal even if only weak secrecy is required (whereas it does provide full-fledged security).

Note that the lower bounds on the alphabet sizes (from our and prior works) hold *individually* for each of the three messages A, B and R, and the above

---

[2] Feige et al. specified a protocol for AND in a model with any number of input players. The version stated here is specialized to the case of two input players, since, like previous works [7,14], our analysis is restricted to the model with two input players.

protocol *simultaneously* meets all of them. For a given function, *a priori* it is not clear that a protocol that is simultaneously optimal for all three messages would exist. A corollary of our result is that indeed, for *all boolean functions in which Alice and Bob have a single bit of input each*, there is such an FKN protocol. This was already known for XOR (even in the case of MPC [9]), and is easily seen to be the case for functions which depend on at most one input. The remaining functions are all "isomorphic" to the AND function[3], for which our current result applies.

1.2 Related Work

Lower bounds on the communication complexity of secure multiparty computation in various models have been the subject of much research spanning three decades [1–3,5–9,12]. The two works that directly addressed the question studied in this work – namely, the optimality of the AND protocol in the FKN model in [8] – are [7] and [14]. The former in fact considered MPC protocols (of which FKN protocols are a special case) for arbitrary functions, and established lower bounds on the *entropy* of the individual messages. When applied to the AND function, these lower bounds are (in bits)

$$H(A) \geq \log_2 3 \qquad H(B) \geq \log_2 3 \qquad H(R) \geq 1.826.$$

While the lower bounds for $H(A)$ and $H(B)$ are achieved by Protocol 1, the lower bound for $H(R)$ leaves a gap (the protocol uses $H(R) = \log_2 6 \approx 2.585$ bits). In [14] this gap was addressed, but restricted to protocols in which Alice and Bob are deterministic (and hence any randomness they need will be included in R). Under this restriction, they showed that $H(R) \geq \log_2 6$, and hence Protocol 1 has optimal alphabet size for all messages. These results, which rely on information-theoretic arguments, not only show that the alphabet sizes for the messages in Protocol 1 are optimal, but also that the distributions of these messages should be uniform when the optimal alphabet size is used; however, they apply only when full-fledged secrecy is required, rather than the weaker secrecy used in this work.

2   Preliminaries

Notation. A *probabilistic map* $\pi : \mathcal{P} \to \mathcal{Q}$ associates a distribution over $\mathcal{Q}$ with each element in $\mathcal{P}$. We write $q \leftarrow \pi(p)$ to denote drawing a sample from the distribution that π associates with p. We write $\text{supp}(\pi(p))$ to denote the support of this distribution. Given two maps $\pi_1 : \mathcal{P}_1 \to \mathcal{Q}_1$ and $\pi_2 : \mathcal{P}_2 \to \mathcal{Q}_2$, and $(p_1, p_2) \in \mathcal{P}_1 \times \mathcal{P}_2$, we write $\text{supp}(\pi_1(p_1), \pi_2(p_2))$ to denote $\text{supp}(\pi_1(p_1)) \times \text{supp}(\pi_2(p_2))$.

FKN Model. Referring to Fig. 1, the three-party secure computation model for a deterministic function $f : \mathcal{X} \times \mathcal{Y} \to \mathcal{Z}$ can be described as follows. Alice and

---

[3] They can be derived from AND by negating the inputs and/or the output.

Bob are provided with a random string R from some fixed distribution. On being given inputs $x \in \mathcal{X}$ and $y \in \mathcal{Y}$, respectively, each of them sends a single message, A and B respectively, to Carol who must compute $z = f(x, y)$, but learn nothing else about (x, y). The security notion employed is information-theoretic security against passively corrupt (honest-but-curious) Carol.

If one considers only the amount of communication received by Carol, then without loss of generality, one may require Alice and Bob to be deterministic, with any randomness they need being part of the message R. (This was the case in [8].) However, when one is interested also in the size of the message R (as in this work), including all the randomness that Alice and Bob may need locally as part of R is not necessarily without loss of generality. Hence, we explicitly model Alice and Bob as being randomized parties. We call this model the Unrestricted FKN model (as opposed to the Restricted FKN model where Alice and Bob are deterministic).

Definition 1 (Unrestricted FKN Protocol). *An* unrestricted FKN proto-col *for a function* $f : \mathcal{X} \times \mathcal{Y} \to \mathcal{Z}$ *with randomness alphabet* $\mathcal{R}$ *and communi-cation alphabets* $\mathcal{A}$ *and* $\mathcal{B}$ *consists of a distribution* π_R *over* $\mathcal{R}$, *and probabilistic maps* $\pi_A : \mathcal{X} \times \mathcal{R} \to \mathcal{A}$, $\pi_B : \mathcal{Y} \times \mathcal{R} \to \mathcal{B}$, *and* $\pi_Z : \mathcal{A} \times \mathcal{B} \to \mathcal{Z}$, *such that the following two conditions hold:*

- **Correctness:** $\forall (x, y) \in \mathcal{X} \times \mathcal{Y}$, $\Pr_{r \leftarrow \pi_R} [\pi_Z(\pi_A(x, r), \pi_B(y, r)) = f(x, y)] = 1$.
- **Secrecy:** $\forall (a, b) \in \mathcal{A} \times \mathcal{B}$, *and* $(x, y), (x', y') \in \mathcal{X} \times \mathcal{Y}$ *s.t.* $f(x, y) = f(x', y')$,

$$\Pr_{r \leftarrow \pi_R} [(\pi_A(x, r), \pi_B(y, r)) = (a, b)] = \Pr_{r \leftarrow \pi_R} [(\pi_A(x', r), \pi_B(y', r)) = (a, b)].$$

Given (π_R, π_A, π_B), note that a necessary and sufficient condition for a π_Z to exist such that the correctness condition is satisfied is that, $\forall (x, y), (x', y') \in \mathcal{X} \times \mathcal{Y}$ s.t. $f(x, y) \neq f(x', y')$,

$$\left(\bigcup_{r \in \mathrm{supp}(\pi_R)} \mathrm{supp}(\pi_A(x, r), \pi_B(y, r)) \right) \cap \left(\bigcup_{r \in \mathrm{supp}(\pi_R)} \mathrm{supp}(\pi_A(x', r), \pi_B(y', r)) \right) = \emptyset.$$

Our lower bound would hold even if the secrecy condition above is weakened as follows:

- **Weak Secrecy:** $\forall (a, b) \in \mathcal{A} \times \mathcal{B}$, *and* $(x, y), (x', y') \in \mathcal{X} \times \mathcal{Y}$ s.t. $f(x, y) = f(x', y')$,

$$\Pr_{r \leftarrow \pi_R} [(\pi_A(x, r), \pi_B(y, r)) = (a, b)] > 0 \Leftrightarrow \Pr_{r \leftarrow \pi_R} [(\pi_A(x', r), \pi_B(y', r)) = (a, b)] > 0.$$

In other words, the weak secrecy condition only requires the following set equality to hold: $\forall (x, y), (x', y') \in \mathcal{X} \times \mathcal{Y}$ s.t. $f(x, y) = f(x', y')$,

$$\bigcup_{r \in \mathrm{supp}(\pi_R)} \mathrm{supp}(\pi_A(x, r), \pi_B(y, r)) = \bigcup_{r \in \mathrm{supp}(\pi_R)} \mathrm{supp}(\pi_A(x', r), \pi_B(y', r)).$$

Note that secrecy implies weak secrecy. Thus, a lower bound proved for weak secrecy also holds for full secrecy. Also note that information theoretic security, i.e. $H(X, Y|A, B, Z) = H(X, Y|Z)$, requires the (strong) secrecy condition. The weak secrecy does not imply information theoretic security because Carol can potentially guess Alice's and Bob's inputs with a probability greater than that of a random guess.

3   Optimality of the FKN Protocol for AND

Consider an unrestricted FKN protocol $(\pi_R, \pi_A, \pi_B, \pi_Z)$ for the AND function, with communication alphabets $\mathcal{A}, \mathcal{B}$. Let $\mathcal{R} = \mathrm{supp}(\pi_R)$. Our goal in this section is to lower bound $|\mathcal{A}|, |\mathcal{B}|$ and $|\mathcal{R}|$, even if the protocol enjoys only weak secrecy (as defined below Definition 1).

For each $x, y \in \{0, 1\}$ and $r \in \mathcal{R}$, we define

$$\mathcal{A}_r^x := \mathrm{supp}(\pi_A(x, r)) \qquad \mathcal{B}_r^y := \mathrm{supp}(\pi_B(y, r)).$$

Note that being supports of distributions, all these sets are non-empty. For brevity, we shall write $\mathcal{A}_r^x \mathcal{B}_r^y$ for $\mathcal{A}_r^x \times \mathcal{B}_r^y$. Since Alice and Bob do not communicate with each other, $\mathrm{supp}((\pi_A(x, r), \pi_B(y, r))) = \mathcal{A}_r^x \mathcal{B}_r^y$. Using this notation, the correctness and weak secrecy conditions (from Definition 1) can be stated as:

$$\text{Let } \mathcal{M}^{xy} := \bigcup_{r \in \mathcal{R}} \mathcal{A}_r^x \mathcal{B}_r^y \qquad\qquad \forall x, y \in \{0, 1\} \qquad (1)$$

$$\mathcal{M}^{xy} \cap \mathcal{M}^{11} = \emptyset \qquad\qquad \forall (x, y) \in \{(0, 0), (0, 1), (1, 0)\} \qquad (2)$$

$$\mathcal{M}^{00} = \mathcal{M}^{01} = \mathcal{M}^{10}. \qquad\qquad\qquad (3)$$

We start with the following lemma about any set system that satisfies the above conditions. This lemma implies that $|\mathcal{R}| \geq 5$ (as it requires that $\mathcal{R} \setminus \{r\}$ has four more elements), and would be key to showing that in fact $|\mathcal{R}| \geq 6$.

Lemma 1. *For any set system $\{\mathcal{A}_r^x, \mathcal{B}_r^y | r \in \mathcal{R}, x, y \in \{0, 1\}\}$ that satisfies (2) and (3), $\forall r \in \mathcal{R}$,*

$$\mathcal{A}_r^0 \cap \mathcal{A}_r^1 = \emptyset, \quad \mathcal{B}_r^0 \cap \mathcal{B}_r^1 = \emptyset, \qquad\qquad (4)$$

$$\mathcal{A}_r^1 \cap \mathcal{A}_{r'}^0 \neq \emptyset \ \Rightarrow\ \mathcal{B}_r^1 \cap (\mathcal{B}_{r'}^0 \cup \mathcal{B}_{r'}^1) = \emptyset \qquad \forall r' \in \mathcal{R} \setminus \{r\}, \qquad (5)$$

$$\mathcal{B}_r^1 \cap \mathcal{B}_{r'}^0 \neq \emptyset \ \Rightarrow\ \mathcal{A}_r^1 \cap (\mathcal{A}_{r'}^0 \cup \mathcal{A}_{r'}^1) = \emptyset \qquad \forall r' \in \mathcal{R} \setminus \{r\}. \qquad (6)$$

Further, $\forall r \in \mathcal{R}, \exists s_1, s_2, t_1, t_2 \in \mathcal{R} \setminus \{r\}$, distinct from each other, s.t.

$$\mathcal{A}_r^1 \cap \mathcal{A}_s^0 \neq \emptyset \qquad\qquad \text{for } s \in \{s_1, s_2\} \qquad (7)$$

$$\mathcal{B}_r^1 \cap \mathcal{B}_t^0 \neq \emptyset \qquad\qquad \text{for } t \in \{t_1, t_2\} \qquad (8)$$

Proof. From (2), $\forall r, r' \in \mathcal{R}$, and $\forall (x, y) \in \{(0, 0), (0, 1), (1, 0)\}$, $\mathcal{A}_r^x \mathcal{B}_r^y \cap \mathcal{A}_{r'}^1 \mathcal{B}_{r'}^1 = \emptyset$. In particular, by considering $r = r'$, and $(x, y) = (0, 1), (1, 0)$, we have $\mathcal{A}_r^0 \mathcal{B}_r^1 \cap$

$\mathcal{A}_r^1\mathcal{B}_r^1 = \emptyset$ and $\mathcal{A}_r^1\mathcal{B}_r^0 \cap \mathcal{A}_r^1\mathcal{B}_r^1 = \emptyset$, from which (4) follows. On the other hand, by considering distinct r, r', and $(x, y) = (0, 0), (0, 1)$, we have $\mathcal{A}_{r'}^0\mathcal{B}_{r'}^0 \cap \mathcal{A}_r^1\mathcal{B}_r^1 = \emptyset$ and $\mathcal{A}_{r'}^0\mathcal{B}_{r'}^1 \cap \mathcal{A}_r^1\mathcal{B}_r^1 = \emptyset$, from which (5) follows. (6) follows symmetrically.

To show (7) and (8), it is enough to show that there exist distinct $s_1, s_2, t_1, t_2 \in \mathcal{R}$ such that $\mathcal{A}_r^1 \cap \mathcal{A}_s^0 \neq \emptyset$ for $s = s_1, s_2$ and $\mathcal{B}_r^1 \cap \mathcal{B}_t^0 \neq \emptyset$ for $t = t_1, t_2$. This is because, by (4), such s, t cannot equal r.

Now, note that since $\mathcal{A}_r^1\mathcal{B}_r^0 \subseteq \mathcal{M}^{10} = \mathcal{M}^{00}$ (by (3)), there exists $s \in \mathcal{R}$ such that $\mathcal{A}_r^1\mathcal{B}_r^0 \cap \mathcal{A}_s^0\mathcal{B}_s^0 \neq \emptyset$, and hence $\mathcal{A}_r^1 \cap \mathcal{A}_s^0 \neq \emptyset$. However, if there is only s such that $\mathcal{A}_r^1 \cap \mathcal{A}_s^0 \neq \emptyset$, then we will have $\mathcal{A}_r^1\mathcal{B}_r^0 \subseteq \mathcal{A}_s^0\mathcal{B}_s^0$ and also $\mathcal{A}_r^1\mathcal{B}_r^0 \subseteq \mathcal{A}_s^0\mathcal{B}_s^1$ (considering $\mathcal{A}_r^1\mathcal{B}_r^0 \subseteq \mathcal{M}^{01}$); but then $\mathcal{B}_r^0 \subseteq \mathcal{B}_s^0 \cap \mathcal{B}_s^1 = \emptyset$ (using (4)), which contradicts the fact that $\mathcal{B}_r^0$ is non-empty. Hence, there are at least two distinct values $s_1, s_2 \in \mathcal{R}$ such that for $s \in \{s_1, s_2\}$, $\mathcal{A}_r^1 \cap \mathcal{A}_s^0 \neq \emptyset$. Similarly, there exist at least two distinct values $t_1, t_2 \in \mathcal{R}$ such that for $t \in \{t_1, t_2\}$, $\mathcal{B}_r^1 \cap \mathcal{B}_t^0 \neq \emptyset$.

It remains to show that $\{s_1, s_2\} \cap \{t_1, t_2\} = \emptyset$. Suppose not. Then there is an r' in this intersection such that $\mathcal{A}_r^1 \cap \mathcal{A}_{r'}^0 \neq \emptyset$ and $\mathcal{B}_r^1 \cap \mathcal{B}_{r'}^0 \neq \emptyset$, contradicting (6). □

From Lemma 1, we see that $|\mathcal{R}| \geq 5$. Our result shows that, in fact, $|\mathcal{R}| \geq 6$.

Theorem 1. *In any weakly secret unrestricted FKN protocol for AND with communication alphabets $\mathcal{A}$, $\mathcal{B}$ and randomness alphabet $\mathcal{R}$, it must be the case that $|\mathcal{A}| \geq 3$, $|\mathcal{B}| \geq 3$ and $|\mathcal{R}| \geq 6$.*

Proof. Consider a weakly secret unrestricted FKN protocol for AND with communication alphabets $\mathcal{A}$, $\mathcal{B}$ and randomness alphabet $\mathcal{R}$. Throughout this proof, we shall use the notation for $\mathcal{A}_r^x$, $\mathcal{B}_r^y$ and $\mathcal{M}^{xy}$ introduced above.

From Lemma 1, it is easy to see that $|\mathcal{A}| \geq 3$ (and symmetrically, $|\mathcal{B}| \geq 3$). Specifically, by (8) and (6), we know that there exist $r, t \in \mathcal{R}$ such that $\mathcal{A}_r^1 \cap (\mathcal{A}_t^0 \cup \mathcal{A}_t^1) = \emptyset$. Since $\mathcal{A}_t^0 \cap \mathcal{A}_t^1 = \emptyset$ (by (4)), and since these sets are non-empty, it must be the case that $|\mathcal{A}_t^0 \cup \mathcal{A}_t^1| \geq 2$. Hence,

$$|\mathcal{A}| \geq |\mathcal{A}_r^1 \cup (\mathcal{A}_t^0 \cup \mathcal{A}_t^1)| = |\mathcal{A}_r^1| + |\mathcal{A}_t^0 \cup \mathcal{A}_t^1| \geq 3,$$

using the fact that $\mathcal{A}_r^1$ is non-empty.

Now we turn to showing that $|\mathcal{R}| \geq 6$. For the sake of contradiction, suppose not. Then, by Lemma 1, $|\mathcal{R}| = 5$, and further we can write $\mathcal{R} = \{r, s_1, s_2, t_1, t_2\}$, that satisfy (7) and (8).

Firstly, using the facts that $\mathcal{A}_r^1 \cap \mathcal{A}_r^0 = \emptyset$ (from (4)) and $\mathcal{A}_r^1 \cap (\mathcal{A}_{t_1}^0 \cup \mathcal{A}_{t_2}^0) = \emptyset$ (from (8) and (6)), the conditions $\mathcal{A}_r^1\mathcal{B}_r^0 \subseteq \mathcal{M}^{0b}$ (for $b \in \{0, 1\}$) can now be rewritten as

$$\mathcal{A}_r^1\mathcal{B}_r^0 \subseteq \mathcal{A}_{s_1}^0\mathcal{B}_{s_1}^b \cup \mathcal{A}_{s_2}^0\mathcal{B}_{s_2}^b \qquad \text{for } b \in \{0, 1\}. \tag{9}$$

Similarly, the conditions $\mathcal{A}_r^0\mathcal{B}_r^1 \subseteq \mathcal{M}^{b0}$ (for $b \in \{0, 1\}$) can be rewritten as

$$\mathcal{A}_r^0\mathcal{B}_r^1 \subseteq \mathcal{A}_{t_1}^b\mathcal{B}_{t_1}^0 \cup \mathcal{A}_{t_2}^b\mathcal{B}_{t_2}^0 \qquad \text{for } b \in \{0, 1\}. \tag{10}$$

Towards deriving a contradiction, in the following claims, we derive a short sequence of conditions implied by the above. Firstly, we can strengthen the conclusions of (7) and (8) as follows:

Claim 1.

$$\mathcal{A}_r^1 \subseteq \mathcal{A}_s^0 \qquad\qquad for\ s \in \{s_1, s_2\}, \tag{11}$$

$$\mathcal{B}_r^1 \subseteq \mathcal{B}_t^0 \qquad\qquad for\ t \in \{t_1, t_2\}. \tag{12}$$

Proof. We shall show $\mathcal{A}_r^1 \subseteq \mathcal{A}_{s_1}^0$, with the other containments following similarly. Suppose $\mathcal{A}_r^1 \not\subseteq \mathcal{A}_{s_1}^0$. Then (9) (with $b = 0$) implies $\mathcal{B}_r^0 \subseteq \mathcal{B}_{s_2}^0$ which in turn implies $\mathcal{B}_r^0 \cap \mathcal{B}_{s_2}^1 = \emptyset$ due to (4). Then, (9) (with $b = 1$) implies $\mathcal{A}_r^1 \subseteq \mathcal{A}_{s_1}^0$ which contradicts our hypothesis. $\qquad\square$

Claim 2. *For all $r' \in \mathcal{R} \setminus \{r\}$, $\mathcal{A}_r^1 \cap \mathcal{A}_{r'}^1 = \emptyset$.*

Proof. For $r' \in \{s_1, s_2\}$, note that by (11), $\mathcal{A}_r^1 \subseteq \mathcal{A}_{r'}^0$ and hence by (4), $\mathcal{A}_r^1 \cap \mathcal{A}_{r'}^1 = \emptyset$. For $r' \in \{t_1, t_2\}$, $\mathcal{B}_r^1 \subseteq \mathcal{B}_{r'}^0$ by (12), and then by (6), $\mathcal{A}_r^1 \cap \mathcal{A}_{r'}^1 = \emptyset$. $\qquad\square$

Claim 3.

$$\mathcal{B}_r^0 \not\subseteq \mathcal{B}_s^0 \qquad\qquad for\ s \in \{s_1, s_2\}, \tag{13}$$

$$\mathcal{A}_r^0 \not\subseteq \mathcal{A}_t^0 \qquad\qquad for\ t \in \{t_1, t_2\}. \tag{14}$$

Proof. We shall prove $\mathcal{B}_r^0 \not\subseteq \mathcal{B}_{s_1}^0$, with the others following symmetrically. Suppose, for the sake of contradiction, $\mathcal{B}_r^0 \subseteq \mathcal{B}_{s_1}^0$. Then $\mathcal{B}_{s_1}^1 \cap \mathcal{B}_r^0 = \emptyset$ due to (4). Also, $\mathcal{A}_r^1 \cap \mathcal{A}_{r'}^1 = \emptyset\ \forall r' \in \mathcal{R} \setminus \{r\}$ by Claim 2. Hence, $\mathcal{A}_r^1 \mathcal{B}_{s_1}^1 \cap \mathcal{M}^{10} = \emptyset$. However, we also have

$$\mathcal{A}_r^1 \mathcal{B}_{s_1}^1 \subseteq \mathcal{A}_{s_1}^0 \mathcal{B}_{s_1}^1 \subseteq \mathcal{M}^{01} \subseteq \mathcal{M}^{10},$$

where the containments follow from (11), (1) and (3) respectively. This contradicts the fact that $\mathcal{A}_r^1$ and $\mathcal{B}_{s_1}^1$ are non-empty. $\qquad\square$

Claim 4.

$$\mathcal{B}_r^0 \cap \mathcal{B}_{s_1}^0 \cap \mathcal{B}_{s_2}^1 \neq \emptyset\ and\ \mathcal{B}_r^0 \cap \mathcal{B}_{s_2}^0 \cap \mathcal{B}_{s_1}^1 \neq \emptyset, \tag{15}$$

$$\mathcal{A}_r^0 \cap \mathcal{A}_{t_1}^0 \cap \mathcal{A}_{t_2}^1 \neq \emptyset\ and\ \mathcal{A}_r^0 \cap \mathcal{A}_{t_2}^0 \cap \mathcal{A}_{t_1}^1 \neq \emptyset. \tag{16}$$

Proof. We shall prove (15), with the other one following symmetrically. From (9) we have, $\mathcal{B}_r^0 \subseteq \mathcal{B}_{s_1}^0 \cup \mathcal{B}_{s_2}^0$ and $\mathcal{B}_r^0 \subseteq \mathcal{B}_{s_1}^1 \cup \mathcal{B}_{s_2}^1$. That is,

$$\mathcal{B}_r^0 \subseteq (\mathcal{B}_{s_1}^0 \cup \mathcal{B}_{s_2}^0) \cap (\mathcal{B}_{s_1}^1 \cup \mathcal{B}_{s_2}^1) = (\mathcal{B}_{s_1}^0 \cap \mathcal{B}_{s_2}^1) \cup (\mathcal{B}_{s_2}^0 \cap \mathcal{B}_{s_1}^1),$$

where we used the fact that $\mathcal{B}_{s_1}^0 \cap \mathcal{B}_{s_1}^1 = \emptyset$ and $\mathcal{B}_{s_2}^0 \cap \mathcal{B}_{s_2}^1 = \emptyset$, due to (4). Now, by (13), $\mathcal{B}_r^0 \not\subseteq \mathcal{B}_{s_1}^0 \cap \mathcal{B}_{s_2}^1$ and $\mathcal{B}_r^0 \not\subseteq \mathcal{B}_{s_2}^0 \cap \mathcal{B}_{s_1}^1$. Hence, (15) follows. $\qquad\square$

Since we have shown the conditions for (9) and (10) to hold, we will now consider the conditions for a similar requirement from (3), $\mathcal{A}_r^0 \mathcal{B}_r^0 \subseteq \mathcal{M}^{10}$.

Claim 5. $\mathcal{B}_r^0 \subseteq \mathcal{B}_t^0$ for $t \in \{t_1, t_2\}$.

Proof. From (3), $\mathcal{A}_r^0 \mathcal{B}_r^0 \subseteq \mathcal{M}^{10}$. But $\mathcal{A}_r^0 \cap \mathcal{A}_r^1 = \emptyset$ due to (4). Also, by (15) $\mathcal{B}_r^0 \cap \mathcal{B}_s^1 \neq \emptyset$ and hence, by (6), $\mathcal{A}_r^0 \cap \mathcal{A}_s^1 = \emptyset$ for $s \in \{s_1, s_2\}$. Therefore, to satisfy $\mathcal{A}_r^0 \mathcal{B}_r^0 \subseteq \mathcal{M}^{10}$ we must have $\mathcal{A}_r^0 \mathcal{B}_r^0 \subseteq \mathcal{A}_{t_1}^1 \mathcal{B}_{t_1}^0 \cup \mathcal{A}_{t_2}^1 \mathcal{B}_{t_2}^0$. Further, from (16), $\mathcal{A}_r^0 \cap \mathcal{A}_t^0 \neq \emptyset$ for $t \in \{t_1, t_2\}$; combined with (4), this implies that $\mathcal{A}_r^0 \not\subseteq \mathcal{A}_t^1$ for $t \in \{t_1, t_2\}$. Hence, $\mathcal{B}_r^0 \subseteq \mathcal{B}_t^0$ for $t \in \{t_1, t_2\}$. $\qquad\square$

Finally, we are ready to derive a contradiction to the assumption that the given protocol, with $|\mathcal{R}| = 5$, is secure.

Claim 6. $\mathcal{A}_{s_1}^1 \cap (\mathcal{A}_r^0 \cup \mathcal{A}_{s_1}^0 \cup \mathcal{A}_{s_2}^0 \cup \mathcal{A}_{t_1}^0 \cup \mathcal{A}_{t_2}^0) = \emptyset$.

Proof. By (15), $\mathcal{B}_r^0 \cap \mathcal{B}_{s_1}^1 \neq \emptyset$ and then by (6), $\mathcal{A}_{s_1}^1 \cap \mathcal{A}_r^0 = \emptyset$. Also, by (15), $\mathcal{B}_{s_2}^0 \cap \mathcal{B}_{s_1}^1 \neq \emptyset$ and then by (6), $\mathcal{A}_{s_1}^1 \cap \mathcal{A}_{s_2}^0 = \emptyset$. We also have $\mathcal{A}_{s_1}^1 \cap \mathcal{A}_{s_1}^0 = \emptyset$ (by (4)). Since $\mathcal{B}_r^0 \cap \mathcal{B}_{s_1}^1 \neq \emptyset$ by (15), Claim 5 implies that $\mathcal{B}_{s_1}^1 \cap \mathcal{B}_t^0 \neq \emptyset$ for $t \in \{t_1, t_2\}$. Then by (6), $\mathcal{A}_{s_1}^1 \cap \mathcal{A}_t^0 = \emptyset$ for $t \in \{t_1, t_2\}$. $\qquad\square$

Now, by Claim 6, $\mathcal{A}_{s_1}^1 \mathcal{B}_{s_1}^0 \cap \mathcal{M}^{00} = \emptyset$ which contradicts the secrecy requirement (3). Thus our assumption that there is a weakly secret protocol with $|\mathcal{R}| = 5$ must be false, completing the proof. $\qquad\square$

4   Conclusion and Future Work

With the above result, for all boolean functions f with boolean inputs for each party, we know FKN protocols that are simultaneously optimal on all messages (even if only weak secrecy is required). Concretely, we have the following optimal alphabet sizes for all 16 functions:

$$|\mathcal{A}| = |\mathcal{B}| = |\mathcal{R}| = 0 \qquad \text{for the 2 constant functions}$$
$$|\mathcal{A}| = 1, |\mathcal{B}| = |\mathcal{R}| = 0 \qquad \text{for the 2 functions of } x \text{ alone}$$
$$|\mathcal{B}| = 1, |\mathcal{A}| = |\mathcal{R}| = 0 \qquad \text{for the 2 functions of } y \text{ alone}$$
$$|\mathcal{A}| = |\mathcal{B}| = |\mathcal{R}| = 1 \qquad \text{for XOR and XNOR}$$
$$|\mathcal{A}| = |\mathcal{B}| = 3, |\mathcal{R}| = 6 \qquad \text{for the remaining 8 functions.}$$

The 8 functions in the last line correspond to the truth table with a single 0 (and three 1s) or a single 1 (and three 0s), which are all "isomorphic" to the AND function (up to negating the inputs and/or the output). Note that the optimality above is exact, and does not hide constant factors or asymptotics.

Our techniques show the potential of elementary set-theoretic arguments in reasoning about protocols. While the arguments currently may appear somewhat unintuitive, we believe that many of the steps used could lead to more general formulations if applied to other problems as well.

We leave several open problems. Firstly, instead of weak secrecy, if we require full-fledged secrecy, then is it the case that for AND, not only is $|\mathcal{R}| = 6$, but R should be uniform over $\mathcal{R}$? This question is relevant when many instances of the AND function are computed, and the randomness (and the other messages) can potentially be compressed. Secondly, if instead of FKN protocol, we consider (honest-but-curious) MPC protocols, do the lower bound on $|\mathcal{R}|$ (or $H(R)$) still hold? In the case of MPC, A, B, R refer to the transcript of the communication between the corresponding pairs of parties. The results in [7] did indeed extend to both these settings, albeit only for the messages A and B. Another dimension to explore is more complex functions where Alice and/or Bob have larger inputs.

Yet another interesting question is the optimality of the AND protocol involving $n > 2$ input players. Feige et al. [8] gave an elegant protocol for this function, which uses a finite field of a prime size $p > n$. It is not clear if such algebraic structure is necessary, or if a more efficient protocol exists.

References

1. Applebaum, B., Holenstein, T., Mishra, M., Shayevitz, O.: The communication complexity of private simultaneous messages, revisited. In: Nielsen, J.B., Rijmen, V. (eds.) EUROCRYPT 2018. LNCS, vol. 10821, pp. 261–286. Springer, Cham (2018). https://doi.org/10.1007/978-3-319-78375-8_9
2. Chor, B., Kushilevitz, E.: A zero-one law for boolean privacy. SIAM J. Discrete Math. **4**(1), 36–47 (1991)
3. Chor, B., Kushilevitz, E.: A communication-privacy tradeoff for modular addition. Inf. Process. Lett. **45**(4), 205–210 (1993)
4. Cramer, R., Damgård, I., Nielsen, J.B.: Secure Multiparty Computation and Secret Sharing. Cambridge University Press, Cambridge (2015). http://www.cambridge.org/de/academic/subjects/computer-science/cryptography-cryptology-and-coding/secure-multiparty-computation-and-secret-sharing?format=HB&isbn=9781107043053
5. Damgård, I., Nielsen, J.B., Polychroniadou, A., Raskin, M.: On the communication required for unconditionally secure multiplication. In: Robshaw, M., Katz, J. (eds.) CRYPTO 2016. LNCS, vol. 9815, pp. 459–488. Springer, Heidelberg (2016). https://doi.org/10.1007/978-3-662-53008-5_16
6. Damgård, I., Nielsen, J.B., Polychroniadou, A., Raskin, M.A.: On the communication required for unconditionally secure multiplication. In: Advances in Cryptology - CRYPTO 2019–39th Annual International Cryptology Conference, Santa Barbara, CA, USA, Proceedings (2019)
7. Data, D., Prabhakaran, M., Prabhakaran, V.M.: On the communication complexity of secure computation. In: Advances in Cryptology - CRYPTO 2014–34th Annual Cryptology Conference, Santa Barbara, CA, USA, 17–21 August 2014, Proceedings, Part II, pp. 199–216 (2014). https://doi.org/10.1007/978-3-662-44381-1_12. Full version in IEEE Trans. Information Theory, 62(7) 2016
8. Feige, U., Killian, J., Naor, M.: A minimal model for secure computation (extended abstract). In: Proceedings of the Twenty-sixth Annual ACM Symposium on Theory of Computing, STOC 1994, pp. 554–563. ACM, New York (1994). https://doi.org/10.1145/195058.195408
9. Franklin, M.K., Yung, M.: Communication complexity of secure computation (extended abstract). In: STOC, pp. 699–710 (1992)
10. Goldreich, O.: Foundations of Cryptography: Basic Applications. Cambridge University Press, Cambridge (2004)

11. Ishai, Y., Kushilevitz, E.: Private simultaneous messages protocols with applications. In: Proceedings of the Fifth Israeli Symposium on Theory of Computing and Systems, pp. 174–183, June 1997. https://doi.org/10.1109/ISTCS.1997.595170
12. Kushilevitz, E.: Privacy and communication complexity. In: 30th Annual Symposium on Foundations of Computer Science, pp. 416–421, October 1989. https://doi.org/10.1109/SFCS.1989.63512
13. Prabhakaran, M., Sahai, A. (eds.): Secure Multi-Party Computation, Cryptology and Information Security Series, vol. 10. IOS Press, Amsterdam (2013)
14. Sundara Rajan S, Rajakrishnan, S., Thangaraj, A., Prabhakaran, V.: Lower bounds and optimal protocols for three-party secure computation. In: 2016 IEEE International Symposium on Information Theory (ISIT), pp. 1361–1365, July 2016. https://doi.org/10.1109/ISIT.2016.7541521

MArBled Circuits: Mixing Arithmetic and Boolean Circuits with Active Security

Dragos Rotaru[1,2]([⊠]) and Tim Wood[1,2]

[1] University of Bristol, Bristol, UK
[2] imec-COSIC KU Leuven, Leuven, Belgium
dragos.rotaru@esat.kuleuven.be, t.wood@kuleuven.be

Abstract. Most modern actively-secure multiparty computation (MPC) protocols involve generating random data that is secret-shared and authenticated, and using it to evaluate arithmetic or Boolean circuits in different ways. In this work we present a generic method for converting authenticated secret-shared data between different fields, and show how to use it to evaluate so-called "mixed" circuits with active security and in the full-threshold setting. A mixed circuit is one in which parties switch between different subprotocols dynamically as computation proceeds, the idea being that some protocols are more efficient for evaluating arithmetic circuits, and others for Boolean circuits.

One use case of our switching mechanism is for converting between secret-sharing-based MPC and garbled circuits (GCs). The former is more suited to the evaluation of arithmetic circuits and can easily be used to emulate arithmetic over the integers, whereas the latter is better for Boolean circuits and has constant round complexity. Much work already exists in the two-party semi-honest setting, but the n-party dishonest majority case was hitherto neglected.

We call the actively-secure mixed arithmetic/Boolean circuit a marbled circuit. Our implementation showed that mixing protocols in this way allows us to evaluate a linear Support Vector Machine with 400 times fewer AND gates than a solution using GC alone albeit with twice the preprocessing required using only SPDZ (Damgård et al., CRYPTO'12), and thus our solution offers a tradeoff between online and preprocessing complexity. When evaluating over a WAN network, our online phase is 10 times faster than the plain SPDZ protocol.

1 Introduction

One of the major modern uses of cryptography is for mutually-distrustful parties to compute a function on their combined secret inputs so that all parties learn

This work has been supported in part by ERC Advanced Grant ERC-2015-AdG-IMPaCT, by the Defense Advanced Research Projects Agency (DARPA) and Space and Naval Warfare Systems Center, Pacific (SSC Pacific) under contract No. N66001-15-C-4070, and by the FWO under an Odysseus project GOH9718N.

© Springer Nature Switzerland AG 2019
F. Hao et al. (Eds.): INDOCRYPT 2019, LNCS 11898, pp. 227–249, 2019.
https://doi.org/10.1007/978-3-030-35423-7_12

the output and no party learns anything more about other parties' inputs than what can be deduced from their own input and the output alone. This is known as secure multiparty computation (MPC) and has recently been shown to be very efficient for evaluating general Boolean [NNOB12,DZ13] and arithmetic [DPSZ12,DKL+13,KOS16,KPR18] circuits.

Many real-world use cases of computing on private data involve some form of statistical analysis, requiring evaluation of arithmetic formulae. Perhaps the most common method of computing arithmetic circuits on private data involves *secret-sharing* (SS), in which secret inputs are split up into several pieces and distributed amongst a set of parties, which then perform computations on these shares (sometimes requiring communication), and recombine them at the end for the result. However, MPC over a finite field or a ring is used to emulate arithmetic over the integers, and consequently, operations such as comparisons between secrets (i.e. $<, >, =$), which we refer to generally as "bit-wise" operations, are an important feature of MPC protocols: one of the shortcomings of MPC based on secret-sharing is that these natural but more complicated procedures require special preprocessing and several rounds of communication.

One way to mitigate these costs would be to use *garbled circuits* (GCs) instead of secret-sharing for circuits involving lots of non-linear operations, since this method has lower round complexity than SS-based MPC solutions (in fact, they can be done in constant rounds). Recent work has shown that multiparty Boolean circuit garbling with active security in the dishonest majority setting can be made very efficient [WRK17,HSS17,KY18]. However, performing general arithmetic computations in Boolean circuits can be expensive since the arithmetic operations must be accompanied by reduction modulo a prime inside the circuit. Moreover, efficient constructions of multiparty constant-round protocols for *arithmetic* circuits remain elusive. Indeed, the best-known optimisations for arithmetic circuits such as using a primorial modulus [BMR16] are expensive even for passive security in the two-party setting. The only work of which the authors are aware in the multiparty setting is the passively-secure honest-majority work by Ben-Efraim [Ben18].

So-called *mixed protocols* are those in which parties switch between secret-sharing (SS) and a garbled circuit (GC) mid-way through a computation, thus enjoying the efficiency of the basic addition and multiplication operations in any field using the former and the low-round complexity of GCs for more complex subroutines using the latter. One can think of mixed protocols as allowing parties to choose the most efficient field in which to evaluate different parts of a circuit.

There has been a lot of work on developing mixed protocols in the two-party passive security setting, for example [HKS+10,KSS13,KSS14,BDK+18]. One such work was the protocol of Demmler et al. [DSZ15] known as ABY, that gave a method for converting between arithmetic, Boolean, and Yao sharings. For small subcircuits, converting arithmetic shares to Boolean shares (of the bit decomposition) of the same secret – i.e. without any garbling – was shown to give efficiency gains over performing the same circuits in with arithmetic shares; for large subcircuits, using garbling allows reducing online costs. Mohassel and

Rindal [MR18] constructed a three-party protocol known as ABY3 for mixing these three types of sharing in the malicious setting assuming at most one corruption.

For mixed protocols to be efficient, clearly the cost of switching between secret-sharing and garbling, performing the operation, and switching back must be more efficient than the method that does not require switching, perhaps achieved by relegating some computation to the offline phase.

1.1 Our Contribution

The main challenge for active security is that it is essential to retain authentication of secrets through the conversion. In this work, we give a simple actively-secure procedure for transforming data that is secret-shared and authenticated in different ways. The motivation is to allow mixed protocols in the dishonest majority setting with active security, with only black-box use of the linear secret sharing scheme (LSSS) and GC subprotocols. The idea behind specifically designing a transformation procedure instead of a whole MPC protocol is that any circuit that makes considerable use of *both* arithmetic operations *and* bit-wise computations is likely to be most efficient when using state-of-the-art SS-based MPC and circuit garbling protocols, assuming the transformation procedure is cheap enough. Our implementation shows that this is achievable with concrete efficiency, and that there is some tradeoff between preprocessing costs and circuit evaluation costs. In the following discussion, we will focus on specific goal of switching between secret-sharing schemes and GCs.

Let $\mathbb{F}_q$ denote the finite field of order q. One of the key observations that allows our generic transformation to be realised is that for many recent protocols in both the SS-based and GC-based MPC paradigms, the starting point is essentially always to create a black-box actively-secure SS-based MPC functionality and to use it either directly to evaluate arithmetic circuits if the field is $\mathbb{F}_p$, or to generate garbled circuits with active security if the field is $\mathbb{F}_2$. At the highest level, the idea of our protocol is to allow data embedded in $\mathbb{F}_p$ to be efficiently transformed into data embedded in $\mathbb{F}_2$ *with authentication*. It is then easy to show that garbled circuits can be used to evaluate on authenticated elements of $\mathbb{F}_p$, as will be demonstrated in this work.

The most obvious way of providing inputs that are secret-shared into a garbled circuit is relatively straightforward: for a given secret, parties can simply input each bit in the bit-decomposition of their share into the GC, and the sum mod p can be computed inside the circuit. The primary technical challenge for a conversion procedure with active security is to maintain *authentication* through the transition from secret-shared inputs and secret inputs inside the GC, and *vice versa*. The naïve way of obtaining authentication is for parties to bit-decompose the shares of the data that provides authentication validating inside the GC: for example, if information-theoretic MACs are used on secrets, parties input their shares of the MACs and the MAC key(s). Final circuit outputs can be sets of bits that represent the bit-decomposition of in $\mathbb{F}_p$, and can be privately opened to different parties. This method requires garbling several additions and multiplications inside the circuit to check the MACs. The advantage of this solution, despite these challenges, is that it requires no additional preprocessing, nor adaptations to the garbling procedure.

Contrasting this approach, our solution makes use of special preprocessing to speed up the conversion. This results in reducing the circuit size by approximately $100,000$ AND gates per conversion for a field with a 128-bit prime modulus (assuming Montgomery multiplication is used). In this work we show how to convert between secret-shared data in $\mathbb{F}_p$, where p is a large prime and is the MPC modulus, and GCs in $\mathbb{F}_{2^k}$ through the use of "double-shared" authenticated **bits** which we dub *daBits*, following the nomenclature set out by [NNOB12]. These doubly-shared secrets are values in $\{0,1\}$ shared and authenticated both in $\mathbb{F}_p$ and $\mathbb{F}_{2^k}$, where by 0 and 1 we mean the additive and multiplicative identity, respectively, in each field. In brief, the conversion of a SS input x into a GC involves constructing a random secret r in $\mathbb{F}_p$ using daBits, opening $x-r$ in MPC, bit decomposing this public value (requiring no communication) and using these as signal bits for the GC, and then in the circuit adding r and computing this modulo p, which is possible since the bit decomposition of r is doubly-shared. This keeps the authentication check outside of the circuit instead requiring that the check happens correctly on the opened value $x - r$. Going the other way around, the output of the circuit is a set of public signal bits whose masking bits are chosen to be daBits. To get the output, parties XOR the public signal bits with the $\mathbb{F}_p$ shares of the corresponding daBit masks, which can be done locally. These shares can then be used to reconstruct elements of $\mathbb{F}_p$ (or remain as bits if desired).

We emphasise that while we focus on allowing conversion between SS and GCs, the conversion is generic in the sense that it is merely a method of converting data embedded into one field into data embedded in another field, with authentication attached. For example, once the bits of $x - r$ are public and the bit decomposition of r is known in $\mathbb{F}_{2^k}$, parties can execute an SS-based MPC protocol on these bits directly, without going through garbled circuits. Thus our work is also compatible with converting classic SPDZ shares in $\mathbb{F}_p$ with the recent protocol SPDZ2k of Cramer et al. [CDE+18].

We remark that several of the multiparty arithmetic garbling techniques of [Ben18] require the use of "multifield shared bits", which precisely correspond to our daBits (albeit in an unauthenticated honest-majority setting), and consequently we suggest that our idea of generating daBits may lead to more efficient actively-secure multiparty garbling of arithmetic circuits.

Related work. Recent work [KSS13, KSS10] deals with conversion between homomorphic encryption (HE) and GC for two parties. In their two-party case, the conversion works by having P_1 encrypt a blinded version of its input $x - r$ using the public key of P_2. Since the second party can decrypt the ciphertext, the share of x held by P_2 is $x - r$ and the share of P_1 is r. They also provide some techniques to convert an additive sharing in a ring to a GC sharing in the malicious case (P_2 only). Unfortunately their solution is insecure in the case of a malicious P_1 without adding some extra zero knowledge proofs. Moreover, it is unclear how to extend their work to convert from an n-party authenticated LSSS sharing of x to an n-party sharing inside a GC with a dishonest majority.

2   Preliminaries

In this section we explain the basics of MPC as required to understand the sequel. In our protocol, one instance of MPC is used to perform the secret-sharing-based MPC over a prime field, and another instance is used to perform another form of MPC – typically, circuit garbling – over a large field of characteristic 2.

2.1   General

We denote the number of parties by n, and the set of indices of parties corrupted by the adversary by A. We write $[j]$ to denote the set $\{1, \ldots, j\}$. We write $\mathbb{F}$ to denote a field, and $\mathbb{F}_q$ to denote the finite field of order q. The arithmetic circuit will be computed in the field $\mathbb{F}_p$ where p is a large prime, and the keys and masks for the garbled circuit in $\mathbb{F}_{2^k}$. By $\log(\cdot)$ we always mean the base-2 logarithm, $\log_2(\cdot)$. We denote by sec and κ the statistical and computational security parameters, respectively. We say that a function $\nu : \mathbb{N} \to \mathbb{R}$ is *negligible* if for every polynomial $f \in \mathbb{Z}[X]$ there exists $N \in \mathbb{N}$ such that $|\nu(X)| < |1/f(X)|$ for all $X > N$. If an event X happens with probability $1 - \nu(\text{sec})$ where ν is a negligible function then we say that X happens with overwhelming probability in sec. We write $x \xleftarrow{\$} S$ to mean that x is sampled uniformly from the set S, and use $x \leftarrow y$ to mean that x is assigned the value y. We will sometimes denote by, for example, $(a - b)_j$ the jth bit in the binary expansion of the integer $a - b$.

2.2   Security

UC Framework. We prove our protocols secure in the universal composability (UC) framework of Canetti [Can01]. We assume the reader's familiarity with this framework. In Fig. 1 we give a functionality $\mathcal{F}_{\mathsf{Rand}}$ for obtaining unbiased random data that we need for our protocol. A protocol realising $\mathcal{F}_{\mathsf{Rand}}$, and other UC functionalities, are given in the full version.

Functionality $\mathcal{F}_{\mathsf{Rand}}$

Random subset On input $(\mathsf{RSubset}, X, t)$ where X is a set satisfying $|X| \geq t$, sample $S \xleftarrow{\$} \{A \subseteq X : |A| = t\}$ and send S to all parties.

Random buckets On input $(\mathsf{RBucket}, X, t)$ where X is a set and $t \in \mathbb{N}$ such that $|X|/t \in \mathbb{N}$, set $n \leftarrow |X|/t$ and then for each $i = 1, \ldots, n$ do the following:

    1. Sample $X_i \xleftarrow{\$} \{A \subseteq X : |A| = t\}$.
    2. Set $X \leftarrow X \setminus X_i$.
    Finally, send $(X_i)_{i=1}^n$ to all parties.

Fig. 1. Functionality $\mathcal{F}_{\mathsf{Rand}}$

We assume an active, static adversary corrupting at most $n - 1$ out of n parties. Adversaries corrupting at most all parties but one are called "full-threshold". An active adversary may deviate arbitrarily from the protocol description, and a static adversary is permitted to choose which parties to corrupt only at the beginning of the protocol, and cannot corrupt more parties later on. Our protocol allows corrupt parties to cause the protocol to abort before honest parties receive output, but if the adversary cheats then the honest parties will not accept an incorrect output. This is known as "security-with-abort" in the literature. While this work focuses on the full-threshold setting, since $\mathcal{F}_{\mathsf{MPC}}$ is used as a black box, the access structure of our protocol is solely dependent on the access structure admitted by the instantiation(s) of $\mathcal{F}_{\mathsf{MPC}}$ - for a complete definition of $\mathcal{F}_{\mathsf{MPC}}$ which is sometimes denoted as $\mathcal{F}_{\mathsf{ABB}}$ or $\mathcal{F}_{\mathsf{AMPC}}$ in the literature check [BDOZ11,SW19].

Communication. We assume point-to-point secure channels, and synchronous communication. Additionally, we assume a broadcast channel, which can be instantiated in the random oracle model over point-to-point secure channels, for example as described in [DPSZ12, App. A.3]. A round of communication is a period of time in which parties perform computation and then send and receive messages. Messages sent in a round cannot depend on messages received during the current round, but messages may depend on messages sent in previous rounds. So-called *constant-round* protocols require $O(1)$ rounds for the entire protocol.

2.3   Garbled Circuits

Essentially all modern dishonest-majority multiparty Boolean circuit garbling protocols, for example [HSS17,WRK17,HOSS18], use some form of secret-sharing based MPC to generate a multiparty garbled circuit, thus following the basic idea of SPDZ-BMR [LPSY15] of using MPC to ensure correctness of the garbling in the classic multiparty garbling protocol by Beaver et al. [BMR90]. The specific garbling protocol is not important for this work: our solution makes use of the garbling subprotocols in a black-box way. For this reason, the explanation of MPC, with authentication for active security, is given below; the explanation of the garbling subprotocols is left to the full version. The important parts of the garbling evaluation are providing inputs from $\mathbb{F}_p$ into a generic multiparty garbled circuit, and extracting $\mathbb{F}_p$ outputs from it, which is dealt with in Sect. 3.2.

2.4   MPC

Our protocol makes use of MPC as a black box, for which the generic functionality is outlined in Fig. 2 as part of the functionality $\mathcal{F}_{\mathsf{Prep}}$. The functionality $\mathcal{F}_{\mathsf{MPC}}$ over a field $\mathbb{F}$ is realised using protocols with statistical security sec if $|\mathbb{F}| = \Omega(2^{\mathsf{sec}})$ and computational security κ depending on the computational primitives being used. We will describe MPC as executed in the SPDZ family of protocols [DPSZ12, DKL+13, KOS16, KPR18, CDE+18]. These protocols are in the preprocessing model in which circuit evaluation is split into a *preprocessing* (or *offline*) phase in which input-independent data is generated, that is then "used up" in an *online* phase which uses the actual circuit inputs. The reason for doing this is that the preprocessed data is expensive to generate, but the online evaluation is cheap as a result.

Note that MPC as used in garbling often offers "less" than full circuit evaluation as described here: for example, [HSS17] defined a protocol $\Pi_{\mathsf{Bit} \times \mathsf{String}}$ that allows bits to be multiplied by bitstrings but is not concerned with multiplication of general field elements in $\mathbb{F}_{2^k}$. However, what follows is enough to understand the main techniques required for SS-based multiparty garbling.

Secret-Sharing. A secret $x \in \mathbb{F}$ is said to be *additively shared*, denoted by $[\![x]\!]$, if a dealer samples a set $\{x^i\}_{i=1}^{n-1} \overset{\$}{\leftarrow} \mathbb{F}$, fixes $x^n \leftarrow x - \sum_{i=1}^{n-1} x^i$, and for all $i \in [n]$ sends x^i to party P_i. Any set of $n-1$ shares is indistinguishable from a set of $n-1$ uniformly-sampled shares, and the sum of all n shares is the secret x. This secret-sharing is linear: the sum of corresponding shares of two secrets is a sharing of the sum of the two secrets, so no communication is required for linear functions. A secret x shared in this way is denoted by $[\![x]\!] = (x^i)_{i=1}^n$.

MPC protocols based on secret-sharing involve secret-sharing all the secret inputs, performing computations on the shares, and recombining at the end to obtain the final result.

Addition of secrets. Addition of secrets is denoted as follows:

$$[\![a]\!] + [\![b]\!] \leftarrow [\![a+b]\!] = (a^i + b^i)_{i=1}^n$$

Thus any linear function on secret-shared data can be evaluated without communication.

Multiplication of secrets. Using a technique due to Beaver [Bea92], multiplication of secrets in the online phase can be computed as a *linear* operation if the parties have access to so-called *Beaver triples* – triples of secret-shared values $([\![a]\!], [\![b]\!], [\![a \cdot b]\!])$, where a and b are uniformly random and unknown to the parties. To multiply $[\![x]\!]$ and $[\![y]\!]$, the parties compute $[\![x-a]\!] \leftarrow [\![x]\!] - [\![a]\!]$ and $[\![y-b]\!] \leftarrow [\![y]\!] - [\![b]\!]$ locally and open them (i.e. they broadcast their shares of $[\![x-a]\!]$ and $[\![y-b]\!]$ so all parties learn $x-a$ and $y-b$), and then compute the product as

$$[\![x \cdot y]\!] \leftarrow [\![a \cdot b]\!] + (x-a) \cdot [\![b]\!] + (y-b) \cdot [\![a]\!] + (x-a) \cdot (y-b).$$

Since a and b are unknown to any party, $x-a$ and $y-b$ reveal nothing about x and y. We refer to protocols that generate Beaver triples as *SPDZ-like*. The main cost of SPDZ-like protocols comes from generating these Beaver triples. The two main ways of doing this are either using somewhat homomorphic encryption (SHE) [DPSZ12, DKL+13, KPR18] or oblivious transfer (OT) [KOS16, CDE+18].

Authentication. Since both addition and multiplication involve only linear operations, computations on shares in the online phase only need to be protected against *additive* errors – that is, a corrupt party P_i changing its share from x_i to $x_i + \varepsilon$. To protect against such errors, linear information-theoretic MACs are used. Since these MACs are linear, parties can maintain MACs on every secret throughout the whole circuit evaluation; then they can run an amortised check of their correctness once at the end of the protocol execution. Though we are not concerned with the specifics of authentication as used in SS-based GC or general MPC in this work, it is helpful to understand how secrets can be authenticated in different ways, and so a brief description of two prevalent forms follows.

SPDZ-style MACs. A secret $a \in \mathbb{F}$ is shared amongst the parties by additively sharing the secret a in $\mathbb{F}$ along with a linear MAC $\gamma(a)$ defined as $\gamma(a) \leftarrow \alpha \cdot a$, where $\alpha \in \mathbb{F}$ is a global MAC key, which is also additively shared. By "global" we mean that every MAC in the protocol uses this MAC key, rather than each party holding their own key and authenticating every share held by every other party. Note that the parties can trivially obtain a MAC on a public value a by computing $[\![\gamma(a)]\!] \leftarrow (\alpha^i \cdot a)_{i=1}^n$.

Now if p is $O(2^{\mathsf{sec}})$ then to introduce an error ε on the sharing requires modifying the corresponding MAC by $\varepsilon \cdot \alpha$ – i.e. the adversary must guess the MAC key. We refer the reader to [DKL+13] for details on the MAC checking procedure.

BDOZ-style MACs. A different type of MAC, sometimes called *pairwise*, used by Bendlin et al. [BDOZ11]. A bit $c \in \mathbb{F}_2$ is shared as $c = \bigoplus_{i=1}^n c^i$ where for each share $c^i \in \mathbb{F}_2$ (held by P_i), for each $j \neq i$, parties P_i and P_j hold a MAC as follows: P_i holds $M_j^i[c] \in \mathbb{F}_{2^k}$ and P_j holds $K_i^j[c] \in \mathbb{F}_{2^k}$ such that $K_i^j[c] \oplus M_j^i[c] = \Delta^j \cdot c^i$, where Δ^j is the MAC key held by P_j and c^i a random bit held by P_i. This MAC scheme is used in the garbling protocols due to Hazay et al. and Wang et al. [HSS17, WRK17].

Sharing Notation. Below we give the precise meaning of the notation $[\![a]\!]_p$ and $[\![c]\!]_{2^k}$. One can think of using SPDZ-style MACs for $\mathbb{F}_p$ and BDOZ-style MACs for $\mathbb{F}_{2^k}$, as described below, but the protocols for conversion are oblivious to the precise method of authentication so these choices are essentially arbitrary. The third type of sharing is the notation that will be used for our special preprocessing called daBits.

$$\text{LSSS Sharing} \quad [\![a]\!]_p = (a^i, \gamma_p(a)^i, \alpha^i)_{i=1}^n$$

$$\text{GC Sharing} \quad [\![c]\!]_{2^k} = (c^i, (K_i^j[c])_{j\neq i}, (M_j^i[c])_{j\neq i}, \Delta^i)_{i=1}^n.$$

$$\text{Sharing in both} \quad [\![b]\!]_{p,2^k} = ([\![b]\!]_p, [\![b]\!]_{2^k}) \text{ where } b \in \{0, 1\}.$$

The sharing $[\![b]\!]_{p,2^k}$ is considered correct if the bit is the same in both fields (either 0 or 1). Creating these bits while guaranteeing active security is one of the contributions of this work.

Conditions on the secret-sharing field. Let $l = \lfloor \log p \rfloor$. Throughout, we assume the MPC is over $\mathbb{F}_p$ where p is some large prime, but we require that one must be able to generate uniformly random field elements by sampling bits uniformly at random $\{[\![r_j]\!]_p\}_{j=0}^{l-1}$ and summing them to get $[\![r]\!]_p \leftarrow \sum_{j=0}^{l-1} 2^j \cdot [\![r_j]\!]_p$. At a high level, this means p must be close to a power of 2. The formal requirement on p is that either $\frac{p-2^l}{p} = O(2^{-\mathsf{sec}})$ or $\frac{2^{l'}-p}{2^{l'}} = O(2^{-\mathsf{sec}})$ where $l' = \lceil \log p \rceil$, which is proved formally in the full version.

Arbitrary Rings vs Fields. Our protocol uses actively-secure MPC as black box, so there is no reason the MPC cannot take place over any ring $\mathbb{Z}/m\mathbb{Z}$ where m is possibly composite, as long as m is (close to) a power of 2. The security of our procedure for generating daBits can tolerate zero-divisors in the ring, so computation may, for example, take place over the ring $\mathbb{Z}/2^l\mathbb{Z}$ for any l, for which actively-secure $\mathcal{F}_{\mathsf{MPC}}$ can be realised using [CDE+18]. Moreover, one can use daBits to convert from a SPDZ $\mathbb{F}_p$ share to a SPDZ2k share: the high level idea of converting between a field and a ring is to generate the same correlated randomness $[\![r]\!]_p \in \mathbb{F}_p$ and $[\![r]\!]_{2^k} \in \mathbb{Z}_{2^k}$ by bit-composing the daBits. Then the conversion from $[\![x]\!]_p$ to $[\![x]\!]_{2^k}$ becomes trivial: parties open $[\![x]\!]_p - [\![r]\!]_p$, assign this to a public y then perform the reduction modulo p in MPC using the public constant y in $\mathbb{Z}_{2^k}$ i.e. $[\![x]\!]_{2^k} \leftarrow (y + [\![r]\!]_{2^k}) \mod p$.

Note on XOR. In our context, we will require heavy use of the (generalised) XOR operation. This can be defined in any field as the function

$$
\begin{aligned}
f : \mathbb{F}_p \times \mathbb{F}_p &\to \mathbb{F}_p \\
(x,y) &\mapsto x + y - 2 \cdot x \cdot y,
\end{aligned}
\tag{1}
$$

which coincides with the usual XOR function for fields of characteristic 2. In SS-based MPC, addition requires no communication, so computing XOR in $\mathbb{F}_{2^k}$ is for free; the cost in $\mathbb{F}_p$ $(p > 2)$ is one multiplication, which requires preprocessed data and some communication. This operation turns out to be the main cost associated with our offline phase (see Table 1).

3 Protocol

The idea behind creating a mixed protocol is to use one instance of $\mathcal{F}_{\mathsf{MPC}}$ over $\mathbb{F}_p$ to perform addition and multiplication in the field, and one instance of $\mathcal{F}_{\mathsf{MPC}}$ over $\mathbb{F}_{2^k}$ is used to perform the garbling, and to allow conversion between the two. Thus the goal is the functionality $\mathcal{F}_{\mathsf{Prep}}$, which is given in Figs. 2 and 3.

Functionality $\mathcal{F}_{\mathsf{Prep}}$

Instances of $\mathcal{F}_{\mathsf{MPC}}$

Independent copies of $\mathcal{F}_{\mathsf{MPC}}$ are identified via session identifiers sid; $\mathcal{F}_{\mathsf{Prep}}$ maintains one dictionary $\mathsf{Val}_{\mathsf{sid}}$ for each instance. Entries cannot be changed, for simplicity. If a party provides an input with an sid which has not been initialised, output 1$eject$ to all parties and awaits another message.

Initialise On input (Initialise, $\mathbb{F}$, sid) from all parties, if sid is a new session identifer then initialise a database of secrets $\mathsf{Val}_{\mathsf{sid}}$ indexed by a set $\mathsf{Val}_{\mathsf{sid}}$.Keys and store the field as $\mathsf{Val}_{\mathsf{sid}}$.Field $\leftarrow \mathbb{F}$. Set the internal flag $\mathsf{Abort}_{\mathsf{sid}}$ to false.

Input On input (Input, i, id, x, sid) from P_i and (Input, i, id, $\bot$, sid) from all other parties, if id $\notin \mathsf{Val}_{\mathsf{sid}}$.Keys then insert it and set $\mathsf{Val}_{\mathsf{sid}}[\mathsf{id}] \leftarrow x$. Then call the procedure **Wait**.

Add On input (Add, id_x, id_y, id, sid), if id_x, $\mathsf{id}_y \in \mathsf{Val}_{\mathsf{sid}}$.Keys then set $\mathsf{Val}_{\mathsf{sid}}[\mathsf{id}] \leftarrow \mathsf{Val}_{\mathsf{sid}}[\mathsf{id}_x] + \mathsf{Val}_{\mathsf{sid}}[\mathsf{id}_y]$.

Multiply On input (Multiply, id_x, id_y, id, sid), if id_x, $\mathsf{id}_y \in \mathsf{Val}_{\mathsf{sid}}$.Keys then set $\mathsf{Val}_{\mathsf{sid}}[\mathsf{id}] \leftarrow \mathsf{Val}_{\mathsf{sid}}[\mathsf{id}_x] \cdot \mathsf{Val}_{\mathsf{sid}}[\mathsf{id}_y]$. Then call the procedure **Wait**.

Random element On input (RElt, id, sid), if id $\notin \mathsf{Val}_{\mathsf{sid}}$.Keys then set $\mathsf{Val}_{\mathsf{sid}}[\mathsf{id}] \xleftarrow{\$} \mathsf{Val}_{\mathsf{sid}}$.Field. Then call the procedure **Wait**.

Random bit On input (RBit, id, sid), if id $\notin \mathsf{Val}_{\mathsf{sid}}$.Keys then set $\mathsf{Val}_{\mathsf{sid}}[\mathsf{id}] \xleftarrow{\$} \{0,1\}$. Then call the procedure **Wait**.

Open On input (Open, i, id, sid) from all parties, if id $\in \mathsf{Val}_{\mathsf{sid}}$.Keys,
- if $i = 0$ then send $\mathsf{Val}_{\mathsf{sid}}[\mathsf{id}]$ to the adversary and run the procedure **Wait**. If the message was (OK, sid), await an error ε from the adversary. Send $\mathsf{Val}_{\mathsf{sid}}[\mathsf{id}] + \varepsilon$ to all honest parties and if $\varepsilon \neq 0$, set the internal flag $\mathsf{Abort}_{\mathsf{sid}}$ to true.
- if $i \in A$, then send $\mathsf{Val}_{\mathsf{sid}}[\mathsf{id}]$ to the adversary and then run **Wait**.
- if $i \in [n] \setminus A$, then call the procedure **Wait**, and if not already halted then await an error ε from the adversary. Send $\mathsf{Val}_{\mathsf{sid}}[\mathsf{id}] + \varepsilon$ to P_i and if $\varepsilon \neq 0$ then set the internal flag $\mathsf{Abort}_{\mathsf{sid}}$ to true.

Check On input (Check, sid) from all parties, run the procedure **Wait**. If not already halted and the internal flag $\mathsf{Abort}_{\mathsf{sid}}$ is set to true, then send the message (Abort, sid) to the adversary and honest parties and ignore all further messages to $\mathcal{F}_{\mathsf{MPC}}$ with this sid; otherwise send the message (OK, sid) and continue.

Internal procedure:

Wait Await a message (OK, sid) or (Abort, sid) from the adversary; if the message is (OK, sid) then continue; otherwise, send the message (Abort, sid) to all honest parties and ignore all further messages to $\mathcal{F}_{\mathsf{MPC}}$ with this sid.

(continued...)

Fig. 2. Functionality $\mathcal{F}_{\mathsf{Prep}}$

Functionality $\mathcal{F}_{\mathsf{Prep}}$ (continued)

Additional commands

daBits On receiving $(\mathsf{daBits}, \mathsf{id}_1, \dots, \mathsf{id}_\ell, \mathsf{sid}_1, \mathsf{sid}_2)$, from all parties where $\mathsf{id}_i \notin \mathsf{Val}.\mathsf{Keys}$ for all $i \in [\ell]$, await a message OK or Abort from the adversary. If the message is OK, then sample $\{b_j\}_{j \in [\ell]} \xleftarrow{\$} \{0, 1\}$ and for each $j \in [\ell]$, set $\mathsf{Val}_{\mathsf{sid}_1}[\mathsf{id}_j] \leftarrow b_j$ and $\mathsf{Val}_{\mathsf{sid}_2}[\mathsf{id}_j] \leftarrow b_j$ and insert the set $\{\mathsf{id}_i\}_{i \in [\ell]}$ into $\mathsf{Val}_{\mathsf{sid}_1}.\mathsf{Keys}$ and $\mathsf{Val}_{\mathsf{sid}_2}.\mathsf{Keys}$; otherwise send the messages $(\mathsf{Abort}, \mathsf{sid}_1)$ and $(\mathsf{Abort}, \mathsf{sid}_2)$ to all honest parties and the adversary and ignore all further messages to $\mathcal{F}_{\mathsf{MPC}}$ with session identifier sid_1 or sid_2.

Fig. 3. Functionality $\mathcal{F}_{\mathsf{Prep}}$ (continued)

Recall from the introduction that the high-level idea of our protocol is to open a secret-shared value, locally bit-decompose it, and use these bits as input bits to the garbled circuit. Once the parties have these, they reveal corresponding secret pseudorandom function keys for circuit evaluation, and the rest of the protocol (including retrieving outputs in secret-shared form) is local.

3.1 Generating daBits Using Bucketing

Any technique for generating daBits require some form of checking procedure to ensure consistency between the two fields. Checking consistency often means checking random linear combinations of secrets produce the same result in both cases. Unfortunately, in our case such comparisons are meaningless since the fields have different characteristic and it seems hard to find a mapping between the two fields which allows to compare random values in $\mathbb{F}_p$ with values in $\mathbb{F}_{2^k}$. We can, however, check XORs of bits, which in $\mathbb{F}_p$ involves multiplication. (See Eq. 1 in Sect. 2.) It is therefore necessary to use a protocol that minimises (as far as possible) the number of multiplications. Consequently, techniques using oblivious transfer (OT) such as [WRK17] to generated authenticated bits require a lot of XORs for checking correctness, so are undesirable for generating daBits.

Our chosen solution uses $\mathcal{F}_{\mathsf{MPC}}$ as a black box. In order to generate the same bit in both fields, each party samples a bit and calls the $\mathbb{F}_p$ and $\mathbb{F}_{2^k}$ instances of $\mathcal{F}_{\mathsf{MPC}}$ with this same input and then the parties compute the n-party XOR. To ensure all parties provided the same inputs in both fields, cut-and-choose and bucketing procedures are required, though since the number of bits necessary to generate is a multiple of $\log p \cdot \mathsf{sec}$ and we can batch-produce daBits, the parameters are modest (for $\mathsf{sec} = 40$ five XORs in $\mathcal{F}_{\mathsf{MPC}}^p$ per daBit are enough).

We use similar cut-and-choose and bucketing checks to those described by Frederiksen et al. [FKOS15, App. F.3], in which "triple-like" secrets can be efficiently checked. The idea behind these checks is the following. One first opens a random subset of secrets so that with some probability all unopened bits are correct. This ensures that the adversary cannot cheat on too many of the daBits.

One then puts the secrets into buckets, and then in each bucket designates one secret as the one to output, uses all other secrets in the bucket to check the last, and discards all but the designated secret. For a single bucket, the check will only pass (by construction) if either all secrets are correct or all are incorrect. Thus the adversary is forced to corrupt whole multiples of the bucket size and hope they are grouped together in the same bucket. Fortunately, (we will show that) there is no leakage on the bits since the parameters required for the parts of the protocol described above already preclude it. The protocol is described in Fig. 4 and 5; we prove that this protocol securely realises the functionality $\mathcal{F}_{\mathsf{Prep}}$ in Figs. 2 and 3 in the $\mathcal{F}_{\mathsf{MPC}}$-hybrid model. To do this, we require Proposition 1.

Protocol $\Pi_{\mathsf{daBits+MPC}}$

This protocol is in the $\mathcal{F}_{\mathsf{MPC}}$-hybrid model.

Initialise
1. Call an instance, $\mathcal{F}_{\mathsf{MPC}}^p$, of $\mathcal{F}_{\mathsf{MPC}}$ with input (Initialise, $\mathbb{F}_p, 0$).
2. Call an instance, $\mathcal{F}_{\mathsf{MPC}}^{2^k}$, of $\mathcal{F}_{\mathsf{MPC}}$ with input (Initialise, $\mathbb{F}_{2^k}, 1$).

Calls to $\mathcal{F}_{\mathsf{MPC}}$ Dealt with by $\mathcal{F}_{\mathsf{MPC}}^p$ or $\mathcal{F}_{\mathsf{MPC}}^{2^k}$, as appropriate.

daBits To generate ℓ bits, do the following:
1. **Generate daBits**
   (a) Let $m \leftarrow CB\ell$ where $C > 1$ and $B > 1$ are chosen so that $C^B \cdot \binom{B\ell}{B} > 2^{\mathsf{sec}}$.
   (b) For each $i \in [n]$,
      i. Party P_i samples a bit string $(b_1^i, \ldots, b_m^i) \xleftarrow{\$} \{0,1\}^m$.
      ii. Call $\mathcal{F}_{\mathsf{MPC}}^p$ where P_i has input (Input, $i, \mathsf{id}_{b_j^i}, b_1^i, 0)_{j=1}^m$ and P_j ($j \neq i$) has input (Input, $i, \mathsf{id}_{b_j^i}, \perp, 0)_{i=1}^m$.
      iii. Call $\mathcal{F}_{\mathsf{MPC}}^{2^k}$ where P_i has input (Input, $i, \mathsf{id}_{b_j^i}, b_1^i, 1)_{j=1}^m$ and P_j ($j \neq i$) has input (Input, $i, \mathsf{id}_{b_j^i}, \perp, 1)_{i=1}^m$.
2. **Cut and Choose**
   (a) Call $\mathcal{F}_{\mathsf{Rand}}$ with input (RSubset, $[CB\ell], (C-1)B\ell$) to obtain a set S.
   (b) Call $\mathcal{F}_{\mathsf{MPC}}^p$ with inputs (Open, $0, \mathsf{id}_{b_j^i}, 0)_{j \in S}$ for all $i \in [n]$.
   (c) Call $\mathcal{F}_{\mathsf{MPC}}^{2^k}$ with inputs (Open, $0, \mathsf{id}_{b_j^i}, 1)_{j \in S}$ for all $i \in [n]$.
   (d) If any party sees daBits which are not in $\{0,1\}$ or not the same in both fields, they send the message Abort to all parties and halt.
3. **Combine** For all $j \in S$, do the following:
   (a) Set $[\![b_j]\!]_p \leftarrow [\![b_j^1]\!]_p$ and then for i from 2 to n compute
      i. $[\![b_j]\!]_p \leftarrow [\![b_j]\!]_p + [\![b_j^i]\!]_p - 2 \cdot [\![b_j]\!]_p \cdot [\![b_j^i]\!]_p$
   (b) Compute $[\![b_j]\!]_{2^k} \leftarrow \bigoplus_{i=1}^n [\![b_j^i]\!]_{2^k}$.

(continued...)

Fig. 4. Protocol $\Pi_{\mathsf{daBits+MPC}}$

Protocol $\Pi_{\mathsf{daBits+MPC}}$

4. **Consistency Check**
   (a) Call $\mathcal{F}_{\mathsf{Rand}}$ with input (RBucket, $[B\ell], B$) and use the returned sets $(S_i)_{i=1}^{\ell}$ to put the $B\ell$ daBits into ℓ buckets of size B.
   (b) For each bucket S_i,
       i. Relabel the bits in this bucket as $b^1, \dots, b^B$.
       ii. For $j = 2$ to B, compute $[\![c^j]\!]_p \leftarrow [\![b^1]\!]_p + [\![b^j]\!]_p - 2 \cdot [\![b^1]\!]_p \cdot [\![b^j]\!]_p$ and $[\![c^j]\!]_{2^k} \leftarrow [\![b^1]\!]_{2^k} \oplus [\![b^j]\!]_{2^k}$.
       iii. Call $\mathcal{F}_{\mathsf{MPC}}^p$ with inputs $(\mathsf{Open}, 0, \mathsf{id}_{c^j}, 0)_{j=2}^B$.
       iv. Call $\mathcal{F}_{\mathsf{MPC}}^{2^k}$ with inputs $(\mathsf{Open}, 0, \mathsf{id}_{c^j}, 1)_{j=2}^B$.
       v. If any party sees daBits which are not in $\{0, 1\}$ or not the same in both fields, they send the message Abort to all parties and halt.
       vi. Set $[\![b_i]\!]_{p,2^k} \leftarrow [\![b^1]\!]_{p,2^k}$.
   (c) Call $\mathcal{F}_{\mathsf{MPC}}^p$ with input $(\mathsf{Check}, 0)$.
   (d) Call $\mathcal{F}_{\mathsf{MPC}}^{2^k}$ with input $(\mathsf{Check}, 1)$.
   (e) If the checks pass without aborting, output $\{[\![b_i]\!]_{p,2^k}\}_{i=1}^{\ell}$ and discard all other bits.

Fig. 5. Protocol $\Pi_{\mathsf{daBits+MPC}}$ (continued)

Proposition 1. *For a given $\ell > 0$, choose $B > 1$ and $C > 1$ so that $C^{-B} \cdot \binom{B\ell}{B}^{-1} < 2^{-\mathsf{sec}}$. Then the probability that one or more of the ℓ daBits output after* **Consistency Check** *by $\Pi_{\mathsf{daBits+MPC}}$ in Figure 5 is different in each field is at most $2^{-\mathsf{sec}}$.*

Proof. Using $\mathcal{F}_{\mathsf{MPC}}^p$ and $\mathcal{F}_{\mathsf{MPC}}^{2^k}$ as black boxes ensures the adversary can only possibly cheat in the input stage. We will argue that:

1. If both sets of inputs from corrupt parties to $\mathcal{F}_{\mathsf{MPC}}^p$ and $\mathcal{F}_{\mathsf{MPC}}^{2^k}$ are bits (rather than other field elements), then the bits are consistent in the two different fields with overwhelming probability.
2. The inputs in $\mathbb{F}_{2^k}$ are bits with overwhelming probability.
3. The inputs in $\mathbb{F}_p$ are bits with overwhelming probability.

We will conclude that the daBits are bits in the two fields, and are consistent.

1. Let c be the number of inconsistent daBits generated by a given corrupt party. If $c > B\ell$ then every set of size $(C-1)B\ell$ contains an incorrect daBit so the honest parties will always detect this in **Cut and Choose** and abort. Since $(C-1)B\ell$ out of $CB\ell$ daBits are opened, on average the probability that a daBit is not opened is $1 - (C-1)/C = C^{-1}$, and so if $c < B\ell$ then we have:

$$\Pr[\text{None of the } c \text{ corrupted daBits is opened}] = C^{-c}. \tag{2}$$

At this point, if the protocol has not yet aborted, then there are $B\ell$ daBits remaining of which exactly c are corrupt.

Suppose a daBit $[\![b]\!]_{p,2^k}$ takes the value $\tilde{b}$ in $\mathbb{F}_p$ and $\hat{b}$ in $\mathbb{F}_{2^k}$. If the bucketing check passes then for every other daBit $[\![b']\!]_{p,2^k}$ in the bucket it holds that $\tilde{b} \oplus \tilde{b}' = \hat{b} \oplus \hat{b}'$, so $\tilde{b}' = (\hat{b} \oplus \hat{b}') \oplus \tilde{b}$, and so $\tilde{b} = \hat{b} \oplus 1$ if and only if $\tilde{b}' = \hat{b}' \oplus 1$. (Recall that we are assuming the inputs are certainly bits at this stage.) In other words, within a single bucket, the check passes if and only if either all daBits are inconsistent, or if none of them are. Thus the probability **Consistency Check** passes without aborting is the probability that all corrupted daBits are placed into the same buckets. Moreover, this implies that if the number of corrupted daBits, c, is not a multiple of the bucket size, this stage never passes, so we write $c = Bt$ for some $t > 0$. Then we have:

$$\Pr[\text{All corrupted daBits are placed in the same buckets}]$$
$$= \frac{\binom{Bt}{B} \cdot \binom{B(t-1)}{B} \cdots \binom{B}{B} \cdot \binom{B\ell-Bt}{B} \cdot \binom{B\ell-Bt-B}{B} \cdots \binom{B}{B}}{\binom{B\ell}{B} \cdot \binom{B\ell-B}{B} \cdots \binom{B}{B}}$$
$$= \frac{(Bt)!}{B!^t} \cdot \frac{(B\ell-Bt)!}{B!^{\ell-t}} \cdot \frac{B!^\ell}{(B\ell)!} = \binom{B\ell}{Bt}^{-1}. \tag{3}$$

Since the randomness for **Cut and Choose** and **Check Correctness** is independent, the event that both checks pass after the adversary corrupts c daBits is the product of the probabilities. To upper-bound the adversary's chance of winning, we compute the probability by maximising over t: thus we need C and B so that

$$\max_t \left\{ C^{-Bt} \cdot \binom{B\ell}{Bt}^{-1} \right\} < 2^{-\mathsf{sec}} \tag{4}$$

The maximum occurs when t is small, and $t \geq 1$ otherwise no cheating occurred; thus since the proposition stipulates that $C^{-B} \cdot \binom{B\ell}{B}^{-1} < 2^{-\mathsf{sec}}$, the daBits are consistent in both fields, if they are indeed bits in both fields.

2. Next, we will argue that the check in **Cut and Choose** ensures that the inputs given to $\mathcal{F}_{\mathsf{MPC}}^{2^k}$ are indeed bits. It follows from Eq. 2 that the step **Cut and Choose** aborts with probability C^{-c} if any element of either field is not a bit, as well as if the element in the two fields does not match. Moreover, in **Consistency Check**, in order for the check to pass in $\mathbb{F}_{2^k}$ for a given bucket, the secrets' higher-order bits must be the same for all shares so that the XOR is always zero when the pairwise XORs are opened. Thus the probability that this happens is the same as the probability above in Eq. 4 since again this can only happen when the adversary is not detected in **Cut and Choose**, that he cheats in some multiple of B daBits, and that these cheating bits are placed in the same buckets in **Consistency Check**.

3. We now show that all of the the $\mathbb{F}_p$ components are bits. To do this, we will show that if the $\mathbb{F}_p$ component of a daBit is not a bit, then the bucket check passes only if all other daBits in the bucket are also not bits in $\mathbb{F}_p$.

If the protocol has not aborted, then in every bucket B, for every $2 \leq j \leq B$, it holds that

$$b^1 + b^j - 2 \cdot b^1 \cdot b^j = c^j \tag{5}$$

where $c^j \in \{0, 1\}$ are determined by the XOR in $\mathbb{F}_{2^k}$. Note that since $c^j = \bigoplus_{i=1}^n b_i^1 \oplus \bigoplus_{i=1}^n b_i^j$ and at least one b_i^j is generated by an honest party, this value is uniform and unknown to the adversary when he chooses his inputs at the beginning.

Suppose $b^1 \in \mathbb{F}_p \setminus \{0, 1\}$. If $b^1 = 2^{-1} \in \mathbb{F}_p$ then by Eq. 5 we have $b^1 = c^j$; but c^j is a bit, so the "XOR" is not the same in both fields and the protocol will abort. Thus we may assume $b^1 \neq 2^{-1}$ and so we can rewrite the equation above as

$$b^j = \frac{b^1 - c^j}{2 \cdot b^1 - 1}. \tag{6}$$

Now if b^j is a bit then it satisfies $b^j(b^j - 1) = 0$, and so

$$0 = \left(\frac{b^1 - c^j}{2 \cdot b^1 - 1}\right) \cdot \left(\frac{b^1 - c^j}{2 \cdot b^1 - 1} - 1\right) = -\frac{(b^1 - c^j)(b^1 - (1 - c^j))}{(2 \cdot b^1 - 1)^2}$$

so $b^1 = c^j$ or $b^1 = 1 - c^j$; thus $b^1 \in \{0, 1\}$, which is a contradiction. Thus we have shown that if b^1 is not a bit then b^j is not a bit for every other b^j in this bucket. Moreover, for each $j = 2, \ldots, B$, there are two distinct values $b^j \in \mathbb{F}_p \setminus \{0, 1\}$ solving Eq. 6 corresponding to the two possible values of $c^j \in \{0, 1\}$, which means that if the bucket check passes then the adversary must *also* have guessed the bits $\{c^j\}_{j=1}^B$, which he can do with probability 2^{-B} since they are constructed using at least one honest party's input. Thus the chance of cheating without detection in this way is at most $2^{-Bt} \cdot C^{-Bt} \cdot \binom{B\ell}{Bt}^{-1}$.

Thus we have shown that the probability that $b^1 \in \mathbb{F}_p \setminus \{0, 1\}$ is given as output for the $\mathbb{F}_p$ component is at most the probability that the adversary corrupts a multiple of B daBits, that these daBits are placed in the same buckets, and that the adversary correctly guesses c bits from honest parties (in the construction of the bits $\{b^j\}_{j \in [B]}$) so that the appropriate equations hold in the corrupted buckets. Indeed, needing to guess the bits ahead of time only *reduces* the adversary's chance of winning from the same probability in the $\mathbb{F}_{2^k}$ case.

We conclude that the daBits are bits in both fields and are the same in both fields except with probability at most $2^{-\mathsf{sec}}$. $\qquad \square$

Theorem 1. *The protocol $\Pi_{\mathsf{daBits+MPC}}$ securely realises $\mathcal{F}_{\mathsf{Prep}}$ in the $(\mathcal{F}_{\mathsf{MPC}}, \mathcal{F}_{\mathsf{Rand}})$-hybrid model against an active adversary corrupting up to $n - 1$ out of n parties.*

The proof is deferred to the full version of the paper.

3.2 Garbling and Switching

In this section we give a high-level description of how our approach can be used to provide input to a garbled circuit from secret-shared data, and convert garbled-circuit outputs into sharings of secrets in $\mathbb{F}_p$.

As was discussed in the preliminaries, many recent garbling protocols use specialised secret-sharing MPC protocols. On this basis, it is straightforward to see that from $\mathcal{F}_{\mathsf{Prep}}$ the parties can both perform secret-sharing-based MPC over a large prime finite field and can garble circuits. A concrete example of this is given in the full version, which modifies the SPDZ-BMR protocol [LPSY15] to allow for our conversion.

From SS to GC. In brief, the parties input a secret-shared $[\![x]\!]_p$ by computing $[\![x-r]\!]_p$ and opening it to reveal $x-r$ where $r = \sum_{j=0}^{\lfloor \log p \rfloor -1} 2^j \cdot [\![r_j]\!]_p$ is constructed from daBits $\{[\![r_j]\!]_{p,2^k}\}_{j=0}^{\lfloor \log p \rfloor -1}$, and $\mathcal{F}_{\mathsf{MPC}}$ is called with input $(\mathsf{Check}, 0)$ either at this point or later on, and then these public values are taken to be input bits to the garbled circuit. To correct the offset r, the circuit $(x-r)+r \bmod p$ is computed inside the garbled circuit. This is possible since the bits of r can be hard-wired into the circuit using the $\mathbb{F}_{2^k}$ sharings of its bit-decomposition. For details, see the full version.

Note that typically for a party to provide input bit b on wire w in a garbled circuit, the parties reveal the secret-shared *wire mask* $[\![\lambda_w]\!]_{2^k}$ to this party, which broadcasts $\Lambda_w \leftarrow b \oplus \lambda_w$, called the associated *signal bit*; then the parties communicate further to reveal keys required for ciphertext decryptions, which is how the circuit is evaluated. This mask thus hides the actual input (and is removed inside the garbled circuit). Since the inputs here are the bits of the public value $x-r$, there is no need mask inputs here, and thus it suffices to set all the corresponding wire mask bits to be 0.

From GC to SS. In standard BMR-style garbling protocols, the outputs of the circuit are a set of public signal bits. These are equal to the actual Boolean outputs XORed with circuit output wire masks, which are initially secret-shared, concealing the actual outputs. Typically in multi-party circuit garbling, the wire masks for output wires are revealed immediately after the garbling stage so that all parties can learn the final outputs without communication after locally evaluating the garbled circuit. When garbling circuits using SS-based techniques, and aiming for computation in which parties can continue to operate on private outputs of a GC, a simple way of obtaining shared output is for the parties not to reveal the secret-shared wire masks for output wires after garbling and instead, after evaluating, to compute the XOR of the secret-shared mask with the public signal bit, in MPC.

In other words, for output wire w they obtain a sharing of the secret output bit b by computing

$$[\![b]\!]_{2^k} \leftarrow \Lambda_w \oplus [\![\lambda_w]\!]_{2^k}.$$

In our case, we want the shared output of the circuit to be in $\mathbb{F}_p$, and to do this it suffices for the masks on circuit output wires to be daBits (instead of random bits shared only in $\mathbb{F}_{2^k}$ as would be done normally) and for the parties to compute (locally)

$$[\![b]\!]_p \leftarrow \Lambda_w + [\![\lambda_w]\!]_p - 2 \cdot \Lambda_w \cdot [\![\lambda_w]\!]_p.$$

To avoid interfering with the description of the garbling subprotocol, we can define an additional layer to the circuit after the output layer which converts output wires with masks only in $\mathbb{F}_{2^k}$ to output wires with masks as daBits, without changing the real values on the wire. To do this, for every output wire w, let $[\![\lambda_w]\!]_{2^k}$ be the associated secret-shared wire mask. Then,

- In the garbling stage take a new daBit $[\![\lambda_{w'}]\!]_{p,2^k}$,
  1. Set $[\![\Lambda_{w_0}]\!]_{2^k} \leftarrow [\![\lambda_w]\!]_{2^k} \oplus [\![\lambda_{w'}]\!]_{2^k}$.
  2. Call $\mathcal{F}_{\mathsf{Prep}}$ with input $(\mathsf{Open}, 0, \mathsf{id}_{\Lambda_{w_0}}, 1)$ to obtain Λ_{w_0}.
- In the evaluation stage, upon obtaining Λ_w,
  1. Compute $\Lambda_{w'} \leftarrow \Lambda_w \oplus \Lambda_{w_0}$.
  2. Compute the final ($\mathbb{F}_p$-secret-shared) output as $[\![b]\!]_p \leftarrow \Lambda_{w'} + [\![\lambda_{w'}]\!]_p - 2 \cdot \Lambda_{w'} \cdot [\![\lambda_{w'}]\!]_p$.

For correctness, observe that $\Lambda_{w'} \oplus \lambda_{w'} = (\Lambda_w \oplus \Lambda_{w_0}) \oplus (\Lambda_{w_0} \oplus \lambda_w) = \Lambda_w \oplus \lambda_w = b$.

4 Implementation

We have implemented daBit generation and the conversion between arithmetic shares and garbled circuits. Our code is developed on top of the MP-SPDZ framework [Ana19] and experiments were run on computers with an identical configuration of i7-7700K CPU and 32 GB RAM connected via a 1 GB/s LAN connection with an average round-trip ping time of 0.3ms. The $\mathcal{F}_{\mathsf{MPC}}^p$ functionality is implemented using LowGear, one of the two variants of Overdrive [KPR18], a SPDZ-like protocol; the $\mathcal{F}_{\mathsf{MPC}}^{2^k}$ functionality is implemented using MASCOT [KOS16] to realise the protocol of [KY18], a variant of SPDZ-BMR multiparty circuit garbling [LPSY15]. In our experiments, $\mathbb{F}_{2^k}$ is always taken with $k = \kappa = 128$ since this is the security of PRF keys used in SPDZ-BMR. The daBits are always generated with $\kappa = 128$ and the same statistical security sec as the protocol for $\mathcal{F}_{\mathsf{MPC}}$.

Primes. We require that p be close to a power of 2 so that $x - r$ is indistinguishable from a uniform element of the field, as discussed in Sect. 2. Since we use LowGear in our implementation, for a technical reason we also require that p be congruent to 1 mod N where $N = 32768$. (This is the amount of packing in the ciphertexts.) Consequently, using LowGear means we always lose $15 = \log 32768$ bits of statistical security if $p > 65537$ since then the k-bit prime must be of the form $2^{k-1} + t \cdot 2^{15} + 1$ for some t where $1 \leq t \leq 2^{k-16} - 1$. We stress that the loss of 15 bits (out of $\log p$) statistical security can be mitigated by executing the conversion only after a check of $r < p$ inside the GC. In this way we guarantee that r is a truly random element modulo p. If we settle for bounded inputs $\log |x| < \log p - \mathsf{sec}$ then the check can be skipped as $x - r$ is close to uniform with distance $2^{-\mathsf{sec}}$ where $r = \sum_{i=0}^{\log |x| + \mathsf{sec}} r_i$.

Cut and choose optimisation. One key observation that enables reduction of the preprocessing overhead in $\mathbb{F}_{2^k}$ is that parties only need to input bits (instead of full $\mathbb{F}_{2^k}$ field elements) into $\mathcal{F}_{\mathsf{MPC}}$ during $\Pi_{\mathsf{daBits+MPC}}$. For a party to input a secret x in MASCOT, the parties create a random authenticated mask r and open it to the party, and the party then broadcasts $x+r$. Since the inputs are just bits, it suffices for the random masks also to be bits. Generating authenticated bits using MASCOT is extremely cheap and comes with a small communication overhead (see Table 1).

Complexity analysis. In LowGear (Overdrive) and MASCOT the authors avoided reporting any benchmarks for random bit masks in $\mathbb{F}_{2^k}$ or random input masks in $\mathbb{F}_p$ since they focused on the entire triple generation protocol. Fortunately their code is open source and easy to modify so we micro-benchmarked their protocols in order to get concrete costs for the procedure **Input** for $\mathcal{F}_{\mathsf{MPC}}^p$ and $\mathcal{F}_{\mathsf{MPC}}^{2^k}$. For example, in the two-party case, to provide a bit as input bit costs overall 0.384 kb with MASCOT in $\mathbb{F}_{2^k}$, whereas for LowGear, providing bits as input costs the same as any arbitrary field element in $\mathbb{F}_p$, requiring 2.048 kb. Hence, with the current state of protocols, inputs are cheap in a binary field whereas triples are cheap in a prime field.

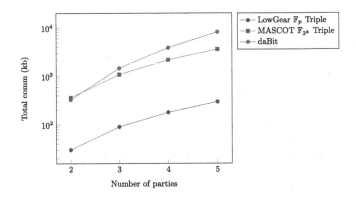

Fig. 6. Total communication costs for all parties per preprocessed element.

Bucketing parameters. Recall that our goal is to minimise the total amount of communication and time spent by parties generating each daBit. By examining the input and triple costs for LowGear and MASCOT the optimal communication for statistical security sec = 64 and $p \approx 2^{128}$ was found to occur when generating $l = 8192$ daBits per loop, a cut-and-choose parameter $C = 5$ and a bucket size $B = 4$. Then we ran the daBit generation along with LowGear and MASCOT for multiple parties on the same computers configuration to get the total communication cost in order to see how the costs scale with the number of parties. Results are given in Fig. 6. While MASCOT triples are not used during the daBit production, we believe that comparing the cost of a daBit to the best triple generation in $\mathbb{F}_{2^k}$ helps to give a rough idea of how expensive a single daBit is. One can check the detailed costs per daBit in Table 1 for various sec. For completeness, with a batch of 8192 elements and sec = 40 then the parameters $C = 2, B = 3$ suffices while for statistical security 80 we use $C = 5$ and $B = 5$.

4.1 Switch Between SPDZ ($\mathbb{F}_p$) to SPDZ-BMR ($\mathbb{F}_{2^k}$)

To reduce the amount of garbling when converting an additive share to a GC one, we assume the $\mathbb{F}_p$ input to the garbled circuit is bounded by $p/2^{\mathsf{sec}}$. In this way the garbled circuit needed to peel off the masked input $x - r$ is smaller: 379 AND gates for a 128 bit prime rather than ≈ 1000 AND gates. Hence, with bounded inputs and sec $= 64$ we need 127 daBits resulting in a total communication cost 2.5MBytes for their preprocessing and an online cost of the SPDZ-BMR garbling of 0.1ms. The preprocessing cost is halved to 1.2 MBytes when going the other way from SPDZ-BMR to SPDZ, as there are only 64 signal bits which need to be locally XORed with daBits.

Table 1. 1 GB/s LAN experiments for two-party daBit generation per party. For all cases, the daBit batch has length 8192.

sec	$\log p$	k	Comm. (kb)			Total (kb)	Time (ms)			Total(ms)
			$\mathcal{F}^p_{\mathsf{MPC}}$	$\mathcal{F}^{2^k}_{\mathsf{MPC}}$	daBitgen		$\mathcal{F}^p_{\mathsf{MPC}}$	$\mathcal{F}^{2^k}_{\mathsf{MPC}}$	daBitgen	
40	128	128	76.60	2.30	6.94	85.84	0.159	0.004	0.004	0.167
64	128	128	146.47	7.68	9.39	163.54	0.303	0.015	0.010	0.328
80	128	128	192.95	4.60	7.32	204.88	0.485	0.009	0.008	0.502

Comparison to semi-honest conversion. Keeping the same security parameters and computers configuration as [RWT+18, DSZ15], when benchmarked with sec $= 40$, the online phase to convert 1000 field elements of size 32 bits takes 193 ms. Our solution benefits from merging multiple conversions at once due to the SIMD nature of operations and that we can perform a single MAC-Check to compute the signal bits for the GC. Note that our conversion from an arithmetic SPDZ share to a SPDZ-BMR GC share takes about 14 times more than the semi-honest arithmetic to an Yao GC conversion in ABY or Chameleon [RWT+18, DSZ15].

4.2 Multiple Class Support Vector Machine

A support vector machine (SVM) is a machine learning algorithm that uses training data to compute a matrix A and a vector $\mathbf{b}$ such that for a so-called *feature vector* $\mathbf{x}$ of a new input, the index of the largest component of the vector $A \cdot \mathbf{x} + \mathbf{b}$ is defined to be its class. We decided to benchmark this circuit using actively-secure circuit marbling as it is clear that there is an operation best suited to arithmetic circuits (namely, $[\![A]\!] \cdot [\![\mathbf{x}]\!] + [\![b]\!]$) and another better for a Boolean circuit (namely, argmax, which computes the index of the vector's largest component).

We have benchmarked the online phase of a multi-class Linear SVM with 102 classes and 128 features over a simulated WAN network (using the Linux tc command) with a round-trip ping time of 100 ms and 50 Mb/s bandwidth with two parties. The SVM structure is the same used by Makri et al. [MRSV19] to classify the Caltech-101 dataset which contains 102 different categories of images such as aeroplanes, dolphins, helicopters and others [FFFP04]. In this dataset, $\mathbf{x} \in \mathbb{F}_p^{128}$, $A \in \mathbb{F}_p^{102 \times 128}$ and $\mathbf{b} \in \mathbb{F}_p^{102}$, and it requires 102 conversions from $\mathbb{F}_p$ to $\mathbb{F}_2^k$ – one for each SVM label. The particular SVM used by Makri et al. has bounded inputs x where $\log|x| \leq 25$, a field size $\log p = 128$ and statistical security sec $= 64$.

We have implemented a special instruction in MP-SPDZ which loads a secret integer modulo p (a SPDZ share) into the SPDZ-BMR machine. To merge all modulo p instructions of SPDZ shares into SPDZ-BMR to form an universal Virtual Machine requires some extra engineering effort: this is why we chose to micro-benchmark in Table 2 the different stages of the online phase: doing $[\![\mathbf{y}]\!]_p \leftarrow [\![A]\!]_p \cdot [\![\mathbf{x}]\!]_p + [\![\mathbf{b}]\!]_p$ with SPDZ, then the instruction converting $[\![\mathbf{y}]\!]_p = ([\![y_1]\!]_p, \ldots, [\![y_{102}]\!]_p)$ to $(\{[\![(y_1)_j]\!]_{2^k}\}_{j=0}^{\log p - 1}, \ldots, \{[\![(y_{102})_j]\!]_{2^k}\}_{j=0}^{\log p - 1})$, ending with the evaluation stage of SPDZ-BMR on

$$\mathsf{argmax}(((\![(y_1)_j]\!]_{2^k})_{j=0}^{\log p - 1}, \ldots, ([\![(y_{102})_j]\!]_{2^k})_{j=0}^{\log p - 1})).$$

We name this construction Marbled-SPDZ.

Online cost. The online phase (Table 2) using Marbled-SPDZ is more than 10 times faster than SPDZ-BMR and about 10 times faster than SPDZ.

Preprocessing cost. The preprocessing effort for the garbling (in AND gates) is reduced by a factor of almost 400 times using our construction. We chose to express the preprocessing costs of Table 2 in terms of AND gates, random triples and bits mainly for the reason that SPDZ-BMR requires much more work for an AND gate than WRK. Based on the concrete preprocessing costs we have in Table 2 we give estimations on the communication where the preprocessing of the garbling is done via WRK: performing an SVM evaluation using i) WRK alone would require 6.6 GB sent per party (3.8 kb per AND gate), ii) SPDZ alone (with LowGear) would require 54MB per party (15 kb per triple/random bit), iii) Marbled-SPDZ would take 160MB per party.

Nevertheless, the main cost in Marbled SPDZ is the daBit generation (119 MB) which is more than 70% of the preprocessing effort. If one chooses sec $= 40$ then we need five triples per daBit and 65 daBits per conversion which amounts to only 119 MB for the entire SVM evaluation (twice the cost of plain SPDZ).

Table 2. Two-party linear SVM: single-threaded (non-amortised) online phase costs and preprocessing costs with sec $= 64$.

Protocol		Online cost			Preprocessing cost		
		Comm. rounds	Time (ms)	Total (ms)	$\mathbb{F}_p$ triples	$\mathbb{F}_p$ bits	AND gates
SPDZ		54	2661	2661	19015	9797	–
SPDZ-BMR		0	2786	2786	–	–	14088217
Marbled- SPDZ	SPDZ	1	133	271.73	13056	0	–
	Conversion	2	137		63546	0	27030
	SPDZ-BMR	0	1.73		–	–	8383

References

[Ana19] N1 Analytics. MP-SPDZ 2019. https://github.com/n1analytics/MP-SPDZ

[BDK+18] Büscher, N., Demmler, D., Katzenbeisser, S., Kretzmer, D., Schneider, T.: HyCC: Compilation of hybrid protocols for practical secure computation. In: Lie, D., Mannan, M., Backes, M., Wang, X. (eds.) ACM CCS 2018, pp. 847–861. ACM Press, October 2018

[BDOZ11] Bendlin, R., Damgård, I., Orlandi, C., Zakarias, S.: Semi-homomorphic encryption and multiparty computation. In: Paterson, K.G. (ed.) EUROCRYPT 2011. LNCS, vol. 6632, pp. 169–188. Springer, Heidelberg (2011). https://doi.org/10.1007/978-3-642-20465-4_11

[Bea92] Beaver, D.: Efficient multiparty protocols using circuit randomization. In: Feigenbaum, J. (ed.) CRYPTO 1991. LNCS, vol. 576, pp. 420–432. Springer, Heidelberg (1992). https://doi.org/10.1007/3-540-46766-1_34

[Ben18] Ben-Efraim, A.: On multiparty garbling of arithmetic circuits. In: Peyrin, T., Galbraith, S. (eds.) ASIACRYPT 2018. LNCS, vol. 11274, pp. 3–33. Springer, Cham (2018). https://doi.org/10.1007/978-3-030-03332-3_1

[BMR90] Beaver, D., Micali, S., Rogaway, P.: The round complexity of secure protocols (extended abstract). In: 22nd ACM STOC, pp. 503–513. ACM Press, May 1990

[BMR16] Ball, M., Malkin, T., Rosulek, M.: Garbling gadgets for boolean and arithmetic circuits. In: Weippl, E.R., Katzenbeisser, S., Kruegel, C., Myers, A.C., Halevi, S. (eds.) ACM CCS 2016, pp. 565–577. ACM Press, October 2016

[Can01] Canetti, R.: Universally composable security: a new paradigm for cryptographic protocols. In: 42nd FOCS, pp. 136–145. IEEE Computer Society Press, October 2001

[CDE+18] Cramer, R., Damgård, I., Escudero, D., Scholl, P., Xing, C.: SPD$\mathbb{Z}_{2^k}$: efficient MPC mod 2^k for dishonest majority. In: Shacham, H., Boldyreva, A. (eds.) CRYPTO 2018. LNCS, vol. 10992, pp. 769–798. Springer, Cham (2018). https://doi.org/10.1007/978-3-319-96881-0_26

[DKL+13] Damgård, I., Keller, M., Larraia, E., Pastro, V., Scholl, P., Smart, N.P.: Practical covertly secure MPC for dishonest majority – or: breaking the SPDZ limits. In: Crampton, J., Jajodia, S., Mayes, K. (eds.) ESORICS 2013. LNCS, vol. 8134, pp. 1–18. Springer, Heidelberg (2013). https://doi.org/10.1007/978-3-642-40203-6_1

[DPSZ12] Damgård, I., Pastro, V., Smart, N., Zakarias, S.: Multiparty computation from somewhat homomorphic encryption. In: Safavi-Naini, R., Canetti, R. (eds.) CRYPTO 2012. LNCS, vol. 7417, pp. 643–662. Springer, Heidelberg (2012). https://doi.org/10.1007/978-3-642-32009-5_38

[DSZ15] Demmler, D., Schneider, T., Zohner, M.: ABY - A framework for efficient mixed-protocol secure two-party computation. In: NDSS 2015. The Internet Society, February 2015

[DZ13] Damgård, I., Zakarias, S.: Constant-overhead secure computation of boolean circuits using preprocessing. In: Sahai, A. (ed.) TCC 2013. LNCS, vol. 7785, pp. 621–641. Springer, Heidelberg (2013). https://doi.org/10.1007/978-3-642-36594-2_35

[FFFP04] Fei-Fei, L., Fergus, R., Perona, P.: Learning generative visual models from few training examples: an incremental Bayesian approach tested on 101 object categories. In: CVPR, p. 178. IEEE (2004)

[FKOS15] Frederiksen, T.K., Keller, M., Orsini, E., Scholl, P.: A unified approach to MPC with preprocessing using OT. In: Iwata, T., Cheon, J.H. (eds.) ASIACRYPT 2015. LNCS, vol. 9452, pp. 711–735. Springer, Heidelberg (2015). https://doi.org/10.1007/978-3-662-48797-6_29

[HKS+10] Henecka, W., Kögl, S., Sadeghi, A.-R., Schneider, T., Wehrenberg, I.: TASTY: tool for automating secure two-party computations. In: Al-Shaer, E., Keromytis, A.D., Shmatikov, V. (eds.), ACM CCS 2010, pp. 451–462. ACM Press, October 2010

[HOSS18] Hazay, C., Orsini, E., Scholl, P., Soria-Vazquez, E.: TinyKeys: a new approach to efficient multi-party computation. In: Shacham, H., Boldyreva, A. (eds.) CRYPTO 2018. LNCS, vol. 10993, pp. 3–33. Springer, Cham (2018). https://doi.org/10.1007/978-3-319-96878-0_1

[HSS17]   Hazay, C., Scholl, P., Soria-Vazquez, E.: Low cost constant round MPC combining BMR and oblivious transfer. In: Takagi, T., Peyrin, T. (eds.) ASIACRYPT 2017. LNCS, vol. 10624, pp. 598–628. Springer, Cham (2017). https://doi.org/10.1007/978-3-319-70694-8_21

[KOS16]   Keller, M., Orsini, E., Scholl, P.: MASCOT: faster malicious arithmetic secure computation with oblivious transfer. In: Proceedings of the 2016 ACM SIGSAC Conference on Computer and Communications Security, pp. 830–842. ACM, 2016

[KPR18]   Keller, M., Pastro, V., Rotaru, D.: Overdrive: making SPDZ great again. In: Nielsen, J.B., Rijmen, V. (eds.) EUROCRYPT 2018. LNCS, vol. 10822, pp. 158–189. Springer, Cham (2018). https://doi.org/10.1007/978-3-319-78372-7_6

[KSS10]   Kolesnikov, V., Sadeghi, A.-R., Schneider, T.: From dust to dawn: practically efficient two-party secure function evaluation protocols and their modular design. IACR Cryptology ePrint Arch. 2010, 79 (2010)

[KSS13]   Kolesnikov, V., Sadeghi, A.-R., Schneider, T.: A systematic approach to practically efficient general two-party secure function evaluation protocols and their modular design. J. Comput. Secur. 21(2), 283–315 (2013)

[KSS14]   Kerschbaum, F., Schneider, T., Schröpfer, A.: Automatic protocol selection in secure two-party computations. In: Boureanu, I., Owesarski, P., Vaudenay, S. (eds.) ACNS 2014. LNCS, vol. 8479, pp. 566–584. Springer, Cham (2014). https://doi.org/10.1007/978-3-319-07536-5_33

[KY18]   Keller, M., Yanai, A.: Efficient maliciously secure multiparty computation for RAM. In: Nielsen, J.B., Rijmen, V. (eds.) EUROCRYPT 2018. LNCS, vol. 10822, pp. 91–124. Springer, Cham (2018). https://doi.org/10.1007/978-3-319-78372-7_4

[LPSY15] Lindell, Y., Pinkas, B., Smart, N.P., Yanai, A.: Efficient constant round multi-party computation combining BMR and SPDZ. In: Gennaro, R., Robshaw, M. (eds.) CRYPTO 2015. LNCS, vol. 9216, pp. 319–338. Springer, Heidelberg (2015). https://doi.org/10.1007/978-3-662-48000-7_16

[MR18]   Mohassel, P., Rindal, P.: Aby 3: a mixed protocol framework for machine learning. In: Proceedings of the 2018 ACM SIGSAC Conference on Computer and Communications Security, pp. 35–52. ACM 2018

[MRSV19] Makri, E., Rotaru, D., Smart, N.P., Vercauteren, F.: EPIC: efficient private image classification (or: learning from the masters). In: Matsui, M. (ed.) CT-RSA 2019. LNCS, vol. 11405, pp. 473–492. Springer, Cham (2019). https://doi.org/10.1007/978-3-030-12612-4_24

[NNOB12] Nielsen, J.B., Nordholt, P.S., Orlandi, C., Burra, S.S.: A new approach to practical active-secure two-party computation. In: Safavi-Naini, R., Canetti, R. (eds.) CRYPTO 2012. LNCS, vol. 7417, pp. 681–700. Springer, Heidelberg (2012). https://doi.org/10.1007/978-3-642-32009-5_40

[RWT+18] Riazi, M.S., Weinert, C., Tkachenko, O., Songhori, E.M., Schneider, T., Koushanfar, F.: Chameleon: a hybrid secure computation framework for machine learning applications. In: Kim, J., Ahn, G.-J., Kim, S., Kim, Y., López, J., Kim, T. (eds.), ASIACCS 18, pp. 707–721. ACM Press, April 2018

[SW19] Smart, N.P., Wood, T.: Error detection in monotone span programs with application to communication-efficient multi-party computation. In: Matsui, M. (ed.) CT-RSA 2019. LNCS, vol. 11405, pp. 210–229. Springer, Cham (2019). https://doi.org/10.1007/978-3-030-12612-4_11

[WRK17] Wang, X., Ranellucci, S., Katz, J.: Global-scale secure multiparty computation. In: Thuraisingham, B.M., Evans, D., Malkin, T., Xu, D. (eds) ACM CCS 2017, pp. 39–56. ACM Press, October/November 2017

A Blind Coupon Mechanism Enabling Veto Voting over Unreliable Networks

Colin Boyd, Kristian Gjøsteen$^{(\boxtimes)}$, Clémentine Gritti, and Thomas Haines

NTNU, Trondheim, Norway
{colin.boyd,kristian.gjosteen,clementine.gritti,thomas.haines}@ntnu.no

Abstract. A Blind Coupon Mechanism (BCM) allows spreading of alerts quietly and quickly over unreliable networks. The BCM primitive ensures that alerts are efficiently broadcast while the nature of these signals are securely hidden. However, current BCM proposals are limited to indicating a single bit of information and also lack natural privacy properties. In this paper, we develop a new BCM solution that allows the transmission of several alerts privately and in one shot. This extension perfectly suits a new kind of applications, that is (absolute) veto voting over unreliable networks, in which multiple decisions are reached using only simple peer-to-peer communications. Our enhanced BCM efficiently supports the spread of votes over unreliable networks while hiding whether these votes contain any or several vetoes. We prove our BCM solution secure and illustrate its use for veto voting protocols in limited communication infrastructures.

Keywords: Blind Coupon Mechanism · Veto voting system · Untraceability

1 Introduction

A *Blind Coupon Mechanism* (BCM) [2,3,5] is a cryptographic primitive allowing confidential signals to be combined in a specific way. A BCM enables a network to distribute a covert signal while ensuring that forging signals is difficult. Signals are embedded in coupons, which are generated by authorities in possession of some secret material. Dummy coupons (without a signal) and signal coupons are exchanged over the network, and combined such that anything joined with a signal coupon becomes a signal coupon.

Such a primitive can prevent an attacker from gaining knowledge about alert transmissions. Suppose an attacker manages to access a network and monitor a sensor-based intrusion detection system. The attacker knows that she is safe until the sensors transmit an alert. Therefore, the system requires a confidential and efficient alert transmission to prevent the attacker from withdrawing and removing her tracks in a timely manner.

The BCM notion was first introduced by Aspnes et al. [2,3] and recently improved by Blazy and Chevalier [5]. A BCM includes a *verification algorithm*

© Springer Nature Switzerland AG 2019
F. Hao et al. (Eds.): INDOCRYPT 2019, LNCS 11898, pp. 250–270, 2019.
https://doi.org/10.1007/978-3-030-35423-7_13

that checks whether a coupon is valid, and a *combining algorithm* that takes as inputs two valid coupons and outputs a coupon. The output coupon is signal (with high probability) if and only if at least one of the inputs is signal. A BCM should satisfy two security properties: *indistinguishability* (an attacker cannot distinguish between dummy and signal coupons) and *unforgeability* (an attacker cannot create a signal coupon unless it has another signal coupon as input).

1.1 Generalized BCMs

Previously proposed BCMs use coupons which can only transmit one bit of information, for example whether an alert has occurred or not. When we consider using BCMs in different applications we may want to have coupons which can signal multiple events. Even in the original application of quietly spreading alerts, it may be useful to be able to indicate additional information on which kind of alert is relevant. We therefore propose a generalized definition of BCMs allowing multiple signals. A trivial way to instantiate our generalized BCM is to use multiple instances of a standard BCM, but we would like also to remain as efficient as possible. Therefore we proposed a construction for a generalized BCM which adds minimally to the overhead for the currently most efficiently known BCM construction.

We are also interested in stronger security for BCMs. Previous BCM analysis [2,3,5] considers only indistinguishability and unforgeability as relevant security properties, ignoring the privacy of the agents contributing coupons. Malicious spotters may attempt to track and follow coupons and thus gain information on individual choices. The original BCM construction [2,3] even suffers from the creation of traceable coupons if key generation is dishonest. Hence, there is a clear lack of privacy notion in [2,3,5], and we therefore add the notion of untraceability to the useful security properties of BCMs.

As a useful new application for our generalized BCM, we propose a novel voting protocol. One way to look at a BCM is that signal coupons override dummy coupons – once a signal coupon has been added, the dummy coupons are irrelevant. In a sense this means that the signal coupons *veto* the effect of dummy coupons. This observation suggests that a BCM is a natural foundation for (absolute) veto voting [4,14,17]. In general, voting systems are designed for elections launched in reliable communication infrastructures to support interaction with central servers. Nevertheless, in some situations, only limited connectivity is available and continuous and local tallying is needed. These restrictive communication infrastructures require to broadcast vetoes quietly and quickly, while the nature of these votes must be securely hidden, allowing us to exploit the untraceability property of our generalized BCM. We depict below a plausible scenario that requires a voting system that fully operates under such conditions.

One could assume that communication channels between system users are secure. Nevertheless, we must defend the system against dishonest participants, who may not forward the received coupons or being curious about others' choices. Hence such an assumption will not help. One could also attempt to encrypt veto coupons and return them to the authorities via peer-to-peer channels, but that would require solving problems related to traceability and privacy similar to those needed in designing a BCM.

1.2   A BCM-Friendly Voting Scenario

A political demonstration is calling for a change of government. The organizers wish demonstrators to express their choices on elements of their new plan. Elements could be whether a demonstration should be scheduled on the coming Saturday. Several parameters may disrupt the voting process and influence the underlying system. For instance, the government may respond to the demonstration by either turning off the mobile phone network or jamming the usable radio frequencies, making radio communication impossible. Although QR-codes with cameras enable a low-bandwidth peer-to-peer communication, the latency is too large to allow reasonable ad-hoc networks. Therefore, the system requires other tools to overcome such communication constraints.

Furthermore, the government must not be able to infiltrate the demonstration network, and to forge a veto canceling any further demonstration. In addition, the organizers running the veto elections may move continuously, and therefore, should sample current veto states from any physical location in the demonstration at any time. Not all demonstrators trust the organizers, and information on who vetoed what may have bad consequences (e.g. being registered in police files as a potential governmental opponent). Hence, privacy and untraceability properties must be guaranteed.

The above scenario motivates the design of a veto voting system in unreliable network infrastructures. During a setup phase, the organizers, seen as *election authorities*, distribute ballots to demonstrators, seen as *voters*. These ballots are pre-marked as either blank or carrying veto(es). During a voting phase, the demonstrators interact using limited peer-to-peer communications, and make their choices, for instance regarding demonstration cessation. They are assured to remain anonymous, hence avoiding political friction among them. Once the voting phase is over, the organizers sample votes by interacting with the demonstrators, and recover the veto results.

Such a veto voting system will enable demonstrators to veto even under the following attacks or constraints from the government. The system will continue to operate successfully, even if the government disturbs the network. Attackers may also attempt to infiltrate the network; however, as an outsider, it will not be able to disrupt the voting process.

1.3   Proposed Solution

Our BCM solution is based on that of Blazy-Chevalier [5] which offers attractive features of strong indistinguishability, unforgeability and applicability to real contexts. We enhance this BCM to allow the transmission of multiple signals in one coupon, only adding one extra group element per signal. We also define a new security property, namely *untraceability*, and prove that our solution satisfies it.

This property precludes an attacker to track, follow and distinguish transmitted coupons.

In addition, we show that veto elections arise as a natural application of BCM. We design a peer-to-peer veto voting system based on our improved BCM, enabling the spread of coupons containing (possibly multiple) veto(es).

- During the setup phase, dummy coupons, representing a *blank* vote, and signal coupons, representing a *veto* vote, are distributed to voters by the authorities via secure communication channels (this is the only phase where such feature must be guaranteed).
- The voters first spread their dummy coupons. Communication channels no longer need to be secure. This is to create a continuous flow of coupons during the entire voting phase, and prevent attackers to distinguish blank and veto votes from a possible discontinuity in spreading them. Whenever a voter decides to veto on some action(s), she uses the appropriate signal coupon and spreads it around her.
- Voters continuously exchange their coupons with their neighbors, ensuring the aforementioned continuous flow. Upon receiving a neighbor's coupon, a voter combines it with her current coupon, and gets an updated coupon, that is then spread around her. One fundamental property of our veto election is that an output coupon is signal (veto) if at least one input is signal. Moreover, one veto is enough to stop an action, and thus vote counting is not required.
- The election authorities intercept coupons at random time from random voters and decode them to obtain veto results. Once a veto is received, this is enough to unilaterally stop the associated action.

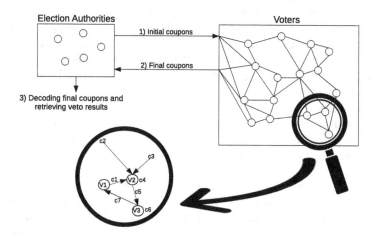

Fig. 1. Veto voting system based on BCM.

Figure 1 illustrates our veto voting system based on BCM. Several election authorities jointly create and distribute initial coupons to the voters. Voters form a network where peer-to-peer communications are possible but limited. Voters spread their coupons around them such that the resulting flow is continuous. From the magnifying glass, we observe that the voter $V2$ has collected coupons $c1$, $c2$ and $c3$ from other voters. She wishes to use her coupon $c4$ for voting. She then emits coupon $c5$ to her neighbors, that is a combination of $c1$, $c2$, $c3$ and $c4$. The voter $V3$ has received coupon $c5$ and combines it with his own coupon $c6$, and spreads the resulting coupon $c7$ around him. Once the voting phase is over, the election authorities intercept final coupons from the voters and jointly decode them to obtain the veto results.

1.4   Related Work

Blind Coupon Mechanism. Aspnes et al. [2,3] introduce BCM as an AND-homomorphic authenticated bit commitment scheme. The authors construct their scheme based on an abstract group structure (U, G, D) such that U is a finite set, $G \subseteq U$ is a cyclic group and D is a proper subgroup of G. The elements in D are dummy coupons and the elements in $G \setminus D$ are signal coupons. The scheme is proved secure with relation to indistinguishability and unforgeability based on the subgroup membership and subgroup escape problems respectively. The subgroup escape problem [2,3] is defined as follows: Given a generator for D (but not G), find an element of $G \setminus D$. The problem seems hard on certain groups with bilinear pairings and on elliptic curves over the ring $\mathbb{Z}_n$.

Recently, Blazy and Chevalier [5] propose a more efficient and more secure scheme compared to that of Aspnes et al. [2,3] by setting their scheme in a group of prime order instead of composite order and by relying on standard assumptions. They design a simple BCM scheme that is OR-homomorphic and combine this scheme with a new version of the linearly homomorphic Structure-Preserving Signature (SPS) scheme [18] to obtain their full, AND-homomorphic BCM scheme. Blazy-Chevalier scheme is proved indistinguishable under the Decisional Diffie-Hellman assumption and is statistically unforgeable.

Nevertheless, implementing a veto protocol over constrained networks using Blazy-Chevalier BCM technique generates computational and communication burdens and impedes its operation. Since we aim to develop veto voting in restrictive peer-to-peer communication infrastructures, we need to extend the aforementioned solution to permit secure and efficient multiple veto broadcast and guarantee practical performance.

Veto Voting. In a reformulation of the famous *Dining Cryptographers* (DC) problem introduced by Chaum [9], Hao and Zieliński [14] consider the following problem. Three cryptographers wish to know among NSA and them, who has not paid for the dinner, such that all the participants are enabled to pay anonymously. If one participant votes with a veto, then one of the cryptographers has paid for the dinner; otherwise, NSA has paid. A protocol for the statement that no cryptographer has paid is thus similar to anonymous veto protocols [7,13,17]. Hao and Zieliński [14] present a protocol, named *Anonymous Veto Network* (AV-net), to solve the reformulated problem. Compared to the DC network solution

[9], AV-net does not require secret channels, does not encounter message collisions and is more resistant to disruptions.

The Kiayias-Yung protocol [17] for veto elections considers a tally without any veto votes as a 0-vote. A voter who wants to veto actually votes on a non-zero random element from $\mathbb{Z}_p$, for a prime p, and if no voter has vetoed, then the tally is 0. One security issue is that any voter can check whether she is the only one who vetoed using her random element [13]. Groth [13] improves the Kiayias-Yung protocol while publishing a smaller amount of data. However, the number of rounds depends on the number of voters, while it is constant in the original Kiayias-Yung protocol [17]. Brandt [7] bases his veto protocol on a technique used for secure multi-party computation applications. While it allows to define a boolean-OR function, solving the function remains complex and expensive.

Hao and Zieliński's AV-net [14] outperforms existing anonymous veto protocols [7,13,17] regarding the number of rounds, computational load and bandwidth usage. Nevertheless, the solution [14] still requires two rounds on voters' side: a first round to send a seed with its proof (preparation phase), and a second round to actually vote (voting and self-tallying phase). To reduce to one round, the preparation phase should be executed only once [11]: voters agree on some parameters before several elections, and use these parameters for all the elections they are participating in.

AV-net [14] also suffers from two issues related to fairness and robustness. First, a voter who has submitted a veto can find out whether there are any other voters who vetoed. Second, the last voter submitting a vote is able to pre-compute the boolean-OR result before submission, allowing the last voter to change the vote according to that pre-computation. Khader et al. [16] propose a variant Hao-Zieliński protocol [14] to provide aforementioned missing properties (by adding a commitment round and a recovery round respectively). Their variant also assumes authenticated public channels to prevent multiple voting and to guarantee voters eligibility. Later, Bag et al. [4] extend further to avoid the fairness and robustness limitations of the previous work, but now maintaining the advantage of a two-round protocol. Indeed, Bag et al.'s solution [4] achieves similar system complexities to AV-net [14], while binding voters to their votes in the very first round, canceling the possibility of runtime changes to any of the inputs. In addition, at the end of the voting phase, voters are not able to learn more than the output of the boolean-OR function and their own votes.

We see that earlier veto voting systems need fairly reliable networks or a sequential round structure in order to work. Neither is available in our scenarios, where connectivity is unreliable and we need continuous and local tallying.

1.5 Contributions

Our paper contains contributions to the design of both a secure BCM scheme and a veto voting system. More precisely, we provide a new BCM construction (Sect. 3) that allows for transmitting multiple signals in one coupon, rather than in separate coupons. We prove it secure according to indistinguishability and unforgeability properties. We also define the notion of untraceability, as an enhancement of the privacy in BCM, and prove that our solution satisfies it. Then, we show that veto voting arises as a straight application of BCM (Sect. 4). We present a peer-to-peer veto voting protocol over unreliable networks based on our solution.

2 Building Blocks

2.1 Preliminaries

In this section, we introduce the mathematical tools and assumptions that our BCM construction and security proofs use.

Bilinear Group and Pairing. Our extended BCM relies on pairing-based cryptography. Let $\mathbb{G}_1$, $\mathbb{G}_2$ and $\mathbb{G}_T$ be three cyclic groups of prime order p. A pairing e is a map $e : \mathbb{G}_1 \times \mathbb{G}_2 \to \mathbb{G}_T$ which satisfies the following properties:

- Bilinearity: Given $g_1 \in \mathbb{G}_1$, $g_2 \in \mathbb{G}_2$ and $a, b \in \mathbb{Z}_p$, $e(g_1^a, g_2^b) = e(g_1, g_2)^{ab}$;
- Non-degeneracy: There exist $g_1 \in \mathbb{G}_1$ and $g_2 \in \mathbb{G}_2$ such that $e(g_1, g_2) \neq 1_{\mathbb{G}_T}$;
- Computability: There exists an efficient algorithm to compute $e(g_1, g_2)$ for all $g_1 \in \mathbb{G}_1$ and $g_2 \in \mathbb{G}_2$.

n-Decisional Diffie-Hellman Exponent (n-DDHE) Assumption. Our scheme is proven untraceable assuming that the n-DDHE problem is hard. Let $\mathbb{G}_1$ be a cyclic group of prime order p and g_1 be a generator of that group. The DDHE assumption [6,15] compares the real and random distributions:

$$\mathsf{DHE}_n = \{\{g_1^{\nu^i}\}_{1 \leq i \leq n}, g_1^{\nu^{n+1}}; \nu \in_R \mathbb{Z}_p\} \quad \mathsf{DHE}_n^\$ = \{\{g_1^{\nu^i}\}_{1 \leq i \leq n}, g_1^{\mu}; \nu, \mu \in_R \mathbb{Z}_p\}$$

A (T, ε)-distinguisher for $\mathbb{G}_1$ is a probabilistic Turing Machine Δ running in time T that, given an element X of either DHE_n or $\mathsf{DHE}_n^\$$, outputs 0 or 1 such that:

$$Adv_{\mathbb{G}_1}^{ddhe_n}(\Delta) = |\Pr[\Delta(X) = 1, X \in \mathsf{DHE}_n] - \Pr[\Delta(X) = 1, X \in \mathsf{DHE}_n^\$]| \geq \varepsilon$$

The DDHE problem is (T, ε)-intractable if no (T, ε)-distinguisher for $\mathbb{G}_1$ exists.

n-Multi-Decisional Diffie-Hellman (n-MDDH) Assumption. Our scheme is proven indistinguishable assuming that the n-MDDH problem is hard. Let $\mathbb{G}_1$ be a cyclic group of prime order p and g_1 be a generator of that group. The MDDH assumption [8] compares the real and random distributions:

$$\mathsf{MDH}_n = \{g_1^{x_0}, \{g_1^{x_j}\}_{1 \leq j \leq n}, \{g_1^{x_0 x_j}\}_{1 \leq j \leq n}; x_0, x_j \in_R \mathbb{Z}_p, 1 \leq j \leq n\}$$
$$\mathsf{MDH}_n^\$ = \{g_1^{x_0}, \{g_1^{x_j}\}_{1 \leq j \leq n}, \{g_1^{r_{0,j}}\}_{1 \leq j \leq n}; x_0, x_j, r_{0,j} \in_R \mathbb{Z}_p, 1 \leq j \leq n\}$$

A (T, ε)-distinguisher for $\mathbb{G}_1$ is a probabilistic Turing Machine Δ running in time T that, given an element X of either MDH_n or $\mathsf{MDH}_n^\$$, outputs 0 or 1 such that:

$$Adv_{\mathbb{G}_1}^{mddh_n}(\Delta) = |\Pr[\Delta(X) = 1, X \in \mathsf{MDH}_n] - \Pr[\Delta(X) = 1, X \in \mathsf{MDH}_n^\$]| \geq \varepsilon$$

The MDDH problem is (T, ε)-intractable if no (T, ε)-distinguisher for $\mathbb{G}_1$ exists.

Double Pairing (DP) Assumption. Our scheme is proven unforgeable assuming that the DP problem is hard. Let $\mathbb{G}_1$, $\mathbb{G}_2$ and $\mathbb{G}_T$ be three cyclic groups of prime order p. Let g_1 be a generator of $\mathbb{G}_1$ and g_2 be a generator of $\mathbb{G}_2$. The DP assumption [1] is defined as follows. A (T, ε)-adversary for $\mathbb{G}_1$ and $\mathbb{G}_2$ is a probabilistic Turing Machine Δ running in time T that given a random pair $X = (g_2, \hat{g}_2)$ in $\mathbb{G}_2^2$, outputs a non-trivial pair $(g_1, \hat{g}_1)$ in $\mathbb{G}_1^2$ satisfying Y : $e(g_1, g_2) \cdot e(\hat{g}_1, \hat{g}_2) = 1_{\mathbb{G}_T}$ such that:

$$Adv_{\mathbb{G}_1, \mathbb{G}_2}^{dp}(\Delta) = |\Pr[X = (g_2, \hat{g}_2) \in \mathbb{G}_2^2; (g_1, \hat{g}_1) \leftarrow \Delta(X) : (g_1, \hat{g}_1) \in \mathbb{G}_1^2 \wedge Y| \geq \varepsilon$$

The DP problem is (T, ε)-intractable if no (T, ε)-adversary for $\mathbb{G}_1$ and $\mathbb{G}_2$ exists.

2.2 Linearly Homomorphic Structure-Preserving Signature

A linearly homomorphic SPS scheme [18] enables verifiable computation mechanisms on encrypted data, by combining homomorphic signature properties with the additional one that signatures and messages only contain group elements with unknown discrete logarithms. Blazy and Chevalier [5] present a linearly homomorphic SPS scheme in an asymmetric setting with groups of prime order, as an extension of the scheme in the symmetric setting given in [18].

Following the idea of Blazy and Chevalier [5], a one-time linearly homomorphic SPS scheme is combined with an OR-homomorphic BCM in the asymmetric setting to guarantee unforgeable signal coupons (the one-time property implies that the tag linked to the to-be-signed message is empty). We extend this combination to the multivariate setting by signing vectors of $n + 1$ elements rather than signing vectors of two elements.

For clarity, we recall the signature scheme introduced in [18]. The one-time linearly homomorphic SPS scheme is composed of the following algorithms:

KeyGen$(1^k) \rightarrow (pk, sik)$. On input of a security parameter 1^k, the algorithm outputs a verification (public) key pk and a signing (secret) key sik.
  Let $(p, \mathbb{G}_1, \mathbb{G}_2, \mathbb{G}_T, g_1, g_2, e)$ be a tuple defined from the bilinear group setting. Pick at random $\alpha \in_R \mathbb{Z}_p$ and compute $\hat{g}_2 = g_2^\alpha$. For $j \in [0, n]$, pick at random $\xi_j, \rho_j \in_R \mathbb{Z}_p$ and compute $hp_j = g_2^{\xi_j} \hat{g}_2^{\rho_j}$. The verification key is $pk = (g_1, g_2, \hat{g}_2, \{hp_j\}_{j \in [0,n]})$ and the signing key is $sik = (\{\xi_j, \rho_j\}_{j \in [0,n]})$.

Sign$(sik, \boldsymbol{m}) \rightarrow \sigma$. On input of a signing key sik and a message vector $\boldsymbol{m} = (m_0, m_1, \cdots, m_n) \in \mathbb{G}_1^{n+1}$, the algorithm outputs a signature σ. Compute $z = \prod_{j=0}^n m_j^{-\xi_j}$ and $u = \prod_{j=0}^n m_j^{-\rho_j}$ and set the signature $\sigma = (z, u)$.

SignDerive$(pk, \{\lambda_i, \sigma_i\}_{i \in [1,l]}) \rightarrow \sigma$. On input of a verification key pk and l pairs of coefficients (arbitrary) and signatures $\{\lambda_i, \sigma_i\}_{i \in [1,l]}$, the algorithm outputs a new signature σ. If all the input signatures are valid, compute $z = \prod_{i=1}^l z_i^{\lambda_i}$ and $u = \prod_{i=1}^l u_i^{\lambda_i}$ and set the new signature $\sigma = (z, u)$.

Verify$(pk, \boldsymbol{m}, \sigma) \rightarrow \{\texttt{valid}, \texttt{invalid}\}$. On input of a verification key pk, a message vector $\boldsymbol{m} = (m_0, m_1, \cdots, m_n) \in \mathbb{G}_1^{n+1}$ and a signature $\sigma = (z, u)$, the algorithm outputs valid or invalid. The signature is valid if and only if $e(z, g_2) \cdot e(u, \hat{g}_2) \cdot \prod_{j=0}^n e(m_j, hp_j) = 1_{\mathbb{G}_T}$ holds.

Correctness. For all key pair $(pk, sik) \leftarrow \mathsf{KeyGen}(1^k)$, for all message vector $\boldsymbol{m}$, if $\sigma \leftarrow \mathsf{Sign}(sik, \boldsymbol{m})$, then $\mathsf{Verify}(pk, \boldsymbol{m}, \sigma) = \mathsf{valid}$.

Let $\{\lambda_i, \boldsymbol{m}_i\}_{i \in [1,l]}$ correspond to $\prod_{i=1}^{l} \boldsymbol{m}_i^{\lambda_i} = (\prod_{i=1}^{l} m_{i,0}^{\lambda_i}, \prod_{i=1}^{l} m_{i,1}^{\lambda_i}, \cdots, \prod_{i=1}^{l} m_{i,n}^{\lambda_i})$. For all key pair $(pk, sik) \leftarrow \mathsf{KeyGen}(1^k)$, for all signatures σ_i on message vectors $\boldsymbol{m}_i$, if $\mathsf{valid} \leftarrow \mathsf{Verify}(pk, \boldsymbol{m}_i, \sigma_i)$ for $i \in [1,l]$, then $\mathsf{valid} \leftarrow \mathsf{Verify}(pk, \{\lambda_i, \boldsymbol{m}_i\}_{i \in [1,l]}, \mathsf{SignDerive}(pk, \{\lambda_i, \sigma_i\}_{i \in [1,l]}))$.

3   New Blind Coupon Mechanism

Our BCM solution extends Blazy-Chevalier scheme [5] into a multivariate setting as follows: in addition to the two elements $g_1, h_1 \in \mathbb{G}_1$, $n-1$ elements $h_2, \cdots, h_n$ are also generated, where n is an integer. This implies that a signal coupon is a tuple of $n+1$ random elements from the group $\mathbb{G}_1$, while a dummy coupon is a tuple $(g_1^r, h_1^r, h_2^r, \cdots, h_n^r)$ of $n+1$ elements where $r \in_R \mathbb{Z}_p^*$ is a random exponent.

3.1   Construction

The extended BCM construction contains the following algorithms:

$\mathsf{BCMGen}(1^k) \to (pk, sk)$. On input a security parameter 1^k, the algorithm outputs the public key pk and the secret key sk.

Let $(p, \mathbb{G}_1, \mathbb{G}_2, \mathbb{G}_T, g_1, g_2, e)$ be a tuple defined from the bilinear group setting. Run the algorithm $\mathsf{KeyGen}(1^k) \to (pk, sik)$ where $pk = (g_1, g_2, \hat{g}_2, \{hp_j\}_{j \in [0,n]})$ and $sik = (\{\xi_j, \rho_j\}_{j \in [0,n]})$. For $j \in [1,n]$, pick at random $\beta_j \in_R \mathbb{Z}_p$ and compute $h_j = g_1^{\beta_j}$. The public key is pk and the secret key is $sk = (sik, \{\beta_j\}_{j \in [1,n]}, \{h_j\}_{j \in [1,n]})$.

$\mathsf{BCMCouponGen}(pk, sk, \boldsymbol{v}) \to c$. On inputs the public key pk, the secret key sk, a vector $\boldsymbol{v} = (v_1, \cdots, v_n) \in \{0,1\}^n$, the algorithm outputs a coupon c.

The integer n corresponds to the number of signal options. For $j \in [1,n]$, each element v_j of the vector $\boldsymbol{v}$ states the nature of the corresponding option opt_j. In particular, a bit $v_j = 0$ states that the option opt_j is set as dummy while a bit $v_j = 1$ states that it is set as signal. Hence, a dummy coupon is defined as $\boldsymbol{v} = (0, 0, \cdots, 0)$ (all 0s) and a coupon with signal on one single option is set as $\boldsymbol{v} = (0, \cdots, 0, 1, 0, \cdots, 0)$ (one 1 and the remaining 0s). We recall that the secret key sk includes the signing key $sik = (\{\xi_j, \rho_j\}_{j \in [0,n]})$. To generate a valid coupon for a dummy or single signal coupon, pick at random $\delta, \delta' \in_R \mathbb{Z}_p$, and then compute $c_{1,0} = g_1^{\delta}$ and for $j \in [1,n]$, $c_{1,j} = h_j^{\delta + v_j \delta'} = g_1^{\beta_j(\delta + v_j \delta')}$. Set $c_1 = \{c_{1,j}\}_{j \in [0,n]}$.

Run the algorithm $\mathsf{Sign}(sik, c_1) \to c_2 = (z, u)$ where:

$$z = \prod_{j=0}^{n} c_{1,j}^{-\xi_j} = g_1^{-\xi_0 \cdot \delta - \sum_{j=1}^{n} \xi_j \beta_j (\delta + v_j \delta')} \qquad u = \prod_{j=0}^{n} c_{1,j}^{-\rho_j} = g_1^{-\rho_0 \cdot \delta - \sum_{j=1}^{n} \rho_j \beta_j (\delta + v_j \delta')}$$

Let the valid coupon be $c = (c_1, c_2)$ where $c_1 = \{c_{1,j}\}_{j \in [0,n]}$ and $c_2 = (z, u)$. We call the pair $c_2 = (z, u)$ the *signature* of the coupon.

BCMVerify(pk, c) → {valid, invalid}. On inputs the public key pk and a coupon c, the algorithm outputs valid if the coupon c is valid; invalid otherwise.

Let a coupon be $c = (c_1, c_2)$ where $c_1 = \{c_{1,j}\}_{j \in [0,n]}$ and $c_2 = (z, u)$. Run $result \leftarrow$ Verify(pk, c_1, c_2) and output $result$ (which is valid or invalid).

BCMCombine($pk, \{c_i\}_{i \in [1,l]}$) → c. On inputs the public key pk, a set $\{c_i\}_{i \in [1,l]}$ of l valid coupons, the algorithm outputs a new valid coupon c combining c_i for $i \in [1, l]$.

Let $c_i = (\{c_{i,1,j}\}_{j \in [0,n]}, (z_i, u_i))$ be a coupon for $i \in [1, l]$. Run the algorithm SignDerive($pk, \{\lambda_i, (z_i, u_i)\}_{i \in [1,l]}$) → c_2 for random exponents λ_i. That algorithm first checks that all the input coupons are valid. If the answer is positive, then it computes $z = \prod_{i=1}^{l} z_i^{\lambda_i}$ and $u = \prod_{i=1}^{l} u_i^{\lambda_i}$ and sets $c_2 = (z, u)$. Moreover, compute $c_{1,j} = \prod_{i=1}^{l} c_{i,1,j}^{\lambda_i}$ for $j \in [0, n]$, and set $c_1 = \{c_{1,j}\}_{j \in [0,n]}$. Finally, set the new, combined coupon $c = (c_1, c_2)$.

BCMDecode(pk, sk, c) → v. On inputs the public key pk, the secret key sk and a valid coupon c, the algorithm outputs a vector $v = (v_1, \cdots, v_n)$. The vector v reveals the nature of the coupon such that each element v_j of the vector v tells whether the corresponding option opt_j is either dummy or signal.

Given a coupon $c = (c_1, c_2)$ where $c_1 = \{c_{1,j}\}_{j \in [0,n]}$, if $c_{1,j} = c_{1,0}^{\beta_j}$ then set $v_j = 0$ for each $j \in [1, n]$; otherwise set $v_j = 1$. Output $v = (v_1, v_2, \ldots, v_n)$.

Correctness on Coupon Decoding. Correctness on coupon decoding focuses on correctness of signature verification. The remaining is easily proved correct. For all key pair $(pk, sk) \leftarrow$ BCMGen(1^k), for all vector v, if $c \leftarrow$ BCMCouponGen(pk, sk, v), then valid $\leftarrow$ BCMVerify(pk, c) and $v \leftarrow$ BCMDecode (pk, sk, c). Let $c = (c_1, c_2) = (\{c_{1,j}\}_{j \in [0,n]}, (z, u))$ be a valid coupon, then we have:

$$e(z, g_2)e(u, \hat{g}_2) \prod_{j=0}^{n} e(c_{1,j}, hp_j) = e(\prod_{j=0}^{n} c_{1,j}^{-\xi_j}, g_2)e(\prod_{j=0}^{n} c_{1,j}^{-\rho_j}, \hat{g}_2) \prod_{j=0}^{n} e(c_{1,j}, g_2^{\xi_j} \hat{g}_2^{\rho_j}) = 1_{\mathbb{G}_T}.$$

Correctness on Combined Coupon Decoding. For all key pair $(pk, sk) \leftarrow$ BCMGen(1^k), for all coupons c_i for $i \in [1, l]$, if valid $\leftarrow$ BCMVerify(pk, c_i), then

$$\text{BCMDecode}(pk, sk, \text{BCMCombine}(pk, \{c_i\}_{i \in [1,l]})) = \bigvee_{i \in [1,l]} \text{BCMDecode}(pk, sk, c_i).$$

Let $c = (c_1, c_2) = (\{c_{1,j}\}_{j \in [0,n]}, (z, u)) = (\{\prod_{i=1}^{l} c_{i,1,j}^{\lambda_i}\}_{j \in [0,n]}, (\prod_{i=1}^{l} z_i^{\lambda_i}, \prod_{i=1}^{l} u_i^{\lambda_i}))$ be a coupon obtained by combining l valid coupons $c_i = (\{c_{i,1,j}\}_{j \in [0,n]}, (z_i, u_i))$, then we have:

$$e(z, g_2) \cdot e(u, \hat{g}_2) \cdot \prod_{j=0}^{n} e(c_{1,j}, hp_j)$$
$$= e(\prod_{j=0}^{n} \prod_{i=1}^{l} c_{i,1,j}^{-\xi_j \cdot \lambda_i}, g_2) \cdot e(\prod_{j=0}^{n} \prod_{i=1}^{l} c_{i,1,j}^{-\rho_j \cdot \lambda_i}, \hat{g}_2) \cdot \prod_{j=0}^{n} e(\prod_{i=1}^{l} c_{i,1,j}^{\lambda_i}, g_2^{\xi_j} \hat{g}_2^{\rho_j}) = 1_{\mathbb{G}_T}$$

3.2 Security

We prove that our extended BCM construction satisfies indistinguishability, unforgeability and untraceability properties. The indistinguishability model in [2,3,5] reflects that, given a valid coupon and oracle access to dummy and signal coupons, the adversary cannot tell whether it is dummy or signal. Our model extends it by considering coupons with signals on different options, in addition to dummy ones.

Experiment $\mathsf{Exp}_{\mathcal{A}}^{\mathrm{Indist}}$

$(pk, sk) \leftarrow \mathsf{BCMGen}(1^k)$
$(\boldsymbol{v_0}, \boldsymbol{v_1}) \leftarrow \mathcal{A}^{\mathcal{O}_{gen}(pk,sk)}(pk)$
$b \leftarrow \{0, 1\}$
$c_b \leftarrow \mathsf{BCMCouponGen}(pk, sk, \boldsymbol{v_b})$
$b' \leftarrow \mathcal{A}^{\mathcal{O}_{gen}(pk,sk)}(pk, c_b)$

Experiment $\mathsf{Exp}_{\mathcal{A}}^{\mathrm{Unforg}}$

$(pk, sk) \leftarrow \mathsf{BCMGen}(1^k)$
$c^* \leftarrow \mathcal{A}^{\mathcal{O}_{gen}(pk,sk)}(pk)$

Note that $\mathcal{A}$ is only allowed to access $\mathcal{O}_{gen}$ once for each single signal vector.

Experiment $\mathsf{Exp}_{\mathcal{A}}^{\mathrm{Untrac}}$

$(pk, sk, l \in \mathbb{N}) \leftarrow \mathsf{BCMGen}(1^k)$
$(\{c_{0,i}\}_{i \in [1,l]}, \{c_{1,i}\}_{i \in [1,l]}) \leftarrow \mathcal{A}^{\mathcal{O}_{gen}(pk,sk)}(pk, l)$ s.t.
    $\mathsf{BCMDecode}(pk, sk, \mathsf{BCMCombine}(pk, \{c_{j,i}\}_{i \in [1,l]}))$ is the same for $j \in \{0,1\}$
$b \leftarrow \{0, 1\}$
$c_b \leftarrow \mathsf{BCMCombine}(pk, \{c_{b,i}\}_{i \in [1,l]})$
$b' \leftarrow \mathcal{A}(pk, c_b)$

Fig. 2. Algorithms defining security experiments $\mathsf{Exp}_{\mathcal{A}}^{\mathrm{Indist}}$ for indistinguishability, $\mathsf{Exp}_{\mathcal{A}}^{\mathrm{Unforg}}$ for unforgeability and $\mathsf{Exp}_{\mathcal{A}}^{\mathrm{Untrac}}$ for untraceability.

As in [18], the unforgeability model prevents an adversary from generating a valid signal coupon which could not be a combination of coupons already seen.

Untraceability is a new BCM security property that encompasses the specific issues encountered in voting applications over unreliable networks, where an attacker should be precluded from tracking and following voters based on the information that coupons store. Given two sets of valid coupons embedding identical signals and oracle access to any coupons, the adversary should not able to tell which set was used to generate the combined coupon.

Indistinguishability Model. In this model, the adversary is provided with a coupon generation oracle, giving it access to as many dummy and signal coupons it wants. Then, given a valid coupon, the adversary cannot tell whether its nature with a non-negligible advantage. The experiment $\mathsf{Exp}_{\mathcal{A}}^{\mathrm{Indist}}$ from Fig. 2 defines the security experiment for indistinguishability.

The adversary wins if $b = b'$ in the experiment. Our scheme is $(T, \varepsilon, q_1 + q_2)$-indistinguishable if there is no T-time adversary $\mathcal{A}$ that succeeds with advantage $|\Pr[b = b'] - 1/2| < \varepsilon$ after making up to $q_1 + q_2$ queries to the coupon generation oracle $\mathcal{O}_{gen}$.

Indistinguishability Proof Sketch. Indistinguishability follows directly from the n-MDDH assumption. We sketch a challenger $\mathcal{B}$ against n-MDDH using an adversary $\mathcal{A}$ against indistinguishability with advantage ε. $\mathcal{B}$ takes as input $g_1^{x_0}$ and two tuples of group elements $\{g_1^{x_j}\}_{1\leq j\leq n}$ and $\{g_1^{t_{0,j}}\}_{1\leq j\leq n}$, where $x_0, x_j \in_R \mathbb{Z}_p$ and $t_{0,j}$ is either equal to $x_0 x_j$ or to a random exponent. When $\mathcal{A}$ submits queries to the coupon generation oracle $\mathcal{O}_{gen}$, $\mathcal{B}$ uses the coupon generation algorithm with its first group element tuple as the secret key. When $\mathcal{A}$ submits two challenged signals, $\mathcal{B}$ uses $g_1^{x_0}$ and its second group element tuple to create the coupon using one of the two challenged signals. If the adversary $\mathcal{A}$ guesses the signal correctly, $\mathcal{B}$ outputs 1; otherwise, it outputs 0.

If the input to $\mathcal{B}$ comes from MDH_n (meaning that $t_{0,j} = x_0 x_j$), the above simulation will be a perfect one of the security game, and the probability that $\mathcal{B}$ outputs 1 equals the probability that the adversary $\mathcal{A}$ guesses correctly in the security experiment. However, if the input to $\mathcal{B}$ comes from $\mathsf{MDH}_n^{\$}$ (meaning that $t_{0,j}$ is a random exponent), the challenged coupon will be independent of the adversary's challenged signals, and the probability that $\mathcal{A}$ guesses correctly is $1/2$. It then follows that $Adv_{\mathbb{G}_1}^{mddh_n}(\mathcal{B}) = \varepsilon$.

Unforgeability Model. In this model, the adversary is given oracle access to dummy coupons and single signal coupons such that the latter are each requested only once. The adversary is not able to create a valid signal coupon that is not a combination of queried coupons with a non-negligible probability. The experiment $\mathsf{Exp}_{\mathcal{A}}^{\mathrm{Unforg}}$ from Fig. 2 defines the security model for unforgeability.

The adversary outputs a valid forged coupon c^* if and only if $\mathsf{BCMDecode}(pk, sk, c^*) = \boldsymbol{v}^* \neq \perp$ and $\boldsymbol{v}^* \notin \{\bigvee_{i\in S} \boldsymbol{v}_i; S \subseteq [1,n]\}$ (i.e. linear span). Our scheme is (T, ε, q)-existentially unforgeable if there is no T-time adversary $\mathcal{A}$ that succeeds with at least probability ε after making up to n queries to the oracle $\mathcal{O}_{gen}$.

Unforgeability Proof Sketch. Before going through the proof for unforgeability, one should notice that signatures (z, u) are part of coupons, hence an adversary asking for signatures is essentially asking for coupons.

Let $\mathcal{A}$ be an adversary that forges a signature with non-negligible advantage. Let $\mathcal{B}$ be the challenger that takes as input a DP instance $(g_2, \hat{g}_2) \in \mathbb{G}_2^2$ and expects $\mathcal{A}$ to find a non-trivial pair $(z, u) \in \mathbb{G}_1^2$ such that $e(z, g_2) \cdot e(u, \hat{g}_2) = 1_{\mathbb{G}_T}$. To do so, $\mathcal{B}$ runs the algorithm KeyGen (when running BCMGen) with random exponents $\xi_j, \rho_j \in_R \mathbb{Z}_p$ for $j \in [0,n]$. When $\mathcal{A}$ requests a signature on $(g_1^{\delta}, \{h_j^{\delta}\}_{j\in[1,n]})$, $\mathcal{B}$ replies by running the algorithm Sign (when running $\mathsf{BCMCouponGen}$). Finally, the adversary $\mathcal{A}$ outputs $(g_1^{\delta^*}, \{h_j^{\delta^*}\}_{j\in[1,n]})$ with signature elements $c_2^* = (z^*, u^*)$. The challenger $\mathcal{B}$ computes a signature on $\mathcal{A}$'s input as $c_2^{\dagger} = (z^{\dagger}, u^{\dagger}) = (g_1^{\delta^{\dagger} \cdot (-\xi_0)} \cdot \prod_{j=1}^n h_j^{\delta^{\dagger} \cdot (-\xi_j)}, g_1^{\delta^{\dagger} \cdot (-\rho_0)} \cdot \prod_{j=1}^n h_j^{\delta^{\dagger} \cdot (-\rho_j)})$. With overwhelming probability, the ratios $\frac{z^*}{z^{\dagger}}$ and $\frac{u^*}{u^{\dagger}}$ are a non-trivial solution to the DP problem. Indeed, any public key pk has exponentially many corresponding secret keys, and thus pk perfectly hides the exponents $\{\xi_j\}_{j\in[0,n]}$ and $\{\rho_j\}_{j\in[0,n]}$. In addition, for a given public key pk, elements $g_1^{\delta^*}$ and $\{h_j^{\delta^*}\}_{j\in[1,n]}$

have an exponential number of valid signatures while Sign algorithm's output is completely determined by the exponents $\{\xi_j\}_{j\in[0,n]}$ and $\{\rho_j\}_{j\in[0,n]}$.

Over the game between $\mathcal{B}$ and $\mathcal{A}$, the latter obtains signatures $\{c_{i,2} = (z_i, u_i)\}_{i\in[1,n]}$ on at most n linearly independent vectors. Hence, given $\{hp_j\}_{j\in[0,n]}$, $\mathcal{A}$ sees at most $2n+1$ linear equations in $2n+2$ unknown values. In $\mathcal{A}$'s view, since $(g_1^{\delta^*}, \{h_j^{\delta^*}\}_{j\in[1,n]})$ must be independent of previously signed vectors, predicting $z^\dagger$ is done only with probability $1/p$. Therefore, with overwhelming probability $1 - \frac{1}{p}$, $z^* \neq z^\dagger$, and thus $\frac{z^*}{z^\dagger}$ and $\frac{u^*}{u^\dagger}$ is a valid solution to the DP problem.

Untraceability Model. In this model, the adversary is provided with a coupon generation oracle, giving it access to as many dummy and signal coupons it wants, such that two distinct sets of these coupons decode to the same vector. Then, given a valid combined coupon, the adversary cannot tell from which set it results from with a non-negligible advantage. The experiment $\mathsf{Exp}_{\mathcal{A}}^{\mathrm{Untrac}}$ from Fig. 2 defines the security model for untraceability.

The adversary wins if $b = b'$. Our scheme is (T, ε, q)-untraceable if there is no T-time adversary $\mathcal{A}$ that succeeds with advantage $|\Pr[b = b'] - 1/2| < \varepsilon$ after making up to q queries to the coupon generation oracle $\mathcal{O}_{gen}$.

Untraceability Proof. Before going through the proof for untraceability, one should notice that Left-or-Right and Real-or-Random notions are equivalent. Since the former is more natural as a security notion, we use it as our security definition. Since the later is easier to work with, we use it as our proof.

Let an adversary $\mathcal{A}$ against untraceability with advantage ε. Using $\mathcal{A}$, we build a challenger $\mathcal{B}$ that solves the n-DDHE problem in $\mathbb{G}_1$. For a generator $g_1 \in \mathbb{G}_1$ and an exponent $\nu \in \mathbb{Z}_p^*$, let $y_j = g_1^{\nu^j} \in \mathbb{G}_1$ for $j \in [1,n]$. The challenger $\mathcal{B}$ is given as input a tuple $(X, T) = ((g_1, y_1, \cdots, y_n), T)$ where T is either equal to $y_{n+1} = g_1^{\nu^{n+1}}$ or to a random element in $\mathbb{G}_1^*$ (such that T is uniform and independent in $\mathbb{G}_1^*$). The challenger's goal is to output 0 when $T = y_{n+1}$ and 1 otherwise. $\mathcal{B}$ interacts with $\mathcal{A}$ as follows.

Let g_2 be a generator of $\mathbb{G}_2$, $\alpha \in_R \mathbb{Z}_p$ and $\hat{g}_2 = g_2^\alpha$. Let $\xi_j, \rho_j \in_R \mathbb{Z}_p$, and $hp_j = g_2^{\xi_j} \hat{g}_2^{\rho_j}$ for $j \in [0,n]$. The challenger sets $h_j = y_j$ for $j \in [1,n]$, meaning that the exponents β_j are implicitly equal to ν^j (and hence, the elements β_j remain unknown to $\mathcal{B}$). The public key $pk = (g_1, g_2, \hat{g}_2, \{hp_j\}_{j\in[0,n]})$ is provided to $\mathcal{A}$. The secret key $sk = (\{\xi_j, \rho_j\}_{j\in[0,n]}, \{h_j\}_{j\in[1,n]})$ is kept by $\mathcal{B}$. The adversary makes queries on vector $\boldsymbol{v}$ to the challenger. The latter replies by generating coupons as follows. First, $\mathcal{B}$ chooses at random exponents $\delta_0, \delta_1, \cdots, \delta_n \in_R \mathbb{Z}_p$. Two or more exponents are equal when there is no signal, while unique exponents represent signals. Then, it computes $c_{1,0} = g_1^{\delta_0}$, $c_{1,j} = y_j^{\delta_j}$ for $j \in [1,n]$, $z = g_1^{-\xi_0 \cdot \delta_0} \cdot \prod_{j=1}^n y_j^{-\xi_j \cdot \delta_j}$ and $u = g_1^{-\rho_0 \cdot \delta_0} \cdot \prod_{j=1}^n y_j^{-\rho_j \cdot \delta_j}$. Such coupons are computable from elements in the tuple given to the challenger.

After the query phase, $\mathcal{A}$ submits two challenged coupon sets $\{c_{0,i}\}_{i\in[1,l]}$ and $\{c_{1,i}\}_{i\in[1,l]}$ such that both sets contain the same signals (if any); and both sets contain the same number of coupons (note that we can pad one set with dummy coupons if needed). $\mathcal{B}$ picks at random a bit $b \in_R \{0,1\}$. For $i \in [1,l]$, we denote a coupon $c_{b,i}$ as $(c_{1,i}^{(b)}, c_{2,i}^{(b)}) = (\{c_{1,j,i}^{(b)}\}_{j \in [0,n]}, (z_i^{(b)}, u_i^{(b)}))$. The challenger computes the coupon c_b that combines $c_{b,i}$ for $i \in [1,l]$ as follows: $c_{1,0}^{(b)} = \prod_{i=1}^{l} y_1^{\delta_{0,i}^{(b)}} = \prod_{i=1}^{l}(g_1)^{\delta_{0,i}^{(b)}} = \prod_{i=1}^{l}(c_{1,0,i}^{(b)})^{\nu}$, $c_{1,j}^{(b)} = \prod_{i=1}^{l} y_{j+1}^{\delta_{j,i}^{(b)}} = \prod_{i=1}^{l}(y_j^{\nu})^{\delta_{j,i}^{(b)}} = \prod_{i=1}^{l}(c_{1,j,i}^{(b)})^{\nu}$ for $j \in [1, n-1]$ and $c_{1,n}^{(b)} = \prod_{i=1}^{l} T^{\delta_{n,i}^{(b)}}$. If $T = y_{n+1}$ then $c_{1,n}^{(b)} = \prod_{i=1}^{l} T^{\delta_{n,i}^{(b)}} = \prod_{i=1}^{l}(y_n^{\nu})^{\delta_{n,i}^{(b)}} = \prod_{i=1}^{l}(c_{1,n,i}^{(b)})^{\nu}$, meaning that the coupon c_b is valid. Indeed, the exponents $\lambda_i \in \mathbb{Z}_p$ are all implicitly set to be equal to ν, and correctness on combined coupon decoding follows. Otherwise, the coupon c_b is independent of b in $\mathcal{A}$'s view.

Finally, $\mathcal{A}$ outputs a bit $b' \in \{0,1\}$. The challenger concludes its own game by outputting a guess as follows. If $b = b'$, then $\mathcal{B}$ outputs 0, meaning that $T = y_{n+1} = g_1^{\nu^{n+1}}$; otherwise, it outputs 1, meaning that T is random in $\mathbb{G}_1$. When $T = y_{n+1} = g_1^{\nu^{n+1}}$, then $\mathcal{A}$'s view is identical to its view in a real attack game, hence $|\Pr[b = b'] - 1/2| \geq \varepsilon$. When T is random in $\mathbb{G}_1$, then $\Pr[b = b'] = 1/2$. Therefore, for g_1 and T uniform in $\mathbb{G}_1$, for ν uniform in $\mathbb{Z}_p$, $|\Pr[\mathcal{B}(X, y_{n+1}) = 0] - \Pr[\mathcal{B}(X, T) = 0]| \geq |(1/2 \pm \varepsilon) - 1/2| = \varepsilon$.

3.3   Efficiency Analysis

Table 1 shows the efficiency results of our extended BCM scheme. The size of components (public key, secret key, coupon) is linear in the number of options, i.e. $O(n)$. The process of checking the validity of a coupon requires $O(n)$ pairing operations, since every element of a coupon is carefully included in the verification. By doing so, any (malicious) modification on a coupon will be notified with a verification failure. The process of decoding a coupon involves $O(n)$ exponentiation operations, since the first $n + 1$ elements of a coupon (excluding the signature part) are required to interpret the veto outcome, which must likely be correct.

Table 1. Size of public/secret keys and coupons, and verification and decoding costs for coupons with n options.

Public key pk (# elements)	Secret key sk (# elements)	Coupon c (# elements)	Verification time (# pairings)	Decoding time (# exponentiations)
$n + 4$	$4n + 2$	$n + 3$	$n + 3$	n

The beneficial feature enabling secure voting over unreliable networks inevitably has an effect on the efficiency of our solution. Yet, while our voting protocol is not optimally efficient, it is practical and can be run in most, if not all, circumstances that require veto elections.

A cost that is linear in the number of vote options is normal in voting systems – for instance, when using homomorphic voting and with a 1-out-of-n scheme involving n encryptions. Our scheme is in some sense a 1-out-of-$\binom{n'}{n}$ scheme for $n' \in [0, n]$ when voters choose to veto on n' options. This means that the ciphertext needs to be of size $O(n)$, and thus the cost of encryption must be at least $O(n)$. Even with such cost, the scheme is practical since it can easily be implemented using terminals, such as reasonably modern smartphones. Clearly, there are more efficient schemes, but they do not have the properties we want.

A parallelization of the protocol may at first seem a promising trade-off between efficiency and security for some scenarios. Indeed, transmitting signals in a parallel way allows voters to only spread coupons containing one signal and no dummies, and thus being of size not depending on the value n. However, in a parallel version of BCM, a coupon with a signal on one option should contain information about which option is considered, increasing the size of the coupon. In addition, a parallel fashion may lose vetoes: coupons with one specific option may be dropped more often, and thus a signal on that option would less likely be noticed. The frequency of spreading coupons containing signals on that particular option may also be higher, and thus noticeable, potentially leaking information to unauthorized entities. In other words, the parallel version does not achieve the desired security goals. On the other hand, transmitting whole coupons with $O(n)$ elements allows to increase the chances to intercept the signals embedded in these coupons, while avoiding leaking information from the frequency of signals on given options.

4   Application: Veto Voting Protocol

The BCM is a primitive originally designed to spread alerts quietly and quickly on wireless networks [2, 3, 5]. We propose a new application from such primitive where our multivariate extension makes it beneficial: peer-to-peer veto voting over unreliable networks. In this section, we describe a protocol where m election authorities are responsible to prepare the veto election and release the veto results, and manifold voters make their choices on n decisions and interact each other during the voting session.

4.1   Description

Setup Phase. The setup phase is managed by m election authorities. First, the election authorities run the algorithm BCMGen in a distributed way to generate the public and secret parameters. To proceed, we assume that election authorities use existing tools such as secret sharing and multi-party computation [10, 12, 19, 20] (this process is out of scope of our paper). Public parameters are made available to all participants, while secret parameters are shared among the m election authorities. Second, the election authorities run the algorithm BCMCouponGen in a distributed way to generate n single veto coupons (corresponding to n single signal coupons) and one blank coupon (corresponding to a dummy coupon) for each voter over secure communication channels.

Every voter (assigned with an index i) hence receives $n + 1$ coupons $c_{i,0}, c_{i,1}, \cdots, c_{i,n}$. There are n options that voters can veto on, where each option refers to the cessation of a demonstration for instance. The coupon $c_{i,0}$ corresponds to a blank vote (no veto) and a coupon $c_{i,j}$, for $j \in [1, n]$, corresponds to a veto on option opt_j. Each voter can combine her coupons to obtain multiple veto option coupons. For instance, by combining the coupon $c_{i,1}$, that corresponds to a veto on option opt_1, and the coupon $c_{i,2}$, that corresponds to a veto on option opt_2, the resulting coupon c is for vetoes on both options opt_1 and opt_2. Once all voters get the public key material and their coupons, the setup phase is over. From this point onwards, secure communication channels between the authorities and voters is not assumed.

Voting Phase. A voter V_A starts the voting phase by generating and spreading blank coupons to her neighbors. We suppose such action from the voter since we want to create a continuous spread of dummy and signal coupons over the voting phase, such that attackers only see the uninterrupted flow while not distinguishing the nature of these coupons.

Thereafter, the voter V_A may decide to veto on either a single option or multiple options. To do so, she distributes a coupon $c1$ that either belongs to $\{c_{i,j}\}_{j \in [1,n]}$ (for vetoing on a single option) or is a combination of single veto coupons from $\{c_{i,j}\}_{j \in [1,n]}$ (for vetoing on multiple options). Combination of coupons is enabled by running the algorithm BCMCombine. Let V_B be one of V_A's neighbors that has received $c1$. At the moment of reception, V_B holds a coupon $c2$ (representing either a blank vote, a single veto vote or a multiple veto vote). First, V_B checks the validity of the coupon $c1$ by running the algorithm BCMVerify. If the output is valid, then he runs the algorithm BCMCombine to combine $c1$ and $c2$ resulting into $c3$, and spreads the latter to his neighbors.

The process of generating and spreading coupons is performed by all voters in the voting network. Each election authority is enabled to communicate with voters individually, allowing the former to intercept emitted coupons and verify with other authorities whether vetoes have been triggered, and on which option(s). The voting phase is over after a certain time that has been agreed among the m election authorities.

Note that a dishonest voter cannot forge a coupon, meaning that no coupon can be created that was not received from the authorities. Therefore a dishonest voter V_A can only deviate from the correct protocol by either spreading coupons with vetoes on additional options, or by not combining received coupons and only transmitting dummy coupons. In the former case, then V_A just expresses her opinion, that is, she is against the chosen propositions. In the second case, then V_A acts as she agrees on all propositions, and other (honest) voters combine her dummy coupons with their own ones, hence possibly inserting some vetoes. We assume that not all the voters act like that since this is in their interest to spread vetoes if they want to raise their voices (anonymously) against their government for example. Therefore, some legitimate coupons are spread anyway and likely intercepted by the authorities.

Sampling Phase. The m election authorities jointly decode the coupons intercepted so far by distributively running the algorithm BCMDecode and obtain the veto results. More precisely, elements in a decoded vector tell whether vetoes have been launched, and on which option(s). Election authorities can repeat the sampling process on multiple coupons in order to enhance the veto results. Depending on the number of collected coupons and the time allocated for voting, the election authorities can attest with overwhelming probability the results of the veto election. Election authorities do not count the number of vetoes since absolute veto is considered, meaning that one veto is enough to stop an action.

We observe that no strong assumption on the reliability of communication channels between the authorities and voters is required. Communication channels are supposed to be functional enough to allow at least one authority to receive one coupon, at the expense of a lower probability on the accuracy of the election result.

A malicious voter may have never combined her neighbors' coupons and only forwarded coupons embedding her own non-veto and veto choices only. Hence, if all voters have acted in such way, then care needs to be taken by the election authorities when sampling. Combination of intercepted coupons can be done by the latter, preventing biased results from dishonest voters. We can also assume that at least one voter is honest and that coupons from this voter has been received and decoded by the election authorities.

4.2 Security

We discuss in this section the security requirements [11] that our veto voting system should meet. Security requirements of the voting protocol reduce to the security of the extended BCM, that has been carefully proven secure in Sect. 3.2. Due to lack of space, we opt for a succinct security description of the resulting veto protocol.

Privacy. For each election, votes should be as secret as possible. An exception exists when a final result only contains non-veto votes, thus no vote can be private. We do not consider such case when discussing about privacy. Privacy comes from indistinguishability: since an attacker cannot distinguish coupons, no information about (non-)veto is leaked. Privacy also derives from untraceability: an attacker cannot find out the path taken by a coupon, assuring that the voting choices made by voters cannot be successfully guessed.

Anonymity and Fairness. Anonymity implies that no one can discover which voter vetoed which option(s). Indeed, an attacker must not be able to reveal the identity of a voter from an intercepted coupon. This requirement is guaranteed by untraceability: an attacker cannot find the path followed by a coupon, and thus cannot locate the voter who emitted the coupon. One can argue that anonymity can lead to potential misuse of the veto power and some kind of accountability on the voter who casts a veto can be desirable. However, in our scenario, we believe anonymity is more important than accountability.

A fairness guarantee should ensure that a given voting method is sensitive to all of the voters' opinions in the right way. Fairness implies that no early results from voting can be obtained. Indeed, none of the voters can learn information on the election outcome before the election authorities officially reveal it. From receiving coupons from neighbors, voters are not able to know whether vetoes are embedded, since any two coupons are indistinguishable and secret key material is required to decode them. This also applies for any external spotters intercepting coupons during the voting phase. Election authorities may intercept coupons during the voting phase and jointly decode them to get a partial result. Nevertheless, we assume that enough election authorities (up to a threshold defined according to the underlying distribution technique [10,12,19,20]) wait for the sampling phase to decode coupons and recover the election results.

Partial Verifiability. Each voter should be able to check that tallying and counting were performed correctly. Unfortunately, our solution does not permit a voter to be aware that her vote has been correctly taken into consideration in the final result. If the voter has vetoed on option opt_j, and if the decoded vector contains a veto for opt_j, then the voter is relieved that her veto choice is included in the election result but cannot be guaranteed that her veto has been assessed. We recall that vote counting is not necessary for absolute veto elections. If the voter has vetoed on option opt_j, and if the decoded vector does not contain a veto for opt_j, then the voter is aware that her veto vote has not been taken into account. In order to increase the probability of having her vote included in the final result, the voter transmits multiple times her veto coupon to her neighbors. We aim to develop a substantive, efficient veto protocol in unreliable communication infrastructures. While verifiability is desirable, it does not seem essential in our scenario.

Correctness and Robustness. Correctness implies that no one should be able to submit incorrect votes. Correctness is enhanced with the algorithm BCMVerify that permits everyone to check the validity of a coupon. Correctness also originates from unforgeability, guaranteeing that an attacker cannot submit a valid fake coupon that successfully decodes to a consistent vote.

Robustness implies that a malicious voter should not prevent the election result from being declared. Even if some voters either fail to vote or abort the voting phase, the election result can still be announced. Election authorities can collect coupons at the time of abortion, and decode them to know what has been vetoed so far.

Functionality. Our voting protocol requires a new setup phase as soon as veto options change. However, if several elections contain the same options, then there is no need to generate and deliver new coupons. Voting and sampling phases should be executed for each election. Nevertheless, both phases can be parallelized: election authorities jointly decode coupons during the voting phase by intercepting them, and agree on a final result once this result is obtained with high probability from collected coupons.

Partial Collusion Resistance. A full collusion against one specific voter involves all other voters in the network. An anonymous protocol is by definition not fully collusion resistant [9,14] since the voter's anonymity cannot be preserved. Nevertheless, having all voters acting maliciously and colluding against one particular voter is not possible in practice; otherwise, this voter would just decide to leave the network. Our voting protocol is partially resistant against colluding voters, such that they cannot discover the result of the veto election and cannot force a result more that what they have been given through their coupons. Such guarantees come from indistinguishability and unforgeability. Our protocol is also resistant against colluding election authorities, up to a given threshold. Such assurance is determined by the distribution technique used at the setup phase [10,12,19,20].

No Self-tallying. The voting protocol is not self-tallying since election authorities must use their secret key shares to decode coupons.

5   Observations and Future Work

We discuss here some observations from both our BCM scheme and veto protocol and possible improvements that can be brought.

Enhancing Unforgeability. Future work will focus on designing a BCM solution that guarantees a stronger unforgeability level while saving its applicability in constrained peer-to-peer communication infrastructures. Our current model restricts the adversary to submit unique coupons with one signal option to the oracle. A desirable extension would be to allow the adversary to request coupons with multiple signal options.

Enhancing Untraceability. Veto elections within a dynamic constrained network should offer untraceability guarantees that would prevent malicious voters and election authorities from tracking, following and distinguishing coupons. We have proven our solution untraceable based on a model where the adversary is only given the public key material and access to a coupon generation oracle. Such model can be strengthened by giving the adversary either the secret key material or access to a coupon decoding oracle. In the full version of the paper, we present three stronger untraceability models and discuss the benefits and limitations of such models regarding our solution and the ones from [2,3,5].

Accountability. For our scenario, we believe anonymity is more important than accountability. However, it is possible to add some accountability to the system. For instance, we can design a threshold system of accountability, such that if fewer voters than the threshold number submit vetoes, then they will be identifiable by someone with the appropriate secret key. On the other hand, if more voters than the threshold number submit vetoes, then they cannot be identified. We discuss this further in the full version.

Unauthorized Voters. Election authorities can forbid some voters to veto by giving them $n + 1$ dummy coupons. Since dummy and signal coupons are indinstinguishable, these voters are not aware of being unauthorized to veto. In our scenario, this setting enables the organizers to specifically authorize experienced demonstrators to decide for demonstration cessation, while inexperienced ones cannot. To go easier on their egos, the latter are not told directly that they have no veto competence. We stress that this is entirely optional.

6 Conclusion

In this paper, we proposed an extension of Blazy-Chevalier BCM scheme [5] to enable the quiet propagation of multiple signals. Our BCM solution is proved secure with relation to indistinguishability and unforgeability properties. We also defined a new security notion, that is untraceability, and showed that our BCM construction satisfies it. Finally, based on our enhanced BCM, we presented an efficient and reliable veto protocol using peer-to-peer communications over unreliable networks.

Acknowledgments. This work was supported by the the Luxembourg National Research Fund and the Research Council of Norway for the joint project SURCVS.

References

1. Abe, M., Fuchsbauer, G., Groth, J., Haralambiev, K., Ohkubo, M.: Structure-preserving signatures and commitments to group elements. J. Cryptol. **29**(2), 363–421 (2016)
2. Aspnes, J., Diamadi, Z., Gjøsteen, K., Peralta, R., Yampolskiy, A.: Spreading alerts quietly and the subgroup escape problem. In: Roy, B. (ed.) ASIACRYPT 2005. LNCS, vol. 3788, pp. 253–272. Springer, Heidelberg (2005). https://doi.org/10.1007/11593447_14
3. Aspnes, J., Diamadi, Z., Yampolskiy, A., Gjøsteen, K., Peralta, R.: Spreading alerts quietly and the subgroup escape problem. J. Cryptol. **28**(4), 796–819 (2015)
4. Bag, S., Azad, M.A., Hao, F.: PriVeto: a fully private two-round veto protocol. IET Inf. Secur. **13**(4), 311–320 (2018)
5. Blazy, O., Chevalier, C.: Spreading alerts quietly: new insights from theory and practice. In: Proceedings of the 13th International Conference on Availability, Reliability and Security, ARES 2018, pp. 30:1–30:6. ACM (2018)
6. Boneh, D., Gentry, C., Waters, B.: Collusion resistant broadcast encryption with short ciphertexts and private keys. In: Shoup, V. (ed.) CRYPTO 2005. LNCS, vol. 3621, pp. 258–275. Springer, Heidelberg (2005). https://doi.org/10.1007/11535218_16
7. Brandt, F.: Efficient cryptographic protocol design based on distributed El Gamal encryption. In: Won, D.H., Kim, S. (eds.) ICISC 2005. LNCS, vol. 3935, pp. 32–47. Springer, Heidelberg (2006). https://doi.org/10.1007/11734727_5
8. Bresson, E., Chevassut, O., Pointcheval, D.: Dynamic group diffie-hellman key exchange under standard assumptions. In: Knudsen, L.R. (ed.) EUROCRYPT 2002. LNCS, vol. 2332, pp. 321–336. Springer, Heidelberg (2002). https://doi.org/10.1007/3-540-46035-7_21

9. Chaum, D.: The dining cryptographers problem: unconditional sender and recipient untraceability. J. Cryptol. **1**(1), 65–75 (1988)
10. Feldman, P.: A practical scheme for non-interactive verifiable secret sharing. In: Proceedings of the 28th Annual Symposium on Foundations of Computer Science, SFCS 1987, pp. 427–438. IEEE Computer Society (1987)
11. Gjøsteen, K.: A latency-free election scheme. In: Malkin, T. (ed.) CT-RSA 2008. LNCS, vol. 4964, pp. 425–436. Springer, Heidelberg (2008). https://doi.org/10.1007/978-3-540-79263-5_27
12. Goldreich, O., Micali, S., Wigderson, A.: How to play any mental game. In: Proceedings of the 19th Annual Symposium on Theory of Computing, STOC 1987, pp. 218–229. ACM (1987)
13. Groth, J.: Efficient maximal privacy in boardroom voting and anonymous broadcast. In: Juels, A. (ed.) FC 2004. LNCS, vol. 3110, pp. 90–104. Springer, Heidelberg (2004). https://doi.org/10.1007/978-3-540-27809-2_10
14. Hao, F., Zieliński, P.: A 2-Round anonymous veto protocol. In: Christianson, B., Crispo, B., Malcolm, J.A., Roe, M. (eds.) Security Protocols 2006. LNCS, vol. 5087, pp. 202–211. Springer, Heidelberg (2009). https://doi.org/10.1007/978-3-642-04904-0_28
15. Herranz, J., Laguillaumie, F., Libert, B., Ràfols, C.: Short attribute-based signatures for threshold predicates. In: Dunkelman, O. (ed.) CT-RSA 2012. LNCS, vol. 7178, pp. 51–67. Springer, Heidelberg (2012). https://doi.org/10.1007/978-3-642-27954-6_4
16. Khader, D., Smyth, B., Ryan, P.Y.A., Hao, F.: A fair and robust voting system by broadcast. In: Proceedings of the 5th International Conference on Electronic Voting, EVOTE 2012, pp. 285–299. Gesellschaft für Informatik (2012)
17. Kiayias, A., Yung, M.: Non-interactive zero-sharing with applications to private distributed decision making. In: Wright, R.N. (ed.) FC 2003. LNCS, vol. 2742, pp. 303–320. Springer, Heidelberg (2003). https://doi.org/10.1007/978-3-540-45126-6_22
18. Libert, B., Peters, T., Joye, M., Yung, M.: Linearly homomorphic structure-preserving signatures and their applications. Des. Codes Crypt. **77**(2–3), 441–477 (2015)
19. Shamir, A.: How to share a secret. Commun. ACM **22**(11), 612–613 (1979)
20. Yao, A.C.: Protocols for secure computations. In: Proceedings of the 23rd Symposium on Foundations of Computer Science, SFCS 1982, pp. 160–164 (1982)

Theory: Oblivious Transfer, Obfuscation and Privacy Amplification

UC Priced Oblivious Transfer with Purchase Statistics and Dynamic Pricing

Aditya Damodaran[1], Maria Dubovitskaya[2], and Alfredo Rial[1(⊠)]

[1] SnT, University of Luxembourg, Esch-sur-Alzette, Luxembourg
{aditya.damodaran,alfredo.rial}@uni.lu
[2] Dfinity, Zurich, Switzerland
maria@dfinity.org

Abstract. Priced oblivious transfer (POT) is a cryptographic protocol that can be used to protect customer privacy in e-commerce applications. Namely, it allows a buyer to purchase an item from a seller without disclosing to the latter which item was purchased and at which price. Unfortunately, existing POT schemes have some drawbacks in terms of design and functionality. First, the design of existing POT schemes is not modular. Typically, a POT scheme extends a k-out-of-N oblivious transfer (OT) scheme by adding prices to the items. However, all POT schemes do not use OT as a black-box building block with certain security guarantees. Consequently, security of the OT scheme needs to be reanalyzed while proving security of the POT scheme, and it is not possible to swap the underlying OT scheme with any other OT scheme. Second, existing POT schemes do not allow the seller to obtain any kind of statistics about the buyer's purchases, which hinders customer and sales management. Moreover, the seller is not able to change the prices of items without restarting the protocol from scratch.

We propose a POT scheme that addresses the aforementioned drawbacks. We prove the security of our POT in the UC framework. We modify a standard POT functionality to allow the seller to receive aggregate statistics about the buyer's purchases and to change prices dynamically. We present a modular construction for POT that realizes our functionality in the hybrid model. One of the building blocks is an ideal functionality for OT. Therefore, our protocol separates the tasks carried out by the underlying OT scheme from the additional tasks needed by a POT scheme. Thanks to that, our protocol is a good example of modular design and can be instantiated with any secure OT scheme as well as other building blocks without reanalyzing security from scratch.

Keywords: Oblivious transfer · UC security · Modular design

1 Introduction

Priced oblivious transfer (POT) [1] is a cryptographic protocol that can be used to protect privacy in e-commerce applications. POT is a protocol between a

© Springer Nature Switzerland AG 2019
F. Hao et al. (Eds.): INDOCRYPT 2019, LNCS 11898, pp. 273–296, 2019.
https://doi.org/10.1007/978-3-030-35423-7_14

seller or vendor $\mathcal{V}$ and a buyer $\mathcal{B}$. $\mathcal{V}$ sells N items (represented as messages) $\langle m_n \rangle_{n=1}^N$ with prices $\langle p_n \rangle_{n=1}^N$ assigned to them. At any transfer phase, $\mathcal{B}$ chooses an index $\sigma \in [1, N]$ and purchases the message m_σ. Security for $\mathcal{B}$ ensures that $\mathcal{V}$ does not learn the index σ or the price p_σ paid by $\mathcal{B}$. Security for $\mathcal{V}$ ensures that $\mathcal{B}$ pays the correct price p_σ for the message m_σ and that $\mathcal{B}$ does not learn any information about the messages that are not purchased.

Typically, POT schemes use a prepaid mechanism [1,2,6,23–25]. $\mathcal{B}$ makes an initial deposit dep to $\mathcal{V}$, revealing the amount dep to $\mathcal{V}$. $\mathcal{B}$ and $\mathcal{V}$ can use an existing payment mechanism of their choice to carry out this transaction. After the deposit phase, when $\mathcal{B}$ purchases a message m_σ, the price p_σ is subtracted from the deposit, but the POT protocol ensures that: (1) $\mathcal{V}$ does not learn the new value $dep' = dep - p_\sigma$ of the deposit and (2) $dep' \geq 0$.

Lack of Modular Design. POT schemes [1,2,6,23–25] have so far been built by extending an existing oblivious transfer (OT) scheme. OT is a protocol between a sender $\mathcal{E}$ and a receiver $\mathcal{R}$. $\mathcal{E}$ inputs N messages $\langle m_n \rangle_{n=1}^N$. At each transfer phase, $\mathcal{R}$ obtains the message m_σ for her choice $\sigma \in [1, N]$. $\mathcal{E}$ does not learn σ, while $\mathcal{R}$ does not learn any information about other messages.

In OT schemes that been used to build POT schemes, the interaction between $\mathcal{E}$ and $\mathcal{R}$ consists of an initialization phase followed by several transfer phases. In the initialization phase, $\mathcal{E}$ encrypts messages $\langle m_n \rangle_{n=1}^N$ and sends the list of ciphertexts to $\mathcal{R}$. In each transfer phase, $\mathcal{R}$, on input σ, computes a blinded request for $\mathcal{E}$. $\mathcal{E}$ sends a response that allows $\mathcal{R}$ to decrypt the ciphertext that encrypts m_σ.

Roughly speaking, to construct a POT scheme from an OT scheme, typically the OT scheme is extended as follows. First, in the initialization phase, the computation of the ciphertexts is modified in order to bind them to the prices of the encrypted messages, e.g. by using a signature scheme. Second, a deposit phase, where $\mathcal{B}$ sends an initial deposit to $\mathcal{V}$, is added. As a result of this deposit phase, $\mathcal{V}$ and $\mathcal{B}$ output a commitment or encryption to the deposit dep. Third, in each transfer phase, the request computed in the OT scheme is extended by $\mathcal{B}$ in order to send to $\mathcal{V}$ an encryption or commitment to the new value dep' of the deposit and to prove to $\mathcal{V}$ (e.g. by using a zero-knowledge proof) that $dep' = dep - p_\sigma$ and that $dep' \geq 0$.

The main drawback of the design of existing POT schemes is a lack of modularity. Although each POT scheme is based on an underlying OT scheme, the latter is not used as a black-box building block. Instead, every OT scheme is modified and extended ad-hoc to create the POT scheme, blurring what components were present in the original OT scheme and what components were added to create the POT scheme.

The lack of modularity has two disadvantages. First, existing POT schemes cannot easily be modified to use another OT scheme as a building block, for example, a more efficient one. Second, every time a new POT scheme is designed, the proofs need to be done from scratch. This means that the security of the underlying OT scheme will be reanalyzed instead of relying on its security guarantees. This is error-prone.

Lack of Purchase Statistics. POT schemes [1,2,6,23–25] effectively prevent $\mathcal{V}$ from learning what messages are purchased by $\mathcal{B}$. Although this is a nice privacy feature for $\mathcal{B}$, the customer and sales management becomes more difficult for $\mathcal{V}$. For example, $\mathcal{V}$ is not able to know which items are more demanded by buyers and which ones sell poorly. As another example, $\mathcal{V}$ is not able to use marketing techniques like giving discounts that depend on the previous purchases of a buyer. It is desirable that, while protecting privacy of each individual purchase, $\mathcal{V}$ gets some aggregate statistics about $\mathcal{B}$'s purchases.

Lack of Dynamic Pricing. In existing POT schemes [1,2,6,23–25], the price of a message is static, i.e. each message is associated with a price in the initialization phase and that price cannot change afterwards. In practical e-commerce settings, this is undesirable because sellers would like to be able to change the price of a product easily. However, modifying existing POT schemes to allow sellers to change the prices of messages at any time throughout the protocol execution is not straightforward and would require rerunning the initialization phase.

1.1   Our Contribution

Functionality $\mathcal{F}_{\text{POTS}}$. We use the universal composability (UC) framework [12] and we describe an ideal functionality $\mathcal{F}_{\text{POTS}}$ for priced oblivious transfer with purchase statistics and dynamic pricing. We modify a standard POT functionality to enable aggregate statistics and dynamic pricing.

Existing functionalities for POT [6,24] consist of three interfaces: an initialization interface where $\mathcal{V}$ sends the messages $\langle m_n \rangle_{n=1}^N$ and the prices $\langle p_n \rangle_{n=1}^N$ to the functionality; a deposit interface where $\mathcal{B}$ sends a deposit *dep* to the functionality, which reveals *dep* to $\mathcal{V}$; and a transfer interface where $\mathcal{B}$ sends an index $\sigma \in [1, N]$ to the functionality and receives the message m_σ from the functionality if the current deposit is higher than the price of the message. The functionality stores the updated value of the deposit.

Our functionality $\mathcal{F}_{\text{POTS}}$ modifies the initialization interface so that $\mathcal{V}$ only inputs the messages $\langle m_n \rangle_{n=1}^N$. Additionally, this interface can be invoked multiple times to send different tuples $\langle m_n \rangle_{n=1}^N$ of messages, where each tuple is associated with a unique epoch identifier *ep*. The idea is that messages of different epochs but with the same message index correspond to the same type or category of items. (This happens, e.g. when using POT to construct a conditional access system for pay-TV [2].) $\mathcal{F}_{\text{POTS}}$ also modifies the transfer interface in order to store the number of times that $\mathcal{B}$ purchases items of each of the types or categories.

Moreover, $\mathcal{F}_{\text{POTS}}$ adds three new interfaces: a "setup price" interface where $\mathcal{V}$ inputs the prices, an "update price" interface where $\mathcal{V}$ modifies the price of a message, and a "reveal statistic" interface where $\mathcal{F}_{\text{POTS}}$ reveals to $\mathcal{V}$ the value of a statistic about the purchases of $\mathcal{B}$.

We propose a scheme Π_{POTS} that realizes $\mathcal{F}_{\text{POTS}}$. Π_{POTS} is designed modularly and provides purchase statistics and dynamic pricing, as described below.

Modular Design. In the UC framework, protocols can be described modularly by using a hybrid model where parties invoke the ideal functionalities of the building blocks of a protocol. For example, consider a protocol that uses as building blocks a zero-knowledge proof of knowledge and a signature scheme. In a modular description of this protocol in the hybrid model, parties in the real world invoke the ideal functionalities for zero-knowledge proofs and for signatures.

We describe Π_{POTS} modularly in the hybrid model. Therefore, $\mathcal{V}$ and $\mathcal{B}$ in the real world invoke only ideal functionalities for the building blocks of Π_{POTS}. Interestingly, one of the building blocks used in Π_{POTS} is the ideal functionality for oblivious transfer $\mathcal{F}_{\text{OT}}$. Thanks to that, Π_{POTS} separates the task that is carried out by the underlying OT scheme from the additional tasks that are needed to create a POT scheme.

The advantages of a modular design are twofold. First, Π_{POTS} can be instantiated with any secure OT scheme, i.e., any scheme that realizes $\mathcal{F}_{\text{OT}}$. The remaining building blocks can also be instantiated with any scheme that realizes their corresponding ideal functionalities, leading to multiple possible instantiations of Π_{POTS}. Second, the security analysis in the hybrid model is simpler and does not need to reanalyze the security of any of the building blocks.

One challenge when describing a UC protocol in the hybrid model is the need to ensure that two or more ideal functionalities receive the same input. For example, in Π_{POTS}, it is necessary to enforce that $\mathcal{B}$ sends the same index $\sigma \in [1, N]$ to the transfer interface of $\mathcal{F}_{\text{OT}}$ and to another functionality $\mathcal{F}_{\text{NHCD}}$ (described below) that binds σ to the price p_σ. Otherwise, if an adversarial buyer sends different indexes σ and σ' to $\mathcal{F}_{\text{OT}}$ and $\mathcal{F}_{\text{NHCD}}$, $\mathcal{B}$ could obtain the message m_σ and pay an incorrect price $p_{\sigma'}$. To address this issue, we use the method proposed in [9], which uses a functionality $\mathcal{F}_{\text{NIC}}$ for non-interactive commitments.

Purchase Statistics. In Π_{POTS}, $\mathcal{V}$ can input multiple tuples $\langle m_n \rangle_{n=1}^{N}$ of messages. We consider that messages associated with the same index σ belong to the same category.

Π_{POTS} allows $\mathcal{B}$ to reveal to $\mathcal{V}$ information related to how many purchases were made for each of the item categories. To do that, $\mathcal{B}$ stores a table Tbl_{st} of counters of how many purchases were made for each category. Tbl_{st} contains position-value entries $[\sigma, v_\sigma]$, where $\sigma \in [1, N]$ is the category index and v_σ is the counter. Any time a message m_σ is purchased, the counter for category σ is incremented in Tbl_{st}. At any time throughout the execution of Π_{POTS}, $\mathcal{B}$ can choose a statistic ST, evaluate it on input Tbl_{st} and reveal to $\mathcal{V}$ the result.

Additionally, $\mathcal{B}$ must prove to $\mathcal{V}$ that the result is correct. To do that, we need a mechanism that allows $\mathcal{V}$ to keep track of the purchases made $\mathcal{B}$, without learning them. For this purpose, Π_{POTS} uses the functionality for a committed database $\mathcal{F}_{\text{CD}}$ recently proposed in [8]. $\mathcal{F}_{\text{CD}}$ stores the table Tbl_{st} of counters and allows $\mathcal{B}$ to read the counters from Tbl_{st} and to write updated counters into Tbl_{st} each time a purchase is made. $\mathcal{V}$ does not learn any information read or written but is guaranteed of the correctness of that information. $\mathcal{F}_{\text{CD}}$ allows $\mathcal{B}$ to hide from $\mathcal{V}$ not only the value of counters read or written, but also the positions where they are read or written into Tbl_{st}. This is a crucial property to construct Π_{POTS}, because the position read or written is equal to the index σ, which needs to be hidden from $\mathcal{V}$ in order to hide what message is purchased. The method in [9] is used to ensure that the index σ is the same both for the counter v_σ incremented in $\mathcal{F}_{\mathrm{CD}}$ and for the message m_σ obtained through $\mathcal{F}_{\mathrm{OT}}$. In [8], an efficient construction for $\mathcal{F}_{\mathrm{CD}}$ based on vector commitments (VC) [15,21] is provided, where a VC commits to a vector x such that $x[\sigma] = v_\sigma$ for $\sigma \in [1, N]$. In this construction, after setup, the efficiency of the read and write operations does not depend on the size of the table, which yields efficient instantiations of Π_{POTS} when N is large.

We note that $\mathcal{V}$ could be more interested in gathering aggregated statistics about multiple buyers rather than a single buyer. Interestingly, Π_{POTS} opens up that possibility. The functionalities $\mathcal{F}_{\mathrm{CD}}$ used between $\mathcal{V}$ and each of the buyers can be used in a secure multiparty computation (MPC) protocol for the required statistic. In this MPC, each buyer uses $\mathcal{F}_{\mathrm{CD}}$ to read and prove correctness of the information about her purchases. With the instantiation of $\mathcal{F}_{\mathrm{CD}}$ based on a VC scheme, $\mathcal{V}$ and the buyers would run a secure MPC protocol where $\mathcal{V}$ inputs one vector commitment for each buyer and each buyer inputs the committed vector and the opening.

Dynamic Pricing. In existing POT schemes [1,2,6,23–25], when $\mathcal{V}$ encrypts the messages $\langle m_n \rangle_{n=1}^N$ in the initialization phase, the price of the encrypted message is somehow bound to the corresponding ciphertext. This binding is done in such a way that, when $\mathcal{B}$ computes a request to purchase a message m_σ, $\mathcal{V}$ is guaranteed that the correct price p_σ is subtracted from the deposit while still not learning p_σ. In some schemes, $\mathcal{V}$ uses a signature scheme to sign the prices in the initialization phase, and $\mathcal{B}$ uses a zero-knowledge proof of signature possession to compute the request.

It would be possible to modify the initialization phase of those schemes so that ciphertexts on the messages $\langle m_n \rangle_{n=1}^N$ are computed independently of the signatures on the prices $\langle p_n \rangle_{n=1}^N$, yet enforcing that requests computed by $\mathcal{B}$ use the right price p_σ for the requested index σ. (For example, both the ciphertext and the signature could embed the index σ, and $\mathcal{B}$, as part of a request, would be required to prove in zero-knowledge that the index in the ciphertext and in the signature are equal.) This would allow $\mathcal{V}$ to modify the prices of messages by issuing new signatures, without needing to re-encrypt the messages. However, this mechanism to update prices would also require some method to revoke the previous signatures, which would heavily affect the efficiency to the Π_{POTS} protocol.

Instead, we use the functionality $\mathcal{F}_{\mathrm{NHCD}}$ for a non-hiding committed database recently proposed in [22]. $\mathcal{F}_{\mathrm{NHCD}}$ stores a table Tbl_{nhcd} with entries $[\sigma, p_\sigma]$, where $\sigma \in [1, N]$ is an index and p_σ is a price. $\mathcal{V}$ sets the initial values of Tbl_{nhcd} and is also able to modify Tbl_{nhcd} at any time. $\mathcal{B}$ knows the content of Tbl_{nhcd} but cannot modify it. When purchasing a message of index σ, $\mathcal{B}$ reads from $\mathcal{F}_{\mathrm{NHCD}}$ the entry $[\sigma, p_\sigma]$. $\mathcal{V}$ does not learn any information about the entry read, yet $\mathcal{V}$ is guaranteed that a valid entry is read. Similarly to the case of $\mathcal{F}_{\mathrm{CD}}$, we stress that $\mathcal{F}_{\text{NHCD}}$ reveals to $\mathcal{V}$ neither the position σ nor the value p_σ, and that the method in [9] is used to prove that the index σ received by $\mathcal{F}_{\text{NHCD}}$ and by $\mathcal{F}_{\text{OT}}$ are the same. In [22], an efficient construction for $\mathcal{F}_{\text{NHCD}}$ based on a non-hiding VC scheme [15,21] is provided, where a non-hiding VC commits to a vector x such that $x[\sigma] = p_\sigma$ for $\sigma \in [1, N]$. In this construction, after setup, the efficiency of the read and write operations does not depend on the size of the table, which yields efficient instantiations of Π_{POTS} when N is large.

It could seem that dynamic pricing undermines buyer's privacy in comparison to existing POT schemes, e.g. when an adversarial $\mathcal{V}$ offers different prices to each of the buyers and changes them dynamically in order to narrow down the messages that a buyer could purchase. However, this is not the case. In existing POT, a seller is also able to offer different prices to each buyer, and to change them dynamically by restarting the protocol. The countermeasure, for both Π_{POTS} and other POT, is to have lists of prices available through a secure bulletin board where buyers can check that the prices they are offered are equal to those for other buyers.

2   Related Work

POT was initially proposed in [1]. The POT scheme in [1] is secure in a half-simulation model, where a simulation-based security definition is used to protect seller security, while an indistinguishability-based security definition is used to protect buyer privacy. Later, POT schemes in the full-simulation model [6] and UC-secure schemes [24] were proposed. The scheme in [6] provides unlinkability between $\mathcal{V}$ and $\mathcal{B}$, i.e., $\mathcal{V}$ cannot link interactions with the same buyer.

We define security for POT in the UC model, like [24], and our protocol does not provide unlinkability, unlike [6] or the PIR-based scheme in [19]. Although unlinkability is important in some settings, an unlinkable POT scheme would require the use of an anonymous communication network and, in the deposit phase, it would hinder the use of widespread payment mechanisms that require authentication. Therefore, because one of the goals of this work is to facilitate sellers' deployment of POT schemes, we chose to describe a scheme that does not provide unlinkability.

The use of POT as building block in e-commerce applications in order to protect buyer privacy has been described, e.g. in the context of buyer-seller watermarking protocols for copyright protection [23] and conditional access systems for pay-TV [2]. Our POT protocol is suitable to be used in any of the proposed settings and it provides additional functionalities to $\mathcal{V}$. In [25], a transformation that takes a POT scheme and produces a POT scheme with optimistic fair exchange is proposed. This transformation can also be used with our POT scheme.

Oblivious transfer with access control (OTAC) [5,16] is a generalization of oblivious transfer where messages are associated with access control policies. In order to obtain a message, a receiver must prove that she fulfils the requirements described in the associated access control policy. In some schemes, access control policies are public [5,16,20,26], while other schemes hide them from the receiver [4,7].

POT could be seen as a particular case of OTAC with public access control policies. In POT, the public access control policy that B must fulfil to get a message is defined as her current deposit being higher than the price of the message. However, existing OTAC schemes cannot straightforwardly be converted into a POT scheme. The reason is that, in adaptive POT, the fulfilment of a policy by B depends on the history of purchases and deposits of B, i.e., whether or not the current deposit of B allows him to buy a message depends on how much B deposited and spent before. Therefore, POT schemes need to implement a mechanism that allows V to keep track of the current deposit of B without learning it, such as a commitment or an encryption of the deposit that is updated by B at each deposit or purchase phase. (Our POT protocol uses functionality $\mathcal{F}_{\mathrm{CD}}$ to store the deposit, in addition to the counters of purchases.) In contrast, existing OTAC schemes do not provide such a mechanism. In those schemes, usually a third party called issuer certifies the attributes of a receiver, and after that the receiver can use those certifications to prove the she fulfils an access control policy.

The oblivious language-based envelope (OLBE) framework in [3] generalizes POT, OTAC and similar protocols like conditional OT. However, similar to the case of OTAC schemes, the instantiation of POT in the OLBE framework is only straightforward for non-adaptive POT schemes, where V does not need to keep track of the deposit of B.

Aside from solutions based on OT, privacy protection in e-commerce can also be provided by protocols that offer anonymity/unlinkability. Here the goal is to protect the identity of B rather than the identity of the items purchased. Most solutions involve anonymous payment methods [10] and anonymous communication networks [18].

3   Universally Composable Security

We prove our protocol secure in the universal composability framework [12]. The UC framework allows one to define and analyze the security of cryptographic protocols so that security is retained under an arbitrary composition with other protocols. The security of a protocol is defined by means of an ideal protocol that carries out the desired task. In the ideal protocol, all parties send their inputs to an ideal functionality $\mathcal{F}$ for the task. $\mathcal{F}$ locally computes the outputs of the parties and provides each party with its prescribed output.

The security of a protocol φ is analyzed by comparing the view of an environment $\mathcal{Z}$ in a real execution of φ against that of $\mathcal{Z}$ in the ideal protocol defined in $\mathcal{F}_\varphi$. $\mathcal{Z}$ chooses the inputs of the parties and collects their outputs. In the real world, $\mathcal{Z}$ can communicate freely with an adversary $\mathcal{A}$ who controls both the network and any corrupt parties. In the ideal world, $\mathcal{Z}$ interacts with dummy parties, who simply relay inputs and outputs between $\mathcal{Z}$ and $\mathcal{F}_\varphi$, and a simulator $\mathcal{S}$. We say that a protocol φ securely realizes $\mathcal{F}_\varphi$ if $\mathcal{Z}$ cannot distinguish the real world from the ideal world, i.e., $\mathcal{Z}$ cannot distinguish whether it is interacting with $\mathcal{A}$ and parties running protocol φ or with $\mathcal{S}$ and dummy parties relaying to $\mathcal{F}_\varphi$.

A protocol $\varphi^{\mathcal{G}}$ securely realizes $\mathcal{F}$ in the $\mathcal{G}$-hybrid model when φ is allowed to invoke the ideal functionality $\mathcal{G}$. Therefore, for any protocol ψ that securely realizes $\mathcal{G}$, the composed protocol φ^{ψ}, which is obtained by replacing each invocation of an instance of $\mathcal{G}$ with an invocation of an instance of ψ, securely realizes $\mathcal{F}$.

In the ideal functionalities described in this paper, we consider static corruptions. When describing ideal functionalities, we use the following conventions as in [9].

Interface Naming Convention. An ideal functionality can be invoked by using one or more interfaces. The name of a message in an interface consists of three fields separated by dots, e.g., pot.init.ini in the priced oblivious transfer functionality described in Sect. 4. The first field indicates the name of the functionality and is the same in all interfaces of the functionality. This field is useful for distinguishing between invocations of different functionalities in a hybrid protocol that uses two or more different functionalities. The second field indicates the kind of action performed by the functionality and is the same in all messages that the functionality exchanges within the same interface. The third field distinguishes between the messages that belong to the same interface, and can take the following different values. A message pot.init.ini is the incoming message received by the functionality, i.e., the message through which the interface is invoked. A message pot.init.end is the outgoing message sent by the functionality, i.e., the message that ends the execution of the interface. The message pot.init.sim is used by the functionality to send a message to $\mathcal{S}$, and the message pot.init.rep is used to receive a message from $\mathcal{S}$.

Network vs Local Communication. The identity of an interactive Turing machine instance (ITI) consists of a party identifier pid and a session identifier sid. A set of parties in an execution of a system of interactive Turing machines is a protocol instance if they have the same session identifier sid. ITIs can pass direct inputs to and outputs from "local" ITIs that have the same pid. An ideal functionality $\mathcal{F}$ has $pid = \bot$ and is considered local to all parties. An instance of $\mathcal{F}$ with the session identifier sid only accepts inputs from and passes outputs to machines with the same session identifier sid. Some functionalities require the session identifier to have some structure. Those functionalities check whether the session identifier possesses the required structure in the first message that invokes the functionality. For the subsequent messages, the functionality implicitly checks that the session identifier equals the session identifier used in the first message. Communication between ITIs with different party identifiers must take place over the network. The network is controlled by $\mathcal{A}$, meaning that he can arbitrarily delay, modify, drop, or insert messages.

Query Identifiers. Some interfaces in a functionality can be invoked more than once. When the functionality sends a message pot.init.sim to $\mathcal{S}$ in such an interface, a query identifier qid is included in the message. The query identifier must also be included in the response pot.init.rep sent by $\mathcal{S}$. The query identifier is used to identify the message pot.init.sim to which $\mathcal{S}$ replies with a message pot.init.rep. We note that, typically, $\mathcal{S}$ in the security proof may not be able to provide an immediate answer to the functionality after receiving a message pot.init.sim. The reason is that $\mathcal{S}$ typically needs to interact with the copy of $\mathcal{A}$ it runs in order to produce the message pot.init.rep, but $\mathcal{A}$ may not provide the desired answer or may provide a delayed answer. In such cases, when the functionality sends more than one message pot.init.sim to $\mathcal{S}$, $\mathcal{S}$ may provide delayed replies, and the order of those replies may not follow the order of the messages received.

Aborts. When an ideal functionality $\mathcal{F}$ aborts after being activated with a message sent by a party, we mean that $\mathcal{F}$ halts the execution of its program and sends a special abortion message to the party that invoked the functionality. When an ideal functionality $\mathcal{F}$ aborts after being activated with a message sent by $\mathcal{S}$, we mean that $\mathcal{F}$ halts the execution of its program and sends a special abortion message to the party that receives the outgoing message from $\mathcal{F}$ after $\mathcal{F}$ is activated by $\mathcal{S}$.

4   Ideal Functionality for POT with Statistics and Dynamic Pricing

We depict our functionality $\mathcal{F}_{\text{POTS}}$ for POT with purchase statistics and dynamic pricing. $\mathcal{F}_{\text{POTS}}$ interacts with a seller $\mathcal{V}$ and with a buyer $\mathcal{B}$ and consists of the following interfaces:

1. $\mathcal{V}$ uses the pot.init interface to send a list of messages $\langle m_n \rangle_{n=1}^N$ and an epoch identifier ep to $\mathcal{F}_{\text{POTS}}$. $\mathcal{F}_{\text{POTS}}$ stores $\langle m_n \rangle_{n=1}^N$ and ep, and sends N and ep to $\mathcal{B}$. In the first invocation of this interface, $\mathcal{F}_{\text{POTS}}$ also initializes a deposit dep' and a table Tbl_{st} with entries of the form $[\sigma, v_\sigma]$, where $\sigma \in [1, \mathcal{N}_{max}]$ is a category and v_σ is a counter of the number of purchases made for that category.
2. $\mathcal{V}$ uses the pot.setupprices interface to send a list of prices $\langle p_n \rangle_{n=1}^{\mathcal{N}_{max}}$ to $\mathcal{F}_{\text{POTS}}$, where $\mathcal{N}_{max}$ is the maximum number of messages in an epoch. $\mathcal{F}_{\text{POTS}}$ stores $\langle p_n \rangle_{n=1}^{\mathcal{N}_{max}}$ and sends $\langle p_n \rangle_{n=1}^{\mathcal{N}_{max}}$ to $\mathcal{B}$.
3. $\mathcal{V}$ uses the pot.updateprice interface to send an index n and a price p to $\mathcal{F}_{\text{POTS}}$. $\mathcal{F}_{\text{POTS}}$ updates the stored list $\langle p_n \rangle_{n=1}^{\mathcal{N}_{max}}$ with p at position n, and sends n and p to $\mathcal{B}$.
4. $\mathcal{B}$ uses the pot.deposit interface to send a deposit dep to $\mathcal{F}_{\text{POTS}}$. $\mathcal{F}_{\text{POTS}}$ updates the stored deposit $dep' \leftarrow dep' + dep$ and sends dep to $\mathcal{V}$.
5. $\mathcal{B}$ uses the pot.transfer interface to send an epoch ep and an index σ to $\mathcal{F}_{\text{POTS}}$. If $dep' \geq p_\sigma$, $\mathcal{F}_{\text{POTS}}$ increments the counter for category σ in Tbl_{st} and sends m_σ for the epoch ep to $\mathcal{B}$.

6. $\mathcal{B}$ uses the pot.revealstatistic interface to send a function ST to $\mathcal{F}_{POTS}$. $\mathcal{F}_{POTS}$ evaluates ST on input table Tbl_{st} and sends the result v and ST to $\mathcal{V}$. ST may be any function from a universe Ψ.

In previous functionalities for POT [6,24], $\mathcal{V}$ sends the messages and prices through the pot.init interface. In contrast, $\mathcal{F}_{POTS}$ uses the pot.setupprices and pot.updateprice interfaces to send and update the prices. This change allows the design of a protocol where $\mathcal{V}$ can update prices without rerunning the initialization phase. We also note that, in $\mathcal{F}_{POTS}$, all the messages m_σ of the same category σ have the same price for any epoch. The idea here is that messages of the same category represent the same type of content, which is updated by $\mathcal{V}$ at each new epoch. Nevertheless, it is straightforward to modify $\mathcal{F}_{POTS}$ so that $\mathcal{V}$ can send a new list of prices for each epoch. Our construction in Sect. 6 can easily be modified to allow different prices for each epoch.

$\mathcal{F}_{POTS}$ initializes a counter ct_v and a counter ct_b in the pot.setupprices interface. ct_v is incremented each time $\mathcal{V}$ sends the update of a price, and ct_b is incremented each time $\mathcal{B}$ receives the update of a price. These counters are used by $\mathcal{F}_{POTS}$ to check that $\mathcal{V}$ and $\mathcal{B}$ have the same list of prices. We note that the simulator $\mathcal{S}$, when queried by $\mathcal{F}_{POTS}$, may not reply or may provide a delayed response, which could prevent price updates sent by $\mathcal{V}$ to be received by $\mathcal{B}$.

The session identifier sid has the structure $(\mathcal{V}, \mathcal{B}, sid')$. This allows any vendor $\mathcal{V}$ to create an instance of $\mathcal{F}_{POTS}$ with any buyer $\mathcal{B}$. After the first invocation of $\mathcal{F}_{POTS}$, $\mathcal{F}_{POTS}$ implicitly checks that the session identifier in a message is equal to the one received in the first invocation.

When invoked by $\mathcal{V}$ or $\mathcal{B}$, $\mathcal{F}_{POTS}$ first checks the correctness of the input. Concretely, $\mathcal{F}_{POTS}$ aborts if that input does not belong to the correct domain. $\mathcal{F}_{POTS}$ also aborts if an interface is invoked at an incorrect moment in the protocol. For example, $\mathcal{V}$ cannot invoke pot.updateprice before pot.setupprices. Similar abortion conditions are listed when $\mathcal{F}_{POTS}$ receives a message from the simulator $\mathcal{S}$.

Before $\mathcal{F}_{POTS}$ queries $\mathcal{S}$, $\mathcal{F}_{POTS}$ saves its state, which is recovered when receiving a response from $\mathcal{S}$. When an interface, e.g. pot.updateprice, can be invoked more than once, $\mathcal{F}_{POTS}$ creates a query identifier qid, which allows $\mathcal{F}_{POTS}$ to match a query to $\mathcal{S}$ to a response from $\mathcal{S}$. Creating qid is not necessary if an interface, such as pot.setupprices, can be invoked only once, or if it can be invoked only once with a concrete input revealed to $\mathcal{S}$, such as pot.init, which is invoked only once per epoch.

Compared to previous functionalities for POT, $\mathcal{F}_{POTS}$ looks more complex. The reason is that we list all the conditions for abortion and that $\mathcal{F}_{POTS}$ saves state information before querying $\mathcal{S}$ and recovers it after receiving a response from $\mathcal{S}$. These operations are also required but have frequently been omitted in the description of ideal functionalities in the literature. We describe $\mathcal{F}_{POTS}$ below.

Description of $\mathcal{F}_{POTS}$. Functionality $\mathcal{F}_{POTS}$ runs with a seller $\mathcal{V}$ and a buyer $\mathcal{B}$, and is parameterised with a maximum number of messages $\mathcal{N}_{max}$, a message space $\mathcal{M}$, a maximum deposit value dep_{max}, a maximum price $\mathcal{P}_{max}$, and a universe of statistics Ψ that consists of ppt algorithms.

1. On input (pot.init.ini, sid, ep, $\langle m_n \rangle_{n=1}^{N}$) from $\mathcal{V}$:
   - Abort if $sid \notin (\mathcal{V}, \mathcal{B}, sid')$.
   - Abort if $(sid, ep', \langle m_n \rangle_{n=1}^{N}, 0)$, where $ep' = ep$, is already stored.
   - Abort if $N > \mathcal{N}_{max}$, or if for $n = 1$ to N, $m_n \notin \mathcal{M}$.
   - Store $(sid, ep, \langle m_n \rangle_{n=1}^{N}, 0)$.
   - Send (pot.init.sim, sid, ep, N) to $\mathcal{S}$.

S. On input (pot.init.rep, sid, ep) from $\mathcal{S}$:
   - Abort if $(sid, ep, \langle m_n \rangle_{n=1}^{N}, 0)$ is not stored, or if $(sid, ep, \langle m_n \rangle_{n=1}^{N}, 1)$ is already stored.
   - If a tuple (sid, Tbl_{st}) is not stored, initialize $dep' \leftarrow 0$ and a table Tbl_{st} with entries $[i, 0]$ for $i = 1$ to $\mathcal{N}_{max}$, and store $(sid, dep', \mathsf{Tbl}_{st})$.
   - Store $(sid, ep, \langle m_n \rangle_{n=1}^{N}, 1)$.
   - Send (pot.init.end, sid, ep, N) to $\mathcal{B}$.

2. On input (pot.setupprices.ini, sid, $\langle p_n \rangle_{n=1}^{\mathcal{N}_{max}}$) from $\mathcal{V}$:
   - Abort if $sid \notin (\mathcal{V}, \mathcal{B}, sid')$ or if $(sid, \langle p_n \rangle_{n=1}^{\mathcal{N}_{max}}, ct_v)$ is already stored.
   - Abort if, for $n = 1$ to $\mathcal{N}_{max}$, $p_n \notin (0, \mathcal{P}_{max}]$.
   - Initialize a counter $ct_v \leftarrow 0$ and store $(sid, \langle p_n \rangle_{n=1}^{\mathcal{N}_{max}}, ct_v)$.
   - Send (pot.setupprices.sim, sid, $\langle p_n \rangle_{n=1}^{\mathcal{N}_{max}}$) to $\mathcal{S}$.

S. On input (pot.setupprices.rep, sid) from $\mathcal{S}$:
   - Abort if $(sid, \langle p_n \rangle_{n=1}^{\mathcal{N}_{max}}, ct_v)$ is not stored, or if $(sid, \langle p_n \rangle_{n=1}^{\mathcal{N}_{max}}, ct_b)$ is already stored.
   - Initialize a counter $ct_b \leftarrow 0$ and store $(sid, \langle p_n \rangle_{n=1}^{\mathcal{N}_{max}}, ct_b)$.
   - Send (pot.setupprices.end, sid, $\langle p_n \rangle_{n=1}^{\mathcal{N}_{max}}$) to $\mathcal{B}$.

3. On input (pot.updateprice.ini, sid, n, p) from $\mathcal{V}$:
   - Abort if $(sid, \langle p_n \rangle_{n=1}^{\mathcal{N}_{max}}, ct_v)$ is not stored.
   - Abort if $n \notin [1, \mathcal{N}_{max}]$, or if $p \notin (0, \mathcal{P}_{max}]$.
   - Increment ct_v, set $p_n \leftarrow p$ and store them into the tuple $(sid, \langle p_n \rangle_{n=1}^{\mathcal{N}_{max}}, ct_v)$.
   - Create a fresh qid and store (qid, n, p, ct_v).
   - Send (pot.updateprice.sim, sid, qid, n, p) to $\mathcal{S}$.

S. On input (pot.updateprice.rep, sid, qid) from $\mathcal{S}$:
   - Abort if (qid, n, p, ct_v) is not stored, or if $(sid, \langle p_n \rangle_{n=1}^{\mathcal{N}_{max}}, ct_b)$ is not stored, or if $ct_v \neq ct_b + 1$.
   - Increment ct_b, set $p_n \leftarrow p$, and store them into the tuple $(sid, \langle p_n \rangle_{n=1}^{\mathcal{N}_{max}}, ct_b)$.
   - Delete the record (qid, n, p, ct_v).
   - Send (pot.updateprice.end, sid, n, p) to $\mathcal{B}$.

4. On input (pot.deposit.ini, sid, dep) from $\mathcal{B}$:
   - Abort if $(sid, dep', \mathsf{Tbl}_{st})$ is not stored, or if $dep' + dep \notin [0, dep_{max}]$.
   - Create a fresh qid and store (qid, dep).
   - Send (pot.deposit.sim, sid, qid) to $\mathcal{S}$.

S. On input (pot.deposit.rep, sid, qid) from $\mathcal{S}$:

- Abort if (qid, dep) is not stored.
- Set $dep' \leftarrow dep' + dep$ and update $(sid, dep', \mathsf{Tbl}_{st})$.
- Delete the record (qid, dep).
- Send (pot.deposit.end, sid, dep) to $\mathcal{V}$.

5. On input (pot.transfer.ini, sid, ep, σ) from $\mathcal{B}$:
   - Abort if $(sid, ep', \langle m_n \rangle_{n=1}^{N}, 1)$ for $ep' = ep$ is not stored.
   - Abort if $(sid, \langle p_n \rangle_{n=1}^{N_{max}}, ct_b)$ and $(sid, \langle p_n \rangle_{n=1}^{N_{max}}, ct_v)$ are not stored, or if $ct_b \neq ct_v$.
   - Abort if $\sigma \notin [1, N]$, or if $dep' < p_\sigma$, where dep' is stored in $(sid, dep', \mathsf{Tbl}_{st})$.
   - Create a fresh qid and store $(qid, ep, \sigma, m_\sigma)$.
   - Send (pot.transfer.sim, sid, qid, ep) to $\mathcal{S}$.

S. On input (pot.transfer.rep, sid, qid) from $\mathcal{S}$:
   - Abort if $(qid, ep, \sigma, m_\sigma)$ is not stored.
   - Set $dep' \leftarrow dep' - p_\sigma$, increment v_σ for the entry $[\sigma, v_\sigma]$ in Tbl_{st}, and update $(sid, dep', \mathsf{Tbl}_{st})$.
   - Delete the record $(qid, ep, \sigma, m_\sigma)$.
   - Send (pot.transfer.end, sid, m_σ) to $\mathcal{B}$.

6. On input (pot.revealstatistic.ini, sid, ST) from $\mathcal{B}$:
   - Abort if $(sid, dep', \mathsf{Tbl}_{st})$ is not stored.
   - Abort if $\mathsf{ST} \notin \Psi$.
   - Set $v \leftarrow \mathsf{ST}(\mathsf{Tbl}_{st})$.
   - Create a fresh qid and store (qid, v, ST).
   - Send (pot.revealstatistic.sim, sid, qid) to $\mathcal{S}$.

S. On input (pot.revealstatistic.rep, sid, qid) from $\mathcal{S}$:
   - Abort if (qid, v, ST) is not stored.
   - Delete the record (qid, v, ST).
   - Send (pot.revealstatistic.end, sid, v, ST) to $\mathcal{V}$.

5 Building Blocks of Our Construction

Ideal Functionality $\mathcal{F}_{\mathrm{AUT}}$. Our protocol uses the functionality $\mathcal{F}_{\mathrm{AUT}}$ for an authenticated channel in [12]. $\mathcal{F}_{\mathrm{AUT}}$ interacts with a sender $\mathcal{T}$ and a receiver $\mathcal{R}$, and consists of one interface aut.send. $\mathcal{T}$ uses aut.send to send a message m to $\mathcal{F}_{\mathrm{AUT}}$. $\mathcal{F}_{\mathrm{AUT}}$ leaks m to the simulator $\mathcal{S}$ and, after receiving a response from $\mathcal{S}$, $\mathcal{F}_{\mathrm{AUT}}$ sends m to $\mathcal{R}$. $\mathcal{S}$ cannot modify m. The session identifier sid contains the identities of $\mathcal{T}$ and $\mathcal{R}$.

Ideal Functionality $\mathcal{F}_{\mathrm{SMT}}$. Our protocol uses the functionality $\mathcal{F}_{\mathrm{SMT}}$ for secure message transmission described in [12]. $\mathcal{F}_{\mathrm{SMT}}$ interacts with a sender $\mathcal{T}$ and a receiver $\mathcal{R}$, and consists of one interface smt.send. $\mathcal{T}$ uses the smt.send interface to send a message m to $\mathcal{F}_{\mathrm{SMT}}$. $\mathcal{F}_{\mathrm{SMT}}$ leaks $l(m)$, where $l : \mathcal{M} \to \mathbb{N}$ is a function that leaks the message length, to the simulator $\mathcal{S}$. After receiving a response from $\mathcal{S}$, $\mathcal{F}_{\mathrm{SMT}}$ sends m to $\mathcal{R}$. $\mathcal{S}$ cannot modify m. The session identifier sid contains the identities of $\mathcal{T}$ and $\mathcal{R}$.

Ideal Functionality $\mathcal{F}_{\text{NIC}}$. Our protocol uses the functionality $\mathcal{F}_{\text{NIC}}$ for non-interactive commitments in [9]. $\mathcal{F}_{\text{NIC}}$ interacts with parties $\mathcal{P}_i$ and consists of the following interfaces:

1. Any party $\mathcal{P}_i$ uses the com.setup interface to set up the functionality.
2. Any party $\mathcal{P}_i$ uses the com.commit interface to send a message cm and obtain a commitment $ccom$ and an opening $copen$. A commitment $ccom$ is a tuple $(ccom', cparcom, \text{COM.Verify})$, where $ccom'$ is the commitment, $cparcom$ are the public parameters, and COM.Verify is the verification algorithm.
3. Any party $\mathcal{P}_i$ uses the com.validate interface to send a commitment $ccom$ to check that $ccom$ contains the correct public parameters and verification algorithm.
4. Any party $\mathcal{P}_i$ uses the com.verify interface to send $(ccom, cm, copen)$ in order to verify that $ccom$ is a commitment to the message cm with the opening $copen$.

$\mathcal{F}_{\text{NIC}}$ can be realized by a perfectly hiding commitment scheme, such as Pedersen commitments [9]. In [9], a method is described to use $\mathcal{F}_{\text{NIC}}$ in order to ensure that a party sends the same input cm to several ideal functionalities. For this purpose, the party first uses com.commit to get a commitment $ccom$ to cm with opening $copen$. Then the party sends $(ccom, cm, copen)$ as input to each of the functionalities, and each functionality runs COM.Verify to verify the commitment. Finally, other parties in the protocol receive the commitment $ccom$ from each of the functionalities and use the com.validate interface to validate $ccom$. Then, if $ccom$ received from all the functionalities is the same, the binding property provided by $\mathcal{F}_{\text{NIC}}$ ensures that all the functionalities received the same input cm. When using $\mathcal{F}_{\text{NIC}}$, it is needed to work in the $\mathcal{F}_{\text{NIC}}\|\mathcal{S}_{\text{NIC}}$-hybrid model, where $\mathcal{S}_{\text{NIC}}$ is any simulator for a construction that realizes $\mathcal{F}_{\text{NIC}}$.

Ideal Functionality $\mathcal{F}_{\text{ZK}}^R$. Let R be a polynomial time computable binary relation. For tuples $(wit, ins) \in R$ we call wit the witness and ins the instance. Our protocol uses the ideal functionality $\mathcal{F}_{\text{ZK}}^R$ for zero-knowledge in [12]. $\mathcal{F}_{\text{ZK}}^R$ is parameterized by a description of a relation R, runs with a prover $\mathcal{P}$ and a verifier $\mathcal{V}$, and consists of one interface zk.prove. $\mathcal{P}$ uses zk.prove to send a witness wit and an instance ins to $\mathcal{F}_{\text{ZK}}^R$. $\mathcal{F}_{\text{ZK}}^R$ checks whether $(wit, ins) \in R$, and, in that case, sends the instance ins to $\mathcal{V}$. The simulator $\mathcal{S}$ learns ins but not wit. In our POT protocol, we use relations that include commitments as part of the instance, while the committed value and the opening are part of the witness. The relation uses the verification algorithm of the commitment scheme to check correctness of the commitment. This allows us to use the method described in [9] to ensure that an input to $\mathcal{F}_{\text{ZK}}^R$ is equal to the input of other functionalities.

Ideal Functionality $\mathcal{F}_{\text{OT}}$. Our protocol uses the ideal functionality $\mathcal{F}_{\text{OT}}$ for oblivious transfer. $\mathcal{F}_{\text{OT}}$ interacts with a sender $\mathcal{E}$ and a receiver $\mathcal{R}$, and consists of three interfaces ot.init, ot.request and ot.transfer.

1. $\mathcal{E}$ uses the ot.init interface to send the messages $\langle m_n \rangle_{n=1}^N$ to $\mathcal{F}_{\text{OT}}$. $\mathcal{F}_{\text{OT}}$ stores $\langle m_n \rangle_{n=1}^N$ and sends N to $\mathcal{R}$. The simulator $\mathcal{S}$ also learns N.

2. $\mathcal{R}$ uses the ot.request interface to send an index $\sigma \in [1, N]$, a commitment $ccom_\sigma$ and an opening $copen_\sigma$ to $\mathcal{F}_{OT}$. $\mathcal{F}_{OT}$ parses the commitment $ccom_\sigma$ as $(cparcom, ,_\sigma$, COM.Verify$)$ and verifies the commitment by running COM.Verify. $\mathcal{F}_{OT}$ stores $[\sigma, ccom_\sigma]$ and sends $ccom_\sigma$ to $\mathcal{E}$.

3. $\mathcal{E}$ uses the ot.transfer interface to send a commitment $ccom_\sigma$ to $\mathcal{F}_{OT}$. If a tuple $[\sigma, ccom_\sigma]$ is stored, $\mathcal{F}_{OT}$ sends the message m_σ to $\mathcal{R}$.

$\mathcal{F}_{OT}$ is similar to existing functionalities for OT [11], except that it receives a commitment $ccom_\sigma$ to the index σ and an opening $copen_\sigma$ for that commitment. In addition, the transfer phase is split up into two interfaces ot.request and ot.transfer, so that $\mathcal{E}$ receives $ccom_\sigma$ in the request phase. These changes are needed to use in our POT protocol the method in [9] to ensure that, when purchasing an item, the buyer sends the same index σ to $\mathcal{F}_{OT}$ and to other functionalities. It is generally easy to modify existing UC OT protocols so that they realize our functionality $\mathcal{F}_{OT}$.

Ideal Functionality $\mathcal{F}_{CD}$. Our protocol uses the ideal functionality $\mathcal{F}_{CD}$ for a committed database in [8]. $\mathcal{F}_{CD}$ interacts with a prover $\mathcal{P}$ and a verifier $\mathcal{V}$, and consists of three interfaces cd.setup, cd.read and cd.write.

1. $\mathcal{V}$ uses the cd.setup interface to initialize Tbl_{cd}. $\mathcal{F}_{CD}$ stores Tbl_{cd} and sends Tbl_{cd} to $\mathcal{P}$ and to the simulator $\mathcal{S}$.

2. $\mathcal{P}$ uses cd.read to send a position i and a value v_r to $\mathcal{F}_{CD}$, along with commitments and openings $(ccom_i, copen_i)$ and $(ccom_r, copen_r)$ to the position and value respectively. $\mathcal{F}_{CD}$ verifies the commitments and checks that there is an entry $[i, v_r]$ in the table Tbl_{cd}. In that case, $\mathcal{F}_{CD}$ sends $ccom_i$ and $ccom_r$ to $\mathcal{V}$. $\mathcal{S}$ also learns $ccom_i$ and $ccom_r$.

3. $\mathcal{P}$ uses cd.write to send a position i and a value v_w to $\mathcal{F}_{CD}$, along with commitments and openings $(ccom_i, copen_i)$ and $(ccom_w, copen_w)$ to the position and value respectively. $\mathcal{F}_{CD}$ verifies the commitments and updates Tbl_{cd} to store v_w at position i. $\mathcal{F}_{CD}$ sends $ccom_i$ and $ccom_w$ to $\mathcal{V}$. $\mathcal{S}$ also learns $ccom_i$ and $ccom_w$.

Basically, $\mathcal{F}_{CD}$ allows $\mathcal{P}$ to prove to $\mathcal{V}$ that two commitments $ccom_i$ and $ccom_r$ commit to a position and value that are read from a table, and that two commitments $ccom_i$ and $ccom_w$ commit to a position and value that are written into the table. In [8], an efficient construction for $\mathcal{F}_{CD}$ based on hiding vector commitments [15, 21] is proposed. In our POT protocol, $\mathcal{F}_{CD}$ is used to store and update the deposit of the buyer and the counters of the number of purchases for each of the item categories.

Ideal Functionality $\mathcal{F}_{NHCD}$. Our protocol uses the ideal functionality $\mathcal{F}_{NHCD}$ for a non-hiding committed database in [22]. $\mathcal{F}_{NHCD}$ interacts with a party $\mathcal{P}_0$ and a party $\mathcal{P}_1$, and consists of three interfaces nhcd.setup, nhcd.prove and nhcd.write.

1. $\mathcal{P}_1$ uses nhcd.setup to send a table Tbl_{nhcd} with N entries of the form $[i, v]$ (for $i = 0$ to N) to $\mathcal{F}_{NHCD}$. $\mathcal{F}_{NHCD}$ stores Tbl_{nhcd} and sends Tbl_{nhcd} to $\mathcal{P}_0$. The simulator $\mathcal{S}$ also learns Tbl_{nhcd}.

2. $\mathcal{P}_b$ ($b \in [0,1]$) uses nhcd.prove to send a position i and a value v_r to $\mathcal{F}_{\text{NHCD}}$, along with commitments and openings $(ccom_i, copen_i)$ and $(ccom_r, copen_r)$ to the position and value respectively. $\mathcal{F}_{\text{NHCD}}$ verifies the commitments and checks that there is an entry $[i, v_r]$ in the table Tbl_{nhcd}. In that case, $\mathcal{F}_{\text{NHCD}}$ sends $ccom_i$ and $ccom_r$ to $\mathcal{P}_{1-b}$. The simulator $\mathcal{S}$ also learns $ccom_i$ and $ccom_r$.

3. $\mathcal{P}_1$ uses nhcd.write to send a position i and a value v_w to $\mathcal{F}_{\text{NHCD}}$. $\mathcal{F}_{\text{NHCD}}$ updates Tbl_{nhcd} to contain value v_w at position i and sends i and v_w to $\mathcal{P}_0$. The simulator $\mathcal{S}$ also learns i and v_w.

$\mathcal{F}_{\text{NHCD}}$ is similar to the functionality $\mathcal{F}_{\text{CD}}$ described above. The main difference is that the contents of the table Tbl_{nhcd} are known by both parties. For this reason, both parties can invoke the nhcd.prove interface to prove that two commitments $ccom_i$ and $ccom_r$ commit to a position and value stored in Tbl_{nhcd}. In addition, the interface nhcd.write reveals the updates to Tbl_{nhcd} made by $\mathcal{P}_1$ to $\mathcal{P}_0$. In [22], an efficient construction for $\mathcal{F}_{\text{NHCD}}$ based on non-hiding vector commitments is proposed. In our POT protocol, $\mathcal{F}_{\text{NHCD}}$ will be used by the seller, acting as $\mathcal{P}_1$, to store and update the prices of items. The buyer, acting as $\mathcal{P}_0$, uses the nhcd.prove interface to prove to the seller that the correct price for the item purchased is used.

The full description of the ideal functionalities is given in the full version [17].

6   Construction Π_{POTS} for $\mathcal{F}_{\text{POTS}}$

Intuition. For each epoch ep, $\mathcal{V}$ and $\mathcal{B}$ use a new instance of $\mathcal{F}_{\text{OT}}$. In the pot.init interface, $\mathcal{V}$ uses ot.init to create a new instance of $\mathcal{F}_{\text{OT}}$ on input the messages $\langle m_n \rangle_{n=1}^{N}$. In the pot.transfer interface, $\mathcal{B}$ uses ot.request on input an index σ and receives the message m_σ through the ot.transfer interface.

To construct a POT protocol based on $\mathcal{F}_{\text{OT}}$, $\mathcal{V}$ must set the prices, and $\mathcal{B}$ must make deposits and pay for the messages obtained. Additionally, our POT protocol allows $\mathcal{V}$ to receive aggregate statistics about the purchases.

Prices. To set prices, $\mathcal{V}$ uses $\mathcal{F}_{\text{NHCD}}$. In the pot.setupprices interface, the seller $\mathcal{V}$ uses nhcd.setup to create an instance of $\mathcal{F}_{\text{NHCD}}$ on input a list of prices $\langle p_n \rangle_{n=1}^{N_{max}}$, which are stored in the table Tbl_{nhcd} in $\mathcal{F}_{\text{NHCD}}$. In the pot.updateprice interface, $\mathcal{V}$ uses nhcd.write to update a price in the table Tbl_{nhcd}.

Deposits. $\mathcal{F}_{\text{CD}}$ is used to store the current funds dep' of $\mathcal{B}$. In the pot.init interface, $\mathcal{V}$ uses cd.setup to create an instance of $\mathcal{F}_{\text{CD}}$ on input a table Tbl_{cd} that contains a 0 at every position. The position 0 of Tbl_{cd} is used to store dep'. In the pot.deposit interface, $\mathcal{B}$ makes deposits dep to $\mathcal{V}$, which are added to the existing funds dep'. (To carry out the payment of dep, $\mathcal{V}$ and $\mathcal{B}$ use a payment mechanism outside the POT protocol.) $\mathcal{B}$ uses $\mathcal{F}_{\text{ZK}}^{R_{dep}}$ to prove in zero-knowledge to $\mathcal{V}$ that the deposit is updated correctly as $dep' \leftarrow dep' + dep$. The interfaces cd.read and cd.write are used to read dep' and to write the updated value of dep' into Tbl_{cd}.

Payments. In the pot.transfer interface, $\mathcal{B}$ must subtract the price p_σ for the purchased message m_σ from the current funds dep'. $\mathcal{B}$ uses nhcd.prove to read the correct price p_σ from Tbl_{nhcd}. Then $\mathcal{B}$ uses $\mathcal{F}_{\mathrm{ZK}}^{R_{trans}}$ to prove in zero-knowledge that $dep' \leftarrow dep' - p_\sigma$. The interfaces cd.read and cd.write of $\mathcal{F}_{\mathrm{CD}}$ are used to read dep' and to write the updated value of dep' into Tbl_{cd}.

Statistics. $\mathcal{F}_{\mathrm{CD}}$ is used to store counters on the number of purchases of each item category in the positions $[1, \mathcal{N}_{max}]$ of table Tbl_{cd}. In the pot.transfer interface, $\mathcal{B}$ uses cd.read to read the table entry $[\sigma, count_1]$ in Tbl_{cd}, where σ is the index of the message purchased m_σ and $count_1$ is the counter for that category. $\mathcal{B}$ computes $count_2 \leftarrow count_1 + 1$ and uses $\mathcal{F}_{\mathrm{ZK}}^{R_{count}}$ to prove in zero-knowledge that the counter is correctly incremented. Then $\mathcal{B}$ uses cd.write to write the entry $[\sigma, count_2]$ in Tbl_{cd}. In the pot.revealstatistic interface, $\mathcal{B}$ uses $\mathcal{F}_{\mathrm{ZK}}^{R_{\mathrm{ST}}}$ to prove in zero-knowledge to $\mathcal{V}$ that a statistic v is the result of evaluating a function ST on input Tbl_{cd}. For this purpose, $\mathcal{B}$ uses cd.read to read the required table entries in Tbl_{cd}.

Construction Π_{POTS}. Π_{POTS} is parameterised with a maximum number of messages $\mathcal{N}_{max}$, a message space $\mathcal{M}$, a maximum deposit value dep_{max}, a maximum price $\mathcal{P}_{max}$, and a universe of statistics Ψ that consists of ppt algorithms. Π_{POTS} uses the ideal functionalities $\mathcal{F}_{\mathrm{AUT}}$, $\mathcal{F}_{\mathrm{SMT}}$, $\mathcal{F}_{\mathrm{NIC}}$, $\mathcal{F}_{\mathrm{ZK}}^R$, $\mathcal{F}_{\mathrm{OT}}$, $\mathcal{F}_{\mathrm{CD}}$ and $\mathcal{F}_{\mathrm{NHCD}}$. We omit some abortion conditions or some of the messages used to invoke functionalities, which are depicted in the full version [17].

1. On input (pot.init.ini, sid, ep, $\langle m_n \rangle_{n=1}^N$), $\mathcal{V}$ and $\mathcal{B}$ do the following:
   - If this is the first execution of this interface, $\mathcal{V}$ and $\mathcal{B}$ set up $\mathcal{F}_{\mathrm{CD}}$ as follows:
     - $\mathcal{V}$ sets a table Tbl_{cd} of $\mathcal{N}_{max}$ entries of the form $[i, 0]$ for $i = 0$ to $\mathcal{N}_{max}$. $\mathcal{V}$ uses cd.setup to send Tbl_{cd} to a new instance of $\mathcal{F}_{\mathrm{CD}}$.
     - $\mathcal{B}$ receives Tbl_{cd} from $\mathcal{F}_{\mathrm{CD}}$ and stores (sid, Tbl_{cd}). Then $\mathcal{B}$ sends the message $setup$ to $\mathcal{V}$ via $\mathcal{F}_{\mathrm{AUT}}$, so that $\mathcal{V}$ continues the protocol execution.
   - $\mathcal{V}$ uses ot.init to send the messages $\langle m_n \rangle_{n=1}^N$ to a new instance of $\mathcal{F}_{\mathrm{OT}}$ with session identifier $sid_{\mathrm{OT}} \leftarrow (sid, ep)$.
   - $\mathcal{B}$ receives the messages from $\mathcal{F}_{\mathrm{OT}}$, stores (sid, ep, N), and outputs the message (pot.init.end, sid, ep, N).
2. On input (pot.setupprices.ini, sid, $\langle p_n \rangle_{n=1}^{\mathcal{N}_{max}}$), $\mathcal{V}$ and $\mathcal{B}$ do the following:
   - For $n = 1$ to $\mathcal{N}_{max}$, $\mathcal{V}$ sets a table Tbl_{nhcd} with entries $[n, p_n]$ and uses nhcd.setup to send Tbl_{nhcd} to a new instance of $\mathcal{F}_{\mathrm{NHCD}}$.
   - $\mathcal{B}$ receives Tbl_{nhcd} from $\mathcal{F}_{\mathrm{NHCD}}$, parses Tbl_{nhcd} as $[n, p_n]$, for $n = 1$ to $\mathcal{N}_{max}$, stores $(sid, \langle p_n \rangle_{n=1}^{\mathcal{N}_{max}})$ and outputs (pot.setupprices.end, sid, $\langle p_n \rangle_{n=1}^{\mathcal{N}_{max}}$).
3. On input (pot.updateprice.ini, sid, n, p), $\mathcal{V}$ and $\mathcal{B}$ do the following:
   - $\mathcal{V}$ uses nhcd.write to send the index n and the price p to $\mathcal{F}_{\mathrm{NHCD}}$.
   - $\mathcal{B}$ receives n and p from $\mathcal{F}_{\mathrm{NHCD}}$, updates the stored tuple $(sid, \langle p_n \rangle_{n=1}^{\mathcal{N}_{max}})$ and outputs (pot.updateprice.end, sid, n, p).

4. On input (pot.deposit.ini, sid, dep), $\mathcal{V}$ and $\mathcal{B}$ do the following:
   - If this is the first execution of the deposit interface, $\mathcal{B}$ uses com.setup to create a new instance of $\mathcal{F}_{\mathrm{NIC}}$, sets $dep_1 \leftarrow 0$ and uses com.commit to get a commitment $ccom_{dep_1}$ to dep_1 with opening $copen_{dep_1}$ from $\mathcal{F}_{\mathrm{NIC}}$. Otherwise, $\mathcal{B}$ takes the stored commitment to the deposit $(sid, ccom_{dep_2}, copen_{dep_2})$, sets $ccom_{dep_1} \leftarrow ccom_{dep_2}$ and $copen_{dep_1} \leftarrow copen_{dep_2}$, and sets $dep_1 \leftarrow v$ where $[0, v]$ is the deposit stored in the table (sid, Tbl_{cd}).
   - $\mathcal{B}$ sets $dep_2 \leftarrow dep_1 + dep$ and uses com.commit to get commitments and openings $(ccom_{dep}, copen_{dep})$ and $(ccom_{dep_2}, copen_{dep_2})$ to dep and dep_2.
   - $\mathcal{B}$ sets a witness wit_{dep} as $(dep, copen_{dep}, dep_1, copen_{dep_1}, dep_2, copen_{dep_2})$ and an instance ins_{dep} as $(cparcom, ccom_{dep}, ccom_{dep_1}, ccom_{dep_2})$, stores $(sid, wit_{dep}, ins_{dep})$, and uses zk.prove to send wit_{dep} and ins_{dep} to $\mathcal{F}_{\mathrm{ZK}}^{R_{dep}}$, where relation R_{dep} is

   $$
   \begin{aligned}
   R_{dep} = \{ &(wit_{dep}, ins_{dep}) : \\
   &1 = \mathsf{COM.Verify}(cparcom, ccom_{dep}, dep, copen_{dep}) \wedge \\
   &1 = \mathsf{COM.Verify}(cparcom, ccom_{dep_1}, dep_1, copen_{dep_1}) \wedge \\
   &1 = \mathsf{COM.Verify}(cparcom, ccom_{dep_2}, dep_2, copen_{dep_2}) \wedge \\
   &dep_2 = dep + dep_1 \ \wedge \ dep_2 \in [0, dep_{max}] \}
   \end{aligned}
   $$

   - $\mathcal{V}$ receives $ins_{dep} = (cparcom, ccom_{dep}, ccom_{dep_1}, ccom_{dep_2})$ from $\mathcal{F}_{\mathrm{ZK}}^{R_{dep}}$. If this is the first execution of the deposit interface, $\mathcal{V}$ invokes com.setup of $\mathcal{F}_{\mathrm{NIC}}$ and then uses com.validate to validate $ccom_{dep_1}$. Otherwise, $\mathcal{V}$ takes the stored commitment $(sid, ccom'_{dep_2})$ (which commits to the old value of the deposit) and aborts if $ccom'_{dep_2} \neq ccom_{dep_1}$, because this means that the buyer used an incorrect commitment $ccom_{dep_1}$ to the old value of the deposit.
   - $\mathcal{V}$ uses com.validate to validate $ccom_{dep_2}$ and $ccom_{dep}$ and stores the tuple (sid, ins_{dep}).
   - $\mathcal{V}$ uses aut.send to send $writedeposit$ to $\mathcal{B}$, so that $\mathcal{B}$ continues the protocol.
   - If this is the first execution of the deposit interface, $\mathcal{B}$ uses com.commit to get a commitment and opening $(ccom_0, copen_0)$ to 0, which is the position where the deposit is stored in the table of $\mathcal{F}_{\mathrm{CD}}$.
   - $\mathcal{B}$ stores $(sid, ccom_{dep_2}, copen_{dep_2})$ and uses the cd.write interface to send $(ccom_0, 0, copen_0)$ and $(ccom_{dep_2}, dep_2, copen_{dep_2})$ in order to write an entry $[0, dep_2]$ into the table of $\mathcal{F}_{\mathrm{CD}}$.
   - $\mathcal{V}$ receives (cd.write.end, sid, $ccom_0$, $ccom_{dep_2}$) from $\mathcal{F}_{\mathrm{CD}}$.
   - $\mathcal{V}$ aborts if the commitment $ccom_{dep_2}$ stored in (sid, ins_{dep}) is not the same as that received from $\mathcal{F}_{\mathrm{CD}}$. If this is not the first execution of the deposit interface, $\mathcal{V}$ aborts if $(sid, ccom_0)$ is not the same as the commitment received from $\mathcal{F}_{\mathrm{CD}}$.
   - $\mathcal{V}$ uses aut.send to send a message $revealdeposit$ to $\mathcal{B}$.
   - $\mathcal{B}$ updates (sid, Tbl_{cd}) with $[0, dep_2]$.

- If this is the first execution of the deposit interface, $\mathcal{B}$ uses smt.send to send $\langle dep, copen_{dep}, 0, copen_0, dep_1, copen_{dep_1} \rangle$ to $\mathcal{V}$, and $\mathcal{V}$ uses com.verify to verify $(ccom_0, 0, copen_0)$ and $(ccom_{dep_1}, dep_1, copen_{dep_1})$. Else the buyer $\mathcal{B}$ uses the smt.send interface to send $\langle dep, copen_{dep} \rangle$ to $\mathcal{V}$.
- $\mathcal{V}$ uses com.verify to verify $(ccom_{dep}, dep, copen_{dep})$.
- $\mathcal{V}$ outputs $(\text{pot.deposit.end}, sid, dep)$.

5. On input $(\text{pot.transfer.ini}, sid, ep, \sigma)$, $\mathcal{V}$ and $\mathcal{B}$ do the following:
   - $\mathcal{B}$ retrieves the entry $[0, dep_1]$ from the table (sid, Tbl_{cd}) and the price p_σ from $(sid, \langle p_n \rangle_{n=1}^{\mathcal{N}_{max}})$, and sets $dep_2 \leftarrow dep_1 - p_\sigma$.
   - $\mathcal{B}$ retrieves the stored tuple $(sid, ccom_{dep_2}, copen_{dep_2})$ and sets $ccom_{dep_1} \leftarrow ccom_{dep_2}$ and $copen_{dep_1} \leftarrow copen_{dep_2}$.
   - $\mathcal{B}$ uses com.commit to obtain from functionality $\mathcal{F}_{\text{NIC}}$ the commitments and openings $(ccom_{dep_2}, copen_{dep_2})$ to dep_2, $(ccom_\sigma, copen_\sigma)$ to σ and $(ccom_{p_\sigma}, copen_{p_\sigma})$ to p_σ.
   - $\mathcal{B}$ sets wit_{trans} as $(p_\sigma, copen_{p_\sigma}, dep_1, copen_{dep_1}, dep_2, copen_{dep_2})$ and the instance ins_{trans} as $(cparcom, ccom_{p_\sigma}, ccom_{dep_1}, ccom_{dep_2})$, stores the tuple $(sid, wit_{trans}, ins_{trans})$, and uses zk.prove to send wit_{trans} and ins_{trans} to $\mathcal{F}_{\text{ZK}}^{R_{trans}}$, where R_{trans} is defined as follows

$$R_{trans} = \{(wit_{trans}, ins_{trans}) :$$
$$1 = \text{COM.Verify}(cparcom, ccom_{p_\sigma}, p_\sigma, copen_{p_\sigma}) \wedge$$
$$1 = \text{COM.Verify}(cparcom, ccom_{dep_1}, dep_1, copen_{dep_1}) \wedge$$
$$1 = \text{COM.Verify}(cparcom, ccom_{dep_2}, dep_2, copen_{dep_2}) \wedge$$
$$dep_2 = dep_1 - p_\sigma \wedge dep_2 \in [0, dep_{max}]\}$$

   - $\mathcal{V}$ receives $ins_{trans} = (cparcom, ccom_{p_\sigma}, ccom_{dep_1}, ccom_{dep_2})$ from $\mathcal{F}_{\text{ZK}}^{R_{trans}}$, uses com.validate to validate the commitments $ccom_{p_\sigma}$ and $ccom_{dep_2}$, and aborts if $ccom_{dep_1}$ is not equal to the stored commitment $(sid, ccom_{dep_2})$.
   - $\mathcal{V}$ stores (sid, ins_{trans}) and uses aut.send to send a message $readprice$ to $\mathcal{B}$, so that $\mathcal{B}$ continues the protocol execution.
   - $\mathcal{B}$ uses nhcd.prove to send the position σ and the price p_σ to $\mathcal{F}_{\text{NHCD}}$, along with their respective commitments and openings $(ccom_\sigma, copen_\sigma)$ and $(ccom_{p_\sigma}, copen_{p_\sigma})$.
   - $\mathcal{V}$ receives $ccom_\sigma$ and $ccom_{p_\sigma}$ from $\mathcal{F}_{\text{NHCD}}$, aborts if $ccom_{p_\sigma}$ is not equal to the commitment stored in (sid, ins_{trans}), uses com.validate to validate $ccom_\sigma$ and adds $ccom_\sigma$ to (sid, ins_{trans}).
   - $\mathcal{V}$ uses aut.send to send the message $commitdeposit$ to $\mathcal{B}$.
   - $\mathcal{B}$ uses cd.write to send the position 0 and the deposit dep_2 into $\mathcal{F}_{\text{CD}}$, along with $(ccom_0, copen_0)$ and $(ccom_{dep_2}, copen_{dep_2})$.
   - $\mathcal{V}$ receives $ccom_0$ and $ccom_{dep_2}$ from $\mathcal{F}_{\text{CD}}$, and aborts if the $ccom_{dep_2}$ in (sid, ins_{trans}) is not the same as that received from $\mathcal{F}_{\text{CD}}$, or if $ccom_0$ received from $\mathcal{F}_{\text{CD}}$ is not the same as $(sid, ccom_0)$ stored during the first execution of the deposit interface.
   - $\mathcal{V}$ uses aut.send to send the message $commitcounter$ to $\mathcal{B}$.

- $\mathcal{B}$ stores $(sid, ccom_{dep_2}, copen_{dep_2})$, updates (sid, Tbl_{cd}) with $[0, dep_2]$, then deletes $(sid, wit_{trans}, ins_{trans})$ and stores $(sid, wit_{count}, ins_{count})$.
- $\mathcal{B}$ retrieves $[\sigma, v]$ from Tbl_{cd}, sets $count_1 \leftarrow v$ and $count_2 \leftarrow count_1 + 1$, and uses com.commit to get from $\mathcal{F}_{\mathrm{NIC}}$ commitments and openings $(ccom_{count_1}, copen_{count_1})$ to $count_1$ and $(ccom_{count_2}, copen_{count_2})$ to $count_2$.
- $\mathcal{B}$ sets wit_{count} as $(\sigma, copen_\sigma, count_1, copen_{count_1}, count_2, copen_{count_2})$ and ins_{count} as $(cparcom, ccom_\sigma, ccom_{count_1}, ccom_{count_2})$, and uses zk.prove to send wit_{count} and ins_{count} to $\mathcal{F}_{\mathrm{ZK}}^{R_{count}}$, where R_{count} is

$$\begin{aligned} R_{count} = \{ (wit_{count}, ins_{count}) : \\ 1 = \mathsf{COM.Verify}(cparcom, ccom_\sigma, \sigma, copen_\sigma) \wedge \\ 1 = \mathsf{COM.Verify}(cparcom, ccom_{count_1}, count_1, copen_{count_1}) \wedge \\ 1 = \mathsf{COM.Verify}(cparcom, ccom_{count_2}, count_2, copen_{count_2}) \wedge \\ count_2 = count_1 + 1 \} \end{aligned}$$

- $\mathcal{V}$ receives ins_{count} from $\mathcal{F}_{\mathrm{ZK}}^{R_{count}}$, aborts if the commitment $ccom_\sigma$ in (sid, ins_{trans}) is not equal to the one in ins_{count}, uses com.validate to validate the commitments $ccom_{count_1}$ and $ccom_{count_2}$, and stores (sid, ins_{count}).
- $\mathcal{V}$ uses aut.send to send the message $readcounter$ to $\mathcal{B}$.
- $\mathcal{B}$ uses cd.read to send the position σ and the counter $count_1$ to $\mathcal{F}_{\mathrm{CD}}$, along with $(ccom_\sigma, copen_\sigma)$ and $(ccom_{count_1}, copen_{count_1})$.
- $\mathcal{V}$ receives $ccom_\sigma$ and $ccom_{count_1}$ from $\mathcal{F}_{\mathrm{CD}}$ and aborts if those commitments are not equal to the ones stored in (sid, ins_{count}).
- $\mathcal{V}$ uses aut.send to send the message $writecounter$ to $\mathcal{B}$.
- $\mathcal{B}$ uses cd.write to send the position σ and the value $count_2$ to $\mathcal{F}_{\mathrm{CD}}$, along with $(ccom_\sigma, copen_\sigma)$ and $(ccom_{count_2}, copen_{count_2})$.
- $\mathcal{V}$ receives $ccom_\sigma$ and $ccom_{count_2}$ from $\mathcal{F}_{\mathrm{CD}}$ and aborts if those commitments are not equal to the ones stored in (sid, ins_{count}).
- $\mathcal{V}$ uses aut.send to send the message $transfer$ to $\mathcal{B}$.
- $\mathcal{B}$ updates (sid, Tbl_{cd}) with $[\sigma, count_2]$ and uses ot.request to send the index σ along with $(ccom_\sigma, copen_\sigma)$ to the instance of $\mathcal{F}_{\mathrm{OT}}$ with session identifier $sid_{\mathrm{OT}} = (sid, ep)$.
- $\mathcal{V}$ receives $ccom_\sigma$ from $\mathcal{F}_{\mathrm{OT}}$ and aborts if it is not equal to the one contained in ins_{count}.
- $\mathcal{V}$ uses ot.transfer to send $ccom_\sigma$ to the instance of $\mathcal{F}_{\mathrm{OT}}$ with session identifier $sid_{\mathrm{OT}} = (sid, ep)$.
- $\mathcal{B}$ receives m_σ from $\mathcal{F}_{\mathrm{OT}}$ and outputs $(\mathsf{pot.transfer.end}, sid, m_\sigma)$.
6. On input $(\mathsf{pot.revealstatistic.ini}, sid, \mathsf{ST})$, $\mathcal{B}$ and $\mathcal{V}$ do the following:
   - $\mathcal{B}$ takes the stored (sid, Tbl_{cd}) and computes $result \leftarrow \mathsf{ST}(\mathsf{Tbl}_{cd})$.
   - For all $i \in \mathbb{P}$, where $\mathbb{P}$ is the subset of positions i such that the entry $[i, v_i]$ in Tbl_{cd} was used by $\mathcal{B}$ to compute $result$, $\mathcal{B}$ and $\mathcal{V}$ do the following:
     • $\mathcal{B}$ uses com.commit to get the commitments and openings $(ccom_i, copen_i)$ to i and $(ccom_{v_i}, copen_{v_i})$ to v_i and stores $(sid, ccom_i, ccom_{v_i})$. Then $\mathcal{B}$ uses cd.read to read $(ccom_i, i, copen_i)$ and $(ccom_{v_i}, v_i, copen_{v_i})$ from $\mathcal{F}_{\mathrm{CD}}$.

- $\mathcal{V}$ receives $(ccom_i, ccom_{v_i})$ from $\mathcal{F}_{CD}$, uses com.validate to validate the commitments $ccom_i$ and $ccom_{v_i}$, and uses aut.send to send the following message $\langle OK, ccom_i, ccom_{v_i}\rangle$ to $\mathcal{B}$.

- $\mathcal{B}$ sets $wit_{ST} \leftarrow (\langle i, copen_i, v_i, copen_{v_i}\rangle_{\forall i})$ and $ins_{ST} \leftarrow (result, cparcom, \langle ccom_i, ccom_{v_i}\rangle_{\forall i})$, and uses zk.prove to send wit_{ST} and ins_{ST} to $\mathcal{F}_{ZK}^{R_{ST}}$, where the relation R_{ST} is

$$R_{ST} = \{(wit_{ST}, ins_{ST}) :$$
$$[1 = \mathsf{COM.Verify}(cparcom, ccom_i, i, copen_i) \wedge$$
$$1 = \mathsf{COM.Verify}(cparcom, ccom_{v_i}, v_i, copen_{v_i})]_{\forall i \in \mathbb{P}} \wedge$$
$$result = \mathsf{ST}(\langle i, v_i\rangle_{\forall i \in \mathbb{P}}) \}$$

- $\mathcal{V}$ receives ins_{ST} from $\mathcal{F}_{ZK}^{R_{ST}}$ and aborts if the commitments received from $\mathcal{F}_{CD}$ are not the same as those in ins_{ST}.
- $\mathcal{V}$ outputs (pot.revealstatistic.end, $sid, result, \mathsf{ST}$).

Theorem 1. *Construction Π_{POTS} realizes functionality $\mathcal{F}_{POTS}$ in the $(\mathcal{F}_{AUT}, \mathcal{F}_{SMT}, \mathcal{F}_{NIC}\|\mathcal{S}_{NIC}, \mathcal{F}_{ZK}^R, \mathcal{F}_{OT}, \mathcal{F}_{CD}, \mathcal{F}_{NHCD})$-hybrid model.*

We prove this theorem in the full version [17].

Instantiation and Efficiency Analysis. In previous work [1,2,6,23–25], the computation and communication cost of POT protocols is dominated by the cost of the underlying OT scheme. This is also the case for Π_{POTS}. However, Π_{POTS} has the advantage that it can be instantiated with any OT protocol that realizes $\mathcal{F}_{OT}$. The OT schemes used to construct UC-secure POT schemes [24], and other UC-secure OT schemes are suitable. Moreover, when new more efficient OT schemes are available, they can also be used to instantiate Π_{POTS}.

We also note that the overhead introduced by $\mathcal{F}_{NIC}$ to allow the modular design of Π_{POTS} is small. $\mathcal{F}_{NIC}$ can be instantiated with a perfectly hiding commitment scheme, such as Pedersen commitments [9]. Therefore, the overhead consists in computing a commitment to each of the values that need to be sent to more than one functionality, and ZK proofs of the opening of those commitments.

As discussed above, to construct POT from an OT scheme, $\mathcal{V}$ must set the prices, and $\mathcal{B}$ must make deposits and pay for the messages obtained. Additionally, our POT protocol allows $\mathcal{V}$ to receive aggregate statistics about the purchases. For these tasks, Π_{POTS} uses $\mathcal{F}_{NHCD}$ and $\mathcal{F}_{CD}$. These functionalities can be instantiated with a non-hiding and hiding VC scheme respectively [8,22], equipped with ZK proofs of an opening for a position of the vector. In [8,22], concrete instantiations based on the Diffie-Hellman Exponent (DHE) assumption are provided. These instantiations involve a common reference string that grows linearly with the length of the committed vector, which in Π_{POTS} is the number N of messages. A non-hiding VC and a hiding VC commit to the tables Tbl_{nhcd} and Tbl_{cd} respectively. The vector commitments, as well as openings for each position of the vector, are of size independent of N. The computation of a commitment and of an opening grows linearly with N. However, when the committed vector changes, both the vector commitment and the openings can be updated with cost independent of N. Therefore, they can be updated and reused throughout the protocol, yielding amortized cost independent of N. The ZK proofs of VC openings offer computation and communication cost independent of N. Therefore, with this instantiation, Π_{POTS} remains efficient when the number N of messages is large.

We compare below Π_{POTS} to the UC-secure scheme in [24], but we note that this comparison would be similar for other full-simulation secure POT protocols. We can conclude that Π_{POTS} provides additional functionalities like dynamic pricing and aggregated statistics with cost similar to POT protocols that do not provide them.

Prices. In [24], in the initialization phase, $\mathcal{V}$ encrypts the messages and, for each message, $\mathcal{V}$ computes a signature that binds a ciphertext to the price of the encrypted message. This implies that one signature per message is sent from $\mathcal{V}$ to $\mathcal{B}$, and thus the cost grows linearly with N. In Π_{POTS}, $\mathcal{F}_{\text{NHCD}}$ is used, which can be instantiated with a non-hiding VC scheme. In this instantiation, only one vector commitment, which commits to a vector that contains the list of prices, needs to be sent from $\mathcal{V}$ to $\mathcal{B}$. Nevertheless, adding the size of the common reference string, the cost also grows linearly with N.

However, non-hiding VC schemes provide dynamic pricing at no extra cost. The vector commitment can be updated with cost independent of N. With a signature scheme, $\mathcal{V}$ could also provide a new signature on the price with cost independent of N. However, $\mathcal{V}$ needs to revoke the signature on the old price. The need of a signature revocation mechanism makes dynamic pricing costly in this case.

Deposit. In [24], in the deposit phase, $\mathcal{B}$ sends a commitment to the new value of the deposit and a ZK proof that the deposit is updated. In Π_{POTS}, $\mathcal{F}_{\text{CD}}$ is used, which can be instantiated with a hiding VC that stores the deposit at position 0. The size of commitments, as well as the cost of a ZK proof of deposit updated, does not depend on N in both cases. However, the common reference string (crs) of the VC scheme grows linearly with N. (We recall that $\mathcal{F}_{\text{CD}}$ not only stores the deposit but also the N counters of purchases.) By applying the UC with joint state theorem [14], it could be possible to share crs for the DHE instantiations of the non-hiding and hiding VC schemes, but this affects the modularity of Π_{POTS}.

Payment. In [24], $\mathcal{B}$ proves in ZK that the price of the purchased message is subtracted from her current funds. This involves a ZK proof of signature possession, to prove that the correct price is used, and a ZK proof of commitment opening, to prove that the correct value of the deposit is used. The cost of these proofs is independent of N. In Π_{POTS}, when using non-hiding and hiding VC schemes to instantiate $\mathcal{F}_{\text{NHCD}}$ and $\mathcal{F}_{\text{CD}}$, we need two ZK proofs of a vector commitment opening, one for the non-hiding VC scheme (for the price) and one for the hiding VC scheme (for the deposit). The amortized cost of those ZK proofs is also independent of N. The cost of a ZK proof of commitment opening for the DHE instantiation is similar to the ZK proof of signature possession in [24].

Statistics. Unlike [24], Π_{POTS} allows $\mathcal{V}$ to get aggregate statistics about the purchases of $\mathcal{B}$. $\mathcal{F}_{CD}$ stores the counters of the number of purchases for each category. With the instantiation based on a hiding VC scheme, updating the counters and reading them to compute a statistic involves again ZK proofs of the opening of positions of a VC, whose amortized computation and communication cost is independent of N.

Aggregate Statistics About Multiple Buyers. Π_{POTS} allows $\mathcal{V}$ to gather statistics about the purchases of each buyer separately. Nonetheless, $\mathcal{V}$ is possibly more interested in gathering aggregate statistics about multiple buyers. This is also appealing to better protect buyer's privacy. Fortunately, Π_{POTS} enables this possibility. The functionalities $\mathcal{F}_{CD}$ used in the execution of Π_{POTS} between $\mathcal{V}$ and each of the buyers can be used to run a secure multiparty computation (MPC) protocol for the required statistic. In this protocol, each buyer reads from $\mathcal{F}_{CD}$ the counters needed for the statistic. We note that $\mathcal{F}_{CD}$ provides commitments to the counters read. These commitments can easily be plugged into existing commit-and-prove MPC protocols [13] to run an MPC between the seller and the buyers. We note the previous POT protocols do not provide this possibility because there buyers do not have any means to prove what they purchased before. $\mathcal{F}_{CD}$ acts as a ZK data structure that stores information about what buyers have proven in zero-knowledge, so that this information can be reused in subsequent ZK proofs.

Acknowledgements. This research is supported by the Luxembourg National Research Fund (FNR) CORE project "Stateful Zero-Knowledge" (Project code: C17/11650748).

References

1. Aiello, B., Ishai, Y., Reingold, O.: Priced oblivious transfer: how to sell digital goods. In: Pfitzmann, B. (ed.) EUROCRYPT 2001. LNCS, vol. 2045, pp. 119–135. Springer, Heidelberg (2001). https://doi.org/10.1007/3-540-44987-6_8
2. Biesmans, W., Balasch, J., Rial, A., Preneel, B., Verbauwhede, I.: Private mobile pay-tv from priced oblivious transfer. IEEE Trans. Inf. Forensics Secur. **13**(2), 280–291 (2018)
3. Blazy, O., Chevalier, C., Germouty, P.: Adaptive oblivious transfer and generalization. In: Cheon, J.H., Takagi, T. (eds.) ASIACRYPT 2016. LNCS, vol. 10032, pp. 217–247. Springer, Heidelberg (2016). https://doi.org/10.1007/978-3-662-53890-6_8
4. Camenisch, J., Dubovitskaya, M., Enderlein, R.R., Neven, G.: Oblivious transfer with hidden access control from attribute-based encryption. In: Visconti, I., De Prisco, R. (eds.) SCN 2012. LNCS, vol. 7485, pp. 559–579. Springer, Heidelberg (2012). https://doi.org/10.1007/978-3-642-32928-9_31
5. Camenisch, J., Dubovitskaya, M., Neven, G.: Oblivious transfer with access control. In: Proceedings of the 16th ACM Conference on Computer and Communications Security, pp. 131–140. ACM (2009)

6. Camenisch, J., Dubovitskaya, M., Neven, G.: Unlinkable priced oblivious transfer with rechargeable wallets. In: Sion, R. (ed.) FC 2010. LNCS, vol. 6052, pp. 66–81. Springer, Heidelberg (2010). https://doi.org/10.1007/978-3-642-14577-3_8

7. Camenisch, J., Dubovitskaya, M., Neven, G., Zaverucha, G.M.: Oblivious transfer with hidden access control policies. In: Catalano, D., Fazio, N., Gennaro, R., Nicolosi, A. (eds.) PKC 2011. LNCS, vol. 6571, pp. 192–209. Springer, Heidelberg (2011). https://doi.org/10.1007/978-3-642-19379-8_12

8. Camenisch, J., Dubovitskaya, M., Rial, A.: Concise UC zero-knowledge proofs for oblivious updatable databases. http://hdl.handle.net/10993/39423

9. Camenisch, J., Dubovitskaya, M., Rial, A.: UC commitments for modular protocol design and applications to revocation and attribute tokens. In: Robshaw, M., Katz, J. (eds.) CRYPTO 2016. LNCS, vol. 9816, pp. 208–239. Springer, Heidelberg (2016). https://doi.org/10.1007/978-3-662-53015-3_8

10. Camenisch, J., Hohenberger, S., Lysyanskaya, A.: Compact e-cash. In: Cramer, R. (ed.) EUROCRYPT 2005. LNCS, vol. 3494, pp. 302–321. Springer, Heidelberg (2005). https://doi.org/10.1007/11426639_18

11. Camenisch, J., Neven, G., et al.: Simulatable adaptive oblivious transfer. In: Naor, M. (ed.) EUROCRYPT 2007. LNCS, vol. 4515, pp. 573–590. Springer, Heidelberg (2007). https://doi.org/10.1007/978-3-540-72540-4_33

12. Canetti, R.: Universally composable security: a new paradigm for cryptographic protocols. In: Proceedings 42nd IEEE Symposium on Foundations of Computer Science, pp. 136–145. IEEE (2001)

13. Canetti, R., Lindell, Y., Ostrovsky, R., Sahai, A.: Universally composable two-party and multi-party secure computation. In: Proceedings of the Thirty-Fourth Annual ACM Symposium on Theory of Computing, pp. 494–503. ACM (2002)

14. Canetti, R., Rabin, T.: Universal composition with joint state. In: Boneh, D. (ed.) CRYPTO 2003. LNCS, vol. 2729, pp. 265–281. Springer, Heidelberg (2003). https://doi.org/10.1007/978-3-540-45146-4_16

15. Catalano, D., Fiore, D.: Vector commitments and their applications. In: Kurosawa, K., Hanaoka, G. (eds.) PKC 2013. LNCS, vol. 7778, pp. 55–72. Springer, Heidelberg (2013). https://doi.org/10.1007/978-3-642-36362-7_5

16. Coull, S., Green, M., Hohenberger, S.: Controlling access to an oblivious database using stateful anonymous credentials. In: Jarecki, S., Tsudik, G. (eds.) PKC 2009. LNCS, vol. 5443, pp. 501–520. Springer, Heidelberg (2009). https://doi.org/10.1007/978-3-642-00468-1_28

17. Damodaran, A., Dubovitskaya, M., Rial, A.: UC priced oblivious transfer with purchase statistics and dynamic pricing. http://hdl.handle.net/10993/39424

18. Dingledine, R., Mathewson, N., Syverson, P.: Tor: The second-generation onion router. Technical report, Naval Research Lab Washington DC (2004)

19. Henry, R., Olumofin, F., Goldberg, I.: Practical PIR for electronic commerce. In: Proceedings of the 18th ACM Conference on Computer and Communications Security, pp. 677–690. ACM (2011)

20. Libert, B., Ling, S., Mouhartem, F., Nguyen, K., Wang, H.: Adaptive oblivious transfer with access control from lattice assumptions. In: Takagi, T., Peyrin, T. (eds.) ASIACRYPT 2017. LNCS, vol. 10624, pp. 533–563. Springer, Cham (2017). https://doi.org/10.1007/978-3-319-70694-8_19

21. Libert, B., Yung, M.: Concise mercurial vector commitments and independent zero-knowledge sets with short proofs. In: Micciancio, D. (ed.) TCC 2010. LNCS, vol. 5978, pp. 499–517. Springer, Heidelberg (2010). https://doi.org/10.1007/978-3-642-11799-2_30

22. Rial, A.: UC updatable non-hiding committed database with efficient zero-knowledge proofs. http://hdl.handle.net/10993/39421
23. Rial, A., Balasch, J., Preneel, B.: A privacy-preserving buyer-seller watermarking protocol based on priced oblivious transfer. IEEE Trans. Inf. Forensics Secur. **6**(1), 202–212 (2011)
24. Rial, A., Kohlweiss, M., Preneel, B.: Universally composable adaptive priced oblivious transfer. In: Shacham, H., Waters, B. (eds.) Pairing 2009. LNCS, vol. 5671, pp. 231–247. Springer, Heidelberg (2009). https://doi.org/10.1007/978-3-642-03298-1_15
25. Rial, A., Preneel, B.: Optimistic fair priced oblivious transfer. In: Bernstein, D.J., Lange, T. (eds.) AFRICACRYPT 2010. LNCS, vol. 6055, pp. 131–147. Springer, Heidelberg (2010). https://doi.org/10.1007/978-3-642-12678-9_9
26. Zhang, Y., et al.: Oblivious transfer with access control : realizing disjunction without duplication. In: Joye, M., Miyaji, A., Otsuka, A. (eds.) Pairing 2010. LNCS, vol. 6487, pp. 96–115. Springer, Heidelberg (2010). https://doi.org/10.1007/978-3-642-17455-1_7

Public-Coin Differing-Inputs Obfuscator for Hiding-Input Point Function with Multi-bit Output and Its Applications

Dongxue Pan[1,2,3], Bei Liang[4(✉)] ⓘ, Hongda Li[1,2,3], and Peifang Ni[1,2,3]

[1] State Key Lab of Information Security, Institute of Information Engineering, Chinese Academy of Sciences, Beijing, China
{pandongxue,lihongda,nipeifang}@iie.ac.cn
[2] School of Cyber Security, University of Chinese Academy of Sciences, Beijing, China
[3] Data Assurance and Communication Security Research Center, CAS, Beijing, China
[4] Chalmers University of Technology, Gothenburg, Sweden
lbei@chalmers.se

Abstract. Differing-inputs obfuscation (diO), first introduced by Barak et al. (CRYPTO 2001) and then revisited by Ananth et al. (ePrint 2013) and Boyle et al. (TCC 2014), is a natural extension of indistinguishability obfuscation (iO), which captures a security notion that the obfuscations of two efficiently generated programs C_0 and C_1 are indistinguishable if it is hard for an adversary to find an input x such that $C_0(x) \neq C_1(x)$, even in the presence of auxiliary information aux that is generated together with C_0 and C_1. A variant notion of diO, called *public-coin* diO, introduced by Ishai, Pandey and Sahai (TCC 2015) relaxes the original definition of diO by requiring that only the actual random coins that were used to sample programs C_0 and C_1 can be used as the auxiliary input. Public-coin diO is indeed of great interest, since it not only allows to evade the implausible results of diO, but also yields several useful applications. However, as far as we know, there was no approach known to build a public-coin differing-input obfuscator neither for general-purpose programs/circuits such as NC^1 circuits nor for special-purpose function such as some variant of point function.

In this paper, we propose a public-coin differing-inputs obfuscator for a class of function, namely hiding-input point function with multi-bit output (MB-HIPF). We show that the existence of public-coin diO for MB-HIPF can be implied under the existence of auxiliary input point obfuscation for unpredictable distrins (AIPO) which can be instantiated under different assumptions (TCC 2012), and the conjecture of the existence of a special-purpose obfuscation for MB-HIPF, which has been considered as a falsifiable assumption (CRYPTO 2014). Besides, we show the applications of public-coin diO for MB-HIPF.

We emphasize that even though our result is based on the special-purpose obfuscation conjecture, it at least provides a different mindset on constructing public-coin diO from more concrete building blocks, *i.e.,*

F. Hao et al. (Eds.): INDOCRYPT 2019, LNCS 11898, pp. 297–317, 2019.
https://doi.org/10.1007/978-3-030-35423-7_15

a special-purpose obfuscation for MB-HIPF and AIPO. Then we can turn to investigating these specific primitives with a more focused mindset.

Keywords: Differing-inputs obfuscation · Special-purpose obfuscation · Hiding-input point function with multi-bit output · Auxiliary input point obfuscation

1   Introduction

Differing Inputs Obfuscation. *Differing inputs obfuscation* (diO), first introduced by Barak et al. [4,5] and then revisited by Ananth et al. [1] and Boyle et al. [9], is a natural extension of indistinguishability obfuscation (iO), which intuitively captures a security notion that the obfuscations of two efficiently generated programs C_0 and C_1 are indistinguishable not only if they compute the same function, but also if it is hard for an adversary to find an input x on which the two programs differ, namely x such that $C_0(x) \neq C_1(x)$. Moreover, the indistinguishability requirements should hold even in the presence of auxiliary information aux that is generated together with the programs, which means that given (C_0, C_1, aux) to the attacker, if it is hard to use this information to find an input x on which $C_0(x) \neq C_1(x)$, then it should also be hard to use this information to distinguish the obfuscations of C_0 and C_1. Unfortunately, the impossibility results for diO in [6,10,16] have given rise to some doubt on the existence of general-purpose diO with arbitrary auxiliary inputs.

Public-Coin Differing Inputs Obfuscation. In order to circumvent the impossibility results coming from planting a trapdoor in the auxiliary input, Ishai, Pandey and Sahai [19] introduced a variant notion of diO, called *public-coin* diO, which in some sense relaxes the original definition of diO by requiring that only the actual random coins that were used to sample programs C_0 and C_1 can be used as the corresponding auxiliary input. As demonstrated in [19], public-coin diO is indeed of great interest, since it not only allows to evade the impossibility results of [6,10,16], but also yields several applications, such as for constructing functional encryption schemes for Turing Machines [19] and constant-round concurrent zero-knowledge [23].

Ishai, Pandey and Sahai [19] showed that public-coin diO for Turing Machines with unbounded inputs, running time, and space complexity, is implied from public-coin diO for NC^1 circuits, together with fully homomorphic encryption (FHE) with decryption in NC^1, and public-coin SNARKs (succinct non-interactive arguments of knowledge) with uniformly distributed auxiliary input. However, [19] did not propose any candidate constructions of public-coin diO for NC^1 circuits at all. As we know, Boyle and Pass [10] demonstrated a conflict between public-coin diO for NC^1 circuits and SNARKs. In particular, they show that assuming the existence of public-coin collision-resistant hash functions and FHE with decryption in NC^1, then there exists an efficiently computable distribution $\mathcal{Z}$ such that either SNARKs for NP w.r.t. auxiliary input $\mathcal{Z}$ do not exist, or public-coin diO for NC^1 circuits does not exist. At first glance, the results from [19] and [10] seem contradict with each other, but we emphasize that Boyle and Pass's [10] implausible results, on the one hand does not rule out the existence of SNARKs in the presence of *uniform auxiliary* input; on the other hand it does not give any evidence of impossibility for public-coin diO since to the best of our knowledge, there is no construction of SNARKs for NP w.r.t. such specifically defined distributional auxiliary input $\mathcal{Z}$.

Our Motivation (i). Based on the observation above, we believe the public-coin diO may be the reasonable and plausible notion for differing-inputs obfuscation and it is worthy of further study. On the downside, prior to our work, there was no approach known to build a public-coin differing-input obfuscator *neither* for general-purpose programs/circuits such as NC^1 circuits *nor* for special-purpose function such as a variant of point function. This gives rise to the following question, which is at the center of our work:

Is it possible to construct a public-coin differing-input obfuscator for a special-purpose function such as a variant of point function with multi-bit output, based on plausible assumptions?

Obfuscation for Point Function. We start with a clarification that here the point function is a general designation containing two different types, *i.e.*, plain point functions and point functions with multi-bit output (MBPF). A plain point function I_x is a function that maps all inputs to 0 except for the single input x that is mapped to 1, while a MBPF $I_{x,y}$ returns y on input x and returns 0 otherwise. Plain point function obfuscators in the presence of auxiliary information about the point x is first introduced by Canetti [14], where such auxiliary information z is required to be computationally hard to invert the point x. Bitansky and Paneth [8] provided a clean treatment on auxiliary inputs by restricting them to be sampled from unpredictable distributions, which output point x together with auxiliary information z and are required to computationally infeasible to recover x given auxiliary information z. They also introduced the notion of plain point obfuscation with auxiliary input secure against unpredictable distributions (AIPO), which requires that given an auxiliary input of x, the AIPO of I_x is indistinguishable from AIPO of $I_{x'}$ where x' is chosen uniformly at random. Moreover, Bitansky and Paneth [8] also revisited two constructions of AIPOs based on two different assumptions, the first of which was suggested by Canetti [14] based on a strong variant of DDH. The second AIPO construction is a modified construction of Wee's original obfuscator for plain point functions (non auxiliary input) [24], which is based on a new assumption that strengthens the assumption made by Wee [24] in order to deal with auxiliary inputs.

Similar to AIPO, Brzuska and Mittelbach [13] introduced the notion of multi-bit point function obfuscation in the presence of computationally hard-to-invert auxiliary information, namely the MB-AIPO for MBPF $I_{x,y}$ via an unpredictable distribution. Unfortunately, Brzuska and Mittelbach [13] show that the existence of indistinguishability obfuscation (iO) contradicts the existence of MB-AIPO. More precisely, if iO and pseudo-random generators exist, then MB-AIPO for

MBPF $I_{x,y}$ with auxiliary input z via an unpredictable distribution (consisting of (x, y, z)) cannot exist.

Our Motivation (ii). Considering the negative results on the existence of MB-AIPO for MBPF $I_{x,y}$ with auxiliary input z via an unpredictable distribution, we are motivated to come up with other notions of obfuscation (*i.e.*, public-coin diO) for a variant of multi-bit point function $I_{x,y}$.

Our Results. In this paper, we provide an affirmative answer to our motivated question. More precisely, we propose a public-coin differing-inputs obfuscator for a class of function, called hiding-input point function with multi-bit output (MB-HIPF) [22]. Our construction relies on the existence of AIPO (auxiliary input point obfuscation for unpredictable distributions) which can be instantiated under different assumptions [8], and the conjecture of the existence of a special-purpose obfuscation for MB-HIPF, which has been considered as a falsifiable assumption [16]. Besides, we show the applications of public-coin diO for MB-HIPF, including constructing witness encryption schemes with unique decryption, which has been shown in [22], and constructing two-round statistical witness indistinguishable arguments, which is one of our contributions.

We emphasize that even though our result is based on the special-purpose obfuscation assumption, it at least provides a different mindset on how to construct public-coin diO. Instead of handling public-coin diO for MB-HIPF as a whole we demonstrate a generic way of building it from narrow and more concrete building blocks, *i.e.*, a special-purpose obfuscation for MB-HIPF and AIPO. Then we can turn to exploring solutions to such specific primitives with a more focused mindset.

Indeed, our special-purpose obfuscation conjecture for MB-HIPF is reminiscent of the one that was used by Garg *et al.* [16] to rule out the existence of *general-purpose* diO with auxiliary input. More precisely, under the conjecture that the special-purpose obfuscation for a specific circuit C with specific auxiliary input aux in a way that hides some specific information exists, Garg *et al.* [16] show that general-purpose diO with auxiliary input cannot exist. Whereas, we use the special-purpose obfuscation conjecture for MB-HIPF to show how to construct a public-coin diO for a *specific class* of function, *i.e.*, MB-HIPF, which makes sense since diO for specific functions may still exist under such conjecture.

Our Construction in a Nutshell. The class of function, MB-HIPF that we intend to obfuscate, is related to an instance of the hard problems of an NP language. Let L be an NP language with corresponding NP relation $\mathcal{R}_L$. We say an instance φ is a hard problem of L if there exists a hard problem sampler such that φ is efficiently samplable by the sampler and if given the randomness used to sample φ, no probabilistic polynomial-time (PPT) adversary can obtain a witness w with overwhelming probability such that $\mathcal{R}_L(\varphi, w) = 1$. A MB-HIPF $I_{\varphi,y}$ w.r.t an instance φ of the hard problems of language L, where $y \in \{0, 1\}^n$, is defined as a function that outputs y on input w such that $\mathcal{R}_L(\varphi, w) = 1$ and otherwise outputs 0. We note that when there does not exist any witness of φ satisfying the relation $\mathcal{R}_L$, $I_{\varphi,y}$ outputs 0 on all inputs.

In order to construct a public-coin diO for MB-HIPF $I_{\varphi,y}$, we use a conjecture of the existence of special-purpose obfuscation spO for MB-HIPF $I_{\varphi,x_1||\cdots||x_q}$ (x_i are random strings and independent with y) that outputs $x_1||\cdots||x_q$ on input a witness of φ. We require $spO(I_{\varphi,x_1||\cdots||x_q})$ not only to preserve the functionality of $I_{\varphi,x_1||\cdots||x_q}$, but also to hide all x_i, namely given $(spO(I_{\varphi,x_1||\cdots||x_q}),i)$, it is hard to recover x_i for any $i \in [q]$.

We prove that AIPO is c-self-composable for any constant c, which means that the concatenation of a sequence of AIPOs for the same point function would not reveal more information than a single AIPO for that point function. For detailed proof please refer to Sect. 3.2. Preparing with this observation, we are safe to obfuscate y bit by bit. We divide $y = y_1, y_2, \cdots, y_n$ into q blocks such that $n = q \cdot c$, and then for $i \in [q]$, $v_i = y_{(i-1)c+1}, \cdots, y_{ic}$. Then we uniformly select $x_1, \cdots, x_q \leftarrow_R \{0,1\}^{l(\lambda)}$ and compute $aux = spO(I_{\varphi,x_1||\cdots||x_q})$. For $i \in [q]$, we compute

$$F(I_{x_i,v_i}) = \big(\mathsf{AIPO}(I_{x_i}), \mathsf{AIPO}(I_{u_1}), \cdots, \mathsf{AIPO}(I_{u_c})\big),$$

where for $j \in [c]$, if $v_{i_j} = 1$ set $u_j := x_i$, otherwise randomly choose $u_j \leftarrow_R \{0,1\}^{l(\lambda)}$ ($u_j \neq x_i$). Then our public-coin diO algorithm $diO_L(I_{\varphi,y}) = (M_L, Evaluate_L)$ is defined with an obfuscation algorithm M_L and an evaluation algorithm $Evaluate_L$, where M_L and $Evaluate_L$ are described as follows. We set

$$M_L = \big(aux, F(I_{x_1,v_1}), \cdots, F(I_{x_q,v_q})\big).$$

On input (M_L, w), $Evaluate_L$ proceeds the evaluation $M_L(w)$ as follows: First evaluate $aux(w) = spO(I_{\varphi,x_1||\cdots||x_q})(w)$ and output 0 if $aux(w) = 0$; Otherwise, divide $aux(w)$ into q blocks as $aux(w) = x'_1, \cdots, x'_q$ and output

$$y = \big(F(I_{x_1,v_1})(x'_1), \cdots, F(I_{x_q,v_q})(x'_q)\big).$$

We note that it is important to show the auxiliary input aux defined above is indeed sampled from an *unpredictable distribution*. More precisely, for any $i \in [q]$ such that

$$((aux,i),x_i) = \big\{\big((spO(I_{\varphi,x_1||\cdots||x_q}),i),x_i\big) : x_1, \cdots, x_q \leftarrow_R \{0,1\}^{l(\lambda)}\big\},$$

given $aux = (spO(I_{\varphi,x_1||\cdots||x_q}),i)$ it is hard to recover x_i for any $i \in [q]$, which is guaranteed by the special-purpose obfuscation conjecture for $I_{\varphi,x_1||\cdots||x_q}$. For detailed construction please refer to Sect. 3.4.

Special-Purpose Obfuscation. The conjecture of special-purpose obfuscation is used by Garg et al. [16] to rule out the existence of *general-purpose* diO with auxiliary input. In particular, Garg et al. show that general-purpose diO cannot exist if assuming the existence of the special-purpose obfuscation for a specific circuit C with specific auxiliary input aux in a way that hides some specific information. Moreover, under the same conjecture, they show that extractable witness encryption (with auxiliary input) does not exist. As mentioned in [16], we cannot objectively tell which one of these two probably exists, general-purpose diO with auxiliary input or special-purpose obfuscation for such specific circuit. However, the special-purpose obfuscation conjecture is a falsifiable assumption in the sense that using the existing candidates constructions of obfuscation [3, 11,12,15,18,25], we do not know how to break such conjecture.

Although the special-purpose obfuscation conjecture rules out the existence of the general-purpose diO with auxiliary input, it may still be reasonable to assume that diO security can be achieved for specific classes of functions. Our result confirms that speculation and we demonstrate that the existence of public-coin diO for a class of function, called hiding-input point functions with multi-bit output, can be implied under the conjecture that special-purpose obfuscation exists.

Outline. In Sect. 2, we define the notations and building blocks that are used through the paper. In Sect. 3, we propose a public-coin differing-inputs obfuscator for the class of hiding-input point functions with multi-bit output. In Sect. 4, we show the applications of public-coin diO for hiding-input point function with multi-bit output. In Sect. 5, we make a conclusion of our work.

2   Preliminaries

2.1   Notations

Let $A(\cdot)$ be a probabilistic algorithm and let $A(x)$ be the result of running algorithm A on input x, then we use $y = A(x)$ (or $y \leftarrow A(x)$) to denote that y is set as $A(x)$. Let $A_r(x)$ be the result of running algorithm A on input x with random value r. For a finite set (distribution) $\mathcal{S}$, we use $y \in_R \mathcal{S}$ (or $y \leftarrow_R \mathcal{S}$) to denote that y is uniformly selected from $\mathcal{S}$. For any promise problem (language) $L = (L_Y, L_N)$, where L_Y is the collection of the yes instances and L_N is the collection of the no instances, and for any instance $x \in L$, we denote by $\mathcal{R}_L$ the efficiently computable binary NP relation for L. And for any witnesses w of $x \in L_Y$, $\mathcal{R}_L(x, w) = 1$. We use $[l]$ to denote the set $\{1, 2, \cdots, l\}$. We write $negl(\cdot)$ to denote an unspecified negligible function, $poly(\cdot)$ an unspecified polynomial. We denote by $a||b$ the concatenation of two bit strings a and b. We use "$X \overset{c}{\approx} Y$" to denote that probabilistic distributions X and Y are computationally indistinguishable. Unless otherwise stated, we use λ to denote the security parameter.

2.2   Obfuscation for Point Functions

In this section, we consider obfuscators for the specific class of point functions. A plain point function I_x for some value $x \in \{0, 1\}^*$ is defined as

$$I_x(s) = \begin{cases} 1, & \text{if } s = x; \\ 0, & \text{otherwise.} \end{cases}$$

In this paper, we consider a variant of point function obfuscators with auxiliary input which was introduced by Canetti [14]. Here we make use of the definition from [13]. The first definition is to formalize the unpredictable distributions where the value x of a point function is sampled from. Afterwards, we give the definition of obfuscator for point obfuscation with auxiliary input secure against such unpredictable distributions.

Definition 2.1 (Unpredictable distribution). *A distribution ensemble* $\mathcal{D} = \{\mathcal{D}_\lambda = (\mathcal{Z}_\lambda, \mathcal{X}_\lambda)\}_{\lambda \in N}$ *on pairs of strings is unpredictable if no poly-size circuit family can predict* $\mathcal{X}_\lambda$ *from* $\mathcal{Z}_\lambda$. *That is, for every poly-size circuit sequence* $\{\mathcal{C}_\lambda\}_{\lambda \in N}$ *and for all large enough* λ:

$$\Pr_{(z,x) \leftarrow_R D_\lambda}[\mathcal{C}_\lambda(z) = x] \leq negl(\lambda).$$

Definition 2.2 (Auxiliary input point obfuscation for unpredictable distributions (AIPO)). *A PPT algorithm AIPO is a point obfuscator for unpredictable distributions if on input* (z, x) *it outputs a polynomial-size circuit that returns 1 on* x *and 0 everywhere else and satisfies the following secrecy property: for any (efficiently samplable) unpredictable distribution* $\mathcal{B}_1$ *over* $\{0, 1\}^{poly(\lambda)} \times \{0, 1\}^\lambda$, *it holds for any PPT algorithm* $\mathcal{B}_2$ *that the probability of outputting true by the following experiment for* $(\mathcal{B}_1, \mathcal{B}_2)$ *is negligibly close to* $1/2$:

$$b \leftarrow_R \{0, 1\},$$
$$(z, x_0) \leftarrow_R \mathcal{B}_1(1^\lambda),$$
$$x_1 \leftarrow_R \{0, 1\}^\lambda,$$
$$p \leftarrow_R AIPO(I_{x_b}),$$
$$b' \leftarrow_R \mathcal{B}_2(1^\lambda, p, z),$$
$$return\, b = b'.$$

The probability is over the coins of adversary $(\mathcal{B}_1, \mathcal{B}_2)$, *the coins of AIPO and the choices of* x_1 *and* b.

In [8] Bitansky and Paneth revisited two constructions of AIPOs based on two different assumptions, the first of which was suggested by Canetti [14] based on a strong variant of DDH. The second AIPO construction is a modified construction of Wee's original obfuscator for point functions (non auxiliary input) [24], which is based on a new assumption that strengthens the assumption made by Wee [24] in order to deal with auxiliary inputs. For detailed AIPO constructions please refer to [8].

POINT FUNCTIONS WITH MULTI-BIT OUTPUT. While a plain point function only returns a single bit, a point function with multi-bit output (MBPF) $I_{x,y}$ for values $x, y \in \{0, 1\}^*$ returns a multi-bit string, which is formally defined as

$$I_{x,y}(s) = \begin{cases} y, \text{ if } s = x; \\ 0, \text{ otherwise.} \end{cases}$$

Similar to AIPO, Brzuska and Mittelbach [13] introduced the notion of multi-bit point function obfuscation for an unpredictable distribution, namely the MB-AIPO for MBPF $I_{x,y}$, where the distribution outputs a tuple (x, y) together with auxiliary information z, and it requires to be computationally infeasible to recover x given auxiliary information z. With respect to an MB-AIPO obfuscator, it must ensure that the obfuscation of $I_{x,y}$ is indistinguishable from an obfuscation with a changed point value y' where y' is chosen uniformly at random.

Unfortunately, due to Brzuska and Mittelbach's [13] negative result that if iO exists, then MB-AIPO for MBPF $I_{x,y}$ with auxiliary input z via an unpredictable distribution cannot exist, it is implausible to assume the existence of MB-AIPO and to build schemes relying on it. Therefore, throughout this paper, our schemes are based on the existence of AIPO (obfuscator for plain point function with auxiliary input from unpredictable distributions), which can be instantiated under different assumptions [8].

2.3   General Purpose Obfuscation

Differing-inputs obfuscation (diO) requires that the obfuscations of two efficiently generated programs C_0 and C_1 are indistinguishable if it is hard for an adversary to find an input x on which the two programs differ, namely x such that $C_0(x) \neq C_1(x)$. Since diO requires the security to be held even in the presence of an auxiliary input that is generated together with the programs, it gives rise to some negative results on the existence of diO with respect to general auxiliary inputs [6,10,16]. In order to circumvent the implausibility results coming from planting a trapdoor in the auxiliary input, Ishai, Pandey and Sahai [19] introduced the notion of *public-coin* diO, which restricts the original definition of diO by requiring the auxiliary input to be the actual random coins that were used to sample programs C_0 and C_1. Here we provide the definition of *public-coin* diO following from [19].

Definition 2.3 (Public-coin differing-inputs sampler for circuits). *An efficient non-uniform sampling algorithm $Sam = \{Sam_\lambda\}$ is called a public-coin differing-inputs sampler for the parameterized collection of circuits $\mathcal{C} = \{\mathcal{C}_\lambda\}$ if the output of Sam_λ is distributed over $\mathcal{C}_\lambda \times \mathcal{C}_\lambda$ and for every efficient non-uniform algorithm $A = \{A_\lambda\}$ there exists a negligible function $negl(\cdot)$ such that for all $\lambda \in N$:*

$$\Pr_r[C_0(x) \neq C_1(x) : (C_0, C_1) \leftarrow Sam_\lambda(r), x \leftarrow A_\lambda(r)] \leq negl(\lambda).$$

Definition 2.4 (Public-coin differing-inputs obfuscator for circuits.) *An uniform PPT algorithm diO is a public-coin differing-inputs obfuscator for the parameterized collection of circuits $\mathcal{C} = \{\mathcal{C}_\lambda\}$ if the following requirements hold:*

- *(functionality) For all security parameters $\lambda \in N$, for all $C \in \mathcal{C}_\lambda$, and for all input x we have that*

$$\Pr[C'(x) = C(x) : C' \leftarrow diO(1^\lambda, C)] = 1.$$

- (security) For every public-coin differing-inputs samplers $Sam = \{Sam_\lambda\}$, for the collection $\mathcal{C}$, every PPT distinguishing algorithm $\mathcal{T} = \{\mathcal{T}_\lambda\}$, there exists a negligible function $negl(\cdot)$ such that for all security parameters $\lambda \in N$:

$$\left| \Pr \left[\begin{array}{c} \mathcal{T}_\lambda(r, C') = 1 : (C_0, C_1) \leftarrow Sam_\lambda(r) \\ C' \leftarrow diO(1^\lambda, C_0) \end{array} \right] \right.$$

$$\left. - \Pr \left[\begin{array}{c} \mathcal{T}_\lambda(r, C') = 1 : (C_0, C_1) \leftarrow Sam_\lambda(r) \\ C' \leftarrow diO(1^\lambda, C_1) \end{array} \right] \right| \leq negl(\lambda),$$

where the probability is taken over r and the coins of diO and $\mathcal{T}_\lambda$.

3 Public-Coin Differing-Inputs Obfuscator for Hiding-Input Point Function with Multi-bit Output

In this section, we will show how to construct the public-coin differing-inputs obfuscator for a class of function, called hiding-input point functions with multi-bit output (MB-HIPF) [22]. Our construction relies on the existence of AIPO (auxiliary input point obfuscation for unpredictable distributions) which can be instantiated under different assumptions [8], and the conjecture of the existence of a special-purpose obfuscation for MB-HIPF, which has been considered as a falsifiable assumption [16]. To this end, we begin with the definition of MB-HIPF and the corresponding conjecture of special-purpose obfuscation for MB-HIPF. We show an observation that AIPO is c-self-composable for any constant c. And then we propose an unpredictable distribution. Afterwards, we give our construction of public-coin diO for MB-HIPF.

3.1 Definition of Hiding-Input Point Function with Multi-bit Output and Conjecture of Special-Purpose Obfuscation

In this subsection, we recall the definition for hiding-input point functions with multi-bit output (MB-HIPF) [22] that we intend to obfuscate. MB-HIPF is related to an instance of the hard problems of an NP language.

Let us consider the hard problems of an NP language L with corresponding NP relation $\mathcal{R}_L$. We call an instance φ a hard problem of L if there exists a hard problem sampler Sam_L such that φ is efficiently samplable by Sam_L and for any PPT algorithm A

$$\Pr[\mathcal{R}_L(\phi, w) = 1 : \phi \leftarrow Sam_L(r), w \leftarrow A(r)] < negl(\lambda),$$

where the probability is taken over r and the coins of algorithm A.

Such hard problem can be constructed essentially from any cryptographic assumption. For example, if one-way functions exists, then there exists a pseudorandom generator $G : \{0,1\}^\lambda \rightarrow \{0,1\}^{2\lambda}$. Now, we define L to be the language as

$$\begin{cases} L_Y = \{m : m \in \{0,1\}^{2\lambda}, \exists\ r \in \{0,1\}^\lambda \text{ such that } m = G(r)\} \\ L_N = \{m : m \in \{0,1\}^{2\lambda}, \nexists\ r \in \{0,1\}^\lambda \text{ such that } m = G(r)\} \end{cases}$$

then an instance φ which is a bit-string randomly sampled from $\{0,1\}^{2\lambda}$, is a hard problem of L since it is difficult to find the pre-image of φ no matter $\varphi \in L_Y$ or $\varphi \in L_N$.

A MB-HIPF $I_{\varphi,y}$ w.r.t an instance φ of the hard problems of language L, where $y \in \{0,1\}^n$, is defined as a function that outputs y on input w such that $\mathcal{R}_L(\varphi, w) = 1$ and otherwise outputs 0. We note that when there is no witness of φ satisfying the relation $\mathcal{R}_L$, $I_{\varphi,y}$ outputs 0 on all inputs.

$I_{\varphi,y}$ is called a *hiding-input* point function since it is related to a hard problem φ and given the description of function $I_{\varphi,y}$, it is hard to detect on which input point the output y will be returned, which thereby leads to the difficulty in obfuscating $I_{\varphi,y}$. Whereas given the description of a multi-bit point function $I_{x,y}$, it is obvious to know the input point x where y is returned and thus the difficulty of obfuscating $I_{x,y}$ is slightly less than obfuscating $I_{\varphi,y}$ in some sense.

Definition 3.1 (Hiding-input point function with multi-bit output (MB-HIPF)). *Let $L = (L_Y, L_N)$ be a language and $\mathcal{R}_L$ is the corresponding relation. And there exists a hard problem sampler Sam_L such that for any PPT algorithm A*

$$\Pr[\mathcal{R}_L(\phi, w) = 1 : \phi \leftarrow Sam_L(r), w \leftarrow A(r)] < negl(\lambda),$$

where the probability is taken over r and the coins of algorithm A. Let $\varphi \in L$ be a hard problem that can be efficiently samplable by Sam_L. Then, we define hiding-input point function with multi-bit output as follows:

$$I_{\varphi,y}(w) = \begin{cases} y, & if\ \mathcal{R}_L(\varphi, w) = 1 \\ 0, & otherwise \end{cases},$$

where $y \in \{0,1\}^n$ and n is a polynomial in λ.

Before presenting the conjecture of the special-purpose obfuscation spO, we first define the function that spO will work on. Let $I_{\varphi,x_1||\cdots||x_q}$ be a hiding-input point function with multi-bit output, where $x_i \in \{0,1\}^{l(\lambda)}$ are independent bit-strings and are chosen uniformly at random for each $i \in [q]$ and q is a polynomial in λ. The function $I_{\varphi,x_1||\cdots||x_q}$ outputs $x_1||\cdots||x_q$ on input a witness of φ and outputs 0 otherwise. We require $spO(I_{\varphi,x_1||\cdots||x_q})$ not only to preserve the functionality of $I_{\varphi,x_1||\cdots||x_q}$, but also to hide all x_i, namely given $(spO(I_{\varphi,x_1||\cdots||x_q}), i)$, it is difficult to recover x_i for any $i \in [q]$. We give the conjecture as follows.

Conjecture 3.1 (Special-purpose Obfuscation). *There exist a hard problem φ of a language L, and an obfuscator spO such that the functionality is preserved and the following holds. For any PPT attacker A and for all security parameter $\lambda \in N$ there is a negligible $negl(\lambda)$ such that:*

$$\Pr\left[x \in \{x_1, \cdots, x_q\} \middle| \begin{array}{l} x_1, \cdots, x_q \leftarrow_R \{0,1\}^{l(\lambda)}, \\ \tilde{I} \leftarrow spO(I_{\varphi,x_1||\cdots||x_q}), \\ x \leftarrow A(1^\lambda, \tilde{I}) \end{array}\right] \leq negl(\lambda).$$

3.2   Constant-Self-composability of AIPO

In this paper we consider the composition of point function obfuscator with a special form, namely *composition by concatenation* [20]. A special case of composability is self-composability, which captures the requirement that the concatenation of a sequence of obfuscations for the same point function would not reveal more information than a single obfuscation for that point function. The composability in [20] is referred to virtual-black-box (VBB) obfuscation for point function, while here we consider the self-composability definition of point obfuscation for unpredictable distributions with auxiliary input (AIPO). Bitansky and Canetti [7] show that VBB obfuscation for point function with auxiliary information does imply constant-self-composability (refer to Proposition A.2 in [7]). Below we will show that AIPO is c-self-composable for any constant c by using the similar proof technique as [7].

Definition 3.2 (c-self-composable AIPO (adapted from [20]). *A PPT algorithm O is a c-self-composable point obfuscator for unpredictable distributions if on input (z, x) it outputs a polynomial-size circuit that returns 1 on x and 0 everywhere else and satisfies the following secrecy property: for any unpredictable distribution $\mathcal{D} = \{\mathcal{D}_\lambda = (\mathcal{Z}_\lambda, \mathcal{X}_\lambda)\}_{\lambda \in N}$ over $\{0,1\}^{poly(\lambda)} \times \{0,1\}^\lambda$ it holds that:*

$$\{z, O_{r_1}(I_x), \dots, O_{r_c}(I_x) : (z, x) \leftarrow \mathcal{D}_\lambda\}_{\lambda \in N} \overset{c}{\approx}$$
$$\{z, O_{r_1}(I_{u_1}), \dots, O_{r_c}(I_{u_c}) : z \leftarrow \mathcal{Z}_\lambda, u_i \leftarrow_R \{0,1\}^\lambda \text{ for } \forall\, i \in [c]\}_{\lambda \in N}.$$

Claim 3.1 *Any auxiliary input point obfuscation for unpredictable distributions as Definition 2.2 is c-self-composable for any constant c.*

Proof. For simplicity, we start with the case $c = 2$. Let O be an point obfuscator with auxiliary input for unpredictable distributions, and let A be a binary poly-size adversary and p a polynomial. For any (efficiently samplable) unpredictable distribution $\mathcal{D}_1 = (\mathcal{Z}_1, \mathcal{X}_\lambda)$ over $\{0,1\}^{poly(\lambda)} \times \{0,1\}^{l(\lambda)}$, and for any $(z, x) \in_R \mathcal{D}_1$, we set

$$\mathcal{D}_2 = (\mathcal{Z}_2, \mathcal{X}_\lambda) = \{((O_s(I_x), z), x) : (z, x) \in \mathcal{D}_1, s \in_R \{0,1\}^{poly(\lambda)}\}.$$

Here $O_s(I_x)$ is the result of running algorithm O on input I_x with randomness s.

By the property of point obfuscation with auxiliary input, no poly-size circuit family can predict $\mathcal{X}_\lambda$ from $\mathcal{Z}_2$. Then $\mathcal{D}_2$ is a new unpredictable distribution.

Thus, by the property of point obfuscation with auxiliary input in Definition 2.2, we have that for any $(z, x) \in_R \mathcal{D}_1$ and every $x' \in_R \{0,1\}^\lambda$:

$$\left| \Pr_{A, r, s}[A(O_r(I_x), O_s(I_x), z) = 1] - \Pr_{A, r', s}[A(O_{r'}(I_{x'}), O_s(I_x), z) = 1] \right| \leq 1/2p(\lambda)$$

where we treated the second obfuscation as auxiliary input.

Now we can consider another unpredictable distribution

$$\mathcal{D}_3 = (\mathcal{Z}_3, \mathcal{X}_\lambda) = \left\{ \begin{array}{l} ((O_{r'}(I_{x'}), z), x) : (z, x) \in \mathcal{D}_1, \\ \qquad\qquad x' \in_R \{0,1\}^{l(\lambda)}, \\ \qquad\qquad r' \in_R \{0,1\}^{poly(\lambda)} \end{array} \right\}.$$

Hence, for any $(z, x) \in_R \mathcal{D}_1$, $x', x'' \in_R \{0,1\}^{l(\lambda)}$, and $s' \in_R \{0,1\}^{poly(\lambda)}$, we have that:

$$\left| \Pr_{A, r', s}[A(O_s(I_x), O_{r'}(I_{x'}), z) = 1] - \Pr_{A, r', s'}[A(O_{s'}(I_{x''}), O_{r'}(I_{x'}), z) = 1] \right| \le 1/2p(\lambda)$$

where we regard the obfuscation $O_{r'}(I_{x'})$ as auxiliary input, $((O_{r'}(I_{x'}), z), x) \in_R \mathcal{D}_3$, and $O_{s'}(I_{x''})$ is the result of running AIPO algorithm O on input $I_{x''}$ with randomness s'.

Therefore, for any $(z, x) \in_R \mathcal{D}_1$, $x', x'' \in_R \{0,1\}^{l(\lambda)}$, and $r, r', s, s' \in_R \{0,1\}^{poly(\lambda)}$, we have that:

$$\left| \Pr_{A, r, s}[A(O_r(I_x), O_s(I_x), z) = 1] - \Pr_{A, r', s'}[A(O_{r'}(I_{x'}), O_{s'}(I_{x''}), z) = 1] \right| \le 1/p(\lambda),$$

where the probability is taken over the coins of A and O.

Thus we have that AIPO is 2-self-composable.

The result follows for $c = 2$.   □

3.3 An Unpredictable Distribution

Given a MB-HIPF $I_{\varphi, y}$ ($y \in \{0,1\}^n$) w.r.t a hard problem φ of a language L, we choose a constant c and divide $y = y_1, y_2, \cdots, y_n$ into $q = q(\lambda)$ blocks such that $n = q \cdot c$. Now we present a sequence of unpredictable distributions $\mathcal{D}^i$ over $\{0,1\}^{poly(\lambda)} \times \{0,1\}^{l(\lambda)}$. Let spO be any special-purpose obfuscation of MB-HIPF $I_{\varphi, x_1 || \cdots || x_q}$, where $x_1, \cdots, x_q \in \{0,1\}^{l(\lambda)}$. We make a conclusion that the following distribution

$$\mathcal{D}^i = (\mathcal{Z}_\lambda, \mathcal{X}_\lambda) = \left\{ \left((spO_r(I_{\varphi, x_1 || \cdots || x_q}), i), x_i \right) : \begin{array}{l} x_1, \cdots, x_q \leftarrow_R \{0,1\}^{l(\lambda)}, \\ r \leftarrow_R \{0,1\}^{poly(\lambda)} \end{array} \right\} \quad (1)$$

is unpredictable, where $spO_r(I_{\varphi, x_1 || \cdots || x_q})$ is the result of running algorithm spO on input $I_{\varphi, x_1 || \cdots || x_q}$ with randomness r. This is directly follows from the security of the conjectured special-purpose obfuscation of MB-HIPF $I_{\varphi, x_1 || \cdots || x_q}$.

3.4 Construction of Public-Coin DiO for Hiding-Input Point Function with Multi-bit Output

Let O be an AIPO, *i.e.*, a point obfuscator with auxiliary input for unpredictable distributions, and spO be a special-purpose obfuscation of MB-HIPF $I_{\varphi, x_1 || \cdots || x_q}$ as conjectured in Subsect. 3.1.

Given a MB-HIPF $I_{\varphi,y}$ ($y \in \{0,1\}^n$) w.r.t a hard problem φ of a language L, we choose a constant c and divide $y = y_1, y_2, \cdots, y_n$ into $q = q(\lambda)$ blocks such that $n = q \cdot c$. And then we randomly choose $x_1, \cdots, x_q \in \{0,1\}^{l(\lambda)}$ and compute an auxiliary input as $aux = spO(I_{\varphi,x_1||\cdots||x_q})$. Define the distribution $((aux, i), x_i) \in \mathcal{D}^i$ as in Eq. 1. Following from the result in Sect. 3.3, we have that for all $i \in [q]$ $((aux, i), x_i)$ is an unpredictable distribution.

Let m be a bit string with length c and denote it as $m = m_1, \cdots, m_c$, we define a function F that takes as input a point function with multi-bit output, namely $I_{x_i,m}$ where $x_i \in \{0,1\}^{l(\lambda)}$ and $m \in \{0,1\}^c$, and outputs $c + 1$ AIPOs either for point function I_{x_i} or for I_{u_i}. More precisely, $F(I_{x_i,m})$ is defined as follows:

$$F(I_{x_i,m}) = \big(O(I_{x_i}), O(I_{u_1}), \cdots, O(I_{u_c})\big),$$

where I_{x_i} and I_{u_j} (for $j \in [c]$) are point functions, and for $j \in [c]$, $u_j := x_i$ if $m_j = 1$, otherwise randomly choose $u_j \leftarrow_R \{0,1\}^{l(\lambda)}$ ($u_j \neq x_i$). On any input $s \in \{0,1\}^{l(\lambda)}$, the function $F(I_{x_i,m})(s)$ first checks whether $O(I_{x_i})(s) = 1$, if it is true, outputs $\big(O(I_{u_1})(s), \cdots, O(I_{u_c})(s)\big)$; otherwise, it outputs 0.

Due to the constant-self-composability of the AIPO scheme O for unpredictable distribution $\mathcal{D}^i$, namely the $(c + 1)$-self-composability of O, we have that for any $((aux, i), x_i) \in \mathcal{D}^i$ and for any $m, m' \in \{0,1\}^c$ it holds

$$\big((aux, i), O(I_{x_i,m})\big) \; c \approx \big((aux, i), O(I_{x_i,m'})\big).$$

Based on above definitions, we propose our public-coin diO scheme for $I_{\varphi,y}$ as $diO_L(I_{\varphi,y}) = (M_L, Evaluate_L)$ where algorithms $(M_L, Evaluate_L)$ are defined as follows. We first divide $y = y_1, y_2, \cdots, y_n$ into q blocks such that $n = q \cdot c$. Let

$$v_i = y_{(i-1)c+1}, \cdots, y_{ic}, \text{ for } i = 1, \cdots, q,$$

M_L is defined as

$$M_L = \big(aux, F(I_{x_1,v_1}), \cdots, F(I_{x_q,v_q})\big).$$

On input (M_L, w), the evaluation algorithm $Evaluate_L$ first evaluates $aux(w) = spO(I_{\varphi,x_1||\cdots||x_q})(w)$ and outputs 0 if $aux(w) = 0$. Otherwise, it divides the output $aux(w)$ into q blocks as $aux(w) = x'_1, \cdots, x'_q$ and outputs

$$y = \big(F(I_{x_1,v_1})(x'_1), \cdots, F(I_{x_q,v_q})(x'_q)\big).$$

Our construction for $diO_L(I_{\varphi,y})$ is depicted in Fig. 1.

Theorem 3.1. *Assuming O be a point obfuscator with auxiliary input for unpredictable distributions, and spO be the conjectured special-purpose obfuscation, then the construction in Fig. 1 is a public-coin differing-inputs obfuscator for the class of hiding-input point functions with multi-bit output.*

Proof. It is obvious that the construction in Fig. 1 is a PPT algorithm and it keeps the functionality from $I_{\varphi,y}$, which can be seen from the evaluation algorithm.

Given a MB-HIPF $I_{\varphi,y}$ ($y \in \{0,1\}^n$) w.r.t a hard problem φ of a language L, $diO_L(I_{\varphi,y})$ proceeds as follows:

1. choose a constant c and divide $y = y_1, y_2, \cdots, y_n$ into $q = q(\lambda)$ blocks such that $n = q \cdot c$, and for $i \in [q]$, $v_i = y_{(i-1)c+1}, \cdots, y_{ic}$.
2. Uniformly select $x_1, \cdots, x_q \leftarrow_R \{0,1\}^{l(\lambda)}$.
3. Compute $aux = spO(I_{\varphi, x_1 || \cdots || x_q})$.
4. For $i \in [q]$, compute $F(I_{x_i, v_i}) = \big(O(I_{x_i}), O(I_{u_1}), \cdots, O(I_{u_c}) \big)$, where for $j \in [c]$, if $v_{i_j} = 1$ set $u_j := x_i$, otherwise randomly choose $u_j \leftarrow_R \{0,1\}^{l(\lambda)}$ ($u_j \neq x_i$).
5. Set
$$M_L = \big(aux, F(I_{x_1, v_1}), \cdots, F(I_{x_q, v_q}) \big).$$
6. $Evaluate_L(M_L, w)$ performs as follows: First evaluate
$$aux(w) = spO(I_{\varphi, x_1 || \cdots || x_q})(w)$$
and output 0 if $aux(w) = 0$.
Otherwise, divide $aux(w)$ into q blocks as $aux(w) = x'_1, \cdots, x'_q$ and output
$$y = \big(F(I_{x_1, v_1})(x'_1), \cdots, F(I_{x_q, v_q})(x'_q) \big).$$
7. Output $diO_L(I_{\varphi,y}) = (M_L, Evaluate_L)$.

Fig. 1. Construction of public-coin diO for MB-HIPF $I_{\varphi,y}$.

Fix any public-coin differing-inputs sampler $Sam = \{Sam_\lambda\}$ for the class of multi-bit hiding-input point functions $\mathcal{C} = \{\mathcal{C}_{\varphi,\lambda} = \{I_{\varphi,y}\}_{y \in \{0,1\}^{n(\lambda)}}\}_{\varphi,\lambda}$, where φ is a hard problem that can be efficiently samplable from the distribution of the hard problems of language $L = (L_Y, L_N)$ (see Definition 3.1). We need to prove that for any PPT distinguishing algorithm $\mathcal{A} = \{\mathcal{A}_\lambda\}$, there exists a negligible function $negl(\cdot)$ such that for all security parameters $\lambda \in N$:

$$\left| \Pr \left[\begin{array}{c} \mathcal{A}_\lambda(r, \widetilde{I}) = 1 : (I_{\varphi,y}, I_{\varphi,y'}) \leftarrow Sam_\lambda(r) \\ \widetilde{I} \leftarrow diO_L(1^\lambda, I_{\varphi,y}) \end{array} \right] \right.$$

$$\left. - \Pr \left[\begin{array}{c} \mathcal{A}_\lambda(r, \widetilde{I}) = 1 : (I_{\varphi,y}, I_{\varphi,y'}) \leftarrow Sam_\lambda(r) \\ \widetilde{I} \leftarrow diO_L(1^\lambda, I_{\varphi,y'}) \end{array} \right] \right| \leq negl(\lambda),$$

where the probability is taken over r and the coins of diO_L and $\mathcal{A}_\lambda$.

That is to prove that for any sampled hard problem φ, and for any $y, y' \in \{0,1\}^n$:
$$\{diO_L(I_{\varphi,y})\} \, c = \{diO_L(I_{\varphi,y'})\}.$$

Let $v_i = y_{(i-1)c+1}, \cdots, y_{ic}$ and $v'_i = y'_{(i-1)c+1}, \cdots, y'_{ic}$ for $i \in [q]$. Since the description of the evaluation algorithm is deterministic, for convenience, we do not write it in the obfuscation results in the following proof. For every $x_1, \cdots, x_q \in_R \{0,1\}^{l(\lambda)}$, let $aux = spO(I_{\varphi, x_1 || \cdots || x_q})$, consider the following sequence of hybrid distributions. For $k \in \{0, 1, \cdots, q\}$, we define H_q^k as follows:

$$H_q^k := \left\{ \left(aux, F(I_{x_1, v_1'}), \cdots, F(I_{x_k, v_k'}), F(I_{x_{k+1}, v_{k+1}}), \cdots, F(I_{x_q, v_q}) \right) \right\}.$$

Then we can see that H_q^0 is the distribution $\left\{ diO_L(I_{\varphi, y}) \right\}_{x_1, \cdots, x_q}$ and H_q^q is the distribution $\left\{ diO_L(I_{\varphi, y'}) \right\}_{x_1, \cdots, x_q}$.

To prove that $\left\{ diO_L(I_{\varphi, y}) \right\} \overset{c}{=} \left\{ diO_L(I_{\varphi, y'}) \right\}$, we first need to prove that for every $x_1, \cdots, x_q \in_R \{0,1\}^{l(\lambda)}$,

$$\left\{ diO_L(I_{\varphi, y}) \right\}_{x_1, \cdots, x_q} \overset{c}{=} \left\{ diO_L(I_{\varphi, y'}) \right\}_{x_1, \cdots, x_q},$$

which is to prove $H_q^0 \overset{c}{=} H_q^q$. And thus we need to prove that $H_q^k \overset{c}{=} H_q^{k+1}$ for every $k \in \{0, 1, \cdots, q - 1\}$. Since $x_1, \cdots, x_q$ are independent, the q obfuscations are independent. Therefore, the indistinguishability between H_q^k and H_q^{k+1} follows from the indistinguishability between the distributions: $\left\{ \left(spO(I_{\varphi, x_1 || \cdots || x_q}), O(I_{x_{k+1}, v_{k+1}}) \right) \right\}$ and $\left\{ \left(spO(I_{\varphi, x_1 || \cdots || x_q}), O(I_{x_{k+1}, v_{k+1}'}) \right) \right\}$.

Since $\left\{ diO_L(I_{\varphi, y}) \right\} = \cup_{x_1, \cdots, x_q \in \{0,1\}^{l(\lambda)}} \left\{ diO_L(I_{\varphi, y}) \right\}_{x_1, \cdots, x_q}$, then we can see that for any $\widetilde{I} \in \left\{ diO_L(I_{\varphi, y}) \right\}$, there would be some $x_1, \cdots, x_q \in \{0,1\}^{l(\lambda)}$ such that $\widetilde{I} \in \left\{ diO_L(I_{\varphi, y}) \right\}_{x_1, \cdots, x_q}$. Then no PPT algorithm can distinguish that $\widetilde{I}$ is an obfuscation of $I_{\varphi, y}$ or $I_{\varphi, y'}$. If there is a PPT algorithm A that can distinguish between $\left\{ diO_L(I_{\varphi, y}) \right\}$ and $\left\{ diO_L(I_{\varphi, y'}) \right\}$, there would be a PPT algorithm B that can distinguish between $\left\{ diO_L(I_{\varphi, y}) \right\}_{x_1, \cdots, x_q}$ and $\left\{ diO_L(I_{\varphi, y'}) \right\}_{x_1, \cdots, x_q}$. Upon receiving a circuit pair $(I_{\varphi, y}, I_{\varphi, y'})$ from A, B delivers it to the challenger. Upon receiving a challenge obfuscation $\widetilde{I}$ from the challenger, B delivers $\widetilde{I}$ to A and outputs what A outputs. Then B can invokes A to break the indistinguishability between $\left\{ diO_L(I_{\varphi, y}) \right\}_{x_1, \cdots, x_q}$ and $\left\{ diO_L(I_{\varphi, y'}) \right\}_{x_1, \cdots, x_q}$, which makes a contradiction with the result proved above.

This completes the proof.   □

4   Applications

In this section, we show that together with weak auxiliary input multi-bit output point obfuscation for unpredictable distributions (AIMPO)[21], the public-coin diO for MB-HIPF can be used to construct witness encryption schemes with unique decryption [22] and two-round statistical witness indistinguishable arguments. Before showing the applications we first provide some basic definitions.

Definition 4.1 Unpredictable distribution [8]. *A distribution ensemble $D = \{D_n = (Z_n, M_n, R_n)\}_{n \in N}$ on triple of strings is unpredictable if no poly-size circuit family can predict M_n from Z_n. That is, for every poly-size circuit sequence $\{C_n\}_{n \in N}$ and for all large enough n: $\Pr_{(z,m,r) \leftarrow_R D_n}[C_n(z) = m] \leq negl(n)$.*

Definition 4.2 Weak auxiliary input multi-bit output point obfuscation for unpredictable distributions [21]. *A PPT algorithm $\mathcal{MO}$ is a weak auxiliary input multi-bit output point obfuscator of the circuit class $\mathcal{C} = \{\mathcal{C}_n = \{I_{m,r} | m \in \{0,1\}^n, r \in \{0,1\}^{poly(n)}\}\}$ for unpredictable distributions if it satisfies:*

- *(functionality) For any $n \in N$, any $I_{m,r} \in \mathcal{C}_n$, and any input $x \neq m$, it holds that $\mathcal{MO}(I_{m,r})(x) = I_{m,r}(x)$ and $\Pr[\mathcal{MO}(I_{m,r})(m) \neq r] \leq negl(n)$, where the probability is taken over the randomness of $\mathcal{MO}$.*
- *(polynomial slowdown) For any $n \in N$, $I_{m,r} \in \mathcal{C}_n$, $|\mathcal{MO}(I_{m,r})| \leq poly(|I_{m,r}|)$.*
- *(secrecy) For any unpredictable distribution $D = \{D_n = (Z_n, M_n, R_n)\}_{n \in N}$ over $\{0,1\}^{poly(n)} \times \{0,1\}^n \times \{0,1\}^{poly(n)}$, it holds that for any PPT algorithm A:*

$$\Pr_{(z,m,r) \leftarrow_R D_n}[A(1^n, z, \mathcal{MO}(I_{m,r})) = m] \leq negl(n).$$

Definition 4.3 Witness encryption with unique decryption [21]. *A witness encryption scheme with unique decryption for a language L with corresponding relation $\mathcal{R}_L$ consists of the following two polynomial-time algorithms:*

- **Encryption.** *The algorithm $Encrypt(1^n, x, m)$ takes as input a security parameter 1^n, an unbounded-length string x, and a message $m \in M$ for some message space M, and outputs a ciphertext CT.*
- **Decryption.** *The algorithm $Decrypt(CT, w)$ takes as input a ciphertext CT and an unbounded-length string w, and outputs a message m or the symbol $\perp$.*

These algorithms satisfy the following three conditions:

- **Correctness.** *For any security parameter n, for any $m \in M$, and for any $x \in L$ such that $\mathcal{R}_L(x, w)$ holds, there exists a negligible function $negl(\cdot)$, such that:*

$$\Pr[Decrypt(Encrypt(1^n, x, m), w) = m] \geq 1 - negl(n).$$

- **Soundness Security.** *For any $x \notin L$, for any PPT adversary A and messages $m_0, m_1 \in M$, there exists a negligible function $negl(\cdot)$, such that:*

$$\left| \Pr[A(Encrypt(1^n, x, m_0)) = 1] - \Pr[A(Encrypt(1^n, x, m_1)) = 1] \right| < negl(n).$$

- **Unique Decryption.** *If w_1, w_2 satisfies $(x, w_1) \in \mathcal{R}_L, (x, w_2) \in \mathcal{R}_L$, then for any (possibly invalid) ciphertext CT,*

$$Decrypt(CT, w_1) = Decrypt(CT, w_2).$$

Definition 4.4 Interactive Proof System. *A pair of interactive Turing machines $\langle P, V \rangle$ is called an interactive proof system for a language L if machine V is polynomial-time and the following two conditions hold:*

- *Completeness: There exists a negligible function c such that for every $x \in L$,*

$$\Pr[\langle P, V \rangle(x) = 1] > 1 - c(|x|)$$

- *Soundness: There exists a negligible function s such that for every $x \notin L$ and every interactive machine B, it holds that*

$$\Pr[\langle B, V \rangle(x) = 1] < s(|x|)$$

$c(\cdot)$ *is called the completeness error, and* $s(\cdot)$ *the soundness error.*

If the soundness condition holds against computationally bounded provers, $\langle P, V \rangle$ is an interactive argument system. Let $View_V \langle P(x, w), V(x) \rangle$ denote the view of V in the execution of the protocol with P having witness w for $x \in L$.

Definition 4.5 *Statistical Witness Indistinguishability. An interactive argument $\langle P, V \rangle$ for a language L is said to be statistical witness-indistinguishable if for every unbounded verifier V^*, every polynomially bounded function $l = l(n) \leq poly(n)$, and every $(x_l, w_{1,l}, w_{2,l})$ such that $(x_l, w_{1,l}) \in \mathcal{R}_L$ and $(x_l, w_{2,l}) \in \mathcal{R}_L$ and $|x_l| = l$, the following two ensembles are statistically indistinguishable:*

$$\{View_{V^*} \langle P(x_l, w_{1,l}), V^*(x_l) \rangle\} \text{ and } \{View_{V^*} \langle P(x_l, w_{2,l}), V^*(x_l) \rangle\}.$$

4.1 Witness Encryption Schemes

In a witness encryption scheme [17], the encryption algorithm takes as input a particular problem instance x along with a message m and produces a ciphertext CT. Any user with knowledge of a witness w for $x \in L$ according to the witness relation $\mathcal{R}_L$ is able to decrypt the ciphertext CT and recover m. The unique decryption property of witness encryption, introduced in [21], guarantees that any (possibly *invalid*) ciphertext CT only can be decrypted to a unique message even if decrypting it with different witnesses for $x \in L$. We recall the construction of witness encryption schemes with unique decryption based on public-coin diO for MB-HIPF and weak AIMPO in [22]. Let L be any NP language and let instance φ be any hard problem of L that can be efficiently samplable without knowing any witness for $\varphi \in L$. Then with a public-coin diO algorithm $\mathcal{O}$ for the function families $\{I_{\varphi,y}\}_{y \in \{0,1\}^n}$, and a weak AIMPO algorithm $\mathcal{MO}$, the construction is as follows.

Construction 4.1 Witness encryption scheme with unique decryption for L.

- **Encrypt** $(1^n, x, \cdot, \cdot)$: On input a message $m \in \{0,1\}^n$, it chooses random values $r_d \in \{0,1\}^{poly(n)}$ and $r_e \in \{0,1\}^{poly(n)}$. Then it encrypts m as

$$CT = Encrypt(1^n, x, m, (r_d, r_e)) = \mathcal{O}(I_{x,m}; r_d), \mathcal{MO}(I_{m,r_d}; r_e) = CT_0, CT_1$$

where $I_{x,m}$ outputs m on input a witness w for $x \in L$ and outputs 0 otherwise, and I_{m,r_d} outputs r_d on input a m and outputs 0 otherwise.
- **Decrypt** $(1^n, \cdot, (x, w))$: On input a ciphertext CT, it parses $CT = CT_0, CT_1$, and runs CT_0 on w. If $CT_0(w) = m' \neq 0$, it runs CT_1 on m' and sets $r_d' = CT_1(m')$. Then it computes $CT_0' = \mathcal{O}(I_{\varphi,m'}; r_d')$. If $CT_0' = CT_0$, it outputs m', otherwise it outputs the symbol $\perp$.

4.2 Two-Round Statistical Witness Indistinguishable Argument

In this subsection, we start with presenting our two-round argument and then show its statistical witness indistinguishability. Let L be any language with relation $\mathcal{R}_L$. Let $\mathcal{O}$ be a public-coin diO algorithm for the MB-HIPF family $\{I_{\varphi,y}\}_{y\in\{0,1\}^n}$, where $I_{\varphi,y}$ outputs y on input a witness w for $\varphi \in L$ and outputs 0 otherwise, and φ is a hard problem that can be efficiently samplable from the distribution of the hard problems of language L and thus any PPT algorithm can find a witness for $\varphi \in L$ with at most negligible probability. Let $\mathcal{MO}$ be a weak AIMPO algorithm. Then for any instance $x \in L$ with at least two witnesses, our protocol is described as follows.

The two-round argument system $\langle P(w), V\rangle(x)$ first let the verifier encrypt a random message $m \in \{0,1\}^n$ as $CT = (\mathcal{O}(I_{x,m}; r_1), \mathcal{MO}(I_{m,r_1}; r_2) = (CT_1, CT_2)$ with randomness r_1 and r_2, where the MB-HIPF $I_{x,m}$ outputs m on input a witness w for $x \in L$ and outputs 0 otherwise, and the point function I_{m,r_1} outputs r_1 on input the message m and outputs 0 otherwise. This encryption algorithm is the encryption algorithm of the WE scheme with unique decryption property constructed in [22]. Upon receiving the ciphertext CT from the verifier, the prover decrypts CT with the witness w for $x \in L$ using the decryption algorithm of the specified WE scheme. The prover parses the ciphertext $CT = (CT_1, CT_2)$, runs CT_1 on the witness w to obtain $m' = CT_1(w)$, runs CT_2 on m' to obtain $r_1' = CT_2(m')$, and computes $CT_1' = \mathcal{O}(I_{x,m'}; r_1')$. If $CT_1' \neq CT_1$, the decryption fails and the prover aborts, otherwise the prover decrypts CT to the message m' and sends m', the verifier accepts $x \in L$ if and only if $m' = m$. The detail of our two-round argument protocol is shown in Fig. 2.

Theorem 4.1 *Assuming that there are public-coin differing-inputs obfuscation algorithms for the function family $\{I_{\varphi,y}\}_{y\in\{0,1\}^n}$, where φ is a variable of the hard problems for L. Additionally assuming the existence of weak AIMPO. Then, the construction in Fig. 2 is a statistical witness indistinguishable argument protocol.*

Proof **Completeness and soundness.** The correctness follows from the functionalities of the public-coin diO algorithm $\mathcal{O}$ and the weak AIMPO algorithm $\mathcal{MO}$. The soundness follows from the security of $\mathcal{O}$ and the secrecy of $\mathcal{MO}$. For any instance $x \notin L$, we show the distribution $D = \{D_n = (Z_n, M_n, R_n)\}_{n\in N}$. We set the distributions $M_n = \{0,1\}^n$, $R_n = \{0,1\}^{poly(n)}$, and $Z_n = \{\mathcal{O}(I_{x,m}; r_1) : m \in M_n, r_1 \in R_n\}$. From the security of $\mathcal{O}$, any PPT algorithm can obtain m from $z = \mathcal{O}(I_{x,m}; r_1)$ with at most negligible probability, then the distribution D is an unpredictable distribution. Now from the secrecy of $\mathcal{MO}$, any PPT algorithm can obtain m from $z = \mathcal{O}(I_{x,m}; r_1)$ and $\mathcal{MO}(I_{m,r_1})$ with at most negligible probability. This guarantees the soundness.

Statistical Witness Indistinguishability. Let w_1, w_2 denote two witnesses such that $(x, w_1) \in \mathcal{R}_L$ and $(x, w_2) \in \mathcal{R}_L$. Then we have that for any (possibly invalid) ciphertext $CT = (CT_1, CT_2)$, if the decryption of CT with w_1 is a

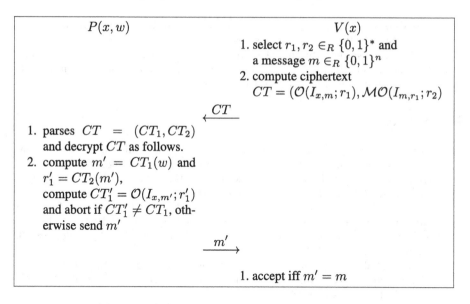

Fig. 2. Two-round argument protocol

message m, then we have $r_1 = CT_2(m)$ and $CT_1 = \mathcal{O}(I_{x,m}; r_1)$. Then form the functionalities of $\mathcal{O}$ and $\mathcal{MO}$, we have $CT_1(w_2) = m$ and $CT_2(m) = r_1$, and thus we have that the decryption of CT with w_2 is the same message m; if the decryption of CT with w_1 is the symbol $\bot$, then it is oblivious that the decryption of CT with w_2 is also the symbol $\bot$. Therefore, the proofs computed for any statement x (with at least two witnesses) using different witnesses are the same except with negligible probability. This guarantees the statistical witness indistinguishability.   □

Remark 1. Combining the Barak's three-round generation protocol [2] with our witness indistinguishable argument, we can obtain a four-round zero-knowledge argument protocol, which has been shown in [22]. The proof follows from the properties of the public-coin diO algorithm $\mathcal{O}$ and the weak AIMPO algorithm $\mathcal{MO}$.

5   Conclusion

In this paper, we construct a public-coin differing-inputs obfuscator for the class of hiding-input point functions with multi-bit output (MB-HIPF) with special-purpose obfuscation for MB-HIPF and AIPO. Besides, we show that together with weak auxiliary input multi-bit output point obfuscation for unpredictable distributions, the public-coin diO for MB-HIPF can be used to construct witness encryption schemes with strong securities [22] and two-round statistical witness indistinguishable arguments. We leave it an open question that whether a public-coin differing-inputs obfuscator for this special function class can be achieved based on some weaker assumptions.

Acknowledgement. This work is supported by National Key R&D Program of China (No. 2017YFB0802500). This work is also partially supported by the Swedish Research Council (Vetenskapsrådet) through the grant PRECIS (621-2014-4845), the National Nature Science Foundation of China (No. 61972124), and the Zhejiang Provincial Natural Science Foundation of China (No. LY19F020019).

References

1. Ananth, P., Boneh, D., Garg, S., Sahai, A., Zhandry, M.: Differing-inputs obfuscation and applications. IACR Cryptology ePrint Archive 2013/689 (2013)
2. Barak, B.: How to go beyond the black-box simulation barrier. In: IEEE Symposium on Foundations of Computer Science (2001)
3. Barak, B., Garg, S., Kalai, Y.T., Paneth, O., Sahai, A.: Protecting obfuscation against algebraic attacks. In: Nguyen, P.Q., Oswald, E. (eds.) EUROCRYPT 2014. LNCS, vol. 8441, pp. 221–238. Springer, Heidelberg (2014). https://doi.org/10.1007/978-3-642-55220-5_13
4. Barak, B., et al.: On the (im)possibility of obfuscating programs. In: Kilian, J. (ed.) CRYPTO 2001. LNCS, vol. 2139, pp. 1–18. Springer, Heidelberg (2001). https://doi.org/10.1007/3-540-44647-8_1
5. Barak, B., et al.: On the (im)possibility of obfuscating programs. J. ACM (JACM) **59**(2), 6 (2012)
6. Bellare, M., Stepanovs, I., Waters, B.: New negative results on differing-inputs obfuscation. In: Fischlin, M., Coron, J.-S. (eds.) EUROCRYPT 2016. LNCS, vol. 9666, pp. 792–821. Springer, Heidelberg (2016). https://doi.org/10.1007/978-3-662-49896-5_28
7. Bitansky, N., Canetti, R.: On strong simulation and composable point obfuscation. J. Cryptol. **27**(2), 317–357 (2014)
8. Bitansky, N., Paneth, O.: Point obfuscation and 3-round zero-knowledge. In: Cramer, R. (ed.) TCC 2012. LNCS, vol. 7194, pp. 190–208. Springer, Heidelberg (2012). https://doi.org/10.1007/978-3-642-28914-9_11
9. Boyle, E., Chung, K.-M., Pass, R.: On extractability obfuscation. In: Lindell, Y. (ed.) TCC 2014. LNCS, vol. 8349, pp. 52–73. Springer, Heidelberg (2014). https://doi.org/10.1007/978-3-642-54242-8_3
10. Boyle, E., Pass, R.: Limits of extractability assumptions with distributional auxiliary input. In: Iwata, T., Cheon, J.H. (eds.) ASIACRYPT 2015. LNCS, vol. 9453, pp. 236–261. Springer, Heidelberg (2015). https://doi.org/10.1007/978-3-662-48800-3_10
11. Brakerski, Z., Dagmi, O.: Shorter circuit obfuscation in challenging security models. In: Zikas, V., De Prisco, R. (eds.) SCN 2016. LNCS, vol. 9841, pp. 551–570. Springer, Cham (2016). https://doi.org/10.1007/978-3-319-44618-9_29
12. Brakerski, Z., Rothblum, G.N.: Virtual black-box obfuscation for all circuits via generic graded encoding. In: Lindell, Y. (ed.) TCC 2014. LNCS, vol. 8349, pp. 1–25. Springer, Heidelberg (2014). https://doi.org/10.1007/978-3-642-54242-8_1
13. Brzuska, C., Mittelbach, A.: Indistinguishability obfuscation versus multi-bit point obfuscation with auxiliary input. In: Sarkar, P., Iwata, T. (eds.) ASIACRYPT 2014. LNCS, vol. 8874, pp. 142–161. Springer, Heidelberg (2014). https://doi.org/10.1007/978-3-662-45608-8_8
14. Canetti, R.: Towards realizing random oracles: hash functions that hide all partial information. In: Kaliski, B.S. (ed.) CRYPTO 1997. LNCS, vol. 1294, pp. 455–469. Springer, Heidelberg (1997). https://doi.org/10.1007/BFb0052255

15. Garg, S., Gentry, C., Halevi, S., Raykova, M., Waters, B.: Candidate indistinguishability obfuscation and functional encryption for all circuits. In: IEEE Symposium on Foundations of Computer Science (2013)
16. Garg, S., Gentry, C., Halevi, S., Wichs, D.: On the implausibility of differing-inputs obfuscation and extractable witness encryption with auxiliary input. In: Garay, J.A., Gennaro, R. (eds.) CRYPTO 2014. LNCS, vol. 8616, pp. 518–535. Springer, Heidelberg (2014). https://doi.org/10.1007/978-3-662-44371-2_29
17. Garg, S., Gentry, C., Sahai, A., Waters, B.: Witness encryption and its applications. In: ACM Symposium on Theory of Computing (2013)
18. Garg, S., Miles, E., Mukherjee, P., Sahai, A., Srinivasan, A., Zhandry, M.: Secure obfuscation in a weak multilinear map model. In: Hirt, M., Smith, A. (eds.) TCC 2016. LNCS, vol. 9986, pp. 241–268. Springer, Heidelberg (2016). https://doi.org/10.1007/978-3-662-53644-5_10
19. Ishai, Y., Pandey, O., Sahai, A.: Public-coin differing-inputs obfuscation and its applications. In: Dodis, Y., Nielsen, J.B. (eds.) TCC 2015. LNCS, vol. 9015, pp. 668–697. Springer, Heidelberg (2015). https://doi.org/10.1007/978-3-662-46497-7_26
20. Lynn, B., Prabhakaran, M., Sahai, A.: Positive results and techniques for obfuscation. In: Cachin, C., Camenisch, J.L. (eds.) EUROCRYPT 2004. LNCS, vol. 3027, pp. 20–39. Springer, Heidelberg (2004). https://doi.org/10.1007/978-3-540-24676-3_2
21. Niu, Q., Li, H., Huang, G., Liang, B., Tang, F.: One-round witness indistinguishability from indistinguishability obfuscation. In: Lopez, J., Wu, Y. (eds.) ISPEC 2015. LNCS, vol. 9065, pp. 559–574. Springer, Cham (2015). https://doi.org/10.1007/978-3-319-17533-1_38
22. Pan, D., Liang, B., Li, H., Ni, P.: Witness encryption with (weak) unique decryption and message indistinguishability: constructions and applications. In: Jang-Jaccard, J., Guo, F. (eds.) ACISP 2019. LNCS, vol. 11547, pp. 609–619. Springer, Cham (2019). https://doi.org/10.1007/978-3-030-21548-4_33
23. Pandey, O., Prabhakaran, M., Sahai, A.: Obfuscation-based non-black-box simulation and four message concurrent zero knowledge for NP. In: Dodis, Y., Nielsen, J.B. (eds.) TCC 2015. LNCS, vol. 9015, pp. 638–667. Springer, Heidelberg (2015). https://doi.org/10.1007/978-3-662-46497-7_25
24. Wee, H.: On obfuscating point functions. In: Proceedings of the Thirty-seventh Annual ACM Symposium on Theory of Computing, pp. 523–532. ACM (2005)
25. Zimmerman, J.: How to obfuscate programs directly. In: Oswald, E., Fischlin, M. (eds.) EUROCRYPT 2015. LNCS, vol. 9057, pp. 439–467. Springer, Heidelberg (2015). https://doi.org/10.1007/978-3-662-46803-6_15

Privacy Amplification from Non-malleable Codes

Eshan Chattopadhyay[1], Bhavana Kanukurthi[2],
Sai Lakshmi Bhavana Obbattu[2], and Sruthi Sekar[3(⊠)]

[1] Cornell University and IAS, Ithaca, USA
eshan.c@gmail.com
[2] Department of Computer Science and Automation, Indian Institute of Science,
Bangalore, India
bhavana.kanukurthi@gmail.com, oslbhavana@gmail.com
[3] Department of Mathematics, Indian Institute of Science, Bangalore, India
sruthi.sekar1@gmail.com

Abstract. Non-malleable Codes give us the following property: their codewords cannot be tampered into codewords of related messages. Privacy Amplification allows parties to convert their weak shared secret into a fully hidden, uniformly distributed secret key, while communicating on a fully tamperable public channel. In this work, we show how to construct a constant round privacy amplification protocol from any augmented split-state non-malleable code. Existentially, this gives us another primitive (in addition to optimal non-malleable extractors) whose optimal construction would solve the long-standing open problem of building constant round privacy amplification with optimal entropy loss and min-entropy requirement. Instantiating our code with the current best known NMC gives us an 8-round privacy amplification protocol with entropy loss $\mathcal{O}(\log(n) + \kappa \log(\kappa))$ and min-entropy requirement $\Omega(\log(n) + \kappa \log(\kappa))$, where κ is the security parameter and n is the length of the shared weak secret. In fact, for our result, even the weaker primitive of Non-malleable Randomness Encoders suffice.

We view our result as an exciting connection between two of the most fascinating and well-studied information theoretic primitives, non-malleable codes and privacy amplification.

1 Introduction

The classical problem of Privacy Amplification was introduced by Bennett, Brassard and Robert in [6]. In this setting, we have two parties, Alice and Bob, who share a common string w, that is only guaranteed to be entropic. The main question that is asked is the following: How can Alice and Bob use w to communicate

E. Chattopadhyay—Research supported by NSF grant CCF-1412958 and the Simons foundation.

B. Kanukurthi—Research supported in part by Department of Science and Technology Inspire Faculty Award.

F. Hao et al. (Eds.): INDOCRYPT 2019, LNCS 11898, pp. 318–337, 2019.
https://doi.org/10.1007/978-3-030-35423-7_16

over a public channel that is fully controlled by a computationally-unbounded adversary, Eve, and still agree on a key K whose distribution is close-to-uniform? This problem has received renewed attention in recent years. While building privacy amplification protocols, there are two main objectives that researchers have tried to meet: (a) build protocols with as low a round complexity as possible and (b) extract a key K that is as long as possible. To achieve the latter objective, a natural goal is therefore to minimize the *"entropy loss"* that occurs due to the protocol.

In the recent times, another interesting information-theoretic primitive that has seen exciting research is Non-malleable codes, which were introduced in the work of Dziembowski, Pietrzak and Wichs [21]. NMCs provide an encoding mechanism with the following guarantee: errors caused to the codeword will render the underlying data either independent of the original encoded message or leave it unchanged. They are defined with respect to a class of tampering families $\mathcal{F}$. The class of tampering families most relevant to this work is the "2-Split-state" family where the codeword consists of two states L and R and the tampering family consists of two functions f and g, each acting independently on L and R respectively. A parameter of importance for any non-malleable coding scheme is its *rate* $(= \frac{\text{message length}}{\text{codeword length}})$. Of late, there has been a lot of research on building non-malleable codes with low-rate for various tampering function families, in particular, the 2-Split-state model. Researchers have also explored connections of other primitives, such as "2-source Non-malleable Extractors" to NMCs. In spite of the exciting research in NMCs, there is no known application of NMCs to information-theoretic primitives which require arbitrary tampering. This isn't surprising: after all, NMCs are secure only with respect to a restricted class of tampering functions (such as 2-split state tampering); when an application requires arbitrary tampering, it is understandably difficult to leverage the usefulness of NMCs. In this work, we overcome this challenge.

Our main result in this work is that we show how to build privacy amplification protocols from non-malleable codes, specifically those with the so-called "augmented" security which we explain later. The protocol has 8 rounds and its entropy loss is related to the rate of the non-malleable code. Furthermore, even though our main protocol is presented in terms of non-malleable codes we can also use the weaker notion of Non-malleable Randomness Encoders in the place of non-malleable codes and get the same parameters. Non-mallebale Randomness Encoders (NMREs) were introduced by Kanukurthi, Obbattu and Sekar [25] and, informally, allow for non-malleable encoding of "pure randomness". There is evidence to suggest that it is easier to build NMREs (with good parameters) than NMCs: specifically, while we know how to build constant-rate NMREs in the 2-Split State Model, a similar result for NMCs has proven elusive in spite of significant interest and effort in the research community. Informally, following are the key results we obtain:

Informal Theorem A: *Assuming the existence of constant rate two-state augmented non-malleable code with optimal error $2^{-\Omega(\kappa)}$, there exists a 8-round privacy amplification protocol with optimal entropy loss $\mathcal{O}(\log(n) + \kappa)$ and min-entropy requirement $\Omega(\log(n) + \kappa)$ (where κ is the security parameter).*

Informal Theorem B: *Assuming the existence of constant rate, two-state augmented non-malleable randomness encoder with optimal error $2^{-\Omega(\kappa)}$ there exists a 8-round privacy amplification protocol with optimal entropy loss $\mathcal{O}(\log(n)+\kappa)$ and min-entropy requirement $\Omega(\log(n)+\kappa)$.*

Further, we instantiate our construction (which gives the above existential results as well) with specific underlying protocols to obtain the following parameters for the privacy amplification protocol:

Informal Theorem C: *Instantiating our construction with the current best known augmented non-malleable code for 2-split-state family [30], we get a 8-round privacy amplification protocol with entropy loss $\mathcal{O}(\log(n)+\kappa\log(\kappa))$ and min-entropy requirement $\Omega(\log(n)+\kappa\log(\kappa)).$[1]*

1.1   Related Work

Recall that the goal of privacy amplification is to enable two parties with a weak (entropic) secret w to agree on a random key K whose distribution is close to uniform. The protocol communication takes place in the presence of a computationally unbounded adversary, Eve, who has complete power to insert, delete or modify messages. Intuitively, a privacy amplification protocol is considered to be secure if any such adversarial tampering of the communication is either detected by one of the honest parties or, if undetected, both parties do agree on the same "secure" key, i.e., one that is guaranteed to be close to uniform from the Eve's point of view. It is no surprise that strong randomness extractors (introduced by Nissan and Zuckerman [34]), which transform non-uniform randomness into uniform randomness by using a short uniformly chosen *seed*, play a huge role in the design of privacy amplification protocols. Specifically, in the setting where Eve is a passive adversary [6,7,32], strong randomness extractors offer a one round solution to the above problem, which is optimal (in terms of entropy loss and min-entropy requirements).

In the setting where Eve is an active adversary, a one-round solution to the problem was first given by Maurer and Wolf [33] with min-entropy requirement of $k_{min} > 2n/3$, where k_{min} is the starting min-entropy requirement and n is the length of w. This was later improved in Dodis, Katz, Reyzin and Smith [17] (with min-entropy requirement of $k_{min} > n/2$). The negative results by [16,20] show that there is no non-interactive (one-round) solution for this problem when the entropy of the weak secret is $k_{min} \leq n/2$. Hence, for $k_{min} \leq n/2$, researchers explored the use of interaction to design privacy amplification protocols.

In the interactive setting with an active adversary, there are two major lines of work. The first line of constructions began with the protocol given by Renner and Wolf [35] who gave a protocol with an entropy loss of $\Theta(\kappa^2)$ and takes $\Theta(\kappa)$ rounds of communication, where κ is the security parameters. This was generalized by Kanukurthi and Reyzin [26]. In [8], Chandran, Kanukurthi, Ostrovsky

---

[1] We can instantiate our construction with recent NMC constructions like [4,31]. We wish to point out that while using [31] slightly improves the entropy loss here (not optimal though), using the constant rate NMC of [4] or [31] results in more entropy loss. This is because the error of their NMC is worse than [30].

and Reyzin, used optimal-rate codes for the edit distance metric to achieve the first protocol with an entropy loss of $\Theta(\kappa)$. The high-level approach of Renner and Wolf's protocol, which was followed in subsequent works, was to first build an "interactive authentication protocol" which authenticates the message bit-by-bit. This authentication protocol is then used to authenticate a seed to a randomness extractor which is then used to extract the final key K, thereby achieving privacy amplification. A natural limitation of this approach is that it is highly interactive and requires $\Theta(\kappa)$ rounds.

The second line of constructions began with the privacy amplification protocol given by Dodis and Wichs [20]. They give an efficient two-round construction (i.e., with optimal round complexity) which has an entropy loss of $\Theta(\kappa^2)$. This work also introduces "seeded Non-malleable extractors (NME)", which has the property that the output of the extractor looks uniform, even given its value on a related seed. Their approach for building two-round privacy amplification protocols roughly works as follows: first, they send a seed to a NME which is used to extract the key (k) to a non-interactive one-time message authentication code. k is then used to authenticate a seed s to an extractor. The final shared key K is evaluated by both parties, unless any tampering is detected, to be $\mathsf{Ext}(w; s)$. In short, the approach of Dodis and Wichs leads to a Privacy amplification protocol with optimal round complexity of 2. Further, [20] give an existential result that if one can efficiently construct non-malleable extractors with optimal parameters, we get a two-round privacy amplification protocol with entropy loss $\Theta(\kappa)$ and min-entropy requirement $\mathcal{O}(\kappa + \log n)$. Subsequent to the existential construction of Privacy Amplification given in [20], there was focus on improving the parameters by giving explicit constructions of seeded non-malleable extractors [9,11,14,15,18,27–30]. While all these constructions give a 2-round privacy amplification protocol with optimal entropy loss, the min-entropy requirement is not optimal (the best known being $\mathcal{O}(\kappa \log \kappa + \log n)$ by [30]).

Even with these existing connections, at the time of writing the original draft of this paper, there was a significant gap between parameters of existing protocols and optimal parameters. In this work, we present an approach to solve the privacy amplification problem with the use of "Non-malleable Randomness encoders (NMRE)" (or "Non-malleable Codes (NMC)"). We offer more details on our techniques in Sect. 1.3. As NMREs are seemingly "easier" to build than NMCs (indeed, we already know how to build 2 state rate-1/2 NMREs from [25]) and NMEs, we only need to additionally make these NMREs have optimal error as well as "augmented" security, in order to build constant round privacy amplification protocols with optimal entropy loss. In fact, the NMRE scheme given in [25] does satisfy the augmented property (as pointed out by [36]), but we still don't know how to get optimal error.

Concurrent and Independent Work. In a recent concurrent and independent work [31], Li obtained a 2 round privacy amplification (PA) protocol with optimal entropy loss and optimal min entropy requirement, thereby closing the biggest open problem in this area. However, even given this very fortunate and important development in the field of privacy amplification, we believe that our work makes several non-trivial contributions. First, our construction techniques differ from the paradigms used in all other papers on privacy amplification. (Li's result, for instance, falls in the Dodis-Wichs paradigm of building PA from NM extractors.) In particular, we leverage the non-malleability of NMCs in the split-state model, to achieve non-malleability in the arbitrary tampering setting of privacy amplification. Further, not only is this is a novel construction of PA, it is also the very first application of non-malleable codes in the split-state model to a model where there is arbitrary tampering. As readers will surely observe, there are many challenges to proving such a result and we overcome them using highly non-trivial proof techniques (described in Sect. 1.3). We believe this contribution will be of independent interest to researchers working in the field of non-malleable codes.

Now that the long standing open problem of achieving asymptotically optimal parameters for privacy amplification protocols has been solved (through Li's result), the next interesting problem would be to optimize the concrete parameters further. Through an approach which is different from all the existing solutions for privacy amplification protocols, we hope to provide a useful direction for achieving this goal.

1.2   Overview of Research on NMCs and NMREs

We now give a brief overview of Non-malleable Codes. NMCs, introduced by Dziembowski, Peitrzak and Wichs, guarantee that a tampered codeword will decode to one of the following:

- $\perp$ i.e., the decoder detects tampering.
- the original message m itself i.e., the tampering did not change the message
- something independent of m

Since, as observed in [21], NMCs cannot be built to be secure against arbitrary, unrestricted tampering, researchers have explored the problem of building NMCs for various classes of tampering families $\mathcal{F}$. The most well-studied model is the "t−split state" model where a codeword consists of t states $(C_1, \ldots C_t)$ and the tampering functions consists of t functions $f_1, \ldots, f_t$. The model permits independent tampering of each C_i via the function f_i. (Each f_i itself is not restricted in any way and, therefore, the model enables arbitrary but independent tampering of each state.) Over a series of works researchers have built NMCs for varying values of t, where $t = 2$ represents the least restrictive model of tampering and $t = n$, for codeword length n, represents the most restrictive model [2–5,12,13,21,24,25,30,31]. At the same time, researchers have also focused on building constructions with good (low) rate. To this date, the problem of building *explicit* constant rate non-malleable codes in the 2-split state model remains open. In [25], the authors introduced a notion called "Non-malleable Randomnes Encoders" which allow for non-malleably encoding "pure randomness". Furthermore, they also present a construction of an NMRE with a constant rate of $\frac{1}{2}$ in the 2-split state model. As we will explain later, the rate of our NMCs/NMREs is closely linked to the entropy loss of the resulting privacy amplification protocol.

Researchers have also explored connections of NMCs to other primitives, as demonstrated by the following picture.

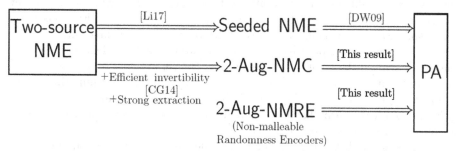

In addition, there have been connections of NMCs with primitives such as Non-malleable secret sharing [22], Non-malleable commitments [23], amongst others. While in the computational setting, taking the split-state tampering model of NMCs to an arbitrary tampering of the commitment is considered in [23], in the information-theoretic setting, the use of split-state NMCs to achieve an arbitrary tampering model in the primitive to be built is not known[2]. One of the reasons for this is that the split-state model doesn't allow for arbitrary tampering when the whole codeword is visible, which most natural applications might require. In this work, we present an application of augmented NMCs (and NMREs) to Privacy Amplification and this requires us to deal with arbitrary tampering. (Augmented non-malleable codes are secure even if one of the states is leaked to the adversary after the tampering). We now give an overview of our techniques to build privacy amplification.

1.3   Technique for Building PA from NMC

In this work, we deviate from the approaches due to Renner and Wolf (of bit-wise authentication) as well as Dodis and Wichs (of using Non-malleable Extractors) and present a new technique to obtain privacy amplification from (augmented) Non-malleable Codes. (We will use certain elements of Renner and Wolf's approach, which we will describe shortly). Just as in prior works, the heart of the protocol consists of an authentication protocol from which we can easily obtain a privacy amplification protocol. So for the rest of this discussion, we restrict our attention to interactive authentication and describe our protocol for the same at a high level. Suppose Bob wants to authentically send a message m to Alice. Alice intiates the protocol by picking a random key k for the MAC, encodes it into (L, R) using a non-malleable code and sends it to Bob. Bob can then authenticate his message using the received key for the MAC and send the message and the tag to Alice. In order to be able to use the MAC security, we must ensure that the MAC key k looks uniform even given the information leaked through the communication channel. It seems natural that the use of non-malleable codes would ensure that even if Eve tampers the channel, Bob would either get the

---

[2] Note that the non-malleable secret sharing schemes using split-state NMCs achieve non-malleability in the independent tampering model, not an arbitrary tampering.

original key or an independent key k. In such a case, the tag evaluated using the MAC key k' will not help Eve in successfully forging a tag for a modified message. While this might seem natural, herein lies the first challenge. In order to use the non-malleability of the NMC, the tampering done by Eve must look like a split-state tampering. If the two states of the non-malleable code are sent directly, the tampering of at least one of them would be dependent on the other, and hence will not be a split-state tampering. Hence, we must find a way to capture this tampering in the interactive setting as a split-state tampering. More intuitively, we need to "amplify" the limited two-state non-malleability to arbitrary unbounded non-malleability. This is the major challenge and the reason for our protocol being a bit complex.

To understand how we overcome this challenge, for the sake of simplicity, we will, for now, assume that the adversary is synchronous. Recall that the protocol starts with Alice encoding a MAC key k into (L, R). Since she can't send both simultaneously to Bob (as it would violate split-state tampering), suppose she first sends the state R. The idea then is that Alice will mask R with a one-time pad that she extracts. Specifically, in this modified protocol, Alice initiates the protocol by picking a seed x_R and sending it to Bob. She then uses this seed (as well as her secret w) to extract a mask y_R to hide R. Alice sends this masked string $Z_R = R \oplus y_R$ to Bob. In the next round, Alice sends the other state L. Finally, Bob uses the received seed in the first step to unmask and get R' and decodes the codeword received to get k'. The main challenge in the security proof is to show that the tampering on L and R can now be captured as two-split-state tamperings. Further, as L is revealed to the adversary, we require the non-malleability to hold, even given the state L. Hence, we require an augmented non-malleable code.

Showing that the above protocol is secure against a synchronous adversary is in itself non-trivial. However, more complications arise when the adversary is asynchronous. Specifically, the order in which the messages are sent to Bob might be altered and hence, the tampering of R itself may end up being dependent on L. To resolve this issue, we borrow the concept of "liveness tests" which was implicit in the protocol due to [35] and made explicit in [26]. A "Liveness Test" is a two round protocol played between Alice and Bob to ensure that Bob is alive in the protocol. It works as follows: Alice sends the seed to a randomness extractor x as a challenge. Bob is expected to respond with $\mathsf{Ext}(w; x)$. The guarantee, which follows from extractor security, is that if Bob doesn't respond to the liveness test, then Eve can't respond to Alice on her own. It can be used to ensure synchrony in the presence of an asynchronous adversary as follows: at the end of each round from Alice to Bob, Bob will be expected to respond to the liveness test. While this is the high level approach, this interleaving of the liveness test and the choice of the messages sent in each round, needs to be done with care to prevent dependency issues from arising.

With high-level intuition behind our construction described above we are able to derive the results (Informal theorems A, B and C) mentioned in the beginning.

1.4   Overview of the Proof Technique

The major challenge in the security proof is to capture the tampering made by Eve as a split-state tampering of the two states. In order to justify this, our first step is to prove that Eve is guaranteed to be caught with high probability, if she behaves asynchronously and gains no more advantage than the synchronous setting. We structure the protocol, so that all the useful information is sent by Alice. This means we only have to ensure, through the liveness tests, that Bob remains alive in between any two messages sent by Alice. Specifically, the protocol begins by Alice sending a liveness test seed for a long extractor output. At every subsequent step, Alice sends a message across to Bob only after Bob responds to the liveness test correctly. Intuitively then, Eve cannot gain any additional advantage in the asynchronous setting than in the synchronous setting because of the following reasons. Firstly, as the useful information (seed of the mask, the masked right state and then the left state) is only sent by Alice, Eve can gain additional advantage if she manages to fool Alice by getting responses from her, acting as Bob. But by extractor security, we show that Eve will not be able to respond to the liveness tests on her own and hence cannot fool Alice except with a negligible probability. On the other hand, if Eve tries to fool Bob by acting as Alice and getting responses from him, then she actually gains no additional information than what she would have in the synchronous setting. This is because, by the nature of the protocol, the only information Bob sends (until the last step) are liveness test responses, which gives no information about the encoded message k.

Once we move into the analysis for the synchronous setting, we wish to use the extractor security to guarantee that Z_R (which is the masked right state, i.e., $R \oplus \mathsf{Ext}(W; X_R)$) looks uniform and hence the tampering on L can be defined independent of R. While intuitively this looks straight forward, the proof requires a careful analysis of the auxiliary information (which are, for example, the liveness test responses), and a suitable use of extractor security to carefully define the correct tampering functions acting on the two states. In particular, once Z_R is replaced by a uniformly chosen string and not the output of an extractor, a challenge is to make the tampering of R consistent with the desired tampering function. We accomplish this by carefully redefining the tampering function acting on R so that it still remains split-state and, at the same time, produces a consistent output as the original tampering function. Once this is done, we use the non-malleability of the underlying NMCs to ensure that the modified key k', if altered, is independent of k. This helps us use the MAC security for the desired robustness.

1.5   Organization of the Paper

We explain the preliminaries and the building blocks required for the main protocol in Sects. 2 and 3. Then, we explain the construction of the protocol in Sect. 4. We give a brief proof sketch of the security analysis in Sect. 5. The detailed proofs are provided in the full version [10].

2 Preliminaries

2.1 Notation

κ denotes security parameter throughout. $s \in_R S$ denotes uniform sampling from set S. $x \leftarrow X$ denotes sampling from a probability distribution X. The notation $\Pr_X[x]$ denotes the probability assigned by X to the value x. $x\|y$ represents concatenation of two binary strings x and y. $|x|$ denotes length of binary string x. U_l denotes the uniform distribution on $\{0,1\}^l$. All logarithms are base 2.

2.2 Statistical Distance and Entropy

Let X_1, X_2 be two probability distributions over some set S. Their *statistical distance* is

$$\mathbf{SD}\,(X_1, X_2) \stackrel{\text{def}}{=} \max_{T \subseteq S}\{\Pr[X_1 \in T] - \Pr[X_2 \in T]\} = \frac{1}{2}\sum_{s \in S}\left|\Pr_{X_1}[s] - \Pr_{X_2}[s]\right|$$

(they are said to be ε-*close* if $\mathbf{SD}\,(X_1, X_2) \leq \varepsilon$ and denoted by $X_1 \approx_\varepsilon X_2$).
For an event E, $\mathbf{SD}_E(A; B)$ denotes $\mathbf{SD}\,(A|E; B|E)$

The *min-entropy* of a random variable W is $\mathbf{H}_\infty(W) = -\log(\max_w \Pr[W = w])$. For a joint distribution (W, E), following [19], we define the *(average) conditional min-entropy* of W given E as

$$\tilde{\mathbf{H}}_\infty(W \mid E) = -\log(\,\underset{e \leftarrow E}{\mathbf{E}}\,(2^{-\mathbf{H}_\infty(W|E=e)}))$$

(here the expectation is taken over e for which $\Pr[E = e]$ is nonzero).

For a random variable W over $\{0,1\}^n$, W is said to be a (n, t)-*source* if $\mathbf{H}_\infty(W) \geq t$.

2.3 Definitions

We now define an interactive authentication protocol. Let Alice and Bob share a secret w, chosen from a distribution W. Through an interactive authentication protocol, the goal is for Alice to be able to authentically send a message m_a to Bob, in the presence of an active adversary Eve. Let m_b denote the message received by Bob. Alice and Bob output "accept" or "reject" after the execution of the protocol, which we denote by t_A and t_B respectively.

Definition 1 *([8]). An interactive protocol (A, B) played by Alice and Bob on a communication channel fully controlled by an adversary Eve, is a (h_W, κ)-* **interactive authentication protocol** *if $\forall m$, it satisfies the following properties whenever $\mathbf{H}_\infty(W) \geq h_W$ and $m_a = m$:*

1. Correctness. If Eve is passive, $\Pr[m_a = m_b] = 1$.

2. *Robustness*. *For any* Eve, *the probability that the following experiment outputs* "Eve *wins*" *is at most* $2^{-\kappa}$: *sample* $w \leftarrow W$; *let* $received_a, received_b$ *be the messages received by Alice and Bob upon execution of* (A, B) *with* Eve *actively controlling the channel, and let* $A(w, received_a, r_a, m_a) = t_A$, $B(w, received_b, r_b) = (m_b, t_B)$. *Output* "Eve *wins*" *if* $(m_b \neq m_a \wedge t_B = "accept")$.

Further, we define a privacy amplification protocol. Let Alice and Bob share a secret w, chosen from a distribution W. The goal of a privacy amplification protocol is for Alice and Bob to agree on a uniform key, in the presence of an active adversary Eve. Let k_A and k_B denote the output of Alice and Bob, after the execution of the protocol.

Definition 2 *([8]). An interactive protocol* (A, B) *played by Alice and Bob on a communication channel fully controlled by an adversary* Eve, *is a* $(h_W, \lambda_k, \delta, \epsilon)$-**privacy amplification protocol** *if it satisfies the following properties whenever* $\mathbf{H}_\infty(W) \geq h_W$:

1. *Correctness*. *If* Eve *is passive,* $\Pr[k_A = k_B] = 1$.
2. *Robustness*. *For any* Eve, *the probability that the following experiment outputs* "Eve *wins*" *is at most* $2^{-\delta}$: *sample* w *from* W; *let* $received_a, received_b$ *be the messages received by Alice and Bob upon execution of* (A, B) *with* Eve *actively controlling the channel, and let* $A(w, received_a, r_a) = k_A$, $B(w, received_b, r_b) = k_B$. *Output* "Eve *wins*" *if* $(k_A \neq k_B \wedge k_A \neq \perp \wedge k_B \neq \perp)$.
3. *Extraction*. *Define* $purify(r)$ *to be a randomized function whose input is either a binary string or* $\perp$. *If* $r = \perp$, *then* $purify(r) = \perp$; *else*, $purify(r)$ *is a uniformly chosen random string of length* λ_k. *Let* $Sent_a, Sent_b$ *be the messages sent by Alice and Bob upon execution of* (A, B) *in presence of* Eve. *Note that the pair* $Sent = (Sent_a, Sent_b)$ *contains an active* Eve's *view of the protocol. We require that for any* Eve,

$$\mathbf{SD}\left((k_A, Sent), (purify(k_A), Sent)\right) \leq \epsilon$$

$$\mathbf{SD}\left((k_B, Sent), (purify(k_B), Sent)\right) \leq \epsilon$$

We now define "Non-malleable randomness encoders"(NMRE), introduced in [25]. NMREs can be viewed as samplers, that would sample a uniform message along with its non-malleable encoding. The security guarantee given by NMREs is that the uniform message output by the NMRE, looks uniform even given the tampered uniform message. The formal definition is given below.

Definition 3. *Let* $(\mathsf{NMREnc}, \mathsf{NMRDec})$ *be s.t.* $\mathsf{NMREnc} : \{0,1\}^r \rightarrow \{0,1\}^k \times (\{0,1\}^{n_1} \times \{0,1\}^{n_2})$ *is defined as* $\mathsf{NMREnc}(r) = (\mathsf{NMREnc}_1(r), \mathsf{NMREnc}_2(r)) = (m, (x, y))$ *and* $\mathsf{NMRDec} : \{0,1\}^{n_1} \times \{0,1\}^{n_2} \rightarrow \{0,1\}^k$.
We say that $(\mathsf{NMREnc}, \mathsf{NMRDec})$ *is a* ϵ-**non-malleable randomness encoder** *with message space* $\{0,1\}^k$ *and codeword space* $\{0,1\}^{n_1} \times \{0,1\}^{n_2}$, *for the distribution* $\mathcal{R}$ *on* $\{0,1\}^r$ *with respect to the 2-split-state family* $\mathcal{F}$ *if the following is satisfied:*

– **Correctness:**

$$\Pr_{r \leftarrow \mathcal{R}}[\mathsf{NMRDec}(\mathsf{NMREnc}_2(r)) = \mathsf{NMREnc}_1(r)] = 1$$

– **Non-malleability:** *For each* $(f, g) \in \mathcal{F}$, $\exists$ *a distribution* $\mathsf{NMRSim}_{f,g}$ *over* $\{0,1\}^k \cup \{same^*, \bot\}$ *such that*

$$\mathsf{NMRTamper}_{f,g} \approx_\epsilon Copy(U_k, \mathsf{NMRSim}_{f,g})$$

where $\mathsf{NMRTamper}_{f,g}$ *denotes the distribution*
$(\mathsf{NMREnc}_1(\mathcal{R}), \mathsf{NMRDec}((f,g)(\mathsf{NMREnc}_2(\mathcal{R})))^3$ *and* $Copy(U_k, \mathsf{NMRSim}_{f,g})$ *is defined as:*

$$u \leftarrow U_k; \ \tilde{m} \leftarrow \mathsf{NMRSim}_{f,g}$$

$$Copy(u, \tilde{m}) = \begin{cases} (u, u), & \text{if } \tilde{m} = same^* \\ (u, \tilde{m}), & \text{otherwise} \end{cases}$$

$\mathsf{NMRSim}_{f,g}$ *should be efficiently samplable given oracle access to* $(f,g)(.)$.

Further, the rate of this code is defined as $k/(n_1 + n_2)$.

We now define a stronger variant of NMREs called "augmented" NMREs. NMREs provide the guarantee that the tampered message can be simulated independent of the original uniform message (barring the $same^*$ case). We now strengthen this guarantee, by requiring that not only the tampered message but also one of the states of the non-malleable encoding, can be simulated independent of the original uniform message.

Definition 4. *Let* $(\mathsf{NMREnc}, \mathsf{NMRDec})$ *be s.t.* $\mathsf{NMREnc} : \{0,1\}^r \rightarrow \{0,1\}^k \times (\{0,1\}^{n_1} \times \{0,1\}^{n_2})$ *is defined as* $\mathsf{NMREnc}(r) = (\mathsf{NMREnc}_1(r), \mathsf{NMREnc}_2(r)) = (m, (x, y))$ *and* $\mathsf{NMRDec} : \{0,1\}^{n_1} \times \{0,1\}^{n_2} \rightarrow \{0,1\}^k$.
We say that $(\mathsf{NMREnc}, \mathsf{NMRDec})$ *is a* ϵ-**augmented non-malleable randomness encoder** *with message space* $\{0,1\}^k$ *and codeword space* $\{0,1\}^{n_1} \times \{0,1\}^{n_2}$, *for the distribution* $\mathcal{R}$ *on* $\{0,1\}^r$ *with respect to the 2-split-state family* $\mathcal{F}$ *if the following is satisfied:*

– **Correctness:**

$$\Pr_{r \leftarrow \mathcal{R}}[\mathsf{NMRDec}(\mathsf{NMREnc}_2(r)) = \mathsf{NMREnc}_1(r)] = 1$$

– **Non-malleability:** *For each* $(f, g) \in \mathcal{F}$, $\exists$ *a distribution* $\mathsf{NMRSim}_{f,g}$ *over* $\{0,1\}^{n_1} \times \{\{0,1\}^k \cup \{same^*, \bot\}\}$ *such that*

$$\mathsf{NMRTamper}^+_{f,g} \approx_\epsilon Copy(U_k, \mathsf{NMRSim}^+_{f,g})$$

---

[3] Here $(f,g)(\mathsf{NMREnc}_2(\mathcal{R}))$ just denotes the tampering by the split-state tampering functions f and g on the corresponding states.

where $\mathsf{NMRTamper}^+_{f,g}$ *denotes the distribution*
$(\mathsf{NMREnc}_1(\mathcal{R}), L, \mathsf{NMRDec}((f(L), g(R))))$ *where* $(L, R) \equiv \mathsf{NMREnc}_2(\mathcal{R})$ *and*
$Copy(U_k, \mathsf{NMRSim}^+_{f,g})$ *is defined as:*

$$u \leftarrow U_k; \; L, \tilde{m} \leftarrow \mathsf{NMRSim}^+_{f,g}$$

$$Copy(u, \tilde{m}) = \begin{cases} (u, L, u), & \text{if } \tilde{m} = same^* \\ (u, L, \tilde{m}), & \text{otherwise} \end{cases}$$

$\mathsf{NMRSim}^+_{f,g}$ *should be efficiently samplable given oracle access to* $(f, g)(.)$.

3 Buliding Blocks

We use information-theoretic message authentication codes, strong average case extractor and an augmented non-malleable code for 2-split-state family, as building blocks to our construction. We define these building blocks below.

3.1 Augmented Non-malleable Codes

Augmented NMCs provide a stronger guarantee (than NMCs) that, both the tampered message and one of the states of the non-malleable encoding of the original message can be simulated independent of the original message. We define augmented non-malleable codes for the 2-split-state family as below.

Definition 5 (Augmented Non-malleable Codes) *[1]. A coding scheme* $(\mathsf{Enc}, \mathsf{Dec})$ *with message and codeword spaces as* $\{0,1\}^\alpha, (\{0,1\}^\beta)^2$ *respectively, is* ϵ- *augmented-non-malleable with respect to the function family* $\mathcal{F} = \{(f_1, f_2) : f_i : \{0,1\}^\beta \to \{0,1\}^\beta\}$ *if* $\forall \ (f_1, f_2) \in \mathcal{F}, \exists$ *a distribution* Sim_{f_1,f_2} *over* $(\{0,1\}^\beta) \times (\{0,1\}^\alpha \cup \{same^*, \bot\})$ *such that* $\forall \ m \in \{0,1\}^\alpha$

$$\mathsf{Tamper}^m_{f_1,f_2} \approx_\epsilon \mathsf{Copy}^m_{Sim_{f_1,f_2}}$$

where $\mathsf{Tamper}^m_{f_1,f_2}$ *denotes the distribution* $(L, \mathsf{Dec}(f_1(L), f_2(R)))$, *where* $\mathsf{Enc}(m) = (L, R)$. $\mathsf{Copy}^m_{Sim_{f_1,f_2}}$ *is defined as*

$$(L, \tilde{m}) \leftarrow Sim_{f_1,f_2}$$

$$\mathsf{Copy}^m_{Sim_{f_1,f_2}} = \begin{cases} (L, m) \text{ if } (L, \tilde{m}) = (L, same^*) \\ (L, \tilde{m}) \text{ otherwise} \end{cases}$$

Sim_{f_1,f_2} *should be efficiently samplable given oracle access to* $(f_1, f_2)(.)$.[4] *We say an* ϵ- *augmented non-malleable code has optimal error, if* $\epsilon \le 2^{-\Theta(\alpha)}$. *We express the rate, of an augmented non-malleable code as a function of* α. *We say the rate is a function* $r(.)$, *if* $2\beta = (\alpha/r(\alpha))$ *i.e codeword length* $= \frac{message\ length}{r(message\ length)}$. *Similarly, the* ϵ-*non-malleable code has error* $2^{-\phi(.)}$, *if* $\epsilon \le 2^{-\phi(.)}$

---

[4] For simplicity in the proof, we may assume here that the decoder Dec never outputs $\bot$. This can be done by replacing $\bot$ with some fixed string, like $00..0$.

3.2 Information-Theoretic One-Time Message Authentication Codes

Message Authentication Codes comprise of keyed functions, Tag and Vrfy. To authenticate a message m, the Tag function is applied on m, which would output tag t. The Vrfy function takes a message m and tag t, outputs either 0 (reject) or 1 (accept). The security guarantee of an information-theoretic one-time message authentication code is that, even an all powerful adversary who has seen atmost one valid message-tag pair, cannot forge a tag that verifies on a different message. The formal definition is as follows:

Definition 6. *A family of pair of functions* $\{\mathsf{Tag}_{k_a} : \{0,1\}^\gamma \to \{0,1\}^\delta,\ \mathsf{Vrfy}_{k_a} : \{0,1\}^\gamma \times \{0,1\}^\delta \to \{0,1\}\}_{k_a \in \{0,1\}^\tau}$ *is said to a* $\mu -$ secure one time MAC *if*

1. *For* $k_a \in_R \{0,1\}^\tau,\ \forall\, m \in \{0,1\}^\gamma,\ \Pr[\mathsf{Vrfy}_{k_a}(m, \mathsf{Tag}_{k_a}(m)) = 1] = 1$
2. *For any* $m \neq m', t, t',\ \Pr_{k_a}[\mathsf{Tag}_{k_a}(m) = t | \mathsf{Tag}_{k_a}(m') = t'] \leq \mu$ *for* $k_a \in_R \{0,1\}^\tau$

3.3 Average-Case Extractors

Extractors output an almost uniform string from a (n, t)-source, using a short uniform string, called *seed*, as a catalyst. Average-case extractors are extractors whose output remains close to uniform, even given the seed and some auxiliary information about the source (but independent of the seed), whenever the source has enough average entropy given the auxiliary information.

Definition 7 [19, Section 2.5]*. Let* $Ext : \{0,1\}^n \times \{0,1\}^d \to \{0,1\}^l$ *be a polynomial time computable function. We say that* Ext *is an efficient average-case* (n, t, d, l, ϵ)*-strong extractor if for all pairs of random variables* (W, I) *such that* W *is an n-bit string satisfying* $\widetilde{\mathbf{H}}_\infty(W|I) \geq t$*, we have* $\mathbf{SD}\left((Ext(W; X), X, I), (U, X, I)\right) \leq \epsilon$*, where* X *is uniform on* $\{0,1\}^d$*.*

4 Protocol

4.1 Notation

- Let Ext' be an $(n, t', d, 3l', \epsilon_1)$- average case extractor.
- Let Ext be an (n, t, d, l, ϵ_2)- average case extractor.
- Let $\mathsf{Enc}, \mathsf{Dec}$ be an ϵ_3- secure two-state augmented non-malleable code with message, codeword spaces being $\{0,1\}^\tau$ and $\{0,1\}^{2l}$.
- Let $\mathsf{Tag}, \mathsf{Vrfy}$ be an ϵ_4-secure one-time MAC with key, message and tag spaces being $\{0,1\}^\tau$, $\{0,1\}^d$, and $\{0,1\}^\delta$ respectively.
- Let Ext'' be an $(n, t'', d, l'', \epsilon_5)$- average case extractor.
- Let λ denote the security parameter w.r.t to the underlying protocols used. We will set the security parameter κ of the main protocol in terms of this λ.

4.2 Protocol

We now describe the Privacy Amplification Protocol below. w is drawn from the entropic source W, and is shared between Alice and Bob. We denote the Interactive Authentication Protocol to authenticate a message m by $\pi_{m,w}^{\mathsf{AUTH}}$ and the Privacy Amplification Protocol by π_w^{PA}.

As described in the introduction, the idea behind the protocol is as follows: For the synchronous setting: Alice picks a MAC key, encodes it using the NMC and sends across the states to Bob. Now, in order to ensure that the tampering done by Eve is captured as a split-state tampering on the states, Alice uses an extractor and masks one of the states before sending it. In the next round, the other state is sent in clear. We require the augmented nature of the NMC to guarantee security even when one state is sent in clear. For the asynchronous setting, we need to add "liveness tests" to the protocol (where an extractor seed is sent by one party as a challenge and the other party has to respond to this correctly). By the nature of the protocol, as the communication is unidirectional (all the "useful information" is only sent by Alice), we only need to include liveness tests to ensure that Bob is alive. For this, Alice sends a liveness test seed for a long extractor output in the first step. This challenge seed is reused for the liveness test responses. The reuse of liveness test seed reduces the number of rounds in the protocol. But, in addition, it is also crucial that this is done to guarantee security of protocol, else dependencies arise.

Theorem 1. *Let* (Enc, Dec), (Tag, Vrfy), Ext′ *and* Ext *be as in Sect. 4.1. Then, the 8-round sub-protocol* π^{AUTH} *in Fig. 1 is a an* (t', κ)-*interactive message authentication protocol.*

Theorem 2.A. *Let* (Enc, Dec), (Tag, Vrfy), Ext′ *and* Ext *be as in Sect. 4.1.*

If (Enc, Dec) *is a two-state, constant rate augmented non-malleable code with optimal error* $2^{-\Omega(\kappa)}$, *then the 8-round protocol* π^{PA} *in Fig. 1 is a* $(t', l'', \kappa, \kappa-1)$-*secure privacy amplification protocol with optimal entropy loss* $\mathcal{O}(\log(n) + \kappa)$ *and with min-entropy requirement* $t' = \Omega(\log(n) + \kappa)$.

Theorem 2.B. *Let* (Enc, Dec), (Tag, Vrfy), Ext′ *and* Ext *be as in Sect. 4.1. If* (Enc, Dec) *is instantiated with the augmented non-malleable code given in [30], then the 8-round protocol* π^{PA} *in Fig. 1 is a* $(t', l'', \kappa, \kappa-1)$-*secure privacy amplification protocol with entropy loss being* $\mathcal{O}(\log(n) + \kappa \log(\kappa))$ *and with min-entropy requirement* $t' = \Omega(\log(n) + \kappa \log \kappa)$.

5 Security Proof Sketch

- Correctness follows easily.

- *Proof sketch of Robustness*: The major challenge in the security proof is to capture the tampering made by Eve as a split-state tampering of the two states. In order to justify this, our first step is to prove that the advantage

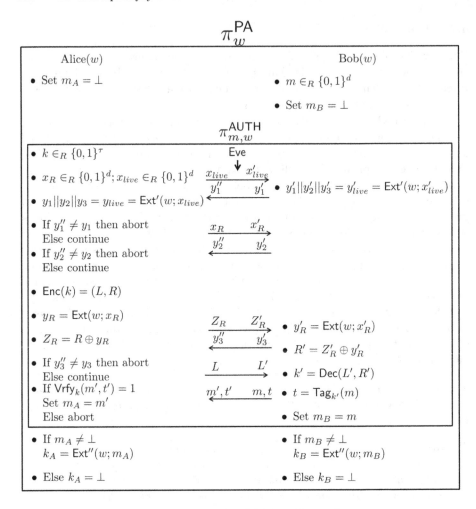

Fig. 1. Privacy Amplification Protocol

that Eve gains by acting asynchronously is no more than that in the synchronous setting (upto a "small" error). By the structure of our protocol, notice that, all the useful information is sent by Alice. Further, in between any two messages sent by Alice, Bob is expected to respond to a liveness test challenge. Intuitively then, Eve cannot gain any additional advantage in the asynchronous setting than in the synchronous setting because of the following reasons. Firstly, as the useful information (seed of the mask, the masked right state and then the left state) is only sent by Alice, Eve can gain additional advantage if she manages to fool Alice by getting responses from her, acting as Bob. But by extractor security, we show that Eve will not be able to respond to the liveness tests on her own and hence cannot fool Alice except with a negligible probability. On the other hand, if Eve tries to fool Bob by acting as Alice and getting responses from him, then she actually gains no additional information than what she would have in the synchronous setting. This is because, by the nature of the protocol, the only information Bob sends (until the last step) are liveness test responses, which gives no information about the encoded message k. We refer the reader to full version [10] for a detailed proof of the following lemma.

Lemma 1. $\Pr[\text{Eve } wins|\text{Async}] \leq \Pr[\text{Eve } wins|\text{Sync, Pass}] + 2^{-l'+1}$

Here, informally the event Async corresponds to Eve acting asynchronously, Sync corresponds to when she acts synchronously and Pass is the event that Eve passes all the liveness tests. Once we move into the analysis for the synchronous setting, we wish to use the extractor security to guarantee that Z_R (which is the masked right state, i.e., $R \oplus \text{Ext}(W; X_R)$) looks uniform and hence the tampering on L can be defined independent of R. While intuitively this looks straight forward, the proof requires a careful analysis of the auxiliary information (which are, for example, the liveness test responses), and a suitable use of extractor security to carefully define the correct tampering functions acting on the two states. In particular, once Z_R is replaced by a uniformly chosen string and not the output of an extractor, a challenge is to make the tampering of R consistent with the desired tampering function. We accomplish this by carefully redefining the tampering function acting on R so that it still remains split-state and, at the same time, produces a consistent output as the original tampering function. Once this is done, we use the non-malleability of the underlying NMCs to ensure that the modified key k', if altered, is independent of k. This helps us use the MAC security for the desired robustness. We refer the reader to full version [10] for a detailed proof of the following lemma.

Lemma 2. $\Pr[\text{Eve } wins|\text{Sync, Pass}] \leq 2^{-\lambda} + 2\epsilon_2 + \epsilon_3 + \epsilon_4$

Combining Lemmata 1 and 2, we complete the proof of robustness. The detailed security analysis of above lemmata are given in full version [10].

Proof Sketch of Theorem 1. After proving that π^{AUTH} is a secure interactive authentication protocol, it is straightforward to prove the correctness and robustness of π^{PA}. Further, by using robustness and the security of Ext'', it is straightforward to show that the extraction error is bounded by $\epsilon_5 + 2^{-\kappa}$, where $2^{-\kappa}$ is the robustness error. The detailed proof and parameter analysis is given in full version [10].

6   Privacy Amplification from Augmented-NMREs

As mentioned in the introduction, we can get the same parameters from our protocol if we replace the use of NMCs by Augmented-NMREs.

Theorem 3. *If* (Enc, Dec) *in* π^{AUTH} *is a two-state, constant rate augmented non-malleable randomness encoder with optimal error* $2^{-\Omega(\kappa)}$, *then the 8-round protocol* π^{PA} *in Fig. 1 is a* $(t', l'', \kappa, \kappa - 1)$-*secure privacy amplification protocol with optimal entropy loss* $\mathcal{O}(\log(n) + \kappa)$ *with min-entropy requirement* $\Omega(\log(n) + \kappa)$.

Proof. The only modification made in this protocol is that instead of picking the MAC key k uniformly at random and then encoding it using NMCs, we use the key k and its encoding output by the NMRE. As augmented-NMREs guarantee the K looks uniform even given L and the modified key K', the proof structure of this theorem follows on the same lines as the security proof in Sect. 5 (details in full version [10]).

7   Conclusion

In this work, we establish the first concrete connection between non-malleable codes and privacy amplification. Further, we provide a framework for obtaining optimal parameters for the privacy amplification protocol from non-malleable codes with appropriate parameters. The novelty in our result is that it gives the first known application (in the *information theoretic setting*) of NMCs in the restricted split-state model to achieve non-malleability in the arbitrary tampering setting of privacy amplification. We believe that this technique might be of independent interest.

References

1. Aggarwal, D., Agrawal, S., Gupta, D., Maji, H.K., Pandey, O., Prabhakaran, M.: Optimal computational split-state non-malleable codes. In: Kushilevitz, E., Malkin, T. (eds.) TCC 2016, Part II. LNCS, vol. 9563, pp. 393–417. Springer, Heidelberg (2016). https://doi.org/10.1007/978-3-662-49099-0_15
2. Aggarwal, D., Dodis, Y., Kazana, T., Obremski, M.: Non-malleable reductions and applications. In: Proceedings of the Forty-Seventh Annual ACM on Symposium on Theory of Computing, STOC 2015, Portland, OR, USA, 14–17 June 2015, pp. 459–468 (2015). https://doi.org/10.1145/2746539.2746544
3. Aggarwal, D., Dodis, Y., Lovett, S.: Non-malleable codes from additive combinatorics. In: Symposium on Theory of Computing, STOC 2014, New York, NY, USA, 31 May–03 June 2014, pp. 774–783 (2014). https://doi.org/10.1145/2591796.2591804
4. Aggarwal, D., Obremski, M.: Inception makes non-malleable codes shorter as well! IACR Cryptology ePrint Archive 2019/399 (2019). https://eprint.iacr.org/2019/399
5. Agrawal, S., Gupta, D., Maji, H.K., Pandey, O., Prabhakaran, M.: A rate-optimizing compiler for non-malleable codes against bit-wise tampering and permutations. In: Dodis, Y., Nielsen, J.B. (eds.) TCC 2015, Part I. LNCS, vol. 9014, pp. 375–397. Springer, Heidelberg (2015). https://doi.org/10.1007/978-3-662-46494-6_16
6. Bennett, C., Brassard, G., Robert, J.M.: Privacy amplification by public discussion. SIAM J. Comput. **17**(2), 210–229 (1988)

7. Bennett, C.H., Brassard, G., Crépeau, C., Maurer, U.M.: Generalized privacy amplification. IEEE Trans. Inf. Theory **41**(6), 1915–1923 (1995)
8. Chandran, N., Kanukurthi, B., Ostrovsky, R., Reyzin, L.: Privacy amplification with asymptotically optimal entropy loss. In: Schulman, L.J. (ed.) Proceedings of the 42nd ACM Symposium on Theory of Computing, STOC 2010, Cambridge, Massachusetts, USA, 5–8 June 2010, pp. 785–794. ACM (2010). https://doi.org/10.1145/1806689.1806796
9. Chattopadhyay, E., Goyal, V., Li, X.: Non-malleable extractors and codes, with their many tampered extensions. In: Proceedings of the 48th Annual ACM SIGACT Symposium on Theory of Computing, STOC 2016, Cambridge, MA, USA, 18–21 June 2016, pp. 285–298 (2016). https://doi.org/10.1145/2897518.2897547
10. Chattopadhyay, E., Kanukurthi, B., Obbattu, S.L.B., Sekar, S.: Privacy amplification from non-malleable codes. Cryptology ePrint Archive, Report 2018/293 (2018). https://eprint.iacr.org/2018/293
11. Chattopadhyay, E., Li, X.: Explicit non-malleable extractors, multi-source extractors, and almost optimal privacy amplification protocols. In: IEEE 57th Annual Symposium on Foundations of Computer Science, FOCS 2016, 9–11 October 2016, Hyatt Regency, New Brunswick, New Jersey, USA, pp. 158–167 (2016). https://doi.org/10.1109/FOCS.2016.25
12. Chattopadhyay, E., Zuckerman, D.: Non-malleable codes against constant split-state tampering. In: 55th IEEE Annual Symposium on Foundations of Computer Science, FOCS 2014, Philadelphia, PA, USA, 18–21 October 2014, pp. 306–315 (2014). https://doi.org/10.1109/FOCS.2014.40
13. Cheraghchi, M., Guruswami, V.: Non-malleable coding against bit-wise and split-state tampering. In: Lindell, Y. (ed.) TCC 2014. LNCS, vol. 8349, pp. 440–464. Springer, Heidelberg (2014). https://doi.org/10.1007/978-3-642-54242-8_19
14. Cohen, G.: Making the most of advice: new correlation breakers and their applications. In: IEEE 57th Annual Symposium on Foundations of Computer Science, FOCS 2016, 9–11 October 2016, Hyatt Regency, New Brunswick, New Jersey, USA, pp. 188–196 (2016). https://doi.org/10.1109/FOCS.2016.28
15. Cohen, G., Raz, R., Segev, G.: Non-malleable extractors with short seeds and applications to privacy amplification. In: Proceedings of the 27th Conference on Computational Complexity, CCC 2012, Porto, Portugal, 26–29 June 2012, pp. 298–308 (2012). https://doi.org/10.1109/CCC.2012.21
16. Dodis, Y., Spencer, J.: On the (non-)universality of the one-time pad. In: 43rd Annual Symposium on Foundations of Computer Science, pp. 376–385. IEEE (2002)
17. Dodis, Y., Katz, J., Reyzin, L., Smith, A.: Robust fuzzy extractors and authenticated key agreement from close secrets. In: Dwork, C. (ed.) CRYPTO 2006. LNCS, vol. 4117, pp. 232–250. Springer, Heidelberg (2006). https://doi.org/10.1007/11818175_14
18. Dodis, Y., Li, X., Wooley, T.D., Zuckerman, D.: Privacy amplification and non-malleable extractors via character sums. In: Ostrovsky, R. (ed.) IEEE 52nd Annual Symposium on Foundations of Computer Science, FOCS 2011, Palm Springs, CA, USA, 22–25 October 2011, pp. 668–677. IEEE (2011). https://doi.org/10.1109/FOCS.2011.67
19. Dodis, Y., Ostrovsky, R., Reyzin, L., Smith, A.: Fuzzy extractors: how to generate strong keys from biometrics and other noisy data. SIAM J. Comput. **38**(1), 97–139 (2008). arXiv:cs/0602007

20. Dodis, Y., Wichs, D.: Non-malleable extractors and symmetric key cryptography from weak secrets. In: Proceedings of the Forty-First Annual ACM Symposium on Theory of Computing, pp. 601–610, Bethesda, Maryland, 31 May–2 Jun 2009 (2009)

21. Dziembowski, S., Pietrzak, K., Wichs, D.: Non-malleable codes. In: Innovations in Computer Science - ICS 2010, Proceedings, Tsinghua University, Beijing, China, 5–7 January 2010, pp. 434–452 (2010). http://conference.itcs.tsinghua.edu.cn/ICS2010/content/papers/34.html

22. Goyal, V., Kumar, A.: Non-malleable secret sharing. IACR Cryptology ePrint Archive 2018/316 (2018). https://eprint.iacr.org/2018/316

23. Goyal, V., Pandey, O., Richelson, S.: Textbook non-malleable commitments. In: Proceedings of the 48th Annual ACM SIGACT Symposium on Theory of Computing, STOC 2016, Cambridge, MA, USA, 18–21 June 2016, pp. 1128–1141 (2016). https://doi.org/10.1145/2897518.2897657

24. Kanukurthi, B., Obbattu, S.L.B., Sekar, S.: Four-state non-malleable codes with explicit constant rate. In: Kalai, Y., Reyzin, L. (eds.) TCC 2017, Part II. LNCS, vol. 10678, pp. 344–375. Springer, Cham (2017). https://doi.org/10.1007/978-3-319-70503-3_11

25. Kanukurthi, B., Obbattu, S.L.B., Sekar, S.: Non-malleable randomness encoders and their applications. In: Nielsen, J.B., Rijmen, V. (eds.) EUROCRYPT 2018, Part III. LNCS, vol. 10822, pp. 589–617. Springer, Cham (2018). https://doi.org/10.1007/978-3-319-78372-7_19

26. Kanukurthi, B., Reyzin, L.: Key agreement from close secrets over unsecured channels. In: Joux, A. (ed.) EUROCRYPT 2009. LNCS, vol. 5479, pp. 206–223. Springer, Heidelberg (2009). https://doi.org/10.1007/978-3-642-01001-9_12

27. Li, X.: Design extractors, non-malleable condensers and privacy amplification. In: Proceedings of the 44th Symposium on Theory of Computing Conference, STOC 2012, New York, NY, USA, May 19–22, 2012. pp. 837–854 (2012). https://doi.org/10.1145/2213977.2214052, https://doi.org/10.1145/2213977.2214052

28. Li, X.: Non-malleable extractors, two-source extractors and privacy amplification. In: 53rd Annual IEEE Symposium on Foundations of Computer Science, FOCS 2012, New Brunswick, NJ, USA, 20–23 October 2012, pp. 688–697 (2012). https://doi.org/10.1109/FOCS.2012.26

29. Li, X.: Non-malleable Condensers for arbitrary min-entropy, and almost optimal protocols for privacy amplification. In: Dodis, Y., Nielsen, J.B. (eds.) TCC 2015, Part I. LNCS, vol. 9014, pp. 502–531. Springer, Heidelberg (2015). https://doi.org/10.1007/978-3-662-46494-6_21

30. Li, X.: Improved non-malleable extractors, non-malleable codes and independent source extractors. In: Symposium on Theory of Computing, STOC 2017, Montreal, Canada, 19–23 June 2017 (2017)

31. Li, X.: Non-malleable extractors and non-malleable codes: partially optimal constructions. In: Computational Complexity Conference, CCC 2019, New Brunswick, 18–20 June 2019 (2019)

32. Maurer, U.M.: Protocols for secret key agreement by public discussion based on common information. In: Brickell, E.F. (ed.) CRYPTO 1992. LNCS, vol. 740, pp. 461–470. Springer, Heidelberg (1993). https://doi.org/10.1007/3-540-48071-4_32

33. Maurer, U., Wolf, S.: Privacy amplification secure against active adversaries. In: Kaliski, B.S. (ed.) CRYPTO 1997. LNCS, vol. 1294, pp. 307–321. Springer, Heidelberg (1997). https://doi.org/10.1007/BFb0052244

34. Nisan, N., Zuckerman, D.: Randomness is linear in space. J. Comput. Syst. Sci. **52**(1), 43–53 (1996)
35. Renner, R., Wolf, S.: Unconditional authenticity and privacy from an arbitrarily weak secret. In: Boneh, D. (ed.) CRYPTO 2003. LNCS, vol. 2729, pp. 78–95. Springer, Heidelberg (2003). https://doi.org/10.1007/978-3-540-45146-4_5
36. Srinivasan, A.: Personal communication

Mathematics: Boolean Functions, Elliptic Curves and Lattices

Vectorial Boolean Functions with Very Low Differential-Linear Uniformity Using Maiorana-McFarland Type Construction

Deng Tang[1,2], Bimal Mandal[3(✉)], and Subhamoy Maitra[4]

[1] School of Mathematics, Southwest Jiaotong University, Chengdu 610031, China
dtang@foxmail.com
[2] State Key Laboratory of Cryptology, P.O. Box 5159, Beijing 100878, China
[3] CARAMBA, INRIA Nancy–Grand Est, Villers-lès-Nancy 54600, France
bimalmandal90@gmail.com
[4] Indian Statistical Institute, Kolkata 700108, India
subho@isical.ac.in

Abstract. The differential-linear connectivity table (DLCT) of a vectorial Boolean function was recently introduced by Bar-On et al. at EUROCRYPT'19. In this paper we construct a new class of balanced vectorial Boolean functions with very low differential-linear uniformity and provide a combinatorial count of hardware gates which is required to implement such circuits. Here, all the coordinate functions are constructed by modifying the Maiorana-McFarland bent functions. Further, we derive some properties of DLCT and differential-linear uniformity of modified inverse functions.

Keywords: Maiorana-McFarland bent function · Vectorial Boolean function · Autocorrelation · Differential-linear uniformity

1 Introduction

To design symmetric ciphers, mainly block ciphers, vectorial Boolean functions play an important role. Cryptanalysis of block ciphers are mainly divided into two directions, one is called differential cryptanalysis which is proposed by Biham and Shamir [3], and another is linear cryptanalysis which is proposed by Matsui [20]. Differential cryptanalysis deals with the probability of the differences between the input vectors and corresponding output vectors. On the other hand, linear cryptanalysis deals with the linear relation between input and outputs vectors. Many block ciphers are attacked by using the differential and linear cryptanalysis, most notable Data Encryption Standard (DES) [31]. To resist the known attacks on each model of block cipher (and hopefully, to resist future attacks), the vectorial Boolean functions used in ciphers should satisfy various design criteria simultaneously. The design criteria on vectorial Boolean functions is depended on the properties of its component functions.

F. Hao et al. (Eds.): INDOCRYPT 2019, LNCS 11898, pp. 341–360, 2019.
https://doi.org/10.1007/978-3-030-35423-7_17

The differential-linear cryptanalysis was first introduced by Langford and Hellman [17]. Many block ciphers [2,12,13,18] are attacked by using this cryptanalytic technique. Recently, Bar-On et al. [1] proposed a new connectivity table, differential-linear connectivity table (DLCT), of vectorial Boolean functions which is focused on the dependency between two sub-ciphers E_0 and E_1. The authors also derived a relation between the DLCT and difference distribution table (DDT) of vectorial Boolean functions. Later, Li et al. [19] investigated the properties of DLCT in more details including the inverse, almost bent (AB), almost perfect nonlinear (APN), Gold and Bracken-Leander power functions and derived the lower bound of differential-linear uniformity. Authors also derived the results on the behavior of DLCT and differential-linear uniformity under different equivalence relations of (n, m)-functions. At the same time, Anne et al. [4] also derived the similar results on DLCT independently. The paper [5] is a merged version of [19] and [4]. It is known that the differential-linear uniformity of a vectorial Boolean function depends on the autocorrelation values of its all component functions. So, the construction of a vectorial Boolean function with very low differential-linear uniformity is same as the construction of a vectorial Boolean function with very low absolute autocorrelation values of its all component functions. Dobbertin [11] first constructed a balanced Boolean function with high nonlinearity by modifying all-zero values on an affine subspace of dimension $\frac{n}{2}$ of a special class of Boolean functions. In this direction, Tang et al. [29], Kavut et al. [15] and Tang et al. [28] also constructed the balanced Boolean functions by modifying the simplest partial spread and Maiorana-McFarland bent functions with low autocorrelation and the absolute indicator strictly lesser than $2^{\frac{n}{2}}$. In this paper our primary focus to construct the balanced vectorial Boolean functions having very low differential-linear uniformity. The technique used in this paper to construct such (n, m)-functions in Construction 1 is given as below, where $n = 2k \geq 4$.

1. Let ϕ_i, $1 \leq i \leq m$, be the permutations over $\mathbb{F}_2^k$ such that for any $(l_1, l_2, \ldots, l_m) \in \mathbb{F}_2^{m*}$ the linear combination $l_1\phi_1 + l_2\phi_2 + \cdots + l_m\phi_m$ is also a permutation over $\mathbb{F}_2^k$ and $l_1\phi_1(\mathbf{0}) + l_2\phi_2(\mathbf{0}) + \cdots + l_m\phi_m(\mathbf{0}) = \mathbf{0}$.
2. Let u_i and v_i, $1 \leq i \leq m$, be Boolean functions over $\mathbb{F}_2^k$ such that for any $(l_1, l_2, \ldots, l_m) \in \mathbb{F}_2^{m*}$ $\mathrm{wt}(l_1u_1 + l_2u_2 + \cdots + l_mu_m) + \mathrm{wt}(l_1v_1 + l_2v_2 + \cdots + l_mv_m) = 2^{k-1}$ and $l_1u_1(\mathbf{0}) + l_2u_2(\mathbf{0}) + \cdots + l_mu_m(\mathbf{0}) = l_1v_1(\mathbf{0}) + l_2v_2(\mathbf{0}) + \cdots + l_mv_m(\mathbf{0}) = 0$.
3. Define an (n, m)-function $G = (g_1, g_2, \ldots, g_m)$ such that $g_i(x, y) = \phi_i(x) \cdot y$ for all $x, y \in \mathbb{F}_2^k$ and $i = 1, 2, \ldots, m$.
4. We construct a balanced (n, m)-function $F = (f_1, f_2, \ldots, f_m)$ by modifying all the coordinate functions of G as follows:

$$f_i(x, y) = \begin{cases} u_i(y), & \text{if } (x, y) \in \{\mathbf{0}\} \times \mathbb{F}_2^k \\ \phi_i(x) \cdot y, & \text{if } (x, y) \in \mathbb{F}_2^{k*} \times \mathbb{F}_2^{k*} \\ v_i(x), & \text{if } (x, y) \in \mathbb{F}_2^{k*} \times \{\mathbf{0}\} \end{cases} ,$$

for all $x, y \in \mathbb{F}_2^k$ and $i = 1, 2, \ldots, m$.

Moreover, we identify such u_i and v_i, $1 \le i \le m$, for $n = 4t \ge 20$ and $m = t - 1$, and construct a balanced $(4t, t-1)$-function having differential-linear uniformity strictly less than 2^{2t-1}. Further, we derive some results on the properties of DLCT.

CONTRIBUTION and ORGANIZATION. Our approach depends on the constructions of coordinate functions of a balanced vectorial Boolean function such that the autocorrelation of all component functions are very low. For that we construct the coordinate functions with very low autocorrelation by modifying the Maiorana-McFarland bent functions. The paper is organized as follows. In Sect. 2, some basic definitions and notations are given. In Sect. 3, some observations on DLCT of vectorial Boolean functions are discussed. In Sect. 4, we derive the differential-linear uniformity of known balanced vectorial Boolean functions. . In Sect. 5, we construct a new class of balanced vectorial Boolean functions by modifying the Maiorana-McFarland functions. In Sect. 6, we construct a balanced $(4t, t-1)$-function $(t \ge 5)$ such that the differential-linear uniformity is strictly less than 2^{2t-1} and nonlinearity is lower bounded by $2^{4t-1} - 2^{2t-1} - 2^{t+1}$. Further, we calculate the total number of gates which is required to implement such circuits in worst case.

Before proceeding further let us present some background material.

2   Preliminaries

Let $\mathbb{F}_2$, $\mathbb{F}_2^n$ and $\mathbb{F}_{2^n}$ be the prime field of characteristic 2, an n-dimensional vector space over $\mathbb{F}_2$ and a finite field of degree of extension n over $\mathbb{F}_2$, respectively. The cardinality of a set A is denoted as $\#A$. Given two integers n and m, a mapping from the vector space $\mathbb{F}_2^n$ to the vector space $\mathbb{F}_2^m$ is often called an (n, m)-function or a vectorial Boolean function if the values n and m are omitted. An (n, m)-function can be viewed as a function S from the finite field $\mathbb{F}_{2^n}$ to the finite field $\mathbb{F}_{2^m}$. Particularly, S is called a Boolean function when $m = 1$, and set of all n-variable Boolean functions is denoted as $\mathcal{B}_n$. Let S be an (n, m)-function, the Boolean functions $s_1, s_2, \ldots, s_m$ in n variables defined by $S(x) = (s_1(x), s_2(x), \ldots, s_m(x))$ are called the *coordinate* functions of S. Further, the Boolean functions, which are the linear combinations, with non all-zero coefficients of the coordinate functions of S, are called *component* functions of S. The component functions of S can be expressed as $\lambda \cdot S$ where $\lambda \in \mathbb{F}_2^{m*}$, all nonzero m-bit vectors. It is known that the vector space $\mathbb{F}_2^n$ is isomorphic to the finite field $\mathbb{F}_{2^n}$ through the choice of some basis of $\mathbb{F}_{2^n}$ over $\mathbb{F}_2$. Indeed, if $\{\lambda_1, \lambda_2, \ldots, \lambda_n\}$ is a basis of $\mathbb{F}_{2^n}$ over $\mathbb{F}_2$, then every vector $x = (x_1, \ldots, x_n)$ of $\mathbb{F}_2^n$ can be identified with the element $x_1\lambda_1 + x_2\lambda_2 + \cdots + x_n\lambda_n \in \mathbb{F}_{2^n}$. The finite field $\mathbb{F}_{2^n}$ can then be viewed as an n-dimensional vector space over $\mathbb{F}_2$. If we identify every element of $\mathbb{F}_2^m$ with an element of finite field $\mathbb{F}_{2^m}$, then the nonzero component functions s_λ of S can be expressed as $\mathrm{Tr}_1^m(\lambda S)$, where $\lambda \in \mathbb{F}_{2^m}^*$ and $\mathrm{Tr}_1^m(x) = \sum_{i=0}^{m-1} x^{2^i}$. For any $(\alpha, \lambda) \in \mathbb{F}_2^n \times \mathbb{F}_2^{m*}$, the Walsh–Hadamard transform of S at (α, λ) is defined as

$$W_{\lambda \cdot S}(\alpha) = \sum_{x \in \mathbb{F}_2^n} (-1)^{\lambda \cdot S(x) + \alpha \cdot x}.$$

If S is defined on a finite field, the Walsh–Hadamard transform of S at $(\alpha, \lambda) \in \mathbb{F}_{2^n} \times \mathbb{F}_{2^m}^*$ is defined as

$$W_{\mathrm{Tr}_1^m(\lambda S)}(\alpha) = \sum_{x \in \mathbb{F}_{2^n}} (-1)^{\mathrm{Tr}_1^m(\lambda S(x)) + \mathrm{Tr}_1^n(\alpha x)}.$$

The nonlinearity $nl(S)$ of an (n, m)-function S is the minimum Hamming distance between all the component functions of S and all affine functions in n variables. According to the definition of Walsh–Hadamard transform, we have

$$nl(S) = 2^{n-1} - \frac{1}{2} \max_{(\alpha, \lambda) \in \mathbb{F}_2^n \times \mathbb{F}_2^{m*}} |W_{\lambda \cdot S}(\alpha)|$$

$$= 2^{n-1} - \frac{1}{2} \max_{(\alpha, \lambda) \in \mathbb{F}_{2^n} \times \mathbb{F}_{2^m}^*} |W_{\mathrm{Tr}_1^m(\lambda S)}(\alpha)|.$$

The nonlinearity $nl(S)$ is upper-bounded by $2^{n-1} - 2^{\frac{n-1}{2}}$ when $m = n$. This upper bound is tight for odd $m = n$. For even $m = n$, the best known value of the nonlinearity of (n, m)-functions is $2^{n-1} - 2^{\frac{n}{2}}$.

Definition 1 ([1]). *For a vectorial Boolean function $S : \mathbb{F}_2^n \to \mathbb{F}_2^m$, the DLCT of S is an $2^n \times 2^m$ table, whose rows correspond to input differences to S and whose columns correspond to bit masks of outputs of S. The value in the cell (Δ, λ), where $\Delta \in \mathbb{F}_2^n$ is a difference and $\lambda \in \mathbb{F}_2^m$ is a mask, is*

$$\mathrm{DLCT}_S(\Delta, \lambda) = \#\{x : \lambda \cdot S(x) = \lambda \cdot S(x + \Delta)\} - 2^{n-1}.$$

It can be seen that $\mathrm{DLCT}_S(\Delta, \lambda) = 2^{n-1}$ if $\Delta = 0$ or $\lambda = 0$. As mentioned in [1], if the DLCT of an Sbox (vectorial Boolean function) used in block ciphers contains many very high/very low values, excluding the cases $\Delta = 0$ or $\lambda = 0$, then this Sbox can be used by an adversary to carry out the differential-linear (DL) attacks. So one can define the differential-linear uniformity of S.

Definition 2. *For a vectorial Boolean function $S : \mathbb{F}_2^n \to \mathbb{F}_2^m$, the differential-linear uniformity of S is defined as*

$$\mathrm{DL}(S) = \max_{(\Delta, \lambda) \in \mathbb{F}_2^{n*} \times \mathbb{F}_2^{m*}} |\mathrm{DLCT}_S(\Delta, \lambda)|.$$

The autocorrelation of a Boolean function $f \in \mathcal{B}_n$ at point $\Delta \in \mathbb{F}_2^n$, $C_f(\Delta)$, is defined as

$$C_f(\Delta) = \sum_{x \in \mathbb{F}_2^n} (-1)^{f(x) + f(x + \Delta)}.$$

It is known [19, Proposition 2.3] that $\text{DLCT}_S(\Delta, \lambda) = \frac{1}{2} C_{\lambda \cdot S}(\Delta)$ and then the differential-linear uniformity of S can be expressed as

$$\text{DL}(S) = \max_{(\Delta, \lambda) \in \mathbb{F}_2^{n*} \times \mathbb{F}_2^{m*}} \frac{1}{2} \left| C_{\lambda \cdot S}(\Delta) \right|. \tag{1}$$

Additionally, for any (n, n)-function S over $\mathbb{F}_{2^n}$, its differential-linear uniformity can be computed as

$$\text{DL}(S) = \max_{(\Delta, \lambda) \in \mathbb{F}_{2^n}^* \times \mathbb{F}_{2^n}^*} \frac{1}{2} \left| C_{\text{Tr}_1^n(\lambda S)}(\Delta) \right|. \tag{2}$$

For any (n, m)-function S, let us define $\delta_S(\Delta, \delta) = \{x \in \mathbb{F}_2^n : S(x) + S(x + \Delta) = \delta\}$, where $\Delta \in \mathbb{F}_2^n$ and $\delta \in \mathbb{F}_2^m$. The differential distribution table (DDT) of S is an $2^n \times 2^m$ matrix such that the coefficient at (Δ, δ) is defined by

$$\text{DDT}_S(\Delta, \delta) = \#\delta_S(\Delta, \delta).$$

It is known that the maximum number of possible distinct δ's is $\min\{2^{n-1}, 2^m\}$, and if $n = m$, $\Delta \neq 0$ and S is permutation, then $\delta \neq 0$. Suppose

$$\delta(S) = \max\{\text{DDT}_S(\Delta, \delta) : \Delta \in \mathbb{F}_2^{n*}, \delta \in \mathbb{F}_2^m\}.$$

Then, $\delta(S) \equiv 0 \pmod 2$ and the function S is called differentially $\delta(S)$-uniform. For $n = m$, $\delta(S) \geq 2$, and if a function S satisfy the equality, then S is called an almost perfect nonlinear (APN) function [6, Definition 9.8]. Bar-On et al. [1] derived the relation between DLCT and DDT as follow.

$$\text{DLCT}_S(\Delta, \lambda) = \frac{1}{2} \sum_{v \in \mathbb{F}_2^m} (-1)^{v \cdot \lambda} \text{DDT}_S(\Delta, v).$$

3 Properties of DLCT

Li et al. [19] and Anne et al. [4,5] recently derived many properties of DLCT along with the bounds of DL of vectorial Boolean functions. They first derived the connection between the DLCT and autocorrelation of vectorial Boolean functions, and then presented generic bounds on the maximum absolute value occurring in the DLCT of vectorial Boolean functions. The properties are mainly related to the connection between DLCT and Walsh–Hadamard transform [19, Proposition 3.1] and DLCT and DDT [19, Proposition 3.3] of vectorial Boolean functions. We further derive some properties of DLCT and provide a necessary and sufficient condition so that $|\text{DLCT}_S(\Delta, \lambda)| = 2^{n-1}$, $\Delta \in \mathbb{F}_2^{n*}$ and $\lambda \in \mathbb{F}_2^{m*}$.

Let us denote $E_a^0 = \{x \in \mathbb{F}_2^n : a \cdot x = 0\}$, $a \in \mathbb{F}_2^n$. We know that for any nonzero $a \in \mathbb{F}_2^n$, E_a^0 is a linear subspace of $\mathbb{F}_2^n$ of dimension $n - 1$. For any (n, m)-function S, it is clear that $\mathbb{F}_2^n = \cup_{\delta \in \mathbb{F}_2^m} \delta_S(\Delta, \delta)$ and $\delta_S(\Delta, \delta) \cap \delta_S(\Delta, \delta') = \emptyset$, if $\delta \neq \delta'$, for all $\Delta \in \mathbb{F}_2^n$.

Proposition 1. *For any* (n,m)*-function* S, $\text{DLCT}_S(\Delta, \lambda) = \sum_{\delta \in E_\lambda^0}$ $\text{DDT}_S(\Delta, \delta) - 2^{n-1}$, *where* $\Delta \in \mathbb{F}_2^n$ *and* $\lambda \in \mathbb{F}_2^m$.

Proof. For any $\Delta \in \mathbb{F}_2^n$ and $\lambda \in \mathbb{F}_2^m$,

$$\text{DLCT}_S(\Delta, \lambda) + 2^{n-1} = \#\{x \in \mathbb{F}_2^n : \lambda(S(x) + S(x+\Delta)) = 0\}$$
$$= \# \bigcup_{\delta \in \mathbb{F}_2^m} \{\delta_S(\Delta, \delta) : \lambda \cdot \delta = 0\} = \sum_{\delta \in E_\lambda^0} \text{DDT}_S(\Delta, \delta).$$

Let us define, $Im(D_\Delta S) = \{y \in \mathbb{F}_2^m : y = S(x) + S(x+\Delta), x \in \mathbb{F}_2^n\}$, $\Delta \in \mathbb{F}_2^n$. Here, $\#Im(D_\Delta S) \le \min\{2^{n-1}, 2^m\} = 2^{\min\{n-1,m\}}$, and for an APN function S, $\#Im(D_\Delta S) = 2^{n-1}$, for all $\Delta \in \mathbb{F}_2^{n*}$.

Corollary 1. *Let* S *be an* (n,m)*-function. For any* $\Delta \in \mathbb{F}_2^{n*}$ *and* $\lambda \in \mathbb{F}_2^{m*}$, $\text{DLCT}_S(\Delta, \lambda) = 2^{n-1}$ *if and only if* $Im(D_\Delta S) \subset E_\lambda^0$. *Moreover,* $\text{DLCT}_S(\Delta, \lambda) = -2^{n-1}$ *if and only if* $Im(D_\Delta S) \subset \mathbb{F}_2^m \setminus E_\lambda^0$.

Proof. Suppose, there exists $\Delta \in \mathbb{F}_2^{n*}$ and $\lambda \in \mathbb{F}_2^{m*}$ such that $\text{DLCT}_S(\Delta, \lambda) = 2^{n-1}$. From Proposition 1, we get $Im(D_\Delta S) \subset E_\lambda^0$. If there exists $\delta \in Im(D_\Delta S)$ but $\delta \notin E_\lambda^0$, then $\sum_{\delta \in E_\lambda^0} \text{DDT}_S(\Delta, \delta) \le 2^n - 2$, and so, $\text{DLCT}_S(\Delta, \lambda) \le 2^{n-1} - 2$. Similarly, we can prove the other claim.

From the above result, it is clear that $DL(S) = 2^{n-1}$ if and only if there exist a $\Delta \in \mathbb{F}_2^{n*}$ and $\lambda \in \mathbb{F}_2^{m*}$ such that $Im(D_\Delta S) \subset E_\lambda^0$ or $Im(D_\Delta S) \subset \mathbb{F}_2^m \setminus E_\lambda^0$.

For example let, $n = m = 4$, $\Delta = 0100, \lambda = 0001$ and $S(x_1, x_2, x_3, x_4) = (x_1 x_2, x_2 x_3, x_3 x_4, x_1 x_4)$. We identify an element $(x_1, x_2, x_3, x_4) \in \mathbb{F}_2^4$ by $x_1 x_2 x_3 x_4$. Then $D_{0100} S(x) = (x_1, x_3, 0, 0)$, and so, $Im(D_{0100} S) = \{0000, 1000, 0100, 1100\} \subset E_{0001}^0$. Thus, $\text{DLCT}_S(0100, 0001) = \sum_{\delta \in E_{0001}^0} \text{DDT}_S(0100, \delta) - 8 = 8$.

From Corollary 1, we get the next result for APN permutations (i.e., $n = m$ and $\#Im(D_\Delta S) = 2^{n-1}$, for all $\Delta \in \mathbb{F}_2^{n*}$). Li et al. [19] proved that $DL(S)$ of S over $\mathbb{F}_2^n$ is lower bounded by $2^{n-1}\sqrt{\frac{1}{2^n-1}}$. We derive the upper bounds of differential-linear uniformity of APN permutations.

Corollary 2. *Let* S *be an APN permutation over* $\mathbb{F}_2^n$. *For any* $\Delta, \lambda \in \mathbb{F}_2^{n*}$,

$$\text{DLCT}_S(\Delta, \lambda) \le 2^{n-1} - 2.$$

Moreover, $\text{DLCT}_S(\Delta, \lambda) + 2^{n-1} = 0$ *if and only if* $Im(D_\Delta S) = \mathbb{F}_2^n \setminus E_\lambda^0$.

Proof. Since $\mathbf{0} \in E_\lambda^0$ but $\mathbf{0} \notin Im(D_\Delta S)$ for any $\Delta \in \mathbb{F}_2^{n*}$, and $\#E_\lambda^0 = \#Im(D_\Delta S) = 2^{n-1}$. From Proposition 1 and Corollary 1, we get the claims.

Form the above corollary it is clear that $DL(S) = 2^{n-1}$ of an APN permutation S over $\mathbb{F}_2^n$ if and only if there exist a $\Delta, \lambda \in \mathbb{F}_2^{n*}$ such that $Im(D_\Delta S) = \mathbb{F}_2^n \setminus E_\lambda^0$. The following problem was proposed by Li et al. [19].

Problem 1 [19, Problem 1]. For an odd integer n, are there (n, n)-functions S other than the Kasami–Welch APN functions that have $\mathrm{DL}(S) = 2^{\frac{n-1}{2}}$?

We observe that it can be possible to find an (n, n)-function other than Kasami–Welch APN that have $\mathrm{DL}(S) = 2^{\frac{n-1}{2}}$. For that $\#E_\lambda^0 \cap Im(D_\Delta S)$ lies between two particular numbers, for all $\Delta, \lambda \in \mathbb{F}_2^{n*}$. We are working on it and try to identify such APN function computationally.

Theorem 1. *Let n be an odd integer. For an APN (n, n)-function S, $\mathrm{DL}(S) = 2^{\frac{n-1}{2}}$ if and only if for any $\Delta, \lambda \in \mathbb{F}_2^{n*}$*

$$2^{n-2} - 2^{\frac{n-1}{2}-1} \le \#E_\lambda^0 \cap Im(D_\Delta S) \le 2^{n-2} + 2^{\frac{n-1}{2}-1}.$$

Proof. Suppose for an APN (n, n)-function S, $\mathrm{DL}(S) = 2^{\frac{n-1}{2}}$. Thus, for any $\Delta, \lambda \in \mathbb{F}_2^{n*}$

$$-2^{\frac{n-1}{2}} \le \mathrm{DLCT}_S(\Delta, \lambda) \le 2^{\frac{n-1}{2}}$$

$$\Leftrightarrow 2^{n-1} - 2^{\frac{n-1}{2}} \le \mathrm{DLCT}_S(\Delta, \lambda) + 2^{n-1} \le 2^{n-1} + 2^{\frac{n-1}{2}}$$

$$\Leftrightarrow 2^{n-1} - 2^{\frac{n-1}{2}} \le \sum_{\delta \in E_\lambda^0} \mathrm{DDT}_S(\Delta, \delta) \le 2^{n-1} + 2^{\frac{n-1}{2}}$$

$$\Leftrightarrow 2^{n-2} - 2^{\frac{n-1}{2}-1} \le \#E_\lambda^0 \cap Im(D_\Delta S) \le 2^{n-2} + 2^{\frac{n-1}{2}-1}.$$

4   On the Differential-Linear Uniformity of Known Balanced Vectorial Boolean Functions

Till date, there are many classes of balanced vectorial Boolean functions with good cryptographic properties have been proposed. These functions are mainly based on the modifications of the inverse function over finite fields and the Maiorana-McFarland bent function over vector spaces. Li et al. [19, Thorem 4.2] and Anne et al. [5, Theorem 4] proved that the differential-linear uniformity of any quadratic (n, n)-function is 2^{n-1} and calculated the possible values of DLCT for the function x^{2^i+1} [19, Corollary 4.3]. In this section we discuss some results on the differential-linear uniformity of known balanced vectorial Boolean functions.

4.1   The Differential-Linear Uniformity of the Inverse Function and Its Modifications

The inverse function $I(x) = x^{2^n-2}$ is bijective on $\mathbb{F}_{2^n}$. The inverse function is differentially 4-uniform when n is even and is APN when n is odd [22]. Li et al. [19] derived the differential-linear uniformity of I, and proved that if $n = 2k$, then $\mathrm{DL}(I) = 2^k$. This class of functions has best known nonlinearity $2^{n-1} - 2^{n/2}$ when n is even and has maximum algebraic degree $n - 1$. It is used as the Sbox of the Advanced Encryption Standard with $n = 8$. Since the inverse function is a differentially 4-uniform bijection when n is even and has best known nonlinearity and maximum algebraic degree, many works on the constructions of new differentially 4-uniform bijections by modifying the inverse function have been done, see for instance [24–27, 30, 32]. There are some differentially 4-uniform functions, which are bijective but not derived from the inverse function [9, 14]. Indeed, those works obtained differentially 4-uniform bijections by permuting the values of the inverse function with even dimensions in two methods. In [27], Qu *et al.* considered differentially 4-uniform bijections in the form of $I_1(x) = x^{2^n-2} + f(x)$, where f are well-choose Boolean functions such that $f(x^{2^n-2}) + f(x^{2^n-2}+1) = 0$. In [30], Tang *et al.* provided differentially 4-uniform bijections in the form of $I_2(x) = (x+g(x))^{2^n-2}$, where g are well-choose Boolean functions such that $g(x) + g(x+1) = 0$.

Let us consider the differential-linear uniformity of the revised inverse functions I_1 and I_2. To this end, we first give some preliminary results which are particularly useful to derive our results. For any integer $n > 0$, the Kloosterman sums over $\mathbb{F}_{2^n}$ are defined as

$$\mathcal{K}(a) = \sum_{x\in\mathbb{F}_{2^n}} (-1)^{\mathrm{Tr}_1^n(x^{2^n-2}+\alpha x)},$$

where $\alpha \in \mathbb{F}_{2^n}$. In fact, the Kloosterman sums are generally defined on the multiplicative group $\mathbb{F}_{2^n}^*$. We extend them to 0 by assuming $(-1)^0 = 1$. The following lemmas are well-known.

Lemma 1 ([16]). *For any positive integer n, the set $\{\mathcal{K}(a) : a \in \mathbb{F}_{2^n}\}$ equals the set of all those values which are divisible by 4 in the range $[-2^{n/2+1}+1, 2^{n/2+1}+1]$.*

Lemma 2 ([8]). *For any positive integer n and any $\Delta \in \mathbb{F}_{2^n}^*$, we have*

$$C_{\mathrm{Tr}_1^n(\lambda I)}(\Delta) = \mathcal{K}\left(\frac{\lambda}{\Delta}\right) + \left(2(-1)^{\mathrm{Tr}_1^n(\frac{\lambda}{\Delta})} - 2\right).$$

We are ready now to present lower bounds on the differential-linear uniformity of the revised inverse functions I_1 and I_2.

Theorem 2. *For any I_1 and I_2, we have $\mathrm{DL}(I_1) \geq 2^{n/2} - 2$ and $\mathrm{DL}(I_2) \geq \frac{1}{2}\left(1 - \sum_{t=0}^{\lfloor n/2\rfloor}(-1)^{n-t}\frac{n}{n-t}\binom{n-t}{t}2^t\right)$.*

Proof. We first consider the differential-linear uniformity of the functions I_1. Note that for any $\Delta \in \mathbb{F}_{2^n}^*$ we have

$$\mathrm{DLCT}_{I_1}(\Delta, 1) = \frac{1}{2}C_{\mathrm{Tr}_1^n(I_1)}(\Delta) = \frac{1}{2}\sum_{x\in\mathbb{F}_{2^n}}(-1)^{\mathrm{Tr}_1^n\left(\frac{1}{x}+\frac{1}{x+\Delta}+f(x)+f(x+\Delta)\right)}$$

$$= \frac{1}{2}\sum_{x\in\mathbb{F}_{2^n}}(-1)^{\mathrm{Tr}_1^n\left(\frac{1}{x}+\frac{1}{x+\Delta}\right)} = \frac{1}{2}C_{\mathrm{Tr}_1^n(I)}(\Delta),$$

where $\mathrm{Tr}_1^n(f(z)) = 0$ for any $z \in \mathbb{F}_{2^n}$ on even n is used in the penultimate identity. Then by Lemmas 1 and 2 we immediately get that $\mathrm{DL}(I_1) \geq 2^{n/2} - 2$.

We shall now discuss the differential-linear uniformity of the functions I_2. Note that

$$\mathrm{DLCT}_{I_2}(1,1) = \frac{1}{2}C_{\mathrm{Tr}_1^n(I_2)}(1) = \frac{1}{2}\sum_{x\in\mathbb{F}_{2^n}}(-1)^{\mathrm{Tr}_1^n\left(\frac{1}{x+g(x)}+\frac{1}{x+1+g(x+1)}\right)}$$

$$= \frac{1}{2}\sum_{x\in\mathbb{F}_{2^n}}(-1)^{\mathrm{Tr}_1^n\left(\frac{1}{x+g(x)}+\frac{1}{x+g(x)+1}\right)} = \frac{1}{2}\sum_{y\in\mathbb{F}_{2^n}}(-1)^{\mathrm{Tr}_1^n\left(\frac{1}{y}+\frac{1}{y+1}\right)}$$

$$= \frac{1}{2}C_{\mathrm{Tr}_1^n(I)}(1),$$

where $g(x) + g(x+1) = 0$ is used in the third identity and $x + g(x)$ are bijective on $\mathbb{F}_{2^n}$ is used in the penultimate identity. It is well-known that (see, e.g., [7]) $\mathcal{K}(1) = 1 - \sum_{t=0}^{\lfloor n/2\rfloor}(-1)^{n-t}\frac{n}{n-t}\binom{n-t}{t}2^t$. Therefore, by Lemma 2 we have $\mathrm{DL}(I_2) \geq \frac{1}{2}\left(1 - \sum_{t=0}^{\lfloor n/2\rfloor}(-1)^{n-t}\frac{n}{n-t}\binom{n-t}{t}2^t\right)$. This completes the proof.

4.2 The Differential-Linear Uniformity of the Maiorana-McFarland Bent Function and Its Modifications

Let us recall the class of Maiorana-McFarland (M-M) bent function, which is defined as

$$h(x,y) = \phi(x) \cdot y + s(x), \tag{3}$$

where $x, y \in \mathbb{F}_2^k$, ϕ is an arbitrary permutation on $\mathbb{F}_2^k$, and s is an arbitrary Boolean function on k variables. Such class of bent functions was discovered independently by Maiorana and McFarland (see [10,21]), which includes a huge numbers of bent functions. The essential of every M-M bent function is a concatenation of 2^k affine functions in k variables and the linear parts of these 2^k affine functions are pairwise distinct. Then h can be written as a concatenation of 2^k affine functions on k variables, i.e.,

$$h = h_0||h_1||\ldots||h_{2^k-1},$$

where $h_i(y) = h(x^i, y)$, for all $y \in \mathbb{F}_2^k$, are affine functions, $x^i \in \mathbb{F}_2^k, 0 \leq i \leq 2^k-1$. The affine function h_i is called a block of length 2^k. It should be noted that every M-M bent function on $2k$ variables is unbalanced since it contains a block of length 2^k with constant values 0 or 1. A basic idea to obtain balanced Boolean function from M-M bent functions is to replace this block by a balanced Boolean function g on k variables. Further, one can obtain balanced vectorial Boolean functions with differently well-chosen mappings ϕ and differently well-chosen functions g on k variables, see for examples [33]. Thus, for obtaining the differential-linear uniformity of such kind of balanced vectorial Boolean functions, it is sufficient to discuss the balanced Boolean functions obtained by replacing the constant block. The all-zero vector of $\mathbb{F}_2^k$ is denoted by $\mathbf{0}$. We consider balanced Boolean functions in the form of

$$f(x,y) = \begin{cases} \phi(x) \cdot y, & \text{if } x \neq \mathbf{0} \\ g(y), & \text{if } x = \mathbf{0} \end{cases}, \tag{4}$$

where $x, y \in \mathbb{F}_2^k$, ϕ is a permutation on $\mathbb{F}_2^k$ such that $\phi(\mathbf{0}) = \mathbf{0}$, and g is a balanced Boolean function on $\mathbb{F}_2^k$.

Lemma 3. *Let f be an $n = 2k$-variable Boolean function generated by (4), then for any $(a, b) \in \mathbb{F}_2^k \times \mathbb{F}_2^k$ we have*

$$C_f(a, b) = \begin{cases} 2^n & \text{if } a = b = \mathbf{0} \\ -2^k + C_g(b), & \text{if } a = \mathbf{0}, b \in \mathbb{F}_2^{k*} \\ 2(-1)^{\phi(a) \cdot b} W_g(\phi(a)), & \text{if } a \in \mathbb{F}_2^{k*}, b \in \mathbb{F}_2^k \end{cases}.$$

Proof. It follows from the definition of autocorrelation function that

$$C_f(a, b) = \sum_{(a,b) \in \mathbb{F}_2^k \times \mathbb{F}_2^k} (-1)^{f(x,y) + f(x+a, y+b)} \tag{5}$$

for any $(a, b) \in \mathbb{F}_2^k \times \mathbb{F}_2^k$. Clearly, we have $C_f(\mathbf{0}, \mathbf{0}) = 2^n$. We now consider the values of $C_f(a, b)$ for all $(a, b) \in \mathbb{F}_2^k \times \mathbb{F}_2^k \setminus \{(\mathbf{0}, \mathbf{0})\}$. Basically, our discussion is built on the facts that $\sum_{x \in \mathbb{F}_2^{k*}} (-1)^{c \cdot x}$ equals -1 if $c \in \mathbb{F}_2^{k*}$, and equals $2^k - 1$ otherwise. We consider the following two cases:

[**Case 1.**] Let $(a, b) \in \{\mathbf{0}\} \times \mathbb{F}_2^{k*}$. It can be easily seen that in this case Eq. (5) becomes

$$\begin{aligned} C_f(a, b) &= \sum_{(x,y) \in \{\mathbf{0}\} \times \mathbb{F}_2^k} (-1)^{f(\mathbf{0},y) + f(\mathbf{0}, y+b)} + \sum_{(x,y) \in \mathbb{F}_2^{k*} \times \mathbb{F}_2^k} (-1)^{f(x,y) + f(x, y+b)} \\ &= \sum_{y \in \mathbb{F}_2^k} (-1)^{g(y) + g(y+b)} + \sum_{(x,y) \in \mathbb{F}_2^{k*} \times \mathbb{F}_2^k} (-1)^{\phi(x) \cdot y + \phi(x) \cdot (y+b)} \\ &= C_g(b) + \sum_{(x,y) \in \mathbb{F}_2^{k*} \times \mathbb{F}_2^k} (-1)^{\phi(x) \cdot b} \\ &= C_g(b) + 2^k \sum_{x \in \mathbb{F}_2^{k*}} (-1)^{\phi(x) \cdot b} \\ &= -2^k + C_g(b). \end{aligned}$$

[**Case 2.**] Let $(a, b) \in \mathbb{F}_2^{k*} \times \mathbb{F}_2^k$. In this case Eq. (5) becomes

$$\begin{aligned} C_f(a, b) &= \sum_{\substack{x \in \{\mathbf{0}, a\} \\ y \in \mathbb{F}_2^k}} (-1)^{f(x,y) + f(x+a, y+b)} + \sum_{\substack{x \in \mathbb{F}_2^k \setminus \{\mathbf{0}, a\} \\ y \in \mathbb{F}_2^k}} (-1)^{f(x,y) + f(x+a, y+b)} \\ &= \sum_{y \in \mathbb{F}_2^k} \left((-1)^{f(\mathbf{0},y) + f(a, y+b)} + (-1)^{f(a,y) + f(\mathbf{0}, y+b)} \right) + \sum_{\substack{x \in \mathbb{F}_2^k \setminus \{\mathbf{0}, a\} \\ y \in \mathbb{F}_2^k}} (-1)^{f(x,y) + f(x+a, y+b)} \\ &= 2 \sum_{y \in \mathbb{F}_2^k} (-1)^{g(y) + \phi(a) \cdot (y+b)} + \sum_{\substack{x \in \mathbb{F}_2^k \setminus \{\mathbf{0}, a\} \\ y \in \mathbb{F}_2^k}} (-1)^{\phi(x) \cdot y + \phi(x+a) \cdot (y+b)} \\ &= 2(-1)^{\phi(a) \cdot b} W_g(\phi(a)) + \sum_{x \in \mathbb{F}_2^k \setminus \{\mathbf{0}, a\}} (-1)^{\phi(x+a) \cdot b} \sum_{y \in \mathbb{F}_2^k} (-1)^{z \cdot y} \end{aligned}$$

$$= 2(-1)^{\phi(a)\cdot b} W_g(\phi(a)),$$

where $z = \phi(a) + \phi(x+a)$ which is nonzero for any $a \in \mathbb{F}_2^{k*}$ and $x \in \mathbb{F}_2^k \setminus \{0, a\}$.

Theorem 3. *Let f be an $n = 2k$-variable Boolean function generated by (4) and there exists $b \in \mathbb{F}_2^{k*}$ such that $C_g(b) = 0$. If f is a component function of an (n, m)-function S, then we have $DL(S) \geq 2^{k-1}$.*

5   A New Class of Balanced Vectorial Boolean Functions from Maiorana-McFarland Functions

We know that the cardinality of the support set of an $2k$-variable bent function f of the form $\phi(x) \cdot y$ is $2^{2k-1} - 2^{k-1}$, where ϕ is a permutation over $\mathbb{F}_2^k$. So if we change the 2^{k-1} outputs values of f from 0 to 1, the modified function become balanced. Tang et al. [28, Construction 1] constructed the balanced Boolean functions having high nonlinearity and very low absolute indicator, the maximum absolute autocorrelation value, by modifying the M-M class of bent functions. We use the same method to construct the coordinate functions of a balanced (n, m)-function. In the next section we identify an $(4t, t-1)$-function ($t \geq 5$) with differential-linear uniformity strictly less than 2^{2t-1} using the Construction 1.

Construction 1. *Let $n = 2k$ be an even integer not less than 4. We construct an (n, m)-function F whose coordinate functions f_i's ($1 \leq i \leq m$) are defined as follows:*

$$f_i(x, y) = \begin{cases} u_i(y), & \text{if } (x, y) \in \{0\} \times \mathbb{F}_2^k \\ \phi_i(x) \cdot y, & \text{if } (x, y) \in \mathbb{F}_2^{k*} \times \mathbb{F}_2^{k*} \\ v_i(x), & \text{if } (x, y) \in \mathbb{F}_2^{k*} \times \{0\} \end{cases},$$

where

(1) $x, y \in \mathbb{F}_2^k$,
(2) ϕ_i's are mappings from $\mathbb{F}_2^k$ to itself satisfying for any $(l_1, l_2, \cdots, l_m) \in \mathbb{F}_2^{m*}$ the linear combination $l_1\phi_1 + l_2\phi_2 + \cdots + l_m\phi_m$ is a permutation on $\mathbb{F}_2^k$ such that $l_1\phi_1(0) + l_2\phi_2(0) + \cdots + l_m\phi_m(0) = 0$, and
(3) u_i's and v_i's are Boolean functions over $\mathbb{F}_2^k$ satisfying for any $(l_1, l_2, \cdots, l_m) \in \mathbb{F}_2^{m*}$ $\text{wt}(l_1u_1 + l_2u_2 + \cdots + l_mu_m) + \text{wt}(l_1v_1 + l_2v_2 + \cdots + l_mv_m) = 2^{k-1}$ and $l_1u_1(0) + l_2u_2(0) + \cdots + l_mu_m(0) = l_1v_1(0) + l_2v_2(0) + \cdots + l_mv_m(0) = 0$.

Theorem 4. *For any $n = 2k \geq 4$, every (n, m)-function F generated by Construction 1 is balanced.*

Proof. The cardinality of the support set of any nonzero component function of F is 2^{n-1}.

Theorem 5. *Let* $n = 2k \geq 4$ *and* F *be an* (n, m)*-function generated by Construction 1. For any* $l = (l_1, l_2, \cdots, l_m) \in \mathbb{F}_2^{m*}$*, we have*

$$
W_{l \cdot F}(a, b) = \begin{cases}
0, & \text{if } (a, b) = (\mathbf{0}, \mathbf{0}) \\
W_{l \cdot U}(b) + W_{l \cdot V}(\mathbf{0}), & \text{if } (a, b) \in \{\mathbf{0}\} \times \mathbb{F}_2^{k*} \\
W_{l \cdot U}(\mathbf{0}) + W_{l \cdot V}(a), & \text{if } (a, b) \in \mathbb{F}_2^{k*} \times \{\mathbf{0}\} \\
(-1)^{(l \cdot \Phi)^{-1}(b) \cdot a} 2^k + W_{l \cdot U}(b) + W_{l \cdot V}(a), & \text{if } (a, b) \in \mathbb{F}_2^{k*} \times \mathbb{F}_2^{k*}
\end{cases},
$$

where $U = (u_1, u_2, \ldots, u_m)$, $V = (v_1, v_2, \ldots, v_m)$, $\Phi = (\phi_1, \phi_2, \ldots, \phi_m)$ *in which* u_i*'s and* v_i*'s are* k*-variable Boolean functions and* ϕ_i*'s are permutations over* $\mathbb{F}_2^k$ *used in Construction 1.*

Proof. For any $l \in \mathbb{F}_2^{m*}$, $l \cdot F(x, y) = l_1 f_1(x, y) + \cdots + l_m f_m(x, y)$, for all $x, y \in \mathbb{F}_2^k$. We know that $\sum_{x \in \mathbb{F}_2^{k*}} (-1)^{u \cdot x}$ equals -1 if $u \in \mathbb{F}_2^{k*}$ and equals $2^k - 1$ otherwise. For any $(a, b) \in \mathbb{F}_2^k \times \mathbb{F}_2^k$, we have

$$
\begin{aligned}
W_{l \cdot F}(a, b) &= \sum_{(x, y) \in \mathbb{F}_2^k \times \mathbb{F}_2^k} (-1)^{l \cdot F(x, y) + a \cdot x + b \cdot y} \\
&= \sum_{(x, y) \in \{\mathbf{0}\} \times \mathbb{F}_2^k} (-1)^{l \cdot F(x, y) + a \cdot x + b \cdot y} + \sum_{(x, y) \in \mathbb{F}_2^{k*} \times \mathbb{F}_2^{k*}} (-1)^{l \cdot F(x, y) + a \cdot x + b \cdot y} \\
&\quad + \sum_{(x, y) \in \mathbb{F}_2^{k*} \times \{\mathbf{0}\}} (-1)^{l \cdot F(x, y) + a \cdot x + b \cdot y} \\
&= W_{l \cdot U}(b) + \sum_{(x, y) \in \mathbb{F}_2^{k*} \times \mathbb{F}_2^{k*}} (-1)^{(l \cdot \Phi)(x) \cdot y + a \cdot x + b \cdot y} + \sum_{x \in \mathbb{F}_2^{k*}} (-1)^{l \cdot V(x) + a \cdot x} \\
&= W_{l \cdot U}(b) + \sum_{x \in \mathbb{F}_2^{k*}} (-1)^{a \cdot x} \sum_{y \in \mathbb{F}_2^{k*}} (-1)^{((l \cdot \Phi)(x) + b) \cdot y} + W_{l \cdot V}(a) - 1 \\
&= \begin{cases}
0, & \text{if } (a, b) = (\mathbf{0}, \mathbf{0}) \\
W_{l \cdot U}(b) + W_{l \cdot V}(\mathbf{0}), & \text{if } (a, b) \in \{\mathbf{0}\} \times \mathbb{F}_2^{k*} \\
W_{l \cdot U}(\mathbf{0}) + W_{l \cdot V}(a), & \text{if } (a, b) \in \mathbb{F}_2^{k*} \times \{\mathbf{0}\} \\
2^k (-1)^{(l \cdot \Phi)^{-1}(b) \cdot a} + W_{l \cdot U}(b) + W_{l \cdot V}(a), & \text{if } (a, b) \in \mathbb{F}_2^{k*} \times \mathbb{F}_2^{k*}
\end{cases}.
\end{aligned}
$$

Theorem 6. *Let the notation be the same as in Theorem 5. Let* $n = 2k \geq 4$ *and* F *be an* (n, m)*-function generated by Construction 1. For any* $l = (l_1, l_2, \cdots, l_m) \in \mathbb{F}_2^{m*}$*, we have*

$$
C_{l \cdot F}(a, b) = \begin{cases}
2^n, & \text{if } (a, b) = (\mathbf{0}, \mathbf{0}) \\
C_{l \cdot U}(b) + 2W_{(l \cdot V)'}(b) - 2^k, & \text{if } (a, b) \in \{\mathbf{0}\} \times \mathbb{F}_2^{k*} \\
C_{l \cdot V}(a) + 2W_{l \cdot U}((l \cdot \Phi)(a)) - 2^k, & \text{if } (a, b) \in \mathbb{F}_2^{k*} \times \{\mathbf{0}\} \\
2(-1)^{(l \cdot \Phi)(a) \cdot b} W_{l \cdot U}((l \cdot \Phi)(a)) + W_{(l \cdot V)''}(b) + 8t, & \text{if } (a, b) \in \mathbb{F}_2^{k*} \times \mathbb{F}_2^{k*}
\end{cases},
$$

where $(l \cdot V)'(x) = (l \cdot V)((l \cdot \Phi)^{-1}(x))$, $(l \cdot V)''(x) = (l \cdot V)((l \cdot \Phi)^{-1}(x) + a)$, *and* t *equals 1 if* $l \cdot V(a) = l \cdot U(b) = 1$ *and equals 0 otherwise.*

Proof. For any $l \in \mathbb{F}_2^{m*}$, the autocorrelation of $l \cdot F$ at $(a, b) \in \mathbb{F}_2^k \times \mathbb{F}_2^k$ is

$$
C_{l \cdot F}(a, b) = \sum_{(x, y) \in \mathbb{F}_2^k \times \mathbb{F}_2^k} (-1)^{l \cdot F(x, y) + l \cdot F(x + a, y + b)}.
$$

Clearly, we have $C_{l \cdot F}(\mathbf{0}, \mathbf{0}) = 2^n$. We consider the following three cases.

[**Case 1.**] Let $a = \mathbf{0}$ and $b \in \mathbb{F}_2^{k*}$. Then $C_{l \cdot F}(\mathbf{0}, b)$ is equal to

$$\sum_{(x,y) \in \{\mathbf{0}\} \times \mathbb{F}_2^k} (-1)^{l \cdot F(\mathbf{0}, y) + l \cdot F(\mathbf{0}, y+b)} + \sum_{(x,y) \in \mathbb{F}_2^{k*} \times \mathbb{F}_2^k} (-1)^{l \cdot F(x,y) + l \cdot F(x, y+b)}$$

$$= \sum_{y \in \mathbb{F}_2^k} (-1)^{l \cdot U(y) + l \cdot U(y+b)} + \sum_{(x,y) \in \mathbb{F}_2^{k*} \times \mathbb{F}_2^k \setminus \{\mathbf{0}, b\}} (-1)^{(l \cdot \Phi)(x) \cdot y + (l \cdot \Phi)(x) \cdot (y+b)}$$

$$+ \sum_{(x,y) \in \mathbb{F}_2^{k*} \times \{\mathbf{0}\}} (-1)^{l \cdot F(x, \mathbf{0}) + l \cdot F(x, b)} + \sum_{(x,y) \in \mathbb{F}_2^{k*} \times \{b\}} (-1)^{l \cdot F(x, b) + l \cdot F(x, \mathbf{0})}$$

$$= C_{l \cdot U}(b) + \sum_{(x,y) \in \mathbb{F}_2^{k*} \times \mathbb{F}_2^k \setminus \{\mathbf{0}, b\}} (-1)^{(l \cdot \Phi)(x) \cdot b} + 2 \sum_{x \in \mathbb{F}_2^{k*}} (-1)^{l \cdot V(x) + (l \cdot \Phi)(x) \cdot b}$$

$$= C_{l \cdot U}(b) + (2^k - 2) \sum_{x \in \mathbb{F}_2^{k*}} (-1)^{(l \cdot \Phi)(x) \cdot b} + 2 \sum_{x \in \mathbb{F}_2^{k*}} (-1)^{l \cdot V \left((l \cdot \Phi)^{-1}(x) \right) + b \cdot x}$$

$$= C_{l \cdot U}(b) + 2 W_{(l \cdot V)'}(b) - 2^k,$$

where $(l \cdot V)'(x) = l \cdot V \left((l \cdot \Phi)^{-1}(x) \right)$ for all $x \in \mathbb{F}_2^k$.

[**Case 2.**] Let $a \in \mathbb{F}_2^{k*}$ and $b = \mathbf{0}$. Then $C_{l \cdot F}(a, \mathbf{0})$ is equal to

$$\sum_{(x,y) \in \{\mathbf{0}, a\} \times \mathbb{F}_2^k} (-1)^{l \cdot F(x,y) + l \cdot F(x+a, y)} + \sum_{(x,y) \in \mathbb{F}_2^k \setminus \{\mathbf{0}, a\} \times \mathbb{F}_2^k} (-1)^{l \cdot F(x,y) + l \cdot F(x+a, y)}$$

$$= \left[\sum_{(x,y) \in \{\mathbf{0}, a\} \times \mathbb{F}_2^{k*}} (-1)^{l \cdot F(x,y) + l \cdot F(x+a, y)} + \sum_{x \in \{\mathbf{0}, a\}} (-1)^{l \cdot F(x, \mathbf{0}) + l \cdot F(x+a, \mathbf{0})} \right] +$$

$$\left[\sum_{(x,y) \in \mathbb{F}_2^k \setminus \{\mathbf{0}, a\} \times \mathbb{F}_2^{k*}} (-1)^{l \cdot F(x,y) + l \cdot F(x+a, y)} + \sum_{x \in \mathbb{F}_2^k \setminus \{\mathbf{0}, a\}} (-1)^{l \cdot F(x, \mathbf{0}) + l \cdot F(x+a, \mathbf{0})} \right]$$

$$= \left[2 \sum_{y \in \mathbb{F}_2^k} (-1)^{l \cdot U(y) + (l \cdot \Phi)(a) \cdot y} - 2 + \sum_{x \in \{\mathbf{0}, a\}} (-1)^{l \cdot V(x) + l \cdot V(x+a)} \right] +$$

$$\left[\sum_{(x,y) \in \mathbb{F}_2^k \setminus \{\mathbf{0}, a\} \times \mathbb{F}_2^k} (-1)^{\left((l \cdot \Phi)(x) + (l \cdot \Phi)(x+a) \right) \cdot y} - (2^k - 2) \right.$$

$$\left. + \sum_{x \in \mathbb{F}_2^k \setminus \{\mathbf{0}, a\}} (-1)^{l \cdot V(x) + l \cdot V(x+a)} \right]$$

$$= C_{l \cdot V}(a) + 2 W_{l \cdot U} \left((l \cdot \Phi)(a) \right) - 2^k.$$

[**Case 3.**] Let $a, b \in \mathbb{F}_2^{k*}$. Then $C_{l \cdot F}(a, b)$ is equal to

$$\sum_{(x,y) \in \{\mathbf{0}, a\} \times \mathbb{F}_2^k} (-1)^{l \cdot F(x,y) + l \cdot F(x+a, y+b)} + \sum_{(x,y) \in \mathbb{F}_2^k \setminus \{\mathbf{0}, a\} \times \mathbb{F}_2^k} (-1)^{l \cdot F(x,y) + l \cdot F(x+a, y+b)}$$

$$= \left[2 \sum_{y \in \mathbb{F}_2^k \setminus \{0,b\}} (-1)^{l \cdot F(0,y) + l \cdot F(a,y+b)} + 2(-1)^{l \cdot F(0,0) + l \cdot F(a,b)} \right.$$

$$+ 2(-1)^{l \cdot F(0,b) + l \cdot F(a,0)} \right] + \left[\sum_{(x,y) \in \mathbb{F}_2^k \setminus \{0,a\} \times \mathbb{F}_2^k \setminus \{0,b\}} (-1)^{l \cdot F(x,y) + l \cdot F(x+a,y+b)} \right.$$

$$+ 2 \sum_{x \in \mathbb{F}_2^k \setminus \{0,a\}} (-1)^{l \cdot F(x,b) + l \cdot F(x+a,0)} \right]$$

$$= \left[2 \sum_{y \in \mathbb{F}_2^k} (-1)^{l \cdot U(y) + (l \cdot \Phi)(a) \cdot (y+b)} - 2(-1)^{l \cdot U(b)} + 2(-1)^{l \cdot U(b) + l \cdot V(a)} \right]$$

$$+ \left[\sum_{(x,y) \in \mathbb{F}_2^k \setminus \{0,a\} \times \mathbb{F}_2^k} (-1)^{(l \cdot \Phi)(x) \cdot y + l \cdot \Phi(x+a) \cdot (y+b)} - 2 \sum_{x \in \mathbb{F}_2^k \setminus \{0,a\}} (-1)^{(l \cdot \Phi)(x) \cdot b} \right.$$

$$+ 2 \sum_{x \in \mathbb{F}_2^k \setminus \{0,a\}} (-1)^{l \cdot V(x) + (l \cdot \Phi)(x+a) \cdot b} \right]$$

$$= 2(-1)^{(l \cdot \Phi)(a) \cdot b} W_{l \cdot U} \big((l \cdot \Phi)(a) \big) - 2(-1)^{l \cdot U(b)} + 2(-1)^{l \cdot U(b) + l \cdot V(a)} + 2$$

$$+ W_{(l \cdot V)''}(b) - 2(-1)^{l \cdot V(a)}$$

$$= 2(-1)^{(l \cdot \Phi)(a) \cdot b} W_{l \cdot U} \big((l \cdot \Phi)(a) \big) + W_{(l \cdot V)''}(b) + 8t,$$

where $(l \cdot V)''(x) = l \cdot V \big((l \cdot \Phi)^{-1}(x) + a \big)$, and t equals 1 if $l \cdot V(a) = l \cdot U(b) = 1$ and equals 0 otherwise.

6   Balanced $(4t, t-1)$-Functions with Very Low Differential-Linear Uniformity

A partial spread of $\mathbb{F}_2^k$ ($k = 2t$) is a set of pairwise supplementary of t-dimensional subspaces of $\mathbb{F}_2^k$. For any $1 \le s \le 2^t + 1$, a partial spread $\mathcal{E}_s$ with $|\mathcal{E}_s| = s$ of $\mathbb{F}_2^k$ can be written as $\mathcal{E}_s = \{E_1, E_2, \ldots, E_s\}$ where E_i's are t-dimensional subspaces of $\mathbb{F}_2^k$ and $E_i \cap E_j = \{0\}$ for any $1 \le i \ne j \le s$. Spreads arise naturally in finite geometry: given a spread of $\mathbb{F}_{2^k}$, the vectors in $\mathbb{F}_{2^k}$ together with the translates of the elements of the spread form the points and lines of an affine plane, called a translation plane. Let us consider the additive group $(\mathbb{F}_{2^k}, +)$ of the finite field $\mathbb{F}_{2^k}$ with $k = 2t$. A classical example of spread of $\mathbb{F}_{2^k}$ is the Desarguesian spread, defined as follows:

- in $\mathbb{F}_{2^k}$ (in univariate form): $\{u\mathbb{F}_{2^t}, \ u \in U\}$ where $U = \{u \in \mathbb{F}_{2^k} : u^{2^t+1} = 1\}$ is the cyclic group of $\mathbb{F}_{2^k}$ with order $2^t + 1$;
- in $\mathbb{F}_{2^k} \approx \mathbb{F}_{2^t} \times \mathbb{F}_{2^t}$ (in bivariate form, thanks to the choice of a basis of the two-dimensional vector space $\mathbb{F}_{2^k}$ over $\mathbb{F}_{2^t}$): $\{E_a : a \in \mathbb{F}_{2^t}\} \cup \{E_\infty\}$ where $E_a = \{(x, ax) : x \in \mathbb{F}_{2^t}\}$ and $E_\infty = \{(0, y) : y \in \mathbb{F}_{2^t}\} = \{0\} \times \mathbb{F}_{2^t}$.

Definition 3. *Let $\mathcal{E} = \{E_1, E_2, \ldots, E_{2^t+1}\}$ be a partial spread of $\mathbb{F}_2^k$ ($k = 2t$). Let linear code $\mathcal{C}$ be a binary one-weight code of length $2^t - 1$, dimension $t - 1$,* *and minimum weight 2^{t-2}, and*

$$G = \begin{bmatrix} g_1 \\ g_2 \\ \vdots \\ g_{t-1} \end{bmatrix}$$

is a generator of $\mathcal{C}$. For every $1 \le i \le 2^{t-2}$, we define a Boolean functions v_i over $\mathbb{F}_2^k$ whose support is $\bigcup_{i \in \mathrm{supp}(g_i)} E_i \setminus \{\mathbf{0}\}$.

Theorem 7. *For any $(l_1, l_2, \cdots, l_{t-1}) \in \mathbb{F}_2^{t-1*}$, the Boolean function $v' = l_1 v_1 + l_2 v_2 + \cdots + l_{t-1} v_{t-1}$, where v_i's are defined in Definition 3, has Hamming weight $2^{k-2} - 2^{t-2}$,*

$$|W_{v'}(a)| \le \begin{cases} 2^{k-1} + 2^{\frac{k}{2}-1}, & \text{if } a = \mathbf{0} \\ 3 \cdot 2^{\frac{k}{2}-1}, & \text{if } a \in \mathbb{F}_2^{k*} \end{cases}$$

and

$$C_{v'}(\omega) \ge \begin{cases} 2^k, & \text{if } \omega = \mathbf{0} \\ 2^{k-2}, & \text{if } \omega \in \mathbb{F}_2^{k*} \end{cases}.$$

Proof. It can be easily seen that the support of v' is a subset of $\{E_1, E_2, \ldots, E_{2^t-1}\}$ with cardinality 2^{t-2}, since $\mathcal{C}$ is a binary one-weight code of length $2^t - 1$, dimension $t - 1$, and minimum weight 2^{t-2}. Then our assertion directly follows from [28, Theorem 9] with $s = 2^{t-2}$.

Definition 4. *Let the notation be the same as in Definition 3. We define $t - 1$ nonzero linear functions $h_1, h_2, \cdots, h_{t-1}$ over E_{2^t+1} such that for any $(l_1, l_2, \cdots, l_{t-1}) \in \mathbb{F}_2^{t-1*}$ the Boolean function $l_1 h_1 + l_2 h_2 + \cdots + l_{t-1} h_{t-1}$ has Hamming weight 2^{t-1}. For every $1 \le i \le t - 1$, we define a Boolean functions u_i over $\mathbb{F}_2^k$ whose support is $\mathrm{supp}(v_i) \cup \mathrm{supp}(h_i)$.*

Clearly, for any $(l_1, l_2, \cdots, l_{t-1}) \in \mathbb{F}_2^{t-1*}$ the Boolean function $l_1 u_1 + l_2 u_2 + \cdots + l_{t-1} u_{t-1}$ has Hamming weight $2^{k-2} + 2^{t-2}$.

Theorem 8. *For any $(l_1, l_2, \cdots, l_{t-1}) \in \mathbb{F}_2^{t-1*}$, the Boolean function $u' = l_1 u_1 + l_2 u_2 + \cdots + l_{t-1} u_{t-1}$, where u_i's are defined in Definition 4, has the following properties:*

$$|W_{u'}(a)| \le \begin{cases} 2^{k-1} + 3 \cdot 2^{\frac{k}{2}-1}, & \text{if } a = \mathbf{0} \\ 5 \cdot 2^{\frac{k}{2}-1}, & \text{if } a \in \mathbb{F}_2^{k*} \end{cases}$$

and

$$C_{u'}(\omega) \ge \begin{cases} 2^k, & \text{if } \omega = \mathbf{0} \\ 2^{k-2} - 2^{\frac{k}{2}+2}, & \text{if } \omega \in \mathbb{F}_2^{k*} \end{cases},$$

Proof. According to the definition of the Walsh–Hadamard transform, we can easily get that $W_{v'}(a) - 2 \cdot 2^{t-1} \leq W_{u'}(a) \leq W_{v'}(a) + 2 \cdot 2^{t-1}$ for any $a \in \mathbb{F}_2^k$. Then by Theorem 7 we have $|W_{u'}(a)| \leq 2^{k-1} + 3 \cdot 2^{\frac{k}{2}-1}$ if $a = \mathbf{0}$ and $|W_{u'}(a)| \leq 5 \cdot 2^{\frac{k}{2}-1}$ otherwise. By the definition of the autocorrelation function, we can obtain that $C_{v'}(a) - 8 \cdot 2^{t-1} \leq C_{u'}(a) \leq C_{v'}(a) + 8 \cdot 2^{t-1}$ for any $\omega \in \mathbb{F}_2^{k*}$. So we have $C_{u'}(\omega) \geq 2^{k-2} - 2^{\frac{k}{2}+2}$ for any $\omega \in \mathbb{F}_2^{k*}$ by Theorem 7. This completes the proof.

Combining Theorems 5, 6, 7 and 8, we have the following theorem.

Theorem 9. *Let $n = 2k = 4t \geq 20$, $m = t - 1$ in Construction 1, v_i's and u_i's are the k-variable Boolean functions defined in Definitions 3 and 4 respectively. For any $(l_1, l_2, \cdots, l_{t-1}) \in \mathbb{F}_2^{t-1*}$, $l_1\phi_1 + l_2\phi_2 + \cdots + l_{t-1}\phi_{t-1}$ is a linear permutation over $\mathbb{F}_2^k$. Then every $(n, t-1)$-function F generated by Construction 1 is balanced and for $f' = l_1 f_1 + l_2 f_2 + \cdots + l_{t-1} f_{t-1}$ we have*

(1) $nl(f') \geq 2^{n-1} - 2^{\frac{n}{2}-1} - 2^{\frac{n}{4}+1}$, and
(2) $\Delta_{f'} \leq 3 \cdot 2^{\frac{n}{2}-2} + 7 \cdot 2^{\frac{n}{4}} < 2^{\frac{n}{2}}$.

Moreover, we have

(3) $nl(F) \geq 2^{n-1} - 2^{\frac{n}{2}-1} - 2^{\frac{n}{4}+1}$, and
(4) $DL(F) \leq 3 \cdot 2^{\frac{n}{2}-3} + 7 \cdot 2^{\frac{n}{4}-1} < 2^{\frac{n}{2}-1}$.

Pasalic et al. [23, Corollary 5] proved that it is possible to construct a special class of (n, m)-functions with nonlinearity $2^{n-1} - 2^{\frac{n}{2}}$, where $n \geq 4m$ and n is even. Further, they identify an $(36, 8)$-function having nonlinearity $2^{35} - 2^{18}$ using a particular linear code. The nonlinearity of $(36, 8)$-functions identified in Theorem 9 is lower bounded by $2^{35} - 2^{17} - 1024$.

6.1   Implementation

The hardware complexity for the direct implementation of an (n, m)-function S is $O(m2^n)$ as the hardware complexity for the direct implementation of each coordinate function of S is $O(2^n)$. In the Construction 1, all coordinate functions are constructed by modifying the M-M bent functions. We know that these bent functions (let $n = 2k$) can be written as a concatenation of 2^k distinct affine functions in k variables. So, the hardware complexity for the implementation of these coordinate functions is $O(k2^k)$, which is much smaller than the direct implementation.

Suppose S be any $(4t, t-1)$-function defined as in Construction 1, where v_i's and u_i's are the $2t$-variable Boolean functions defined as in Definitions 3 and 4, respectively. Let for any fixed $x \in \mathbb{F}_2^{2t}$, $S(x, y) = S_x(y)$, for all $y \in \mathbb{F}_2^{2t}$, and S_x is called a block corresponding to x. Thus, $S_0(y) = (u_1(y), \ldots, u_{t-1}(y))$, and if $x \neq \mathbf{0}$, $S_x(\mathbf{0}) = (v_1(x), \ldots, v_{t-1}(x))$, otherwise $S_x(y) = (\phi_1(x) \cdot y, \ldots, \phi_{t-1}(x) \cdot y)$. We need $t - 1$ decoders for the permutations ϕ_i, $1 \leq i \leq t - 1$, and for hardware implementation of $t-1$ decoders we need $(t-1)2^{2t}$ gates. It is clear that if $x \neq \mathbf{0}$ and $v_i(x) = 0$ then the ith coordinate of S_x is a linear function in $2t$ variables, and so, the implementation of the ith coordinate of S_x we need $2t - 1$ gates in worst case. If $x \neq \mathbf{0}$ and $v_i(x) = 1$, we need to add an extra nonlinear monomial $(y_1 + 1) \cdots (y_{2t} + 1)$, which does not disturb the other output values in the same coordinate of S_x block, so, $4t - 1$ extra gates is required, and so, total number of gates required to implement the ith coordinate of S_x block is $6t - 2$ in worst case. The Hamming weight of u_i and v_i, $1 \leq i \leq t - 1$, are $2^{2t-2} + 2^{t-2}$ and $2^{2t-2} - 2^{t-2}$, respectively. Thus, they are not balanced, so, they are nonlinear functions. To implement the S_0 block, we need $(t - 1)2^{2t}$ gates in worst case, and for other $2^{2t} - 1$ block, we need

$$(t - 1)\{(6t - 2)(2^{2t-2} - 2^{t-2}) + (2t - 1)(2^{2t} - 1 - 2^{2t-2} + 2^{t-2})\}$$
$$= (t - 1)\{(2t - 1)(2^{2t} - 1) + (4t - 1)(2^{2t-2} - 2^{t-2})\}$$

gates in worst case. Thus, the implementation the function S defined as in Construction 1 requires $(t - 1)\{(3t + 1)2^{2t} - (2^{2t-2} + (4t - 1)2^{t-2} + 2t - 1)\}$ gates in worst case.

Table 1. $(4, 2)$-function S'.

(x_1, x_2, y_1, y_2)	$S'(x_1, x_2, y_1, y_2)$
$(0, 0, 0, 0)$	$(0, 0)$
$(0, 0, 0, 1)$	$(0, 0)$
$(0, 0, 1, 0)$	$(0, 0)$
$(0, 0, 1, 1)$	$(0, 0)$
$(0, 1, 0, 0)$	$(0, 0)$
$(0, 1, 0, 1)$	$(1, 1)$
$(0, 1, 1, 0)$	$(0, 1)$
$(0, 1, 1, 1)$	$(1, 0)$
$(1, 0, 0, 0)$	$(0, 0)$
$(1, 0, 0, 1)$	$(0, 1)$
$(1, 0, 1, 0)$	$(1, 0)$
$(1, 0, 1, 1)$	$(1, 1)$
$(1, 1, 0, 0)$	$(0, 0)$
$(1, 1, 0, 1)$	$(1, 0)$
$(1, 1, 1, 0)$	$(1, 1)$
$(1, 1, 1, 1)$	$(0, 1)$

For example let, $n = 4$ and S' be an $(4, 2)$-function defined in Table 1. The coordinate functions of S' are simple Maiorana-McFarland bent functions in 4 variables, where the permutations are $\phi_1(x_1, x_2) = (x_1, x_2)$ and $\phi_2(x_1, x_2) = (x_2, x_1 + x_2)$, $x_i \in \mathbb{F}_2$, $i = 1, 2$. Now we modify the function S' by suitable choices of u_i's and v_i's, $1 \leq i \leq 2$ and construct a balanced $(4, 2)$-function S. Suppose $supp(u_1) = \{(1, 1)\}$, $supp(v_1) = \{(1, 1)\}$, $supp(u_2) = \{(1, 1)\}$ and

Table 2. Modified $(4,2)$-functions S defined as in Construction 1.

(x_1,x_2,y_1,y_2)	$s_1'(x,y)$		$s_1(x,y)$		$s_2'(x,y)$		$s_2(x,y)$	
$(0,0,0,0)$	0		$u_1(0,0)=0$		0		$u_2(0,0)=0$	
$(0,0,0,1)$	0	0	$u_1(0,1)=0$	y_1y_2	0	0	$u_2(0,1)=0$	y_1y_2
$(0,0,1,0)$	0		$u_1(1,0)=0$		0		$u_2(1,0)=0$	
$(0,0,1,1)$	0		$u_1(1,1)=1$		0		$u_2(1,1)=1$	
$(0,1,0,0)$	0		$v_1(0,1)=0$		0		$v_2(0,1)=1$	
$(0,1,0,1)$	1	y_2	1	y_2	1	y_1+y_2	1	y_1y_2+1
$(0,1,1,0)$	0		0		1		1	
$(0,1,1,1)$	1		1		0		0	
$(1,0,0,0)$	0		$v_1(1,0)=0$		0		$v_2(1,0)=0$	
$(1,0,0,1)$	0	y_1	0	y_1	1	y_2	1	y_2
$(1,0,1,0)$	1		1		0		0	
$(1,0,1,1)$	1		1		1		1	
$(1,1,0,0)$	0		$v_1(1,1)=1$		0		$v_2(1,1)=0$	
$(1,1,0,1)$	1	y_1+y_2	1	y_1y_2+1	0	y_1	0	y_1
$(1,1,1,0)$	1		1		1		1	
$(1,1,1,1)$	0		0		1		1	

$supp(v_2) = \{(0,1)\}$. Then modified function S is given as in Table 2 and for the hardware implementation of S we need $3 + 3 = 6$ gates, without taking the decoders into account. In the Table 2, s_j' and s_j are the jth coordinate functions of S' and its modified $(4,2)$-function S, $j = 1, 2$, respectively. To implement the coordinate functions s_1, we need 1 XOR and 2 AND gates, and for s_2, 1 XOR and 2 AND gates, which are much smaller than the original calculation. For the other choices of u_i's and v_i's, we may need more gates to implement the function.

7   Conclusion

In the paper we first derive some properties of DLCT of an (n, m)-function and the differential-linear uniformity of known balanced vectorial Boolean functions. Further, we construct the balanced $(4t, t-1)$-function using Construction 1 which have very low differential-linear uniformity. Towards implementation, we count the number of gates that are required to implement such circuits. Our functions can be implemented for large Sboxes with significantly improved cryptographic properties. Obtaining constructions for (n, m)-functions with different choices of n, m, having efficient hardware implementation and good cryptographic properties are of significant interest in this direction.

Acknowledgments. We would like to thank the anonymous reviewers of Indocrypt 2019 for their valuable suggestions and comments, which considerably improved the quality of our paper. The work of Deng Tang was supported by the National Natural Science Foundation of China (grants 61872435 and 61602394).

References

1. Bar-On, A., Dunkelman, O., Keller, N., Weizman, A.: DLCT: a new tool for differential-linear cryptanalysis. In: Ishai, Y., Rijmen, V. (eds.) EUROCRYPT 2019. LNCS, vol. 11476, pp. 313–342. Springer, Cham (2019). https://doi.org/10.1007/978-3-030-17653-2_11

2. Biham, E., Dunkelman, O., Keller, N.: Enhancing differential-linear cryptanalysis. In: Zheng, Y. (ed.) ASIACRYPT 2002. LNCS, vol. 2501, pp. 254–266. Springer, Heidelberg (2002). https://doi.org/10.1007/3-540-36178-2_16

3. Biham, E., Shamir, A.: Differential cryptanalysis of DES-like cryptosystems. J. Cryptol. 4(1), 3–72 (1991)

4. Canteaut, A., Kölsch, L., Wiemer, F.: Observations on the DLCT and absolute indicators. Cryptology ePrint Archive (2019). https://eprint.iacr.org/2019/848.pdf

5. Canteaut, A., et al.: On the differential-linear connectivity table of vectorial boolean functions. CoRR (2019). http://arxiv.org/abs/1907.05986

6. Carlet, C.: Vectorial Boolean Functions for Cryptography. In: Crama, Y., Hammer, P.L. (eds.) Chapter of the Monograph: Boolean Models and Methods in Mathematics, Computer Science, and Engineering, pp. 398–470. Cambridge University Press (2010)

7. Carlitz, L.: Kloosterman sums and finite field extensions. Acta Arith. 2(16), 179–194 (1969)

8. Charpin, P., Helleseth, T., Zinoviev, V.: Propagation characteristics of $x \to x^{-1}$ and Kloosterman sums. Finite Fields Appl. 13(2), 366–381 (2007)

9. Charpin, P., Kyureghyan, G.M., Suder, V.: Sparse permutations with low differential uniformity. Finite Fields Appl. 28, 214–243 (2014)

10. Dillon, J.F.: Elementary Hadamard difference sets. Ph.D. thesis, University of Maryland (1974)

11. Dobbertin, H.: Construction of bent functions and balanced Boolean functions with high nonlinearity. In: Preneel, B. (ed.) FSE 1994. LNCS, vol. 1008, pp. 61–74. Springer, Heidelberg (1995). https://doi.org/10.1007/3-540-60590-8_5

12. Dunkelman, O., Indesteege, S., Keller, N.: A differential-linear attack on 12-round serpent. In: Chowdhury, D.R., Rijmen, V., Das, A. (eds.) INDOCRYPT 2008. LNCS, vol. 5365, pp. 308–321. Springer, Heidelberg (2008). https://doi.org/10.1007/978-3-540-89754-5_24

13. Huang, T., Tjuawinata, I., Wu, H.: Differential-linear cryptanalysis of ICEPOLE. In: Leander, G. (ed.) FSE 2015. LNCS, vol. 9054, pp. 243–263. Springer, Heidelberg (2015). https://doi.org/10.1007/978-3-662-48116-5_12

14. Kyureghyan, G.M., Zieve, M.: Permutation polynomials of the form $x + y(x^k)$. In: Contemporary Developments in Finite Fields and Applications, pp. 178–194. World Scientific Publication, Hackensack (2016)

15. Kavut, S., Maitra, S., Tang, D.: Construction and search of balanced Boolean functions on even number of variables towards excellent autocorrelation profile. Des. Codes Crypt. 87(2–3), 261–276 (2019)

16. Lachaud, G., Wolfmann, J.: The weights of the orthogonals of the extended quadratic binary goppa codes. IEEE Trans. Inf. Theory 36(3), 686–692 (1990)

17. Langford, S.K., Hellman, M.E.: Differential-linear cryptanalysis. In: Desmedt, Y.G. (ed.) CRYPTO 1994. LNCS, vol. 839, pp. 17–25. Springer, Heidelberg (1994). https://doi.org/10.1007/3-540-48658-5_3

18. Leurent, G.: Improved differential-linear cryptanalysis of 7-round chaskey with partitioning. In: Fischlin, M., Coron, J.-S. (eds.) EUROCRYPT 2016. LNCS, vol.

9665, pp. 344–371. Springer, Heidelberg (2016). https://doi.org/10.1007/978-3-662-49890-3_14

19. Canteaut, A., et al.: On the differential linear connectivity table of vectorial Boolean functions. arXiv:1907.05986 [cs.IT] (2019)

20. Matsui, M.: Linear cryptanalysis method for DES cipher. In: Helleseth, T. (ed.) EUROCRYPT 1993. LNCS, vol. 765, pp. 386–397. Springer, Heidelberg (1994). https://doi.org/10.1007/3-540-48285-7_33

21. McFarland, R.L.: A family of difference sets in non-cyclic groups. J. Comb. Theory Ser. A **15**(1), 1–10 (1973)

22. Nyberg, K.: Differentially uniform mappings for cryptography. In: Helleseth, T. (ed.) EUROCRYPT 1993. LNCS, vol. 765, pp. 55–64. Springer, Heidelberg (1994). https://doi.org/10.1007/3-540-48285-7_6

23. Pasalic, E., Maitra, S.: Linear codes in generalized construction of resilient functions with very high nonlinearity. IEEE Trans. Inf. Theory **48**(8), 2182–2191 (2002)

24. Peng, J., How Tan, C.: New differentially 4-uniform permutations by modifying the inverse function on subfields. Cryptogr. Commun. **9**(3), 363–378 (2017)

25. Peng, J., How Tan, C.: New explicit constructions of differentially 4-uniform permutations via special partitions of $\mathbb{F}_{2^{2k}}$. Finite Fields Appl. **40**, 73–89 (2016)

26. Qu, L., Tan, Y., Li, C., Gong, G.: More constructions of differentially 4-uniform permutations on $\mathbb{F}_{2^{2k}}$. Des. Codes Crypt. **78**(2), 391–408 (2016)

27. Qu, L., Tan, Y., How Tan, C., Li, C.: Constructing differentially 4-uniform permutations over $\mathbb{F}_{2^{2k}}$ via the switching method. IEEE Trans. Inf. Theory **59**(7), 4675–4686 (2013)

28. Tang, D., Kavut, S., Mandal, B., Maitra, S.: Modifying Maiorana-McFarland type bent functions for good cryptographic properties and efficient implementation. SIAM J. Discrete Math. (SIDMA) **33**(1), 238–256 (2019)

29. Tang, D., Maitra, S.: Constructions of n-variable ($n \equiv 2 \mod 4$) balanced Boolean functions with maximum absolute value in autocorrelation spectra $<2^{\frac{n}{2}}$. IEEE Trans. Inf. Theory **64**(1), 393–402 (2018)

30. Tang, D., Carlet, C., Tang, X.: Differentially 4-uniform bijections by permuting the inverse function. Des. Codes Crypt. **77**(1), 117–141 (2015)

31. US National Bureau of Standards, Data Encryption Standard. Federal Information Processing Standards Publications, vol. 46 (1977)

32. Zha, Z., Hu, L., Sun, S.: Constructing new differentially 4-uniform permutations from the inverse function. Finite Fields Appl. **25**, 64–78 (2014)

33. Zhang, W., Pasalic, E.: Highly nonlinear balanced S-boxes with good differential properties. IEEE Trans. Inf. Theory **60**(12), 7970–7979 (2014)

On the Relationship Between Resilient Boolean Functions and Linear Branch Number of S-Boxes

Sumanta Sarkar[1]([⊠]), Kalikinkar Mandal[2], and Dhiman Saha[3]

[1] TCS Innovation Labs, Hyderabad, India
sumanta.sarkar1@tcs.com
[2] University of Waterloo, Waterloo, Canada
kmandal@uwaterloo.ca
[3] Indian Institute of Technology, Bhilai, India
dhiman@iitbhilai.ac.in

Abstract. Differential branch number and linear branch number are critical for the security of symmetric ciphers. The recent trend in the designs like PRESENT block cipher, ASCON authenticated encryption shows that applying S-boxes that have nontrivial differential and linear branch number can significantly reduce the number of rounds. As we see in the literature that the class of 4×4 S-boxes have been well-analysed, however, a little is known about the $n \times n$ S-boxes for $n \geq 5$. For instance, the complete classification of 5×5 affine equivalent S-boxes is still unknown. Therefore, it is challenging to obtain "the best" S-boxes with dimension ≥ 5 that can be used in symmetric cipher designs. In this article, we present a novel approach to construct S-boxes that identifies classes of $n \times n$ S-boxes ($n = 5, 6$) with differential branch number 3 and linear branch number 3, and ensures other cryptographic properties. To the best of our knowledge, we are the first to report 6×6 S-boxes with linear branch number 3, differential branch number 3, and with other good cryptographic properties such as nonlinearity 24 and differential uniformity 4.

Keywords: S-box · Resilient Boolean function · Linear branch number · Differential branch number · Nonlinearity · Differential uniformity · Lightweight cipher

1 Introduction

A basic design principle of a block cipher consists of confusion and diffusion as suggested by Shannon [15]. The confusion layer makes the relation between the key and the ciphertext as complex as possible, whereas the diffusion layer spreads the plaintext statistics across the ciphertext. Over the years, several block ciphers have been constructed, and the most notable one is AES [6]. Later on, a lot of interest grew in lightweight cryptography, as the requirement of security of

© Springer Nature Switzerland AG 2019
F. Hao et al. (Eds.): INDOCRYPT 2019, LNCS 11898, pp. 361–374, 2019.
https://doi.org/10.1007/978-3-030-35423-7_18

Internet of Things (IoT) was felt. In this regard, lightweight block ciphers like PRESENT [4], CLEFIA [17] were standardized by ISO/IEC 29192. NIST too has taken an initiative to standardize lightweight cryptography algorithms [10]. With the advent of lightweight cryptography, a lot of effort has been devoted to find lightweight S-boxes with good cryptographic properties. There is also a considerable amount of literature available on lightweight MDS matrices which are used to build the diffusion layer.

In practice, S-boxes are used to build the confusion layer. An $n \times m$ S-box is a mapping from $\mathbb{F}_2^n$ to $\mathbb{F}_2^m$. In most cases S-boxes with $n = m$ are used, however there are some S-boxes where $n \neq m$, for instance DES [7] uses $(6, 4)$ S-boxes. In order to build a secure block cipher, the S-box should have high nonlinearity, high differential uniformity, high degree. Additionally, to reduce the number of rounds, it is desired that the number of active S-boxes increase as quickly as possible, and to achieve this goal, the S-boxes should have high differential and linear branch numbers. In case of AES, the number of active S-boxes increases due to the choice of ShiftRow and MixColumn operation. However, in the case of PRESENT or ASCON, this depends largely on the branch numbers of the S-box itself. PRESENT has removed the usual diffusion layer that is normally implemented by an MDS matrix. Thus saving a considerable amount of hardware cost. It uses a 4×4 S-box that has the following properties: differential branch number is 3; differential uniformity is 4; nonlinearity is 4; algebraic degree is 3.

The round function of PRESENT is comprised of 16 such S-boxes followed by a bit-permutation $L : \mathbb{F}_2^{64} \to \mathbb{F}_2^{64}$, where the role of the bit-permutation is to mix up the outputs of the S-boxes which become the input to the next round. As a bit-permutation can be implemented by wires only, this reduces the hardware implementation cost (in gates) for the entire design.

In [14], the upper bounds on linear and differential branch numbers were derived. For an $n \times n$ S-box $\mathcal{S}$, its linear branch number, denoted by $\mathcal{LBN}(\mathcal{S})$, satisfies $\mathcal{LBN}(\mathcal{S}) \leq n-1$, and its differential branch number, denoted by $\mathcal{DBN}(\mathcal{S})$, satisfies $\mathcal{DBN}(\mathcal{S}) \leq \lceil \frac{2n}{3} \rceil$. It is also interesting to note that ASCON [8] and SYCON [13] use 5×5 S-boxes that have differential branch number 3 and linear branch number 3. The block cipher SC2000 [16] used a 6×6 S-box, however, it has both linear and differential branch number 2.

1.1   Our Contribution

It is easy to observe that the trivial lower bound for differential and linear branch number is 2. However, constructing an S-box that has both differential and linear branch number greater than 2 along with other cryptographic properties is a non-trivial task. In this article, we investigate the problem of constructing S-boxes with both differential and linear branch number greater than 2. Our idea is to apply the relationship between resilient Boolean functions and the linear branch number to construct S-boxes that ensure linear branch number at least 3. In Sect. 3, we present Algorithm 1 that produces S-boxes with linear branch number 3. Further, we present Algorithm 2 which produces S-boxes with linear branch number 3 and differential branch number 3. Then, in Sect. 4, we consider some known classes of permutations over $\mathbb{F}_{2^6}$ with well-known cryptographic properties, and applying Algorithms 1 and 2, we obtain 6×6 S-boxes with both linear and differential branch number 3, nonlinearity 24, and differential uniformity 4. The hardware implementation cost of such S-boxes are also provided. To the best of our knowledge, this is the first time such 6×6 S-boxes with good cryptographic properties are reported. We also show how to construct efficient 5×5 S-boxes that have low hardware implementation overheads.

2   Preliminaries

Denote by $\mathbb{F}_2$, the finite field of two elements $\{0, 1\}$. Let $\mathbb{F}_{2^n}$ be the finite field with 2^n elements and $\mathbb{F}_2^n$ be the n-dimensional vector space over $\mathbb{F}_2$. For any $x \in \mathbb{F}_2^n$, the Hamming weight of x, denoted by $wt(x)$ is the number of 1's in x. Bitwise XOR is denoted by $\oplus$ and for any $x, y \in \mathbb{F}_2^n$ their dot product $x \cdot y$ is simply the usual inner product $x_0 y_0 \oplus \cdots \oplus x_{n-1} y_{n-1}$. An $n \times n$ S-box is a permutation $\mathcal{S} : \mathbb{F}_2^n \to \mathbb{F}_2^n$. We denote by $\mathbb{GL}(n, \mathbb{F}_2)$, the set of all linear permutations of $\mathbb{F}_2^n$. Clearly $\mathbb{GL}(n, \mathbb{F}_2)$ is a proper subset of the set of all permutations over $\mathbb{F}_2^n$. The S-box $\mathcal{S}$ can also be viewed as an n-tuple of Boolean functions in n-variable, i.e., $\mathcal{S} = (f_1, \ldots, f_n)$, where $f_i : \mathbb{F}_2^n \to \mathbb{F}_2$, here f_i is called a *coordinate* function of $\mathcal{S}$ and any linear combination of coordinate functions is called a *component* function of $\mathcal{S}$.

For a secure design, S-box needs to satisfy several properties such as high nonlinearity, high differential uniformity, high algebraic degree, etc. [5]. Basically the nonlinearity of $\mathcal{S}$ is the minimum nonlinearity that is obtained by any component function of $\mathcal{S}$. The algebraic degree of $\mathcal{S}$ is the maximum degree of its coordinate functions. Let $\mathcal{S}(\delta, \Delta) = \{\#x \in \mathbb{F}_2^n : \mathcal{S}(x) \oplus \mathcal{S}(x \oplus \delta) = \Delta\}$. Then the differential uniformity of $\mathcal{S}$ is defined as

$$\mathcal{DU}_\mathcal{S} = \max_{\delta \neq 0, \Delta} \{\mathcal{S}(\delta, \Delta)\}.$$

Lower the differential uniformity, better the resistance is against the differential attack [3]. The least possible differential uniformity is 2, and S-boxes with 2 differential uniformity are called Almost Perfect Nonlinear (APN) functions. The differential distribution table (DDT) of $\mathcal{S}$ is a matrix of order $2^n \times 2^n$ constructed as follows: the (δ, Δ)-th element of DDT is $\mathcal{S}(\delta, \Delta)$. In Table 1, we present the difference distribution table of the S-box $\mathcal{S} = 408235B719A6CDEF$.

We now recall the notions of correlation matrices, linear and differential branch numbers. Consider an $n \times n$ S-box $\mathcal{S}$. For any $\alpha, \beta \in \mathbb{F}_2^n$ the correlation coefficient of $\mathcal{S}$ with respect to (α, β) is given by

$$C_\mathcal{S}(\alpha, \beta) = \sum_{x \in \mathbb{F}_2^n} (-1)^{\beta \cdot \mathcal{S}(x) + \alpha \cdot x}. \tag{1}$$

If $\mathcal{S}(x) = (f_1(x), \ldots, f_n(x))$, then $\beta \cdot \mathcal{S}(x)$ is a Boolean function that is a linear combination of $\{f_1(x), \ldots, f_n(x)\}$, and $\alpha \cdot x$ is a linear Boolean function of the form $\ell_1 x_1 \oplus \ldots \oplus \ell_n x_n$.

Table 1. DDT of S-Box 408235B719A6CDEF

δ	Δ															
	0	1	2	3	4	5	6	7	8	9	A	B	C	D	E	F
0	16	0	0	0	0	0	0	0	0	0	0	0	0	0	0	0
1	0	4	0	0	2	0	2	0	2	0	2	0	4	0	0	0
2	0	0	8	0	0	0	0	0	2	0	0	2	2	0	0	2
3	0	0	0	6	2	0	2	2	2	0	0	0	0	0	2	0
4	0	0	0	2	4	4	0	2	0	2	0	0	0	2	0	0
5	0	2	0	2	0	4	0	0	2	2	0	0	2	0	0	2
6	0	0	0	0	0	0	4	4	0	0	0	4	0	0	0	4
7	0	2	0	2	0	0	0	4	0	0	2	2	0	2	2	0
8	0	0	2	0	2	4	0	0	4	2	0	0	0	0	0	2
9	0	2	0	0	2	0	0	0	2	4	0	0	0	2	4	0
A	0	0	0	0	0	0	2	2	0	2	4	2	0	2	2	0
B	0	2	2	2	0	0	2	0	0	0	2	4	2	0	0	0
C	0	4	2	0	0	0	2	0	2	0	0	0	2	4	0	0
D	0	0	0	0	2	0	0	2	0	2	2	0	4	4	0	0
E	0	0	0	2	2	0	0	0	0	2	4	0	0	0	2	4
F	0	0	2	0	0	4	2	0	0	0	0	2	0	0	4	2

It is easy to see that $-2^n \leq \mathsf{C}_{\mathcal{S}}(\alpha, \beta) \leq 2^n$. The correlation matrix $\mathsf{C}_{\mathcal{S}}$ of $\mathcal{S}$ is the $2^n \times 2^n$ matrix indexed by $\alpha, \beta \in \mathbb{F}_2^n$ in which the entry in the cell (α, β) is given by $\mathsf{C}_{\mathcal{S}}(\alpha, \beta)$:

$$\mathsf{C}_{\mathcal{S}} = [C_{\alpha,\beta}]_{2^n \times 2^n} \quad \text{where } C_{\alpha,\beta} = \mathsf{C}_{\mathcal{S}}(\alpha, \beta) \tag{2}$$

Next we recall some definitions related to the differential branch number and linear branch number.

Definition 1. *For any $n \times n$ S-box $\mathcal{S}$, its differential branch number (respectively linear branch number) is denoted by $\mathcal{DBN}(\mathcal{S})$ (respectively $\mathcal{LBN}(\mathcal{S})$) and defined as*

$$\mathcal{DBN}(\mathcal{S}) := \min_{x,x' \in \mathbb{F}_2^n,\, x \neq x'} \{wt(x \oplus x') + wt(\mathcal{S}(x) \oplus \mathcal{S}(x'))\},$$

and

$$\mathcal{LBN}(\mathcal{S}) := \min_{\alpha, \beta \in \mathbb{F}_2^n,\, \mathsf{C}_{\mathcal{S}}(\alpha, \beta) \neq 0} \{wt(\alpha) + wt(\beta)\},$$

where $\mathsf{C}_{\mathcal{S}}(\alpha, \beta)$ is the correlation coefficient as in (1).

If $\mathcal{S}$ is a linear permutation of $\mathbb{F}_2^n$, then there exists a binary $n \times n$ invertible matrix M such that $\mathcal{S}(x) = \mathrm{M}x$ for every $x \in \mathbb{F}_2^n$. In this case $\mathcal{DBN}(\mathcal{S})$ and $\mathcal{LBN}(\mathcal{S})$ can be simplified as done in the following fact taken from [6, Ch 9].

Fact 1. *Let S be a linear permutation of $\mathbb{F}_2^n$ given by $M \in \mathrm{GL}(n, \mathbb{F}_2)$. Then,*

$$\mathcal{DBN}(S) = \min_{\alpha \in \mathbb{F}_2^n, \alpha \neq 0} \{wt(\alpha) + wt(M\alpha)\}$$

$$\mathcal{LBN}(S) = \min_{\alpha \in \mathbb{F}_2^n, \alpha \neq 0} \{wt(\alpha) + wt(M^t\alpha)\}.$$

For any S-box S it is easy to see that $\mathcal{DBN}(S)$ is ≥ 2 and $\mathcal{LBN}(S) \geq 2$. Also,

$$\mathcal{DBN}(S) = \mathcal{DBN}(S^{-1}) \qquad \text{and} \qquad \mathcal{LBN}(S) = \mathcal{LBN}(S^{-1}).$$

It is interesting to note that the differential branch number is related to DDT. The differential branch number can be redefined as

$$\mathcal{DBN}(S) := \min_{\delta \neq 0, \Delta \neq 0, \mathcal{D}_S(\delta, \Delta) \neq 0} \{wt(\delta) + wt(\Delta)\}.$$

For example, it is clear from the DDT (Table 1), the differential branch number of 408235B719A6CDEF is 2.

One important classification of S-boxes is partitioning them into *affine equivalence* classes. For sake of completeness, we define the affine equivalence of S-boxes below.

Definition 2 (Affine Equivalence). *Let S, S' be two permutations of $\mathbb{F}_2^n$. We say that S is affine equivalent to S' if there exist matrices $A, B \in \mathrm{GL}(n, \mathbb{F}_2)$, and $c, d \in \mathbb{F}_2^n$ such that*

$$S'(x) = B \cdot S[A\,x \oplus c] \oplus d, \qquad \text{for all } x \in \mathbb{F}_2^n. \tag{3}$$

Affine equivalence preserves some cryptographic properties of S-boxes, such as differential uniformity, nonlinearity, degree, but it does not preserve branch numbers in general. For instance, the two S-boxes $S = $ C56B90AD3EF84712 and $S' = $ CD6310A5BE784F92 are affine equivalent, but they have different differential branch number: $\mathcal{DBN}(S) = 3$, whereas $\mathcal{DBN}(S') = 2$. The S-box S is used in PRESENT.

On the other hand, if A and B are permutation matrices[1] then the corresponding affine equivalence class preserves the branch number [12]. We state this as the following lemma.

Lemma 1. *If S and S_1 are two affine equivalent $n \times n$ S-boxes, such that $S_1(x) = B \cdot S[A\,x \oplus c] \oplus d$, for all $x \in \mathbb{F}_2^n$, where A and B are $n \times n$ permutation matrices, and $c, d \in \mathbb{F}_2^n$, then $\mathcal{DBN}(S) = \mathcal{DBN}(S_1)$ and $\mathcal{LBN}(S) = \mathcal{LBN}(S_1)$.*

---

[1] A matrix obtained by permuting rows (or columns) of an identity matrix.

3   Relation Between Resilient Boolean Function and Linear Branch Number

Let us define the resilient Boolean function first.

Definition 3. *A Boolean function $f : \mathbb{F}_2^n \to \mathbb{F}_2$ is called r-resilient if*

$$\sum_{x \in \mathbb{F}_2^n} (-1)^{f(x) \oplus \alpha \cdot x} = 0,$$

for all $\alpha \in \mathbb{F}_2^n$ such that $0 \le wt(\alpha) \le r$.

The relation between resilient Boolean functions and linear branch number was first noticed in [14]. We reiterate it here for the sake of clarity.

Lemma 2. *Let $\mathcal{S} : \mathbb{F}_2^n \to \mathbb{F}_2^n$ be an S-box. Then all the coordinate functions are $(\mathcal{LBN}(\mathcal{S}) - 2)$-resilient and also the algebraic $\deg(\mathcal{S}) \le n - \mathcal{LBN}(\mathcal{S}) + 1$.*

Proof. Let us assume $\mathcal{LBN}(\mathcal{S}) = r$. Then for all β with $wt(\beta) = 1$ and for all α with $1 \le wt(\alpha) \le r - 2$

$$C_{\mathcal{S}}(\alpha, \beta) = \sum_{x \in \mathbb{F}_2^n} (-1)^{\beta \cdot \mathcal{S}(x) + \alpha \cdot x} = 0.$$

As $wt(\beta) = 1$, so $\beta \cdot \mathcal{S}(x)$ is a coordinate function of $\mathcal{S}$, and every coordinate function of an S-box is necessarily balanced.

The degree of an n-variable r-resilient function is bounded by $n - 1 - r$, which proves the second part of the lemma.   □

Suppose the S-box S has $\mathcal{LBN}(S) = 3$, then every coordinate function of S will be 1-resilient. The differential and linear branch numbers are not invariant in an affine equivalence class unlike nonlinearity or differential uniformity. So if by some construction method one can get an S-box with high nonlinearity and high differential uniformity, but with $\mathcal{DBN} = \mathcal{LBN} = 2$, then one naive idea would be to search in the affine equivalent class of that S-box for $\mathcal{DBN} \ge 3$ and $\mathcal{LBN} \ge 3$. However, this search may not conclude as the size of affine equivalence is huge to exhaust for dimensions more than 4. For instance, cardinality of $\mathbb{GL}(5, \mathbb{F}_2)$ is around 2^{24}. In this case we can apply the necessary condition that every coordinate function should be resilient, to reject many S-boxes without checking their whole affine equivalence class. Based on this, we develop an algorithm which takes an S-box as an input and efficiently checks the possibility of the existence of any S-box with linear branch number 3 in its affine equivalence class.

Algorithm 1 is an heuristic one that we apply to construct a collection of affine equivalent S-boxes with linear branch number 3. The input S-box S could have linear branch number 3 or 2. However, the effectiveness of this algorithm can be realized if we take S such that $\mathcal{LBN}(S) = 2$, then we show how it can lead to an affine equivalent S-box(es) with $\mathcal{LBN}(S) = 3$. First it forms all possible 1-resilient component functions of S out of all $2^n - 1$ component

---

Algorithm 1. Construction of S-boxes with linear branch number 3

Input: S-box $S : \mathbb{F}_2^n \to \mathbb{F}_2^n$

Output: $\emptyset$ or S-boxes with linear branch number 3

1: Construct B as the set of all possible nonzero component functions of S
2: Extract the subset $\mathcal{R} \subset B$ which is the set of 1-resilient component functions of S.
3: **if** $|\mathcal{R}| < n$ **then**
4:     return $\emptyset$
5: **else**
6:     $\mathcal{T} = \emptyset$ ▷ Empty Set
7:     Form a new set $\{f_1, \ldots, f_n\}$; $f_i \in \mathcal{R}$
8:     **if** $\mathcal{U} = (f_1, \ldots, f_n)$ is a permutation of $\mathbb{F}_2^n$ **then**
9:         $\mathcal{T} \leftarrow \mathcal{T} \cup \{\mathcal{U}\}$ and go to Step 7
10: **return** $\mathcal{T}$

---

functions in Step 2. If $\mathcal{R}$ does not have at least n numbers of 1-resilient functions, the algorithm quits as, to ensure the linear branch number 3, all n-coordinate functions must be 1-resilient. On the other hand, if there are at least n numbers of 1-resilient component functions available, then every time n of them are chosen as coordinate functions in Step 7. Then it all remains to check whether $\mathcal{U}$ is a permutation or not. If yes, it is an S-box with $\mathcal{LBN} = 3$. Obviously, $\mathcal{U}$ is an affine equivalent of S and thus the nonlinearity and differential uniformity are preserved in $\mathcal{U}$.

We now apply the degree bound in order to show a nonexistence result related to 4×4 S-boxes.

Theorem 1. *There is no 4×4 S-box with $\mathcal{LBN} = 3$ and nonlinearity nonzero.*

Proof. If a 4×4 S-box S has $\mathcal{LBN} = 3$, then by Lemma 2, we know $\deg(S) \leq 2$. There are 302 affine equivalent 4×4 S-boxes, and among them only 6 classes have degree 2. Each of these 6 S-boxes have nonlinearity zero. Thus the proof. □

The degree bound of S-box with $\mathcal{LBN} = 3$ has been very effective in the above proof. Out of 302 affine equivalent S-boxes, there are 244 S-boxes with nonzero nonlinearity and nontrivial differential uniformity (<16). Then in order to prove the same result, one had to check the full class of each of these 244 S-boxes.

3.1 Adding $\mathcal{DBN} = 3$ Criterion

It is clear that ensuring $\mathcal{LBN}(S) = 3$ will harden the linear cryptanalysis [9], on the other hand it is also desired that $\mathcal{DBN}(S) > 2$, which gives better protection against the differential cryptanalysis.

For lightweight ciphers, 4×4 S-boxes have been very popular choice, for example, PRESENT [4], SKINNY [2], and GIFT [1]. In [14], the upper bounds on linear and differential branch number were derived. For an $n \times n$ S-box S, $\mathcal{LBN}(S) \leq n - 1$, and $\mathcal{DBN}(S) \leq \lceil \frac{2n}{3} \rceil$. Thus for 4×4 S-boxes the maximum

$\mathcal{LBN}$ and $\mathcal{DBN}$ values are exactly 3. However, as per Theorem 1, there is no scope of using 4×4 S-box with $\mathcal{LBN} = 3$. Lightweight ciphers namely ASCON [8] and SYCON [13] have used 5×5 S-boxes with $\mathcal{LBN} = \mathcal{DBN} = 3$.

We now introduce another heuristic in Algorithm 2 which takes an S-box with $\mathcal{LBN} = 3$ and $\mathcal{DBN} = 2$, and then applies linear transformation on both input and output to get an affine equivalent S-box which preserves the linear branch number, however, makes $\mathcal{DBN} = 3$.

Algorithm 2. Construction of S-boxes with linear branch number 3 and differential branch number 3

    Input: S-box $S : \mathbb{F}_2^n \to \mathbb{F}_2^n$ with $\mathcal{LBN}(S) = 3$
    Output: $\emptyset$ or S-boxes with linear branch number 3 and differential branch number 3

 1: Take a set of matrices $\mathcal{M}_1 \subset \mathbb{GL}(n, \mathbb{F}_2)$
 2: $\mathcal{A}_S = \emptyset$
 3: **for** A **in** $\mathcal{M}_1$ **do**
 4:    **if** $\mathcal{LBN}(S \circ A) = 3$ **then**
 5:        $\mathcal{A}_S \leftarrow \mathcal{A}_S \cup A$
 6: Take a set of matrices $\mathcal{M}_2 \subset \mathbb{GL}(n, \mathbb{F}_2)$
 7: $\mathcal{B}_S = \emptyset$
 8: **for** B **in** $\mathcal{M}_2$ **do**
 9:    **if** $\mathcal{DBN}(B \circ S) = 3$ **then**
10:        $\mathcal{B}_S \leftarrow \mathcal{B}_S \cup B$
11: $\mathcal{T} = \emptyset$
12: **for** $A \in \mathcal{A}_S$ **do**
13:    **for** B **in** $\mathcal{B}_S$ **do**
14:        **if** $\mathcal{LBN}(B \circ S \circ A) = 3$ and $\mathcal{DBN}(B \circ S \circ A) = 3$ **then**
15:           $\mathcal{T} \leftarrow \mathcal{T} \cup \{B \circ S \circ A\}$
16: **return** $\mathcal{T}$

One can apply Algorithm 1 to get an S-box with $\mathcal{LBN} = 3$, which will be the input to Algorithm 2. One naive way to look for S-boxes with $\mathcal{LBN} = \mathcal{DBN} = 3$ is to search in an affine equivalence class of an S-box. As the dimension grows, the size of the affine equivalence class also grows making it impossible to exhaust. So we apply the heuristic that takes a subset of matrices A of $\mathbb{GL}(n, \mathbb{F}_2)$ which acts on the input variables of S with $\mathcal{LBN}(S) = 3$, and also preserves the $\mathcal{LBN}$. Then it takes another subset of matrices B of $\mathbb{GL}(n, \mathbb{F}_2)$ which acts on the output of $S \circ A$, and also increases $\mathcal{DBN}$ to $\mathcal{DBN} = 3$. After that combining these two submatrices, if $\mathcal{LBN}(B \circ S \circ A) = \mathcal{DBN}(B \circ S \circ A) = 3$, then $B \circ S \circ A$ is added to the collection $\mathcal{T}$. For a fixed $\mathcal{M}_1$ and $\mathcal{M}_2$, the worst-case time complexity of Algorithm 2 in terms of bit operations is $O(|\mathcal{M}_1| \cdot |\mathcal{M}_2| \cdot (n^2 2^n + 2^{2n} + n2^{3n})) = O(|\mathcal{M}_1| \cdot |\mathcal{M}_2| \cdot n2^{3n})$ where $O(n^2 2^n)$ is the time complexity of constructing an affine equivalent S-box, $O(2^{2n})$ is for computing differential branch number, and $O(n2^{3n})$ is for computing linear branch number.

We do not want to consider $\mathcal{M}_1 = \mathcal{M}_2 = \mathbb{GL}(n, \mathbb{F}_2)$, as the complexity will be too high. For instance, $|\mathbb{GL}(5, \mathbb{F}_2)| \approx 2^{24}$, so one can imagine the vastness involved in this case. We carefully choose some subclass of $\mathbb{GL}(n, \mathbb{F}_2)$. We also want to keep the $n \times n$ identity matrix $\mathcal{I}_{n \times n}$ in both $\mathcal{M}_1$ and $\mathcal{M}_2$. If the input S-box is already a lightweight one, then ideally we want a minimum overhead for the input and output linear transformation so that the overall implementation does not scale much. In that case one of A and B being equal to $\mathcal{I}_{n \times n}$ will serve the purpose.

4   Leveraging the Known Classes of S-Boxes with Good Cryptographic Properties

As we aimed at constructing S-boxes with good cryptographic properties along with high branch numbers, we leverage the existing classes of S-boxes that are known to have good cryptographic properties. We achieve this by applying Algorithms 1 and 2 to the known classes of S-boxes with good cryptographic properties. We start with the power functions, which are defined over finite fields $\mathbb{F}_{2^n}$ and are of the form $F(x) = x^d$ for some d such that F is a permutation of $\mathbb{F}_{2^n}$. There are several known classes of power functions which have good cryptographic properties. We consider the simplest one, the Gold functions.

4.1   Gold Function

Definition 4. *Let n be odd. The function $F : \mathbb{F}_{2^n} \to \mathbb{F}_{2^n}$, defined by*

$$F(x) = x^{2^k + 1}$$

is known as Gold function where $\gcd(k, n) = 1$.

Note that the Gold functions are quadratic. For odd n and $\gcd(k, n) = 1$, then it becomes APN [11]. In the case of even n and $\gcd(2^k + 1, 2^n - 1) = 1$, the Gold functions can have the best differential uniform 4. For example, for $k = 2$ and $n = 6$, Gold function $F(x) = x^5$ is 4 differentially uniform, the nonlinearity is 24, which is also high. Therefore, this function is interesting to the cipher designers. However, $\mathcal{LBN}(F) = \mathcal{DBN}(F) = 2$, and that makes it a weaker choice for the design. We now apply Algorithm 1 hoping that it would yield an S-box that has $\mathcal{LBN} = 3$. In order to do that first we consider all the nonzero component functions of F. As this is defined over finite fields, so the set of component functions is $C_F = \{Tr(\lambda F(x)) : \lambda \in \mathbb{F}_{2^n}^*\}$, where $\mathbb{F}_{2^n}^*$ consists of all nonzero elements from $\mathbb{F}_{2^n}$. Note that the Trace function (Tr) is defined by

$$Tr(x) = x + x^2 + \ldots + x^{2^{n-1}},$$

and the range of Tr is in $\mathbb{F}_2$, that means it is a Boolean function.

By computing C_F for $F(x) = x^5$, we notice that there exist only 10 1-resilient component functions. For As there are 6 coordinate functions for a 6×6 S-box, thus enough combinations of 1-resilient functions are available to construct an affine equivalent S-box with $\mathcal{LBN} = 3$ as per Algorithm 1. The only thing that we need to care about is that while taking 6 component functions as the coordinate functions, they should form an S-box, that is a permutation of $\mathbb{F}_2^6$. Then we are ensured to have a 6×6 S-box with linear branch number 3 and nonlinearity 24. Following is an example of a set of 6 1-resilient component functions of x^5 defined over $\mathbb{F}_{2^6}$, which yield the S-box with $\mathcal{LBN} = 3$.

$$y_0 = x_0x_5 \oplus x_1x_2 \oplus x_1x_3 \oplus x_2x_4 \oplus x_2x_5 \oplus x_3x_4 \oplus x_3x_5 \oplus x_3 \oplus x_4x_5 \oplus x_4 \oplus x_5$$

$$y_1 = x_0x_4 \oplus x_0 \oplus x_1x_2 \oplus x_1x_4 \oplus x_1 \oplus x_2x_4 \oplus x_2x_5 \oplus x_3 \oplus x_4 \oplus x_5$$

$$y_2 = x_0x_1 \oplus x_0x_3 \oplus x_1x_3 \oplus x_1x_4 \oplus x_1 \oplus x_2x_3 \oplus x_2x_4 \oplus x_3x_4 \oplus x_4 \oplus x_5$$

$$y_3 = x_0x_2 \oplus x_0x_3 \oplus x_0x_4 \oplus x_1x_2 \oplus x_1x_4 \oplus x_1 \oplus x_2x_3 \oplus x_2x_5 \oplus x_3x_4 \oplus x_3x_5$$
$$\oplus x_3 \oplus x_4x_5 \oplus x_4 \oplus x_5$$

$$y_4 = x_0x_1 \oplus x_0x_2 \oplus x_0 \oplus x_1x_2 \oplus x_1x_4 \oplus x_1x_5 \oplus x_1 \oplus x_2x_3 \oplus x_2x_4 \oplus x_3x_4 \oplus x_4x_5 \oplus x_4$$

$$y_5 = x_0x_1 \oplus x_0x_3 \oplus x_0x_4 \oplus x_1 \oplus x_2 \oplus x_3x_4 \oplus x_3x_5 \oplus x_3 \oplus x_4x_5 \oplus x_4$$

4.2 6×6 Quadratic S-Box with $\mathcal{LBN} = 3$ and $\mathcal{DBN} = 3$

We consider the class $F(x) = x^{10} + \alpha x$ defined over $\mathbb{F}_{2^6}$. First we find by using Algorithm 1, 6×6 S-boxes with $\mathcal{LBN} = 3$ of this form. Then we apply Algorithm 2 to get an S-box with $\mathcal{LBN} = \mathcal{DBN} = 3$. Essentially we will form a subclass of affine equivalent S-boxes. In order to shorten the search effort, we choose a small class of invertible matrices. We choose 6×6 nonsingular Toeplitz matrices.

Definition 5. *A matrix is called Toeplitz if every descending diagonal from left to right is constant.*

Following is an example of a Toeplitz matrix of order $n \times n$

$$\begin{bmatrix} a_0 & a_1 & a_2 & \cdots & a_{n-2} & a_{n-1} \\ a_{-1} & a_0 & a_1 & \cdots & a_{n-3} & a_{n-2} \\ \vdots & \vdots & \vdots & \vdots & \vdots & \vdots \\ a_{-(n-1)} & a_{-(n-2)} & a_{-(n-3)} & \cdots & a_{-1} & a_0 \end{bmatrix}. \tag{4}$$

A Toeplitz matrix is defined by its first row and first column. For instance $\{a_0, a_1, \ldots, a_{n-1}, a_{-1}, a_{-2}, \ldots, a_{-(n-1)}\}$ defines the Toeplitz matrix as in (4).

We consider the S-box $\mathcal{S} = [0, 54, 47, 48, 3, 5, 24, 55, 23, 56, 32, 38, 46, 49, 45, 27, 61, 14, 62, 36, 16, 19, 39, 13, 1, 43, 26, 25, 22, 12, 57, 10, 30, 58, 17, 28, 9, 29, 50, 15, 8, 53, 31, 11, 37, 40, 6, 34, 2, 35, 33, 41, 59, 42, 44, 20, 63, 7, 4, 21, 60, 52, 51, 18]$. For this S-box we have $\mathcal{LBN}(\mathcal{S}) = 3$, but $\mathcal{DBN}(\mathcal{S}) = 2$. The hardware cost of this S-box is 79.68 GE.

We take $\mathcal{S}$ as an input to Algorithm 2. Let $\mathbb{T}_6$ denote the set of all nonsingular 6×6 Toeplitz matrices. Then $|\mathbb{T}_6| = 1024$. To keep the search space small, we choose $\mathcal{M}_1 = \mathcal{M}_2 = \mathbb{T}_6$. As a result we see that among the possible Toeplitz matrices, by applying the following Toeplitz matrix M on the output, it is possible to obtain an affine equivalent S-box $\mathcal{S}'$ with $\mathcal{LBN}(\mathcal{S}') = 3$ and $\mathcal{DBN}(\mathcal{S}') = 3$.

$$M = \begin{bmatrix} 1 & 0 & 0 & 0 & 0 & 0 \\ 0 & 1 & 0 & 0 & 0 & 0 \\ 0 & 0 & 1 & 0 & 0 & 0 \\ 0 & 0 & 0 & 1 & 0 & 0 \\ 0 & 0 & 0 & 0 & 1 & 0 \\ 1 & 0 & 0 & 0 & 0 & 1 \end{bmatrix}. \tag{5}$$

In Table 2, we present this S-box $\mathcal{S}'$, and its hardware cost is 86.71 GE. The cost of this derived S-box does not scale much as it comes through by applying such a low cost matrix M in Eq. (5).

Table 2. 6×6 S-box $\mathcal{S}'$ with $\mathcal{LBN}(\mathcal{S}') = 3$, $\mathcal{DBN}(\mathcal{S}') = 3$. nonlinearity = 24, differential uniformity = 4, degree = 2

x	0	1	2	3	4	5	6	7	8	9	10	11	12	13	14	15	16	17	18	19	20	21	22	23	24	25	26	27	28	29	30	31
$S(x)$	0	58	47	28	3	29	24	15	23	53	32	11	46	40	45	34	61	35	62	41	16	42	39	20	1	7	26	21	22	52	57	18
x	32	33	34	35	36	37	38	39	40	41	42	43	44	45	46	47	48	49	50	51	52	53	54	55	56	57	58	59	60	61	62	63
$S(x)$	30	54	17	48	9	5	50	55	8	56	31	38	37	49	6	27	2	14	33	36	59	19	44	13	63	43	4	25	60	12	51	10

We would like to point out that as far as we know the existence of 6×6 S-box that have significant cryptographic properties and at the same time has $\mathcal{LBN} = \mathcal{DBN} = 3$ has never been reported. This function is the first in the literature.

4.3 Cubic Function

Next we consider the function $F : \mathbb{F}_{2^6} \to \mathbb{F}_{2^6}$, defined by

$$F(x) = x^{19},$$

S-box derived from this function has degree 3, nonlinearity 24 and differential uniformity 4. We apply the same technique as in Algorithm 1, however, we extend the input by considering the Extended Affine (EA) equivalent[2] class of x^{19}. Then

Table 3. 6×6 S-box $\mathcal{S}$ with $\mathcal{LBN}(\mathcal{S}) = 3$, $\mathcal{DBN}(\mathcal{S}) = 3$. nonlinearity = 24, differential uniformity = 4, degree = 3

x	0	1	2	3	4	5	6	7	8	9	10	11	12	13	14	15	16	17	18	19	20	21	22	23	24	25	26	27	28	29	30	31
$S(x)$	0	45	48	15	58	32	14	49	13	7	41	12	3	54	55	26	42	25	22	34	60	38	53	31	21	51	4	24	27	28	43	33
x	32	33	34	35	36	37	38	39	40	41	42	43	44	45	46	47	48	49	50	51	52	53	54	55	56	57	58	59	60	61	62	63
$S(x)$	39	19	30	63	16	1	59	8	57	62	29	50	6	44	36	17	23	10	56	37	9	47	5	20	40	52	35	2	18	61	46	11

---

[2] $\mathcal{S}$ and $\mathcal{S}'$ are EA equivalent if $\mathcal{S}' = B \circ \mathcal{S} \circ A + L$ for some linear function L and affine permutations A and B.

Table 4. 5×5 S-box $\mathcal{S}$ with $\mathcal{LBN}(\mathcal{S}) = 3$, $\mathcal{DBN}(\mathcal{S}) = 3$. nonlinearity = 8, differential uniformity = 8, degree = 2

x	0	1	2	3	4	5	6	7	8	9	10	11	12	13	14	15	16	17	18	19	20	21	22	23	24	25	26	27	28	29	30	31
$S(x)$	0	14	27	17	22	24	15	5	30	25	7	4	11	12	16	19	3	9	8	6	21	31	28	18	20	23	29	26	1	2	10	13

$y_0 = x_0x_3 \oplus x_1 \oplus x_2x_3 \oplus x_3x_4 \oplus x_4$
$y_1 = x_0 \oplus x_1x_2 \oplus x_1x_3 \oplus x_1 \oplus x_2x_3 \oplus x_2 \oplus x_3 \oplus x_4$
$y_2 = x_0x_1 \oplus x_0x_4 \oplus x_0 \oplus x_2 \oplus x_3$
$y_3 = x_0x_3 \oplus x_0 \oplus x_1 \oplus x_3x_4 \oplus x_3$
$y_4 = x_1x_4 \oplus x_1 \oplus x_2 \oplus x_3$

Hardware cost = 38.28 GE

x	0	1	2	3	4	5	6	7	8	9	10	11	12	13	14	15	16	17	18	19	20	21	22	23	24	25	26	27	28	29	30	31
$S(x)$	0	27	22	15	14	17	24	5	30	7	11	16	25	4	12	19	3	8	21	28	9	6	31	18	20	29	1	10	23	26	2	13

$y_0 = x_0 \oplus x_1x_3 \oplus x_2x_3 \oplus x_3x_4 \oplus x_4$
$y_1 = x_0x_1 \oplus x_0x_3 \oplus x_0 \oplus x_1x_3 \oplus x_1 \oplus x_2 \oplus x_3 \oplus x_4$
$y_2 = x_0x_2 \oplus x_1 \oplus x_2x_4 \oplus x_2 \oplus x_3$
$y_3 = x_0 \oplus x_2x_3 \oplus x_2 \oplus x_3x_4 \oplus x_3$
$y_4 = x_0x_4 \oplus x_0 \oplus x_1 \oplus x_3$

Hardware cost = 38.28 GE

x	0	1	2	3	4	5	6	7	8	9	10	11	12	13	14	15	16	17	18	19	20	21	22	23	24	25	26	27	28	29	30	31
$S(x)$	0	27	14	17	22	15	24	5	30	7	25	4	11	16	12	19	3	8	9	6	21	28	31	18	20	29	23	26	1	10	2	13

$y_0 = x_0 \oplus x_1x_3 \oplus x_2x_3 \oplus x_3x_4 \oplus x_4$
$y_1 = x_0x_2 \oplus x_0x_3 \oplus x_0 \oplus x_1 \oplus x_2x_3 \oplus x_2 \oplus x_3 \oplus x_4$
$y_2 = x_0x_1 \oplus x_1x_4 \oplus x_1 \oplus x_2 \oplus x_3$
$y_3 = x_0 \oplus x_1x_3 \oplus x_1 \oplus x_3x_4 \oplus x_3$
$y_4 = x_0x_4 \oplus x_0 \oplus x_2 \oplus x_3$

Hardware cost = 44.53 GE

we get a 6×6 S-box $\mathcal{S}$ such that $\mathcal{LBN}(\mathcal{S}) = 3$ and $\mathcal{DBN}(S) = 3$. The S-box is given in Table 3 and its hardware cost is 158.59 GE.

5   Lightweight 5×5 S-Boxes

In another direction we use the relationship between resilient Boolean functions and S-boxes with linear branch number 3 to come up with lightweight S-boxes with $\mathcal{LBN} = 3$ and $\mathcal{DBN} = 3$. In particular we restrict to 5×5 quadratic S-boxes.

We give a little tweak to Algorithm 1, and start with 1-resilient functions in the first place in order to get S-boxes with $\mathcal{LBN} = 3$. First we enumerate all the 5-variable quadratic 1-resilient Boolean functions, the total number of such functions is 2868. However, if we restrict the quadratic resilient functions to have only 4 terms, then there are 285 such functions; and with only 5 terms, there are 330 such functions. We consider this type of resilient functions and combine them as coordinate functions of S-boxes. If these coordinate functions form an S-box, then $\mathcal{LBN} = 3$ is ensured. Then we apply the idea of Algorithm 2, however with a little tweak. We randomly select matrices from $\mathbb{GL}(5, \mathbb{F}_2)$, and apply on input and output of the S-boxes in order to get S-boxes with $\mathcal{LBN} = 3$ and $\mathcal{DBN} = 3$. We give some examples of S-boxes that are obtained in this way in

Table 4. We also measure their hardware cost. Implementation of all the S-boxes in this article are done using Verilog HDL for ASIC. Mentor LeonardoSpectrum Level 3 (2018a.2) is used for synthesis with the UMC 65 nm Low-Power RVT (Regular VT) Standard Performance Generic Core Cell Library from Faraday.

6 Conclusions

We have studied the relationship between the resilient Boolean functions and S-boxes with linear branch number 3. We have shown how efficiently and systematically S-boxes with linear and differential branch number 3 can be constructed. We have presented such 5×5 and 6×6 S-boxes with good cryptographic properties such as nonlinearity and differential uniformity. The hardware costs of these S-boxes are provided. We think these S-boxes are interesting and can be used in cipher design, for instance, by following the design principle of ASCON. This idea can also be explored further in order to construct new hardware-friendly S-boxes.

References

1. Banik, S., Pandey, S.K., Peyrin, T., Sasaki, Y., Sim, S.M., Todo, Y.: GIFT: a small present. In: Fischer, W., Homma, N. (eds.) CHES 2017. LNCS, vol. 10529, pp. 321–345. Springer, Cham (2017). https://doi.org/10.1007/978-3-319-66787-4_16
2. Beierle, C., et al.: The skinny family of block ciphers and its low-latency variant mantis. In: Robshaw, M., Katz, J. (eds.) CRYPTO 2016. LNCS, vol. 9815, pp. 123–153. Springer, Heidelberg (2016). https://doi.org/10.1007/978-3-662-53008-5_5
3. Biham, E., Shamir, A.: Differential cryptanalysis of DES-like cryptosystems. In: Menezes, A.J., Vanstone, S.A. (eds.) CRYPTO 1990. LNCS, vol. 537, pp. 2–21. Springer, Heidelberg (1991). https://doi.org/10.1007/3-540-38424-3_1
4. Bogdanov, A., et al.: PRESENT: an ultra-lightweight block cipher. In: Paillier, P., Verbauwhede, I. (eds.) CHES 2007. LNCS, vol. 4727, pp. 450–466. Springer, Heidelberg (2007). https://doi.org/10.1007/978-3-540-74735-2_31
5. Carlet, C.: Vectorial Boolean functions for cryptography. In: Hammer, P., Crama, Y. (eds.) Boolean Methods and Models. Cambridge University Press, Cambridge (2010)
6. Daemen, J., Rijmen, V.: The Design of Rijndael: AES - The Advanced Encryption Standard. Information Security and Cryptography. Springer, Heidelberg (2002). https://doi.org/10.1007/978-3-662-04722-4_1
7. DES: Data encryption standard. In: FIPS PUB 46, Federal Information Processing Standards Publication, pp. 46–52 (1977)
8. Dobraunig, C., Eichlseder, M., Mendel, F., Schläffer, M.: Ascon v1.2. Submission to NIST lightweight cryptography project (2019)
9. Matsui, M.: Linear cryptanalysis method for DES cipher. In: Helleseth, T. (ed.) EUROCRYPT 1993. LNCS, vol. 765, pp. 386–397. Springer, Heidelberg (1994). https://doi.org/10.1007/3-540-48285-7_33
10. NIST: NIST lightweight cryptography project (2019)

11. Gold, R.: Maximal recursive sequences with 3-valued recursive crosscorrelation functions. IEEE Trans. Inf. Theory **14**(1), 154–156 (1968)
12. Saarinen, M.-J.O.: Cryptographic analysis of all 4 × 4-bit S-boxes. In: Miri, A., Vaudenay, S. (eds.) SAC 2011. LNCS, vol. 7118, pp. 118–133. Springer, Heidelberg (2012). https://doi.org/10.1007/978-3-642-28496-0_7
13. Sarkar, S., Mandal, K., Saha, D.: Sycon v1.0. Submission to the NIST lightweight cryptography project (2019)
14. Sarkar, S., Syed, H.: Bounds on differential and linear branch number of permutations. In: Susilo, W., Yang, G. (eds.) ACISP 2018. LNCS, vol. 10946, pp. 207–224. Springer, Cham (2018). https://doi.org/10.1007/978-3-319-93638-3_13
15. Shannon, C.E.: Communication theory of secrecy systems. Bell Syst. Tech. J. **28**, 656–715 (1949)
16. Shimoyama, T., et al.: The block cipher SC2000. In: Matsui, M. (ed.) FSE 2001. LNCS, vol. 2355, pp. 312–327. Springer, Heidelberg (2002). https://doi.org/10.1007/3-540-45473-X_26
17. Shirai, T., Shibutani, K., Akishita, T., Moriai, S., Iwata, T.: The 128-bit blockcipher CLEFIA (extended abstract). In: Biryukov, A. (ed.) FSE 2007. LNCS, vol. 4593, pp. 181–195. Springer, Heidelberg (2007). https://doi.org/10.1007/978-3-540-74619-5_12

The Complete Cost of Cofactor $h = 1$

Peter Schwabe[(✉)] and Amber Sprenkels[(✉)]

Digital Security Group, Radboud University,
P.O. Box 9010, 6500 Nijmegen, GL, The Netherlands
peter@cryptojedi.org, amber@electricdusk.com

Abstract. This paper presents optimized software for constant-time variable-base scalar multiplication on prime-order Weierstraß curves using the complete addition and doubling formulas presented by Renes, Costello, and Batina in 2016. Our software targets three different microarchitectures: Intel Sandy Bridge, Intel Haswell, and ARM Cortex-M4. We use a 255-bit elliptic curve over $\mathbb{F}_{2^{255}-19}$ that was proposed by Barreto in 2017. The reason for choosing this curve in our software is that it allows most meaningful comparison of our results with optimized software for Curve25519. The goal of this comparison is to get an understanding of the cost of using cofactor-one curves with complete formulas when compared to widely used Montgomery (or twisted Edwards) curves that inherently have a non-trivial cofactor.

Keywords: Elliptic curve cryptography · SIMD · Curve25519 · Scalar multiplication · Prime-field arithmetic · Cofactor security

1 Introduction

Since its invention in 1985, independently by Koblitz [34] and Miller [38], elliptic-curve cryptography (ECC) has widely been accepted as the state of the art in asymmetric cryptography. This success story is mainly due to the fact that attacks have not substantially improved: with a choice of elliptic curve that was in the 80s already considered conservative, the best attack for solving the elliptic-curve discrete-logarithm problem is still the generic Pollard-rho algorithm (with minor speedups, for example by exploiting the efficiently computable negation map in elliptic-curve groups [14]).

One of the main developments since the first generation of elliptic-curve cryptography has been in the choice of curves. Until 2006, the widely accepted choice of elliptic curve was a prime-order Weierstraß curve. In 2006, Bernstein proposed the Montgomery curve "Curve25519"[1] as an alternative offering multiple security and performance features. Most importantly—at least in the context of this paper—it featured highly efficient *complete formulas*, which enable fast arithmetic without any checks for special cases. These complete formulas are

---

[1] In the 2006 paper, Curve25519 referred to the ECDH key-exchange protocol; Bernstein later recommended to use X25519 for the protocol and Curve25519 for the underlying curve [7].

© Springer Nature Switzerland AG 2019
F. Hao et al. (Eds.): INDOCRYPT 2019, LNCS 11898, pp. 375–397, 2019.
https://doi.org/10.1007/978-3-030-35423-7_19

somewhat limited, because they only cover differential addition. This is not a problem for the X25519 elliptic-curve Diffie-Hellman key exchange presented in [6], but it makes implementation of more advanced protocols (like signature schemes) somewhat inconvenient.

This issue was addressed through a sequence of three papers. In [23], Edwards introduced a new description of elliptic curves; in [13], Bernstein and Lange presented very efficient complete formulas for group arithmetic on these curves (and introduced the name "Edwards curves"); and in [8], Bernstein, Birkner, Joye, Lange, and Peters generalized the concept to twisted Edwards curves and showed that this class of elliptic curves is birationally equivalent to Montgomery curves. The twisted Edwards form of Curve25519 was subsequently used in [9,10] for the construction of the Ed25519 digital-signature scheme.

The simplicity and efficiency of X25519 key exchange and Ed25519 signatures resulted in quick adoption in a variety of applications, such as SSH, the Signal protocol, and the Tor anonymity project. Both schemes are also used in TLS 1.3.

Complete Addition or Prime Order. Unfortunately, the advantages of Montgomery and twisted Edwards curves—most notably the very efficient complete addition formulas— have to be weighed against a disadvantage: the group of points cannot have prime order as it always has a cofactor of a multiple of 4. Consequently, a somewhat simplified view on choosing curves for cryptographic applications is that we have to choose between either efficient complete formulas through Montgomery or (twisted) Edwards curves, or prime-order groups through Weierstraß curves.

The design of X25519 and Ed25519 carefully takes the non-trivial cofactor into account. However in more involved protocols, a non-trivial cofactor may complicate the protocol's design, potentially leading to security issues. In the last years, we saw at least two examples of protocols deployed in real-world applications that had catastrophic vulnerabilities because they did not carefully handle the cofactor.

The first example was a vulnerability in the Monero cryptocurrency, that allowed for arbitrary double spending [36]. Monero requires that "key images"— which bind transactions to their sender's public key—should be non-malleable, i.e. for a transaction to be valid, its public key must be unique. Unfortunately, due to the cofactor, an attacker could construct different key images that were bound to the same public key, therefore allowing arbitrary double-spending. This issue was mitigated by checking the order of the key image, which involves a full scalar multiplication, ironically diminishing the performance that Curve25519 was meant to provide.

The second example was recently discovered by Cremers and Jackson, who found more vulnerabilities in protocols caused by the non-trivial cofactor [22]. These vulnerabilities allowed attackers to bypass the authentication properties of the Secure Scuttlebutt Gossip protocol and Tendermint's secure handshake.

Why not both? In 2015, Hamburg presented the "Decaf" technique [28], which removes the cofactor of twisted Edwards curves through a clever encoding. He later refined the technique to "Ristretto" (see [1]), which is now proposed in the crypto forum research group (CFRG) of IETF for standardization [46]. The Decaf and Ristretto encodings come at some computational cost and also added complexity of the implementation, but it eliminates the burden of handling the cofactor in protocol design.

However, there is another, much more obvious, approach to complete addition in prime-order elliptic-curve groups. It is long known that complete addition formulas also exist for Weierstraß curves [18], but those formulas were long regarded as too inefficient to offer an acceptable tradeoff. The situation changed in 2016, when Renes, Costello, and Batina revisited the approach from [18] and presented much more efficient complete addition formulas for Weierstraß curves [42]. Unfortunately, these formulas are still considerably less efficient than the incomplete addition formulas that possibly require handling of special cases. The performance gap is even larger compared to the complete addition formulas for twisted Edwards curves, and the complete differential additional used in the scalar-multiplication ladder on Montgomery curves.

Contributions of this Paper. If we assume the usage of complete addition formulas for both—twisted Edwards or Montgomery curves on one hand and Weierstraß curves on the other hand—the choice of curve becomes a tradeoff between performance and protocol simplicity. To fully understand this tradeoff, we need to know how large exactly the performance penalty is for using Weierstraß curves with the complete addition formulas from [42]. The standard approach to understand performance differences is to compare the speed of optimized implementations, ideally on different target architectures. Almost surprisingly however, there are no such optimized implementations of elliptic-curve scalar multiplication using complete formulas on Weierstraß curves. In this paper we present such implementations and answer the question about the actual cost of complete cofactor-1 ECC arithmetic using the formulas from [42].

More specifically, we present highly optimized software targeting three different microarchitectures for variable-basepoint scalar multiplication on a 255-bit Weierstraß curve over the field $\mathbb{F}_{2^{255}-19}$, the same field underlying Curve25519. Choosing a curve over the same field eliminates possible effects that are not due to the choice of curve shape and corresponding addition formulas, but due to differences in speed of the field arithmetic.

The three microarchitectures we are targeting are Intel's 64-bit Haswell generation of processors featuring AVX2 vector instructions; the earlier Intel Ivy Bridge processors that feature AVX vector instructions, but not yet the AVX2 integer-vector instruction set; and the ARM Cortex M4 family of 32-bit embedded microcontrollers. All our implementations follow the "constant-time" approach of avoiding secret branch conditions and secretly indexed memory access.

We compare our results to scalar multiplication from highly optimized X25519 software on the same microarchitectures. Perhaps surprisingly the performance penalty heavily depends on the microarchitecture; it ranges between a factor of only 1.47 on Intel Haswell and a factor of 2.87 on ARM Cortex M4.

Disclaimer. This paper revisits the discussion of the performance of Curve-25519 (and Curve448) relative to the old Weierstraß curves. We see a certain risk that the results in this paper may be misinterpreted one way or another, so we would like to clarify our intentions, and how we see the results of this paper:

- The motivation for this work has been that we saw a potentially interesting missing data point in the context of choosing elliptic curves for cryptographic applications.
- We do not think that any elliptic-curve standardization discussion should be re-opened. No result in this paper suggests that this would be useful and we believe that the choice of Curve25519 and Curve448 by IETF was a very sensible one. All effort that the community can invest in standardization is better placed in, for example, efforts to choose sensible post-quantum primitives.
- We see a rather common misconception of Weierstraß curves not having any (practical) complete addition formulas. For example, the book "Serious Cryptography" by Aumasson describes the ANSSI and Brainpool curves (both prime-order Weierstraß curves) as *"two families of curves that don't support complete addition formulas [...]"* [2, page 231]. In similar spirit, Bernstein and Lange on their "SafeCurves" website [12], dismiss Weierstraß curves entirely as a viable option for cryptographic applications based on the ground that complete addition is so much less efficient than incomplete addition formulas (and even less efficient than complete addition on twisted Edwards curves). In our opinion, a sensibly chosen Weierstraß curve using the complete addition formulas from [42] or [45] may well be the *safer* choice for protocols and applications that can live with the performance penalty.
- While we think that it is always preferable to use complete addition formulas for implementing Weierstraß-curve arithmetic, we would like to articulate that by no means we recommend the use of the Renes-Costello-Batina formulas above the use of Curve25519 with Ristretto for *new* protocols. Indeed, we support the proposal brought into CRFG by de Valence, Grigg, Tankersley, Valsorda, and Lovecruft [46] for the standardization of the Ristretto encoding.

Related Work. The most relevant related work for this paper can be grouped in two categories: papers presenting optimized implementations of Curve25519 and papers investigating performance of complete group addition on Weierstraß curves.

In the first category, the directly related papers present results for optimized scalar multiplication on Curve25519 targeting the same microarchitectures that we target in this paper. To the best of our knowledge, the current speed record for X25510 on Intel Sandy Bridge and Ivy Bridge processors is held by the "Sandy2x" software by Chou [19]. The speed record for the Intel Haswell microarchitecture is held by the software by Oliveira, López, Hışıl, Faz-Hernández, Rodríguez-Henríquez presented in [40]. This paper also presents even higher speeds for the Intel Skylake microarchitecture; that software makes use of the MULX and ADCX/ADOX instructions that are not available on Haswell. Finally, the speed record for scalar multiplication on Curve25519 on Cortex-M4 is held by software presented by Haase and Labrique in [27]. We provide a comparison of our results with the results from those papers in Sect. 4.

In the second category we are aware of only three results: In [42], Renes Costello, and Batina provide benchmarks of scalar multiplication on various NIST-P curves [32] in OpenSSL [41] using their complete formulas and compare them with the "standard" incomplete formulas used by default in OpenSSL. This comparison shows a performance penalty of a factor of about 1.4. However, the figures in [42, Table 2] strongly suggest that the comparison did not use the optimized implementation of scalar multiplication on the NIST curves that would need to be enabled with the configure option `enable-ec_nistp_64_gcc_128` when building OpenSSL. In [37], Costa Massolino, Renes, and Batina present an FPGA implementation of scalar multiplication on arbitrary Weierstraß curves over prime-order fields using the complete formulas from [42]. They claim that their results are "competitive with current literature", but also state that "it is not straightforward to do a well-founded comparison among works in the literature". This is because hardware implementations have a much larger design space, not only with tradeoffs between area and speed, but also flexibility with regards to the supported elliptic curves (e.g., through different curve shapes or support for specialized or generic field arithmetic). Finally, in [45] Susella and Montrasio estimate performance of different scalar-multiplication approaches. They report estimates in terms of multiplications per scalar bit, assuming that multiplication costs as much as squaring and multiplication by (small) constants, and that addition costs 10% of a multiplication. In this metric the ladder from [45] is very slightly cheaper at 19.1 than scalar multiplication using the formulas from [42] at 19.33. However, if we understand correctly, the estimates for [42] are computed without taking into account *signed* fixed-window scalar multiplication. In this metric, the Montgomery ladder used in X25519 software would come at a cost of 10.8.

Notation. We use abbreviations $\mathbf{M}$ to refer to the cost of a finite-field multiplication, use $\mathbf{S}$ to refer to the cost of a squaring, $\mathbf{a}$ to refer to the cost of an addition, and $\mathbf{m_c}$ to refer to the cost of multiplication by a constant c.

Availability of Software. We place all software related to this paper into the public domain (to the maximum extent possible, using the Creative Commons CC0 waiver). The code packages are published through the public archive at https://doi.org/10.5281/zenodo.7494621.

Organization of this Paper. In Sect. 2 we give a brief review of the mathematical background on elliptic curves and in particular motivate our choice of curve, which we call Curve13318. In Sect. 3 we provide details of our implementations of constant-time variable-basepoint scalar multiplication on Curve13318 for Intel Sandy Bridge, Intel Haswell, and ARM Cortex M4. Section 4 presents the performance results and compares to state-of-the-art implementations of scalar multiplication on Curve25519. We conclude the paper and give an overview of possible future work in Sect. 5.

2   Preliminaries

2.1   Weierstraß, Montgomery, and Twisted Edwards Curves

The typical way to introduce elliptic curves over a field $\mathbb{F}$ with large characteristic is through the *short Weierstraß equation*

$$E_W : y^2 = x^3 + ax + b,$$

where $a, b \in \mathbb{F}$. As long as the discriminant $\delta = -16(4a^3 + 27b^2)$ is nonzero, this equation describes an elliptic curve and any elliptic curve over a field $\mathbb{F}$ with characteristic not equal to two or three can be described through such an equation. For cryptography we typically choose a field of large prime order p; the relevant group in the cryptographic setup is the group of $\mathbb{F}_p$-rational points $E(\mathbb{F}_p)$. Whenever we talk about "the order of an elliptic curve" in this paper we mean the order of this group. The typical way to use Weierstraß curves in cryptography is to pick curve parameter $a = -3$ for somewhat more efficient arithmetic and to represent a point $P = (x, y)$ in Jacobian coordinates $(X : Y : Z)$ with $(x, y) = (X/Z^2, Y/Z^3)$. Point addition is using the formulas from [13] (improving on [20]) and uses $11\mathbf{M} + 5\mathbf{S} + 9\mathbf{a}$. Most efficient doubling uses formulas from [4] that use $3\mathbf{M} + 5\mathbf{S} + 8\mathbf{a}$. Alternatively, one can use a ladder with differential additions, for example using the approach from [33] that costs $6\mathbf{M} + 6\mathbf{S} + 20.5\mathbf{a}$ per ladder step.

Using a ladder for scalar multiplication is also what Montgomery proposed in [39] for a different class of elliptic curves, so-called *Montgomery curves*. These are described through an equation of the form

$$E_M : by^2 = x^3 + ax^2 + x,$$

again with $a, b \in \mathbb{F}$. The "ladder step" consisting of one differential addition and one doubling costs $5\mathbf{M} + 4\mathbf{S} + 8\mathbf{a}$. The formulas were shown to be complete by Bernstein in the Curve25519 paper [6]. One peculiarity of the formulas is that they only involve the x-coordinate of a point. For Diffie-Hellman protocols this has the advantage of free point compression and decompression, but for signatures this involves extra effort to recover the y-coordinate.

The most efficient complete formulas for full addition (and doubling) are on *twisted Edwards* curves [8], i.e., curves with equation

$$E_{tE} : x^2 + y^2 = 1 + dx^2y^2.$$

For the special case of $a = -1$, the formulas from [29] need only $8\mathbf{M} + 8\mathbf{a}$ for addition and $4\mathbf{M} + 4\mathbf{S} + 6\mathbf{a}$ for doubling. If -1 is a square in $\mathbb{F}_p$ then the formulas are complete. Every twisted Edwards curves is birationally equivalent to a Montgomery curve [8, Thm. 3.2] and in the case of Curve25519 both shapes are used in protocols: the Montgomery shape and corresponding ladder for X25519 key exchange and the twisted Edwards shape for Ed25519 signatures.

2.2 Curve13318

The goal of this paper is to investigate the performance of complete addition and doubling on a Weierstraß curve and compare it to the performance of Curve25519. Many aspects contribute to the performance of elliptic-curve arithmetic and as we are mainly interested in the impact of formulas implementing the group law, we decided to choose a curve that is as similar to Curve25519 as possible, except that it is in Weierstraß form and has prime order. This means that in particular, we want a curve that

- is defined over the field $\mathbb{F}_p$ with $p = 2^{255} - 19$;
- is twist secure (for a definition, see [6] or [12]);
- has parameter $a = -3$ to support common speedups of the group law; and
- has small parameter b.

A curve with precisely these properties was proposed in May 2017 by Barreto on Twitter [3]. Specifically, he proposed the curve with equation

$$E : y^2 = x^3 - 3x + 13318,$$

defined over $\mathbb{F}_{2^{255}-19}$. In a follow-up tweet Barreto clarified that the selection criteria for this curve were "all old SafeCurves properties (with recent improvements) plus prime order". Barreto did not name this curve; we will in the following refer to it as Curve13318. This name at the same time points to the curve parameter b and its intended similarities to Curve25519. The order of the group of $\mathbb{F}_p$-rational points on Curve13318 is

$$N = \ell = 2^{255} + 325610659388873400306201440571661405155.$$

2.3 The Renes-Costello-Batina Formulas

In 2016, Renes, Costello, and Batina published a set of formulas for doubling and addition on short Weierstraß curves [42], based on previous work by Bosma and Lenstra [18]. The formulas are complete for all elliptic curves defined over a field with characteristic not equal to 2 or 3. Together with the formulas published by Susella and Montrasio in 2017 [45], the Renes-Costello-Batina formulas are the only set of addition formulas for prime-order Weierstraß curves that is proven to be complete.

Because we implement variable-basepoint scalar multiplication on a curve with $a = -3$, we will use the algorithms for addition and doubling from [42, Section 3.2]. The relevant complete formulas for (projective) point addition are

$$
\begin{aligned}
X_3 &= (X_1Y_2 + X_2Y_1)(Y_1Y_2 + 3(X_1Z_2 + X_2Z_1 - bZ_1Z_2)) \\
&\quad - 3(Y_1Z_2 + Y_2Z_1)(b(X_1Z_2 + X_2Z_1) - X_1X_2 - 3Z_1Z_2), \\
Y_3 &= 3(3X_1X_2 - 3Z_1Z_2)(b(X_1Z_2 + X_2Z_1) - X_1X_2 - 3Z_1Z_2) \\
&\quad + (Y_1Y_2 - 3(X_1Z_2 + X_2Z_1 - bZ_1Z_2))(Y_1Y_2 + 3(X_1Z_2 + X_2Z_1 - bZ_1Z_2)), \\
Z_3 &= (Y_1Z_2 + Y_2Z_1)(Y_1Y_2 - 3(X_1Z_2 + X_2Z_1 - bZ_1Z_2)) \\
&\quad + (X_1Y_2 + X_2Y_1)(3X_1X_2 - 3Z_1Z_2).
\end{aligned}
$$

In [42], the formula for addition is implemented through 43 distinct operations, specifically $12\mathbf{M}+2\mathbf{m_b}+29\mathbf{a}$. The algorithm used to compute the addition (ADD) is listed in Algorithm 1.

Algorithm 1 Renes-Costello-Batina formula for $a = -3$. Used for exception-free addition on Curve13318.

---

procedure $\text{ADD}((X_1 : Y_1 : Z_1), (X_2 : Y_2 : Z_2))$

$v_1 \leftarrow X_1 \cdot X_2$	$v_{17} \leftarrow v_1 + v_3$	$v_{31} \leftarrow v_{30} + v_{29}$
$v_2 \leftarrow Y_1 \cdot Y_2$	$v_{18} \leftarrow v_{16} - v_{17}$	$v_{33} \leftarrow v_1 + v_1$
$v_3 \leftarrow Z_1 \cdot Z_2$	$v_{19} \leftarrow b \cdot v_3$	$v_{33} \leftarrow v_{32} + v_1$
$v_4 \leftarrow X_1 + Y_1$	$v_{20} \leftarrow v_{19} - v_{18}$	$v_{34} \leftarrow v_{33} - v_{27}$
$v_5 \leftarrow X_2 + Y_2$	$v_{21} \leftarrow v_{20} + v_{20}$	$v_{35} \leftarrow v_{13} \cdot v_{31}$
$v_6 \leftarrow v_4 \cdot v_5$	$v_{22} \leftarrow v_{20} + v_{21}$	$v_{36} \leftarrow v_{31} \cdot v_{34}$
$v_8 \leftarrow v_6 - v_7$	$v_{23} \leftarrow v_2 - v_{22}$	$v_{37} \leftarrow v_{23} \cdot v_{24}$
$v_9 \leftarrow Y_1 + Z_1$	$v_{24} \leftarrow v_2 + v_{22}$	$v_{38} \leftarrow v_{36} + v_{37}$
$v_{10} \leftarrow Y_2 + Z_2$	$v_{25} \leftarrow b \cdot v_{18}$	$v_{39} \leftarrow v_8 \cdot v_{24}$
$v_{11} \leftarrow v_9 \cdot v_{10}$	$v_{26} \leftarrow v_3 + v_3$	$v_{40} \leftarrow v_{39} - v_{35}$
$v_{13} \leftarrow v_{11} - v_{12}$	$v_{27} \leftarrow v_{26} + v_3$	$v_{41} \leftarrow v_{13} \cdot v_{23}$
$v_{14} \leftarrow X_1 + Z_1$	$v_{28} \leftarrow v_{25} - v_{27}$	$v_{42} \leftarrow v_8 \cdot v_{33}$
$v_{15} \leftarrow X_2 + Z_2$	$v_{29} \leftarrow v_{28} - v_1$	$v_{43} \leftarrow v_{41} + v_{42}$
$v_{16} \leftarrow v_{14} \cdot v_{15}$	$v_{30} \leftarrow v_{29} + v_{29}$	

$X_3 \leftarrow v_{40}$
$Y_3 \leftarrow v_{38}$
$Z_3 \leftarrow v_{43}$

return $(X_3 : Y_3 : Z_3)$

Correspondingly, the complete formulas for doubling are

$$X_3 = 2XY(Y^2 + 3(2XZ - bZ^2)) - 6XZ(2bXZ - X^2 - 3Z^2),$$
$$Y_3 = (Y^2 - 3(2XZ - bZ^2))(Y^2 + 3(2XZ - bZ^2))$$
$$+ 3(3X^2 - 3Z^2)(2bXZ - X^2 - 3Z^2),$$
$$Z_3 = 8Y^3 Z.$$

The cost of the doubling formulas is $8\mathbf{M} + 3\mathbf{S} + 2\mathbf{m_b} + 21\mathbf{a}$. The algorithm for doubling (DOUBLE) is listed in Algorithm 2.

We can reduce the cost of the doubling algorithm by erasing (some of) the multiplications v_1, v_4, v_6, v_{28}, using the rule that $2\alpha\beta = (\alpha + \beta)^2 - \alpha^2 - \beta^2$. By applying this rule, we trade $1\mathbf{M} + 1\mathbf{a}$ for $1\mathbf{S} + 3\mathbf{a}$. As we will describe in Sect. 3, this trick is beneficial only on the *Haswell* platform,

3   Implementation

In order to get a comprehensive benchmark for the performance of complete arithmetic on Curve13318, we optimized variable-basepoint scalar multiplication

---

Algorithm 2 Renes-Costello-Batina formula for $a = -3$. Used for exception-free doubling on Curve13318.

---

procedure DOUBLE$((X : Y : Z))$

$v_1 \leftarrow X \cdot X$	$v_{13} \leftarrow v_2 + v_{11}$	$v_{25} \leftarrow v_{24} - v_{17}$
$v_2 \leftarrow Y \cdot Y$	$v_{14} \leftarrow v_{12} \cdot v_{13}$	$v_{26} \leftarrow v_{22} \cdot v_{25}$
$v_3 \leftarrow Z \cdot Z$	$v_{15} \leftarrow v_5 \cdot v_{12}$	$v_{27} \leftarrow v_{14} + v_{26}$
$v_4 \leftarrow X \cdot Y$	$v_{16} \leftarrow v_3 + v_3$	$v_{28} \leftarrow Y \cdot Z$
$v_5 \leftarrow v_4 + v_4$	$v_{17} \leftarrow v_3 + v_{16}$	$v_{29} \leftarrow v_{28} + v_{28}$
$v_6 \leftarrow X \cdot Z$	$v_{18} \leftarrow b \cdot v_7$	$v_{30} \leftarrow v_{22} \cdot v_{29}$
$v_7 \leftarrow v_6 + v_6$	$v_{19} \leftarrow v_{18} - v_{17}$	$v_{31} \leftarrow v_{15} - v_{30}$
$v_8 \leftarrow b \cdot v_3$	$v_{20} \leftarrow v_1 - v_{19}$	$v_{32} \leftarrow v_2 \cdot v_{34}$
$v_9 \leftarrow v_8 - v_7$	$v_{21} \leftarrow v_{20} + v_{20}$	$v_{33} \leftarrow v_{32} + v_{32}$
$v_{10} \leftarrow v_9 + v_9$	$v_{22} \leftarrow v_{20} + v_{21}$	$v_{34} \leftarrow v_{33} + v_{33}$
$v_{11} \leftarrow v_{10} - v_9$	$v_{23} \leftarrow v_1 + v_1$	
$v_{12} \leftarrow v_2 - v_{11}$	$v_{24} \leftarrow v_{23} + v_1$	

$X_3 \leftarrow v_{31}$
$Y_3 \leftarrow v_{27}$
$Z_3 \leftarrow v_{34}$

return $(X_3 : Y_3 : Z_3)$

---

on the Intel *Sandy Bridge* and *Haswell* microarchitectures, as well as the ARM *Cortex M4* processor.

The high-level structure of the scalar multiplication is shared among all three implementations. First—before operating on the key k—we validate the input point P, by checking whether P satisfies $y_P^2 = x_P^3 - 3x_P + 13318$. Because we have not defined any encoding for the neutral element $\mathcal{O}$, this check will implicitly validate that $P \neq \mathcal{O}$.

For the scalar-multiplication core, we use a left-to-right signed-window double-and-add algorithm, with $w = 5$. This algorithm is listed in Algorithm 3. The subroutine RECODESIGNEDWINDOW$_5$ computes a vector of coefficients $k' = (k'_0, \ldots, k'_{50})$, such that $k = k'_0 + 32k'_1 + \ldots, +2^{250}k'_{50}$ and $k'_i \in \{-16, \ldots, 15\}$.

The table lookup is implemented in a traditional scanning fashion: selecting the required value using a bitwise AND operation. Where we use an unsigned representation, we compute the conditional negation of Y by negating Y and selecting the correct result using bitwise operations. When using floating points, we use a single XOR operation to conditionally flip the sign bit. These operations are—as well as the rest of the code—implemented in constant-time.

At the end of the double-and-add algorithm, we end up with a representation of $R = [k]P$ in projective coordinates. We compute the affine representation of x_R and y_R by computing the inverse of Z_R. Like most implementations of Curve25519 scalar multiplication, we use Fermat's little theorem and raise Z_R to the power $2^{255} - 21$ to obtain Z_R^{-1}. We chose not to exploit the optimization described in [16], because previous implementations have not had the

---

Algorithm 3 Signed double-and-add describe the used functions

---

1: **function** DOUBLEANDADD(k, P)
2:     $\mathbf{T} \leftarrow (\mathcal{O}, P, \ldots, [16]P)$ ▷ Precompute ($[2]P, \ldots, [16]P$)
3:     $k' \leftarrow$ RECODESIGNEDWINDOW$_5(k)$
4:     $R \leftarrow \mathcal{O}$
5:     **for** i **from** 50 **down to** 0 **do**
6:         $R \leftarrow [32]R$ ▷ 5 point doublings
7:         $Q \leftarrow \mathbf{T}_{|k'_i|}$ ▷ Constant-time lookup from $\mathbf{T}$
8:         $Q \leftarrow (-1)^{k'_i}Q$ ▷ Constant-time conditional negation
9:         $R \leftarrow R + Q$ ▷ Point addition
10:     **return** R ▷ $R = (X_R : Y_R : Z_R)$

---

opportunity to implement this technique; exploiting this invention would give us an unfair advantage.

In the following subsections we describe the architecture-specific optimizations of field arithmetic required to implement the Renes-Costello-Batina formulas and in particular our vectorization strategy on Intel processors.

3.1 Sandy Bridge

The first implementation we present is based on the *Sandy Bridge* microarchitecture. Sandy Bridge is Intel's first microarchitecture featuring *Advanced Vector Extensions* (AVX). In addition to 2×-parallel 64-bit integer arithmetic, AVX supports 4×-parallel double-precision floating-point arithmetic. Because the multiplications and squarings in the Renes-Costello-Batina formulas can be conveniently grouped in batches of 4, we will be using the 4×-parallel floating-point arithmetic on 256-bit ymm vector registers.

Representation of Prime-Field Elements. Using doubles with 53-bit mantissa, we can emulate integer registers of 53 bits. To guarantee that no rounding errors occur in the underlying floating-point arithmetic, we use carry chains[2] to reduce the amount of bits in each register before performing operations that might overflow. Building on this approach, [6] recommends—but does not implement—*radix-$2^{21.25}$* redundant representation, based on the arithmetic described in [5].

We use precisely this representation and represent a field element f through 12 signed double-precision floating-point values $f_0, \ldots, f_{11}$. For every f_i, its base b_i is defined by $b_i = 2^{\lceil 21.25i \rceil}$. Doubles already store their base in the exponent, which is large enough for our purposes. Therefore, we do not have to consider the base when evaluating f's value. Indeed, the value is computed by just computing the sum of the limbs:

$$f = \sum_{i=0}^{11} f_i$$

---

[2] Also called "coefficient reduction".

Coefficient Reduction. The Intel architecture supports no native modulo operation on floating points. Instead we extract a limb f_i's top bits by subsequently adding and subtracting a large constant $c_i = 3 \cdot 2^{51} b_{i+1}$, forcing the processor to discard the lower mantissa bits.

In code, each carry step needs 5 instructions to perform this routine. In Listing 1, the 4×-vectorized carry step from f_0 to f_1 is shown. To reduce f_{12} back to f_0, we multiply by $19 \cdot 2^{-255}$, which is implemented using a regular `vmulpd ymmX, [rel .reduceconstant]` instruction.

Listing 1 Single carry step for radix $2^{21.25}$ from limb f_0 to limb f_1.

```
1   ; Inputs:
2   ;   - ymm0: f0
3   ;   - [rel .precisionloss0]: times 4 dq 0x3p73 (c0 = 3·2^51·2^22)
4   ; Outputs:
5   ;   - ymm0: f0
6   ;   - ymm1: f1
7   vmovapd ymm14, yword [rel .precisionloss0]   ; load c0
8   vaddpd ymm15, ymm0, ymm14                    ; z' ← round(f0 + c0)
9   vsubpd ymm15, ymm15, ymm14                   ; t ← round(z' − c0)
10  vaddpd ymm1, ymm1, ymm15                     ; f1 ← round(f1 + t)
11  vsubpd ymm0, ymm0, ymm15                     ; f0 ← round(f0 − t)
```

All micro-operations (µops) corresponding to the arithmetic instructions in Listing 1 execute on port 1 of Sandy Bridge's back end. Furthermore, every v{add,sub}pd instruction has a latency of 3 cycles (cc). Consequently, the latency of one carry step is the sum of the latencies of instructions 2–4, i.e. the latency is $3 + 3 + 3 = 9$cc. Still, the reciprocal throughput is only 4cc.

In a sequential carry chain the back end is stalled most of the time due to data hazards. We expect a single carry chain to use $9 \cdot 14 = 126$cc or 31.5cc per lane. Even in a twice interleaved carry chain, the latency is still 63cc, while the reciprocal throughput is still only 56cc. In other words, the twice interleaved case still suffers from data hazards.

To overcome this, we implement a triple interleaved carry chain, as displayed in Fig. 1. In this case, the latency is reduced to 45cc, while the reciprocal throughput is 60cc. Conversely the bottleneck is not the latency, but the reciprocal throughput of the carry chain, of which the lower bound is 15cc per lane.

$$f_0 \to f_1 \to f_2 \to f_3 \to f_4 \to f_5,$$
$$f_4 \to f_5 \to f_6 \to f_7 \to f_8 \to f_9,$$
$$f_8 \to f_9 \to f_{10} \to f_{11} \to f_0 \to f_1$$

Fig. 1. Triple interleaved 12-limb carry chain.

Multiplication. For radix-$2^{21.25}$, we use basic $4\times$ parallel Karatsuba multiplication [31], using inspiration from [30]. An inconvenience introduced by implementing Karatsuba using floating points, is that the shift-by-128-bit operations cannot be optimized out. Instead, we have to explicitly multiply some limbs by $2^{\pm 128}$. This costs 23 extra multiplication ops (implemented using 12 vmulpds, and 11 vandpds). Still, the Karatsuba implementation, which contains 131 vmulpd instructions, was measured to be 8% faster than the schoolbook method (which contains 155 vmulpd instructions).

Vectorization Strategy. We group the multiplications from both algorithms in three batches each, which have been chosen such that the complexity of the operations in-between the multiplications minimized. The resulting algorithms are given in Algorithms 4 and 5.

In particular, we cannot optimize the squaring operations in DOUBLE using the $2\alpha\beta = (\alpha + \beta)^2 - \alpha^2 - \beta^2$ rule, because $\alpha + \beta$ has too little headroom to be squared without doing an additional carry chain.

Because we cannot perform shift operations on floating-point values, and because the reciprocal throughput of vmulpd and v{add,sub}pd are both 1cc, we replace all chained additions by multiplications. This substitutes 8a for 4m in ADD, and 10a for 5m in DOUBLE.

Last, we found that shuffling the ymm registers turns out to be relatively weak and expensive. That is because Sandy Bridge has no arbitrary shuffle instruction (like the vpermq instruction in AVX2). To shuffle every value in a ymm register into the correct lane, we would need at least two μops on port 5. Then it is cheaper to put all the values in the first lane, and accept that most of the additions and subtractions are not batched.

3.2   Haswell

The more recent *Haswell* microarchitecture from Intel supports *Advanced Vector Extensions 2* (AVX2). Haswell's AVX2 is more powerful than its predecessor. First, because AVX2 allows for $4\times$ parallel 64-bit integer arithmetic; and second, because addition and subtraction operations—using the vp{add,sub}q instructions—have a reciprocal throughput of only 0.5cc. Together with the other instructions in AVX2, Haswell lends itself for efficient $4\times$ parallel 64-bit integer arithmetic.

Algorithm 4 Algorithm for point addition for Curve13318 as implemented on the Sandy Bridge microarchitecture. A rule (＿) denotes a "dead" value, i.e. one that has no meaning and is unused. RED executes a coefficient-reduction chain.

---

procedure ADD(X_1, Y_1, Z_1, X_2, Y_2, Z_2)

$v_{14} \leftarrow X_1 + Z_1$	$v_4 \leftarrow X_1 + Y_1$	$v_4 \leftarrow X_1 + Y_1$	$v_9 \leftarrow Y_1 + Z_1$
$v_{15} \leftarrow X_2 + Z_2$	$v_5 \leftarrow X_2 + Y_2$	$v_5 \leftarrow X_2 + Y_2$	$v_{10} \leftarrow Y_2 + Z_2$
$v_{16} \leftarrow v_{14} \cdot v_{15}$	$v_1 \leftarrow X_1 \cdot X_2$	$v_2 \leftarrow Y_1 \cdot Y_2$	$v_3 \leftarrow Z_1 \cdot Z_2$
$v_{16} \leftarrow \text{RED}(v_{16})$	$v_1 \leftarrow \text{RED}(v_1)$	$v_2 \leftarrow \text{RED}(v_2)$	$v_3 \leftarrow \text{RED}(v_3)$
$v_7 \leftarrow v_2 + v_1$	$v_{12} \leftarrow v_2 + v_3$		
$v_{17} \leftarrow v_1 + v_3$			
$v_{18} \leftarrow v_{16} - v_{17}$			
$v_{19} \leftarrow b \cdot v_3$			
$v_{20} \leftarrow v_{19} - v_{18}$			
$v_{25} \leftarrow b \cdot v_{18}$			
$v_{27} \leftarrow 3 \cdot v_3$			
$v_{28} \leftarrow v_{25} - v_{27}$			
$v_{29} \leftarrow v_{28} - v_1$	$v_{v_1-v_3} \leftarrow v_1 - v_3$		
$v_{22} \leftarrow 3 \cdot v_{20}$		$v_{31} \leftarrow 3 \cdot v_{29}$	$v_{34} \leftarrow 3 \cdot v_{v_1-v_3}$
$v_{22} \leftarrow \text{RED}(v_{22})$		$v_{31} \leftarrow \text{RED}(v_{31})$	$v_{34} \leftarrow \text{RED}(v_{34})$
$v_{23} \leftarrow v_2 - v_{22}$			
$v_{24} \leftarrow v_2 + v_{22}$			
$v_{37} \leftarrow v_{23} \cdot v_{24}$	$v_{36} \leftarrow v_{31} \cdot v_{34}$	$v_6 \leftarrow v_4 \cdot v_5$	$v_{11} \leftarrow v_9 \cdot v_{10}$
$v_{37} \leftarrow \text{RED}(v_{37})$	$v_{36} \leftarrow \text{RED}(v_{36})$	$v_6 \leftarrow \text{RED}(v_6)$	$v_{11} \leftarrow \text{RED}(v_{11})$
$v_{37} \leftarrow v_{37} - 0$	$v_{36} \leftarrow v_{36} - 0$	$v_8 \leftarrow v_6 - v_7$	$v_{13} \leftarrow v_{11} - v_{12}$
$v_{38} \leftarrow v_{36} + v_{37}$			
$v_{39} \leftarrow v_{24} \cdot v_8$	$v_{42} \leftarrow v_{33} \cdot v_8$	$v_{41} \leftarrow v_{23} \cdot v_{13}$	$v_{35} \leftarrow v_{31} \cdot v_{13}$
$v_{39} \leftarrow \text{RED}(v_{39})$	$v_{42} \leftarrow \text{RED}(v_{42})$	$v_{41} \leftarrow \text{RED}(v_{41})$	$v_{35} \leftarrow \text{RED}(v_{35})$
$v_{43} \leftarrow v_{41} + v_{42}$			
$v_{40} \leftarrow v_{39} - v_{35}$			

$X_3 \leftarrow v_{40}$
$Y_3 \leftarrow v_{38}$
$Z_3 \leftarrow v_{43}$

Representation of Prime-Field Elements. We use the *radix*-$2^{25.5}$ redundant representation, which was introduced in [15]. The representation stores an integer f into 10 *unsigned*[3] 64-bit limbs, with each base $b_i = 2^{\lceil 25.5i \rceil}$. Then the value of f is given by

---

[3] When we use *signed* limbs, we need—for the coefficient reduction—an instruction that shifts packed quadwords to the right while shifting in sign bits. Such an arithmetic shift operation—which would be called `vpsraq`—has never been implemented for the Haswell microarchitecture. Indeed, the first occurrence of the `vpsraq`-instruction was in AVX-512, in the Knight's Landing and Skylake-X microarchitectures.

Algorithm 5 Algorithm for point doubling for Curve13318 as implemented on the Sandy Bridge microarchitecture. A rule (——) denotes a "dead" value, i.e. one that has no meaning and is unused. RED executes a coefficient-reduction chain.

procedure DOUBLE(X, Y, Z)

$Y \leftarrow Y + 0$	$v_{2x} \leftarrow X + X$	——	——
$v_1 \leftarrow X \cdot X$	$v_6 \leftarrow X \cdot Z$	$v_3 \leftarrow Z \cdot Z$	$v_{28} \leftarrow Y \cdot Z$
$v_1 \leftarrow \text{RED}(v_1)$	$v_6 \leftarrow \text{RED}(v_6)$	$v_3 \leftarrow \text{RED}(v_3)$	$v_{28} \leftarrow \text{RED}(v_{28})$
$v_{24} \leftarrow 3 \cdot v_1$	$v_{18} \leftarrow 2b \cdot v_6$	$v_8' \leftarrow -\frac{b}{2} \cdot v_3$	$v_{17} \leftarrow 3 \cdot v_3$
$v_{25} \leftarrow v_{24} - v_{17}$	$v_{19} \leftarrow v_{18} - v_{17}$	——	——
$v_{20} \leftarrow v_1 - v_{19}$	——	——	——
$v_{22} \leftarrow -3 \cdot v_{20}$	——	——	——
$v_9 \leftarrow v_8' + v_6$	——	——	——
$v_{11} \leftarrow -6 \cdot v_9$	$v_{34} \leftarrow 8 \cdot v_{28}$	——	——
$v_{11} \leftarrow \text{RED}(v_{11})$	$v_{34} \leftarrow \text{RED}(v_{34})$	$v_{22} \leftarrow \text{RED}(v_{22})$	$v_{25} \leftarrow \text{RED}(v_{25})$
$v_{29} \leftarrow v_{28} + v_{28}$	——	——	——
$v_{30} \leftarrow v_{22} \cdot v_{29}$	$v_{26} \leftarrow v_{22} \cdot v_{25}$	$v_2 \leftarrow Y \cdot Y$	$v_5 \leftarrow v_{2x} \cdot Y$
$v_{30} \leftarrow \text{RED}(v_{30})$	$v_{26} \leftarrow \text{RED}(v_{26})$	$v_2 \leftarrow \text{RED}(v_2)$	$v_5 \leftarrow \text{RED}(v_5)$
$v_{12} \leftarrow v_2 - v_{11}$	——	——	——
$v_{13} \leftarrow v_2 + v_{11}$	——	——	——
$v_{32} \leftarrow v_2 \cdot v_{34}$	$v_{15} \leftarrow v_5 \cdot v_{12}$	$v_{14} \leftarrow v_{12} \cdot v_{13}$	——
$v_{32} \leftarrow \text{RED}(v_{32})$	$v_{15} \leftarrow \text{RED}(v_{15})$	$v_{14} \leftarrow \text{RED}(v_{14})$	——
$v_{31} \leftarrow v_{15} - v_{30}$	——	——	——
$v_{27} \leftarrow v_{14} + v_{26}$	——	——	——

$X_3 \leftarrow v_{31}$
$Y_3 \leftarrow v_{27}$
$Z_3 \leftarrow v_{34}$

$$f = \sum_{i=0}^{9} b_i f_i.$$

Coefficient Reduction. For coefficient reduction in radix $2^{25.5}$, we use the carry chain described by Sandy2x [19], adapted to AVX2. It is shown in Listing 2.

One carry step uses only 3 μops, each of which can execute on a separate port. Consequently, the reciprocal throughput of a single carry step is 1cc, while the latency of a carry step is 2cc. Therefore, it is optimal to implement the coefficient reduction using a twice interleaved carry chain, as visualized in Fig. 2.

$$f_0 \rightarrow f_1 \rightarrow f_2 \rightarrow f_3 \rightarrow f_4 \rightarrow f_5 \rightarrow f_6,$$
$$f_5 \rightarrow f_6 \rightarrow f_7 \rightarrow f_8 \rightarrow f_9 \rightarrow f_0 \rightarrow f_1$$

Fig. 2. Twice interleaved 10-limb carry chain.

Listing 2 Single carry step for radix $2^{25.5}$.

```
1  ; Inputs:
2  ;   - ymm0: f0
3  ;   - [rel .MASK26]: times 4 dq 0x3FFFFFF
4  ; Outputs:
5  ;   - ymm0: f0
6  ;   - ymm1: f1
7  vpsrlq ymm15, ymm0, 26                    ; t ← ⌊2⁻²⁶f0⌋
8  vpaddq ymm1, ymm1, ymm15                  ; f1 ← f1 + t
9  vpand ymm0, ymm0, yword [rel .MASK26]     ; f0 ← f0 mod 2²⁶
```

Multiplication and Squaring. For the multiplication of numbers in radix $2^{25.5}$, we adapt the multiplication routine from Sandy2x for AVX2. The multiplication routine uses the schoolbook method of multiplication. It contains 109 `vpmuludq` instructions. Of these 109 instructions, 9 `vpmuludq`s are used to precompute $19 \cdot \{g_1, g_2, \ldots, g_9\} \equiv 2^{255} \cdot \{g_1, g_2, \ldots, g_9\}$, where g is the second input operand. These values will be used for the limbs in the result that wrap around the field modulus, as is described in the Sandy2x paper ([19]).

In addition to the multiplication routine, we implement an optimized routine for squaring operations, based on the multiplication routine, that we will use in the next section.

Furthermore, we looked at the possibility of using Karatsuba multiplication, instead of using the schoolbook method. In this endeavor, we chose the Karatsuba *base* $B = 2^{153}$, i.e. we split the inputs into one part of 6 limbs, and one part of 4 limbs. We execute the Karatsuba algorithm to obtain a 19-limb value h_u, which is the *uncarried* result. To carry the high limbs from h_u onto the lower limbs, we multiply the high limbs by 19 using 3 `vpaddq`s and 1 `vpsllq` per limb; then we accumulate the results onto the lower limbs, yielding our carried product h.

In the Karatsuba routine, the port pressure is better divided, with 97 μops on port 0 and 149 μops on ports 1 and 5, relative to the schoolbook method, with 109 μops on port 0 and 90 on ports 1 and 5. However, the Karatsuba multiplication routine performs considerably worse than the Schoolbook method. Presumably, the CPU's front end cannot keep up with the added bulk of instructions.

Why not `mulx`? In [40], Oliveira et al. make use of the Bit Manipulation Instruction Set 2 (BMI2) extension in Haswell. BMI2 introduces the instruction `mulx`, which allows for unsigned multiply with arbitrary destination registers (instead of always storing the result in `rdx:rax`). Using this with a packed radix-2^{64} representation, field multiplication and squaring can be sped up quite a lot. However, experiments showed that the penalty introduced by more expensive additions/subtractions beat the performance gain achieved by using `mulx`.

Vectorization Strategy. Similar as in the implementation for Sandy Bridge, we batched all multiplications in the ADD algorithm into three different batches. The complete vectorization strategy is given in Algorithms 6 and 7.

In the implementation of DOUBLE, we applied the squaring trick described in Sect. 2.3, and rewrite $v_7 = 2XZ = (X + Z)^2 - X^2 - Z^2$. After replacing the multiplication v_6 by a squaring, we can replace the first of the three multiplication batches in DOUBLE with a batched squaring operation, that computes the values $\{(X + Z)^2, v_1, v_2, v_3\}$.

We realize that in both algorithms we can reduce the amount of shuffle operations needed, by unpacking the values from their SIMD registers after the first batched operations, and using the general-purpose instructions for many cheap operations, i.e. additions, subtractions, triplings[4], and multiplies with b. This way, we eagerly compute the core of the algorithm, leaving only two batched multiplications and a few additions. After repacking the values into the ymm-bank, we execute the remainder of the algorithm, including the two other multiplication batches.

3.3   ARM Cortex M4

Field Arithmetic. For the ARM Cortex M4, we reused the finite field arithmetic from Haase and Labrique [27]. For field elements, they use a packed representation in radix 2^{32}. We refer to their paper for the details of the field arithmetic, which can be summarized as cleverly exploiting the magnificent powers of the umlal and umaal instructions.

One function we added was fe25519_mul_u32_asm, used for multiplication with small constants. It was based on Fujii's code [25, Listing 3.2], which was in turn based on [43].

Application of Formulas. On top of the field arithmetic, we implemented the ADD and DOUBLE algorithms using function calls to the underlying field operations. Because—compared to multiplications—field additions are relatively expensive, there is no benefit in using the $2\alpha\beta = (\alpha + \beta)^2 - \alpha^2 - \beta^2$ trick. However, multiply-with-small-constant operations are relatively cheap, so we replaced any chained additions (like the $v_b \leftarrow v_a + v_a$; then $v_a \leftarrow v_b + v_a$ pattern) by multiplications (i.e. $v_a \leftarrow 3v_a$). No other modifications were introduced. Even the order of the operations has been kept to the original.

---

[4] Using lea r64, [2*r64 + r64] instructions.

Algorithm 6 Algorithm for point addition for Curve13318 as implemented on the Haswell microarchitecture. A rule ($\_\_$) denotes a "dead" value, i.e. one that has no meaning and is unused. RED executes a coefficient-reduction chain. The additions/subtractions with large constants ($2^{32}p$, $4p$ and $2^{37}p$) are to ensure that all the values are in the positive domain after subtraction.

procedure ADD($X_1, Y_1, Z_1, X_2, Y_2, Z_2$)

$Y_1 \leftarrow \text{RED}(Y_1)$	$Y_2 \leftarrow \text{RED}(Y_2)$	$Y_1 \leftarrow \text{RED}(Y_1)$	$Y_2 \leftarrow \text{RED}(Y_2)$
$v_{14} \leftarrow X_1 + Z_1$	$v_4 \leftarrow X_1 + Y_1$	$v_4 \leftarrow X_1 + Y_1$	$v_9 \leftarrow Y_1 + Z_1$
$v_{15} \leftarrow X_2 + Z_2$	$v_5 \leftarrow X_2 + Y_2$	$v_5 \leftarrow X_2 + Y_2$	$v_{10} \leftarrow Y_2 + Z_2$
$v_{16} \leftarrow v_{14} \cdot v_{15}$	$v_1 \leftarrow X_1 \cdot Y_2$	$v_2 \leftarrow Y_1 \cdot Z_2$	$v_3 \leftarrow Z_1 \cdot Z_2$
$v_{16} \leftarrow \text{RED}(v_{16})$	$v_1 \leftarrow \text{RED}(v_1)$	$v_2 \leftarrow \text{RED}(v_2)$	$v_3 \leftarrow \text{RED}(v_3)$
$v_{17} \leftarrow v_1 + v_3$			
$v_7 \leftarrow v_1 + v_2$			
$v_{12} \leftarrow v_2 + v_3$			
$v_{18} \leftarrow v_{16} - v_{17}$			
$v_{19} \leftarrow b \cdot v_3$			
$v_{25} \leftarrow b \cdot v_{18}$			
$v_{20} \leftarrow v_{18} - v_{19}$			
$v_{22} \leftarrow 3 \cdot v_{20}$			
$v_{24} \leftarrow v_{22} + v_2$			
$v_{23} \leftarrow v_2 - v_{22}$			
$v_{27} \leftarrow 3 \cdot v_3$			
$v_{v_{25}-v_1} \leftarrow v_{25} - v_1$			
$v_{29} \leftarrow v_{v_{25}-v_1} - v_{27}$			
$v_{31} \leftarrow 3 \cdot v_{29}$			
$v_{33} \leftarrow 3 \cdot v_1$			
$v_{34} \leftarrow v_{33} - v_{27}$			
$v_{34} \leftarrow v_{34} + 2^{32}p$	$v_{24} \leftarrow v_{24} + 2^{32}p$	$v_{31} \leftarrow v_{31} + 2^{32}p$	$v_{23} \leftarrow v_{23} + 2^{32}p$
$v_{34} \leftarrow \text{RED}(v_{34})$	$v_{24} \leftarrow \text{RED}(v_{24})$	$v_{31} \leftarrow \text{RED}(v_{31})$	$v_{23} \leftarrow \text{RED}(v_{23})$
$v_{36} \leftarrow v_{34} \cdot v_{31}$	$v_{37} \leftarrow v_{24} \cdot v_{23}$	$v_6 \leftarrow v_4 \cdot v_5$	$v_{11} \leftarrow v_9 \cdot v_{10}$
$v_{36} \leftarrow \text{RED}(v_{36})$	$v_{37} \leftarrow \text{RED}(v_{37})$	$v_6 \leftarrow \text{RED}(v_6)$	$v_{11} \leftarrow \text{RED}(v_{11})$
$v_{38} \leftarrow v_{36} + v_{37}$			
$_____$	$_____$	$v_7 \leftarrow v_7 - 4p$	$v_{12} \leftarrow v_{12} - 4p$
$_____$	$_____$	$v_8 \leftarrow v_6 - v_7$	$v_{13} \leftarrow v_{11} - v_{12}$
$v_{42} \leftarrow v_8 \cdot v_{34}$	$v_{39} \leftarrow v_8 \cdot v_{24}$	$v_{35} \leftarrow v_{13} \cdot v_{31}$	$v_{41} \leftarrow v_{13} \cdot v_{23}$
$_____$	$v_{39} \leftarrow v_{39} + 2^{37}p$	$_____$	$_____$
$_____$	$v_{40} \leftarrow v_{39} - v_{35}$	$_____$	$_____$
$v_{43} \leftarrow v_{42} + v_{41}$	$_____$	$_____$	$_____$
$v_{43} \leftarrow \text{RED}(v_{43})$	$v_{40} \leftarrow \text{RED}(v_{40})$	$_____$	$_____$

$X_3 \leftarrow v_{40}$
$Y_3 \leftarrow v_{38}$
$Z_3 \leftarrow v_{43}$

4   Performance Results

The complete scalar multiplication algorithm was tested and benchmarked on Intel Core i7-2600 (Sandy Bridge), Intel Core i5-3210 (Ivy Bridge), Intel Core i7-4770 (Haswell), and the ARM STM32F407 (Cortex-M4). On the Intel processors, all measurements were done with Turbo Boost disabled, all Hyper-Threading cores shut down, and with the CPU clocked at the maximum nominal frequency. The STM32F407 device was run with its default settings, as listed in the datasheet [44] (i.e. clocked from the 16MHz internal RC-oscillator). We list the benchmarking results in Table 1. As expected, none of our implementations exceed the performance of Curve25519.

Algorithm 7 Algorithm for point doubling for Curve13318 as implemented on the Haswell microarchitecture.   A rule (——) denotes a "dead" value, i.e. one that has no meaning and is unused. RED executes a coefficient-reduction chain. The additions/subtractions with large constants ($2^{32}p$, $4p$ and $2^{37}p$) are to ensure that all the values are in the positive domain after subtraction.

---

procedure DOUBLE(X, Y, Z)

$v_{X+Z} \leftarrow X + Z$	$v_{X+Z} \leftarrow X + Z$	$v_{X+Z} \leftarrow X + Z$	$v_{X+Z} \leftarrow X + Z$
$v_{2Y} \leftarrow Y + Y$	$v_{2Y} \leftarrow Y + Y$	$v_{2Y} \leftarrow Y + Y$	$v_{2Y} \leftarrow Y + Y$
$v_{(X+Z)^2} \leftarrow v_{X+Z}^2$	$v_1 \leftarrow X^2$	$v_2 \leftarrow Y^2$	$v_3 \leftarrow Z^2$
$v_{(X+Z)^2} \leftarrow \text{RED}(v_{(X+Z)^2})$	$v_1 \leftarrow \text{RED}(v_1)$	$v_2 \leftarrow \text{RED}(v_2)$	$v_3 \leftarrow \text{RED}(v_3)$

$v_{Z^2+2XZ} \leftarrow v_{(X+Z)^2} - v_1$
$v_7 \leftarrow v_{Z^2+2XZ} - v_3$
$v_{18} \leftarrow b \cdot v_7$
$v_8 \leftarrow b \cdot v_3$
$v_{17} \leftarrow 3 \cdot v_3$
$v_{19} \leftarrow v_{18} - v_{17}$
$v_9 \leftarrow v_8 - v_7$
$v_{24} \leftarrow 3 \cdot v_1$
$v_{11} \leftarrow 3 \cdot v_9$
$v_{20} \leftarrow v_{19} - v_1$
$v_{22} \leftarrow 3 \cdot v_{20}$
$v_{12} \leftarrow v_2 - v_{11}$
$v_{13} \leftarrow v_2 + v_{11}$
$v_{25} \leftarrow v_{24} - v_{17}$
$v_{4v_2} \leftarrow 4 \cdot v_2$

$v_{22} \leftarrow v_{22} + 2^{32}p$	$v_{12} \leftarrow v_{12} + 2^{32}p$	$v_{25} \leftarrow v_{25} + 2^{32}p$	$v_{13} \leftarrow v_{13} + 2^{32}p$
$v_{22} \leftarrow \text{RED}(v_{22})$	$v_{12} \leftarrow \text{RED}(v_{12})$	$v_{25} \leftarrow \text{RED}(v_{25})$	$v_{13} \leftarrow \text{RED}(v_{13})$
$v_{26} \leftarrow v_{22} \cdot v_{25}$	$v_{14} \leftarrow v_{12} \cdot v_{13}$	$v_{28} \leftarrow v_{2Y} \cdot Z$	$v_4 \leftarrow v_{2Y} \cdot X$
$v_{26} \leftarrow \text{RED}(v_{26})$	$v_{14} \leftarrow \text{RED}(v_{14})$	$v_{28} \leftarrow \text{RED}(v_{28})$	$v_4 \leftarrow \text{RED}(v_4)$
$v_{27} \leftarrow v_{26} + v_{14}$	————	————	————
$v_{30} \leftarrow v_{28} \cdot v_{22}$	$v_{15} \leftarrow v_4 \cdot v_{12}$	$v_{34} \leftarrow v_{4v_2} \cdot v_{28}$	————
$v_{30} \leftarrow v_{30} - 2^{37}p$	————	————	————
$v_{31} \leftarrow v_{15} - v_{30}$	————	————	————
$v_{31} \leftarrow \text{RED}(v_{31})$	$v_{34} \leftarrow \text{RED}(v_{34})$	————	————

$X_3 \leftarrow v_{31}$
$Y_3 \leftarrow v_{27}$
$Z_3 \leftarrow v_{34}$

Table 1. Measured cycle counts of the variable-basepoint scalar-multiplication routines on the Sandy Bridge (SB), Ivy Bridge (IB), Haswell (H) and Cortex M4 (M4) architectures.

Implementation	SB	IB	H	M4
Chou16 [19]	159 128[a]	156 995[a]	155 823[b]	–
Faz-Hernández-Lopez15 [24]	–	–	≈ 156 500[c]	–
OLHF18 [40]	–	–	138 963[a]	–
Fujii-Aranha19 [26]	–	–	–	907 240[a]
Haase-Labrique19 [27]	–	–	–	625 358[a]
Curve13318 (**this work**)	389 546[b]	382 966[b]	204 643[b]	1 797 451[b]
Ed25519 verify	221 988[d]	206 080[d]	184 052[d]	–
slowdown	2.45×	2.44×	1.47×	2.87×

[a] As reported in the respective publication.

[b] From own measurements.

[c] As reported in [24]. This publication expressed their benchmarks in kcc. As such, this value has been padded with zeros.

[d] Cycle counts reported on Bernstein and Lange's eBACS website [11]; included for the sake of completeness. The SB, IB and H measurements were selected from the tables for the `h6sandy`, `manny613` and `genji202` machines respectively. At the moment of writing, it is unclear to the authors which implementations were used to construct these cycle counts.

It can immediately be seen that the slowdown factor is dependent on the platform. In particular, the Haswell implementation of scalar multiplication on Curve13318 performs, also relatively speaking, much better than the others. The source of this is seems to be that Algorithms 1 and 2 lend themselves for very efficient 4-way parallelization, which is not supported by Curve25519's ladder algorithm. Through AVX2, 4-way parallelization is very powerful on Haswell, whereas on the other platforms it is not, at least not to the same extent. This makes it possible to write a Haswell implementation that is significantly faster than the others.

The Cost of Completeness

Another question we might be able to answer is if the factor-1.4 penalty claimed in [42]—for complete formulas vs. incomplete formulas—is realistic also for optimized implementations.

In [17], Bos, Costello, Longa, and Naehrig present performance results for scalar multiplication on a prime-order Weierstraß curve over $\mathbb{F}_{2^{256}-189}$ using parameter $a = -3$. The curve is very similar to Curve13318 and the implementation uses non-complete formulas for addition and doubling. The authors report 278 000 cycles for variable-base scalar multiplication on Intel Sandy Bridge. The software in [17] is seriously optimized, and claimed to run in constant time, so these 278 000 cycles are reasonably comparable to our 389 546 cycles with complete formulas. In other words, this comparison affirms the factor-1.4 performance-penalty claim from [42].

5   Future Work and Conclusion

Future work. Of course it might be possible to improve on our results for optimized arithmetic using the Renes-Costello-Batina formulas, but we would be surprised to see such improvements change the big picture and conclusion we draw in this paper. What would be interesting to explore is carefully optimized software for the complete ladder formulas presented in [45]. Our intuition is that in practice they will end up slightly slower than the signed fixed-window scalar multiplication using Renes-Costello-Batina formulas we employed here, but settling this question clearly needs more implementation effort.

Conclusion. The analysis in this paper shows that using prime-order Weierstraß curves with complete addition formulas is between ≈1.5 times and ≈2.9 times slower than using state-of-the-art Montgomery curve arithmetic. In an area where even a 10% improvement in performance is often considered important and worth publication in major venues, this is a pretty heavy price to pay; at least for some applications that are bottlenecked by ECC performance.

However, for applications that primarily aim at simplicity and safety against subgroup attacks, the performance penalty might be acceptable. This point of view is supported, for example, also by the fact that the attempt to standardize the high-performance "FourQ" curve [21] in CFRG [35] was only very short lived. The discussion around this proposal acknowledged that FourQ offers considerably faster arithmetic than Curve25519, but questioned that there are any applications that really need that performance[5].

In our opinion, for the design of new protocols, the most efficient, simple, and safe choice of elliptic curve remains Curve25519 in twisted Edwards form with the Ristretto encoding to remove the non-trivial cofactor.

References

1. Arcieri, T., de Valence, H., Lovecruft, I.: The Ristretto Group. https://ristretto.group/ristretto.html. Accessed 31 July 2019
2. Aumasson, J.P.: Serious Cryptography: A Practical Introduction to Modern Encryption. No Starch Press, San Francisco (2017)
3. Barreto, P.S.L.M.: Tweet (2017). https://twitter.com/pbarreto/status/869103226276134912
4. Bernstein, D.J.: A software implementation of NIST P-224. In: Talk at the Workshop on Elliptic Curve Cryptography - ECC 2001 (2001). http://cr.yp.to/talks.html#2001.10.29
5. Bernstein, D.J.: Floating-point arithmetic and message authentication (2004). http://cr.yp.to/papers.html#hash127
6. Bernstein, D.J.: Curve25519: new Diffie-Hellman speed records. In: Yung, M., Dodis, Y., Kiayias, A., Malkin, T. (eds.) PKC 2006. LNCS, vol. 3958, pp. 207–228. Springer, Heidelberg (2006). https://doi.org/10.1007/11745853_14. http://cr.yp.to/papers.html#curve25519

---

[5] For the full discussion, see https://mailarchive.ietf.org/arch/msg/cfrg/sCqu86nFiAw_9beBXVqBM_zES_k.

7. Bernstein, D.J.: 25519 naming. Posting to the CFRG mailing list (2014). https://www.ietf.org/mail-archive/web/cfrg/current/msg04996.html

8. Bernstein, D.J., Birkner, P., Joye, M., Lange, T., Peters, C.: Twisted Edwards curves. In: Vaudenay, S. (ed.) AFRICACRYPT 2008. LNCS, vol. 5023, pp. 389–405. Springer, Heidelberg (2008). https://doi.org/10.1007/978-3-540-68164-9_26. http://cr.yp.to/papers.html#twisted

9. Bernstein, D.J., Duif, N., Lange, T., Schwabe, P., Yang, B.-Y.: High-speed high-security signatures. In: Preneel, B., Takagi, T. (eds.) CHES 2011. LNCS, vol. 6917, pp. 124–142. Springer, Heidelberg (2011). https://doi.org/10.1007/978-3-642-23951-9_9. See also full version [10]

10. Bernstein, D.J., Duif, N., Lange, T., Schwabe, P., Yang, B.Y.: High-speed high-security signatures. J. Cryptogr. Eng. **2**(2), 77–89 (2012). http://cryptojedi.org/papers/#ed25519. See also short version [9]

11. Bernstein, D.J., Lange, T.: eBACS: ECRYPT Benchmarking of Cryptographic Systems. https://bench.cr.yp.to/results-sign.html. Accessed 03 Oct 2019

12. Bernstein, D.J., Lange, T.: SafeCurves: choosing safe curves for elliptic-curve cryptography. https://safecurves.cr.yp.to. Accessed 31 July 2019

13. Bernstein, D.J., Lange, T.: Faster addition and doubling on elliptic curves. In: Kurosawa, K. (ed.) ASIACRYPT 2007. LNCS, vol. 4833, pp. 29–50. Springer, Heidelberg (2007). https://doi.org/10.1007/978-3-540-76900-2_3. https://cr.yp.to/papers.html#newelliptic

14. Bernstein, D.J., Lange, T., Schwabe, P.: On the correct use of the negation map in the Pollard rho method. In: Catalano, D., Fazio, N., Gennaro, R., Nicolosi, A. (eds.) PKC 2011. LNCS, vol. 6571, pp. 128–146. Springer, Heidelberg (2011). https://doi.org/10.1007/978-3-642-19379-8_8. https://cryptojedi.org/papers/#negation

15. Bernstein, D.J., Schwabe, P.: NEON crypto. In: Prouff, E., Schaumont, P. (eds.) CHES 2012. LNCS, vol. 7428, pp. 320–339. Springer, Heidelberg (2012). https://doi.org/10.1007/978-3-642-33027-8_19. https://cryptojedi.org/papers/#neoncypto

16. Bernstein, D.J., Yang, B.Y.: Fast constant-time GCD computation and modular inversion. IACR Trans. Cryptogr. Hardw. Embed. Syst. **2019**(3), 340–398 (2019). https://tches.iacr.org/index.php/TCHES/article/view/8298

17. Bos, J.W., Costello, C., Longa, P., Naehrig, M.: Selecting elliptic curves for cryptography: an efficiency and security analysis. J. Cryptogr. Eng. **6**(4), 259–286 (2016). https://www.microsoft.com/en-us/research/wp-content/uploads/2016/02/selecting.pdf

18. Bosma, W., Lenstra, H.W.: Complete systems of two addition laws for elliptic curves. J. Number Theory **53**(2), 229–240 (1995). http://www.sciencedirect.com/science/article/pii/S0022314X85710888

19. Chou, T.: Sandy2x: new Curve25519 speed records. In: Dunkelman, O., Keliher, L. (eds.) SAC 2015. LNCS, vol. 9566, pp. 145–160. Springer, Cham (2016). https://doi.org/10.1007/978-3-319-31301-6_8. https://www.win.tue.nl/~tchou/papers/sandy2x.pdf

20. Cohen, H., Miyaji, A., Ono, T.: Efficient elliptic curve exponentiation using mixed coordinates. In: Ohta, K., Pei, D. (eds.) ASIACRYPT 1998. LNCS, vol. 1514, pp. 51–65. Springer, Heidelberg (1998). https://doi.org/10.1007/3-540-49649-1_6

21. Costello, C., Longa, P.: FourQ: four-dimensional decompositions on a $\mathbb{Q}$-curve over the Mersenne prime. In: Iwata, T., Cheon, J.H. (eds.) ASIACRYPT 2015. LNCS, vol. 9452, pp. 214–235. Springer, Heidelberg (2015). https://doi.org/10.1007/978-3-662-48797-6_10. https://eprint.iacr.org/2015/565.pdf

22. Cremers, C., Jackson, D.: Prime, order please! Revisiting small subgroup and invalid curve attacks on protocols using Diffie-Hellman. Cryptology ePrint Archive, Report 2019/526 (2019). https://eprint.iacr.org/2019/526
23. Edwards, H.M.: A normal form for elliptic curves. Bull. (New Series) Am. Math. Soc. **44**(3), 393–422 (2007). https://www.ams.org/journals/bull/2007-44-03/S0273-0979-07-01153-6/S0273-0979-07-01153-6.pdf
24. Faz-Hernández, A., López, J.: Fast implementation of Curve25519 using AVX2. In: Lauter, K., Rodríguez-Henríquez, F. (eds.) LATINCRYPT 2015. LNCS, vol. 9230, pp. 329–345. Springer, Cham (2015). https://doi.org/10.1007/978-3-319-22174-8_18
25. Fujii, H.: Efficient Curve25519 implementation for ARM microcontrollers. Master's thesis, Universidade Estadual de Campinas (2018). http://taurus.unicamp.br/bitstream/REPOSIP/332957/1/Fujii_Hayato_M.pdf
26. Fujii, H., Aranha, D.F.: Curve25519 for the Cortex-M4 and beyond. In: Lange, T., Dunkelman, O. (eds.) LATINCRYPT 2017. LNCS, vol. 11368, pp. 109–127. Springer, Cham (2019). https://doi.org/10.1007/978-3-030-25283-0_6. http://www.cs.haifa.ac.il/~orrd/LC17/paper39.pdf
27. Haase, B., Labrique, B.: AuCPace: Efficient verifier-based PAKE protocol tailored for the IIoT. IACR Trans. Cryptogr. Hardw. Embed. Syst. 1–48 (2019). https://tches.iacr.org/index.php/TCHES/article/view/7384
28. Hamburg, M.: Decaf: eliminating cofactors through point compression. In: Gennaro, R., Robshaw, M. (eds.) CRYPTO 2015. LNCS, vol. 9215, pp. 705–723. Springer, Heidelberg (2015). https://doi.org/10.1007/978-3-662-47989-6_34. https://www.shiftleft.org/papers/decaf/
29. Hisil, H., Wong, K.K.-H., Carter, G., Dawson, E.: Twisted Edwards curves revisited. In: Pieprzyk, J. (ed.) ASIACRYPT 2008. LNCS, vol. 5350, pp. 326–343. Springer, Heidelberg (2008). https://doi.org/10.1007/978-3-540-89255-7_20. http://eprint.iacr.org/2008/522/
30. Hutter, M., Schwabe, P.: Multiprecision multiplication on AVR revisited. J. Cryptogr. Eng. **5**(3), 201–214 (2015). http://cryptojedi.org/papers/#avrmul
31. Karatsuba, A., Ofman, Y.: Multiplication of multidigit numbers on automata. Soviet Physics Doklady **7**, 595–596 (1963). Translated from Doklady Akademii Nauk SSSR, **145**(2), 293–294, July 1962
32. Kerry, C.F., Director, C.R.: FIPS PUB 186–4 federal information processing standards publication digital signature standard (DSS) (2013). http://nvlpubs.nist.gov/nistpubs/FIPS/NIST.FIPS.186-4.pdf
33. Kim, K.H., Choe, J., Kim, S.Y., Kim, N., Hong, S.: Speeding up elliptic curve scalar multiplication without precomputation. Cryptology ePrint Archive, Report 2017/669 (2017). https://eprint.iacr.org/2017/669.pdf
34. Koblitz, N.: Elliptic curve cryptosystems. Math. Comput. **48**, 209–209 (1987). https://www.ams.org/journals/mcom/1987-48-177/S0025-5718-1987-0866109-5/S0025-5718-1987-0866109-5.pdf
35. Ladd, W., Longa, P., Barnes, R.: Curve4Q. IETF CFRG Internet Draft (2017). https://tools.ietf.org/html/draft-ladd-cfrg-4q-00. Accessed 18 Aug 2019
36. luigi1111, Spagni, R. ("fluffypony"): Disclosure of a major bug in CryptoNote based currencies. Post on the Monero website (2017). https://www.getmonero.org/2017/05/17/disclosure-of-a-major-bug-in-cryptonote-based-currencies.html. Accessed 31 Aug 2019

37. Massolino, P.M.C., Renes, J., Batina, L.: Implementing complete formulas on Weierstrass curves in hardware. In: Carlet, C., Hasan, M.A., Saraswat, V. (eds.) SPACE 2016. LNCS, vol. 10076, pp. 89–108. Springer, Cham (2016). https://doi.org/10.1007/978-3-319-49445-6_5. https://eprint.iacr.org/2016/1133.pdf
38. Miller, V.S.: Use of elliptic curves in cryptography. In: Williams, H.C. (ed.) CRYPTO 1985. LNCS, vol. 218, pp. 417–426. Springer, Heidelberg (1986). https://doi.org/10.1007/3-540-39799-X_31
39. Montgomery, P.L.: Speeding the Pollard and elliptic curve methods of factorization. Math. Comput. **48**(177), 243–264 (1987). http://www.ams.org/journals/mcom/1987-48-177/S0025-5718-1987-0866113-7/S0025-5718-1987-0866113-7.pdf
40. Oliveira, T., López, J., Hışıl, H., Faz-Hernández, A., Rodríguez-Henríquez, F.: How to (pre-)compute a ladder. In: Adams, C., Camenisch, J. (eds.) SAC 2017. LNCS, vol. 10719, pp. 172–191. Springer, Cham (2018). https://doi.org/10.1007/978-3-319-72565-9_9. https://eprint.iacr.org/2017/264.pdf
41. OpenSSL: Cryptography and SSL/TLS toolkit. http://www.openssl.org/. Accessed 18 Aug 2019
42. Renes, J., Costello, C., Batina, L.: Complete addition formulas for prime order elliptic curves. In: Fischlin, M., Coron, J.-S. (eds.) EUROCRYPT 2016. LNCS, vol. 9665, pp. 403–428. Springer, Heidelberg (2016). https://doi.org/10.1007/978-3-662-49890-3_16. http://eprint.iacr.org/2015/1060
43. Santis, F.D., Sigl, G.: Towards side-channel protected X25519 on ARM Cortex-M4 processors. In: SPEED-B – Software performance enhancement for encryption and decryption, and benchmarking (2016). https://ccccspeed.win.tue.nl/papers/SPEED-B_Final.pdf
44. STMicroelelectronics: RM0090 reference manual (2019). https://www.st.com/content/ccc/resource/technical/document/reference_manual/3d/6d/5a/66/b4/99/40/d4/DM00031020.pdf/files/DM00031020.pdf/jcr:content/translations/en.DM00031020.pdf
45. Susella, R., Montrasio, S.: A compact and exception-free ladder for all short Weierstrass elliptic curves. In: Lemke-Rust, K., Tunstall, M. (eds.) CARDIS 2016. LNCS, vol. 10146, pp. 156–173. Springer, Cham (2017). https://doi.org/10.1007/978-3-319-54669-8_10
46. de Valence, H., Grigg, J., Tankersley, G., Valsorda, F., Lovecruft, I.: The ristretto255 group. IETF CFRG Internet Draft (2019). https://tools.ietf.org/html/draft-hdevalence-cfrg-ristretto-01. Accessed 31 July 2019

Revisiting Approximate Polynomial Common Divisor Problem and Noisy Multipolynomial Reconstruction

Jun Xu[1,2], Santanu Sarkar[3(✉)], and Lei Hu[1,2]

[1] State Key Laboratory of Information Security,
Institute of Information Engineering, Chinese Academy of Sciences,
Beijing 100093, China
[2] Data Assurance and Communications Security Research Center,
Chinese Academy of Sciences, Beijing 100093, China
{xujun,hulei}@iie.ac.cn
[3] Indian Institute of Technology, Sardar Patel Road, Chennai 600036, India
sarkar.santanu.bir1@gmail.com

Abstract. In this paper, we present a polynomial lattice method to solve the approximate polynomial common divisor problem. This problem is the polynomial version of the well known approximate integer common divisor problem introduced by Howgrave-Graham (Calc 2001). Our idea can be applied directly to solve the noisy multipolynomial reconstruction problem in the field of error-correcting codes. Compared to the method proposed by Devet, Goldberg and Heninger in USENIX 2012, our approach is faster.

Keywords: Approximate polynomial common divisor problem · Noisy multipolynomial reconstruction · Polynomial lattice

1 Introduction

It is well known that the common divisor of given integers can be easily computed by using the extended Euclidean algorithm. However, computing common divisor becomes hard when given integers are the sums of some unknown noises and multiples of the desired common divisor. Such a problem, firstly introduced by Howgrave-Graham [22], is called the approximate integer common divisor (Integer-ACD) problem, which is the integer version of approximate common divisor (ACD) problem and has seen plenty of applications in fully homomorphic encryption (FHE) schemes [2,3,10–12,37]. In fact, the strategy that transforming an easy problem into a hard one by adding noise has been widely used in cryptography, e.g., the celebrated learning with errors (LWE) problem [35].

The approximate common divisor problem admits a polynomial version, which is called the approximate polynomial common divisor (Polynomial-ACD) problem [4]. It contains the general approximate polynomial common divisor

© Springer Nature Switzerland AG 2019
F. Hao et al. (Eds.): INDOCRYPT 2019, LNCS 11898, pp. 398–411, 2019.
https://doi.org/10.1007/978-3-030-35423-7_20

(Polynomial-GACD) problem and the partial approximate polynomial common divisor (Polynomial-PACD) problem. To be specific, for given nonnegative integers γ, η, ρ satisfying $\gamma > \eta > \rho$, a (γ, η, ρ)-Polynomial-GACD problem is stated as follows:

Definition 1 $((\gamma, \eta, \rho)$-Polynomial-GACD problem). *Let $\mathbb{F}[x]$ be the polynomial ring over a finite field $\mathbb{F}$. Let $r_1(x), \cdots, r_n(x)$ be n random polynomials where degrees of all $r_i(x)$ lie in $[0, \rho]$. Let $p(x) = (x - p_1) \cdots (x - p_\eta)$, where $p_1, \cdots, p_\eta$ are random elements in $\mathbb{F}$. Suppose n polynomials $a_1(x), \cdots, a_n(x)$ with degree at most γ and with at least one has degree γ in $\mathbb{F}[x]$ are given with*

$$a_i(x) \equiv r_i(x) \bmod p(x) \text{ for } 1 \leq i \leq n, \tag{1}$$

where $a_1(x), \cdots, a_n(x)$ are called n samples. The goal is to output the approximate common divisor $p(x)$.

The definition of a (γ, η, ρ)-Polynomial-PACD problem is the same as that of a (γ, η, ρ)-Polynomial-GACD problem except that an exact multiple of γ-degree polynomial $a_n(x)$ of $p(x)$ is given with all roots of $a_n(x)$ are in $\mathbb{F}$.

There are efficient algorithms for computing a common divisor of given polynomials. However, the presence of noises leads to that given polynomials may be inexact and changes the nature of such a question, which is the so-called Polynomial-ACD problem. Its various variants have been investigated by many researchers such as [8,9,14–16,20,21,23,25,26,32,33,36,38]. The Polynomial-ACD problem is a key research topic in the symbolic-numeric computing area.

In the coding field, codewords are often affected by noises during transmission. Therefore, one needs to design an efficient decoding algorithm in order to recover the corrupted codewords. The Reed-Solomn code is a classical group of error-correcting codes, which is based on univariate polynomials over finite fields and has been many prominent applications. In STOC 1999, Naor and Pinkas [30] first proposed the noisy polynomial reconstruction problem, which is closely connected to the list decoding of Reed-Solomon codes. In EUROCRYPT 2000, Bleichenbacher and Nguyen [1] distinguished the noisy polynomial reconstruction problem from the noisy polynomial interpolation problem. In ANTS 2012, Cohn and Heninger [5] further considered the multivariate version of this problem, which is called noisy multipolynomial reconstruction problem and defined as follows:

Definition 2 (Noisy Multipolynomial Reconstruction Problem). *Suppose $r_1(x), \cdots, r_n(x)$ are n univariate polynomials with at most ρ-degree in $\mathbb{F}[x]$. For given γ distinct points $x_1, \cdots, x_\gamma$ in $\mathbb{F}$, there exist the following γ vectors:*

$$\big(r_1(x_1), \cdots, r_n(x_1)\big), \cdots, \big(r_1(x_\gamma), \cdots, r_n(x_\gamma)\big).$$

Suppose that η vectors are not corrupted in the received γ vectors, the goal is to reconstruct each polynomial $r_i(x)$.

In fact, this problem for $n = 1$ corresponds to a list decoding algorithm of Reed-Solomon codes. In order to increase the feasible decoding radius of these codes, Guruswami and Sudan [19] gave a list-decoding algorithm that outputs a list of polynomially many solutions. In [6], Cohn and Heninger proposed a faster variant of the Guruswami-Sudan algorithm, which was inspired by Howgrave-Graham's approach [22] for solving the Integer-PACD problem.

Parvaresh-Vardy codes [34] are based on the noisy multipolynomial reconstruction problem. Guruswami-Rudra codes [18] achieved the improved rates by transmitting less symbols. Recently, Devet, Goldberg and Heninger [13] pointed out that the connections between the noisy multipolynomial reconstruction problem and some kind of private information retrieval (PIR) and further designed an optimally robust PIR based on this problem.

Based on the Lagrange interpolation technique, a polynomial with degree at most ρ can be reconstructed when at least $\rho + 1$ points and the corresponding evaluations are given. It implies that the number η of correct codewords should be greater than or equal to $\rho + 1$ for solving the noisy multipolynomial reconstruction problem in the polynomial time. By utilizing clever polynomial constructions to decode the codewords, Parvaresh and Vardy [34] and Guruswami and Rudra [18] approach such an asymptotic limit of $\eta \geq \rho+1$. Later, Cohn and Heninger [5] heuristically analyzed the noisy multipolynomial reconstruction problem based on the algebraic independence hypothesis and obtained the bound $\eta > \rho^{\frac{n}{n+1}} \gamma^{\frac{1}{n+1}}$ by using the idea of Coppersmith's method [7] for finding small solutions of multivariate polynomial equations. In [13], Devet, Goldberg and Heninger proposed a heuristic lattice method and presented the bound $\eta \geq \gamma - \frac{n}{n+1}(\gamma - \rho - 1)$ to solve the noisy polynomial reconstruction problem.

Our Work: In this paper, a method to solve the Polynomial-ACD problem is proposed. This method can be used for solving the noisy multipolynomial reconstruction problem. We modify slightly the lattice of Devet, Goldberg and Heninger [13]. This modification reduces time complexity.

Organization: In Sect. 2, we present some notations and preliminary knowledge. In Sect. 3, we give an attack for solving Polynomial-ACD problems and present the experiment results. We analyze the noisy multipolynomial reconstruction problem in Sect. 4. Section 5 concludes the paper.

2   Preliminaries

Notations: Let $\mathbb{F}[x]$ be the polynomial ring over the finite field $\mathbb{F}$. The components or entries of the involved row vectors and matrices in this paper are all polynomials in $\mathbb{F}[x]$. Row vectors are denoted by lowercase bold letters and matrices by uppercase bold letters. Let $\mathbf{a}$ be the vector $(a_1(x), \cdots, a_n(x))$ then the i-th component of $\mathbf{a}$ is the polynomial $a_i(x)$. We write $\deg(a_i(x))$ for the degree of the polynomial $a_i(x)$ and the degree of the vector $\mathbf{a}$ is $\deg(\mathbf{a}) = \max_i \deg(a_i(x))$.

Moreover, for polynomials $a(x)$, $b(x) \in \mathbb{F}[x]$, the quotient after $a(x)$ is divided by $b(x)$ is denoted by $\lfloor \frac{a(x)}{b(x)} \rfloor \in \mathbb{F}[x]$. Moreover, the transpose of the vector or matrix is denoted by the symbol T as usual.

Polynomial Lattices: Let $\mathbf{b}_1, \cdots, \mathbf{b}_n$ in $\mathbb{F}[x]^n$ be n linearly independent row vectors. A polynomial lattice L is $\mathbb{F}[x]$-spanned by $\mathbf{b}_1, \cdots, \mathbf{b}_n$ as follows,

$$L = \left\{ \sum_{i=1}^{n} k_i(x) \cdot \mathbf{b}_i \mid k_i(x) \in \mathbb{F}[x] \right\},$$

where $\{\mathbf{b}_1, \cdots, \mathbf{b}_n\}$ is a basis for L and $\mathbf{B} = [\mathbf{b}_1^T, \cdots, \mathbf{b}_n^T]^T$ is the corresponding basis matrix. The rank or dimension of L is denoted as $\dim(L) = n$. The determinant of L is computed as $\det(L) = \det(\mathbf{B})$, which is a polynomial in $\mathbb{F}[x]$.

Polynomial lattices have been well studied in [24]. There are several polynomial lattice basis reduction algorithms such as [17,29] that run in polynomial time and output a reduced basis $\{\mathbf{v}_1, \cdots, \mathbf{v}_n\}$ for L satisfying

$$\deg(\mathbf{v}_1) + \cdots + \deg(\mathbf{v}_n) = \deg(\det(L)). \tag{2}$$

If the reduced basis has been ordered such that $\deg(\mathbf{v}_1) \leq \cdots \leq \deg(\mathbf{v}_n)$, then $\deg(\mathbf{v}_1) \leq \frac{\deg(\det(L))}{n}$. Furthermore, based on (2), one can obtain the following properties:

$$\deg(\mathbf{v}_i) \leq \frac{\deg(\det(L)) - \sum\limits_{j=1}^{i-1} \deg(\mathbf{v}_j)}{n - (i-1)} \text{ for } 2 \leq i \leq n.$$

Here $\mathbf{v}_1$ is a minimal vector in polynomial lattice L. However, in the case of integer lattices [31], finding a shortest vector is an NP-hard problem and efficient lattice reduction algorithms such as LLL [27] only get an exponential approximation.

3 An Algorithm for Solving Polynomial-ACD Problem

In this section, we present a method to solve the Polynomial-ACD problem. For given n samples $a_1(x), \cdots, a_n(x)$, according to (1), i.e., $a_i(x) \equiv r_i(x) \bmod p(x)$ for $1 \leq i \leq n$, there exist polynomial $q_i(x)$ subject to

$$a_i(x) = p(x)q_i(x) + r_i(x) \text{ for } i = 1, \cdots, n.$$

Without loss of generality denote $\deg a_n(x) = \gamma$. For the case of the Polynomial-PACD problem, let $a_n(x)$ be an exact multiple of γ-degree polynomial of $p(x)$, i.e., $a_n(x) \equiv 0 \bmod p(x)$. Let $\beta(x)$ be a polynomial such that $0 \leq \deg \beta(x) < \gamma$.

Algorithm 1. Solving Polynomial-ACD problem

Input: (γ, η, ρ)-Polynomial-ACD samples $a_1(x), \cdots, a_n(x)$ where $\gamma > \eta > \rho + 1$
Output: $p(x)$ or the $(\gamma - \rho)$ most significant coefficients of $p(x)$
1: Construct the $n \times n$ polynomial matrix

$$\mathbf{M}(x^\rho) = \begin{pmatrix} 1 & & \lfloor \frac{a_1(x)}{x^\rho} \rfloor \\ & \ddots & \vdots \\ & & 1 \lfloor \frac{a_{n-1}(x)}{x^\rho} \rfloor \\ & & \lfloor \frac{a_n(x)}{x^\rho} \rfloor \end{pmatrix}.$$

2: Run a polynomial lattice basis row reduction algorithm on $\mathbf{M}(x^\rho)$
3: Rearrange rows of the reduced matrix according to the degrees from small to large and write it as matrix $\mathbf{M}'(x^\rho)$
4: If the degrees of at least two rows in $\mathbf{M}'(x^\rho)$ are larger than or equal to $\eta - \rho$, abort
5: Write $\mathbf{U}$ such that $\mathbf{U} \cdot \mathbf{M}(x^\rho) = \mathbf{M}'(x^\rho)$, where $\mathbf{U}$ is a unimodular $n \times n$ matrix. Write the last column of matrix $\mathbf{U}^{-1}$ as $(w_{1n}(x), \cdots, w_{nn}(x))^T$
6: **if** it is a case of Polynomial-PACD problem **then**
7:     Calculate $d^{-1} \frac{a_n(x)}{w_{nn}(x)}$, where d is some constant such that $d^{-1} \frac{a_n(x)}{w_{nn}(x)}$ is monic.
8:     Set $p(x) = d^{-1} \frac{a_n(x)}{w_{nn}(x)}$
9:     **return** $p(x)$
10: **else**
11:     Compute $d^{-1} \lfloor \frac{a_n(x)}{w_{nn}(x)} \rfloor$, where d is some constant satisfying $d^{-1} \lfloor \frac{a_n(x)}{w_{nn}(x)} \rfloor$ is monic.
12:     **if** $\gamma > \eta + \rho$ **then**
13:         Set $p(x) = d^{-1} \lfloor \frac{a_n(x)}{w_{nn}(x)} \rfloor$
14:         **return** $p(x)$
15:     **else**
16:         **return** the $(\gamma - \rho)$ most significant coefficients of $d^{-1} \lfloor \frac{a_n(x)}{w_{nn}(x)} \rfloor$
17:     **end if**
18: **end if**

Let $L(\beta)$ be the polynomial lattice spanned by the row vectors of the following $n \times n$ matrix

$$\mathbf{M}(\beta) = \begin{pmatrix} 1 & & \lfloor \frac{a_1(x)}{\beta(x)} \rfloor \\ & \ddots & \vdots \\ & & 1 \lfloor \frac{a_{n-1}(x)}{\beta(x)} \rfloor \\ & & \lfloor \frac{a_n(x)}{\beta(x)} \rfloor \end{pmatrix}$$

Then, we present the Algorithm 1 for solving Polynomial-ACD problem.

3.1 Main Result

In this subsection, we explain Algorithm 1. First, we give the following theorem.

Theorem 1. *Given a vector* $\mathbf{v} = (u_1(x), \cdots, u_{n-1}(x), \sum_{i=1}^{n} u_i(x)\lfloor \frac{a_i(x)}{\beta(x)} \rfloor) \in L(\beta)$, *we have*

$$\deg\left(\sum_{i=1}^{n} u_i(x)q_i(x)\right) \leq \deg \mathbf{v} + \max\left\{\deg \beta(x), \rho\right\} - \eta.$$

Proof. According to $a_i(x) = p(x)q_i(x) + r_i(x)$ for $i = 1, \cdots, n$, we get the following equation $p(x)\sum_{i=1}^{n} u_i(x)q_i(x) = \sum_{i=1}^{n} u_i(x)a_i(x) - \sum_{i=1}^{n} u_i(x)r_i(x)$. Since $\deg p(x) = \eta$, we have

$$\eta + \deg\left(\sum_{i=1}^{n} u_i(x)q_i(x)\right) = \deg\left(\sum_{i=1}^{n} u_i(x)a_i(x) - \sum_{i=1}^{n} u_i(x)r_i(x)\right). \quad (3)$$

Let us analyze the upper bound of $\deg\left(\sum_{i=1}^{n} u_i(x)q_i(x)\right)$ as follows. First, since $\mathbf{v} = \left(u_1(x), \cdots, u_{n-1}(x), \sum_{i=1}^{n} u_i(x)\lfloor \frac{a_i(x)}{\beta(x)} \rfloor\right)$, we easily acquire

$$\deg\left(\sum_{i=1}^{n} u_i(x)\lfloor \frac{a_i(x)}{\beta(x)} \rfloor\right) \leq \deg \mathbf{v}. \quad (4)$$

Note that $\deg a_i(x) = \deg(\beta(x)\lfloor \frac{a_i(x)}{\beta(x)} \rfloor)$, we have $\deg\left(\sum_{i=1}^{n} u_i(x)a_i(x)\right) = \deg\left(\beta(x)\sum_{i=1}^{n} u_i(x)\lfloor \frac{a_i(x)}{\beta(x)} \rfloor\right)$. Hence from (4), we have

$$\deg\left(\sum_{i=1}^{n} u_i(x)a_i(x)\right) \leq \deg \mathbf{v} + \deg \beta(x). \quad (5)$$

Since $\deg u_i(x) \leq \deg \mathbf{v}$ and $\deg r_i(x) \leq \rho$ for $1 \leq i \leq n-1$, we have

$$\deg\left(\sum_{i=1}^{n-1} u_i(x)r_i(x)\right) \leq \deg \mathbf{v} + \rho. \quad (6)$$

As $u_n(x)\lfloor \frac{a_n(x)}{\beta(x)} \rfloor = \left(\sum_{i=1}^{n} u_i(x)\lfloor \frac{a_i(x)}{\beta(x)} \rfloor\right) - \left(\sum_{i=1}^{n-1} u_i(x)\lfloor \frac{a_i(x)}{\beta(x)} \rfloor\right)$, $\deg\left(u_n(x)\lfloor \frac{a_n(x)}{\beta(x)} \rfloor\right) \leq \max\left\{\deg\left(\sum_{i=1}^{n} u_i(x)\lfloor \frac{a_i(x)}{\beta(x)} \rfloor\right), \deg\left(\sum_{i=1}^{n-1} u_i(x)\lfloor \frac{a_i(x)}{\beta(x)} \rfloor\right)\right\}$. Since $\deg\lfloor \frac{a_i(x)}{\beta(x)} \rfloor \leq \gamma - \deg \beta(x)$ and $\deg u_i(x) \leq \deg \mathbf{v}$ for $1 \leq i \leq n-1$, we obtain

$$\deg\left(\sum_{i=1}^{n-1} u_i(x)\lfloor \frac{a_i(x)}{\beta(x)} \rfloor\right) \leq \deg \mathbf{v} + \gamma - \deg \beta(x).$$

We have obtained (4), i.e., $\deg\left(\sum_{i=1}^{n} u_i(x)\lfloor\frac{a_i(x)}{\beta(x)}\rfloor\right) \leq \deg\mathbf{v}$, therefore we have

$\deg\left(u_n(x)\lfloor\frac{a_n(x)}{\beta(x)}\rfloor\right) \leq \max\left\{\deg\mathbf{v}, \deg\mathbf{v}+\gamma-\deg\beta(x)\right\}$. As $0 \leq \deg\beta(x) \leq \gamma$,

we get $\deg\left(u_n(x)\lfloor\frac{a_n(x)}{\beta(x)}\rfloor\right) \leq \deg\mathbf{v} + \gamma - \deg\beta(x)$. Note that $\deg\left(\lfloor\frac{a_n(x)}{\beta(x)}\rfloor\right) = \gamma - \deg\beta(x)$, we get $\deg u_n(x) \leq \deg\mathbf{v}$. From $\deg r_n(x) \leq \rho$, we further have

$$\deg\left(u_n(x)r_n(x)\right) \leq \deg\mathbf{v} + \rho. \tag{7}$$

According to (5), (6) and (7), we get $\deg\left(\sum_{i=1}^{n} u_i(x)a_i(x) - \sum_{i=1}^{n} u_i(x)r_i(x)\right) \leq \deg\mathbf{v} + \max\{\deg\beta(x), \rho\}$.

Plugging this inequality into (3), we obtain

$$\deg\left(\sum_{i=1}^{n} u_i(x)q_i(x)\right) \leq \deg\mathbf{v} + \max\left\{\deg\beta(x), \rho\right\} - \eta.$$

$\square$

For finding polynomial equations on $q_1(x), \cdots, q_n(x)$, we implement the lattice basis row reduction algorithm on $\mathbf{M}(\beta)$. Then we rearrange the row vectors of the reduced matrix according to the degrees from small to large and let the corresponding matrix be $\mathbf{M}'(\beta)$. Based on Theorem 1, we directly have the following result.

Corollary 1. *Let* $\mathbf{v}_i = \left(u_{i1}(x), \cdots, u_{i,n-1}(x), \sum_{j=1}^{n} u_{ij}(x)\lfloor\frac{a_j(x)}{\beta(x)}\rfloor\right)$ *be the i-th row vector of* $\mathbf{M}'(\beta)$. *Then*

$$\deg\left(\sum_{j=1}^{n} u_{ij}(x)q_j(x)\right) \leq \deg\mathbf{v}_i + \max\left\{\deg\beta(x), \rho\right\} - \eta.$$

Furthermore, if

$$\max\mathbf{v}_i + \left\{\deg\deg\beta(x), \rho\right\} \leq \eta - 1, \tag{8}$$

we get $\sum_{j=1}^{n} u_{ij}(x)q_j(x) = 0$.

3.2   Recovering $q_1(x), \cdots, Q_n(x)$

Suppose that the condition (8) holds for the first $n-1$ row vectors of $\mathbf{M}(\beta)$, we can obtain $n-1$ linearly independent homogeneous equations $\sum_{j=1}^{n} u_{ij}(x)q_j(x) =$

0 for $i = 1, \cdots, n - 1$. Let $d_n(x) = \sum_{j=1}^{n} u_{nj}(x)q_j(x)$ and denote $\mathbf{U}$ as matrix $(u_{ij}(x))_{n \times n}$. We have $\mathbf{U} \cdot \mathbf{M}(\beta) = \mathbf{M}'(\beta)$ and $\mathbf{U}(q_1(x), \cdots, q_n(x))^T = (0, \cdots, 0, d_n(x))^T$. Note that $\mathbf{M}(\beta)$ and $\mathbf{M}'(\beta)$ are lattice basis matrices of $L(\beta)$, hence $\mathbf{U}$ and $\mathbf{U}^{-1}$ are both unimodular matrices. Left multiply $\mathbf{U}^{-1}$ by both sides of the above equation and get

$$(q_1(x), \cdots, q_n(x))^T = \mathbf{U}^{-1}(0, \cdots, 0, d_n(x))^T.$$

Let $(w_{1n}(x), \cdots, w_{nn}(x))^T$ be the last column of matrix $\mathbf{U}^{-1}$, which can be publicly computed. According to the above equation, we get

$$q_i(x) = d_n(x)w_{in}(x) \tag{9}$$

for $1 \leq i \leq n$. It implies that $d_n(x)$ is a common divisor of $q_1(x), \cdots, q_n(x)$. With probability $1 - \frac{1}{|\mathbb{F}|^{n-1}}$ [28], polynomials $q_1(x), \cdots, q_n(x)$ are coprime, that is, $d_n(x)$ is a unit in field $\mathbb{F}$. We denote the nonzero constant d as $d_n(x)$ for the sake of discussion.

From $a_i(x) = p(x)q_i(x) + r_i(x)$, $\deg r_i(x) < \deg p(x)$ and $p(x)$ is monic, we get that the leading coefficient of $q_i(x)$ is equal to that of the corresponding $a_i(x)$. Therefore, we can determine $d_n(x)$ by comparing the leading coefficients of both sides in (9). Furthermore, $q_1(x), \cdots, q_n(x)$ are acquired.

3.3   Recovering $p(x)$

The Case of Polynomial-PACD. Note that $a_n(x) = p(x)q_n(x)$. From (9), we deduce $p(x) = d^{-1}\frac{a_n(x)}{w_{nn}(x)}$. Moreover, we recover $r_i(x)$ $(1 \leq i \leq n)$ according to $r_i(x) = a_i(x) \bmod p(x)$.

The Case of Polynomial-GACD. According to $a_n(x) = p(x)q_n(x) + r_n(x)$ and (9), we obtain

$$d^{-1}\left\lfloor \frac{a_n(x)}{w_{nn}(x)} \right\rfloor = p(x) + d^{-1}\left\lfloor \frac{r_n(x)}{w_{nn}(x)} \right\rfloor. \tag{10}$$

Note that $\deg a_n(x) = \gamma$ and $\deg p(x) = \eta$, we have $\deg q_n(x) = \deg w_{nn}(x) = \gamma - \eta$. From $\deg r_n(x) \leq \rho$, we derive $\deg\lfloor \frac{r_n(x)}{w_{nn}(x)} \rfloor \leq \rho - (\gamma - \eta) = \eta - (\gamma - \rho)$.

If $\gamma > \eta + \rho$, we have $\deg\lfloor \frac{r_n(x)}{w_{nn}(x)} \rfloor < 0$, i.e., $\lfloor \frac{r_n(x)}{w_{nn}(x)} \rfloor = 0$. Plugging it into (10), we get $p(x) = d^{-1}\lfloor \frac{a_n(x)}{w_{nn}(x)} \rfloor$. Furthermore, the $r_i(x)$ $(1 \leq i \leq n)$ are obtained due to $r_i(x) = a_i(x) \bmod p(x)$.

If $\gamma \leq \eta + \rho$, according to (10), $\deg\lfloor \frac{r_n(x)}{w_{nn}(x)} \rfloor \leq \eta - (\gamma - \rho)$ and $\deg p(x) = \eta$, we obtain that the $(\gamma - \rho)$ most significant coefficients of $p(x)$ are respectively equal to those of $d^{-1}\lfloor \frac{a_n(x)}{w_{nn}(x)} \rfloor$.

3.4 Optimizing $\beta(x)$

Note that the key point that our strategy can work is to get the following polynomial equations:

$$\sum_{j=1}^{n} u_{ij}(x)q_j(x) = 0 \text{ for } i = 1, \cdots, n-1 \text{ and } \sum_{j=1}^{n} u_{nj}(x)q_j(x) = d$$

where d is some nonzero constant. According to Corollary 1, we obtain that the above equations hold under the condition

$$\begin{cases} \deg \mathbf{v}_1 + \max\big\{\deg \beta(x), \rho\big\} \le \eta - 1 \\ \qquad \vdots \\ \deg \mathbf{v}_{n-1} + \max\big\{\deg \beta(x), \rho\big\} \le \eta - 1 \\ \deg \mathbf{v}_n + \max\big\{\deg \beta(x), \rho\big\} = \eta \end{cases} \tag{11}$$

Remark 1. The motivation of (11) is based upon the assumption that the degrees of the reduced basis vectors $\mathbf{v}_1, \ldots, \mathbf{v}_n$ are relatively average. In essence, we assume that the first reduced basis vector $\mathbf{v}_1$ satisfies $\deg \mathbf{v}_1 \approx \frac{\deg(\det(L(\beta)))}{n}$. In fact, if the above relation holds, according to (2), it is easy to deduce that $\deg \mathbf{v}_i \approx \frac{\deg(\det(L(\beta)))}{n}$ for all $1 \le i \le n$.

When $0 \le \deg \beta(x) \le \rho$, the condition (11) becomes

$$\deg \mathbf{v}_i \le \eta - \rho - 1 \text{ for } 1 \le i \le n - 1$$
$$\text{and } \deg \mathbf{v}_n = \eta - \rho. \tag{12}$$

When $\deg \beta(x) \ge \rho$, (11) becomes

$$\deg \mathbf{v}_i \le \eta - 1 - \deg \beta(x) \text{ for } 1 \le i \le n-1 \text{ and } \deg \mathbf{v}_n = \eta - \deg \beta(x). \tag{13}$$

Note that $\dim L(\beta) = n$ and $\deg \det L(\beta) = \gamma - \deg \beta(x)$.
Thus from (2) we get

$$\deg \mathbf{v}_1 + \cdots + \deg \mathbf{v}_n = \gamma - \deg \beta(x). \tag{14}$$

Thus from (14) respectively, we deduce that

$$n \ge \begin{cases} \frac{\gamma + \rho - \eta - \deg \beta(x)}{\eta - \rho - 1} + 1, & 0 \le \deg \beta(x) \le \rho, \\ \frac{\gamma - \eta}{\eta - \deg \beta(x) - 1} + 1, & \deg \beta(x) \ge \rho. \end{cases}$$

It is easy to see that the above condition is optimal when $\deg \beta(x) = \rho$. For the sake of simplicity, we take $\beta(x) = x^\rho$. In this situation, the above condition is

$$n \ge \frac{\gamma - \eta}{\eta - \rho - 1} + 1. \tag{15}$$

Table 1. Analysis of the polynomial-PACD problem instances over finite field $\mathbb{F}_p$.

n	η	γ	ρ	$\frac{\gamma-\eta}{\eta-\rho-1}+1$	Our algorithm
					Average reduction time (sec.)
4	11	20	7	4.0	0.01
6	10	20	7	6.0	0.03
12	9	20	7	12.0	0.18
15	84	165	77	14.5	2.84
18	86	170	80	17.8	4.75

3.5 Analysis of the Attack Complexity

The dominant calculation of our algorithms is the polynomial lattice reduction for finding equations on $q_1(x), \cdots, q_n(x)$. Mulders and Storjohann [29] presented a simple algorithm in time $O(n^3\delta^2)$. Later, Giorgi et al. [17] proposed another algorithm which runs in time $O(n^{\omega+o(1)}\delta)$, where δ is the maximum degree of the input basis matrix, n is the dimension, and ω is a valid exponent for matrix multiplication.

Corresponding to lattice $L(x^\rho)$ in Algorithm 1, the smallest number of samples $\lceil \frac{\gamma-\eta}{\eta-\rho-1} \rceil + 1$ satisfying (15) is taken as the dimension n, the maximum degree of the input basis matrix $\mathbf{M}(\beta)$ is $\gamma - \rho$. Therefore, the involved running time of the lattice reduction algorithm is $O\left((\lceil \frac{\gamma-\eta}{\eta-\rho-1} \rceil + 1)^{\omega+o(1)}(\gamma - \rho)\right)$ for Giorgi et al.'s algorithm.

3.6 Experimental Verification

In this section, we present experimental results in Table 1. The experiments are done in Sage 8.4 on Linux Ubuntu 14.04 on a desktop with Intel(R) Xeon(R) CPU E5-2670 v3 @ 2.30 GHz, 3 GB RAM and 3 MB Cache. We take $\mathbb{F}_p$ as the underlying finite field $\mathbb{F}$, where p is a random 128-bit prime. The runtime in Table 1 refers to the consuming time in second on the polynomial lattice reduction algorithm. The obtained reduced basis matrix by using the polynomial lattice reduction algorithm is the weak Popov form [29]. We run 100 experiments for each parameter. In each case, we see that the success rate is 100 percent. However, if we take $n < \frac{\gamma-\eta}{\eta-\rho-1} + 1$, our idea always fails to find $p(x)$.

4 Relation Between Polynomial-ACD Problem and Noisy Multipolynomial Reconstruction

In this section, we discuss the relation between the Polynomial-ACD problem and the noisy multipolynomial reconstruction. This relation has been proposed in [5,13].

Consider n univariate polynomials $r_1(x), \ldots, r_n(x)$ of degree ρ over a finite field $\mathbb{F}$. Suppose these polynomials are evaluated at points $x_1, \cdots, x_\gamma$. Let $z_{is} = r_s(x_i)$ for $1 \le i \le \gamma$ and $1 \le s \le n$. Now suppose y_{is} are given for $1 \le i \le \gamma$ and $1 \le s \le n$ where $y_{is} = z_{is}$ for $i \in \{i_1, i_2, \ldots, i_\eta\}$ for each values of s. Our target is to find $r_1(x), \ldots, r_n(x)$ from the knowledge of x_i and y_{is}. This problem has an application in error correcting code [13]. One algorithm is given to solve this problem in [13, Algorithm 1, Page 4]. Now we show that one can use Polynomial-ACD Problem to solve this problem.

Let us assume without loss of generality $y_{is} = z_{is}$ for $1 \le i \le \eta$ and $1 \le s \le n$. One can use Lagrange interpolation to construct n polynomial $a_s(x)$ with degree $\gamma - 1$ such that $a_s(x_i) = y_{is}$ for $1 \le i \le \gamma$ and $1 \le s \le n$. Note that

$$a_s(x_j) = y_{is} = z_{is} = r_s(x_j) \text{ with } s = 1, \cdots, n \text{ and } j = 1, \cdots, \eta.$$

Let $p(x) = (x - x_1) \cdots (x - x_\eta)$. Hence, we have $a_s(x) \equiv r_s(x) \bmod p(x)$ for $s = 1, \cdots, n$. Moreover, there is another relation $N(x) = (x - x_1) \cdots (x - x_\gamma) \equiv 0 \bmod p(x)$. Thus there are polynomials $q_1(x), \cdots, q_n(x), q_{n+1}(x)$ in $\mathbb{F}[x]$ such that $a_s(x) = p(x)q_s(x) + r_s(x)$ for $s = 1, \cdots, n$ and $N(x) = p(x)q_{n+1}(x)$. Once the approximate common divisor $p(x)$ is found out, the desired $r_s(x)$ can be obtained according to $r_s(x) = a_s(x) \bmod p(x)$ if $\eta > \rho$ for $1 \le s \le n$.

From the condition (15), we get that the noisy multipolynomial reconstruction problem can be solved under the condition $n + 1 \ge \frac{\gamma - \eta}{\eta - \rho - 1} + 1$, i.e.,

$$\eta \ge \frac{\gamma + n(\rho + 1)}{n + 1}. \tag{16}$$

Table 2. Noisy multipolynomial reconstruction over finite field $\mathbb{F}_p$.

n	η	γ	ρ	$\mathbb{F}_p$	
				Algorithm 1 [13]	
				Average reduction time (sec.)	
14	87	100	85	<1	<1
22	27	90	23	6.33	11.13
20	97	200	90	9.86	32.44
25	86	200	80	19.95	63.48
40	83	163	80	41.04	135.19
54	97	150	95	57.73	173.00
70	75	145	73	156.63	484.02

The condition (16) is the same as that in [13], which is close to the theoretical limit $\eta \ge \rho + 1$ when n is sufficiently large.

Remark 2. Devet, Goldberg and Heninger [13] considered the lattice spanned by the row vectors of matrix $\begin{pmatrix} x^\rho & & a_1(x) \\ & \ddots & \vdots \\ & & x^\rho & a_n(x) \\ & & & N(x) \end{pmatrix}$, whereas we consider matrix

$$\begin{pmatrix} 1 & & \lfloor \frac{a_1(x)}{x^\rho} \rfloor \\ & \ddots & \vdots \\ & & 1 & \lfloor \frac{a_n(x)}{x^\rho} \rfloor \\ & & & \lfloor \frac{N(x)}{x^\rho} \rfloor \end{pmatrix}.$$

Remark 3. There is slight error in Algorithm 1 of [13]. Step 7 in Algorithm 1 of [13] "b" should be replaced by "$-b$".

Some experimental results are given in Table 2. Here a random 128-bit prime p has been taken. We run 100 experiments for each parameters. From Table 2, it is clear that our method is faster than that of [13]. When $\gamma - \rho$ is small, reduction time in our approach is significantly less than the existing idea. This is because that the degrees of polynomials of the involved input matrix are smaller than [13].

5   Conclusion

In this paper, the Polynomial-ACD problem has been analyzed and lattice attack has been proposed. Our attack idea is used to solve the noisy multipolynomial reconstruction problem. In our attack, the polynomials of the involved lattice are reduced so that experimentally execution time is faster than the existing approach.

Acknowledgments. The authors would like to thank the anonymous reviewers for their helpful comments and suggestions. This work was supported by the National Natural Science Foundation of China (Grants 61732021, 61502488). J. Xu is supported by Introducing Excellent Young Talents of Institute of Information Engineering, Chinese Academy Sciences and China Scholarship Council (No. 201804910206). S. Sarkar thanks Department of Science & Technology, India for partial support.

References

1. Bleichenbacher, D., Nguyen, P.Q.: Noisy polynomial interpolation and noisy Chinese remaindering. In: Preneel, B. (ed.) EUROCRYPT 2000. LNCS, vol. 1807, pp. 53–69. Springer, Heidelberg (2000). https://doi.org/10.1007/3-540-45539-6_4
2. Cheon, J.H., et al.: Batch fully homomorphic encryption over the integers. In: Johansson, T., Nguyen, P.Q. (eds.) EUROCRYPT 2013. LNCS, vol. 7881, pp. 315–335. Springer, Heidelberg (2013). https://doi.org/10.1007/978-3-642-38348-9_20
3. Cheon, J.H., Stehlé, D.: Fully homomorphic encryption over the integers revisited. In: Oswald, E., Fischlin, M. (eds.) Advances in Cryptology - EUROCRYPT 2015. Lecture Notes in Computer Science, vol. 9056, pp. 513–536. Springer, Berlin Heidelberg (2015)

4. Cheon, J.H., Hong, H., Lee, M.S., Ryu, H.: The polynomial approximate common divisor problem and its application to the fully homomorphic encryption. Inf. Sci. **326**, 41–58 (2016)
5. Cohn, H., Heninger, N.: Approximate common divisors via lattices. Open Book Ser. **1**(1), 271–293 (2013)
6. Cohn, H., Heninger, N.: Ideal forms of Coppersmith's theorem and Guruswami-Sudan list decoding. Adv. Math. Comm. **9**(3), 311–339 (2015)
7. Coppersmith, D.: Small solutions to polynomial equations, and low exponent RSA vulnerabilities. J. Cryptol. **10**(4), 233–260 (1997)
8. Corless, R.M., Gianni, P.M., Trager, B.M., Watt, S.M.: The singular value decomposition for polynomial systems. In: Proceedings of the 1995 International Symposium on Symbolic and Algebraic Computation, pp. 195–207. ACM (1995)
9. Corless, R.M., Watt, S.M., Zhi, L.: QR factoring to compute the GCD of univariate approximate polynomials. IEEE Trans. Sig. Process. **52**(12), 3394–3402 (2004)
10. Coron, J.-S., Lepoint, T., Tibouchi, M.: Scale-invariant fully homomorphic encryption over the integers. In: Krawczyk, H. (ed.) PKC 2014. LNCS, vol. 8383, pp. 311–328. Springer, Heidelberg (2014). https://doi.org/10.1007/978-3-642-54631-0_18
11. Coron, J.-S., Mandal, A., Naccache, D., Tibouchi, M.: Fully homomorphic encryption over the integers with shorter public keys. In: Rogaway, P. (ed.) CRYPTO 2011. LNCS, vol. 6841, pp. 487–504. Springer, Heidelberg (2011). https://doi.org/10.1007/978-3-642-22792-9_28
12. Coron, J.-S., Naccache, D., Tibouchi, M.: Public key compression and modulus switching for fully homomorphic encryption over the integers. In: Pointcheval, D., Johansson, T. (eds.) EUROCRYPT 2012. LNCS, vol. 7237, pp. 446–464. Springer, Heidelberg (2012). https://doi.org/10.1007/978-3-642-29011-4_27
13. Devet, C., Goldberg, I., Heninger, N.: Optimally robust private information retrieval. In: Proceedings of the 21st USENIX Conference on Security Symposium, Security 2012, Berkeley, CA, USA, p. 13. USENIX Association (2012)
14. Eliaš, J.: Approximate polynomial greatest common divisor. Ph.D. thesis, Master thesis, Charles University in Prague (2012)
15. Emiris, I.Z., Galligo, A., Lombardi, H.: Numerical univariate polynomial GCD. Lect. Appl. Math. Am. Math. Soc. **32**, 323–344 (1996)
16. Giesbrecht, M., Haraldson, J., Kaltofen, E.: Computing approximate greatest common right divisors of differential polynomials (2017). CoRR, abs/1701.01994
17. Giorgi, P., Jeannerod, C.-P., Villard, G.: On the complexity of polynomial matrix computations. In: Proceedings of Symbolic and Algebraic Computation, International Symposium, ISSAC 2003, Drexel University, Philadelphia, Pennsylvania, USA, 3–6 August 2003, pp. 135–142 (2003)
18. Guruswami, V., Rudra, A.: Explicit codes achieving list decoding capacity: error-correction with optimal redundancy. IEEE Trans. Inf. Theory **54**(1), 135–150 (2008)
19. Guruswami, V., Sudan, M.: Improved decoding of Reed-Solomon and algebraic-geometry codes. IEEE Trans. Inf. Theory **45**(6), 1757–1767 (1999)
20. Halikias, G., Galanis, G., Karcanias, N., Milonidis, E.: Nearest common root of polynomials, approximate greatest common divisor and the structured singular value. IMA J. Math. Control Inf. **30**(4), 423–442 (2013)
21. Hough, D.G.: Explaining and ameliorating the ILL condition of zeros of polynomials. Ph.D. thesis (1977). AAI7731401

22. Howgrave-Graham, N.: Approximate integer common divisors. In: Silverman, J.H. (ed.) CaLC 2001. LNCS, vol. 2146, pp. 51–66. Springer, Heidelberg (2001). https:// doi.org/10.1007/3-540-44670-2_6
23. Hribernig, V., Stetter, H.J.: Detection and validation of clusters of polynomial zeros. J. Symb. Comput. **24**(6), 667–681 (1997)
24. Kailath, T.: Linear Systems, vol. 156. Prentice-Hall, Englewood Cliffs (1980)
25. Kaltofen, E., Yang, Z., Zhi, L.: Approximate greatest common divisors of several polynomials with linearly constrained coefficients and singular polynomials. In: Proceedings of the 2006 International Symposium on Symbolic and Algebraic Computation, pp. 169–176. ACM (2006)
26. Karmarkar, N.K., Lakshman, Y.N.: On approximate GCDs of univariate polynomials. J. Symb. Comput. **26**(6), 653–666 (1998)
27. Lenstra, A.K., Lenstra, H.W., Lovasz, L.: Factoring polynomials with rational coefficients. Math. Ann. **261**(4), 515–534 (1982)
28. Morrison, K.E.: Random polynomials over finite fields. https://web.calpoly.edu/ ~kmorriso/Research/RPFF.pdf
29. Mulders, T., Storjohann, A.: On lattice reduction for polynomial matrices. J. Symb. Comput. **35**(4), 377–401 (2003)
30. Naor, M., Pinkas, B.: Oblivious transfer and polynomial evaluation. In: Proceedings of the Thirty-First Annual ACM Symposium on Theory of Computing, STOC 1999, New York, NY, USA, pp. 245–254. ACM (1999)
31. Nguyen, P.Q., Stern, J.: The two faces of lattices in cryptology. In: Silverman, J.H. (ed.) CaLC 2001. LNCS, vol. 2146, pp. 146–180. Springer, Heidelberg (2001). https://doi.org/10.1007/3-540-44670-2_12
32. Noda, M.-T., Sasaki, T.: Approximate GCD and its application to ill-conditioned equations. J. Comput. Appl. Math. **38**(1–3), 335–351 (1991)
33. Pan, V.Y.: Numerical computation of a polynomial GCD and extensions. Ph.D. thesis, Inria (1996)
34. Parvaresh, F., Vardy, A.: Correcting errors beyond the Guruswami-Sudan radius in polynomial time. In: Proceedings of 46th Annual IEEE Symposium on Foundations of Computer Science (FOCS 2005), 23–25 October 2005, Pittsburgh, PA, USA, pp. 285–294 (2005)
35. Regev, O.: On lattices, learning with errors, random linear codes, and cryptography. In: Proceedings of the Thirty-Seventh Annual ACM Symposium on Theory of Computing, STOC 2005, New York, NY, USA, pp. 84–93. ACM (2005)
36. Schönhage, A.: Quasi-GCD computations. J. Complex. **1**(1), 118–137 (1985)
37. van Dijk, M., Gentry, C., Halevi, S., Vaikuntanathan, V.: Fully homomorphic encryption over the integers. In: Gilbert, H. (ed.) EUROCRYPT 2010. LNCS, vol. 6110, pp. 24–43. Springer, Heidelberg (2010). https://doi.org/10.1007/978-3-642-13190-5_2
38. Winkler, J.R., Yang, N.: Resultant matrices and the computation of the degree of an approximate greatest common divisor of two inexact Bernstein basis polynomials. Comput. Aided Geom. Des. **30**(4), 410–429 (2013)

Quantum: Algorithms, Attacks and Key Distribution

Efficient Quantum Algorithms Related to Autocorrelation Spectrum

Debajyoti Bera[1][(✉)], Subhamoy Maitra[2], and Sapv Tharrmashastha[1]

[1] Computer Science and Engineering Department, IIIT-D, New Delhi 110020, India
{dbera,tharrmashasthav}@iiitd.ac.in
[2] Applied Statistics Unit, Indian Statistical Institute,
203 B T Road, Kolkata 700108, India
subho@isical.ac.in

Abstract. In this paper, we propose efficient probabilistic algorithms for several problems regarding the autocorrelation spectrum. First, we present a quantum algorithm that samples from the Walsh spectrum of any derivative of $f()$. Informally, the autocorrelation coefficient of a Boolean function $f()$ at some point a measures the average correlation among the values $f(x)$ and $f(x \oplus a)$. The derivative of a Boolean function is an extension of autocorrelation to correlation among multiple values of $f()$. The Walsh spectrum is well-studied primarily due to its connection to the quantum circuit for the Deutsch-Jozsa problem. We extend the idea to "Higher-order Deutsch-Jozsa" quantum algorithm to obtain points corresponding to large absolute values in the Walsh spectrum of a certain derivative of $f()$. Further, we design an algorithm to sample the input points according to squares of the autocorrelation coefficients. Finally we provide a different set of algorithms for estimating the square of a particular coefficient or cumulative sum of their squares.

Keywords: Autocorrelation · Boolean function · Cryptology · Quantum computing · Walsh spectrum

1 Introduction

Boolean functions are very important building blocks in cryptology, learning theory and coding theory. Different properties of Boolean functions can be well understood by different spectra; specifically, Walsh and autocorrelation spectra are two most important tools for cryptographic purposes. For a Boolean function $f()$, these spectra can be thought as the list of all values of the Walsh transform and autocorrelation transform, respectively, of $f()$. We use Walsh coefficients and autocorrelation coefficients to indicate the individual values in those spectra.

Shannon related these spectra to confusion and diffusion of cryptosystems long ago [16]. Confusion of a Boolean function used in a cryptosystem can be characterized by a Walsh spectrum with low absolute values – such functions are known to resist linear cryptanalysis [3]; similarly, functions with less diffusion

© Springer Nature Switzerland AG 2019
F. Hao et al. (Eds.): INDOCRYPT 2019, LNCS 11898, pp. 415–432, 2019.
https://doi.org/10.1007/978-3-030-35423-7_21

(high absolute value in the autocorrelation spectrum) may make a cryptosystem vulnerable against differential attacks (see for example [17] and the references therein). Walsh spectrum (often referred to as Fourier spectra for Boolean functions) has been shown to be useful for learning Boolean functions as well [14].

Analyzing these spectra and designing functions with specific spectral properties are therefore important tasks. This problem becomes challenging for large functions. Such large functions may arise while modelling a complete stream or block cipher as a Boolean function with number of inputs equal to the key size in bits. Modelling such a complicated Boolean function by analysing the spectra is clearly elusive [15]. In classical domain, for an n-input 1-output Boolean function, generation of complete Walsh or autocorrelation spectrum requires $O(2^n)$ space and $O(n2^n)$ time. Needless to mention that for analysing a cipher or learning a Boolean function, it is easier to locate the points if there are high coefficients in a spectrum. Thus it makes sense to design techniques for sampling points with high coefficients and estimate the high coefficients in which a Boolean function can be used only as a black-box.

The motivation in cipher design is to obtain a Boolean function for which the maximum absolute value in both the spectra is minimized (for autocorrelation we consider non-zero points only). While there are many such examples and constructions of such functions in literature related to combinatorics, cryptography and coding theory, such Boolean functions are not implemented in a straightforward manner such as simple circuits or truth/look-up tables. This is because it is very hard to implement a complex Boolean function on large number of variables (say 160) in this manner due to exponential circuit size. For example, in stream cipher (one may also consider the specific example of Grain v1 [8]), LFSR/NFSRs (Linear/Nonlinear Feedback Shift Registers) are used. The secret key (say 80 bits) and the public IV (Initialization Vector, say 80 bits again) are loaded in the initial state. Then the initial state is evolved as a Deterministic Finite Automaton for many (say 160 or 200) steps. The output bit is generated by combining some selected bits (say 15) from the LFSR/NFSRs. Then we start generating the output bits which is used as key stream bits for cryptographic purposes. Now if you consider the initial key and IV as the inputs to a Boolean function and the key stream bit at any instance as an output, this is a Boolean function with 160 input bits and one output bit. Modelling such a complicated Boolean function by analysing the spectra is practically not possible. For more details, one may refer to [15]. However, if the complete circuit can be implemented in quantum paradigm, then one may have much better efficiency in mounting the attacks.

The situation is well settled for the Walsh spectrum. Walsh spectrum of a function $f : \{0,1\}^n \longrightarrow \{0,1\}$ is defined as the following function[1] from $\{0,1\}^n$

---

[1] The normalization factor used depends upon the application but has no bearing on properties of interest.

to $\mathbb{R}[-1,1]$ in which $x \cdot y$ stands for the 0–1 valued expression $\oplus_{i=1...n} x_i y_i$:

$$\text{for } y \in \{0,1\}^n, \quad \hat{f}(y) = \frac{1}{2^n} \sum_{x \in \{0,1\}^n} (-1)^{f(x)}(-1)^{y \cdot x}$$

Fig. 1. Circuit for Deutsch-Jozsa algorithm (without measurement)

The Deutsch-Jozsa algorithm [5], even though usually described as solving a different problem, makes only *one* query to U_f (a standard unitary implementation of $f()$) and at the end, puts the second register in the state $|1\rangle$ and the first register in the state $\sum_{z \in \mathbb{F}_2^n} \hat{f}(z)|z\rangle$; the quantum circuit for the same is illustrated in Fig. 1. Measuring the second register in the standard basis generates a state $|z\rangle$ with probability $\hat{f}(z)^2$. Note that Walsh coefficients do satisfy $\sum_z \hat{f}(z)^2 = 1$ (this is due to Parseval's theorem); thus the Deutsch-Jozsa algorithm can be considered as an efficient sampling algorithm for Walsh coefficients [13]. So if one can implement a stream cipher (a Boolean function) as a quantum oracle [6], then it is possible to sample high points in a Walsh spectrum in constant time with linear number of gates and that enables us to answer several questions related to the spectrum [18].

In contrast to the Walsh spectrum, the autocorrelation spectrum is less studied. It is defined as the following transformation (see footnote 1) from $\{0,1\}^n$ to $\mathbb{R}[-1,1]$.

$$\text{for } a \in \{0,1\}^n, \quad \check{f}(a) = \frac{1}{2^n} \sum_{x \in \{0,1\}^n} (-1)^{f(x)}(-1)^{f(x \oplus a)}$$

The entire autocorrelation spectrum can be obtained by first computing the Walsh spectrum (using the well-known "fast Walsh-Hadamard transform" algorithm), then squaring each of the coefficients, and finally applying the same transform once more on this squared spectrum. This approach requires 2^n many calls to $f()$, $n2^n$ other operations and space complexity of 2^n.

However, a question remains that *what* can be found out about the autocorrelation spectrum in $o(2^n)$, preferably polynomial, time.

- Especially, can we identify the points with high coefficients?
- Can we estimate a particular coefficient?

Counting and sampling often go hand-in-hand, so one would also like to sample from a distribution proportional to the coefficients. It should be noted that $\sum_a \breve{f}(a)^2 \in [1, 2^n]$ unlike Walsh coefficients, therefore, it appears difficult to get a quantum sampling algorithm like Deutsch-Jozsa as an immediate corollary.

The quantum algorithms we propose in this paper address these questions. Naturally, in terms of autocorrelation spectrum, such algorithms will be able to expose the weaknesses of a Boolean function (used in a cryptographic primitive) better than the classical approaches. There are quite a few important research results related to quantum cryptanalysis of symmetric ciphers [4,9,10]. A recent work [12] in this direction considered merging the ideas from Grover's [7] and Simon's [2] algorithms. However, there has been no specific attempt to solve concrete problems related to the autocorrelation spectrum. This we present in this paper.

One of the ideas used by us is that of amplitude amplification which is the underlying engine behind Grover's algorithms. However, our approach is very different from that of Simon's algorithm even though it is tempting to use this algorithm since $\breve{f}(a) = 1$ iff $f(x) = f(x \oplus a)$ for all x and the latter is one of main promises held by f in the Simon's problem. First, another condition on f, i.e., if $f(x) = f(y)$ then $x = y \oplus a$, may not necessarily hold for 1-bit functions and secondly, Simon's algorithm is specifically designed for finding any such a and not sampling according to a distribution proportional to $\breve{f}(a)$.

Another important measure related to autocorrelation spectrum is the sum-of-squares indicator. Naturally it is better if this value is low.

Definition 1 (Sum-of-squares indicator). *The sum-of-squares indicator for the characteristic of f is defined as*

$$\sigma_f = \sum_{a \in \mathbb{F}_2^n} \breve{f}(a)^2$$

It is known that $1 \leq \sigma_f \leq 2^n$. In particular, $\sigma_f = 1$ if f is a Bent function and $\sigma_f = 2^n$ if f is a linear function. A small σ_f indicates that a function satisfies the *global avalanche criteria* (GAC).

1.1 Outline

The results in this paper answer the questions of sampling and estimation that were raised above.

In Sect. 2 we present a generalization of the Deutsch-Jozsa problem that we name as "Higher-order Deutsch-Jozsa" (HoDJ), which is related to the derivatives of a Boolean function. Higher-order derivatives capture the correlation among multiple output values of the same function and is important for constructing cryptographic hash functions that are resistant to linear attack, differential attack, cube attack, etc.

We then discuss a quantum algorithm whose output is a random sample from a distribution that is proportional to the Walsh coefficients of any specific higher-order derivative. For k-th order derivative, the algorithm uses only $n + 1$ *additional* qubits, makes 2^k calls to the function and uses altogether $O(n2^k)$

gates that is a meagre fraction compared to the usual exponential (in n) time and space complexity seen in classical algorithms.

The first-order derivative is also known as the autocorrelation spectrum so this sampling algorithm can be used to generate samples according to the distribution of the *Walsh coefficients* of the autocorrelation coefficients. By making a subtle observation, we show how to actually sample according to the autocorrelation spectrum itself. We are not aware of any classical sampling algorithm for the autocorrelation spectrum and the only algorithm known for generating the entire spectrum, which involves computing Walsh transformation twice and is no doubt an overkill for the task of sampling, incurs $\Theta(2^n)$ space complexity and $\Theta(n2^n)$ time complexity. In comparison to it, our quantum algorithm has $O\left(n\frac{2^{n/2}}{\sqrt{\sigma_f}}\log\frac{1}{\delta}\right)$ time complexity (exhibiting a quadratic speedup) and $2n + 1$ space complexity; here δ indicates the probability of failure. If σ_f is not too small, say $\frac{2^n}{poly(n)}$, then the time complexity shows an exponential speedup over the classical one. We explain this algorithm for autocorrelation sampling and discuss its properties in Sect. 3.

We next move on to estimating algorithms in Sect. 4. First, in Subsect. 4.1 we give a quantum algorithm to estimate the autocorrelation coefficient at any given point with high accuracy, denoted ϵ, and low error, denoted δ. Our algorithm makes $\Theta\left(\frac{1}{\epsilon}\log\frac{1}{\delta}\right)$ calls to the function (rather, a quantum oracle for the same). This is almost square-root of the known classical complexity of $O\left(\frac{1}{\epsilon^2}\log\frac{1}{\delta}\right)$. We explain why the sampling techniques that we designed *cannot* be used to design an efficient estimation algorithm, and instead, design our algorithm using the idea of a "swap-test".

Our final contribution is a quantum algorithm to estimate the sum-of-squares σ_f; this we describe in Subsect. 4.2. We explain that a classical sampling based approach requires $O\left(\frac{2^{2n}}{\epsilon^2}\log\frac{1}{\delta}\right)$ calls to f (ϵ would generally be greater than 1 for estimating σ_f since $\sigma_f \in [1, 2^n]$) and then describe a quantum approach that displays quadratic speedup and only makes $O\left(\frac{2^n}{\epsilon}\log\frac{1}{\delta}\right)$ calls.

2 Sampling from Higher-Order Derivative

Higher-order derivatives of a Boolean function was explicitly introduced, in the context of cryptanalysis, by Lai [11].

Definition 2 (Derivative). *Given a point $a \in \{0,1\}^n$, the (first-order) derivative of an n-bit function f at a is defined as*

$$\Delta f_a(x) = f(x \oplus a) \oplus f(x)$$

For a list of points $\mathcal{A} = (a_1, a_2, \ldots, a_k)$ (where $k \leq n$) the k-th derivative of f at $(a_1, a_2, \ldots, a_k)$ is recursively defined as

$$\Delta f_{\mathcal{A}}^{(k)}(x) = \Delta f_{a_k}(\Delta f_{a_1,a_2,\ldots,a_{k-1}}^{(k-1)}(x)),$$

where $\Delta f_{a_1,a_2,\ldots,a_{k-1}}^{(k-1)}(x)$ is the $(k-1)$-th derivative of f at points $(a_1, a_2, \ldots, a_{k-1})$. The 0-th derivative of f is defined to be f itself.

Higher-order derivatives form the basis of many cryptographic attacks, especially those that generalize the differential attack technique against block ciphers such as Integral attack, AIDA, cube attack, zero-sum distinguisher, etc. These attacks mostly revolve around the algebraic degree of a higher-order derivative. Let $deg(f)$ denote the algebraic degree of some function f. It is known that $deg(\Delta f^{(i+1)}) \leq deg(\Delta f^{(i)}) - 1$ and if f is an n-bit function then $\Delta f^{(n)}$ is a constant function. Thus if a function has the degree of its i-th order derivative, at some $(a_1, a_2, \ldots a_i)$, to be a constant, then this fact is essentially a beacon for mounting an attack if $i \ll n$. Therefore, it is central to study the algebraic degree and other properties of higher-order derivatives, and to the best of our knowledge, we provide the first algorithms for these tasks.

Specifically, we show how to efficiently sample from the Walsh-Hadamard spectrum of the i-th order derivative. This allows us to estimate if a higher-order derivative of f is biased towards any linear function, thereby partly answering the question above since the Walsh-Hadamard transform of a linear function is constant.

Despite the complicated expression for computing $\Delta f^{(k)}$, it has an equivalent expression that we shall use for our results. For any multiset S of points (including $S = \emptyset$), define the notations $X_s = \bigoplus_{a \in S} a$ and $f(x \oplus S) = f(x \oplus X_s)$. In the case of $S = \emptyset$, it can be noted that X_s is the empty string and hence $f(x \oplus S) = f(x)$. The i-th derivative of f at $\mathcal{A} = (a_1, a_2, \ldots a_i)$ can be shown[2] to be

$$\Delta f_{\mathcal{A}}^{(i)}(x) = \bigoplus_{S \subseteq \mathcal{A}} f(x \oplus S)$$

where $S \subseteq \mathcal{A}$ indicates all possible sub-lists of $\mathcal{A}$ (including duplicates, if any, in $\mathcal{A}$). For example, the second-order derivative at a pair of points (a, b) can be written as

$$\Delta f_{(a,b)}^{(2)} = f(x) \oplus f(x \oplus a) \oplus f(x \oplus b) \oplus f(x \oplus a \oplus b).$$

For the sake of brevity, we will drop the superscript (i) if it is clear from the list $\mathcal{A}$.

Now we describe a quantum circuit that generates the Walsh-Hadamard spectrum of the k-derivative of an n-bit function f at some set of points $\mathcal{A} = (a_1, a_2, \ldots a_k)$. We refer to the circuit as $HoDJ_n^k$ ("Higher-order Deutsch-Jozsa").

For calling f we use the standard unitary operator $U_f : |x\rangle|b\rangle \mapsto |x\rangle|b \oplus f(x)\rangle$ where $x \in \{0,1\}^n$ and $b \in \{0,1\}$. We use $|+\rangle$ and $|-\rangle$ to denote the states $\frac{1}{\sqrt{2}}(|0\rangle + |1\rangle)$ and $\frac{1}{\sqrt{2}}(|0\rangle - |1\rangle)$, respectively; observe that $U_f|x\rangle|+\rangle = |x\rangle|+\rangle$ and $U_f|x\rangle|-\rangle = (-1)^{f(x)}|x\rangle|-\rangle$.

The circuit for $HoDJ_n^k$ acts on $k + 2$ registers, $R_1, \ldots R_k, R_{k+1}, R_{k+2}$ that are initialized as

– R_1 has one qubit that is initialized to $|1\rangle$,

---

[2] The proof is present in [11].

- R_2 consists of n-qubits that is initialized to $|0^n\rangle$,
- and each of $R_3 \ldots R_{k+2}$ consists of n-qubits in which R_{2+t} is initialized to a_t of $\mathcal{A}$.

The circuit itself is a generalization of the quantum circuit for the Deutsch-Jozsa problem [5] and uses the ability of this circuit to generate a distribution of Walsh-Hadamard coefficients that was explained earlier.

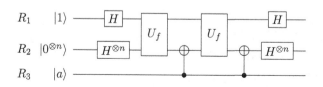

Fig. 2. Circuit for 1st-order Walsh-Hadamard derivative sampling

Figure 2 shows the quantum circuit for $HoDJ_n^1$; for this problem, $\mathcal{A}$ is a singleton set, say $\{a\}$. The evolution of the quantum state as the operators are applied is as follows:

Initial State : $|1\rangle|0^n\rangle|a\rangle$

$$\xrightarrow{H \otimes H^n} \frac{1}{\sqrt{2^n}} \sum_x |-\rangle|x\rangle|a\rangle$$

$$\xrightarrow{U_f} \frac{1}{\sqrt{2^n}} \sum_x (-1)^{f(x)}|-\rangle|x\rangle|a\rangle$$

$$\xrightarrow{CNOT_2^3} \frac{1}{\sqrt{2^n}} \sum_x (-1)^{f(x)}|-\rangle|x \oplus a\rangle|a\rangle$$

$$\xrightarrow{U_f} \frac{1}{\sqrt{2^n}} \sum_x (-1)^{f(x) \oplus f(x \oplus a)}|-\rangle|x \oplus a\rangle|a\rangle$$

$$\xrightarrow{CNOT_2^3} \frac{1}{\sqrt{2^n}}|-\rangle \sum_x (-1)^{f(x) \oplus f(x \oplus a)}|x\rangle|a\rangle$$

$$\xrightarrow{H \otimes H^n} |1\rangle \sum_y \left[\frac{1}{2^n} \sum_x (-1)^{(x \cdot y)} (-1)^{f(x) \oplus f(x \oplus a)} \right] |y\rangle|a\rangle$$

$$= |1\rangle \sum_y \widehat{\Delta f_a}(y)|y\rangle|a\rangle$$

Therefore, at the end of the circuit R_2 can be found to be in a state $|y\rangle$ with probability $\widehat{\Delta f_a}(y)^2$ thus accomplishing the objective of sampling according to the Walsh-Hadamard distribution of the 1st-order derivative of f.

Next, an illustration of $HoDJ_n^2$ corresponding to the 2nd-order derivative is presented in Fig. 3 in which we use $\mathcal{A} = (a, b)$. We show the state of this circuit

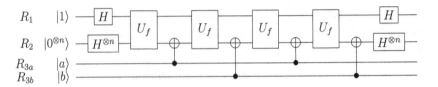

Fig. 3. Circuit for Walsh-Hadamard sampling of 2nd-order derivative

after each layer of operators.

Initial State : $|1\rangle|0^n\rangle|a\rangle|b\rangle$

$$\xrightarrow{H\otimes H^n} \frac{1}{\sqrt{2^n}}\sum_{x\in\{0,1\}^n}|-\rangle|x\rangle|a,b\rangle$$

$$\xrightarrow{U_f} \frac{1}{\sqrt{2^n}}\sum_x(-1)^{f(x)}|-\rangle|x,a,b\rangle$$

$$\xrightarrow{CNOT_2^3} \frac{1}{\sqrt{2^n}}\sum_x(-1)^{f(x)}|-\rangle|x\oplus a\rangle|a,b\rangle$$

$$\xrightarrow{U_f} \frac{1}{\sqrt{2^n}}\sum_x(-1)^{f(x)\oplus f(x\oplus a)}|-\rangle|x\oplus a\rangle|a,b\rangle$$

$$\xrightarrow[U_f]{CNOT_2^4,} \frac{1}{\sqrt{2^n}}\sum_x(-1)^{f(x)\oplus f(x\oplus a)\oplus f(x\oplus a\oplus b)}|-\rangle|x\oplus a\oplus b\rangle|a,b\rangle$$

$$\xrightarrow[U_f]{CNOT_2^3} \frac{1}{\sqrt{2^n}}\sum_x(-1)^{\oplus_{S\subseteq\{a,b\}}f(x\oplus S)}|-\rangle|x\oplus b\rangle|a,b\rangle$$

$$\xrightarrow{CNOT_2^4} \frac{1}{\sqrt{2^n}}\sum_x(-1)^{\oplus_{S\subseteq\{a,b\}}f(x\oplus S)}|-\rangle|x,a,b\rangle$$

$$\xrightarrow{H\otimes H^n} |1\rangle\sum_y\left[\frac{1}{2^n}\sum_x(-1)^{x\cdot y}(-1)^{\oplus_{S\subseteq\{a,b\}}f(x\oplus S)}\right]|y\rangle|a,b\rangle$$

Measuring R_2 at the end will collapse it into $|y\rangle$ for some $y\in\{0,1\}^n$ with probability $\Pr[y] = \left[\frac{1}{2^n}\sum_x(-1)^{x\cdot y}\Delta f_{(a,b)}(x)\right]^2 = \widehat{\Delta f_{(a,b)}}(y)^2$ that is the square of the Walsh coefficient of $\Delta f_{(a,b)}$ (2nd-order derivative function) at the point y.

The circuit can be generalized to higher values of k in a straight forward manner. The following theorem formalizes this result where we ignore the first register since that contains an ancillary qubit which is reset to its initial state at the end of the computation. For counting the number of gates, please note that each of the CNOT gates shown in Fig. 3 actually consists of n 2-qubit CNOT gates applied in parallel.

Theorem 1. *For any $\mathcal{A} = (a_1, a_2, \ldots a_k)$ such that $a_i \in \{0,1\}^n$ $\forall i$, the HoDJ$_n^k$ circuit uses $n+1$ initialized ancilla qubits, employs k registers corresponding to* *the points in* $\mathcal{A}$*, makes* 2^k *calls to* U_f*,* $\Theta(n2^k)$ *calls to* H *and* $CNOT$ *gates, has a depth of* $2(2^k + 1)$ *and operates as follows*

$$|0^n\rangle|a_1\rangle\ldots|a_k\rangle \xrightarrow{HoDJ_n^k} \sum_y \widehat{\Delta f_{\mathcal{A}}}(y)|y\rangle|a_1\rangle\ldots|a_k\rangle$$

Proof. The circuit is a generalization of those illustrated in Figs. 2 and 3. At the core is a sub-circuit that we denote by C' and which acts as

$$|x\rangle|a_1\rangle\ldots|a_k\rangle|b\rangle \xrightarrow{C'} |x\rangle|a_1\rangle\ldots|a_k\rangle|b \oplus \Delta f_{\mathcal{A}}\rangle(x) = |x\rangle|a_1\rangle\ldots|a_k\rangle|b \oplus \bigoplus_{S\subseteq\mathcal{A}} f(x \oplus S)\rangle$$

Construction of C' uses a *binary reflected Gray code* (BRGC, or "Gray code" in short) for the set of integers $\{0, 1, \ldots, 2^k - 1\}$. Such a BRGC will be a sequence of k-bit strings (codes) $(g_1, g_2, \ldots, g_{2^k})$ such that each g_i is unique and every adjacent code differ at exactly one position. Integer 0 is encoded by the code 0^n and without loss of generality, let $g_{2^k} = 0^n$. Due to the cyclic property of BRGC, g_1 must be some k-bit string with Hamming weight 1.

C' operates in 2^k stages. We will use $|\mathcal{A}\rangle$ as a shorthand for $|a_1\rangle\ldots|a_k\rangle$. The initial state of the qubits, before stage 1, is $|x\rangle|\mathcal{A}\rangle|b\rangle$. Observe that $\bigoplus_{S\subseteq\mathcal{A}} f(x \oplus S) = \bigoplus_{i=1}^{2^k} f(x \oplus (g_j \cdot \mathcal{A}))$ in which we used the notation $g_j \cdot \mathcal{A} = (g_j)_1 a_1 \oplus (g_j)_2 a_2 \oplus \ldots (g_j)_k a_k$ to denote a linear combination of some of the a_i's.

The j-th stage of C' creates the state $|x \oplus (g_j \cdot \mathcal{A})\rangle |\mathcal{A}\rangle |b \oplus \bigoplus_{i=1}^j f(g_i \cdot \mathcal{A})\rangle$ by making the following transformations.

$$|x \oplus (g_{j-1} \cdot \mathcal{A})\rangle |\mathcal{A}\rangle |b \oplus \bigoplus_{i=1}^{j-1} f(g_i \cdot \mathcal{A})\rangle$$

$$\xrightarrow{CNOT} |x \oplus (g_j \cdot \mathcal{A})\rangle |\mathcal{A}\rangle |b \oplus \bigoplus_{i=1}^{j-1} f(g_i \cdot \mathcal{A})\rangle$$

$$\xrightarrow{U_f} |x \oplus (g_j \cdot \mathcal{A})\rangle |\mathcal{A}\rangle |b \oplus \bigoplus_{i=1}^{j-1} f(g_i \cdot \mathcal{A}) \oplus f(g_j \cdot \mathcal{A})\rangle$$

The $CNOT$ operation above is justified since $g_{j-1} \cdot \mathcal{A}$ and $g_j \cdot \mathcal{A}$ are both linear combinations of some of the a_i's differing by exactly one a_t. The $CNOT$ uses the corresponding register $|a_t\rangle$ as the control register and the first register qubit as the target register. This also holds true for stage 1 since g_1 has Hamming weight 1. Lastly, observe that the final state after the 2^k-th stage matches the one specified above: $|x\rangle |\mathcal{A}\rangle |b \oplus \bigoplus_{S\subseteq\mathcal{A}} f(x \oplus S)\rangle$.

It is not hard to calculate that C' also makes the following transformation if $|b\rangle$ is replaced by $|-\rangle$.

$$|x\rangle|a_1 \ldots a_k\rangle|-\rangle \xrightarrow{C'} (-1)^{\oplus_{S\subseteq\mathcal{A}} f(x \oplus S)}|x\rangle|a_1 \ldots a_k\rangle|-\rangle = (-1)^{\Delta f_{\mathcal{A}}(x)}|x\rangle|a_1 \ldots a_k\rangle|-\rangle$$

The circuit for $HoDJ_n^k$ is constructed as

$$|-\rangle|0^n\rangle|a_1 \ldots a_k\rangle$$

$$\xrightarrow{H^n} \frac{1}{\sqrt{2^n}}\sum_x |-\rangle|x\rangle|a_1 \ldots a_k\rangle$$

$$\xrightarrow{C'} \frac{1}{\sqrt{2^n}}\sum_x |-\rangle(-1)^{\Delta f_A(x)}|x\rangle|a_1 \ldots a_k\rangle = |-\rangle\frac{1}{\sqrt{2^n}}\sum_x (-1)^{\Delta f_A(x)}|x\rangle|a_1 \ldots a_k\rangle$$

$$\xrightarrow{H^n} |-\rangle\sum_y \widehat{\Delta f_A}(y)|y\rangle|a_1 \ldots a_k\rangle$$

For computing the resource usage of $HoDJ_n^k$, observe that C' is implemented above using a depth $2 \cdot 2^k$ circuit and each of its stages employ one U_f gate and n $CNOT$ gates (that act in parallel on all the n qubits of the first register and is shown as a single $CNOT$ operation above). This completes the proof of the theorem. □

A quick observation is that $HoDJ_n^0$ essentially generates $\sum_y \hat{f}(y)|y\rangle$ that is exactly the same output as that of the Deutsch-Jozsa circuit and in fact, the circuit for $HoDJ_n^0$ is exactly same as that of the Deutsch-Jozsa circuit for n-bit functions.

3   Autocorrelation Sampling

In Sect. 2 we explained how to sample from the higher order derivatives of a Boolean function. In this section we present an algorithm to sample according to a distribution that is proportional to the autocorrelation coefficients of a function; specifically, we would like to output $|a\rangle$ with probability proportional to $\check{f}(a)^2$. We will use the technique presented in Sect. 2 for doing so and will use a key observation stated in this lemma.

Lemma 1. $\check{f}(a) = \widehat{\Delta f_a^{(1)}}(0^n)$

Proof. LHS is equal to $\frac{1}{2^n}\sum_x(-1)^{f(x)}(-1)^{f(x\oplus a)} = \frac{1}{2^n}\sum_x \Delta f_a^{(1)}(x)$. Now observe that $\widehat{\Delta f_a^{(1)}}(0^n) = \frac{1}{2^n}\sum_x \Delta f_a^{(1)}(x)$ and this proves the lemma. □

The circuit used in Algorithm 1 is illustrated in Fig. 4.

Theorem 2. *The observed outcome returned by Algorithm 1 is a random sample from the distribution $\{\check{f}(a)^2/\sigma_f\}_{a\in\mathbb{F}_2^n}$ with probability at least $1-\delta$. The algorithm makes $O(\frac{2^{n/2}}{\sqrt{\sigma_f}}\log\frac{2}{\delta})$ queries to U_f and uses $O(n\frac{2^{n/2}}{\sqrt{\sigma_f}}\log\frac{2}{\delta})$ gates altogether.*

Algorithm 1. Algorithm for autocorrelation sampling

1: Start with three registers initialized as $|1\rangle$, $|0^n\rangle$, and $|0^n\rangle$.
2: Apply H^n to R_3 to generate the state $\frac{1}{\sqrt{2^n}}\sum_{b\in\mathbb{F}_2^n}|1\rangle|0^n\rangle|b\rangle$.
3: Apply $HoDJ_n^1$ on the registers R_1, R_2 and R_3 to generate the state
$$|\Phi\rangle = \frac{1}{\sqrt{2^n}}|1\rangle\sum_{b\in\mathbb{F}_2^n}\sum_{y\in\mathbb{F}_2^n}\widehat{\Delta f_b^{(1)}}(y)|y\rangle|b\rangle.$$
4: Apply fixed-point amplitude amplification [19] on $|\Phi\rangle$ to amplify the probability of observing R_2 in the state $|0\rangle$ to $1-\delta$ for any given constant δ
5: Measure R_3 in the standard basis and return the observed outcome

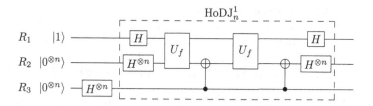

Fig. 4. Circuit for autocorrelation sampling

Proof. We can write the final state of the circuit in Fig. 4 as

$$|\Phi\rangle = \frac{1}{\sqrt{2^n}}|1\rangle\sum_{b\in\mathbb{F}_2^n}\sum_{y\in\mathbb{F}_2^n}\widehat{\Delta f_b^{(1)}}(y)|y\rangle|b\rangle$$

$$= |1\rangle\otimes|0^n\rangle\otimes\left(\frac{1}{\sqrt{2^n}}\sum_b\widehat{\Delta f_b}(0^n)|b\rangle\right) + \sum_y|1\rangle|y\rangle\otimes\left(\frac{1}{\sqrt{2^n}}\sum_b\widehat{\Delta f_b}(y)|b\rangle\right)$$

$$= |1\rangle\otimes|0^n\rangle\otimes\left(\frac{1}{\sqrt{2^n}}\sum_b\check{f}(b)|b\rangle\right) + \sum_y|1\rangle|y\rangle\otimes\left(\frac{1}{\sqrt{2^n}}\sum_b\widehat{\Delta f_b}(y)|b\rangle\right)$$

Suppose we denote the normalized state $\frac{1}{\sqrt{\sigma_f}}\sum_b\check{f}(b)|b\rangle$ by $|\Phi'\rangle$ and the state $\frac{1}{\sqrt{2^n}}\sum_b\widehat{\Delta f_b}(y)|b\rangle$ by $|\Phi_y''\rangle$. Then, using Lemma 1 we can rephrase $|\Phi\rangle$ as

$$|\Phi\rangle = \sqrt{\frac{\sigma_f}{2^n}}|1\rangle\otimes|0^n\rangle\otimes|\Phi'\rangle + \sum_y|1\rangle|y\rangle|\Phi_y''\rangle$$

and the probability of observing R_2 in state $|0^n\rangle$ as $\sigma_f/2^n$.

Fixed-point amplitude amplification will make $O(\frac{2^{n/2}}{\sqrt{\sigma_f}}\log\frac{2}{\delta})$ calls to the circuit in Fig. 4 and ensure that the amplitude of the state $|1\rangle|0^n\rangle|\Phi'\rangle$ is at least $\sqrt{1-\delta}$. Therefore, after amplification R_3 will be in the state $|\Phi'\rangle$ with probability at least $1-\delta$, and when that happens, the observed state upon measuring R_3 would be some $|b\rangle$ with probability $\check{f}(b)^2/\sigma_f$—that is, a sample from the autocorrelation distribution.

The number of queries required for the whole process is the number of times that amplitude amplification calls the circuit ($O(\frac{2^{n/2}}{\sqrt{\sigma_f}} \log \frac{2}{\delta})$) multiplied by the number of calls to U_f made by the circuit (which is only two). The total number of gates involved is also obtained in a similar manner along with the observation that the circuit uses $\Theta(n)$ which is evident from Fig. 4.   □

4   Estimation Algorithms

The main problem here is to estimate, with high accuracy and small error (if any), important functions of an autocorrelation spectrum.

For these algorithms we use the quantum technique of amplitude estimation. We use a particular version that was recently presented for estimating the probability of "success" of a quantum circuit (where success corresponds to the output state of the circuit to be in a certain subspace) with additive accuracy.

Lemma 2 ([1]). *Let $\mathcal{A}$ be a quantum circuit without any measurement and let p denote the probability of observing its output state in a particular subspace. There is a quantum algorithm that makes a total of $\Theta(\frac{\pi}{\epsilon} \log \frac{1}{\delta})$ calls to (controlled)-$\mathcal{A}$ and returns an estimate $\tilde{p}$ such that,*

$$\Pr[\tilde{p} - \epsilon \leq p \leq \tilde{p} + \epsilon] \geq 1 - \delta$$

for any accuracy $\epsilon \leq \frac{1}{4}$ and error $\delta < 1$.

4.1   Autocorrelation Estimation

The objective of this section is to estimate the value of $|\check{f}(a)|$ for any particular $a \in \{0,1\}^n$; this is identical to estimating $|\check{f}(a)|^2$.

First, observe that $\check{f}(a) = \frac{1}{2^n} \sum_x (-1)^{f(x)}(-1)^{f(x \oplus a)} = \mathbb{E}_x[X_x]$ where the ± 1-valued random variable $X_x = (-1)^{f(x) \oplus f(x \oplus a)}$ is defined for x chosen uniformly at random from $\{0,1\}^n$. Therefore, the number of samples needed if we were to classically estimate $\check{f}(a)$ with accuracy ϵ and error δ is $O(\frac{1}{\epsilon^2} \log \frac{1}{\delta})$.

The quantum circuit in Fig. 4 can also be used to estimate $|\check{f}(a)|$, rather, $\check{f}(a)^2/2^n$. Recall that the probability of observing R_2 in the state $|0^n\rangle$ and R_3 in the state $|a\rangle$ (without any amplification) is $\frac{\check{f}(a)^2}{2^n}$ (refer to the proof of Theorem 2). Let F denote $\frac{\check{f}(a)^2}{2^n}$, ϵ denote the desired accuracy and δ denote the desired probability of error. Call the algorithm in Lemma 2 to obtain an estimate F' of F with an accuracy ϵ' and error probability δ. We know from the lemma that with high probability $F' - \epsilon' \leq F \leq F' + \epsilon'$ which implies that $2^n F' - 2^n \epsilon' \leq \check{f}(a)^2 \leq 2^n F' + 2^n \epsilon'$. Therefore, if we use $\epsilon' = \frac{\epsilon}{2^n}$ then $2^n F'$ is an ϵ-accurate estimate of $\check{f}(a)^2$.

However, the number of calls to the circuit will be $\Theta(\frac{1}{\epsilon'} \log \frac{1}{\delta}) = \Theta(\frac{2^n}{\epsilon} \log \frac{1}{\delta})$ which is $\Omega(2^n)$; this is clearly undesirable and begging to be bettered.

It may be tempting to improve the above method by first amplifying the probability of observing R_2 in the state $|0^n\rangle$ and *then* estimating the probability of observing R_3 in the state $|a\rangle$. However, for amplitude estimation at this stage the probability of R_2, R_3 to be in the state $|0^n\rangle \otimes |a\rangle$ should be exactly $c\breve{f}(a)^2$ for some known constant c; since σ_f is not known, fixed-point amplitude amplification cannot guarantee a knowledge of the exact probability after amplification. Thus it is unclear if amplitude amplification followed by amplitude estimation can lead to a better estimation algorithm.

Now we will describe a quantum algorithm for the aforementioned task aiming for a better query complexity. Our technical objective will be to generate a state with a probability that is related to $|\breve{f}(a)|^2$ but much higher than that in the earlier approach and our main tool will be the quantum technique of "swap test".

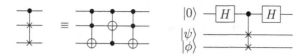

Fig. 5. Swap-gate (left) and quantum circuit for swap-test (right)

Suppose we have two registers over the same number of qubits that are in states denoted by $|\psi\rangle$ and $|\phi\rangle$. The swap test circuit, denoted by ST and illustrated in Fig. 5, uses an additional qubit initialized to $|0\rangle$ and applies a conditional swap-gate in a clever manner such that if the first (single-qubit) register is measured, then $|0\rangle$ is observed with probability $\frac{1}{2}[1 + |\langle\psi|\phi\rangle|^2]$. It is easy to show that the circuit performs the following transformation.

$$|0\rangle|\psi\rangle|\phi\rangle \xrightarrow{ST} |0\rangle \otimes \frac{1}{2}\Big[|\psi\rangle|\phi\rangle + |\phi\rangle|\psi\rangle\Big] + |1\rangle \otimes \frac{1}{2}\Big[|\psi\rangle|\phi\rangle - |\phi\rangle|\psi\rangle\Big]$$

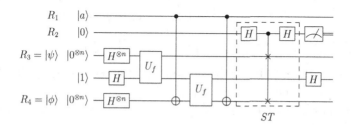

Fig. 6. Circuit for estimation of autocorrelation coefficient at a point a

Our algorithm for estimation of $|\breve{f}(a)|^2$ is presented in Algorithm 2 and a circuit diagram is given in Fig. 6. We do not show the $|1\rangle$ qubit in the algorithm; it is merely used, in the form $|-\rangle$, to apply the U_f gate in a phase-version.

Algorithm 2. Autocorrelation estimation at point a

Require: Parameters: ϵ (confidence), δ (error)

1: Start with four registers of which R_1 is initialized to $|a\rangle$, R_2 to $|0\rangle$, and R_3, R_4 to $|0^n\rangle$.

2: Apply these transformations.

$$|a\rangle|0\rangle|0^n\rangle|0^n\rangle$$

$$\xrightarrow{H^n \otimes H^n} |a\rangle|0\rangle\left(\tfrac{1}{\sqrt{2^n}}\sum_x |x\rangle\right)\left(\tfrac{1}{\sqrt{2^n}}\sum_y |y\rangle\right)$$

$$\xrightarrow{CNOT} |a\rangle|0\rangle\left(\tfrac{1}{\sqrt{2^n}}\sum_x |x\rangle\right)\left(\tfrac{1}{\sqrt{2^n}}\sum_y |y \oplus a\rangle\right)$$

$$\xrightarrow{U_f \otimes U_f} |a\rangle|0\rangle\left(\tfrac{1}{\sqrt{2^n}}\sum_x (-1)^{f(x)}|x\rangle\right)\left(\tfrac{1}{\sqrt{2^n}}\sum_y (-1)^{f(y \oplus a)}|y \oplus a\rangle\right)$$

$$\qquad\qquad\qquad\qquad\qquad\qquad\qquad\qquad\qquad \triangleright \text{ Uses reusable } |-\rangle$$

$$\xrightarrow{CNOT} |a\rangle|0\rangle\left(\tfrac{1}{\sqrt{2^n}}\sum_x (-1)^{f(x)}|x\rangle\right)\left(\tfrac{1}{\sqrt{2^n}}\sum_y (-1)^{f(y \oplus a)}|y\rangle\right)$$

$$= |a\rangle|0\rangle|\psi\rangle|\phi_a\rangle$$

- Normalized state $\tfrac{1}{\sqrt{2^n}}\sum_x (-1)^{f(x)}|x\rangle$ denoted ψ
- Normalized state $\tfrac{1}{\sqrt{2^n}}\sum_y (-1)^{f(y \oplus a)}|y\rangle$ denoted ϕ_a

3: Apply ST on R_2, R_3 and R_4 to obtain

$$|a\rangle\left[|0\rangle \otimes \tfrac{1}{2}\big(|\psi\rangle|\phi_a\rangle + |\phi_a\rangle|\psi\rangle\big) + |1\rangle \otimes \tfrac{1}{2}\big(|\psi\rangle|\phi_a\rangle - |\phi_a\rangle|\psi\rangle\big)\right]$$

4: $\ell \leftarrow$ estimate the probability of observing R_2 in the state $|0\rangle$ with accuracy $\pm\tfrac{\epsilon}{2}$ and error δ

5: Return $2\ell - 1$ as the estimate of $|\breve{f}(a)|^2$

Obviously, an accurate estimation of $\tfrac{1}{2}[1 + |\breve{f}(a)|^2]$ will automatically lead to an accurate estimation of $|\breve{f}(a)|^2$. Observe that $\tfrac{1}{2}[1 + |\breve{f}(a)|^2] \gg |\breve{f}(a)|^2/2^n$ and therefore, estimation using Algorithm 2 is more efficient compared to that obtained from autocorrelation sampling (describe earlier in this section).

Theorem 3. *Algorithm 2 makes* $\Theta\left(\tfrac{\pi}{\epsilon}\log\tfrac{1}{\delta}\right)$ *calls to* U_f *and returns an estimate* α *such that*

$$\Pr\left[\alpha - \epsilon \leq \breve{f}(a)^2 \leq \alpha + \epsilon\right] \geq 1 - \delta$$

Proof. Let $|\chi_a^0\rangle$ denote the state $\tfrac{1}{2}|\psi\rangle|\phi_a\rangle + \tfrac{1}{2}|\phi_a\rangle|\psi\rangle$. Observe that

$$\big\||\chi_a^0\rangle\big\|^2 = \tfrac{1}{4}\left[2\||\psi\rangle\| \cdot \||\phi_a\rangle\| + 2\langle\psi|\phi_a\rangle|^2\right] = \tfrac{1}{2}\left[1 + |\langle\psi|\phi_a\rangle|^2\right]$$

From Step-3 of the algorithm, the probability of observing R_2 in the state $|0\rangle$, say denoted p_0, can be expressed as $\big\||\chi_a^0\rangle\big\|^2$.

Further observe that $\langle\psi|\phi\rangle = \tfrac{1}{2^n}\sum_x (-1)^{f(x)}(-1)^{f(x \oplus a)} = \breve{f}(a)$. Therefore, $p_0 = \tfrac{1}{2} + \tfrac{1}{2}\breve{f}(a)^2$ and ℓ is an estimate of p_0 such that,

$$1 - \delta \leq \Pr\left[\ell - \tfrac{\epsilon}{2} \leq p_0 \leq \ell + \tfrac{\epsilon}{2}\right]$$
$$= \Pr[2\ell - \epsilon \leq 2p_0 \leq 2\ell + \epsilon]$$
$$= \Pr[2\ell - 1 - \epsilon \leq 2p_0 - 1 \leq \ell - 1 + \epsilon]$$
$$= \Pr[\alpha - \epsilon \leq \breve{f}(a)^2 \leq \alpha + \epsilon] \qquad\qquad (\because \alpha = 2\ell - 1)$$

This shows that $2\ell - 1$ is an ϵ-accurate estimate of $\check{f}(a)^2$.

For analysing the number of queries to U_f, first observe that the circuit to obtain the state in Step-3 of the algorithm (see Fig. 6) uses only two calls to U_f. The amplitude estimation procedure of Lemma 2 shall make $\Theta\left(\frac{\pi}{\epsilon}\log\frac{1}{\delta}\right)$ calls to this circuit, giving a total of $\Theta\left(\frac{\pi}{\epsilon}\log\frac{1}{\delta}\right)$ calls to U_f. $\square$

The above theorem shows how to estimate $\check{f}(a)^2$ using a quantum algorithm that shows a quadratic speedup over a classical sampling-based algorithm. However, there remains the question of estimating $\check{f}(a)$ when its value is 0. In the above approach, p_0 shall be $\frac{1}{2}$, and therefore, $\ell \leq \frac{1}{2} + \epsilon/2$. This implies that the estimate for $\check{f}(a)^2$ shall only satisfy $\alpha \leq \epsilon$. A minor improvement may be added to Algorithm 2 to handle this situation that we now describe.

First apply the previously mentioned technique of applying amplitude estimation on the output state of sampling algorithm from Sect. 3 but using a very high ϵ. Note that amplitude estimation does not err when the probability it is estimating is 0. Then run Algorithm 2 as usual and return the minimum of the two estimates. In case $\check{f}(a) = 0$, the first amplitude estimation will correctly return 0 as the estimate. We skip the details due to lack of space in this paper.

4.2   Estimation of Sum-of-Squares Indicator

In this section we consider the problem of estimating the sum-of-squares indicator σ_f. As before the objective will be to obtain an estimate with ϵ accuracy and δ probability of error. Since $\sigma_f \geq 1$, typical values of ϵ will be 1 or more.

We first discuss a classical sampling-based approach. Let a, b, c be three random variables chosen uniformly at random from $\mathbb{F}_2^n$ such that $b \neq c$ and let $X_{a,b,c}$ be the ± 1-valued random variable $(-1)^{f(a \oplus b)}(-1)^{f(a \oplus c)}$. We first express σ_f as the expectation of these random variables.

$$\sigma_f = \sum_{a \in \mathbb{F}_2^n} \check{f}(a)^2 = \sum_{a \in \mathbb{F}_2^n} \left[\frac{1}{2^n}\sum_{b \in \mathbb{F}_2^n}(-1)^{f(b)\oplus f(b\oplus a)}\right]^2$$

$$= \frac{1}{2^{2n}}\sum_{a \in \mathbb{F}_2^n}\left[2^n + \sum_{\substack{b \neq c \\ b,c \in \mathbb{F}_2^n}}(-1)^{f(a\oplus b)\oplus f(a\oplus c)}\right]$$

$$= 1 + \frac{1}{2^{2n}}\sum_{\substack{a \in \mathbb{F}_2^n \\ b \neq c}}(-1)^{f(a\oplus b)\oplus f(a\oplus c)}$$

$$= 1 + (2^n - 1)\mathbb{E}_{a,b,c}[X_{a,b,c}]$$

Note that $\mathbb{E}[X_{a,b,c}] = \frac{\sigma_f - 1}{2^n - 1} \approx \frac{\sigma_f}{2^n}$. One way to estimate $\mathbb{E}[X_{a,b,c}]$ is to use multiple independent samples of a, b, c. Since each sample of $X_{a,b,c}$ requires 2 calls to $f()$, therefore $O(\frac{1}{\epsilon'^2}\log\frac{1}{\delta})$ calls to $f()$ would be sufficient to estimate $\mathbb{E}[X_{a,b,c}]$ with ϵ' accuracy and δ error. Suppose $\tilde{X}$ is the estimate that we obtain; since it satisfies

$$\Pr[\tilde{X} - \epsilon' \leq \mathbb{E}[X_{a,b,c}] \leq \tilde{X} + \epsilon'] \geq 1 - \delta$$

then an estimate of $\sigma_f = 1 + (2^n - 1)\mathbb{E}[X_{a,b,c}]$ can be obtained by $1 + (2^n - 1)\tilde{X}$. It follows that

$$\Pr\left[1 + (2^n - 1)\tilde{X} - \epsilon'(2^n - 1) \leq \sigma_f \leq 1 + (2^n - 1)\tilde{X} + \epsilon'(2^n - 1)\right] \geq 1 - \delta$$

Thus, if we want to estimate σ_f with accuracy ϵ, we have to set $\epsilon' = \frac{\epsilon}{2^n - 1} \approx \frac{\epsilon}{2^n}$. The number of calls to $f()$ then becomes $O(\frac{2^{2n}}{\epsilon^2} \log \frac{1}{\delta})$ which is only marginally better than the $\Theta(2^{2n})$ classical non-randomized process of computing all autocorrelation values and then summing them up.

On the quantum side, the circuit in Fig. 4 can help us in estimating the sum-of-squares indicator of f. Since the probability of observing R_2 (in Fig. 4) to be in the state $|0^n\rangle$ is $\sigma_f/2^n$, Lemma 2 can be used to efficiently estimate $\sigma_f/2^n$. The number of calls to U_f shall be $\Theta\left(\frac{2^n}{\epsilon} \log \frac{1}{\delta}\right)$ following the same analysis that was done in Sect. 4.1. Thus we get a quadratic improvement over the classical sampling algorithm.

We tried to improve upon this method by using the swap-test technique of Sect. 4.1 and running Algorithm 2 with initial state $\frac{1}{\sqrt{2^n}} \sum_x |x\rangle|0\rangle|0^n\rangle|0^n\rangle$. We can estimate the probability of observing the output qubit in the state $|0\rangle$ using a *relative accuracy* quantum estimation approach. However, the number of calls to U_f remained the same $\Theta\left(\frac{2^n}{\epsilon} \log \frac{1}{\delta}\right)$.

5   Conclusion

Autocorrelation spectrum is a very important tool for designing Boolean functions with good cryptographic properties and also for mounting differential attacks of cryptosystems. In this paper we design several efficient quantum algorithms that analyse different aspects of Boolean functions that are related to their autocorrelation spectra. We first show that the Deutsch-Jozsa algorithm can be suitably extended to sample the Walsh spectrum of any derivative. Further, we specifically concentrate on the autocorrelation spectrum of a Boolean function. We present an algorithm to sample according to a distribution that is proportional to the autocorrelation coefficients of a Boolean function. Finally we consider the estimation of some values or some functions of autocorrelation coefficients with high accuracy and small error. Our algorithms will have applications to evaluate the cryptographic properties of a Boolean function in a significantly faster manner than in classical paradigm.

Acknowledgements. The second author acknowledges the support from the project "Cryptography & Cryptanalysis: How far can we bridge the gap between Classical and Quantum Paradigm", awarded under DAE-SRC, BRNS, India.

References

1. Bera, D., Tharrmashastha, P.V.: Error reduction of quantum algorithms. Phys. Rev. A **100**, 012331 (2019)

2. Brassard, G., Hoyer, P.: An exact quantum polynomial-time algorithm for Simon's problem. In: Proceedings of the Fifth Israel Symposium on the Theory of Computing Systems (ISTCS 1997), Washington, DC, USA, p. 12. IEEE Computer Society (1997)

3. Chabaud, F., Vaudenay, S.: Links between differential and linear cryptanalysis. In: De Santis, A. (ed.) EUROCRYPT 1994. LNCS, vol. 950, pp. 356–365. Springer, Heidelberg (1995). https://doi.org/10.1007/BFb0053450

4. Chailloux, A., Naya-Plasencia, M., Schrottenloher, A.: An efficient quantum collision search algorithm and implications on symmetric cryptography. In: Takagi, T., Peyrin, T. (eds.) ASIACRYPT 2017. LNCS, vol. 10625, pp. 211–240. Springer, Cham (2017). https://doi.org/10.1007/978-3-319-70697-9_8

5. Deutsch, D., Jozsa, R.: Rapid solution of problems by quantum computation. Proc. R. Soc. Lond. Ser. A **439**, 553–558 (1992)

6. Grassl, M., Langenberg, B., Roetteler, M., Steinwandt, R.: Applying Grover's algorithm to AES: quantum resource estimates. In: Takagi, T. (ed.) PQCrypto 2016. LNCS, vol. 9606, pp. 29–43. Springer, Cham (2016). https://doi.org/10.1007/978-3-319-29360-8_3

7. Grover, L.K.: Quantum computers can search rapidly by using almost any transformation. Phys. Rev. Lett. **80**, 4329–4332 (1998)

8. Hell, M., Johansson, T., Meier, W.: Grain: a stream cipher for constrained environments. Int. J. Wirel. Mob. Comput. **2**(1), 86–93 (2007)

9. Kaplan, M., Leurent, G., Leverrier, A., Naya-Plasencia, M.: Breaking symmetric cryptosystems using quantum period finding. In: Robshaw, M., Katz, J. (eds.) CRYPTO 2016. LNCS, vol. 9815, pp. 207–237. Springer, Heidelberg (2016). https://doi.org/10.1007/978-3-662-53008-5_8

10. Kaplan, M., Leurent, G., Leverrier, A., Naya-Plasencia, M.: Quantum differential and linear cryptanalysis. IACR Trans. Symmetric Cryptol. **2016**(1), 71–94 (2016)

11. Lai, X.: Higher order derivatives and differential cryptanalysis. In: Blahut, R.E., Costello, D.J., Maurer, U., Mittelholzer, T. (eds.) Communications and Cryptography. The Springer International Series in Engineering and Computer Science (Communications and Information Theory), vol. 276, pp. 227–233. Springer, Boston (1994). https://doi.org/10.1007/978-1-4615-2694-0_23

12. Leander, G., May, A.: Grover meets Simon – quantumly attacking the FX-construction. In: Takagi, T., Peyrin, T. (eds.) ASIACRYPT 2017. LNCS, vol. 10625, pp. 161–178. Springer, Cham (2017). https://doi.org/10.1007/978-3-319-70697-9_6

13. Maitra, S., Mukhopadhyay, P.: The Deutsch-Jozsa algorithm revisited in the domain of cryptographically significant Boolean functions. Int. J. Quantum Inf. **03**(02), 359–370 (2005)

14. Mansour, Y.: Learning Boolean functions via the Fourier transform. In: Roychowdhury, V., Siu, K.Y., Orlitsky, A. (eds.) Theoretical Advances in Neural Computation and Learning, pp. 391–424. Springer, Boston (1994). https://doi.org/10.1007/978-1-4615-2696-4_11

15. Sarkar, S., Maitra, S., Baksi, A.: Observing biases in the state: case studies with Trivium and Trivia-SC. Des. Codes Crypt. **82**(1), 351–375 (2017)

16. Shannon, C.E.: A mathematical theory of communication. SIGMOBILE Mob. Comput. Commun. Rev. **5**(1), 3–55 (2001)

17. Tang, D., Maitra, S.: Construction of n-variable ($n \equiv 2 \bmod 4$) balanced Boolean functions with maximum absolute value in autocorrelation spectra $<2^{\frac{n}{2}}$. IEEE Trans. Inf. Theory **64**(1), 393–402 (2018)

18. Xie, Z., Qiu, D., Cai, G.: Quantum algorithms on Walsh transform and Hamming distance for Boolean functions. Quantum Inf. Process. **17**(6), 139 (2018)
19. Yoder, T.J., Low, G.H., Chuang, I.L.: Fixed-point quantum search with an optimal number of queries. Phys. Rev. Lett. **113**, 210501 (2014)

Quantum Attacks Against Type-1 Generalized Feistel Ciphers and Applications to CAST-256

Boyu Ni[1,2], Gembu Ito[3], Xiaoyang Dong[4(✉)], and Tetsu Iwata[3(✉)]

[1] Key Laboratory of Cryptologic Technology and Information Security,
Shandong University, Ministry of Education, Qingdao, People's Republic of China
[2] School of Cyber Science and Technology, Shandong University,
Qingdao, People's Republic of China
[3] Nagoya University, Nagoya 464-8603, Japan
g_itou@echo.nuee.nagoya-u.ac.jp, tetsu.iwata@nagoya-u.jp
[4] Institute for Advanced Study, Tsinghua University,
Beijing 100084, People's Republic of China
xiaoyangdong@tsinghua.edu.cn

Abstract. Generalized Feistel Schemes (GFSs) are important components of symmetric ciphers, which have been extensively studied in the classical setting. However, detailed security evaluations of GFS in the quantum setting still remain to be explored.

In this paper, we give improved polynomial-time quantum distinguishers on Type-1 GFS in quantum chosen-plaintext attack (qCPA) setting and quantum chosen-ciphertext attack (qCCA) setting. In qCPA setting, we give a new quantum polynomial-time distinguisher on $(3d-3)$-round Type-1 GFS with branches $d \geq 3$, which gains $(d-2)$ more rounds than the previous distinguishers. This leads us to obtain a better key-recovery attack with reduced time complexities by a factor of $2^{\frac{(d-2)n}{2}}$, where n is the bit length of the branch. We also show a quantum distinguishing attack against $(d^2 - d + 1)$-round version in qCCA setting, and this gives a key-recovery attack with much lower time complexity.

In addition, based on a 14-round quantum distinguisher, we give quantum key-recovery attacks on round-reduced CAST-256 block cipher. For the 256-bit key version, we could attack up to 20-round CAST-256 in time 2^{111}, which is faster than the quantum brute-force attack by a factor of 2^{17}. For the 128-bit key version, we could attack 17 rounds in time $2^{55.5}$, while the best previous classical or quantum attacks are no more than 16 rounds.

Keywords: Generalized Feistel scheme · Quantum attack · Simon's algorithm · CAST-256

1 Introduction

Feistel block ciphers are featured by the efficient Feistel network, whose encryption and decryption processes are based on similar operations. This design

© Springer Nature Switzerland AG 2019
F. Hao et al. (Eds.): INDOCRYPT 2019, LNCS 11898, pp. 433–455, 2019.
https://doi.org/10.1007/978-3-030-35423-7_22

has been extensively studied [8,15,20,27] and adopted in many standard block ciphers, including DES, Triple-DES, Camellia [3], and GOST [12]. Feistel network was also generalized to form Generalized Feistel Networks (GFNs) or Generalized Feistel Schemes (GFSs). GFSs adopt more than two branches and different operations between the branches. At CRYPTO 1989, Zheng et al. [46] summarized several types of GFSs, called Type-1, Type-2, and Type-3 GFSs. In addition, some other GFSs were invented by Anderson and Biham [2], Lucks [32] and Schneier and Kelsey [38]. Many important primitives employ GFSs, such as block ciphers CAST-256 [1] (Type-1), CLEFIA [39] (Type-2), Simpira [14] (Type-2), as well as hash functions MD5 and SHA-1 (Type-1). GFSs inherit the advantages of Feistel network. Besides, it allows a small round function to construct a cipher with a larger block size, which is beneficial to lightweight implementations.

Classically, Luby and Rackoff [31] proved that the 3-round Feistel scheme is a secure pseudo-random permutation. At CRYPTO 1989, Zheng et al. [46] showed that the $(2d - 1)$-round Type-1 GFS is secure against chosen-plaintext attacks. Moriai and Vaudenay pointed out that $(d^2 - d)$-round Type-1 GFS is not secure against chosen-ciphertext attacks [33]. See also the analysis by Hoang and Rogaway [17]. Generic attacks on these constructions are also widely studied, such as birthday attack [23], meet-in-the-middle attack [16], differential attacks [34,41], and Patarin et al.'s attacks [35,36,42].

It was a common belief that quantum attacks on symmetric primitives are of minor concern, as they mainly consist of employing Grover's algorithm [13] to generically speed up search (sub-)problems. However, Kuwakado and Morii [28] found the first polynomial-time quantum distinguisher on 3-round Feistel block ciphers by using Simon's algorithm [40]. This result proves that there is a case that quantum attacks can exponentially improve classical attacks. Later, various quantum attacks against symmetric primitives were invented, such as key-recovery attacks against Even-Mansour constructions [29], forgery or key-recovery attacks against block cipher based MACs [5,24], key-recovery attacks against the FX construction [30], and so on.

At FOCS 2012, Zhandry et al. [45] classified the quantum cryptanalysis into two models, i.e., the standard security (Q1 model) and quantum security (Q2 model). In Q1 model, adversaries could only collect data classically and process them with local quantum computers. In contrast to this, in Q2 model, the adversaries could query the oracle with quantum superpositions of inputs, and obtain the corresponding superposition of outputs. Adversaries from Q2 model are more powerful, while Q2 model is not realistic for the foreseeable future. However, Q2 model is still theoretically interesting. Moreover, as stated by Ito et al. [22], *"the threat of this attack model becomes significant if an adversary has access to its white-box implementation. Because arbitrary classical circuit can be converted into quantum one, the adversary can construct a quantum circuit from the classical source code given by the white-box implementation"*. In this paper, we assume that the adversaries are in the Q2 model.

There have already been papers investigating Feistel schemes or GFSs against Q2 adversaries. Besides Kuwakado and Morii [28]'s work, Ito et al. [22] extended the quantum distinguisher to 4-round Feistel scheme under quantum chosen-ciphertext attack setting. Based on the Grover-meets-Simon algorithm by Leander and May [30], Hosoyamada et al. [19] and Dong et al. [11] introduced some quantum key-recovery attacks on Feistel schemes. Dong et al. [10] gave some quantum distinguishers and key-recovery attacks on some GFSs. Dong et al. [9] and Bonnetain et al. [6] studied 2K-/4K-Feistel schemes against quantum slide attacks. Notably, Hosoyamada and Iwata [18] proved a quantum security bound of the 4-Round Luby-Rackoff construction recently.

Our Contributions. We continue the work of Dong, Li, and Wang [10] to evaluate the security of Type-1 GFSs against quantum attacks. We focus on Type-1 GFSs, as the structure is employed in the above mentioned practical designs[1]. We give some improved attacks on Type-1 GFSs in Q2 model with both quantum chosen-plaintext attack (qCPA) setting and quantum chosen-ciphertext attack (qCCA) setting. Then, some applications to CAST-256 block ciphers are given. We have three contributions:

- First, in qCPA setting, we give new quantum polynomial-time distinguishers on $(3d - 3)$-round Type-1 GFS with branches $d \geq 3$, which gain $(d - 2)$ more rounds than the previous distinguishers. The improvement is obtained by shifting the position of α_b, which is a constant used to define a period, so that the period is preserved for longer rounds. It turns out that the observation is simple, but effective to improve the number of rounds that we can attack. Based on Leander and May's algorithm [30], we could get better key-recovery attacks, whose time complexities gain a factor of $2^{\frac{(d-2)n}{2}}$, where n is the bit length of the branch.
- Second, assuming that we are in the qCCA setting, we show a distinguishing attack against the $(d^2 - d + 1)$-round version. The number of rounds is significantly larger than the above, and this follows the intuition in the classical setting where the diffusion of Type-1 GFS in the decryption direction is slow, which is pointed out in [33]. The distinguishers in both qCPA and qCCA settings and the key-recovery attacks are summarized in Tables 1 and 2.
- Third, we also evaluate CAST-256 block cipher against quantum attacks. We find 14-round polynomial-time quantum distinguishers in qCPA setting. Note that the best previous one is 7 rounds [10]. Based on this, we could derive quantum key-recovery attack on 20-round CAST-256. Compared to this, the best previous quantum key-recovery attack is on 16 rounds. The results are summarized in Table 3. We also compare our quantum attacks with classical attacks in Table 4. When the key size of CAST-256 is 128, our result also reaches 17 rounds, which gains one more round than before.

---

[1] Dong, Li, and Wang also analyzed Type-2 GFSs [10], and we do not know if quantum attacks on Type-2 GFSs can be improved.

Table 1. Rounds of quantum distinguishers on Type-1 GFS

Source	Setting	Distinguisher	$d=3$	$d=4$	$d=5$	$d=6$	$d=7$	...
[10]	qCPA	$2d-1$	5	7	9	11	13	...
Sect. 4	qCPA	$3d-3$	6	9	12	15	18	...
Sect. 5	qCCA	d^2-d+1	7	13	21	31	43	...

Table 2. Key-recovery attacks on Type-1 GFS ($d \geq 3$) in quantum settings

Setting	Distinguisher	Key-recovery rounds	Complexity (log)
qCPA	$2d-1$ [10]	$r \geq d^2-d+2$	$(\frac{1}{2}d^2 - \frac{3}{2}d + 2) \cdot \frac{k}{2} + \frac{(r-d^2+d-2)k}{2}$
qCPA	$3d-3$ [Ours]	$r \geq d^2$	$(\frac{1}{2}d^2 - \frac{3}{2}d + 2) \cdot \frac{k}{2} + \frac{(r-d^2)k}{2}$
qCCA	d^2-d+1 [Ours]	$r \geq d^2-d+1$	$\frac{(r-(d^2-d+1))k}{2}$

Table 3. Quantum attacks on CAST-256†

Source	Setting	Distinguisher	Attacked rounds					
			$r=15$	$r=16$	$r=17$	$r=18$	$r=19$	$r=20$
[10]	qCPA	7	$2^{92.5}$	2^{111}	–	–	–	–
Sect. 7	qCPA	14	$2^{18.5}$	2^{37}	$2^{55.5}$	2^{74}	$2^{92.5}$	2^{111}

†: Note that for CAST-256 with 256-bit key, the trivial bound is 2^{128} by Grover's algorithm.

Table 4. Comparison between classical and quantum attacks on CAST-256

Source	Key	Attack	Rounds	Data	Time
[43]	128	boomerang	16	$2^{49.3}$	–
[10]	128	qCPA	12	–	$2^{55.5}$
Sect. 7	128	qCPA	17	–	$2^{55.5}$
[44]	192	linear	24	$2^{124.1}$	$2^{156.52}$
Sect. 7	192	qCPA	18	–	2^{74}
[4]	256	multidim.ZC	28	$2^{98.8}$	$2^{246.9}$
[10]	256	qCPA	16	–	2^{111}
Sect. 7	256	qCPA	20	–	2^{111}

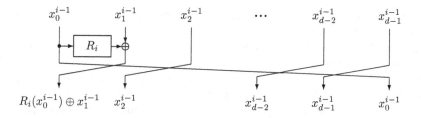

Fig. 1. The i-th round of Type-1 GFS

2 Preliminaries

2.1 Notation

For a positive integer n, let $\{0,1\}^n$ be the set of all strings of n bits. Let $\mathrm{Perm}(n)$ be the set of all permutations on $\{0,1\}^n$, and let $\mathrm{Func}(n)$ be the set of all functions from $\{0,1\}^n$ to $\{0,1\}^n$. For vectors a and b of the same dimension, we denote their inner product by $a \cdot b$. In this paper, e denotes Napier's number.

2.2 Type-1 Generalized Feistel Schemes

In this section, we describe Type-1 generalized Feistel schemes (GFSs) [46]. In Type-1 GFS, we divide the dn-bit state into d branches, where $d \geq 3$ and each branch constitutes an n-bit sub-block. Let Φ_r denote the encryption algorithm of the r-round Type-1 GFS, and Φ_r^{-1} denote its decryption algorithm. Let $R_1, R_2, \ldots, R_r \in \mathrm{Func}(n)$ be the keyed round functions of Φ_r. We assume that the function R_i takes a k-bit key k_i as input (thus the total key length of Φ_r is rk bits). Φ_r takes a plaintext $(x_0^0, x_1^0, \ldots, x_{d-1}^0) \in (\{0,1\}^n)^d$ as input, and outputs a ciphertext $(x_0^r, x_1^r, \ldots, x_{d-1}^r) \in (\{0,1\}^n)^d$, where the i-th round is defined as

$$(x_0^i, x_1^i, \ldots, x_{d-1}^i) = (R_i(x_0^{i-1}) \oplus x_1^{i-1}, x_2^{i-1}, x_3^{i-1}, \ldots, x_{d-1}^{i-1}, x_0^{i-1}).$$

The decryption is naturally defined by reversing the direction of the shift of the branches. Figure 1 shows the i-th round of Type-1 GFS.

2.3 Simon's Algorithm

Here we review Simon's algorithm [40] that is the basis of our distinguishers. Simon's algorithm solves the following problem efficiently.

Problem 1. Given a function $f : \{0,1\}^n \to \{0,1\}^n$ that has a non-zero period $s \in \{0,1\}^n$ such that

$$f(x) = f(x') \Leftrightarrow x' = x \oplus s$$

for any distinct $x, x' \in \{0,1\}^n$, the goal is to find the period s.

In the classical setting, $O(2^{n/2})$ queries are needed to find s, while Simon's algorithm finds s with $O(n)$ quantum queries.

In what follows, we recall how Simon's algorithm works. Assume that we have access to the quantum oracle U_f, which is defined as $U_f |x\rangle |z\rangle = |x\rangle |z \oplus f(x)\rangle$. For an n-qubit state $|x\rangle$, Hadamard transformation $H^{\otimes n}$ is defined as $H^{\otimes n} |x\rangle = \frac{1}{\sqrt{2^n}} \sum_{y \in \{0,1\}^n} (-1)^{x \cdot y} |y\rangle$. Simon proposed a circuit $\mathcal{S}_f$ that computes a vector that is orthogonal to s for a periodic function f, which is defined as $\mathcal{S}_f = (H^{\otimes n} \otimes I_n) \cdot U_f \cdot (H^{\otimes n} \otimes I_n)$ and works as follows.

$$\mathcal{S}_f |0^n\rangle |0^n\rangle = (H^{\otimes n} \otimes I_n) \cdot U_f \cdot (H^{\otimes n} \otimes I_n) |0^n\rangle |0^n\rangle$$

$$= (H^{\otimes n} \otimes I_n) \cdot U_f \frac{1}{\sqrt{2^n}} \sum_x |x\rangle |0^n\rangle$$

$$= (H^{\otimes n} \otimes I_n) \frac{1}{\sqrt{2^n}} \sum_x |x\rangle |f(x)\rangle$$

$$= \frac{1}{2^n} \sum_{x,y} (-1)^{x \cdot y} |y\rangle |f(x)\rangle \tag{1}$$

If f satisfies $f(x) = f(x') \Leftrightarrow x' = x \oplus s$, then Eq. (1) can be rearranged as

$$\frac{1}{2^n} \sum_{x \in V, y} ((-1)^{x \cdot y} + (-1)^{(x \oplus s) \cdot y}) |y\rangle |f(x)\rangle \,,$$

where V is a linear subspace of $\{0,1\}^n$ of dimension $(n-1)$ that partitions $\{0,1\}^n$ into cosets V and $V+s$. The vector y such that $y \cdot s \equiv 1 \pmod 2$ satisfies $(-1)^{x \cdot y} + (-1)^{(x \oplus s) \cdot y} = 0$. Therefore, the vector y that we obtain by measuring the first n qubits of $\mathcal{S}_f |0^n\rangle |0^n\rangle$ satisfies $y \cdot s \equiv 0 \pmod 2$. By repeating this measurement for $O(n)$ times, we obtain $(n-1)$ linearly independent vectors that are all orthogonal to s with a high probability. Then we can recover s by solving the system of linear equations with $O(n^3)$ classical steps.

2.4   Quantum Distinguisher Based on Simon's Algorithm

Next, we introduce a quantum distinguisher based on Simon's algorithm. We follow the approach of Kaplan et al. [24] and Santoli and Schaffner [37], and the formalization by Ito et al. [22]. To recover s with Simon's algorithm, the function f has to satisfy $f(x) = f(x') \Leftrightarrow x' = x \oplus s$. However, for distinguishers, the condition can be relaxed.

In more detail, suppose that we are given an oracle $\mathcal{O} : \{0,1\}^n \to \{0,1\}^n$, which is either an encryption algorithm $E_K \in \mathrm{Perm}(n)$ or a random permutation $\Pi \in \mathrm{Perm}(n)$, and our goal is to distinguish the two cases. We assume that the quantum oracles $U_\mathcal{O}$ and $U_{\mathcal{O}^{-1}}$ are given. The distinguisher in [22] can be applied to a function $f^\mathcal{O} : \{0,1\}^\ell \to \{0,1\}^m$, where there exists a non-zero period s when $\mathcal{O} = E_K$, i.e., $f^\mathcal{O}$ such that $f^{E_K}(x) = f^{E_K}(x \oplus s)$ holds for all x. We expect that, with a high probability, f^Π does not have any period. The distinguisher works as follows:

1. Prepare an empty set $\mathcal{Y}$.
2. Measure the first ℓ qubits of $\mathcal{S}_{f^{\mathcal{O}}} |0^{\ell+m}\rangle$ and add the obtained vector y to $\mathcal{Y}$ for η times.
3. Calculate the dimension d of the vector space spanned by $\mathcal{Y}$.
4. If $d = \ell$, then output $\mathcal{O} = \Pi$, otherwise output $\mathcal{O} = E_K$.

If $f^{\mathcal{O}}$ has the period s, the obtained vector y is orthogonal to s. Therefore the dimension d of the vector space spanned by $\mathcal{Y}$ is at most $\ell - 1$. On the other hand, if $f^{\mathcal{O}}$ has no period, the dimension can reach ℓ. Thus we can distinguish the two cases by checking the dimension.

This distinguisher fails only if $\mathcal{O} = \Pi$ and the dimension of the vector space spanned by $\mathcal{Y}$ is less than ℓ. To analyze the success probability of the distinguisher, define a parameter ϵ_f^{π} as

$$\epsilon_f^{\pi} = \max_{t \in \{0,1\}^{\ell} \setminus \{0^{\ell}\}} \Pr_x \left[f^{\pi}(x) = f^{\pi}(x \oplus t) \right],$$

where $\pi \in \mathrm{Perm}(n)$ is a fixed permutation. This parameter shows how the dimension of y is biased when $\Pi = \pi$. If this parameter is large (i.e., there exists t that is close to a period), then with a high probability, the vector space spanned by $\mathcal{Y}$ is orthogonal to t. Thus, we take a small constant $0 \le \delta < 1$ arbitrarily, and we say that a permutation π is irregular if $\epsilon_f^{\pi} > 1 - \delta$. In addition, define the set of the irregular permutations irr_f^{δ} as

$$\mathrm{irr}_f^{\delta} = \{\pi \in \mathrm{perm}(n) \mid \epsilon_f^{\pi} > 1 - \delta\}.$$

The following theorem was proved in [22].

Theorem 1 ([22]). *Let ℓ and m be positive integers that are $O(n)$. Assume that we have a quantum circuit with $O(poly(\ell, m))$ qubits which computes $f^{\mathcal{O}} : \{0,1\}^{\ell} \to \{0,1\}^m$ by making $O(1)$ queries to $\mathcal{O}$, and runs in time $T(\ell, m)$. The distinguisher makes $O(\eta)$ quantum queries, and distinguishes E_K from Π with probability at least*

$$1 - \frac{2^{\ell}}{e^{\delta\eta/2}} - \Pr_{\Pi}[\Pi \in \mathrm{irr}_f^{\delta}].$$

This shows that the distinguisher succeeds if $\Pr_{\Pi}[\Pi \in \mathrm{irr}_f^{\delta}]$ is a small value.

2.5 Hosoyamada and Sasaki's Method to Truncate Outputs of Quantum Oracles

At ISIT 2010, Kuwakado and Morii [28] introduced a quantum distinguishing attack on 3-round Feistel scheme by using Simon's algorithm. As shown in Fig. 2, let α_0 and α_1 be arbitrary constants, and define f as:

$$f : \{0,1\} \times \{0,1\}^n \to \{0,1\}^n$$
$$(b, x) \mapsto \alpha_b \oplus x_1^3,$$
$$\text{where } (x_0^3, x_1^3) = E(\alpha_b, x).$$

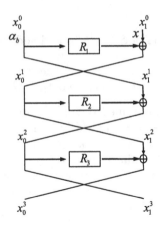

Fig. 2. 3-round Feistel cipher

E is the 3-round Feistel scheme and f can be written as $f(b,x) = R_2(R_1(\alpha_b) \oplus x))$. It is easy to see that f is a periodic function that satisfies $f(b,x) = f(b \oplus 1, x \oplus R_1(\alpha_0) \oplus R_1(\alpha_1))$ for any (b,x). Then by using Simon's algorithm, one obtains the period $s = 1 \| R_1(\alpha_0) \oplus R_1(\alpha_1)$ in polynomial time.

In the above distinguisher, one has to truncate the $2n$-bit output of E to obtain the right half n bits, namely x_1^3. However, Kaplan et al. [24] and Hosoyamada et al. [19] pointed out that in quantum setting, it is non-trivial to truncate the entangled $2n$ qubits to n qubits, since the usual truncation destroys entanglements.

At SCN 2018, Hosoyamada and Sasaki [19] introduced a method to simulate truncation of outputs of quantum oracles without destroying quantum entanglements. Here, we review their method. Let $\mathcal{O} : |x\rangle|y\rangle|z\rangle|w\rangle \mapsto |x\rangle|y\rangle|z \oplus \mathcal{O}_L(x,y)\rangle|w \oplus \mathcal{O}_R(x,y)\rangle$ be the encryption oracle E_K, where $\mathcal{O}_L$, $\mathcal{O}_R$ denote the left and right n bits of the complete encryption, respectively. The goal is to simulate the oracle $\mathcal{O}_R : |x\rangle|y\rangle|w\rangle \mapsto |x\rangle|y\rangle|w \oplus \mathcal{O}_R(x,y)\rangle$. Hosoyamada and Sasaki first try to simulate a tweaked $\mathcal{O}_R$, i.e., $\mathcal{O}_R' : |x\rangle|y\rangle|w\rangle|0^n\rangle \mapsto |x\rangle|y\rangle|w \oplus \mathcal{O}_R(x,y)\rangle|0^n\rangle$ with ancilla qubits. Let $|+\rangle := H^{\otimes n}|0^n\rangle = \frac{1}{\sqrt{2^n}}\sum_z |z\rangle$, where $H^{\otimes n}$ is an n-qubit Hadamard gate. Thus,

$$\mathcal{O}|x\rangle|y\rangle|+\rangle|w\rangle = \mathcal{O}(|x\rangle|y\rangle[\frac{1}{\sqrt{2^n}}\sum_z |z\rangle]|w\rangle)$$

$$= |x\rangle|y\rangle[\frac{1}{\sqrt{2^n}}\sum_z |z \oplus \mathcal{O}_L(x,y)\rangle]|w \oplus \mathcal{O}_R(x,y)\rangle. \qquad (2)$$

Let $z' = z \oplus \mathcal{O}_L(x,y)$. Then Eq. (2) becomes

$$|x\rangle|y\rangle[\frac{1}{\sqrt{2^n}}\sum_z |z'\rangle]|w \oplus \mathcal{O}_R(x,y)\rangle = |x\rangle|y\rangle[\frac{1}{\sqrt{2^n}}\sum_{z'} |z'\rangle]|w \oplus \mathcal{O}_R(x,y)\rangle$$

$$= |x\rangle|y\rangle|+\rangle|w \oplus \mathcal{O}_R(x,y)\rangle.$$

So $\mathcal{O}|x\rangle|y\rangle|+\rangle|w\rangle = |x\rangle|y\rangle|+\rangle|w \oplus \mathcal{O}_R(x,y)\rangle$. Hosoyamada and Sasaki define $\mathcal{O}'_R := (I \otimes H^{\otimes n}) \circ \mathtt{Swap} \circ \mathcal{O} \circ \mathtt{Swap} \circ (I \otimes H^{\otimes n})$, where $\mathtt{Swap}$ is an operator that swaps the last $2n$ bits: $|x\rangle|y\rangle|z\rangle|w\rangle \mapsto |x\rangle|y\rangle|w\rangle|z\rangle$. So we have

$$
\begin{aligned}
\mathcal{O}'_R|x\rangle|y\rangle|w\rangle|0^n\rangle &= (I \otimes H^{\otimes n}) \circ \mathtt{Swap} \circ \mathcal{O} \circ \mathtt{Swap} \circ (I \otimes H^{\otimes n})|x\rangle|y\rangle|w\rangle|0^n\rangle \\
&= (I \otimes H^{\otimes n}) \circ \mathtt{Swap} \circ \mathcal{O}|x\rangle|y\rangle|+\rangle|w\rangle \\
&= (I \otimes H^{\otimes n}) \circ \mathtt{Swap}|x\rangle|y\rangle|+\rangle|w \oplus \mathcal{O}_R(x,y)\rangle \\
&= (I \otimes H^{\otimes n})|x\rangle|y\rangle|w \oplus \mathcal{O}_R(x,y)\rangle|+\rangle \\
&= |x\rangle|y\rangle|w \oplus \mathcal{O}_R(x,y)\rangle|0^n\rangle \, .
\end{aligned}
$$

Hence, $\mathcal{O}_R$ could be simulated given the complete encryption oracle $\mathcal{O}$ using ancilla qubits. Intuitively, Hosoyamada and Sasaki first randomize the left part by using the Hadamard transformation, and then force it to become $|0^n\rangle$ by applying the Hadamard transformation again.

2.6 Combining Grover Search and Distinguishers

Leander and May combined Grover search and Simon's algorithm to show a key recovery attack against the FX construction [30]. Hosoyamada and Sasaki [19], and Dong and Wang [11] showed key recovery attacks against Feistel schemes by using this combining technique.

Grover Search. Grover search provides a quadratic speed up on unsorted-database search [13]. Let N be the number of elements in the database, and assume that there exists only one target element. In the classical setting, we can find the target element in time $O(N)$. However, in the quantum setting, Grover's algorithm can find it in time $O(\sqrt{N})$.

This algorithm was generalized later as quantum amplitude amplification by Brassard et al. [7] as in the following theorem.

Theorem 2 ([7]). *Let $\mathcal{A}$ be any quantum algorithm on q qubits that uses no measurement. Let $\mathcal{B} : \{0,1\}^q \to \{0,1\}$ be a function that classifies outcomes of $\mathcal{A}$ as good or bad. Let $p > 0$ be the initial success probability that a measurement of $\mathcal{A}|0\rangle$ is good. Set $m = \lfloor \pi/4\theta_p \rfloor$, where θ_p is defined so that $\sin^2(\theta_p) = p$ and $0 < \theta_p \le \pi/2$. Moreover, define the unitary operator $Q = -\mathcal{A}S_0\mathcal{A}^{-1}S_\mathcal{B}$, where the operator $S_\mathcal{B}$ conditionally changes the sign of the amplitudes of the good states,*

$$
|x\rangle \mapsto \begin{cases} -|x\rangle & \text{if } \mathcal{B}(x) = 1, \\ |x\rangle & \text{if } \mathcal{B}(x) = 0, \end{cases}
$$

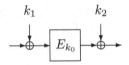

Fig. 3. The FX construction

while the operate S_0 changes the sign of the amplitude if and only if the state is the zero state $|0\rangle$. Then, after the computation of $Q^m \mathcal{A} |0\rangle$, a measurement is good with probability at least $\max\{1 - p, p\}$.

Key Recovery Attack Against the FX Construction. The FX construction by Killian and Rogaway is a way to extend the key length of a block cipher [25,26]. Let E be an n-bit block cipher that takes an m-bit key k_0 as input. The FX construction under two additional n-bit keys k_1, k_2 is described as

$$\text{Enc}(x) = E_{k_0}(x \oplus k_1) \oplus k_2.$$

Figure 3 shows the FX construction.

Leander and May constructed a function $f(k, x)$ that is defined as

$$f(k, x) = \text{Enc}(x) \oplus E_k(x) = E_{k_0}(x \oplus k_1) \oplus k_2 \oplus E_k(x).$$

If $k = k_0$, $f(k, x)$ satisfies $f(k, x) = f(k, x \oplus k_1)$ for all $x \in \{0, 1\}^n$. That is, the function $f(k_0, \cdot)$ has a period k_1. However, if $k \neq k_0$, with a high probability, the function $f(k, \cdot)$ does not have any period. Then they apply Grover search over $k \in \{0, 1\}^m$. They construct the classifier $\mathcal{B}$ that identifies the states as good if $k = k_0$ by using Simon's algorithm to $f(k, \cdot)$. The time complexity of Grover search is $O(2^{m/2})$ and Simon's algorithm runs in time $O(n)$ in the classifier $\mathcal{B}$. Thus this attack runs in time $O(2^{m/2})$. For more details, see [30].

3   Previous Attacks

In this section, we review the quantum attacks against Type-1 GFSs by Dong et al. [10]. They showed a $(2d-1)$-round distinguishing attack and a (d^2-d+2)-round key recovery attack.

We first review the distinguishing attack. Let $\alpha_0, \alpha_1 \in \{0, 1\}^n$ be two arbitrary distinct n-bit constants, and $x_1^0, x_2^0, \ldots, x_{d-2}^0 \in \{0, 1\}^n$ be arbitrary n-bit constants. Given the oracle $\mathcal{O}$, they define a function $f^{\mathcal{O}}$ as

$$f^{\mathcal{O}} : \{0, 1\} \times \{0, 1\}^n \to \{0, 1\}^n$$
$$(b, x) \mapsto \alpha_b \oplus y_1,$$
where $(y_0, y_1, \ldots, y_{d-1}) = \mathcal{O}(\alpha_b, x_1^0, x_2^0, \ldots, x_{d-2}^0, x). \tag{3}$

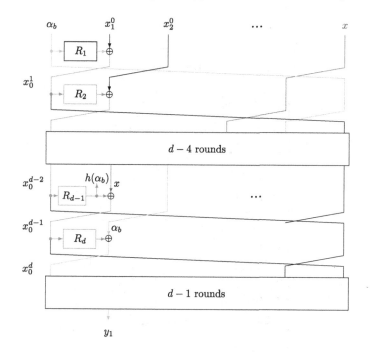

Fig. 4. $(2d-1)$-round distinguishing attack

Let the intermediate state value after the first i rounds be $(x_0^i, x_1^i, \ldots, x_{d-1}^i)$. If $\mathcal{O}$ is $\varPhi_{2d-1}$, then the function $f^{\mathcal{O}}$ is described as

$$
\begin{aligned}
f(b, x) &= \alpha_b \oplus x_1^{2d-1} \\
&= \alpha_b \oplus x_0^d \\
&= \alpha_b \oplus R_d(x_0^{d-1}) \oplus \alpha_b \\
&= R_d(R_{d-1}(R_{d-2}(\cdots R_2(R_1(\alpha_b) \oplus x_1^0) \oplus x_2^0 \cdots) \oplus x_{d-2}^0) \oplus x), \quad (4)
\end{aligned}
$$

where in the second equality, we use the fact that $x_i^i = x_{d-1}^{i+1} = x_{d-2}^{i+2} = \cdots = x_1^{i+d-1}$ (See Fig. 4). Let $h(\cdot) = R_{d-1}(R_{d-2}(\cdots R_2(R_1(\cdot) \oplus x_1^0) \oplus x_2^0 \cdots) \oplus x_{d-2}^0)$. We see that $h(\cdot)$ is a function that is independent of the input (b, x), since $x_1^0, x_2^0, \ldots, x_{d-2}^0$ are constants. By using $h(\cdot)$, we can describe Eq. (4) as $f^{\mathcal{O}} = R_d(h(\alpha_b) \oplus x)$, and $f^{\mathcal{O}}$ satisfies

$$
\begin{aligned}
f(b, x) &= R_d(h(\alpha_b) \oplus x) \\
&= R_d(h(\alpha_{b\oplus 1}) \oplus h(\alpha_0) \oplus h(\alpha_1) \oplus x) \\
&= f(b \oplus 1, x \oplus h(\alpha_0) \oplus h(\alpha_1)).
\end{aligned}
$$

This implies that the function $f^{\mathcal{O}}$ has the period $(1, h(\alpha_0) \oplus h(\alpha_1))$.

If $\mathcal{O}$ is $\varPi$, then with a high probability, $f^{\mathcal{O}}$ does not have any period. Therefore, $\Pr_{\varPi}[\varPi \in \mathsf{irr}_f^{\delta}]$ is a small value and we can distinguish the two cases.

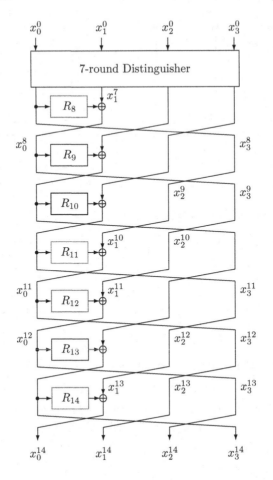

Fig. 5. $(d^2 - d + 2)$-round key recovery attack for $d = 4$

We next review the key recovery attack. We recover the key of the $(d^2 - d + 2)$-round Type-1 GFS by appending $(d^2 - 3d + 3)$ rounds after the $(2d - 1)$-round distinguisher (See Fig. 5). For each x_1^i, where $d \geq 3$, we have $x_1^i = R_{i+1}(x_d^{i+1}, k_{i+1}) \oplus x_0^{i+1}$. This implies that when we need the value of x_1^i, we have to recover k_{i+1}. From the property of Feistel cipher, we have $x_j^i = x_{j-1}^{i+1} = \cdots = x_1^{i+j-1}$ for $3 \leq j \leq d$, and $x_0^i = x_1^{i+d-1}$. For d branches, it holds that $x_1^{2d-1} = R_{2d}(x_{d-1}^{2d}, k_{2d}) \oplus x_0^{2d}$, and thus we need to recover one sub-key k_{2d}, and since $x_0^{2d} = x_1^{3d-1}$ and $x_{d-1}^{2d} = x_1^{3d-2}$ hold, we need two sub-keys k_{3d-1} and k_{3d}. By parity of this reasoning, the subkey length that we need to recover becomes $[1 + 2 + 3 + \cdots + (d - 2)]k + k = (\frac{d^2}{2} - \frac{3d}{2} + 2)k$ bits. Thus, the time complexity of the exhaustive search for $(d^2 - d + 2)$ rounds by Grover search is $O(2^{(\frac{d^2}{2} - \frac{3d}{2} + 2) \cdot \frac{k}{2}})$. The distinguisher runs in time $O(n)$ and the time complexity of this attack is $O(2^{(\frac{d^2}{2} - \frac{3d}{2} + 2) \cdot \frac{k}{2}})$.

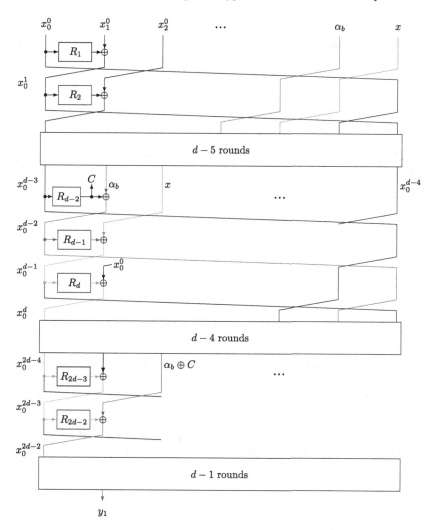

Fig. 6. $(3d-3)$-round distinguishing attack

This attack is better than the direct application of Grover search to the entire $(d^2 - d + 2)k$-bit subkey. If we recover the subkey of r rounds for $r > d^2 - d + 2$, the time complexity is $O(2^{(\frac{d^2}{2} - \frac{3d}{2} + 2) \cdot \frac{k}{2} + \frac{(r-d^2+d-2)k}{2}})$, since the subkey length that we need to recover becomes $(\frac{d^2}{2} - \frac{3d}{2} + 2)k + (r - d^2 + d - 2)k$ bits in total.

4 $(3d-3)$-Round Distinguishing Attack in qCPA Setting

In this section, we present our distinguishing attacks against $(3d - 3)$-round Type-1 GFSs. We improve the number of rounds that we can distinguish from $(2d-1)$ rounds to $(3d-3)$ rounds by shifting the position of α_b in the plaintext.

As before, we first fix two arbitrary distinct constants $\alpha_0, \alpha_1 \in \{0,1\}^n$ and fix arbitrary constants $x_0^0, x_1^0, \ldots, x_{d-3}^0 \in \{0,1\}^n$. Given the oracle $\mathcal{O}$, we define a function $f^{\mathcal{O}}$ as

$$f^{\mathcal{O}} : \{0,1\} \times \{0,1\}^n \to \{0,1\}^n$$
$$(b, x) \mapsto \alpha_b \oplus y_1,$$
$$\text{where } (y_0, y_1, \ldots, y_{d-1}) = \mathcal{O}(x_0^0, x_1^0, \ldots, x_{d-3}^0, \alpha_b, x).$$

Observe that the difference from Eq. (3) is the position of α_b.

If $\mathcal{O}$ is Φ_{3d-3}, let $(x_0^i, x_1^i, \ldots, x_{d-1}^i)$ be the intermediate state value after the first i rounds. Now $f^{\mathcal{O}}$ is described as:

$$f^{\mathcal{O}}(b, x) = \alpha_b \oplus y_1$$
$$= \alpha_b \oplus x_1^{3d-3}$$
$$= \alpha_b \oplus x_0^{2d-2}, \tag{5}$$

since $x_0^i = x_{d-1}^{i+1} = x_{d-2}^{i+2} = \cdots = x_1^{i+d-1}$ (See Fig. 6).

Our main observation is the following lemma.

Lemma 1. *If $\mathcal{O}$ is Φ_{3d-3}, then for any $b \in \{0,1\}$ and $x \in \{0,1\}^n$, the function $f^{\mathcal{O}}$ satisfies*

$$f^{\mathcal{O}}(b, x) = f^{\mathcal{O}}(b \oplus 1, x \oplus R_{d-1}(C \oplus \alpha_0) \oplus R_{d-1}(C \oplus \alpha_1)),$$

where $C = R_{d-2}(R_{d-3}(\cdots R_1(x_0^0) \oplus x_1^0 \cdots) \oplus x_{d-3}^0)$. That is, $f^{\mathcal{O}}$ has the period $s = (1, R_{d-1}(C \oplus \alpha_0) \oplus R_{d-1}(C \oplus \alpha_1))$.

Proof. We first consider the intermediate state value after the first $(d-2)$ rounds in which α_b reaches the leftmost position (See Fig. 6). The value is described as

$$(x_0^{d-2}, x_1^{d-2}, \ldots, x_{d-1}^{d-2}) = \Phi_{d-2}(x_0^0, x_1^0, \ldots, x_{d-3}^0, \alpha_b, x)$$
$$= (R_{d-2}(x_0^{d-3}) \oplus \alpha_b, x, x_0^0, x_0^1, \ldots, x_0^{d-3}).$$

For $1 \leq i \leq d-3$, x_0^i is described as

$$x_0^i = R_i(R_{i-1}(\cdots R_1(x_0^0) \oplus x_1^0 \cdots) \oplus x_{i-1}^0) \oplus x_i^0.$$

We see that x_0^i is a constant that is independent of the input (b, x), since $x_0^0, x_1^0, \ldots, x_{d-3}^0$ are constants. Let $C = R_{d-2}(x_0^{d-3})$, which is independent of (b, x) and hence can be treated as a constant. The output after one more round, which is the output after the first $(d-1)$ rounds, is described as

$$(x_0^{d-1}, x_1^{d-1}, \ldots, x_{d-1}^{d-1}) = (R_{d-1}(C \oplus \alpha_b) \oplus x, x_0^0, x_0^1, \ldots, x_0^{d-3}, C \oplus \alpha_b).$$

Now we consider the value of x_0^{2d-2}. This is the intermediate state value after the first $(2d-2)$ rounds in which $\alpha_b \oplus C$ reaches the leftmost position again, and is described as

$$x_0^{2d-2} = R'(R_{d-1}(C \oplus \alpha_b) \oplus x) \oplus \alpha_b \oplus C, \tag{6}$$

where $R'(\cdot) = R_{2d-2}(R_{2d-3}(\cdots R_{d+1}(R_d(\cdot) \oplus x_0^0) \oplus x_0^1 \cdots) \oplus x_0^{d-3})$ (See Fig. 6). $R'(\cdot)$ is a function that is independent of the input (b,x), since $x_0^0, x_0^1, \ldots, x_0^{d-3}$ are constants. From Eqs. (5) and (6), the function $f^{\mathcal{O}}$ is described as

$$f^{\mathcal{O}}(b,x) = \alpha_b \oplus R'(R_{d-1}(C \oplus \alpha_b) \oplus x) \oplus \alpha_b \oplus C$$
$$= R'(R_{d-1}(C \oplus \alpha_b) \oplus x) \oplus C.$$

The function $f^{\mathcal{O}}$ has the claimed period since it satisfies

$$f^{\mathcal{O}}(b \oplus 1, x \oplus R_{d-1}(C \oplus \alpha_0) \oplus R_{d-1}(C \oplus \alpha_1))$$
$$= R'(R_{d-1}(C \oplus \alpha_{b\oplus 1}) \oplus R_{d-1}(C \oplus \alpha_0) \oplus R_{d-1}(C \oplus \alpha_1) \oplus x) \oplus C$$
$$= R'(R_{d-1}(C \oplus \alpha_b) \oplus x) \oplus C$$
$$= f^{\mathcal{O}}(b,x),$$

and hence the lemma follows. $\qquad\qquad\qquad\qquad\qquad\qquad\qquad\qquad\qquad\square$

Therefore, we can distinguish the $(3d-3)$-round Type-1 GFS by using the function $f^{\mathcal{O}}$. The success probability of the distinguishing attack with measuring $(4n+4)$ times is at least $1 - (2/e)^{n+1} - \Pr[\Pi \in \mathrm{irr}_f^{1/2}]$, where we use $\delta = 1/2$ and $\eta = 4n+4$. Note that $\Pr[\Pi \in \mathrm{irr}_f^{1/2}]$ is a small value, since with a high probability, the function $f^{\mathcal{O}}$ does not have any period when $\mathcal{O}$ is Π, since Π is a random permutation.[2]

5 $(d^2 - d + 1)$-Round Distinguishing Attack in qCCA Setting

If we can use the decryption oracle in the quantum setting, we can construct a distinguishing attack against the $(d^2 - d + 1)$-round Type-1 GFS. We write the i-th round function in decryption as R_i. Note that this is different from the notation in Sect. 4.

We fix two distinct constants α_0, α_1 and $(d-2)$ constants $x_1^0, x_2^0, \ldots, x_{d-2}^0$, which are all n bits. Given the decryption oracle $\mathcal{O}^{-1}$, we define $f^{\mathcal{O}^{-1}}$ as

$$f^{\mathcal{O}^{-1}} : \{0,1\} \times \{0,1\}^n \to \{0,1\}^n$$
$$(b,x) \mapsto \alpha_b \oplus y_0,$$
$$\text{where } (y_0, y_1, \ldots, y_{d-1}) = \mathcal{O}^{-1}(x, x_1^0, x_2^0, \ldots, x_{d-2}^0, \alpha_b).$$

---

[2] This is intuitively obvious. However, precise computation of the probability is not known. See [21, Appendix C] (full version of [22]) for experimental computation of a related setting of Feistel cipher for small values of n.

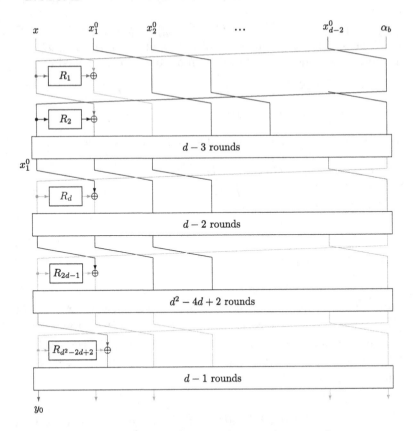

Fig. 7. $(d^2 - d + 1)$-round distinguishing attack

Consider the case $\mathcal{O}^{-1} = \Phi^{-1}_{d^2-d+1}$, and let the intermediate state value after the first i rounds be $(x_0^i, x_1^i, \ldots, x_{d-1}^i)$. $f^{\mathcal{O}^{-1}}$ is described as:

$$\begin{aligned} f^{\mathcal{O}^{-1}}(b, x) &= \alpha_b \oplus y_0 \\ &= \alpha_b \oplus x_0^{d^2-d+1} \\ &= \alpha_b \oplus x_1^{d^2-2d+2}, \end{aligned} \tag{7}$$

since $x_1^i = x_2^{i+1} = x_3^{i+2} = \cdots = x_0^{i+d-1}$ (See Fig. 7).

The following lemma holds.

Lemma 2. *If $\mathcal{O}^{-1}$ is $\Phi^{-1}_{d^2-d+1}$, then for any $b \in \{0,1\}$ and $x \in \{0,1\}^n$, the function $f^{\mathcal{O}^{-1}}$ satisfies*

$$f^{\mathcal{O}^{-1}}(b, x) = f^{\mathcal{O}^{-1}}(b \oplus 1, x \oplus R_1(\alpha_0) \oplus R_1(\alpha_1)).$$

That is, $f^{\mathcal{O}^{-1}}$ has the period $s = (1, R_1(\alpha_0) \oplus R_1(\alpha_1))$.

Proof. In the first round, $R_1(\alpha_b)$ is xored into x. In the d-th round, the value $R_1(\alpha_b) \oplus x$ is used as the input of R_d, and the output of R_d is xored into x_1^0. This implies that x_1^d is

$$x_1^d = R_d(R_1(\alpha_b) \oplus x) \oplus x_1^0. \tag{8}$$

See Fig. 7. The function $R(\cdot) = R_d(\cdot) \oplus x_1^0$ is independent of the input (b, x), since x_1^0 is a constant. Therefore, Eq. (8) can be described as

$$x_1^d = R(R_1(\alpha_b) \oplus x)$$

with some function $R \in \mathrm{Func}(n)$. After additional $(d - 1)$ rounds, this value is used as the input of R_{2d-1}, and the output of R_{2d-1} is xored into the sub-block which was x_2^0 at the input. The sub-block which was x_2^0 at the input is a constant because it is not xored by the value that includes b nor x (Specifically, it depends only on x_1^0). Therefore, for some function $R' \in \mathrm{Func}(n)$, the value of x_1^{2d-1} is described as

$$x_1^{2d-1} = R'(R_1(\alpha_b) \oplus x).$$

After that, for each $(d - 1)$ rounds, this value is used as the input to the round function and the output is xored into the sub-block which was x_i^0 at the input, for $i = 3, 4, \ldots, d - 2$. We see that the sub-block itself depends on $x_1^0, \ldots, x_{i-1}^0$, but it is a constant that is independent of the input (b, x) since a value related to (b, x) is not xored into the sub-block. Therefore, the value of $x_1^{2d-1+(d-1)\times(d-4)} = x_1^{d^2-3d+3}$ is described as

$$x_1^{d^2-3d+3} = R''(R_1(\alpha_b) \oplus x)$$

for some function $R'' \in \mathrm{Func}(n)$.

In the $(d^2 - 2d + 2)$-th round, $R_{d^2-2d+2}(R''(R_1(\alpha_b) \oplus x))$ is xored into the sub-block which was α_b at the input. Since only the value that does not include b nor x is xored into the sub-block which was α_b, with some function $R''' \in \mathrm{Func}(n)$, the value of $x_1^{d^2-2d+2}$ is described as

$$x_1^{d^2-2d+2} = R'''(R_1(\alpha_b) \oplus x) \oplus \alpha_b. \tag{9}$$

From Eqs. (7) and (9), the function $f^{\mathcal{O}^{-1}}$ can be written as

$$f^{\mathcal{O}^{-1}}(b, x) = \alpha_b \oplus R'''(R_1(\alpha_b) \oplus x) \oplus \alpha_b$$
$$= R'''(R_1(\alpha_b) \oplus x).$$

The function $f^{\mathcal{O}}$ satisfies

$$f^{\mathcal{O}^{-1}}(b \oplus 1, x \oplus R_1(\alpha_0) \oplus R_1(\alpha_1)) = R'''(R_1(\alpha_{b\oplus 1}) \oplus x \oplus R_1(\alpha_0) \oplus R_1(\alpha_1))$$
$$= R'''(R_1(\alpha_b) \oplus x)$$
$$= f^{\mathcal{O}^{-1}}(b, x),$$

and hence we have the lemma. □

The success probability of the distinguishing attack using the function $f^{\mathcal{O}^{-1}}$ with measuring $(4n + 4)$ times is at least $1 - (2/e)^{n+1} - \Pr[\Pi \in \text{irr}_f^{1/2}]$, where we use $\delta = 1/2$ and $\eta = 4n + 4$. We see that $\Pr[\Pi \in \text{irr}_f^{1/2}]$ is a small value, and hence the attack succeeds with a high probability.

6   Key Recovery Attacks on Type-1 GFSs

Similarly to the previous key recovery attacks by Dong et al. [10] that combine Grover search and the distinguisher, we can construct key recovery attacks against Type-1 GFSs based on our distinguishers.

With the $(3d - 3)$-round distinguisher in qCPA setting, we can recover the key of the d^2-round Type-1 generalized Feistel cipher in time $O(2^{(\frac{d^2}{2} - \frac{3d}{2} + 2) \cdot \frac{k}{2}})$ by replacing the $(2d - 1)$-round distinguisher in Dong et al.'s attack with our $(3d - 3)$-round distinguisher. In general, the key recovery attack against the r-round version, where $r \geq d^2$, runs in time $O(2^{(\frac{d^2}{2} - \frac{3d}{2} + 2) \cdot \frac{k}{2} + \frac{(r - d^2)k}{2}})$.

With the $(d^2 - d + 1)$-round distinguisher in qCCA setting, by using the decryption oracle, we can recover the key of the r-round Type-1 GFS for $r > d^2 - d + 1$ in time $O(2^{\frac{(r - (d^2 - d + 1))k}{2}})$, because the subkey length that we need to recover is $(r - d^2 + d - 1)k$ bits.

If $d = 3$, the time complexity of these two key recovery attacks is the same because $(\frac{d^2}{2} - \frac{3d}{2} + 2) \cdot \frac{k}{2} + \frac{(r - d^2)k}{2} - \frac{(r - (d^2 - d + 1))k}{2} = \frac{k(d - 2)(d - 3)}{4}$. If $d > 3$, the key recovery attack with the $(d^2 - d + 1)$-round distinguisher is better than the one with the $(3d - 3)$-round distinguisher.

7   Quantum Attacks on Round-Reduced CAST-256 Block Cipher in qCPA Setting

CAST-256 block cipher [1] is a first-round AES candidate. It has 48 rounds, including 24 rounds Type-1 GFS and 24 rounds inverse Type-1 GFS. The block size is 128 bits, which are divided into four 32-bit branches and the key size can be 128, 192 or 256 bits. Each round function absorbs 37-bit subkey. Our attack is quite general and does not need any other details of the cipher.

In this section, we introduce a new 14-round quantum distinguisher in qCPA on CAST-256 shown in Fig. 8. The distinguisher, started from the 24th round, is composed of 1-round Type-1 GFS and 13-round inverse Type-1 GFS. It is derived based on the result presented in Sect. 5. When $d = 4$, $(d^2 - d + 1) = 13$ round distinguisher is obtained (from round R_{25} to R_{37} of CAST-256). Thanks to the special structure of CAST-256, we could add one more round R_{24} to the 13-round distinguisher for free. Hence, the 14-round distinguisher is derived.

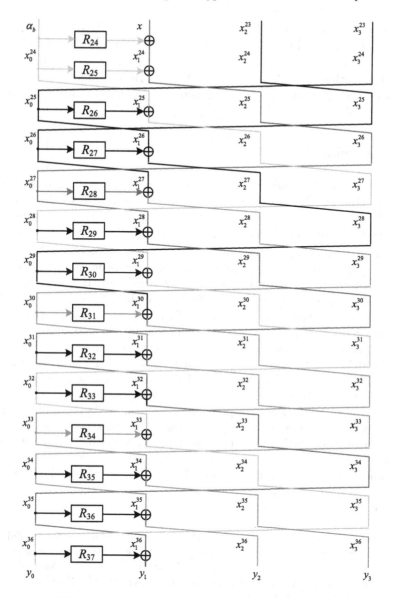

Fig. 8. 14-round distinguishing attack on CAST-256

We also fix two distinct constants α_0, α_1 and 2 constants x_2^{23}, x_3^{23}, which are all n bits. Given the 14-round CAST-256 encryption oracle $\mathcal{O}$, we define $f^{\mathcal{O}}$ as

$$f^{\mathcal{O}} : \{0,1\} \times \{0,1\}^n \to \{0,1\}^n$$
$$(b, x) \mapsto \alpha_b \oplus y_0 \, ,$$
$$\text{where } (y_0, y_1, y_2, y_3) = \mathcal{O}(\alpha_b, x, x_2^{23}, x_3^{23}) \, .$$

According to Lemma 2, $f^{\mathcal{O}}$ has the period $s = (1, R_{24}(\alpha_0) \oplus R_{25}(\alpha_0) \oplus R_{24}(\alpha_1) \oplus R_{25}(\alpha_1))$. As is shown in Sect. 6, we could add or append several rounds to attack $r > 14$ rounds CAST-256 in time $\mathcal{O}(2^{\frac{37(r-14)}{2}})$, because the subkey length that we need to recover is $37(r - 14)$ bits. Thus we could attack 20-round CAST-256 with 256-bit key in time 2^{111}, which is faster than Grover's algorithm by a factor of $2^{128-111} = 2^{17}$.

8   Conclusions

In this paper, we give some improved polynomial-time quantum distinguishers on Type-1 GFS in qCPA and qCCA settings. First, we give new qCPA quantum distinguishers on $(3d - 3)$-round Type-1 GFS with branches $d \geq 3$, which gain $(d - 2)$ more rounds than the previous distinguishers. Hence, we could get better key-recovery attacks, whose time complexities gain a factor of $2^{\frac{(d-2)n}{2}}$. We also obtain $(d^2 - d + 1)$-round qCCA quantum distinguishers on Type-1 GFS, which gain many more rounds than the previous distinguishers. In addition, we also discuss the quantum attack on CAST-256 block cipher.

As an open question, the tight bound of the number of rounds that we can distinguish is not known. There is a possibility that we can distinguish more than $(3d - 3)$ rounds in qCPA setting, and we may distinguish more than $(d^2 - d + 1)$ rounds in qCCA setting. Moreover, we may distinguish more than 14 rounds of CAST-256 when considering its special structure, which applies both Type-1 GFS and its inverse as the round functions. We anticipate the analysis with respect to the provable security approach in [18] can settle the problem, while this is beyond the scope of this paper. We also note that we do not know the impact of combining qCPA and qCCA as applied against 4-round Feistel block ciphers in [22].

Another open question is that, we could apply $(d^2 - d + 1)$-round qCCA quantum distinguishers to other block ciphers. Note that when the branch number is large, the distinguisher becomes very long.

Acknowledgments. The authors thank the anonymous reviewers for helpful comments. Boyu Ni and Xiaoyang Dong are supported by the National Key Research and Development Program of China (No. 2017YFA0303903), the National Natural Science Foundation of China (No. 61902207), the National Cryptography Development Fund (No. MMJJ20180101, MMJJ20170121).

References

1. Adams, C., Gilchrist, J.: The CAST-256 encryption algorithm. RFC 2612, June 1999
2. Anderson, R.J., Biham, E.: Two practical and provably secure block ciphers: BEAR and LION. In: Gollmann, D. (ed.) FSE 1996. LNCS, vol. 1039, pp. 113–120. Springer, Heidelberg (1996). https://doi.org/10.1007/3-540-60865-6_48

3. Aoki, K., et al.: *Camellia*: a 128-bit block cipher suitable for multiple platforms—design and analysis. In: Stinson, D.R., Tavares, S. (eds.) SAC 2000. LNCS, vol. 2012, pp. 39–56. Springer, Heidelberg (2001). https://doi.org/10.1007/3-540-44983-3_4

4. Bogdanov, A., Leander, G., Nyberg, K., Wang, M.: Integral and multidimensional linear distinguishers with correlation zero. In: Wang, X., Sako, K. (eds.) ASIACRYPT 2012. LNCS, vol. 7658, pp. 244–261. Springer, Heidelberg (2012). https://doi.org/10.1007/978-3-642-34961-4_16

5. Bonnetain, X.: Quantum key-recovery on full AEZ. In: Adams, C., Camenisch, J. (eds.) SAC 2017. LNCS, vol. 10719, pp. 394–406. Springer, Cham (2018). https://doi.org/10.1007/978-3-319-72565-9_20

6. Bonnetain, X., Naya-Plasencia, M., Schrottenloher, A.: On quantum slide attacks. Cryptology ePrint Archive, Report 2018/1067 (2018). https://eprint.iacr.org/2018/1067

7. Brassard, G., Hoyer, P., Mosca, M., Tapp, A.: Quantum amplitude amplification and estimation. Contemp. Math. **305**, 53–74 (2002)

8. Dinur, I., Dunkelman, O., Keller, N., Shamir, A.: New attacks on Feistel structures with improved memory complexities. In: Gennaro, R., Robshaw, M. (eds.) CRYPTO 2015. LNCS, vol. 9215, pp. 433–454. Springer, Heidelberg (2015). https://doi.org/10.1007/978-3-662-47989-6_21

9. Dong, X., Dong, B., Wang, X.: Quantum attacks on some Feistel block ciphers. Cryptology ePrint Archive, Report 2018/504 (2018). https://eprint.iacr.org/2018/504

10. Dong, X., Li, Z., Wang, X.: Quantum cryptanalysis on some generalized Feistel schemes. Sci. China Inf. Sci. **62**(2), 022501 (2019)

11. Dong, X., Wang, X.: Quantum key-recovery attack on Feistel structures. Sci. China Inf. Sci. **61**(10), 102501:1–102501:7 (2018)

12. National Soviet Bureau of Standards: Information processing system - cryptographic protection - cryptographic algorithm GOST 28147–89

13. Grover, L.K.: A fast quantum mechanical algorithm for database search. In: Proceedings of the Twenty-Eighth Annual ACM Symposium on the Theory of Computing, Philadelphia, Pennsylvania, USA, May 22–24, 1996, pp. 212–219 (1996)

14. Gueron, S., Mouha, N.: Simpira v2: a family of efficient permutations using the AES round function. In: Cheon, J.H., Takagi, T. (eds.) ASIACRYPT 2016. LNCS, vol. 10031, pp. 95–125. Springer, Heidelberg (2016). https://doi.org/10.1007/978-3-662-53887-6_4

15. Guo, J., Jean, J., Nikolić, I., Sasaki, Y.: Meet-in-the-middle attacks on generic Feistel constructions. In: Sarkar, P., Iwata, T. (eds.) ASIACRYPT 2014. LNCS, vol. 8873, pp. 458–477. Springer, Heidelberg (2014). https://doi.org/10.1007/978-3-662-45611-8_24

16. Guo, J., Jean, J., Nikolic, I., Sasaki, Y.: Meet-in-the-middle attacks on classes of contracting and expanding Feistel constructions. IACR Trans. Symmetric Cryptol. **2016**(2), 307–337 (2016)

17. Hoang, V.T., Rogaway, P.: On generalized Feistel networks. In: Rabin, T. (ed.) CRYPTO 2010. LNCS, vol. 6223, pp. 613–630. Springer, Heidelberg (2010). https://doi.org/10.1007/978-3-642-14623-7_33

18. Hosoyamada, A., Iwata, T.: 4-round Luby-Rackoff construction is a qPRP. In: Galbraith, S., Moriai, S. (eds.) ASIACRYPT 2019. LNCS, Springer, Cham (2019). To appear

19. Hosoyamada, A., Sasaki, Y.: Quantum Demiric-Selçuk meet-in-the-middle attacks: applications to 6-round generic Feistel constructions. In: Catalano, D., De Prisco, R. (eds.) SCN 2018. LNCS, vol. 11035, pp. 386–403. Springer, Cham (2018). https://doi.org/10.1007/978-3-319-98113-0_21

20. Isobe, T., Shibutani, K.: Generic key recovery attack on Feistel scheme. In: Sako, K., Sarkar, P. (eds.) ASIACRYPT 2013. LNCS, vol. 8269, pp. 464–485. Springer, Heidelberg (2013). https://doi.org/10.1007/978-3-642-42033-7_24

21. Ito, G., Hosoyamada, A., Matsumoto, R., Sasaki, Y., Iwata, T.: Quantum chosen-ciphertext attacks against Feistel ciphers. Cryptology ePrint Archive, Report 2018/1193 (2018). https://eprint.iacr.org/2018/1193

22. Ito, G., Hosoyamada, A., Matsumoto, R., Sasaki, Y., Iwata, T.: Quantum chosen-ciphertext attacks against Feistel ciphers. In: Matsui, M. (ed.) CT-RSA 2019. LNCS, vol. 11405, pp. 391–411. Springer, Cham (2019). https://doi.org/10.1007/978-3-030-12612-4_20

23. Jutla, C.S.: Generalized birthday attacks on unbalanced Feistel networks. In: Krawczyk, H. (ed.) CRYPTO 1998. LNCS, vol. 1462, pp. 186–199. Springer, Heidelberg (1998). https://doi.org/10.1007/BFb0055728

24. Kaplan, M., Leurent, G., Leverrier, A., Naya-Plasencia, M.: Breaking symmetric cryptosystems using quantum period finding. In: Robshaw, M., Katz, J. (eds.) CRYPTO 2016. LNCS, vol. 9815, pp. 207–237. Springer, Heidelberg (2016). https://doi.org/10.1007/978-3-662-53008-5_8

25. Kilian, J., Rogaway, P.: How to protect DES against exhaustive key search. In: Koblitz, N. (ed.) CRYPTO 1996. LNCS, vol. 1109, pp. 252–267. Springer, Heidelberg (1996). https://doi.org/10.1007/3-540-68697-5_20

26. Kilian, J., Rogaway, P.: How to protect DES against exhaustive key search (an analysis of DESX). J. Cryptol. **14**(1), 17–35 (2001)

27. Knudsen, L.R.: The security of Feistel ciphers with six rounds or less. J. Cryptol. **15**(3), 207–222 (2002)

28. Kuwakado, H., Morii, M.: Quantum distinguisher between the 3-round Feistel cipher and the random permutation. In: IEEE International Symposium on Information Theory, ISIT 2010, June 13–18, 2010, Austin, Texas, USA, Proceedings, pp. 2682–2685 (2010)

29. Kuwakado, H., Morii, M.: Security on the quantum-type Even-Mansour cipher. In: Proceedings of the International Symposium on Information Theory and its Applications, ISITA 2012, Honolulu, HI, USA, October 28–31, 2012, pp. 312–316 (2012)

30. Leander, G., May, A.: Grover meets Simon – quantumly attacking the FX-construction. In: Takagi, T., Peyrin, T. (eds.) ASIACRYPT 2017. LNCS, vol. 10625, pp. 161–178. Springer, Cham (2017). https://doi.org/10.1007/978-3-319-70697-9_6

31. Luby, M., Rackoff, C.: How to construct pseudorandom permutations from pseudorandom functions. SIAM J. Comput. **17**(2), 373–386 (1988)

32. Lucks, S.: Faster Luby-Rackoff ciphers. In: Gollmann, D. (ed.) FSE 1996. LNCS, vol. 1039, pp. 189–203. Springer, Heidelberg (1996). https://doi.org/10.1007/3-540-60865-6_53

33. Moriai, S., Vaudenay, S.: On the pseudorandomness of top-level schemes of block ciphers. In: Okamoto, T. (ed.) ASIACRYPT 2000. LNCS, vol. 1976, pp. 289–302. Springer, Heidelberg (2000). https://doi.org/10.1007/3-540-44448-3_22

34. Nachef, V., Volte, E., Patarin, J.: Differential attacks on generalized Feistel schemes. In: Abdalla, M., Nita-Rotaru, C., Dahab, R. (eds.) CANS 2013. LNCS, vol. 8257, pp. 1–19. Springer, Cham (2013). https://doi.org/10.1007/978-3-319-02937-5_1

35. Patarin, J., Nachef, V., Berbain, C.: Generic attacks on unbalanced Feistel schemes with contracting functions. In: Lai, X., Chen, K. (eds.) ASIACRYPT 2006. LNCS, vol. 4284, pp. 396–411. Springer, Heidelberg (2006). https://doi.org/10.1007/11935230_26

36. Patarin, J., Nachef, V., Berbain, C.: Generic attacks on unbalanced Feistel schemes with expanding functions. In: Kurosawa, K. (ed.) ASIACRYPT 2007. LNCS, vol. 4833, pp. 325–341. Springer, Heidelberg (2007). https://doi.org/10.1007/978-3-540-76900-2_20

37. Santoli, T., Schaffner, C.: Using Simon's algorithm to attack symmetric-key cryptographic primitives. Quantum Inf. Comput. 17(1&2), 65–78 (2017)

38. Schneier, B., Kelsey, J.: Unbalanced Feistel networks and block cipher design. In: Gollmann, D. (ed.) FSE 1996. LNCS, vol. 1039, pp. 121–144. Springer, Heidelberg (1996). https://doi.org/10.1007/3-540-60865-6_49

39. Shirai, T., Shibutani, K., Akishita, T., Moriai, S., Iwata, T.: The 128-bit blockcipher CLEFIA (extended abstract). In: Biryukov, A. (ed.) FSE 2007. LNCS, vol. 4593, pp. 181–195. Springer, Heidelberg (2007). https://doi.org/10.1007/978-3-540-74619-5_12

40. Simon, D.R.: On the power of quantum computation. SIAM J. Comput. 26(5), 1474–1483 (1997)

41. Tjuawinata, I., Huang, T., Wu, H.: Improved differential cryptanalysis on generalized Feistel schemes. In: Patra, A., Smart, N.P. (eds.) INDOCRYPT 2017. LNCS, vol. 10698, pp. 302–324. Springer, Cham (2017). https://doi.org/10.1007/978-3-319-71667-1_16

42. Volte, E., Nachef, V., Patarin, J.: Improved generic attacks on unbalanced Feistel schemes with expanding functions. In: Abe, M. (ed.) ASIACRYPT 2010. LNCS, vol. 6477, pp. 94–111. Springer, Heidelberg (2010). https://doi.org/10.1007/978-3-642-17373-8_6

43. Wagner, D.: The boomerang attack. In: Knudsen, L. (ed.) FSE 1999. LNCS, vol. 1636, pp. 156–170. Springer, Heidelberg (1999). https://doi.org/10.1007/3-540-48519-8_12

44. Wang, M., Wang, X., Hu, C.: New linear cryptanalytic results of reduced-round of CAST-128 and CAST-256. In: Avanzi, R.M., Keliher, L., Sica, F. (eds.) SAC 2008. LNCS, vol. 5381, pp. 429–441. Springer, Heidelberg (2009). https://doi.org/10.1007/978-3-642-04159-4_28

45. Zhandry, M.: How to construct quantum random functions. In: 53rd Annual IEEE Symposium on Foundations of Computer Science, FOCS 2012, New Brunswick, NJ, USA, October 20–23, 2012, pp. 679–687 (2012)

46. Zheng, Y., Matsumoto, T., Imai, H.: On the construction of block ciphers provably secure and not relying on any unproved hypotheses. In: Brassard, G. (ed.) CRYPTO 1989. LNCS, vol. 435, pp. 461–480. Springer, New York (1990). https://doi.org/10.1007/0-387-34805-0_42

Device Independent Quantum Key Distribution Using Three-Party Pseudo-Telepathy

Jyotirmoy Basak[1], Arpita Maitra[2], and Subhamoy Maitra[1(✉)]

[1] Applied Statistics Unit, Indian Statistical Institute,
203 B T Road, Kolkata 700108, India
bjyotirmoy.93@gmail.com, subho@isical.ac.in
[2] C R Rao Advanced Institute for Mathematics, Statistics and Computer Science,
Hyderabad 500046, India
arpita76b@gmail.com

Abstract. Removing trustworthiness from the devices is the motivation towards device independent quantum key distribution (DI-QKD). The only assumption in this case is that the devices obey the laws of quantum mechanics and are spatially isolated from each other. The security of the protocol can be achieved by certain tests based on various statistical analysis. Recently, Vidick and Vazirani (VV) proposed a DI-QKD scheme (Phys. Rev. Lett., 2014) exploiting the CHSH game. In a similar direction, here we present a simple proposal that exploits the idea of multi-party pseudo-telepathy game to certify device independent security. The relative advantages of our protocol are also discussed.

Keywords: Quantum Key Distribution (QKD) · Device Independence (DI) · Multi Party Pseudo Telepathy (MPPT)

1 Introduction

Since the very first protocol for Quantum Key Distribution (QKD) by Bennet and Brassard [6] a large number of variants and extensions are proposed till date. For a non-exhaustive list, one may refer to [4,7,8,11,13,14,17,19]. The security of all these protocols rely on the assumption that the legitimate parties, Alice and Bob, use single photon source or maximally entangled states. The assumption on single photon source is necessary for the security analysis of the Preparation and Measure protocols [6–8,13]. Further, the assumption that the legitimate parties need to share the maximally entangled states is essential for the security analysis of entanglement-based QKD protocols [11,14]. In this case the security is guaranteed from the property called monogamy of entanglement [15]. Removing such trustful assumptions is the motivation towards Device Independence (DI). In device independent protocols, it is assumed that the entangled states are available from the Third Party (TP) and thus they need to be tested to check

© Springer Nature Switzerland AG 2019
F. Hao et al. (Eds.): INDOCRYPT 2019, LNCS 11898, pp. 456–471, 2019.
https://doi.org/10.1007/978-3-030-35423-7_23

whether they are actually so. The black boxes are operated non-locally to certify the entanglement. Each box accepts certain inputs and produce outputs in each run of the testing procedure. After enough iterations, observing certain specific input-output statistics, one can certify whether the states shared between two legitimate parties are indeed maximally entangled along with the functionality of the measurement devices. In this direction various protocols [1–3,22] are proposed. In 2014, Vazirani and Vidick [25] published a DI-QKD protocol where they exploited the CHSH game [12] to certify the maximality of entanglement. In [16], the idea of multiparty games (such as magic square guessing game) have been considered in the context of parallel Device-Independent QKD.

In this initiative, instead of CHSH game, we exploit the multi-party pseudo-telepathy game [9,10] to certify the maximality of entanglement. We also perform a comparison between the VV [25] and our protocol to underline the advantages. We exploit this game to certify the device independent security of our protocol as well as to generate the raw key bits simultaneously.

1.1 Multi-party Pseudo Telepathy Game

Before proceeding further, let us briefly describe the Multi Party Pseudo Telepathy game [9,10]. For any n-party pseudo telepathy ($n \geq 3$), the game G_n consists of n players. The input bit string $x_1 \ldots x_n$ contains even number of 1's. Each player A_i receives a single input bit x_i and is requested to produce an output bit y_i. One may interpret it as $x_1 \ldots x_n$ is the question and $y_1 \ldots y_n$ is the answer. The game G_n will be won by this team of n players if $\sum_{i=1}^{n} y_i \equiv \frac{1}{2} \sum_{i=1}^{n} x_i \pmod 2$. Here, no communication is allowed among the n participants after receiving the inputs and before producing the outputs. It has been proved in [9] that no classical strategy for the game G_n can be successful with a probability better than $\frac{1}{2} + 2^{-\lceil n/2 \rceil}$. However, quantum entanglement serves to eliminate the classical need to communicate and it is shown that there exists a perfect quantum protocol where the n parties will always win the game. Let us define

$$|\Phi_n^+\rangle = \frac{1}{\sqrt{2}}|0^n\rangle + \frac{1}{\sqrt{2}}|1^n\rangle \text{ and } |\Phi_n^-\rangle = \frac{1}{\sqrt{2}}|0^n\rangle - \frac{1}{\sqrt{2}}|1^n\rangle.$$

While describing the quantum strategy in [9], they consider that H denotes Hadamard transform, and S the unitary transformation such that $S|0\rangle \mapsto |0\rangle$, $S|1\rangle \mapsto i|1\rangle$. They also consider that the players are allowed to share a prior entanglement, the state $|\Phi_n^+\rangle$. According to the strategy in [9], if $x_i = 1$, A_i applies transformation S to his qubit; otherwise he does nothing. He applies H to his qubit and then measures his qubit in $\{|0\rangle, |1\rangle\}$ basis in order to obtain y_i. He finally produces y_i as his output. It can be checked that the game G_n is always won by the n distributed parties without any communication among themselves. For our protocol, we will consider three-party pseudo telepathy game.

1.2 Contribution, Caveat and Organization

In this paper, we claim Device Independence (DI) Security with a very simple QKD protocol. We use lesser qubits than the Vidick-Vazirani [25] (VV-QKD) protocol. Instead of the CHSH game [12], we use Multi-Party Pseudo-Telepathy (MPPT) for checking DI. This happens with probability 1 (compared to 0.85 in CHSH). Several bases are considered in VV-QKD as it uses the CHSH game for checking the DI, but the key is generated in a different basis. In our approach, the MPPT game (as described in Sect. 1.1) itself is again used to derive the raw secret key and thus no additional basis is required. This is achieved by carefully considered logical operations. The complete protocol description is presented in Sect. 2. We have justified the security issues with certain results in Sect. 3.

While discussing the security of a protocol, there are two directions.

- We may devise certain schemes with algorithmic details as well as certain justifications towards security. Then we may wait for further cryptanalytic results. This mostly happens for the actual implementations in secure applications. Indeed, the cryptanalytic efforts continue and once certain weaknesses are identified, necessary counter-measures are taken or the scheme is dumped. For example, design of commercial stream or block ciphers successfully follow this path of research. This was the scenario when BB84 protocol [6] was first proposed as, at that time, the security claims were justified from certain laws of Physics only.
- The other direction is to provide schemes with complete security proofs. Here, a few basic assumptions are considered and based on that there are formal-looking security proofs. These are mostly popular in theoretical world, though there are serious implications to security applications too. However, several systems are arriving in market where security proofs are advertised. Unfortunately, even with the security proofs, in certain cases flaws are identified at a later date. A detailed "another look" towards the security proofs is available at [23]. In fact, larger the proofs, lesser is the confidence, as many of the long proofs require more serious attention. Further, many popular schemes do not appear with the formal security proofs, and later such proofs are presented for previously designed schemes. For example, after the publication of the BB84 protocol [6], in last three decades researchers have noted many important theoretical proofs justifying several security aspects of BB84 and its variants.

In this paper, we present our idea with certain theoretical justifications. We do not claim a complete security proof covering all the aspects of this protocol. However, so far we did not identify any cryptanalytic results on our scheme. We believe publication of this protocol will attract further cryptanalytic efforts or theorems to explain formal security results.

2 Protocol Description

In the proposed protocol, we assume Alice to possess the two black boxes denoted by D_1^A and D_2^A. Bob has the remaining one denoted by D_1^B. Each box can take an input $x \in \{0,1\}$ and can output $y \in \{0,1\}$. In each run $i \in \{1, \cdots, n\}$ of the protocol, Alice selects two random bits $x_1, x_2 \in \{0,1\}$ as input to her devices D_1^A and D_2^A respectively. Bob selects a random bit $x_3 \in \{0,1\}$ as input to his device D_1^B. Just like other device independent protocols, our assumption here is that the devices obey the laws of quantum mechanics and they are specially isolated from each other and from any adversary.

At the beginning of the protocol, we consider Alice and Bob share n many GHZ states $\frac{1}{\sqrt{2}}(|000\rangle + |111\rangle)$ that are supplied by some TP. The first two particles of each GHZ state are retained by Alice and the remaining one is sent to Bob through a public quantum channel where Eve have an access. Alice and Bob randomly choose the inputs for their respective devices. In this phase they do not communicate among themselves. After getting the inputs, they perform respective operations based upon their input choices as mentioned in the multi-party pseudo-telepathy game [9]. After the corresponding operation, if the measurement result is $|0\rangle$, they output 0, and 1 otherwise.

Table 1. Strategy for key generation

Input		Possible output		Operation		Extracted key	
Alice (x_1x_2)	Bob (x_3)	Alice (y_1y_2)	Bob (y_3)	Alice $(x_1 \vee x_2) \oplus y_1 \oplus y_2$	Bob (y_3)	Alice	Bob
00	0	00	0	$(0 \vee 0) \oplus 0 \oplus 0 = 0$	0	0	0
		11	0	$(0 \vee 0) \oplus 1 \oplus 1 = 0$	0	0	0
		01	1	$(0 \vee 0) \oplus 0 \oplus 1 = 1$	1	1	1
		10	1	$(0 \vee 0) \oplus 1 \oplus 0 = 1$	1	1	1
11	0	10	0	$(1 \vee 1) \oplus 1 \oplus 0 = 0$	0	0	0
		01	0	$(1 \vee 1) \oplus 0 \oplus 1 = 0$	0	0	0
		00	1	$(1 \vee 1) \oplus 0 \oplus 0 = 1$	1	1	1
		11	1	$(1 \vee 1) \oplus 1 \oplus 1 = 1$	1	1	1
01	1	10	0	$(0 \vee 1) \oplus 1 \oplus 0 = 0$	0	0	0
		01	0	$(0 \vee 1) \oplus 0 \oplus 1 = 0$	0	0	0
		00	1	$(0 \vee 1) \oplus 0 \oplus 0 = 1$	1	1	1
		11	1	$(0 \vee 1) \oplus 1 \oplus 1 = 1$	1	1	1
10	1	10	0	$(1 \vee 0) \oplus 1 \oplus 0 = 0$	0	0	0
		01	0	$(1 \vee 0) \oplus 0 \oplus 1 = 0$	0	0	0
		00	1	$(1 \vee 0) \oplus 0 \oplus 0 = 1$	1	1	1
		11	1	$(1 \vee 0) \oplus 1 \oplus 1 = 1$	1	1	1

After the measurement, Alice and Bob will discuss their respective input choices publicly and discard all the cases where the number of 1's in the input string is odd. They have to discard an expected $\frac{n}{2}$ number of inputs. Let the remaining set be $\mathcal{A}$. Alice chooses a random subset of size $\gamma|\mathcal{A}|$ and shares it publicly with Bob, where $0 < \gamma < 1$. They publicly discuss the inputs and the corresponding outputs for the states in $\gamma|\mathcal{A}|$ and check what fraction of these inputs satisfy the multi-party pseudo telepathy (parity) condition. If the success probability is less than $1 - \eta$ (where η is the amount of tolerable noise), then they abort the protocol. Otherwise, they proceed further and generate shared secret key from the rest $(1 - \gamma)|\mathcal{A}|$ states. Conditional on the event that the measurement data has passed the pseudo-telepathy phase successfully, Alice and Bob proceed for key generation.

Algorithm 1. Proposed DI-QKD protocol

---

1. Inputs: $n = $ total number of samples (GHZ states) provided by the third party, $\eta = $ noise tolerance
2. For rounds $i \in \{1, \cdots, n\}$, Alice picks $x_1, x_2 \in \{0, 1\}$, and Bob picks $x_3 \in \{0, 1\}$, uniformly at random. They input x_1, x_2, x_3 into their respective devices and obtain output $y_1, y_2, y_3 \in \{0, 1\}$ respectively. According to the strategy in [9], if $x_i = 1$, the transformation S is applied on the qubit; otherwise nothing is done. Then H is applied on this qubit and the qubit is measured in $\{|0\rangle, |1\rangle\}$ basis in order to obtain y_i.
3. They discuss about their inputs publicly for each of the n cases and discard all those cases where the number of 1's in the input bit string is odd. Let the set $\mathcal{A}$ contains all those cases which are not discarded.
4. **Testing:** Alice chooses a random subset $\mathcal{B} \subseteq \mathcal{A}$ of size $\gamma|\mathcal{A}|$ where $0 < \gamma < 1$. Alice then shares the identity of each element in the set publicly with Bob. They discuss the inputs and the corresponding outputs publicly and compute the fraction of inputs in $\mathcal{B}$ that satisfy the parity condition $\sum_{i=1}^{3} y_i \equiv \frac{1}{2} \sum_{i=1}^{3} x_i \pmod 2$. If this fraction is smaller than $(1 - \eta)$, they abort the protocol.
5. **Extraction:** For the rest of the states (i.e., for the states in $\mathcal{A} \setminus \mathcal{B}$), Alice computes $(x_1 \vee x_2) \oplus y_1 \oplus y_2$. They perform error correction followed by privacy amplification to finalize the secret key.

Alice performs the operation $(x_1 \vee x_2) \oplus y_1 \oplus y_2$ in her side and generate a single output bit for each run of the remaining set. From the Table 1, it is clear that for each possible values of input-output pairs, the classical bit generated at Alice's end will be exactly same as the classical bit produced as a output (y_3) by Bob's device. They now proceed for error correction and perform information reconciliation followed by privacy amplification to generate the shared secret key. The proposed protocol is described in Algorithm 1.

2.1   Bitwise Advantage over the VV Protocol

In the QKD protocol [25], Alice and Bob perform n successive steps with their respective devices. At each step, Alice privately chooses a random input x_i from $\{0, 1, 2\}$ and Bob privately chooses a random input $y_i \in \{0, 1\}$ for their devices. They share the Bell state $|\Phi^+\rangle = \frac{1}{\sqrt{2}}[|00\rangle + |11\rangle]$ apriori and measure their qubits according to the values of x_i and y_i.

After n steps are completed, Alice and Bob publicly announce their inputs (x_i, y_i) and outputs (a_i, b_i) corresponding to a subset B of size γn for some $\gamma \in (0, 1)$. From this, they compute the fraction of inputs that satisfies the CHSH condition. If this is not within a threshold, the protocol is aborted. Otherwise, they continue to announce their remaining input choices. Let C be the subset of the n steps for which $x_i = 2$ and $y_i = 1$. They further discuss the output for the set $B \cap C$ and check what fraction of this outputs are equal. If this value also lies within a certain range, they proceed for the remaining set of states and generate the key. Note that the case $(x_i, y_i) = (2, 0)$ is not considered in the protocol. When Alice and Bob announce the values of (x_i, y_i), they throw away the results corresponding to $(2, 0)$.

According to the VV protocol, the key is generated for the input tuple $(2, 1)$. That is, for the key generation part, expected $\frac{1}{6}$-th portion of the n entangled states are valid (as Alice and Bob choose inputs uniformly at random). The tuple $(0, 0), (0, 1), (1, 0), (1, 1)$ are exploited to check the error (i.e., to check the CHSH condition) and for the tuple $(2, 0)$ the states are thrown away.

Let us assume that the VV protocol starts with n_1 number of entangled states and uses $\gamma_1 n_1$ $(0 < \gamma_1 < 1)$ number of states for CHSH testing. Consider that our protocol starts with n_2 number of entangled states and uses γ_2 $(0 < \gamma_2 < 1)$ fractions of the remaining states (i.e., the states for which the input choices are valid with respect to the pseudo-telepathy game) for DI testing. To validate the performance comparison of our protocol with VV protocol [25], we have to consider that both the protocol starts with same number of initial states and let this number be n (i.e., $n_1 = n_2 = n$). Then, for VV protocol, $\gamma_1 n$ number of states will be used for error checking purpose and raw key bits will be generated from the rest $(n - \gamma_1 n)$ of the states. For our protocol, first $\frac{n}{2}$ number of states will be discarded for invalid input choice and from the remaining $\frac{n}{2}$ states, $\gamma_2 \frac{n}{2}$ number of states will be used for error checking purpose and rest $(\frac{n}{2} - \gamma_2 \frac{n}{2})$ states will be used for key generation.

In case of VV protocol, as the inputs are chosen randomly, only $\frac{1}{6}$th portion of the remaining $(n - \gamma_1 n)$ number of states will generate the raw key bits. So, the length of the initial key (before privacy amplification and information reconciliation phase) generated by VV protocol from n number of states will be $\frac{1}{6} \times (n - \gamma_1 n) = \frac{(n - \gamma_1 n)}{6}$.

In case of our protocol, all the valid input choices will generate key bits. So, for our protocol, all the remaining $(\frac{n}{2} - \gamma_2 \frac{n}{2})$ states will generate the raw key bits. This implies that the length of the raw key generated by our protocol from n number of states will be equal to $\frac{1}{2}(n - \gamma_2 n)$. Now, if we consider that the chosen value of γ_1 and γ_2 are same for both the protocol and consider this value as γ, then it is clear from the above expressions that the length of the generated raw key for our protocol will be 3 times more as compared to the VV protocol.

Since we are using three qubit entangled states (GHZ) in comparison to two-qubit entangled states in VV protocol, in terms of exact number of particles, our protocol provides a $3 \times \frac{2}{3} = 2$ fold advantage.

3   Security of the Proposed Scheme

Towards establishing the security of our protocol, we will enumerate some assumptions and define some security notions below. Our security claims depend on the following assumptions.

1. Devices follow the laws of quantum mechanics and they are causally independent, i.e., each use of a devices is independent of the previous use and they behave the same in all trials. This also implies that the devices are memoryless.
2. Alice and Bob's laboratories are perfectly secured, i.e., no information is leaked from their laboratories.

First we need to clarify one issue regarding the MPPT protocol modified for two parties. Note that if two bits are with one party (here Alice) and one bit is with another party (here Bob), then they can always win the game. The strategy is that if Alice receives 00, 01 or 10, then she will output 00 and if she receives 11, then she will produce 01. On the other hand Bob will produce what he receives, i.e., if he receives 0, he will produce 0 and if he receives 1, he will produce 1. Thus in this case, there is a classical strategy, where without any entanglement, Alice and Bob can win the game with probability 1. This happens as the inputs are from the set $\{000, 011, 101, 110\}$ only, where the first two bits go to Alice and the third to Bob. Note that when the input string is of Hamming weight 0 mod 4 (bit string 000), then the output is also 000 (Hamming weight even). When the input string is of Hamming weight 2 mod 4 (bit strings 011, 101, or 110), then the outputs are 001, 001 and 010 respectively (Hamming weight odd).

However, this is not the case for the Three Party Pseudo Telepathy game, where the three parties are separated and the success probability in the classical case is bounded by 0.75. However, the motivation for the QKD scheme is to check whether

- the supplied states from the third party are indeed $\frac{1}{\sqrt{2}}(|000\rangle + |111\rangle)$, and
- the quantum devices from the third party honestly execute the following steps
  - to apply the S gate on the input particle if the classical input is 1, else it does nothing,
  - to apply the H gate on the particle generated,
  - to measure in $\{|0\rangle, |1\rangle\}$ basis.

Since Alice, by herself, will only consider procuring two separate devices for each of the two particles she possesses in each GHZ state, and there is in no way Alice and Bob will try to cheat each other, the quantum supremacy over the classical experiments will not suffer. That is though Alice will have two particles at her disposal, she will use them separately. There should not be any classical communication between the two devices used by Alice. The quantum devices from the third party will be procured as independent items for the requirements mentioned above and not considering that Alice will handle two particles together on her own.

Definition 1. *Given a security parameter $\epsilon \geq 0$, a key distribution protocol between Alice and Bob is said to be ϵ-correct iff Alice and Bob both agree on a m-bit key $K \in \{0,1\}^m$, except with some failure probability at most ϵ. That is, both Alice and Bob achieve the keystreams K_A, K_B respectively such that $\Pr(K_A \neq K_B) \leq \epsilon$.*

We now show the correctness of our protocol.

Theorem 1. *The proposed QKD scheme is ϵ-correct, where $\epsilon = \left[1 - (1 - \eta)^l\right]$. Here, l denotes the length of the entire raw key and η is the tolerable noise parameter.*

Proof. In our QKD scheme, Alice and Bob share n copies of GHZ states in such a way so that the first two particles of each state belong to Alice and the third one belongs to Bob. Alice picks $x_1, x_2 \in \{0,1\}$, and Bob picks $x_3 \in \{0,1\}$, uniformly at random. They input $x_1, x_2, x_3 \in \{0,1\}$ into their respective devices and obtain output $y_1, y_2, y_3 \in \{0,1\}$ respectively. They discuss about their inputs publicly for each of the n cases and discard all those cases where the number of 1's in the input bit string is odd. Let the set $\mathcal{A}$ contains all those cases which are not discarded. Alice chooses a random subset $\mathcal{B} \subseteq \mathcal{A}$ of size $\gamma|\mathcal{A}|$ where $0 < \gamma < 1$. Alice then shares the identity of each element in the set publicly with Bob. They discuss the inputs and the corresponding outputs publicly and compute the fraction of inputs in $\mathcal{B}$ that satisfy the parity condition $\sum_{i=1}^{3} y_i \equiv \frac{1}{2} \sum_{i=1}^{3} x_i$ (mod 2). If this fraction is smaller than $(1 - \eta)$, they abort the protocol.

For the rest of the states (i.e., for the states in $\mathcal{A} \setminus \mathcal{B}$), Alice computes $(x_1 \vee x_2) \oplus y_1 \oplus y_2$. They perform error correction followed by privacy amplification to finalize the secret key.

Hence, in the i-th instance of our QKD scheme, the raw key bit at Alice's side will be $R_{A_i} = (x_1 \vee x_2) \oplus y_1 \oplus y_2$ and the raw key bit at Bob's side will be $R_{B_i} = y_3$. From Table 1, it is clear that irrespective of inputs and outputs, whenever Alice and Bob win the pseudo telepathy game with probability 1, the raw key bit generated in each instance at Alice's and Bob's side will be equal i.e., $\Pr(R_{A_i} = R_{B_i}) = 1$.

Now, this situation occurs in noiseless condition when the communication channel is absolutely noiseless and the devices involved in the protocol are absolutely perfect. However, in reality, the channel as well as the devices are inherently erroneous. Moreover, the presence of adversary (if any) will be reflected in the measurement result by the law of physics. As η proportion of deviation is allowed in the testing phase of our scheme, each raw key bit of Alice and Bob will mismatch with probability atmost η, i.e., for the i-th raw key bit of Alice (R_{A_i}) and Bob (R_{B_i}), $\Pr(R_{A_i} \neq R_{B_i}) \leq \eta$. This implies that each raw key bit of Alice and Bob will match with probability atleast $(1 - \eta)$. So, if Alice and Bob share an l bit raw key in this scheme, then the entire raw key of Alice (R_A) will match with the entire raw of Bob (R_B) with probability atleast $(1 - \eta)^l$, i.e., $\Pr(R_A = R_B) \geq (1 - \eta)^l$. This implies that, $\Pr(R_A \neq R_B) \leq 1 - (1 - \eta)^l$. Let $\epsilon = \left[1 - (1 - \eta)^l\right]$. Hence, the proposed scheme is ϵ-correct. $\qquad\square$

Next, we try to establish the security of our protocol. The security of the entire protocol relies on two phases, the security of DI testing phase and the security of QKD phase.

In an entanglement based quantum cryptographic scheme, the most common attack strategy is through correlation where the adversary Eve creates a correlated system (entangled state) and shares some particles of this correlated system with the parties so that Eve can get some information about the measurement (done by the parties) and corresponding measurement outcome. This attack strategy will also work for the proposed QKD scheme where Eve can create an m particle GHZ state and distribute any three out of m entangled qubits between Alice and Bob. Without loss of generality, we assume that the first three particles are distributed among Alice and Bob and the remaining $m - 3$ particles are retained by Eve. Eve then plays the game together with Alice and Bob, but remains silent when both the inputs and the measurement results are announced publicly. That is, instead of GHZ states (3 qubit), the TP distributes the 3 particles of an m-qubit GHZ state that will be used in our protocol. After adopting this strategy, if the success probability p still lies in the range $[1 - \eta, 1]$, then the protocol will no longer be device independent.

Theorem 2. *If an m-party pseudo-telepathy game is played among m players and any t out of these players broadcast their inputs and the corresponding outputs, then for these t players, the outcome will be successful with probability $\frac{1}{2}$.*

Proof. Let us consider m-particle GHZ states $|\phi_m^+\rangle = \frac{1}{\sqrt{2}}(|0^m\rangle + |1^m\rangle)$. In terms of density matrix it becomes $\rho = \frac{1}{2}(|0^m\rangle + |1^m\rangle)(\langle 0^m| + \langle 1^m|)$. We can write it as

$$\rho = \frac{1}{2}(|0^t\rangle |0^{m-t}\rangle + |1^t\rangle |1^{m-t}\rangle)(\langle 0^t| \langle 0^{m-t}| + \langle 1^t| \langle 1^{m-t}|) = \rho_{ABE},$$

where t particles are possessed by system A and system B and remaining $m - t$ particles are possessed by system E. In case of t out of m-party pseudo-telepathy game, the game can be viewed as a t-party pseudo-telepathy game played on the subsystem AB. Taking the trace on system E, we get the reduced density matrix for the sub-system AB as

$$\rho_{AB} = tr_E(\rho_{ABE}) = \frac{1}{2}(|0^t\rangle \langle 0^t| + |1^t\rangle \langle 1^t|) = \frac{I}{2}.$$

This is a mixed state since $tr((\frac{I}{2})^2) = \frac{1}{2} < 1$. Thus, the problem now boils down to the game played by t parties by sharing a mixed state instead of a maximally entangled state.

Let us proceed by choosing a valid input string. Let there be j number of 1's in the input string, such that $j \equiv 0 \mod 2$. Then the S operation (as mentioned in the quantum strategy of pseudo telepathy game [9]) will be applied for j parties and consequently we obtain

$$\rho'_{AB} = \frac{1}{2}(|0^t\rangle \langle 0^t| + |1^t\rangle \langle 1^t|).$$

Now, after $H^{\otimes t}$ operation on ρ'_{AB} we get,

$$\rho^1_{AB} = \frac{1}{2}\frac{1}{2^t}\Big(\sum_{k=0}^{2^t-1}\sum_{l=0}^{2^t-1}|k\rangle\langle l| + (-1)^{f(x)}\sum_{k=0}^{2^t-1}\sum_{l=0}^{2^t-1}|k\rangle\langle l|\Big),$$

where $|x\rangle = |k\rangle \otimes |l\rangle = |kl\rangle$ and

$$f(x) = \begin{cases} 0 & \text{if wt}(x) \equiv 0 \mod 2; \\ 1 & \text{if wt}(x) \equiv 1 \mod 2. \end{cases}$$

When one measures the above state, i.e., ρ^1_{AB} in computational basis, i.e., in $\{|0\rangle, |1\rangle\}^t$ basis, we get non zero probability if and only if $k = l$. There are 2^t possibilities when $k = l$. That means for any valid input string, the output string may take any value from the 2^t exhaustive possibilities. Out of these, the participating t parties will be successful in half of the cases. Hence, the success probability of the game reduces to $\frac{1}{2}$. □

Moreover, instead of GHZ state, if the third party (adversary) provides some non maximally entangled states of the form $\cos\theta|000\rangle + \sin\theta|111\rangle$, then the corresponding success probability of the multi-party pseudo telepathy game will be $\frac{1}{2}(1+\sin 2\theta)$ which becomes maximum (i.e., 1) for GHZ states (i.e., when $\theta = \frac{\pi}{4}$). Hence, observing the success probability of the pseudo telepathy game one can certify if the states are perfectly GHZ state. If the states are perfectly GHZ state, then from the monogamy relation of maximally entangled state [24], one can certify that Eve can never be correlated with Alice or Bob's sub-systems. One may refer to [5, 20] towards more detailed analysis related of device independence security in multipartite systems.

Our next effort is to analyze the security of QKD phase. In case of a classical cryptographic primitive, the security is defined in the context of random systems [21] by measuring its distance from the ideal (random) system which is secure by definition. In the case of classical key distribution scheme, the ideal system is the one that produces a uniform and random key at one end and for which all the interfaces are completely independent of its previous interfaces. This key is secure by construction as each string from the set of all possible key strings are equally likely and adversary has to guess randomly from the set of possible keys. If the real system generating a key is indistinguishable from this ideal one, then this key is assumed to be secure.

However, in the quantum setting, the adversary may create a correlated system to get some information about the measurement and corresponding key bits shared by the parties. But Eve will not get any information if her system (state) is uncorrelated with the system (state) shared by the parties. So, in this setting, if the system of Eve is uncorrelated with the system of the parties and the system shared by the parties seems maximally mixed state to Eve then the overall system is assumed to be secure.

Definition 2. *A QKD protocol is said to be ϵ-secure if an adversary Eve is almost ignorant about the key i.e., if ρ_{KE}^{real} denotes the real system of Eve and ρ_{KE}^{ideal} denotes the ideal system of Eve then $\rho_{KE}^{real} \approx_\epsilon \rho_{KE}^{ideal}$ where $\rho_{KE}^{ideal} = \frac{\mathcal{I}_k}{2^m} \otimes \rho_E$.*

Let us assume that ρ_{ABE} denotes the joint system shared by Alice, Bob and Eve and ρ_E denotes the marginal state on the system of the adversary. Now, to show that the proposed QKD scheme is secure, we have to show that the trace distance $\frac{1}{2}\|\rho_{ABE} - \frac{\mathcal{I}_k}{2^m} \otimes \rho_E\|$ is negligible. According to the definition, if it can be shown that $\frac{1}{2}\|\rho_{ABE} - \frac{\mathcal{I}_k}{2^m} \otimes \rho_E\| \leq \epsilon$, then the proposed scheme will be ϵ-secure.

Now refer to Theorem 2. If Eve creates any correlation with Alice and Bob's system, she will be identified in pseudo telepathy phase. Conditioning on the event that pseudo telepathy game is successful with probability 1, Alice and Bob share maximally entangled (here, GHZ state) state. From the monogamy relation of maximally entangled state [24], one can certify that Eve can never be correlated with Alice or Bob's sub-systems. In other words, the testing phase of the protocol actually certifies that Eve's system has no (or almost negligible) correlation with Alice's and Bob's system and the states shared by Alice and Bob are (close to) the GHZ states. So, the success in testing phase implies that Eve gets no information about the measurements and corresponding outcomes. This implies that Eve has to guess the outcomes and corresponding raw key bits for each instances. How easily Eve can guess the raw key bits will depend on the closeness of the generated key with a random bit string of equal length. Sometimes, this closeness measure is also termed as distinguishability, i.e., how well one can distinguish a real system from an ideal system. The measurement of this closeness can be done either in terms of statistical distance or by introducing a *distinguisher* $\mathcal{D}$ which will distinguish between the real system $(\mathcal{S}')$ and the ideal system $(\mathcal{S}')$.

In the distinguisher setting, the distinguisher $\mathcal{D}$ has to guess whether it has interacted with system $\mathcal{S}$ or $\mathcal{S}'$. The distinguishing advantage between system $\mathcal{S}$ and $\mathcal{S}'$ will be the maximum guessing probability that Eve can have in this game.

The distinguishing advantage between the systems $\mathcal{S}$ and $\mathcal{S}'$ can be defined by the expression,

$$\delta(\mathcal{S}, \mathcal{S}') = \max_{\mathcal{D}}[\Pr(E|\mathcal{S}) - \Pr(E|\mathcal{S}')],$$

where E is a distinguishing event and $\Pr(E|\mathcal{S})(\Pr(E|\mathcal{S}'))$ signifies the probability that the event E is satisfied given the distinguisher is interacting with system $\mathcal{S}$ $(\mathcal{S}')$.

As an alternative approach, this closeness measure can also be done in terms of statistical distance which can be defined as follows. Let X_0 and X_1 be two random variables over a finite set $\mathcal{C}$. Then the statistical distance $\Delta(X_0, X_1)$ is defined as:

$$\Delta(X_0, X_1) = \frac{1}{2} \sum_{x \in \mathcal{C}} |\Pr[X_0 = x] - \Pr[X_1 = x]|.$$

Based on this notions of closeness measure, the following theorem can be concluded which shows the security of the generated raw key.

Theorem 3. *Each raw key bit generated in our protocol (Algorithm 1) is atmost η-distinguishable from a random bit where η is the tolerable noise parameter for the protocol.*

Proof. We formulate this proof in terms of the distinguishing advantage. For our quantum key distribution scheme, two parties choose three classical bits as input where the inputs must belong to the set $\{000, 011, 101, 110\}$ (even weight) and from the output bits, each party produce a single bit which is considered as a raw key bit. So, in this setting, each of the real system ($\mathcal{S}'$) and the ideal system ($\mathcal{S}$) will receive three classical bits as input and produce one classical bit as output.

So, there are two possible distinguishing event based on the output. The first one denotes the event where the system will generate 0 as output bit for the set of valid inputs (this event is expressed by E_0) and the second one denotes the event where the system will generate 1 as output bit for the set of valid inputs (this event is expressed by E_1).

Now, from Table 1, it is evident that for our key generation system ($\mathcal{S}'$), irrespective of the input (where the input must be from the set $\{000, 011, 101, 110\}$), the system will output 0 in two out of four times and will output 1 in two out of four times.

In the testing phase, atmost η proportion of deviation is allowed, i.e., Alice and Bob will pass the testing phase if the pseudo telepathy game violates the winning condition in atmost η proportion. Now, for the instances where the pseudo telepathy game violates the winning condition, Alice and Bob will get different key bits. So, in the worst case, atmost η proportion of bits get flipped from the original one (i.e., the key bits may flip from 0 to 1 or vice versa for atmost η proportion of instances). On the other hand, the ideal system will always produce 0 and 1 as output with equal probability irrespective of the input.

Thus, for event E_0, the distinguishing advantage between the two system $\mathcal{S}$ and $\mathcal{S}'$ will be, $\Pr(E_0 = 1|\mathcal{S}) - \Pr(E_0 = 1|\mathcal{S}') = \frac{1}{2} - (\frac{2}{4} - \eta) = \eta$.

Similarly, for event E_1, the distinguishing advantage between this two system $\mathcal{S}$ and $\mathcal{S}'$ will be, $\Pr(E_1 = 1|\mathcal{S}) - \Pr(E_1 = 1|\mathcal{S}') = \frac{1}{2} - (\frac{2}{4} - \eta) = \eta$.

Therefore, the maximum distinguishing advantage that can be achieved by the distinguisher for each event will be equal to η. Hence, according to the definition, the overall distinguishing advantage between this two systems $\mathcal{S}$ and $\mathcal{S}'$ will be $\delta(\mathcal{S}, \mathcal{S}') = \eta$.

Alternatively, while performing this closeness measure in terms of statistical distance, we assume that the random variable $X_{\mathcal{S}}$ denotes the outcome of the ideal system ($\mathcal{S}$) and the random variable $X_{\mathcal{S}'}$ denotes the outcome of the real system ($\mathcal{S}'$). The two random variables are defined over the set $\mathcal{C}' = \{0, 1\}$. The statistical distance between these two random variables $X_{\mathcal{S}}$ and $X_{\mathcal{S}'}$ will be,

$$\frac{1}{2} \sum_{x \in \mathcal{C}'} |\Pr(X_S = x) - \Pr(X_{S'} = x)|$$

$$= \frac{1}{2} |\Pr(X_S = 0) - \Pr(X_{S'} = 0)| + \frac{1}{2} |\Pr(X_S = 1) - \Pr(X_{S'} = 1)|$$

$$= \frac{1}{2} \left(\left| \frac{1}{2} - \left(\frac{2}{4} - \eta \right) \right| + \left| \frac{1}{2} - \left(\frac{2}{4} - \eta \right) \right| \right) = \eta$$

From this calculation, it is evident that the statistical distance $\Delta(X_S, X_{S'}) = \eta$. Now, if we consider any distinguisher Algorithm $\mathcal{A}$ that distinguishes between these two random variables and $Adv_{\mathcal{A}}(X_S, X_{S'})$ denotes the advantage of $\mathcal{A}$ in distinguishing X_S and $X_{S'}$, then it can be shown that $Adv_{\mathcal{A}}(X_S, X_{S'}) \leq \Delta(X_S, X_{S'})$. As the statistical distance $\Delta(X_S, X_{S'}) = \eta$, the distinguishing advantage $Adv_{\mathcal{A}}(X_S, X_{S'})$ will be less than or equals to η.   □

This implies that it is not possible to distinguish a key bit generated in our protocol from a random bit with probability more than η. So, each raw key bit generated in our protocol is η-distinguishable. Our system works identically with the ideal system when $\eta = 0$, i.e., when the channel is completely noiseless and no error is incorporated by the adversary. To summarize, the raw key generated in our protocol is almost random as the value of η is very small in practice.

Lemma 1. *In the proposed scheme, the adversary Eve (E) will guess the shared raw key (of Alice) R_A with conditional min entropy $\mathrm{H}_{\min}(R_A|E) \geq l \log(\frac{2}{1+2\eta})$ where η is the tolerable noise parameter.*

Proof. From the result of Theorem 2, it is clear that if Eve has strong correlation with the system shared between Alice and Bob then it will be detected in the testing phase and Alice and Bob will abort the protocol. So, the successful completion of testing phase implies that Eve has no (or negligible) correlation with the system shared between Alice and Bob.

Similarly, from the result of Theorem 3, it is also clear that the raw key bits generated in our protocol is almost η distinguishable from the random one. So, Eve can guess each raw key bit with probability almost $(\frac{1}{2} + \eta)$ i.e., $\Pr_{\mathrm{guess}}(R_{A_i}|E_i) \leq \frac{1}{2} + \eta$ where R_{A_i} denotes i-th raw key bit at Alice's side and E_i denotes Eve's subsystem corresponding to i-th shared state.

From the operational interpretation of min-entropy [18], we can rewrite the guessing probability as $\Pr_{\mathrm{guess}}(R_{A_i}|E_i) = 2^{-\mathrm{H}_{\min}(R_{A_i}|E_i)}$. This implies that the conditional min-entropy of each raw key bit R_{A_i} is $\mathrm{H}_{\min}(R_{A_i}|E_i) \geq -\log(\frac{1}{2} + \eta)$.

In this scheme, the outcome of pseudo telepathy game in each instance is independent of the previous instances. So, all the raw key bits R_{A_i} are independent. If l denotes the length of the entire raw key then from the additive property of the conditional min-entropy we have,

$$\mathrm{H}_{\min}(R_A|E) = \sum_{i=1}^{l} \mathrm{H}_{\min}(R_{A_i}|E_i) \geq -l \log\left(\frac{1}{2} + \eta \right) = l \log\left(\frac{2}{1 + 2\eta} \right).$$

□

After the extraction phase of the protocol, each of Alice and Bob will have a raw key (R_A and R_B respectively) of length l. Due to channel noise, Bob's raw key might not be exactly same with Alice's raw key. So, Alice and Bob then perform information reconciliation where Alice sends the syndrome (which is generated by multiplying the raw key with a parity check matrix) of her raw key to Bob through an authenticated classical channel so that Bob can detect the error in his key and generate an estimate of Alice's key (say $\hat{R}_A$).

Alice and Bob then perform privacy amplification to further reduce the correlation of Eve's system (with the shared system of Alice and Bob) and also to reduce Eve's information about the shared key. Alice then generates a (small length) random seed y and share this to Bob through the classical channel. They input their raw key and the seed to a strong seeded randomness extractor and consider the output as the final key. As after the error correction phase, Alice and Bob have the same key, the final output of their extractor function will be equal i.e., $Ext(R_A, y) = Ext(\hat{R}_A, y)$.

From the proof of Lemma 1, it is clear that Eve can guess each raw key bit correctly with probability atmost $\left(\frac{1}{2} + \eta\right)$. So, Eve can guess the entire l bit raw key correctly with probability atmost $\left(\frac{1}{2} + \eta\right)^l$.

This guessing probability is very small and close to the random guess. As Eve can not guess the entire raw key with certainty, whenever she applies her guessed key to the extractor function, she comes up with a different key. So, Eve can not get any information about the final key and Alice and Bob can securely share a key between them.

4   Conclusion

In the present effort, we propose a simple device independent quantum key distribution protocol exploiting the multi (three)-party pseudo-telepathy game. The simplicity of the protocol relies on the fact that it does not require different measurement bases and one simple test is sufficient for both the device independence checking as well as the security of the generated key bits. The security of the protocol is guaranteed from the estimation of the success probability of the multi-party pseudo-telepathy game. Conditional on the event that the game is successful with probability $1 - \eta$ where η is sufficiently small, the security of the key distribution part is guaranteed. Moreover, we show that our protocol has advantage in terms of the length of the generated raw key as compared to the VV protocol [25]. Further cryptanalytic study on this protocol will be interesting research work in this direction.

Acknowledgments. The authors like to thank the anonymous reviewers for their comments that improved the technical as well as editorial quality of the paper. The third author acknowledges the support from the project "Cryptography & Cryptanalysis: How far can we bridge the gap between Classical and Quantum Paradigm", awarded under DAE-SRC, BRNS, India.

References

1. Acín, A., Gisin, N., Masanes, L.: From Bell's theorem to secure quantum key distribution. Phys. Rev. Lett. **97**, 120405 (2006)
2. Acín, A., Massar, S., Pironio, S.: Efficient quantum key distribution secure against no-signalling eavesdroppers. New J. Phys. **8**(8), 126 (2006)
3. Acín, A., Brunner, N., Gisin, N., Masanes, L., Pino, S., Scarani, V.: Secrecy extraction from no-signalling correlations. Phys. Rev. A **74**(4), 042339 (2006)
4. Acín, A., Gisin, N., Ribordy, G., Scarani, V.: Quantum cryptography protocols robust against photon number splitting attacks for weak laser pulse implementations. Phys. Rev. Lett. **92**, 057901 (2004)
5. Acín, A., Baccari, F., Cavalcanti, D., Wittek, P.: Efficient device-independent entanglement detection for multipartite systems. Phys. Rev. X **7**, 021042 (2017)
6. Bennett, C.H., Brassard, G.: Quantum cryptography: public key distribution and coin tossing. In: Proceedings of IEEE International Conference on Computers, Systems and Signal Processing, vol. 175, p. 8 (1984)
7. Bennett, C.H.: Quantum cryptography using any two non orthogonal states. Phys. Rev. Lett. **68**, 3121–3124 (1992)
8. Boyer, M., Gelles, R., Kenigsberg, D., Mor, T.: Semiquantum key distribution. Phys. Rev. A **79**, 032341 (2009)
9. Brassard, G., Broadbent, A., Tapp, A.: Multi-party pseudo-telepathy. In: Dehne, F., Sack, J.-R., Smid, M. (eds.) WADS 2003. LNCS, vol. 2748, pp. 1–11. Springer, Heidelberg (2003). https://doi.org/10.1007/978-3-540-45078-8_1
10. Brassard, G., Broadbent, A., Tapp, A.: Quantum pseudo-telepathy. Found. Phys. **35**(11), 1877–1907 (2005). https://doi.org/10.1007/s10701-005-7353-4
11. Braunstein, S.L., Pirandola, S.: Side-channel-free quantum key distribution. Phys. Rev. Lett. **108**, 130502 (2012)
12. Clauser, J.F., Holt, R.A., Horne, M.A., Shimony, A.: Proposed experiment to test local hidden-variable theories. Phys. Rev. Lett. **23**, 880 (1969)
13. Curty, M., Lo, H.K., Qi, B.: Measurement-device-independent quantum key distribution. Phys. Rev. Lett. **108**, 130503 (2012)
14. Ekert, A.K.: Quantum cryptography based on Bell's theorem. Phys. Rev. Lett. **67**, 661 (1991)
15. Tomamichel, M., Fehr, S., Kaniewski, J., Wehner, S.: One-sided device-independent QKD and position-based cryptography from monogamy games. In: Johansson, T., Nguyen, P.Q. (eds.) EUROCRYPT 2013. LNCS, vol. 7881, pp. 609–625. Springer, Heidelberg (2013). https://doi.org/10.1007/978-3-642-38348-9_36
16. Jain, R., Miller, C.A., Shi, Y.: Parallel device-independent quantum key distribution (2017). https://arxiv.org/abs/1703.05426
17. Jo, Y., Bae, K., Son, W.: Enhanced Bell state measurement for efficient measurement-device-independent quantum key distribution using 3-dimensional quantum states. Nat. Sci. Rep. **9**, 687 (2019). https://www.nature.com/articles/s41598-018-36513-x
18. Konig, R., Renner, R., Schaffner, C.: The operational meaning of min- and max-entropy. IEEE Trans. Inf. Theory **55**(9), 4337–4347 (2009)
19. Liu, Y., et al.: Experimental measurement-device-independent quantum key distribution. Phys. Rev. Lett. **111**, 130502 (2013)
20. Mančinska, L.: Maximally entangled state in pseudo-telepathy games. In: Calude, C.S., Freivalds, R., Kazuo, I. (eds.) Computing with New Resources. LNCS, vol. 8808, pp. 200–207. Springer, Cham (2014). https://doi.org/10.1007/978-3-319-13350-8_15

21. Maurer, U.: Indistinguishability of random systems. In: Knudsen, L.R. (ed.) EUROCRYPT 2002. LNCS, vol. 2332, pp. 110–132. Springer, Heidelberg (2002). https://doi.org/10.1007/3-540-46035-7_8
22. Mayers, D., Yao, A.: Quantum cryptography with imperfect apparatus. In: Proceedings of the 39th Annual Symposium on Foundations of Computer Science (FOCS 98), pp. 503–509. IEEE Computer Society, Washington 1998
23. Koblitz, N., Menezes, A.: Another look at provable security. http://cacr.uwaterloo.ca/~ajmeneze/anotherlook/index.shtml. Accessed 1 Oct 2019
24. Tomamichel, M., Fehr, S., Kaniewski, J., Wehner, S.: A monogamy-of-entanglement game with applications to device-independent quantum cryptography. New J. Phys. **15**, 103002 (2013)
25. Vazirani, U., Vidick, T.: Fully device-independent quantum key distribution. Phys. Rev. Lett. **113**, 140501 (2014)

Generalized Approach for Analysing Quantum Key Distribution Experiments

Arpita Maitra[1][(✉)] and Suvra Sekhar Das[2]

[1] C R Rao Advanced Institute of Mathematics Statistics and Computer Science,
Hyderabad 500046, India
arpita76b@gmail.com
[2] G.S Sanyal School of Telecommunication, Indian Institute of Technology
Kharagpur, Kharagpur 721302, India
suvra@gssst.iitkgp.ac.in

Abstract. In this initiative, a generalized approach towards step by step synthesis of Quantum Key Distribution (QKD) experiments is presented. Schematic diagram of the optical setup of any QKD protocol is easily available in the literature whereas step by step synthesis of the circuit needs further attention. For practical implementation, this understanding is necessary. In the current effort, we describe a disciplined methodology to synthesize the optical experimental setup of QKD protocols. This approach can be extended towards any optical experiment. The beam splitter and phase retarders are described in terms of annihilation and creation operators. We represent the polarization of photon in the Fock state basis. We consider two QKD protocols; Passive BB84 with coherent light (Progress in Informatics, 2011) and Reference Frame Independent 6–4 QKD (RFI-QKD) (https://arxiv.org/abs/1905.09197) to test the methodology. We observe that this disciplined methodology can successfully describe the experiments. This can be exploited to build a convenient synthesis tool for modelling any optical arrangement for security analysis.

Keywords: Synthesis tool · Quantum Cryptography · Wave-particle superposition · Passive BB84 QKD · Reference Frame Independent 6–4 QKD

1 Introduction

Since the pioneering result of Shor [23], extensive attention is given towards post quantum cryptography. Lattice based [4, 15, 17, 19] and code based [3, 16, 21] cryptography are believed to be secure against quantum adversary. Another avenue is quantum cryptography [2, 6, 9, 14, 28, 29]. In the last two decades enormous proliferation has occurred in this domain. Abstract theoretical models have been implemented in practice. On the other hand, various experimental observations give birth to new theories. However, synthesis of a given experimental setup remains comparatively less explored. For example, experimentally it has been

© Springer Nature Switzerland AG 2019
F. Hao et al. (Eds.): INDOCRYPT 2019, LNCS 11898, pp. 472–491, 2019.
https://doi.org/10.1007/978-3-030-35423-7_24

shown that one can create a photon which can lie in the superposition state of wave and particle [1,10,12,18,20,22,24]. Further, entanglement has also been demonstrated between these two behavioural nature of a photon [25]. These results might have great impact in quantum cryptology. Schematic diagram for all such optical setup are available in the literatures. However, step by step synthesis of the circuits requires futher attention.

For involved understanding of a circuit towards practical implementation purpose, stepwise synthesis is mandatory. In the present draft, we describe a convenient methodology which can serve this purpose, specially for cryptographic application. In this direction, we exploit second quantization of photon.

Different kind of Beam Splitters (BS) and various Phase Retarders (PR) are used in any kind of optical experimental setup. We describe different BSs and PRs in terms of annihilation and creation operators. Such description provides us an easier way to analyze any optical setup. One may use Jones matrix algebra to describe any optical device. However, this approach becomes cumbersome when number of photons increase. On the other hand, if we describe the optical devices using second quantization, it becomes handy to model any optical setup for arbitrary number of photons. In this regard, we pick up three optical set-ups which are significant from cryptological view point. First one is wave-particle superposition [25] experiment. Second one is Passive BB84 with coherent light [7] source and the third one is very recently demonstrated 6–4 Reference Frame Independent Quantum Key Distribution (RFI-QKD) [26,27] protocol.

We believe that our methodology pave a pathway towards automation, i.e., given an input state and a circuit diagram one may generate an automated algorithm which provides the output result instantly. This methodology might have been exploited in security analysis for optics based cryptographic protocols.

2 Preliminaries

In this section we provide the quantum mechanical description of beam splitter and various phase retarders [13].

2.1 Beam Splitter

The description of quantum Beam Splitter (BS) is available in many literatures [5,11,13]. The figure (Fig. 1) of a beam splitter is taken from [5].

Non Polarizing Beam Splitter. In case of Classical Non Polarizing Beam Splitter (NBS) the input fields are related to the output fields with the following expression.

$$\begin{pmatrix} E_3 \\ E_4 \end{pmatrix} = \begin{pmatrix} t_0 & r_1 \\ r_0 & t_1 \end{pmatrix} \cdot \begin{pmatrix} E_1 \\ E_2 \end{pmatrix}$$

where t_0 (resp. t_1) is the transmission coefficient of port 1 (resp. port 2) and r_0 (resp. r_1) is the reflection coefficient of port 1 (resp. port 2).

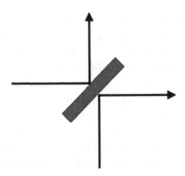

Fig. 1. Figure shows the schematic diagram of a beam splitter [5, page2]. Here, incoming ray which is projected on the beam splitter through port 1 is reflected through port 4 (vertical arrow) and transmitted through port 3 (horizontal arrow). The incoming ray which is projected on the beam splitter through port 2 is reflected through port 3 (horizontal arrow) and transmitted through port 4 (vertical arrow).

Now, the relation between r_0, t_0, r_1, t_1 can be obtained from the following formula [13]:

$$\arg(r_0) + \arg(r_1) - \arg(t_0) - \arg(t_1) = \pm\pi$$

Based on the construction of the BS, the sign of the phase has to be determined. The conventional choice for a BS cube is $\arg(r_0) = \arg(r_1) = \arg(t_0) = 0$, but $\arg(t_1) = \pi$ [13]. Thus, for a 50 : 50 BS splitter one can write,

$$E_3 = \frac{E_1 + E_2}{\sqrt{2}}, \quad E_4 = \frac{E_1 - E_2}{\sqrt{2}}$$

In case of Quantum NBS, the electric fields are replaced by annihilation operator and creation operator, i.e., in case of quantum NBS, we can write

$$\begin{pmatrix} c \\ d \end{pmatrix} = \begin{pmatrix} t_0 & r_1 \\ r_0 & t_1 \end{pmatrix} \cdot \begin{pmatrix} a \\ b \end{pmatrix}$$

where, c, d are annihilation operator at port 3 and 4 respectively and a, b are the annihilation operator at the input ports 1 and 2 respectively. Similarly, the same expression can be written for creation operators $a^\dagger, b^\dagger, c^\dagger$ and $d^\dagger$.

If we set $r_0 = r_1 = \sqrt{\eta}$ and $t_0 = t_1 = \sqrt{1-\eta}$, then with analogy to classical case one may write,

$$c = \sqrt{1-\eta}a + \sqrt{\eta}b, \quad d = \sqrt{\eta}a - \sqrt{1-\eta}b$$

Alternatively, we can write

$$a = \sqrt{1-\eta}c + \sqrt{\eta}d, \quad b = \sqrt{\eta}c - \sqrt{1-\eta}d$$

Same expression can be drawn for $a^\dagger$ and $b^\dagger$.

If we consider polarization along with the photon number, then an extra index has to be added with the operators, i.e., instead of a (resp. b) we use a_j (resp. b_k), where j, k each indicates either horizontal or vertical polarization. Similarly, for creation operator instead of $a^\dagger$ or $b^\dagger$, we use $a_j^\dagger$, $b_k^\dagger$. Hence, from now on we will write, for annihilation operator

$$a_j = \sqrt{1 - \eta}c_j + \sqrt{\eta}d_j, \quad b_k = \sqrt{\eta}c_k - \sqrt{1 - \eta}d_k$$

And for creation operator, we will write

$$a_j^\dagger = \sqrt{1 - \eta}c_j^\dagger + \sqrt{\eta}d_j^\dagger, \quad b_k^\dagger = \sqrt{\eta}c_k^\dagger - \sqrt{1 - \eta}d_k^\dagger$$

The same expression can be drawn if we consider the following BS operator

$$\hat{B} = e^{i\theta(a^\dagger b + b^\dagger a)}$$

In this notation, the relationship between the output ports and the input ports of a BS is expressed as follows.

$$\begin{pmatrix} c \\ d \end{pmatrix} = \hat{B}^\dagger \begin{pmatrix} a \\ b \end{pmatrix} \hat{B}$$

Expanding $\hat{B}$ in Taylor series we will get the above expressions for a ($a^\dagger$) and b ($b^\dagger$), where $|r_0| = |r_1| = \cos\theta$ and $|t_0| = |t_1| = \sin\theta$. Here, we assume symmetric BS. In case of $50 : 50$ BS, θ will be $\pi/4$.

Polarizing Beam Splitter. In case of Polarizing Beam Splitter (PBS), Horizontal polarization is transmitted completely where as Vertical polarization is completely reflected. If we assume that the photons which incident on port 1 transmitted through port 3 and the photons which incident on port 2 is transmitted through port 4, then for Horizontal polarization we can write

$$a_H = c_H, \quad b_H = d_H$$

Similarly, if the photon at port 1 is reflected through port 4 and the photon at port 2 is reflected through port 3, then for Vertical polarization we can write

$$a_V = d_H, \quad b_V = c_V$$

2.2   Phase Retarders

A schematic diagram of a phase retarder is given in Fig. 2. The figure is taken from [13].

In case of classical phase retarder (PR), relationship amongst input polarizations and output polarizations can be expressed as

$$\begin{pmatrix} E_x' \\ E_y' \end{pmatrix} = \begin{pmatrix} 1 & 0 \\ 0 & e^{-i\theta} \end{pmatrix} \cdot \begin{pmatrix} E_x \\ E_y \end{pmatrix}$$

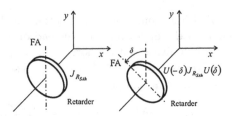

Fig. 2. Figure shows the schematic diagram of a phase retarder [13, page 2]. The left one shows Fast axis parallel to conventional Y axis whereas the right one shows Fast axis making an angle δ with conventional Y axis.

where, E'_x (resp. E'_y) is the output polarization along X (resp. Y) axis and E'_x (resp. E_y) is the input polarization along X (resp. Y) axis [13].

In case of quantum PR, we can modify the above expression as

$$\begin{pmatrix} a'_x \\ a'_y \end{pmatrix} = \begin{pmatrix} 1 & 0 \\ 0 & e^{-i\theta} \end{pmatrix} \cdot \begin{pmatrix} a_x \\ a_y \end{pmatrix}$$

where, a'_x (resp. a'_y) is the annihilation operator at output port along X (resp. Y) axis and a_x (resp. a_y) is the annihilation operator at input port along X (resp. Y) axis. Thus, we can write

$$a'_x = a_x, \ a'_y = e^{-i\theta} a_y$$

where, θ is the angle made by the PR with its fast axis.

If we assume Horizontal polarization is along X axis and Vertical polarization is along Y axis, then the above equation can be rewritten as

$$a'_H = a_H, \ a'_V = e^{-i\theta} a_V$$

2.3 Analysis of Wave-Particle Superposition

Based on the above description, in this section, we analyze mathematically the experimental setup for generating wave-particle superposition of photon in the light of second quantization of matter.

Quantum superposition is one of the fundamental pillars of quantum cryptography. This has wide applications in quantum random number generation, quantum key distribution, quantum secure communication etc. The range of such applicability motivates us to analyze the optical set-up (Fig. 3).

Here, we define two mode polarization basis Fock state $|n_H, n_V\rangle$, where n_H represents the number of horizontally polarized photons and n_V represents vertically polarized photons with $n_H + n_V = n$ [30]. The basis state can be written in terms of annihilation and creation operator as follows.

$$|n_H, n_V\rangle = \frac{(a_H^\dagger)^{n_H} (a_V^\dagger)^{n_V}}{\sqrt{n_H! n_V!}} |0\rangle.$$

Here, $a^\dagger$ stands for creation operator whereas a stands for annihilation operator. An n photon state can be expressed as the superposition of the basis states. That is an n photon state can be written as

$$|\psi^n\rangle = \sum_{n_H=0}^{n} C_{n_H} |n_H, n_V\rangle |_{n_V = n - n_H}$$

where, $\sum_{n_H=0}^{n} |C_{n_H}|^2 = 1$.

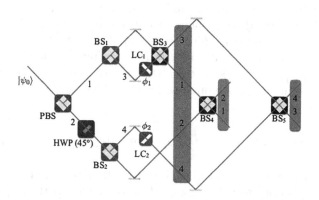

Fig. 3. Figure shows the layout of the experimental implementation of the wave-particle toolbox (the diagram is taken from the supplementary material [32, page 1])

Now, consider the following schematic diagram of the experimental arrangement for generating wave-particle superposition of photon. The diagram is taken from supplementary material of [25]. The initial photon was prepared in a superposition state of horizontal (H) and vertical (V) polarization, i.e.,

$$|\psi^1\rangle_{in} = \cos\alpha |V\rangle + \sin\alpha |H\rangle.$$

In Fock state basis this can be rewritten as

$$|\psi^1\rangle_{in} = \cos\alpha |0_H, 1_V\rangle + \sin\alpha |1_H, 0_V\rangle$$
$$= (\cos\alpha\, a_V^\dagger + \sin\alpha\, a_H^\dagger) |0_H, 0_V\rangle$$

This photon is then passed through a Polarization Beam Splitter (PBS). According to the specification given in [25], we define

$$a_H^\dagger = c_H^\dagger,\ a_V^\dagger = d_V^\dagger,\ b_H^\dagger = d_H^\dagger,\ b_V^\dagger = c_V^\dagger$$

where $a_H^\dagger, b_H^\dagger$ (resp. $a_V^\dagger, b_V^\dagger$) represent creation operators at port 1 and port 2 for horizontal (Vertical) polarization. Similarly, $c_H^\dagger, d_H^\dagger$ (resp. $c_V^\dagger, d_V^\dagger$) represent creation operators at port C and port D for horizontal (resp. vertical) polarization.

After PBS the state becomes $|\psi^1\rangle_{PBS} = (\cos\alpha\, d_V^\dagger + \sin\alpha\, c_H^\dagger)\, |0_H, 0_V\rangle$. To make the current discussion compatible with [25] we define the path of photon which emitted from port D as path 1 and the path of photon emitted from port C as path 2. Thus, we rewrite $|\psi^1\rangle_{PBS}$ as $|\psi^1\rangle_{PBS} = (\cos\alpha\, (d_V^\dagger)_1 + \sin\alpha\, (c_H^\dagger)_2)\, |0_H, 0_V\rangle$.

The photon in path 1 is further bifurcated by $50 : 50$ Beam Splitter (BS_1) whereas the photon in path 2 is passed through a Half Wave Plate (HWP) making an angle of $45°$ with the fast axis. From Sect. 2.2 we get that H polarised light passes through the HWP without introducing any phase in the path whereas V polarised light introduce $45°$ phase angle into the path. As path 2 stands for H polarised light, no phase is introduced. Hence, after BS_1 and HWP the state becomes $|\psi^1\rangle_{BS_1+HWP} = (\frac{1}{\sqrt{2}}\cos\alpha\,((c_V^\dagger)_1 + (d_V^\dagger)_3) + \sin\alpha\,(c_H^\dagger)_2)\,|0_H, 0_V\rangle$.

Now, photon in path 2 is bifurcated by BS_2. Thus, the resultant state after BS_1, HWP and BS_2 is written as

$$|\psi^1\rangle_{BS} = \frac{1}{\sqrt{2}}(\cos\alpha\,((c_V^\dagger)_1 + (d_V^\dagger)_3) + \sin\alpha\,((c_H^\dagger)_2 + (d_H^\dagger)_4))\,|0_H, 0_V\rangle.$$

Here, path 3 denotes the photon which is emitted from port D of BS_1 and path 4 represents the photon emitted from port D of BS_2. Then both the photon travelling through path 3 and 4 are passed through two phase retarders introducing the phase ϕ_1 in path 3 and the phase ϕ_2 in path 4 respectively. The resultant state now becomes

$$|\psi^1\rangle_{BS} = \frac{1}{\sqrt{2}}(\cos\alpha\,((c_V^\dagger)_1 + e^{i\phi_1}(d_V^\dagger)_3) + \sin\alpha\,((c_H^\dagger)_2 + e^{i\phi_2}(d_H^\dagger)_4))\,|0_H, 0_V\rangle.$$

Path 1 and 3 now recombined by another $50 : 50$ Beam Splitter BS_3 giving rise to a new state as follows

$$\begin{aligned}
|\psi^1\rangle_{BS} &= \frac{1}{\sqrt{2}}(\cos\alpha\,\frac{1}{\sqrt{2}}((c_V^\dagger + d_V^\dagger)_1 + e^{i\phi_1}(c_V^\dagger - d_V^\dagger)_3) + \sin\alpha\,((c_H^\dagger)_2 \\
&\quad + e^{i\phi_2}(d_H^\dagger)_4))\,|0_H, 0_V\rangle \\
&= \frac{1}{\sqrt{2}}(\cos\alpha\,\frac{1}{\sqrt{2}}((1 + e^{i\phi_1})(c_V^\dagger)_1 + (1 - e^{i\phi_1})(d_V^\dagger)_3) + \sin\alpha\,((c_H^\dagger)_2 \\
&\quad + e^{i\phi_2}(d_H^\dagger)_4))\,|0_H, 0_V\rangle \\
&= \frac{1}{\sqrt{2}}(\cos\alpha\,\sqrt{2}e^{\frac{i\phi_1}{2}}(\cos\frac{\phi_1}{2}(c_V^\dagger)_1 - i\sin\frac{\phi_1}{2}(d_V^\dagger)_3) + \sin\alpha\,((c_H^\dagger)_2 \\
&\quad + e^{i\phi_2}(d_H^\dagger)_4))\,|0_H, 0_V\rangle
\end{aligned}$$

This can be written as

$$|\psi^1\rangle_{BS} = \cos\alpha\,|wave\rangle + \sin\alpha\,|particle\rangle$$

where,

$$|wave\rangle = e^{\frac{i\phi_1}{2}}(\cos\frac{\phi_1}{2}(c_V^\dagger)_1 - i\sin\frac{\phi_1}{2}(d_V^\dagger)_3)$$

$$|particle\rangle = \frac{1}{\sqrt{2}}((c_H^\dagger)_2 + e^{i\phi_2}(d_H^\dagger)_4)$$

Note that in case of *wave* the probability amplitudes of path 1 and 3 depend on phase angle ϕ_1 whereas in case of *particle*, the probability amplitudes of path 2 and 4 do not depend on phase angle ϕ_2.

To observe wave-particle morphing as function of α, path 1 and 2 are synchronised on beam splitter BS_4. Similarly, path 3 and 4 are synchronised on beam splitter BS_5 resulting the state

$$|\psi^1\rangle_{BS} = \frac{1}{\sqrt{2}}\Big[\Big(\cos\alpha e^{\frac{i\phi_1}{2}}\Big(\cos\frac{\phi_1}{2}((c_V^\dagger)_1 + (d_V^\dagger)_2) - i\sin\frac{\phi_1}{2}((c_V^\dagger)_3 + (d_V^\dagger)_4)\Big)\Big)$$

$$+ \sin\alpha\Big(\frac{1}{\sqrt{2}}((c_H^\dagger)_1 - (d_H^\dagger)_2) + e^{i\phi_2}((c_H^\dagger)_3 - (d_H^\dagger)_4)\Big)\Big]|0_H, 0_V\rangle$$

where,

$$|wave - det\rangle = e^{\frac{i\phi_1}{2}}\Big(\cos\frac{\phi_1}{2}((c_V^\dagger)_1 + (d_V^\dagger)_2) - i\sin\frac{\phi_1}{2}((c_V^\dagger)_3 + (d_V^\dagger)_4)\Big)$$

$$|particle - det\rangle = \frac{1}{2}\Big(((c_H^\dagger)_1 - (d_H^\dagger)_2) + e^{i\phi_2}((c_H^\dagger)_3 - (d_H^\dagger)_4)\Big)$$

One should note that the expression of the final state is also available in [25]. However, we present the step wise synthesis for better understanding as that was not available in [25]. For the following two protocols, we show how one can reach at the final output by exploiting similar kind of analysis, that had not been presented earlier.

3   Passive Coherent State BB84

Quantum Key Distribution (QKD) is an algorithmic description of a secure key exchange methodology between two spatially distant parties. In QKD protocol, security comes from the laws of quantum physics, specifically from no-cloning [8, 31] and Heisenberg uncertainty principle. The famous BB84 [2] protocol is the first protocol in this domain. Till date more than 1000 QKD protocols are proposed.

Like any QKD protocol, passive coherent state BB84 [7] can be subdivided into two phases. First one is state preparation and the second one is the measurements at Alice and Bob's side. In state preparation phase, Alice starts with two phase randomized strong coherent pluses, prepared in $+45°$ and $-45°$ linear polarization respectively (Fig. 4). The figure is taken from [7]. In the figure the state is described in terms of density matrix. In the current draft we consider the

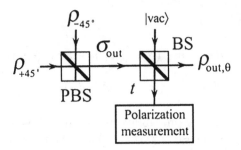

Fig. 4. Figure shows the schematic diagram of a passive BB84 QKD source with coherent light [7, page 58]).

vector form of the state, i.e., in our case we will assume that $|\alpha_{+45°}\rangle$ is entering from port 1 of the PBS and $|\alpha_{+45°}\rangle$ is entering from port 2 of the PBS. These states can be written as

$$|\alpha_{\pm45°}\rangle = e^{-\frac{|\alpha|^2}{2}} \sum_{0}^{\infty} \frac{\alpha^n}{\sqrt{n!}} |n_{\pm45°}\rangle$$

where n is the number of photons in $\pm45°$ angle polarization and α is the mean photon number.

The above expression can be further written as

$$|\alpha_{\pm45°}\rangle = e^{-\frac{|\alpha|^2}{2}} \sum_{0}^{\infty} \frac{\alpha^n}{\sqrt{n!}} (a^\dagger)^n |0\rangle$$

which is equivalent to

$$|\alpha_{\pm45°}\rangle = D(\alpha) |0\rangle = e^{\alpha a^\dagger - \alpha^* a} |0\rangle$$

where, $D(\alpha)$ is a unitary operator.

Thus, we can write

$$|\alpha_{+45°}\rangle |\alpha_{-45°}\rangle = D(\alpha_{+45°})D(\alpha_{-45°}) |0\rangle_1 |0\rangle_2$$
$$= \exp(\alpha a^\dagger_{+45°} - \alpha^* a_{+45°})$$
$$\exp(\alpha b^\dagger_{-45°} - \alpha^* b_{-45°}) |0\rangle_1 |0\rangle_2$$

This is equivalent to express the state in the following form.

$$|\alpha_{+45°}\rangle |\alpha_{-45°}\rangle = \exp(\frac{\alpha}{\sqrt{2}}(a^\dagger_H + a^\dagger_V) - \frac{\alpha^*}{\sqrt{2}}(a_H + a_V))$$
$$\exp(\frac{\alpha}{\sqrt{2}}(b^\dagger_H - b^\dagger_V) - \frac{\alpha^*}{\sqrt{2}}(b_H - b_V)) |0\rangle_1 |0\rangle_2$$

After Polarization Beam Splitter (PBS) the resultant photon states can be written as

$$|\beta\rangle_3 \, |\beta'\rangle_4 = \exp(\frac{\alpha}{\sqrt{2}}(c_H^\dagger + d_V^\dagger) - \frac{\alpha^*}{\sqrt{2}}(c_H + d_V))$$
$$\exp(\frac{\alpha}{\sqrt{2}}(d_H^\dagger - c_V^\dagger) - \frac{\alpha^*}{\sqrt{2}}(d_H - c_V)) \, |0\rangle_3 \, |0\rangle_4$$

Now, rearranging the states we get,

$$|\beta\rangle_3 \, |\beta'\rangle_4 = \exp(\frac{\alpha}{\sqrt{2}}(c_H^\dagger - c_V^\dagger) - \frac{\alpha^*}{\sqrt{2}}(c_H - c_V))$$
$$\exp(\frac{\alpha}{\sqrt{2}}(d_H^\dagger + d_V^\dagger) - \frac{\alpha^*}{\sqrt{2}}(d_H + d_V)) \, |0\rangle_3 \, |0\rangle_4$$

This is equivalent to writing the state as

$$|\beta\rangle_3 \, |\beta'\rangle_4 = D(\frac{\alpha}{\sqrt{2}})D(\frac{\alpha}{\sqrt{2}}) \, |0\rangle_3 \, |0\rangle_4$$

Note that here, $\beta = \beta' = \frac{\alpha}{\sqrt{2}}$.

$|\beta\rangle_3$ is inserted through port 1 of a Beam Splitter (BS) with very low transmission coefficient t ($t \ll 1$). In port 2 of the BS a vacuum state is inserted. Thus we can write,

$$|\beta\rangle_1 \, |0\rangle_2 = D(\frac{\alpha}{\sqrt{2}}) \, |0\rangle_1 \, |0\rangle_2$$

is the input state of BS. After BS, the state becomes

$$|\gamma\rangle_3 \, |\gamma'\rangle_4 = \exp(\frac{\alpha}{\sqrt{2}}(\sqrt{t}c_H^\dagger + \sqrt{1-t}d_H^\dagger - \sqrt{t}c_V^\dagger - \sqrt{1-t}d_V^\dagger)$$
$$- \frac{\alpha^*}{\sqrt{2}}(\sqrt{t}c_H + \sqrt{1-t}d_H - \sqrt{t}c_V - \sqrt{1-t}d_V)) \, |0\rangle_3 \, |0\rangle_4$$

Rearranging the state we get

$$|\gamma\rangle_3 \, |\gamma'\rangle_4 = \exp(\frac{\alpha\sqrt{t}}{\sqrt{2}}(c_H^\dagger - c_V^\dagger) - \frac{\alpha^*\sqrt{t}}{2}(c_H - c_V))$$
$$\exp(\frac{\alpha\sqrt{1-t}}{\sqrt{2}}(d_H^\dagger - d_V^\dagger) - \frac{\alpha^*\sqrt{1-t}}{\sqrt{2}}(d_H - d_V)) \, |0\rangle_3 \, |0\rangle_4$$
$$= D\left(\frac{\alpha\sqrt{t}}{\sqrt{2}}\right)D\left(\frac{\alpha\sqrt{1-t}}{\sqrt{2}}\right) \, |0\rangle_3 \, |0\rangle_4$$

where, $\gamma = \frac{\alpha\sqrt{t}}{\sqrt{2}}$ and $\gamma' = \frac{\alpha\sqrt{1-t}}{\sqrt{2}}$. Now, $|\gamma\rangle$ is sent to Bob where as $|\gamma'\rangle$ is retained by Alice for polarization measurement.

The measurement setup at Alice's place is described in Fig. 5. The figure is taken from [7].

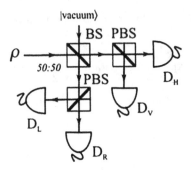

Fig. 5. Figure shows the schematic diagram of the polarization measurement in a passive BB84 QKD with coherent light [7, page 59]).

In our case, ρ in the figure describes the density matrix of $|\gamma'\rangle$. According to the figure, the initial state before 50 : 50 BS is

$$|\gamma'\rangle_1 |0\rangle_2 = D\left(\frac{\alpha\sqrt{1-t}}{\sqrt{2}}\right) |0\rangle_1 |0\rangle_2 \tag{1}$$

Now, let the annihilation and creation operator at port 1 of BS be a and $a^\dagger$ respectively. Similarly, let the annihilation and creation operator at port 2 of BS be b and $b^\dagger$ respectively. Then Eq. 1 can be rewritten as

$$|\gamma'\rangle_1 |0\rangle_2 = \exp\left(\frac{\alpha\sqrt{1-t}}{\sqrt{2}}(a_H^\dagger - a_V^\dagger) - \frac{\alpha^*\sqrt{1-t}}{\sqrt{2}}(a_H - a_V)\right) |0\rangle_1 |0\rangle_2$$

After beam splitter, the state becomes

$$|\delta\rangle_3 |\delta'\rangle_4 = \exp\left(\frac{\alpha\sqrt{1-t}}{2}(c_H^\dagger + d_H^\dagger - c_V^\dagger - d_V^\dagger)\right.$$
$$\left. - \frac{\alpha^*\sqrt{1-t}}{2}(c_H + d_H - c_V - d_V)\right) |0\rangle_3 |0\rangle_4$$

Rearranging the state we get

$$|\delta\rangle_3 |\delta'\rangle_4 = \exp\left(\frac{\alpha\sqrt{1-t}}{2}(c_H^\dagger - c_V^\dagger) - \frac{\alpha^*\sqrt{1-t}}{2}\right.$$
$$(c_H - c_V)\left)\exp\left(\frac{\alpha\sqrt{1-t}}{2}(d_H^\dagger - d_V^\dagger)\right.$$
$$\left. - \frac{\alpha^*\sqrt{1-t}}{2}(d_H - d_V)\right) |0\rangle_3 |0\rangle_4$$

According to the Fig. 5, $|\delta\rangle$ enters in PBS associated with $\{|H\rangle, |V\rangle\}$ basis, whereas $|\delta'\rangle$ enters in PBS associated with $\{|R\rangle, |L\rangle\}$ basis. Thus, the initial states of the PBS associated with $\{|H\rangle, |V\rangle\}$ basis will be

$$|\delta\rangle_1 |0\rangle_2 = \exp\left(\frac{\alpha\sqrt{1-t}}{2}(a_H^\dagger - a_V^\dagger) - \frac{\alpha^*\sqrt{1-t}}{2}(a_H - a_V)\right) |0\rangle_1 |0\rangle_2 .$$

And the out-coming state from the PBS associated with $\{|H\rangle, |V\rangle\}$ basis will be

$$|\mu\rangle_3 |\mu'\rangle_4 = \exp(\frac{\alpha\sqrt{1-t}}{2}(c_H^\dagger - d_V^\dagger) - \frac{\alpha^*\sqrt{1-t}}{2}(c_H - d_V)) |0\rangle_3 |0\rangle_4.$$

Rearranging the state we can write,

$$|\mu\rangle_3 |\mu'\rangle_4 = \exp(\frac{\alpha\sqrt{1-t}}{2}c_H^\dagger - \frac{\alpha^*\sqrt{1-t}}{2}c_H)$$
$$\exp(-\frac{\alpha\sqrt{1-t}}{2}d_V^\dagger + \frac{\alpha^*\sqrt{1-t}}{2}d_V) |0\rangle_3 |0\rangle_4.$$

This implies that at port 3 of the PBS, we get horizontally polarized coherent state with mean photon number $\frac{\alpha\sqrt{1-t}}{2}$. And at port 4, we get vertically polarized coherent state with mean photon number $\frac{\alpha^*\sqrt{1-t}}{2}$.

Proceeding in the similar way, one may write the out-coming states from the PBS associated with $\{|R\rangle, |L\rangle\}$ basis as

$$|\nu\rangle_3 |\nu'\rangle_4 = \exp(\frac{\alpha\sqrt{1-t}}{2}c_H^\dagger - \frac{\alpha^*\sqrt{1-t}}{2}c_H)$$
$$\exp(-\frac{\alpha\sqrt{1-t}}{2}d_V^\dagger + \frac{\alpha^*\sqrt{1-t}}{2}d_V) |0\rangle_3 |0\rangle_4.$$

Describing in $\{|R\rangle, |L\rangle\}$ basis, one gets

$$|\nu\rangle_3 |\nu'\rangle_4 = \exp(\frac{\alpha\sqrt{1-t}}{2\sqrt{2}}(c_R^\dagger + c_L^\dagger) - \frac{\alpha^*\sqrt{1-t}}{2\sqrt{2}}(c_R + c_L))$$
$$\exp(-\frac{\alpha\sqrt{1-t}}{2\sqrt{2}}(d_R^\dagger - d_L^\dagger) + \frac{\alpha^*\sqrt{1-t}}{2\sqrt{2}}(d_R - d_L)) |0\rangle_3 |0\rangle_4.$$

This implies that at each of the output ports of the PBS, we get a linear combination of $|L\rangle$ and $|R\rangle$. Now, we set a detector which detects $|R\rangle$ at port 3 and a detector which detects $|L\rangle$ at port 4. So, at port 3, we can only detect the coherent light with R polarization with mean photon number $\frac{\alpha\sqrt{1-t}}{2\sqrt{2}}$. Similarly, at port 4 we can only detect the coherent light with L polarization with mean photon number $\frac{\alpha^*\sqrt{1-t}}{2\sqrt{2}}$.

One should note that in the current draft the ideal scenario has been considered, i.e., we assume that the detectors are flawless and there is no noise in the channel. However, in practice, due to the detector inefficiency and the presence of noise in the channel, the observed mean photon number will differ from the theoretical value. Considering the deviation as a result of eavesdropping, one may calculate the mutual information extracted by the adversary and based on that, the parameters for classical post-processing should be determined.

4   Reference Frame Independent 6–4 QKD Protocol

In this section we try to model the optical setup for 6-4 Reference frame independent quantum key distribution protocol [26]. Entangled source like Spontaneous Parametric Down Conversion (SPDC) type-II is used in the actual experiment. In the present draft, for simplicity, we assume noise-free single photon source, i.e., we assume that it emits $\frac{1}{\sqrt{2}}(|H\rangle|V\rangle + |V\rangle|H\rangle)$. First particle is given to Alice whereas the second particle is given to Bob. Both the particles are sent through Polarization Maintaining Fibre (PMF) and hence introducing an overall phase ϕ. Thus, the resultant state can be written as

$$|\psi\rangle_{AB} = \frac{1}{\sqrt{2}}(|H\rangle_A|V\rangle_B + e^{-i\phi}|V\rangle_A|H\rangle_B)$$

where, the subscript A stands for Alice and subscript B stands for Bob. In terms of number state basis $|\psi\rangle_{AB}$ can be written as

$$|\psi\rangle_{AB} = \frac{1}{\sqrt{2}}(|1_H,0_V\rangle_A|0_H,1_V\rangle_B + e^{-i\phi}|0_H,1_V\rangle_A|1_H,0_V\rangle_B)$$

The schematic diagram for the optical setup at Bob's end and Alice's end are given in Figs. 6 and 7 respectively. The diagrams are taken from [26]. Based on the diagrams, we analyze the path of photons in terms of annihilation and creation operators. We now focus on Bob's setup. From the diagram it is seen that Bob's photon is passed through a half wave plate (HWP1). After this step, $|\psi\rangle_{AB}$ becomes

$$|\psi\rangle_{AB}^{HWP1_B} = \frac{1}{\sqrt{2}}(e^{-i\theta_1}|1_H,0_V\rangle_A|0_H,1_V\rangle_B + e^{-i\phi}|0_H,1_V\rangle_A|1_H,0_V\rangle_B).$$

Here, we assume that HWP1 makes an angle θ_1 with its fast axis. Now, the photon is passed through a 50 : 50 beam splitter. The reflected path is tagged

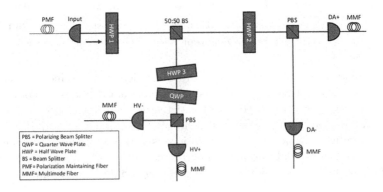

Fig. 6. Figure shows the schematic diagram of optical setup at Bob's end [26]

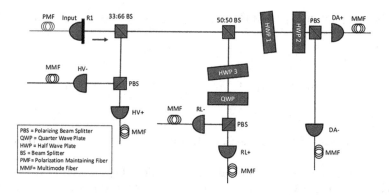

Fig. 7. Figure shows the schematic diagram of optical setup at Alice's end [26]

as 1 whereas the transmitted path is tagged as 2. Thus, the resultant state can be written in terms of annihilation and creation operators as

$$|\psi\rangle_{AB}^{BS_B} = \frac{1}{2}(e^{-i\theta_1}|1_H, 0_V\rangle_A ((c_V^\dagger)_1 + (d_V^\dagger)_2) + e^{-i\phi}|0_H, 1_V\rangle_A ((c_H^\dagger)_1 + (d_H^\dagger)_2))$$
$$|0_H, 0_V\rangle_B.$$

In path 1, the photon has to pass two retarders. One is HWP3 and another is quarter wave plate (QWP). The resultant photon after QWP can be expressed as

$$|\psi\rangle_{AB}^{QWP_B} = \frac{1}{2}(e^{-i\theta_1}|1_H, 0_V\rangle_A (e^{-i\theta_3}e^{-i\mu}(c_V^\dagger)_1 + (d_V^\dagger)_2) + e^{-i\phi}|0_H, 1_V\rangle_A$$
$$((c_H^\dagger)_1 + (d_H^\dagger)_2))|0_H, 0_V\rangle_B.$$

Here we assume that HWP3 and QWP are making angles θ_3 and μ respectively with their respective fast axes. The photon is then passed through a polarizing beam splitter (PBS). After PBS, the photon state can be described as

$$|\psi\rangle_{AB}^{QWP_B} = \frac{1}{2}(e^{-i\theta_1}|1_H, 0_V\rangle_A (e^{-i\theta_3}e^{-i\mu}(HV^-)_1 + (d_V^\dagger)_2) + e^{-i\phi}|0_H, 1_V\rangle_A$$
$$((HV^+)_1 + (d_H^\dagger)_2))|0_H, 0_V\rangle_B.$$

In path 2, photon is passed through HWP2 resulting the state

$$|\psi\rangle_{AB}^{HWP2_B} = \frac{1}{2}(e^{-i\theta_1}|1_H, 0_V\rangle_A (e^{-i\theta_3}e^{-i\mu}(HV^-)_1 + e^{-i\theta_2}(d_V^\dagger)_2)$$
$$+ e^{-i\phi}|0_H, 1_V\rangle_A ((HV^+)_1 + (d_H^\dagger)_2))|0_H, 0_V\rangle_B.$$

Here, we assume that HWP2 is making an angle θ_2 with its fast axis.

Next, the photon is passed through a PBS giving rise to the resultant state

$$|\psi\rangle_{AB}^{PBS_B} = \frac{1}{2}(e^{-i\theta_1}|1_H, 0_V\rangle_A (e^{-i\theta_3}e^{-i\mu}(HV^-)_1 + e^{-i\theta_2}\frac{1}{\sqrt{2}}(DA^+ - DA^-)_2)$$

$$+ e^{-i\phi}|0_H, 1_V\rangle_A ((HV^+)_1 + \frac{1}{\sqrt{2}}(DA^+ + DA^-)_2))|0_H, 0_V\rangle_B.$$

Now, path 1 is measured in $\{HV^+, HV^-\}$ basis whereas path 2 is measured in $\{DA^+, DA^-\}$ basis. For each basis, each state can be obtained with probability $\frac{1}{4}$.

We now will focus on the optical setup of Alice. The photon in Alice's place first passes through 33 : 66 beam splitter (BS_A^1) generating the resultant state

$$|\psi\rangle_{AB}^{BS_A^1} = \frac{1}{2}(e^{-i\theta_1}(\alpha(c_H^\dagger)_2 + \beta(d_H^\dagger)_1)(e^{-i\theta_3}e^{-i\mu}(HV^-)_1$$

$$+ e^{-i\theta_2}\frac{1}{\sqrt{2}}(DA^+ - DA^-)_2) + e^{-i\phi}(\alpha(c_V^\dagger)_2 + \beta(d_H^\dagger)_1)$$

$$((HV^+)_1 + \frac{1}{\sqrt{2}}(DA^+ + DA^-)_2))|0_H, 0_V\rangle_A|0_H, 0_V\rangle_B,$$

where $\alpha = \sqrt{\frac{2}{3}}$ and $\beta = \sqrt{\frac{1}{3}}$.

In reflected path (path 1 in case of Alice) the photon is passed through a PBS generating the following state

$$|\psi\rangle_{AB}^{PBS_A^1} = \frac{1}{2}(e^{-i\theta_1}(\alpha(c_H^\dagger)_2 + \beta(HV^+)_1)(e^{-i\theta_3}e^{-i\mu}(HV^-)_1 + e^{-i\theta_2}\frac{1}{\sqrt{2}}(DA^+$$

$$-DA^-)_2) + e^{-i\phi}(\alpha(c_V^\dagger)_2 + \beta(HV^-)_1)((HV^+)_1 + \frac{1}{\sqrt{2}}(DA^+$$

$$+DA^-)_2))|0_H, 0_V\rangle_A|0_H, 0_V\rangle_B.$$

In path 2 (transmitted path in Alice's place), the photon is passed through a 50:50 BS. Thus the resultant state should be

$$|\psi\rangle_{AB}^{BS_A^2} = \frac{1}{2}(e^{-i\theta_1}(\frac{\alpha}{\sqrt{2}}((c_H^\dagger)_2 + (d_H^\dagger)_3) + \beta(HV^+)_1)(e^{-i\theta_3}e^{-i\mu}(HV^-)_1$$

$$+ e^{-i\theta_2}\frac{1}{\sqrt{2}}(DA^+ - DA^-)_2) + e^{-i\phi}(\frac{\alpha}{\sqrt{2}}((c_V^\dagger)_2 + (d_V^\dagger)_3)$$

$$+ \beta(HV^-)_1)((HV^+)_1 + \frac{1}{\sqrt{2}}(DA^+ + DA^-)_2))|0_H, 0_V\rangle_A|0_H, 0_V\rangle_B.$$

Here, path 3 indicates reflected path of photon after 50:50 BS. In path 3, the photon is passed through HWP and then QWP resulting the photon in following form. Here, we assume that the HWP and QWP make angle η_1 and ϕ_1

respectively with their respective fast axes.

$$|\psi\rangle_{AB}^{(H+Q)_A^2} = \frac{1}{2}(e^{-i\theta_1}(\frac{\alpha}{\sqrt{2}}((c_H^\dagger)_2 + (d_H^\dagger)_3) + \beta(HV^+)_1)(e^{-i\theta_3}e^{-i\mu}(HV^-)_1$$

$$+ e^{-i\theta_2}\frac{1}{\sqrt{2}}(DA^+ - DA^-)_2) + e^{-i\phi}(\frac{\alpha}{\sqrt{2}}((c_V^\dagger)_2 + e^{-i\eta_1}e^{-i\phi_1}(d_V^\dagger)_3)$$

$$+ \beta(HV^-)_1)((HV^+)_1 + \frac{1}{\sqrt{2}}(DA^+ + DA^-)_2))|0_H, 0_V\rangle_A |0_H, 0_V\rangle_B.$$

The photon is then passed through a PBS resulting the state

$$|\psi\rangle_{AB}^{PBS_A^2} = \frac{1}{2}(e^{-i\theta_1}(\frac{\alpha}{\sqrt{2}}((c_H^\dagger)_2 + \frac{1}{\sqrt{2}}(RL^+ + RL^-)_3) + \beta(HV^+)_1)$$

$$(e^{-i\theta_3}e^{-i\mu}(HV^-)_1 + e^{-i\theta_2}\frac{1}{\sqrt{2}}(DA^+ - DA^-)_2) + e^{-i\phi}(\frac{\alpha}{\sqrt{2}}((c_V^\dagger)_2$$

$$+ e^{-i\eta_1}e^{-i\phi_1}\frac{1}{\sqrt{2}}(RL^+ - RL^-)_3) + \beta(HV^-)_1)((HV^+)_1 + \frac{1}{\sqrt{2}}(DA^+$$

$$+ DA^-)_2))|0_H, 0_V\rangle_A |0_H, 0_V\rangle_B.$$

In path 2 the photon is passed through two HWPs resulting the state

$$|\psi\rangle_{AB}^{PBS_A^2} = \frac{1}{2}(e^{-i\theta_1}(\frac{\alpha}{\sqrt{2}}((c_H^\dagger)_2 + \frac{1}{\sqrt{2}}(RL^+ + RL^-)_3) + \beta(HV^+)_1)$$

$$(e^{-i\theta_3}e^{-i\mu}(HV^-)_1 + e^{-i\theta_2}\frac{1}{\sqrt{2}}(DA^+ - DA^-)_2) + e^{-i\phi}(\frac{\alpha}{\sqrt{2}}$$

$$(e^{-i(\eta_2+\eta_3)}(c_V^\dagger)_2 + e^{-i\eta_1}e^{-i\phi_1}\frac{1}{\sqrt{2}}(RL^+ - RL^-)_3) + \beta(HV^-)_1)$$

$$((HV^+)_1 + \frac{1}{\sqrt{2}}(DA^+ + DA^-)_2))|0_H, 0_V\rangle_A |0_H, 0_V\rangle_B.$$

After PBS the state can be written as

$$|\psi\rangle_{AB}^{PBS_A^2} = \frac{1}{2}(e^{-i\theta_1}(\alpha\frac{1}{2}((DA^+ + DA^-)_2 + (RL^+ + RL^-)_3) + \beta(HV^+)_1)$$

$$(e^{-i\theta_3}e^{-i\mu}(HV^-)_1 + e^{-i\theta_2}\frac{1}{\sqrt{2}}(DA^+ - DA^-)_2)$$

$$+ e^{-i\phi}(\frac{\alpha}{2}(e^{-i(\eta_2+\eta_3)}(DA^+ - DA^-)_2 + e^{-i\eta_1}e^{-i\phi_1}RL^+ - RL^-)_3)$$

$$+ \beta(HV^-)_1)((HV^+)_1 + \frac{1}{\sqrt{2}}(DA^+ + DA^-)_2))|0_H, 0_V\rangle_A |0_H, 0_V\rangle_B.$$

As the phases do not contribute at the time of measurements, we can set all the phases equal to zero. Hence, we get

$$|\psi\rangle_{AB}^{PBS_A^2} = \frac{1}{2}(\frac{\alpha}{2}((DA^+ + DA^-)_2 + (RL^+ + RL^-)_3) + \beta(HV^+)_1)((HV^-)_1$$

$$+ \frac{1}{\sqrt{2}}(DA^+ - DA^-)_2) + (\frac{\alpha}{2}((DA^+ - DA^-)_2 + (RL^+ - RL^-)_3)$$

$$+ \beta(HV^-)_1)((HV^+)_1 + \frac{1}{\sqrt{2}}(DA^+ + DA^-)_2))|0_H, 0_V\rangle_A |0_H, 0_V\rangle_B.$$

Simplifying the above equation we get

$$
\begin{aligned}
|\psi\rangle_{AB}^{PBS_A^2} = &\frac{1}{2}((\frac{\alpha}{2}((DA^+ + DA^-)_2 + (RL^+ + RL^-)_3) + \beta(HV^+)_1)(HV^-)_1 \\
&+ \frac{1}{2}((\frac{\alpha}{2}(RL^+ + RL^-)_3) + \beta(HV^+)_1)\frac{1}{\sqrt{2}}(DA^+ - DA^-)_2 \\
&+ \frac{1}{2}(\frac{\alpha}{2}((DA^+ - DA^-)_2 + (RL^+ - RL^-)_3) + \beta(HV^-)_1) \\
&(HV^+)_1 + \frac{1}{2}(\frac{\alpha}{2}(RL^+ - RL^-)_3) + \beta(HV^-)_1)(\frac{1}{\sqrt{2}}(DA^+ + DA^-)_2 \\
&+ \frac{\alpha}{2\sqrt{2}}(DA^+ DA^+ + DA^- DA^-)_2
\end{aligned}
\tag{2}
$$

The conditional probability for the coincident events can be calculated from Eq. 2. In Table 1, $A = +$ (resp. $B = +$) implies Alice (resp. Bob) measures HA^+ or DA^+ or RL^+ in $\{HA^+, HA^-\}$, $\{DA^+, DA^-\}$, $\{RL^+, RL^-\}$ basis respectively. Similarly, $A = -$ (resp. $B = -$) implies Alice (resp. Bob) measures HA^- or DA^- or RL^- in $\{HA^+, HA^-\}$, $\{DA^+, DA^-\}$, $\{RL^+, RL^-\}$ basis respectively.

Table 1. Conditional Probability for coincident events

Alice	Bob	Pr(A = +, B = +)	Pr(A = +, B = -)	Pr(A = -, B = +)	Pr(A = -, B = -)
$\{HA^+, HA^-\}$	$\{HA^+, HA^-\}$	0	0	0	0
		0	$\frac{1}{4}\cdot\frac{1}{3}$	0	0
		0	0	$\frac{1}{4}\cdot\frac{1}{3}$	0
		0	0	0	0
$\{DA^+, DA^-\}$	$\{DA^+, DA^-\}$	$\frac{1}{8}\cdot\frac{2}{3}$	0	0	0
		0	0	0	0
		0	0	0	0
		0	0	0	$\frac{1}{8}\cdot\frac{2}{3}$
$\{HA^+, HA^-\}$	$\{DA^+, DA^-\}$	$\frac{1}{8}\cdot\frac{1}{3}$	0	0	0
		0	$\frac{1}{8}\cdot\frac{1}{3}$	0	0
		0	0	$\frac{1}{8}\cdot\frac{1}{3}$	0
		0	0	0	$\frac{1}{8}\cdot\frac{1}{3}$
$\{DA^+, DA^-\}$	$\{HA^+, HA^-\}$	$\frac{1}{16}\cdot\frac{2}{3}$	0	0	0
		0	$\frac{1}{16}\cdot\frac{2}{3}$	0	0
		0	0	$\frac{1}{16}\cdot\frac{2}{3}$	0
		0	0	0	$\frac{1}{16}\cdot\frac{2}{3}$
$\{RL^+, RL^-\}$	$\{HA^+, HA^-\}$	$\frac{1}{16}\cdot\frac{2}{3}$	0	0	0
		0	$\frac{1}{16}\cdot\frac{2}{3}$	0	0
		0	0	$\frac{1}{16}\cdot\frac{2}{3}$	0
		0	0	0	$\frac{1}{16}\cdot\frac{2}{3}$
$\{RL^+, RL^-\}$	$\{DA^+, DA^-\}$	$\frac{1}{16}\cdot\frac{2}{3}$	0	0	0
		0	$\frac{1}{16}\cdot\frac{2}{3}$	0	0
		0	0	$\frac{1}{16}\cdot\frac{2}{3}$	0
		0	0	0	$\frac{1}{16}\cdot\frac{2}{3}$

Comparing the theoretical value with the observed one, we may calculate the detectors' inefficiency and noise in the channel. These two parameters play important role in choosing error correction code and hash function for classical post-processing in practical implementation.

5 Proposed Algorithm

In this section we summarize our methodology in form of an algorithm. The algorithm is described in Algorithm 1.

Algorithm 1. Algoritm for step wise synthesis

---

1. Inputs: initial photon state, circuit diagram.
2. Represent the initial photon state in Fock state basis, i.e., in terms of

$$|n_H, n_V\rangle = \frac{(a_H^\dagger)^{n_H}(a_V^\dagger)^{n_V}}{\sqrt{n_H! n_V!}}|0\rangle. \tag{3}$$

3. If the photon passes through a BS, then for
   - port 1 and Horizontal polarization H, write $a_H = \sqrt{1-\eta}c_H + \sqrt{\eta}d_H$, where η is reflection coefficient and c_H and d_H represent outer ports of the BS.
   - port 2 and Horizontal polarization H, write $b_H = \sqrt{\eta}c_H - \sqrt{1-\eta}d_H$.
   - port 1 and Vertical polarization V, write $a_V = \sqrt{1-\eta}c_V + \sqrt{\eta}d_V$, where c_V and d_V represent outer ports of the BS.
   - port 2 and Vertical polarization V, write $b_V = \sqrt{\eta}c_V - \sqrt{1-\eta}d_V$.
4. If the photon passes through PBS, then for
   - H polarization,
     - write $a_H = c_H$
     - write $b_H = d_H$
   - V polarization,
     - write $a_V = d_V$
     - write $b_V = c_V$
5. If the photon passes through a PR making an angle θ with its fast axis, then for
   - H polarization, write $a_H = c_H$
   - V polarization write $a_V = e^{-i\theta}c_V$,
   where a stands for input port and c stands for output port.
6. Output: resultant state

---

6 Conclusion

Quantum key distribution protocols have been implemented in practice [26,27]. Commercial QKD devices are also available in the international market [33]. In the current effort, we propose a methodology towards step wise synthesis of the optical set-up. Our methodology may open up an avenue for automation where given an optical circuit and an initial state, the generated output will combine all optical operations that the photon passes through. In other words, the generated output will carry the information about the paths it travels. The motivation behind this is to build up a simulator which replace the optical laboratory set-up. In the current initiative, we consider the pure states only. Exploiting Stokes formalism (density matrix approach that includes mixed states), one may extend the simulator including the parameters for instrumental error. This might be an interesting future research direction.

References

1. Auccaise, R., et al.: Experimental analysis of the quantum complementarity principle. Phys. Rev. A **85**, 032121 (2012)
2. Bennett, C.H., Brassard, G.: Quantum cryptography: public key distribution and coin tossing. In: Proceedings of IEEE International Conference on Computers, Systems and Signal Processing, vol. 175, issue 8 (1984)
3. Bernstein, D.J., Chou, T., Schwabe, P.: McBits: fast constant-time code-based cryptography. In: Bertoni, G., Coron, J.-S. (eds.) CHES 2013. LNCS, vol. 8086, pp. 250–272. Springer, Heidelberg (2013). https://doi.org/10.1007/978-3-642-40349-1_15
4. Brakerski, Z., Langlois, A., Peikert, C., Regev, O., Stehlé, D.: Classical hardness of learning with errors. In: Proceedings of the Forty-fifth Annual ACM Symposium on Theory of Computing, STOC 2013, pp. 575–584. ACM, New York (2013)
5. Brańczyk, A.M.: Hong-Ou-Mandel Interference (2017). arXiv:1711.00080v1
6. Braunstein, S.L., Pirandola, S.: Side-channel-free quantum key distribution. Phys. Rev. Lett. **108**, 130502 (2012)
7. Curty, M., Ma, X., Lo, H.-K., Lütkenhaus, N.: Passive preparation of BB84 signal states with coherent light. Prog. Inf. (8), 57–63 (2011)
8. Dieks, D.: Communication by EPR devices. Phys. Lett. A **92**(6), 271272 (1982)
9. Ekert, A.K.: Quantum cryptography based on Bell's theorem. Phys. Rev. Lett. **67**(6), 661 (1991)
10. Ionicioiu, R., Terno, D.R.: Proposal for a quantum delayed-choice experiment. Phys. Rev. Lett. **107**, 230406 (2011)
11. Jennewein, T., Weihs, G., Zeilinger, A.: Photon statistics and quantum teleportation experiments. J. Phys. Soc. Jpn. **72**, 168–173 (2003). Proceedings Waseda International Symposium on Fundamental Physics-New Perspectives in Quantum Physics
12. Kaiser, F., Coudreau, T., Milman, P., Ostrowsky, D.B., Tanzilli, S.: Entanglement-enabled delayed choice experiment. Science **338**, 637640 (2012)
13. Kučra, P.: Quantum description of optical devices used in interferometry. Radioengineering **16**, 1–6 (2007)
14. Lo, H.K., Curty, M., Qi, B.: Measurement-device-independent quantum key distribution. Phys. Rev. Lett. **108**, 130503 (2012)
15. Nguyen, P.Q.: Lattice reduction algorithms: theory and practice. In: Paterson, K.G. (ed.) EUROCRYPT 2011. LNCS, vol. 6632, pp. 2–6. Springer, Heidelberg (2011). https://doi.org/10.1007/978-3-642-20465-4_2
16. Overbeck, R., Sendrier, N.: Code-based cryptography. In: Bernstein, D.J., Buchmann, J., Dahmen, E. (eds.) Post-Quantum Cryptography, pp. 95–145. Springer, Heidelberg (2009). https://doi.org/10.1007/978-3-540-88702-7_4

17. Peikert, C.: Public-key cryptosystems from the worst-case shortest vector problem: extended abstract. In: Proceedings of the Forty-first Annual ACM Symposium on Theory of Computing, STOC 2009, pp. 333–342. ACM, New York (2009)
18. Peruzzo, A., Shadbolt, P.J., Brunner, N., Popescu, S., O'Brien, J.L.: A quantum delayed choice experiment. Science **338**, 634–637 (2012)
19. Regev, O.: On lattices, learning with errors, random linear codes, and cryptography. In: Proceedings of the Thirty-seventh Annual ACM Symposium on Theory of Computing, STOC 2005, pp. 84–93. ACM, New York (2005)
20. Roy, S., Shukla, A., Mahesh, T.S.: NMR implementation of a quantum delayed-choice experiment. Phys. Rev. A **85**, 022109 (2012)
21. Sendrier, N.: Code-based cryptography: state of the art and perspectives. IEEE Secur. Priv. **15**(4), 44–50 (2017)
22. Shadbolt, P., Mathews, J.C.F., Laing, A., O'Brien, J.L.: Testing foundations of quantum mechanics with photons. Nat. Phys. **10**, 278286 (2014)
23. Shor, P.W.: Algorithms for quantum computation: discrete logarithms and factoring. In: Foundations of Computer Science (FOCS) 1994, pp. 124–134. IEEE Computer Society Press (1994)
24. Tang, J.S., et al.: Realization of quantum Wheelers delayed choice experiment. Nat. Photon **6**, 600604 (2012)
25. Rab, A.S., et al.: Entanglement of photons in their dual wave-particle nature. Nat. Commun. **8**, 915 (2017)
26. Tannous, R.: Polarization entangled photon sources for free-space quantum key distribution, Master Thesis, University of Waterloo (2018)
27. Tannous, R., Ye, Z., Jin, J., Kuntz, K.B., Lütkenhaus, N., Jennewein, T.: Demonstration of a 6–4 state reference frame independent channel for quantum key distribution (2019). https://arxiv.org/pdf/1905.09197.pdf
28. Tomamichel, M., Fehr, S., Kaniewski, J., Wehner, S.: One-sided device-independent QKD and position-based cryptography from monogamy games. In: Johansson, T., Nguyen, P.Q. (eds.) EUROCRYPT 2013. LNCS, vol. 7881, pp. 609–625. Springer, Heidelberg (2013). https://doi.org/10.1007/978-3-642-38348-9_36
29. Vazirani, U., Vidick, T.: Fully device-independent quantum key distribution. Phys. Rev. Lett. **113**, 140501 (2014)
30. Vintskevich, S.V., Grigoriev, D.A., Miklin, N.I., Fedorov, M.V.: Entanglement of multiphoton polarization Fock states and their superpositions. arXiv:1812.11462v2 (2019)
31. Wootters, W.K., Zurek, W.H.: A single quantum cannot be cloned. Nature **299**, 802803 (1982)
32. Supplementary material of [26]. https://doi.org/10.1038/s41467-017-01058-6
33. https://www.idquantique.com

Hardware: Efficiency, Side-Channel Resistance and PUFs

Efficient Hardware Implementations of Grain-128AEAD

Jonathan Sönnerup[(✉)], Martin Hell[(✉)], Mattias Sönnerup,
and Ripudaman Khattar

Department of Electrical and Information Technology, Lund University,
Lund, Sweden
{jonathan.sonnerup,martin.hell}@eit.lth.se, syntaxnone@gmail.com,
ripudaman11@gmail.com

Abstract. We implement the Grain-128AEAD stream cipher in hardware, using a 65 nm library. By exploring different optimization techniques, both at RTL level but also during synthesis, we first target high throughput, then low power. We reach over 33 GB/s targeting a high-speed design, at expense of power and area. We also show that, when targeting low power, the design only requires 0.23 μW running at 100 kHz. By unrolling the design, the energy consumed when encrypting a fixed length message decreases, making the 64 parallelized version the most energy efficient implementation, requiring only 11.2 nJ when encrypting a 64 kbit message. At the same time, the best throughput/power ratio is achieved at a parallelization of 4.

Keywords: Grain · Stream cipher · ASIC · Hardware design · NIST

1 Introduction

Due to the growth and widespread use of resource-constrained connected devices, e.g., in the Internet of Things (IoT), the need for protection against security threats has increased. RFID devices, smart cards, and sensor networks often require low power consumption as they are driven by batteries. The cost of manufacturing an IC chip is correlated to the area. Hence, area efficient designs are needed to reduce the cost when producing large quantities. This puts a demand, not only on the architectural design, but also on the implementation. The implementation may vary largely depending on what techniques are being utilized, both during programming (HDL), but also during synthesis, if aiming for an ASIC. At the same time, high-speed implementations are required for environments with much data, and where low latency is needed.

There are a large number of proposed cryptographic algorithms and several attempts have been made towards identifying suitable algorithms for widespread adoption, e.g., NESSIE, ECRYPT, CRYPTREC and the NIST AES contest. The successful standardization of AES has been followed by more NIST initiatives, most notably the SHA-3 competition, the Post-Quantum Cryptography

© Springer Nature Switzerland AG 2019
F. Hao et al. (Eds.): INDOCRYPT 2019, LNCS 11898, pp. 495–513, 2019.
https://doi.org/10.1007/978-3-030-35423-7_25

Standardization Process and the recent Lightweight Cryptography Standardization Process. The latter particularly addresses the need for algorithms that are specifically targeting resource constrained environments [1].

Grain-128AEAD is an instance of the Grain family of stream ciphers. Grain was first proposed in 2005, as an 80-bit stream cipher. The 128-bit variant Grain-128 was presented in 2006 [7], and was successfully cryptanalyzed in [5]. Building upon previous analysis results, a new 128-bit variant with authentication (MAC) support, Grain-128a, was proposed in 2011 [2]. It has also been adopted as an ISO standard [10]. Most recently, Grain-128AEAD supporting Authenticated Encryption with Associated Data, was proposed in 2019 and also submitted to the above mentioned NIST Lightweight Cryptography Standardization Process [8,9]. It is built upon the Grain-128a cipher, but with some added features. There have been several implementations of Grain-128a, most notably the work in [11], where the authors utilize Galois transforms, pipelining and multiple clocks, targeting a high-throughput implementation. While this is important in high-speed applications such as 5G (and beyond) and in servers and gateways which handle multiple connections simultaneously, low energy consumption for certain packet sizes is essential for constrained devices. In [4], the authors target low-energy implementations of stream ciphers, including Grain-128a, discussing multiple techniques for reducing power consumption. In this paper, we discuss several optimization techniques applied to Grain-128AEAD, targeting both high-speed implementations and low-power implementations. Optimizations are considered in both the RTL and at the synthesis level. A small area does not necessarily mean low energy consumption for encrypting a network packet. Adding some area to Grain will reduce the energy for encrypting a packet, even though the power consumption is slightly higher. Our results can be used to better understand the trade-offs between area, power, energy and throughput for the Grain-128AEAD stream cipher. They also provide new benchmark figures for its hardware performance, allowing better and more transparent comparison with other ciphers supporting AEAD. The code is made available at https://github.com/Grain-128AEAD.

The paper is outlined as follows. In Sect. 2, a high-level overview of the Grain-128AEAD design is presented. Section 3 presents a straightforward implementation providing results from where optimization strategies are derived. In Sect. 4, the utilized RTL optimizations are discussed, whereas in Sect. 5, different synthesis level optimizations are introduced. Finally, the results are presented in Sect. 6 and the conclusions are given in Sect. 7.

2   Grain-128AEAD

This section will provide a brief overview of the Grain-128AEAD design in order to support the optimization approaches discussed later. For a comprehensive design description, we refer to the specification [8,9].

Grain-128AEAD is a cipher in the Grain family. It supports Authenticated Encryption with Associated Data (AEAD) to simultaneously assure confidentiality and authenticity of the data. The overall design is similar to the other ciphers in the family, in particular Grain-128a. It consists of two main building blocks. The first is a pre-output generator consisting of a Linear Feedback Shift Register (LFSR) with feedback function f, a Non-linear Feedback Shift Register (NFSR) with feedback function g, and a pre-output function denoted h. The pre-output generator outputs a stream y_t. The second block is the authentication block consisting of a shift register and an accumulator. A multiplexer (MUX) is used to control if the pre-output stream y_t is used for authentication, z_i', or for keystream, z_i. The architectural overview of Grain-128AEAD is depicted in Fig. 1.

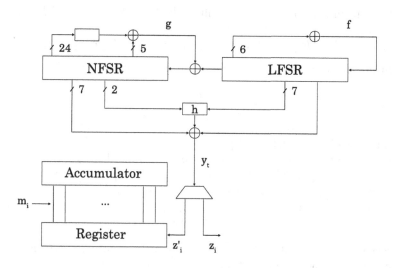

Fig. 1. An architectural overview of Grain-128AEAD.

2.1 Phases of Grain-128AEAD

For the hardware implementation, we logically divide the cipher into three phases. The first phase is the *loading phase*, in which the shift registers are loaded with the key and the nonce. Next, Grain-128AEAD enters the *initialization phase* in which the registers and the authentication module are initialized. Finally, the cipher enters the *running phase*, in which pre-output is generated both for encryption and authentication.

2.2 Pre-output Generation

The pre-output generator uses a 128-bit LFSR and a 128-bit NFSR. The content, at instance t, of the LFSR is denoted as $S_t = [s_0^t, s_1^t, \ldots, s_{127}^t]$, and similarly for the NFSR, $B_t = [b_0^t, b_1^t, \ldots, b_{127}^t]$. Together, the two FSRs form the 256-bit state of the generator. The feedback polynomial of the LFSR, f, may be written as the recurrence relation given by

$$s_{127}^{t+1} = s_0^t + s_7^t + s_{38}^t + s_{70}^t + s_{81}^t + s_{96}^t$$
$$= \mathcal{L}(S_t).$$

The feedback polynomial of the NFSR, g, may be written as the recurrence relation given by

$$
\begin{aligned}
b_{127}^{t+1} = \; & s_0^t + b_0^t + b_{26}^t + b_{56}^t + b_{91}^t + b_{96}^t + b_3^t b_{67}^t + b_{11}^t b_{13}^t \\
& + b_{17}^t b_{18}^t + b_{27}^t b_{59}^t + b_{40}^t b_{48}^t + b_{61}^t b_{65}^t + b_{68}^t b_{84}^t \\
& + b_{22}^t b_{24}^t b_{25}^t + b_{70}^t b_{78}^t b_{82}^t + b_{88}^t b_{92}^t b_{93}^t b_{95}^t \\
= \; & s_0^t + \mathcal{F}(B_t).
\end{aligned}
$$

The Boolean function h_t uses bits from both the LFSR and the NFSR, and is defined as

$$
h_t = b_{12}^t s_8^t + s_{13}^t s_{20}^t + b_{95}^t s_{42}^t + s_{60}^t s_{79}^t + b_{12}^t b_{95}^t s_{94}^t.
$$

The output, y_t, from the pre-output generator is given by

$$
y_t = h_t + s_{93}^t + \sum_{j \in \mathcal{A}} b_j^t,
$$

where $\mathcal{A} = \{2, 15, 36, 45, 64, 73, 89\}$.

After the initialization phase, the pre-output is used to generate keystream bits z_i for encryption and authentication bits z_i' to update the register in the accumulator generator. The keystream is generated as

$$
z_i = y_{384+2i},
$$

i.e., every even bit (counting from 0) from the pre-output generator is taken as a keystream bit. The authentication bits are generated as

$$
z_i' = y_{384+2i+1},
$$

i.e., every odd bit from the pre-output generator is taken as an authentication bit.

2.3 Authentication Module

The authenticator generator consists of a 64-bit shift register and a 64-bit accumulator. The content of the shift register, at instance i, is denoted $R_i = [r_0^i, r_1^i, \ldots, r_{63}^i]$, and similarly for the accumulator, the content is denoted $A_i = [a_0^i, a_1^i, \ldots, a_{63}^i]$. The accumulator is updated as

$$
a_j^{i+1} = a_j^i + m_i r_j^i, \qquad 0 \le j \le 63, \quad 0 \le i \le L, \tag{1}
$$

where m_i is the ith message bit, and the shift register is updated as

$$
\begin{aligned}
r_{63}^{i+1} &= z_i', \\
r_j^{i+1} &= r_{j+1}^i, \qquad 0 \le j \le 62.
\end{aligned}
$$

2.4   Loading and Initialization

After reset, the cipher must be loaded and initialized. The loading is performed as follows. Let k_i be the key bits where $0 \leq i \leq 127$, and let IV_i be the nonce (IV) bits where $0 \leq i \leq 95$. The NFSR is loaded with the key, i.e., $b_i^0 = k_i$, $0 \leq i \leq 127$. The first 96 bits of the LFSR is loaded with the nonce, i.e., $s_i^0 = IV_i$, $0 \leq i \leq 95$, and the last 32 bits are filled with 31 ones and a zero, i.e., $s_i^0 = 1$, $96 \leq i \leq 126$, $s_{127}^0 = 0$. Next, in the initialization phase, the cipher is clocked 256 times, feeding back the pre-output adding it with the input to the NFSR and LFSR, using the XOR operation, i.e.,

$$s_{127}^{t+1} = \mathcal{L}(S_t) + y_t, \quad 0 \leq t \leq 255,$$
$$b_{127}^{t+1} = s_0^t + \mathcal{F}(B_t) + y_t, \quad 0 \leq t \leq 255.$$

Next, the shift register and accumulator in the authenticator are initialized with the pre-output stream as

$$a_j^0 = y_{256+j}, \quad 0 \leq j \leq 63,$$
$$r_j^0 = y_{320+j}, \quad 0 \leq j \leq 63.$$

At the same time, the key is added to the feedback of the LFSR as

$$s_{127}^{t+1} = \mathcal{L}(S_t) + k_{t-256}, \quad 256 \leq t \leq 383,$$

while the NFSR is updated as

$$b_{127}^{t+1} = s_0^t + \mathcal{F}(B_t), \quad 256 \leq t \leq 383.$$

The loading phase and the initialization phase are summarized in Fig. 2.

3   A Straightforward Approach

The stream cipher is implemented in hardware using RTL design in VHDL. For synthesis and power simulation, the Synopsys Design Compiler 2013.12 is used along with a 65 nm library from ST Microelectronics, stm065v536. The number of required gates, and the number of transistors in a gate depends on the library used and may vary by a large degree. In this paper, the area of the designs are given in gate equivalents (GE), which is the physical area divided by the area of a 2-input NAND gate for the given library.

A straightforward approach is taken when implementing the cipher, closely following the proposed architectural design in [8,9] - the FSRs are in Fibonacci configuration parallelized at most 32 times. The key and nonce are simultaneously loaded serially, and the accumulator is loaded by first loading the shift register, then moving the values to the accumulator. For the parallelized implementations, the loading phase is sped up by a factor n, where n is the parallelization level. A simple Finite State Machine (FSM) is used to keep track of

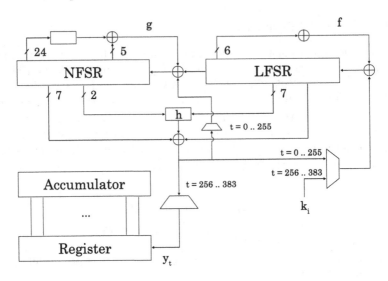

Fig. 2. An architectural overview of the initialization in Grain-128AEAD.

the different phases, or states, in order to control the data paths. Finally, we let the synthesizing tool optimize for speed. This implementation and synthesis is used for benchmarking and comparison with our optimized implementations.

In order to improve the bottlenecks in the synthesized design, we must analyze the critical paths. Similar to [11], we define the following delays:

- D_n: the maximal delay from any NFSR or LFSR flip-flop to any other NFSR or LFSR flip-flop.
- D_y: the maximal delay from any NFSR or LFSR flip-flop to the output, via the y function.
- D_{ya}: the maximal delay from any NFSR or LFSR flip-flop to any accumulator flip-flip, via the y function.
- D_a: the maximal delay from any flip-flop in the authentication section to any accumulator flip-flop, or output.
- D_{yn}: the maximal delay from a flip-flop of the NFSR or LFSR through the y function to the first flip-flop of the NFSR. This path only exists during initialization of the cipher, via a MUX.

The critical paths are highlighted in Fig. 3. Note that y_{out}, after initialization, corresponds to z as in Fig. 1. Similarly, y_{accum}, after initialization, corresponds to z'.

Synthesizing the design yields the results shown in Table 1, where the propagation delay of the critical path is listed. D_{yn} is only available during initialization. In the running state of the cipher, it is instead D_n which is the critical path. These critical delays, together with D_{ya}, will be targeted in the next section.

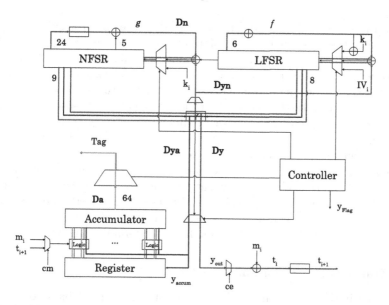

Fig. 3. Architectural overview of Grain-128AEAD with the following potential critical paths highlighted: D_n (blue), D_y (purple), D_{ya} (green), D_a (yellow), and D_{yn} (red). (Color figure online)

Table 1. Clock periods and critical paths of the straightforward implementation, for different levels of parallelization.

	x1	x2	x4	x8	x16	x32
Period (ns)	490	610	640	690	770	840
Critical Path	D_{yn}	D_{yn}	D_{yn}	D_{yn}	D_{ya}	D_{ya}

4 RTL Level Optimizations

Here, we present the architectural optimization techniques utilized when targeting speed, area, and power. In particular, for speed improvements, we aim to lower the delay induced by the critical paths in Table 1. We start by presenting a general optimization technique, Galois transform, to reduce the D_n path. Then, we utilize a similar technique in order to reduce the path D_{yn}, discussed in Sect. 4.2.

4.1 Galois Transformation

As described earlier, the D_n path lies between two flip-flops (any flip-flop to the right most flip-flop in Fig. 1) in the FSRs, for the 1, 2, 4, and 8 parallelized versions, causing a bottleneck in the running mode. The usual strategy would be to pipeline the FSRs by inserting flip-flops at well chosen positions. In order to pipeline a design, the delay elements can only be inserted in the feed-forward cutset of the corresponding graph [12]. This is not possible for the FSRs due to their intrinsic feedback property. In order to decrease the propagation delay in the D_n path, the cipher may be transformed from its normal Fibonacci configuration to a Galois configuration. In the Fibonacci configuration, the flip-flops are updated with the value of the previous flip-flop every clock cycle, i.e., $x_i = x_{i+1}$, except for x_{n-1} which gets updated with the result of the feedback polynomial, i.e., $x_{n-1} = f(x)$. In the Galois configuration, some of the flip-flops get updated with the result of a function of other flip-flops, i.e., $x_i = g(x)$. The Galois configuration leads to shorter propagation delays due to the feedback function in Fibonacci being split up and put in between flip-flops.

For an LFSR, the Fibonacci to Galois transform is a one-to-one mapping. For an NFSR, multiple Galois configurations exist for a given Fibonacci configuration [6]. The Galois transform is identical to Grain-128a, hence we refer to [11] for details. Grain-128a can not be transformed to a Galois configuration for a parallelization level above 16. The same holds for Grain-128AEAD.

4.2 Transforming the y Function

During the initialization phase, the y function is being fed back to the shift registers, forming an FSR. As in the previous section, it is not possible to insert pipelines due to the lack of a feed-forward cutset. Instead, similar to the Galois transform, it is possible to transform the y function in such way that it is split up and fed back to different registers, which reduces the critical path, D_{yn}. The transformed functions are denoted as Y_{125}, Y_{126}, and Y_{127}. For a parallelization level of 8 and 16, only Y_{126} and Y_{127} may be used. As an example for the non-parallelized version, the functions are given by

$$Y_{127} = b_{12}s_8 + s_{13}s_{20} + b_{95}s_{42},$$
$$Y_{126} = b_{11}b_{94}s_{93} + b_{72} + b_1 + s_{50}s_{78},$$
$$Y_{125} = s_{91} + b_{87} + b_{13} + b_{34} + b_{43} + b_{62}.$$

After initialization, during the running state, the feedback loop is disconnected. This allows for insertion of pipelines steps. By combining both Galois-like transformation and pipelining, both D_{yn} and D_y may be reduced, see Fig. 4. The controller switches between the two methods when required.

4.3 Isolating the Authentication Module

The accumulator is updated using the values in the shift register as in Eq. (1). When parallelizing the design, the accumulator is updated with the corresponding shift register plus values from the shift registers with larger index as

$$a_j^{i+1} = a_j^i + \sum_{k=0}^{\frac{p}{2}-1} m_{i+k} \cdot r_{j+k}^i, \qquad p \geq 4,$$

where p is the parallelization level. For $p = 2$, the update expression is equivalent to Eq. (1), since 1 bit is generated every clock cycle for authentication. Note that

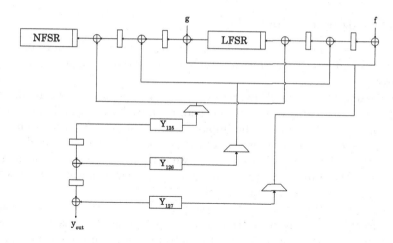

Fig. 4. The transformation of the y function along with pipeline steps and control logic.

for a parallelization level of 4 and above, some values have not yet been shifted in to the shift register, e.g., for $p = 4$, the register a_{63} is updated as

$$a_{63}^{i+1} = a_{63}^i + \left(m_i \cdot r_{63}^i\right) + \left(m_{i+1} \cdot r_{64}^i\right),$$

where r_{64} has been generated but is not located in the shift register. This can be seen as a future value, and requires extra combinational logic to handle. This means that the path D_{ya} becomes longer and, for the higher levels of parallelization, affects the timing of the design, as seen in Table 1.

In order to make the D_{ya} path shorter, a pipeline step is inserted between the y function and the accumulator logic, as shown in Fig. 5. This allows for the throughput to increase due to a higher clock frequency, but adds a 1 clock cycle delay to the accumulator calculation. Note that this does not affect the security.

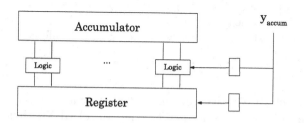

Fig. 5. Isolating the authentication module using pipelining.

4.4 Optimizing the Controller

A controller is a unit responsible for managing the data flow and operations, such as the feedback loop, when to accumulate data, and when to encrypt the plaintext.

The straightforward implementation of the controller is a finite state machine (FSM) with states corresponding to loading, initialization, and the running phase. The controller can also be implemented using a LFSR with some combinational logic. Experiments with LFSRs gave roughly the same results as the FSM generated by the synthesizer. Here, we explore an alternative strategy to keep track of the state by using a clock divider and a shift register, which often, but not always, gave better performance.

The idea is to start from an empty shift register (all zeroes), and shifting in a 1 each clock cycle. This means that after n clock cycles, there is a 1 at index n in the shift register. We can use this to control the logic in the cipher via, e.g., MUXes. However, Grain requires 512 clock cycles before it produces the first bit, i.e., 128 for loading key and nonce plus 384 for the initialization rounds. This results in a shift register with 512 flip-flops, which is not desirable due to the huge increase in size. Instead, note that the resolution given by 512 registers is not fully utilized, since we ignore most of the intermediate values, hence we can reduce the size. With a reduced size, we must compensate with a lower clock frequency for controlling the design at the correct time instances. This is done using a clock divider to slow the shift register down by a factor 2^k. The value of $2^k p$ can not exceed 128, since the least amount of clock cycles that we need to keep track of are 128, for loading key and nonce. The number of registers required depends on the level of parallelization, p, and the k value as $512/(2^k p)$. Taking the clock divider registers into account gives an expression for the total number of registers required as

$$\frac{512}{2^k p} + k.$$

This design does not require much hardware, e.g., letting $p = 16, k = 3$ results in 7 flip-flops. In this paper, the largest value of k is selected, for every level of parallelization, i.e., $k = \log_2(128/p)$.

The index of the shift register corresponding to the different phases are calculated as

$$i_{\text{load}} = \frac{128}{kp}, \quad i_{\text{init}} = \frac{128 + 256}{kp}, \quad i_{\text{run}} = \frac{512}{kp}.$$

For the control MUXes that remain in their state after being activated may be directly connected to the controller. For the control MUXes that are only activated during a single state, an inverter together with an AND-gate is required.

4.5 Unrolling

Grain natively supports parallelization up to 32 times by using multiple feedback and output functions, f, g and y. However, there is nothing preventing us to go further, at RTL level. Consider AES, where multiple rounds of the AES round function is executed one after the other, in a loop structure. The block is fed back via MUXes to realize successive iterations. Unrolling the AES rounds to a level L means that we put L AES round functions serially in a single combinational block as done in [13].

When unrolling Grain, we do not utilize multiple instances of the FSRs, but rather the feedback functions. When reaching a parallelization level above 32, the feedback functions start to interact. Revising the feedback function f of the LFSR, we can extend this to include multiple copies of f, denoted as f_k. The index k is related to the level of parallelization, where the highest k value plus 1 $(\max(k) + 1)$ equals the parallelization level. Expressing the bits as a sequence, we can write the expression as

$$s_{i+128+k} = s_{i+0+k} + s_{i+7+k} + s_{i+38+k} + s_{i+70+k} + s_{i+81+k} + s_{i+96+k}.$$

With $k = 31$, the bit with the highest index in f_{31} is $s_{i+96+31} = s_{i+127}$, by design. However, $k = 32$ includes bit index s_{i+128} in f_{32}, which is not a register index, but rather the output from the function f_0. Thus, the two feedback functions are connected, as seen in Fig. 6. Increasing k leads to more interconnection between the feedback functions, thus increasing the propagation delay. Parallelization of higher degrees for the authentication module continues the approach described in Sect. 4.3.

Apart from an increase in throughput, unrolling also allows for energy saving as more data is processed in a single clock cycle which reduces the total switching activity and the number of clock cycles it takes to complete a computation [3].

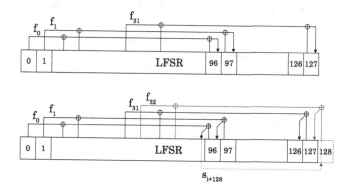

Fig. 6. Example of unrolling above the specified level of 32. The bottom picture shows the structure when using a parallelization level of 33. The last feedback function, f_{32}, needs to read the value from a flip flop that does not exist, the register index 128. Instead, this value is the output from f_0, which would have been stored in register index 128 if it existed. We can therefore take the output from f_0 as an input to f_{32}. From this it is clear that the propagation delay increases when exceeding the specified level of parallelization.

5   Synthesis Level Optimization

Synthesis is the process where high-level RTL code, like VHDL and Verilog, is used to generate a gate-level netlist. There are 3 steps involved during synthesis:

1. Translation: The RTL code is converted to a technology-independent representation of Boolean expressions.
2. Optimization: The Boolean expressions are minimized, with respect to gates, using a minimization algorithm.
3. Technology mapping: The Boolean expressions are mapped to a library, based on the used technology, in order to produce a gate-level netlist.

Design Vision requires the RTL code, design constraints, and a standard cell library, in order to generate a netlist. Design Vision offers two commands used for compiling - `compile` and `compile_ultra`. The `compile_ultra` command is used for designs with tight timing constraints, and produces better quality of results compared to `compile`. Hence, only `compile_ultra` is used during synthesis.

There are several compiler options to be utilized during synthesis. Here, we highlight some of the most commonly used features:

- **Structuring** - The process where intermediate variables are added to the design, in order to reduce area. The synthesis tool factors out common sub functions that mostly reduces the area and turn them into intermediate variables.
- **Flattening** - Here, the tool converts combinational logic paths into a sum-of-products representation. This often leads to a faster design due to the combinational logic requiring only two levels. Consequently, it may lead to an increase in area.
- **Ungrouping** - A common strategy when implementing a design is to group different parts of the code, to have a hierarchical design. This leads to well structured design and it is easy to analyze the synthesized design. By ungrouping, the tool is less constrained and may reorganize the design as it see fits, which may lead to a faster design, at the expense of area.
- **Clock Gating** - Insert control logic in order to regulate the clock signal, either to shut it down at time instances, or to modify the clock pulse. This may be used to save energy.

5.1   Transistor Types

In a complementary MOS (CMOS) design, both NMOS and PMOS are used. When one is conducting, the other is not, resulting in very small static power consumption, given by

$$P_s = V_{dd} \cdot I_{\text{leakage}},$$

where V_{dd} is the supply voltage. The leakage current depends on the threshold voltage, V_{th}, and a transistor with low V_{th}, LVT, has higher leakage current than a transistor with a high V_{th}, HVT. To minimize leakage current, HVT transistors are most suitable for power efficient implementations. For the high-speed implementations, LVT transistors are most suitable since they allow to increase the switching speed.

6   Synthesis Results

Providing results for all possible combinations of implementations, synthesis options and transistors would become very verbose. Instead, to facilitate a more clear and concise presentation and basis for comparison, the implementations considered will be as follows.

- **Straightforward implementation.** This implementation will closely follows the architectural design, using no optimization techniques. The design is synthesized for high speed utilizing LVT transistors, and different synthesis flags to achieve the best result.
- **High speed implementation.** Here, we apply all viable optimizations at RTL and synthesis level and synthesize for high speed using LVT transistors.
- **Low Power implementation.** In the low power scenario, we cut back the clock frequency, employing only unrolling and the improved controller as optimization techniques. Both the LVT and HVT transistors are used for comparison of power consumption.

6.1   Straightforward Implementation

Results for the straightforward implementation are shown in Table 2, using no RTL optimizations, but synthesized for maximum speed. Synthesis options such as flattening, structuring, and ungrouping were utilized. Neither flattening nor structuring affected the result significantly. Only the grouping/ungrouping option made a difference. This difference was typically in the order of 0.02 ns for the period. In the result tables, the best result is presented, and we also highlight whether grouping (G) or ungrouping (U) yielded the result.

Similar to [4], we also calculate the energy consumed when encrypting 1 block of data (64 bits) and 1000 blocks, shown in Table 3. For example, encrypting 1 block of data, in the non-parallelized ($n = 1$) version at 2.04 GHz, requires 128 (loading key and IV) + 384 (initialization) + 128 (64 keystream bits + 64 bits for authentication) = 640 clock cycles. The energy consumed results in 640×0.49 ns $\times 170\,\mu W = 0.053$ nJ. Note that the number of clock cycles required for encryption is inversely proportional to n.

The non-parallelized version has the highest clock frequency, but the lowest throughput (thrp). The clock period does not scale at the same rate as n, which allows the higher levels of parallelization to have higher throughput. Between $n = 1$ and $n = 32$, the throughput increases by a factor 19, whereas the area only increases by a factor 3.8. For $n = 32$, we achieve the highest throughput to area ratio. For $n = 4$, the highest throughput to power is reached along with the lowest energy consumption, making it the most power efficient version.

Table 2. Straightforward implementation synthesized for high speed. The throughput per area is given in kbit/s per GE. The throughput per power is given in GB/s per mW. The synthesis optimization (Opt.) shows whether grouping (G) or ungrouping (U) gave the best result.

n	Period	Freq.	Thrp.	Area	Power	Thrp. / Area	Thrp. / Power	Opt.
	(ns)	(GHz)	(Gb/s)	(GE)	(mW)			
1	0.49	2.04	1.02	2689	0.17	182	5.99	U
2	0.61	1.64	1.64	2776	0.14	284	11.76	G
4	0.64	1.56	3.12	3333	0.21	450	14.93	G
8	0.69	1.44	5.76	4324	0.42	640	13.70	G
16	0.77	1.29	10.32	6265	0.92	792	11.24	G
32	0.84	1.19	19.04	10226	2.54	895	7.52	G

Table 3. This shows the energy consumption for the straightforward implementation, processing 1 and 1000 blocks of data. 1 block equals 64 bits of data.

Energy (nJ)	x1	x2	x4	x8	x16	x32
1 Block	0.053	0.027	0.022	0.023	0.028	0.042
1000 Blocks	10.70	5.48	4.31	4.65	5.69	8.57

The ungrouping option seems to be worse for all versions except $n = 1$. Using the ungrouping option led to a higher clock frequency, but the tool reported fanout violations which it could not resolve. Choosing to only consider results without any violations, these results were omitted.

6.2 High Speed Implementation

Here, we apply the techniques described earlier in order to increase the throughput of the design. For the parallelization levels 1, 2, 4, 8 and 16, Galois transform together with y transform, isolation of authentication module, and the optimized controller are utilized. For the 32 (parallelized) and 64 (unrolled) versions, only isolation of authentication and the optimized controller are possible. Transformation of the y function is not applicable due to similar constraints as for the Galois transformation of the shift registers.

The results for the optimized implementation are presented in Table 4. The energy consumption for a given message length is given in Table 5, where the highest speed at each level of parallelization from Table 4 is used. Table 4 shows an increase in throughput for every level of parallelization, at the expense of increased power consumption. However what is interesting is that the optimized controller actually reduces the power consumption while increasing the throughput for $n = 32$ and $n = 64$. For $n = 32$, the power consumption is lower than the straightforward implementation, while for $n = 64$, it is just 0.22 mW more than the straightforward, 32 parallelized version, but with a 76% increase in

Table 4. Results for the high-speed implementation, with optimized controller on greyed background and regular controller on white. The throughput per area is given in kbit/s per GE. The throughput per power is given in GB/s per mW.

n	Period	Freq.	Thrp.	Area	Power	Thrp. / Area	Thrp. / Power	Opt.
	(ns)	(GHz)	(Gb/s)	(GE)	(mW)			
1	0.43	2.3	1.15	2791	0.24	412	4.79	U
	0.40	2.5	1.25	2645	0.25	472	5.00	U
2	0.46	2.17	2.17	2800	0.21	776	10.33	G
	0.43	2.32	2.32	2695	0.23	861	10.09	G
4	0.47	2.13	4.26	3335	0.29	1277	14.69	G
	0.48	2.08	4.16	3199	0.29	1300	14.34	U
8	0.48	2.08	8.32	4537	0.67	1834	12.42	G
	0.46	2.17	8.68	4448	0.67	1951	12.96	G
16	0.50	2.00	16.00	6270	1.44	2552	11.11	G
	0.48	2.08	16.64	7118	1.55	2338	10.74	U
32	0.69	1.45	23.20	9148	2.66	2536	8.72	G
	0.64	1.56	24.96	9206	1.78	2710	14.02	U
64	1.00	1.00	32.00	16618	4.76	1926	6.72	G
	0.95	1.05	33.60	16958	2.76	1982	12.17	U

Table 5. This shows the energy consumption for the high-speed implementation, processing 1 and 1000 blocks of data. 1 block equals 64 bits of data.

Energy (nJ)	x1	x2	x4	x8	x16	x32	x64
1 Block	0.064	0.032	0.022	0.025	0.030	0.023	0.026
1000 Blocks	12.85	6.35	4.38	4.95	5.98	4.58	5.26

throughput. We can again note that a parallelization level of 4 yields the highest throughput per power along with the lowest energy consumption. The optimized controller also affects the throughput per power the most for $n = 32$ and $n = 64$.

As also seen in Table 4, ungrouping the design led to a higher throughput when using the optimized controller.

It is clear that the area increases with higher throughput, due to higher levels of parallelization. An important metric is the throughput per area, which measures area efficiency. From the table, we find that the most area efficient implementation occurs when $n = 32$, using the improved controller. This is not surprising since increasing parallelization should only require a "small" increase in area, by design. This is an important feature in the Grain family of stream ciphers.

6.3 Low Power Implementation

When targeting low power, a clock period must be specified. Many low-power devices run at frequencies around 10 MHz. The ISO standard for contactless smart cards, ISO/IEC 15693, defines the frequency to be 13.56 MHz. Older proximity cards operate at 125 kHz. Thus, for low power applications, we choose to synthesize the design at the clock frequencies 100 KHz and 10 MHz, shown in Tables 6 and 7, respectively.

The synthesis script utilizes compile_ultra with clock gating and low power transistors (HVT). For comparison, we also synthesize the design using the high speed scripts and select the best result, for comparison. The RTL optimization implemented for low power is unrolling along with the optimized controller.

Table 6. Result for the low power implementation running at 100 kHz. Here, we compare the speed script (S_s), the power (P_s) script, and the power script using the optimized controller (P_{opt}). 1 block equals 64 bits of data.

n	Area (GE)			Power (μW)			Energy (nJ)	
	S_s	P_s	P_{opt}	S_s	P_s	P_{opt}	1 block	1000 blocks
1	2509	2375	2337	2.29	0.23	0.26	1.47	296
	-	-5%	-7%	-	-89%	-88%	-	-
2	2592	2588	2511	2.33	0.28	0.30	0.90	180
	-	0%	-3%	-	-87%	-86%	-	-
4	2952	2950	2862	2.33	0.29	0.32	0.46	93.2
	-	0%	-3%	-	-87%	-86%	-	-
8	3695	3692	3594	2.76	0.31	0.35	0.25	49.8
	-	0%	-2%	-	-88%	-87%	-	-
16	5168	5158	5053	3.77	0.42	0.39	0.16	31.3
	-	0%	-2%	-	-89%	-90%	-	-
32	8168	8126	7950	5.93	0.62	0.46	0.09	18.5
	-	0%	-3%	-	-90%	-92%	-	-
64	14100	14093	13800	10.89	1.08	0.63	0.06	12.7
	-	0%	-2%	-	-90%	-94%	-	-

Overall, there was very little difference in area when synthesizing for high speed and low power using the standard controller. For such low frequencies, the timing is easily met and the tool optimizes for area in both cases, thus there is not much to improve. For the power however, there is a clear difference using HVT transistors compared to LVT. There is a 86–92% reduction in power consumption for all levels of parallelization running at 100 kHz, and a 19–37% power reduction for 10 MHz. In the design paper of Grain [8,9], the authors used HVT transistors when synthesizing for high speed. This led to a lower

Table 7. Result for the low power implementation running at 10 MHz. Here, we compare the speed script (S_s), the power (P_s) script, and the power script using the optimized controller (P_{opt}). 1 block equals 64 bits of data.

n	Area (μm^2)			Power (μW)			Energy (nJ)	
	S_s	P_s	P_{opt}	S_s	P_s	P_{opt}	1 block	1000 blocks
1	2510	2375	2337	33.66	22.07	25.21	1.41	283
	-	-5%	-6%	-	-34%	-25%	-	-
2	2592	2589	2511	33.96	26.93	29.13	0.86	173
	-	0%	-3%	-	-21%	-14%	-	-
4	2952	2951	2862	34.43	27.38	31.05	0.44	88.0
	-	0%	-3%	-	-20%	-10%	-	-
8	3695	3693	3595	36.83	29.38	33.59	0.24	47.2
	-	0%	-3%	-	-20%	-9%	-	-
16	5168	5162	5057	44.02	39.49	36.93	0.15	29.7
	-	0%	-2%	-	-10%	-16%	-	-
32	8172	8128	7951	66.02	57.08	41.66	0.08	16.7
	-	0%	-2%	-	-13%	-37%	-	-
64	14101	14093	13810	117.4	97.39	55.93	0.06	11.2
	-	0%	-2%	-	-17%	-52%	-	-

clock frequency and a higher power consumption than the figures in Table 4. Hence, HVT should only be used for lower frequencies where power is the main concern, whereas LVT should be used for higher frequencies where the target is speed.

Even though the power consumption increases with increasing n, the energy cost decreases since the computation can be done in much shorter time. This leads to the unrolled 64-parallelized version being the most energy efficient implementation for a given message length.

The optimized controller reduces the area in all cases at expense of higher power consumption for $n = 1, 2, 4, 8$. For $n = 16, 32, 64$, the power consumption is reduced when using the optimized controller.

7   Conclusions

In this paper, we implemented Grain-128AEAD and investigated the impact of different implementation strategies, from RTL to synthesis-level design, to either achieve high throughput or low power consumption.

By utilizing different optimization techniques, we reduced the power by up to 94% compared to a straightforward implementation. By unrolling the design, the power consumption increases while the energy for encrypting a message of fixed size decreases. The 64-level parallelization implementation requires only 11.2 nJ when encrypting 64 kbits of data compared to 283 nJ for the non-parallelized version. For the high-speed implementation, the maximum throughput reached is 33.6 GB/s. It is not obvious in which cases the (un)grouping option yields the best result, hence both options should be analyzed in order to find the best result. We notice that a parallelization level of 4 yields the most power efficient implementation, both for the straightforward implementation and the high-speed one. The experiments show that Grain is well suited both in high-speed applications as well as on constrained devices requiring low power consumption.

Acknowledgements. This paper was supported by the Swedish Foundation for Strategic Research, grant RIT17-0032.

References

1. National Institute of Standards and Technology: Proposed submission requirements and evaluation criteria for the post-quantum cryptography standardization process (2018). https://csrc.nist.gov/CSRC/media/Projects/Lightweight-Cryptography/documents/final-lwc-submission-requirements-august2018.pdf
2. Ågren, M., Hell, M., Johansson, T., Meier, W.: Grain-128 a: a new version of Grain-128 with optional authentication. Int. J. Wireless Mobile Comput. **5**(1), 48–59 (2011)
3. Banik, S., Bogdanov, A., Regazzoni, F.: Exploring energy efficiency of lightweight block ciphers. In: Dunkelman, O., Keliher, L. (eds.) SAC 2015. LNCS, vol. 9566, pp. 178–194. Springer, Cham (2016). https://doi.org/10.1007/978-3-319-31301-6_10
4. Banik, S., et al.: Towards low energy stream ciphers. IACR Trans. Symmetric Cryptol. **2018**(2), 1–19 (2018). https://doi.org/10.13154/tosc.v2018.i2.1-19. https://tosc.iacr.org/index.php/ToSC/article/view/886
5. Dinur, I., Shamir, A.: Breaking Grain-128 with dynamic cube attacks. In: Joux, A. (ed.) FSE 2011. LNCS, vol. 6733, pp. 167–187. Springer, Heidelberg (2011). https://doi.org/10.1007/978-3-642-21702-9_10
6. Dubrova, E.: A transformation from the Fibonacci to the Galois NLFSRs. IEEE Trans. Inf. Theory **55**(11), 5263–5271 (2009). https://doi.org/10.1109/TIT.2009.2030467
7. Hell, M., Johansson, T., Maximov, A., Meier, W.: A stream cipher proposal: Grain-128. In: 2006 IEEE International Symposium on Information Theory, pp. 1614–1618, July 2006. https://doi.org/10.1109/ISIT.2006.261549
8. Hell, M., Johansson, T., Meier, W., Sönnerup, J., Yoshida, H.: An AEAD variant of the grain stream cipher. In: Carlet, C., Guilley, S., Nitaj, A., Souidi, E.M. (eds.) C2SI 2019. LNCS, vol. 11445, pp. 55–71. Springer, Cham (2019). https://doi.org/10.1007/978-3-030-16458-4_5
9. Hell, M., Johansson, T., Meier, W., Sönnerup, J., Yoshida, H.: Grain-128AEAD - a lightweight AEAD streamcipher. NIST Lightweight Cryptography, Round 1 Submission (2019)
10. ISO/IEC 29167–13:2015 information technology—automatic identification and data capture techniques—part 13: Crypto suite Grain-128A security services for air interface communications (2015)
11. Mansouri, S.S., Dubrova, E.: An improved hardware implementation of the Grain-128a stream cipher. In: Kwon, T., Lee, M.-K., Kwon, D. (eds.) ICISC 2012. LNCS, vol. 7839, pp. 278–292. Springer, Heidelberg (2013). https://doi.org/10.1007/978-3-642-37682-5_20

12. Proakis, J.G., Manolakis, D.K.: Digital Signal Processing, 4th edn. Prentice-Hall Inc., Upper Saddle River (2006)
13. Zambreno, J., Nguyen, D., Choudhary, A.: Exploring area/delay tradeoffs in an AES FPGA implementation. In: Becker, J., Platzner, M., Vernalde, S. (eds.) FPL 2004. LNCS, vol. 3203, pp. 575–585. Springer, Heidelberg (2004). https://doi.org/10.1007/978-3-540-30117-2_59

Exploring Lightweight Efficiency of **ForkAES**

Fatih Balli$^{(\boxtimes)}$ and Subhadeep Banik

LASEC, Ecole Polytechnique Fédérale de Lausanne, Lausanne, Switzerland
{fatih.balli,subhadeep.banik}@epfl.ch

Abstract. Recently the ForkAES construction was proposed by Andreeva et al. for efficiently performing authenticated encryption of very short messages on next generation IoT devices. The ForkAES tweakable block cipher uses around one and a half AES encryption calls to produce a pair of ciphertexts for any given plaintext. However the only downside of the construction is that it needs to store an extra state of 128 bits in addition with the storage elements required to perform AES encryption. Thus a hardware implementation of ForkAES would require additional circuit area to accommodate the extra state.

In this paper, we first show that it is possible to implement ForkAES without any additional storage elements other than those required to implement AES, if the AES circuit can additionally perform decryption. Such an implementation naturally requires more clock cycles to perform ForkAES operations. We extend the recently proposed Atomic AES v2.0 architecture to realize ForkAES and compare the area-latency trade-offs incurred with and without an additional storage. The area of the most compact ForkAES design takes about 1.2 times that of AES.

In the second part of the paper we look at another important parameter of lightweight efficiency, i.e. energy. It is well known that round based constructions for AES are the most energy efficient ones. We extend the so-called "S_3K_2" construction of Banik et al. (IEEE HOST 17) to realize ForkAES in an energy-preserving manner, and compare the effects of some design choices. The energy consumption of our best ForkAES design takes about 2 times that of AES. From lightweight design perspective, our results hence demonstrate that although ForkAES lives up to its promise (of being roughly 1.5 times that of AES) in terms of its area, the same does not hold for its energy consumption.

Keywords: Energy efficiency · ForkAES · Serialized implementation

1 Introduction

In the past few years, lightweight cryptography has indeed become an important research discipline. A number of lightweight block ciphers like Clefia [2] and

---

The source code for our implementations are provided at [1].

© Springer Nature Switzerland AG 2019
F. Hao et al. (Eds.): INDOCRYPT 2019, LNCS 11898, pp. 514–534, 2019.
https://doi.org/10.1007/978-3-030-35423-7_26

Present [3] have become popular and have been well-studied with respect to their security and implementation. Both ciphers have been standardized in ISO/IEC 29192 "Lightweight Cryptography". The Simon and Speck family of block ciphers [4] was proposed very recently by researchers of the NSA with the goal of reducing hardware area. While the above ciphers have mostly targeted optimization of hardware area, there have been other block ciphers aimed at optimizing other lightweight design metrics. The principal among them is energy. The block cipher Midori [5] was designed to specifically optimize energy consumption. It has also been found that for energy efficient encryption of large quantities of data, stream cipher based constructions like Trivium [6] are more energy efficient [7]. However, AES still remains the de-facto encryption standard worldwide for a number of sectors like banking and e-commerce. It is a part of several internet protocols like HTTPS, FTPS, SFTP, WebDAVS, OFTP, and AS2.

Efficient encryption and authentication of short messages (with maximum message length of 64 bytes) is an essential requirement for enabling security in constrained computation and communication scenarios such as next generation IoT devices. Accordingly, the recently started NIST lightweight cryptography project specifies that AEAD submissions should be "optimized to be efficient for short messages (e.g., as short as 8 bytes)" [8]. ForkAES was proposed by Andreeva et al. in [9] as a solution for the above. ForkAES is a **tweakable forkcipher**, which is basically a tweakable blockcipher that uses the AES round function to produce two blocks of ciphertext. It is based on the tweakable blockcipher KIASU [10], which relies on the round function of AES and uses the TWEAKEY framework to derive round keys from a 128-bit secret key and a 64-bit tweak. Finally, the authors proposed several nonce-based AEAD modes of operations like FAEP and SAEP, optimized to be efficient for short messages. There has been sufficient interest in the community as evident from the cryptanalytic attempt on round reduced ForkAES [11]. Furthermore, the forking construction [12] with a more lightweight SPN block cipher Skinny [13], is also a submission to the NIST lightweight cryptography project [8].

1.1 Contribution and Organization

As acknowledged by the authors, forking a block cipher to produce two ciphertext blocks in the manner that they propose requires one additional storage element of size equal to the AES blocksize, meant for storing an intermediate block cipher state during the computation. This naturally comes at a cost to the circuit size, since an additional storage component needs to be integrated in the design. In this paper, we show that it is possible to implement ForkAES without any additional storage elements other than those required to implement AES, if the AES circuit can perform both the encryption and decryption operations. A very good candidate for the implementation is the Atomic-AES architectures designed in [14,15] that can perform both encryption and decryption operations with a datapath width of 8-bits. Atomic-AES v2.0 performs encryption/decryption using 246/326 cycles respectively and occupies only around 2060 GE when implemented with the standard cell library of the STM 90 nm CMOS logic process. However an implementation that does not have an extra storage element requires more clock cycles to perform ForkAES operations. This will be clear when we delve into the circuit level description of ForkAES. In the first part of the paper we implement ForkAES both with and without additional storage and compare the area-latency tradeoffs incurred in implementing the circuit.

In the second part of the paper we look at the energy consumption aspect of lightweight efficiency when applied to ForkAES. The fundamental questions then become how expensive is a ForkAES call (in terms of energy) and what type of implementation leads to the most energy-efficient ForkAES realization. It is well known that round based constructions for AES are the most energy efficient, hence we naturally follow the round-based implementation paradigm to realize energy-efficient ForkAES implementations. The freedom of choices in the design, such as whether or not to add a new temporary register, or reorganize the decryption datapath, leads to a few different realizations. Hence we pursue those ideas, which generally involve some trade-off, to find the most energy-efficient implementation with this paradigm. We report our findings and briefly explain the intuition behind design choices. We point out that unlike in circuit area, there is a gap between the energy consumption of ForkAES and AES. We hope that our results draw attention to the energy-consumption perspective of being lightweight and can be used to improve the idea of forkciphers.

The paper is organized as follows. Section 2 contains mathematical descriptions of ForkAES. In Sect. 3, we show that it is possible to implement ForkAES without additional storage. We explore the circuit level challenges required to implement ForkAES both with and without additional storage and present a detailed comparison. Section 4 focuses on the energy consumption aspects of ForkAES and compares the results of multiple design choices. Section 5 concludes the paper.

2 ForkAES Tweakable Blockcipher

FORKCIPHERS. Let $\mathcal{B}$, $\mathcal{K}$, and $\mathcal{T}$ be non-empty sets or spaces. A tweakable fork-cipher $\mathbf{E}$ is a tuple of three deterministic algorithms:

1. An encryption algorithm $\mathbf{E} : \mathcal{K} \times \mathcal{T} \times \mathcal{B} \rightarrow (\mathcal{B})^2$;
2. A decryption algorithm $\mathbf{D} : \mathcal{K} \times \mathcal{T} \times \mathcal{B} \times \{0,1\} \rightarrow \mathcal{B}$;
3. A tag-reconstruction algorithm $\mathbf{R} : \mathcal{K} \times \mathcal{T} \times \mathcal{B} \times \{0,1\} \rightarrow \mathcal{B}$.

We define $\mathbf{E}_K^T(P)[0] = C_0$ and $\mathbf{E}_K^T(P)[1] = C_1$ Decryption and tag reconstruction take a bit b such that it holds $\mathbf{D}_K^{T,b}(\mathbf{E}_K^T(P)[b]) = P$, for all $K, T, P, b \in \mathcal{K} \times \mathcal{T} \times \mathcal{B} \times \{0,1\}$. The tag-reconstruction takes K, T, C_b, and b as input, and produces $C_{b \oplus 1}$. When K and T are omitted, we simply write $\mathbf{D}^b$ and $\mathbf{R}^b$ for these pair of algorithms.

ROUND FUNCTION OF AES. We recall that AES-128 is a substitution-permutation network over 128-bit inputs, which transforms the input through ten rounds consisting of SubBytes (SB), ShiftRows (SR), MixColumns (MC), and a round-key addition with a round key K_i. At the start, a whitening key K_0 is XORed to the state; the final round omits the MixColumns operation. We write

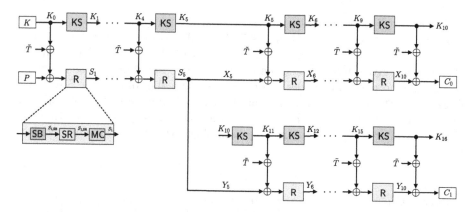

Fig. 1. ForkAES tweakable block cipher. SB, SR, MC are SubBytes, ShiftRows and Mix-Columns operations of AES-128 respectively; KS is a one round key schedule operation. Formal descriptions of algorithms are given in Fig. 2.

S_i for the state after Round i, and $S_i[j]$ for the j-th byte, for $0 \leq i \leq 10$ and $0 \leq j \leq 15$. Further, we use $S_{r,SB}$, $S_{r,SR}$, and $S_{r,MC}$ for the states in the r-th round directly after the SubBytes, ShiftRows, and MixColumns operations, respectively. The byte ordering is given by:

$$\begin{bmatrix} 0 & 4 & 8 & 12 \\ 1 & 5 & 9 & 13 \\ 2 & 6 & 10 & 14 \\ 3 & 7 & 11 & 15 \end{bmatrix} .$$

We adopt a similar convention for the round keys K_i and their bytes $K_i[j]$, for $0 \leq i \leq 16$; for both, we also use often a matrix-wise indexing of the bytes from $0,0$ to $3,3$. More details can be found in [16].

KIASU-BC [10] is a tweakable block cipher that differs from the AES-128 only in the fact that it XORs a public 64-bit tweak T to the topmost two rows of the state whenever a round key is XORed. We denote the tweak by T and by $T[j]$, $0 \leq j \leq 7$, the bytes of T. The bytes are ordered as

$$\begin{bmatrix} 0 & 1 & 2 & 3 \\ 4 & 5 & 6 & 7 \end{bmatrix} .$$

Alternatively one can consider as if $\mathsf{Transpose}(T||0^{64})$ is XORed to each of the round keys, where $\mathsf{Transpose}$ is a matrix transposition.

ForkAES. It is a forkcipher based on KIASU-BC. It forks the state after five rounds and transforms it twice to two ciphertexts C_0 and C_1. Denote by $\tilde{T} = \mathsf{Transpose}(T||0^{64})$. We denote the states of the first branch by $X_i =^{\mathrm{def}} S_i$, for $0 \leq i \leq 10$, where $X_0 = S_0$ denotes the plaintext P and $X_{10} \oplus K_{10} \oplus \tilde{T} = C_0$.

Moreover, we denote the states of the second branch by Y_i, for $5 \leq i \leq 10$, where $Y_5 = S_5$ and $C_1 = Y_{10} \oplus K_{16} \oplus \tilde{T}$. We will also write R for the sequence MC $\circ$ SR $\circ$ SB and KS for an iteration of the AES-128 key schedule. A schematic illustration is given in Fig. 1, and more details can be found in [9]. The designers of ForkAES propose two modes of operations using the fork cipher SAEF and PAEF. In both these modes of operation, the only functionalities of ForkAES required are (a) Encryption $\mathbf{E}$, (b) Decryption $\mathbf{D}^0$ and (c) Reconstruction $\mathbf{R}^0$. Thus in this paper we will concentrate on implementing these three functions in hardware.

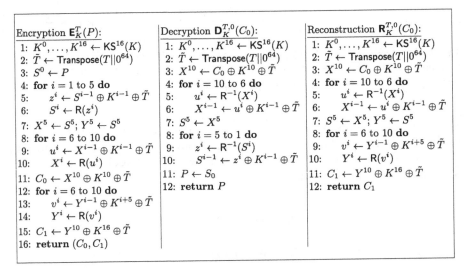

Fig. 2. Exact descriptions of the three algorithms $\mathbf{E}, \mathbf{D}^0, \mathbf{R}^0$ used in SAEF and PAEF forkable modes of operations from [9]. Here, R denotes the round function, i.e. $\mathsf{R}(x) = \mathsf{MC}(\mathsf{SR}(\mathsf{SB}(x)))$ and KS^{16} denotes successive applications of key schedule algorithm 16 times, i.e. $K_{i+1} \leftarrow \mathsf{KS}(K_i)$ for $0 \leq i \leq 16$ where $K_0 = K$.

3   Serial Implementation of ForkAES

The three functions that any ForkAES circuit must accommodate in order to execute the FAEP and SAEP modes of operation are Encryption $\mathbf{E}$, Decryption $\mathbf{D}^0$ and Reconstruction $\mathbf{R}^0$. To begin with, we will show that it is possible to execute these functions without the use of an extra register. To do so we first examine the case when the circuit does utilize an additional register.

First of all, from Figs. 1 and 2 it is straightforward to see that Decryption $\mathbf{D}^0$ operation is the simple AES decryption with an additional tweak. Thus any circuit that performs AES decryption can perform $\mathbf{D}^0$ with or without an additional register in the same number of clock cycles. Thus we concentrate on the $\mathbf{E}, \mathbf{R}^0$ functions.

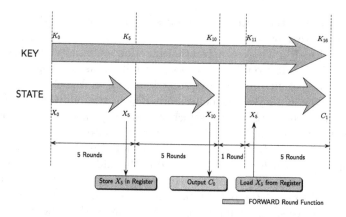

Fig. 3. Executing **E** on an AES circuit with an additional register

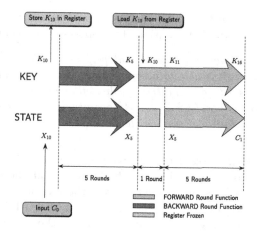

Fig. 4. Executing **R**[0] on an AES circuit with an additional register

Encryption E. As shown pictorially in Fig. 3, encryption on an AES circuit would proceed as follows. In the first 5 rounds, the circuit would proceed in the forward direction, i.e. execute the forward keyschedule function on the key registers and the forward AES round functions on the state registers. After this, the intermediate state X_5 is stored in the additional register, parallelly while the circuit continues to execute the forward functions on both the key and state registers for another 5 rounds. At this point the first ciphertext $C_0 = X_{10} \oplus K_{10} \oplus \tilde{T}$ is output from the state side.

Thereafter there needs to be one blank round in which the key registers executes the forward keyschedule to compute the 12th roundkey K_{11}, during which the state registers could either be frozen using clock gating techniques, or let to operate normally (it does not make any difference to the eventual circuit output). After this the state X_5 that was stored in the extra register is loaded back on to the state registers and the circuit operates in the forward direction in both the state and key sides for another 5 rounds to output the second ciphertext block C_1.

Reconstruction R^0. The reconstruction function essentially outputs C_1 when the input is C_0. It would be executed as follows as per Fig. 4. The initial inputs to the circuit are the ciphertext block $C_0 = X_{10} \oplus K_{10} \oplus \tilde{T}$ and the 11th roundkey K_{10}. We parallelly store K_{10} in the additional register and execute the inverse AES round functions and keyschedule for 5 rounds. At this point the state and key registers store the intermediate states X_5 and K_5 respectively. We freeze the state register for one round at this point and simultaneously load K_{10} that was stored in the additional register back on to key registers. After this round the key registers compute the 12th roundkey K_{11} required to start the bottom branch of the reconstruction process. After this the state registers are unfrozen and both run in the forward direction for 5 more rounds to compute C_1.

We now try to prove that both encryption and reconstruction can be performed on an AES circuit that additionally supports decryption.

Proposition 1. *Consider any circuit that performs both AES encryption and decryption. If the circuit is able to accommodate an additional 64 bit tweak register and a mechanism to add the tweak value efficiently to the state, then it is possible to perform the ForkAES E and R^0 operations on such a circuit without requiring any other additional storage elements.*

Proof Idea 1. We first look at encryption as explained in Fig. 5. The AES circuit first runs for 10 rounds without interruption, and the ciphertext block $C_0 = X_{10} \oplus K_{10} \oplus \tilde{T}$ is output. Thereafter the circuit is made to operate in the backward direction for 5 rounds, i.e. the inverse AES round functions and keyschedule operations are performed so that at the end of this, the circuit returns to having X_5, K_5 in the state and key registers. At this point we freeze

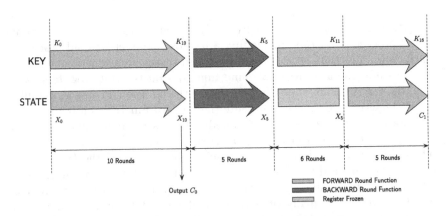

Fig. 5. Executing **E** on an AES circuit without an additional register

the state registers for 6 rounds and let the key registers run in the forward direction this time for 6 rounds, so that the 12th roundkey K_{11} is computed by this time. After this both the state and key registers are both run in the forward direction for 5 rounds so that after this the ciphertext block C_1 would have been computed.

We next look at reconstruction $\mathbf{R}^0$. Reconstruction is essentially getting the circuit to output C_1, given C_0 and K_{10} as inputs. This is essentially how the circuit functions in the last 16 rounds in the encryption operation as is evident from Figs. 5 and 6. This completes the proof sketch.   □

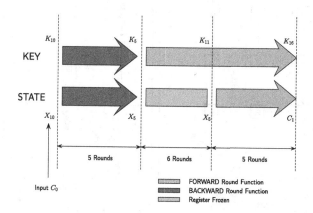

Fig. 6. Executing $\mathbf{R}^0$ on an AES circuit without an additional register

3.1   Implementing **ForkAES** with the **Atomic AES V 2.0** architecture

The Atomic AES v2.0 architecture was proposed in [15]. It is an 8-bit serial circuit that accommodates both encryption and decryption operations. One forward round is executed in 23 clock cycles and an inverse round is executed in 31 clock cycles. It occupies an area of only 2060 GE when implemented with the standard cell library of the STM 90 nm CMOS logic process and thus a very good candidate for a lightweight implementation of **ForkAES** both with and without the use of additional storage elements.

We first look at the circuit without an additional register, and refer this implementation as **Configuration A**. Before getting into circuit details of the implementation let us look at the changes we need to make to the original circuit to accommodate **ForkAES** operations. They are highlighted in purple in Fig. 7.

A: The original circuit had a an additional 32 bit multiplexer, for the mixcolumn circuit. This is because the last round in AES encryption does not employ a MixColumns operation. However all **ForkAES** round functions are identical: none of them omit the MixColumns function. Thus the 32 bit multiplexer can be omitted.

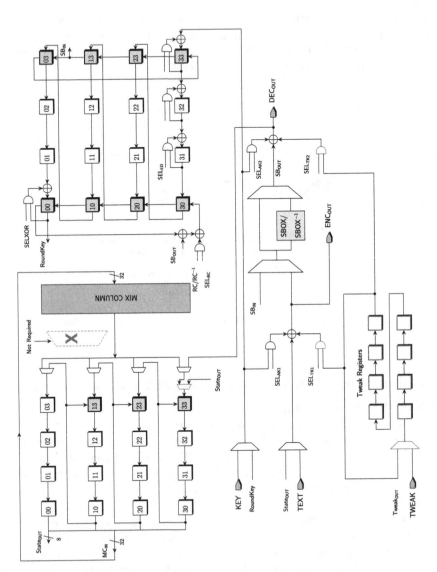

Fig. 7. ForkAES on the Atomic-AES v 2.0 circuit without an additional register

B: Additional 64 bit tweak register, to accommodate the tweak addition operation. Also additional 8-bit and gates are required to prevent tweak addition in clock cycles when it is not required.

C: One additional 8-bit multiplexer to cycle back the bytes coming out of the state registers back into the state.

D: Additional circuitry to generate more round constants.

E: Additional circuitry to generate control signals to employ a more fine-grained control over the circuit.

F: Additional circuitry to generate gated clock signals to periodically stop data movement in registers as and when required.

We now look at register level operations for a clearer picture of the movement of data in and out of the registers. Note that we do not delve into circuit level details of how the AES round and key functions operate. The readers are referred to [15] for a more detailed and comprehensive analysis of clock by clock operations involved in the actual round functions/keyschedule functions the circuit. However before we proceed it would be helpful to have an idea of the sequence of operations performed by the Atomic AES circuit while performing encryption/decryption. An encryption round consists of the following sequence of operations:

ShiftRows (3 cycles), MixColumns (4 cycles), AddRoundKey + SubBytes of next round (16 cycles)

Thus given $SB(X_i \oplus K_i)$ as input a forward round on this circuit produces $SB(X_{i+1} \oplus K_{i+1})$. A decryption round consists of the following operations:

MixColumns $^{-1}$ (12 cycles), ShiftRows $^{-1}$ (3 cycles), SubBytes $^{-1}$ + AddRoundKey (16 cycles)

Thus an inverse round would produce $X_i \oplus K_i$ given $X_{i+1} \oplus K_{i+1}$ as input. Now let us look at the sequence of operations in ForkAES **E** operation:

Cycles 0 to 222. The first $16 + 9 \cdot 23 = 223$ cycles are used for loading of key/plaintext on to the registers (16 cycles) and executing the first 9 rounds of AES (207 cycles) and the 10th round substitution layer. Of course the initial data loaded onto the state register after cycle 15 is $SB(X_0 \oplus K_0)$ so that every forward round can function seamlessly.

Cycles 223 to 229. The next $3 + 4 = 7$ cycles are used to execute the 10th round ShiftRows (3 cycles) and the subsequent MixColumns (4 cycles). Thus the content of the state register at this point is basically equal to $Y = MC \circ SR \circ SB(X_9 \oplus K_9)$.

Cycles 230 to 245. These 16 cycles are used to do the final key addition to generate the first ciphertext block C_0. At the same time the bytes coming out of the state register (which are the individual bytes of Y) are driven back into the state register via the additional multiplexer mentioned in item C of the above list. Since the inverse round operations of Atomic-AES v 2.0 circuit start with the MixColumns $^{-1}$ operation this will nicely help us invert round function to get back X_5. Note that at the same time K_{10} is recycled back into the key registers.

Cycles 246 to 400. The next $31 \cdot 5 = 155$ cycles are used to perform 5 inverse AES round operations.

Cycles 401 to 515. At this point of time the state registers store the signal X_5 and are frozen by gating the clock signal feeding them. The key registers store K_5, and so the next $5 \cdot 23 = 115$ cycles are used to operate the keyschedule in the forward direction to compute K_{10}.

Cycles 516 to 538. The key registers function normally so that from cycles 523–538 the 12th roundkey K_{11} are available for key addition. The state registers are frozen till cycle 522. From cycles 523 to 538 the bytes are taken out of the state register added to the individual bytes of K_{11}, passed through the S-box and driven back into the state registers. In this way at the end of this set of cycles, the state registers hold $\mathsf{SB}(X_5 \oplus K_{11})$, which is exactly the value required to operate the subsequent forward rounds.

Cycles 539 to 653. The next $5 \cdot 23 = 115$ cycles, 5 forward AES rounds are executed in a normal way, so that it is able to output the final ciphertext block C_1.

All the above description implicitly assumes that the Tweak register essentially operates as a circularly shifting register that makes the tweak bytes available for addition as and when required. We already know that decryption $\mathbf{D}^0$ is performed in a manner exactly same as the AES decryption function on the Atomic AES circuit in 326 cycles. As per Proposition 1, the reconstruction $\mathbf{R}^0$ is simply achieved by executing the operations from cycles 230 to 653. Thus encryption, decryption and reconstruction takes 654, 326 and 424 cycles respectively. This completes the analysis for **Configuration A**. Due to space constraints, we omit similar detailed circuit level analysis for the case when an extra register is used (call it **Configuration B**). However it is not too difficult to see that the clock-by-clock analysis is pretty similar to the arguments outlined right at the beginning of the section.

3.2   Implementation Results

In order to perform a fair performance evaluation, we first implemented the circuits using VHDL. Thereafter the following design flow was adhered to for all the circuits: a functional verification at the RTL level was first done using Mentor Graphics Modelsim software. The designs were synthesized using the standard cell library of the 90 nm logic process of STM (CORE90GPHVT v 2.1.a) with the Synopsys Design Compiler, with the compiler being specifically instructed to optimize the circuit for area. A timing simulation was done on the synthesized netlist to confirm the correctness of the design, by comparing the output of the timing simulation with known test vectors. The switching activity of each gate of the circuit was collected while running post-synthesis simulation. The average power was obtained using *Synopsys Power Compiler*, using the back annotated switching activity. The results are tabulated in Table 1. We can achieve an implementation of 2476 gates in **Configuration A**, which is only around 400 GE larger than the original AES circuit.

Table 1. Performance comparison of ForkAES implemented with Atomic-AES v2.0 circuit. For comparison Atomic-AES v2.0 consumes 2060 GE of area.

#	Configuration	Area (GE)	Operation	Latency (cycles)	Power (μW)	Energy (nJ)	TP_{max} (Mbps)
1	**A**	2476	Encryption	654	118.8	7.77	54.90
			Decryption	326		3.87	55.07
			Reconstruction	424		5.04	42.34
2	**B**	2911	Encryption	384	134.8	5.18	91.74
			Decryption	326		4.39	54.03
			Reconstruction	309		4.17	57.00

In Fig. 8, we present a componentwise breakdown of the areas occupied in the 2 configurations. It can be seen that most of the area is occupied by the registers (state and key), s-box, mixcolumn and other control signals required in the core AES circuit. The additional area requirement is accounted for by the tweak registers, clock gating circuit, and the additional register used in **Configuration B.**

4   Energy Consumption of **ForkAES** Architectures

During its functionality, the energy spent by a circuit can be divided into two parts: leakage energy and dynamic energy. The former roughly scales with the number of gates constituting the circuit, where each gate is associated with a constant power leakage due to its implementation in the CMOS technology. The latter, on the other hand, essentially stems from state changes of wires, as each component of the circuit receives and further propagates glitches, until both its input and output values are stabilized. This repeats each time the input of components change that coincides with the rising edge of the clock signal.

Hence, minimizing the circuit size does not necessarily align with the goal of reducing energy consumption. Following the work of Banik et al. [17], a circuit that performs one round of AES per clock cycle leads to the most energy efficient design. Then the follow-up question is how one can transform that particular one round per clock cycle AES circuit to obtain most energy efficient implementation for ForkAES. Since converting a plain AES architecture that supports both decryption and encryption into ForkAES circuit reveals a number of free design choices, we consider and compare each one of the possible designs below.

4.1   Generic Architecture

On a higher level, the architectures we propose share the common structure with some further tweaks that let us pick the most energy efficient architecture. The following summary of the design refers to the most energy efficient design on average and it is obtained through a combination of compartmentalized components SC#1, KC#1, TC explained below. Further modifications we make lead to

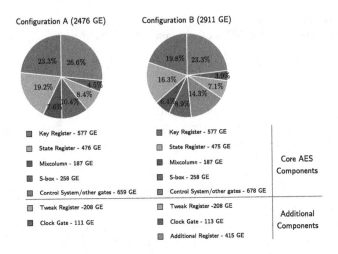

Fig. 8. Component-wise breakdown of areas in the 2 configurations of ForkAES

slight changes in the precise description of these components and as well as the main circuit as seen in Fig. 9. We present the power and energy consumption results of the modifications in Table 2.

In comparison to Atomic AES that uses 8-bit data and key path, the designs below utilize 128-bit data and key paths. All mainly consist of three components, that handle the states S_i, the round keys K_i and the temporary register.

STATE COMPONENT. It consists of three parts (see SC#1 in Fig. 9):

- At its core, 128-bit Register$_{St}$ is used to keep the plaintext/ciphertext state of each ForkAES round. At the rising edge of the clock, its content is updated to the next state with the help of the multiplexer described below.
- The multiplexer placed at the input of Register$_{St}$ supports three basic operations, by selecting which value should be loaded into this register. First, it can load the next plaintext/ciphertext state from the wire St, as it is computed by the round function circuit. Secondly, it can load the initial state, e.g. S_0 during encryption. And lastly, it can load the contents of the temporary register Register$_{Tmp}$.
- Round function bus consists of two series of 128-bit combinatorial circuits arranged to perform either the round function R or its inverse R^{-1}, as well as the tweaked key addition. This dual circuit is complemented with masking AND gates (denoted with symbol $\longrightarrow$) that disable the unused part of the circuit, i.e. either the encryption or the decryption path, to reduce energy consumption. The final output of the circuit is selected by the output multiplexer.

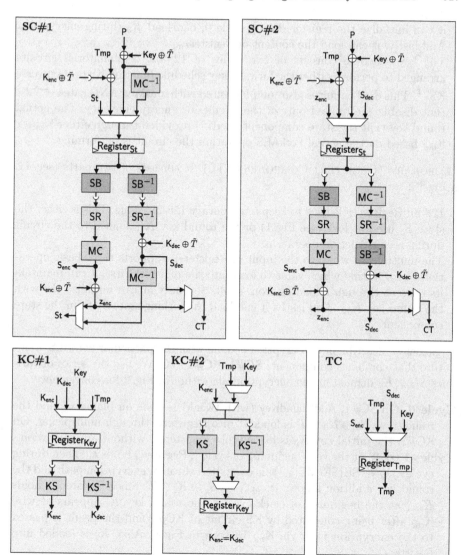

Fig. 9. The state components SC#1, SC#1; the key components KC#1, KC#2, and the temporary register component TC of ForkAES circuit.

KEY COMPONENT (KC). The key component KC works in a quite similar fashion to the state component. It also consists of three parts (see KC#1 in Fig. 9):

- 128-bit $\mathsf{Register_{Key}}$ is used to keep the current round key (more precisely it keeps K_{i-1} at round i). It is updated with the rising edge of the clock.
- The multiplexer wired to the input of $\mathsf{Register_{Key}}$ supports three different basic operations, by selecting which value to load into the register. First, it can load the next round key computed by the key schedule circuit. Secondly,

it can initialize the register during cycle 0, e.g. load K_0 during encryption. And lastly, it can load the content of $\text{Register}_{\text{Tmp}}$.

- The key schedule consists of two series of 128-bit combinatorial circuits arranged to perform either the forward key schedule function KS or its inverse KS^{-1}. This dual circuit is also complemented with masking AND gates ($\longrightarrow\!\!\!\!\!\rightarrow$) that disable the unused part of the circuit for energy efficiency. The actual round key that the state component needs is provided through either K_{enc} or K_{dec} based on the actual ForkAES operation the circuit is performing.

TEMPORARY (REGISTER) COMPONENT (TC). It consists of two parts (see TC in Fig. 9):

- 128-bit $\text{Register}_{\text{TC}}$ is used to keep a temporary 128-bit value. This is either the state S_5 used at fork (see Fig. 1) or the round key K_{10} loaded to the circuit during reconstruction operation.
- The multiplexer wired to the input of $\text{Register}_{\text{TC}}$ supports three basic operations, by selecting which value to load into the register. First, it can maintain its content through reloading from itself. Secondly, it can initialize the with the round key K_{10}. And lastly, it can load the forking state S_5 from the state component.

Below we describe how encryption is done with the particular ForkAES architecture that combines components SC#1, KC#1, TC. We use the series of variables S_i, z_i, K_i defined in the encryption algorithm in Fig. 2 for convenience.

Cycle 0. On SC#1, AddRoundKey (with tweak) is done on plaintext, and the result $z_1 = S_0 \oplus K_0 \oplus \tilde{T}$ is loaded[1] into $\text{Register}_{\text{St}}$ through multiplexer. On KC#1, the initial key K_0 is loaded into $\text{Register}_{\text{Key}}$ without any operation.

Cycles 1 to 4. At the very beginning of cycle i, $\text{Register}_{\text{St}}$ holds z_i. Then during cycle i, $S_i \leftarrow \text{SB}(\text{SR}(\text{MC}(z_i)))$ is computed through encryption path and the round key addition follows it: $z_{i+1} \leftarrow S_i \oplus K_i \oplus \tilde{T}$. Since $\text{Register}_{\text{Key}}$ holds K_{i-1} at the beginning of clock cycle i, the round key K_i appears at wire K_{enc} after being computed by KS circuit of KC#1 and the result is passed to the encryption path via K_{enc} as seen in Fig. 9. Also, K_i is loaded into $\text{Register}_{\text{Key}}$.

Cycle 5. Works similar to cycles 1–4. The only difference is that the forking state S_5 from the encryption path is stored into the temporary register $\text{Register}_{\text{Tmp}}$.

---

[1] More precisely, the value is loaded into $\text{Register}_{\text{St}}$ during the rising edge that marks the end of cycle 0, hence the value itself becomes available at the output of the register at cycle 1. We rather say the value is loaded into the register at clock cycle 0.

Cycles 6 to 9. Similar to cycles 1 to 4.

Cycle 10. Works similar to cycles 1 to 4. The difference is that C_0 becomes available at the output wire CT during this clock cycle. Also, the control bits of multiplexer before Register$_{St}$ is set to load the forking state S_5 for the next clock cycle from the temporary register Register$_{Tmp}$.

Cycle 11. At the beginning of this cycle, Register$_{St}$ receives $v_6 = S_5 \oplus K_{11} \oplus \tilde{T}$. Similar to cycle 1, the computation $Y_6 \leftarrow \mathsf{SB}(\mathsf{SR}(\mathsf{MC}(v_6)))$ is done first, and then the key addition: $v_7 \leftarrow Y_6 \oplus K_{12} \oplus \tilde{T}$. v_7 is stored back into Register$_{St}$, and the round key K_{12} is stored into Register$_{Key}$.

Cycles 12 to 15. Similar to cycles 1 to 4.

Cycle 16. Similar to cycle 10, with the difference that C_1 becomes available at CT.

Below we describe how ForkAES reconstruction is performed by the circuit, which involves some parts of encryption and decryption operations. We assume that at the beginning of the operation, the ciphertext C_0 is loaded into P, and the round key K_{10} is loaded into Key.

Cycle 0. On SC#1, AddRoundKey (with tweak) and MC^{-1} is computed on the ciphertext C_0, and the result $X_{10,\mathsf{SR}}$ is loaded into Register$_{St}$ through multiplexer. On KC#1, the initial key K_{10} is loaded both into Register$_{Key}$ and Register$_{Tmp}$ without any operation.

Cycles 1 to 4. At the beginning of cycle i, Register$_{St}$ holds $X_{11-i,\mathsf{SR}}$. Then during cycle i, $u_{11-i} \leftarrow \mathsf{SB}^{-1}(\mathsf{SR}^{-1}(z_i))$ is first computed through decryption path[2] and the round key addition follows it: $X_{10-i} \leftarrow u_{11-i} \oplus K_{10-i} \oplus \tilde{T}$. And finally, $X_{10-i,\mathsf{SR}} \leftarrow \mathsf{MC}^{-1}(X_{10-i})$. In the same fashion, at the beginning of the clock cycle i, Register$_{Key}$ holds K_{11-i}, hence the round key K_{10-i} is calculated with the combinatorial KS^{-1} circuit of KC#1 and the result is passed to the decryption path via K$_{dec}$ as seen in Fig. 9; and also loaded back into Register$_{Key}$.

Cycle 5. Works similar to cycles 1–4. The difference is that the forking state S_5 from the decryption path appears at S$_{dec}$ and hence it is loaded into the temporary register Register$_{Tmp}$ at the end of this clock cycle. Moreover, the round key K_{10} is loaded back into Register$_{Key}$ from Register$_{Tmp}$.

Cycle 6. No decryption or encryption operation is done on SC#1, because an operation that must follow is a round key addition (see Fig. 1). Therefore, the forking state S_5 is read from Register$_{Tmp}$ and the round key addition is done on the wire: $v_6 \leftarrow S_5 \oplus K_{11} \oplus \tilde{T}$, where the round key K_{11} is computed with KS circuit in KC#1. The result v_6 is loaded into Register$_{St}$.

Cycles 7 to 11. Works similar to cycles 12 to 16 of ForkAES encryption operation above, and the result C_1 becomes available at clock cycle 11.

---

[2] Note that $\mathsf{SB}^{-1}(\mathsf{SR}^{-1}(x)) = \mathsf{SR}^{-1}(\mathsf{SB}^{-1}(x))$ for all x.

We skip the description of decryption, as it can be easily constructed by repeating the cycles 1 to 4 of ForkAES reconstruction above.

4.2 Modified Implementations

We explore possible modifications to the generic circuit, and compare their results in Table 2. In order to derive a single metric for strict comparison, we take the average of energy consumed by each ForkAES encryption $\mathbf{E}$, decryption $\mathbf{D}^0$ and reconstruction $\mathbf{R}^0$ operations. Our choice of this metric is justified by the fact that the proposed modes of operations SAEF and PAEF by Andreeva et al. [9] make the following number of ForkAES calls for a message of m blocks and an associated data of a blocks[3]:

- encryption: $(m + a) \cdot \mathbf{E}$,
- decryption: $a \cdot \mathbf{E} + m \cdot \mathbf{D}^0 + m \cdot \mathbf{R}^0$.

Hence the average energy spent per message block roughly converges to our metric assuming $m \gg a$.

CLOCK GATING (DESIGN #2). One might notice that during encryption the control bits and contents of $\mathsf{Register_{Tmp}}$ is irrelevant for 12 clock cycles, and used as a storage for 4 cycles. Similarly, during reconstruction, the $\mathsf{Register_{Tmp}}$ stores its value for many cycles without receiving a new value. The register stores its value through a multiplexer that feeds the register's own value back into its input (see TC in Fig. 9). Hence one might wonder if freezing the register by micromanaging its clock signal yields a better design instead of reloading the register with the same value multiple times. We implemented this version. This implementation (#2 in Table 2) is dubbed with an extra cg, i.e. clock gating. Even though there is a small energy gain in decryption, the encryption becomes more costly. That might be explained with the inherent glitches on additional clock signals of registers, as adding more control leads to more complicated circuit in front of this signal. The glitch on this clock signal incurs further wasted computation in other components. In conclusion, this modification leads to a less efficient implementation on average.

REORGANIZED DECRYPTION PATH (#3). One of the benefits of the state component SC#1 (see Fig. 9) is that both SB and SB^{-1} has the same input, which allows them to be implemented as a single circuit and share a demultiplexer. This idea is due to Banik et al. [14]. As a disadvantage, this design requires an extra MC^{-1} circuit attached to the input wire P, as ForkAES does not skip a MixColumns operation at the last round in contrast to the original AES-128. In order to understand this trade-off better, we compare it with another state component design, i.e. SC#2. The latter organizes MC^{-1}, SR^{-1}, SB^{-1} circuits

---

[3] This metric omits the additional higher-level circuitry such as control blocks to handle multiple associated data and message blocks in SAEF and PAEF, as we only focus on the ForkAES implementation.

in a more intuitive fashion in the decryption path, and eliminates the need to append an extra MC^{-1} to the input (see Fig. 9). In conclusion, this leads to a slightly less efficient implementation as reported in Table 2, because the energy consumption caused by duplication of some S-box circuitry due to separation beats the energy gain by removal of MC^{-1}.

REMOVING TEMPORARY REGISTER (#4). We have shown in Sect. 3 that even without a temporary register to store the forking state S_5, one can still realize ForkAES operations. This would apparently require more clock cycles, and therefore more energy. In order to understand this trade-off, we consider the design that is a combination of SC#1, KC#1 without temporary component. In order to micromanage the registers, we use clock gating. It can be seen in the Table 2 that this design is at least 20% less efficient than its counterpart with temporary components (due to clock gating based implementation, comparison of #2 versus #4 is more reasonable).

FLIPPED KEY SCHEDULER (#5). Our final tweaked design is based on the following observation: during each clock cycle, the round key is computed either through KS or KS^{-1} circuit. Because it takes few nanoseconds for these circuits to compute the final round key, the output wires K_{enc} and K_{dec} propagate glitches into SC#1 circuit. That is due to the fact that $Register_{Key}$ actually stores the previous round key instead of the exact round key needed by the state component. In comparison, if the key component were to be updated as such that the particular round key was stored in the key register precisely when it was needed by the state component, then K_{enc} and K_{dec} would be glitch-free. The modified key component is given as KC#2 in Fig. 9. This modification decreases the energy spent during encryption operation, but surprisingly incurs more for decryption and reconstruction operations. The energy results of this modification can be seen by comparing designs #1 versus #5 in Table 2 (Fig. 10).

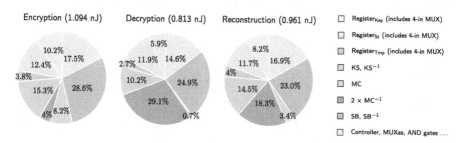

Fig. 10. Component-wise breakdown of the energy consumption of the most energy-efficient architecture, i.e. implementation #1 with SC#1, KC#1, TC components, during ForkAES encryption, decryption and reconstruction operations.

Table 2. Results for various energy-efficient architectures. For comparison, note that the most efficient AES-128 circuit "S_3K_2" of [14] consumes 0.484 nJ on average with 22729 GE area, making the most efficient ForkAES implementation at least twice more expensive.

#	Configuration	Area (GE)	Operation	Latency (cycles)	Power (μW)	Energy (nJ)	TP_{max} (Mbps)
1	SC#1, KC#1, TC (described in text)	27155	Encryption	17	643.6	1.094	2671
			Decryption	11	739.2	0.813	2064
			Reconstruction	12	800.8	0.961	1892
			Average	–	–	**0.956**	–
2	SC#1, KC#1, TC, cg	27182	Encryption	17	713.5	1.213	2892
			Decryption	11	735.3	0.809	2234
			Reconstruction	12	809.7	0.972	2048
			Average	–	–	**0.998**	–
3	SC#2, KC#1, TC	30908	Encryption	17	748.3	1.272	3042
			Decryption	11	618.8	0.681	2351
			Reconstruction	12	849.3	1.019	2155
			Average	–	–	**0.991**	–
4	SC#1, KC#1, cg	26480	Encryption	25	713.7	1.784	2112
			Decryption	11	695.3	0.765	2408
			Reconstruction	15	760.3	1.140	1766
			Average	–	–	**1.230**	–
5	SC#1, KC#2, TC	27137	Encryption	17	630	1.071	3790
			Decryption	11	759.1	0.835	2929
			Reconstruction	12	849.5	1.019	2684
			Average	–	–	**0.975**	–

5   Conclusion

The recently proposed ForkAES cipher would normally require an additional register to store an intermediate state during computation. Thus an implementation of ForkAES in hardware would require additional circuit area to accommodate the extra state. In this paper, we first showed that it was possible to implement ForkAES without any additional storage elements other than those required to implement AES, if the AES circuit could additionally perform decryption. As a proof of concept, using the Atomic AES v2.0 architecture as a building block, we implemented the ForkAES circuit both with and without an additional register and present a tradeoff in terms of area of circuit and number of clock cycles required to perform encryption/decryption/reconstruction operations of ForkAES. Without an additional register, the circuit occupies 2476 GE which is only around 400 GE more than the core AES circuit. In the second part of the paper we looked at the energy-efficiency of ForkAES implementations. We extended the so-called "S_3K_2" construction of Banik et al. [17] to realize ForkAES in an energy-preserving manner, and compared the effects of some design choices. We found that the energy consumption of the most energy-efficient implementation of ForkAES consumed about 2 times that of AES. From lightweight design perspective, our results present various tradeoffs involved in the design space of ForkAES that can be useful in determining the implementation most suitable to meeting any given area/power/energy budget.

Acknowledgments. The authors are supported by the Swiss National Science Foundation (SNSF) through the Ambizione Grant PZ00P2_179921.

References

1. Lightweight forkaes implementations. https://c4science.ch/source/lightforkaes/
2. Shirai, T., Shibutani, K., Akishita, T., Moriai, S., Iwata, T.: The 128-bit blockcipher CLEFIA (extended abstract). In: Biryukov, A. (ed.) FSE 2007. LNCS, vol. 4593, pp. 181–195. Springer, Heidelberg (2007). https://doi.org/10.1007/978-3-540-74619-5_12
3. Bogdanov, A., et al.: PRESENT: an ultra-lightweight block cipher. In: Paillier, P., Verbauwhede, I. (eds.) CHES 2007. LNCS, vol. 4727, pp. 450–466. Springer, Heidelberg (2007). https://doi.org/10.1007/978-3-540-74735-2_31
4. Beaulieu, R., Shors, D., Smith, J., Treatman-Clark, S., Weeks, B., Wingers, L.: The SIMON and SPECK families of lightweight block ciphers. IACR Cryptology ePrint Archive, 2013:404 (2013)
5. Banik, S., et al.: Midori: a block cipher for low energy. In: Iwata, T., Cheon, J.H. (eds.) ASIACRYPT 2015. LNCS, vol. 9453, pp. 411–436. Springer, Heidelberg (2015). https://doi.org/10.1007/978-3-662-48800-3_17
6. De Cannière, C., Dunkelman, O., Knežević, M.: KATAN and KTANTAN—a family of small and efficient hardware-oriented block ciphers. In: Clavier, C., Gaj, K. (eds.) CHES 2009. LNCS, vol. 5747, pp. 272–288. Springer, Heidelberg (2009). https://doi.org/10.1007/978-3-642-04138-9_20

7. Banik, S., et al.: Towards low energy stream ciphers. IACR Trans. Symmetric Cryptol. **2018**(2), 1–19 (2018)

8. Nist lightweight cryptography project. https://csrc.nist.gov/projects/lightweight-cryptography

9. Andreeva, E., Reyhanitabar, R., Varici, K., Vizár, D.: Forking a blockcipher for authenticated encryption of very short messages. IACR Cryptology ePrint Archive, 2018:916 (2018)

10. Jean, J., Nikolić, I., Peyrin, T.: Tweaks and keys for block ciphers: the TWEAKEY framework. In: Sarkar, P., Iwata, T. (eds.) ASIACRYPT 2014. LNCS, vol. 8874, pp. 274–288. Springer, Heidelberg (2014). https://doi.org/10.1007/978-3-662-45608-8_15

11. Banik, S., et al.: Cryptanalysis of ForkAES. In: Deng, R.H., Gauthier-Umaña, V., Ochoa, M., Yung, M. (eds.) ACNS 2019. LNCS, vol. 11464, pp. 43–63. Springer, Cham (2019). https://doi.org/10.1007/978-3-030-21568-2_3

12. Andreeva, E., Lallemand, V., Purnal, A., Reyhanitabar, R., Roy, A., Vizár, D.: Forkae v.1. NIST Lightweight Cryptography Project (2019)

13. Beierle, C., et al.: The SKINNY family of block ciphers and its low-latency variant MANTIS. In: Robshaw, M., Katz, J. (eds.) CRYPTO 2016. LNCS, vol. 9815, pp. 123–153. Springer, Heidelberg (2016). https://doi.org/10.1007/978-3-662-53008-5_5

14. Banik, S., Bogdanov, A., Regazzoni, F.: Atomic-AES: a compact implementation of the AES encryption/decryption core. In: Dunkelman, O., Sanadhya, S.K. (eds.) INDOCRYPT 2016. LNCS, vol. 10095, pp. 173–190. Springer, Cham (2016). https://doi.org/10.1007/978-3-319-49890-4_10

15. Banik, S., Bogdanov, A., Regazzoni, F.: Atomic-AES v 2.0. IACR Cryptology ePrint Archive, 2016:1005 (2016)

16. Daemen, J., Rijmen, V.: The Design of Rijndael: AES - The Advanced Encryption Standard. Information Security and Cryptography. Springer, Heidelberg (2002). https://doi.org/10.1007/978-3-662-04722-4

17. Banik, S., Bogdanov, A., Regazzoni, F.: Efficient configurations for block ciphers with unified ENC/DEC paths. In: 2017 IEEE International Symposium on Hardware Oriented Security and Trust, HOST 2017, McLean, VA, USA, 1–5 May 2017, pp. 41–46 (2017)

FPGA Implementation and Comparison of Protections Against SCAs for RLWE

Timo Zijlstra[1(✉)], Karim Bigou[2], and Arnaud Tisserand[1]

[1] CNRS, Lab-STICC UMR 6285 and Université Bretagne Sud, Lorient, France
{timo.zijlstra,arnaud.tisserand}@univ-ubs.fr
[2] Université Bretagne Occidentale and Lab-STICC UMR 6285, Brest, France
karim.bigou@univ-brest.fr

Abstract. We present various FPGA implementations of protections against SCAs for RLWE-based PKE. We implemented the main solutions from the state of the art with improved variants. We also propose a new protection based on a redundant representation of the ring elements to randomize computations. We compare the implementation results of all these solutions.

Keywords: Ring learning with errors · Side channel attack · Blinding · Masking · Shuffling · Randomization

1 Introduction

The algorithms currently used in *public-key cryptography* (PKC) in most of applications are not secure against *quantum computers* using Shor's algorithm [28]. *Post-quantum cryptography* (PQC) relies on mathematical problems for which known quantum algorithms offer no significant speed-up. *Lattice* problems such as *learning with errors* (LWE) and *ring*-LWE (RLWE) received a lot of attention. A standardization project for post-quantum encryption and signatures has been launched by NIST in 2016 [8]. Its goal is to select and standardize post-quantum solutions to replace RSA and ECC. The second round started in January 2019, it includes 17 *public-key encryption* (PKE) submissions [1], and 9 of them are based on lattice problems.

While PQC is resistant against quantum computers, its implementation must be protected against *physical attacks*. Side channel attacks (SCAs) exploit the leakage of secret information through the analysis of the power consumption, electromagnetic radiation or computation timings of the cryptographic device. For instance, *correlation power analysis* (CPA) uses a set of *traces* obtained by measuring the power consumption of the device for different inputs.

The *secret key* in RLWE based cryptosystems consists of a polynomial in a finite ring. Decryption involves a multiplication with the secret polynomial. This multiplication is the ideal target for SCAs. One way to prevent such attacks is

© Springer Nature Switzerland AG 2019
F. Hao et al. (Eds.): INDOCRYPT 2019, LNCS 11898, pp. 535–555, 2019.
https://doi.org/10.1007/978-3-030-35423-7_27

to *randomize* the operands to remove the correlation between the power traces and the secret polynomial coefficients.

In this work, we implement in hardware various countermeasures from the state of the art against SCAs. We also improve some of them and propose a new one. We consider the *masking* scheme from [25] for which we propose a new masked decoder. Our decoder is deterministic and does not add to the decryption failure probability, as opposed to the one from [25]. We also implement two randomization techniques proposed by [27]: *blinding*, *shifting*; and a combination of the two. To the best of our knowledge, these are the first FPGA implementations of these techniques. We also propose a new countermeasure based on a *redundant representation* of the ring elements to randomize the computations during the decryption algorithm. Our new protection leads to a small overhead in terms of time and area. We also propose two methods to shuffle the operations during the point-wise multiplications. Finally, we compare all those solutions implemented on the same FPGA and using the same *high-level synthesis* (HLS) tools for fair comparison. HLS allows us to quickly evaluate several architectures and parameters. Our results show that HLS tools lead to implementations with similar, or even better, performances than VHDL or Verilog ones from the literature but for a significantly reduced design cost.

2   Definitions and Notations

- For q a prime number and n a power of two, let $\mathbb{Z}_q = \mathbb{Z}/q\mathbb{Z}$ and $\mathcal{R}_q = \mathbb{Z}_q[x]/(x^n + 1)$.
- Lower case bold variables (*e.g.* $\mathbf{a}$) are polynomials in $\mathcal{R}_q$ of degree $< n$.
- $\mathcal{B}_\lambda$ denotes the symmetric binomial distribution centered around 0 with integer parameter λ.
- $\mathbf{a} \xleftarrow{\$} \mathcal{B}_\lambda(\mathcal{R}_q)$ is a polynomial in $\mathcal{R}_q$ whose coefficients are sampled from $\mathcal{B}_\lambda$.
- $\odot$ is used for point-wise multiplication of polynomials and vectors.

3   State of the Art Analysis

3.1   Learning with Errors Based PKE

The LWE problem and LWE based cryptography have been introduced by Regev in [24], where it is shown that LWE is at least as hard as some worst case lattice problems. The introduction of RLWE by [17] gives rise to more efficient cryptographic applications by adding an algebraic structure to the lattices. The matrices and vectors from Regev's cryptosystem are replaced by polynomials in finite rings, reducing the size of the public key and allowing fast multiplication algorithms. This speed-up has been studied by [11] in hardware implementation. The definition of RLWE we give here is a practical instantiation of the more general definition from [17].

Definition 1 (RLWE [17]**).** *For some (secret key) polynomial* $\mathbf{s} \xleftarrow{\$} \mathcal{B}_\lambda(\mathcal{R}_q)$, *a RLWE sample is generated by sampling a polynomial* $\mathbf{a}$ *from the uniform distribution over* $\mathcal{R}_q$, *and sampling* $\mathbf{e} \xleftarrow{\$} \mathcal{B}_\lambda(\mathcal{R}_q)$ *and computing the output* $(\mathbf{a}, \mathbf{b})$ *where* $\mathbf{b} = \mathbf{a} \cdot \mathbf{s} + \mathbf{e}$. *The search variant of the RLWE problem is to find* $\mathbf{s}$ *given a number of samples for* $\mathbf{s}$.

We describe the framework used for instance by NewHope. Other schemes may use deterministic errors ("Learning with Rounding") or Gaussian noise instead of using the binomial distribution. RLWE based submissions still present in the second round of the NIST standardization project include NewHope [2], LAC [15] and Round5 [4].

1. Key generation. Let $\mathbf{s} \xleftarrow{\$} \mathcal{B}_\lambda(\mathcal{R}_q)$ be the private key. Sample a uniform random $\mathbf{a} \in \mathcal{R}_q$ and $\mathbf{e}_0 \xleftarrow{\$} \mathcal{B}_\lambda(\mathcal{R}_q)$. The public key is given by the RLWE sample $(\mathbf{a}, \mathbf{b})$ where $\mathbf{b} := \mathbf{as} + \mathbf{e}_0$.
2. Encryption. Let the plaintext $\mathbf{m} \in \mathcal{R}_q$ be a polynomial with coefficients in the set $\{0, 1\}$ only. Sample 3 polynomials $\mathbf{e}_1, \mathbf{e}_2, \mathbf{e}_3 \xleftarrow{\$} \mathcal{B}_\lambda(\mathcal{R}_q)$. The ciphertext is given by $(\mathbf{c}_1, \mathbf{c}_2)$, where $\mathbf{c}_1 \leftarrow \mathbf{ae}_1 + \mathbf{e}_2$ and $\mathbf{c}_2 \leftarrow \mathbf{be}_1 + \mathbf{e}_3 + \lfloor \frac{q}{2} \rfloor \cdot \mathbf{m}$.
3. Decryption. Let $\mathbf{d} \leftarrow \mathbf{c}_2 - \mathbf{c}_1 \mathbf{s}$. For each coefficient of $\mathbf{d}$, decode to 0 if it is closer to 0 than to $\lfloor \frac{q}{2} \rfloor$, else decode to 1.

3.2   Components of the Cryptosystem

Encoding/Decoding. The maps between the message space $\{0, 1\}^n$ and $\mathcal{R}_q$ are called ENCODE and DECODE. A string of bits is encoded by mapping 0 to 0 and 1 to $\lfloor \frac{q}{2} \rfloor$, resulting in a polynomial with coefficients in $\mathbb{Z}_q$. To decode a polynomial in $\mathcal{R}_q$, a coefficient is mapped to 0 if it is closer to 0 than to $\lfloor \frac{q}{2} \rfloor$ in $\mathbb{Z}_q$, else it is mapped to 1. That is, if $c \in \left[\lfloor \frac{q}{4} \rfloor, \lfloor \frac{3q}{4} \rfloor \right)$ then $c \mapsto 1$, else $c \mapsto 0$.

Binomial Sampling. The $\mathcal{B}_\lambda$ distribution over $\mathbb{Z}_q$ is sampled by generating 2λ uniformly random bits $a_1, \ldots, a_\lambda, b_1, \ldots, b_\lambda$ and returning $\sum_{i=1}^{\lambda}(a_i - b_i) \bmod q$.

Polynomial Multiplication and NTT. The encryption and decryption functions both rely on polynomial multiplication in $\mathcal{R}_q$. The polynomial multiplication is a costly operation. Hardware implementations of RLWE schemes such as [20] tend to use the Number Theoretic Transform (NTT) to compute this operation. It has also been suggested to use the schoolbook algorithm for area optimization [21], but in general the NTT seems to yield better performance and highly area-optimized implementations exist [26].

To compute a polynomial multiplication using the NTT, the polynomials should be mapped to the NTT domain where the polynomial multiplication is a point-wise operation taking only n modular multiplications in $\mathbb{Z}_q$. Addition and subtraction can also be performed point-wise in the NTT domain. The inverse NTT is applied to bring the result back in the time domain.

Definition 2 (NTT). *Let $\omega \in \mathbb{Z}_q$ be a primitive n-th root of unity and $\mathbf{a}(x) = \sum_{i=0}^{n-1} a_i x^i$ an element in $\mathcal{R}_q$. Then the image of $\mathbf{a}$ under the NTT is given by $\hat{\mathbf{a}} = \sum_{j=0}^{n-1} \hat{a}_j x^j$, where $\hat{a}_j = \mathbf{a}(\omega^j)$.*

To use the NTT for multiplication in $\mathcal{R}_q$, the polynomials have to be pre-processed using the *negative wrapped convolution* (NWC) [16]. Let $\mathbf{a}, \mathbf{b}, \mathbf{c}, \mathbf{d} \in \mathcal{R}_q$ such that $\mathbf{a}(x)\mathbf{b}(x) = \mathbf{c}(x) + \mathbf{d}(x)(x^n + 1)$ in $\mathbb{Z}_q[x]$ for some $\mathbf{c}(x)$ of degree smaller than n. Let $\phi \in \mathbb{Z}_q$ be a primitive $2n$-th root of unity such that $\phi^n = -1 \bmod q$. Then, in $\mathbb{Z}_q[x]$ and for $i \geq 0$, one has:

$$\mathbf{a}(\phi\omega^i)\mathbf{b}(\phi\omega^i) \equiv \mathbf{c}(\phi\omega^i) + \mathbf{d}(\phi\omega^i)((\phi\omega^i)^n + 1) \bmod q$$
$$\equiv \mathbf{c}(\phi\omega^i) + \mathbf{d}(\phi\omega^i)(-1 + 1) \bmod q$$
$$= \mathbf{c}(\phi\omega^i)$$

This means that $\mathrm{NTT}(\mathbf{a}(\phi x)) \odot \mathrm{NTT}(\mathbf{b}(\phi x)) = \mathrm{NTT}(\mathbf{c}(\phi x))$. In other words, one gets the reduction $\bmod(x^n + 1)$ for free by applying the NTT to $\mathbf{a}(\phi x)$ instead of $\mathbf{a}(x)$. To obtain the correct result from the polynomial multiplication, the inverse of the NWC should be applied to $\mathrm{NTT}^{-1}(\mathrm{NTT}(\mathbf{c}))$. That is, each coefficient has to be multiplied by a power of ϕ^{-1}. Therefore, the values of $\phi^i \bmod q$ have to be precomputed for $0 < i < n$ and $-n < i < 0$.

The transform is efficiently computed in $\log_2(n)$ stages of n multiplications using the Cooley-Tukey algorithm [9]. Several optimizations have been proposed to accelerate this computation. The multiplication by the powers of the $2n$-th root of unity can be merged with the twiddle factors in the first stage or the scaling multiplication by $n^{-1} \bmod q$ [26]. Instead of precomputing n^{-1} and the powers of ϕ^{-1}, the values of $n^{-1}\phi^{-i}$ for $0 \leq i < n$ can be precomputed directly. A similar result merging the NWC with the final stage of the inverse NTT was described by [22]. By making clever use of the Decimation-In-Time (DIT) and Decimation-In-Frequency (DIF) transforms, [22] shows that the bit reversal can be avoided. The DIT NTT is used to compute the inverse transformation. The DIT NTT takes an input in bit-reversed order and returns the output in the original order. The bit-reversal resulting from the DIF forward transformation is thus automatically undone by the inverse NTT. All the operations in the NTT domain are computed on the bit-reversed coefficient vectors. The public and private keys are therefore stored in bit-reversed order in the NTT domain. To limit the amount of modular reductions during the NTT, [14] allows variables to grow slightly larger than q.

Not counting symmetric primitives, the NTT is the most expensive operation in the scheme with a complexity of $\mathcal{O}(n \log n)$. To reduce the number of NTTs to be computed, the public and private keys can be stored in the NTT domain. The ciphertext part c_1 must also be sent in the NTT domain. During the encryption, 2 forward NTTs and 1 inverse NTT have to be computed and during the decryption only 1 inverse NTT is needed.

Using the constant geometry variant [19] of the NTT algorithm, the memory access pattern is independent of the stage. The values are not read from the same memory as the one that the updated variables are written to, therefore 2

BRAMs are needed in the implementation. At each iteration of the stage loop, 2 values are read from the memory, a butterfly operation is computed and the 2 results are written to the memory. A detailed description of the stage is given by Algorithm 1. All arithmetic operations are performed in $\mathbb{Z}_q$.

Algorithm 1. i-th stage of the NTT [19]

1: **function** STAGE(X, i)
2:     **for** $j \leftarrow 0$ to $\frac{n}{2} - 1$ **do**
3:         $\theta \leftarrow \omega^{\lfloor \frac{j}{2^i} \rfloor \cdot 2^i}$ ▷ Get twiddle factor from memory
4:         $(x_0, x_1) \leftarrow (X[2j], X[2j+1])$ ▷ Read from memory X
5:         $\left(Y[j], Y[j + \frac{n}{2}]\right) \leftarrow (x_0 + x_1, (x_0 - x_1)\theta)$ ▷ Write to memory Y
6:     **return** Y

Modular Reduction. Modular reduction for moduli of the form $q = 2^{l_1} - 2^{l_2} + 1$ can be efficiently computed using algorithms in the style of [29]. Using the fact that $2^{l_1} \equiv 2^{l_2} - 1 \bmod q$, a modular reduction can be computed using only bitwise shifts, additions and subtractions.

3.3 Side Channel Analysis

Power analysis attacks on cryptographic implementations have first been described by [12]. Side channel attacks on LWE cryptography exploit vulnerabilities in Gaussian sampling algorithms [6,10], polynomial multiplication [3] or the NTT [23]. The decryption algorithm makes use of the secret key and is therefore vulnerable to statistical and machine learning attacks on side channels such as power consumption (for instance differential power analysis, DPA) or electromagnetic radiations (differential electromagnetic analysis, DEMA).

3.4 Protections

All the operations in the decryption handle inputs that depend on the secret key. To protect it against DPA, these inputs should be randomized at the start of each decryption. The decryption algorithm decodes the coefficients of some polynomial $\mathbf{d}$ where $\mathbf{d}$ is defined by $\mathbf{d} = \mathbf{c}_2 - \text{NTT}^{-1}(\mathbf{c}_1 \odot \mathbf{s})$. It should be noted that knowledge of the coefficients of $\mathbf{d}$ leads to complete key recovery in the chosen plaintext attack model. Since $\mathbf{c}_1$ and $\mathbf{c}_2$ are known inputs and $\mathbf{c}_1$ is invertible in $\mathcal{R}_q$ with high probability, one can compute $\mathbf{c}_1^{-1} \cdot (\mathbf{c}_2 - \mathbf{d}) = \mathbf{s}$. To prevent SCAs on the coefficients of $\mathbf{d}$, these coefficients should not be computed directly. Instead, a randomized or masked version of $\mathbf{d}$ is used. The decoder should therefore be able to decode randomized or masked inputs. We now present the main countermeasures from literature against statistical attacks on RLWE.

Masking. In [25] the secret key is split in two shares: $\mathbf{s} = \mathbf{s}' + \mathbf{s}''$ for some uniformly random $\mathbf{s}'$ at the start of each decryption. The linear part of the decryption function is computed twice: first the ciphertext is decrypted (but not decoded) using secret key $\mathbf{s}'$ and then using secret key $\mathbf{s}''$, yielding two polynomials $\mathbf{d}'$ and $\mathbf{d}''$. The final step consists of decoding the coefficients of $\mathbf{d} = \mathbf{d}' + \mathbf{d}''$ to bits. This is a non linear operation, that is, $\mathrm{DECODE}(a + b)$ is not necessarily equal to $\mathrm{DECODE}(a) + \mathrm{DECODE}(b)$. As an example, if $a = b = \lfloor \frac{q}{6} \rfloor$, $2 \times \mathrm{DECODE}\left(\lfloor \frac{q}{6} \rfloor\right) = 0$ but $\mathrm{DECODE}\left(2 \times \lfloor \frac{q}{6} \rfloor\right) = 1$. This means that one cannot simply apply the decoder to the coefficients of $\mathbf{d}'$ and $\mathbf{d}''$ separately and then add the results in $\mathbb{Z}_2$ to obtain the correct plaintext.

Because of the DPA scenario mentioned above, the two shares $\mathbf{d}'$ and $\mathbf{d}''$ should not be recombined before decoding to bits. Let d' and d'' denote a coefficient (of some fixed index) of polynomials $\mathbf{d}'$ and $\mathbf{d}''$ respectively. A *masked decoder* takes as input two coefficients $(d', d'') \in \mathbb{Z}_q^2$ and computes the value of $\mathrm{DECODE}(d' + d'')$ without computing $d' + d''$. The solution from [25] makes use of the fact that for some $(d', d'') \in \mathbb{Z}_q^2$ it is easy to deduce the value of $\mathrm{DECODE}(d' + d'')$. For instance, if $0 \leq d' < \frac{q}{4}$ and $\frac{q}{4} \leq d'' < \frac{q}{2}$ then it must hold that $\frac{q}{4} \leq (d' + d'') < \frac{3q}{4}$, therefore the coefficient decodes to 1. Similar "easy cases" exist, but not all $(d', d'') \in \mathbb{Z}_q^2$ can be resolved in this way. If both d' and d'' lie between 0 and $\frac{q}{4}$, all we know is that $0 \leq (d' + d'') < \frac{q}{2}$ and this can decode to either 0 or 1.

The idea from [25] to solve the hard cases is to *reshare* the two shares: for any $\delta \in \mathbb{Z}_q$ one has $d' + \delta + d'' - \delta = d' + d'' = d$. It is therefore possible to add any constant to one of the shares and subtract the same constant from the other one. However, there is no guarantee that $(d' + \delta, d'' - \delta)$ is an easy case. If the new shares still do not form an easy case, the shares have to be reshared again. In [25] a list of constants $\{\delta_1, \ldots, \delta_{16}\}$ is presented that is supposed to minimize the number of resharings to be performed. Their implementation refreshes the shares 16 times such that with high probability an easy case is obtained in at least one of the 16 iterations.

The computation time overhead due to the 16 iterations and the additional decoding failures are important drawbacks to this solution. [18] propose an alternative masked decoding. Their method effectively decodes without additional decoding failures. The comparison that they make between this decoder and their re-implementation of the one from [25] however shows only a very limited improvement in terms of performance. Their masked decryption takes over 3 times more cycles to compute than the unmasked version. The same implementation also uses a blinding countermeasure proposed by [27].

Blinding. With the blinding countermeasure [27] the polynomials $\mathbf{s}$ and $\mathbf{c}_1$ are multiplied by scalars a and b in $\mathbb{Z}_q$ respectively. The blinded polynomial multiplication is then computed: $(a\mathbf{s}) \cdot (b\mathbf{c}_1) = (ab)\mathbf{s} \cdot \mathbf{c}_1$. The inverse $(ab)^{-1}$ should be computed to obtain $\mathbf{s} \cdot \mathbf{c}_1$. [27] suggested to use (pre-computed) powers of ω and ω^{-1} as blinding factors to avoid the modular inversion. The decoding process cannot be protected from DPA with the scalar blinding method. The blinding multiplication has to be inverted before the coefficients can be decoded.

Shifting. It is also suggested in [27] to apply a random anti-cyclic shift to the coefficients vector of the polynomials before multiplying. Due to the ring structure, this anti-cyclic shift corresponds to a multiplication by some power of x. For some random $i, j < n$, $(x^j \mathbf{s}(x)) \cdot (x^i \mathbf{c}_1(x)) = x^{i+j} \mathbf{s}(x) \mathbf{c}_1(x)$ is computed and $\mathbf{s}(x) \mathbf{c}_1(x)$ can be recovered by inversing the shift.

In practice it is not possible to obtain $x^i \mathbf{s}$ and $x^j \mathbf{c}_1$ by applying anti-cyclic shifts to their coefficients vectors, because they are represented in the NTT domain. To multiply by x^i in the NTT domain, observe that

$$\text{NTT}(x^i) = (1, \omega^i, \omega^{2i}, \ldots, \omega^{(n-1)i}), \tag{1}$$

and $\text{NTT}((\phi x)^i) = \phi^i \cdot \text{NTT}(x^i)$. All of the coefficients of $\text{NTT}(x^i)$ are already pre-computed, since they are exactly the n powers of ω. Multiplication by x^i can thus be done by a pointwise multiplication with the powers of ω and ϕ^i (for the NWC). This multiplication has to be performed in bit-reversed order, since $\mathbf{s}$ and $\mathbf{c}_1$ are in the NTT domain.

Shuffling. Masking, blinding and shifting offer little to no protection against single trace attacks. The single trace attack by [23] exploits leakage from the operations performed during the NTT. In that paper, it is suggested to counter the attack by randomizing the order in which the butterfly operations are computed. During each stage, the $\frac{n}{2}$ butterfly operations can be computed in a random order. The same shuffling methods can also be applied to all the pointwise operations in the decryption.

4 Unprotected FPGA Implementation of RLWE

In this section, we present our implementation of the encryption and decryption algorithms described in the previous section on an Artix XC7A200 FPGA using Vivado HLS (version 2018.1). Our decryption architecture is the basis for the protected implementations proposed in the next sections. We compare our unprotected RLWE implementations with results from literature. One of our goals is to show that competitive results can be obtained using HLS from C code for a reduced design cost compared to VHDL or Verilog design.

Figure 1 presents the high-level architecture of our *accelerator*. For encryption, the public keys are first loaded into the local *RAM*, then the computations are performed by the *functional units* (FUs, see below). During encryption/decryption our accelerator is isolated for security reasons, it does not take any input or generate any output. After encryption/decryption, the result is sent out through the interface. In the paper, all the communications through the interface are included in our results. Depending on parameter n, the typical time spent for interfacing represents about 12% to 21% of the total encryption/decryption time.

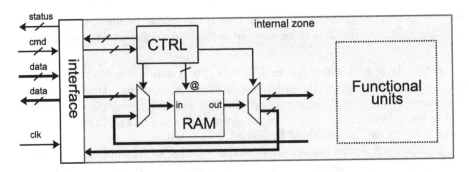

Fig. 1. High level architecture of our accelerator.

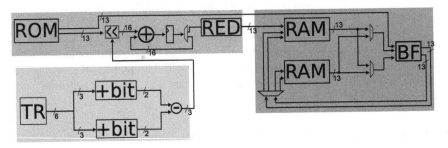

Fig. 2. Architecture computing the error polynomials in the NTT domain. The yellow part uses the PRNG (TR unit) to generate samples from the $\mathcal{B}_\lambda$ distribution (here: $\lambda = 3$). The +bit operator computes the sum of λ input bits. The NWC (upper left) is computed using a shift-based multiplier and modular reduction (RED). The NTT is computed on the right, using one Gentlemen-Sande butterfly (BF) operator. (Color figure online)

Parameters. In order to compare with literature results, we implement RLWE for the parameter sets $(n, q, \lambda) = (1024, 12289, 8)$ and $(256, 7681, 3)$. For $n = 1024$, we use a simplification of the CPA-secure version of NewHope1024 PKE with key reuse. We do not implement the key refreshing, ciphertext compression/decompression and key encoding/decoding in this paper. For simplicity we use the Trivium stream cipher as PRNG.

Encryption and Decryption. Following [22], we avoid the bit-reversal step by implementing both the DIF and DIT NTT. The stage loop is fully pipelined, such that it takes just over $\frac{n}{2}$ clock cycles to complete one stage. The complete forward transformation is computed in few more than $\frac{n}{2} \log n$ cycles.

The error polynomials e_1, e_2 and e_3 are sampled from the binomial distribution $\mathcal{B}_\lambda(\mathcal{R}_q)$. The required random bits are provided by the PRNG. Since the ciphertext part $c_1 = ae_1 + e_2$ will be sent in the NTT domain, the NTT has to be applied to both e_1 and e_2. The NWC must be computed for both polynomials. To compute these multiplications, we use the fact that the coefficients are sampled from $\mathcal{B}_\lambda$ and therefore are bounded by $-\lambda$ and λ. The multiplications can be computed using only a few shifts and additions, without using a DSP block.

Table 1. FPGA implementation results for our RLWE solutions (denoted V1, V2 and V3) and literature solutions. If specified, encryption/decryption and server/client/ server (for a 3-step key exchange) timing results are shown separately. Separate area results for server and client are indicated with +.

Source	FPGA	Latency (clock cycles)	MHz	Time (μs)	Slice, DSP, LUT, BRAM
$n = 256$					
[20]	XC6VLX75	6861/4404	262	26.2/16.8	1506, 1, 4549, 12
[26]	XC6VLX75	6300/2800	313	20.1/9.1	n.a., 1, 1349, 2
V1	XC7A200	5039/2188	208	24.2/10.5	1624, 1, 4365, 5
V2	XC7A200	3764/2239	250	15.1/9.0	2122, 6, 5616, 8
$n = 1024$					
[13]	XC7Z020	6900/10300/2800	133/131	51.9/78.6/21.1	n.a., $(8+8)$, $(18756+20826)$, $(14+14)$
[30]	XC7A035	171124/179292	125/117	1369/1532	0, $(2+2)$, $(5142+4498)$, $(4+4)$
V3	XC7A200	16146/9586	250	64.6/38.3	4106, 7, 11164, 12

The NTT is then applied to e_1 and e_2 simultaneously, using two parallel NTT units each consisting of one butterfly unit and two BRAMs. The architecture for sampling e_1 (or e_2) and mapping it to the NTT domain is shown in Fig. 2.

The architecture for decryption is shown in Fig. 3. The area and timing implementation results for RLWE are shown in Table 1 with similar solutions from the literature.

Our small implementation is denoted by V1. This implementation with only 1 DSP block is comparable in size and speed to [20] but is larger and 15 to 20% slower than the cryptoprocessor from [26]. By computing the forward NTTs in parallel in V2, we are faster than both, but more DSP blocks are needed. For $n = 1024$, the key exchange implementation by [13] is comparable with our V3 results in terms of speed, but the V3 implementation uses 50% less DSP blocks and BRAMs. We conclude that results obtained using HLS are comparable or, in the best case, even better in terms of speed (up to 25%) and/or area (up to 50%) than results from works based on VHDL or Verilog implementations.

5   New Variants of State of the Art Protections

The protections proposed in this section and the next one are implemented by modifying our base architecture from Fig. 3 for $n = 256$ and $q = 7681$. In real-world applications these protections should be part of an architecture

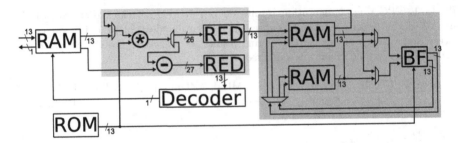

Fig. 3. Architecture for the decryption. The ciphertext is completely loaded in the RAM before starting the computations. The two pointwise operations (one before and one after the inverse NTT) in the blue region share a DSP block. (Color figure online)

implementing the CCA2-secure version of the scheme, including a re-encryption of the decrypted ciphertext and several evaluations of some hash function.

5.1 Masking with a New Masked Decoder

We implement a variant of the masking scheme described in the state of the art [25], improving the masked decoding process. We propose a simple masked decoder that does not need 16 iterations and that does not increase the decoding failure probability. Let $d', d'' \in \left[0, \frac{q}{4}\right)$, then $d' + d'' \in \left[0, \frac{q}{2}\right)$. If either d' or d'' were to be shifted by exactly the right amount (cf. Fig. 4), then we would be able to determine if either $d' + d'' \in \left(\frac{-q}{4}, \frac{q}{4}\right)$ or $d' + d'' \in \left(\frac{q}{4}, \frac{3q}{4}\right)$. The trick is then to find a $\delta \in \left[\frac{-q}{4}, \frac{q}{4}\right]$ such that $d' + \delta$ changes quadrant while $d'' - \delta$ does not (or the other way around). Suppose that $d' \geq d''$ and let $\delta = 1 + \min(\lfloor \frac{q}{4} \rfloor - d', d'')$. Then, depending on the value of δ, there are two possibilities for the new shares $d' + \delta$ and $d'' - \delta$:

1. $d' + \delta = \lfloor \frac{q}{4} \rfloor + 1 \in \left[\frac{q}{4}, \frac{q}{2}\right)$ and $d'' - \delta$ is in the same interval as d''. Then $d' + d''$ must be in the interval $\left(\frac{q}{4}, \frac{3q}{4}\right)$, therefore we decode to 1.
2. $d' + \delta$ is in the same interval as d' and $d'' - \delta = -1 \in \left[\frac{-q}{4}, 0\right)$. Then $d' + d''$ must be in the interval $\left[0, \frac{q}{4}\right) \cup \left(\frac{-q}{4}, 0\right]$ and therefore we decode to 0.

Similar solutions can be found for the other hard cases. Let Q_i denote the interval $\left[\frac{iq}{4}, \frac{(i+1)q}{4}\right)$ for $0 \leq i \leq 3$, that we will refer to as "quadrants". The property that allows to solve the easy cases is the following:

Property 1. If $d' \in Q_i$ and $d'' \in Q_j$ then $(d' + d'') \in Q_{i+j \bmod 4} \cup Q_{i+j+1 \bmod 4}$.

In the remainder of this section, we let i and j be the quadrant indices of d' and d'' respectively. For $i + j = 1 \bmod 4$ it follows from Property 1 that $(d' + d'') \in Q_1 \cup Q_2$. In other words, the sum lies in the left half of $\mathbb{Z}_q$ and therefore decodes to 1. Similarly, the $(d', d'') \in \mathbb{Z}_q^2$ for which $i + j = 3 \bmod 4$ are easy cases and decode to 0.

The hard cases are given by $(d', d'') \in \mathbb{Z}_q^2$ for which $i + j = 0 \bmod 4$ or $i + j = 2 \bmod 4$, that is, $(d' + d'') \in Q_0 \cup Q_1$ or $(d' + d'') \in Q_2 \cup Q_3$ respectively.

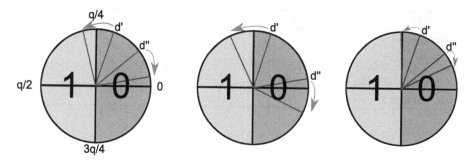

Fig. 4. Left: given that $d', d'' \in [0, \frac{q}{4})$, there is no simple way to determine if $d' + d'' \in (\frac{q}{4}, \frac{3q}{4})$, *i.e.* this is a hard case. Adding some δ to d' while subtracting the same δ from d'' yields a new pair (d', d'') which is an easy case. Middle: for some hard cases, adding and subtracting a constant δ does not give a solution: the new pair (d', d'') is another hard case. Right: d' is closer to $\frac{q}{4}$ than d'' is to 0. We therefore let $\delta = 1 + \lfloor \frac{q}{4} \rfloor - d'$. Then by construction, $d' + \delta$ changes quadrant while $d'' - \delta$ does not. It follows that $d = d' + \delta + d'' - \delta > \frac{q}{4}$ and $d < \frac{3q}{4}$. Therefore (d', d'') decodes to 1.

To reduce to an easy case, it suffices to move either (but not both) d' or d'' to an adjacent quadrant. Then for the new pair $(d' + \delta, d'' - \delta)$ exactly 1 mod 4 is added to or subtracted from the sum $i + j$. Then for the updated i, j it holds that $i + j = 1 \bmod 4$ or $i + j = 3 \bmod 4$ and Property 1 applies (Fig. 4).

It is always possible to modify the sum $i + j$ for the i, j corresponding to the shares by exactly 1. Assume w.l.o.g. that $d' \geq d''$. If $d' \in Q_i$, $d'' \in Q_j$ and d' is closer to $\frac{iq}{4}$ than d'' is to $\frac{(j-1)q}{4}$, then there is a δ such that $d' + \delta \in Q_{i+1}$ and $d'' - \delta \in Q_j$. If the opposite holds, then d'' can be moved to Q_{j-1} by subtracting a δ while d' stays in Q_i. The new pair $(d' + \delta, d'' - \delta)$ forms an easy case. This method does not work when the distance δ'' between d'' and $\frac{(j-1)q}{4}$ is equal to the distance δ' between d' and $\frac{iq}{4}$. However, these are exactly the cases for which $d' + d''$ is equal to either $\lfloor \frac{q}{4} \rfloor$ or $\lfloor \frac{3q}{4} \rfloor$. This means that even an unmasked decoder would not be able to decode these cases correctly. The parameters in LWE-based cryptoschemes are usually chosen such that such cases appear with negligible probability.

The comparison operation $\delta' < \delta''$ has to be implemented with caution. Generally, comparisons are performed by checking the bit sign of the subtraction of its operands. Since $\delta' - \delta'' = -(d' + d'') + \lfloor \frac{kq}{4} \rfloor$ for some integer $k < 4$, this operation leaks information about the unmasked value of d.

Instead of implementing a combinatory circuit, we have implemented successive accesses to a look-up table to perform the comparison. The implemented algorithm is described in Algorithm 2, where the bits of a and b are denoted $(a_0, \ldots, a_{w-1})$ and $(b_0, \ldots, b_{w-1})$ respectively. The look-up table implements the function T defined by $T(a_i, b_i, Y) = (a_i \wedge (\overline{b_i} \vee Y)) \vee (\overline{b_i} \wedge Y)$.

Note that it is not necessary to assume that $d' > d''$. Given (d', d'') and their corresponding quadrant indices $(i, j) = index(d', d'')$, the distances $\delta' = \lfloor \frac{(i+1)q}{4} \rfloor - d'$ and $\delta'' = d'' - \lfloor \frac{iq}{4} \rfloor$ are computed and compared. We have that:

Algorithm 2. Returns *True* if and only if $a > b$

1: **function** COMPARE(a, b)
2:    $Y \leftarrow$ *False*
3:    **for** $i = 0$ to $w - 1$ **do**
        $Y \leftarrow T'(a_i, b_i, Y)$
4:    **return** Y

$$\delta' < \delta'' \iff \left\lfloor \frac{(i+1)q}{4} \right\rfloor - d' < d'' - \left\lfloor \frac{jq}{4} \right\rfloor$$
$$\iff \left\lfloor \frac{(j+1)q}{4} \right\rfloor - d'' < d' - \left\lfloor \frac{iq}{4} \right\rfloor,$$

which means that swapping d' and d'' (and their corresponding indices) does not change the boolean outcome of the comparison. The complete masked decoder is given by Algorithm 3. The new reshared parts $d' + \delta$ and $d'' - \delta$ do not need to be computed explicitly. The comparison of δ' and δ'' yields sufficient information to update the indices (i, j) and determine the decoded bit.

Algorithm 3. Proposed masked decoder for (d', d'')

1: **function** DECODE(d', d'')
2:    $r \xleftarrow{\$} \{0, 1\}$ ▷ Mask for output
3:    $(i, j) \leftarrow \mathbf{index}(d', d'')$ ▷ Quadrant indices
4:    **if** $i + j \equiv 1 \bmod 4$ **then**
5:        **return** $(r, \bar{r})$ ▷ Easy cases $i + j \equiv 1$ or 3.
6:    **else if** $i + j \equiv 3 \bmod 4$ **then**
7:        **return** (r, r)
8:    **else**
9:        $\delta' \leftarrow \left\lfloor \frac{(i+1)q}{4} \right\rfloor - d'$ ▷ Distance to interval boundaries
10:       $\delta'' \leftarrow d'' - \left\lfloor \frac{iq}{4} \right\rfloor$
11:       **if** COMPARE(δ'', δ') **then**
12:           **if** $i + j + 1 \equiv 1 \bmod 4$ **then**
13:               **return** $(r, \bar{r})$
14:           **else**
15:               **return** (r, r)
16:       **else**
17:           **if** $i + j - 1 \equiv 1 \bmod 4$ **then**
18:               **return** $(r, \bar{r})$
19:           **else**
20:               **return** (r, r)

In order to make this masked decoder compatible with CCA2-secure implementations, the output is also masked. Instead of returning the plaintext bit, a random bit is generated and XORed with the unmasked decoding result. The decoder returns both the mask and the masked value.

A total of $2^{n \log q} = 2^{3328}$ different masks can be obtained. The security of the masking scheme with its original decoder is experimentally evaluated by [25]. They also mention the (small) possibility of horizontal DPA attacks targeting the 16 iterations of their masked decoder. Our proposed decoder does not have this vulnerability since it does not use 16 iterations.

5.2   Shifting

In [27] there is no mention of any masked decoder. To secure the complete decryption function, we propose to apply the (normal) decoder to the shifted polynomial $x^{i+j}\mathbf{c}_2(x) - x^{i+j}\mathbf{s}(x)\mathbf{c}_1(x)$, meaning that $\mathbf{c}_2(x)$ should be shifted separately. The plaintext can then be obtained by applying the inverse shift to the decoded polynomial. The minus sign that comes with the anti-cyclic shift does not change the value of the decoded coefficient, because $\forall a \in \mathbb{Z}/q\mathbb{Z}$ it holds that $\text{DECODE}(a) = \text{DECODE}(-a)$. The decryption procedure for a ciphertext $(\mathbf{c}_1, \mathbf{c}_2)$ can then be described as follows:

1. Generate random $i, j < n$.
2. Compute $\text{NTT}(x^i) \odot \mathbf{s}$ and $\text{NTT}(x^j) \odot \mathbf{c}_1$ by multiplying $\mathbf{s}$ and $\mathbf{c}_1$ by the powers of ω and ϕ in an order determined by i and j respectively.
3. Compute the pointwise product to obtain $x^{i+j}\mathbf{s} \cdot \mathbf{c}_1$ and apply in the inverse NTT.
4. Apply the anti-cyclic $(i+j)$- shift to $\mathbf{c}_2$ and obtain $x^{i+j}\mathbf{c}_2$.
5. Compute the subtraction $x^{i+j}\mathbf{c}_2 - x^{i+j}\mathbf{s} \cdot \mathbf{c}_1 = x^{i+j}(\mathbf{c}_2 - \mathbf{s} \cdot \mathbf{c}_1)$.
6. Decode to obtain the shifted plaintext. Shift $i + j$ positions to the left.

5.3   Blinding

The blinding countermeasure is implemented by generating two random indices $0 \le i, j < n$ and multiplying $\mathbf{c}_1$ and $\mathbf{s}$ by ω^i and ω^j respectively.

5.4   Shifting and Blinding Combined

Both shifting and blinding involve multiplication by the powers of ω and ϕ. To shift the polynomial $\mathbf{s}(x)$ by $i < n$ positions, we compute $\phi^i \cdot \text{NTT}(x^i) \odot \mathbf{s}(x)$. With almost no additional costs, this operation can be combined with the blinding operation by simply modifying the exponents of ω. To shift the polynomial by i positions and blind using ω^{-j} for some $j < n$, we use:

$$\omega^{-j}\phi^i \cdot \text{NTT}(x^i) \odot \mathbf{s}(x) = (\phi^i \omega^{-j}, \phi^i \omega^{i-j}, \dots, \phi^i \omega^{(n-1)i-j}) \odot \mathbf{s}(x) \quad (2)$$

Both $\mathbf{s}$ and $\mathbf{c}_1$ are shifted and blinded. The combined blinding factor has to be removed before the decoding. The combination of the two countermeasures is therefore somewhat more expensive than shifting alone. The decoding is performed in the shifted order.

Both shifting and blinding use two $\log(n)$-bit randomization factors. As pointed out by [27], the total amount of added noise entropy for shifting and blinding combined is $4 \log(n)$ bits. For $n = 256$ this is equal to 32.

6   New Protections

6.1   Shuffling

The first of the two shuffling methods proposed in this paper consists of replacing loop counters by linear feedback shift registers (LFSR). An LFSR is parametrized by an irreducible polynomial $f \in \mathbb{F}_2[x]$ and its degree k. It computes $x^i a \bmod f$ for $0 \leq i < 2^k - 1$ and some initial state $a \in \mathbb{F}_2[x]/f$. The computed values are exactly all the $2^k - 1$ invertible elements of the finite field $\mathbb{F}_2[x]/f$. The order in which they are computed is determined by the initial state a. Multiplication by x in $\mathbb{F}_2[x]/f$ is very fast and can be computed using only 1 shift and a XOR on bit positions depending on f. Our second shuffling method consists of generating a random permutation using a permutation network in the style of [5].

LFSR Method. Let an LFSR be parametrized by some irreducible polynomial f of degree $\frac{n}{2}$. We let $k = \log_2(n) - 1$ and consider the coefficients vectors of polynomials in $\mathbb{F}_2[x]/f$ to be the binary representations of integers ranging from 0 to $\frac{n}{2} - 1$. The LFSR thus generates a sequence of $\frac{n}{2} - 1$ integers that will serve as indices for the loop counter in Algorithm 1. Instead of computing the i-th butterfly operation at the i-th loop iteration, we compute the butterfly operation that is on the j-th position, where j is the index corresponding to the i-th element generated by the LFSR. In other words, the normal loop counter is replaced by an LFSR. The LFSR has only $2^k - 1$ outputs, whereas we need 2^k for the $\frac{n}{2}$ butterfly operations. Therefore the first operation of each stage is not shuffled: it is always computed in the first loop iteration of the stage.

To obtain a meaningful permutation, we use the PRNG to generate a new initial state a at the start of each stage. Since $a = 0$ is not allowed as initial state, we set $a = 1$ as the default state in the case that the PRNG outputs 0. The initial state is thus set to default state with probability $\frac{4}{n}$. All the other initial states appear with probability $\frac{2}{n}$. This slight bias could be reduced by having the PRNG generate multiple initial states and selecting a non-zero state.

The $2^k - 1$ possible initial states determine $2^k - 1$ unique sequences. The operations of a complete $\log_2(n)$ stage NTT can then be computed in $(2^k - 1)^{\log_2(n)}$ different ways. For $n = 256$ and $k = 7$ this is more than 2^{55}. With the LFSR method applied to the pointwise operations outside the NTT as well, the total number of random bits added is equal to 71. A single trace attack like [23] that requires all of the $\log_2(n)$ stages seems unlikely to succeed on an implementation using the LFSR countermeasure as described.

We use an LFSR of degree $k = \log_2(n)$ in a similar manner to shuffle the order of the n pointwise multiplications outside the NTT.

Drawbacks to the LFSR loop counter include a limited permutation space, a slightly biased outcome and the fact that the first element is not permuted.

Permutation Network Method. We propose to use a permutation network generator in the style of [5]. Their permutation generator is designed for use in

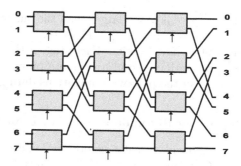

Fig. 5. Permutation network for $N = 8$. Each box is controlled by a random bit and swaps the inputs if this bit is equal to 1.

AES and is impractical for larger ($N = 256$) permutations. It is also biased. We simplify their permutation network to obtain a permutation generator that can generate $N^{N/2}$ permutations and that is uniform on its range. In the remainder of this section, the parameter N is the size of the permutation, which is equal to n for the shuffling of the pointwise operations. To shuffle the butterfly operations during the computation of the NTT, N is substituted by $\frac{n}{2}$.

For $b \in \{0, 1\}$, let the operators $T_b : \{0, \ldots, N-1\} \rightarrow \{0, \ldots, N-1\}$ be defined by the mapping $x \mapsto \lfloor \frac{x}{2} \rfloor + b\frac{N}{2}$. Then T_0 is a bitwise shift erasing the least significant bit (LSB), and T_1 applies the same shift and sets the MSB to 1.

The permutation network consists of $k = \log_2(N)$ stages and takes as input $(x_0, \ldots, x_{N-1}) = (0, \ldots, N-1)$. During each stage, $\frac{N}{2}$ random bits $b_1, \ldots, b_{N/2}$ are generated and for all pairs (x_{2i}, x_{2i+1}) the images $T_{b_i}(x_{2i})$ and $T_{\bar{b}_i}(x_{2i+1})$ are computed. In other words, for each pair (x_{2i}, x_{2i+1}), one is sent to position i, while the other is mapped to $i + \frac{N}{2}$. This is equivalent to writing one bit of the image of x_{2i} under the generated permutation and writing its complement to the image of x_{2i+1}. The network is shown for $N = 8$ in Fig. 5. It is exactly the same as the computation scheme of the constant geometry NTT, in which the butterfly operators are replaced by controlled swap operators.

For any integer $0 \leq x < N$ the image of x under the generated permutation can be written as $T_{b_1} \circ \cdots \circ T_{b_k}(x)$ and is equal to the value corresponding to the binary representation $(b_1, \ldots, b_k)_2$. The $\frac{kN}{2}$ control bits thus determine the image of each index under the generated permutation. By uniqueness of binary representation it follows that any modification to any subset of the $\frac{kN}{2}$ control bits would modify the generated permutation as well. The permutation generator is therefore an injective map from $\{0, 1\}^{Nk/2}$ into the set of all permutations Σ_N. This means that the number of possible configurations of the $\frac{kN}{2}$ control bits, which is equal to $N^{N/2}$, is exactly the number of permutations that can be generated by the network. The number of different permutations that can be obtained is 2^{1024} for the pointwise operations and 2^{256} for the NTT. Moreover, the output of the permutation network is uniform on its range given uniformly random input.

Since the permutation space is much larger than the one we obtain with the LFSR, we will only generate one $\{0, \ldots, \frac{n}{2} - 1\} \rightarrow \{0, \ldots, \frac{n}{2} - 1\}$ permutation for the NTT at the start of each decryption. Each stage is then computed in the order defined by this permutation. We also compute only one permutation of size n that will be used for all the pointwise operations during one decryption.

6.2   Randomization Using Redundant Number Representation

In RSA and ECC, some exponent or scalar randomization countermeasures have been proposed against SCAs (see for instance [7]). A secret exponent or scalar can be randomized without loss of information by adding a random multiple of the group order to it. The corresponding power traces are thus randomized, removing correlation between the side channel traces and the secret key. A similar concept can be applied to RLWE.

We can add random multiples of the modulus q to the secret key coefficients without invalidating the secret key. This is done at the start of each decryption. The PRNG is used to generate small r-bit random numbers for some integer parameter r. These numbers are multiplied by q and then added to the input and to the secret key. We then continue using arithmetic operations in $\mathbb{Z}/(2^r q)\mathbb{Z}$ instead of in $\mathbb{Z}_q$. The fact that for all $a, b \in \mathbb{Z}$ we have that $ab \bmod (2^r q) \equiv ab \bmod q$, ensures us that the result is in the correct equivalence class.

The redundancy is not removed for the decoding. Instead we modify the algorithm to decode the coefficients directly from $\mathbb{Z}/(2^r q)\mathbb{Z}$ to $\{0, 1\}$. The new decoder returns 0 if the input lies in the union of sets $\bigcup_{i=0}^{2^r} \left[\frac{-q}{4} + iq, \frac{q}{4} + iq \right)$ and returns 1 if the input is in $\bigcup_{i=0}^{2^r} \left[\frac{q}{4} + iq, \frac{3q}{4} + iq \right)$.

At each execution of the algorithm, the multipliers, adders and decoder are handling different inputs. The computations (and the corresponding traces) are thus randomized. A total of $256r$ random bits are added to the operands (Fig. 6).

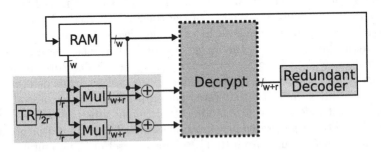

Fig. 6. Architecture with our redundant representation countermeasure. Before the decryption, small r-bit random multiples of q are added to the coefficients of $\mathbf{c}_1$ and $\mathbf{s}$. The operations in the decryption function are performed in $\mathbb{Z}/(2^r q)\mathbb{Z}$.

Validation Through Correlation Power Analysis Simulations. We evaluate the robustness of our countermeasure based on a redundant representation by simulating CPAs. The polynomial multiplication in the NTT domain consists of n independent multiplications in $\mathbb{Z}/q\mathbb{Z}$. They are of the form $c \cdot s \bmod q$, where s is a coefficient of the secret key and c is a coefficient of the input ciphertext. We simulate correlation attacks on one modular multiplication of a known input coefficient c with an unknown secret key coefficient s.

We assume that the attacker observes the modular multiplication $c \cdot s \bmod q$ for a number of different (known) inputs c. For each modular multiplication she/he obtains the exact Hamming weight (HW) of the result. The attacker computes the "predictions": the HW of the value $c \cdot s \bmod q$ for all subkey candidates $s \in \mathbb{Z}_q$ and for all inputs c. She/he evaluates the correlation between the observed HW and the predictions. For each subkey possibility $\tilde{s} \in \mathbb{Z}_q$, the Pearson's correlation coefficient between the observed HW and the predictions is computed. Without countermeasures, the highest correlation is obtained for the correct subkey guess.

The inputs are randomized by adding a multiple of q and used in computations in $\mathbb{Z}/(2^r q)\mathbb{Z}$ for some redundancy parameter r. The impact of our countermeasure on the effectiveness of the CPA can be seen (for $q = 7681$) in Fig. 7. Without redundancy ($r = 0$), the attacker observes the exact HW of the value $c \cdot s \bmod q$ for different values of c. These HWs coincide with the predictions for the correct subkey guess, resulting in a correlation coefficient of 1. For higher levels of redundancy, the average of the correlation coefficient for the correct subkey guess decreases.

The right side of Fig. 7 shows that the maximum correlation is obtained for incorrect subkey guesses for all $r \geq 1$. We refer to subkey guesses that yield to a higher correlation coefficient than the correct subkey guess as *false positives*. The number of these false positives increases with the redundancy level. For $r = 8$ and $r = 9$ there are on average around $\frac{q}{2}$ subkey guesses, for one coefficient of the secret key, that yield to a higher correlation coefficient than the correct key guess. Our countermeasure ensures that an exponential number of up to $\left(\frac{q}{2}\right)^n$ guesses have to be tested to recover the complete secret key.

7 Comparison of All Protections

FPGA implementation results for RLWE solutions with various countermeasures are presented in Table 2. Results from [25] are reported, and we also re-implemented their solution on an Artix-7 XC7A200 (denoted "A7") to provide fair comparisons. We also implemented the blinding and shifting methods from [27] and our shuffling methods. To the best of our knowledge, these are the first FPGA implementations for these countermeasures. Finally, the results for masking with our new masked decoder and our redundant randomized countermeasures are reported. The amount of randomness added for each countermeasure is specified in the second column of the table.

We cannot directly compare our re-implementation of the masking from [25] and their original results on a Virtex-II XC2VP7 (denoted "V2"). However, it

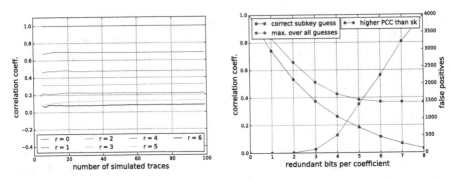

Fig. 7. Mean correlation over 1000 simulations between the correct subkey guess and the observed HW as a function of the number of traces (left) and the number of redundant bits per coefficient (right). Right: average (1000 simulations of 100 traces each) of the maximum correlation over all subkey guesses is shown in red and the number of subkey guesses with higher correlation than the correct secret key in green. (Color figure online)

can be seen that the impact of masking on the performance of their V2 implementation is very high compared to our A7 re-implementation. The computation time for decryption is tripled. This is probably because the number of arithmetic operations in $\mathbb{Z}_q$ is doubled while no parallelism is used. Moreover, it seems that their masked decoder is implemented sequentially. In our re-implementation of the masked decoder from [25], we use parallelism to significantly reduce the performance penalty of their 16-step decoder. This increases the area.

Our new masked decoder is relatively simple and requires a small area (about 20% reduction compared to the re-implementation of the decoder from [25]), with almost the performance of the unprotected implementation. Compared to the unprotected solution, we use extra DSP blocks and BRAMs to compute the decryptions of the two shares in parallel.

The blinding implementation gives a slightly slower solution. Its area overhead is smaller than for both masking techniques. However, we stress that this blinding countermeasure should be used in combination with another countermeasure (as specified in [18]), since the blinding factor is removed before the decoding step. The shifting implementation yields to similar overhead (although with lower frequency) and its combination with blinding seems to be worthwhile. The permutation network is relatively costly in area. The LFSR loop counter is cheaper and slightly faster.

Finally, our redundant randomized countermeasure does not need additional DSPs or BRAMs to be implemented for small redundancy parameters ($r \leq 4$) and can therefore be used as a cheap way to secure the decryption. For higher redundancy levels the multiplication cannot be computed within a single 18×25 bits multiplier, as the ones hardwired in the Artix DSP blocks. A few additional DSP blocks and BRAMs are needed.

Table 2. FPGA results for RLWE with various countermeasures and $(q, n) = (7681, 256)$. The source column refers to the work in which the countermeasure was first proposed in LWE context. Timing and area results are for the decryption only.

Counter-measure	Entropy added (bits)	Src.	Impl.	FPGA	Lat.	Clk. (ns)	Time (μs)	Slice, LUT, DSP, BRAM
None	0	-	[25]	V2	2800	8.3	23.5	-, 1713, 1, -
Masking	3328	[25]	[25]		7500	10	75.2	-, 2014, 1, -
None	0	-			2357	3.3	7.8	483, 1163, 2, 3
Blinding	16	[27]			2768	3.8	10.6	941, 2284, 3, 4
Shifting	16	[27]			3138	4.7	14.8	832, 2150, 3, 4
Shift + Blind	32	[27]			3183	4.6	14.7	1063, 2781, 3, 4
Masking	3328	[25]			2517	4.0	10.1	2187, 5500, 5, 6
Our Mask.	3328				2510	4.0	10.1	1722, 4269, 5, 6
Permutation	1280				2521	4.5	11.4	3183, 7385, 2, 4
LFSR ctr.	71		this work	A7	2846	3.6	10.3	1069, 2861, 2, 3
$r = 1$	256				2272	3.7	8.5	629, 1599, 2, 3
$r = 2$	512				2273	3.6	8.2	611, 1664, 2, 3
$r = 3$	768	this work			2333	3.8	8.9	807, 2067, 2, 3
$r = 4$	1024				2338	3.6	8.5	872, 2285, 2, 3
$r = 5$	1280				2352	3.8	9.0	990, 2677, 2, 6
$r = 6$	1536				2394	3.9	9.4	1254, 3466, 3, 6
$r = 7$	1792				2410	3.9	9.4	1713, 5017, 3, 6
$r = 8$	2048				2426	3.9	9.5	2544, 7837, 3, 6

8   Conclusion

In this work, we compared several countermeasures against SCAs for RLWE from [25, 27] and proposed new ones. Our first proposed countermeasure is an adaptation of [25] with a new masked decoder which is deterministic. Our second one uses a redundant representation to randomize polynomial coefficients. We also implemented two different methods for shuffling. All the countermeasures (from literature and our ones) have been implemented on FPGA to evaluate the overhead compared to a common reference implementation on the same FPGA. Our new decoder uses over 20% less slices and LUTs than the one from [25]. To the best of our knowledge, we also present the first FPGA implementations for the blinding and shifting countermeasures from [27], and a combination of the two. Finally, our protection based on redundancy at ring level provides a cheap randomization method with an adjustable security/overhead trade-off.

In the future, we will explore other types of architectures, operators, algorithms and countermeasures (*e.g.* at architecture level). We also plan to use our solutions in the context of application benchmarks and evaluate their security against SCAs using a hardware setup under development in our research group.

Acknowledgment. This work has been supported by a PhD grant from PEC/DGA/Région Bretagne.

References

1. Alagic, G., et al.: Status report on the first round of the NIST post-quantum cryptography standardization process. Technical report (2019)
2. Alkim, E., Ducas, L., Pöppelmann, T., Schwabe, P.: Post-quantum key exchange - a new hope. In: Proceedings 25th USENIX Security Symposium, pp. 327–343 (2016)
3. Aysu, A., Tobah, Y., Tiwari, M., Gerstlauer, A., Orshansky, M.: Horizontal side-channel vulnerabilities of post-quantum key exchange protocols. In: Proceedings IEEE International Symposium on Hardware Oriented Security and Trust (HOST), pp. 81–88, May 2018
4. Baan, H., et al.: Round5: compact and fast post-quantum public-key encryption. In: Ding, J., Steinwandt, R. (eds.) PQCrypto 2019. LNCS, vol. 11505, pp. 83–102. Springer, Cham (2019). https://doi.org/10.1007/978-3-030-25510-7_5
5. Bayrak, A.G., Velickovic, N., Ienne, P., Burleson, W.: An architecture-independent instruction shuffler to protect against side-channel attacks. ACM Trans. Archit. Code Optim. 8(4), 20:1–20:19 (2012)
6. Groot Bruinderink, L., Hülsing, A., Lange, T., Yarom, Y.: Flush, gauss, and reload – a cache attack on the BLISS lattice-based signature scheme. In: Gierlichs, B., Poschmann, A.Y. (eds.) CHES 2016. LNCS, vol. 9813, pp. 323–345. Springer, Heidelberg (2016). https://doi.org/10.1007/978-3-662-53140-2_16
7. Chabrier, T., Tisserand, A.: On-the-fly multi-base recoding for ECC scalar multiplication without pre-computations. In: Proceedings 21st Symposium on Computer Arithmetic (ARITH), pp. 219–228. IEEE Computer Society, April 2013
8. Chen, L., et al.: Report on post-quantum cryptography. Technical report (2016)
9. Cooley, J.W., Tukey, J.W.: An algorithm for the machine calculation of complex fourier series. Math. Comput. 19(90), 297–301 (1965)
10. Espitau, T., Fouque, P.-A., Gérard, B., Tibouchi, M.: Side-channel attacks on BLISS lattice-based signatures: exploiting branch tracing against strongswan and electromagnetic emanations in microcontrollers. In: Proceedings ACM SIGSAC Conference on Computer and Communications Security (CCS), pp. 1857–1874, November 2017
11. Göttert, N., Feller, T., Schneider, M., Buchmann, J., Huss, S.: On the design of hardware building blocks for modern lattice-based encryption schemes. In: Prouff, E., Schaumont, P. (eds.) CHES 2012. LNCS, vol. 7428, pp. 512–529. Springer, Heidelberg (2012). https://doi.org/10.1007/978-3-642-33027-8_30
12. Kocher, P., Jaffe, J., Jun, B.: Differential power analysis. In: Wiener, M. (ed.) CRYPTO 1999. LNCS, vol. 1666, pp. 388–397. Springer, Heidelberg (1999). https://doi.org/10.1007/3-540-48405-1_25
13. Kuo, P.-C., et al.: Post-quantum key exchange on FPGAs. IACR Cryptology ePrint Archive, 2017:690 (2017)
14. Longa, P., Naehrig, M.: Speeding up the number theoretic transform for faster ideal lattice-based cryptography. In: Foresti, S., Persiano, G. (eds.) CANS 2016. LNCS, vol. 10052, pp. 124–139. Springer, Cham (2016). https://doi.org/10.1007/978-3-319-48965-0_8
15. Lu, X., et al.: LAC: practical ring-LWE based public-key encryption with byte-level modulus. IACR Cryptology ePrint Archive, 2018:1009 (2018)
16. Lyubashevsky, V., Micciancio, D., Peikert, C., Rosen, A.: SWIFFT: a modest proposal for FFT hashing. In: Nyberg, K. (ed.) FSE 2008. LNCS, vol. 5086, pp. 54–72. Springer, Heidelberg (2008). https://doi.org/10.1007/978-3-540-71039-4_4

17. Lyubashevsky, V., Peikert, C., Regev, O.: On ideal lattices and learning with errors over rings. In: Gilbert, H. (ed.) EUROCRYPT 2010. LNCS, vol. 6110, pp. 1–23. Springer, Heidelberg (2010). https://doi.org/10.1007/978-3-642-13190-5_1

18. Oder, T., Schneider, T., Pöppelmann, T., Güneysu, T.: Practical CCA2-secure and masked ring-LWE implementation. IACR Trans. Cryptographic Hardw. Embed. Syst. (TCHES) **2018**(1), 142–174 (2018)

19. Pease, M.C.: An adaptation of the fast Fourier transform for parallel processing. J. ACM **15**(2), 252–264 (1968)

20. Pöppelmann, T., Güneysu, T.: Towards practical lattice-based public-key encryption on reconfigurable hardware. In: Lange, T., Lauter, K., Lisoněk, P. (eds.) SAC 2013. LNCS, vol. 8282, pp. 68–85. Springer, Heidelberg (2014). https://doi.org/10.1007/978-3-662-43414-7_4

21. Pöppelmann, T., Güneysu, T.: Area optimization of lightweight lattice-based encryption on reconfigurable hardware. In: Proceedings IEEE International Symposium on Circuits and Systemss (ISCAS), pp. 2796–2799, June 2014

22. Pöppelmann, T., Oder, T., Güneysu, T.: High-performance ideal lattice-based cryptography on 8-bit ATxmega microcontrollers. In: Lauter, K., Rodríguez-Henríquez, F. (eds.) LATINCRYPT 2015. LNCS, vol. 9230, pp. 346–365. Springer, Cham (2015). https://doi.org/10.1007/978-3-319-22174-8_19

23. Primas, R., Pessl, P., Mangard, S.: Single-trace side-channel attacks on masked lattice-based encryption. In: Fischer, W., Homma, N. (eds.) CHES 2017. LNCS, vol. 10529, pp. 513–533. Springer, Cham (2017). https://doi.org/10.1007/978-3-319-66787-4_25

24. Regev, O.: On lattices, learning with errors, random linear codes, and cryptography. In: Proceedings 37th Annual ACM Symposium on Theory of Computing, pp. 84–93, May 2005

25. Reparaz, O., Sinha Roy, S., Vercauteren, F., Verbauwhede, I.: A masked ring-LWE implementation. In: Güneysu, T., Handschuh, H. (eds.) CHES 2015. LNCS, vol. 9293, pp. 683–702. Springer, Heidelberg (2015). https://doi.org/10.1007/978-3-662-48324-4_34

26. Roy, S.S., Vercauteren, F., Mentens, N., Chen, D.D., Verbauwhede, I.: Compact ring-LWE cryptoprocessor. In: Batina, L., Robshaw, M. (eds.) CHES 2014. LNCS, vol. 8731, pp. 371–391. Springer, Heidelberg (2014). https://doi.org/10.1007/978-3-662-44709-3_21

27. Saarinen, M.-J.O.: Arithmetic coding and blinding countermeasures for lattice signatures - engineering a side-channel resistant post-quantum signature scheme with compact signatures. J. Cryptographic Eng. **8**(1), 71–84 (2018)

28. Shor, P.W.: Polynomial time algorithms for prime factorization and discrete logarithms on a quantum computer. SIAM J. Sci. Stat. Comput. **26**, 1484 (1997)

29. Solinas, J.A.: Generalized mersenne numbers. Technical report CORR-99-39, Center for Applied Cryptographic Research, University of Waterloo (1999)

30. Oder, T., Güneysu, T.: Implementing the NewHope-simple key exchange on low-cost FPGAs. In: Lange, T., Dunkelman, O. (eds.) LATINCRYPT 2017. LNCS, vol. 11368, pp. 128–142. Springer, Cham (2019). https://doi.org/10.1007/978-3-030-25283-0_7

Analysis of the Strict Avalanche Criterion in Variants of Arbiter-Based Physically Unclonable Functions

Akhilesh Anilkumar Siddhanti[1], Srinivasu Bodapati[2],
Anupam Chattopadhyay[3], Subhamoy Maitra[4], Dibyendu Roy[5(⊠)],
and Pantelimon Stănică[6]

[1] Georgia Institute of Technology, Atlanta, USA
akhilesh@gatech.edu
[2] Indian Institute of Technology Mandi, Mandi, India
srinivasu@iitmandi.ac.in
[3] Nanyang Technological University, Singapore, Singapore
anupam@ntu.edu.sg
[4] Indian Statistical Institute, Kolkata, India
subho@isical.ac.in
[5] ERTL(E), STQC, Kolkata, India
roydibyendu.rd@gmail.com
[6] Naval Postgraduate School, Monterey, USA
pstanica@nps.edu

Abstract. Arbiter-based Physically Unclonable Functions (Arbiter PUF) were introduced to generate cryptographically secure secret keys during runtime, rather than storing it in Non-Volatile Memory (NVM) which are vulnerable to physical attacks. However, its construction was a target to several statistical and modeling attacks. One such statistical weakness of the Arbiter PUF is that it leaks information to the adversary, if some challenge-response pairs are known. The response is heavily biased towards the effect of flipping certain bits of the input, a widely studied property, known as the Strict Avalanche Criterion (SAC). Several variants of Arbiter PUFs have been proposed since then, with varying degrees of success against SAC. In this paper, we provide a generalized framework to analyze any Arbiter PUF variant against SAC. Building on this analysis, we propose a new Arbiter PUF variant which is not only highly resistant to SAC but also has very good reliability.

Keywords: Arbiter PUF · Boolean function · Bias · SAC

1 Introduction

It is a well-known fact that storing cryptographic keys in Non-Volatile Memory (NVM) is insecure and is subject to physical attacks [7]. As an alternative, Arbiter-based Physically Unclonable Functions (PUFs) were introduced in [4], generating a huge interest in the cryptology community. An Arbiter-based PUF

© Springer Nature Switzerland AG 2019
F. Hao et al. (Eds.): INDOCRYPT 2019, LNCS 11898, pp. 556–577, 2019.
https://doi.org/10.1007/978-3-030-35423-7_28

is a physical one-way function from an n-dimension space, referred to as *challenge* to a one bit output, called *response*. This function, when instantiated on a silicon chip, uses the inherent manufacturing process variations of the chip and transforms into an unknown Boolean function. This means that an instantiated PUF cannot be cloned – even by the manufacturer. This has led to many interesting applications of Arbiter PUFs like identification and authentication [2,6,8], key generation and storage, and have even found their ways to commercially available products like RFID tags and smart cards [1]. But, there are some performance metrics an ideal Arbiter PUF should exhibit:

Uniqueness. When same challenges are given to different PUFs, the responses should be different as well. However, this does not happen in practice. There have been several works which show that when an Arbiter PUF is implemented on Xilinx Virtex-5/Kintex-7 FPGAs, the responses exhibit a very low value of uniqueness [10,12].

Uniformity. An Arbiter PUF should be uniform (or balanced), i.e., 50% of challenges should produce 0 as response, while the other 50% produce 1.

Reliability. An Arbiter PUF should produce the same response for a given input challenge. In practice, this fails due to several environmental variations, instabilities and aging in the circuit.

However, Arbiter PUFs have long been known to be susceptible to model building attacks using linear programming and ML techniques like Logistic Regression and SVM [15]. In a model building attack, the adversary develops a software model of the Physically Unclonable Function which gives the same response as output as the real PUF would generate (for the same challenge input). The model is built using the knowledge of several thousands of Challenge-Response pairs (CRPs) generated from the real PUF. Consequently, XOR [3] and Feedforward PUFs [8] were introduced. Several attacks have been reported on XOR PUFs since then, with [15] reporting attacks on up to 6-XOR PUFs, and several works have shown that an exponential increase in the number of challenge-response pairs (CRPs) is required for every additional XOR. Note that it has been reported in [18] that only a maximum of 12 XORs can be combined to provide a reliable response. However, it was recently shown in [1] that using a combination of reliability and CMA-ES, only a linear increase in CRPs is required to successfully clone XOR PUFs.

A statistical weakness prevalent in most of the Arbiter PUF variants has been reported in [14]. For an Arbiter PUF, there is a clear bias between the responses of two challenges which differ at 1 or more positions. This shows that the Boolean function, irrespective of the PUF construction, is *weak* in nature, since an Arbiter PUF can be distinguished from a random source by collection of very few samples. This gives a significant advantage to the adversary. This bias affects the XOR PUF and Feedforward PUF as well. In fact, we go on to show that the bias affects any general variant of Arbiter PUF. Based on this, we then develop a new variant of Arbiter PUF exhibiting very good properties of Strict Avalanche Criterion, while still maintaining reliability better than a XOR PUF with same number of Arbiter PUFs.

One of the first works to highlight a bias in the output for Arbiter-based PUFs was [14]. New Arbiter-based constructions were developed to mitigate bias and improve reliability [16], albeit under two different constructions, cMPUF and rMPUF. The authors in [16] also claim that the constructions withstand the reliability-based attack presented by Becker in [1] and ML attacks like [15].

Our Contribution. The primary goal of this paper is to analyze several existing PUFs and propose an improved construction of PUF. An overview of our contribution is described below.

- We first discuss a theoretical derivation for a bias in an n-bit Arbiter PUF and n-bit k-XOR PUF (in Sect. 3).
- Next we discuss how the bias prevails in a Feedforward PUF construction (in Sect. 4).
- In Sect. 5, we provide a general framework to theoretically analyze bias and reliability of any Arbiter-based PUF construction.
- In Sect. 6 we introduce a new construction, S-PUF, and theoretically prove that the bias reduces significantly. We then combine several S-PUFs to build S_n-PUF with negligible bias and very high reliability and discuss its security against conventional machine learning attacks and Becker's reliability based attack [1] in Sect. 7, showing that it is the best PUF construction as far as we know.

2 Background

2.1 Description of Arbiter-Based Physically Unclonable Functions and Their Variants

Using variations in a manufacturing process, Arbiter-based Physically Unclonable Functions generate a pseudorandom output based on an n-bit input. The input is commonly referred to as *challenge*, and 1-bit output as *response*. The function is said to be *reliable*, if it can produce the same response for every n-bit input. Several studies have discussed the reliability of Arbiter-based PUFs [1,2,16,18]. We are going to treat Arbiter-based PUFs from a Boolean function perspective, but before that we will explore the construction of Arbiter-based PUFs as known by the research community [3,8,15].

Arbiter PUF. A general Arbiter PUF consists of two symmetrically placed electrical paths consisting of n switches. A common pulse is transmitted at the same time on both the paths and received at the end by an arbiter. Every switch has a 1-bit input. If the input supplied to a switch is 0, the paths are not affected, whereas an input of 1 will swap the two paths (see Fig. 1). Due to process variations, the pulse will traverse one path faster than the other. The arbiter simply generates the output as 0/1 depending on which pulse arrives first - the top or the bottom. Since the inception of Arbiter PUFs, they have been shown to be vulnerable against modeling attacks. One can model an arbiter PUF using machine learning techniques like Logistic Regression and Neural Networks [15], given enough challenge-response pairs. This prompted the introduction of XOR-based Arbiter PUFs and Feedforward PUFs.

k-XOR PUF. An k-XOR PUF combines the output of k Arbiter PUFs, each fed with the same challenge vector C, by a simple XOR (see Fig. 2). The Arbiter PUF can be seen as a XOR PUF with $k = 1$.

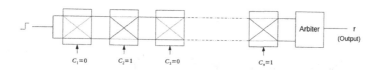

Fig. 1. An Arbiter PUF with n inputs.

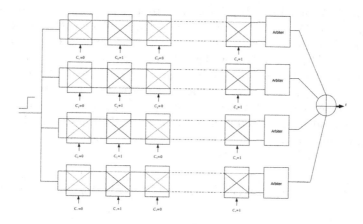

Fig. 2. k-XOR n-bit Arbiter PUF

Feedforward PUF. Another approach to construct Arbiter PUFs is to use additional arbiters as feedforward links [8]. The delay differences between the two paths after stage t_1 are checked using an arbiter, the output of which is fed as an input to an additional switch t_2. The input to the switch t_2 is denoted as C_{t_2}. The construction has been described in Fig. 3.

2.2 Modeling Arbiter-Based PUFs as Boolean Functions

Arbiter PUF. An Arbiter PUF can be represented as a function of the challenge and path delays due to the n switches. Here we follow the similar modeling

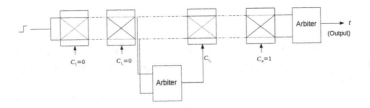

Fig. 3. Design of a Feedforward PUF

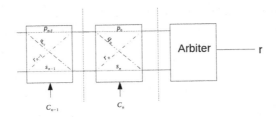

Fig. 4. The four possible delays a switch can introduce.

as described in [9]. Let $\Delta(n)$ be the difference between the top and bottom paths of an n-length Arbiter PUF. It is customary to map the challenge and response bits using $f : \{0,1\} \rightarrow \{-1,1\}$ using the signature $f(x) = (1 - 2 \cdot x)$ for all $x \in \{C \cup r\}$. From here, we will assume $C_i \in \{-1,1\}$ and $r \in \{-1,1\}$ using the same mapping. The time taken by the pulse to traverse the two paths, *top* and *bottom*, will be denoted as $\delta_{top}(n)$ and $\delta_{bottom}(n)$ respectively. At each switch i, four fixed, different values are introduced into the circuit, as shown in Fig. 4. We denote these four delay values as p_i, q_i, r_i and s_i respectively. These p_i, q_i, r_i and s_i are randomly selected from a same normal distribution. So if the delay values $\delta_{top}(i)$ and $\delta_{bottom}(i)$ are known for some intermediate switch i, we can write $\delta_{top}(i + 1)$ and $\delta_{bottom}(i + 1)$ as:

$$\delta_{top}(i + 1) = \frac{1 + C_{i+1}}{2}(p_{i+1} + \delta_{top}(i)) + \frac{1 - C_{i+1}}{2}(s_{i+1} + \delta_{bottom}(i)) \quad (1)$$

$$\delta_{bottom}(i + 1) = \frac{1 + C_{i+1}}{2}(q_{i+1} + \delta_{bottom}(i)) + \frac{1 - C_{i+1}}{2}(r_{i+1} + \delta_{top}(i)). \quad (2)$$

The difference between the top and bottom paths is $\Delta(i)$. Subtracting Eqs. (1) and (2) will give us the following relation:

$$\Delta(i + 1) = C_{i+1} \cdot \Delta(i) + \alpha_{i+1}C_{i+1} + \beta_{i+1}, \quad (3)$$

where $\alpha_i = \frac{(p_i - q_i)}{2} + \frac{(r_i - s_i)}{2}, \beta_i = \frac{(p_i - q_i)}{2} - \frac{(r_i - s_i)}{2}$. To simplify our expression, we denote the parity of challenge bits, P_k as: $P_k = \prod_{i=k+1}^{n} C_i$. By iteratively using integers $i \geq 0$ in Eq. (3) and observing the pattern, the nth term can be written as a function of parity bits and the delay values p_i, q_i, r_i and s_i:

$$\Delta(n) = \alpha_1 P_0 + (\alpha_2 + \beta_1)P_1 + \ldots + (\alpha_n + \beta_{n-1})P_{n-1} + \beta_n P_n, \quad (4)$$

where $P_k = \prod_{i=k+1}^{n} C_i$, for $k = 0, 1, \ldots, n-1$ and $P_n = 1$. Thus, an Arbiter PUF with n-bit input can be expressed as polynomial expression of the following form, $\Delta(C) = \langle P, D \rangle$. Here P and D are the two vectors of $n+1$ length and $\langle \cdot, \cdot \rangle$ denotes the standard inner product. The explicit form of P, D are $P = (P_0, P_1, \ldots, P_n)$, $D = (\alpha_1, \alpha_2 + \beta_1, \alpha_3 + \beta_2, \ldots, \alpha_n + \beta_{n-1}, \beta_n)$.

In the Eq. (4) it can be observed that $P_i \in \{-1, 1\}$ for $i = 0, 1, \ldots, n-1$. Now if the sign of $\Delta(C)$ is negative the PUF outputs 0 and if sign of $\Delta(C)$ is positive then PUF outputs 1. We use the transformation $Q_i = \frac{1-P_i}{2}$ on Eq. (4) for $i = 0, 1, \ldots, n-1$ and $Q_n = P_n$. After substituting $P_i = 1 - 2Q_i$ for $i = 0, 1, \ldots, n-1$ in Eq. (4) we have the following.

$$\Delta(C) = \alpha_1(1 - 2Q_0) + (\alpha_2 + \beta_1)(1 - 2Q_1) + (\alpha_3 + \beta_2)(1 - 2Q_2)$$
$$+ \cdots + (\alpha_n + \beta_{n-1})(1 - 2Q_{n-1}) + \beta_n Q_n. \tag{5}$$

The response bit, r, is simply the sign value of $\Delta(n)$, that is, $r = sgn(\Delta(n))$. From Eq. (5) it can be noticed that, after the above mentioned transformation, the PUF becomes a function which takes 0 or 1 as input and depending upon the sign of $\Delta(C)$ it outputs either 0 or 1. Complete PUF with n input can be seen as a Boolean function $f : \{0,1\}^n \to \{0,1\}$ involving n variables. The number of variables will be n as P_n is always a constant equal to 1, so the total number of variable Q_n is essentially n.

k-**XOR PUF.** The XOR PUF is equivalent to an arbiter PUF for $k = 1$. The response bit r can be represented as: $r = \bigoplus_{i=1}^{k} sgn(\Delta^i(n))$.

Feedforward PUF. A feedforward PUF uses an arbiter over the first t_1 stages, and feeds the input to the switch t_2 as C_{t_2}. We can represent this relation as: $C_{t_2} = sgn(\Delta(C_1, C_2, \ldots, C_{t_1}))$. We denote the response bit as: $z = sgn(\Delta(C_\mathbf{x}))$, where

$$\Delta(C_\mathbf{x}) = \alpha_1(C_1 C_2 \cdots C_{t_1} \cdots C_{t_2} \cdots C_n) + (\alpha_2 + \beta_1)(C_2 \cdots C_{t_1} \cdots C_{t_2} \cdots C_n)$$
$$+ \cdots + (\alpha_{t_1} + \beta_{t_1-1})(C_{t_1} \cdots C_{t_2} \cdots C_n) + \cdots +$$
$$+ (\alpha_{t_2} + \beta_{t_2-1})(C_{t_2} \cdots C_n) + \cdots + (\alpha_n + \beta_{n-1})C_n + \beta_n \tag{6}$$

3 Theoretical Estimation of the Experimental Bias Observed on r XOR PUF in [16]

In this section, we provide the exact theoretical estimation of the bias observed in [16]. We first recall the algebraic expression of the PUF which is described in Eq. (4), namely $\Delta(C) = \langle P, D \rangle = \alpha_1 P_0 + (\alpha_2 + \beta_1)P_1 + \cdots + (\alpha_n + \beta_{n-1})P_{n-1} + \beta_n P_n$. Here, $P_k = \prod_{i=k+1}^{n} C_i$ for $k = 0, 1, \ldots, n-1$ and $P_n = 1$. In our model, we construct two inputs to the PUF by modifying the sign of C_1. We use $\Delta C_\mathbf{x}$, $\Delta C_{\widetilde{\mathbf{x}}}$ to denote ΔC corresponding to $\mathbf{x}$ and $\widetilde{\mathbf{x}}$ respectively. It can be noticed that all the monomials of $\Delta C_\mathbf{x}$ and $\Delta C_{\widetilde{\mathbf{x}}}$ have the same sign, except the first one $\alpha_1 P_0$, as C_1 is only involved in $\alpha_1 P_0$. It can be observed that $\Delta C_{\mathbf{x}}$ and $\Delta C_{\tilde{\mathbf{x}}}$ will be of same sign if the following condition holds:

$$|\alpha_1 P_0| < |(\alpha_2 + \beta_1)P_1 + (\alpha_3 + \beta_2)P_2 + \cdots + (\alpha_n + \beta_{n-1})P_{n-1} + \beta_n P_n|$$

$$\Rightarrow |\alpha_1| < |(\alpha_2 + \beta_1)P_1 + (\alpha_3 + \beta_2)P_2 + \cdots + (\alpha_n + \beta_{n-1})P_{n-1} + \beta_n P_n| \quad (7)$$

$$\Rightarrow |\alpha_1| < |X|, \quad \text{where } X = (\alpha_2 + \beta_1)P_1 + (\alpha_3 + \beta_2)P_2$$

$$+ \cdots + (\alpha_n + \beta_{n-1})P_{n-1} + \beta_n P_n. \quad (8)$$

Here, $\alpha_i = \frac{p_i - q_i}{2} + \frac{r_i - s_i}{2}$ and $\beta_i = \frac{p_i - q_i}{2} - \frac{r_i - s_i}{2}$ and p_i, q_i, r_i, s_i follows $\mathcal{N}(\mu, \sigma)$ (i.e., normal distribution with mean μ and standard deviation σ). As p_i, q_i, r_i and s_i follows the same normal distribution $\mathcal{N}(\mu, \sigma)$, so $p_i - q_i, r_i - s_i$ will follow $\mathcal{N}(0, \sqrt{2}\sigma)$. Hence α_i, β_i will follow $\mathcal{N}(0, \sqrt{2}\sigma)$. We use σ_1 to denote $\sqrt{2}\sigma$, so α_i and β_i will follow $\mathcal{N}(0, \sigma_1)$. From Eq. (4) it can be seen that, $P_i \in \{-1, 1\}$, so $(\alpha_2 + \beta_1)P_1 + (\alpha_3 + \beta_2)P_2 + \ldots + (\alpha_n + \beta_{n-1})P_{n-1} + \beta_n P_n$ will follow $\mathcal{N}(0, \sqrt{2n - 1}\sigma_1)$ i.e., $X \sim \mathcal{N}(0, \sqrt{2n - 1}\sigma_1)$.

From Eq. (8) we need to find the probability $Pr\left[|\alpha_1| < |X|\right]$. This is equivalent to find $Pr\left[\left|\frac{\alpha_1}{X}\right| < 1\right]$. In the following lemma we will find the required probability.

Lemma 1. If $\alpha_1 \sim \mathcal{N}(0, \sigma_1)$ and $X \sim \mathcal{N}(0, \sqrt{2n - 1}\sigma_1)$, then $Pr\left[\left|\frac{\alpha_1}{X}\right| < 1\right] = 1 - \frac{2}{\pi} \tan^{-1}\left(\frac{1}{\sqrt{2n-1}}\right)$.

Proof. Here $\alpha_1 \sim \mathcal{N}(0, \sigma_1)$ and $X \sim \mathcal{N}(0, \sqrt{2n - 1}\sigma_1)$. Firstly, we are interested to check the distribution of $\frac{\alpha_1}{X}$. For simplicity, we use σ_2 to denote $\sqrt{2n - 1}\sigma_1$. Now, the probability density functions of the distribution of α_1 and X, denoted by $f_{\alpha_1}(\alpha_1)$ and $f_X(x)$, respectively, are given below $f_{\alpha_1}(\alpha_1) = \frac{1}{\sqrt{2\pi}\sigma_1}e^{-\frac{\alpha_1^2}{2\sigma_1^2}}$, $-\infty < \alpha_1 < \infty$; $f_X(x) = \frac{1}{\sqrt{2\pi}\sigma_2}e^{-\frac{x^2}{2\sigma_2^2}}$, $-\infty < x < \infty$. We consider $\mathbf{y}_1 = \frac{\alpha_1}{X}$ and $\mathbf{y}_2 = X$, so $\alpha_1 = \mathbf{y}_1\mathbf{y}_2$ and $X = \mathbf{y}_2$. If $-\infty < \alpha_1, x < \infty$, then $-\infty < y_1, y_2 < \infty$. As the two distribution are mutually independent, the joint distribution of α_1, X will be $f_{\alpha_1, X}(\alpha_1, x) = \frac{1}{2\pi\sigma_1\sigma_2}e^{-\left(\frac{\alpha_1^2}{2\sigma_1^2} + \frac{x^2}{2\sigma_2^2}\right)}$. The joint distribution of $\mathbf{y}_1, \mathbf{y}_2$ will be, $f_{\mathbf{y}_1, \mathbf{y}_2}(y_1, y_2) = \frac{1}{2\pi\sigma_1\sigma_2}e^{-\left(\frac{y_1^2 y_2^2}{2\sigma_1^2} + \frac{y_2^2}{2\sigma_2^2}\right)}y_2$, where $-\infty < y_1, y_2 < \infty$. Now we are interested to find the distribution of $\mathbf{y}_1$ i.e., $f_{\mathbf{y}_1}(y_1)$, which is described below,

$$f_{\mathbf{y}_1}(y_1) = \int_{-\infty}^{\infty} f_{\mathbf{y}_1, \mathbf{y}_2}(y_1, y_2)dy_2 = \int_{-\infty}^{\infty} \frac{1}{2\pi\sigma_1\sigma_2}e^{-\left(\frac{y_1^2 y_2^2}{2\sigma_1^2} + \frac{y_2^2}{2\sigma_2^2}\right)}y_2 dy_2 = \frac{1}{\pi}\frac{\frac{\sigma_1}{\sigma_2}}{y_1^2 + (\frac{\sigma_1}{\sigma_2})^2}.$$

Our aim is to find the probability $Pr[|\frac{\alpha_1}{X}| < 1]$ i.e., for that we need to find $Pr[|\mathbf{y}_1| < 1]$. To find this, we do the following,

$$Pr[|\mathbf{y}_1| < 1] = \left|\int_{-1}^{1} \frac{1}{\pi}\frac{\frac{\sigma_1}{\sigma_2}}{y_1^2 + (\frac{\sigma_1}{\sigma_2})^2}dy_1\right| = \frac{1}{\pi}\left|\left\{\tan^{-1}\left(\frac{1}{\frac{\sigma_1}{\sigma_2}}\right) - \tan^{-1}\left(\frac{-1}{\frac{\sigma_1}{\sigma_2}}\right)\right\}\right|$$

$$= \frac{2}{\pi} \tan^{-1}\left(\frac{\sigma_2}{\sigma_1}\right) = \frac{2}{\pi} \tan^{-1}(\sqrt{2n-1}) = 1 - \frac{2}{\pi} \tan^{-1}\left(\frac{1}{\sqrt{2n-1}}\right),$$

where $\sigma_2 = \sqrt{2n-1}\sigma_1$. Hence $Pr[|\frac{\alpha_1}{X}| < 1] = 1 - \frac{2}{\pi} \tan^{-1}\left(\frac{1}{\sqrt{2n-1}}\right)$. $\qquad\square$

From the result of the Lemma 1 the following result follows.

Lemma 2. *Let* x *and* $\tilde{x}$ *be two inputs to an* n *inputs PUF, where the first coordinates of* x *and* $\tilde{x}$ *are of opposite in sign. Let* z *and* $\tilde{z}$ *be the outputs corresponding to* x *and* $\tilde{x}$. *Then* $Pr[z = \tilde{z}] = 1 - \frac{2}{\pi} \tan^{-1}\left(\frac{1}{\sqrt{2n-1}}\right)$.

From the Lemma 2 we have $Pr[z = \tilde{z}] = 1 - \frac{2}{\pi} \tan^{-1}\left(\frac{1}{\sqrt{2n-1}}\right) = \frac{1}{2} + \left(\frac{1}{2} - \frac{2}{\pi} \tan^{-1}\left(\frac{1}{\sqrt{2n-1}}\right)\right)$.

Now let us observe the bias for flipping t^{th} bit of the input. Revisiting Eq. (4), we have (without any flips):

$$\Delta(C) = \alpha_1(C_1 \cdots C_t \cdots C_n) + (\alpha_2 + \beta_1)(C_2 \cdots C_t \cdots C_n) + \cdots$$
$$+ (\alpha_t + \beta_{t-1})(C_t \cdots C_n) + (\alpha_{t+1} + \beta_t)(C_{t+1} \cdots C_n) + \cdots$$
$$+ (\alpha_n + \beta_{n-1})P_{n-1} + \beta_n P_n.$$

Flipping the tth bit results in the following expression:

$$\Delta(C) = -[\alpha_1(C_1 \cdots C_t \cdots C_n) + (\alpha_2 + \beta_1)(C_2 \cdots C_t \cdots C_n) + \cdots$$
$$+ (\alpha_t + \beta_{t-1})(C_t \cdots C_n)] + (\alpha_{t+1} + \beta_t)(C_{t+1} \cdots C_n) + \cdots$$
$$+ (\alpha_n + \beta_{n-1})P_{n-1} + \beta_n P_n.$$

We know that $\alpha \sim (0, \sigma_1\sqrt{2t-1})$ and $X \sim (0, \sigma_1\sqrt{2n-2t+1})$, where $\alpha = \alpha_1(C_1 \cdots C_t \cdots C_n) + (\alpha_2 + \beta_1)(C_2 \cdots C_t \cdots C_n) + (\alpha_t + \beta_{t-1})(C_t \cdots C_n)$ and $X = (\alpha_{t+1} + \beta_t)(C_{t+1} \cdots C_n) + \ldots + (\alpha_n + \beta_{n-1})P_{n-1} + \beta_n P_n$.

Thus, the bias can be written as:

$$Pr[z = \tilde{z}] = 1 - \frac{2}{\pi} \tan^{-1} \sqrt{\frac{2t-1}{2n-2t+1}}. \qquad (9)$$

Lemma 3. *For two inputs* x *and* $\tilde{x}$ *differing in the* t^{th} *coordinate, we have* $Pr[z = \tilde{z}] = 1 - \frac{2}{\pi} \tan^{-1} \sqrt{\frac{2t-1}{2n-2t+1}}$.

Further, we are interested in finding the bias of r-XOR PUFs. For that we use a Piling-up lemma, which is stated in Lemma 4 below.

Lemma 4. [13] *If* $Pr[X_i = 0] = p_i = \frac{1}{2} + \epsilon_i$, *for* $i = 1, \ldots, r$, *then* $Pr\left[\bigoplus_{i=1}^{r} X_i = 0\right] = \frac{1}{2} + 2^{r-1} \prod_{i=1}^{r} \epsilon_i$.

For a single PUF, we obtained that $Pr[z = \tilde{z}] = \frac{1}{2} + \left(\frac{1}{2} - \frac{2}{\pi} \tan^{-1} \left(\frac{1}{\sqrt{2n-1}} \right) \right)$
i.e., $Pr[z = \tilde{z}] = \frac{1}{2} + \epsilon$, where $\epsilon = \left(\frac{1}{2} - \frac{2}{\pi} \tan^{-1} \left(\frac{1}{\sqrt{2n-1}} \right) \right)$. Now if we consider
r-XOR PUF with n inputs, then the bias of the same can be calculated from
Lemma 4, which is stated in the following lemma.

Lemma 5. *Let* $\mathbf{x}$ *and* $\tilde{\mathbf{x}}$ *be two inputs to an* n *inputs* r-XOR PUF, *where the*
first coordinates of $\mathbf{x}$ *and* $\tilde{\mathbf{x}}$ *are of opposite in sign. If* z *and* $\tilde{z}$ *are the outputs*
corresponding to $\mathbf{x}$ *and* $\tilde{\mathbf{x}}$, *then* $Pr[z = \tilde{z}] = \frac{1}{2} + 2^{r-1}\epsilon^r$, *where* $\epsilon = \left(\frac{1}{2} - \frac{2}{\pi} \tan^{-1} \left(\frac{1}{\sqrt{2n-1}} \right) \right)$.

This theoretical bias obtained in Lemma 5 is exactly the same as the experimental bias observed in [16] for several r XOR PUFs with n inputs.

4   Theoretical Estimation of the Bias in Feedforward PUF

Let us assume we have an n-bit feedforward PUF with a single feedforward link.
The challenge vector is denoted by $C_{\mathbf{x}} = (C_1, C_2, \ldots, C_n)$. We will assume the
input to the feedforward loop is taken after t_1 stages, and fed to switch t_2 so that
$C_{t_2} = sgn(\Delta(C_1, C_2, \ldots, C_{t_1}))$. We denote the response bit as: $z = sgn(\Delta(C_{\mathbf{x}}))$

$$\Delta(C_{\mathbf{x}}) = \alpha_1(C_1 C_2 \cdots C_{t_1} \cdots C_{t_2} \cdots C_n) + (\alpha_2 + \beta_1)(C_2 \cdots C_{t_1} \cdots C_{t_2} \cdots C_n)$$
$$+ \cdots + (\alpha_{t_1} + \beta_{t_1-1})(C_{t_1} \cdots C_{t_2} \cdots C_n) + \cdots +$$
$$+ (\alpha_{t_2} + \beta_{t_2-1})(C_{t_2} \cdots C_n) + \cdots + (\alpha_n + \beta_{n-1})C_n + \beta_n. \qquad (10)$$

We are interested in calculating the bias of $\Delta z = z \oplus \tilde{z}$, where z corresponds to
the input $\mathbf{x}$ and $\tilde{z}$ corresponds to the input $\tilde{\mathbf{x}}$. Here $\mathbf{x}$ and $\tilde{\mathbf{x}}$ differ only at the
first position. The following lemma proves the result.

Lemma 6. *Let* $\mathbf{x}$ *and* $\tilde{\mathbf{x}}$ *be two inputs to a feed forward PUF which takes feed-*
back from the t_1 *stage and feds to switch* t_2. *If the first coordinates of* $\mathbf{x}$ *and* $\tilde{\mathbf{x}}$
are of opposite signs and the others are of the same sign, then

$$Pr[z = \tilde{z}] = 1 - \frac{2}{\pi} \tan^{-1} \frac{1}{\sqrt{2n-1}}$$
$$- \frac{4}{\pi^2} \tan^{-1} \frac{1}{\sqrt{2t_1-1}} \tan^{-1} \frac{\sqrt{\frac{2t_2-2}{2n-2t_2+1}} - \frac{1}{\sqrt{2n-1}}}{1 + \sqrt{\frac{2t_2-2}{(2n-2t_2+1)(2n-1)}}},$$

where z *and* $\tilde{z}$ *correspond to the output bit corresponding to* $\mathbf{x}$ *and* $\tilde{\mathbf{x}}$.

Proof. Flipping the first bit we have, $\tilde{C}_1 = C_1 \times -1$ and $C_{t_2} = \Delta(C_1, C_2, \ldots,$
$C_{t_1})$, where $\mathbf{x} = (C_1, C_2, \ldots, C_{t_2}, \ldots, C_n)$ and $\tilde{\mathbf{x}} = (\tilde{C}_1, C_2, \ldots, \tilde{C}_{t_2}, \ldots, C_n)$.
Hence, the sign of C_{t_2} will be different corresponding to $\mathbf{x}$ and $\tilde{\mathbf{x}}$ as C_1
changes its sign. One may note that the sign of C_{t_2} will change with proba-
bility $\frac{2}{\pi} \tan^{-1}(\frac{1}{\sqrt{2t_1-1}})$ when the first bit C_1 changes its sign (see Lemma 2). We
consider two cases.

Case 1 (The sign of C_{t_2} is altered). Here $\widetilde{C}_1 = -C_1$ and $\widetilde{C}_{t_2} = -C_{t_2}$. The Eq. (10) becomes:

$$\Delta(C_{\mathbf{x}}) = \alpha_1(C_1 C_2 \cdots C_{t_1} \cdots C_{t_2} \cdots C_n) - [(\alpha_2 + \beta_1)(C_2 \cdots C_{t_1} \cdots C_{t_2} \cdots C_n)$$
$$+ \cdots + (\alpha_{t_2} + \beta_{t_2 - 1})(C_{t_2} \cdots C_n)] + (\alpha_{t_2 + 1} + \beta_{t_2})(C_{t_2 + 1} \cdots C_n)$$
$$+ \cdots + (\alpha_n + \beta_{n-1})C_n + \beta_n.$$

It can be observed that the sign of $\Delta(C_{\mathbf{x}})$ and $\Delta(C_{\widetilde{\mathbf{x}}})$ will remain the same for $\mathbf{x}$ and $\widetilde{\mathbf{x}}$ iff $|\alpha| < |X|$, where $\alpha = (\alpha_2 + \beta_1)(C_2 \cdots C_{t_1} \cdots C_{t_2} \cdots C_n) + \cdots + (\alpha_{t_2} + \beta_{t_2 - 1})(C_{t_2} \cdots C_n)$ and $X = \alpha_1(C_1 C_2 \cdots C_{t_1} \cdots C_{t_2} \cdots C_n) + (\alpha_{t_2 + 1} + \beta_{t_2})(C_{t_2 + 1} \cdots C_n) + \cdots + (\alpha_n + \beta_{n-1}) C_n + \beta_n$. If $\alpha_i, \beta_i \sim \mathcal{N}(0, \sigma_1)$ then $\alpha \sim \mathcal{N}(0, \sigma_\alpha)$ and $X \sim \mathcal{N}(0, \sigma_X)$, where $\sigma_\alpha = \sigma_1 \sqrt{2t_2 - 2}$, $\sigma_X = \sigma_1 \sqrt{2n - 2t_2 + 1}$. This leads to, $\frac{\sigma_\alpha}{\sigma_X} = \frac{\sqrt{2t_2 - 2}}{\sqrt{2n - 2t_2 + 1}}$. Hence, under this scenario $Pr[z = \widetilde{z}|\text{Case 1 holds}] = 1 - \frac{2}{\pi} \tan^{-1} \frac{\sqrt{2t_2 - 2}}{\sqrt{2n - 2t_2 + 1}}$ (see Lemma 2).

Case 2 (The sign of C_{t_2} is not altered). Here $\widetilde{C}_1 = -C_1$ and $\widetilde{C}_{t_2} = C_{t_2}$. Now Eq. (10) becomes:

$$\Delta(C_{\mathbf{x}}) = -[\alpha_1(C_1 C_2 \cdots C_{t_1} \cdots C_{t_2} \cdots C_n)]$$
$$+ (\alpha_2 + \beta_1)(C_2 \cdots C_{t_1} \cdots C_{t_2} \cdots C_n) + \cdots + (\alpha_{t_2} + \beta_{t_2 - 1})(C_{t_2} \cdots C_n)$$
$$+ (\alpha_{t_2 + 1} + \beta_{t_2})(C_{t_2 + 1} \cdots C_n) + \cdots + (\alpha_n + \beta_{n-1}) C_n + \beta_n.$$

Here we have $\alpha = \alpha_1(C_1 C_2 \cdots C_{t_1} \cdots C_{t_2} \cdots C_n)$ and $X = (\alpha_2 + \beta_1)(C_2 \cdots C_{t_1} \cdots C_{t_2} \cdots C_n) + \cdots + \beta_n$. As we know $\alpha \sim \mathcal{N}(0, \sigma_1)$ and $X \sim \mathcal{N}(0, \sigma_1 \sqrt{2n - 1})$, $Pr[z = \widetilde{z}|\text{Case 2 holds}] = 1 - \frac{2}{\pi} \tan^{-1} \frac{1}{\sqrt{2n - 1}}$ (see Lemma 2).

It can be observed that $Pr[\text{Case 1 holds}] = \frac{2}{\pi} \tan^{-1} \frac{1}{\sqrt{2t_1 - 1}}$ and $Pr[\text{Case 2 holds}] = 1 - \frac{2}{\pi} \tan^{-1} \frac{1}{\sqrt{2t_1 - 1}}$. Combining Case 1 and Case 2 we have,

$$Pr[z = \widetilde{z}] = Pr[z = \widetilde{z}|\text{Case 1 holds}] \times Pr[\text{Case 1 holds}]$$
$$+ Pr[z = \widetilde{z}|\text{Case 2 holds}] \times Pr[\text{Case 2 holds}]$$
$$= \left[\left(1 - \frac{2}{\pi} \tan^{-1} \frac{\sqrt{2t_2 - 2}}{\sqrt{2n - 2t_2 + 1}} \right) \left(\frac{2}{\pi} \tan^{-1} \left(\frac{1}{\sqrt{2t_1 - 1}} \right) \right) \right]$$
$$+ \left[\left(1 - \frac{2}{\pi} \tan^{-1} \frac{1}{\sqrt{2n - 1}} \right) \left(1 - \frac{2}{\pi} \tan^{-1} \frac{1}{\sqrt{2t_1 - 1}} \right) \right]$$
$$= 1 - \frac{2}{\pi} \tan^{-1} \frac{1}{\sqrt{2n - 1}} + \frac{4}{\pi^2} \tan^{-1} \frac{1}{\sqrt{2n - 1}} \tan^{-1} \frac{1}{2t_1 - 1}$$
$$- \frac{4}{\pi^2} \tan^{-1} \frac{\sqrt{2t_2 - 2}}{\sqrt{2n - 2t_2 + 1}} \tan^{-1} \frac{1}{\sqrt{2t_1 - 1}}$$
$$= 1 - \frac{2}{\pi} \tan^{-1} \frac{1}{\sqrt{2n - 1}}$$
$$- \frac{4}{\pi^2} \tan^{-1} \frac{1}{\sqrt{2t_1 - 1}} \left(\tan^{-1} \frac{\sqrt{2t_2 - 2}}{\sqrt{2n - 2t_2 + 1}} - \tan^{-1} \frac{1}{\sqrt{2n - 1}} \right)$$
$$= 1 - \frac{2}{\pi} \tan^{-1} \frac{1}{\sqrt{2n - 1}}$$

$$-\frac{4}{\pi^2} \tan^{-1} \frac{1}{\sqrt{2t_1-1}} \tan^{-1} \frac{\sqrt{\frac{2t_2-2}{2n-2t_2+1}} - \frac{1}{\sqrt{2n-1}}}{1+\sqrt{\frac{2t_2-2}{(2n-2t_2+1)(2n-1)}}}.$$

The lemma is shown.   □

5   Theoretical Proof for a Bias in Any Arbiter PUF Variant

In this section we will show several results on biases in any variant of Arbiter PUF. Here, we assume that the variant is constructed by placing k arbiters in parallel, each supplied by the same challenge input $C = \{C_1, \ldots, C_n\}$, whereas the outputs $r_1, r_2, \ldots, r_n$ are combined to give a singular output r by a combiner function f. First, we will develop a more general form of Piling-up Lemma that will give us a way to handle the weight of an Arbiter PUF.

Theorem 1. *Let $I = \{I_k\}_{k=1}^s$ be a partition of a set of n independent variables, say, $\{x_1, x_2, \ldots, x_n\} = I_1 \cup I_2 \cup I_3 \ldots \cup I_s$ such that $I_k \cap I_j = \phi$. Let $f : \{0,1\}^n \to \{0,1\}$, defined as $f = \sum_{k=1}^s \prod_{i \in I_k} x_i$ and $Pr[x_i = 0] = p_i = \frac{1}{2} + \epsilon_i$, where ϵ_i represents the bias in x_i. Then we have: $Pr(f(x_1, x_2, \ldots, x_n) = 0) = Pr\left[\sum_{k=1}^s \prod_{i \in I_k} x_i = 0\right] = \frac{1}{2} + 2^{s-1} \prod_{k=1}^s \epsilon_{I_k}$, where $\epsilon_{I_k} = P_{I_k} - \frac{1}{2}$, $P_{I_k} = 1 - \prod_{i \in I_k} (1 - p_i)$.*

Proof. We denote $Pr[x_i = 0] = p_i \; \forall i \in \{1, \ldots, n\}$. Now since x_i and x_j are independent, $Pr[x_i x_j = 0] = 1 - Pr[x_i x_j = 1] = 1 - [Pr[x_i = 1]Pr[x_j = 1]] = 1 - [(1 - p_i)(1 - p_j)]$. Similarly,

$$Pr\left[\prod_{i \in I_k} x_i = 0\right] = 1 - Pr\left[\prod_{i \in I_k} x_i = 1\right] = 1 - \prod_{i \in I_k} Pr[x_i = 1]$$

$$= 1 - \prod_{i \in I_k} (1 - Pr[x_i = 0]) = 1 - \prod_{i \in I_k} (1 - p_i).$$

In terms of bias, $Pr\left[\prod_{i \in I_k} x_i = 0\right] = 1 - \prod_{i \in I_k} (\frac{1}{2} - \epsilon_i)$.

We will now use mathematical induction on the sum of product terms to arrive at our result. Let us observe the behavior for the sum of two product terms:

$$Pr\left[\prod_{i \in I} x_i + \prod_{j \in J} x_j = 0\right]$$

$$= Pr\left[\prod_{i \in I} x_i = 0\right] Pr\left[\prod_{j \in J} x_j = 0\right] + Pr\left[\prod_{i \in I} x_i = 1\right] Pr\left[\prod_{j \in J} x_j = 1\right]$$

$$= P_I P_J + (1 - P_I)(1 - P_J) = 1 - P_I - P_J + 2P_I P_J = \frac{1}{2} + 2\epsilon_I \epsilon_J.$$

Let us assume the following holds true for r product terms: $Pr\left[\sum_{j=1}^{r}\prod_{i\in I_j} x_i = 0\right] = \frac{1}{2} + 2^{r-1}\prod_{j=1}^{r}\epsilon_{I_j}$. For the $(r+1)^{th}$ term we have:

$$Pr\left[\sum_{j=1}^{r}\prod_{i\in I_j} x_i + \prod_{i\in I_r} x_i = 0\right]$$

$$= Pr\left[\sum_{j=1}^{r}\prod_{i\in I_j} x_i = 0\right] Pr\left[\prod_{i\in I_r} x_i = 0\right] + Pr\left[\sum_{j=1}^{r}\prod_{i\in I_j} x_i = 1\right] Pr\left[\prod_{i\in I_r} x_i = 1\right]$$

$$= \left(\frac{1}{2} + 2^{r-1}\prod_{j=1}^{r}\epsilon_{I_j}\right)\left(\frac{1}{2} + \epsilon_{I_{r+1}}\right) + \left(1 - \left(\frac{1}{2} + 2^{r-1}\prod_{j=1}^{r}\epsilon_{I_j}\right)\right)\left(1 - \left(\frac{1}{2} + \epsilon_{I_{r+1}}\right)\right)$$

$$= \left(\frac{1}{2} + 2^{r-1}\prod_{j=1}^{r}\epsilon_{I_j}\right)\left(\frac{1}{2} + \epsilon_{I_{r+1}}\right) + \left(\frac{1}{2} - 2^{r-1}\prod_{j=1}^{r}\epsilon_{I_j}\right)\left(\frac{1}{2} - \epsilon_{I_{r+1}}\right)$$

$$= \frac{1}{4} + 2^{r-2}\prod_{j=1}^{r}\epsilon_{I_j} + \frac{\epsilon_{I_{r+1}}}{2} + 2^{r-1}\prod_{j=1}^{r+1}\epsilon_{I_j} + \frac{1}{4} - 2^{r-2}\prod_{j=1}^{r}\epsilon_{I_j} - \frac{\epsilon_{I_{r+1}}}{2} + 2^{r-1}\prod_{j=1}^{r+1}\epsilon_{I_j}$$

$$= \frac{1}{2} + 2^{r}\prod_{j=1}^{r+1}\epsilon_{I_j}.$$

Hence, for s partitions on the set I, we have: $Pr\left[\sum_{k=1}^{s}\prod_{i\in I_k} x_i\right] = \frac{1}{2} + 2^{s-1}\prod_{k=1}^{s}\epsilon_{I_k}$, and the theorem is shown. $\square$

Corollary 1. *When $Pr[x_i = 0] = p$, for all x_i, $1 \le i \le n$, then $Pr[f(x_1, x_2, \ldots, x_n) = 0] = \frac{1}{2} + 2^{s-1}\prod_{k=1}^{s}\epsilon_{I_k}$, where $\epsilon_{I_k} = P_{I_k} - \frac{1}{2}$, $P_{I_k} = 1 - (1-p)^{|I_k|}$.*

We next concentrate on finding the bias of the output of several PUFs combined via a Boolean function under the assumption that the probability of output of each PUF changes is constant p.

Theorem 2. *Let $f : \{0,1\}^n \to \{0,1\}$ be a Boolean function with the 0-support of f at $a \in \{0,1\}^n$ given by $\Omega_{f,a}^{(k)} = \{z \in \{0,1\}^n : C_f(a) = -2^n + 2k\}$. Let $\Omega_{f,a}^{(k,w)} = \{z \in \Omega_{f,a}^{(k)} : wt(z) = k\}$. Further, we assume that the probability of any two input changes is $Pr[x_i + \tilde{x}_i = 0] = p$, for all i, where $\tilde{x}_i = x_i + a_i$, for $a_i \in \{0,1\}^n$. Then*
$Pr[f(x_1, \ldots, x_n) = f(\tilde{x}_1, \ldots, \tilde{x}_n)] = \frac{1}{2^n}\sum_{k=1}^{2^{n+1}}\sum_{w=0}^{n} kp^{n-w}(1-p)^w \left|\Omega_f^{(-2^n+2k,w)}\right|$.

Proof. We will start with an example to clear up the following argument. We take $f(x_1, x_2, x_3, x_4) = x_1 x_2 + x_3 x_4 + x_1 x_3 x_4$, which has the autocorrelation spectrum $(16, 0, 0, 0, 8, 0, -8, 0, 8, 0, -8, 0, 8, 0, -8, 0)$ (the domain is ordered lexicographically). Therefore, taking into account the changes in the output for every possible value of a_i, where $\tilde{x}_i = x_i + a_i$, we see that for $a = (0, 0, 0, 0)$, there are 16 values of x where $f(x) = f(\tilde{x})$, for $a = (0, 0, 0, 1), (0, 0, 1, 0), (0, 0, 1, 1)$, $(0, 1, 0, 1)$, $(0, 1, 1, 1)$, $(1, 0, 0, 1), (1, 0, 1, 1), (1, 1, 0, 1), (1, 1, 1, 1)$ since the autocorrelation coefficient is 0, it means that there are 8 values of x (for each case), where $f(x) = f(\tilde{x})$, for $a = (0,1,0,0)$, $(1,0,0,0)$, $(1,1,0,0)$, since the auto-correlation coefficient is 8, there are 12 values of x, where $f(x) = f(\tilde{x})$ (and consequently, 4 values of x where $f(x) = f(\tilde{x})+1$), for $a = (0,1,1,0)$, $(1,0,1,0)$, $(1,1,1,0)$, since the autocorrelation coefficient is -8, there are 4 values of x, where $f(x) = f(\tilde{x})$. Recall now that $Pr[x_i = \tilde{x}_i] = p$, and so partitioning the set of vectors a into vectors of the same weight whose autocorrelation coefficient is constant $2^4 - 2k \in \{-8, 0, 8\}$ (observe that for the autocorrelation coefficient -16 there are no values of x such that $f(x) = f(\tilde{x})$). Precisely,

$$\Omega_f = \Omega_f^{(-8,2)} \cup \Omega_f^{(-8,3)} \cup \Omega_f^{(-8,2)} \cup \Omega_f^{(0,1)} \cup \Omega_f^{(0,2)} \cup \Omega_f^{(0,3)} \cup \Omega_f^{(0,4)} \cup \Omega_f^{(8,1)}$$
$$\cup\, \Omega_f^{(8,2)} \cup \Omega_f^{(16,0)},$$

where the first label represents the autocorrelation coefficient and the second is the weight of the vectors, for example $\Omega_f^{(-8,2)} = \{(0,1,1,0),(1,0,1,0)\}$, we get

$$16 \cdot Pr[f(x_1,x_2,x_3,x_4) + f(\tilde{x}_1,\tilde{x}_2,\tilde{x}_3,\tilde{x}_4)]$$
$$= 4 \cdot p^2(1-p)^2 \left|\Omega_f^{(-8,2)}\right| + 4 \cdot p(1-p)^3 \left|\Omega_f^{(-8,3)}\right| + 8 \cdot p^3(1-p) \left|\Omega_f^{(0,1)}\right|$$
$$+ 8 \cdot p^2(1-p)^2 \left|\Omega_f^{(0,2)}\right| + 8 \cdot p(1-p)^3 \left|\Omega_f^{(0,3)}\right| + 8 \cdot (1-p)^4 \left|\Omega_f^{(0,4)}\right|$$
$$+ 12 \cdot p^3(1-p) \left|\Omega_f^{(8,1)}\right| + 12 \cdot p^2(1-p)^2 \left|\Omega_f^{(8,1)}\right| + 16 \cdot p^4 \left|\Omega_f^{(16,0)}\right|$$
$$= 40p^3(1-p) + 44p^2(1-p)^2 + 28p(1-p)^3 + 8(1-p)^4 + 16p^4.$$

Now, for the general case, we let, for $k \geq 1$ (recall that the autocorrelation coefficients are all even) $\Omega_f^{(-2^n+2k,w)} = \{a : C_f(a) = -2^n + 2k, wt(a) = w\}$, and reasoning exactly as in the example above, we get the probability

$$Pr[f(x_1,\ldots,x_n) = f(\tilde{x}_1,\ldots,\tilde{x}_n)] = \frac{1}{2^n} \sum_{k=1}^{2^n} \sum_{w=0}^{n} kp^{n-w}(1-p)^w \left|\Omega_f^{(-2^n+2k,w)}\right|.$$

We will now conduct experiments and verify Theorem 2 on various combiner functions.

5.1   Experimental Verification with Variants of Arbiter PUFs

We have verified Theorem 2 for various combiner functions and few of them are mentioned in this section. The experiments have been conducted using C programming. One may note that theoretical parameters do not depend on the delay parameters (i.e., distribution parameters), so for our experiments we have considered standard pseudorandom generators like lrand(), srand().

PUF type	Combiner function and parameters	Experimental bias	Theoretical bias (Theorem 2)
k-XOR	$f = x_1 + x_2 + x_3 + x_4$, $n = 10$ and $k = 4$	0.630	0.629
(n,k)-MPUF [16]	$f = x_1 x_5 x_6 + x_2 x_5 x_6 + x_2 x_5 + x_3 x_5 x_6$ $+x_3 x_6 + x_4 x_5 x_6 + x_4 x_5 + x_4 x_6 + x_4$ $n = 10$ and $k = 2$	0.759	0.760

6 S-PUF Construction: Improving the SAC Property

In this section, we propose a new Arbiter-based PUF construction to improve its SAC property, using only two Arbiter PUFs. The construction not only shows a significant improvement in the SAC property over other PUF constructions but also has a reliability of an 2-XOR PUF. We denote this new construction as S-PUF, since it involves a circular 'shift' of the challenge vector.

The construction involves two n-bit Arbiter PUFs, where the input $C = \{C_1, C_2, \ldots, C_n\}$ of the first Arbiter PUF is shifted by $n/2$ positions and fed to the second Arbiter PUF as the input:

$$\tilde{C} = \{C_{n/2}, C_{n/2+1}, \ldots, C_n, C_1, \ldots, C_{n/2-1}\}, \tag{11}$$

where $\tilde{C}$ is the input to the second Arbiter. The output of two PUFs is simply XORed to produce the output.

6.1 Design Rationale

The motivation arises from Lemma 3, where we try to find the value of t with minimum bias: $Pr[z = \tilde{z}] = 1 - \frac{2}{\pi} \tan^{-1} \sqrt{\frac{2t-1}{2n-2t+1}} = \frac{1}{2} + \frac{1}{2} - \frac{2}{\pi} \tan^{-1} \sqrt{\frac{2t-1}{2n-2t+1}} = \frac{1}{2} + \epsilon'$, where $\epsilon' = \frac{1}{2} - \frac{2}{\pi} \tan^{-1} \sqrt{\frac{2t-1}{2n-2t+1}}$. Putting $\epsilon' = 0$ we have: $\epsilon' = \frac{1}{2} - \frac{2}{\pi} \tan^{-1} \sqrt{\frac{2t-1}{2n-2t+1}} = 0 \implies \tan^{-1} \sqrt{\frac{2t-1}{2n-2t+1}} = \frac{\pi}{4} \implies t = \lceil \frac{n+1}{2} \rceil$ or $\lfloor \frac{n+1}{2} \rfloor$. For even n we have experimentally observed that $t = \lfloor \frac{n+1}{2} \rfloor$ i.e., $t = \frac{n}{2}$ provides the lowest bias. For odd n the bias will be lowest for $t = \frac{n+1}{2}$. As in general n is even, we assume $t = \frac{n}{2}$.

For a k-XOR PUF, when a challenge bit is flipped, the same bias is observed in every participant Arbiter PUF contributing to the XOR. However, in the S-PUF construction we move the flip position to a different location for the second Arbiter PUF to reduce the bias as much as possible. Note that since it is not possible to move every bit flip to $(\frac{n}{2})$ in the second Arbiter PUF, we choose the next best available position for the same. This construction comes with no additional requirement of hardware or memory, as shown in Fig. 5.

6.2 Bias in the S-PUF Construction

Now let us observe the bias in the S-PUF, as proposed. Using the Piling-up Lemma and Eq. (3), we have:

$$Pr[z = \tilde{z}] = \frac{1}{2} + \epsilon_1 \epsilon_2$$

$$= \frac{1}{2} + \left(\frac{1}{2} - \frac{2}{\pi} \tan^{-1} \sqrt{\frac{2t_1 - 1}{2n - 2t_1 + 1}} \right) \left(\frac{1}{2} - \frac{2}{\pi} \tan^{-1} \sqrt{\frac{2t_2 - 1}{2n - 2t_2 + 1}} \right)$$

$$= \frac{1}{2} + \epsilon'. \tag{12}$$

We take $t_2 = ((t_1 + (\frac{n}{2}) - 2) \bmod n) + 1$.

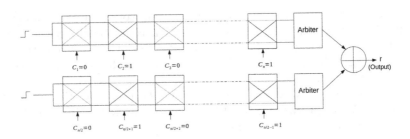

Fig. 5. S-PUF construction with only two Arbiter PUFs

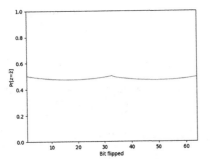
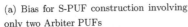
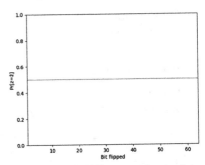

(a) Bias for S-PUF construction involving only two Arbiter PUFs

(b) Bias for S-PUF construction involving 4 Arbiter PUFs

7   Constructions of S_n-PUFs

An S-PUF construction consisting of 2 Arbiter PUF has very good SAC property, but is very weak against model-building attacks. An S-PUF will have a similar level of security as that of a 2-XOR PUF against linear programming and ML attacks. Hence, we need to use multiple Arbiter PUFs to fend off model building attacks. We will describe a special combiner function which will take inputs from several S-PUFs and produce a 1-bit response. Combined together, we call this new PUF construction, an S_n-PUF. Therefore, an S_n-PUF is composed of n S-PUFs (where each S-PUF is as mentioned in Sect. 6). For the following combiner functions: $f_1(x) = x_1 + x_2x_3 + x_4x_5x_6 + x_7x_8x_9x_{10} + x_{11}x_{12}x_{13}x_{14}x_{15}$,

$f_2(x) = x_1x_2x_3x_4x_5 + x_6x_7x_8x_9x_{10} + x_{10}x_{11}x_{12}x_{13}x_{14}x_{15}$, $f_3(x) = x_{14} + x_{15} + x_1x_2x_3x_4x_5 + x_6x_7x_8x_9x_{10} + x_{10}x_{11}x_{12}x_{13}$, the reliabilities have been described in Table 1. We notice that the functions mentioned in Table 1 provide good reliabilities. We also observe that other cryptographic properties of the functions f_1, f_2 and f_3 are not very good. We mention some cryptographic properties of these function in Table 2. Note that the functions f_1, f_2 and f_3 are either highly biased towards 0 or do not have good nonlinearity even if they produce good reliability. We need a function which has good nonlinearity and produces reasonable good reliability. We observed that the M-M (Maiorana-McFarland) bent functions [11] which have the highest nonlinearity produce reasonable good reliability. The general algebraic normal form of an M-M bent function involving $2n$ number of variables is $f(x,y) = \phi(x) \cdot y + g(x)$, where $x, y \in \{0,1\}^n$, $\phi(y)$ is a permutation and g is a Boolean function on n variables. For our combiner function we assume $g(y) = 0$ (as it provides good reliability), i.e., the combiner function is $f(x,y) = \phi(x) \cdot y$. In Table 3 we provide reliabilities of different S-PUFs, when we consider $f(x,y) = \phi(x) \cdot y$ as the combiner function. Here, our prime assumption is that the input to the combiner function must be even.

Table 1. Reliability for S-PUF with combiner

Arbiters used	Combiner function	Reliability of single PUF	Overall reliability
30	f_1	0.96	0.87
30	f_2	0.96	0.97
30	f_3	0.96	0.89

Table 2. Cryptographic properties of combiner functions

Function	Variables	Nonlinearity	Bias
f_1	15	11344	0.5
f_2	15	2404	0.073
f_3	15	3664	0.5

Table 3. S-PUF with $f(x,y) = \phi(x) \cdot y$ as combiner function

Arbiters used	Input to the combiner	Reliability	Nonlinearity	Bias
24	12	0.81	2016	0.4922
28	14	0.78	8128	0.4960
32	16	0.76	32640	0.4980

7.1 Security Discussions on S_n-PUFs

All Arbiter-based PUFs are susceptible to model-building attacks through Machine Learning techniques like LR and SVM [15]. In [1], it was shown that only a linear increase in the number of CRPs is required to build a robust model to cryptanalyze XOR PUFs. Keeping these results in mind, we stand in the favor of S_n-PUFs using a two-fold argument:

Security Against Conventional Machine Learning Attacks. Note that current ML techniques (apart from Becker's reliability attack reported in [1]) have only been able to attack up to 6-XOR PUFs (as reported in [15]). Hence, we choose S_{12} PUF (involving 24 Arbiter XOR PUFs) to be sufficiently safe against any modern machine learning attack known to us. A 24-XOR PUF will have very low reliability, while S_{12}-PUF performs very well in terms of reliability (see Table 3) and the SAC property (see Sect. 6).

Security Against Becker's Attack in [1]. Becker's attack uses the randomness of CMA-ES algorithm to converge at a solution. The attacks proceeds with measuring reliability values of each PUF in the n-XOR PUF as $h_0, h_1, \ldots, h_{n-1}$ and generating a random n-XOR PUF model and measuring the reliability of each of its constituent PUFs as $\tilde{h}_0, \tilde{h}_1, \ldots, \tilde{h}_{n-1}$. Note that we cannot obtain reliability values of constituent PUFs in a n-XOR PUF directly. For this, the author explains in [1, Section 5.2]: *"Let us assume for a PUF model $\overrightarrow{\omega}$ and for a challenge $\overrightarrow{\Phi_i}$ of one of the n Arbiter PUFs, the expected reliability is low, i.e., $\tilde{h} = 0$. Then the measured reliability h_i should also be low, since a bit flip of one of the response bits that are XORed directly results in a bit flip of the output of an XOR PUF. Hence, in this case the measured reliability h_i matches with the computed reliability $\tilde{h}_i$. If the computed reliability for the challenge Φ_i is high, i.e., $\tilde{h}_i = 1$, and the observed reliability is also high, the computed and observed reliability vectors match each other."* Note that a "bit flip" in any constituent Arbiter PUFs for an S_n-PUF does not mean a necessary effect in the output, due to the nature of the M-M type construction. Thus the reliability parameters cannot be obtained to mount the attack. Further, the reliability of each PUF is not equally represented in the output reliability of S_n-PUF due to high nonlinearity of the combiner function, making it even more difficult to model. Combining this with several factors such as the ability to use as large number of Arbiter PUFs (increasing n) is possible while maintaining very good reliability (PUFs exhibiting higher reliability make Becker's attack even more difficult), S_n-PUF can defend reliability based attacks quite well if not completely circumvent it.

8 Experimental Results

The proposed S-PUF is implemented in Verilog with placement constraints. The designed PUF is tested on Nexys-4 DDR Artix-7 FPGA board. The responses for a given challenge to the PUF are recorded using a serial communication UART protocol. Next, we will discuss about the performance metrics of the PUF and the implications of those in deriving a security key.

The main functionality of a PUF is it should be able to generate all possible combinations of the output in the response. In an ideal case, for a PUF with 16-bit challenge should be able to produce different 2^{16} combinations of outputs. That means each challenge should have a unique response. To validate this behavior, the *Hamming distance* of the response is plotted to check the distribution of the response. A test case of challenges with a one-bit flip in consecutive challenges are given to the PUF and the responses are recorded. This Hamming distance is also known as the *Intra Hamming distance* and can be expressed as *Intra Hamming distance* $= \sum_{i=1}^{k} \frac{HD(R_i, R_{i+1})}{n} \times 100$; here, k is the total number of challenges given to the PUF, R_i and R_{i+1} are the responses to the challenges C_i and C_{i+1}, respectively. Figure 6 is the plot displaying the Hamming distance of the responses with the iterations. The plot is like a Gaussian plot with a maximum at the half of its response length. Moreover, the plot shows that the proposed S-PUF is able to generate different combinations of the responses over its length.

The response from the PUF is mostly used as a security key or as an encryption key. The key must have few properties such as the key must be uniformly distributed in nature and it should be noise free. Based on these requirements, the few parameters for the PUF are defined as *uniqueness, uniformity, bit-aliasing and reliability.*

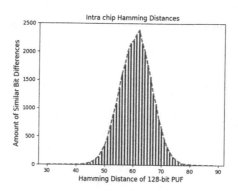

Fig. 6. Hamming distance of a 128-bit S-PUF on a Nexys-4 DDR Artix-7 FPGA

Uniqueness. The physical significance of uniqueness is how uniquely the PUF can distinguish its output from one device to the other of same configuration. That is, the same PUF design on two different chips (or devices) of the same configuration should not give the same output. The uniqueness of the PUF design is evaluated using the inter chip Hamming distance and the same is expressed as *Uniqueness* $= \sum_{i=1}^{k-1} \sum_{j=i+1}^{k} \frac{HD(R_i, R_j)}{n} \times 100$. Here, k is the number of chips considered for experiment. The inter chip Hamming distance is calculated as the

Hamming distance between R_i and R_j, where R_i and R_j are the responses of the PUF to the same challenge C from two different chips (FPGA) $FPGA_i$ and $FPGA_j$. The ideal value of uniqueness is 50%, that is, half of the bits should be different. From the plot (Fig. 7) it is clear that the proposed S-PUF has a maximum Inter Hamming distance at half of its response length, therefore, the uniqueness of the PUF is 50%. Uniqueness is calculated over two FPGAs of same family.

Uniformity. The response of the PUF should satisfy the condition of having an equal number of 0's and 1's in the response, to use it as a security key. The uniformity of a chip is calculated as $Uniformity = \frac{1}{n} \sum_{k=1}^{n} R[k] \times 100$. Here, k is the bit position and n is the length of the response. The ideal value of the uniformity is 50%. Since all possible responses are considered to calculate the average, the value might deviate slightly. The maximum, minimum and average values of the uniformity can be considered, while evaluating the design.

Bit-Aliasing. The physical significance of the bit-aliasing parameter is whether any particular bit position in the response is permanently sourced to either 0 or 1. The response bit must be derived from the applied challenge and the physical properties of the circuit. When bit-aliasing happens, different chips produce the same response irrespective of the challenge given. The bit aliasing of a particular bit position over different chips is calculated as $bit\text{-}alising_p = \frac{1}{n} \sum_{i=1}^{k} R_i[p]$. Here, k is the number of chips used for experiment, $R_i[p]$ is the pth-bit of the response (R_i) of chip i. The ideal value of bit$-$aliasing is 50%, which indicates the equal distribution of 0 and 1.

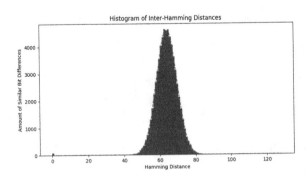

Fig. 7. Uniqueness of a 128-bit S-PUF on two Nexys-4 DDR Artix-7 FPGA's with same challenge set

Reliability. Reliability is one of the main concerns in today's electronic devices and systems. Similarly, the reliability of the PUF is an important metric to use PUF as a security primitive. The significance of the reliability of PUF translates to how efficiently a PUF can reproduce the same response bits under different situations. The situations can be the aging effect, the heating of the device or variations in the voltage levels of the output. Since, today's electronic circuits are more prone to the noise, any variation in the response bits will not serve the purpose of the PUF:

$$IHD = \frac{1}{m} \frac{\sum_{t=1}^{m} HD(R_i, R_i^t)}{n} \times 100 \qquad (13)$$

$$reliability = (100 - IHD)\%. \qquad (14)$$

The reliability of the PUF is calculated by using the *intra Hamming distance* of the response for same challenge given for several iterations. The reliability can be calculated from the Eqs. (13) and (14); here, n is the length of the response R_i and m is the total number of iterations. The ideal value of the reliability is 100%. Usually, for a good PUF design, the reliability is varied by a few error bits.

From the plot shown in Fig. 8, it can be observed that the reliability of the PUF is very good. The maximum error in a response is about 20 bits, which can be recovered using some error correction mechanism. The error occurred can be easily recovered using an error correction code scheme such as BCH, or Reed-Solomon codes.

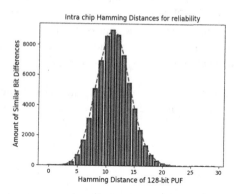

Fig. 8. Reliability of a 128-bit S-PUF on a Nexys-4 DDR Artix-7 FPGA

8.1 Comparison of the S-PUF Results

The comparison of the PUF metrics studied above are summarized here with few existing designs. The designs presented in [5] have two variations one with the post characterization (CHAR) and other one including the error correction capability (CHAR & MAJ). Table 4 summarizes the metrics and it is evident that the proposed S-PUF has a good performance.

Table 4. Comparison of the S-PUF with few existing designs; Reliability of the design is without ECC while the other designs with ECC

Parameter	Proposed S-PUF	Ring oscillator PUF [17]	Original Design [5]	CHAR	CHAR & MAJ
Uniqueness	50%	49.22	48.52	45.60	45.60
Uniformity	49.9%	48.5	51.06	50.60	50.54
Reliability	92%	99.99	92.00	98.87	99.58
Bit-aliasing	51.7%	47.89	43.52	43.52	43.52

9   Conclusion

In this paper, we have provided a theoretical estimation of the previously observed experimental bias. We noticed that these biases do not depend on the parameters of the distribution. These theoretical proofs of biases are also experimentally verified by doing several experiments in hardware, as well as in software. From our theoretical estimates, the biases of several PUFs with large inputs can be determined, which is not possible, computationally. Further, we introduce a new construction of a PUF, which overcomes these biases. We want to point out that our new construction is secure against existing attack techniques. The proposed S-PUF is implemented in an Artix-7 FPGA and we observe that the S-PUF has a good uniqueness, bit-aliasing and uniformity. The design also has a good reliability of 92%, where the error can be recovered using some error correction mechanism.

Acknowledgments. We would like to thank the anonymous reviewers of Indocrypt 2019 for their valuable suggestions and comments, which considerably improved the quality of our paper.

References

1. Becker, G.T.: The gap between promise and reality: on the insecurity of XOR arbiter PUFs. In: Güneysu, T., Handschuh, H. (eds.) CHES 2015. LNCS, vol. 9293, pp. 535–555. Springer, Heidelberg (2015). https://doi.org/10.1007/978-3-662-48324-4_27
2. Delvaux, J., Gu, D., Schellekens, D., Verbauwhede, I.: Secure lightweight entity authentication with strong PUFs: mission impossible? In: Batina, L., Robshaw, M. (eds.) CHES 2014. LNCS, vol. 8731, pp. 451–475. Springer, Heidelberg (2014). https://doi.org/10.1007/978-3-662-44709-3_25
3. Devadas, S.: Physical unclonable functions and secure processors. In: Clavier, C., Gaj, K. (eds.) CHES 2009. LNCS, vol. 5747, p. 65. Springer, Heidelberg (2009). https://doi.org/10.1007/978-3-642-04138-9_5
4. Gassend, B., Clarke, D., Van Dijk, M., Devadas, S.: Silicon physical random functions. In: Proceedings of the 9th ACM Conference on Computer and Communications Security, pp. 148–160. ACM (2002). https://dl.acm.org/citation.cfm?id=586132

5. Gu, C., Hanley, N., O'neill, M.: Improved reliability of FPGA-based PUF identification generator design. ACM Trans. Reconfigurable Technol. Syst. **10**(3), 20:1–20:23 (2017)
6. Hammouri, G., Sunar, B.: PUF-HB: a tamper-resilient HB based authentication protocol. In: Bellovin, S.M., Gennaro, R., Keromytis, A., Yung, M. (eds.) ACNS 2008. LNCS, vol. 5037, pp. 346–365. Springer, Heidelberg (2008). https://doi.org/10.1007/978-3-540-68914-0_21
7. Kömmerling, O., Kuhn, M.G.: Design principles for tamper-resistant smartcard processors. In: Smartcard 99, pp. 9–20 (1999). http://static.usenix.org/events/smartcard99/full_papers/kommerling/kommerling.pdf
8. Lee, J.W., Lim, D., Gassend, B., Suh, G.E., Van Dijk, M., Devadas, S.: A technique to build a secret key in integrated circuits for identification and authentication applications. In: 2004 Symposium on VLSI Circuits, Digest of Technical Papers (IEEE Cat. No. 04CH37525), pp. 176–179. IEEE (2004). https://people.csail.mit.edu/devadas/pubs/vlsi-symp-puf.pdf
9. Lim, D., Lee, J.W., Gassend, B., Suh, G.E., Van Dijk, M., Devadas, S.: Extracting secret keys from integrated circuits. IEEE Trans. Very Large Scale Integr. Syst. (VLSI) **13**(10), 1200–1205 (2005)
10. Machida, T., Yamamoto, D., Iwamoto, M., Sakiyama, K.: A new mode of operation for arbiter PUF to improve uniqueness on FPGA. In: 2014 Federated Conference on Computer Science and Information Systems, pp. 871–878. IEEE (2014)
11. Maiorana, J.A.: A class of bent functions. R41 Technical Paper, August 1970
12. Maiti, A., Gunreddy, V., Schaumont, P.: A systematic method to evaluate and compare the performance of physical unclonable functions. In: Athanas, P., Pnevmatikatos, D., Sklavos, N. (eds.) Embedded Systems Design with FPGAs, pp. 245–267. Springer, New York (2013). https://doi.org/10.1007/978-1-4614-1362-2_11
13. Menezes, A.J., van Oorschot, P.C., Vanstone, S.A.: Handbook of Applied Cryptography. CRC Press, Boca Raton (1996). ISBN: 0-8493-8523-7
14. Nguyen, P.H., Sahoo, D.P., Chakraborty, R.S., Mukhopadhyay, D.: Security analysis of arbiter PUF and its lightweight compositions under predictability test. ACM Trans. Des. Autom. Electron. Syst. (TODAES) **22**(2), 20 (2017)
15. Rührmair, U., Sehnke, F., Sölter, J., Dror, G., Devadas, S., Schmidhuber, J.: Modeling attacks on physical unclonable functions. In: Proceedings of the 17th ACM Conference on Computer and Communications Security, pp. 237–249. ACM (2010). https://eprint.iacr.org/2010/251.pdf
16. Sahoo, D.P., Mukhopadhyay, D., Chakraborty, R.S., Nguyen, P.H.: A multiplexer-based arbiter PUF composition with enhanced reliability and security. IEEE Trans. Comput. **67**(3), 403–417 (2017)
17. Srinivasu, B., Vikramkumar, P., Chattopadhyay, A., Lam, K.-Y.: CoLPUF: a novel configurable LFSR-based PUF. In: IEEE Asia Pacific Conference on Circuits and Systems (APCCAS), pp. 358–361 (2018)
18. Meng-Day, Y., Hiller, M., Delvaux, J., Sowell, R., Devadas, S., Verbauwhede, I.: A lockdown technique to prevent machine learning on PUFs for lightweight authentication. IEEE Trans. Multi-scale Comput. Syst. **2**(3), 146–159 (2016)

Author Index

Printed in the United States
by Baker & Taylor Publisher Services